Web Services Foundations

Athman Bouguettaya · Quan Z. Sheng
Florian Daniel
Editors

Web Services Foundations

Foreword by Michael P. Papazoglou

 Springer

Editors
Athman Bouguettaya
School of Computer Science
  and Information Technology
RMIT University
Melbourne, VIC
Australia

Florian Daniel
Dipartimento di Ingegneria e Scienza
  dell'Informazione
Università di Trento
Povo, Trento
Italy

Quan Z. Sheng
School of Computer Science
University of Adelaide
Adelaide, SA
Australia

ISBN 978-1-4939-4878-9   ISBN 978-1-4614-7518-7   (eBook)
DOI 10.1007/978-1-4614-7518-7
Springer New York Heidelberg Dordrecht London

To my parents, Horia and Mahmoud, and my wife Malika

Athman Bouguettaya

To my parents Shuilian and Jianwu, my brothers Guanzheng and Xinzheng, my wife Yaping and my daughters Fiona and Phoebe

Quan Z. Sheng

To Cinzia, my family, my friends

Florian Daniel

Foreword

Service-Oriented Computing (SOC) is the computing paradigm that utilizes software services as fundamental elements for developing and deploying distributed software applications. Services are self-describing, platform-agnostic computational elements that support rapid, low-cost composition of distributed applications. They perform functions, which can be anything from simple requests to complicated business processes. Services allow organizations to expose their core competencies programmatically via a self-describing interface based on open standards over the Internet (or intranet) using standard (XML-based) languages and protocols. Because services provide a uniform and ubiquitous information distributor for wide range of computing devices (such as handheld computers, PDAs, cellular telephones, or appliances) and software platforms (e.g., UNIX or Windows), they constitute a major transition in distributed computing.

A Web service is a specific kind of service that is identified by a URI that exposes its features programmatically over the Internet using standard Internet languages and protocols, and can be implemented via a self-describing interface based on open Internet standards (e.g., XML interfaces which are published in network-based repositories).

Understanding the conceptual underpinnings and mastering the technical intricacies of Web services is anything but trivial and is absolutely necessary to construct a well-functioning service-based system or application. Web service technology is undergoing continuous, rapid evolution, thanks to both standardization efforts pushed forward by industry and the research efforts of the scientific community.

Web services standards are still evolving. However, they seem to converge today on a handful of standards: the Simple Object Access Protocol (SOAP) for service communication, Web Services Description Language (WSDL) for service description, Universal Description, Discovery, and Integration Infrastructure (UDDI) for registering and discovering services, and the Business Process Execution Language (BPEL) for service composition. A plethora of WS-* specifications also exists to describe the full spectrum of activities related to Web services in topics such as reliable messaging, security, privacy, policies, event processing, and coordination, to name but a few.

Leading international conferences, such as the International Conference on Service-Oriented Computing (ICSOC), the International Conference on Web Services (ICWS), the International Conference on Service Computing (SCC), and others, have spearheaded groundbreaking research efforts. This has led to the emergence of novel topics such as semantic Web services, automated Web service composition, Web service recommendations, quality of service, trust, and a range of other interesting themes. Related conference series such as Web Engineering, Cloud Computing, Business Process Management, HCI, and Database related conferences, have all been strongly influenced by the emergence of Web services and consistently feature Web service related topics in their calls for papers. These conferences contribute to the wealth of knowledge that is growing exponentially around Web services.

The content of this book and that of its companion book *Advanced Web Services* (Springer, 2013) reflect such activities. It is a testimonial of the leading role of its editors and their highly influential work in the area of Web services. Together, both books cover an enormous wealth of important topics and technologies that mirror the evolution of Web services. They provide an exhaustive overview of the challenges and solutions of all major achievements pertaining to Web services. Each chapter is an authoritative piece of work that synthesizes all pertinent literature and highlights important accomplishments and advances in its subject matter.

To my knowledge, this is the first attempt of its kind, providing complete coverage of the key subjects in Web services. I am not aware of any other book that is as thorough, comprehensive and ambitious in explaining the current state of the art of scientific research and in synthesizing the perspectives and know-how of so many experts in the field. Both books are a must-read for everyone interested in the field. They cater for the needs of both novices to the field as well as seasoned researchers and practitioners. They are a major step in this field's maturation and will serve to unify, advance, and challenge the scientific community in many important ways.

It is a real pleasure to have been asked to provide the foreword for this book collection. I am happy to commend the editors and authors on their accomplishment, and to inform the readers that they are looking at a landmark in the development of the Web services field. Anybody serious about Web services ought to have handy a copy of *Web Services Foundations* and *Advanced Web Services* in their private library!

Tilburg, The Netherlands   Michael P. Papazoglou
December 2012

Preface

Web Service technology is undeniably the preferred delivery method for the Service-Oriented Computing (SOC) paradigm. It has evolved over the years to be a comprehensive, interdisciplinary approach to modern software development. Web services have gone beyond software componentization technology to embody and express the software manifestation of a general trend transforming our modern society from an industrial, production-centric economy into a digital, service-centric economy. Web services aim to provide the missing conceptual links that unify a variety of different disciplines, such as networking, distributed systems, cloud computing, autonomic computing, data and knowledge management, knowledge-based systems, and business process management. Web services are the technological proxies of services that power much of the developed and increasingly developing economies. In this respect, Web services play a central role in enabling and sustaining the growth of service-centric economies and help modernizing organizations, companies and institutions also from an IT perspective.

Over the last decade, Web services have become a thriving area of research and academic endeavors. Yet, despite a substantial body of research and scientific publications, the Web services community has been hitherto missing a one stop-shop that would provide a consolidated understanding of the scientific and technical progress of this important subject. This book (the second of a two-book collection) is a serious attempt to fill this gap and serve as a primary point of reference reflecting the pervasive nature of Web services.

This book is the first installment of a two-book collection (we discuss the advanced topics in the second book, *Advanced Web Services*, Springer, 2013). Together, they comprise approximately 1,400 pages covering state-of-the-art theoretical and practical aspects as well as experience using and deploying Web services. The collection offers a comprehensive overview of the scientific and technical progress in Web services technologies, design, architectures, applications, and performance. The first book of the collection consists of two major parts:

I   Foundations of Web Services (12 chapters)—It explores the most representative theoretical and practical approaches to Web services, with a special focus on the general state-of-the-art approaches to Web service composition;

II Service Selection and Assisted Composition (16 chapters)—It focuses on other aspects of Web service composition problem, specifically takes a deep look at non-functional aspects (e.g., quality of service), Web service recommendations, and how Web service composition is made easy for less expert developers.

The second book (*Advanced Web Services*, Springer, 2013) consists of three major parts:

I   Advanced Services Engineering and Management (11 chapters)—It explores advanced engineering problems, such as Web service transactions and recovery, security and identity management, trust and contracts, and Web service evolution and management;

II Web Service Applications and Case Studies (5 chapters)—It covers concrete scenarios of the use of Web service technology and reports on empirical studies of real-world Web service ecosystems;

III Novel Perspectives and Future Directions (10 chapters)—It surveys approaches of the applications on how the Web service paradigm can be applied to novel contexts, such as human-centric computing, human work and the Internet of Things, and discusses the value of Web services in the context of mobile and cloud computing.

The topics covered in the collection are reflective of their intent: they aim to become the primary source for all pertinent information regarding Web service technologies, research, deployment and future directions. The purpose of the two books is to serve as a trusted and valuable reference point to researchers and educators who are working in the area of Web services, to students who wish to learn about this important research and development area, and to practitioners who are using Web services and the service paradigm daily in their software development projects.

This collection is the result of an enormous community effort, and their production involved more than 100 authors, consisting of the worlds leading experts in this field. We would like to thank the authors for their high-quality contributions and the reviewers for their time and professional expertise. All contributions have undergone a rigorous review process, involving three independent experts in two rounds of review. We are also very grateful to Springer for their continuous help and assistance.

Melbourne, Australia, December 2012   Athman Bouguettaya
Adelaide, Australia   Quan Z. Sheng
Trento, Italy   Florian Daniel

Contents

Contributors

Dhaminda B. Abeywickrama Faculty of IT, Monash University, Clayton Campus, Wellington Road, Clayton, VIC 3800, Australia, e-mail: dhaminda. abeywickrama@gmail.com

Mohammed AbuJarour SAP AG, Potsdam, Germany, e-mail: mohammed. abujarour@sap.com

Amal Alhosban Wayne State University, Detroit, MI, USA, e-mail: ea1179@ wayne.edu

Mohsen Asadi Simon Fraser University, Burnaby, BC, Canada, e-mail: masadi@ sfu.ca

Ahmed Awad Faculty of Computers and Information, Cairo University, Giza, Egypt, e-mail: a.gaafar@fci-cu.edu.eg

Boualem Benatallah CSE, University of New South Wales, Sydney, NSW, Australia, e-mail: boualem@cse.unsw.edu.au

Salima Benbernou Université Paris Descartes, Paris, France, e-mail: salima. benbernou@parisdescartes.fr

Swapan Bhattacharya Jadavpur University, Kolkata, India, e-mail: bswapan2000@yahoo.co.in

M. Brian Blake Graduate School, University of Miami, Coral Gables, FL 33124-3220, USA, e-mail: m.brian.blake@miami.edu

Steffen Bleul Munich, Germany, e-mail: stbleul@gmx.de

Fabio Casati University of Trento, Via Sommarive 5, 38123 Trento, Italy, e-mail: casati@disi.unitn.it

Jayeeta Chanda BPPIMT, 137, VIP Road, Kolkata, India, e-mail: jayeeta. chanda@gmail.com

Min Chen Concordia University, Montreal, QC, Canada, e-mail: minchen2008 halifax@yahoo.com

Xi Chen Schlumberger Technologies (Beijing) Ltd., Beijing, China, e-mail: bargittachen@gmail.com

Alan Colman Faculty of Information and Communication Technology, Swinburne University of Technology, Melbourne, VIC, Australia, e-mail: acolman@swin.edu.au

Florian Daniel University of Trento, Via Sommarive 5, Trento, Italy, e-mail: daniel@disi.unitn.it

Joseph G. Davis School of Information Technologies, University of Sydney, Sydney, NSW 2006, Australia, e-mail: joseph.davis@sydney.edu.au

Giuseppe De Giacomo Dipartimento di Ingegneria Informatica Automatica e Gestionale Antonio Ruberti, Sapienza Università di Roma, via Ariosto 25, 00185 Rome, Italy, e-mail: degiacomo@dis.uniroma1.it

Khalil Drira CNRS, LAAS, University of Toulouse, 7 avenue du colonel Roche, 31400 Toulouse, France, e-mail: khalil.drira@laas.fr

Zaiwen Feng State Key Laboratory of Software Engineering, School of Computer, Wuhan University, Wuhan, China, e-mail: fengzaiwen@whu.edu.cn

Dragan Gašević Athabasca University, Athabasca, AB, Canada; Simon Fraser University, Burnaby, BC, Canada, e-mail: dgasevic@acm.org

Claude Godart LORIA-INRIA-UMR 7503, 54506 Vandoeuvre-les-Nancy, France, e-mail: claude.godart@loria.fr

Nawal Guermouche CNRS, LAAS, University of Toulouse, 7 avenue du colonel Roche, 31400 Toulouse, France, e-mail: nawal.guermouche@laas.fr

Claudio Guidi Dipartimento di Matematica, University of Padua, Via Trieste 63, 35121 Padua, Italy, e-mail: cguidi@math.unipd.it

Riadh Ben Halima ReDCAD, University of Sfax, 3038 Sfax, Tunisia, e-mail: riadh.benhalima@enis.rnu.tn

Jun Han Faculty of Information and Communication Technology, Swinburne University of Technology, Melbourne, VIC, Australia, e-mail: jhan@swin.edu.au

Khayyam Hashmi Wayne State University, Detroit, MI, USA, e-mail: eh2304@wayne.edu

Keqing He State Key Laboratory of Software Engineering, School of Computer, Wuhan University, Wuhan, China, e-mail: hekeqing@whu.edu.cn

Patrick C. K. Hung University of Ontario Institute of Technology, Oshawa, ON, Canada, e-mail: patrick.hung@uoit.ca

Vu Hung University of New South Wales, Sydney, NSW, Australia, e-mail: vthung@gmail.com

Fuyuki Ishikawa National Institute of Informatics, 2-1-2 Hitotsubashi, Chiyoda-ku, Tokyo 101-8430, Japan, e-mail: f-ishikawa@nii.ac.jp

Ananya Kanjilal BPPIMT, 137, VIP Road, Kolkata, India, e-mail: ag_k@rediffmail.com

Georgia Kleanthous Manchester Centre for Service Research, University of Manchester, Manchester M60 1QD, UK, e-mail: georgia.kleanthous@gmail.com

Woralak Kongdenfha ECPE, Naresuan University, Phitsanulok, Thailand, e-mail: woralakk@gmail.com

Freddy Lecue IBM Research, Dublin, Ireland, e-mail: freddy.lecue@ie.ibm.com

Jaejoon Lee Lancaster University, Lancashire, UK, e-mail: j.lee@comp.lancs.ac.uk

Angel Lagares Lemos University of New South Wales, Sydney, NSW, Australia, e-mail: angell@cse.unsw.edu.au

Niels Lohmann University of Rostock, Rostock, Germany, e-mail: niels.lohmann@uni-rostock.de

Michael R. Lyu Department of Computer Science and Engineering, The Chinese University of Hong Kong, Shatin, Hong Kong, China, e-mail: lyu@cse.cuhk.edu.hk

Zaki Malik Department of Computer Science, Wayne State University, Detroit, MI, USA, e-mail: zaki@cs.wayne.edu

Massimo Mecella Dipartimento di Ingegneria Informatica Automatica e Gestionale Antonio Ruberti, Sapienza Università di Roma, via Ariosto 25, 00185 Rome, Italy, e-mail: mecella@dis.uniroma1.it

Brahim Medjahed Department of Computer and Information Science, University of Michigan, Dearborn, MI, USA, e-mail: brahim@umich.edu

Nikolay Mehandjiev Manchester Centre for Service Research, University of Manchester, Manchester M60 1QD, UK, e-mail: n.mehandjiev@manchester.ac.uk

Emna Mezghani CNRS, LAAS, University of Toulouse, 7 avenue du colonel Roche, 31400 Toulouse, France; ReDCAD, University of Sfax, 3038 Sfax, Tunisia, e-mail: emna.mezghani@laas.fr

Mahboobeh Moghaddam School of Information Technologies, University of Sydney, Sydney, NSW 2015, Australia; National ICT Australia, Australian Technology Park, Sydney, NSW, Australia, e-mail: mahboobe@it.usyd.edu.au

Bardia Mohabbati Simon Fraser University, Burnaby, BC, Canada, e-mail: mohabbati@sfu.ca

Fabrizio Montesi IT University of Copenhagen, Rued Langgaards Vej 7, 2300 Copenhagen, Denmark, e-mail: fmontesi@itu.dk

Hamid R. Motahari-Nezhad HP Labs, Palo Alto, CA, USA, e-mail: hamidreza.motahari-nezhad@hp.com

Abdallah Namoun Manchester Centre for Service Research, University of Manchester, Manchester M60 1QD, UK, e-mail: abdallah.namoune@mbs.ac.uk

Tuan Nguyen Faculty of Information and Communication Technology, Swinburne University of Technology, Melbourne, VIC, Australia, e-mail: tmnguyen@swin.edu.au

Fabio Patrizi Dipartimento di Ingegneria Informatica Automatica e Gestionale Antonio Ruberti, Sapienza Università di Roma, via Ariosto 25, 00185 Rome, Italy, e-mail: patrizi@dis.uniroma1.it

Cesare Pautasso Faculty of Informatics, University of Lugano, via Buffi 13, 6900 Lugano, Switzerland, e-mail: c.pautasso@ieee.org

Pascal Poizat LRI UMR CNRS, 8623 Orsay, France, e-mail: pascal.poizat@lri.fr

Carlos Rodríguez University of Trento, Via Sommarive 5, 38123 Trento, Italy, e-mail: crodriguez@disi.unitn.it

Soudip Roy Chowdhury University of Trento, Via Sommarive 5, 38123 Trento, Italy, e-mail: rchowdhury@disi.unitn.it

Regis Saint-Paul Oceanet Technology, Nantes, France, e-mail: regis.saintpaul@gmail.com

Sabnam Sengupta BPPIMT, 137, VIP Road, Kolkata, India, e-mail: sabnamsg@gmail.com

Stefano Soi University of Trento, Via Sommarive 5, 38123 Trento, Italy, e-mail: soi@disi.unitn.it

Christian Stahl Department of Mathematics and Computer Science, Technische Universiteit Eindhoven, 5600 MB Eindhoven, 513, Eindhoven, The Netherlands, e-mail: C.Stahl@tue.nl

Wil M. P. van der Aalst Department of Mathematics and Computer Science, Technische Universiteit Eindhoven, 5600 MB Eindhoven, 513, Eindhoven, The Netherlands, e-mail: W.M.P.v.d.Aalst@tue.n

Usman Wajid Manchester Centre for Service Research, University of Manchester, Manchester M60 1QD, UK, e-mail: usman.wajid@manchester.ac.uk

Jian Wang State Key Laboratory of Software Engineering, School of Computer, Wuhan University, Wuhan, China, e-mail: jianwang@whu.edu.cn

Thomas Weise School of Computer Science and Technology, University of Science and Technology of China, 230027 Hefei, Anhui, China, e-mail: tweise@ustc.edu.cn

Karsten Wolf University of Rostock, Rostock, Germany, e-mail: karsten.wolf@uni-rostock.de

Hua Xiao IBM Canada Laboratory, Markham, ON, Canada, e-mail: huaxiao@ca.ibm.com

Yuhong Yan Concordia University, Montreal, QC, Canada, e-mail: yuhong@encs.concordia.ca

Jian Yang Macquarie University, Sydney, NSW 2109, Australia, e-mail: jian.yang@mq.edu.au

Qi Yu Rochester Institute of Technology, Rochester, NY, USA, e-mail: qi.yu@rit.edu

Gianluigi Zavattaro INRIA Focus Research Team, University of Bologna, Mura A. Zamboni 7, 40127 Bologna, Italy, e-mail: zavattar@cs.unibo.it

Jia Zhang Carnegie Mellon University, Silicon Valley, Mountain View, CA, USA, e-mail: jia.zhang@sv.cmu.edu

Liang-Jie Zhang Kingdee International Software Group Co. Ltd., Shenzhen, China, e-mail: zhanglj@ieee.org

Weiliang Zhao University of Wollongong, Wollongong, NSW 2522, Australia, e-mail: wzhao@uow.edu.au

Huiyuan Zheng Macquarie University, Sydney, NSW 2109, Australia, e-mail: huiyuan.zheng@mq.edu.au

Zibin Zheng Department of Computer Science and Engineering, The Chinese University of Hong Kong, Shatin, Hong Kong, China, e-mail: zbzheng@cse.cuhk.edu.hk

Ying Zou Department of Electrical and Computer Engineering, Queen's University, Kingston, ON, Canada, e-mail: ying.zou@queensu.ca

Part I
Foundations of Web Services

Chapter 1
Web Services and Business Processes: A Round Trip

Mohammed AbuJarour and Ahmed Awad

Abstract Service-oriented Architecture (SOA) is considered as an implementation for business processes (BP). However, the relation between SOA and BPs is usually inspected in one direction only. In this chapter, we investigate the *bi-directional* relation between web services and business processes, and explore potential benefits therefrom. In particular, we introduce a novel approach to generate additional information about web services based on the configurations of business processes that consume these web services. This information is then used to enhance and smooth the modeling and configuration of future business processes. Through our approach, we can generate three types of information from consumers' business processes, namely annotations, context, and relations among web services. To evaluate our approach, we use the SAP reference model and we show the results in this chapter.

1.1 The Relation Between Business Processes and Web Services

Service-oriented Architecture (SOA) has been considered as an implementation platform for business processes (BP), nevertheless, each of them is typically investigated separately. Investigating both worlds (i.e., SOA and BP) together is expected to result in several benefits for both SOA and BP communities. For instance, getting a running instance of a business process model requires mapping its *service* tasks to (web) services. This mapping step requires sufficient information about the used web

M. AbuJarour (✉)
SAP AG, Potsdam, Germany
e-mail: mohammed.abujarour@sap.com

A. Awad
Faculty of Computers and Information,
Cairo University, Giza, Egypt
e-mail: a.gaafar@fci-cu.edu.eg

A. Bouguettaya et al. (eds.), *Web Services Foundations*,
DOI: 10.1007/978-1-4614-7518-7_1,
© Springer Science+Business Media New York 2014

services that is understandable by process engineers or business people who create such mappings. Finding candidate web services to execute each service task is one of the key challenges in SOA, e.g., due to poor service descriptions [10]. We consider the configurations of BPs as a rich source of information about their consuming web services that enhance service discovery and future BP configurations.

Due to the increasing number of BPs, service consumers in several application domains maintain repositories of business process models (BPM) for their daily activities, e.g., "ship ordered item". Each business process is composed of a set of manual (i.e., performed by employees) or service tasks (i.e., performed through web services). Building a new BPM incorporates three steps: (1) creating and labeling its tasks (2) determining the interaction between them, i.e., data and control flow (3) configuring the created model, i.e., *selecting* web services to perform service tasks. The built BPM is typically stored in the consumer's repository for future requests.

Using the aforementioned scenario in practice involves several challenges, such as, service discovery, service selection, BP configuration. *Service discovery* is one of the main challenges in Service-oriented Computing (SOC), where a list of candidate web services are returned to service consumer as a result for their queries. Choosing a particular web service to invoke from this list is known as *service selection* [18], which has become a complex task due to several factors, e.g., lack of rich service descriptions. Therefore, additional information about web services— e.g., annotations, relations among web services, etc.—is expected to help meet this challenge [7]. *Business process configuration* represents the service selection step, where each service task is assigned a web service to execute it. Performing this task dynamically requires sufficient information about web services so that process engineers configure their BPMs accordingly. Technical information only is not sufficient, because it does not fit their backgrounds and knowledge [19].

Using web services within distributed business processes brings the challenges of service discovery and selection to business processes. In this work, we introduce a novel approach to bridge both worlds (SOA and BPM), where we use business process configurations to derive additional information about their implementing web services that reflect service consumers' perspective (business view) to enrich their technical descriptions released by their providers. We are able to generate three types of information about web services, namely annotations, context, and relations among web services. Annotations for web services are generated from tasks' labels and documentations, whereas context is derived from models' titles and descriptions. We discover *additional* realistic and rich relations among web services in the form of linkage patterns using behavioral profiles [24] of their consuming business processes. Additionally, we derive a global representation of all relations among web services that are derived from multiple business processes. We use this global representation to predict relations among web services that are not used together in a single business process using the gained knowledge in this global representation.

The contributions of the work introduced in this chapter are:

1. Supporting smooth configuration of business processes by enabling context-aware service selection.

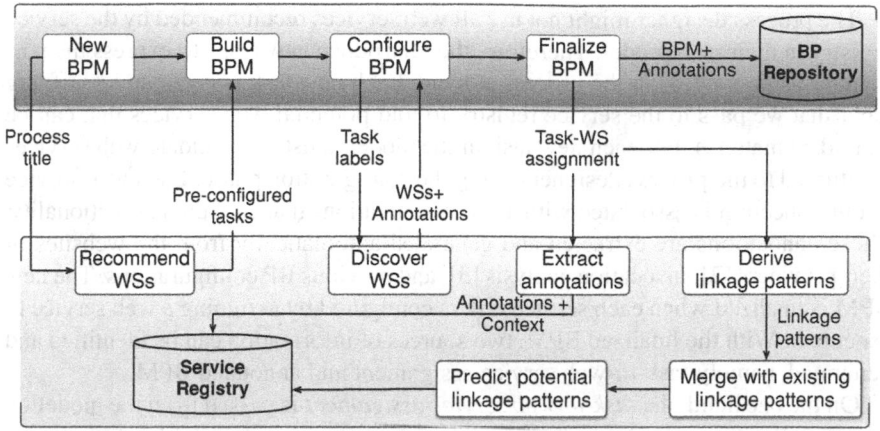

Fig. 1.1 An overview of our approach of integrating business processes and web services

2. Finding realistic, rich relations among web services as *linkage patterns*.
3. Disambiguating exclusive relations between web services using lexical ontologies, e.g., WordNet.
4. Merging behavioral profiles of BPs into a single global behavioral profile.
5. Revealing relations among web services that have not yet been used together.

The rest of this chapter is organized as follows: We give an overview of our approach in Sect. 1.2. Then, we introduce the fundamental concepts that are used throughout this chapter in Sect. 1.3. After that, we present our approach to generate annotations for web services from business process configurations in Sect. 1.4. In Sect. 1.5, we describe our approach to derive rich relations among web services in the form of linkage patterns. Deriving global behavioral profiles among web services is described in Sect. 1.6. Implementation details and experiments are introduced in Sect. 1.7. Related work is summarized in Sect. 1.8. We summarize this chapter in Sect. 1.9.

1.2 Overview of Our Approach

In this section we give an overview of our approach that represents a round trip between web services and business processes as shown in Fig. 1.1. The scenario starts when a business process designer creates a new BPM. At that point, the designer gives a descriptive name and summary for the new process, e.g., *establish a company in Germany*. Behind the scene, a request is sent to a service registry to find relevant web services that have been used in similar models, e.g., *establish a company in UK*. The returned recommended services are provided as *pre-configured* tasks that are made available to the designer to accelerate the process design.

The process designer might not use all web services recommended by the service registry in their new model. Therefore, they introduce new tasks to express the particular business needs in the process at hand. Each new task is given an identifying label that we pass to the service registry to find potential web services that can be candidate matches. For each new task in the model, a list of candidate web services is returned to the process designer during the configuration phase. Each web service in our collection is associated with a set of annotations that explain its functionality. These annotations are extracted and generated automatically from the websites of their providers [2], invocation analysis [3], and previous BP configurations. The new BPM is finalized when each service task is configured by assigning a web service to execute it. With the finalized BPM, two sources of information can be identified and generated, namely task-to-web service assignment and annotated BPM.

On the one hand, the *task-to-web service assignment* is passed from the modeling framework to the service registry, where annotations, context, and relations are generated therefrom. On the other hand, the tasks in the created BPM are automatically annotated with the annotations of the web services they are bound with, resulting in an *annotated BPM*. These annotations are crucial for BPM lookup, because not only task labels are used to index and find tasks, but enriched annotations are also used to achieve this goal [4] leading to better discovery of models from process repositories.

We use this assignment list also to generate behavioral profiles, based on which we derive rich relations among web services. Even more, we discover *hidden* relations among services that have not been used together in any business process configuration yet. The notion of behavioral profiles is developed by Weidlich et al. [24] to give a behavioral abstraction over business processes. We use this notion and extend it according to requirements for discovering relations among web services.

1.3 Fundamentals: Business Process Knowledge

Researchers have proposed several approaches that investigate the behavioral relations among tasks within a process model. For instance, the α-algorithm [22], causal footprints [23] and behavioral profiles [24].[1] Although these approaches are developed for different purposes, they have a fundamental common feature; generating a set of behavioral relations among tasks in a process model. We use these behavioral relations in our approach to derive rich relations among web services. Causal footprints [23] and behavioral profiles [24] take as input a process model, represented as a WF-net [21]. Whereas the α-algorithm requires as input a set of process execution traces (i.e., log). We use the behavioral profiles approach as a starting point, because we have process models as input and because the behavioral profile approach is much more efficient than causal footprints. Nevertheless, our approach is independent of this selection and works with process behavior abstraction approaches that support the fundamental behavioral relations.

---

[1] There are other related approaches that share similar underlying concepts.

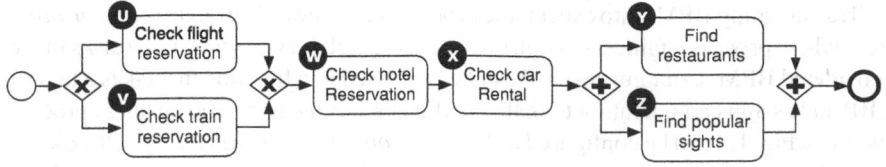

Fig. 1.2 A journey organizer business process modeled in BPMN 1.0

Behavioral profiles represent an abstract description of a business process and identifies the behavioral relationship between any pair of its nodes. This relationship can be: (1) strict order $\rightsquigarrow$, (2) concurrent $\|$, (3) exclusive #, or (4) inverse order $\leftsquigarrow$. The formal definition of behavioral profiles is introduced in Definition 1.1.

Definition 1.1 *(Behavioral Profile)* Let N be the set of nodes within a business process model. The *behavioral profile* of a business process model is a function $bhp: N \times N \rightarrow \{\rightsquigarrow, \leftsquigarrow, \|, \#\}$ that assigns a behavioral property, strict order, inverse order, parallel, or exclusive, between each pair of nodes within the business process model.

If two tasks a, b appear in strict order, $bhp(a, b) = \rightsquigarrow$, then task a always executes before task b. Similarly, if two tasks are concurrent then they can be executed in any order. Exclusiveness means that at most one of the two tasks can execute within a process instance. The behavioral profile of the BP shown in Fig. 1.2 includes several behavioral properties, such as: $bhp(U, V) = \#, bhp(W, X) = \rightsquigarrow, bhp(X, W) = \leftsquigarrow, bhp(Y, Z) = \|, bhp(U, X) = \rightsquigarrow, bhp(Y, V) = \leftsquigarrow$, etc.

The definition of behavioral profiles is not sufficient to achieve our goal of discovering fine-grained linkage patterns among web services, in particular assigning *weights* to the discovered linkage patterns. Therefore, we extend it by incorporating the shortest distance between each pair of tasks in addition to their behavioral property. The distance between a pair of tasks is calculated by counting the number of edges between them in the considered BPM. A preliminary definition of the extended behavioral profile is given in Definition 1.2. A comprehensive definition of the "Extended Behavioral Profile" is introduced in Definition 1.3.

Definition 1.2 *(Extended Behavioral Profile)* Let N be a set of nodes within a business process model. The *extended behavioral profile* of a business process model is a function $bhp': N \times N \rightarrow \{\rightsquigarrow, \leftsquigarrow, \|, \#\} \times \mathbb{N}$ that assigns a behavioral property, strict order, inverse order, parallel, or exclusive, and a *distance*, between each pair of nodes within the business process model.

For instance, the extended behavioral profile of the BP in Fig. 1.2 includes several pairs, such as: $bhp'(U, V) = (\#, 0), bhp'(W, X) = (\rightsquigarrow, 1), bhp'(X, W) = (\leftsquigarrow, 1), bhp'(Y, Z) = (\|, 0), bhp'(U, X) = (\rightsquigarrow, 3), bhp'(Y, V) = (\leftsquigarrow, 5)$, etc. To derive useful behavioral properties between tasks of a BP, we remove cyclic edges, because their existence makes all tasks inside each BP concurrent.

Transforming BPMs into executable processes is achieved through a *configuration* step, where process engineers assign operations of web services to *service* tasks in the considered BPM. Configuring a BP can be expressed as a function that takes a task of a BP and assigns an operation to that task if it is a *service* task. The business process shown in Fig. 1.2 can be configured as follows: $conf(U) =$ BookFlightTicket, $conf(V) =$ BookTrainTicket, $conf(W) =$ HotelReservation, $conf(X) =$ CarRental, $conf(Y) =$ FindRestaurants, and $conf(Z) =$ FindSights. Where values to the right of the $conf$ function are operations of web services.

1.4 Annotating Web Services Using Business Process Knowledge

In this section, we describe our approach to generate annotations and derive contexts for web services based on the configurations of their consuming business processes. From each finalized (i.e., configured) BPM, we generate a *task-to-web service assignment* list, based on which we generate annotations for web services from the tasks of their consuming business processes. Task labels and documentation are extracted and their assigned web services are annotated with this extracted information. These labels and documentations are created by service consumers that represent the application level, i.e., business people. Additionally, the title of the created BPM is used to derive the context in which these web services are typically used. This information is then used to enable context-aware service selection for similar cases in the future.

Sharing information about business processes and web services used to execute them is not usually desired by service consumers, because this information might be considered one aspect of their competitive advantage. Nevertheless, our approach can be valuable in several scenarios and application domains, in particular, where high potentials for collaboration are expected and low potentials for competition among service consumers exist, such as government services, education and research, online modeling platforms, and quality-based service brokers.

Figure 1.3 shows a process model using BPMN for establishing a UK limited company. The first six activities of the process are services of the UK Companies

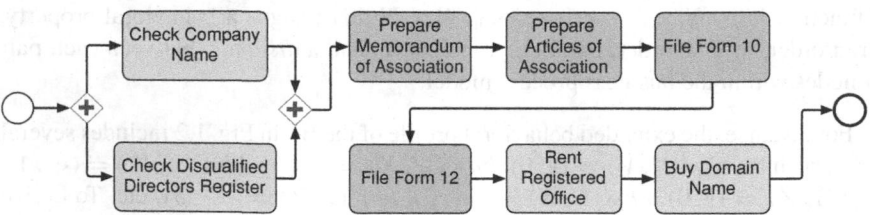

Fig. 1.3 Example process model of establishing a UK limited company

House. In the beginning, it has to be checked whether the desired company name is not already in use and the directors are not disqualified from leading a company. For the remaining steps, electronic forms are provided in the Portable Document Format (PDF). The last two activities in the model are web services offered by private service providers, e.g., "Buy domain name" can be executed using the whois web service (http://www.webservicex.net/whois.asmx).

Using our approach, a process engineer can configure their BPM to establish a company in UK using the existing annotations for web services and their operations used in such a model. These annotations are generated from the websites of their providers and through invocation analysis. Although they might be not rich enough, such annotation can be helpful in some cases. Generating additional annotations for such web services and operations from this BPM enrich their descriptions. In this particular use case, all used operations are associated with the context "establish a company in UK". Additionally, each operation is annotated with the label and documentation of each task that uses it. For instance, the whois web service is annotated with "buy domain name".

According to the German Federal Ministry of Economics and Technology, establishing a company in Germany incorporates 9 major steps.[2] For instance, check the company name, notarize the articles of association and foundation agreement, notify the Office of Business and Standards, register at the Trade Office (involves check manager's qualifications), etc. Some of these steps are similar to the ones involved in establishing a limited company in UK, such as "check the company name", "check qualified managers", "rent office", "buy domain name". For instance, whois web service (http://www.webservicex.net/whois.asmx), that is used to execute the "buy domain name" task in the case of UK company, can be suggested to execute its counterpart task in the German case.

Saving this model adds additional information to the service registry about the considered web services, such as the new labels and the current context. This additional information helps the service registry provide better results in future similar business processes, such as "Establishing a company in France".

1.5 Fine-Grained Linkage Patterns Among Web Services

Relations among web services are important to understand the functionalities of these web services and the interaction among them. We discover preliminary relations among web services from their WSDL files, and derive additional fine-grained ones in the form of linkage patterns using their consuming BPs (Fig. 1.1). Each of these linkage patterns has one of these types: *Predecessors, successors, similar, complementary*, and *related*. Moreover, we assign weights to such relations based on the usage of their web services in the corresponding BP. This weight is used to rank web services that have the same linkage pattern, e.g., rank web services that have

---

[2] http://www.existenzgruender.de/englisch/

the *predecessor* relation with a particular web service. In this section, we describe the types and weights of linkage patterns that we find based on business process knowledge.

1.5.1 Types of Linkage Patterns

Traditional approaches to discover relations among operations of web services usually give binary decisions whether two web services are related or not, without providing control flow dependency, e.g., parallel, sequence, etc. Such relations are not sufficient given the increasing number and complexity of web services and business processes. In our approach—based on extended behavioral profiles—we are able to identify five types of relations among operations of web services based on their usage in BPMs. Consider two tasks, A and B, that are configured with OP_1 and OP_2, respectively. Based on their behavioral properties, the following five types of linkage patterns can be identified:

1. **Predecessor**: An operation OP_1 is a predecessor of another operation OP_2 if it appears *before* OP_2 in the configurations of BPMs where both operations have been used, i.e., $bhp(A, B) = \leadsto$.
2. **Successor**: An operation OP_1 is a successor of another operation OP_2 if it appears *after* OP_2 in the configurations of BPMs where both operations have been used, i.e., $bhp(A, B) = \reverseleadsto$.
3. **Similar**: An operation OP_1 is similar to another operation OP_2 if it appears within exclusive relations with OP_2 in the configurations of BPMs where both operations have been used (i.e., $bhp(A, B) = \#$) and there is a high semantic similarity between the terms used to label both tasks and their executing operations, e.g., *"rent a bike"* and *"buy a bike"*.
4. **Complementary**: An operation OP_1 is complementary to another operation OP_2 if it appears within exclusive relations with OP_2 in the configurations of BPMs where both operations have been used (i.e., $bhp(A, B) = \#$) but there is *no high* semantic similarity between the terms used to label both tasks and their executing operations, e.g., *accept* and *reject*.
5. **Related**: An operation OP_1 is related to another operation OP_2 if it appears *concurrently* to OP_2 in the configurations of BPMs where both operations have been used, i.e., $bhp(A, B) = \|$. For instance, *"validate address"* and *"validate email address"*.

1.5.2 Weights of Linkage Patterns

Existing approaches of discovering relations among web services give binary decisions on whether there is a relation between two web services or not. Such decisions are based on the co-occurrence of both services in service compositions, for instance. In our approach, we are able to discover fine-grained relations and assign a weight (between 0 and 1) to each relation to reflect its strength.

The first type of information that we use to calculate the weight of a relation between two web services is the distance between their consuming tasks in the corresponding BP. This information is provided in the extended behavioral profile of the BP. The distance between any two tasks in a BP is greater than 0 if their behavioral property is either strict order or inverse order. Therefore, the distance is used to assign a weight to predecessor and successor linkage patterns only. The weight, ω, of a linkage pattern, r, between two operations where the distance between their consuming tasks is d, and the maximum distance between any pair of tasks in their BP is len, is given by Eq. 1.1.

$$\omega(r) = \frac{len - d}{len} \tag{1.1}$$

Exclusive tasks can be similar (doing the same functionality) or complementary to each other (doing different functionalities). For instance, "Get weather by city" and "Get weather by post code" are *similar* tasks. Whereas, "Send acceptance" and "Send rejection" are *complementary*. To determine the linkage pattern between two web services whose consuming tasks are exclusive to each other, we investigate the semantics of terms appearing in their names and their consuming tasks. We use WordNet [13] to find `synsets` for these terms and calculate the average distance, (syn_dist), among their *nearest common ancestors (NCA)* in WordNet [26]. The special value (-1) means that there is no similarity between both terms, i.e., they do not have a common ancestor in WordNet, e.g., acceptance and rejection. If the average distance, (syn_dist), is between 0 and a predefined threshold, then the linkage pattern between both services is *similar* and its weight is calculated using the same equation above, where len is replaced by our threshold value, and d is replaced by syn_dist. For instance, syn_dist ("bookFlightTicket", "BookTrainTicket") = 16. Based on our experiments, we set the value of the maximum WordNet distance threshold to 20. Given this value, the aforementioned web services are *similar* and the weight of their linkage pattern is 0.2. Linkage patterns are classified as *complementary* if the semantic similarity is low, i.e., syn_dist is higher than the predefined threshold. Linkage patterns *complementary* and *related* are assigned the weight 1.

Whenever a new BPM is created by a service consumer, we discover all possible linkage patterns from that BPM and store them in the database of the service registry. Frequencies and weights of linkage patterns are used to derive scores for these patterns to rank recommended web services within each type of recommendation. The score of each linkage pattern is the aggregation of weights of all instances of this pattern that are typically discovered from multiple BPMs. In practice, web services are used by different service consumers in multiple business processes with different arrangements. These differences result in incompatible relations among web services, i.e., ws_1 is a predecessor for ws_2 in one business process, but ws_1 is similar to ws_2 in another business process. To handle such situations, we merge all behavioral profiles of business process in a single global profile. Additionally, we use gained knowledge in this global profile to predict relations among web services that are not used together in the same business process, yet (Sect. 1.6.).

1.5.3 Example: Linkage Patterns of Purchase Order Processing

In this section, we apply our approach to a real-world purchase order processing scenario from the SAP Reference Model, whose BP is shown in Fig. 1.4. When this process is configured, we assume that a single operation of a web service is assigned to each task in this model. For instance, operation A is assigned to task "process purchase requisition order". Following the traditional approaches of discovering relations among web services, we get the result that there is a relation between A and B. No further information about the type and strength of this relation is provided. In our approach, we get the extended behavioral profile that encapsulates business process knowledge for these operations as shown previously. This extended behavioral profile is shown in Table 1.1.

From Table 1.1, we notice that operations A and E are exclusive and also are the operations A and B. We refine this relation further as either *similar* or *complementary*. To achieve this refinement, we analyze the semantics of the terms in the labels of their corresponding tasks. Based on our experiments, we set our threshold maximum WordNet distance to 20 to control the similarity search in WordNet. We repeat this step for each pair of operations that are exclusive to each other. With result obtained, we establish the linkage patterns among the operations as shown in Table 1.2. Based on the semantic analysis, the *exclusive* relation between operations A, E—obtained from the profile—is refined to a complementary linkage pattern. On the other hand, the exclusive relation between A, B is identified as similar, because of the high similarity between terms appearing in the labels of their counterpart tasks.

Using these linkage patterns, users who search for a particular service, e.g., A, get useful lists of recommendations. These recommendations represent inter-links among web services that help service consumers explore web service comfortably.

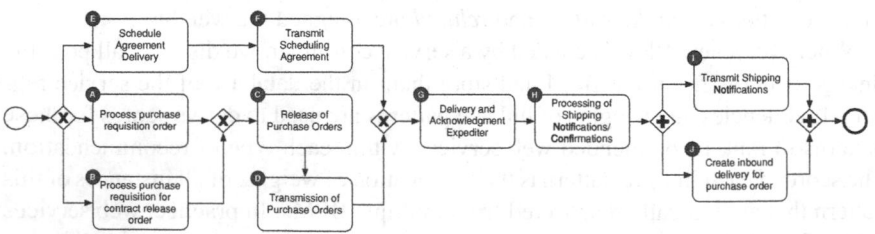

Fig. 1.4 A business process for "purchase order processing" from *SAP* reference model represented in BPMN 1.0

Table 1.1 Extended behavioral profile for business process in Fig. 1.4

	A	B	C	D	E	F	G	H	I	J
A	(‖, 0)	(#, 0)	(⇝, 2)	(⇝, 3)	(#, 0)	(#, 0)	(⇝, 5)	(⇝, 6)	(⇝, 8)	(⇝, 8)
B	(#, 0)	(‖, 0)	(⇝, 2)	(⇝, 3)	(#, 0)	(#, 0)	(⇝, 5)	(⇝, 6)	(⇝, 8)	(⇝, 8)
C	(⇝, 2)	(⇝, 2)	(‖, 0)	(⇝, 1)	(#, 0)	(#, 0)	(⇝, 3)	(⇝, 4)	(⇝, 6)	(⇝, 6)
D	(⇝, 3)	(⇝, 3)	(⇝, 1)	(‖, 0)	(#, 0)	(#, 0)	(⇝, 2)	(⇝, 3)	(⇝, 5)	(⇝, 5)
E	(#, 0)	(#, 0)	(#, 0)	(#, 0)	(‖, 0)	(⇝, 1)	(⇝, 3)	(⇝, 4)	(⇝, 6)	(⇝, 6)
F	(#, 0)	(#, 0)	(#, 0)	(#, 0)	(⇝, 1)	(‖, 0)	(⇝, 2)	(⇝, 3)	(⇝, 5)	(⇝, 5)
G	(⇝, 5)	(⇝, 5)	(⇝, 3)	(⇝, 2)	(⇝, 3)	(⇝, 2)	(‖, 0)	(⇝, 1)	(⇝, 3)	(⇝, 3)
H	(⇝, 5)	(⇝, 5)	(⇝, 3)	(⇝, 2)	(⇝, 4)	(⇝, 3)	(⇝, 1)	(‖, 0)	(⇝, 2)	(⇝, 2)
I	(⇝, 8)	(⇝, 8)	(⇝, 6)	(⇝, 5)	(⇝, 6)	(⇝, 5)	(⇝, 3)	(⇝, 2)	(‖, 0)	(‖, 0)
J	(⇝, 8)	(⇝, 8)	(⇝, 6)	(⇝, 5)	(⇝, 6)	(⇝, 5)	(⇝, 3)	(⇝, 2)	(‖, 0)	(‖, 0)

Table 1.2 Linkage patterns for business process in Fig. 1.4. *P* Predecessor, *S* Successor, *M* Similar, *C* Complementary, *R* Related

	A	B	C	D	E	F	G	H	I	J
A	–	(M, 0.300)	(S, 0.875)	(S, 0.750)	(C, 1.000)	(C, 1.000)	(S, 0.500)	(S, 0.375)	(S, 0.125)	(S, 0.125)
B	(M, 0.300)	–	(S, 0.875)	(S, 0.750)	(C, 1.000)	(C, 1.000)	(S, 0.500)	(S, 0.375)	(S, 0.125)	(S, 0.125)
C	(P, 0.875)	(P, 0.875)	–	(S, 1.000)	(C, 1.000)	(C, 1.000)	(S, 0.750)	(S, 0.625)	(S, 0.375)	(S, 0.375)
D	(P, 0.750)	(P, 0.750)	(P, 1.000)	–	(C, 1.000)	(C, 1.000)	(S, 0.875)	(S, 0.750)	(S, 0.500)	(S, 0.500)
E	(C, 1.000)	(C, 1.000)	(C, 1.000)	(C, 1.000)	–	(S, 1.000)	(S, 0.750)	(S, 0.625)	(S, 0.375)	(S, 0.375)
F	(C, 1.000)	(C, 1.000)	(C, 1.000)	(C, 1.000)	(P, 1.000)	–	(S, 0.875)	(S, 0.750)	(S, 0.500)	(S, 0.500)
G	(P, 0.500)	(P, 0.500)	(P, 0.750)	(P, 0.875)	(P, 0.750)	(P, 0.875)	–	(S, 1.000)	(S, 0.750)	(S, 0.750)
H	(P, 0.500)	(P, 0.500)	(P, 0.750)	(P, 0.875)	(P, 0.625)	(P, 0.750)	(P, 1.000)	–	(S, 0.875)	(S, 0.875)
I	(P, 0.125)	(P, 0.125)	(P, 0.375)	(P, 0.500)	(P, 0.375)	(P, 0.500)	(P, 0.750)	(P, 0.875)	–	(R, 1.000)
J	(P, 0.125)	(P, 0.125)	(P, 0.375)	(P, 0.500)	(P, 0.375)	(P, 0.500)	(P, 0.750)	(P, 0.875)	(R, 1.000)	–

1.6 Global Behavioral Profiles

Several approaches have been proposed to find relations among web services [5, 9, 12, 15], whose main goal is finding whether two web services are related or not, without further refinement of the suggested relations. Additionally, these approaches are not able to find *indirect* relations among web services, because they use knowledge about web services that are used together only. Relations between web services that are not used together remain missing.

Missing relations between web services do not necessarily indicate their independence. Several reasons can lead to such missing relations, such as lack of knowledge about web services and their functionalities, multiple web services with equivalent functionalities, and non-functional requirements (e.g., price, quality). We consider such missing relations as *hidden* ones and aim at revealing (part of) them. One approach of revealing such hidden relations is using knowledge concealed in the configurations of business processes that use these web services. Each configuration is considered an identifier for its tasks and its web services. Multiple tasks that have different labels are similar if they are bound with the same web service. Similarly, web services that have different names are considered similar if they are bound with tasks that share the same label.

In Sect. 1.5, we introduced an approach to discover rich relations among web services in the form of linkage patterns using business process knowledge that is contained in a single business process. As different consumers use web services in multiple business processes with different relations among them, multiple configurations over the same set of web services appear. These configurations are *local* to each individual process. In this section, we develop an approach to derive a *global* behavioral profile over the entire set of web services in a service registry and reveal *hidden* relations among web services within this global profile.

To validate our approach, we use a set of business processes from the SAP reference model [8]. These models represent possibilities to configure SAP R/3 ERP systems. Thus, it is analogous to business process configurations over a service landscape.

1.6.1 Extending Behavioral Profiles

Revealing hidden relations among web services requires a global behavioral profile, where all services in the considered registry are involved. A global profile is the result of *merging* all individual behavioral profiles of business processes. Merging two relations from two profiles results in *unknown* relations between web services that do not appear together in one business process. Moreover, this merging step might result in *contradicting* relations, e.g., merging $a \#_x b$ and $a \leadsto_y b$. Therefore, the four basic behavioral relations of the original behavioral profile in Definition 1.1 are not sufficient. We *extend* the four basic relations to capture such situations when merging individual profiles by introducing two additional relations: Unknown (?) and contradicts (✳). These two relations do not appear on the level of individual raw profiles. They appear only when profiles are merged as we show in Sect. 1.6.2. We record the *distance* between tasks bound to web services in the process configuration similar to Definition 1.2. This distance is used in the derived linkage patterns among web services to rank services during service discovery. We obtain this distance by counting the edges on the shortest path between the nodes representing the tasks in the process graph of each BP. In this section, we present the formal notion of *extended* behavioral profiles. Additionally, we introduce a business process with its extended behavioral profile that is used as a running example in the rest of this section.

1.6.1.1 Formal Model

The original definition of behavioral profiles is concerned with behavioral relations among tasks within a business process. However, in our approach, we are interested in discovering relations among web services used in such business processes. Therefore, we extend the notion of behavioral profiles and generalize the one introduced in Definition 1.2 to capture this requirement.

Definition 1.3 *(Extended Behavioral Profile)*[3] Let $\mathcal{W}$ be the set of web services within a service registry. The *extended behavioral profile* of web services in $\mathcal{W}$ is a function $xbhp : \mathcal{W} \times \mathcal{W} \to \mathcal{P}(\{\rightsquigarrow, \leftsquigarrow, \|, \#, ?, ✳\} \times \mathbb{N})$ that assigns a set of pairs of a behavioral property (strict order, inverse order, parallel, exclusive, unknown, or contradicts) and a distance between each pair of web services within the service registry.

Comparing Definitions 1.2 and 1.3 of the extended behavioral profile with Definition 1.1, we notice that the behavioral relations are leveraged from the level of tasks within individual process models (configurations) to the level of web services within the service registry. Moreover, the extended profile records the distance between web services consumed within an individual profile. This distance is greater than zero if the behavioral relation is either $\rightsquigarrow$ or $\leftsquigarrow$ and zero otherwise. Finally, Definition 1.3 allows multiple behavioral properties to exist between two web services in the global behavioral profile where two additional behavioral relations (✳&?) are introduced. An individual behavioral profile (Definition 1.1) of a process can be turned into an extended profile by adding all web services in the service registry to the services consumed by that process where their behavioral relations are set to unknown. For simplicity, we ignore these unknown relations for input behavioral profiles.

Definition 1.4 *(Projections over an Extended Behavioral Profile)* Let $\mathcal{W}$ be the set of web services within a service registry and let x be an extended behavioral profile. The function $rel_x : \mathcal{W} \times \mathcal{W} \to \{\rightsquigarrow, \leftsquigarrow, \|, \#, ?, ✳\}$ projects the behavioral relation between two web services a and b in the registry with respect to profile x. Similarly

---

[3] This is a comprehensive definition for Definition 1.2

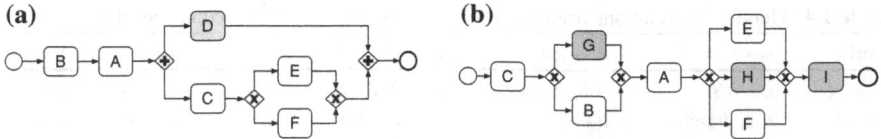

Fig. 1.5 Two anonymized business processes from SAP reference model

Table 1.3 The *extended* behavioral profile of BP_1 shown in Fig. 1.5a

	A	B	C	D	E	F
A	($\parallel$, 0)	($\leftarrow$, 1)	($\rightsquigarrow$, 2)	($\rightsquigarrow$, 2)	($\rightsquigarrow$, 4)	($\rightsquigarrow$, 4)
B	($\rightsquigarrow$, 1)	($\parallel$, 0)	($\rightsquigarrow$, 3)	($\rightsquigarrow$, 3)	($\rightsquigarrow$, 5)	($\rightsquigarrow$, 5)
C	($\leftarrow$, 2)	($\leftarrow$, 3)	($\parallel$, 0)	($\parallel$, 0)	($\rightsquigarrow$, 2)	($\rightsquigarrow$, 2)
D	($\leftarrow$, 2)	($\leftarrow$, 3)	($\parallel$, 0)	($\parallel$, 0)	($\parallel$, 0)	($\parallel$, 0)
E	($\leftarrow$, 4)	($\leftarrow$, 5)	($\leftarrow$, 2)	($\parallel$, 0)	($\parallel$, 0)	(#, 0)
F	($\leftarrow$, 4)	($\leftarrow$, 5)	($\leftarrow$, 2)	($\parallel$, 0)	(#, 0)	($\parallel$, 0)

$dist_x : \mathcal{W} \times \mathcal{W} \rightarrow \mathbb{N}$ projects the distance between the two services with profile x. For simplicity, we express $rel_x(a, b) = \{*\}$ as $a *_x b$ where $* \in \{\rightsquigarrow, \leftarrow, \parallel, \#, ?, \circledast\}$.

1.6.1.2 Running Example of Global Profiles

In Fig. 1.5, we introduce two anonymized business processes from the SAP reference model that are used as a running example throughout this section. The common anonymized labels between both business processes indicate using the same service in their configuration. BP_1 has 6 tasks where only task D is not a common task with BP_2. On the other hand, BP_2 has 8 tasks among which 3 tasks are not common with BP_1, namely G, H, and I.

The extended behavioral profile of BP_1 is shown in Table 1.3, and that of BP_2 can be generated similarly, we omit it. It is worth mentioning that both BPs are configured such that each task is bound with a web service to execute it. According to Table 1.3, $xbhp_{BP_1}(E, F) = \{(\#, 0)\}$ and $xbhp_{BP_1}(A, D) = \{(\rightsquigarrow, 2)\}$. Relations that are not shown in this profile are implicitly *unknown*, e.g., $xbhp_{BP_1}(A, G) = \{(?, 0)\}$.

1.6.2 Deriving Global Behavioral Profiles

Knowledge about relations among web services is usually scattered in disparate profiles of business processes. Collecting this knowledge into a single profile is essential to reveal hidden relations among these web services. We call the result of this step a *global* behavioral profile. The global profile might include unknown or contradicting relations among some pairs of web services. We inspect the gained knowledge in the

Table 1.4 Merging the relations from two profiles x and y into an intermediate profile t

Profile	$a \rightsquigarrow_x b$	$a \leftsquigarrow_x b$	$a \parallel_x b$	$a \#_x b$	$a ?_x b$	$a ⨳_x b$
$a \rightsquigarrow_y b$	$a \rightsquigarrow_t b$	$a \parallel_t b\ a⨳_t b$	$a \parallel_t b\ a⨳_t b$	$a⨳_t b$	$a \rightsquigarrow_t b$	$a⨳_t b$
$a \leftsquigarrow_y b$	$a \parallel_t b\ a⨳_t b$	$a \leftsquigarrow_t b$	$a \parallel_t b\ a⨳_t b$	$a⨳_t b$	$a \leftsquigarrow_t b$	$a⨳_t b$
$a \parallel_y b$	$a \parallel_t b\ a⨳_t b$	$a \parallel_t b\ a⨳_t b$	$a \parallel_t b$	$a⨳_t b$	$a \parallel_t b$	$a⨳_t b$
$a \#_y b$	$a⨳_t b$	$a⨳_t b$	$a⨳_t b$	$a \#_t b$	$a \#_t b$	$a⨳_t b$
$a ?_y b$	$a \rightsquigarrow_t b$	$a \leftsquigarrow_t b$	$a \parallel_t b$	$a \#_t b$	$a ?_t b$	$a⨳_t b$
$a ⨳_y b$	$a⨳_t b$	$a⨳_t b$	$a⨳_t b$	$a⨳_t b$	$a⨳_t b$	$a⨳_t b$

global profile to *predict* possible resolutions for its unknown relations. Both steps, i.e., deriving a global profile and predicting unknown relations are of incremental nature. That is, at the point that a new process configuration is available, this new profile is merged with the global profile, to obtain a new global profile, and the prediction of unknown relations is performed again.

Given a set of behavioral profiles, we want to derive a global profile that contains pairwise relations between all web services. We achieve this by merging all individual profiles iteratively in a pairwise manner. The result of each merging iteration is an intermediate profile that is merged with another profile. This step is repeated until all individual profiles are incorporated. Merging individual profiles might result in unknown or contradicting relations among web services. Unknown relations appear between web services that are not used together in the same business process, whereas contradicting relations appear due to *conflicting* relations in source profiles. For instance, the relations ($a \#_x b$) (i.e., a and b are exclusive in profile x) and ($a \rightsquigarrow_y b$) (i.e., a precedes b in profile y) might imply that one of these relations is wrong, i.e., used incorrectly by a process engineer. Exclusiveness usually means that web services do similar or complementary jobs [1]. Currently, we propagate such conflicts to the resulting intermediate profile by adding two relations ($a ⨳_z b$) and ($b ⨳_z a$) that represent a contradiction to the resulting intermediate profile z.

We merge two relations between web services a and b that appear in both input profiles x and y into the global profile t according the rules that are summarized in Table 1.4. These rules can be grouped as follows:

1. Merging ($a *_x b$) with ($a *_y b$) gives ($a *_t b$), where $*$ is the same type of relation.
2. Merging ($a \leftsquigarrow_x b$) with ($a \rightsquigarrow_y b$) gives ($a \parallel_t b$) and ($a ⨳_t b$).
3. Merging ($a *_x b$) with ($a \bullet_y b$) gives ($a \parallel_t b$) and ($a ⨳_t b$), where $* \in \{\rightsquigarrow, \leftsquigarrow\}$ and $\bullet = \parallel$.
4. Merging ($a *_x b$) with ($a \#_y b$) gives ($a \#_t b$) if $* = \#$, and $a ⨳_t b$ otherwise.
5. Merging ($a ?_x b$) with ($a *_y b$) gives ($a *_t b$), where $*$ is a basic relation.
6. Merging ($a ⨳_x b$) with ($a *_y b$) gives $a ⨳_t b$.

Some merging rules are non-deterministic, i.e., produce multiple alternatives (Table 1.4). For instance, merging ($a \rightsquigarrow_x b$) and ($a \leftsquigarrow_y b$) gives two options: ($a \parallel_t b$) and ($a ⨳_t b$). Parallelism means that there is no dependency between a and b, i.e., they can be used in any order. On the other hand, a dependency between a and b means that either profile x or y is incorrect, where it includes a data anomaly, e.g., missing data [20]. In this case, we conclude that there is a contradiction ($a \divideontimes_t b$). To resolve such uncertainties, a human intervention is needed, which is out of scope of this work.

An important property of these rules is *associativity*, where the order of merging behavioral profiles of business processes does not affect the global behavioral profile. Consider three profiles of three business processes, where two tasks appear in all three profiles. We can identify the following cases:

1. Three *similar* relations in all three profiles: According to the first rule, the result will always be the same relation in the global profile.
2. Three *different* ordering relations: According to the second rule, at least one of the merging steps results in a parallel relation. This resulting parallel relation occurs either as an intermediate (first merging two different ordering relations) or a final one (first merging two similar ordering relations). As an intermediate relation is further merged with the remaining order relation. This last merging step results in a parallel relation in the global profile according to the third rule. This shows that such merging steps always result in a parallel relation in the global profile.
3. Parallel and ordering: Merging three relations that include parallel and ordering relations results in a parallel relation in the global profile according to the third rule.
4. Exclusive and others: Merging three relations that include exclusive and ordering or parallel relations results in a contradiction relation in the global profile according to the fourth rule.
5. Unknown and others: Unknown relations do not affect the result of such merging steps according to fifth rule.
6. Contradicts and others: Contradicts relations always result in a contraction relation in the global profile according to the sixth rule.

The second component in the extended behavioral profile (besides the relation's type) is *distance* between services. This distance between two services in an intermediate profile is calculated as the shortest distance in the corresponding profiles unless one of both distances is zero, i.e., # or ∥. In that case, we use the non-zero distance from both input relations.

1.6.2.1 Example Revisited

Assuming that the two processes from Fig. 1.5 are the only individual profiles in our knowledge base. By applying our merging rules shown in Table 1.4, we get the global profile shown in Table 1.5. This global profile has 9 web services that represent the union of all services in its source profiles, i.e., BP_1 and BP_2. For instance, merging relations ($\leftarrow\!\!\sim$, 1) and ($\leftarrow\!\!\sim$, 2) between web services A and B from BP_1 and BP_2, receptively, gives the relation ($\leftarrow\!\!\sim$, 1) in the global profile. The distance of the relation in the global profile is the minimum distance from input relations. Some merging

Table 1.5 Merging profiles of BP_1 and BP_2 (Fig. 1.5a,b) in one global profile

	A	B	C	D	E	F	G	H	I
A	(‖, 0)	(⇜, 1)	(‖, 0) (⊛, 0)	(⇝, 2)	(⇝, 2)	(⇝, 2)	(⇜, 2)	(⇝, 2)	(⇝, 8)
B	(⇝, 1)	(‖, 0)	(‖, 0) (⊛, 0)	(⇝, 3)	(⇝, 4)	(⇝, 4)	(#, 0)	(⇝, 4)	(⇝, 10)
C	(‖, 0) (⊛, 0)	(‖, 0) (⊛, 0)	(‖, 0)	(‖, 0)	(⇝, 2)	(⇝, 2)	(⇝, 2)	(⇝, 8)	(⇝, 14)
D	(⇜, 2)	(⇜, 3)	(‖, 0)	(‖, 0)	(‖, 0)	(‖, 0)	**(?, 0)**	**(?, 0)**	**(?, 0)**
E	(⇜, 2)	(⇜, 4)	(⇜, 2)	(‖, 0)	(‖, 0)	(#, 0)	(⇜, 4)	(#, 0)	(⇝, 2)
F	(⇜, 2)	(⇜, 4)	(⇜, 2)	(‖, 0)	(#, 0)	(‖, 0)	(⇜, 4)	(#, 0)	(⇝, 2)
G	(⇝, 2)	(#, 0)	(⇜, 2)	**(?, 0)**	(⇝, 4)	(⇝, 4)	(‖, 0)	(⇝, 4)	(⇝, 10)
H	(⇜, 2)	(⇜, 4)	(⇜, 8)	**(?, 0)**	(#, 0)	(#, 0)	(⇜, 4)	(‖, 0)	(⇝, 2)
I	(⇜, 8)	(⇜, 10)	(⇜, 14)	**(?, 0)**	(⇜, 2)	(⇜, 2)	(⇜, 10)	(⇜, 2)	(‖, 0)

rules produce multiple alternatives. For instance, A and C has the relation $(⇝, 2)$ and $(⇜, 4)$ in BP_1 and BP_2, respectively. Merging both relations gives two alternatives in the global profile between A and C: $(‖, 0)$ and $(⊛, 0)$. The remaining relations can be derived in the same way. Merging extended behavioral profiles of BPs that do *not* have the same exact set of web services results in unknown relations between web services that do not appear in the same BP. For instance, relations between D from one side and G, H, and I on the other side in the global profile. In the sequel, we aim at using the knowledge gained from merging both profiles to reveal such unknown relations.

1.6.3 Predicting Unknown Relations (a ? b)

Merging two profiles that do not have the same set of web services results in a global profile with unknown relations among web services that do not appear in both source profiles. In this section, we describe our approach to reveal such *unknown* relations by predicting potential resolutions for them.

We predict potential resolutions for the unknown relation between web services a and b in the global profile g with the help of a common service between them, e.g., c. Having more than one common service is resolved by intersecting all predicted relations from each common service according to Alg. 1. Our goal is to resolve the relation $(a\ ?_g\ b)$ into $(a\ ⇜_g\ b)$, $(a\ ⇝_g\ b)$, $(a\ ‖_g\ b)$, or $(a\ \#_g\ b)$ by investigating the relations between a and c on the one hand and between b and c on the other hand. We select a common service c such that we can derive useful information from its relations with the considered services. For instance, selecting c such that $(a\ ⊛_g\ c)$ is not of value. Therefore, the common service c has to be in one of the basic four relations with both a and b. Furthermore, the predicted relation has to be consistent

Table 1.6 Resolving the unknown relation $a \ ?_g \ b$ via a common service c

Relation	$a \leadsto c$	$a \leftsquigarrow c$	$a \parallel c$	$a \# c$
$b \leadsto c$	$a \leadsto b$ $a \leftsquigarrow b$ $a \parallel b$ $a \# b$	$a \leftsquigarrow b$	$a \parallel b$ $a \leftsquigarrow b$	$a \# b$ $a \leftsquigarrow b$
$b \leftsquigarrow c$	$a \leadsto b$	$a \leftsquigarrow b$ $a \leadsto b$ $a \parallel b$ $a \# b$	$a \parallel b$ $a \leadsto b$	$a \# b$ $a \leadsto b$
$b \parallel c$	$a \parallel b$ $a \leadsto b$	$a \parallel b$ $a \leftsquigarrow b$	$a \parallel b$ $a \leadsto b$ $a \leftsquigarrow b$	$a \parallel b$ $a \# b$
$b \# c$	$a \# b$ $a \leadsto b$	$a \# b$ $a \leftsquigarrow b$	$a \parallel b$ $a \# b$	$a \# b$ $a \leadsto b$ $a \leftsquigarrow b$

with existing relations in the global profile. Finding a useful resolution for unknown relations depends on the used knowledge, therefore it is not always possible to predict such a resolution. In such cases, the unknown relation between a and b ($a \ ?_g \ b$) in the global profile g remains and a human expert is informed about the situation to find a resolution manually if necessary.

We predict potential resolutions for each unknown relation between web services a and b in the global profile g—i.e., ($a \ ?_g \ b$)—using a common service, c, according to the set of rules that is summarized in Table 1.6. For instance, resolving ($a *_g c$) and ($b *_g c$) gives ($a \leadsto_g b$), ($a \leftsquigarrow_g b$), ($a \parallel_g b$), and ($a \#_g b$), where $* = \leadsto$ or $* = \leftsquigarrow$. Each of these predicted relations still preserves the existing relations ($a \leadsto c$) and ($b \leadsto c$) or ($a \leftsquigarrow c$) and ($b \leftsquigarrow c$). Resolving ($a \leadsto_g c$) and ($b \leadsto_g c$) gives ($a \leftsquigarrow_g b$). Any other relation, e.g., ($a \leadsto b$), does not preserve the existing relation between a, b on the one hand and c on the other hand. For instance, ($a \leadsto b$) means that b executes *before* a, that contradicts ($a \leftsquigarrow c$). Similarly, we cannot deduce that ($a \# b$) as it contradicts ($b \leadsto c$), since that implies either ($c \leftsquigarrow b$) or ($c \# b$), which is not the case.

Distances of the predicted $\leadsto$ and $\leftsquigarrow$ relations in the global profile are calculated according to the functions shown in Table 1.7. Distances are used to rank relevant web services during service discovery [1]. Additionally, we use them to prune possible resolutions. For some cases, the new distance is the absolute value of the difference of two distance. As an example, consider the case where we have ($a \leadsto c$) and ($b \leadsto c$). According to Table 1.6, all four basic relations are valid resolutions. For the predicted ($a \parallel b$) and ($a \# b$) we set distance to zero. However, for the two remaining cases, i.e. ($a \leadsto b$) and ($a \leftsquigarrow b$), the distance is the absolute value of the difference in input distances. When we have no information to calculate the distance, we set it to an artificial value infinity, e.g., the case of ($a \parallel c$) and ($b \parallel c$). For the

Table 1.7 Distances of the predicted relation $a\,?\,b$ via a common service c

Relation	$a \rightsquigarrow c$	$a \leftsquigarrow c$	$a \parallel c$	$a \# c$
$b \rightsquigarrow c$	$|diff()|$	$sum()$	$dist(b,c)$	$dist(b,c)$
$b \leftsquigarrow c$	$sum()$	$|diff()|$	$dist(b,c)$	$dist(b,c)$
$b \parallel c$	$dist(a,c)$	$dist(a,c)$	∞	N/A
$b \# c$	$dist(a,c)$	$dist(a,c)$	N/A	∞

cases where there is no order in the predicted relation between a and b, we express this using N/A in the table.

According to our rules of resolution shown in Table 1.6, possible resolutions to an unknown relation $a\,?\,b$ can include both $a \rightsquigarrow b$ and $a \leftsquigarrow b$. We use the distance information to prune one or both of these resolutions according to the following rules. Consider two relations $(a *_x b)$ and $(b \bullet_y c)$ with distances d_x and d_y, respectively, where $*$ and $\bullet$ are either $\rightsquigarrow$ or $\leftsquigarrow$, and Δd is defined as $d_x - d_y$, we identify three cases:

1. $\Delta d = 0$: The unknown relation $(a\,?\,b)$ cannot be predicted to $(a \rightsquigarrow b)$ or $(a \leftsquigarrow b)$.
2. $\Delta d > 0$: The unknown relation $(a\,?\,b)$ can be predicted to $(a \rightsquigarrow b)$, but not to $(a \leftsquigarrow b)$.
3. $\Delta d < 0$: The unknown relation $(a\,?\,b)$ can be predicted to $(a \leftsquigarrow b)$, but not to $(a \rightsquigarrow b)$.

Table 1.6 shows possible resolutions of $a\,?\,b$ using one common service c. However, a and b might have a set of common services, which includes services that have useful behavioral relations ($\rightsquigarrow$, $\leftsquigarrow$, $\parallel$, or $\#$) with both a and b. In Algorithm 1, we show the steps we follow to achieve this resolution. We use each element in this set to predict the unknown relation between a, b according to the rules in Table 1.6 (Line 7). After that, we do an intersection among all possible resolutions deduced from each element in that set (Line 11). The resulting relations from this intersection are then used as potential resolutions to that unknown relation between a and b. If this intersection gives an empty set (e.g., due to contradictions), we are unable to predict resolutions for $a\,?\,b$ (Lines 12–13). These steps are repeated for all unknown relations in the global profile until no further resolutions are found.

1.6.3.1 Example Revisited

In Table 1.5, we show the global profile that we get by merging the extended global profiles of BP_1 (Fig. 1.5a) and BP_2 (Fig. 1.5b). That global profile has three unknown relations between service D on the one hand and services G, H, and I on the other hand, because these services are not used in the same BP. However, BP_1 and BP_2 have other common web services, e.g., A, B and C. We use such common services to predict resolutions for (part of) these three unknown relations.

Algorithm 1: Predicting unknown relations in the global profile

---

Require: g the global profile
Ensure: g' the global profile with some unknown relations revealed
1: $pred \leftarrow \emptyset$
2: **for all** $a?b \in g$ **do**
3:    $CT \leftarrow getCommonTasks(a, b)$
4:    **for all** $c \in CT$ **do**
5:       $ac \leftarrow rel_g(a, c)$
6:       $bc \leftarrow rel_g(b, c)$
7:       $tmp \leftarrow predictRelaton(ac, bc)$ {According to Tables 1.6 and 1.7}
8:       **if** $pred = \emptyset$ **then**
9:          $pred \leftarrow tmp$
10:      **else**
11:         $pred \leftarrow intersect(pred, temp)$
12:         **if** $pred = \emptyset$ **then**
13:            break
14:         **end if**
15:      **end if**
16:   **end for**
17:   $g \leftarrow merge(g, pred)$ {According to Table 1.4}
18: **end for**
19: $g' \leftarrow g$
20: **return** g'

Table 1.8 Possible relations between services D & G via common services {A, B, C, E, F}

Common task	A	B	C	E	F
Relation with D	D ↤ A	D ↤ B	D ‖ C	D ‖ E	D ‖ F
Relation with G	G ↝ A	G # B	G ↤ C	G ↝ E	G ↝ F
Deduced relation	D ↤ G	D ↤ G	D ↝ G	D ↤ G	D ↤ G
		D # G	D ‖ G	D ‖ G	D ‖ G

To predict $(D \, ? \, G)$, we select the set of common tasks among them. In this example, this set is {A, B, C, E, F}. Because $(D \leftharpoondown A)$ and $(G \leadsto A)$, we deduce that $(D \leftharpoondown G)$ according to the transitivity rule. Similarly, we deduce all potential relations between D and G using their common services as shown in Table 1.8. The intersection of these alternatives is ϕ, i.e., there is no common relation among potential relations. Therefore, the relation between D and G in the global profile remains unknown.

We follow the same steps to predict the relation $(D \, ? \, H)$. The set of common tasks is the same. Intersecting all potential relations between D and H gives the new relation $(D \parallel H)$. Again, the same set of common tasks is used to reveal the $(D \, ? \, I)$. In this case, the intersection of all potential relations between these tasks gives two alternatives: $(D \parallel I)$ and $(D \leadsto I)$. The distance in the new strict order relation is the minimum distance between I and the common tasks. In this case, the distance is 2. The global profile after revealing potential hidden relations is shown in Table 1.9.

Table 1.9 Revealing hidden relations in the global profile of BP_1 and BP_2

	A	B	C	D	E	F	G	H	I
A	(‖, 0)	(←, 1)	(‖, 0) (✻, 0)	(⇝, 2)	(⇝, 2)	(⇝, 2)	(←, 2)	(⇝, 2)	(⇝, 8)
B	(⇝, 1)	(‖, 0)	(‖, 0) (✻, 0)	(⇝, 3)	(⇝, 4)	(⇝, 4)	(#, 0)	(⇝, 4)	(⇝, 10)
C	(‖, 0) (✻, 0)	(‖, 0) (✻, 0)	(‖, 0)	(‖, 0)	(⇝, 2)	(⇝, 2)	(⇝, 2)	(⇝, 8)	(⇝, 14)
D	(←, 2)	(←, 3)	(‖, 0)	(‖, 0)	(‖, 0)	(‖, 0)	**(?, 0)**	(‖, 0)	(‖, 0) (⇝, 2)
E	(←, 2)	(←, 4)	(←, 2)	(‖, 0)	(‖, 0)	(#, 0)	(←, 4)	(#, 0)	(⇝, 2)
F	(←, 2)	(←, 4)	(←, 2)	(‖, 0)	(#, 0)	(‖, 0)	(←, 4)	(#, 0)	(⇝, 2)
G	(⇝, 2)	(#, 0)	(←, 2)	**(?, 0)**	(⇝, 4)	(⇝, 4)	(‖, 0)	(⇝, 4)	(⇝, 10)
H	(←, 2)	(←, 4)	(←, 8)	(‖, 0)	(#, 0)	(#, 0)	(←, 4)	(‖, 0)	(⇝, 2)
I	(←, 8)	(←, 10)	(←, 14)	(‖, 0) (←, 2)	(←, 2)	(←, 2)	(←, 10)	(←, 2)	(‖, 0)

1.7 Implementation and Evaluation

In this section, we describe the implementation of our prototype to validate our proposed approach, in addition to a set of experiments using a subset of the BPs from the SAP reference model.

1.7.1 Implementation: Integrating Depot and Oryx

We have developed a prototype that implements our approach to enrich service descriptions using business process configurations. In this section, we give details about the implementation of this prototype that integrates *Oryx*—a business process modeling platform and repository—and *Depot*—a web service registry.[4] The front-end of our prototype is Oryx, whereas Depot represents the backend. Figure 1.6 shows a screenshot of using our prototype to design a business process for establishing a company in Germany.

To create a new model for this process in Oryx, a proper title, such as "Establishing a company in Germany" is given by the process designer. The area labeled with *A* in Fig. 1.6 shows a list of web services discovered in Depot that have been used is similar contexts and are relevant to this process. For instance, the whois web services used in the UK example can be shown in this example despite the fact that there is no high similarity between terms appearing in "establish a company in Germany" and "whois". Each of these web services is already configured and can be simply dragged-

---

[4] The authors conducted this work during their stay at Hasso-Plattner-Institut at University of Potsdam, Germany

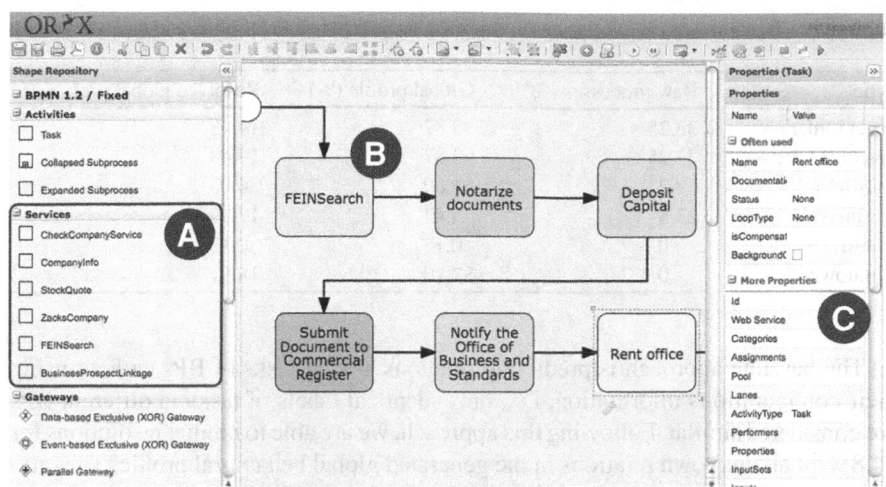

Fig. 1.6 A screenshot of our prototype used to model the process of establishing a company in Germany. *A* Suggested web services, *B* A pre-configured task from *A*, *C* Task properties

and-dropped to the design area. Indeed, the task labeled with *B* "FEINSearch" is an example of such pre-configured tasks. The web service assigned to this task gives company's details by its name or address. If the provided name does not exist, this hints that this name can be used as a name for the new company to be established.

1.7.2 Experiments

In this section, we show a set of experiments to evaluate our approach of predicting potential relations among web services using business process knowledge. We use a set of business processes from the SAP reference model [8], because these models represent possibilities to configure SAP R/3 ERP systems. Thus, it is analogous to business process configurations over a service landscape. We use 18 BPs with related missions from the SAP reference model. In particular, they are concerned with purchase order/requisition processing. These processes include 146 tasks in total. On average, each BP has about 8 tasks. Among the 146 tasks, 81 tasks are distinct, i.e., bound (configured) with distinct web services. We performed this configurations manually and verified the results manually as well. We analyzed the labels of the tasks and decided which labels (tasks) that can be bound to the same web service. Additionally, we had to manually restructure the models to have a single start and a single end node so that the behavioral profile calculation algorithm can be applied to them. Moreover, we excluded loops to obtain useful behavioral relations among tasks. A loop yields relations among all nodes within that loop concurrent.

Table 1.10 Types and ratios of relations in raw profiles, derived global profile, and resolved profile

Type	Raw processes (%)	Global profile (%)	Resolved global profile (%)
Strict Order ⤳	33.25	3.87	14.48
Inverse Order ⬳	33.25	3.87	14.48
Parallel ‖	9.7	1.60	34.03
Exclusive #	23.8	3.42	17.97
Conflict ※	0	0.15	0.12
Unknown ?	0	87.10	18.91

The baseline approach is predicting relations among tasks of BPs *without* using their configurations information, i.e., only identical labels of tasks in different BPs are considered similar. Following this approach, we are able to predict resolutions for 54.8 % of all unknown relations in the generated global behavioral profile. The ratio of resolved relations using labels of tasks depends considerably only on the degree of similarity and cohesion among labels. Using the configurations of these BPs where semantically similar tasks are bound to a single web services, we are able to predict resolutions for around 72 % of all unknown relations among tasks used in our experiments.

We are able to reveal different types of relations among web services. In Table 1.10, we show the ratio of each type of relations with respect to the total number of relations in source profiles, their derived global profile, and after revealing part of the hidden relations in that global profile. Note that percentages in this table are local to each column. The majority of relations in the revealed global profile are parallel (34 %). Additional knowledge about such tasks and their bound web services can be used to resolve such relations in more concrete ones. This further resolution is part of our future work. Conflicting relations appear due to inaccurate configurations of BPs or due to lack of sufficient knowledge about tasks and web services. Unknown relations are still in the global profile even after applying our resolutions approach. Either the used knowledge is not sufficient to reveal such relations or there are no such useful relations. For instance, a music web service and a web service for Gene analysis.

1.8 Related Work

Bringing SOA and BPMs has been an active research topic. For instance Buchwald et al. propose an approach to bridge the gap between business process models and service compositions [6]. The proposed approach introduces an intermediate layer between business process models (business view) and executable models, service compositions (technical view). The authors identify the need to store and maintain the relationship between business view tasks and technical view ones. To this point, the middle layer provides several types of transformation rules from the business to the technical view. However, this knowledge is kept in the middle layer and it is not the intention of that approach to reuse this knowledge to either enhance process modeling and/or service discovery.

The fact of having process repositories with hundreds to thousands of process models has attracted researchers to reuse-based process modeling. Smirnov et al. use so-called behavioral profiles of business process models to extract association rules and action patterns among tasks [17]. Based thereon, process modeling tools can suggest to the user the insertion of certain tasks, if the user inserts other tasks within the model. Moreover, the approach can suggest a structuring relationship among the inserted tasks, e.g., tasks *A* and *B* should be exclusive to each other.

In our work, we make an explicit bi-directional link between business processes and web services. This link is used to discover fine-grained linkage patterns among web services used in BPs. The goal of this approach is to use these linkage patterns to enhance service discovery during the configuration of business process models.

Finding relations among web services has been considered by several researchers in the community. Approaches that tackle this problem can be grouped roughly in four groups:

- *Input/output matching approaches*: These approaches match inputs and outputs of operations of web services to find relations among them [9]. The main goal of these approaches is to investigate composability among web services [14, 16].
- *Semantic approaches*: These approaches apply Artificial Intelligence planning techniques to find valid compositions of web services [11, 12]. They are based on the assumption that web services are described formally using ontologies, such as OWL-S, WSMO, etc.
- *Service compositions-based approaches*: These approaches are based on the idea that web services used in a service composition are related [5, 25]. Compared to our approach, these approaches are unable to reveal hidden relations among web services that were never used in the same process model.
- *Consumer-consumer similarity approaches*: These approaches use the idea that similar service consumers usually use the same web services [15].

1.9 Summary

In this chapter, we introduced a novel approach to enrich poor service descriptions with information extracted from the configurations of BPs that consume them. We use business process configurations to discover fine-grained relations among web services used in such processes in the form of linkage patterns. The required business process knowledge is captured using the notion of extended behavioral profiles. Based on these profiles, we can determine five types of linkage patterns among web services, namely predecessor, successor, similar, complementary, and related. Additionally, each linkage pattern is assigned a weight that reflects its strength. These weights are used to rank service recommendations that enables service exploration.

Additionally, we introduced an approach to reveal hidden relations among web services by exploiting process configurations over these services. Typically, several process configurations exist. Therefore, we merge these individual profiles into a single global profile. After that, unknown relations within the global profiles were input to our prediction approach to reveal possible behavioral relations that might exist among them. To reveal these relations, we use common services between the two services with an unknown relation. We applied our approach to a subset of the SAP reference models and our experiments show that we could reveal about 72 % of the unknown relations in the global profile.

References

1. AbuJarour, M., Awad, A.: Discovering linkage patterns among web services using business process knowledge. In: Proceeding of the 8th International Conference on Services Computing, SCC (2011)
2. AbuJarour, M., Naumann, F., Craculeac, M.: Collecting, annotating, and classifying public web services. In: Proceedings of the 2010 International Conference on On-the-Move to Meaningful Internet Systems, OTM (2010)
3. AbuJarour, M., Oergel, S.: Automatic sampling of web services. In: Proceeding of the 9th International Conference on Web Services, ICWS (2011)
4. Awad, A.: BPMN-Q: A language to query business processes. In: Proceedings of the 2nd International Workshop on Enterprise Modelling and Information Systems Architectures, EMISA (2007)
5. Basu, S., Casati, F., Daniel, F.: Toward web service dependency discovery for SOA management. In: Proceedings of the 5th International Conference on Services Computing, SCC (2008)
6. Buchwald, S., Bauer, T., Reichert, M.: Bridging the Gap Between Business Process Models and Service Composition Specifications, Chap. Methods, Trends and Advances, Int'l Handbook on Service Life Cycle Tools and Technologies (2011)
7. Buchwald, S., Tiedeken, J., Reichert, M.: Anforderungen an ein Metamodell für SOA-Repositories. In: Proceedings of the 2nd Central-European Workshop on Services and their Composition (Services und ihre Komposition), ZEUS (2010)
8. Curran, T.A., Keller, G., Ladd, A.: SAP R/3 Business Blueprint: Understanding the Business Process Reference Model, 1st edn. Prentice Hall (1997)
9. Dong, X., Halevy, A., Madhavan, J., Nemes, E., Zhang, J.: Similarity search for web services. In: Proceedings of the Thirtieth International Conference on Very Large Data Bases, VLDB, (2004)
10. Fensel, D., Keller, U., Lausen, H., Polleres, A., Toma, I.: WWW or what is wrong with web service discovery? In: Proceedings of the W3C Workshop on Frameworks for Semantics in Web Services (2005)
11. Lecue, F., Leger, A.: Semantic web service composition based on a closed world assumption. In: Proceedings of the 2006 European Conference on Web Services (2006)
12. Lin, L., Arpinar, I.B.: Discovery of semantic relations between web services. In: Proceedings of the 2006 International Conference on Web Services, ICWS (2006)
13. Miller, G.A.: WordNet: a lexical database for english. Commun. ACM **38**, 38–41 (1995)
14. Omer, A.M., Schill, A.: Web service composition using input/output dependency matrix. In: Proceedings of the 3Rd Workshop on Agent-Oriented Software Engineering Challenges for Ubiquitous and Pervasive Computing, AUPC 09 (2009)
15. Rong, W., Liu, K., Liang, L.: Personalized web service ranking via user group combining association rule. In: Proceedings of the 2009 International Conference on Web Services, ICWS (2009)
16. Segev, A.: Circular context-based semantic matching to identify web service composition. In: Proceedings of the 2008 International Workshop on Context Enabled Source and Service Selection, Integration and Adaptation, CSSSIA (2008)

17. Smirnov, S., Weidlich, M., Mendling, J., Weske, M.: Action patterns in business process models. In: Proceedings of the 7th International Conference on Service-Oriented Computing, ICSOC/ServiceWave (2009)
18. Sreenath, R.M., Singh, M.P.: Agent-based service selection. J. Web Sem. 1(3), 0–0 (2004)
19. Stein, S., Barchewitz, K., El Kharbili, M.: Enabling business experts to discover web services for business process automation. In: Proceedings of the 2nd Workshop on Emerging Web Services Technology, WEWST (2007)
20. Sun, S.X., Zhao, J.L., Nunamaker, J.F., Liu Sheng, O.R.: Formulating the data-flow perspective for business process management. Info. Sys. Research 17(4), 374–391 (2006)
21. van der Aalst, W.M.P., van Hee, K.M.: Workflow management: models, methods, and systems. MIT Press, London (2002)
22. van der Aalst, W.M.P., Weijters, T., Maruster, L.: Workflow mining: discovering process models from event logs. IEEE Trans. Knowl. Data Eng. 16(9), 1128–1142 (2004)
23. van Dongen, B.F., Mendling, J., van der Aalst, W.M.P.: Structural patterns for soundness of business process models. In: EDOC, pp. 116–128. IEEE Computer Society (2006)
24. Weidlich, M., Polyvyanyy, A., Mendling, J., Weske, M.: Efficient computation of causal behavioural profiles using structural decomposition. In: Proceedings of the 31st International Conference on Applications and Theory of Petri Nets, Petri Nets (2010)
25. Winkler, M., Springer, T., Trigos, E.D., Schill, A.: Analysing dependencies in service compositions. In: Proceedings of the 2009 International Conference on Service-Oriented Computing, ICSOC/ServiceWave (2009)
26. Weikum G. et al.: The YAGO-NAGA project: harvesting, searching, and ranking knowledge from the web. http://www.mpi-inf.mpg.de/yago-naga/

Chapter 2
RESTful Web Services: Principles, Patterns, Emerging Technologies

Cesare Pautasso

Abstract RESTful Web services are software services which are published on the Web, taking full advantage and making correct use of the HTTP protocol. This chapter gives an introduction to the REST architectural style and how it can be used to design Web service APIs. We summarize the main design constraints of the REST architectural style and discuss how they impact the design of so-called RESTful Web service APIs. We give examples on how the Web can be seen as a novel kind of software connector, which enables the coordination of distributed, stateful and autonomous software services. We conclude the chapter with a critical overview of a set of emerging technologies which can be used to support the development and operation of RESTful Web services.

2.1 Introduction

REST stands for REpresentational State Transfer [13]. It is the architectural style that explains the quality attributes of the World Wide Web, seen as an open, distributed and decentralized hypermedia application, which has scaled from a few Web pages in 1990 up to billions of addressable Web resources today [4, 6]. Even if it is no longer practical to take a global snapshot of the Web architecture, seen as a large set of Web browsers, Web servers, and their collective state, it is nevertheless possible to describe the style followed by such Web architecture. The REST architectural style includes the design constraints which have been followed to define the HTTP protocol [12], the fundamental standard together with URI and HTML which has enabled to build the Web [5]. These constraints make up the REST architectural style and have been distilled by Roy Fielding in his PhD dissertation [11].

C. Pautasso (✉)
Faculty of Informatics, University of Lugano, via Buffi 13, Lugano CH-6900, Switzerland
e-mail: c.pautasso@ieee.org

A. Bouguettaya et al. (eds.), *Web Services Foundations*,
DOI: 10.1007/978-1-4614-7518-7_2,
© Springer Science+Business Media New York 2014

Over the last decade, the Web has grown from a large-scale hypermedia application for publishing and discovering documents (i.e., Web pages) into a programmable medium for sharing data and accessing remote software components delivered as a service. As the Web became widespread, TCP/IP port 80 started to be left open by default on most Internet firewalls, making it possible to use the HTTP protocol [12] (which by default runs on port 80) as a universal mean for tunneling messages in business to business integration scenarios. RESTful Web services—as opposed to plain (or Big [22]) Web services—emphasize the correct and complete use of the HTTP protocol to publish software systems on the Web [24]. More and more services published on the Web are claiming to be designed using REST. As we are going to discuss, even if all make use of the HTTP protocol natively, not all of them do so in full compliance with the constraints of the REST architectural style [16].

In this chapter we present how the Web can be seen as a novel kind of software connector, which enables the coordination of distributed, stateful and autonomous software services. We summarize the main design constraints of the REST architectural style and discuss how they impact the design of so-called RESTful Web service APIs. We conclude the chapter with a critical overview of a set of emerging technologies which can be used to support the development and operation of RESTful Web services.

2.2 Principles

Understanding the architectural principles underlying the World Wide Web can lead to improving the design of other distributed systems, such as integrated enterprise architectures. This is the claim of RESTful Web services, designed following the REST architectural style [11], which emphasizes the scalability of component interactions, promotes the reuse and generality of component interfaces, reduces coupling between components, and makes use of intermediary components to reduce interaction latency, enforce security, and encapsulate legacy systems.

2.2.1 Design Constraints

The main design constraints of the REST architectural style are: global addressability through resource identification, uniform interface shared by all resources, stateless interactions between services, self-describing messages, and hypermedia as a mechanism for decentralized resource discovery by referral.

1. *Addressability* All resources that are published by a Web service should be given a unique and stable identifier [17]. These identifiers are globally meaningful, so that no central authority is involved in minting them, and they can be dereferenced independently of any context. The concept of a resource is kept very general

as REST intentionally does not make any assumptions on the corresponding implementation. A resource can be used to publish some service capability, a view over the internal state of a service, as well as any source of machine-processable data, which may also include meta-data about the service.

2. *Uniform Interface* All resources interact through a uniform interface, which provides a small, generic and functionally sufficient set of methods to support all possible interactions between services. Each method has a well defined semantics in terms of its effect on the state of the resource. In the context of the Web and its HTTP protocol, the uniform interface comprises the methods (e.g., GET, PUT, DELETE, POST, HEAD, OPTIONS, etc.) that can be applied to all Web resource identifiers (e.g., URIs which conform to the HTTP scheme). The set of methods can be extended if necessary (e.g., PATCH has been recently proposed as an addition to deal with partial resource updates [8]) and other protocols based on HTTP such as WebDAV include additional methods [14].

3. *Stateless Interactions* Services do not establish any permanent session between them which spans across more than a single interaction. This ensures that requests to a resource are independent from each other. At the end of every interaction, there is no shared state that remains between clients and servers. Requests may result in a state change of the resource, whose new state becomes immediately visible to all of its clients.

4. *Self-Describing Messages* Services interact by exchanging request and response messages, which contain both the data (or the representations of resources) and the corresponding meta-data. Representations can vary according to the client context, interests and abilities. For example, a mobile client can retrieve a low-bandwidth representation of a resource. Likewise, a Web browser can request a representation of a Web page in a particular language, according to its user preferences. This greatly enhances the degree of intrinsic interoperability of a REST architecture, since a client may dynamically negotiate the most appropriate representation format (also called media type) with the resource as opposed to forcing all clients and all resources to use the same format. Request and response messages also should contain explicit meta-data about the representation so that services do not need to assume any kind of out-of-band agreement on how the representation should be parsed, processed and understood.

5. *Hypermedia* Resources may be related to each other. Hypermedia is about embedding references to related resources inside resource representations or in the corresponding meta-data. Clients can thus discover the identifiers (or hyper-links) of related resources when processing representations and choose to follow the link as they navigate the graph built out of relationships between resources. Hypermedia helps to deal with decentralized resource discovery and is also used for dynamic discovery and description of interaction protocols between services. Despite its usefulness, it is also the constraint that has been the least used in most Web service APIs claiming to be RESTful. Thus, sometimes Web service APIs which also comply with this constraint are also named "Hypermedia APIs" [3].

2.2.2 Maturity Model

The main design constraints of the REST architectural style can also be adopted incrementally, leading to the definition of a maturity model for RESTful Web services as proposed by Leonard Richardson. This has led to a discussion on whether only services that are fully mature can be actually called RESTful. In the state of the practice, however, many services which are classified in the lower levels of maturity already present themselves as making use of REST.

- *Level 0: HTTP as a tunnel* These are all services which simply exchange XML documents (sometimes referred to as Plain-Old-XML documents as opposed to SOAP messages) over HTTP POST request and responses, effectively following some kind of XML-RPC protocol [28]. A similar approach is followed by services which replace the XML payloads with JSON, YAML or other formats which are used to serialize the input and output parameters of a remote procedure call, which happens to be tunneled through an open HTTP endpoint. Even if such services are not making use of SOAP messages, they are not really making full use of the HTTP protocol according to the REST constraints either. In particular, since all messages go to the same endpoint URL, a service can distinguish between different operations only by parsing such information out of the XML (or JSON) payload.
- *Level 1: Resources* As opposed to using a single endpoint for tunneling RPC messages through the HTTP protocol, services on maturity level 1 make use of multiple identifiers to distinguish different resources. Each interaction is addressed to a specific resource, which can however still be misused to identify different operations or methods to be performed on the payload, or to identify different instances of object of a given class, to which the request payload is addressed.
- *Level 2: HTTP Verbs* In addition to fine-grained resource identification, services of maturity level 2 also make proper use of the REST uniform interface in general and of the HTTP verbs in particular. This means that not only clients can perform a GET, DELETE, PUT on a resource, in addition to POSTing to it, but also do so in compliance with the semantics of such methods. For example, service designers ensure that GET, PUT and DELETE requests to their service are idempotent. Since we can assume that the HTTP methods are used according to their standard semantics, we can use the corresponding safety and idempotency properties to optimize the system by introducing intermediaries. For example, the results of safe and side-effect free GET requests can be cached and failed PUT and DELETE requests can be automatically retried. Additionally, services make use of HTTP status codes correctly to, e.g., indicate whether methods are applicable to a given resource or to assign blame between which party is responsible for a failed interaction.
- *Level 3: Hypermedia* These are the fully mature RESTful Web services, which in addition to exposing multiple addressable resources which share the same uniform interface also make use of hypermedia to model relationship between resources. This is achieved by embedding so-called *hypermedia controls* within resource representations [19]. Depending on the chosen media type, hypermedia controls

such as links or forms can be parsed, recognized and interpreted by clients to drive their navigation within the graph of related resources. Hypermedia controls will be typed according to the semantics of the relationship and contain all information necessary for a client to formulate a request to a related resource. As opposed to knowing in advance all the addresses of the resources that will be used, a client can thus dynamically discover with which resource it should interact by following links of a certain type. Key to achieving this level of maturity is the choice of media types which support hypermedia controls (e.g., XML or JSON do not, while ATOM, XHTML or JSON-LD do.). The ability of a service to change the set of links that are given to a client based on the current state of a resource is also known with the ugly HATEOAS (Hypertext As The Engine Of Application State) acronym, to which now the simpler "hypermedia" term is preferred [23].

The maturity level of a service also affects the quality attributes of the architecture in which the service is embedded. Tunneling messages through an open HTTP port (level 0) leads only to the basic ability to communicate and exchange data, but—security issues notwithstanding—is likely to result in brittle integrated systems, which are difficult to evolve and scale. Distinguishing multiple resources helps to apply divide and conquer techniques to the design of a service interface and enable services to use global identifiers to address each resource that is being published. Applying a standardized and uniform interface to each resource removes unnecessary variations (as there are only a few universally accepted methods applicable to a resource) and enables all services to interact with all resources within the architecture, thus promoting interoperability and serendipitous reuse [29]. Additionally the semantics of the methods that make up the uniform interface can be adjusted so that the scalability and reliability of the architecture are enhanced. However, only the dynamic discoverability of resources provided by hypermedia contributes to minimize the coupling within the resulting architecture.

2.2.3 Comparing REST Versus WS-*

The maturity model can also be used to give a rough comparison between RESTful Web services and WS-* Web Services (Fig. 2.1). A more detailed comparison can be found in [22].

As the maturity level increases, the service will switch from using a single communication endpoint to many URIs (on the resource identification axis). Likewise, the set of possible methods (or operations) will be limited to the ones of the uniform interface as opposed to designing each service with its own set of operations explicitly described in a WSDL document. From a REST perspective, all WSDL operations are tunneled through a single HTTP verb (POST), thus reducing the expressiveness of HTTP seen as an application protocol, which is used as a transport protocol for tunneling messages. In WSDL several communication endpoints can be associated with the same service although these endpoints are not intended for distinguishing

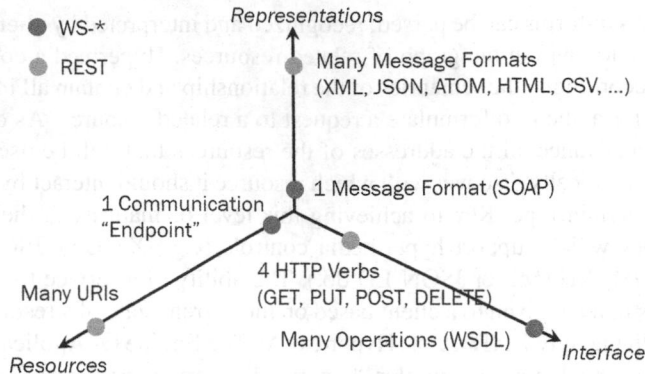

Fig. 2.1 Design space: RESTful web services versus WS-* web services

HTTP resources but may be used to access the same service through alternative communication mechanisms.

The third axis is not directly reflected in the maturity model but is also important for understanding the difference between the two technology stacks, one having a foundation in the SOAP protocol and the XML format, while the other leaves open the choice of which message format should be used (shown on the representations axis) so that clients and services can negotiate the most suitable format to achieve interoperability.

2.3 Example

As inspiration for this example we use the Doodle REST API, which gives programmatic access to the Doodle poll Web service available at (http://www.doodle.ch). Doodle is a very popular service, which allows to minimize the number of emails exchanged in order to find an agreement among a set of people. The service allows to initiate polls by configuring a set of options (which can be a set of dates for scheduling a meeting, but can also be a set of arbitrary strings). The link to the poll is then mailed out to the participants, who are invited to answer the poll by selecting the preferred options. The current state of the poll can be polled at any time by the initiator, who will typically inform the participants of the outcome with a second email message.

The Simple Doodle REST API (Fig. 2.2) publishes two kinds of resources: polls (a set of options once can choose from) and votes (choices of people within a given poll). There is a natural containment relationship between the two kinds of resources, which fits naturally into the convention to use / as a path separator in URIs. Thus the service publishes a /poll root resource, which contains a set of /poll/{id} poll instances, which include the corresponding set of votes /poll/{id}/vote/{id}.

1. Resources:
   polls and votes
2. Containment Relationship:

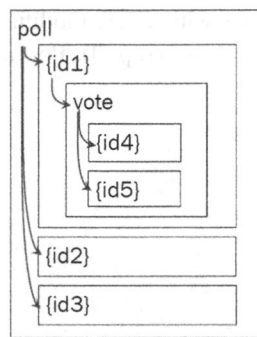

	GET	PUT	POST	DELETE
/poll	✓	✗	✓	✗
/poll/{id}	✓	✓	✗	✓
/poll/{id}/vote	✓	✗	✓	✗
/poll/{id}/vote/{id}	✓	✓	✗	?

3. URIs embed IDs of "child" instance resources
4. POST on the container is used to create child resources
5. PUT/DELETE for updating and removing child resources

Fig. 2.2 Simple Doodle REST API

2.3.1 Listing Active Polls

The root /poll resource is used to retrieve (with GET) the list of links to the polls which have been instantiated:

```
⇒GET /poll
  Accept: text/uri-list

⇐200 OK
  Content-Type: text/uri-list

  http://doodle.api/poll/201204301
  http://doodle.api/poll/201204302
  http://doodle.api/poll/201205011
```

2.3.2 Creating New Polls

The same /poll resource acts as factory resource which accepts POST requests to create new poll instances. The identifier of the newly created poll is returned as a link associated with the Location response header.

```
⇒POST /poll
  Content-Type: application/xml
  <options>A,B,C</options>

⇐201 Created
  Location: /poll/201205012
```

2.3.3 Fetching the Current State of a Poll

The current state of a poll instance can be read with GET, modified with PUT (e.g., to change the set of possible options or to close the poll). Poll instances can also be removed with DELETE.

```
⇒GET /poll/201205012
  Accept: application/xml
```

```
⇐200 OK
  Content-Type: application/xml

  <poll>
  <options>A,B,C</options>
  <votes href="/poll/201205012/vote"/>
  </poll>
```

The representation of a newly created poll resource, in addition to the set of options provided by the client, also contains a link to the resource used to cast votes. Clients can follow the link to express their opinion and make a choice. The nested vote resource acts as a factory resource for individual votes.

2.3.4 Casting Votes

```
⇒POST /poll/201205012/vote
  Content-Type: application/xml
  <vote>
  <name>C. Pautasso</name>
  <choice>B</choice>
  </vote>
```

```
⇐201 Created
  Location: /poll/201205012/vote/1
```

After the previous request has been processed a new vote has been cast and the state of the poll has changed. Retrieving it will now return a different representation, which includes the information about the vote.

```
⇒GET /poll/201205012
  Accept: application/xml
```

```
⇐200 OK
  Content-Type: application/xml

  <poll>
  <options>A,B,C</options>
  <votes href="/poll/201205012/vote">
  <vote id="1">
  <name>C. Pautasso</name>
  <choice>B</choice>
  </vote>
  </votes>
  </poll>
```

2.3.5 Changing Votes

Since each vote gets its own URI it is also possible to manipulate its state with PUT and DELETE. For example, clients may want to retract a vote (with DELETE) or modify the choice (with PUT) as in the following example.

```
⇒PUT /poll/201205012/vote/1
  Content-Type: application/xml
  <vote>
  <name>C. Pautasso</name>
  <choice>C</choice>
  </vote>

⇐200 OK
```

2.3.6 Interacting with Votes

In general, it is not always possible nor it is necessary for a resource to respond to requests which make use of all possible methods of the uniform interface. In the context of the Simple Doodle REST API, as shown in Fig. 2.2, it has been chosen not to support PUT and DELETE on the /poll and /poll/{id}/vote resources. Also POST requests to individual instances /poll/{id} or /poll/{id}/vote/ {id} are not supported. Such requests do not have a meaningful effect on the state of the resource and are thus disallowed. Clients attempting to issue them will receive an erroneous response:

```
⇒POST /poll/201205012/vote/1

⇐405 Method not allowed
```

Clients can also inquire which methods are allowed before attempting to perform them on a resource making use of the OPTIONS method as follows

⇒OPTIONS /poll/201205012/vote/1

⇐204 No Content
  Allow: GET, PUT, DELETE

An OPTIONS request will return a list of the methods which are currently applicable to a resource in the response Allow header. The set of allowed methods may change depending on the state of the resource.

2.3.7 Removing a Poll

Once a poll has received enough votes and a decision has been made, its state will be kept indefinitely by the service until an explicit request to remove it is made by a client.

⇒DELETE /poll/201205012

⇐200 OK

Subsequent requests directed to the delete poll instance will also receive an erroneous response.

⇒GET /poll/201205012

⇐404 Not Found

2.4 Patterns

Once the basic architectural principles for the design of RESTful Web services are established, it remains sometimes difficult to apply them directly to the design of specific Web service APIs. In this Section we collect a small number of design patterns, which provide some guidance on how to deal with resource creation, long running operations and concurrent updates. Additional known patterns address features such event notifications, enhancing the reliability of interactions, atomicity and transactions and supporting the evolution of service interfaces. In general, applying one of these patterns requires to make use of some existing feature of the standard HTTP protocol, which may need to be augmented with some conventions and shared assumptions on how to interpret its status code and headers. The current understanding within the REST community is that it should be possible to design fully functional service APIs that do not require any non-standard extension to the HTTP protocol.

The example patterns included in this chapter is not intended to be complete, for additional guidance on how to design RESTful Web services, we refer the interested reader to [1, 7, 10, 25, 30].

2.4.1 Resource Creation

The instantiation of resources is a key feature of most RESTful Web services, which enable clients to create new resource identifiers and set the corresponding state to an initial value. The resource identifier can either be set by the client or by the service. It is easier to guarantee that URIs created by the service are unique, while it is possible that multiple clients will generate the same identifier.

When using a single HTTP interaction to create a resource, there are two possible verbs that can be used: PUT or POST. The basic semantics of PUT requests is to update the state of the corresponding resource with the provided payload. If no resource is found with the given identifier, a new resource is created. This has the advantage of using idempotent requests to create a resource, but requires clients to avoid mixing up resource identifiers. POST on the other hand assumes that the server will create a new resource identifier. Since POST is not idempotent, there have been a number of patterns that have been proposed to address this limitation and avoid the so-called "duplicated POST submission" problem. The convention is to use some kind of "factory" resource, to which POST requests are directed for creating new resources. However, repeating such requests in case of failure would lead to potentially multiple, different instances to be created by the factory.

The pattern is based on the idea of splitting the centralized generation of the new resource identifier on the service-side from the initialization of its state with the payload provided by the client. The pattern makes combined usage of both POST and PUT requests as follows.

```
⇒POST /factory
  <Empty Payload>

⇐303 See Other
  Location: /factory/id

⇒PUT /factory/id
  <Initialization Payload>

⇐200 OK
```

The first POST request returns a new unique resource identifier /factory/id but does not initialize its corresponding resource since the payload is empty. The second request PUTs the initial state on the new resource. In the worst case, failures during the first POST request will lead to lost resource identifiers, which however can be garbage collected by the server since the corresponding resource has not been initialized. Likewise, clients may fail between the two requests and thus could forget to follow up with the PUT request. The designer of the service needs to make reasonable assumptions on the maximum allowed delay between the two interactions. If a client is too late and the resource identifier has been already garbage collected by the server, then another one can be simply retrieved by repeating the first POST request.

Variations of this pattern have been proposed which replace the initial POST with a GET request, which in the same way returns a new unique identifier every time it is invoked. Similarly, the response payload of the first request could be used to provide the client with a representation template, i.e., a form to be completed with the information required to initialize the new resource.

2.4.2 Long Running Operations

HTTP is a client/server protocol which does not assume that every request is followed by a response indicating that the work has completed. For long running operations, which may result in a timeout of the network communication, it is possible to break the connection and avoid blocking the client for too long. This is particularly useful to invoke service operations that—depending on the size of the input provided by clients or by the complexity of their internal implementation—may require a long time to complete processing it.

The pattern is based on turning the long running operation into a resource, whose identifier can be returned immediately to the client submitting the corresponding job.

```
⇒POST /job
  Input data payload
⇐202 Accepted
  Content-Location: /job/201205019

  <job>
  <status>pending</status>
  <message>Your job has been queued for processing</message>
  <ping-time>2012-05-01T05:22:12Z</ping-time>
  </job>
```

The 202 Accepted status code implies that the service has verified the request input payload and has accepted it, but no immediate response can be given. The client should follow the link given in the Content-Location header to inquire (with GET) about the status of the pending request.

```
⇒GET /job/201205019
```

```
⇐200 OK
 <job>
 <status>processing</status>
 <message>Your job is being processed</message>
 <ping-time>2012-05-01T06:22:09Z</ping-time>
 </job>
```

Clients can send GET requests to the job resource at any time to track its progress. In addition to the status, the response also contains a hint (in the `ping-time` element) on when the next poll request should be performed in order to reduce network traffic and service load due to excessive polling.

Once the job has been completed, the response to the poll request will redirect the client to another resource from which the final result can be retrieved.

```
⇒GET /job/201205019
```

```
⇐303 See Other
 Location: /job/201205019/output
 <job>
 <status>done</status>
 <message>Your job has been successfully
 completed</message>
 </job>
```

The client can then follow the link found in the `Location` header to retrieve (with GET) the output of the completed job. The link could also be shared among different clients interested in reading the output of the original POST request.

```
⇒GET /job/201205019/output
```

```
⇐200 OK
 Output data payload
```

In case the client is no longer interested in retrieving the results, it is possible to cancel the resource job and thus remove it from the queue of pending requests. The client thus issues a DELETE request on the job resource, which will be allowed as long as the job has not yet completed its execution.

```
⇒DELETE /job/201205019
```

```
⇐200 OK
```

After a request has completed it is no longer possible to cancel it. In this case, a similar DELETE request can be performed on the resource representing the output results of the job when the client has completed downloading them and it is no longer interested in keeping the results stored on the server.

```
⇒DELETE /job/201205019/output
```

⇐200 OK

If clients do not remember to clean up after themselves the server can end up storing a copy of all long running requests and potentially run out of space. Still, a garbage collection mechanism can be implemented to automatically remove old results through the same DELETE request.

This pattern shows how to deal with long running operations by applying a general design principle of turning "everything into a resource" [24]. In this case the resource represents the long running request which is managed by the client through the HTTP uniform interface.

2.4.3 Optimistic Locking

RESTful Web services are stateful services, which associate to each resource URI a representation which is produced based on the current state of the corresponding resource. It is thus important to deal with concurrent state modifications without violating the stateless constraint, which prevents clients to establish a session with a service in which the resource is updated.The problem addressed by this pattern is thus the one of dealing with concurrent resource updates in compliance with the stateless constraint.The solution adopted by the HTTP protocol makes use of a form of optimistic locking, as follows.

1. The client retrieves the current state of a resource.

   ⇒GET /resource

   ⇐200 OK
     ETag: 1

     Current representation

   Together with the representation of the resource, the client is given through the ETag header some meta-data which identifies the current version of the resource.
2. The client updates the state of a resource. While doing so, the client uses the If-Match header to make the request conditional.

   ⇒PUT /resource
     If-Match: 1

     New representation

   ⇐200 OK
     ETag: 2

     Updated representation

The server will execute the PUT request only if the version of the resource (on the server-side) matches the version provided within the client request. If there is a mismatch, another client has already updated the resource in the meanwhile and an update conflict has been detected. This is indicated using the standard 409 Conflict status code. To recover the client should start again from step 1. by retrieving the latest state of the resource. After recomputing the change locally, the client can once again attempt to update the resource.

As with most optimistic protocols, this solution works well if the ratio of updates (PUT or POST) to reads (GET) is small. The pattern should not be used for resources that are hotly contested between multiple clients, or in case the cost of re-trying a failed update is expensive.

2.5 Technologies

Over the past few years, REST has evolved from the original state in which an apparent lack of tooling support was limiting the adoption of the technology [27] and there have been quite a few frameworks that have been proposed for most programming languages and service delivery platforms (Table 2.1). Indeed, as a reaction to the complexity of WS-* technology stacks, REST was initially positioned as a lightweight alternative where no tools beyond a Web browser and some standard HTTP library were necessary to develop RESTful Web services. The situation has changed and with the growth in popularity of REST also a number of development frameworks have appeared.

2.5.1 Frameworks

Most frameworks support both client-side consumption of resources as well as server-side publishing of resources. However, some frameworks are starting to appear which specifically target the development of loosely coupled clients (e.g., RESTAgent or Guzzle). Some frameworks (e.g., ActiveResource, Compojure-rest, the Django REST Framework) are built as an extension of existing Web/MVC application development frameworks. Others (e.g., Persevere) come with a standalone HTTP server stack. Concerning the Java language, the oldest framework is RESTlet, while others (e.g., Jersey, RESTEasy, ApacheCXF) implement the JSR-311 [15] standard, which defines how to publish Java code as a RESTful Web service using source code annotations. With the 3.5 release of the .NET framework, also the Windows Communication Framework (WCF) technology stack supports REST. Likewise many existing WS-* technology frameworks (e.g., ApacheCXF) have begun to offer SOAP-less bindings to plain HTTP and started to support the use of JSON inside HTTP payloads.

Table 2.1 Technology: Frameworks for developing and hosting RESTful web services (homepage links verified as of 1st October 2012)

Framework	Language/ Platform	Project Homepage
ActiveResource	Ruby/Rails	http://api.rubyonrails.org/classes/ActiveResource/Base.html
apache2rest	PERL	http://code.google.com/p/apache2rest/
ApacheCXF	Java	http://cxf.apache.org/
Bowler	Scala	http://bowlerframework.org/
C2Serve	C++	http://www.c2serve.eu/
Compojure-rest	Clojure	http://github.com/ordnungswidrig/compojure-rest
Crochet	Scala	https://github.com/xllora/Crochet
Django REST	Python/Django	http://django-rest-framework.org/
Exyus	.NET	http://code.google.com/p/exyus/
FRAPI	PHP/Zend	http://getfrapi.com/
Guzzle	PHP	http://guzzlephp.org/
Jersey	Java	http://jersey.java.net/
OpenRASTA	.NET	https://github.com/openrasta/openrasta/wiki
Persevere	JavaScript	http://www.persvr.org/
Pinky	Scala	https://github.com/pk11/pinky/wiki
Piston	Python/Django	https://bitbucket.org/jespern/django-piston/wiki/Home
Prestans	Python/WSGI	http://prestans.googlecode.com/
Recess	PHP	http://www.recessframework.org/
RESTAgent	Java	http://restagent.codeplex.com/
RESTEasy	Java	http://www.jboss.org/resteasy.html
RESTfulie	Ruby, Java, C#	http://restfulie.caelum.com.br/
RESTify	JavaScript/Node	http://mcavage.github.com/node-restify/
RESTlet	Java	http://www.restlet.org/
RESTSharp	.NET	http://restsharp.org/
Scotty	Haskell	https://github.com/xich/scotty
Spray	Scala/Akka	http://spray.cc/
Taimen	Java, Clojure	https://bitbucket.org/kumarshantanu/taimen/
Tonic	PHP	http://peej.github.com/tonic/
Webmachine	Erlang	http://wiki.basho.com/Webmachine.html
Yesod	Haskell	http://www.yesodweb.com/
WCF	.NET	http://msdn.microsoft.com/en-us/library/vstudio/ bb412169.aspx
WebPy	Python	http://webpy.org/
Wink	Java	http://incubator.apache.org/wink/

2.5.2 Guidelines for Framework Selection

In general, it currently remains challenging to find a suitable framework which gives simple and correct guidance [32] to the service developer according to the REST constraints and which at the same time gives full access and control over the raw HTTP interactions. Even if it is possible to reuse or extend existing Web application development frameworks based on the Model-View-Controller (MVC) pattern, these may only offer limited support for processing both incoming and outgoing representations in customized non-HTML media types. Like in [26], we collect and discuss here a set of basic features that should be supported by a fully featured framework for developing RESTful Web services.

- Can requests be routed to the corresponding service logic based on both resource identifiers and HTTP methods? Some frameworks only use resource identifiers and ignore methods, leaving it up to the developer to run different logic based on the request method.
- Are custom or extended HTTP verbs supported? Can the framework support different URI schemes or is it tied to HTTP/HTTPS URIs? Even if REST does not make any assumption about the actual uniform interface, most frameworks are tightly coupled with the HTTP protocol and thus assume that only the HTTP methods will be used.
- Does the framework enforce the semantics of the HTTP uniform interface (i.e., read-only GET, idempotent PUT and DELETE)?
- What is the abstraction level required to handle content type negotiation? Can the same service logic be easily reused for responses returned using different representation formats? Is the developer required to manually work with HTTP headers? Can custom media types be defined?
- Are ETags headers automatically computed and checked? How does the framework deal with conflicting updates?
- What are the assumptions made by the framework concerning the lifecycle of a resource? Can different business logic be invoked depending on the state of a resource? Is the state of a resource persisted implicitly or explicitly across server reboots?
- How easy is it to embed links to related resources in a representation being sent back to the client?
- Are URI templates supported for request routing and link generation? Must URI templates be embedded in the source code, or can they be read from configuration files, or can they be dynamically discovered and remotely updated?
- Does the framework transparently handles redirects to new resource identifiers?
- How easy is it to configure caching support without rebuilding the service logic and without relying on external caching proxies?
- How does the framework map internal exceptions of the service logic to HTTP status codes? Can such mapping be customized?
- Does the framework present REST as an optional "transport protocol binding" next to WS-* technology, or is REST the default, or the only option?
- How difficult is to configure the framework to use HTTPS?
- Does the framework support some notion of service interface description? Can such description be generated automatically for documentation purposes? Can code be generated from the description?
- Does the framework allow to automatically scale-out the service on multiple parallel processing units in a multicore or a cluster environment? How does the framework deal with concurrency?

These questions should be considered when evaluating the adoption of one of the currently emerging frameworks for supporting the development and operation of RESTful Web service APIs. Due to space limitations and given the current state of flux of the technology, we have chosen not to include any assessment on how the various frameworks listed in Table 2.1 would comply with the features mentioned in the previous checklist. A very good survey addressing a subset of the features and of the frameworks has recently appeared in [32].

2.6 Discussion

Service-oriented architectures promote the design of distributed and integrated systems out of the composition of reusable and autonomous services [9, 18]. The goal is not only to reduce integration costs through the standardization of interface contracts and the interoperability of middleware tools [2], but also to lower the efforts needed to manage the evolution of the integrated systems thanks to the loose coupling that is established among its constituent services. The design constraints of the REST architectural style help to achieve such quality attributes not only in the context of the Web but also when applied to the design of Web service APIs. In particular, reuse [29] and loose coupling [21] are emphasized by employing a uniform interface for all elements within the same architecture; performance and scalability are supported by ensuring the visibility of the interactions, which are kept stateless, and introducing intermediary caching layers where appropriate; interoperability is fostered by the wide-reaching standardization of the underlying technologies (i.e., HTTP, URIs, SSL) as well as the opportunity for dynamic negotiation of the most understandable representation format; reliability is enhanced through the use of idempotent interactions, which can be automatically retried in case of failures.

In the context of service oriented architectures, REST promotes the use of a novel (or different) kind of software connector to coordinate the interactions between a set of distributed services. As opposed to traditional bus connectors for services which enable to use primitives such as synchronous remote procedure calls (RPC) or asynchronous messaging (à la publish/subscribe), REST resources enable the reliable transfer and sharing of state between multiple services. As illustrated in this chapter's example, the state of a poll resource can be shared by multiple participants by means of its resource identifier. By initializing a new poll, one client can post information—literally on the Web—with the intention of sharing this information with other clients, which can then manipulate it to find an agreement. Whereas each interaction between the client and the resource makes use of synchronous HTTP request/response rounds, the overall end-to-end interaction between multiple clients mediated by the resource is completely asynchronous. As long as the various clients can discover the identifier of the shared resource, they can exchange information through it without ever being directly in contact with one another. To this extent, REST introduces a different interaction style between services that is more similar to the one enabled by a blackboard or a tuple-space software connector, rather than a messaging and publish/subscribe system used in most traditional service-oriented architectures.

2.7 Conclusion

The Web can be seen as an existence proof that it is known how to build highly scalable, decentralized and loosely coupled distributed systems. The architectural principles explaining how the Web works can thus be adopted to build integrated, service-oriented systems that could also be expected to feature similar quality attributes. This is the claim of RESTful Web services, which advocate the correct and complete use of the HTTP protocol for the design and the delivery of Web service APIs. Over time a number of patterns have appeared to complement the basic guidance found within the original design constraints of the REST architectural style. These patterns describe conventional solutions for specific design problems within the context of the existing standard HTTP protocol. From the technology perspective, a clear need for supporting the automated development and hosting of RESTful Web services has been addressed by the growing number of emerging frameworks with variable degrees of stability and maturity.

2.8 More information

In addition to the original formulation of REST in Dr. Fielding's dissertation [11], more information about REST and RESTful Web services can be found in several books that have been published on the subject in the past few years. Richardson and Ruby [24] introduces the term RESTful Web services; Allamaraju [1] provides a collection of best practices explaining how to make correct usage of the HTTP protocol; Webber et al. [30] gives an extensive and well written discussion on how to use the Web as an integration platform; Tilkov [25] has a similar goal but targets the German-speaking audience; Wilde and Pautasso [31] is a collection of research-oriented, application-oriented and practice-oriented writings on REST; Amundson [3] promotes the term Hypermedia API, focusing on the least known aspects of REST. Erl et al. [10] gives an in-depth discussion of the relationship between SOA and REST. More design patterns for RESTful Web services can be found in Daigneau [7].

Acknowledgments Many thanks to Erik Wilde for all the help in preparing and running four editions of a successful WWW and ICWE tutorial on RESTful Web Services.

References

1. Allamaraju, S.: RESTful Web Services Cookbook. O'Reilly and Associates Sebastopol, California (2010)
2. Alonso, G.: Myths around web services. Bull. Tech. Committee Data Eng **25**(4), 3–9 (2002)
3. Amundsen, M.: Building Hypermedia APIs with HTML5 and Node. O'Reilly, USA (2011)
4. Berners-Lee, T.: Long live the web. Sci. Am. (12) (2010)
5. Berners-Lee, T., Cailliau, R., Luotonen, A., Frystyk Nielsen, H., Secret, A.: The world wide web. Communications of the ACM 37(8), 76–82 (1994). doi:10.1145/179606.179671
6. Berners-Lee, T., Fischetti, M., Dertouzos, M.: Weaving the Web. Harper Collins, San Francisco (1999)
7. Daigneau, R.: Service Design Patterns: Fundamental Design Solutions for SOAP/WSDL and RESTful Web Services. Addison Wesley, Upper Saddle River (2011)
8. Dusseault, L., Snell, J.M.: Patch method. http. Internet RFC 5789 (2010)
9. Erl, T.: Service-Oriented Architecture: Concepts, Technology, and Design. Prentice Hall, Upper Saddle River (2005)
10. Erl, T., Carlyle, B., Pautasso, C., Balasubramanian, R.: SOA with REST: Principles, Patterns and Constraints for Building Enterprise Solutions with REST. Prentice Hall, Upper Saddle River (2012)
11. Fielding, R.T.: Architectural styles and the design of network-based software architectures. Ph.D. thesis, University of California, Irvine, Irvine, California (2000)
12. Fielding, R.T., Gettys, J., Mogul, J.C., Frystyk Nielsen, H., Masinter, L., Leach, P.J., Berners-Lee, T.: Hypertext transfer protocol. http/1.1. Internet RFC 2616 (1999)
13. Fielding, R.T., Taylor, R.N.: Principled design of the modern web architecture. ACM Trans. Internet Technol. **2**(2), 115–150 (2002). doi:10.1145/337180.337228
14. Goland, Y.Y., Whitehead, E.J., Faizi, A., Carter, S., Jensen, D.: Http extensions for distributed authoring—webdav. Internet RFC 2518 (1999)
15. Hadley, M., Sandoz, P.: JAX-RS: The java api for restful web services. Java Specification Request (JSR) 311 (2009)
16. Maleshkova, M., Pedrinaci, C., Domingue, J.: Investigating web apis on the world wide web. In: Proceedings of the 8th IEEE European Conference on Web Services (ECOWS2010), pp. 107–114 (2010). doi:10.1109/ECOWS.2010.9
17. Nielsen, J.: User interface directions for the web. Commun. ACM **42**(1), 65–72 (1999). doi:10.1145/291469.291470
18. Papazoglou, M.P., van den Heuvel, W.J.: Service oriented architectures: approaches, technologies and research issues. VLDB J. **16**, 389–415 (2007)
19. Parastatidis, S., Webber, J., Silveira, G., Robinson, I.: The role of hypermedia in distributed system development. In: Pautasso et al. [21], pp. 16–22. doi:10.1145/1798354.1798379
20. Pautasso, C., Wilde, E., Marinos, A. (eds.): First International Workshop on RESTful Design (WS-REST 2010). Raleigh, North Carolina (2010)
21. Pautasso, C., Wilde, E.: Why is the web loosely coupled? a multi-faceted metric for service design. In: Quemada, J., León, G., Maarek, Y.S., Nejdl, W. (eds.) 18th International World Wide Web Conference, pp. 911–920. ACM Press, Madrid, Spain (2009)
22. Pautasso, C., Zimmermann, O., Leymann, F.: Restful web services vs. "big" web services: Making the right architectural decision. In: Huai, J., Chen, R., Hon, H.W., Liu, Y., Ma, W.Y., Tomkins, A., Zhang X. (eds.) 17th International World Wide Web Conference, pp. 805–814. ACM Press, Beijing, China (2008)
23. Richardson, L.: Developers like hypermedia, but they don't like web browsers. In: Pautasso et al. [21], pp. 4–9. doi:10.1145/1798354.1798377
24. Richardson, L., Ruby, S.: RESTful Web Services. O'Reilly & Associates, Sebastopol (2007)
25. Tilkov, S.: REST und HTTP: Einsatz der Architektur des Web für Integrationsszenarien. dpunkt.verlag, Heidelberg, Germany (2009)
26. Tilkov, S.: REST litmus test for web frameworks (2010). http://www.innoq.com/blog/st/2010/07/rest_litmus_test_for_web_frame.html

27. Vinoski, S.: Restful web services development checklist. IEEE Internet Comput. **12**(6), 94–96 (2008). doi:10.1109/MIC.2008.130
28. Vinoski, S.: Rpc and rest: Dilemma, disruption, and displacement. IEEE Internet Comput. **12**(5), 92–95 (2008)
29. Vinoski, S.: Serendipitous reuse. IEEE Internet Comput. **12**(1), 84–87 (2008). doi:10.1109/MIC.2008.20
30. Webber, J., Parastatidis, S., Robinson, I.: REST in Practice: Hypermedia and Systems Architecture. O'Reilly & Associates, Sebastopol (2010)
31. Wilde, E., Pautasso, C. (eds.): REST: From Research to Practice. Springer, Heidelberg (2011)
32. Zuzak, I., Schreier, S.: Arrested development: guidelines for designing REST frameworks. Internet Comput. **16**(4), 26–35 (2012)

Chapter 3
Conceptual Design of Sound, Custom Composition Languages

Stefano Soi, Florian Daniel and Fabio Casati

Abstract Service composition, web mashups, and business process modeling are based on the composition and reuse of existing functionalities, user interfaces, or tasks. Composition tools typically come with their own, purposely built composition languages, based on composition techniques like data flow or control flow, and only with minor distinguishing features—besides the different syntax. Yet, all these composition languages are developed from scratch, without reference specifications (e.g., XML schemas), and by reasoning in terms of low-level language constructs. That is, there is neither reuse nor design support in the development of custom composition languages. We propose a conceptual design technique for the construction of custom composition languages that is based on a generic composition reference model and that fosters reuse. The approach is based on the abstraction of common composition techniques into high-level language features, a set of reference specifications for each feature, and the assembling of features into custom languages by guaranteeing their soundness. We specifically focus on mashup languages.

3.1 Introduction

The proliferation of composition instruments like mashup platforms or web service composition environments, which allow one to integrate Web-accessible APIs and data into value-adding, composite applications or services, also led to the proliferation

S. Soi (✉) · F. Daniel · F. Casati
University of Trento, Via Sommarive 5, 38123 Trento, Italy
e-mail: soi@disi.unitn.it

F. Casati
e-mail: casati@disi.unitn.it

F. Daniel
Dipartimento di Ingegneria e Scienza dell'Informazione, Università di Trento, Povo, Trento, Italy
e-mail: daniel@disi.unitn.it

A. Bouguettaya et al. (eds.), *Web Services Foundations*,
DOI: 10.1007/978-1-4614-7518-7_3,
© Springer Science+Business Media New York 2014

of respective *composition languages*. Depending on the type of API or data source (we call them collectively components), the type of application or service (e.g., data mashup vs. UI mashup vs. service composition, and similar), and the target user of the application or service, composition languages differ in the features they offer to the developer—not only in their syntax. While in many cases language differences among tools actually don't seem to be necessary, in other cases these differences may indeed "make the difference". This is, for instance, the case of domain-specific mashup platforms [1], which aim to provide more effective development support (compared to generic tools) by tailoring their composition language to a specific domain and its very own needs. That is, despite the existence of standard languages like BPEL, there are good reasons for having different languages for different uses and different users.

Designing a composition language is however *not an easy task*. There are lots of conceptual and technological choices to be made, such as (i) which *components* to support (e.g., SOAP services, RESTful services, UI widgets, or proprietary component technologies); (ii) which *composition logic* to adopt (e.g., event-based, control flow, data flow, blackboard-like data exchange, and so on); (iii) which *data integration* capabilities to support (e.g., parameter mapping, template-based transformations, scripts, etc.); and (iv) which *presentation* features to provide, if any (e.g., UI templates, UI widgets, single pages, multiple pages). All these choices do not only affect the structure of the composition language, but eventually they determine the complexity and viability of the composition platform built on top. A careless selection of features and constructs inevitably results in inconsistent languages and tools. Even worse, oftentimes developers are not even aware of which choices need to be made and which options are available, or they do not understand which implications an individual choice has on another choice. For example, it does not make sense to support both control flow and data flow based composition logics in one and a same language, as both paradigms specify the order in which component operations are to be invoked. The former explicitly defines this order independently of how data is passed from one component to another; the latter defines the order implicitly focusing instead on how data is passed among components. Having both together could thus lead to duplicate—possibly inconsistent—definitions of the operations' invocation order.

Recognizing this difficulty, which we experience ourselves in the development of our mashup tools, with this paper we would like to lay the foundation for the *conceptual design of custom composition languages* for mashup tools, an approach that aims to modularize and reuse language construction knowledge. The idea is to enable a developer to reason at a high level of abstraction about the composition language he would like to obtain and to allow him to interactively construct his language by specifying the set of composition features that characterize his target language—everything by guaranteeing the soundness, i.e., consistency, of the final result. With the help of a hosted design tool, we would like to provide custom composition language design *as a service* and equip the design tool with an according, hosted runtime environment (an execution engine) that is able to execute compositions/mashups expressed in any of the languages constructed with the tool. The final objective is very ambitious. The approach is to start with a set of core functionalities and to extend this set over time as new requirements emerge. The *contributions* we provide in this paper are:

- We provide a comprehensive conceptualization of the most important *composition features* that characterize todays most prominent composition languages.
- We derive a *generic, extensible composition language meta-model*, which expresses how the identified features can be used together for the construction of custom composition languages.
- We modularize the identified composition features into *reusable language patterns*, and equip the patterns with a simple logic-based language to express feature composition constraints and to guarantee consistency.
- We generate *custom composition languages* and according custom component description languages from the developer's selection of composition features.

The *structure* of the remainder of the paper is as follows. Next, we provide an example scenario and some background knowledge on composition language features. Then, in Sect. 3.4, we describe key requirements and our problem statement. In Sect. 3.5, we outline our approach. In Sect. 3.6, we describe our generic composition language meta-model, and in Sect. 3.7 we describe the structure of composition features. In Sect. 3.8 we show two composition language definition examples, in Sect. 3.9 we discuss related works and in Sect. 3.10 we conclude.

3.2 Scenario

Let's assume we need to develop a custom composition language with specific properties. Specifically, let's assume we want to develop a mashup language presenting the same characteristics of the language used by the mashArt mashup platform [5], which we developed from scratch in the context of the mashArt project. A simple example of a composition instance that the language must be able to support is the one presented in Fig. 3.1: we want to allow any user to search for a given—user-selected—object in a specific—user-selected—geographical area and to get a list of results. Then, by selecting one of the results the user will see its location displayed on a map and will be provided with the traffic information related to the geographical area around this location. For example, a user must be able to look for hotels in Miami, get a list of hotels in the city and, when selecting one of them, visualize its location on a map and have the traffic information regarding the area around the selected hotel. This example shows the need for the integration and synchronization of data, business logic and user interfaces.

Concretely, we need a mashup language allowing one to integrate data, application logic (e.g., through Web services) and graphical UI components. This is what we called *universal integration* in the context of the mashArt project. Moreover, as shown in Fig. 3.1, the language has to support the presentation of the UI components inside a single Web page, manage their synchronization (considering the event-based

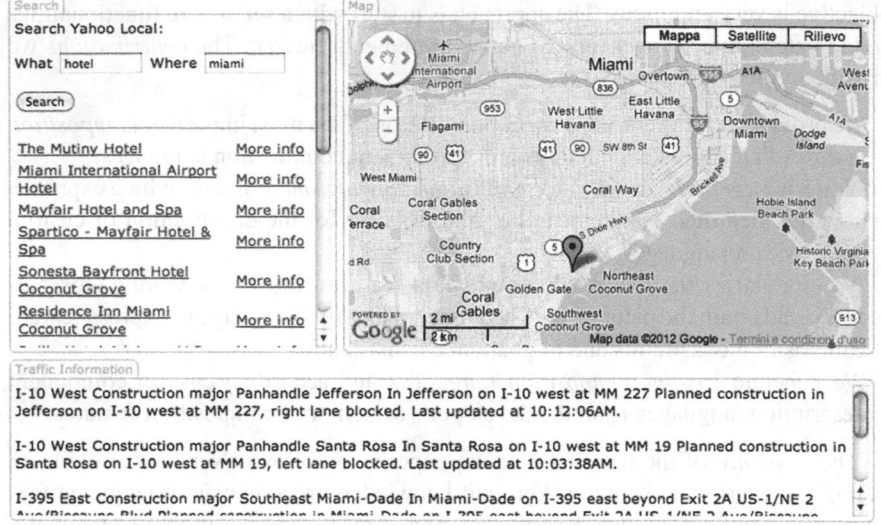

Fig. 3.1 Example of mashup application the mashArt language must support

nature of UIs), and allow for the explicit definition of the data flow schema enabling components to exchange data. Propagating data among components may require conditional execution of flows, as well as branching and merging of parallel flows. UI components, which are implemented in JavaScript, can possibly have parameters for their configuration and one or more operations including an arbitrary number of input and output parameters. Web services are typically SOAP-based or RESTful. The resulting mashups are accessible to any user in a single-user fashion; thus, no user management or collaboration support by the language is needed.

3.3 Background: Software Composition

The scenario shows that mashup development is an intricate software integration and composition endeavor. As highlighted in [1], next to the integration of data and application logic, mashups also feature integration of user interface, i.e., UI integration. Figure 3.2 graphically illustrates the situation from a conceptual point of view and contextualizes the three integration layers in the domain of the Web with its very own component technologies

Data level integration. When the focus is on the integration of data, we have specific needs to address. Typically, solutions for retrieving, combining, splitting and transforming data are needed. In addition, when more than one entity is involved in the data integration process data exchange among the involved parties may be needed. In the context of Web mashups, we have specific conditions and constraints.

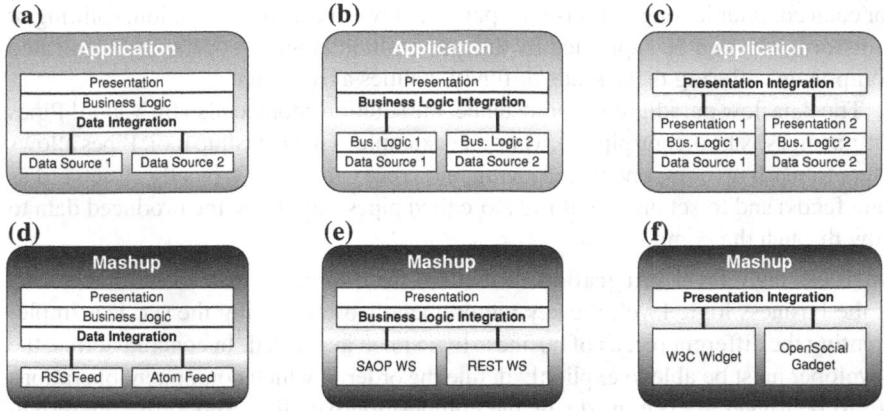

Fig. 3.2 The different levels of integration in general and in the specific context of web mashups

Data sources are typically not fully accessible, i.e., the standard way of retrieving data on the Web is through Web services or Web APIs. This means that we can only access the data provided by the service and we cannot make arbitrary complex, free queries over the data source, as we could do with conventional databases. The key problem of data integration is understanding which data items are semantically similar to which other data items and solving possible formatting differences. Mashups aren't any different. They usually integrate data coming from completely independent sources, which were not designed to work together; thus, data format and structure mismatches must be solved. Mechanisms to address these kinds of problems span from simple data mapping solutions, allowing one, e.g., to map part of the output of one service onto (part of) the input of another service, to more powerful solutions supporting data transformation languages and processors (like, e.g., XSLT). On the other side, though, on the Web there are official and de-facto standards that are often-times adopted (e.g., RSS and Atom feeds, XML and JSON formats), which simplify data integration in that they standardize the syntax and partly also the semantics of data (e.g., RSS and Atom).

In the mashup context, considering also the usual intent to keep the tools' complexity as low as possible, a well-known and widely adopted paradigm for data integration is *data flow* integration. Specifying a data flow among components means explicitly expressing (e.g., visually modeling) how data flows from one component to one or more other components, thereby also stating an order of invocation of components (the flow) and respective activation conditions (the availability of input data). In other words, a data flow based composition logic implies also a control flow logic, i.e., an execution order of components. With the term component we specifically refer to software artifacts (e.g., Web services) exposing public functions (also called operations) providing for data provisioning or processing. Data travelling along a flow are visible only to the component involved in the flow. Data flows allow the easy implementation of data mappings, e.g., by creating separate data flow connections for each communicating output-input pair. Features like data aggregation, splitting or transformation can be supported by the composition language or through dedicated components offering these kinds of functionalities as a service.

The data flow paradigm is, for instance, the solution adopted also by Yahoo! Pipes (http://pipes.yahoo.com/pipes/), a popular example of data mashup tool. Pipes allows users to mash up components retrieving and processing data (typically structured as data feeds) and to set up data flows (so-called pipes), allowing the produced data to flow through the composition.

Business logic level integration. When the main target is instead the integration at the business logic level, the key requirement is orchestrating the services implementing the different pieces of business logic to be integrated. In concrete terms, the developer must be able to explicitly define the order in which component operations are to be triggered. The most suitable composition paradigm supporting these features is the *control flow* paradigm. Specifying a control flow means specifying when to enact which component inside a composition. Doing so may require the definition of conditional flows, of flow branching (i.e., parallel flows) and flow merging (i.e., parallel flows synchronization).

Examples of pure control flow based compositions can be developed, e.g., in BPMN, which offers many control flow related constructs including conditions, loops, parallel flows and so forth. Although the focus of the control flow paradigm is on the order of tasks or components, executing them usually requires complementary data passing mechanisms to feed them with the necessary inputs. In combination with the control flow paradigm, the *blackboard approach*, i.e., global variables holding data produce and consumed at runtime, is typically used for this (note that the "data flow" constructs of BPMN do not express a data flow based composition logic, but rather the writing and reading of business data). This scheme is also used in the BPEL language, where the main target is the integration of SOAP-based Web services.

Presentation level integration. As mentioned, in other cases the main focus is on the integration of user interfaces at the presentation layer. In this case the composition language must support the graphical representation of UI components with suitable constructs. Also in this case, our focus on Web mashups sets specific constraints. UI presentation takes place inside the browser, normally in standard HTML pages. As shown by the example of Fig. 3.1, typically a Web page may contain one or more UI components. UI components are software artifacts that have two main functions: show a graphical user interface and provide users with a point of direct interaction with the composition through their interfaces. UI components usually require synchronization, in order to have them show related content. Typically the interaction mechanism implementing UI synchronization is event-based, since UI development is intrinsically event-based and it is just not possible to predict when and in which order user interactions will take place (which makes asynchronous events a good instrument to manage communication among components). Support for data passing among UI components may also be needed and can be implemented following either the data flow or the blackboard paradigms.

Concretely, in the mashup world, languages supporting presentation features typically include two additional concepts to lay out UI components: *pages* and *viewports*. A viewport is a placeholder where a UI component is hosted and rendered (e.g., a `div` or `iframe` element contained in an HTML page). A page can contain one or more viewports, allowing for the presentation of integrated user interfaces. These concepts are present in the models of several mashup tools, e.g., mashArt and JackBe Presto, as well as in the W3C Widgets family of specifications (where the term viewport itself comes from).

Having user interfaces oriented toward human users opens to the introduction of other composition features, such as user authorization and management mechanisms in the case of mashups with multiple pages. Individual pages may be assigned to specific user roles, allowing for the definition of multi-user, collaborative mashup applications where several users can work on a shared mashup instance acting on the pages they have access to. This is, for instance, one of the main features in the MarcoFlow platform [2].

3.4 Requirements and Problem Statement

What does it now mean to develop a *custom* composition language for mashup design and to support its execution? In order to answer this question, first of all we define a *custom composition language* as a composition language that is specifically tailored to a given combination of component types and a target application/service type (mashup type). We represent a language (we use the terms *language* and *composition language* interchangeably) by means of its meta-model or XSD schema. Standard languages like BPEL [7] or BPMN [8] are very focused languages that are generally not able to satisfy the requirements of a mashup platform, since mashups typically go much beyond the orchestration of SOAP web services or human tasks.

In order to develop a custom language, we generally have different *design options* that allow us to achieve the desired expressive power:

- *Development from scratch*: This is the current practice that we want to prevent. Developing a language from scratch means designing the language without any reference by looking at the composition problem to be solved and by deriving suitable, ad-hoc composition constructs. This task is more complex than it looks like and often leads to poorly designed, inconsistent languages, which can only be run by specifically tailored runtime environments.
- *Selection of off-the-shelf language*: This is the other, ideal extreme, in which for each component and mashup type combination we have a pre-defined language that supports all features of the given combination. Implementing all these languages is not feasible, in that the number of potential languages (and execution engines) grows combinatorially with the number of component types and features of the target mashups. Also, the introduction of a new component type or feature would require the update of the whole languages library.

- *Extension of existing language*: A practice that works in many situations is to take an existing language, e.g., BPEL, and to extend it with new constructs and semantics, so as to support custom features. Starting from a known language eases the adoption of the extended language, but it is typically hard to identify a suitable language, and changes to the original language may involuntarily introduce inconsistencies into the custom extension. Even with small extensions, the language's own engine can usually no longer be used for execution.
- *Customization of reference language*: Another option is to provide a set of reference languages with predefined extension mechanisms. For instance, we could have reference languages for data-flow-based, control-flow-based, UI-based mashups, and combinations thereof. Yet, it is hard to predict all possible customization requirements and to maintain the library of reference languages and execution engines up to date with changing technologies and applications.
- *Modular composition of language*: Finally, we can provide a set of basic language features, such as control flow, data flow, UI synchronization, and the like and allow the developer to compose his own language. Newly emerging features can be added to the feature library without invalidating prior language specifications. Given a library of language features, it suffices to implement only one execution engine that is able to understand all the features, in order to be able to execute a large set of custom mashups.

In this paper we specifically focus on the problem of developing custom languages, while our vision is also to provide runtime support for custom languages; the modular composition approach seems therefore most suitable. But which is a good granularity for *reusable language modules*? We again have several options:

- *Individual language constructs* (with the term *construct* we generically refer to both meta-model and XSD constructs): Constructs like components, pages, ports, inputs, outputs, connectors, and similar are the basic ingredients for every language. Yet, constructs represent the lowest level of granularity of a language. It is therefore hard to encode reusable language construction knowledge, if not in the form of a library of typical composition constructs. How to use each construct, in which combination with other constructs, for which typical modeling situation, and so on can however not be expressed.
- *Composite constructs*: Modules may express composite constructs, such as the structured elements sequence, parallel flow, and loop, typically used for the construction of well-formed models. This technique aids the development of composition languages that are sound, but it is still very syntactic and does not support reuse of more complex language construction knowledge.
- *Language patterns*: Modules may also express more complex usage patterns of constructs that represent semantically meaningful composition language properties, such as control flow, data flow, UI synchronization, component types, asynchronous versus synchronous communications, etc. If such patterns are further equipped with suitable language composition constraints, it is also possible to guarantee their sound composition.

Given our experience with the reuse of modeling knowledge [3], we advocate the use of semantically meaningful language patterns to represent reusable language composition knowledge. We call these patterns *language features*, since they allow us to represent composition features in an abstract fashion. The question that remains to be answered is therefore which language features must be provided, so as to support the construction of a reasonably wide set of possible languages. Looking at set of existing mashup approaches [4–6] and standard composition languages [7, 8] and without trying to crack the whole problem at once, we identify five key aspects (groups of features) that influence the expressive power of a composition language:

1. *Component types*: First and foremost, the *object* of the composition, i.e., the types of components, influences the whole logic of the language most prominently. There are many possible component technologies to take into account, such as SOAP web services, RESTful services, UI widgets, JavaScript classes, plain XML or CSV data sources, and similar. Composing UI widgets is, for example, fundamentally different from orchestrating web services.
2. *Control flow logic*: Next, it is important to define how the *computation* of a composite application or service is enacted, that is, how and when individual components are processed. Components may be enacted in parallel (e.g., in the case of simple UI widgets placed in a web page), they may be executed sequentially, their execution may be subject to conditions, and so on. The possibility to integrate heterogeneous component technologies (e.g., UI widgets and web services) further increases the number of available control flow options, if the control flow paradigm is required at all.
3. *Data passing logic*: In addition to the control flow logic, the language must be able to express how data is *propagated* among components. While data flow paradigms typically bring together aspects of both control flow and data passing, other paradigms like pure control flow or UI synchronization may rather adopt a blackboard approach with global variables.
4. *Presentation logic*: One of the distinguishing features of mashups is that they also feature *integration of user interfaces*, not only services and data sources. This however asks for specific techniques to lay out and render UI elements. For instance, we may make use of HTML templates with placeholders or we may have automatic arrangements of UI widgets, there might be the need of special visualization components for data sources, and so on.
5. *Collaboration support*: Finally, mashups can be much more than simple, one-page applications. We can have mashups that implement *collaborative* business processes with different actors per task, or we can have mashups that support the *concurrent* use of individual pages by multiple users. Supporting these features requires the possibility to express at least roles of users and to assign them to pages, while more complex logics can be envisioned.

The *problem* we want to solve in this paper is to *enable developers to design custom composition languages in an abstract, conceptual fashion*, supporting the five above feature types and guaranteeing that the final languages come without internal inconsistencies, i.e., that they are *sound*. Our focus is on imperative mashup languages that can be executed by a mashup engine.

3.5 Approach

Figure 3.3 graphically illustrates how we decompose the problem into artifacts and how we finally obtain a custom language. The idea is to express a *custom composition language* as a set of *composition features* that give the language its expressive power. Features come with a set of *feature constraints*, which express feature compatibilities, conflicts, and subsumptions. For each of the five types of composition features discussed above, we provide a set of concrete features (we discuss them next). Each feature has a *reference specification*, i.e., a pattern of language constructs, which implements the feature and represents reusable language composition knowledge. Patterns are based on a *generic composition language meta-model*. The meta-model does not yet represent an executable language. It syntactically puts composition constructs and features in relation with each other, but it also contains constructs and features that are not compatible with each other (e.g., control flow and data flow constructs). The meta-model determines which features are supported and how they are syntactically integrated; the sensible design of feature constraints provides for soundness. Hence, given a set of non-conflicting composition features, the custom composition language is represented by the *union* of the respective reference specifications. Similarly, we derive a *custom component description language*, which can be used as guide for the implementation of components and to describe their external interfaces.

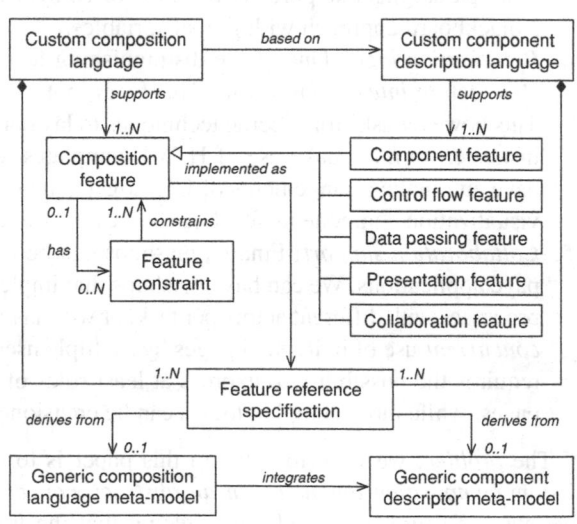

Fig. 3.3 Conceptual approach to the development of custom composition languages

In the following, we first construct the generic meta-model, then we describe how we define composition features on top using patterns and constraints and how patterns can be used and integrated for the development of custom languages.

3.6 The Generic Composition Meta-Model

Before going into the details of the language meta-model, we introduce the meta-meta-model it complies with, as such is also the basis for the final code generation.

3.6.1 Language Meta-Meta-Model

To design the meta-model for the composition languages, we use a notation and modeling language derived from the UML Class Diagram with some peculiarities. Specifically, we impose some constraints on the allowed types of modeling constructs, tailoring them to the expressive power required by our modeling needs. As detailed in Sect. 3.6.3, applying these constraints allows for an unambiguous translation of the meta-model into a formal—and machine-readable—language schema definition, which is then needed for the definition of other artifacts of the system. In addition, using this constrained modeling language also opens to future extensions of the meta-model by third parties, making them aware of the implications of each model extension or modification on the resulting language definition (since deterministic translation rules are defined). Concretely, as defined by the meta-meta-model depicted in Fig. 3.4, the meta-model may consist of:

- *Entities.* Represent main constructs of the composition language. They are identified by a name.
- *Attributes.* Each entity can have a set of related attributes characterizing it. Attributes have a name and a type. The type can be stated through its name or

Fig. 3.4 Composition language meta-meta-model

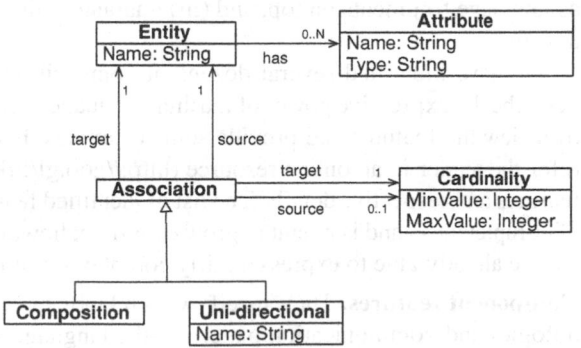

can be explicitly defined in form of enumeration of possible values. To be noticed, each entity in our meta-model must contain an attribute named *id*, representing a unique identifier for the instances of the entity used to reference them.

- *Associations*. Relations among the entities are expressed through associations. Only two possible types of associations are needed: *composition* and *uni-directional* association. The composition is used to state that an entity is contained in another one, while the uni-directional association states that an entity simply refers to another entity, but it is not contained in it.
- *Cardinalities*. Represent associations' multiplicities. The target cardinality represents the multiplicity of the association when reading it following the specified association direction, while the source cardinality represents the multiplicity when reading the association in the opposite direction.

3.6.2 The Generic Meta-Model

In essence, our approach is to *compose* composition languages out of composition features represented as language patterns. Just like in any other composition approach, the core problem is therefore the identification and formalization of the "components" to work with. In our case, these components are *language patterns* (e.g., XSD fragments). However, these patterns have a distinctive feature that makes our problem very different form generic component-based development (next to the fact that we do not handle software modules but document/model fragments): unlike, for example, web services, *language patterns are not independent*. That is, the reference specifications of different composition features may overlap (e.g., interacting with a *SOAP service* is very similar to interacting with a *RESTful service*), include other features (e.g., the *data flow* paradigm generally subsumes the presence of *data source components*), or exclude others (e.g., the *data flow* paradigm does not make use of *variables*). This asks for a thorough design of the language patterns and their mutual interaction points, a task that we achieve by mapping each composition feature into the *generic composition meta-model* (see Fig. 3.5), which (i) integrates all basic language constructs syntactically, (ii) allows us to define composition features as language fragments on top, and (iii) guarantees that fragments are compatible by design.

We have identified several dozens of composition features that can be used to describe the expressive power of mashup languages. In the following paragraphs, we overview the features and provide some examples. For space reasons, however, we refer the reader to an online resource (http://goo.gl/hfkLO) for the list of supported features and respective details. The list of identified features comes without the claim of completeness and is meant to grow over time; however, as we will see in Sect. 3.8, we are already able to express a fairly complex set of mashup languages.

Component features. They specify which kinds of components—in terms of technologies and communication patterns—the language should support. For instance,

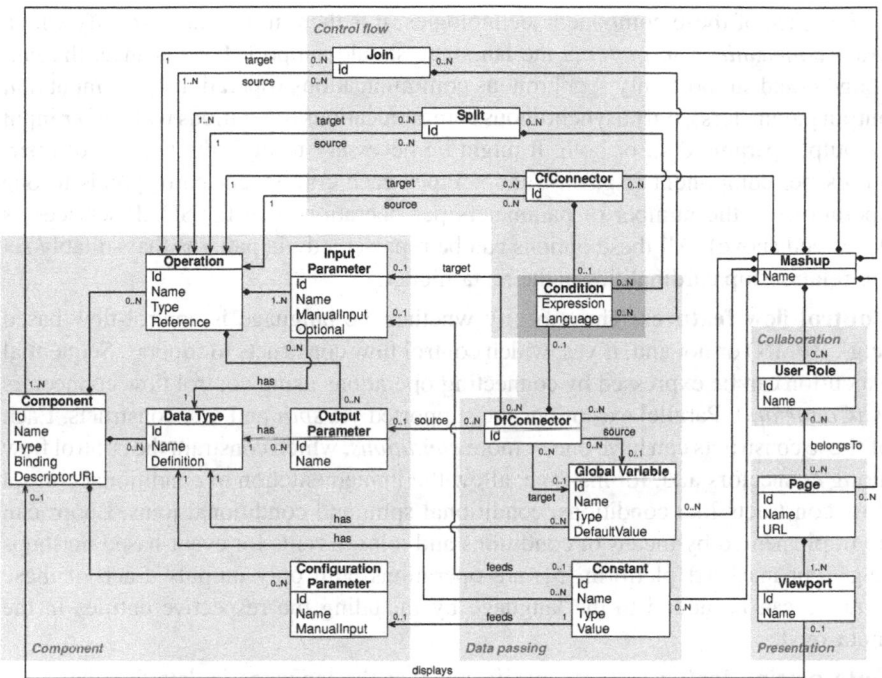

Fig. 3.5 The generic composition meta-model for custom languages. *Gray boxes* group entities into feature types. The component group is also used to derive component descriptor languages

a SOAP web service may come with message-based operations of four different types (request-response, solicit-response, one-way, notification), custom data formats for each input and output message, a service endpoint, and a protocol binding (e.g., SOAP). We represent such a service in the meta-model as a *component* that has a set of *operations* with different input/output parameter patterns (implementing the four different operation types), only single *input/output parameters* per operation to represent input/output messages, an own *data type* for each parameter, and respective *binding* and *endpoint* attribute values. Similarly, a W3C UI widget [9] can be seen as a *component* with some *configuration parameters* but without operations, which can be displayed in a *viewport* of a *page* of the mashup.

Analogously, the meta-model so far conciliates the following *technologies*, which are the basis of many types of mashups and, as such, widely used and accepted (component technologies are tracked by the *type* attribute of the *component* entity):

- Data source components: RSS feeds, Atom feeds, RESTful data components, SOAP data components, JavaScript data components.
- Web service components: Atom services, RESTful services, SOAP services, JavaScript components.
- UI components: W3C UI widgets [9], JavaScript UI components [5] (our own).

For each of these component technologies, it is then important to specify which exact *communication patterns* the language should support. For instance, the language could support only synchronous communications (operations with input *and* output parameters), only asynchronous communications (operations with *either* input *or* output parameters), or both. It might be necessary to limit the number of operations per component (e.g., in Yahoo! Pipes each component corresponds to one operation) or the number of parameters per operation (like for SOAP services as described above). All these options can be represented via patterns that suitably set the relationship cardinalities in the meta-model.

Control flow features. They specify whether the language is control-flow-based (e.g., BPMN) or not and, if yes, which control flow constructs to support. Sequential execution can be expressed by connecting operations using control flow connectors (*CfConnetors*). Parallel executions are supported via *split* and *join* constructs. Each of these constructs can have one or more *conditions*, which constrain the control flow along connectors and, for instance, allow the implementation of conditional control flow constructs like conditions, conditional split, and conditional joins. Loops can be implemented by means of conditions and joins. Events for event-based mashups (e.g., our mashArt platform [5]) are operations with only outputs. Each of these features can be added to the language by including the respective entities in the meta-model.

Data passing features. They specify whether the language is data-flow-based or not and how data is propagated among components. In data-flow-based languages (e.g., Yahoo! Pipes) it suffices to connect two operations using a data flow connector (*DfConnector*), in order to propagate the output of the first operation as input to the second operation. Implicitly, data flow connectors also determine how components are enacted and, hence, do not require any additional control flow construct. Data flows may however be subject to conditional execution. Control-flow-based languages, instead, require additional constructs to specify how data are passed among components. The most common technique is to write/read *global variables* (blackboard feature), which are accessible during the execution of a composition (e.g., as in BPEL). The meta-model represents the writing/reading operations with a data flow connector between the variable and its target/source parameter. UI-based mashups, such as widget portals, typically run all widgets in parallel, and data is passed via global variables or events (operation with only outputs). Configuration parameters are instead typically set once at the startup of a component (e.g., the background color of a UI widget); we support this by means of *constants*. Data passing may also require mapping output parameters to input parameters, a feature that can be achieved by specifying data flow connectors between parameters instead of between operations.

Presentation features. They specify whether the language is UI-based or not and how UI widgets are laid out into web pages. Unlike service compositions, mashups typically also come with an own user interface that renders UI components and data from UI-less components. The minimum support required to express this capability in the meta-model is represented by the *page* and *viewport* entities, which allow the ordering of UI components into pages (HTML web pages) and their rendering in selected areas inside these pages (typically div or iframe HTML elements). We assume the HTML pages are given and already linked to each other as necessary.

Collaboration features. They specify whether the language describes single-user or multi-user mashups and how user roles collaborate. Single-user mashups (the most common type of mashups) do not require any user management. Multi-user mashups, instead, may restrict the visibility of individual *pages* to selected *user roles* only. Users may have different views on a mashup (e.g., via different pages) or they may have the same view (e.g., via the concurrent use of a same page). For the time being, we start with a simple, role-based user management logic and do not say anything about how such is implemented, as this is a runtime choice.

The above features and examples show that developing a good generic meta-model is a *trade-off* between the simplicity and usability of the final language (the fewer individual constructs the better) and the ease of mapping features onto the meta-model (the more constructs the better; in the extreme case, each feature could have its own construct). The challenge we try to solve in this paper is exactly that of identifying the right balance between the two, so as to be able to map all relevant features and to do so in an as elegant as possible fashion from the resulting language point of view.

3.6.3 Mapping the Generic Meta-Model to XSD

The information represented by the generic meta-model constitutes the basis for the definition of the feature reference specifications (see Sect. 3.7.1) and is required by the language generation algorithm (see Sect. 3.7.3). Therefore, we need to serialize the generic meta-model in a machine-readable format. To this aim, also considering the context where mashup languages are used (i.e., the Web), we map the meta-model onto an equivalent XSD definition. As introduced in Sect. 3.6.1, we impose some simple conventions and constraints to the admitted modeling constructs for the meta-model so that we can define a set of rules which guarantees an unambiguous translation of the model.

Figure 3.6 exemplifies how the generic meta-model is translated into an equivalent XSD definition applying the following translation rules:

- Entities (e.g., *page*) are translated as XSD elements having the same name of the entity.
- Entity attributes (e.g., a page's URL) are translated as XSD attributes of the related element having the same name of the entity's attribute.
- Composition associations (e.g., the one having *viewport* as source and *page* as target) are translated defining within the element associated to the target entity an XSD child element (with zero or more possible occurrences depending on the specified cardinality) having the name of the source entity (e.g., the element *page*

Fig. 3.6 Example of translation of a meta-model fragment into XSD

has 1 to N child elements *viewport*). As shown in the example in the figure, the child elements are contained and defined within the parent element.

- Uni-directional associations (e.g., the one having *page* as source and *userRole* as target) are translated defining within the element associated to the source entity an XSD child element (with zero or more possible occurrences depending on the specified cardinality) having the name of the form "association-Name_targetEntityName" and including an attribute *ref* designed to contain a reference (i.e., the ID) to a target entity instance (e.g., the element *page* may have 0 to N child elements *belongsTo_userRole*). The child elements only refer to the target entity and do not define it.

Applying the above translation rules to the meta-model presented in Fig. 3.5 we obtain an equivalent XSD definition that we use as base for the production of the artifacts and algorithm presented in the next section. The complete schema definition can be inspected at http://goo.gl/hfkLO.

3.7 Representing and Assembling Composition Features

The meta-model in Fig. 3.5 solves the problem of integrating the composition language constructs needed to specify a varied set of composition features. Designing the meta-model required both the analysis of the features to be supported and knowledge about their implementation in terms of language constructs. We aim to abstract away from low-level language constructs and represent concrete composition features on top of the generic meta-model so as to allow the language developer to focus on the selection of features only, in order to design his custom language.

We define a composition feature as $f = \langle name, label, desc, spec, Constr \rangle$, where *name* is a text label that uniquely identifies the feature (e.g., data_flow); label briefly describes the feature and expresses its semantics; *desc* is a natural language verbose description of the feature for human consumption; *spec* is the reference specification of the feature; and $Constr = constr_i$ is a set of feature constraints.

```
<feature name="condition" label="Conditions">

    <description> Conditions can be set for each connector to define the
        possible flows of the composition. Conditions are supported both for
        control flow and data flow composition paradigms.
    </description>

    <specification>

        <include fragments="conditionForCf" if="control_flow"/>
        <include fragments="conditionForDf" if="data_flow"/>
        <include fragments="conditionForSplit" if="split"/>
        <include fragments="conditionForJoin" if="join"/>

    </specification>

    <constraints>
        (control_flow AND blackboard) OR data_flow
    </constraints>

</feature>
```

Listing 3.1 XML reference specification of the condition composition feature

The XML code in Listing 3.1 shows an example of how we serialize, for instance, the condition feature in our *feature knowledge base* of the form $F = f_j$. The example shows the two core ingredients that allow us to collapse the assembling of features into a simple selection of feature names: First, the *reference specification* of the feature expresses which specific language constructs—out of all those represented in the generic meta-model—are needed to implement the feature. From the XSD representation of the generic meta-model (see Sect. 3.6.3), we identify given subsets of the schema definition representing semantically meaningful parts of it. An ID uniquely identifies each of these fragments in the XSD. Second, the *feature constraints* state feature compatibilities or incompatibilities. They are simple Boolean conditions. We detail these two aspects in the following.

3.7.1 Feature Specification Language

In order for feature specifications to be composable, we adopt a constructive approach that starts with an empty language specification (we call it the *base language*), which contains only the basic XSD structure (e.g., name space definitions and types) for the language to be generated, and then incrementally adds new constructs based on the specifications the of selected features. Since a given feature may span multiple constructs of the meta-model, a feature reference specification generally requires multiple language fragments (identified through manually assigned IDs) to be included in the final custom language definition. For instance, the specification of the `blackboard` feature requires several fragments to be included, e.g., those related to the specification of the *Global Variable* construct and those related to the specification of the *DfConnector* construct used to connect variables and parameters. The syntax to require the *inclusion of the fragments* referenced by a given feature is as follows:

```
<include
     fragments="[comma separated list of fragments IDs]"
     if="[condition]" />
```

Each feature specification contains one or more `include` elements that are composed by an attribute `fragments` listing the fragments needed to implement the feature in the custom language XSD definition. The referenced IDs relate to XSD fragments defining elements, attributes, enumerations and similar. In addition, the `include` element may optionally contain an attribute `if` that can be used to require a conditional inclusion of the referenced fragment(s). In particular, the condition can require the selection or non-selection of other features for the inclusion to be performed (as exemplified in Listing 3.1). The fragments come with default values for cardinalities (i.e., values for the `minOccur` and `maxOccur` XSD attributes), as specified in the meta-model in Figure 3.5. Some features, such as the `max_1_operation_per_component` or the `single_page` features, may need to modify them. In order to change cardinality values, we provide a dedicated cardinality setting function with the following syntax:

```
<setCardinality
     element="[elementID]"
     minOccurs="[value]"
     maxOccurs="[value]" />
```

The function has three attributes, which allow us to select which XSD `element` in the current language specification to modify and which `minOccurs` and/or `maxOccurs` values to assign to the element. It can be noticed that an association's cardinality setting involves only one XSD element. This is because, according to our translation rules, associations are translated in one element that is nested into the associated element and, therefore, the cardinality setting needs only to set the number of possible occurrences of one element, i.e., the nested one.

3.7.2 Feature Constraints Language

Feature constraints are *Boolean conditions* that check (i) whether all features *required* by a given selection of features are contained in the selection and (ii) whether the selection contains *conflicting* features. Feature constraints therefore guarantee for the semantic soundness of a selection of features. Feature constraints are of the form: *constr* ::= *fbool* | ¬*constr* | *constr op constr*.
fbool ∈ *FB* is a Boolean variable representing the selection (or not) of a feature,

$FB = \{fb_j | fb_j = \langle name, val \rangle, name = f_j.name, f_j \in F, val = true|false\}$ is the set of Boolean variables representing all features, and $op \in \{\wedge, \vee, \oplus\}$ is one of the logical AND, OR, and XOR operators.

For example, in Listing 3.1 we have the constraint (control_flow AND blackboard) OR data_flow, since for the definition of conditions it is required the presence of some data passing mechanism in the mashup model. This is an example of constraint assessing the presence of the features required for the selected one. An example of constraint preventing conflicting features is the one associated to the feature max_0_operation_per_component (e.g., used for simple UI widget portals), which may state: NOT(data_flow OR control_flow). It would not make sense to support any of these paradigms in a language that by definition does not allow communication among components.

In addition to assigning constraints to individual features, we assign a set of base constraints to the base language, in order to enforce global constraints that guarantee the integrity of the overall language. For instance, the constraint (control_flow XOR data_flow) OR user_interface asks for the selection of at least one basic mashup paradigm (e.g., a simple state machine or UI widget portal).

3.7.3 Language Generation Algorithm

Algorithm 1 summarizes the language generation logic. It takes as input a set of feature names and produces as output either an according combination of composition and component description languages or *null* (in case of constraint conflicts). After initializing the variables holding the language to be generated and the constraints to be evaluated (lines 2–3), the algorithm loads the complete feature specifications of each feature in input from the feature knowledge base (line 4) and sets the respective Boolean variables to *true* and all the remaining variables (those associated to non-selected features) to *false* (lines 5–6). This enables the processing of the checkSoundness function, which checks whether all the constraints associated to the selected features are satisfied. For this purpose, the function evaluates the Boolean formula contained in *CONSTR* based on the variable values assigned in lines 5–6. If the evaluation returns *false*, the function stops processing and returns *null* (lines 7–10). Otherwise, the algorithm constructs the list of IDs of all the fragments required by the selected features and the set of *setCardinality* instructions needed to update the default cardinalities (lines 11–13). Based on these sets the algorithm constructs the actual output composition language including all the fragments in the *FRAGMENTS* set and then updates the cardinalities of the elements of the resulting composition language based on the instructions contained in the *SETCARDINS* set (lines 14–15). Finally the algorithm returns the composition language definition and the component description language definition, which is extracted by the former (line 17).

Our current prototype of the language generator comes as a simple command line tool, which takes as input a text file with the list of desired language features and, if successful, produces as output two XSD files for the composition and component description languages. The feature knowledge base F is a plain XML file, which can easily be extended with new features.

Algorithm 1. generateLanguage

Data:	Set of selected feature names *FnameSel*
Results:	⟨*compositionLang, componentDescLang*⟩ containing the generated composition language specification in XSD and the according component description language specification in XSD, or *null* if the there are conflicts among the constraints of the selected features

1   // the knowledge base F and the set of Boolean variables FB are accessible through global variables
2   *compositionLang = languageBase*; //languageBase is a global variable
3   *CONSTR = baseConstraints*; //baseConstraints is global variable
4   *Fsel* = {*f*ⱼ | *f*ⱼ ∈ *F, f*ⱼ*.name* ∈ *FnameSel*}; //load sel. features from knowledge base F
5   for each *fb* ∈ *FB* //set values of Boolean variables in FB
6   *fb.val* = (*fb.name* ∈ *FnameSel*) ? true : false;
7   for each *f* ∈ *Fsel* //construct set of constraints to be checked
8   *CONSTR* = *CONSTR* ∪ *f.Constr*;
9   if (**checkSoundness**(*CONSTR, FB*) == false) then //check soundness
10   return null; //interrupt processing if constraint conflicts occur
11   for each *f* ∈ *Fsel*
12   *FRAGMENTS* = *FRAGMENTS* ∪ **returnIncludes**(f); //construct set of fragments IDs
13   *SETCARDINS* = *SETCARDINS* ∪ **returnSets**(f); //construct set of setCardin. opers
14   **includeFragments**(*FRAGMENTS, compositionLang*); //construct composition language
15   **updateCardinalities**(*SETCARDINS, compositionLang*); //update cardinalities
16   //construct result set by generating also the component description language
17   return ⟨*compositionLang*, **extractDescLang**(*compositionLang*)⟩;

3.8 Examples

In the following sections, we apply the conceptual design approach introduced above to two concrete examples with different requirements.

3.8.1 *mashArt*

In Sect. 3.2, we stated a set of requirements for the mashArt composition language. In the following, starting from these requirements, we derive the set of features (emphasized in `Courier` font in the following paragraphs) to be given as input to our generation algorithm to produce a mashup language supporting our scenario.

As said, mashArt aims at integrating data, business logic and user interfaces. Therefore, `data_component`, `service_component` and `ui_component` features are required to support all the different types of needed components. All the components must be implemented through JavaScript, therefore the features

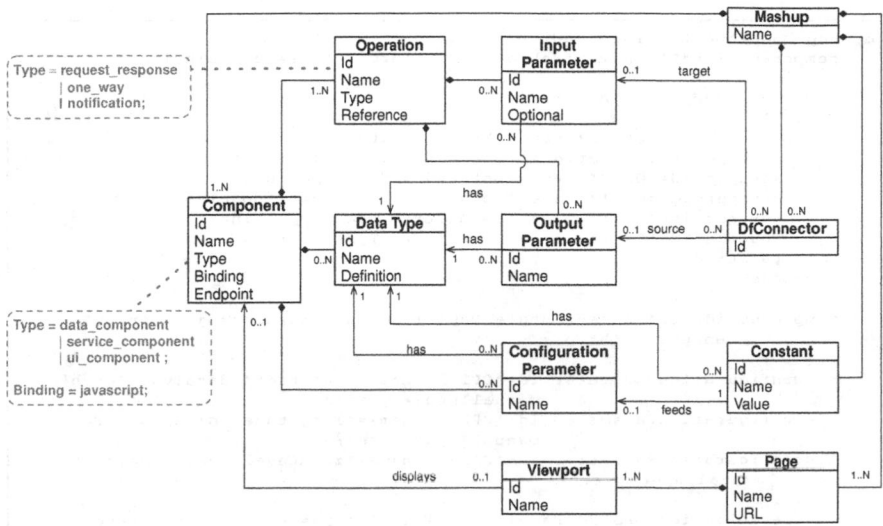

Fig. 3.7 A composition language meta-model supporting the discussed features set

javascript_for_data, javascript_for_service and javascript_
for_ui have to be included. In particular, data components must support only
request_response_for_data operations, service components both
request_response_for_service, one_way_for_service and
notification_for_service operations and UI components only one_way_
for_ui and notification_for_ui operations. The requirements do not
include isolated UI components (i.e., widgets), so all components will have minimum
one operation, while no maximum number of operations per component is required
(max_N_operation_per_component). Also the number of input and output
parameters per operation should not be constrained to any limit (max_N_input_
param_per_oper and max_N_output_param_per_operation). Clearly,
it is also required to support the display and layout of UI components, which is fulfilled by the user_interface feature. In particular, we require compositions to
be constituted by a single_page. The components' intercommunication, according to the requirements, must be supported through the data_flow mechanisms.
In addition, merge and branch features are explicitly required.

The above paragraph provides the list of features supporting our scenario (the
only design artifact to be produced) to be given as input to the language generation algorithm shown in Algorithm 1. Doing so produces an XSD specification
for the composition language that is equivalent to the meta-model illustrated in
Fig. 3.7.

For space reasons we cannot include the whole XSD specification, which can
be inspected at http://goo.gl/hfkLO. Listing 3.2, though, provides an excerpt of the
XML definition—compliant to this specification—representing the example scenario
introduced in Sect. 3.2 (i.e., geo-localized search with traffic information).

```
<mashup name="GeoLocalSearchWithTraffic">
   <component id="C1" name="Yahoo Local Search" type="ui" binding="
      javascript"
                  endpoint="http://...">
      [...]
      <operation id="OP2-1" name="Item Selected"
            type="notification" reference="itemSelected">
         <output id="O2-1" name="Latitude" dataType="double"/>
         <output id="O3-1" name="Longitude" dataType="double"/>
         <output id="O4-1" name="Zoom Level" dataType="int"/>
         <output id="O5-1" name="Label" dataType="string"/>
      </operation>
   </component>

   <component id="C2" name="Google Map" type="ui" binding="javascript"
                  endpoint="http://...">
      [...]
      <configurationParameter id="CP1-2" name="latitude" dataType="double"
                              manualInput="yes"/>
      <configurationParameter id="CP2-2" name="longitude" dataType="double"
                              manualInput="yes"/>
      <configurationParameter id="CP3-2" name="zoomLevel" dataType="int"
         manualInput="yes"/>
      [...]
      <operation id="OP1-2" name="Show Point" type="one-way" reference="
         showPoint">
         <input id="I1-2" name="longitude" dataType="double" optional="no"
            />
         <input id="I2-2" name="latitude" dataType="double" optional="no" /
            >
      </operation>
   </component>

   <component id="C3" name="Geo Names" type="service" binding="javascript"
                  endpoint="http>//...">
      [...]
      <operation id="OP1-3" name="Get address" type="request-response"
                  reference="getAddress">
         <input id="I1-3" name="longitude" dataType="double" optional="no"
            />
         <input id="I2-3" name="latitude" dataType="double" optional="no" /
            >
         <output id="O1-3" name="city" dataType="string"/>
         <output id="O2-3" name="street" dataType="string"/>
      </operation>

   </component>

   [...]
   <constant id="CNST1" name="Latitude" dataType="double" value="46.0667"
            feeds_configurationParameter="CP1-2"/>
   <constant id="CNST2" name="Longitude" dataType="double" value="11.1333"
            feeds_configurationParameter="CP2-2"/>
   <constant id="CNST3" name="Zoom Level" dataType="int" value="13"
            feeds_configurationParameter="CP3-2"/>
   [...]

   <dfConnector id="DF1" source_output="O2-1" target_input="I1-2" />
   <dfConnector id="DF2" source_output="O3-1" target_input="I2-2" />
   <dfConnector id="DF3" source_output="O1-1" target_input="I1-3" />
   <dfConnector id="DF4" source_output="O2-1" target_input="I2-3" />
</mashup>
```

Listing 3.2 XML definition of the example mashup application presented in Sect. 3.2

Figure 3.8 shows how the example scenario can be modeled using the graphical syntax we adopt in the mashArt editor. It can be noticed that all the main composition

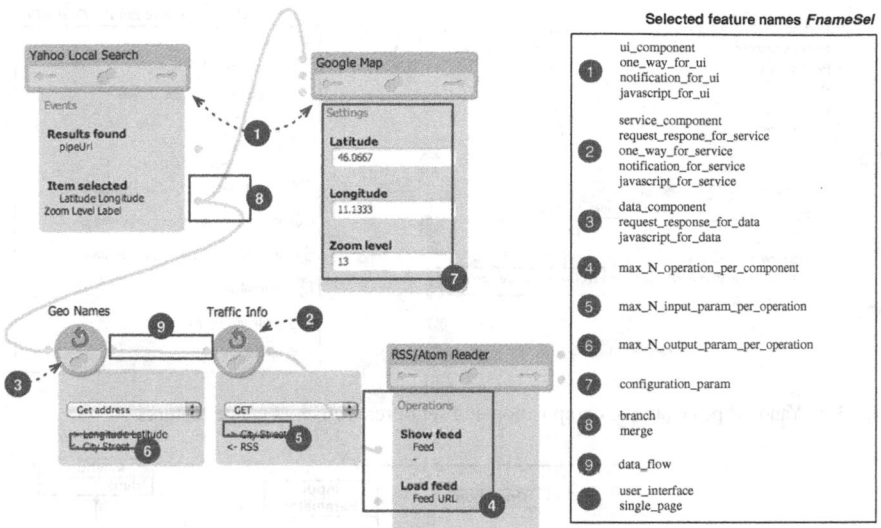

Fig. 3.8 mashArt example composition model and the set of respective language features

features supported by the existing editor are also supported by the language produced by our system, which are summarized on the right side of this figure.

3.8.2 Yahoo! Pipes

In the following, we derive part of the mashup language underlying the popular mashup platform Yahoo! Pipes from an example modeled in its graphical editor. Pipes is a data mashup tool for the retrieval and processing of web data feeds. Figure 3.9 shows an example Pipes model, which we use to analyze Pipes' language features.

Pipes is based on the `data_flow` paradigm. It supports `data_component` and `service_component` types to retrieve and process data, respectively. Specifically, data source components types are `RSS_for_data` or `atoms_for_data`, while the only supported service component type is `REST_for_service`. Each component in Pipes provides exactly one function, that is, each component represents one single operation. Therefore `max_1_operation_per_component`. All operations are of type request-response (`request_response_for_data` and `request_response_for_service`). Each operation may have one or more inputs (`max_N_input_param_per_operation`) but one and only one output (`max_1_output_param_per_operation`). Manual inputs (`manual_input`) are used to fill the values of input fields, i.e., of `configuration_parameter`(s). Some inputs can be fed with both an input pipe and a manually set constant value. Also in this example, the output of a component can be the source

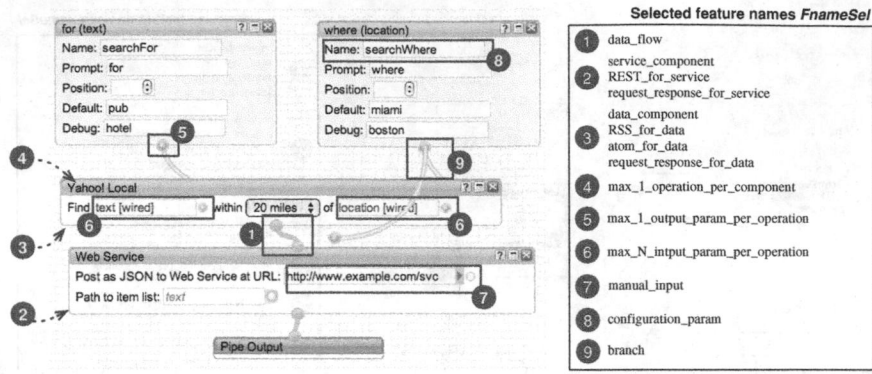

Fig. 3.9 Yahoo Pipes example composition and set of respective language features

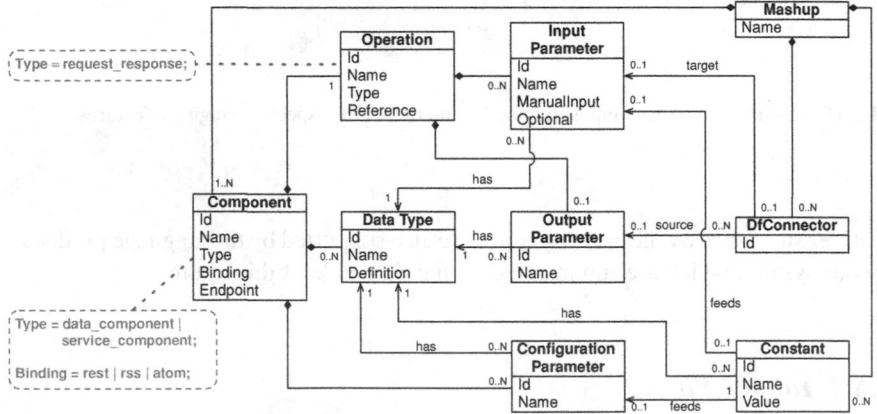

Fig. 3.10 A composition language meta-model supporting the discussed features set

for an arbitrary number of dataflow connectors, allowing one to branch the data flow into parallel flows. Input parameters, instead, have at most one input pipe; so, there is not need for any merge.

The language produced by the language generation algorithm (defined in Algorithm 1) giving as input to it the described features is equivalent to the meta-model illustrated in Fig. 3.10. The respective language XSD specifications and the XML model of the scenario can be inspected online at http://goo.gl/hfkLO.

3.9 Related Work

The problem we aim to solve in this paper, i.e., supporting the design of custom mashup/composition languages, has not been addressed before. Most contributions in the area of mashup and service-oriented computing focus on the design of specific languages taking into account, for example, quality of service [10], adaptivity or context-awareness [11], energy efficiency [12], and similar. We instead propose a language (the composition features) for the design of languages—*a model weaving approach* (at the meta-model level) for *black-box composition* languages (e.g., mashups), in the terminology of Heidenreich et al. [13]. The problem is very complex, but our analysis of a large set of mashup tools and practices has shown that the design space for non-mission-critical mashups (without fault handling, compensations, transactions, etc.) is limited and manageable, up to the point where we can provide mashup execution as a service for a large class of custom languages.

If we compare the meta-model in Fig. 3.5 with, for example, that of BPEL [7] (see also http://www.ebpml.org/wsper/wsper/ws-bpel20b.png) or XPDL, we notice a bias toward *simplicity*. The reason for this is that mashup platforms (our target) aim to simplify composition, typically moving complexity from the composition to the components. For instance, it is common practice to have a dedicated *data filter* component, instead of a filter construct at language level (see, for example, Yahoo! Pipes). The meta-model we propose in this paper shares this interpretation for both the component model and the composition model. Also Saeed and Pautasso [14] have a similar perspective, but they focus on the design of a generic mashup component description language only and do not elaborate on their composition. Their model contains technology aspects (e.g., component wrappers), which are instead a runtime aspect. We only propose the use of component types and bindings.

A proposal toward the standardization of a generic mashup language, covering as many different uses as possible, is represented by the Open Mashup Alliance's EMML (Enterprise Mashup Markup Language) specification [15]. The target of the initiative is however different: data mashups. In our view the key novelty mashups brought to software integration is integration at the UI layer. Hence, the focus on data mashups only is too narrow, yet the language has already grown very complex and has not been adopted so far by vendors outside the Alliance itself.

However, especially with the growing importance of cloud computing and composition as a service providers (such as mashup platforms or scientific workflows [16]), we expect the importance of customization of composition languages—as a means of diversification—to grow. Also Trummer and Faltings [17] work toward composition as a service; yet, instead of focusing on custom language design, they approach the problem from the provider side and study the optimal selection of service composition algorithms—a task that could be eased if customers were allowed to tailor the composition language to be executed to their very specific needs.

3.10 Conclusion and Future Work

Component-based development and composition tools, such as mashup tools, are an increasingly important reality in today's software development landscape. With this paper, we aim to lower the barriers to the development of *good* composition tools by approaching a relevant and central aspect of composition, i.e., the design of *composi-*

tion languages. We specifically focus on the problem of developing *custom* mashup languages and show that a sensible design of suitable abstractions and reference specifications enables a *conceptual* development paradigm for mashup languages that is based on the assisted selection of desired composition features and allows developers to neglect low-level details. The paradigm improves *awareness* of design choices and fosters *reuse* of language design knowledge.

In approaching this methodological problem, we also solve a relevant, non-conventional composition problem per se, i.e., the composition of components (the language patterns) that are *not independent* of each other and that require an integration that is much tighter than that of traditional component technologies, such as web services, already *before* composing them. The key to solve this problem is mapping composition features to a generic language meta-model, an artifact that aim to refine and evolve *collectively* with the help of the scientific community.

The idea is to make the meta-model, the feature reference specifications, and the language generator open source and to share it with the community. In this context, we also want to equip the language design paradigm with an interactive language design tool and a hosted execution engine that is able to run compositions developed with any variation of language developed on top of the common meta-model. The final goal is to provide mashup execution *as a service*. This will eventually lower the barriers to the development of custom mashup platforms.

References

1. Daniel, F., Yu, J., Benatallah, B., Casati, F., Matera, M., Saint-Paul, R.: Understanding UI integration: a survey of problems, technologies and opportunities. IEEE Internet Comput. **11**(3)(May/June 2007), 59–66 (2007)
2. Daniel, F., Soi, S., Tranquillini, S., Casati, F., Heng, C., Yan, L.: Distributed orchestration of user interfaces. Inf. Syst. **37**(6)(September 2012, Elsevier), 539–556 (2012)
3. Daniel, F., Rodriguez, C., Roy Chowdhury, S., Motahari Nezhad, H.R., Casati, F.: Discovery and reuse of composition knowledge for assisted mashup development. WWW 2012 Companion, pp. 493–494
4. Daniel, F., Imran, M., Kling, F., Soi, S., Casati, F., Marchese, M.: Developing domain-specific mashup tools for end users. WWW 2012 Companion, pp. 491–492
5. Daniel, F., Casati, F., Benatallah, B., Shan, M.C.: Hosted universal composition: models, languages and infrastructure in mashArt. ER 2009, pp. 428–443
6. Baresi, L., Guinea, S.: Mashups with mashlight. ICSOC 2010, pp. 711–712
7. OASIS: Web Services Business Process Execution Language, Version 2.0, April 2007. http://docs.oasis-open.org/wsbpel/2.0/OS/wsbpel-v2.0-OS.html
8. OMG: Business Process Model and Notation, Version 2.0, January 2011. http://www.omg.org/spec/BPMN/2.0/
9. W3C: Widget Packaging and Configuration. W3C Working Draft, March 2011. http://www.w3.org/TR/widgets/
10. Mohabbati, B., Gasevic, D., Hatala, M., Asadi, M., Bagheri, E., Boskovic, M.: A quality aggregation model for service-oriented software product lines based on variability and composition patterns. ICSOC 2011, pp. 436–451
11. Hermosillo, G., Seinturier, L., Duchien, L.: Creating context-adaptive business processes. ICSOC 2010, pp. 228–242

12. Hoesch-Klohe, K., Ghose, A.K.: Carbon-aware business process design in Abnoba. ICSOC 2010, pp. 551–556
13. Heidenreich, F., Johannes, J., Aßmann, U., Zschaler, S.: A close look at composition languages. ACoM 2008
14. Saeed, A., Pautasso, C.: The mashup component description language. iiWAS 2011, pp. 311–316
15. Open Mashup Alliance: Enterprise Mashup Markup Language (EMML), May 2012. http://www.openmashup.org/omadocs/v1.0/index.html
16. Blake, M.B., Tan, W., Rosenberg, F.: Composition as a service. IEEE Internet Comput. **14**(1), 78–82 (2010)
17. Trummer, I., Faltings, B.: Dynamically selecting composition algorithms for economical composition as a service. ICSOC 2011, pp. 513–522

Chapter 4
Service-Oriented Programming with Jolie

Fabrizio Montesi, Claudio Guidi and Gianluigi Zavattaro

Abstract The wide adoption of service-oriented computing has led to a heterogeneous scenario formed by different technologies and specifications. Examples can be found both at the design level—the frameworks for defining services and those for defining their coordination feature fundamentally different primitives—and at the implementation level—different communication technologies are used depending on the context. In this chapter we present Jolie, a fully-fledged service-oriented programming language. Jolie addresses the aforementioned heterogeneity in two ways. On the one hand, it combines computation and composition primitives in an intuitive and concise syntax. On the other hand, the behaviour and deployment of a Jolie program are orthogonal: they can be independently defined and recombined as long as they have compatible typing.

4.1 Introduction

Service-Oriented Computing (SOC) is a design methodology that focuses on the composition of autonomous entities in a system, called *services*. SOC abstracts from the implementation details of services by imposing a standard communication mechanism between the entities in an SOA (Service-Oriented Architecture). For instance, the Web Services specifications [1] impose the use of the SOAP protocol [2],

F. Montesi (✉)
IT University of Copenhagen, Rued Langgaards Vej 7, DK-2300 Copenhagen S, Denmark
e-mail: fmontesi@itu.dk

C. Guidi
Dipartimento di Matematica, University of Padova, Via Trieste 63, 35121 Padova, Italy
e-mail: cguidi@math.unipd.it

G. Zavattaro
INRIA Focus Research Team, University of Bologna, Mura A. Zamboni 7, 40127 Bologna, Italy
e-mail: zavattar@cs.unibo.it

A. Bouguettaya et al. (eds.), *Web Services Foundations*,
DOI: 10.1007/978-1-4614-7518-7_4,
© Springer Science+Business Media New York 2014

which builds on XML as a data format and HTTP as the transport. Applying such a restriction, it is possible to have SOAs where each service is potentially implemented in a different technology, such as Java, C, or C#.

SOC is widely adopted in many different settings; here we list some notable examples. Web Services are widespread and supported by many industrial technologies, such as Java and .NET; they are especially used in enterprise software development. Applications in modern Linux distributions, e.g., hardware information services and desktop environment components as in the KDE SC [3] and GNOME [4], communicate locally using the D-Bus technology [5]; in the Windows operating system, DCOM was created to address the same issue. Many web applications expose REST APIs to allow external applications to interact with them. All of the aforementioned technologies make it possible for applications to communicate by means of loosely coupled messaging systems. The adoption of SOC, however, has led to a problem of fragmentation. Many different service-oriented technologies and specifications, such as the ones listed above, target specific requirements and cannot be integrated without ad-hoc interventions, which usually imply the writing of some adapters for the message formats and the communication semantics. In other words, there are many technologies and applications based on common conceptual ground that are unable to interoperate without ad-hoc interventions, which can be very costly, hard to maintain, and prone to breaking wrt future system modifications.

From the perspective of the methodologies and tools for composing SOAs the situation is less fragmented, but there is a marked separation between *behavioural* and *architectural* composition. Behavioural composition deals with the specific series of interactions (message exchanges) to be performed in order to reach a goal. For example, an E-Commerce service supporting the purchase of some products may offer a buy functionality implemented by composing a warehouse service for sending the product to the client and a bank service for handling the payment. Services that behaviourally compose other services are usually called *orchestrators*. The most renowned technology for performing behavioural composition is WS-BPEL [6], a language based on the Web Services specifications. Architectural composition, on the other hand, deals with the topological structure of an SOA, managing its execution and integration. For example, an application server may manage the execution of multiple applications in the same environment; or, a proxy may be used to bridge two SOAs that run in separate networks. A more generic approach to bridging is represented by *mediators*. These may work on different levels, e.g., by allowing a service available on Bluetooth or a LAN to communicate with another service on the Internet, or by performing data format conversion. Notable examples of mediators are all the Enterprise Service Bus (ESB) technologies [7] and the aforementioned D-Bus [5]. Differently from the case of behavioural composition, we are not aware of programming languages supporting architectural composition: the latter is usually obtained through tools that are specific to some architectural patterns.

To the best of our knowledge, the literature lacks proposals of languages that enable SOA designers to deal effectively with both behavioural and architectural aspects, by providing a satisfactory support for solving the technological fragmentation problem reported above. We argue that offering such a language would simplify greatly the design of SOAs, since designers would have to deal with a single and homogeneous set of concepts instead of many different tools.

In this chapter we present the Jolie programming language [8], our proposal for filling this gap. Jolie is the result of our attempt to obtain a common denominator that coherently offers the main features of SOC and their integration with existing technologies. We aim at offering a programming language for defining the base services, their organization in an SOA, and the behaviour of the orchestrators responsible for the supervision of the interactions among the services, possibly using different communication technologies. In our opinion, Jolie is the first language that positively responds to the problems of heterogeneity of both service communication technologies and compositional aspects.

A Jolie program defines a service and is a composition of two parts, called *behaviour* and *deployment*. A behaviour defines the implementation of the functionalities offered by a service; behavioural primitives include communication and computation constructs. However, these do not deal with how communications are supported: they abstractly refer to *communication ports*, which are assumed to be correctly defined in the deployment part. The latter deals with the actual definition of the necessary information for supporting communications. Therefore, communication ports establish a notion of compatibility between the behaviour and deployment parts of a program. This separation of concerns addresses the first form of heterogeneity mentioned above: a behaviour can be deployed using various communication media and data protocol combinations.

The deployment part can also make use of architectural primitives for handling the structure of an SOA. For instance, Jolie supports *embedding* and *aggregation*. Embedding deals with the structure of the execution contexts in which services operate, establishing a hierarchy of services. It allows a service to run another one as a sub-service. An embedder can communicate with an embedded service through an ordinary communication port: its behaviour abstracts from embedding, so if the programmer decides in the future not to embed a service and instead to refer to an external one, the behaviour does not need to be changed. Embedding has also some performance benefits. Aggregation, on the other hand, deals with the architecture of the connections in an SOA. It allows for the creation of proxy services that can forward invocations to other services. Aggregation is purely related to deployment, since it takes only communication ports as parameters and creates bridges between them. The flexible aggregation and embedding mechanisms are examples of how Jolie addresses the second form of heterogeneity mentioned above. Remarkably, their design also elicits that the behavioural and architectural composition mechanisms can abstractly interact through the shared concept of communication ports.

Structure of the chapter. Sect. 4.2 presents the basic constructs of the language; Sect. 4.3 shows how Jolie handles complex behavioural composition by supporting stateful sessions and error recovery; Sect. 4.4 introduces architectural composition with embedding and aggregation; we show a practical example that uses our main composition primitives in Sect. 4.5; Sect. 4.6 discusses related work; Sect. 4.7 reports conclusions, references to additional resources, and future work.

4.2 Language Basics: Behaviour and Deployment

A Jolie program defines an entity in an SOA (a service). Programs are run by the Jolie interpreter, and are usually stored inside files with the .ol extension.[1] A program is made by two parts, called *behaviour* and *deployment*.

The behavioural part defines the actions to be performed by the service, such as internal computations and input/output communications. This part abstracts from *how* communications will actually be supported. For example, a behavioural primitive may express the action "ask the calculator service to add the numbers 2 and 6 and then get a result back", without knowing exactly how to reach this calculator service (or which kind of communication protocol it uses).

The deployment part complements the behavioural part, introducing the necessary information for establishing communication links between services. It can also be used to define the structure of an SOA, as we will show later.

The structure of a Jolie *Program* is thus given by the following syntax:

$$Program \quad := \quad D \ \mathtt{main}\,\{B\}$$

where D represents the deployment part and B the behavioural part. The main procedure is the execution entry point.

4.2.1 Behaviours

The syntax for expressing service behaviours in Jolie combines the message-passing and the imperative programming styles. The former models composition of the behaviours of other services, whereas the latter enables internal computation. Fig. 4.1 reports a selection of the syntax for behaviours.

Communications. Rules *(input)*, *(output)*, and *(input choice)* implement communications. An input η can either be a one-way or a request-response. Statement *(one-way)* receives a message for operation o and stores its content in variable x. *(request-response)* receives a message for operation o in variable x, executes behaviour B (called the *body* of the request-response input), and then sends the value of the evaluation of expression e to the invoker. *(notification)* and *(solicit-response)* dually implement the outputs towards the input primitives. *(notification)* sends a message containing the value of the evaluation of expression e. *(solicit-response)* sends a message with the evaluation of e and then waits for a response from the invoked service; the response value will be assigned to variable y. In the output statements, OP is an *output port name*. This name acts as a reference to an output port (cf. Sect. 4.2.2) specified in the deployment definition D of the same service in which the behaviour is defined. Output port OP will contain the information (e.g., a URL) for contacting the target service. Finally, *(input choice)* implements input-guarded choice. Namely,

---

[1] A Jolie program definition may even be retrieved from URLs or local memory.

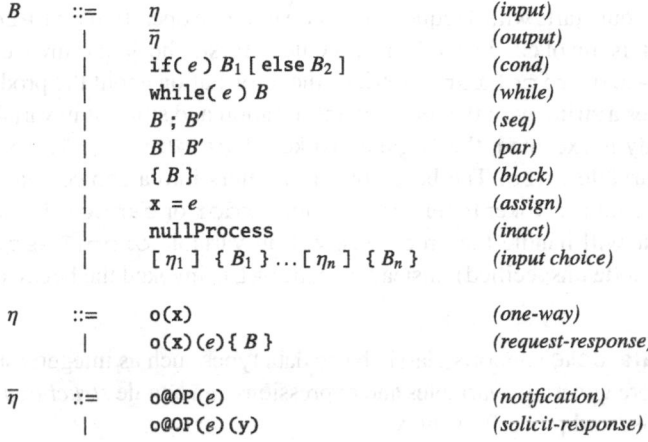

B	$::=$	η	(input)
	$\mid$	$\bar{\eta}$	(output)
	$\mid$	if(e) B_1 [else B_2]	(cond)
	$\mid$	while(e) B	(while)
	$\mid$	B ; B'	(seq)
	$\mid$	$B \mid B'$	(par)
	$\mid$	{ B }	(block)
	$\mid$	$\mathbf{x} = e$	(assign)
	$\mid$	nullProcess	(inact)
	$\mid$	[η_1] { B_1 } ... [η_n] { B_n }	(input choice)
η	$::=$	o(x)	(one-way)
	$\mid$	o(x)(e){ B }	(request-response)
$\bar{\eta}$	$::=$	o@OP(e)	(notification)
	$\mid$	o@OP(e)(y)	(solicit-response)

Fig. 4.1 Jolie behavioural syntax (selected rules)

it supports the receiving of a message for any of the operations in the inputs in the choice. When a message for an input η_i can be received, then all the other branches are deactivated and η_i is executed. Afterwards, the related branch behaviour B_i is also executed. A static check enforces all the η_i in an input choice to have different operations, so to avoid ambiguity.

Statement compositions. Rules (*cond*) and (*while*) implement the standard conditional and iteration constructs. In (*cond*), the else block is optional (denoted by its enclosure in square brackets). Rule (*seq*) enables the sequential composition of behaviours: B is executed, waited for termination, and then B' is executed. Rule (*par*) runs B and B' in parallel. The sequential operator ; binds tighter than the parallel operator | . Operator precedence can be overridden using the (*block*) construct.

Assignments and empty behaviour. Rule (*assign*) evaluates expression e and assigns its value to variable x. Term nullProcess denotes the empty behaviour.

Remark 4.1 (*Sequence-Parallel interaction*). Despite its C/Java-like syntax, it is interesting to observe that the constructs for behaviour composition in Jolie follow the workflow tradition. For instance, it is easy to program the fork-join pattern, as in { $B_1 \mid B_2$ } ; B_3, which is not natively supported, e.g., by Java.   □

Example 4.1 (*Store service*). We give an implementation example of the behaviour of a store service. The service allows for retrieving information about a product (available quantity and price) and then placing an order for buying it.

```
getProductInfo( prod )( info ) {
  { getQuantity@Warehouse( prod )( q ) |
    getPrice@PriceList( prod )( price )
}; info = "Price: " + price + "; Quantity: " + q
}; [ order( orderDesc ) ] { /* handle order */ }
  [ cancel() ] { nullProcess }
```

The behaviour starts with a request-response input on operation `getProductIn fo`. When it is invoked, its body is executed. First, the latter invokes services `Warehouse` and `PriceList` to retrieve the information about the product. Then, it concatenates a string with the retrieved information and stores it in variable `info`. After the body is executed, the original invoker of `getProductInfo` is sent the content of variable `info`. The behaviour now enters into a choice, waiting for an input from the same invoker for either operation `order` or `cancel`. In the first case the behaviour will handle the order, received on variable `orderDesc` (we leave the handling code unspecified); instead, if `cancel` is invoked the behaviour simply terminates.   □

Handling data. Jolie supports classic basic data types such as integers, strings, and booleans. More generally, variables and expressions can handle *structured data trees* using a concise and powerful syntax.

The variable state of a Jolie program is organised as a data tree. A variable then is simply a *path* for traversing the state and obtaining a subtree. Variables are dynamically allocated at runtime. It is easy to understand how this works by making a comparison to XML trees.[2] Consider the following behaviour:

```
x = 5 ; y = 10
```

Executing the code above would yield a state with two subnodes, x and y, respectively containing the integers 5 and 10. An XML representation would be:

```
<state> <x>5</x> <y>10</y> </state>
```

Executing now the statement z = y / x would yield the following state:

```
<state> <x>5</x> <y>10</y> <z>2</z> </state>
```

State traversing is obtained through the dot operator ., which can be used to specify paths. For instance, we can store information on a `person`:

Listing 4.1 A tree with personal information
```
person.name = "John"; person.age = 42;
person.contact.email = "john@smith.org";
person.contact.phoneNumber[0] = "123";
person.contact.phoneNumber[1] = "456"
```

The code above shows two features. The first is nesting: `email` is a subnode of `contact` which is a subnode of `person`. The second is vectors, obtained with the usual square bracket notation. An XML representation would be:

```
<state> <person> <name>John</name> <age>42</age> <contact>
        <email>john@smith.org</email>
        <phoneNumber>123</phoneNumber>
```

---

[2] We observe, however, that Jolie trees are different from XML trees, as they are designed for performance. For example, Jolie tree nodes store typed values (strings, integers, ...), whereas XML does not: all XML node values are strings, and their type is just an optional annotation.

```
<phoneNumber>456</phoneNumber> </contact> </person>
</state>
```

Jolie also comes with some native operators for manipulating data trees. In the following we show the deep copy operator « and the vector size operator #. Assume that the following code is run with the state represented above:

```
x << person.contact ; numbers = #x.phoneNumber
```

In the resulting state x would then contain a copy of the tree pointed by person.con
tact and numbers the size of the vector phoneNumber inside that tree.

In the rest of the chapter, we will simply refer to paths as variables.

4.2.2 Deploying Services

We introduce now the syntax for deployment. The basic deployment primitives are *input ports* and *output ports*, which support input and output communications with other services. Ports are based on *interfaces* and *data types*.

A deployment D is simply a list of *deployment instructions* among which we can have input and output ports, type definitions, and interfaces:

$$D \quad ::= \quad D\,D \quad | \quad IP \quad | \quad OP \quad | \quad T_{\mathsf{def}} \quad | \quad I \quad | \quad \ldots$$

We leave this definition open with . . . as it will be extended in the next sections.
Communication ports. Communication ports define how communications with other services are supported. There are two kinds of ports. *Input ports* deal with exposing input operations to other services. *Output ports*, instead, define how to invoke the operations of other services. Input and output ports are dual concepts and their syntaxes are quite similar. Ports are based upon the three fundamental concepts of *location*, *protocol* and *interface*. The former two define the concrete binding information between a Jolie program and other services. The last, instead, defines type information that is expected to be satisfied by the behaviour that uses the ports.

A location expresses the communication medium, along with its configuration parameters, that a service uses for exposing its interface (in the case of an input port) or contacting another service (in the case of an output port). A protocol defines how data to be sent or received should be, respectively, encoded or decoded following an isomorphism. Finally, a port must specify the interface that is accessible through it. The syntax for input and output ports is in Fig. 4.2 where URI is a URI (Uniform Resource Identifier), defining the location of the port; id, p, and iface$_i$ are identifiers representing, respectively, the name of the port, the data protocol to use, and the interfaces accessible through the port

A location must indicate the communication medium the port has to use and its related parameters, in this form: medium [:parameters], where medium is a medium identifier and the optional parameters is a medium-specific string. Jolie

Fig. 4.2 Input and output
ports syntax

$IP ::=$ inputPort id {
    Location: URI
    Protocol: p
    Interfaces: iface$_1$, ..., iface$_n$
}

$OP ::=$ outputPort id {
    Location: URI
    Protocol: p
    Interfaces: iface$_1$, ..., iface$_n$
}

currently supports four mediums: bt12cap (Bluetooth L2CAP), localsocket (Unix local sockets), rmi (Java RMI), and socket (TCP/IP sockets). An example of a valid location is: "socket://www.mysite.com:80/", where socket is the medium and the following part represents the parameters.

Protocols are referred to by name. Examples of valid protocol names are http, https, soap, sodep [9] (a binary protocol specifically developed for Jolie), and xmlrpc. The HTTP protocol implementation, http, can dynamically detect client invocations using different formats (e.g., GWT-RPC [10] and JSON [11]).

Data types and interfaces. Communication ports require interfaces to be defined. An interface is a collection of operation types. The latter define the data types of the values that can be communicated over each specified operation.

We start from data types. We remind that Jolie values are data trees. A data type specifies (i) the structure of a data tree, (ii) the type of the content of its nodes, and (iii) the allowed number of occurences of each node. Let us see an example first. We write a type for the data tree pointed by person in Listing 4.1.

```
type Person:void { .name:string .age:int
                   .contact[0,1]:void
                        { .email:string .phoneNumber*:string } }
```

A value of type Person must not contain anything in its root node (it is void). It *must* have the subnodes name (which must contain a string) and age (an integer). It *may* have a subnode contact (this is specified by the notation [0,1], to be read as "from zero to one occurrences"). If it does, subnode contact must not contain anything in its root node (void), but it must have an email subnode and *any* number of phoneNumber subnodes (specified by the * notation).

The syntax for data types T_{def} is as follows:

$$T_{def} ::= \text{type id } T$$
$$T ::= : BT\ [\ \{\ .id_1\ R_1\ T_1\ ...\ .id_n\ R_n\ T_n\}]|\ \text{undefined}$$
$$R ::= [\ min, max]\ |*|\ ?\ \ BT ::= \text{int}\ |\ \text{string}\ |\ \text{void}...$$

Type definitions assign a type T to a name id. Each type T comprehends a basic type BT and (optionally) a list of named subnode types or the undefined keyword, which makes the type accepting any subtree. Each subtype comes with a range R, which specifies the allowed number of occurences of the subnode in a value. A range R can be an interval from min (an integer major or equal than zero) to max (an integer major or equal than its associated min), or *, meaning any number of occurences. ? is a shortcut for [0,1].

The syntax for interfaces I is:

$$
\begin{array}{rcl}
I & ::= & \text{interface id } \{ \ [\text{OneWay}: \ OW^+ \,] \,[\, \text{RequestResponse}: \ RR^+ \,] \ \} \\
OW & ::= & \text{id}(\ OT\ ) \\
RR & ::= & \text{id}(\ OT_{\text{req}}\ )\ (\ OT_{\text{resp}}\ ) \\
OP_T & ::= & BT \mid \text{type}
\end{array}
$$

An interface I is a list of one-way and request-response operation declarations, respectively OW and RR. OW maps an operation id to an operation type OT, which can be either a basic type BT or a reference to a user-defined type. RR is similar, but it distinguishes between the type for the request OT_{req} and the response OT_{resp}.

Remarkably, it is possible to define multiple input ports that expose the same interface through different communication technologies. This way, for example, a Jolie program may expose the same set of functionalities through a web interface and over Bluetooth, retaining simplicity in the behaviour.

Deployment introduces runtime type checking to behaviours. Whenever a message is sent or received through a port, its type is checked against that specified for its operation in the port's interface. An invoker sending a message with a wrong type receives a TypeMismatch fault. Also, an output statement may throw the same fault when trying to send a message with wrong type.

4.2.3 Putting it All Together

We can finally use the syntax shown so far to implement working Jolie programs, defining their behavioural and deployment parts. The following examples are complete, and therefore executable. The next listing defines a service that offers an operation for performing the summation of some numbers.

```
type SumRequest:void { .number[2,*]:int }
interface SumInterface { RequestResponse: sum(SumRequest)(int) }
inputPort SumInput { Location: "socket://localhost:8000/"
                          Protocol: soap Interfaces: SumInterface }
main {
  sum( req )( result ) { i = 0;
    while( i < #req.number ) { result = result + req.number[i++]
        }
    } }
```

The code above implements a service that exposes an operation sum that takes at least two number nodes in its request message and then replies with the sum of the numbers. The service is deployed accepting `socket` connections at TCP port 8000 and uses the `soap` protocol. Let us see a program that invokes the service above. Below, we use the `include` primitive for importing the output port `Console` from the Jolie standard library unit `console.iol` and print the result.

```
include "console.iol"
type SumRequest:void { .number[2,*]:int }
interface SumInterface { RequestResponse: sum(SumRequest)(int) }
outputPort SumServ { Location: "socket://localhost:8000/"
                     Protocol: soap Interfaces: SumInterface }
main {
    request.number[0] = 3; request.number[1] = 5;
    sum@SumServ( request )( response );
    println@Console( response )() /* will print 8 */ }
```

We can already see how the separation between behaviour and deployment helps in addressing the heterogeneity of communication technologies. For example, if we want to invoke our service from a web browser it is sufficient to change its communication protocol to `http`, without considering the behaviour:

```
inputPort SumInput { Location: "socket://localhost:8000/"
                     Protocol: http Interfaces: SumInterface }
```

Now we can sum numbers from a web browser by opening a URL such as: http://localhost:8000/sum?number=10\&number=2\&number=4

Remark 4.2 (*Automatic Type Casting*) In the example above, we pass some integer parameters to our service through a *query string* in an HTTP URL, which does not carry data typing. In this case, Jolie is actually casting such string parameters to integers, referring to the operation type. Automatic type casting for untyped data also allows for rejecting immediately messages with a wrong type. For example, browsing the following URL would get and display a `TypeMismatch` error: http://localhost:8000/sum?number=wrong   □

4.3 Sessions and Error Recovery

Until now we have presented services that run their behaviours only once. We also never accounted for errors in their executions. However, in service-oriented computing, services should be available multiple times and engage in *sessions*, i.e. stateful conversations with other entities with a shared goal. For example, a web browser, an E-Commerce service, and a bank service may start a session to perform a payment. Then, they would need to handle possible errors in such an activity. In this section, we introduce the Jolie primitives for programming sessions and error recovery.

4.3.1 Behaviour Instances

A service participates in a session by executing an instance of its behaviour. So far we have executed behaviours a single time; e.g., the sum service in Sect. 4.2.3 supports a single session with a client for receiving some numbers and replying with their summation. The service must be executed again manually if it is needed again.

Jolie allows to reuse behavioural definition multiple times with the *execution modality* deployment primitive [12]:

$$D \; ::= \; ... \; | \; \text{execution} \, \{ \, M \, \}$$
$$M \; ::= \; \text{single} \, | \, \text{sequential} \, | \, \text{concurrent}$$

single is the default execution modality (so the execution construct may be omitted in this case), which runs the program behaviour once. sequential, instead, causes the program behaviour to be made available again after the current instance has terminated. This is useful, for instance, for modelling services that need to guarantee exclusive access to a resource. Finally, concurrent causes a program behaviour to be instantiated and executed *whenever its first input statement can receive a message*. Jolie also supports special procedures for initialising a service before it makes its behaviour available, omitted here. The interested reader may refer to [13].

In the sequential and concurrent cases, the behavioural definition inside the main procedure must be an input statement (an input η or an input choice, cf. Sect. 4.2, Fig. 4.1); we refer to the operations in such input statements as *starting operations*.

Variable state. A crucial aspect of behaviour instances is that each instance has its own private state, determining variable scoping. This lifts programmers from worrying about race conditions in most cases. For instance, we could simply add the deployment instruction execution { concurrent } to the sum service in Sect. 4.2.3 to make it supporting multiple clients at the same time. Access to variables would be safe since each behaviour instance would have its private state.

Jolie also provides *global variables* to support sharing of data among different behaviour instances. These can be accessed using the global prefix:

```
global.myGlobalVariable = 3; // Global variable
myLocalVariable = 1 // Local to this behaviour instance
```

Concurrent access to global variables can be restricted through synchronized blocks, similarly to Java: $B::= ... | \text{synchronized(id)} \, \{ B \}$ which allows only one process at a time to enter any synchronized block sharing the same id.

Dynamic binding. Jolie allows output ports to be dynamically bound, i.e., their locations and protocols (called *binding information*) can change at runtime. Changes to the binding information of an output port is local to a behaviour instance: output ports are considered part of the local state of each instance. Dynamic binding is obtained by treating output ports as variables. For instance, the following would print the location and protocol name of output port `Printer`

```
include "console.iol"     include "Printer.iol"
outputPort Printer { Location: "socket://p:80/"
    Protocol: sodep   Interfaces: PrinterInterface }
main { println@Console( P.location )();
        println@Console( P.protocol )() }
```

where the file `Printer.iol` contains the interface:

```
interface PrinterInterface { OneWay: printText(string) }
```

Binding information may be entered at runtime by making simple assignments:

```
include "Printer.iol"
outputPort P { Interfaces: PrinterInterface }
main { P.location = "socket://p:80/"; P.protocol = "sodep" }
```

Example 4.2 (*Binding registry*). We show a usage example of dynamic binding and binding transmission by implementing a binding registry, i.e., a service that shares binding information. The registry offers a request-response operation, `getBinding`, that returns the binding information for contacting a service. We identify services by simple names. The interface of the registry is thus:

```
interface RIf { RequestResponse: getBinding(string)(Binding) }
```

where `Binding` is the type of port bindings defined in the standard Jolie library. Below we implement the registry behaviour, which supplies binding information for an inkjet printer and a laser printer (whose services we leave unspecified).

```
main {
    getBinding( name )( b ) {
        if ( name == "LaserPrinter" ) {
        b.location = "socket://p1.com:80/"; b.protocol = "sodep"
        } else if ( name == "InkJetPrinter" ) {
        b.location = "socket://p2.it:80/"; b.protocol = "soap"
        }
    }}
```

Finally, we define a client that calls `getBinding` for discovering the laser printer:

```
outputPort Registry { /* omitted */ }
outputPort Printer { Interfaces: PrinterInterface }
main { getBinding@Registry( "LaserPrinter" )( Printer );
        printText@Printer( "My text" ) }
```

4.3.2 Message Routing with Correlation Sets

Having multiple instances of a behaviour running in a service introduces the problem of routing incoming messages to the right instances. Let us clarify with an example. Assume that an E-Commerce service has two behaviour instances opened for buying two products, respectively product A and product B. If a message for performing a payment comes from the network, how can we determine if the payment is for A or it is for B? Supposedly, we should require that the payment message contains some information that allows us to relate it to the correct behaviour instance, e.g., a serial number. In common web application frameworks this issue is covered by the *sid* session identifier, a unique key usually stored as a browser cookie.

Jolie supports incoming message routing to behaviour instances by means of *correlation sets* [14]. Correlation sets are a generalisation of session identifiers: instead of referring to a single variable for identifying behaviour instances, a correlation set allows the programmer to refer to the combination of multiple variables, called *correlation variables*. Correlation set programming deals both with the deployment and behavioural parts. The former must declare the correlation sets, instructing the interpreter on how to relate incoming messages to internal behaviour instances. The latter instead has to assign the concrete values to the correlation variables.

Correlation set declaration. Correlation sets are declared in the deployment part of a program using the following syntax:

$$D \quad ::= \quad \ldots \mid C \qquad\qquad C \quad ::= \quad \texttt{cset} \ \{ \ C_{Var}^{+} \ \}$$
$$C_{Var} \quad ::= \quad \texttt{x} : \mathsf{T_{path}}^{+}$$

A correlation set declaration C is a list of correlation variable declarations. A correlation variable declaration C_{Var} links a correlation variable $\texttt{x}$ to a list of aliases. A correlation alias $\mathsf{T_{path}}$ is a path (using the same syntax for variable paths) starting with a message type name, indicating where the value for comparing the correlation variable can be retrieved within the message. Aliases ensure loose coupling between the names of the correlation variables and the data structures of incoming messages.

The fact that correlation aliases are defined on message types makes correlation definitions statically strongly typed. A static checker verifies that each alias points to a node that will surely be present in every incoming message of the referenced type; technically, this means that the node itself and all its ancestor nodes are not optional in the type. As an example, the following is an invalid correlation set definition:

```
type MyType:void { .a:int { .b?:string } }
cset { myVar: MyType.a.b }
```

because node b is optional under a in type MyType. Hereafter we refer to a path such as a.b, i.e., the path that follows after the type name, as the aliasing path for the correlation variable for the relative type (MyType above).

Jolie performs many other static checks for ensuring correctness of correlation set declarations (see [14]). Here we highlight that, for services using `sequential` or `concurrent` execution modalities, for each operation used in an input statement in the behaviour there is exactly one correlation set that links all its variables to the type of the operation. Since there is *exactly one* correlation set referring to an operation, we can unambiguosly call it the correlation set for the operation. We can now define how correlation works (see [14] for a formal definition).

> Let o be an operation and C be the correlation set for o. We say that an incoming message for o *correlates* with a behaviour instance if, for every variable x with y as aliasing path for the input type of o in C, we have that the value of x in the state of the behaviour instance is the same as the value of y in the message.

Whenever a service receives a message through an input port (and the message is correctly typed wrt the port's interface) there are three possibilities, defined below.

- The message correlates with a behaviour instance. In this case the message is received and given to the behaviour instance, which will be able to consume it through an input statement for the related operation of the message.
- The message does not correlate with any behaviour instance and its operation is a starting operation in the behavioural definition. In this case, a new behaviour instance is created and the message is assigned to it. If the starting operation has an associated correlation set, all the correlation variables in the correlation set are atomically assigned (from the values of the aliases in the message) to the behaviour instance before starting its executing.
- The message does not correlate with any behaviour instance of its operation is not a starting operation in the behavioural definition. In this case, the message is rejected and a `CorrelationError` fault is sent back to the invoker.

Correlation values. In the behavioural part of a program, correlation variables must be explicitly prefixed with the `csets` keyword. So, for instance, assigning the value `"MyValue"` to the correlation variable `myVar` looks like:

```
csets.myVar = "MyValue"
```

It is often useful to assign a *fresh* value to a correlation variable, to ensure unambiguity between behaviour instances. The primitive `new` addresses this point:

```
csets.myVar = new
```

We observe that a programmer can make mistakes when programming correlation. As an example, assume that in the following code snippet operation `close` (for closing a behaviour instance) has input type `CloseType`:

```
cset { x: CloseType.closeIdentifier } main { open(); close() }
```

The code above is wrong because `x` is not instantiated before the input statement `close()`. This would case a deadlock since no input message would be able to correlate for that input. Jolie comes with a static checker that can detect some common problems in correlation programming [14], such as this one.

Example 4.3 (*Distributed authentication*). We report an example from [14] inspired by the OpenID Authentication specifications [15], a largely adopted decentralised Single Sign-On protocol that allows a service, called *relying party*, to authenticate a user, the *client*, by relying on another external service that is responsible for handling identities, the *identity provider*. Therefore, OpenID specifies a *multiparty session*. When the client requests access to the relying party, the latter starts an authentication session with the identity provider and redirects the client to it. The client then sends its authentication credentials to the identity provider, which will inform the relying party on the result of the authentication attempt. The example can be downloaded at [16]. Here, we show an implementation sketch for the relying party.

```
cset { clientToken: /* ... */ }
cset { secureToken: AuthMessage.secureToken }
interface RelyingPartyInterface {
OneWay: authSucceeded(AuthMessage), authFailed(AuthMessage)
RequestResponse: login(LoginRequest)(Redirection) }
main {
    login( loginRequest )( redirection ) {
        openRequest.clientToken = csets.clientToken = new;
        openRequest.secureToken = csets.secureToken = new;
        openRequest.relyingPartyIdentifier = MY_IDENTIFIER;
        openAuth@IdentityProvider( openRequest );
        /* ... build redirection message for client ... */
    }; [ authSucceeded( message ) ] { /* ... */ }
        [ authFailed( message ) ] { /* ... */ }           }
```

The service receives a request on the starting operation `login` from the client for initiating the protocol. The body of `login` generates two fresh correlation tokens, `clientToken` and `secureToken`, and also stores them under the `openRequest` variable. We will use `clientToken` for receiving messages from the client and `secureToken` for receiving messages from the identity provider. The client is not informed about `secureToken`, preventing it to maliciously act as the identity provider. The body of `login` performs a call to the identity provider, starting an authentication session and communicating `secureToken`. The reply will redirect the client to the identity provider. The relying party will then wait for a notification about the result of the authentication attempt, hence the input choice on `authSucceeded` and `authFailed`, which correlate through `secure Token`.   □

4.3.3 Fault Handling

Fault handling in Jolie involves four basic concepts: *scope, fault, termination* and *compensation*. We now describe the first three concepts: the reader interested in compensation handling can refer to [17]. A scope is a behaviour container denoted by a unique name and able to manage faults. A fault is a signal raised by a behaviour towards the enclosing scope when an error state is reached, in order to allow for its recovery. Termination is a mechanism used to recover from errors: it is automatically triggered when a scope is unexpectedly terminated from a parallel behaviour and must be smoothly stopped. We say that a scope terminates successfully if it does not raise any fault signal; a scope obtains this by handling all the faults thrown by its internal behaviour. Recovery mechanisms are implemented by exploiting *handlers*, which contain the code to execute when faults or terminations are triggered.

We extend the syntax of behaviours with the primitives for fault handling:

$$
\begin{array}{llll}
B & ::= \dots \mid & \mathtt{scope(\,s\,)\ \{\,}B\,\} & (scope) \\
  & \mid & \mathtt{install(\,}h_1 \mathtt{\,=>\,} B_1 \mathtt{\,,\ \dots,\ } h_n \mathtt{\,=>\,} B_n \mathtt{\,)} & (inst) \\
  & \mid & \mathtt{cH} & (cH) \\
  & \mid & \mathtt{throw(\,f\,[\,,\ x\,]\,)} & (throw)
\end{array}
$$

Above, *(scope)* defines a scope with a unique scope name s and a behaviour B. *(inst)* dynamically installs the handlers B_i for their respective names h_i in the enclosing scope, where h can be either a fault name or one of the special keywords $\mathtt{this}$ and $\mathtt{default}$. If it is a fault name, then the handler is installed as a fault handler; if it is $\mathtt{this}$, then the handler is installed as a termination handler for the enclosing scope; if, finally, it is $\mathtt{default}$, then the handler is installed as a fallback fault handler for all faults that do not have a specific fault handler. Installing a handler overwrites the previous one for the same fault or scope name; however, handlers can be composed by using the $\mathtt{cH}$ placeholder, which is replaced by the code of the previously installed handler. Finally, *(throw)* throws a fault f with some optional data x.

Automatic fault transmission. Uncaught fault signals in a request-response body are automatically sent to the invoker. Hence, invokers are always notified of unhandled faults. We update the syntax for request-response operation types (cf. Sect. 4.2.2) to declare the faults f_i that could be sent back to invokers with data of type OT_i:

$$
RR \quad ::= \quad \mathtt{id(\,} OT_{\mathsf{req}} \mathtt{\,)\,(\,} OT_{\mathsf{resp}} \mathtt{\,)\ [\,throws\,} f_1 \mathtt{(\,} OT_1 \mathtt{\,)} \ \dots\ f_n \mathtt{(\,} OT_n \mathtt{\,)\,]}
$$

It follows from the fact that request-response operations may return a fault, that now the solicit-response output statement may throw the received fault.

Handler composition. The $\mathtt{cH}$ element allows for the dynamic composition of behavioural code. Consider the following example:

```
scope(s) { install( f => i = i+2 ); install( f => i++; cH ) }
```

The second $\mathtt{install}$ uses $\mathtt{cH}$ in its handler. At runtime, $\mathtt{cH}$ will be replaced with the previously installed handler. So the second install instruction is equivalent to:

```
install( f => i++; i = i + 2 )
```

Install statement priority. An install statement may execute in parallel to other behaviours that may throw a fault. This introduces a problem of nondeterminism:

how can the programmer ensure that the correct handlers are installed regardless of the scheduling of the parallel activities? Jolie solves this issue by giving priority to the install primitive wrt fault processing, making handler installation predictable. As an example, consider the following code:

```
scope(s) { throw(f) | install( f => println@Console("Hi")() ) }
```

where, inside the scope s, we have a parallel composition of a throw statement for fault f and an installation of a handler for the same fault. The priority given to the install primitive guarantees that the handler will be installed before the fault signal for f reaches the scope construct and its handler is searched for.

4.4 Architectural Composition

Until now we have shown how a behaviour can compose other behaviours abstracting from its deployment. In this section we show how composition can be obtained from the opposite perspective. Namely, we present *architectural composition*, a different kind of composition that a deployment definition can obtain abstracting from the specific behavioural definitions of the involved services.

Architectural composition can be roughly divided in two main categories. The first deals with the structuring of the execution contexts in which services operate. For instance, a service may execute other sub-services in the same execution engine, in order to gain advantages in terms of resource control. Other examples can be the *wrapping* and *hiding* of an entity in an SOA. The second category deals with the topology of the connections between services in an SOA. Jolie supports mechanisms for both categories [18, 13]. Here we introduce two representatives, respectively *embedding* [13] and *aggregation* [13, 19].

4.4.1 Embedding

Embedding is a mechanism for executing multiple services in the same virtual machine. A service, called *embedder*, can *embed* another service, called *embedded* service, by targetting it with the embedded primitive. The syntax for embedding is:

$$
\begin{array}{rcl}
D & ::= & \dots \mid E \\
E & ::= & \text{embedded} \, \{ \, E_{\text{type}} : \textsf{path} \, [\, \textsf{in} \, \text{OP} \,] \, \} \\
E_{\text{type}} & ::= & \text{Jolie} \mid \text{Java} \mid \text{JavaScript}
\end{array}
$$

where E is the embedding construct, E_{type} specifies the type (technology) of the service to embed, and path is a URL (possibly in simple form) pointing to the definition of the service to embed. Jolie currently supports the embedding of Jolie, Java, and JavaScript service definitions; this support can be modularly extended [13].

Embedding may optionally specify an output port OP; in this case, as soon as the service is loaded, the output port OP is bound to the "local" communication input port of the embedded service. The meaning of local communication input port is dependent on the embedding type; we will show examples for Jolie and Java services. This makes embedding a *cross-technology* mechanism: it can load services defined using different languages. Embedding produces a hierarchy of services where the embedder is the parent service of the embedded ones; this hierarchy handles termination: whenever a service terminates all its embedded services are recursively terminated. The hierarchy is also useful for enhancing performance: services in the same virtual machines may communicate using fast local memory communication channels.

When embedding a Jolie service, the path URL must point to a file containing a Jolie program (provided as source code or in binary form). Command line parameters can also be passed. Local in-memory communication between embedder and embedded is enabled by means of the local communication medium, which must be specified by the embedded service. In this case no protocol definition is needed.

Example 4.4 (*Embedded Jolie service*). We embed the sum service from Sect. 4.2.3. First, we add the following input port to allow for local communications:

```
inputPort LocalIn { Location: "local" Interfaces: SumInterface }
```

Now we can design a modified version of the client program in Sect. 4.2.3 to embed the sum service (whose definition we assume to be stored in file sum_service.ol) and call it using an output port bound by embedding. We omit interfaces.

```
outputPort SumService { Interfaces: SumInterface }
embedded { Jolie: "sum_service.ol" in SumService }
main {  request.number[0] = 3; request.number[1] = 5;
        sum@SumService( request )( response )        }
```

□

When embedding a Java service, the path URL must unambiguously identify a Java class, which can also be in the Java classpath of the Jolie interpreter. The class must extend the JavaService abstract class, offered by the Jolie Java library for supporting the automatic conversion between Java values and their Jolie representations. Each method of the embedded class is seen as an operation from the embedder, which will instantiate an object using the class and bind it to the output port. Embedding Java services is particularly useful for interacting with existing Java code, or perform some task where computational performance is important. Many services of the Jolie standard library (like Console) are Java services.

Example 4.5 (*Java service embedding*). We embed a simple Java service that offers a length Request-Response operation that takes a string as request and replies with the length of the string. Consider the following Java code:

```
package example; import jolie.runtime.JavaService;
public class MyService extends JavaService {
    public Integer length( String request )
```

```
        { return request.length(); }              }
```

We can embed and use the code above from a Jolie program such as the following:

```
interface MyServiceIface { RequestResponse: length(string)(int) }
outputPort MyService { Interfaces: MyServiceIface }
embedded { Java: "example.MyService" in MyService }
main { length@MyService( "Hi" )( l ) }
```

□

We end our presentation of embedding by showing how to use it at runtime. *Dynamic embedding* can be used to implement features such as code mobility (an important aspect in cloud computing middleware) and service adaptation.

Example 4.6 (Platform-as-a-service). We report a sketch, from [13], of a simple platform-as-a-service solution, where customers can load services by service mobility. Each customer has a certain amount of allowed execution time: a loaded service cannot run for more than the customer's allowed time, and when the service terminates the allowed time is decreased. We use the MetaService service from the Jolie standard library, which can dynamically embed and unload services respectively through the loadEmbeddedService and unloadEmbeddedService operations.

```
execution { concurrent } csets { sid: /* ... */ }
main {
  login( l )( csets.sid )
          { auth@AccountManager( l )( account ); csets.sid = new };
  startService( s )() { loadEmbeddedService@MetaService( s )();
              setNextTimeout@Time( account.allowedTime ) };
  [ timeout() ] { nullProcess } [ stop( sid ) ] { nullProcess };
  { unloadEmbeddedService@MetaService( s.resourceName )() |
      updateAllowedTime@AccountManager( account )() }          }
```

The service supports multiple sessions (execution{concurrent}). First, the customer is required to login, creating a behaviour instance. An AccountMana ger service is composed for handling authentication; if auth fails, we rely on automatic fault transmission (cf. Sect. 4.3.3) to send the fault to the customer through login. If auth succeeds, we assign a fresh token to the correlation variable sid and send it back to the customer. The startService operation is then made available, which can be called to start a new service; the latter is loaded by composing MetaService. After the service is embedded, a Time service is used to start a timer set to the customer's allowed time. The timer is used in the following input choice, where either the timeout occurs or the stop operation gets called first. In any case the service gets unloaded and, concurrently, the account allowed time gets updated.   □

4.4.2 Aggregation

Aggregation is a generalisation of network proxies that allows a service to expose operations without implementing them in its behaviour, but instead delegating them to other services. Aggregation can also be used for programming various architectural patterns—such as load balancers, reverse proxies, and adapters—omitted here (see [13, 19]). The syntax for aggregation extends that for input ports, by introducing an Aggregates primitive that expects a list of output port names:

$$IP ::= \text{inputPort id } \{ \text{ Location: } URI \text{ Protocol: } p$$
$$\text{Interfaces: iface}_1, ..., \text{iface}_n \text{ [Aggregates: } OP^+] \{ \} $$

The interfaces of the output ports must not share any operation name. We can now define how aggregation works. Let *IP* be an input port. Whenever a message for operation o is received through *IP* we have the three following possibilities.

- o is an operation declared in one of the interfaces of *IP*. In this case, the message is normally received by the program as described in Sect. 4.3.2.
- o is not declared in one of the interfaces of *IP* and is declared in the interface of an output port *IP* aggregated by *IP*. In this case, the message is forwarded to *OP* as an output from the aggregator.
- o is not declared in any interface of *IP* or of its aggregated output ports. Then, the message is rejected and an IOException fault is sent to the caller.

From the second item above, we can observe that aggregation *merges* the interfaces of the aggregated output ports and makes them accessible through a single input port. Thus, an invoker would see all the aggregated services as a single one.

Remarkably, aggregation handles the request-response pattern seamlessly: when forwarding a request-response invocation to an aggregated service, the aggregator will automatically also take care of relaying the response to the original invoker.

Example 4.7 (Forwarder). Aggregation can be used for system integration, e.g. bridging services that use different communication technologies or protocols [13]. The deployment snippet below creates a service that forwards incoming SODEP calls on TCP port 8000 to the output port MyOP, converting the received messages to SOAP.

```
outputPort MyOP { Location: "socket://someurl.ex:80/"
                  Protocol: soap Interfaces: MyIface }
inputPort MyInput { Location: "socket://localhost:8000/"
                    Protocol: sodep Aggregates: MyOP }
```

$\square$

Example 4.8 (Aggregation and embedding). We give an example where three servi ces—A, B, and C—are aggregated by a service M, which also embeds C. The code follows, where we have an output port for each service with the same name:

Fig. 4.3 The aggregator M exposes the union of all the interfaces of the services it aggregates (A, B, C). Service C executes inside the virtual machine of M, by embedding. Interfaces are represented with *dotted rectangles*

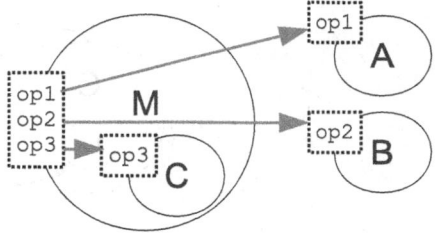

```
outputPort A { Location:  "socket://someurlA.com:80/"
                Protocol:  soap Interfaces: InterfaceA }
outputPort B { Location:  "socket://someurlC.com:80/"
                Protocol:  xmlrpc Interfaces: InterfaceB }
outputPort C { Interfaces: InterfaceC }
embedded      { Java: "example.serviceB" in B }
inputPort M { Location:"socket://urlM.com:8000/"
                Protocol: sodep Aggregates: A, B, C }
```

Observe that the code for aggregating service C abstracts from the fact that it is actually embedded and not external; this abstraction is given by using output ports for aggregating, creating a dependency only on the interface instead of the implementation and location of the target service. The obtained architecture is graphically represented in Fig. 4.3, where we assume that the aggregated interfaces are singletons.

The grey arrows represent how the messages will be forwarded. E.g., an incoming message for operation op3 will be forwarded to the embedded service C.   □

4.5 Example: An Automotive Case Study

We present a Jolie implementation of the automotive case study in the EU project SENSORIA [20]. We describe the main aspects of the implementation. A complete description and executable source code can be found at [21].

In the automotive case study a car experiments a failure during a travel. An onboard computer helps the driver in finding and booking some services for handling the situation: a garage for receiving the car, a tow truck for towing the car to the garage, and a car rental for renting a replacement car. We describe the execution flow of the system. All entities are coded in Jolie, unless otherwise stated.

Getting assistance after a failure. When the Jolie program running in the car onboard computer (called *car service*) detects a failure, it sends the failure description to the *assistance service* of the car manufacturer. The latter analyses the description and sends back to the car service a Jolie program, called *local assistant*, that is specific for the kind of failure. The car service now dynamically embeds the local assistant (similarly to Example 4.6), and starts interacting with it. Both the car service and the

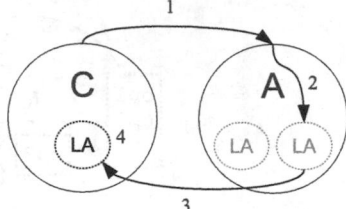

Fig. 4.4 (*Local assistant retrieval*). The car service C calls the assistance service A (1), which selects the appropriate local assistance code LA (2) and sends it back to C (3). C can now dynamically embed and run LA (4)

local assistant implement predefined static interfaces that define the operations they will use to interact. The mechanism is depicted in Fig. 4.4.

Local assistant behaviour. The behaviour of the local assistant depends on the kind of failure. For instance, we distinguish between failures that make the car unable to move or not. Here we describe only the case in which the car is unable to move, where we need to find a garage, a tow truck, and a car rental to handle the situation. First, the local assistant asks the car service for the GPS coordinates of the car. The car service actually aggregates a secondary service, the *sensors service*, for making some read-only instrumentation data transparently available to the local assistant. Then, it will use such information for building an ordered list of suitable garage, tow truck, and car rental services, which are dynamically discovered through a registry provided on the public network. The assistant asks now the car service to display the list to the user, which also contains price information. The list is shown through an embedded Java User Interface. The assistant is then notified of the user's selection.

Bookings and payments. The local assistant has now to book and pay for the selected garage, tow truck, and car rental services. For each service, we perform the booking and then the payment. Here we exploit dynamic fault handling for elegantly adapting our error recovery strategy based on the reached point of execution. Consider for instance the following (simplified) code sketch:

```
scope( s ) { book@Garage( gb )( gr );
         install( default => cancelBook@Garage( gr ) );
         pay@Bank( gr )( gp );
         install( default => cH | cancelPay@Bank( gp ) );
         book@TowTruck( tb )( tr );
         install( default => cH | cancelBook@TowTruck( tr ) );
         /* ... */ }
```

Above, scope s takes care of the bookings and payments. Whenever one of those is successfully carried out, we update the fault handler for the scope by adding the code for reverting it (in parallel, for efficiency). So, for example, if the booking of the tow truck fails we would revert both booking and payment for the garage.

Bank transactions. There are different bank services that could be involved in the payments. Here we describe the case for garage payment, depicted in Fig. 4.5. Let us

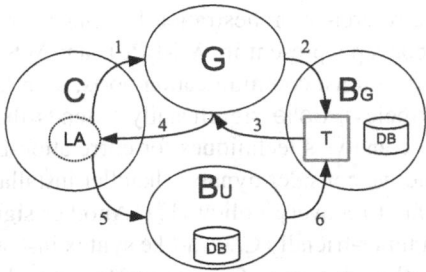

Fig. 4.5 (*Payment workflow*). The local assistant LA inside the car service C calls the garage G (1), which opens a bank transaction T inside its bank B_G (2) and obtains a transaction identifier (3), forwarded to LA (4). LA then asks C to send the identifier to the user's bank B_U (5), which finally closes the money transfer correlating with T (6)

call B_U the bank service handling the user's bank account and B_G the bank service handling the bank account of the garage. When the local assistant books the garage, the latter opens a behaviour instance in B_G for handling the bank transaction, gets back a transaction identifier (which is a correlation value for the behaviour instance in B_G) and returns it to the assistant. The assistant now delegates the payment to the car service, which handles the user's private data. In order to perform the payment, the car service contacts B_U passing the user's account data, the binding information to B_G, and the transaction identifier. B_U can now close the transaction by contacting B_G, using the binding information for reaching its input port and the transaction identifier for correlating with the right behaviour instance. All the provided bank implementations use SQL-based DBMSs through the Jolie standard library.

4.6 Related Work

Related work can be found in orchestration languages and integration middleware for SOAs. Our deployment language allows Jolie to apply the service-oriented paradigm also to other domains; here we briefly consider the programming of web applications. Table 4.1 gives a systematic overview of our discussion.

Table 4.1 Comparison of natively supported features in Jolie and related technologies

Name \ Feature	Behavioural composition	Termination handling	Architectural composition	Formal specifications	Web development
Jolie	Yes	Yes (dynamic)	Yes	Yes	Yes
WS-BPEL	Yes	Yes (static)	No	No	No
Orc	Yes	No	No	Yes	No
ESB	No	No	Yes	No	No
Web frameworks	No	No	No	No	Yes

WS-BPEL [6] is the reference orchestration language for Web Services. Jolie takes inspiration from concepts present in WS-BPEL and WSDL, such as one-way and request-response operations, communication ports, correlation sets, and termination handling. Nevertheless, Jolie significantly extends them. For instance, (i) we have developed static analysis techniques for correlation-based message delivery [14], and (ii) in Jolie we consider dynamic handler installation to guarantee the execution of the right fault recovery policy [17]. Another significant difference is that Jolie uses a programmer-friendly C/Java-like syntax instead of the XML-based syntax of WS-BPEL; although some of our examples (e.g., Example 4.1) may be encoded as WS-BPEL programs, the latter would be much longer and complex due to the verbose XML syntax and additional declarative parts. Furthermore, WS-BPEL does not come with formal semantics, making it ambiguous in some cases and leading to different execution behaviour in different implementations [22]. Jolie, on the other hand, is a formally specified language (see Sect. 4.7) and offers a reference implementation. Some other orchestration languages in the literature come equipped with a formal semantics. Blite [22] is a language that formally captures a subset of WS-BPEL. Differently from Jolie, Blite does not have its own interpreter but compiles its programs to WS-BPEL. HomeBPEL [23] is an extension of WS-BPEL for handling stateful code mobility. Differently, Jolie supports stateless service mobility through dynamic embedding (state mobility can be obtained, but it must be coded manually by the programmer). PiDuce [24] is an implementation of a pi-like process language equipped with powerful pattern-based primitives used to deconstruct XML documents. Finally, Orc [25] is an orchestration language that follows a data-flow oriented approach. The pruning operator found in Orc elegantly captures the "speculative parallelism" pattern, which invokes several services in parallel and considers only the first reply. An initial study of how this can be obtained in Jolie is presented in [26].

We now move to integration middlewares for SOAs, which cover architectural composition. In this context the Enterprise Application Integration (EAI) framework [27] is often used, along with the Enterprise Service Bus (ESB) model [7]. These solutions cover a similar role to that of aggregation, as reported in [19] (where a more powerful version of aggregation is also presented). Embedding, on the other hand, is usually supported through specific application servers which can, in practice, be difficult to compose. In Jolie, instead, embedder services can be seamlessly re-embedded by others to form a hierarchy. Finally, differently from our approach all these tools are specific to some application domain (e.g., Web Services) and are thus less general.

Jolie can be used as a self-contained web server through its http protocol [28], making it an alternative to other web server technologies (e.g., Apache Tomcat) and programming frameworks (e.g. PHP, JSP, Ruby on Rails). Noteworthingly, Jolie natively supports structured behaviours and multiparty sessions (cf. Sect. 4.3, Example 4.3), which are usually encoded manually with bookkeeping code in web applications.

4.7 Conclusions

We have introduced Jolie, a programming language that synthesises a coherent programming paradigm from the technologies and practices that emerged in service-oriented computing in the recent years. It deals with both the heterogeneity of communication technologies and that of composition mechanisms. We addressed the former by separating the behavioural and deployment definitions of Jolie programs and reducing their coupling to communication ports. We covered composition mechanisms by offering behavioural composition primitives for managing complex workflows and more high-level architectural primitives that build system topologies.

Jolie comes with formal specifications (in terms of a process calculus) of its semantics, omitted in this chapter [13, 29, 30]. This formal approach has been instrumental for reasoning on the underlying model of many constructs of the language. For instance, correlation sets and their properties are formalised in [14]. Dynamic fault handling has been developed purposefully for Jolie; its formalisation is reported in [17]. A formal account of aggregation can be found in [19].

Jolie has also been a source of inspiration for other work. For example, dynamic fault handling has been proven to be more expressive than classic static fault handling [31]. Montesi and Sangiorgi [32] reports some programming patterns for component-based systems that can be implemented in Jolie [13]. Guidi and Montesi [18] presents some engineering concepts that have been generalised from practical experience in Jolie programming.

Applications. The design of Jolie has been validated (and influenced) by covering a broad spectrum of applications, from low-level software tightly combined with hardware to enterprise SOAs. Jorba [33] is a framework for context-aware distributed applications, based on dynamic embedding. Leonardo [28] is a Web Server written in pure Jolie. Vision [34] is a push-enabled peer-to-peer application for sharing slides during presentations. Anedda et al. [35] presents a distributed architecture for the management of virtual machines written in Jolie. Jolie is also used in industrial development. SAP Connector is a tool for the seamless integration of SAP ECC installations with Jolie programs; it exploits the Jolie deployment language to integrate with numerous third-party information systems. Web Catalogue is an enterprise catalogue with web and smartphone frontends, based on Leonardo. Central Watcher is a software for managing and monitoring phone centrals, which uses embedding to integrate with native hardware management libraries. SAP Connector, Web Catalogue, and Central Watcher are some of the proprietary products of italianaSoftware s.r.l. [36], a software development company that uses Jolie as main development language and contributes to its code base regularly. A survey of the performance of the Jolie interpreter goes out of the scope of this chapter (which concentrates on the language). Roughly, it can be outlined as appropriate for many industrial deployments. For instance, stable deployments of SAP Connector have processed hundreds of thousands of transactions. Or, Web Catalogue uses embedding and aggregation heavily to compose a system of more than 30 SOAs, and a set of about 400 services dynamically run for various tasks; e.g., user access, pictures, news, and localisation are all handled by different inner SOAs.

Tool support. Jolie comes with many supporting tools (see [8]). Examples are: joliedoc, a documentation generator; jolie2dummy, a tool for the quick prototyping of Jolie code with "dummy" data generated from an interface; jolie2java, a converter from Jolie data types to Java class definitions; jolie2wsdl, which generates WSDL [37] documents from Jolie interfaces; vice versa, wsdl2jolie generates a Jolie output port for calling a Web Service from its WSDL descriptor. Joliepse is a prototype IDE for Jolie. jEye [38] is a graphical editor for Jolie programs. Finally, QtJolie is a C++ integration library for Jolie services, developed in the KDE SC [3].

Future Work. We plan to implement a type system for dynamic binding to guarantee that output ports are always bound to the expected interfaces. A similar study is planned for dynamic embedding. Another future work is to develop a static analysis for verifying the absence of "dangling bindings", i.e., a service should never bind an output port to a location where there is no available service.

We will investigate how Jolie can be combined with techniques for the specification of protocols such as those based on session types, contracts, and choreographies [39–41]. Our aim is to produce tools for supporting the verification and sound implementation of SOAs wrt global descriptions of system behaviour. The granularity introduced by embedding in SOAs make it interesting to consider analysis techniques where services can play multiple roles, like [42]. More generally, we intend to explore how the architectural primitives of Jolie may influence the design of protocol specification languages, e.g. by considering network topologies.

References

1. W3C. Web Services Architecture. http://www.w3.org/TR/ws-arch/
2. W3C. SOAP Specifications. http://www.w3.org/TR/soap/
3. K Desktop Environment. http://www.kde.org/
4. GNOME. http://www.gnome.org/
5. D-Bus website. http://www.freedesktop.org/wiki/Software/dbus/
6. OASIS. WS-BPEL Version 2.0. http://docs.oasis-open.org/wsbpel/
7. Chappell, D.A.: Enterprise Service Bus—Theory in Practice. O'Reilly, Sebastopol (2004)
8. Jolie website. http://www.jolie-lang.org/
9. SODEP protocol. http://www.jolie-lang.org/wiki.php?page=Sodep
10. Google Web Toolkit. http://code.google.com/webtoolkit/
11. JavaScript Object Notation. http://www.json.org/
12. Montesi, F., Guidi, C., Zavattaro, G.: Composing services with JOLIE. In: Proceedings of ECOWS 2007, pp. 13–22 (2007)
13. Montesi, F.: Jolie: a service-oriented programming language. Master's thesis, Department of Computer Science, University of Bologna (2010)
14. Montesi, F., Carbone, M.: Programming services with correlation sets. In: ICSOC, pp. 125–141 (2011)
15. OpenID Specifications. http://openid.net/developers/specs/
16. OpenID implementation. http://www.jolie-lang.org/files/ws_handbook2012/openid.zip
17. Guidi, C., Lanese, I., Montesi, F., Zavattaro, G.: Dynamic error handling in service oriented applications. Fundamenta Informaticae **95**(1), 73–102 (2009)

18. Guidi, C., Montesi, F.: Reasoning about a service-oriented programming paradigm. In: Proceedings of YR-SOC 2009, pp. 67–81 (2009)
19. Preda, M.D., Gabbrielli, M., Guidi, C., Mauro, J., Montesi, F.: Interface-based service composition with aggregation. In: ESOCC, pp. 48–63 (2012)
20. SENSORIA. Software Engineering for Service-Oriented Overlay Computers. http://www.sensoria-ist.eu/
21. Automotive example. http://www.jolie-lang.org/files/ws_handbook2012/automotive.zip
22. Lapadula, Alessandro, Pugliese, Rosario, Tiezzi, Francesco: Using formal methods to develop ws-bpel applications. Sci. Comput. Program. **77**(3), 189–213 (2012)
23. Bundgaard, M., Glenstrup, Hildebrandt, A.J., Højsgaard, T.T., Niss, H.: Formalizing higher-order mobile embedded business processes with binding bigraphs. In: Proceedings of COORDINATION 2008, pp. 83–99 (2008)
24. Carpineti, Samuele, Laneve, Cosimo, Padovani, Luca: Piduce—a project for experimenting web services technologies. Sci. Comput. Program. **74**(10), 777–811 (2009)
25. Kitchin, D., Quark, A., Cook, W.R., Misra, J.: The Orc programming language. In: Proceedings of FMOODS/FORTE 2009, pp. 1–25 (2009)
26. Preda, M.D., Gabbrielli, M., Lanese, I., Mauro, J., Zavattaro, G.: Graceful interruption of request-response service interactions. In: ICSOC, pp. 590–600 (2011)
27. Sherif, M.H.: Handbook of Enterprise Integration. Auerbach Publishers, Boca Raton (2009)
28. Leonardo Web Server. http://www.sourceforge.net/projects/leonardo/
29. Guidi, C., Lucchi, R., Gorrieri, R., Busi, N., Zavattaro, G.: SOCK: a calculus for service oriented computing. In: Proceedings of ICSOC 2006, pp. 327–338 (2006)
30. Guidi, C.: Formalizing languages for service oriented computing. Ph.D. thesis, University of Bologna (2007). http://www.cs.unibo.it/pub/TR/UBLCS/2007/2007-07.pdf
31. Lanese, I., Vaz, C., Ferreira, C.: On the expressive power of primitives for compensation handling. In: ESOP, pp. 366–386 (2010)
32. Montesi, F., Sangiorgi, D.: A model of evolvable components. In: Proceedings of Fifth Symposium on Trustworthy Global Computing (TGC 2010) (2010)
33. Ivan L., Bucchiarone, A., Montesi, F.: A framework for rule-based dynamic adaptation. In: Proceedings of TGC, pp. 284–300 (2010)
34. Vision framework. https://jolie.svn.sourceforge.net/svnroot/jolie/trunk/playground/
35. Anedda, P., Gaggero, M., Manca, S., Schiaratura, O., Leo, S., Montesi, F., Zanetti, G.: A general service oriented approach for managing virtual machines allocation. In: Proceedings of ACM Symposium on Applied Computing (SAC) 2009, pp. 2154–2161 (2009)
36. italianaSoftware s.r.l. italianaSoftware. http://www.italianasoftware.com/
37. W3C. Web Services Description Language. http://www.w3.org/TR/wsdl
38. jEye. A graphical designer for Jolie. http://sourceforge.net/projects/jeye/
39. Honda, K., Yoshida, N., Carbone, M.: Multiparty asynchronous session types. In: Proceedings of POPL'08, vol. 43(1), pp. 273–284. ACM Press (2008)
40. Castagna, G., Gesbert, N., Padovani, L.: A theory of contracts for web services. ACM Trans. Program. Lang. Syst., **31**(5), 1–61 (2009)
41. Lanese, I., Guidi, C., Montesi, F., Zavattaro, G.: Bridging the gap between interaction—and process-oriented choreographies. In: SEFM, pp. 323–332 (2008)
42. Baltazar, P., Caires, L., Vasconcelos, V.T., Vieira, H.T.: A type system for flexible role assignment in multiparty communicating systems. In TGC (2012, to appear)

Chapter 5
From Artifacts to Activities

Niels Lohmann and Karsten Wolf

Abstract We consider services as units in interorganizational business processes. Following trends in the business process management community, we switch from an activity-centric description of processes to artifact-centric descriptions. In the interorganizational setting, unique problems arise. For instance, an artifact hub that is crucial for present-day enactment of artifact-centric processes, can hardly be shared between different organizations since the stored information may be subject to trade secrets. We propose a solution that involves the translation of an artifact-centric model into an activity-centric model. In this course, we consider artifacts as entities that may be sent around between organizations. The location of an artifact may imply access restrictions for one or the other organization. We propose both a formal model and algorithms to show the effectiveness of our approach.

5.1 Introduction

Different communities are concerned with web services. Consequently, there exist several different views on the topic. Some emphasize technical issues while others focus on business aspects. In the area of business process management (BPM), a web service is often understood as a substructure in an interorganizational business process. The idea is that the service describes one party's share in the overall process. In this context, a service is typically a (local) business process where some tasks are communication activities with other parties. Communication may be arbitrarily complex thus distinguishing these services from the frequently advocated simple invoke/response scheme. Furthermore, these services have a meaningful internal state

N. Lohmann (✉) · K. Wolf
University of Rostock, Rostock, Germany
e-mail: niels.lohmann@uni-rostock.de

K. Wolf
e-mail: karsten.wolf@uni-rostock.de

A. Bouguettaya et al. (eds.), *Web Services Foundations*,
DOI: 10.1007/978-1-4614-7518-7_5,

determined by the respective state of the local business process. Hence, techniques such as reasoning about preconditions and postconditions are less appropriate than for simple invoke/response services. In addition, unique problems pop up such as the deadlock freedom of the communication between organizations.

A typical business process model consists of activities that are arranged using control flow primitives such as sequential or parallel execution, exclusive or inclusive branches, and loops. We shall refer to such a process representation as an *activity-centric* process. Currently, this is the dominating way of describing business processes and most workflow engines and modeling notations rely on activity-centric process models. However, alternative representations have been discussed as well. One of these alternatives are so-called *artifact-centric* processes. Promoters claim that artifact-centric models are better comprehendible by business analysts (which typically have little background in computer science). An artifact-centric process explicitly represents business-relevant artifacts such as documents, database states, etc. together with their distinguished life cycle and certain goals (or milestones). The actual activities remain implicit. An example for an artifact would be an application form which may have the simple life cycle not filled/filled but not signed/signed. If the goal is to get a signed form, we can derive the sequence of activities *fill/sign*. In most proposals for enacting artifact-centric processes, the derivation of activities is left to an AI planner that runs on the data of the actual process instance. To this end, all process relevant data need to be stored in a single database that is called *artifact hub*.

We consider this approach as quite problematic for several reasons. First, problems of unsoundness of the overall approach are detected only at run time which may cause severe threats for real business relations. Second, AI planning is a computationally challenging problem, so the execution of a planner at run time may cause unacceptable delays in process execution. Third, and most relevant in our interorganizational setting, trade secrets between the involved companies may inhibit a central artifact hub. The contribution of this chapter is to address these problems. First, we propose to automatically translate an artifact-centric process into an activity-centric process. This way, we keep the advantages of an artifact-centric view to the business analyst while being able to map execution to existing and mature workflow engines. Time expenses are shifted from run time (as for the AI planner) to preparation time (for the translation) which is less time-critical. Moreover, translation inherently includes a check for soundness of the derived model. This part of our contribution is presented in Sect. 5.4. Then, in Sect. 5.5, we propose techniques that allow us to abandon the artifact hub. In our approach, an artifact may be a mobile entity; that is, one that may be sent from one organization to another. This way, we can model artifacts that are invisible or inaccessible to some organization for certain points in time. We can further directly derive the necessity to perform communication activities from the artifact model. As an example, consider the above-mentioned application form. If filling and signing the form is performed by different business units, we observe that both filling and signing is only possible if the form is physically present in the respective unit. Under the assumption that the empty form is initially available for the filling unit, we would be able to come up with the activity-centric model *fill/send to other unit* for the one business unit and *receive filled form/sign* for the other. Consequently, we first propose a model for mobility of artifacts, cf. Sect. 5.5.1. Then, we augment this model with other information that is useful for deriving faithful activity-centric models from a given artifact-centric model. An example would be the enforcement of compliance rules, cf. Sect. 5.5.2. Finally, we discuss related work (Sect. 5.6) and conclude (Sect. 5.7).

All together, we thus outline an approach for an artifact-centric service collaboration. This presentation is based on previous papers of the authors [37, 38, 43].

5.2 Running Example: Insurance Claim Handling

We use a simple insurance claim handling process (based on [52]) as running example for this chapter. In this process, a customer submits a claim to an insurer who then prepares a fraud detection check offered by an external service. Based on the result of this check, the claim is either (1) assessed and the settlement estimated, (2) detected fraudulent and reported, or (3) deemed incomplete. In the last case, further information are requested from the customer before the claim is resubmitted to the fraud detection service. In this situation, the customer can alternatively decide to withdraw the claim. On successful assessment, a settlement case is processed by a financial clerk. The claim is settlement paid in several rates or all at once. A single complete payment further requires an authorization of the controlling officer. When the settlement is finally paid, the claim is archived.

5.3 A Formal Model for Artifacts

Being concerned with an interorganizational setting, we assume that there is a set $\mathcal{A}$ of *agents* (or roles, organizations, etc.). In our approach, agents are principals in a role-based access control for artifacts.

Informally, an artifact consists of data fields that can be manipulated (changed) by agents. Thereby, the change of data is constrained by the role-based access control. Hence, we model an artifact as a state machine. States represent the possible valuations of the data fields whereas transitions are the potential atomic changes that can happen to the data fields. In this paper, we use Petri nets for implicitly representing state machines. When data fields in an artifact evolve independently of each other, the size of a Petri net grows much slower than the number of represented states.

Definition 1 *(Petri net)* A *Petri net* $N = [P, T, F, m_0]$ consists of two finite and disjoint sets P (*places*) and T (*transitions*), a *flow relation* $F \subseteq (P \times T) \cup (T \times P)$, and an *initial marking* m_0. A marking $m : P \to \mathbb{N}$ represents a state of the Petri net and is visualized as a distribution of tokens on the places. Transition t is enabled in marking m iff, for all $[p, t] \in F$, $m(p) > 0$. An enabled transition t can fire,

(a)

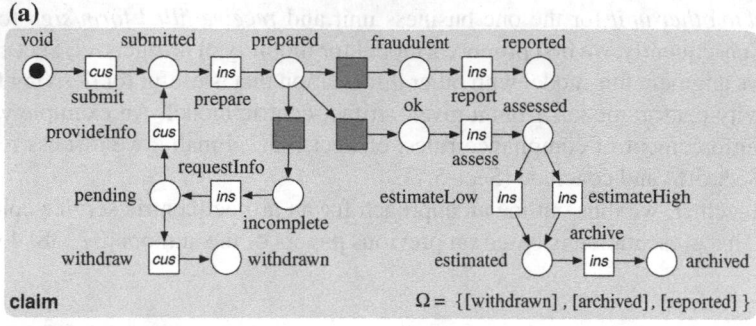

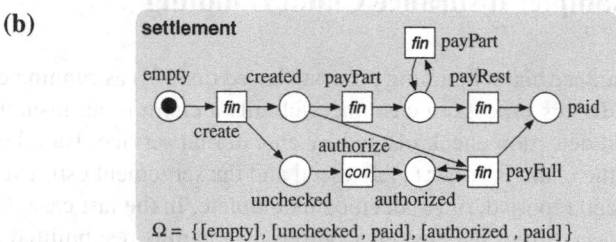

(b)

Fig. 5.1 Running example process. **a Claim** artifact. **b Settlement** artifact

transforming m into the new state m' with $m'(p) = m(p) - W(p, t) + W(t, p)$ where $W([x, y]) = 1$ if $[x, y] \in F$, and $W([x, y]) = 0$, otherwise.

Transitions are triggered by *actions*. The available actions form the *interface* to the artifact. For modeling role based access control, each action is associated to an agent, meaning that this agent is permitted to perform that action.

Throughout this chapter fix a set $\mathcal{L} = \mathcal{L}_c \cup \mathcal{L}_u$ of *action labels*. This set is partitioned into a set $\mathcal{L}_c$ of *controllable actions* that are executed by agents and a set $\mathcal{L}_u$ of *uncontrollable actions* that are not controllable by any agent, but are under the influence of the environment. Such uncontrollable actions are suitable to model choices that are external to the business process model, such as the outcome of a service call (e.g., to a fraud detection agency) or just choices whose decision process is not explicitly modeled at this level of abstraction. We further define a mapping $c : \mathcal{L} \to \mathcal{A}$ representing the *access control*. This access control can be canonically extended [38] to sets of agents (i.e., *roles*), yielding a sophisticated role-based access control.

Running example (cont.) Figure 5.1 depicts the claim and the settlement artifacts. Each transition is labeled by the agent that executes it (*ins*urer, *cus*tomer, *con*troller, and *fin*ancial clerk) or is shaded gray in case of uncontrollable actions.

Definition 2 *(Artifact)* An *artifact* $A = [N, \ell, \Omega]$ consists of

- A Petri net $N = [P, T, F, m_0]$;
- a transition labeling $\ell : T \rightarrow \mathcal{L}$ associating actions with Petri net transitions;
- a set Ω of markings of N representing endpoints in the life cycle of the artifact.

Action $x \in \mathcal{L}$ is enabled in marking m iff some transition $t \in T$ with $l(t) = x$ is enabled in m. Executing the enabled action x amounts to firing any (nondeterministically chosen) such transition.

Nondeterminism in an artifact may sound unusual at first glance but may occur due to prior abstraction. The final markings of the **claim** artifact include the markings [withdrawn], [reported], and [archived] modeling the different outcomes of the claim handling. The **settlement** artifact also has three final markings: [empty] (no settlement has been created), [unchecked, paid] (unchecked payment), and [authorized, paid] (authorized payment).

5.4 Executing Artifact-Centric Business Processes

In this section, we present the first part of our approach: the translation of an artifact-centric model into an activity-centric one. For the moment, we ignore the interorganizational aspects of our setting. These aspects are added in the next section.

At first glance, execution of an artifact-centric process amounts to a sequence of activities that transforms all artifacts into their respective goal states. A second view, however, shows that additional aspects need to be taken into consideration.

1. Even if every artifact reaches its local final state, the respective global state might still model an unreasonable and undesired situation. For instance, a beer order together with a wine-loaded cargo is reachable in the running example but certainly unwanted.
2. Even if a global sequence of activities is reasonable with respect to every artifact in isolation, it may introduce problems such as deadlocks (nonfinal markings without successors) or livelocks (infinite runs without reachable final marking).
3. Even if a sequence of activities is formally correct from the control flow perspective, it may not be meaningful from a semantic perspective. For instance, a shipper must not load the cargo before the ordered goods have been paid although that sequence would perfectly transform all artifacts into their final states while avoided deadlocks or lovelocks.

In the course of this section, we address these three problems as follows. With a specification of *goal states*, we restrict the set of all possible final states to a subset of desired global final states. This addresses the first problem. To avoid deadlocks and livelocks, the artifacts' actions need to be *controlled* by the environment, resulting in an interaction model (i.e., a choreography) which may serve as a contract between the agents. This interaction model provides the necessary coordination to deal with the

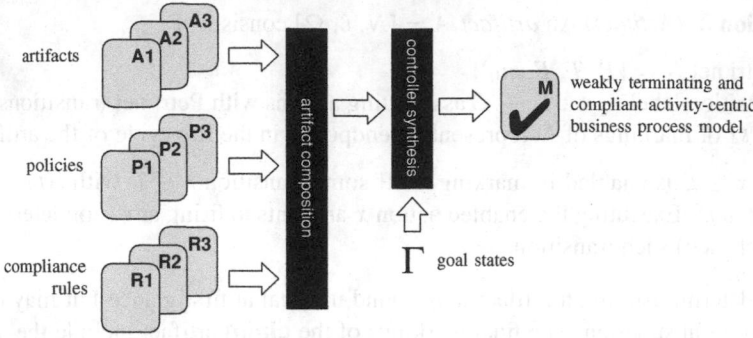

Fig. 5.2 Overview: Artifact composition and controller synthesis (Sect. 5.4.1) derive a choreography from artifacts, policies (Sect. 5.4.2), and compliance rules (Sect. 5.5)

second problem. Finally, we introduce *policies* to further refine the interdependencies between artifacts. This tackles the third problem. Later, in Sect. 5.5 we further discuss how compliance rules can be integrated into this approach. Figure 5.2 provides an overview.

5.4.1 Goal States and Controller Synthesis

To simplify subsequent definitions, we first unite the artifacts. The union of a set of artifacts is again an artifact.

Definition 3 *(Artifact union)* Let $A_1, \ldots, A_n$ be artifacts with pairwise disjoint Petri nets $N_1, \ldots, N_n$. Define the *artifact union* $\bigcup_{i=1}^n A_i = [N, \ell, \Omega]$ to be the artifact consisting of

- $N = [\bigcup_{i=1}^n P_i, \bigcup_{i=1}^n T_i, \bigcup_{i=1}^n F_i, m_{0_1} \oplus \cdots \oplus m_{0_n}]$,
- $\ell(t) = \ell_i(t)$ iff $t \in T_i$ $(i \in \{1, \ldots, n\})$, and
- $\Omega = \{m_1 \oplus \cdots \oplus m_n \mid m_i \in \Omega_i \wedge 1 \leq i \leq n\}$

Thereby, $\oplus$ denotes the composition of markings: $(m_1 \oplus \cdots \oplus m_n)(p) = m_i(p)$ iff $p \in P_i$.

The previous definition is of rather technical nature. The only noteworthy property is that the set of final markings of the union consists of all combinations of final markings of the respective artifacts. We shall later restrict this set of final markings to a subset of *goal states*.

The next definition captures the interplay between two artifacts A_1 and A_2 and uses their interfaces (i.e., the labels associated to artifact transitions) to synchronize artifacts. In the resulting *composition*, each pair of transitions t_1 and t_2 of artifact A_1 and A_2, respectively, with the same label (i.e., $\ell_1(t_1) = \ell_2(t_2)$) is replaced by a new

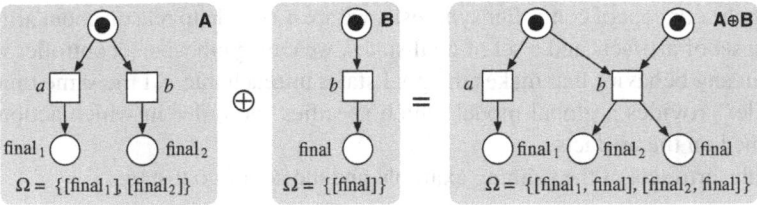

Fig. 5.3 Example for the composition of two artifacts.

transition $[t_1, t_2]$ which models synchronous firing of t_1 and t_2. Consequently, the composition of two artifacts restricts their behavior by synchronization.

Definition 4 *(Artifact composition)* Let A_1 and A_2 be artifacts. Define their *shared labels* as $S = \mathcal{L}_c \setminus \{l \mid \exists t_1 \in T_1, \exists t_2 \in T_2 : \ell(t_1) = \ell(t_2) = l\}$. The *composition* of A_1 and A_2 is the artifact $A_1 \oplus A_2 = [N, \ell, \Omega]$ consisting of:

- $N = [P, T, F, m_{0_1} \oplus m_{0_2}]$ with

  - $P = P_1 \cup P_2$;
  - $T = (T_1 \cup T_2 \cup \{[t_1, t_2] \in T_1 \times T_2 \mid \ell(t_1) = \ell(t_2)\}) \setminus (\{t \in T_1 \mid \ell_1(t) \in S\} \cup \{t \in T_2 \mid \ell_2(t) \in S\})$,
  - $F = ((F_1 \cup F_2) \cap ((P \times T) \cup (T \times P))) \cup \{[[t_1, t_2], p] \mid [t_1, p] \in F_1 \vee [t_2, p] \in F_2\} \cup \{[p, [t_1, t_2]] \mid [p, t_1] \in F_1 \vee [p, t_2] \in F_2\}$,

- for all $t \in T \cap T_1$: $\ell(t) = \ell_1(t)$, for all $t \in T \cap T_2$: $\ell(t) = \ell_2(t)$, and for all $[t_1, t_2] \in T \cap (T_1 \times T_2)$: $\ell([t_1, t_2]) = \ell_1(t_1)$, and
- $\Omega = \{m_1 \oplus m_2 \mid m_1 \in \Omega_1 \wedge m_2 \in \Omega_2\}$.

The composition $A_1 \oplus A_2$ is *complete* if for all $t \in T_i$ holds: if $\ell_i(t) \notin S$, then $\ell_i(t) \in \mathcal{L}_u$ $(i \in \{1, 2\})$.

Figure 5.3 depicts an example for the composition of two artifacts. Final markings of the composition are built just like in the union. We call a composition *complete* if for each transition in one artifact exists a transition in the other artifact that carries the same label. Intuitively, a complete composition does not contain "unsynchronized" transitions. To avoid undesired behavior, a complete composition plays an important role.

Given an artifact A and a set $\Gamma \subseteq \Omega$ of goal states of A, we call another artifact A' a *controller* for A iff (1) their composition $A \oplus A'$ is complete and (2) for each reachable markings of the composition, a marking $m \oplus m'$ is reachable such that $m \in \Gamma$ and m' is a final marking of A'. Intuitively, this controller synchronizes with A such that a goal state $m \in \Gamma$ of A always remains reachable.

The existence of controllers (also called *controllability* [57]) is a fundamental correctness criterion for communicating systems such as services. It can be decided constructively [57]: If a controller for an artifact exists, it can be constructed automatically.

With the concept of controller synthesis, we are now able to reason about artifacts. Given a set of artifacts and a set of goal states, we can synthesize a controller which rules out any behavior that makes the goal states unreachable. At the same time, the controller provides a global model which specifies the order in which actions are performed on the artifacts.

For the artifacts of the running example and the set of goal states

$$\Gamma = \{[\text{withdrawn, empty}], [\text{reported, empty}],$$
$$[\text{archived, unchecked, paid}], [\text{archived, authorized, paid}]\}$$

expressing withdrawn and reported claims as well as unchecked and authorized payments. Although free of deadlocks and livelocks, it still contains undesired behavior which we rule out with policies in the next subsection.

5.4.2 Policies

Artifact-centric approaches follow a declarative modeling style. Consequently, the order of actions in the generated choreography is only constrained to avoid deadlocks and livelocks with respect to goal states. As a downside of this approach, a lot of unreasonable behavior is exposed. For instance, paying a settlement before the claim is assessed would be possible.

To rule out this undesired behavior, we employ *policies* (also called *behavioral constraints* [40]). For keeping notations slim, we also model policies with artifacts; that is, labeled Petri nets with a set of final markings. These artifacts have no physical counterpart and are only used to model dependencies between actions of different artifacts. The application of policies then boils down to the composition of the artifacts with these policies. In principal, goal states can be expressed by policies as well. We still decided to split these concepts, because the former conceptionally express liveness properties whereas the latter express safety properties.

For the running example, we use two policies:

P1 The claim may be archived only if the settlement is paid.
P2 A settlement may only be created after the claim has been estimated.

Figures 5.4a, b depict the artifacts for the policies **P1** and **P2**. The union with the artifacts **claim** and **settlement** is depicted in Fig. 5.4c where the policies are highlighted with bold strokes. By applying more and more policies to the artifacts, we add more dependencies between artifacts and exclude more and more unintended behavior.

Figure 5.5 depicts the Petri net representing the final activity-centric model. Each transition is labeled with an action (what is done), an artifact (which data are accessed;

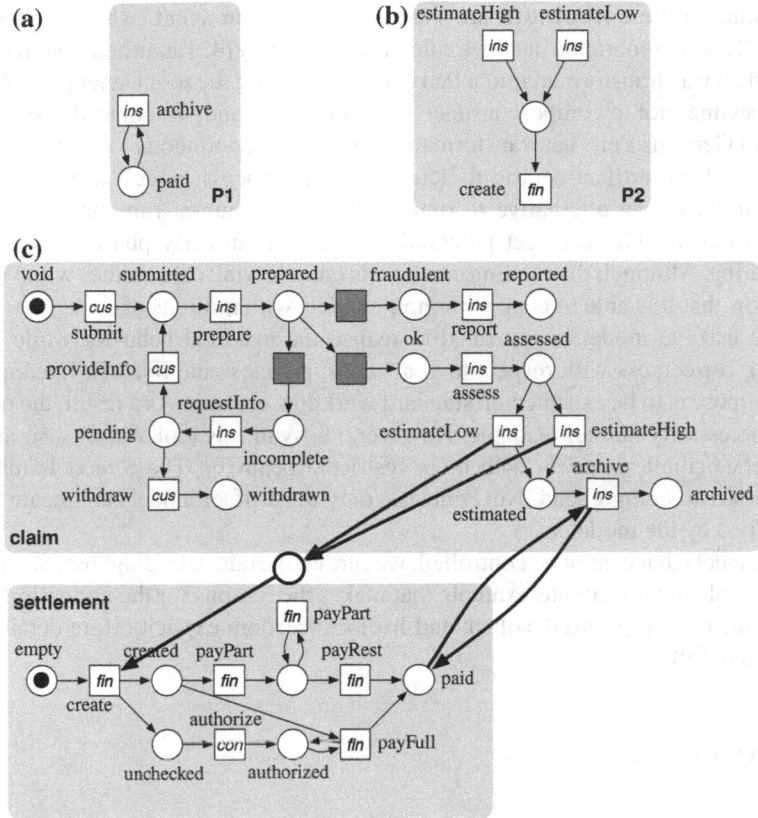

Fig. 5.4 Application of policies to artifacts. **a** Policy P1. **b** Policy P2. **c** Policy P2 and P3 applied to artifacts **claim** and **settlement**

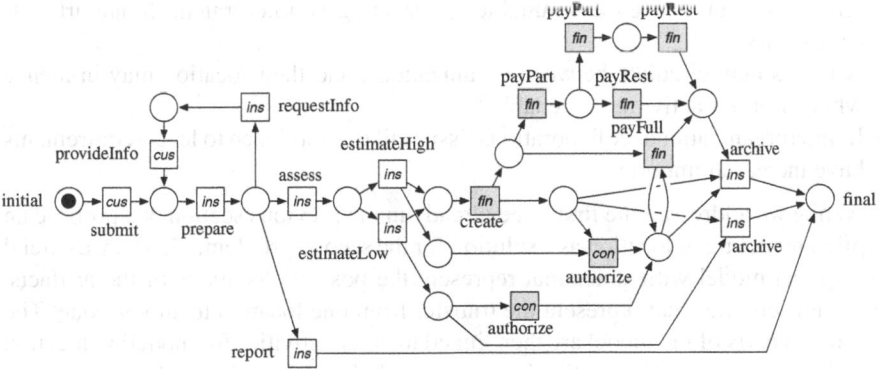

Fig. 5.5 Resulting choreography between agents *customer*, *insurer*, *controller* and *financial clerk*

the actions on the **settlement** are shaded grey), and an agent (who performs the action). This choreography has been calculated by Wendy [42] as an automaton model which then was transformed into a Petri net model using the tool Genet [15]. With a preprocessing tool to compose artifacts and policies, Wendy as controller synthesis tool, and Genet as Petri net transformation, we have a continuous tool chain for the translation from artifact-centric to activity-centric process models available. This tool chain offers an alternative to running an artifact hub at runtime. Especially, the approach is able to detect potential problems in an early phase of workflow engineering. Although the running example is rather trivial, case studies with Wendy [42] show that it is able to cope with input models with millions of states.

Note that the model is generated to realize the maximal behavior while guaranteeing correctness with respect to goal states, policies, and livelock freedom. Its main purpose is to be executed on standard workflow engines. As a result, the model is not necessarily human-readable. However, the synthesis tool Wendy also allows to generate smaller models with more restricted behavior. These models may be much easier to comprehend. Nevertheless, only the artifact models are meant to be understood by the modeler.

For models that cannot be controlled, we further introduced a diagnosis algorithm [36] that calculates a counterexample that makes the reasons for the impossibility to control the model toward deadlock and livelock freedom explicit. More details can be found in [38].

5.5 Extensions

Now we turn to the main contribution of this paper and approach the interorganizational aspects of artifact-centric processes. These aspects include the following issues:

- An artifact hub is even less suitable for enacting an interorganizational artifact-centric process;
- Artifacts may circulate between organizations, and their location may influence whether or not activities are enabled;
- In interorganizational collaborations, issues like compliance to legal requirements have increased importance.

While we addressed the first issue already in the previous section, we propose an explicit modeling of location as a solution for the second problem. That is, we extend the artifact model with states that represent the possible locations of the artifacts, and with activities that represent the transfer from one location to another one. The additional parts of the model are then linked to other activities for modeling location based restrictions for their activation. In the end, the extended model can be treated in the same way as proposed in the previous section. The resulting activity-centric model is a global business process model that provides a global view. It can serve as a contract (or a choreography, or a protocol) for the overall activity behavior. In the same style, we propose model extensions for coping with compliance requirements.

5.5.1 Interorganizational Business Processes

5.5.1.1 Location-Aware Artifacts

If we want to derive a protocol from a set of given artifacts, we have to understand the reasons for which messages are sent around in an artifact context. It turns out that there exist different shapes of artifacts which cause interorganizational interaction for different reasons. We give a few examples.

Consider first an artifact that is materialized as, say, a physical form. Actions in this artifact correspond to filling in fields in this form. Still, some actions may be bound to particular agents (e.g., signatures), so the artifact itself must be passed to that agent. Passing the artifact corresponds to sending a message. The act of sending would, at the same time, disable any actions bound to the sending agent. In another scenario, an artifact manifests itself as a database record. In this case, the artifact is not passed, but a message may be required to announce the existence of the artifact and to transmit some kind of access link which then enables the other agent to perform actions on the artifact by remote access to the data base.

Taking the artifact-centric approach seriously, we propose to include the acts of sending a message, receiving a message, and synchronous communication steps as specific actions of the artifact. Likewise, the current location of the artifact (at an agent or "in transit") becomes an additional data field. The additional data field can be used for modeling the actual effect of the messaging activity such as enabling or disabling other actions.

Running example (cont.) Figure 5.6 depicts an location-aware extension of the **claim** artifact. Two additional places ("@insurer" and "@controller") model the *locaction* of the insurance claim file. In our example, we assume that after submitting the claim, a physical file is created by the insurer which can be sent to the controlling officer by executing the respective action "send to controller". We further assume that the **settlement** artifact is a data base entry that can be remotely accessed by the insurer, the financial clerk, and the controlling officer. Hence, we do not need to extend it with location information and keep the model in Fig. 5.1b as is.

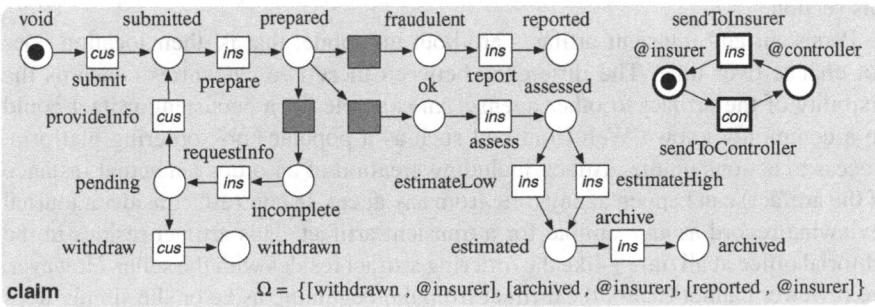

Fig. 5.6 Location-aware **claim** artifact. Added nodes are depicted with *bold lines*

We see that the extension to the functional artifact model may vary a lot. Hence, it is reasonable to provide this information as part of the artifact. One possible approach is to make the modeler fully responsible for modeling location-specific information about the artifact. Another option would be to automatically generate an extension of the model from a more high level specification. The latter approach has the advantage that the added information is consistent by construction (e.g., a message can only be received after it has been sent). However, our subsequent treatment of location-aware artifacts does not depend on the way they have been obtained.

For the sake of automatically generating location information, we observe that the necessary extension to an artifact model can be reduced to applying a reasonably sized set of recurring patterns. In consequence, we suppose that it is possible to automatically derive the extension from a few general categories. In the next subsection, we make a preliminary proposal for such a categorization.

5.5.1.2 Categorization of Location Information

In this subsection, we propose a two-dimensional categorization of artifacts and discuss the consequences on the derivation of a location-aware extension of an artifact. The first dimension is concerned with the possible changes of ownership and remote visibility of the artifact. The second dimension deals with remote accessibility to actions.

In the first dimension, we distinguish *mobile*, *persistent*, and *transient* artifacts.

A mobile artifact may change its location over time. A typical example is a physical form that is exchanged between agents, for instance for collecting information or just signatures from different agents. The direct debit authorization discussed in previous sections is a particular instance of a mobile artifact. Messages caused by a mobile artifact typically correspond to a change of location of the artifact. This can be modeled using an additional data element that records the location which may be at a particular agent or "in transit" between two agents. Actions correspond to sending an artifact (move the location field from "at X" to "in transit from X to Y" and receiving an artifact (move the location field from "in transit from X to Y" to "at Y"). The location field may then be used for constraining remote access as discussed later in this section.

Persistent and transient artifacts are both immobile; that is, their location does not change over time. The difference between these two categories concerns the visibility of the artifact to other agents. An example for a persistent artifact could be a commonly known Web front-end such as a popular book-ordering platform. Access to actions on the artifact, including creation of an order (an actual instance of the artifact) can happen at any time from any agent. In contrast, consider a journal reviewing record as an example for a transient artifact. This artifact resides in the editorial office at all time—like the ordering artifact resides with the seller. However, the reviewer cannot access the artifact from the beginning as he or she simply does not know of its existence. Only after having been invited to review the paper, the reviewer can start to act on the artifact (including downloading the paper and filling in

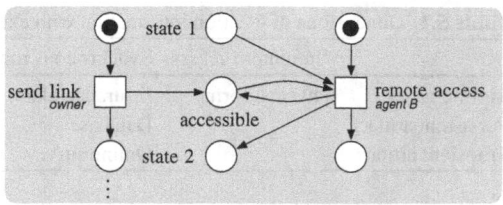

Fig. 5.7 Excerpt of a transient artifact whose *owner* needs to send a link prior to remote access of *agent B*

the fields in the recommendation form). In essence, the reviewer invitation contains a *link* to the artifact, possibly in the form of login information thus announcing the existence to the artifact. This link message makes the artifact remotely accessible. For a persistent artifact, no such information is required. At least, passing the link to the artifact to the remote (customer) agent, is typically not part of the interorganizational business process model for book selling.

Persistent artifacts basically do not require any location-specific extension (such as the **settlement** example). It is just necessary to be aware of the particular location for the purpose of distinguishing remote from local access to the artifact. For a transient model, we propose to add a place for each agent that is marked as soon as the artifact is visible to that agent. An action "send link" marks that place thus modeling the fact that the artifact can be accessed after having received the link (or login) information. Once a place is marked, the artifact can be accessed indefinitely by the respective agent. See Fig. 5.7 for an example.

The second dimension determines, whether and how an artifact can be accessed by remote agents. For a mobile artifact, an agent is remote if it is not currently owning the artifact. For a persistent or transient artifact, all agents are remote, except the one that possesses it. Remote accessibility may differ between actions, so we suggest to specify this information for each action separately.

We distinguish three options for remote accessibility of an action: *none, synchronous,* and *asynchronous*. For a real paper form, the standard option would be none. The form is not remote accessible. Performing an action requires physical presence of the artifact. An exception may be a situation where two agents are actually present in a single location such as in the case of a contract that is signed by a customer directly at a desk which does not require passing the contract from the clerk to the customer. Synchronous transfer is an obvious option for artifacts with interactive Web forms as front-end. An example for an asynchronously accessible artifact can be found in the once popular tool *Majordomo*[1] for managing electronic mailing lists. Participants could manipulate their recorded data (like subscription and unsubscription) by writing e-mails containing specific commands to a particular e-mail address.

Although there is a certain correlation between the dimensions, we can think of examples for all possible combinations of values for the two discussed dimensions. Even for a mobile artifact, asynchronous remote access may be reasonable. Think of a product that is about to be assembled where the delivery and mounting of a part

---

[1] http://www.greatcircle.com/majordomo/

Table 5.1 Dimensions of location information with examples

	No remote access	Synchronous remote access	Asynchronous remote access
Mobile artifact	Physical form	Insurance claim with delegation	
Persistent artifact	–	Database	Majordomo
Transient artifact	–	Online survey	Review form

from a supplier may be modeled as an asynchronous access to the artifact. Thus, there is a need to explicitly state the remote accessibility scheme for each action.

We do not claim that the above categorization (see Table 5.1 for an overview) is complete. However, discussions subsequent to the presentation of the original article [43] did not reveal any further categories. Further investigations of more involved scenarios such as Enterprise Integration Patterns [27] or Service Interaction Patterns [6] are subject of future work. It is this safe to assume for the remainder of this paper that a location-aware artifact model be given.

Running example (cont.) Locations can be used to refine the policies of our insurance process:

P1 The claim may be archived only if it resides at the insurer and the settlement is paid.

P2 A settlement may only be created after the claim has been estimated.

P3 To authorize the complete payment of the settlement, the claim artifact must be at hand to the controlling officer.

P4 The claim artifact may only be sent to the controller if it has been estimated and the settlement has not been checked.

P5 The claim artifact may only be sent back to the insurer if the settlement has been authorized.

Figure 5.8 depicts the resulting location-aware choreography. Note the highlighted transitions modeling the required message exchange between the insurer and the controlling officer to satisfy policy P3–P5.

5.5.2 Compliance Rules

Compliance rules are often *declarative* and describe *what* should be achieved rather than *how* to achieve it. Temporal logics such as CTL [10], LTL [50] or PLTL [51] are common ways to formalize such declarative rules. To make these logics approachable for nonexperts, also graphical notations have been proposed [5, 7]. Given such rules, compliance of a business process model can be verified using model checking techniques [16]. These checks can be classified as *compliance by detection*, also called after the fact or retrospective checking [53]. Their main goal is to provide a rigorous proof of compliance. In case of noncompliance, diagnosis information may help to fix the business process toward compliance. This step can be very complicated, because the rules may affect various parts and agents of the business process

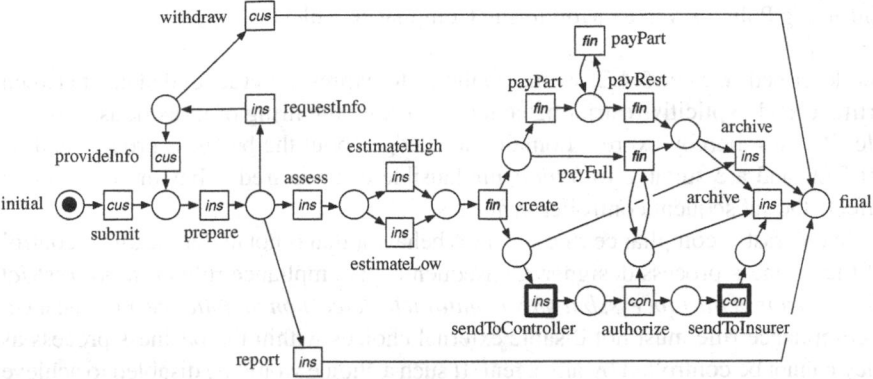

Fig. 5.8 Location-aware choreography with highlighted message exchange that satisfies policies P1–P5

(e. g., financial staff and the press team). Furthermore, the declarative nature of the rules does not provide recipes on how to fix the business process. To meet the previous example rule, an action "send information to press team" needs to be added to the process and must be executed at most 2 weeks after the execution of an action "sign financial report". Compliance can be eventually reached after iteratively adjusting and checking the business process model. The main advantage of this approach is the fact that it can be applied to already running business processes.

An alternative approach focuses on the early design phases and takes a business process model and the compliance rules as input and automatically generates a business process model that is *compliant by design* [53], cf. Fig. 5.2. This has several advantages: First, a subsequent proof and potential corrections are not required. This may speed up the modeling process. Second, the approach is flexible as the generation can be repeated when rules are added, removed, or changed. Third, the approach is complete in the sense that an unsuccessful model generation can be interpreted as "the business process cannot be *made* compliant" rather than "the current model is not compliant". Fourth, compliance is not only detected, but actually enforced. That is, noncompliant behavior becomes technically impossible.

5.5.2.1 Modeling Compliance Rules

This subsection investigates to what extend compliance rules can be integrated into the artifact-centric approach. Before we present different shapes of compliance rules and their formalization with Petri nets, we first discuss the difference between a policy and a compliance rule.

Enforcing Policies Versus Monitoring Compliance Rules

As described in Sect. 5.4.2, we use policies to express interdependencies between artifacts and explicitly restrict behavior by making the firing of transitions impossible. Policies thereby express domain knowledge about the business process and its artifacts and are suitable to *inhibit* implausible or undesired behavior. This finally affects the subsequent controller synthesis.

In contrast, a compliance rule specifies behavior that is not under the direct control of the business process designer. Consequently, a compliance rule *must not restrict the behavior of the process, but only monitor it to detect noncompliance.* For instance, a compliance rule must not disable external choices within the business process as they cannot be controlled by any agent. If such a choice would be disabled to achieve compliance, the resulting business process model would be spurious as the respective choice could not be disabled in reality. Therefore, compliance rules must not restrict the behavior of the artifacts, but only restrict the final states of the model. This may classify behavior as undesired (viz. noncompliant), but this behavior remains reachable. Only if this behavior can be circumvented by the controller synthesis, we faithfully found a compliant business process which can be actually implemented. We formalize this nonrestricting nature as *monitor property* [40, 57]. Intuitively, this property requires that in every reachable marking of an artifact, it holds that for each action label of that artifact a transition with that label is activated. This rules out situations in which the firing of a transition in a composition is inhibited by a compliance rule.

Expressiveness of Compliance Rules

Conceptually, we model compliance rules by artifacts with the monitor property. Again, adding a compliance rule to an artifact-centric model boils down to composition, cf. Def 4. The monitor property ensures that the compliance rule's transitions are synchronized with the other artifacts, but without restricting (i. e., disabling) actions. That is, the life cycle of a compliance rule model evolves together with the artifacts' life cycles, but may only affect the final states of the composed model.

In a finite-state composition of artifacts, the set of runs reaching a final state forms a regular language. The terminating runs of a compliance rule (i. e., sequences of transitions that reach a final marking) describe compliant runs. This set again forms a regular language. In the composition of the artifacts and the compliance rules, these regular languages are synchronized—viz. intersected—yielding a subset of terminating runs. Regular languages allow to express a variety of relevant scenarios. In fact, we can express all patterns listed by Dwyer et al. [19], including:

- enforcement and existence of actions (e. g., *"Every compliant run must contain an action 'archive claim'."*),
- absence/exclusion of actions (e. g., *"The action 'withdraw claim' must not be executed."*),

- ordering (precedence and response) of actions (e. g., *"The action 'create settlement' must be executed after 'submit claim', but before 'archive claim'."*), and
- numbering constraints/bounded existence of actions (e. g., *"The action "partially pay settlement" must not be executed more than three times."*).

The explicit model of data states of the artifacts further allows to express rules concerning data flow, such as:

- enforcement/exclusion of data states (e. g., *"The claim's state 'fraud reported' and the settlement's state 'paid' must never coincide."*), or
- data and control flow concurrency (e.g., *"The action 'publish review' may only be executed if the review artifact is in state 'reviewers blinded'."*).

Additionally, the explicit modeling of the location of the artifacts allows to express spacial constraints:

- enforcement/exclusion of actions at specific locations (e. g., *"The task 'sign' may only be executed if the contract artifact is at the human resources department"*), or
- enforcement/exclusion of the transport/transfer of an artifact in a certain state (e. g., *"iPhone prototypes must not leave the company premises after the operating system is installed."*).

On top of that, any combinations are possible, allowing to express complex compliance rules.

Limitations

Apart from the conceptual richness, the presented approach has some theoretical limits. First, it is not applicable to nonregular languages. For instance, a rule requiring that a compliant run must have an arbitrary large, but equal number of *a* and *b* actions or that *a* and *b* actions must be properly balanced (Dyck languages) cannot be expressed with a finite-state models. Second, rules that affect infinite runs (e. g., certain LTL formulae [50]) cannot be expressed. Infinite runs are predominantly used to reason about reactive systems. A business process, however, is usually designed to eventually reach a final state—this basically is the essence of the soundness property. Therefore, we shall focus on an interpretation of LTL which only considers finite runs, similar to a semantics described by Havelund and Roşu [26]. Third, just like Awad et al. [8], we also do not consider the **X** (next state) operator of CTL*, because we typically discuss distributed systems in which states are not partially ordered. Forth, we do not use timed Petri nets and hence can make no statements on temporal properties of business processes. However, we can abstract the variation of time by events such as "time passes" or data states such as "expired" as in [24, 46]. Conceptually, an extension toward more expressive constraints would be possible. For instance, pushdown automata could be used to express Dyck languages, a yielding context-free language as product. However, this extension would need further

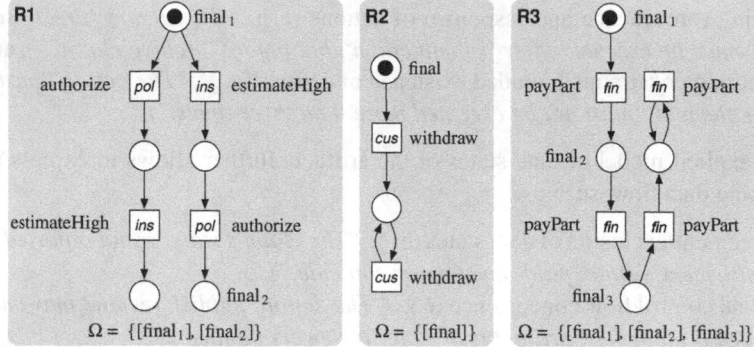

Fig. 5.9 Compliance rules modeled as Petri nets

theoretical consideration as, for instance, controllability is undecidable in case of infinite state systems [47].

Example Formalizations of Compliance Rules

As mentioned earlier, we again use artifacts (i. e., Petri nets with final markings and action labels) that satisfy the monitor property to model compliance rules. As an example, we consider the following compliance rules for our example insurance claim process:

R1   All insurance claims with an estimated high settlement must be authorized.
R2   Customers must not be allowed to withdraw insurance claims.
R3   Settlements should be paid in at most three parts.

Figure 5.9 shows the Petri net formalizations of these compliance rules. In rule R1, we exploited the fact that the actions "authorize" and "estimateHigh" are executed at most once. In rule R2 and R3, the monitor property is achieved by allowing "withdraw" and "payPart" to fire in any reachable state. Without restriction of the behavior, the final markings classify executions as compliant or not. For instance, executing "estimateHigh" in rule R1 without eventually executing "authorize" does not reach the final marking [final$_2$]. Other examples can be formalized similarly.

Discussion

We conclude this section by a discussion of the implications of using Petri nets to formalize compliance rules.

- *Single formalism.* We can model artifacts, policies, and compliance rules with the same formalism. Though we do not claim that Petri nets should be used by domain experts to model compliance regulations, using a single formalism still facilitates the modeling and verification process. Furthermore, each rule implicitly models compliant behavior which can be simulated. This is not possible if, for instance, arbitrary LTL formulae are considered.
- *Level of abstraction.* Rules can be expressed using minimal overhead. Each rule contains only those places and transitions that are affected by the rule and plus some additional places to model further causalities. In particular, no placeholder elements (e. g., anonymous activities in BPMN-Q [7]) are required. These placeholder elements must not be confused with "wildcard" dependencies, for instance requiring input from artifact *A*, *B*, or *C*. To formalize such dependencies with our artifact model, they need to be unfolded explicitly. Of course, syntactic extensions may be introduced to modeling languages to compact the models.
- *Independent design.* The rules can be formulated independently of the artifact and policy models. That is, the modeler does not need to be confronted with the composite model. This modular approach is more likely to scale, because the rules can also be validated independently of the other rules.
- *Reusability.* The composition is defined in terms of action labels. Therefore, rules may be reused in different business process models as long as the labels match. This can be enforced using standard naming schemes or ontologies.
- *Runtime monitoring.* The monitor property ensures that the detection of noncompliant behavior is transparent to the process as no behavior is restricted. Therefore, the models of the compliance rules can be also used to check compliance during or after runtime, for instance by inspecting execution logs.
- *Rule generation.* Finally, the structure of the Petri nets modeling compliance rules is very generic. Therefore, it should be possible to automatically generate Petri nets for standard scenarios or to provide templates to which only the names of the constrained actions need to be filled. Also, the monitor property can be automatically enforced.

5.5.2.2 Compliance By Design

This section presents the second ingredient of this contribution: the construction of business process models that are compliant by design. Beside the construction, we also discuss the diagnosis of noncompliant business process models.

Constructing Compliant Models

None of the compliance rules discussed in the previous section hold in the example process depicted in Fig. 5.8. This noncompliance can be detected by standard model checking tools. They usually provide a counterexample which describes how a noncompliant situation can be reached. For instance, the action sequence "1. submit, 2.

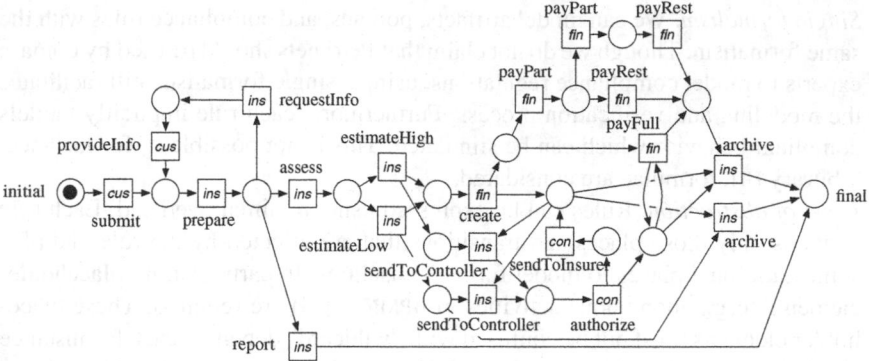

Fig. 5.10 Operational business process satisfying the compliance rules R1–R3

prepare, 3. requestInfo, 4. withdraw" is a witness that the process does not comply with rule R2 from Sect. 5.5.2.1. To satisfy this requirement, the transition "withdraw" can be simply removed. However, implementing the other rules is more complicated, and each modification would require another compliance check.

We propose to *synthesize* a compliant model instead of verifying compliance. By composing the Petri net models of the artifacts, the policies, and the compliance rules and by taking the goal states into account, we derive a Petri net that models the artifacts' life cycles that are restricted by the policies and whose final states are constrained by the goal states and the compliance rules. *Compliant behavior is now reduced to weak termination*, and we can apply the same algorithm [57] and tool [42] to synthesize a controller. If such a controller exists, it provides an operational model that specifies the order in which the agents need to perform their actions. This model is *compliant by design*—a subsequent verification is not required. Beside weak termination (and hence, compliance), the synthesis algorithm further guarantees the resulting model is *most permissive* [57]. That is, exactly that behavior has been removed that would violate weak termination. Another important aspect of the approach is its flexibility to add further compliance rules. That is, we do not need to edit the existing model, but we can simply repeat the synthesis for the new rule set.

Running example (cont.) Figure 5.10 depicts the resulting business process model. It obviously contains no transition labeled with "withdraw", but the implementation of the other rules yielded a whole different structure of the part modeling the settlement processing. *It is important to stress that the depicted business process model has been synthesized completely automatically* using the partner synthesis tool Wendy [42] and the Petri net synthesis tool Petrify [17]. Admittedly, it is a rather complicated model, but any valid implementation of the compliance rules would yield the same behavior or a subset. Though our running example is clearly a toy example, experimental results [42] show that controller synthesis can be effectively applied to models with millions of states.

5.6 Related Work

Artifact-centric approaches have recently received broad attention from both academia and industry. This section sketches related work in the context of several categories touched by this chapter.

GSM. The guard-stage-milestone model (GSM) [28, 29] is the result of IBM's long-standing effort of promoting the artifact-centric view on business processes. GSM follow a clearly declarative way which allows for greater flexibility. Milestones can be compared to our goal states. However, GSM has a stronger focus on modeling and further allows for elegant hierarchical models. Artifact-centric models are often formalized using infinite state systems (cf. [28, 18, 25]) whereas our approach heavily relies synthesis and hence on finite state models. GSM further assumes active artifacts that may perform service calls and has no concept of locations.

Artifacts and service orientation. The idea of encapsulating functionality as services also influenced artifact-centric approaches. Several authors investigated how services can be used to manipulate the state of artifacts. Keeping a declarative modeling style, services are described by preconditions and postconditions formulated in different logics. Bhattacharya et al. [12] study several questions related to artifacts and services, including reachability of goal states, absence of deadlocks, and redundancy of data. Their employed logics is similar to OWL-S. Similar settings are investigated by Calvanese et al. [14] and Fritz et al. [22] for first order logics. Gerede and Su [23] language based on CTL to specify artifact behaviors in artifact-centric process models. Each paper provides complexity and decidability results for the respective problems. These approaches share the idea of using service calls to manipulate artifacts. The artifact itself, however, is assumed to be immobile, resulting in orchestrating workflows rather than our choreography-like setting.

Artifact hosting. Hull et al. [30] introduce *artifact-centric hubs* as central infrastructure hosting data that can be read and written by participants. The authors motivate that, compared to autonomous settings such as choreographies, the centralized storage of data has the advantage of providing a conceptual rendezvous point to exchange status information of the aggregate. This centralized approach can be mimicked by our location-aware approach by remotely accessible immobile artifacts. However, to tackle potential problems arising with the hosting of sensible data in a centralized data hub, we propose to derive explicit message flow from an location-aware artifact model.

Execution. For the execution of artifact-centric processes exist different approaches: Li and Wu [34] assume that each artifact has a service interface and propose a translation into WS-BPEL. They assume, however, an existing workflow that coordinates the artifact execution—such a workflow could be the result of our partner synthesis approach. Opposed to the transformation of the artifacts, Ngamakeur et al. [48] promote the direct execution of artifacts as a translation is less flexible and is potentially connected with information loss. In our approach, we also do not change the artifacts, but only derive a workflow that coordinates the executing agents. Finally, Liu et al. [35] translate the ECA tules of Artiflow to WS-BPEL.

Conformance. Fahland et al. [21] extend conformance checking to artifact-centric business processes. Their approach bases on comparing recorded data base states with a process model and can be applied similarly to our model. Yongchareon et al. [58] study private and shared artifacts. Based on this distinction, public and private views can be defined. To support refinement of executable process models, we rely on existing results [2, 3, 56] which need to be extended toward an artifact-centric model.

Proclets. Aalst et al. [1, 4] introduce *proclets* to specify business processes in which object life cycles can be modeled in different levels of granularity and cardinality. Consequently, proclets are well-suited to deal with settings in which several instances of data objects are involved. Being introduced as workflow models, proclets have no concept of locations.

Compliance by detection. Awad et al. [8] investigate a pattern-based compliance check based on BPMN-Q [7]. They also cover the compliance rule classes defined by Dwyer et al. [19] and give a CTL formalization as well as an antipattern for each rule. These antipatterns are used to highlight the compliance violations in a BPMN model. Such a visualization is very valuable for the process designer and it would be interesting to see whether such antipatterns are also applicable to the artifact-centric approach. Sadiq et al.[54] use a declarative specification of compliance rules from which they derive compliance checks. These checks are then annotated to a business process and monitored during its execution. These checks are similar to the nonblocking compliance rule models that only monitor behavior rather than constraining it. Lu et al. [46] compare business processes with compliance rules and derive a compliance degree. This is an interesting approach, because it replaces yes/no answers by numeric values which could help to easier diagnose noncompliance. Knuplesch et al. [31] analyze data aspects of operational business process models. Similar to the artifact-centric approach, data values are abstracted into compact life cycles.

Compliance by design. Goedertier and Vanthienen [24] introduce the declarative language PENELOPE to specify compliance rules. From these rules, a state space and a BPMN model is generated which is compliant by design. This approach is limited to acyclic process models. Furthermore, the purpose of the generated model is rather the validation of the specified rules than the execution. Küster et al. [33] study the interplay between control flow models and object life cycles. The authors present an algorithm to automatically derive a sound process model from given object life cycles. The framework is, however, not designed to express dependencies between life cycles and therefore cannot specify complex policies or compliance rules.

5.7 Conclusion

We extended the idea of artifact-centric process design to an interorganizational setting where artifacts cannot be gathered in artifact hubs. We observed that in such a setting the actual location of the artifact has a significant impact on executability of actions and on the message flow in a corresponding activity-centric process. We propose to enhance artifacts with explicit information on location and its impact on remote access to actions. This information can be modeled manually or derived systematically from a high level description. We suggest a principal two-dimensional categorization into mobile, persistent, and transient artifacts on one hand, and no, synchronous, or asynchronous remote access to actions on the other as an initial proposal for a high level description. From location-aware artifacts and goal states for the artifacts, we can derive a global interaction model that may serve as a contract between the involved agents. The interaction model can be derived in such a way that it respects specified policies of the involved agents. We can further appropriately integrate compliance requirements. The whole approach relies on only one simple formalism. Petri nets express the functional part of an artifacts, location information, as well as policies. This way, it is possible to employ existing tools for the automated construction of an activity-centric models and the invocation of policies. These tools have already proven their capability to cope with nontrivial problem instances.

In our modeling approach to artifacts, we did not include mechanisms for creating new artifact instances. If the overall number of artifacts in the system is bounded, this is not a serious problem since the creation of a new artifact instance can be modeled by a transition from a state "not existing" to the actual initial state of the artifact. This approach does not work in the case of an unbounded number of artifacts. Similar problems are known in the area of verification of parameterized programs where parts of the program may spawn a finite but not a priori bounded number of threads which run identical programs. There exist ways to finitely model such systems and several verification problems turn out to be decidable [20, 9]. Future research is required to find out whether the methodology used there extends to the problems and solutions proposed in this paper.

Another interesting issue is the further transformation of the global activity-centric model derived in this paper into local processes for the agents. We see two potential directions which need to be further explored. First, we could exploit existing research on *accordance* (e.g., [11, 13, 56]). In [3], we showed that it is possible for each agent to replace its part of a contract by an accordant private process. Relying on the accordance criterion, soundness of the original interaction model is inherited by the collaboration of private processes. The approach requires a suitable decision procedure for checking accordance [56, 55] or powerful transformation rules which preserve accordance [32]. Both appear to be more advanced for establishing deadlock freedom than for livelock freedom, so more progress needs to be made there.

A second opportunity for deriving local processes is to use the *realizability* approach proposed in [44, 45]. There, local processes are constructed from a choreography for the sake of proving that the choreography can be implemented (realized). To this end, the choreography is transformed into a service where the local processes are computed as correctly interacting partners. Adding results from [57] to this approach, we can even compute a finite representation of a *set* of processes for each agent such that each combination of one process per agent yields a correct set of realizing partners for the choreography. The concept was called *autonomous controllability* in [57]. In the artifact setting, such a finite representation of a set of processes could be used to derive, at least to some degree, a local process that not only respects the artifacts and policies known to all involved agents, but also artifacts and policies that are hidden from the other agents. Again, past research focused on deadlock freedom, so further work is required to make that technology available in the context of this paper. Nevertheless, the discussion suggests that the chosen approach connects artifact-centric choreographies to promising methods for further tool support.

We believe that we can further exploit ideas for bridging the gap between the global interaction model and the local processes of the agents. It is also worth to explore ideas known from program verification for the purpose of supporting unbounded creation of artifact instances. Furthermore, a reverse translation from activity-centric to artifact-centric models could be a promising direction of research. This could promote the artifact-centric modeling style to an equitable view on the process under investigation.

The main practical limitation is the lack of a proper modeling language, because the presented Petri net formalization is only a conceptual modeling language. We recently developed an extension [41] for BPMN [49] to provide a graphical notation that is more accessible for domain experts to model artifacts, policies, and compliance rules. A canonic next step would then be the integration of the approach into a modeling tool and an empirical evaluation thereof. Furthermore, we concentrated on the early design of a business process and did not consider its execution. For business processes that are already in execution, our approach is currently not applicable as the translations from conceptual models to industrial languages are still very immature [39].

References

1. Aalst, WMPvd, Barthelmess, P., Ellis, C.A., Wainer, J.: Proclets: a framework for lightweight interacting workflow processes. Int. J. Cooperative Inf. Syst. **10**(4), 443–481 (2001)
2. Aalst, W.M.P.v.d., Lohmann, N., Massuthe, P., Stahl, C., Wolf, K.: From public views to private views—correctness-by-design for services. In: WS-FM 2007, LNCS 4937, pp. 139–153. Springer (2008)
3. Aalst, W.M.P.v.d., Lohmann, N., Massuthe, P., Stahl, C., Wolf, K.: Multiparty contracts: agreeing and implementing interorganizational processes. Comput. J. **53**(1), 90–106 (2010)
4. Aalst, W.M.P.v.d., Mans, R.S., Russell, N.C.: Workflow support using proclets: divide, interact, and conquer. IEEE Data Eng. Bull. **32**(3), 16–22 (2009)
5. Aalst, W.M.P.v.d., Pesic, M.: DecSerFlow: towards a truly declarative service flow language. In: WS-FM 2006, LNCS 4184, pp. 1–23. Springer (2006)

6. Alistair Barros, M.D., ter Hofstede, A.: Service interaction patterns. In: BPM 2005, vol. LNCS 3649, pp. 302–318. Springer (2005)
7. Awad, A.: BPMN-Q: a language to query business processes. In: EMISA 2007, LNI P-119, pp. 115–128. GI (2007)
8. Awad, A., Weidlich, M., Weske, M.: Visually specifying compliance rules and explaining their violations for business processes. J. Vis. Lang. Comput. **22**(1), 30–55 (2011)
9. Ball, T., Chaki, S., Rajamani, S.K.: Parameterized verification of multithreaded software libraries. In: TACAS 2001, LNCS 2031, pp. 158–173. Springer (2001)
10. Ben-Ari, M., Manna, Z., Pnueli, A.: The temporal logic of branching time. In: POPL '81, pp. 164–176. ACM (1981)
11. Benatallah, B., Casati, F., Toumani, F.: Representing, analysing and managing Web service protocols. Data Knowl. Eng. **58**(3), 327–357 (2006)
12. Bhattacharya, K., Gerede, C.E., Hull, R., Liu, R., Su, J.: Towards formal analysis of artifact-centric business process models. In: BPM 2007, LNCS 4714, pp. 288–304. Springer (2007)
13. Bravetti, M., Zavattaro, G.: Contract based multi-party service composition. In: FSEN 2007, LNCS 4767, pp. 207–222. Springer (2007)
14. Calvanese, D., Giacomo, G.D., Hull, R., Su, J.: Artifact-centric workflow dominance. In: ICSOC/ServiceWave 2009, LNCS 5900, pp. 130–143. Springer (2009)
15. Carmona, J., Cortadella, J., Kishinevsky, M.: Genet: A tool for the synthesis and mining of petri nets. In: ACSD 2009, pp. 181–185. IEEE Computer Societey (2009)
16. Clarke, E.M., Grumberg, O., Peled, D.A.: Model Checking. MIT Press, Cambridge (1999)
17. Cortadella, J., Kishinevsky, M., Kondratyev, A., Lavagno, L., Yakovlev, A.: Petrify: A tool for manipulating concurrent specifications and synthesis of asynchronous controllers. Trans. Inf. and Syst. **E80-D**(3), 315–325 (1997)
18. Damaggio, E., Hull, R., Vaculín, R.: On the equivalence of incremental and fixpoint semantics for business artifacts with guard-stage-milestone lifecycles. In: BPM 2011, LNCS 6896, pp. 396–412. Springer (2011)
19. Dwyer, M.B., Avrunin, G.S., Corbett, J.C.: Patterns in property specifications for finite-state verification. In: ICSE 1999, pp. 411–420. IEEE (1999)
20. Emerson, E.A., Kahlon, V.: Reducing model checking of the many to the few. In: CADE 2000, LNCS 1831, pp. 236–254. Springer (2000)
21. Fahland, D., de Leoni, M., van Dongen, B.F., van der Aalst, W.M.P.: Behavioral conformance of artifact-centric process models. In: BIS 2011, LNBIP 87, pp. 37–49. Springer (2011)
22. Fritz, C., Hull, R., Su, J.: Automatic construction of simple artifact-based business processes. In: ICDT 2009, ACM International Conference Proceeding Series, vol. 361, pp. 225–238. ACM (2009)
23. Gerede, C.E., Su, J.: Specification and verfication of artifact behaviors in business process models. In: ICSOC 2007, LNCS 4749, pp. 181–192. Springer (2007)
24. Goedertier, S., Vanthienen, J.: Designing compliant business processes with obligations and permissions. In: BPM Workshops 2006, LNCS 4103, pp. 5–14. Springer (2006)
25. Hariri, B.B., Calvanese, D., Giacomo, G.D., Masellis, R.D., Felli, P.: Foundations of relational artifacts verification. In: BPM 2011, LNCS 6896, pp. 379–395. Springer (2011)
26. Havelund, K., Roşu, G.: Testing linear temporal logic formulae on finite execution traces. Technical Report 01.08, RIACS (2001)
27. Hohpe, G., Woolf, B.: Enterprise Integration Patterns: Designing, Building, and Deploying Messaging Solutions. Addison-Wesley, New York (2003)
28. Hull, R., Damaggio, E., Fournier, F., Gupta, M., Heath, F.T., Hobson, S., Linehan, M.H., Maradugu, S., Nigam, A., Sukaviriya, P., Vaculín, R.: Introducing the guard-stage-milestone approach for specifying business entity lifecycles. In: WS-FM 2010, LNCS 6551, pp. 1–24. Springer (2011)
29. Hull, R., Damaggio, E., Masellis, R.D., Fournier, F., Gupta, M., Heath, F.T., Hobson, S., Linehan, M.H., Maradugu, S., Nigam, A., Sukaviriya, P.N., Vaculín, R.: Business artifacts with guard-stage-milestone lifecycles: managing artifact interactions with conditions and events. In: DEBS 2011, pp. 51–62 (2011)

30. Hull, R., Narendra, N.C., Nigam, A.: Facilitating workflow interoperation using artifact-centric hubs. In: ICSOC/ServiceWave 2009, pp. 1–18 (2009)
31. Knuplesch, D., Ly, L.T., Rinderle-Ma, S., Pfeifer, H., Dadam, P.: On enabling data-aware compliance checking of business process models. In: ER 2010, LNCS 6412, pp. 332–346. Springer (2010)
32. König, D., Lohmann, N., Moser, S., Stahl, C., Wolf, K.: Extending the compatibility notion for abstract WS-BPEL processes. In: WWW 2008, pp. 785–794. ACM (2008)
33. Küster, J.M., Ryndina, K., Gall, H.: Generation of business process models for object life cycle compliance. In: BPM 2007, LNCS 4714, pp. 165–181. Springer (2007)
34. Li, D., Wu, Q.: Translating artifact-based business process model to BPEL. In: CSEE (2), Communications in Computer and Information Science, vol. 215, pp. 482–489. Springer (2011)
35. Liu, G., Liu, X., Qin, H., Su, J., Yan, Z., Zhang, L.: Automated realization of business workflow specification. In: ICSOC/ServiceWave Workshops, LNCS 6275, pp. 96–108. Springer (2009)
36. Lohmann, N.: Why does my service have no partners? In: WS-FM 2008, LNCS 5387, pp. 191–206. Springer (2009)
37. Lohmann, N.: Compliance by design for artifact-centric business processes. In: BPM 2011, LNCS 6896, pp. 99–115. Springer (2011)
38. Lohmann, N.: Compliance by design for artifact-centric business processes. Inf. Syst. **38**, 606–618 (2012) (Accepted for publication in March 2012)
39. Lohmann, N., Kleine, J.: Fully-automatic translation of open workflow net models into simple abstract BPEL processes. In: Modellierung 2008, Lecture Notes in Informatics (LNI), vol. P-127, pp. 57–72. GI (2008)
40. Lohmann, N., Massuthe, P., Wolf, K.: Behavioral constraints for services. In: BPM 2007, LNCS 4714, pp. 271–287. Springer (2007)
41. Lohmann, N., Nyolt, M.: Artifact-centric modeling using BPMN. In: ICSOC 2011 Workshops, LNCS, vol. 7221, pp. 54–65. Springer (2012)
42. Lohmann, N., Weinberg, D.: Wendy: a tool to synthesize partners for services. In: PETRI NETS 2010, LNCS 6128, pp. 297–307. Springer (2010). http://service-technology.org/wendy
43. Lohmann, N., Wolf, K.: Artifact-centric choreographies. In: ICSOC 2010, LNCS 6470, pp. 32–46. Springer (2010)
44. Lohmann, N., Wolf, K.: Realizability is controllability. In: WS-FM 2009, LNCS 6194, pp. 110–127. Springer (2010)
45. Lohmann, N., Wolf, K.: Decidability results for choreography realization. In: ICSOC 2011, LNCS 7084, pp. 92–107. Springer (2011)
46. Lu, R., Sadiq, S.W., Governatori, G.: Compliance aware business process design. In: BPM 2007 Workshops, LNCS 4928, pp. 120–131. Springer (2007)
47. Massuthe, P., Serebrenik, A., Sidorova, N., Wolf, K.: Can I find a partner? Undecidablity of partner existence for open nets. Inf. Process. Lett. **108**(6), 374–378 (2008)
48. Ngamakeur, K., Yongchareon, S., Liu, C.: A framework for realizing artifact-centric business processes in service-oriented architecture. In: DASFAA 2012, LNCS 7238, pp. 63–78. Springer (2012)
49. OMG: Business Process Model and Notation (BPMN). Version 2.0, Object Management Group (2011). http://www.omg.org/spec/BPMN/2.0
50. Pnueli, A.: The temporal logic of programs. In: FOCS 1977, pp. 46–57. IEEE (1977)
51. Pnueli, A.: In transition from global to modular temporal reasoning about programs. In: Logics and models of concurrent systems, volume F-13 of NATO Advanced Summer Institutes, pp. 123–144. Springer (1985)
52. Ryndina, K., Küster, J.M., Gall, H.: Consistency of business process models and object life cycles. In: MoDELS Workshops, LNCS 4364, pp. 80–90. Springer (2006)
53. Sackmann, S., Kähmer, M., Gilliot, M., Lowis, L.: A classification model for automating compliance. In: CEC/EEE 2008, pp. 79–86. IEEE (2008)
54. Sadiq, S.W., Governatori, G., Namiri, K.: Modeling control objectives for business process compliance. In: BPM 2007, LNCS 4714, pp. 149–164. Springer (2007)

55. Stahl, C.: Service substitution—a behavioral approach based on Petri nets. Ph.D. thesis, Humboldt-Universität zu Berlin, Mathematisch-Naturwissenschaftliche Fakultät II; Eindhoven University of Technology (2009)
56. Stahl, C., Massuthe, P., Bretschneider, J.: Deciding substitutability of services with operating guidelines. LNCS T. Petri Nets and Other Models of Concurrency 2(5460), 172–191 (2009)
57. Wolf, K.: LNCS Trans. Petri Nets Other Models Concurr. Does my service have partners? 5460(2), 152–171 (2009)
58. Yongchareon, S., Liu, C., Zhao, X.: An artifact-centric view-based approach to modeling inter-organizational business processes. In: WISE 2011, LNCS 6997, pp. 273–281. Springer (2011)

Chapter 6
On the Composability of Semantic Web Services

Brahim Medjahed, Zaki Malik and Salima Benbernou

Abstract In this chapter, we propose a multilevel composability model for automatically checking the composability of semantic Web services. The model is defined by a set of rules called composability rules. Each rule specifies the constraints and requirements for checking horizontal and vertical composability. The model provides support for partial and total composability via the notions of composability degree and τ-composability. Then, we describe rules dealing with static semantic, dynamic semantic, and business process composability. Finally, we discuss future research directions in the area of service composition.

6.1 Introduction

Service computing is slated to shape modern societies in vital areas such as health, government, science, and business [1]. It utilizes services as the building blocks for developing and integrating applications distributed within and across organizations. The most common realization of service-based systems relies on Web services. Web services may wrap a wide range of resources such as programs, sensors, databases, storage devices, and visualization facilities. A key plank of the service computing agenda is service composition. *Web service composition* refers to the process of

B. Medjahed (✉)
Department of Computer and Information Science, University of Michigan–Dearborn,
Dearborn, USA
e-mail: brahim@umich.edu

Z. Malik
Department of Computer Science, Wayne State University, Detroit, USA
e-mail: zaki@cs.wayne.edu

S. Benbernou
LIPADE, Université Paris Descartes, Paris, France
e-mail: salima.benbernou@parisdescartes.fr

A. Bouguettaya et al. (eds.), *Web Services Foundations*,
DOI: 10.1007/978-1-4614-7518-7_6,
© Springer Science+Business Media New York 2014

combining several Web services to provide a value-added service. It is emerging as the technology of choice for building cross-organizational applications on the Web [26].

Service composition has recently taken a central stage as an emerging research area (e.g., [4, 8, 19]). However, existing service composition techniques and standards provide little or no support for the semantics of participant services, their messages, and interactions. Additionally, they require dealing with low level programming details which may lead to unexpected failures at run-time. A promising approach uses *ontology* to automate the tedious composition process [25]. An *ontology* is a *formal* and *explicit* specification of a *shared conceptualization* [5, 12]. Ontologies are expected to play a central role to empower Web services with semantics. The combination of these powerful concepts (i.e., Web services and ontologies) has resulted in the emergence of a new generation of Web services called *Semantic Web services* [25].

To illustrate the complexity of the composition process, let us consider the example of users willing to translate a word from Chinese to Urdu. Assume that no Chinese-Urdu translation service is available. One solution would be to combine two simple services WS_1 = Chinese-English and WS_2 = English-Urdu. The tasks performed by users to compose WS_1 and WS_2 include the following. They first have to determines which services are relevant to their requests (i.e., WS_1 and WS_2). For that purpose, they need to delve into a large space of heterogeneous services. Those services are related to different domains of interest such as insurance, translation, and stock market. Users then should understand the exact format, content, and semantics of messages exchanged between WS_2 and WS_2. They must also "manually" specify the way WS_1's and WS_2's messages are mapped to each other. Finally, they should find out how WS_2 and WS_2 can together define an overall business process (e.g., define the order of messages). As shown in this example, service composition involves going through several complex stages. One important, yet tedious, stage is the *composability* of interacting services [30]. *Composability* refers to the process checking whether participant services can actually work together, hence avoiding unexpected failure at run time. The "manual" checking of service composability would clearly be unrealistic. What is needed is a framework where composability would be checked *automatically* and transparently.

We identify three avenues in the area of service composition that could benefit from checking composability: composition analysis, automatic composition, and operation outsourcing. In the first case, composability is checked *a posteriori*. Composers first specify their composite service (e.g., using BPEL4WS). The composition engine then checks the "correctness" of the composite service using composability rules. In the second case, the composition engine uses the composability rules to generate composite service descriptions from high-level specifications of composition requests. The engine needs to determine the set of participants relevant to the composition request while making sure that they are composable. In the third case, composability rules are used to "replace" an operation by a "compatible" one. This could be useful to enable the subcontracting of operations or substitutability of a participant by another.

Several techniques have been proposed to deal with service composability. *LARKS* defines five techniques for service matchmaking: context matching, profile comparison, similarity matching, signature matching, and constraint matching [40]. These techniques mostly compare text descriptions, signatures (inputs and outputs), and logical constraints about inputs and outputs. The *ATLAS* matchmaker defines two methods to compare service capabilities described in DAML-S [31]. The first method compares functional attributes to check whether advertisements support the required type of service or deliver sufficient quality of service. The second compares the functional capabilities of Web services in terms of inputs and outputs. No evaluation study is presented to determine the effectiveness and speed of *ATLAS* matchmaker. In this chapter, we propose a multilevel *composability model* for semantic Web service composition. We introduce the concepts of *composability degree* and *τ-composability* to cater for *partial* and *total* composability. Finally, we discuss directions for future research in Web service composition.

The remainder of this chapter is organized as follows. Section 6.2 overviews current research in Web service composition. Section 6.3 presents our approach for the semantic description of Web services. Section 6.4 describes the proposed composability model. Sections 6.5 and 6.6 give details about static semantic and dynamic semantic composability, respectively. Section 6.7 is devoted to business process composability. Section 6.8 summarized future research directions in service composition. Section 6.9 provides concluding remarks.

6.2 Web Service Composition: Background

Web service composition is a process that combines outsourced Web services to offer *value-added* services [38]. The benefits offered by service composition lie in four major aspects. First, it enables organizations to outsource existing Web services, which avoids developing new applications from scratch and ensures a rapid time-to-market. Second, it reduces the complexity, because complicated services can be incrementally constructed out of relatively simple ones. Third, application development based on Web services reduces business risks since reusing existing services avoids the introduction of new errors. Finally, the possibility of outsourcing the "best-in-their-class" services allows companies to increase their revenue.

Service composition can be conducted in three different fashions: process/programming, interaction, and planning. In the rest of this section, we overview these three different approaches.

6.2.1 Process-Based Composition

Most existing Web service composition techniques require programming to some extent for constructing the orchestration model [1, 26, 27]. Composers first need to study the component services that are described using WSDL or some ontology languages and understand the functionalities of the services and the supported operations. A further step analysis requires to identify the way operations are interconnected, services are invoked, and messages are mapped to one another. The process-based composition scheme makes the process of composing service demanding for composers. Composers need to be domain experts who are familiar with the service description language, the service orchestration algebra, and the corresponding programming skills. Since common users cannot act as a service composer, the programming-based scheme hinders common users from composing Web services at large.

BPEL4WS models the behavior of a business process based on the interactions with the involved business partners [3]. It uses WSDL to model the services in the process flow and describe the external services that are needed by the process. A major design goal of BPEL4WS is to separate the public aspects of business process behavior from the internal ones. The separation helps businesses conceal their internal decisions from their business partners. Moreover, internal changes of the process implementation no longer affects the public business protocol. ebXML provides a set of common business process specifications that are shared by multiple industries [10]. These specifications, stored in the business library, can be used by companies to build customized business processes. Interactions between business processes are represented through choreographies. To model collaboration in which companies can engage, ebXML defines Collaboration Protocol Agreements.

CMI's *coordination model* extends the traditional workflow coordination primitives with advanced primitives such as *placeholder* [13, 36]. The concept of placeholder enables the dynamic establishment of trading relationships. A placeholder activity is replaced at runtime with a concrete activity having the same input and output as those defined as part of the placeholder. *eFlow* models a composite service a graph that defines the order of execution among the nodes in the process [8]. Service nodes represent the invocation of a basic or composite service. The definition of a service node contains a *search recipe* represented in a query language. When a service node is invoked, a search recipe is executed to select a reference to a specific service. *SELF-SERV* [4] adopts *state charts* for composite service specification. It also defines a *peer-to-peer* Web service execution model in which the responsibility of coordinating the execution of a composite service is distributed across several peer components called *coordinators*. The coordinator is a lightweight scheduler which determines when a state within a state chart should be entered and what should be done when the state is entered. It also determines when should a state be exited and what should be done after the state is exited.

6.2.2 Interactive Composition

The interactive composition scheme blurs the distinction between composers and common users. Composers are required to have a clear goal and know the tasks that need to be performed to accomplish the composition. Common users can be guided through a set of steps to finish a composer's task. The composition scheme will work interactively with the common users to help them achieve the orchestration model. The orchestration process can start from users' goals and work backward by chaining all related services. It can also start from some initial states and achieve the users' goals by adding services in the forward direction. At each step, the scheme will choose a new service based on the task specified by the users. The interactive scheme can also capture the constraints and preferences during the interaction process. The constraints and preferences can serve as additional criteria to select services for the composition.

An interactive composition approach is proposed in [39]. It adopts the OWL ontologies to model the component services. The service model specifies the input, output, precondition, and effects (IOPE) of services. The proposed approach also implements a tool for automatic translation from WSDL to OWL-S, which enables the support of WSDL-based component services. The data types are defined by XML-schema and message exchange between component services relies on the data flow approach. The composed service are specified using OWL-S. The interactive composition can be performed by chaining component services in either the forward or the backward directions. At each step, the composition scheme adds a new service based on the users' selection. Existing component service in the orchestration model can serve as a criterion to filter candidate services. Only the services that match the IOPE properties of existing services can be selected by the system and presented to the users. *Ninja* [15] introduces a technique called Automatic Path creation (APC) to cater for interactive service composition. When an APC receives requests for composite service execution, the APC creates a path that includes a sequence of operators that perform computation on data and connectors that provide data transport between operators. *Ninja* mostly focuses on fault tolerance by replicating services on multiple workstations. It uses a limited operator functional classification to automate the selection of operators. It is also mainly based on input-output matching of services.

6.2.3 Planning-Based Composition

The planning-based composition scheme aims to relieve users from the composition processes as much as possible. It relies on AI planning techniques for automatic service composition. In this context, users are allowed to submit a declarative query specifying the goal he/she wants the composite service to achieve together with some the constraints and preferences that need to be satisfied. Based on the user's query, the composition scheme can derive a corresponding orchestration model with all constraints and preferences satisfied. The planning scheme regards services as actions that are applicable in states. State transitions are specified using the preconditions of some actions. A transition will lead to some new states, in which the effects of some actions are valid. Based on this, the composition scheme recursively adds new services until users' goals have been achieved. The states of existing service in the orchestration will determine the selection of the new services. For example, the preconditions of the new services should be satisfied via the effect of some existing services.

A representative planning-based composition approached is presented in [24]. It is based on situation calculus to compose Web services. More specifically, it adopts Golog, which is a logic programming language, and makes some extensions to adapt it to Web services. The situation calculus enables software agents to reason about Web services. Web services are modeled as actions, which is similar to the classical AI planning problem. Web services are associated with some preconditions and generate some effect under these preconditions. Simple Web services are categorized into two groups. Web services in the first group perform information collection actions. Web services in the second group perform world-altering actions. Composite Web services perform complex actions by composing simple Web services from both groups. Users can specify their requests and constraints, which can be transformed using situation calculus. Users' constraints can be used to customize the predefined generic composition templates. This helps generate the specific composition plans that fulfill users' requirements. *SWORD* [32] uses a rule-base expert system to automatically determine whether a desired composite service can be achieved using existing services. SWORD does not seem to focus on service composability and semantic description of Web services. *SHOP2* adopts the concept of HTN (Hierarchical Task Network) as a planning methodology [42]. It decomposes tasks into smaller and smaller subtasks, until primitive tasks are found that can be performed directly. *Estimated-regression* is another planning technique for service composition [23]. The situation-space search is guided by a heuristic estimator obtained by backward chaining in a relaxed problem space. The resulting space is so much smaller than situation space that a planner can build complete representation of it, called a regression graph. The regression graph reveals, for each conjunct of a goal, the minimal sequence of actions that could achieve it.

6.3 Semantic Description of Web Services

The semantic description of Web services is an important requirement for checking their composability. The large scale and heterogeneity of Web services may hinder any attempt for "understanding" their semantics and hence composing them. We define a *metadata ontology*, called *operation ontology*, used as a template to define Web service operations. A *metadata ontology* provides concepts that allow the description of other concepts (operations in our case) [12].

Each operation is an instance of the operation ontology. It is defined by a set of *non-functional* and *functional* attributes. *Non-functional* (or *qualitative*) attributes include a set of metrics that measure the quality of the operation. *Functional* attributes describe syntactic and semantic features of an operation. We identify three groups of functional attributes: *syntactic*, *static semantic*, and *dynamic semantic*. *Syntactic* attributes represent the structure of a service operation. The *static semantics* of an operation models "non-computational" properties of an operation, that is properties that are independent of the execution of the operation. Static semantics is described at two "granularities": operation and messages. *Dynamic semantics* refers to the way and constraints under which an operation is executed.

The concept of *vertical ontology* is key for defining the content of static semantic attributes. It captures the knowledge valid for a particular domain (e.g., government, medical) [12]. Service providers may adopt different vertical ontologies to specify the content of a given parameter. The use of different ontologies requires dealing with the issue of ontology mapping [9] which is out of the scope of this chapter.

6.3.1 Static Semantics of Operations

The static semantics at the operation granularity is defined by the following attributes: *provider and consumer types*, *category*, and *purpose*.

The provider of an operation may be governmental ("federal", "state", "local", etc.) or non-governmental ("non-profit" and "business") agencies. The *consumer type* specifies the group of consumers (users or other Web services) that are eligible to invoke the operation. For instance, certain government welfare services may be eligible to certain citizens. In the United States, WIC (Women, Infant, and Children) is a program for pregnant women, lactating mothers, and children.

The *category* C_{ik} of an operation op_{ik} describes the area of interest of op_{ik}. It is defined by a tuple $(Dom_{ik}, Syn_{ik}, Spec_{ik}, Overlap_{ik})$. Dom_{ik} gives the area of interest of the community (e.g., "healthcare"). It takes its value from a vertical ontology for domain names. Syn_{ik} contains a set of alternative domain names for C_{ik}. For example "medical" is a synonym of "healthcare". $Spec_{ik}$ is a set of specializations of C_{ik}'s domain. For example, "insurance" and "children" are specializations of "healthcare". This means that C_{ik} provides health insurance services for children. $Overlap_{ik}$ contains the list of categories that *overlap* with C_{ik}'s category. It is used to provide a peer-to-peer topology for connecting operations with "related" categories. We say that $category_{ik}$ overlaps with $category_{jl}$ if composing op_{ik} with op_j's is "meaningful". By meaningful, we mean that the composition provides a *value-added* service (in terms of categories). For example, an operation that has *healthcare* as a domain may be composed with another operation whose domain is *insurance*. This would enable providing health insurance for needy families.

The *purpose* describes the goal of the operation. It is defined by four attributes: *Func, Syn, Spec,* and *Overlap*. The *Func* describes the business functionality offered by the operation. Examples of functions are "eligibility", "registration", and "mentoring". The *Syn, Spec,* and *Overlap* attributes work as they do for categories. The *Overlap* contains the list of purposes that are related to the purpose of the current operation.

6.3.2 Static Semantics of Messages

Each message within an operation is semantically described via a *message type* $\mathcal{MT}$. The message type gives the general semantics of the message. For example, a message may represent a "purchase order" or an "invoice". However, message types do not capture the semantics of parameters within a message. We define below a set of attributes to model the semantics of message parameters: *data type*, *business role*, *unit*, and *language*.

The *data type* gives the range of values that may be assigned to the parameter. We use XML Schema's *built-in* data types as the typing system. *Built-in* (or simple) types are pre-defined in the XML Schema specification. They can be either *primitive* or *derived*. Unlike *primitive* types, *derived* types are defined in terms of other types. For example, *integer* is derived from the *decimal* primitive type. Complex data types can also be adopted in our model but are out of the scope of this chapter [18]. The *business role* gives the type of information conveyed by the message parameter. For example, an `address` parameter may refer to the first (street address and unit number) or second (city and zip code) line of an address. Business roles take their values from a pre-defined taxonomy. Every parameter would have a well-defined meaning according to that taxonomy. An example of such taxonomy is *RosettaNet*'s business dictionary [26]. It contains a common vocabulary that can be used to describe business properties. The *unit* refers to the measurement unit in which the parameter's content is provided. For example, a *weight* parameter may be expressed in "Kilograms" or "Pounds". An *eligibility period* parameter may be specified in days, weeks, or months. We use standard measurement units (length, area, weight, money code, etc.) to assign values to parameters' units. If a parameter does not have a unit (e.g., *address*), its unit is equal to "none". The content of a message parameter may be specified in different languages. For example, an `English-Urdu-translation` operation takes as input an English word, and returns as output its translation in Urdu. We adopt the standard taxonomy for languages to specify the value of the *language* attribute.

6.3.3 Dynamic Semantics

The *dynamic semantics* or *business logic* of an operation op_{ik} refers to the outcome expected after executing op_{ik} given a specific condition. It is defined by a set of *rules* where each rule R_{ik}^m has the following format:

$$R_{ik}^m = \frac{(PreParameters_{ik}^m, PreCondition_{ik}^m)}{(PostParameters_{ik}^m, PostCondition_{ik}^m)}$$

$PreParameters_{ik}^m$ and $PostParameters_{ik}^m$ are sets of parameters. Each parameter is defined by name, data type, business role, unit, and language as stated in Sect. 6.3.2. The elements of $PreParameters_{ik}^m$ and $PostParameters_{ik}^m$ generally refer to op_{ik}'s input and output parameters. However, they may in some cases refer to parameters that are neither input nor output of op_{ik}. For example, assume that the *address* of every citizen registered with the Department on the Aging is stored in the department's database. In this case, this parameter should not be required as input for the `orderMeal` operation since its value could be retrieved from the database.

PreCondition$_{ik}^m$ and PostCondition$_{ik}^m$ are conditions over the parameters in PrePara meters$_{ik}^m$ and PostParameters$_{ik}^m$ respectively. They are specified as predicates in first-order logic. The rule R_{ik}^m specifies that if PreCondition$_{ik}^m$ holds when the operation op_{ik} starts, then PostCondition$_{ik}^m$ holds after op_{ik} reaches its End state. If PreCondition$_{ik}^m$ does not hold, there are no guarantees about the outcome of the operation. The following is an example of the pre and post condition of a rule associated with the operation `registerFoodCheck` (to receive food assistance from a government welfare program):

$$\frac{income < 22{,}090 \wedge size \geq 2 \wedge zip = 22044}{approved = true \wedge duration = 6}$$

The rule uses *income* (unit = {year, US dollar}), *familySize*, *zip*, *approved* and *duration* (unit = {month}) as parameters. It states that citizens with a yearly income less than 22,090 US dollars, a minimum household size 2, and living in area code 22044 are eligible for food checks for a 6-month period.

6.4 The Composability Model

In this section, we describe our composability model for semantic Web services. The model is based on the semantic description of Web services presented in Sect. 6.3.

6.4.1 Composability Stack

The proposed model for composability contains rules organized into five levels (Fig. 6.1). Each rule CR_{pq} at a level CL_p ($p = 0, 4$) compares a specific feature of services within CL_p.

The first level CL_0 compares syntactic attributes such as the number of message parameters (CR_{00}). The second level CL_1 compares static semantic attributes. We define two groups of rules at this level. The first group compares the static semantics of messages. The second group compares the static semantics of operations. The third level CL_2 compares dynamic semantic attributes. The fourth composability level CL_3 focuses on quality of operation attributes. It contains three groups of rules. The first group compares security attributes. The second group checks business attributes. The third group deals with runtime attributes. The fifth composability level CL_4 It contains rules that check the soundness of a composite service, that is, whether

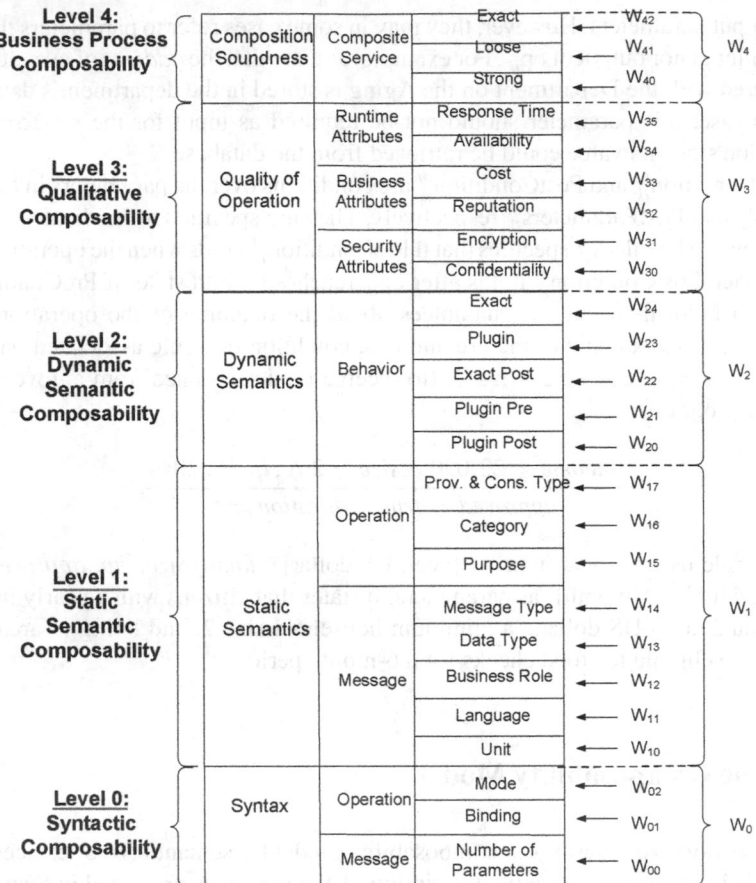

Fig. 6.1 Web service composability stack

that service provides a value-added. Our focus in this chapter is on *static semantic*, *dynamic semantic*, and *business process* composability. Details about syntactic and qualitative rules can be found in [28].

6.4.2 Operation Mode and States

Service composition involves the combination of several operations that belong to the same or different Web services. Each operation op_{ik} has an input and output message. Input and output messages contain parameters. The order according to which op_{ik}'s input and output messages are sent and received defines the operation *mode*. The mode indicates whether the operation initiates interactions or simply replies to invocations from other services. We define two modes: *In/Out* or *Out/In*.

In/Out operation first receives an input message by a client, processes it, and then returns an output message to the client. *Out/In* first sends an output message to a server and receives an input message as a result. As specified in WSDL standard, some operations may be limited to an input or output message (e.g., notification operation) [1, 28]. Such operations may be considered as *In/Out* or *Out/In* operations where the input or output message is empty.

The execution of an operation op_{ik} generally goes through four major observable states: *Ready*, *Start*, *Active*, and *end*. We define a precedence relationship between states, noted $\longrightarrow_t$, as follows: $S_1 \longrightarrow_t S_2$ if S_1 occurs before S_2. The execution states are totally ordered according to $\longrightarrow_t$ as follows: *Ready* $\longrightarrow_t$ *Start* $\longrightarrow_t$ *Active* $\longrightarrow_t$ *End*. The execution of op_{ik} is in the *Ready* state if the request for executing op_{ik} has not been made yet. The *Start* state means that op_{ik} execution has been initiated. op_{ik} is in the *Active* state if op_{ik} has already been initiated and the corresponding request is being processed. After processing the request, the operation reaches the *End* state during which results are returned.

6.4.3 Horizontal and Vertical Composition

We define two ways of combining operations: *horizontal* and *vertical*. Each composability rule may be applicable to horizontal composition, vertical composition, or both.

Horizontal composition models a "supply chain"-like combination of operations (Fig. 6.2). Let op_{ik} and op_{jl} be two operations that are horizontally composed. We call op_{ik} and op_{jl} *source* and *target* operations respectively. op_{ik} is first executed, followed by op_{jl}'s execution. op_{ik}'s messages are used to *feed* op_{jl}'s input message.

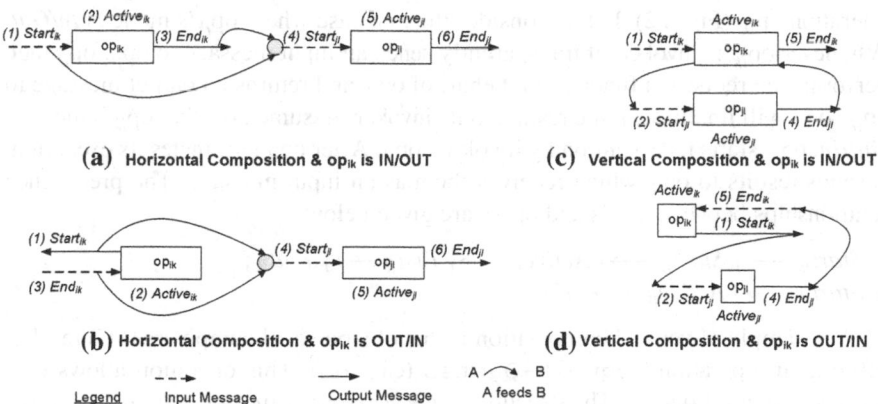

Fig. 6.2 Horizontal and vertical composition: **a** horizontal composition and op_{ik} is IN/OUT; **b** horizontal composition and op_{ik} is OUT/IN; **c** vertical composition and op_{ik} is IN/OUT; **d** vertical composition and op_{ik} is OUT/IN

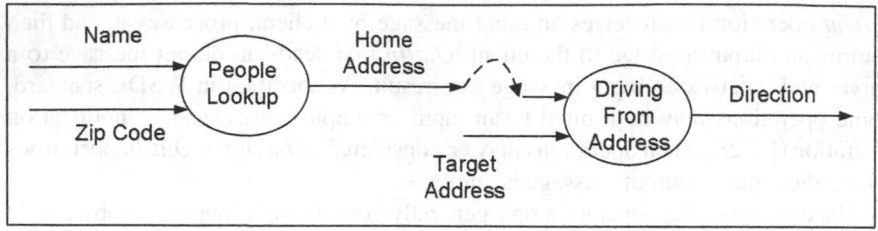

Fig. 6.3 Example of horizontal and vertical composition

Let $\mathcal{M}$ be a set of messages and $Input_{jl}$ the input message of op_{jl}. We say that $\mathcal{M}$ *feeds* $Input_{jl}$ if parameters in $\mathcal{M}$'s messages are used as $Input_{jl}$'s parameters. As depicted in Fig. 6.2, In_{ik} and Out_{ik} messages feed In_{jl}. The precedence relationships between op_{ik}'s and op_{jl}'s states are given below:

- $Start_{ik} \longrightarrow_t Active_{ik} \longrightarrow_t End_{ik}$;
- $End_{ik} \longrightarrow_t Start_{jl} \longrightarrow_t Active_{jl} \longrightarrow_t End_{jl}$.

As example of the horizontal composition (case (a)), assume that op_{ik} provides translation from Chinese to English and op_{jl} provides translation from English to Urdu. The operations op_{ik} and op_{jl} may be horizontally composed to provide translation from Chinese to Urdu. In this case, the output of op_{ik} (English translation) is used as input by op_{jl}. The second case of horizontal composition (case (b)) refers to the situation where op_{ik} outsources from another operation (i.e., op_{ik} is vertically composed with a third operation). op_{ik} is then horizontally composed with op_{jl}. For example, a `get_directions` (Out/In) operation may be executed by outsourcing from other operations `People_Lookup` and `Direction-From-Address` (Fig. 6.3). The `get_directions` operation is then horizontally composed with `Notify-Citizens` (In/Out operation).

Vertical Composition models the "subcontracting" of an operation op_{jl} by another operation op_{ik} (Fig. 6.2). Let us consider the first case where op_{ik}'s mode is *In/Out*. Whenever op_{ik} is invoked, it transparently sends an input message to op_{jl}. op_{jl} then performs the requested function on behalf of op_{ik} and returns an output message to op_{ik}. op_{ik} will finally send the results to its invoker. Assume now that op_{ik}'s mode is *Out/In*. op_{ik} starts its execution by invoking op_{jl}. After op_{jl} terminates its execution, it sends results to op_{ik} which receives them as an input message. The precedence relationships between op_{ik}'s and op_{jl}'s are given below:

- $Start_{ik} \longrightarrow_t Start_{jl} \longrightarrow_t Active_{jl} \longrightarrow_t End_{jl} \longrightarrow_t End_{ik}$;
- $Start_{ik} \longrightarrow_t Active_{ik} \longrightarrow_t End_{ik}$.

An example of vertical composition is that of a personal computers (PC) reseller offering an operation `Request-Quotes` (case (c)). This operation allows customers to request quotes. The execution of `Request-Quotes` requires the invocation of another operation provided by a PC manufacturer to get the latest prices. The second case of vertical composition (case (d)) models "request-response" interactions.

6.4.4 Composability Rules Classification

Composability rules check whether two operations op_{ik} and op_{jl} are composable from different perspectives. We characterize composability rules by their *level*, *granularity*, *attribute*, *symmetry*, and *composition type*. Table 6.1 summarizes the different composability rules. We organize these rules into five levels: *syntactic*, *static semantic*, *dynamic semantic*, *qualitative*, and *business process*. These levels check composability at the message and operation *granularity*. Each rule in a given level compares a specific pair of *attributes* of op_{ik} and op_{jl} (e.g., mode, binding, purpose, and cost). A rule is either *symmetric* or *asymmetric*. It is *symmetric* if the order in which it is checked (from op_{ik} to op_{jl} or op_{jl} to op_{ik}) is not important. This is in contrast with *asymmetric* rules; if an asymmetric rule is satisfied from op_{ik} to op_{jl} then it is not necessarily satisfied from op_{jl} to op_{ik}. Finally, a rule may be applicable for horizontal composition (e.g., *Plugin Prematch*), vertical composition (e.g., *Exact Postmach*), both (e.g., *purpose* and *category*), or hybrid (e.g., composition soundness).

Table 6.1 Composability rules classification

Level	Granularity	Attribute	Symmetry	Horizontal	Vertical	Hybrid
Syntactic	Message	Number of parameters	✓	✓	✓	
	Operation	Binding	✓	✓	✓	
		Mode		✓	✓	
Static semantics	Message	Data type	✓	✓	✓	
		Unit	✓	✓	✓	
		Language	✓	✓	✓	
		Business role	✓	✓	✓	
		Message type	✓		✓	
	Operation	Purpose		✓	✓	
		Category		✓	✓	
		Prov. & cons. type		✓	✓	
Dynamic semantics	Operation	Plugin Postmatch			✓	
		Plugin Prematch		✓		
		Exact Postmatch	✓		✓	
		Plugin			✓	
		Exact	✓		✓	
Qualitative	Operation	Confidentiality			✓	
		Encryption	✓		✓	
		Reputation			✓	
		Cost			✓	
		Availability			✓	
		Response time			✓	
Business process	Composite	Exact				✓
		Loose				✓
		Strong				✓

6.4.5 Composability Degree

Composers may have different views on composability rules. One may, for example, give higher importance to syntactic composability while another may focus on semantic rules. To capture this aspect, we associate a *weight* W_p to each level CL_p. We also define a *weight* W_{pq} for each rule CR_{pq} in that level. A weight is an estimate of the significance of the corresponding level or rule from the composer's point of view. Composers assign a weight to each level and rule. The higher is a weight, the more important is the corresponding level or rule. W_p (≥ 0 and ≤ 1) compares CL_p to the other levels in terms of their importance. The total of weights assigned to the different levels equals 1. Similarly, W_{pq} (≥ 0 and ≤ 1) compares CR_{pq} to the other rules at level CL_p. The total of weights assigned to rules within a level equals 1. Formally, the different weights must respect the following constraints, where $|CL_p|$ is the number of rules at level p:

1. $\forall p, q \,|\, 0 \leq p \leq 4$ and $0 \leq q \leq |CL_p| - 1$: $(0 \leq W_p \leq 1) \wedge (0 \leq W_{pq} \leq 1)$; and

2. $\left(\sum_{p=0}^{4} W_p = 1 \right) \wedge \left(\forall p: \sum_{q=0}^{|CL_p|-1} W_{pq} = 1 \right)$.

Due to the heterogeneity of Web services, it is not always possible to find operations that are fully composable with source operations. Composers may, in this case, select operations that are partially composable and then, adapt their operations based on the results returned by the composability process. For example, the composer may modify the data type of a parameter if it is not compatible with the data type of the corresponding target's parameter. For that purpose, we introduce the notion of composability *degree*.

The *degree* of op_{ik} and op_{jl} gives the ratio of composability rules that are satisfied between op_{ik} and op_{jl}. It takes its values from 0 to 1 (≥ 0 and ≤ 1). We define a function *satisfied*$_{pq}(op_{ik}, op_{jl})$ that returns 1 if the rule CR_{pq} is satisfied between op_{ik} and op_{jl} and 0 otherwise. To reflect the composer's view on each rule CR_{pq}, we adjust the value returned by the function *satisfied*$_{pq}(op_{ik}, op_{jl})$ with the weight W_{pq}. The degree at a given level CL_p is obtained by adding the adjusted values returned by the function *satisfied* applied on each CL_p's rule. Once the degree at CL_p is computed, we adjust it with the weight W_p assigned to CL_k. We give below the definition of degree(op_{ik}, op_{jl}).

Definition 6.1. Let op_{ik} and op_{jl} be two operations. The *degree* of op_{ik} and op_{jl} is obtained by summing composability degrees at all levels $CL_p (p = 0, 4)$:

$$\text{Degree}(op_{ik}, op_{jl}) = \sum_{p=0}^{4} \left(W_p \times \sum_{q=0}^{|CL_p|-1} \left(W_{pq} \times satisfied_{pq}(op_{ik}, op_{jl}) \right) \right)$$

where W_p is the weight of composability level CL_p; W_{pq} is the weight of composability rule CR_{pq}; and *satisfied*$_{pq}(op_{ik}, op_{jl})$ is a boolean function that returns 1 if the rule CR_{pq} is satisfied between op_{ik} and op_{jl} and 0 otherwise.   ◇

During a composition process, the composer assigns weights to each level and rule by providing a vector called *level weight* (LW) and matrix called *rule weight* (RW). The element LW_p ($p = 0, 4$) gives the weight assigned to level CL_p. The element CW_{pq} gives the weight assigned to rule CR_{pq}. If a rule CR_{pq} is undefined, then CW_{pq} is automatically assigned the value 0. Additionally, if the weight of a given level is equal to 0, then the weight of each rule within that level is also equal to 0. As an illustration, let us consider case study 1 (e-government). Let us assume that a user provides the weights given below to his/her source operation op_i:

$$LW = \begin{pmatrix} 0.2 \ 0.3 \ 0.2 \ 0.1 \ 0.2 \end{pmatrix}$$

$$RW = \begin{pmatrix} 0.25 & 0.25 & 0.3 & 0 & 0 & 0 & 0 & 0 \\ 0.1 & 0.1 & 0.1 & 0.1 & 0.1 & 0.1 & 0.2 & 0.2 \\ 0.1 & 0.1 & 0.1 & 0.1 & 0.6 & 0 & 0 & 0 \\ 0.1 & 0.1 & 0.1 & 0.1 & 0.6 & 0 & 0 & 0 \\ 0 & 0.5 & 0.5 & 0 & 0 & 0 & 0 & 0 \end{pmatrix}$$

This example shows that the composer gives more importance to static semantic composability since the corresponding weight is greater than the other levels' weights. Among dynamic semantic properties, the composer gives higher priority to the *exact* behavioral rule. Assume now that op_i is compared to another operation op_j using the composability model and that the composability rules for the following rules are satisfied: CR_{00}, CR_{01}, CR_{02}, CR_{10}, CR_{15}, CR_{16}, CR_{20}, CR_{21}, CR_{22}, CR_{23}, CR_{24}, CR_{33}, CR_{35}, CR_{36}. The composability degree is computed as follows:

$Degree(op_i, op_j)$

$= 0.2 \times (0.25 + 0.25 + 0.3) + 0.3 \times (0.1 + 0.1 + 0.2)$

$+ 0.2 \times (0.1 + 0.1 + 0.1 + 0.1 + 0.6) + 0.1 \times (0.1) = 0.49 = 49\%$.

Based on the degree of op_i and op_j, we can decide about the composability of those operations. If *degree* $= 0$ then no rule is satisfied and the operations are *non composable*. If *degree* $= 1$ then all composability rules (with a positive level and rule weight) are satisfied and the operations are *fully* composable. Otherwise, a subset of rules are satisfied. In this case, op_i and op_j are *partially* composable.

6.4.6 τ-Composability

Composers may have different expectations about the composability degree of their operations. For that purpose, they provide a *composability threshold* τ ($0 < \tau \leq 1$) which gives the minimum value allowed for a composability degree. All operations op_{jl} so that $degree(op_{ik}, op_{jl}) \geq \tau$ are candidates to be composed with op_{ik}. If the threshold is greater than $degree(op_{ik}, op_{jl})$ then op_{ik} is not composable with op_{jl}.

Based on the notions of degree and threshold, we introduce a "relaxed" definition of composability called τ-*composability*. τ-*composability* compares the composability degree and threshold to decide whether an operation is composable with another from composers' perspectives. Below is the definition of τ-composability.

Definition 6.2. Let op_{ik} and op_{jl} be two operations and let τ ($0 < \tau \leq 1$) be the composability threshold. We say that op_{ik} is τ-*composable* with op_{jl} if *degree* $(op_{ik}, op_{jl}) \geq \tau$. $\diamond$

The composability threshold is given by composers as part of their *profile*. Composers personalize the composability checking process via their profile. They assign values to the level weights vector (LW), rule weights matrix (RW), and τ. Other variables such as the maximum number of target operations can also be initialized. The way users create their profile depends on their level of expertise. We identify three types of users: *casual* (i.e., with minimal expertise), *expert* (i.e., with high expertise), and *regular* (i.e., with average expertise). *Casual* users may leave LW and RW unassigned in their profile. The system automatically distributes weights between levels and rules in a uniform way. The composability threshold will also be set to 1. In this case, full composability will be required. *Expert* users are knowledgable about the meaning of all operation and message attributes. They may customize the composability process by assigning the desired values to LW, RW, and τ. If the degree exceeds the threshold but not equals to 1, users change the specification of their operations based on the feedback returned by the system (e.g., which rules are not satisfied) to increase the degree. The third type of users, called *regular* users, includes those that have *some* knowledge about operation and message attributes. They may assign values to parts of LW and RW. In this case, the system automatically distributes weights between unassigned levels and rules. If τ was not assigned by a user, it is automatically set to 1 by the system.

6.5 Static Semantic Composability

For two operations op_{ik} and op_{jl} to be "plugged" together, they must be semantically "compliant". In this section, we present composability rules at the static semantic levels. We define each rule with regard to vertical and horizontal composability. We consider composability at both operation and message granularities.

6.5.1 Operation Granularity

We define three static semantic rules at the operation granularity. The first rule compares op_{ik}'s and op_{jl}'s *provider* and *consumer types*. If the composition is vertical, op_{ik} and op_{jl} must have at least one common provider type and one common consumer type. For example, if op_{ik} expects to outsource from a federal agency's operation then op_{jl}'s agency should include the type "federal". Additionally, if op_{ik} provides benefits for children and pregnant women then op_{jl} should provide benefits for at least those two groups. If op_{ik} is horizontally composed with op_{jl}, then it should be viewed as a consumer of op_{jl}. Hence, op_{jl}'s consumer type should include at least one value from op_{ik}'s provider types.

The third rule compares operations' *categories*. Assume that op_{ik} is vertically composed with op_{jl}. Since op_{ik} is meant to "replace" op_{jl}, the following two conditions should be true: (i) op_{ik}'s and op_{jl}'s domains of interest are similar or synonyms, and (ii) all characteristics (i.e., elements of the "spec" attribute) of op_{ik}'s category are provided by op_{jl}'s. For example, assume that op_{ik}'s category provides health insurance for children (i.e., Dom_{ik}="healthcare" and $Spec_{ik}$={"children", "insurance"}). The operation op_{jl} should not only deal with healthcare but also *at least* provide insurance for children as well. Assume now that op_{ik} is horizontally composed with op_{jl}. Category$_{ik}$ and category$_{jl}$ should be defined so that op_{ik} and op_{jl} "can" be combined. This is captured by the *Overlap* attribute of a category. Hence, category$_{ik}$ is composable with category$_{jl}$ if Overlap$_{ik}$ contains category$_{jl}$.

The last rule compares operations' *purposes*. The *purpose composability* rule is defined in the same way as *category composability* where Dom is replaced by Func.

6.5.2 Message Granularity

We define five static semantic rules at the message granularity. The first rule compares op_{ik}'s and op_{jl}'s message types. This rule is applicable only to vertical composition since horizontal composition does not involve replacing op_{ik}'s messages with op_{jl}'s or vice versa. Assume that op_{ik} is vertically composed with op_{jl}. As depicted in Fig. 6.2, we identify two cases based on the mode of op_{ik}. If op_{ik}'s mode is *In/Out*, then In$_{ik}$'s (resp. Out$_{ik}$'s) and In$_{jl}$'s (Out$_{jl}$'s) types should be similar. If op_{ik}'s mode is *Out/In*, then Out$_{ik}$'s (resp. In$_{ik}$'s) and In$_{jl}$'s (Out$_{jl}$'s) types should be similar.

The second composability rule compares parameters' data types. It is based on the notion of *compatibility* between data types (XML Schema). Two parameters are *data type compatible* if they have the same built-in type. Compatibility of derived types and complex data types can also be adopted. However, these issues are out of the scope of this chapter. A discussion about typing in XML can be found in [18].

Data type composability depends on the composition type (horizontal or vertical) and operations' modes. As depicted in Fig. 6.2, we identify the following four cases. If op_{ik} is vertically composed with op_{jl} and $Mode_{ik}$ = "In/Out", then In_{ik} is "plugged" with In_{jl} and Out_{jl} is "plugged" with Out_{ik} (Fig. 6.2c). The data type of each parameter in In_{jl} (Out_{ik}) should be compatible with the data type of a corresponding parameter in In_{ik} (Out_{jl}). If op_{ik} is vertically composed with op_{jl} and $Mode_{ik}$ = "Out/In", then Out_{ik} is "plugged" with In_{jl} and Out_{jl} is "plugged" with In_{ik} (Fig. 6.2d). The data type of each parameter in In_{jl} (resp. In_{ik}) should be compatible with the data type of a corresponding parameter in Out_{ik} (Out_{jl}). If op_{ik} is horizontally composed with op_{jl}, then In_{ik} and Out_{ik} are "plugged" with In_{jl} independently of op_{ik}'s mode (Fig. 6.2a, b). The data type of each parameter in In_{jl} should be compatible with the data type of a corresponding parameter in In_{ik} or Out_{ik}.

The remaining three rules compare parameters' *business role*, *language*, and *unit* respectively. They are defined similarly to data type composability, except that the data type is replaced by *business role*, *language*, and *unit*, respectively.

6.6 Dynamic Semantic Composability

The *dynamic semantic* composability (or *B-Composability*) compares the business logic rules of source and target operations. Let us consider two rules $R_{ik}^n = (PreC_{ik}^n, PostC_{ik}^n)$ and $R_{jl}^m = (PreC_{jl}^m, PostC_{jl}^m)$ that belong to op_i and op_j respectively. B-composability relates $PreC_{ik}^n$ to $PreC_{jl}^m$ and $PostC_{ik}^n$ to $PostC_{jl}^m$. We define several forms of B-composability depending on the relationships between post- and pre-conditions. Each form is an instantiation of the general form of B-composability, called *generic B-composability*. We say that op_{ik} is *Generically B-composable* with op_{jl} if:

$$\forall R_{ik}^n \in Rules(op_{ik}) \exists R_{jl}^m \in Rules(op_{jl})|$$
$$(\widetilde{PreC}_{ikn} \mathcal{R}_1 PreC_{jl}^m) \wedge (PostC_{jl}^m \mathcal{R}_2 PostC_{ik}^n)$$

The relations $\mathcal{R}_1$ and $\mathcal{R}_2$ relate preconditions and postconditions, respectively. Each relation is either equivalence ($\Leftrightarrow$), implication ($\Rightarrow$), or *nil* (meaning that the corresponding term is dropped). As illustrated in this section, we may need to include information about the postcondition in the precondition clause. To allow this flexibility, we define $\widetilde{PreC}_{ikn}$ as either $PreC_{ik}^n$ or $PreC_{ik}^n \wedge PostC_{ik}^n$ in the generic B-composability rule. Note that techniques for comparing pre and post-conditions have been presented in [44]. However, these techniques deal with component-based environments *not* Web services.

Figure 6.4 depicts the different forms of B-Composability rules. We first give the strongest rule and then weaken the rules by relaxing $\mathcal{R}_1$ and $\mathcal{R}_2$ from $\Leftrightarrow$ to $\Rightarrow$, and *nil*. We also vary $\widetilde{PreC}_{ikn}$ from $PreC_{ik}^n$ to $PreC_{ik}^n \wedge PostC_{ik}^n$. Relaxing the rules enables the comparison of less closely related operations.

Exact—Exact B-composability instantiates $\mathcal{R}_1$ and $\mathcal{R}_2$ to $\Leftrightarrow$ and $\widetilde{PreC}_{ikn}$ to $PreC_{ik}^n$ (Fig. 6.4a). If two operations are exactly B-composable, then their business logics are equivalent. Hence, whenever one operation is used, it could be replaced by the other with no change in observable business logic. This rule is suitable for vertical composition since op_{ik} and op_{jl} are in their *active* state simultaneously.

Plugin—This rule relaxes both $\mathcal{R}_1$ and $\mathcal{R}_2$ from $\Leftrightarrow$ to $\Rightarrow$. It also instantiates $\widetilde{PreC}_{ikn}$ to $PreC_{ik}^n$. The rule R_{ik}^n is matched by any rule R_{jl}^m whose precondition is weaker to allow *at least* all of the conditions that R_{ik}^n allows. The post-condition of R_{jl}^m is

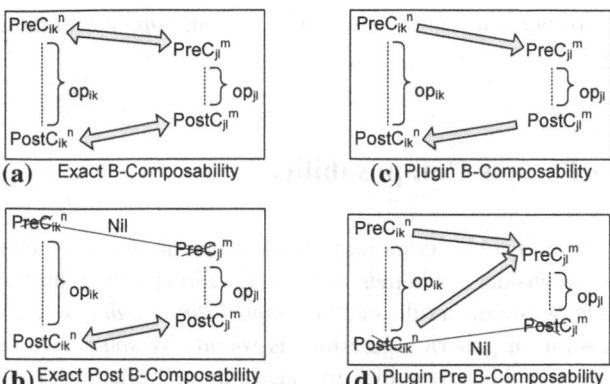

Fig. 6.4 B-composability rules: **a** Exact B-composability; **b** Plugin B-composability; **c** Exact Post B-composability; **d** Plugin Pre B-composability;

stronger than R_{ik}^n's to provide a condition *at least* as strong as R_{ik}^n's. As depicted in Fig. 6.4b, this rule is suitable for vertical composition since op_{ik} and op_{jl} are in their *active* state simultaneously.

Exact Post—In some cases, composers are concerned only with the effects of operations. For example, a composer may be interested in an operation that provides a social benefit independently of any precondition of that operation. Thus, a useful relaxation of the exact B-composability is to consider only the postcondition part of the conjunction. *Exact post* is also an instance of the generic B-composability, with $\mathcal{R}_2$ instantiated to ⇔ and dropping both $\widetilde{PreC}_{ikn}$ and $PreC_{jl}^m$ (Fig. 6.4c). Since only equivalence relationship is used, the exact post is symmetric. Because op_{ik} and op_{jl} are in their *active* state simultaneously (Fig. 6.4c), this rule is suitable for vertical composition.

Plugin Pre—Plugin Pre includes information about op_i's postcondition in the precondition and drops the relationship between postconditions. It is an instantiation of generic B-composability where $\mathcal{R}_1$ is instantiated to ⇒, $\mathcal{R}_2$ to *nil*, and $\widetilde{PreC}_{ikn}$ to $PreC_{ik}^n \wedge PostC_{ik}^n$. This rule is particularly useful to check horizontal composability that is, whether the execution of op_i can be followed by the execution of op_j. Figure 6.4d shows that op_{ik} and op_{jl} enter their *active* states sequentially ($Active_{ik} \longrightarrow_t Active_{jl}$). Since op_i is executed (according to R_{ik}^n) before op_j, $PreC_{ik}^n$ and $PostC_{kl}$ are by definition true. In order for op_j to be executable according to R_{jl}^m, its precondition $PreC_{jl}^m$ should be true. One way to ensure this is to check that the implication $PreC_{ik}^n \wedge PostC_{ik}^n \Rightarrow PreC_{jl}^m$ is true.

Plugin Post—Plugin Postmatch is a relaxation of exact Postmatch where the relationship between postconditions is equal to ⇒. Thus, Plugin Postmatch is an instance of the generic B-composability, with $\mathcal{R}_1$ and $\mathcal{R}_2$ instantiated to *nil* and ⇒ respectively (Fig. 6.4d). In contrast to exact Postmatch, Plugin Postmatch is asymmetric because of the use of implication between postconditions. As stated in Fig. 6.4d, this rule is suitable for vertical composition since op_{ik} and op_{jl} are in their *active* state simultaneously.

6.7 Business Process Composability

Service composition involves combining a set of operations in a specific way. One important issue to consider is whether such combination provides an added value. To address this issue, we define a rule, called *composition soundness*, to check whether a given composition of generic operations is *sound*. By *sound*, we mean that the way operations are combined provides an added value. The definition of *composition soundness* is based on the notions of *composition* and *stored templates* defined below.

Composition Template—A *composition template* is built for each composite service *CS* and gives its general structure. It is modeled by a directed graph (V, E) where *V* is a set of operation IDs and *E* is a set of edges. If an operation *op* is vertically composed with another operation op' in CS, then *op* and op' represent the same node in *V* since the execution of *op* is "replaced" by the execution of op'. Edges in *E* model horizontal composition relationships between *E*'s operations. An edge (op_{ik}, op_{jl}) belongs to E if op_{ik} is horizontally composed with op_{jl}.

Stored Template—*Stored templates* are defined by directed graphs similar to those used for composition templates. The difference between stored and composition templates is twofold. First, stored templates are saved in a *stored template repository* (*ST-repository*) while composition are computed for each composite service and then discarded. Second, the interpretation given to composition and stored templates are different. Composition templates model actual composite services as defined by users. Hence they may or may not provide added values. Stored template model "potential" composite services. They are generally pre-defined by domain experts (i.e., community providers). Hence, they inherently provide added values. Stored templates may also be "learned" by the system. Each time a composite service is defined by a user, the system saves the corresponding composition template in the *ST-repository* if the template does not already exist in the repository.

Composition Soundness—Because stored templates intrinsically provide added values, they can prove or disprove the soundness of a composite service *CS*. The idea is to compare the composition template of *CS* (*template*(*CS*)) with the existing stored templates. The following four cases are then possible:

1. *Case 1*: If *template*(*CS*) is equal to a given stored template *ST*, then *CS* provides *exactly* the same functionalities as the functionalities modeled by *ST*. We say that *CS* is *exactly sound* with respect to *ST*.
2. *Case 2*: If *template*(*CS*) is a *subgraph* of a given stored template *ST*, then *CS* provides a subset of the functionalities modeled by *ST*.
3. *Case 3*: If a given stored template *ST* is a *subgraph* of *template*(*CS*), then *CS* provides all the functionalities modeled by *ST*. *CS* also provides functionalities not offered by *ST*. We say that *CS* is *strongly sound* with respect to *ST*.

4. *Case 4*: If none of the previous cases is possible, then *CS* is not *sound*.

Process templates and *reference processes* are defined in [8] and [37] respectively. However, these notions are different from the notion of stored templates. Indeed, process templates and reference processes are used as *a priori* "canvas" when defining composite services. In contrast, stored templates are used *a posteriori* to check the soundness of composite services.

6.8 Research Directions in Service Composition

We identify the following directions for future research in Web service composition: service mashup, autonomic composition of Web services, cloud services, and dynamic composition of Web services.

Service Mashup—One of the goals of Web 2.0 is to make it easy to create, use, describe, share, and reuse resources on the Web [7, 22]. Mashup is an application development approach that allows users to aggregate multiple services (e.g., Google Map and Amazon.com) to create a service that serves a new purpose. Unlike Web services composition where the focus is on the composition of business (process) services only, the mashup process goes further in that it allows more functionalities and can compose heterogeneous resources such as data services and User Interface services [22]. Much of the current work in service mashup involves tools and techniques that instrument the mashup process and subsequently visualize the results [17, 34]. Another issue is to define techniques for predicting or mining meaningful mashups.

Autonomic Composition of Web Services—Autonomic computing identifies four fundamental "self" properties: self-healing, self-configuring, self-optimizing, and self-protecting [41]. Self-configuring compositions are composite services that are capable of automatically discovering new participant services, selecting among available service providers, and choosing among different options available for contracts [30]. Self-optimizing compositions automatically select participants that would maximize Quality of Service [33, 43]. Self-healing compositions automatically detect that some composition requirements (e.g., regulatory or business requirements) are no longer satisfied and react to requirement violations [2, 14]. Self-adapting compositions are able to function in spite of changes in behaviors of external services; they reduce as much as possible the need of human intervention for adapting services to changes.

Cloud Services—Cloud computing allows users to access applications running on large-scale remote computing environments. Cloud computing precursors include grid computing, which links disparate computers to form one large infrastructure; and utility computing, a metered service in which individuals work with programs kept on shared servers and, like a public utility, pay based on their usage level [16, 20, 29]. Tools and techniques are needed to simplify the development, debugging, testing, change management, customization and integration of cloud services. Other research thrusts include complex event processing (e.g., real-time data feeds such as location information for mobile devices) [11], cloud monitoring and management (e.g., failure prediction) [35], and security [6, 21].

Dynamic Composition of Web Services—The support of dynamic composition will facilitate the establishment of *on demand* and *real-time* partnerships. Services will not statically be bound to each other. New partners with relevant features should be dynamically discovered and assembled. Currently, relationships among component services are mostly established at development time. While current service-oriented technologies provide capabilities for defining Web services, they clearly are not sufficient to facilitate the establishment of dynamic business relationships. More research effort is needed to enable the creation of dynamic relationships.

6.9 Conclusion

In this chapter, we proposed a *composability model* to ascertain that Web services can safely be combined, hence avoiding unexpected failures at run time. Composability is checked through a set of *rules* organized into five *levels*: *syntactic*, *static semantic*, *dynamic semantic*, *qualitative*, and *business process* levels. We introduced the concepts of *composability degree* and *τ-composability* to cater for *partial* and *total* composability. Finally, we discussed four directions for future research in Web service composition: service mashup, autonomic composition of Web services, cloud services, and dynamic composition of Web services.

References

1. Alonso, G., Casati, F., Kuno, H., Machiraju, V.: Web Services: Concepts, Architecture, and Applications. Springer, Berlin, ISBN: 3540440089 (2003)
2. Baresi, L., Guinea, S.: An introduction to self-healing web services. In: International Conference on Engineering of Complex Computer Systems, p. 4, June 2005
3. BEA, IBM, Microsoft: Business Process Execution Language for Web Services (BPEL4WS). http://xml.coverpages.org/bpel4ws.html
4. Benatallah, B., Dumas, M., Shen, M., Ngu, A.H.H.: Declarative composition and peer-to-peer provisioning of dynamic web services. In: ICDE Conference, pp. 297–308, CA, USA, Feb 2002
5. Berners-Lee, T., Hendler, J., Lassila, O.: The semantic web. Sci. Am. **284**(5), 34–43 (2001)
6. Bertino, E., Paci, F., Ferrini, R., Shang, N.: Privacy-preserving digital identity management for cloud computing. IEEE Data Eng. Bull. **32**(1), 21–27 (2009)
7. Bouguettaya, A., Nepal, S., Sherchan, W., Zhou, X., Wu, J., Chen, S., Liu, D., Li, L., Wang, H., Liu, X.: End-to-end service support for mashups. IEEE Trans. Serv. Comput. **3**(3), 250–263 (2010)
8. Casati, F., Ilnicki, S., Jin, L., Krishnamoorthy, V., Shan, M.-C.: Adaptive and dynamic service composition in eFlow. In: CAiSE Conference, pp. 13–31, Stockholm, Sweden, June 2000
9. Doan, A., Madhavan, J., Dhamankar, R., Domingos, P., Halevy, A.: Learning to match ontologies on the semantic web. VLDB J. **12**(4), 309–319 (2003)

10. ebXML.: http://www.ebxml.org, 2003
11. Eugster, P.Th., Felber, P., Guerraoui, R., Kermarrec, A.-M.: The many faces of publish/subscribe. ACM Comput. Surv. **35**(2), 114–131 (2003)
12. Fensel, D.: Ontologies: A Silver Bullet for Knowledge Management and Electronic Commerce. Springer, Berlin, ISBN: 3540003029 (2003)
13. Georgakopoulos, D., Schuster, H., Cichocki, A., Baker, D.: Managing process and service fusion in virtual enterprises. Inf. Syst. **24**(6), 429–456 (1999)
14. Ghosh, D., Sharman, R., Rao, H.R., Upadhyaya, S.: Self-healing systems—survey and synthesis. Decis. Support Syst. **42**, 2164–2185 (2007)
15. Gribble, S.D., Brewer, E.A., Hellerstein, J.M., Culler, D.: Scalable, distributed data structures for internet service construction. In: Proceedings of the Symposium on Operating Systems Design and Implementation, pp. 319–332, San Diego, CA, USA, Oct 2000
16. Hayes, B.: Cloud computing. Commun. ACM **51**(7), 9–11 (2008)
17. Jhingran, A.: Enterprise information mashups: integrating information, simply. In: VLDB, pp. 3–4, 2006
18. Kuper, G.M., Simeon, J.: Subsumption for XML types. In: ICDT Conference, pp. 331–345, London, UK, Jan 2001
19. Lazcano, A., Alonso, G., Schuldt, H., Schuler, C.: The WISE approach to electronic commerce. Int. J. Comput. Syst. Sci. Eng. **15**(5), 343–355 (2000)
20. Leavitt, N.: Is cloud computing really ready for prime time? IEEE Comput. **42**(1), 15–20 (2009)
21. Lin, D., Squicciarini, A.C.: Data protection models for service provisioning in the cloud. In: SACMAT, pp. 183–192, 2010
22. Di Lorenzo, G., Hacid, H., Paik, H.-Y., Benatallah, B.: Data integration in mashups. SIGMOD Rec. **38**(1), 59–66 (2009)
23. McDermott, D.V.: Estimating-regression planning for interactions with web services. In: International Conference on Artificial Intelligence Planning Systems, pp. 204–211, Toulouse, France, Apr 2002
24. McIlraith, S.A., Son, T.C.: Adapting Golog for composition of semantic web services. In: 8th International Conference on Principles and Knowledge Representation and Reasoning (KR-02), pp. 482–496, Toulouse, France, 2002
25. McIlraith, S.A., Son, T.C., Zeng, H.: Semantic web services. IEEE Intell. Syst. **16**(2), 46–53 (2001)
26. Medjahed, B., Benatallah, B., Bouguettaya, A., Ngu, A., Elmagarmid, A.: Business-to-business interactions: issues and enabling technologies. VLDB J. **12**(1), 59–85 (2003)
27. Medjahed, B., Bouguettaya, A.: Service Composition for the Semantic Web. Springer, Berlin, ISBN: 9781441984647 (2011)
28. Medjahed, B., Bouguettaya, A., Elmagarmid, A.: Composing web services on the semantic web. VLDB J. **12**(4), 333–351 (2003)
29. Mika, P., Tummarello, G.: Web semantics in the clouds. IEEE Intell. Syst. **23**(5), 82–87 (2008)
30. Papazoglou, M.P., Traverso, P., Dustdar, S., Leymann, F.: Service-oriented computing: a research roadmap. Int. J. Cooperative Inf. Syst. **17**(2), 223–255 (2008)
31. Payne, T.R., Paolucci, M., Sycara, K.: Advertising and matching DAML-S service descriptions (position paper). In: International Semantic Web Working Symposium, pp. 76–78, CA, USA, July 2001
32. Ponnekanti, S.R., Fox, A.: SWORD: a developer toolkit for web service composition. In: Proceedings of the International World Wide Web Conference, pp. 83–107, Honolulu, Hawaii, USA, May 2002
33. Rosenberg, F., Müller, M.B., Leitner, P., Michlmayr, A., Bouguettaya, A., Dustdar, S.: Meta-heuristic optimization of large-scale QoS-aware service compositions. In: IEEE SCC, pp. 97–104, 2010
34. Sabbouh, M., Higginson, J., Semy, S., Gagne, D.: Web mashup scripting language. In: WWW, pp. 1305–1306, 2007
35. Salfner, F., Lenk, M., Malek, M.: A survey of online failure prediction methods. ACM Comput. Surv. **42**(3), Article 3, 1–42 (2010)

36. Schuster, H., Baker, D., Cichocki, A., Georgakopoulos, D., Rusinkiewicz, M.: The collaboration management infrastructure. In: Proceedings of the IEEE International Conference on Data Engineering, pp. 485–487, San Jose, CA, USA, Mar 2000
37. Schuster, H., Georgakopoulos, D., Cichocki, A., Baker, D.: Modeling and composing service-based and reference process-based multi-enterprise processes. In: CAiSE Conference, pp. 247–263, Stockholm, Sweden, June 2000
38. Singh, M.P.: Physics of service composition. IEEE Internet Comput. 5(3), 6 (2001)
39. Sirin, E., Parsia, B., Hendler, J.: Filtering and selecting semantic web services with interactive composition techniques. IEEE Intell. Syst. 19(4), 42–49 (2004)
40. Sycara, K., Klush, M., Widoff, S.: Dynamic service matchmaking among agents in open information environments. ACM SIGMOD Rec. 28(1), 47–53 (1999)
41. Want, R., Pering, T., Tennenhouse, D.L.: Comparing autonomic and proactive computing. IBM Syst. J. 42(1), 129–135 (2003)
42. Wu, D., Parsia, B., Hendler, J., Nau, D.: Automating DAML-S web services composition using SHOP2. In: International Semantic Web Conference, pp. 195–210, FL, USA, Oct 2003
43. Yu, Q., Bouguettaya, A.: Framework for web service query algebra and optimization. TWEB 2(1), 1–35 (2008)
44. Zaremski, A.M., Wing, J.M.: Specification matching of software components. ACM Trans. Softw. Eng. Methodol. 6(4), 333–369 (1997)

Chapter 7
Semantic Web Service Composition: The Web Service Challenge Perspective

Thomas Weise, M. Brian Blake and Steffen Bleul

Abstract Service-oriented architecture (SOA) is a software design paradigm for creating highly modular, distributed applications. Web services can implement well-defined, atomic functions which can be composed into high-level business processes. The composition of clearly separable modules is one of the key advantages of SOAs. This article provides an overview of research, challenges, and competitions in this domain. We first define and discuss the general notions of syntactical and semantic discovery/composition and the corresponding quality of service (QoS) features. One focus of this chapter is the Web Service Challenge (WSC), which has established an extensive body of knowledge and community of researchers in the area of web service composition. We discuss the structure, requirements, and utilities provided in the scope of this competition. The paper furthermore includes a detailed literature review of the activities of the WSC event in context of the related initiatives.

7.1 Introduction

Service-oriented architectures (SOAs) [39, 79, 129] represent a promising paradigm for realizing business processes within enterprise software systems. The modularity of services that underlie SOAs enable an infrastructure that is easy to maintain,

T. Weise (✉)
Nature Inspired Computation and Applications Laboratory, School of Computer Science and Technology, University of Science and Technology of China (USTC), Hefei 230027, Anhui, China
e-mail: tweise@ustc.edu.cn

M. B. Blake
University of Miami, Graduate School, Coral Gables, FL 33124-3220, USA
e-mail: m.brian.blake@miami.edu

S. Bleul
Munich, Germany
e-mail: stbleul@gmx.de

A. Bouguettaya et al. (eds.), *Web Services Foundations*,
DOI: 10.1007/978-1-4614-7518-7_7,
© Springer Science+Business Media New York 2014

extend, improve, and interconnect. To fully enable the flexibility of SOA environments, approaches must be developed that compose multiple services into higher-level business processes. Services are building blocks in implementing business processes in companies and to integrate heterogeneous resources and external systems [186].

The composition of services within companies implements processes such as ordering, billing, accounting, and information dissemination. Each service within the process realizes a specific task. The communication between services is realized with messages, either directly or by using a middleware. Compositions of services are normally defined in a process execution language such WS-BPEL [24, 102] and a message choreography language like WS-CDL [106]. The automatic execution of specifications provided in such languages is then performed by process execution engines.

Service oriented architectures evolve by replacing services with more effective substitutes. These substitutes may offer extended functionality or enhanced quality of service (QoS) (i.e., reduced response time or higher throughput). When organizations collaborate on their offerings, services offer flexibility in outsourcing software capabilities to external entities.

Consequently, service discovery and service composition [62, 186] are essential functionalities in service oriented architectures. In this paper, we review the developments in automated web service composition during the last five years. This work leverages the research activities and results of the Web Service Challenge (WSC) [30]. The WSC initiative was the first effort that attempts to enhance the state-of-the-art in service composition through annual "side-by-side" community evaluation.

7.2 Automatic Web Service Composition

7.2.1 Syntactic Discovery

The syntactic description of a function in an imperative language like C, Java, or C# contains the input and output data types, as sketched in Listing 7.1. From a simplified perspective, a web service w can be described in the same way, by a set $w.T_I$ of input types t_i and a set $w.T_O$ of output data types t_o. Syntactic web service discovery means finding web services whose input and output parameter types *exactly* fit to the types T_G of available input data and which produce output data *exactly* fitting to a set of required types T_N (Fig. 7.1).

Fig. 7.1 Example for a syntactical interface

```
Title getBookTitle(ISBN bookId) {
    ...
}
```

A discovery request R can be fully specified as a tuple $R = (R.T_G, R.T_N, R.W)$ of the set $R.T_G$ of types of the known data elements, the set $R.T_N$ of types which should be found, and a web service repository $R.W$. Notice that in a software system, the service repository is not part of the user's request, but part of the data accessible by the algorithm. From algorithmic perspective, however, it is part of the input of the discovery procedure. The goal of solving the request R is to discover a service $w \in R.W$ for which can be executed with the given parameters and produces instances of the wanted types as output, i.e., fulfills the predicate $valid_{synD} (w, R)$ defined in Eq. (7.1).

$$valid_{synD} (w, R) \Leftrightarrow (w \in R.W) \wedge (\forall t_i \in w.T_I$$
$$\Rightarrow t_i \in R.T_G) \wedge (\forall t_o \in R.T_N \Rightarrow t_o \in w.T_O) \quad (7.1)$$

7.2.2 Syntactical Composition

Service composition also permits combining multiple services in order to fulfill the requirements of a user-based request. Such a composition C is a directed acyclic graph (DAC) describing the order in which the services must be executed. It consists of a set $C.W$ of services and a strict partial order $C.pred$ defined on them (where $w' \in C.pred (w)$ means that $w' \in C.W$ must be executed before $w \in C.W$). For a valid syntactic composition $valid_{synC} (C, R)$ defined in Eq. (7.2) must hold. In [165], the authors show that the syntactical service composition is NP-complete.

$$valid_{synC} (C, R) \Leftrightarrow (\forall w \in C.W \Rightarrow w \in R.W) \qquad \qquad \wedge$$
$$\left(\forall w \in C.W, t_i \in w.T_I \Rightarrow t_i \in \left[R.T_G \cup \bigcup_{\forall w' \in C.pred(w)} w'.T_O\right]\right) \wedge$$
$$(\forall t_o \in R.T_N \Rightarrow t_o \in [\bigcup_{\forall w \in C.W} w.T_O])$$
$$(7.2)$$

7.2.3 Semantic Composition

Semantic composition takes into account that besides primitive types (such as numbers or Boolean values), type systems usually support hierarchical compositions of types.[1] In Eq. (7.1), the parameter type ISBN could be a class. In the publishing industry, the ISBNs are used to uniquely identify media. Because of the shortage of remaining unused identifies the ten-digit ISBN-10 have been superseded by the new thirteen-digit ISBN-13s. The ISBN class could be subclassed to ISBN-10 and ISBN-13. Instances of all three classes could be passed to the function getBookTitle.

---

[1] Also, formal representations of pre and post conditions may be considered during the matching process.

Semantic composition takes such type hierarchies into account by representing the types as concepts in an ontology. This ontology can again be described as DAG. The composition request is thus complemented with a subsumption predicate $R.subs$ where $t' \in R.subs\,(t)$ means that type t' subsumes type t. In a class hierarchy known from Object Oriented Programming, the type ISBN could subsume both, ISBN-10 and ISBN-13. ISBN-10 and ISBN-13 are then specializations of ISBN.

A service w can be executed if for each of input types $t'_i \in w.T_I$, at least one instance of either t'_i directly or any type t_i with $t'_i \in subs\,(t_i)$ is available. For simplicity, let us $R.subs^\star\,(T)$ be the joint set of all subsumed types of the types $t \in T$. Then, a valid solution for the semantic service composition request R fulfills Eq. (7.3). A syntactic composer can be extended to support semantic composition by replacing the "equals" operation applied to (syntactical) parameter names with a subsumption check. Such a check can be performed in $\mathbf{O}(1)$ if all the subsumed concepts are stored in a hash map built upon loading the type taxonomy.

$$valid_{semC}\,(C, R) \Leftrightarrow (\forall w \in C.W \Rightarrow w \in R.W) \qquad\qquad\qquad\qquad \wedge$$
$$\left(\forall w \in C.W, t_i \in w.T_I \Rightarrow t_i \in subs^\star\left(R.T_G \cup \bigcup\nolimits_{\forall w' \in C.pred(w)} w'.T_O\right)\right) \wedge$$
$$\left(\forall t_o \in R.T_N \Rightarrow t_o \in subs^\star\left(\bigcup\nolimits_{\forall w \in C.W} w.T_O\right)\right)$$
$$\tag{7.3}$$

7.2.4 QoS-Based Composition

Currently, discovery and composition tasks predominantly consist of AI *planning problems* [190] which can be solved with informed (heuristic) or uninformed (exhaustive) local search methods [50, 203]. However, in a SOA, not only the functionality of a business process itself is of interest but also nonfunctional criteria such as quality of service (QoS) [46, 47]. This especially holds for enterprise mash-up, i.e., software systems which partly rely on services provided by external vendors. QoS may be modeled with semantic conditions, but can also be considered as orthogonal objective—i.e., it is possible to perform syntactic composition with regard to QoS. In usual composition scenarios, however, QoS and semantics are closely linked together.

When QoS is considered together with functionality, service composition becomes a (constrained combinatorial) *optimization problem* [200]. The validity criterion *valid* now becomes a feasibility constraint whereas the QoS parameters can be considered as objective functions. Both, the constraint and the objectives can be combined to a single heuristic guiding, for example, an A^* search. However, depending on the size of the service repository $R.W$, the number of non-functional criteria, and the expected number of involved services, optimization algorithms such as Evolutionary Algorithms [28, 29, 70, 200], Simulated Annealing [108, 161, 200], Tabu Search [84, 93, 200], or other metaheuristics [83, 152, 200] become feasible approaches. Especially multi-objective Evolutionary Algorithms are promising, since they are able to return multiple solutions in one run which can represent a trade-off between the objectives (i.e., one composition could have a high runtime at lower costs whereas another one may be more costly but also faster) from which a human operator might pick the most suitable one(s).

7.3 History and Impact of the WSC

7.3.1 History

The Web Service Challenge (WSC) is an event for researchers investigating software engineering concerns in the area of efficient automatic web service composition algorithms. Since 2005, this annual forum has attracted 44 contributions from 97 authors. As shown in Table 7.1, the challenges proposed in the WSC evolved from the general concept of syntactical web service composition in 2005 to semantic composition involving QoS optimization in 2009. At the same time, the forum leverages standardized data formats such as WSDL [51], OWL [35, 94], WS-BPEL [24, 102], and WSLA [107, 136].

The first Web Service Challenge in 2005 focused on syntactic service composition. Simple XML [58] data formats were used to describe the challenge. Techniques from Artificial Intelligence, often based on heuristic or uninformed searches, were prevalent. In the following year, a semantic composition challenge was added. The type taxonomy was represented as XSD schema [80]. The solutions to these challenges were sequences of services. In 2007, the WSC further developed—the type taxonomies were represented in the OWL format and the challenge included the ability to evaluate services that can be executed in parallel. Another major change was that the composition systems were required to be implemented as Web Services.

Generally, semantic web service composition [186] has been achieved with hierachical task network planning [191, 192], Petri Nets [159], situation calculus (e.g., with Golog) [147, 148, 159], uninformed search [150], with planning based on rule-based expert systems [179], via model checking [177, 196], with semi-automatic procedures [187], and Genetic Programming [27]. As can be seen in Table 7.1, the techniques developed within the framework of the Web Service Challenge are even more wide spread and include, for example, agent-based methodologies [60], but also more low-level techniques from AI such as heuristic search [48] which proved to be especially efficient.

In 2008, the WSC event introduced challenge datasets with structured data types. More importantly, the solutions could contain arbitrarily nested and parallel processes, as well as choices between different possible processes. Therefore, WS-BPEL was adopted as solution format. From this point on, the entries to the WSC—composition services—could theoretically be plugged directly into existing SOAs. Finally in 2009, QoS criteria were introduced. The goal was extended beyond the synthesis of valid compositions to also find valid compositions with maximal throughput and minimal response time. WSLA was chosen in order to represent these quality dimensions in the input data. In 2010, the WSC event featured much

Table 7.1 The Web Service Challenge (WS-Challenge, WSC) [41]

I. Web Service Challenge 2005 [41, 5]

Syntactical Web Service Composition

1. [98]: Hashing, Depth-limited Search
2. [162]: Bloom Filter Hash, A* search
3. [38]: Agents, Modal Logic, Prolog
4. [86]: Topic Map, Multi-Agent System
5. [77]: Partial Order Planning

II. Web Service Challenge 2006 [42]

Semantic Web Service Composition, Taxonomy represented as XSD

6. [20]: Hashing, Greedy Seach
7. [48]: Hashing, Tree Data Structures, Multi-Threading, Greedy Search, Interative Deepening
   Depth-First Search
8. [110]: Depth-First Search, Prolog
9. [163]: AI, Planning, Breadth-First Search
10. [78]: Answer Set Programming
11. [185]: Hashing, Bi-Directional Search Depth-First Search
12. [71]: Description Logic Reasoning
13. [23]: Hashing, Metric Planning via Greedy Search
14. [207]: Inverted Table Index, Breadth-First Search
15. [219]: Trees, String Prefix Matching, Breadth-First Search
16. [140]: Syntactic Composition only, Hashing, Depth-limited Search

III. Web Service Challenge 2007 [43]

WSC'06 + OWL for Taxonomy, Concurrency, Composer as Service

17. [103]: Table-based Index, Greedy Search
18. [88]: Inverted Table Index, Breadth-First Search
19. [49]: Hashing, Tree Data Structures, Multi-Threading, Greedy Search, Genetic Algorithm,
    Iterative Deepening Depth-First Search
20. [111]: Breadth-First Search, Prolog, Constraint Logic Programming over Finite Domains
    (CLP(FD))
21. [220]: Breadth-First Search, Greedy Search, Indexing using B-Trees, Least Recently Used
    Memory Management
22. [60]: Triple-Store, Memetic Algorithms
23. [164]: Inverted Index, AI, Planning

IV. Web Service Challenge 2008 [31]

WSC'07 + Structured Data Types, BPEL, Multi-Objective Composition

24. [157]: Tranformation to Satisfieability (SAT)Problem, Iterative Application of a SAT Solver
25. [209]: And/Or Graph, Depth-First Search
26. [208]: Breadth-First Search in a Planning Graph
27. [59]: Triple-Store, Memetic Algorithms
28. [212]: Integer Linear Programming, Non-Functional Objectives, Constraints
29. [204]: Hashing, Tree Data Structures, Multi-Threading, Greedy Search, Genetic Algorithm,
    Iterative Deepening Depth-First Search
30. [21]: Greedy Depth-First Search
31. [184]: Greedy Search, Indexing using B-Trees, Least Recently Used Memory Management

Table 7.1 (continued)

I. Web Service Challenge 2005 [41, 5]
Syntactical Web Service Composition
V. Web Service Challenge 2009 [112]
WSC'08 + Quality of Service, WSLA
32. [22]: Greedy Search, Priority Queue
33. [33]: Depth-First Search
34. [217]: Service Classes, Indexing using B-Trees, Greedy Search, Iterative Deepening Depth-First Search
35. [182]: Planning Domain Description Language (PDDL), Graphplan
36. [158]: Planning, Dynamic Programming, Learning Depth-First Search
37. [72]: Matrix Representation, Topological Network Analysis, Multi-Criteria Integer Programming, Depth-First Search
38. [166]: Planning, A*
39. [99]: Dynamic Programming, Integer Programming, Pruning, Multi-Threading
40. [210]: Service Layer Representation, Two Steps: Solution Finding, Service Number Reduction

VI. Web Service Challenge 2010 [45]
WSC'09 + Larger Scale Test Sets
41. [137]: Greedy Search
42. [75]: Greedy Search, Priority Queue
43. [138]: Service Layer Representation, Two Steps:Solution Finding, Service Number Reduction; Dynamic Programming

larger and complex challenge tasks whereas the involved formats remained the same. Since 2005, the scale of the challenge datasets has steadily increased, leading to rather large-scale testsets comprising service repositories with 40000 services, ontologies with 20000 concepts, and compositions comprising a minimum of 50 services.

7.3.2 Impact

Because of its structure, evolution, and relevance, the Web Service Challenge has become a major reference in both, the research and the industrial service composition community. The developers of widely-recognized systems such as ADDO [47, 49], MOVE [97], and jUDDI+ [71] used the WSC as reference for their work.

In 2012, checking Google Scholar (and Microsoft Academic Search) for citations of the competition lead papers and entries reveales 119 (72) references to the 2005 challenge, 119 (67) for the 2006 one, 85 (31) for 2007, 62 (23) for 2008, and 70 (20) for 2009. Adding up these numbers, there are more than 450 (210) citations of the WSC or works that competed in its context—which emphasizes its large influence on the community.

Table 7.2 The semantic web service challenge (SWS-Challenge) [175]

I. 1st Semantic Web Services Challenge Workshop (Stanford, USA, 2006) [6]

Phase I: Discovery, Interoperability, Mediation

1. [54]: WebL + Glue: Visual Modeling, Automatic Code Generation, WSMO Ontology, Service Discovery
2. [68]: OWL-P: Business Processes in Open Systems, Memetic Algorithms, Business Partners = Agents, OWL
3. [69]: WSMX: WSMO, Data Mediation, Semantic Lifting and Lowering of Messages
4. [85]: METEOR-S: Protocol and Data Mediation
5. [178]: Service Mediation
6. [115]: jABC:UML, Web Service Wrappers for Mediation, Visual Modeling
7. [124]: DIANE: Description Language (DSD), Interaction Modeling, Service Mediation, BPEL
8. [145]: Human-based Service Mediation, Data and Process Abstraction

II. 2nd Semantic Web Services Challenge Workshop (Budva, Republic of Montenegro, 2006) [8]

Phase II: Adaptation, Changes in SOA

9. [92]: WSMX Middleware: Semantic Enriching of Schemas, Data and Process Mediation, WSMO, WSML
10. [55]: WebML + Glue: Visual Modeling, Service Discovery
11. [125]: DIANE: Description Language (DSD), Matchmaking, Middleware
12. [114]: jABC: Web Service Wrappers for Mediation

III. 3rd Semantic Web Services Challenge Workshop (Athens, USA, 2006) [9]

Phase III: Same as Phase II

13. [53]: WebML + Glue: Entity Relationship, UML, WSMO, WebRatio, F-Logic
14. [214]: WSMX Middleware: WSMO, WSML, WSMX
15. [120]: DIANE: Description Language (DSD), Matchmaking, Middleware
16. [113]: jABC + jETI: GraphSIB, AXIS, miAamics

IV. 4th Semantic Web Services Challenge Workshop (Innsbruck, Austria, 2007) [10]

SWS Phase III + Composition

17. [123]: DIANE: Description Language (DSD), Matchmaking, Middleware, Temporal Reasoning
18. [117]: jABC + jETI: AXIS, Velocity, JAXB, Java
19. [56]: WebML + Glue: Entity Relationship, UML, WSMO, WebRatio WS
20. [155]: WSMX Middleware: WSMO, WSML, WSMX

V. Special Session at ICEIS (Madeira, Portugal, 2007) [172, 173]

21. [215]: WSMX Middleware: WSMO, WSML, Entity Relationship Model, Service Mediation
22. [142]: WebML + Webratio vs. jABC +jETI
23. [128]: DIANE (Fuzzy Sets) vs. SWE-ET (Glue + WebRatio, F-Logic); Modeling, Matchmaking, Dynamics
24. [146]: Swashup: Ruby on Rails Mashup
25. [206]: METEOR-S: SAWSDL, GraphPlan

(contienued)

Table 7.2 (contiued)

I. 1st Semantic Web Services Challenge Workshop (Stanford, USA, 2006) [6]
Phase I: Discovery, Interoperability, Mediation
VI. 5th Semantic Web Services Challenge Workshop (Silicon Valley, USA, 2007) [44]

26. [121, 122]: DIANE Middleware: Mediation, Fuzzy Sets, Service Discovery and Composition
27. [116]: jABC + jETI: Mediation, AXIS, GeneSys, JAXB
28. [57]: WebML/WebRatio + Glue:Entity Relationship, UML, WSMO
29. [118]: jABC + miAamics: Service Discovery
30. [154]: Service Discovery, WSMO, Constraint-based Service Composition

VII. 6th Semantic Web Services Challenge Workshop (Tenerife, Spain, 2008) [82, 171]
31. [195]: Debugging of Ontologies: MUPSter, DION, RADON, Protegee, SWOOP
32. [32]: Semantic Mediation, Semantic Bridges
33. [65]: New Scenario Proposal: Logistics, Functional/Non-Functional Properties
34. [143]: jABC: ABC/ETI, Mediator Synthesis, Semantic Linear-time Temporal Logic
35. [119]: jABC: Semantic Linear-time Temporal Logic, Abductive Logic Programming, Event Calculus, Model Checking, SAP's Goal-oriented Enterprise Management (GEM)
36. [216]: WSMX Middleware: WSMO, WSML, WSMX, KAON2 Reasoner, IRIS Reasoner, Service Mediation

VIII. 7th Semantic Web Services Challenge Workshop (Karlsruhe, Germany, 2008) [14, 171]
New Discovery Scenario
37. [181]: COSMO: Model-Driven Architecture, Model Transformations
38. [130]: jABC + GEM: Service Mediation for "Purchase Order Mediation v2" and "Payment Problem"

IX. 8th Semantic Web Services Challenge Workshop (Eindhoven, The Netherlands, 2009) [174]
39. [26]: COSMO: Model-Driven Architecture, Model Transformation, Goal Modeling
40. [169]: Glue2: Semantic Service Discovery for the Logistics Management Scenario

Fig. 7.2 The relation between WSC, SWS, and SC Contest

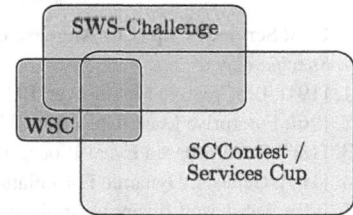

7.4 Related Events

Since the conception of the WSC approach, other derivative events have emerged: the SWS Challenge and the SC Contest. The later events have focused on other aspects of the service composition. In total, 293 researchers are involved in the three challenges, but only five of them contributed to more than one family of competitions. The relation of the challenge themes is illustrated in Fig. 7.2.

Table 7.3 The IEEE International Services Computing Contest (SCContest) and Services Cup

I. First IEEE International Services Computing Contest (Chicago, USA, 2006) [66]
Theme: SOA Methodologies and Tools to Better Solve Business Issues
1. [199]: Geospatial Data, Grid Computing, Replication, Security, BPEL, SOA
2. [52]: Home Automation, OSGi, Smart Home, Ubiquitous Computing, Central Gateways
3. [189]: VIDRE: Business Rules, Rules Engine, RuleML, Supply Chain Management
4. [135]: Self-Adaptive Web Service Integration (SAWI): Personal Mobility Manager, Self-Adaptation, WSDL
5. [104]: MIDAS: Supply Chain Management, SOA
6. [74]: SOAR: SOA for Real-Estate Industry, Trust and Security Architecture

II. Second IEEE International Services Computing Contest (Salt Lake City, USA, 2007) [218]
Theme: SOA Methodologies and Tools to Better Solve Business Issues
7. [105]: e-Healthcare, Medicin, Multimedia, Security, Speech Recognition, Atom/RSS
8. [73]: (Dynamic) Supply Chain Management, Knowledge-Driven SOA

III. Third IEEE International Services Computing Contest (Honolulu, USA, 2008) [15]
Theme: Business SOA and Services Mash-up
9. [76]: Domain-Specific Query Language (DSQL) for Services Mash-Up, OWL-D, SQL-like language
10. [221]: Rich Internet Application, Naval Shipping and Logistics, BPEL, Web 2.0
11. [198]: Semantic Mash-Up: Bayesian Networks, Ontologies, Tourism
12. [100]: Mash-Up: News Industry, Data Augumentation for Celibrities, Text Mining, Web Crawling
13. [25]: University-wide Web 2.0 Information/Service System, Service Mash-Ups
14. [89]: Open Service Process Platform: Web 2.0, Orchestration OSGi
15. [101]: Mash-Up: Home Library Management System, Bar Code Scanning, ISBN
16. [139]: Combination of Geographical Information Systems (GIS) and Data, BPEL, XML, AJAX
17. [91]: Mash-Up: Forest Fires, GIS, Simulation
18. [134]: Rental Advising System, GIS, Service Wrappers and Mash-Ups
19. [160]: Mash-Up of Travel Planning Services: Bus, Flight, Train, Hotel
20. [67]: E-Commerce: Illustration of Products via Second Life, HTML Wrapping, REST

IV. First Services Cup (Los Angeles, USA, 2009) [16]
No Specific Theme
21. [194]: BioCreative MetaServer, BC-VisCon, Text Mining, Bioinformatics, Genetics
22. [96]: Enterprise Mash-Up, SAP, GUI, E-Commerce, Marketplaces
23. [180]: Stream-based Event Processing in a SOA, Selling and Buying Stocks
24. [109]: Genesis: Dynamic Formulation of Abstract Business Processes, Business-OWL
25. [90]: Web-based Business Application, Behavior Model Inference, SPIN, Promela, Weka, GraphViz
26. [19]: Posr: Automatic Generation of User Interfaces and Services Wrapping existing Applications, Travel Planning

(continued)

Table 7.3 (continued)

I. First IEEE International Services Computing Contest (Chicago, USA, 2006) [66]
Theme: SOA Methodologies and Tools to Better Solve Business Issues
V. Second Services Cup (Miami, USA, 2010) [18]
Theme: Cloud Computing
27. [132]: SIR: Text Correction, Human as a Service, REST-based SOA, Cloud Computing
28. [211]: Accountability, Cloud Computing, Logging
29. [188]: Cloud Computing, Cost Approximation: Neural Networks, MapReduce
30. [197]: TAPoR: Text Mining, Digital Humanities, MapReduce
31. [151]: Service Security Lab, Model Driven Architecture, Cloud Computing

---

The Semantic Web Service Challenge (SWS) has attracted 40 contributions from 72 authors, as listed in Table 7.2. It propagates the interaction of services, processes, and e-businesses in one specific scenario. Web service discovery and composition is involved in so far that, in order to wire two SOAs with each other and to adapt processes to changing requirements, services matching to the (new) requirements must be discovered and, if necessary, combined. These discovery or competition tasks are, however, of much smaller scale. Furthermore, the challenge requires the complete implementation of an application scenario. While this, on one hand, allows researchers to study "a system in action", it also requires much more work and does not allow for the research on singular, specific aspects of a SOA.

While earlier Web Service Challenges lacked rich semantics as compared to the Semantic Web Service Challenges [126, 127], in 2007, the WSC has supported OWL taxonomies and later, with WSC'08 , structured data types. The WSC represents a challenge which is theoretical enough to allow researchers to construct solutions as modules without needing to deal with the complete enterprise architecture at once. It is, however, also realistic enough to represent the challenges in such an architecture.

The International Services Computing Contest (SCContest), renamed to Services Cup in 2008, has attracted 31 contributions from 129 authors, as listed in Table 7.3. The SWS is more general than the WSC as it provides a well-defined task, although the task is less precise. The Services Cup, on the other hand, gives much more freedom to its participants: the organizers introduce a theme such as "Services Mash-Ups" or "Cloud Computing", from which the participants demonstrate capabilities. This challenge thus creates a venue for researchers from different areas in Web Services, it also makes the comparison of systems much more subjective.

In 2004, the first workshop entirely dedicated to service composition took place co-located with ICWS in San Diego (see Table 7.4). This workshop merged into the conference as sessions into the following years.

Table 7.4 The International Workshop on Semantic Web Services and Web Process Composition (SWSWPC)

I. First International Workshop on Semantic Web Services and Web Process Composition (San Diego, USA, 2004) [62]
1. [61]: Semantic Web Service Composition: Travel Industry, QoS
2. [63]: Comparison: Academic and Industrial Research on Web Service Composition
3. [37]: Semantic Service Interoperability: Content, Conversation, Policy
4. [144]: OWL-S
5. [186]: Automated Web Service Composition: Survey
6. [183]: METEOR-S: WSDL-S, Web Service Description and Discovery
7. [40]: End-User input for Compensations (Undoing) in Transactions composed of Web Services
8. [168]: Semantics for Dynamic Service Discovery, WSMO
9. [193]: Service Discovery, Matching: OWL-S/UDDI
10. [141]: Protocols for E-Businesses: Reasoning, Aggregation, Refinement/Subsumption
11. [213]: Web Portal Discovery, Semantic Web, Ontologies, UDDI, P2P
12. [167]: METEOR-S: Annotation, Machine Learning, Weka, Classification of WSDL Descriptions

7.5 The 2010 WSC

The 2010 WSC adopts the idea of Semantic Web Services with functional and non-functional characteristics. Web Services are specified with a semantic interface description as well as quality of service aspects. The task is to find a composition of services that produces a set of queried output parameters from a set of provided input parameters which is optimal in terms of (at least) one of the two QoS dimensions "Throughput" and "Response Time".

7.5.1 Software Suite

The WSC software suite (implemented in Java) is not limited to the competition, but it is also suitable for the evaluation of general web service composition systems. This suite includes:

- A challenge generator [112, 201] which can generate composition tasks consisting of arbitrary numbers of services, semantic concepts, QoS annotations, and solutions (consisting of arbitrary numbers of services). This program creates both the challenge as well as suitable solutions (for reference).
- A verifier/checker software [112, 201] that can check whether a given WS-BPEL process specification fulfills a composition task as well as computes its QoS properties.

- Ten pre-defined composition challenges [201], ranging from small-scale to large-scale composition problems, along with example solutions obtained from three state-of-the art systems [75, 137, 138].
- A GUI which can communicate which a composer via a SOAP-based Web Service Interface [153].
- A skeleton implementation of a composition system in Java including an example competition system.
- A full specification and documentation of all formats, protocols, and processes involved in the above.

The composer software is placed on the server side of the suite and started with a bootstrap procedure. First, the system is provided with the locations of the service descriptions. The WSDL file contains a set $R.W$ of semantically annotated services w along with annotations $w.T_I$ and $w.T_O$ of their respective input- and output parameters (see Sect. 7.2.3). Every service has an arbitrary number of parameters. The annotation with semantic individuals will not only be used for message parts, but for whole message structures specified with XSD. These structures can consist of simple elements, SOAP-Arrays [153], Lists, Structures, and Enumerations. The number of services ranged from 500 to 20000 in the ten challenge tasks provided.

In addition to the WSDL file, the addresses of the OWL file and the WSLA data are also provided during the bootstrapping process. The OWL file contains the taxonomy of concepts, in other words, holds the type subsumption relationships $R.subs$. The 2010 WSC features ontologies with between 5000 and 100000. Each WSLA file contains the QoS description of a Web Service as outlined in Sect. 7.2.4. During the

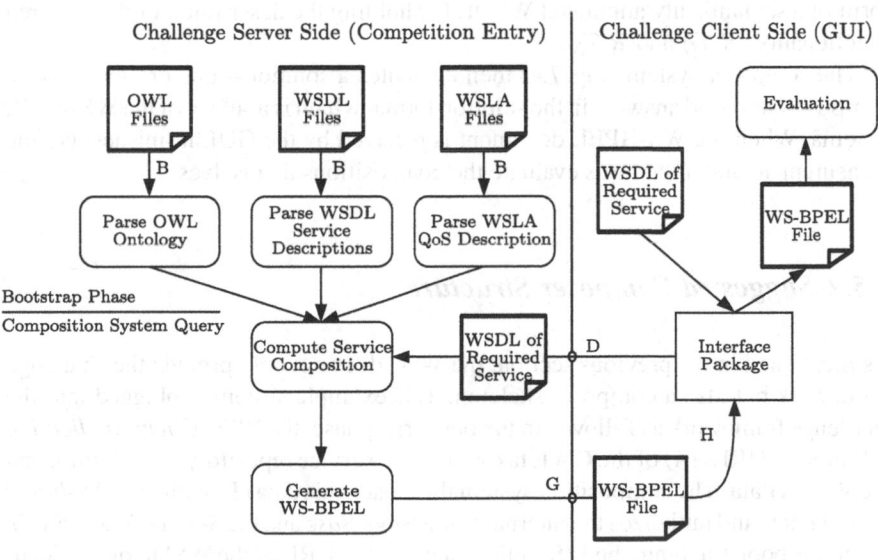

Fig. 7.3 Overview on the WSC system

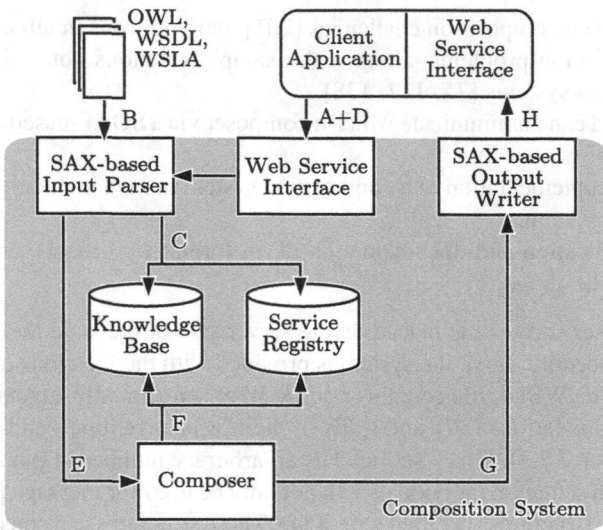

Fig. 7.4 The blueprint of the example composition system

bootstrapping process—sketched in the upper part of Fig. 7.3—the composers load the relevant information from these files.

The composition task will then be sent to the composer via a client-side GUI. After the bootstrapping on the server side is finished, the GUI queries the composition system with the challenge problem definition. The problem definition is provided in form of a semantically annotated WSDL file holding the description of the required functionality ($R.T_G$ and $R.T_N$).

The composer system (Fig. 7.4) then computes a solution—one or more service compositions—and answers in the solution format which is a subset of the WS-BPEL schema. When the WS-BPEL document is received by the GUI, it finishes its time measurement and afterwards evaluate the compositions themselves.

7.5.2 Suggested Composer Structure

As mentioned in the previous section, the WSC does not only provide the challenge framework but also a composer skeleton. This example system is plugged into the challenge framework as follows. In the bootstrap phase, the WSC *Client Application* submits the URLs *(A)* of the OWL taxonomy, the service repository WSDL files, and the WSLA data. The composition system then loads this data *(B)* with the *SAX-based Input Parser* and initializes the internal *Knowledge Base* and the *Service Registry (C)*. After this bootstrapping, the WSC client submits the URL of the WSDL query document *(D)*. Starting from this point, the parser loads the information to the *Composer*

(E) which computes a solution *(F)*. The solutions are passed to the *SAX-based Output Writer (G)*. The client UI offers an internal Web Service as a callback interface (which is necessary to avoid communication timeouts). The composition system calls this callback Web Service in order to stream the composition result to the *Client Application (H)*. The evaluation of the result is done with the verifier/checker software.

7.6 WSC-Based Survey of Semantic Web Service Composition Techniques

As can be seen in Table 7.1, a wide variety of approaches to semantic web service composition have been applied and tested within the framework of the WSC. They can roughly be divided into the following categories:

7.6.1 Uninformed Search

Uninformed search algorithms [190] exhaustively search the space possible solutions until a valid composition is found. Here, depth-first search [33, 110, 209], breadth-first search [207, 208, 219], depth-limited search [98, 140], iterative deepening depth-first search [48, 49, 217], and bi-directional searches [185] are most commonly applied in Web Service Composition. In general, these methods implement the composition task as a graph search problem. Usually, the search is conducted backwards. Initially, the set N of needed parameters, i.e., the parameters required as output of the composition, is defined as:

$$N = R.T_N \tag{7.4}$$

Then, the set of promising services, services which can produce at least one of the needed parameters as output, is computed as:

$$P = \{w : (w \in R.W) \land \exists (t_o \in N) \land (t_o \in subs^\star(w.T_O))\} \tag{7.5}$$

According to the search pattern applied, e.g., depth-first search, breadth-first search, interative deepening depth-first search etc., service w is expanded, i.e., added to the composition and the set N of needed parameters is modified as follows:

$$N' = N \cap subs^\star(w.T_O) \cup \{t_i : (t_i \in w.t_i) \land (t_i \notin subs^\star(R.T_G))\} \tag{7.6}$$

At the end of this process, all parameters which can be covered by the outputs of the service no longer require additional processes, i.e., are not members of the new version N' of the set N. At this point, the input parameters of the service which are not provided by $R.T_G$ now become members of N' and are processed in the same manner as the wanted output parameters.

Breadth-first search methods first expends all services of the same depth before transitioning to another level. Depth-first search and its derived methods always expand the most recently discovered (unexpanded) service. This process is repeated iteratively until all services in the composition can be executed, i.e., until $N = \emptyset$. Uninformed algorithms therefore do not make use of any priority or heuristic information. For larger composition or problems with many alternative services that can produce required concepts, the runtime of these methods quickly increases and they become infeasible [202, 203].

7.6.2 Informed/Heuristic Search

Heuristic search methods, such as greedy search [20, 23, 48, 103, 184, 220] and A* [162, 166] are usually applied in a way similar to the uninformed search methods. These approaches initially find services w able to produce the wanted, user-specified composition output. They then traverse backwards in order to find services w' that can produce the inputs needed for w. However, while uninformed searches process the services in the order in which they are discovered, informed methods incorporate heuristics into their decision about which service should be expanded next. A common heuristic is to give priority to services that contain the largest number of parameters that may lead to the deletion of the most needed concepts or which lead to the fewest new needed concepts. The utilization of such heuristics can accelerate the search process by several orders of magnitude [202, 203].

7.6.3 Techniques from AI and Planning

A more high-level point of view is to consider Web Service Composition as a planning problem [158, 163, 164, 182, 208]. Partial order planning [77] and metric planning [23] are two leading techniques for planning. The partial order planning approach initially creates set of *actions* (which represent subsets of the overall composition solution) and a *partial order* of these actions. A metric planning approach creates a set of *states* defined by a set of propositional variables (a triple of propositions create an action). The assignment of numeric values for these variables allows an overall plan to be valuated based on a set of actions. AI planning methods require the translation of the composition problem into a representation which can be processed by a planning software. The advantage of this approach is that planners incorporate efficient and optimized algorithms. The drawback is that they cannot utilize knowledge like the web service composition-specific heuristics mentioned before. The leading approaches to web service composition use heuristic approaches to prune the search space prior to executing the planning algorithms. Strategies for increased performance would include removing web services with duplicative outputs or limit the expansion of planning graphs immediately after a proposition layer contains the necessary goal propositions.

7.6.4 Metaheuristic and Centralized Approaches

Metaheuristics [83, 152, 200] are randomized optimization methods which try to find solutions which are optimal according to one or multiple objective functions. They are similar to heuristic search algorithms in that they employ functions which evaluate and rate candidate solutions according to their utility. Different from the algorithms discussed in Sect. 7.6.2, however, they do not construct their solutions in a strictly iterative way.

A good example in the domain of Web Service Composition is the use of evolutionary algorithms (EAs) by [49, 202–204]. EAs are population-based metaheuristics which, in a cycle, refine a set (the population) of candidate solutions. [203] first create a set of random initial compositions. Each composition is evaluated with a heuristic. In a randomized selection step, the best candidate solutions are chosen for further extension with a highest probability. Each composition then is either randomly mutated (by, e.g., expanding one of their services in order to satisfy its input parameters) or combined with another composition. After this reproduction step, the next cycle (generation) of the EA begins.

Such metaheuristics tend to be one order of magnitude slower than greedy search in the semantic composition problem [202, 203]. For QoS-based composition, however, they may be the most attractive approaches.

Dynamic Programming [99, 138, 158] is an approach which divides a problem into smaller sub-problems, solves these problems, and combines their solutions to a final result [36, 131]. These approaches are quite similar to divide and conquer strategies. Dynamic Programming can be used as programming paradigm to reduce the runtime of uninformed search significantly and reach the effectiveness of heuristic search methods [158].

Similar to metaheuristics, Integer (Linear) Programming (ILP) [72, 99, 212] can be used to treat the composition problem as a constrained optimization task with linear objective function(s). Here, a composition is represented as a vector of integer values. There exists a variety of highly-efficient algorithms for ILP [34].

7.6.5 Multi-Agent and Decentralized Approaches

So far, all approaches discussed assume the existence of one central repository and one central computer executing the algorithm. Multi-agent systems, in contrast, are decentralized by nature. Agents can synthesize compositions via cooperation in parallel [59, 60, 86]. Decentralized systems can more effectively adapt to (dynamic) distributed environments where services enter and exit the system unpredictably, can exploit the geographic distributions of computing resources, and are likely to scale better. Available and high capacity systems can be used to execute search algorithms, on-demand. However, decentralized approaches do not outperform centralized heuristic search approaches if the system is centralized and a single computer performs the composition.

7.7 Discussion

In this article, we presented a review on the Web Service Challenge, a competition that has had significant impact in the evolution of Service Oriented Architectures. We compared this challenge with related competitions and provided a survey of the works submitted to all competitions, in tabular and textual form.

The Web Service Challenge created a research community for automated semantic service composition and implementations of fast performing composition engines. After 2007, the focus of the challenge gradually changed from a solely scientific service indexing competition to a comprehensive and practice-oriented solution for Service-oriented Architectures.

As of 2009, it fosters the implementation of composers in a way that could directly be reused in an actual SOA. It now solely adopts standardized data formats such as WS-BPEL, WSDL, OWL, and WSLA. Its tasks are already highly practical, requiring the compositions to fulfill both functional and non-functional constraints.

References

1. Second IEEE International Conference on Engineering of Complex Computer Systems (ICECCS'96), IEEE (1996)
2. Eleventh International Conference on World Wide (WWW'02), ACM (2002)
3. IEEE International Conference on E-Technology, E-Commerce, and E-Service (IEEE'05), IEEE (2005)
4. IEEE International Conference on Web Services: Bridge the Gap between Business Services and IT Services (ICWS'05), IEEE (2005)
5. Web Service Challenge at ICEBE'05 (2005)
6. First Workshop of the Semantic Web Service Challenge: Challenge on Automating Web Services Mediation, Choreography and Discovery, 2006. The Digital Enterprise Research Institute (DERI), Stanford (2006). http://sws-challenge.org/wiki/index.php/Workshop_Stanford
7. IEEE International Conference on Web Services (ICWS'06), IEEE (2006)
8. Second Workshop of the Semantic Web Service Challenge: Challenge on Automating Web Services Mediation, Choreography and Discovery, 2006. DERI, Standford (2006). http://sws-challenge.org/wiki/index.php/Workshop_Budva
9. Third Workshop of the Semantic Web Service Challenge: Challenge on Automating Web Services Mediation, Choreography and Discovery, 2006. DERI, Standford (2006). http://sws-challenge.org/wiki/index.php/Workshop_Athens

10. Kweb, SWS Challenge Workshop, 2007. Semantic Technology Institute Innsbruck, Innsbruck (2007). http://sws-challenge.org/wiki/index.php/Workshop_Innsbruck

11. IEEE Joint Conference on E-Commerce Technology (9th CEC) and Enterprise Computing, E-Commerce and E-Services (4th EEE) (CEC/EEE'07), IEEE (2007)

12. Second IEEE International Services Computing Contest (SCContest'07), IEEE (2007)

13. IEEE Joint Conference on E-Commerce Technology (10th CEC) and Enterprise Computing, E-Commerce and E-Services (5th EEE) (CEC/EEE'08), IEEE (2008)

14. Seventh Semantic Web Services Challenge Workshop (SWSC'08). Springer, Berlin (2008). http://sws-challenge.org/wiki/index.php/Workshop_Karlsruhe

15. Third IEEE International Services Computing Contest, IEEE (2008)

16. SERVICES Cup'09, IEEE (2009)

17. IEEE International Conference on Service-Oriented Computing and Applications (SOCA'10), IEEE (2010)

18. SERVICES Cup'10 (2010)

19. AbuJarour, M., Craculeac, M., Menge, F., Vogel, T., Schwarz, J.: Posr: a comprehensive system for aggregating and using web services. In [16], pp. 139–146 (2009)

20. Aiello, M., Platzer, C., Rosenberg, F., Tran, H., Vasko, M., Dustdar, S.: Web service indexing for efficient retrieval and composition. In [205], pp. 424–426 (2006)

21. Aiello, M., van Benthem, N., el Khoury, E.: Visualizing compositions of services from large repositories. In [13], pp. 359–362 (2008)

22. Aiello, M, el Khoury, E., Lazovik, A., Ratelband, P.: Optimal QoS-aware web service composition. In [95], pp 491–494 (2009)

23. Akkiraju, R., Srivastava, B., Ivan, A., Goodwin, R., Syeda-Mahmood, T.: Semantic matching to achieve web service discovery and composition. In [205], pp. 445–447 (2006)

24. Andrews, T., Curbera, F., Dholakia, H., Goland, Y., Klein, J., Leymann, F., Liu, K., Roller, D., Smith, D., Thatte, S., Trickovic, I., Weerawarana, S.: BPEL4WS, business process execution language for web services version 1.1. (2003). http://www.ibm.com/developerworks/library/specification/ws-bpel/

25. Ariga, R.K.R., Akula, K., Gujjala, S.R., Karim, M., Ramesh, S., Zhang, J.: iNIU a services portal for NIU students. In [15], pp. 144–151 (2008)

26. Asuncion, C.H., Quartel, D.A.C., Pokraev, S.: Applying goal-oriented and model-driven approaches to solve the payment problem scenario. In [174] (2009)

27. Aversano, L., di Penta, M., Taneja, K.: A genetic programming approach to support the design of service compositions. Int. J. Comput. Syst. Sci. Eng. (CSSE) 21(4), 247–254 (2006)

28. Bäck, T.: Evolutionary Algorithms in Theory and Practice: Evolution Strategies, Evolutionary Programming, Genetic Algorithms. Oxford University Press, Oxford (1996)

29. Bäck, T., Fogel, D.B., Michalewicz, Z. (eds.): Handbook of Evolutionary Computation. Oxford University Press, Oxford (1997)

30. Bansal, A., Bansal, S., Blake, M.B., Bleul, S., Weise, T.: Overview of the web services challenge (WSC): discovery and composition of semantic web services. In: Blake, M.B., Cabral, L., König-Ries, B., Küster, U., Martin, D. (eds.) Semantic Web Services: Advancement Through Evaluation. Springer, Heidelberg (2012)

31. Bansal, A., Blake, M.B., Kona, S., Bleul, S., Weise, T., Jäger, M.C.: WSC-08: Continuing the web service challenge. In [13], pp. 351–354 (2008)

32. Barnickel, N., Weinand, R., Fluegge, M.: Semantic system integration: incorporating rule based semantic bridges into BPEL processes. In [82] (2008)

33. Bartalos, P., Bieliková, M.: Semantic web service composition framework based on parallel processing. In [95], pp. 495–498 (2009)

34. Beasley, J.E. (ed.): Advances in Linear and Integer Programming. Oxford University Press, Oxford (1996)

35. Bechhofer, S., van Harmelen, F., Hendler, J., Horrocks, I., McGuinness, D.L., Patel-Schneider, P.F., Stein, L.A.: OWL web ontology language reference. In: W3C recommendation, W3C (2004). http://www.w3.org/TR/2004/REC-owl-ref-20040210/

36. Bellman, R.E.: Dynamic Programming Dover Books on Mathematics. Princeton University Press, Princeton (1957)
37. Benatallah, B., Nezhad, H.M.: Interoperability in semantic web services. In [62], pp. 22–25 (2004)
38. Bharadwaj, R., Mukhopadhyay, S., Padh, N.: Service composition in a secure agent-based architecture. In [3], pp. 787–790 (2005)
39. Bieberstein, N., Bose, S., Fiammante, M., Jones, K., Shah, R.: Service-Oriented Architecture (SOA) Compass: Business Value, Planning, and Enterprise Roadmap. DeveloperWorks. Pearson Education, Indianapolis (2005)
40. Biswas, D.: Compensation in the world of web services composition. In [62], pp. 69–80 (2004)
41. Blake, M.B., Tsui, K.C., Wombacher, A.: The EEE-05 challenge: a new web service discovery and composition competition. In [3], pp. 780–783 (2005)
42. Blake, M.B., Cheung, W.K., Jäger, M.C., Wombacher, A.: WSC-06: The web service challenge. In [205], pp. 505–508 (2006)
43. Blake, M.B., Cheung, W.K., Jäger, M.C., Wombacher, A.: WSC-07: evolving the web service challenge. In [11], pp. 505–508 (2007)
44. Blake, M.B., Petrie, C.J., Roman, D.: Workshop on service composition & SWS challenge (SerComp & SWS challenge 2007). In [133], pp. xxi–xxii (2007)
45. Blake, M.B., Weise, T., Bleul, S.: WSC-2010: web services composition and evaluation. In [17] (2010)
46. Bleul, S., Weise, T.: An ontology for quality-aware service discovery. In [222], vol. RC23821 (2005)
47. Bleul, S., Weise, T., Geihs, K.: An ontology for quality-aware service discovery. Int. J. Comput. Syst. Sci. Eng. (CSSE) 21(4), 227–234 (2006)
48. Bleul, S., Weise, T., Geihs, K.: Large-scale service composition in semantic service discovery. In [205], pp. 427–429 (2006)
49. Bleul, S., Weise, T., Geihs, K.: Making a fast semantic service composition system faster. In [11], pp. 517–520 (2007)
50. Bleul, S., Weise, T., Geihs, K.: The web service challenge: a review on semantic web service composition. In: Wagner, M., Hogrefe, D., Geihs, K., David, K. (eds.) Service-Oriented Computing (SOC'2009), vol. 17. European Association of Software, Science and Technology (2009)
51. Booth, D., Liu, C.K.: Web services description language (WSDL) version 2.0 part 0: primer. In: W3C Recommendation, W3C (2007). http://www.w3.org/TR/2007/REC-wsdl20-primer-20070626
52. Bourcier, J., Chazalet, A., Desertot, M., Escoffier, C., Marin, C.: A dynamic-SOA home control gateway. In [66], pp. 463–470 (2006)
53. Brambilla, M., Celino, I., Ceri, S., Cerizza, D., Della Valle, E., Facca, F.M., Tziviskou, C.: Improvements and future perspectives on web engineering methods for automating web services mediation, choreography and discovery. In [9] (2006)
54. Brambilla, M., Ceri, S., Cerizza, D., Della Valle, E., Facca, F.M., Fraternali, P., Tziviskou, C., Web modeling-based approach to automating web services mediation, choreography and discovery. In [6] (2006)
55. Brambilla, M., Ceri, S., Cerizza, D., Della Valle, E., Facca, F.M., Tziviskou, C.: Coping with requirements changes: SWS-challenge phase II. In [8] (2006)
56. Brambilla, M., Celino, I., Ceri, S., Cerizza, D., Della Valle, E., Facca, F.M., Turati, A., Tziviskou, C.: WebML and glue: an integrated discovery approach for the SWS challenge. In [10] (2007)
57. Brambilla, M., Ceri, S., Facca, F.M., Tziviskou, C., Celino, I., Cerizza, D., Della Valle, E., Turati, A.: WebML and glue: an integrated discovery approach for the SWS challenge. In [133], pp 148–151 (2007)
58. Bray, T., Paoli, J., Sperberg-McQueen, C.M., Maler, E., Yergeau, F.: Extensible markup language (XML) 1.0, 4th edn. In: W3C Recommendation, W3C (2007). http://www.w3.org/TR/2006/REC-xml-20060816

59. Buhler, P.A., Thomas, R.W.: Experiences building a standards-based service description repository. In [13], pp. 343–346 (2008)
60. Buhler, P.A., Greenwood, D., Weichhart, G.: A multiagent web service composition engine, revisited. In [11], pp. 529–532 (2007)
61. Cardoso, J., Sheth, A.P.: Introduction to semantic web services and web process composition. In [62], pp. 1–13 (2004)
62. Cardoso, J., Sheth, A.P. (eds.): Revised Selected Papers from the First International Workshop on Semantic Web Services and Web Process Composition (SWSWPC'04). Springer, Berlin (2004)
63. Cardoso, J., Miller, J.A., Su, J., Pollock, J.: Academic and industrial research: do their approaches differ in adding semantics to web services? In [62] (2004)
64. Cardoso, J., Cordeiro, J., Filipe, J. (eds.): Nineth International Conference on Enterprise Information Systems (ICEIS'07), vol. SAIC. Institute for Systems and Technologies of Information Control and Communication (INSTICC) Press, Miami (2007)
65. Carenini, A., Cerizza, D., Comerio, M., Della Valle, E., De Paoli, F., Maurino, A., Palmonari, M., Sassi, M., Turati, A.: Semantic web service discovery and selection: a test bed scenario. In [82] (2008)
66. Chen, Z., Shoniregun, C.A., You, Y. (eds.): First IEEE international services computing contest (SCContest'06), IEEE (2006). http://iscc.servicescomputing.org/2006/
67. Chodos, D., Stroulia, E.: Second life gift registry: bringing retail web applications into the metaverse. In [15], pp. 199–206 (2008)
68. Chopra, A.K., Desai, N., Singh, M.P.: Business processes interoperation using OWL-P. In [6] (2006)
69. Cimpian, E., Kotinurmi, P., Mocan, A., Moran, M., Vitvar, T., Zaremba, M.: Dynamic RosettaNet integration on the semantic web services. In [6] (2006)
70. Coello Coello, C.A., Lamont, G.B., van Veldhuizen, D.A.: Evolutionary Algorithms for Solving Multi-Objective Problems. Springer, New York (2002)
71. Colasuonno, F., Coppi, S., Ragone, A., Scorcia, L.L.: jUDDI+: a semantic web services registry enabling semantic discovery and composition. In [205], pp. 442–444 (2006)
72. Cui, L.Y., Kumara, S.R.T., Yoo, J.J., Cavdur, F.: Large-scale network decomposition and mathematical programming based web service composition. In [95], pp. 511–514 (2009)
73. Dai, W., Moynihan, P., Gou, J., Zou, P., Yang, X., Chen, T., Wan, X.: Services oriented knowledge-based supply chain application. In [12], pp. 660–667 (2007)
74. de Mello, E.R., Parastatidis, S., Reinecke, P., Smith, C., van Moorsel, A., Webber, J.: Secure and provable service support for human-intensive real-estate processes. In [66], pp. 495–504 (2006)
75. Degeler, V., Georgievski, I., Lazovik, A., Aiello, M.: Concept mapping for faster QoS-aware web service composition. In [17] (2010)
76. Ding, W., Cheng, J., Qi, K., Li, Y., Zhao, Z., Fang, J.: A domain-specific query language for information services mash-up. In [15], pp. 113–119 (2008)
77. Dorn, J., Hrastnik, P., Rainer, A.: Web service discovery and composition with MOVE. In [3], pp. 791–792 (2005)
78. Dorn, J., Rainer, A., Hrastnik, P.: Toward semantic composition of web services with MOVE. In [205], pp. 437–438 (2006)
79. Erl, T.: Service-Oriented Architecture: Concepts, Technology, and Design. Prentice Hall International Inc Professional Technical References, Upper Saddle River (2006)
80. Fallside, D.C., Walmsley, P.: XML schema part 0: primer, 2nd edn. In: W3C Recommendation, W3C (2004). http://www.w3.org/TR/2004/REC-xmlschema-0-20041028/
81. Fensel, D., Giunchiglia, F., McGuinness, D.L., Williams, M. (eds.): Eighth International Conference on Knowledge Representation and Reasoning (KR'02). Morgan Kaufmann Publishers (2002)
82. García-Castro, R., Gómez-Pérez, A., Petrie, C.J., Della Valle, E., Küster, U., Zaremba, M., Shafiq, O. (eds.): Sixth International Workshop on Evaluation of Ontology-Based Tools and the Semantic Web Service Challenge (EON-SWSC'08), CEUR Workshop Proceedings, vol.

359. RWTH Aachen, Aachen (2008). http://sunsite.informatik.rwth-aachen.de/Publications/
     CEUR-WS/Vol-359/
83. Glover, F., Kochenberger, G.A. (eds.): Handbook of Metaheuristics. Kluwer Academic,
     Boston (2003)
84. Glover, F., Taillard, É.D., de Werra, D.: A user's guide to tabu search. Ann. Oper. Res. **41**(1),
     3–28 (1993)
85. Gomadam, K., Lathem, J., Miller, J.A., Nagarajan, M., Pennington, C., Sheth, A.P., Verma,
     K., Wu, Z.: Semantic web services challenge 2006-phase I. In [6] (2006)
86. Greenwood, D., Buhler, P.A., Reitbauer, A.: Web service discovery and composition using
     the web service integration gateway. In [3], pp. 789–790 (2005)
87. Gschwind, T., Pautasso, C. (eds.): Second Workshop on Emerging Web Services Technology
     (WEWST'07). Birkhäuser (2007)
88. Gu, Z., Xu, B., Li, J.: Inheritance-aware document-driven service composition. In [11], pp.
     513–516 (2007)
89. Habich, D., Richly, S., Rümpel, A., Bücke, W., Preißler, S.: Open service process platform
     2.0. In [15], pp. 152–159 (2008)
90. Hallal, H.H., Dury, A., Petrenko, A.: Web-FIM: automated framework for the inference of
     business software models. In [16], pp. 130–138 (2009)
91. Harzallah, Y., Michel, V., Liu, Q., Wainer, G.: Distributed simulation and web map mash-up
     for forest fire spread. In [15], pp. 176–183 (2008)
92. Haselwanter, T., Kotinurmi, P., Moran, M., Vitvar, T., Zaremba, M.: Dynamic B2B integration
     on the semantic web services: SWS challenge phase 2. In [8] (2006)
93. Hertz, A., Taillard, É.D., de Werra, D.: A tutorial on tabu search. In [176], pp. 13–24 (1995)
94. Hitzler, P., Krötzsch, M., Parsia, B., Patel-Schneider, P.F., Rudolph, G.: OWL 2 web ontol-
     ogy language primer. In: W3C Recommendation, W3C (2009). http://www.w3.org/TR/2009/
     REC-owl2-primer-20091027/
95. Hofreiter, B. (ed.): Eleventh IEEE Conference on Commerce and Enterprise Computing
     (CEC'09), IEEE (2009)
96. Hoyer, V., Gilles, F., Janner, T., Stanoevska-Slabeva, K.: SAP research roof top market place:
     putting a face on service-oriented architectures. In [16], pp. 107–114 (2009)
97. Hrastnik, P., Rainer, A.: Web service discovery and composition for virtual enterprises. Int.
     J. Web Serv. Res. (IJWSR) **4**(1), 23–29 (2007)
98. Huang, S., Wang, X., Zhou, A.: Efficient web service composition based on syntactical match-
     ing. In [3], pp. 782–783 (2005)
99. Huang, Z., Jiang, W., Hu, S., Liu, Z.: Effective pruning algorithm for QoS-aware service
     composition. In [95], pp. 519–522 (2009)
100. Jacob, M., Kuscher, A., Plauth, M., Thiele, C.: Automated data augmentation services using
     text mining, data cleansing and web crawling techniques. In [15], pp. 136–143 (2008)
101. Jeyaverasingam, S., Yan, Y.: A mash up home library management system. In [15], pp. 160–
     167 (2008)
102. Jordan, D., Evdemon, J., Alves, A., Arkin, A., Askary, S., Barreto, C., Bloch, B., Curbera,
     F., Ford, M., Goland, Y., Guízar, A., Kartha, N., Liu, C.K., Khalaf, R., König, D., Marin, M.,
     Mehta, V., Thatte, S., van der Rijn, D., Yendluri, P., Yiu, A.: Web Services Business Process
     Execution Language Version 2.0: OASIS Standard, OASIS (2007). http://docs.oasis-open.
     org/wsbpel/2.0/wsbpel-v2.0.pdf
103. Juszcyk, L., Michlmayer, A., Platzer, C.: Large scale web service discovery and composition
     using high performance in-memory indexing. In [11], pp. 509–512 (2007)
104. Kart, F., Shen, Z., Gerede, C.E.: The MIDAS system: a service oriented architecture for
     automated supply chain management. In [66], pp. 487–494 (2006)
105. Kart, F., Miao, G., Moser, L.E., Melliar-Smith, P.M.: A distributed e-healthcare system based
     on the service oriented architecture. In [12], pp. 652–659 (2007)
106. Kavantzas, N., Burdett, D., Ritzinger, G., Fletcher, T., Lafon, Y.: Web services choreography
     description language version 1.0: W3C candidate recommendation. In: W3C Recommenda-
     tion, W3C (2005). http://www.w3.org/TR/2005/CR-ws-cdl-10-20051109/

107. Keller, A., Ludwig, H.: The WSLA framework: specifying and monitoring service level agreements for web services. J. Netw. Syst. Manag. **11**(1), 57–81 (2003)
108. Kirkpatrick, S., Gelatt Jr, C.D.: Optimization by simulated annealing. Sci. Mag. **220**(4598), 671–680 (1983)
109. Ko, R.K.L., Jusuf, A., Lee, S.G.S.: Genesis: dynamic collaborative business process formulation based on business goals and criteria. In [16], pp. 123–129 (2009)
110. Kona, S., Bansal, A., Gupta, G., Hite, T.D.: Web service discovery and composition using USDL. In [205], pp. 430–432 (2006)
111. Kona, S., Bansal, A., Gupta, G., Hite, T.D.: Semantics-based web service composition engine. In [11], pp. 521–524 (2007)
112. Kona, S., Bansal, A., Blake, M.B., Bleul, S., Weise, T.: WSC-2009: a quality of service-oriented web services challenge. In [95], pp. 487–490 (2009)
113. Kubczak, C., Margaria, T., Steffen, B.: Semantic web services challenge 2006: an approach to mediation and discovery with jABC and miAamic. In [9] (2006)
114. Kubczak, C., Margaria, T., Steffen, B.: Semantic web services challenge 2006: the jABC approach to mediation and choreography. In [8] (2006)
115. Kubczak, C., Nagel, R., Margaria, T., Steffen, B.: The jABC approach to mediation and choreography. In [6] (2006)
116. Kubczak, C., Margaria, T., Steffen, B., Naujokat, S.: Service-oriented mediation with jETI/jABC: verification and export. In [133], pp. 144–147 (2007)
117. Kubczak, C., Margaria, T., Winkler, C., Steffen, B.: Semantic web services challenge 2007: an approach to discovery with miAamics and jABC. In [10] (2007)
118. Kubczak, C., Winkler, C., Margaria, T., Steffen, B.: an approach to discovery with miAamics and jABC. In [133], pp. 157–160 (2007)
119. Kubczak, C., Margaria, T., Kaiser, M., Lemcke, J., Knuth, B.: Abductive synthesis of the mediator scenario with jABC and GEM. In [82] (2008)
120. Küster, U., König-Ries, B.: Discovery and mediation using the DIANE service description. In [9] (2006)
121. Küster, U., König-Ries, B.: Semantic mediation between business partners: a SWS-challenge solution using DIANE service descriptions. In [133], pp. 139–143 (2007)
122. Küster, U., König-Ries, B.: Semantic service discovery with DIANE service descriptions. In [133], pp. 152–156 (2007)
123. Küster, U., König-Ries, B.: Service discovery using DIANE service descriptions: a solution to the SWS-challenge discovery scenarios. In [10] (2007)
124. Küster, U., Klein, C., König-Ries, B.: Discovery and mediation using the DIANE service description. In [6] (2006)
125. Küster, U., König-Ries, B., Klein, M.: Discovery and mediation using DIANE service descriptions. In [8] (2006)
126. Küster, U., König-Ries, B., Klein, M., Stern, M.: DIANE: a matchmaking-centered framework for automated service discovery, composition, binding and invocation. Int. J. Electron. Commer. (IJEC) **12**(2), 41–68 (2007)
127. Küster, U., Lausen, H., König-Ries, B.: Evaluation of semantic service discovery: a survey and directions for future research. In [87], pp. 41–58 (2007)
128. Küster, U., Turati, A., Zaremba, M., König-Ries, B., Cerizza, D., Della Valle, E., Brambilla, M., Ceri, S., Facca, F.M., Tzviskou, C.: Service discovery with SWE-ET and DIANE: a comparative evaluation by means of solutions to a common scenario. In [64], pp. 430–437 (2007)
129. Lawler, J.P., Howell-Barber, H.: Service-Oriented Architecture: SOA Strategy, Methodology, and Technology. Auerbach Publications, New York (2007)
130. Lemcke, J., Kaiser, M., Kubczak, C., Margaria, T., Knuth, B.: Advances in Solving the Mediator Scenario with jABC and jABC/GEM. In [14, 171], Stanford Logic Group, Computer Science Department, Stanford University, pp. 89–102 (2008)
131. Lew, A., Mauch, H.: Dynamic Programming: A Computational Tool. Springer, Berlin (2006)

132. Li, W., Svärd, P.: REST-based SOA application in the cloud: a text correction service case study. In [18], pp. 84–90 (2010)
133. Li, Y., Raghavan, V.V. (eds.): 2007 IEEE/WIC/ACM International Conferences on Web Intelligence and Intelligent Agent Technology Workshops (WI/IAT Workshops'07), IEEE (2007)
134. Liang, J., Zhang, Y., Lu, J., Sathulla, S., Chen, D., Wang, S.: A rental advising system based on service oriented architecture. In [15], pp. 184–190 (2008)
135. Lorenzoli, D., Mussino, S., Pezzé, M., Sichel, A., Tosi, D., Schilling, D.: A SOA based self-adaptive personal mobility manager. In [66], pp. 479–486 (2006)
136. Ludwig, H., Keller, A., Dan, A., King, R.P., Franck, R.: Web Service Level Agreement (WSLA) Language Specification. IBM, New York (2003). http://www.research.ibm.com/wsla/WSLASpecV1-20030128.pdf
137. Luo, S., Xu, B., Yan, Y.: An accumulated-QoS-first search approach for semantic web service composition. In [17] (2010)
138. Ma, H., Jiang, W., Hu, S., Huang, Z., Liu, Z.: Two-phase graph search algorithm for QoS-aware automatic service composition. In [17] (2010)
139. Ma, S., Li, M., Du, W.: Service composition for GIS. In [15], pp. 168–175 (2008)
140. Makhzan, M.A., Lin, K.: Solution to a complete web service discovery and composition. In [205], pp. 455–457 (2006)
141. Mallya, A.U., Singh, M.P.: A semantic approach for designing e-business protocols. In [62], pp. 111–123 (2004)
142. Margaria, T., Winkler, C., Kubczak, C., Steffen, B., Brambilla, M., Ceri, S., Cerizza, D., Della Valle, E., Facca, F.M., Tziviskou, C.: SWS mediator with WEBML/WEBRATIO and JABC/JETI: a comparison. In [64], pp. 422–429 (2007)
143. Margaria, T., Bakera, M., Raffelt, H., Steffen, B.: Synthesizing the mediator with jABC/ABC. In [82] (2008)
144. Martin, D., Paolucci, M., McIlraith, S.A., Burstein, M., McDermott, D., McGuinness, D.L., Parsia, B., Payne, T., Sabou, M., Solanki, M., Srinivasan, N., Sycara, K.: Bringing semantics to web services: the OWL-S approach. In [62], pp. 26–42 (2004)
145. Maximilien, E.M.: Human-based semantic web services: phase 1. In [6] (2006)
146. Maximilien, E.M.: A partial solution to the semantic web services challenge problem using swashup: the ruby on rails services mashup approach. In [64], pp. 438–446 (2007)
147. McIlraith, S.A., Son, T.C.: Adapting Golog for composition of semantic web services. In [81], pp. 482–496 (2002)
148. McIlraith, S.A., Son, T.C., Zeng, H.: Semantic web services. IEEE Intell. Syst. Mag. 16(2), 46–53 (2001)
149. McIlraith, S.A., Plexousakis, D., van Harmelen, F. (eds.): Third International Semantic Web Conference (ISWC'04). Springer (2004)
150. Medjahed, B., Bouguettaya, A., Elmagarmid, A.K.: Composing web services on the semantic web. VLDB J.: Int. J. Very Large Data Bases 12(4), 333–351 (2003)
151. Menzel, M., Warschofsky, R., Thomas, I., Willems, C., Meinel, C.: The service security lab: a model-driven platform to compose and explore service security in the cloud. In [18], pp. 115–122 (2010)
152. Michalewicz, Z., Fogel, D.B.: How to Solve It: Modern Heuristics. Springer, Berlin (2004)
153. Mitra, N., Lafon, Y.: SOAP version 1.2 part 0: primer, 2nd edn. In: W3C Recommendation, W3C (2007). http://www.w3.org/TR/2007/REC-soap12-part0-20070427/
154. Moran, M., Vitvar, T., Zaremba, M.: Towards constraint-based composition with incomplete service descriptions. In [133], pp. 161–165 (2007)
155. Moran, M., Zaremba, M., Vitvar, T.: Service discovery and composition with WSMX for SWS challenge workshop IV. In [10] (2007)
156. Morse, J.N. (ed.) Fourth International Conference on Multiple Criteria Decision Making: Organizations, Multiple Agents With Multiple Criteria (MCDM'80). Springer (1980)
157. Nam, W., Kil, H., Lee, D.: Type-aware web service composition using Boolean satisfiability solver. In [13], pp. 331–334 (2008)

158. Nam, W., Kil, H., Lee, J.: QoS-driven web service composition using learning-based depth first search. In [95], pp. 507–510 (2009)
159. Narayanan, S., McIlraith, S.A.: Simulation, verification and automated composition of web services. In [2], pp. 77–88 (2002)
160. Navabpour, S., Ghoraie, L.S., Malayeri, A.A., Chen, J., Lu, J.: An intelligent traveling service based on SOA. In [15], pp. 191–198 (2008)
161. Nolte, A., Schrader, R.: A note on the finite time behaviour of simulated annealing. Math. Oper. Res. (MOR) 25(3), 476–484 (2000)
162. Oh, S., On, B., Larson, E.J., Lee, D.: BF*: web services discovery and composition as graph search problem. In [3], pp. 784–786 (2005)
163. Oh, S., Kil, H., Lee, D., Kumara, S.R.T.: Algorithms for web services discovery and composition based on syntactic and semantic service descriptions. In [205], pp. 433–435 (2006)
164. Oh, S., Yoo, J.J., Kil, H., Lee, D., Kumara, S.R.T.: Semantic web-service discovery and composition using flexible parameter matching. In [11], pp. 533–536 (2007)
165. Oh, S., Lee, D., Kumara, S.R.T.: Effective web service composition in diverse and large-scale service networks. IEEE Trans. Serv. Comput. (TSC) 1(1), 15–16 (2008)
166. Oh, S., Lee, J., Cheong, S., Lim, S., Kim, M., Lee, S., Park, J., Noh, S., Sohn, M.M.: WSPR*: web-service planner augmented with A* algorithm. In [95], pp. 515–518 (2009)
167. Oldham, N., Thomas, C., Sheth, A.P., Verma, K.: METEOR-S web service annotation framework with machine learning classification. In [62], pp. 137–146 (2004)
168. Olmedilla, D., Lara, R., Polleres, A., Lausen, H.: Trust negotiation for semantic web services. In [62], pp. 81–95 (2004)
169. Palmonari, M., Comerio, M., Carenini, A., Cerizza, D., Panziera, L.: A solution to the logistics management scenario with the GLUE2 web service discovery engine. In [174] (2009)
170. Payne, T., Tamma, V. (eds.): AAAI fall symposium on agents and the semantic web, vol. FS-05-01. AAAI Press (2005)
171. Petrie, C.J. (ed.): Semantic web services challenge workshop, LG-2009-01, Stanford Logic Group, Computer Science Department, Stanford University (2009). http://logic.stanford.edu/reports/LG-2009-01.pdf
172. Petrie, C.J., Lausen, H., Zaremba, M.: SWS challenge: first year overview. In [64], pp. 407–412 (2007). http://sws-challenge.org/wiki/index.php/Special_Session_at_ICEIS2007
173. Petrie, C.J., Margaria, T., Küster, U., Lausen, H., Zaremba, M.: SWS challenge: status, perspectives, lessons learned so far. In [64], pp. 447–452 (2007)
174. Petrie, C.J., Küster, U., Cabral, L., Facca, F.M. (eds.): Eighth Semantic Web Services Challenge Workshop (SWSC'09). DERI, Stanford (2009). http://sws-challenge.org/wiki/index.php/Workshop_ECOWS_2009
175. Petrie, C.J., Margaria, T., Lausen, H., Zaremba, M. (eds.): Semantic Web Services Challenge: Results from the First Year. Semantic Web and Beyond: Computing for Human Experience. Springer (2009)
176. Pezzella, F. (ed.): Giornate di Lavoro (Entreprise Systems: Management of Technological and Organizational Changes, "Gestione del cambiamento tecnologico ed organizzativo nei sistemi d'impresa") (AIRO'95). Associazione Italiana di Ricerca Operativa (1995)
177. Pistore, M., Traverso, P.: Automated synthesis of composite BPEL4WS web services. In [4], pp. 293–301 (2005)
178. Pokraev, S., Quartel, D.A.C., Wombacher, A.: SWS challenge. In [6] (2006)
179. Ponnekanti, S.R., Fox, A.: SWORD: a developer toolkit for web service composition. In [2] (2002)
180. Preißler, S., Habich, D., Lehnert, W.: Standing processes in service-oriented environments. In [16], pp. 115–122 (2009)
181. Quartel, D.A.C., Pokraev, S., Dirgahayu, T., Mantovaneli Pessoa, R., van Sinderen, M.: Model-driven service integration using the COSMO framework. In [14, 171], Computer Science Department, Stanford University, pp. 77–88 (2008)
182. Rainer, A., Dorn, J.: MOVE: a generic service composition framework for service oriented architectures. In [95], pp. 503–506 (2009)

183. Rajasekaran, P., Miller, J.A., Verma, K., Sheth, A.P.: Enhancing web services description and discovery to facilitate composition. In [62], pp. 55–68 (2004)
184. Raman, K., Zhang, Y., Panahi, M., Lin, K.: Customizable business process composition with query optimization. In [13], pp. 363–366 (2008)
185. Ramasamy, V.: Syntactical & semantical web services discovery and composition. In [205], pp. 439–441 (2006)
186. Rao, J., Su, X.: A survey of automated web service composition methods. In: Cardoso, J., Sheth, A.P. (eds.) Revised Selected Papers from the First International Workshop on Semantic Web Services and Web Process Composition (SWSWPC'04), pp. 43–54. Springer (2004)
187. Rao, J., Dimitrov, D., Hofmann, P., Sadeh, N.: A mixed initiative approach to semantic web service discovery and composition: SAP's guided procedures framework. In [7], pp. 401–410 (2006)
188. Richly, S., Püschel, G., Habich, D., Götz, S.: MapReduce for scalable neural nets training. In [18], pp. 99–106 (2010)
189. Rosenberg, F., Nagl, C., Dustdar, S.: Applying distributed business rules: the VIDRE approach. In [66], pp. 471–478 (2006)
190. Russell, S.J., Norvig, P.: Artificial Intelligence: A Modern Approach (AIMA). Prentice Hall, Upper Saddle River (2002)
191. Sirin, E., Parsia, B., Wu, D., Hendler, J., Nau, D.: HTN planning for web service composition using SHOP2. Web Semant.: Sci. Serv. Agents World Wide Web 1(4), 377–396 (2004)
192. Sirin, E., Parsia, B., Hendler, J.: Template-based composition of semantic web services. In [170], pp. 85–92 (2005)
193. Srinivasan, N., Paolucci, M., Sycara, K.: An efficient algorithm for OWL-S based semantic search in UDDI. In [62], pp. 96–110 (2004)
194. Starlinger, J., Leitner, F., Valencia, A., Leser, U.: SOA-based integration of text mining services. In [16], pp. 99–106 (2009)
195. Stuckenschmidt, H.: Debugging OWL ontologies: a reality check. In [82] (2008)
196. Traverso, P., Pistore, M.: Automated composition of semantic web services into executable processes. In [149], pp. 380–394 (2004)
197. Vashishtha, H., Smit, M., Stroulia, E.: Moving text analysis tools to the cloud. In [18], pp. 107–114 (2010)
198. Wang, W., Zeng, G., Zhang, D., Huang, Y., Qiu, Y., Wang, X.: An intelligent ontology and Bayesian network based semantic mashup for tourism. In [15], pp. 128–135 (2008)
199. Wei, Y., Yue, P., Dadi, U., Min, M., Hu, C., Di, L.: Active acquisition of geospatial data products in a collaborative grid environment. In [66], pp. 455–462 (2006)
200. Weise, T.: Global Optimization Algorithms: Theory and Application. self-published (2009). http://www.it-weise.de/
201. Weise, T.: Web Service Challenge 2010 (2010). http://www.it-weise.de/documents/files/W2010WSC_data.rar
202. Weise, T., Bleul, S., Geihs, K.: Web Service Composition Systems for the Web Service Challenge: A Detailed Review. Technical Report 2007, 7, Fachbereich 16: Elektrotechnik/Informatik, University of Kassel (2007)
203. Weise, T., Bleul, S., Comes, D.E., Geihs, K.: Different approaches to semantic web service composition. In: Mellouk, A., Bi, J., Ortiz, G., Chiu, D.K.W., Popescu, M. (eds.) Third International Conference on Internet and Web Applications and Services (ICIW'08), IEEE, pp. 90–96 (2008)
204. Weise, T., Bleul, S., Kirchhoff, M., Geihs, K.: Semantic web service composition for service-oriented architectures. In [13], pp. 355–358 (2008)
205. Wombacher, A., Huemer, C., Stolze, M. (eds.): IEEE Joint Conference on E-Commerce Technology and Enterprise Computing, E-Commerce and E-Services (CEC/EEE'06), IEEE (2006)
206. Wu, Z., Gomadam, K., Ranabahu, A., Sheth, A.P., Miller, J.A.: Automatic composition of semantic web services using process mediation. In [64], pp. 453–462 (2007)
207. Xu, B., Li, T., Gu, Z., Wu, G.: SWSDS: quick web service discovery and composition in SEWSIP. In [205], pp. 449–451 (2006)

208. Yan, Y., Zheng, X.: A planning graph based algorithm for semantic web service composition. In [13], pp. 339–342 (2008)
209. Yan, Y., Xu, B., Gu, Z.: Automatic service composition using AND/OR graph. In [13], pp. 335–338 (2008)
210. Yan, Y., Xu, B., Gu, Z., Luo, S.: A QoS-driven approach for semantic service composition. In [95], pp. 523–526 (2009)
211. Yao, J., Chen, S., Wang, C., Levy, D., Zic, J.: Accountability as a service for the cloud: from concept to implementation with BPEL. In [18], pp. 91–98 (2010)
212. Yoo, J.J., Kumara, S.R.T., Lee, D.: A web service composition framework using integer programming with non-functional objectives and constraints. In [13], pp. 347–350 (2008)
213. Yu, H., Mine, T., Amamiya, M.: Towards automatic discovery of web portals semantic description of web portal capabilities. In [62], pp. 124–136 (2004)
214. Zaremba, M., Vitvar, T., Moran, M., Haselwanter, T., Sirbu, A.: WSMX discovery for SWS challenge. In [9] (2006)
215. Zaremba, M., Vitvar, T., Moran, M., Brambilla, M., Ceri, S., Cerizza, D., Della Valle, E., Facca, F.M., Tziviskou, C.: Towards semantic interoperabilty: in-depth comparison of two approaches to solving semantic web service challenge mediation tasks. In [64], pp. 413–421 (2007)
216. Zaremba, M., Herold, M., Zaharia, R., Vitvar, T.: Data and process mediation support for B2B integration. In [82] (2008)
217. Zhang, J., Nie, W., Panahi, M., Chang, Y., Lin, K.: Business process composition with QoS optimization. In [95], pp. 499–502 (2009)
218. Zhang, L., van der Aalst, W., Hung, P.C.K. (eds.): IEEE International Conference on Services Computing (SCC'07), IEEE (2007)
219. Zhang, Y., Yu, T., Raman, K., Lin, K.: Strategies for efficient syntactical and semantic web services discovery and composition. In [205], pp. 452–454 (2006)
220. Zhang, Y., Raman, K., Panahi, M., Lin, K.: Heuristic-based service composition for business processes with branching and merging. In [11], pp. 525–528 (2007)
221. Zhu, P., Zhan, D., Zhu, C., Li, D., Song, T., Huang, B.: A rich internet application based on BPEL services composition for port logistics. In [15], pp. 120–127 (2008)
222. Zirpins, C., Ortiz, G., Lamersdorf, W., Emmerich, W.: Engineering Service Compositions: First International, Workshop (WESC'05) (2005)

Chapter 8
Automated Service Composition Based on Behaviors: The Roman Model

Giuseppe De Giacomo, Massimo Mecella and Fabio Patrizi

Abstract During the last years, many approaches have been proposed in order to address the issue of automated service composition. In this chapter, we discuss the so-called "Roman model", in which services are abstracted as transition systems and the objective is to obtain a composite service that preserves a desired interaction, expressed as a (virtual) target service. We will also outline its deployment in the challenging applications of smart houses, i.e., buildings pervasively equipped with sensors and actuators making their functionalities available according to the service-oriented paradigm.

8.1 Introduction

Services are software artifacts, possibly distributed and built on top of different technologies, that export a description of themselves, are accessible to external clients and communicate through a commonly known, standard interface which enables interoperability. More in general, Service Oriented Computing (SOC) is a computing paradigm whose basic elements are services, that can be used as building blocks to devise other services. A classical example of such a paradigm is provided by *Web services*, i.e., applications published over the Internet and self-described, usually built by different companies and relying on different technologies, which share a same communication protocol, namely SOAP. For instance, many online travel

G. De Giacomo · M. Mecella (✉) · F. Patrizi
Dipartimento di Ingegneria Informatica Automatica e Gestionale Antonio Ruberti,
Sapienza Università di Roma, Via Ariosto 25, 00185 Roma, Italy
e-mail: degiacomo@dis.uniroma1.it

M. Mecella
e-mail: mecella@dis.uniroma1.it

F. Patrizi
e-mail: patrizi@dis.uniroma1.it

A. Bouguettaya et al. (eds.), *Web Services Foundations*,
DOI: 10.1007/978-1-4614-7518-7_8,
© Springer Science+Business Media New York 2014

agencies integrate different Web services offered by hotels, airlines, restaurants, etc., to provide final users with a complete service, combining all functionalities of its basic components. No constraints are required over the *internal* structure of each Web service, but they are all required to be published, compliant with the same communication protocol and to export a description of their interface, so as to facilitate access and communication.

Abstracting from this example, services can be thought as generic programs, publicly available and wrapped so as to mutually interact and communicate over a common platform. As such, the SOC paradigm makes easier code re-use and extension, as, in a sense, each service is interpreted as a procedure/method in programming languages and, thus, a set of services as a sort of *programming library*. This similarity can be taken as the basis of *service composition*: as exactly as in a programming language procedures/methods are combined to produce more complex procedures/methods, so services can be combined to build more complex services.

This chapter focuses on *automated service composition*, that is, the problem of automatically combining a set of available services, so as to meet a desired specification. To this end, we start from the classical architecture for Web services. The parties typically involved include a client, that can be a service itself, the *directory*, and a set of *service providers*. The directory is a central, publicly available registry storing service descriptions which allow clients to search for some desired service; service providers are organizations, typically companies, that publish actual running services, advertised in registries. A typical session is as follows: (i) a client searches for a desired service, e.g., weather forecasting, in a directory; (ii) if the service is found, the client is redirected to the provider that deploys the service; (iii) the client contacts the desired service and interacts with it, according to its needs. This simple scenario is already sufficient to raises two classical questions in SOC: (i) *how to describe services?* (ii) *what if the desired service is not found?* The first one concerns *service modeling*, i.e., the definition of a suitable abstraction of services, able to capture aspects that can be relevant to clients; the second one raises the problem of finding a constructive alternative to the trivial answer: "the request cannot be fulfilled". As one may expect, there exist many reasonable, correct answers to them. In this work we discuss both problems. We first present a model, sometime referred to as the "Roman Model", that substantially enriches existing ones, by providing an abstraction of the *conversations* a service can carry on with clients; then, on top of this model, we describe a technique for *building* a solution that fulfills a client request by suitably combining the available services. In addition, we show that such techniques is in fact *best one can do*, in the sense of returning the most general solution, while being optimal with respect to worst-case time complexity.

8.1.1 Modeling Behaviors

In the literature, several approaches to service modeling have been proposed. Rather than actual languages widely used to describe Web services, such as WSDL, we focus on their conceptual model. A WSDL description exports a *functional* specification of a service, that is, from an abstract standpoint, the set of operations provided by the service, along with the corresponding format of messages exchanged. We can say that WSDL has an underlying *atomic* conceptual model, specified in terms of input-output requirements. For instance, a service providing stock quotes of some market can be successfully described this way, with a single operation that returns the list of quotes. However, when more complex specifications need to be exported, it shows severe limitations. For instance, let us consider the same Web service for stock quotes and assume that it provides quotations only to authenticated clients. In an input-output approach, one would describe two operations, `auth` and `quote`, as well as the respective data format necessary for interaction. Unfortunately, the input-output approach does not allow for *conversation specification*, i.e., for putting constraints on the order that operations should be executed in. A very natural constraint would be, e.g., requiring clients to authenticate before requesting quotes. Observe also that cases may exist where two services export a same set of operations but allow different execution sequences. Since this last constraint is not captured by input-output approaches, such services would appear to clients as the same. In a word, atomic conceptual models export services' *interface* but not their *behavior*.

The need for a *behavioral* description of services has been already recognized in the literature, e.g., [3], yet the community suffers from a lack of standard languages for this purpose. In this work, we present the so-called *Roman Model* (as named by [23]), originally introduced in [6], and oriented to describe all *conversations* supported by services, that includes (in its various variants) relevant features, such as nondeterminism and shared memory.

In our model, services export their behavioral features by means of a language that represents transition systems, i.e., Kripke structures whose transitions are labeled by service's operations, under the assumption that each legal run of the system corresponds to a conversation supported by the service. To clarify this, consider Fig. 8.1. The former is a graphical representation of an input–output description of the stock quote service with authentication, which provides information about operations that can be requested; the latter is a behavioral representation of the same service, providing more information: indeed, it tells clients that they (i) must authenticate before requesting a `quote` operation and, then, (ii) may request any number of quotes. Of course, more sophisticated examples do exist, where several operations, even nondeterministic, can be executed in a state, with nondeterminism modeling partial knowledge about service's internal logic. Also, there are settings relying on the same approach, where operations have parameters and are able to exchange data with other clients and even with an underlying database (cf. [5]).

Fig. 8.1 Service descriptions.
a Input–output. **b** Behaviors

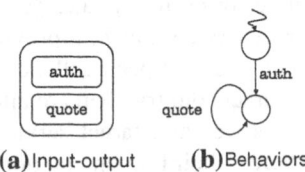

(a) Input-output   **(b)** Behaviors

A first advantage brought by such a model is its *generality* with respect to service integration, in the sense that it is abstract enough to serve as conceptual model for several classes of scenarios. As an example, it can be used to model Web service applications as well as multi-agent system ones. As a consequence, results obtained on this model are also relevant to areas different from SOC. Second, from the SOC viewpoint, it provides a behavioral, stateful, service representation, which allows for describing those inter-operation constraints that current languages, e.g., WSDL, do not capture. We remark the importance of such a feature in a perspective of composition automatization: indeed, composition engines are intended to replace human operators, who compose services based on their informal description, often provided in natural language, which include behavioral information. Importantly, when dealing with a behavioral model, we can look at services as high-level descriptions of software artifacts. Indeed, they are characterized by states and state transitions triggered by inputs, which, specifically, represent requested operations. This interpretation suggests, hence, to see service (possibly finite) runs as computation fragments, that can be suitably combined to generate more complex services.

8.1.2 Composing Services

Many works exist which deal with automated composition of services (see Sect. 8.2 for a survey). Our problem can be informally stated as follows:

> Consider a set of available services, a.k.a. *community*, and an additional *target service*, all exporting their conversational behaviors. Is it possible to coordinate the available services so to support, at execution time, all conversations supported by the target service?

In other words, the problem amounts to realize a (virtual) target service, by resorting only to (actual) available services. Obviously, how services are combined in the practice depends on the exported behavioral models. To see how this can be done, consider the following example.

Example 8.1 Figure 8.2 shows a service composition problem instance in the Roman Model, which includes two available services, represented in subfigures (a) and (b), and a target one, in subfigure (c). The one in subfigure (a), say S_a, provides login/logout capabilities, allowing a client to be authenticated and to close an authenticated session, whereas the one in subfigure (b), say S_b, provides market stock quotes from all over the world. Clients willing to interact with S_b are, first, required to input the market country of their interest and, then, are allowed to request either stock quotes or currency rates (versus, e.g., euro and dollar) for that market. As for the target service, say T, it provides stock quotes of a selected market only to authenticated clients. Specifically, clients of such a service need first to login, then to select a market country, then are allowed to request quotes and, finally, to logout.

As we said, target services are *virtual*, that is, only their specification exists, whereas their implementation is missing. However, it is easily seen that, by resorting

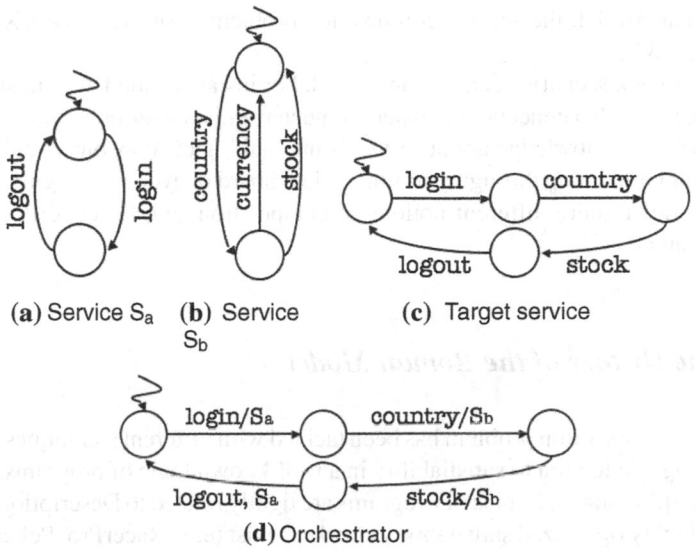

Fig. 8.2 A service composition example in the Roman Model. **a** Service S_a. **b** Service S_a. **c** Target service. **d** Orchestrator

to available services, this example's target service can be built. Indeed, it is enough *delegating* login/logout operations to S_a and country selection and stock requests to S_b. Observe that the target service not only provides a set of operations, but imposes a set of constraints over their executions, e.g., stock can be requested only after country has been executed. Since, on their side, also available service operations are subject to such a kind of constraints, when a target service is to be realized, they must be met. For instance, had not T required operation country be executed before stock, it would be not realizable, as S_b is the only service that provides stock and it requires country to be executed first.

The composition can be realized by a machine which, on one side, receives client's operation requests and, on the other side, forwards them to an appropriate available service which executes it and, consequently, changes its state, where a new set of operations becomes available. Such a machine, similar to a Mealy machine but that can be, in general, infinite-state, is called *orchestrator*. A possible orchestrator is shown in subfigure (d). Each state of the machine corresponds to a state of the target service and each transition is labeled by a pair of the form *operation/service*, with an intuitive semantics: the requested operation is assigned to the output service. For instance, operation login is delegated to service S_a.

The example above shows how the existence of temporal constraints among operation executions makes the problem non trivial: each time an operation is to be delegated to some available service, one needs to check whether all constraints are fulfilled, i.e., whether the service chosen for delegation is in a state where the operation is actually executable. This makes the orchestrator construction an hard task:

in the Roman Model, the service composition problem is shown to be EXPTIME-complete [6, 32].

More complex scenarios can be considered. For instance, nondeterministic available services are also conceivable, where nondeterminism over operation execution represents partial knowledge about service's internal logic. Also, one could think of services communicating through a common blackboard or even exchanging data. All these scenarios require different notions of composition and, hence, different kind of orchestrators.

8.1.3 The History of the Roman Model

The specific composition problem has been tackled with different techniques, starting by exploiting a reduction to satisfiability in a well-known logic of programs, namely PDL [6, 8, 9].[1] Notably, Logics of Programs are tightly related to Description Logics, for which highly optimized satisfiability checkers exist (e.g., RacerPro, Pellet, FACT, etc.). This framework has been then extended to consider interesting variants, e.g.: forms of target service loose specifications [7], trust-aware services [13], distributed orchestrators [35], shared environments [18], data-aware services [5].

More recently, another approach has been proposed based on computing compositions by exploiting (variants of) the formal notion of simulation [10, 34]. Interestingly, through this, the case where the state of services is only partially observable has been also addressed [16]. The solution technique directly appeals to techniques for Linear Time Logic (LTL) synthesis, to model-check a game structure representing a so-called *safety-game*. Since this can be realized in practice on top of symbolic model checking technologies, the approach gained a high level of scalability, and has been effectively realized in the context of an EU research project (see Sect. 8.4). In the following we will focus on this latter approach.

8.2 State-of-the-art on Automated Service Composition

In order to discuss *automated* service composition, and compare different approaches, we introduce here a sort of conceptual framework for "semantic service integration", that is constituted by the following elements[2]: (i) the *community ontology*, which represents the common understanding on an agreed upon reference semantics between

---

[1] The reader should note that [6] has been historically one of the most cited papers in the automated service composition field, cf. more than 390 citations according to Google Scholar—September 2012. The same for [5] (cf. more than 250 citations).

[2] Such a framework is inspired by the research on "semantic data integration" [27]. Obviously that research has dealt with data (i.e., static aspects) and not with computations (i.e., dynamic aspects) that are of interest in composition of services. Still many notions and insights developed in that field may have a deep impact in service composition. An example is the distinction that we make later

the services,[3] concerning the meaning of the offered operations, the semantics of the data flowing through the service operations, etc; (ii) the set of *available services*, which are the actual Web services available to the community; (ii) the *mapping* for the available services to the community ontology, which expresses how services expose their behavior in terms of the community ontology; and (iv) the *client service request*, to be expressed by using the community ontology.

In general, the community ontology comprises several aspects: on one side, it describes the semantics of the information managed by the services, through appropriate semantic standards and languages; on the other side, it should consider also some specification of the service behaviors, on possible constraints and dependencies between different service operations, not limited solely to pre- and post-conditions, but considering also the process of the service. In building such a "semantic service integration" system, two general approaches can be followed. (i) In the *service-tailored* approach, the community ontology is built mainly taking into account the available services, by suitably reconciling them; indeed the available services are directly mapped as elements of the community ontology, and the service request is composed by directly applying the mappings for accessing concrete computations. (ii) Conversely in the *client-tailored* one, the community ontology is built mainly taking into account the client, independently from the services available; they are described (i.e., mapped) by using the community ontology, and the service request is composed by reversing these mappings for accessing concrete computations.

In fact, most of the research on automated service composition has adopted a service-tailored approach. For example, the works based on Planning in AI (e.g., [38, 40, 33]) consider services as atomic actions—only I/O behavior is modeled, and the community ontology is constituted by propositions/formulas (facts that are known to be true) and actions (which change the truth-value of the propositions); available services are mapped into the community ontology as atomic actions with pre- and post-conditions. In order to render a service as an atomic action, the atomic actions, as well as the propositions for pre- and post-conditions, must be carefully chosen by analyzing the available services, thus resulting in a service-tailored approach.

Other works (e.g., Papazoglou's et al. [39], Bouguettaya et al. [30], Sheth et al. [12]) have essentially considered available services as atomic actions characterized by the I/O behavior and possibly effects. But differently from those based on planning, instead of concentrating on the automatic composition, they have focused more on modeling issues and automated discovery of services described making use of rich ontologies.

Also the work of McIlraith et al. [29] can be classified as service-tailored: services are seen as (possibly infinite) transition systems, the common ontology is a Situation Calculus Theory (therefore is semantically very rich) and service names, and each

---

between "service-tailored" and "client-tailored" service integration systems, which roughly mimic the distinction between Global As View (GAV) and Local As View (LAV) in data integration.

[3] Note that many scenarios of cooperative information systems, e.g., *e*-Government or *e*-Business, consider preliminary agreements on underlying ontologies, yet yielding a high degree of dynamism and flexibility.

service name in the common ontology is mapped to a service seen as a procedure in Golog/Congolog Situation Calculus; the client service request is a Golog/Congolog program having service names as atomic actions with the understatement that it specifies acceptable sequences of actions for the client (as in planning) and not a transition system that the client wants to realize.

Finally, the work by Hull et al. [11] describes a setting where services are expressed in terms of atomic actions (communications) that they can perform, and channels linking them with other services. The aim of the composition is to refine the behavior of each service so that the conversations realized by the overall system satisfy a given goal (dynamic property) expressed as a formula in LTL. Although possibly more on choreography synthesis than on composition of the form discussed here, we can still consider it a service-tailored approach, since there is no effort in hiding the service details from the client that specifies the goal formula.

Much less research has been done following a client-tailored approach, but some remarkable exceptions should be mentioned: the work of Knoblock et al. [31] is basically a data integration approach, i.e., the community ontology is the global schema of an integrated data system, the available services are essentially data sources whose contents is mapped as views over the global schema, and the client request is basically a parameterized query over such a schema; therefore the approach is client-tailored, but neither the ontology nor mappings consider service behavior at all.

The work of Traverso et al. [33] can be classified also as client-tailored: services are seen as (finite) transition systems, the common ontology is a set of atomic actions and propositions, as in Planning; a service is mapped to the community ontology as a transition system using the alphabet of the community and defining how transitions affect the propositions, and the client service request asks for a sequence of actions to achieve GOAL1 (main computation), with guarantees that upon failure GOAL2 is reached (exception handling).

Finally, the line of research taken in [6–9], but also in [21], has the dynamic behavior of services at the center of its investigation. In order to study the impact of such dynamics on automatic composition, all these works make simplifying assumptions on the community ontology, which essentially becomes an alphabet of actions. Still the notion of community ontology is present, and in fact all these works adopt a client-tailored approach. A fundamental issue that arises is whether such rich descriptions of the dynamic behavior of the services can be combined with rich (non propositional) descriptions of the information exchanged by the services, while keeping automated composition feasible. The first results on this issue were reported in [5], where available services that operate on a shared world description (in a form of a database) are considered. Such services can either operate on the world through some atomic processes as in OWL-S, or exchange information through messages. While the available services themselves are with finite states, the world description is not. Under suitable assumptions on how the world can be queried and modified, decidability of service composition is shown. Interestingly [5] shows that even if the available services can be modeled as deterministic transition systems, the presence

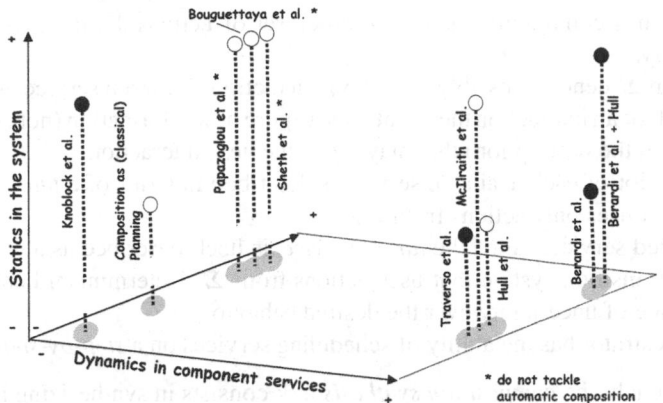

Fig. 8.3 Comparison of the various approaches

of a world description whose state is not known at composition time, requires dealing with nondeterminism.

Figure 8.3 summarizes, on the basis of the previous discussion, the considered works. The three axis represent the levels of detail according to which the community ontology and the mappings and the client request can be modeled. Namely, (i) *statics in the system* represents how fine grained is the modeling of the static semantics (i.e., ontologies of data and/or services, inputs and outputs, alphabet of actions, etc.); (ii) *dynamics in component services* represents how fine grained is the modeling of the processes and behavioral features of the services (only atomic actions, transition systems, etc.); and (iii) *dynamics in client service request* represents how fine grained is the modeling of the process required by the client, varying from a single step (as in the case of services consisting essentially of queries over a data integration system) to a (set of) sequential steps, to a (set of) conditional steps, to including loops, up to running under the full control of the client (as in our approach). *Black/white lollipops* represent service-tailored (white) versus client-tailored (black) approaches.

Finally, in the last years, many works (e.g., [1, 19, 26, 36] consider how to perform composition by taking into account Quality-of-Service (QoS) of the composite and component services. Moreover, some works consider non classical techniques (e.g., [37] adopts learning approaches) for solving the composition problem.

8.3 The Roman Approach

The approach to service composition described here falls into the client-tailored class. Its distinguishing features can be summarized as follows:

- The available services are grouped together into a so-called *community* (many other approaches, e.g., [4], consider the notion of community as central in the composition process).

- Services in a community share a common set of actions Σ, the *actions of the community*.
- Actions in Σ denote (possibly complex) interactions between service and clients. As a result of an interaction the client may acquire new information (not necessarily modeled in the description) that may affect the next interaction.
- The behavior of each available service is described in terms of a *finite transition system* that uses only actions from Σ.
- The desired service, called the *target service*, is itself described as a finite, deterministic transition system that uses actions from Σ. Determinism here captures the absence of uncertainty over the desired behavior.
- The orchestrator has the ability of scheduling services on a *step-by-step* basis.

In this approach, the *composition synthesis* task consists in synthesizing an *orchestrator* able to coordinate the community services so as to mimic the behavior of the target service. Differently put, the behavior obtained by coordinating the services should present no differences, from the client perspective, with the target service.

To describe this setting in terms of the framework previously discussed, we identify the following correspondences:

- the community ontology is simply Σ;
- the available services are the actual services in the community;
- the mapping from the available services to the community ontology is represented by the transition systems that describe the available services (built from community actions);
- the client request is the target service (again, built from community actions).

In [6, 8], the simple case where available services are modeled as deterministic finite transition systems is addressed, while in [9], (diabolic) nondeterminism has been introduced, to account for those situations where the orchestrator cannot control the outcome of interactions. The presence of nondeterministic conversations stems naturally when services offer interactions with an unforeseeable result. For instance consider a service that allows one to purchase items with a credit card. After obtaining the credit card details, the service interacts with the bank, to request payment authorization. If it is granted, the service offers the client the option to confirm the payment, while in case of denial the service offers the possibility of entering the details again. As it can be seen, the next options made available to clients depend on the outcome of the authorization request, which, from the outside perspective, is nondeterministic. As a result, the service itself is nondeterministic, from the perspective of its clients. Notice that after an interaction has taken place, its result becomes observable, that is, clients can know the state that the service has moved to. This feature can thus be exploited by the orchestrator (which is in fact a particular client), that can observe the current state of the available services and choose how to carry on a certain task.[4]

---

[4] The reader should observe that also the standard proposal WSDL 2.0 adopts a similar approach: an operation can have multiple output messages (the `out message` and various `outfault`

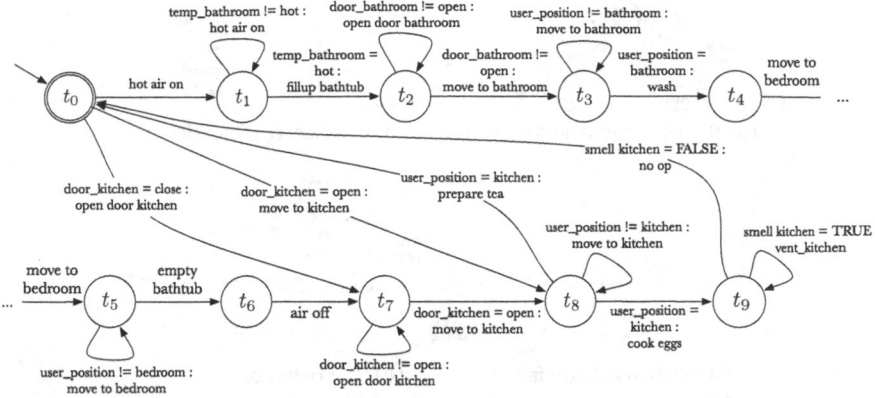

Fig. 8.4 Target service for the smart-house scenario

In the following, we present some technical details of the Roman approach, by considering non-deterministic services and the presence of data. In doing so, we use a running example from the context of smart houses, an interesting application scenario that our approach has been fully implemented in, proving effective. In this context, the composition goal is to generate an orchestrator that realizes some desired *routines* requested by the user, i.e., predefined sequences of operations that the house is intended to execute by suitably exploiting some devices (considered as services). For instance, a typical request issued in the morning could require heating the bathroom, lifting the shutters, and preparing a coffee, while at night, a user might request closing the shutters, locking the door, and switching the lights off.

8.3.1 The Framework

Technically, the behavior of services and the state of the house, called *environment*, are abstracted as finite-state transition systems. In details: each service is represented as a nondeterministic transition system (to model partial controllability); the user request, called *target*, is represented as a deterministic transition system (to model full controllability); and the environment is represented as a nondeterministic transition system (to model partial predictability). The state of the environment is assumed fully observable by all services, including the target. Our ultimate goal is to *simulate* the target by suitably delegating actions to the available services, as they are requested by the client.

For an example consider Fig. 8.4, which shows a fragment of a target behavior for the smart house scenario. It captures some requests typically issued by a user in

---

messages), and the client observes how the service behaved only after receiving a specific output message.

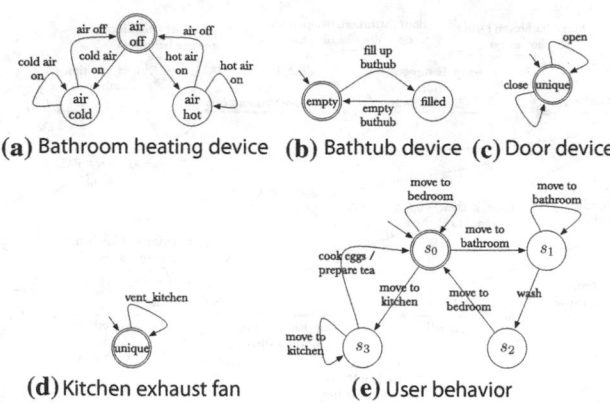

(a) Bathroom heating device **(b)** Bathtub device **(c)** Door device

(d) Kitchen exhaust fan device   **(e)** User behavior

Fig. 8.5 Service community for the smart-house scenario. **a** Bathroom heating device. **b** Bathtub device. **c** Door device. **d** Kitchen exhaust fan device. **e** User behavior

the morning: having a shower and breakfast. States t_1, t_2, and t_3 contain the requests for heating the bathroom ("hot air on"), filling up the bathtub, opening the bathroom door, etc., that is, all the actions necessary to have a shower; the remaining states correspond to the actions to execute in order to have a breakfast ready. Checking whether these requests can be fulfilled in the proper order and, if so, which devices can be used to perform the actions, is exactly the objective of the synthesis task.

Figure 8.5 shows the set of available services, i.e., the *community*, for the same scenario. Notice that also the user is represented as a service. This is because users can in general execute actions that contribute to the realization of a target. Obviously, when this is not desired, a user can be simply excluded themselves from the community. For the environment, we consider the following state variables, with respective domain:

- *temp_bathroom* : {*warm, hot, cold*};
- *user_position* : {*bedroom, bathroom, kitchen*};
- *door_bathroom* : {*closed, open*};
- *door_kitchen* : {*closed, open*};
- *smell_kitchen* : *boolean*;

in which every state variable assignment corresponds to a different environment state.

8.3.1.1 Environment and Behaviors

Formally, we have a shared nondeterministic, fully observable environment, which provides an abstract account of action preconditions and effects, and a mean of communication among services. In details, an *environment* is a tuple $\mathcal{E} = \langle \mathcal{A}, E, e_0, \rho \rangle$, where:

- $\mathcal{A}$ is a finite set of shared actions;
- E is the finite set of environment states;
- $e_0 \in E$ is the initial state;
- $\rho \subseteq E \times \mathcal{A} \times E$ is the transition relation among states: $\langle e, a, e' \rangle \in \rho$, or $e \xrightarrow{a} e'$ in $\mathcal{E}$, denotes that action a performed in state e may lead the environment to a successor state e'.

Services stand for the interface that available devices expose. At each step, a service offers a set of executable actions that can be chosen by the client. The client selects one, the service executes it, and a new step starts. In general service executions affect the environment (cf. above), hence they are equipped with the ability to test conditions (i.e., guards) on the environment, when needed. A (service) _behavior_ over an environment $\mathcal{E} = \langle \mathcal{A}, E, e_0, \rho \rangle$ is a tuple $\mathcal{B} = \langle B, b_0, G, \varrho \rangle$, where:

- B is the finite set of behavior states;
- $b_0 \in B$ is the initial state;
- G is a set of _guards_, that is, boolean functions $g : E \mapsto \{\texttt{true}, \texttt{false}\}$;
- $\delta \subseteq B \times G \times \mathcal{A} \times B$ is the behavior transition relation, where $\langle b, g, a, b' \rangle \in \varrho$, or $b \xrightarrow{g,a} b'$ in $\mathcal{B}$, denotes that action a executed in state b, when the environment is in a state e such that $g(e) = \texttt{true}$, may lead the behavior to state b'.

The target in Fig. 8.4 has guarded actions, e.g., $temp\_bathroom\ ! = hot\ :\ hot\ air\ on$, meaning that action $hot\ air\ on$ can be requested only if the environment is in a state where $temp\_bathroom\ ! = hot$ holds. We then decouple the state of physical device from that of the house, coping with unpredictable situations. Suppose the plan is running and the orchestration module instructs the bath heating device to switch the hot air on, while a tenant is switching the air off when leaving the bathroom: thanks to guards, the plan does not progress until hot temperature is reached. In other words, the fact that the bath heating device is in state $hot\ air\ on$ does not yield that the bathroom temperature is actually hot.

As discussed, behaviors are _nondeterministic_. That is, given a state and an action, there may be several transitions whose guards evaluate to $\texttt{true}$. We say that a behavior $\mathcal{B}$ over $\mathcal{E}$ is _deterministic_ if for no behavior state $b \in B$ and no environment state $e \in E$ there exist two transitions $b \xrightarrow{g_1,a} b'$ and $b \xrightarrow{g_2,a} b''$ in $\mathcal{B}$ such that $b' \neq b''$ and $g_1(e) = g_2(e) = \texttt{true}$. Obviously, given a state of a deterministic behavior and a legal action, we know exactly _the_ next behavior state, while this is not the case for nondeterministic behaviors. Thus, we say that the former are _fully controllable_ while the latter are only _partially controllable_.

Finally, we define a _system_ $\mathcal{S} = \langle \mathcal{B}_1, \ldots, \mathcal{B}_n, \mathcal{E} \rangle$ as an environment $\mathcal{E}$ and n predefined _available behaviors_ $\mathcal{B}_i$ over $\mathcal{E}$. A _target behavior_ is a _deterministic_ behavior over $\mathcal{E}$ that represents the fully controllable desired behavior to be obtained through the available behaviors.

Let us analyze the target of Fig. 8.4. The transition system represents the actions that a user may ask at each moment in time. In state t_0, the initial one, the user can make a choice: either to have a shower and then to have breakfast, or to have a breakfast only. In the first case he asks for action $hot\ air\ on$, otherwise, he can _move to kitchen_ only if the kitchen door is open, or, if not, ask for *open door kitchen*. Let us suppose he decides to have a shower. In state t_1 he may request to *fillup bathtub* (guarded action) only if the bathroom temperature is reasonably hot. Then he may ask to *open door bathroom* (guarded) and only when it is opened he can move to the bathroom, wash and go back to the bedroom. Unless the system is sure that the user is back in the bedroom, the bathtub cannot be emptied, and the hot air cannot be switched off in the bathroom. After having a shower, the user is supposed to have breakfast. So, when the kitchen door is open, he can decide to either prepare a tea or cook eggs. In the latter case, the house system should vent the kitchen until the smell is gone. After these activities, the target returns in its starting state, allowing the tenants to repeat infinitely many times the same sequences of actions.

8.3.2 Enacted Behaviors

To show how the composition task is automatically carried out, we introduce some intermediate notions. Given a behavior B over $\mathcal{E}$, the *enacted behavior* of B over $\mathcal{E}$ is the tuple $T_B = \langle S, \mathcal{A}, s_0, \delta \rangle$, where:

- $S = B \times E$ is the (finite) set of T_B states—given a state $s = \langle b, e \rangle$, we denote b by $beh(s)$ and e by $env(s)$;
- $\mathcal{A}$ is the set of actions in $\mathcal{E}$;
- $s_0 \in S$, with $beh(s_0) = b_0$ and $env(s_0) = e_0$, is the initial state of T_B;
- $\delta \subseteq S \times \mathcal{A} \times S$ is the enacted transition relation, where $\langle s, a, s' \rangle \in \delta$, or $s \xrightarrow{a} s'$ in T_B, iff: (i) $env(s) \xrightarrow{a} env(s')$ in $\mathcal{E}$; and (ii) $beh(s) \xrightarrow{g,a} beh(s')$ in B, with $g(env(s)) = \texttt{true}$ for some $g \in G$.

Technically, T_B is the synchronous product of the behavior and the environment, and represents all the possible executions obtainable by executing B, once guards are evaluated and actions are performed on $\mathcal{E}$. Observe that both the environment and the behavior are possible sources of nondeterminism for an enacted behavior.

All available behaviors in a system act concurrently, in an interleaved fashion, in the same environment. For simplicity, we assume that behaviors are *asynchronous*, that is, exactly one moves at each step.[5] The behavior emerging from the joint execution of all the available behaviors on an environment is referred to as the *enacted system behavior*. Let $\mathcal{S} = \langle B_1, \ldots, B_n, \mathcal{E} \rangle$ be a system, where $\mathcal{E} = \langle \mathcal{A}, E, e_0, \rho \rangle$ and $B_i = \langle B_i, b_{i0}, G_i, \varrho_i \rangle$ ($i \in \{1, \ldots, n\}$). The *enacted system behavior* of $\mathcal{S}$ is the tuple $T_{\mathcal{S}} = \langle S_{\mathcal{S}}, \mathcal{A}, \{1, \ldots, n\}, s_{\mathcal{S}0}, \delta_{\mathcal{S}} \rangle$, where:

- $S_{\mathcal{S}} = B_1 \times \cdots \times B_n \times E$ is the finite set of $T_{\mathcal{S}}$ states; when $s_{\mathcal{S}} = \langle b_1, \ldots, b_n, e \rangle$, we denote b_i by $beh_i(s_{\mathcal{S}})$, for $i \in \{1, \ldots, n\}$, and e by $env(s_{\mathcal{S}})$;

---

[5] In fact, it is possible to extend the approach and results presented here, to the case in which at each step more than one available behaviors acts as in [35].

- $s_{S0} \in S_S$ with $beh_i(s_{S0}) = b_{i0}$, for $i \in \{1, \ldots, n\}$, and $env(s_{S0}) = e_0$, is the initial state of T_S;
- $\delta_S \subseteq S_S \times \mathcal{A} \times \{1, \ldots, n\} \times S_S$ is the T_S transition relation, where $\langle s_S, a, k, s'_S \rangle \in \delta_S$, or $s_S \xrightarrow{a,k} s'_S$ in T_S, iff:

  - $env(s_S) \xrightarrow{a} env(s'_S)$ in $\mathcal{E}$;
  - $beh_k(s_S) \xrightarrow{g.a} beh_k(s'_S)$ in $\mathcal{B}_k$, with $g(env(s_S)) = \texttt{true}$, for some $g \in G_k$; and
  - $beh_i(s_S) = beh_i(s'_S)$, for $i \in \{1, \ldots, n\} \setminus \{k\}$.

Note that the enacted system behavior T_S is the synchronous product of the environment with the asynchronous product of the available behaviors. It is essentially the same form as any other enacted behavior, except for the presence of the index k in transitions. This makes explicit which behavior is the one that performs the action in the transition (while all other remain still).

8.3.3 Orchestrator and Composition

We can now introduce the notion of *orchestrator*, and define when it is a composition of the desired target service. The *orchestrator* is a component intended to activate, stop, and resume the available services (behaviors), and to instruct them to execute an action among those allowed in the current state. The orchestrator has *full observability* on the available behaviors and the environment, that is, it can keep track (at runtime) of their current states.

To formally define orchestrators, some technical notions are needed. A _trace_ for an enacted behavior T_B is a possibly infinite sequence of the form $s^0 \xrightarrow{a^1} s^1 \xrightarrow{a^2} \cdots$ such that (i) $s^0 = s_0$ and (ii) $s^j \xrightarrow{a^{j+1}} s^{j+1}$ in T_B, for all $j > 0$. A _history_ is a finite prefix $h = s^0 \xrightarrow{a^1} \cdots \xrightarrow{a^\ell} s^\ell$ of a trace. We denote s^ℓ by $last(h)$, and ℓ by $length(h)$. The notions of trace and history extend immediately to enacted system behaviors: system traces have the form $s^0 \xrightarrow{a^1,k^1} s^1 \xrightarrow{a^2,k^2} \cdots$, and system histories have the form $s^0 \xrightarrow{a^1,k^1} \cdots \xrightarrow{a^\ell,k^\ell} s^\ell$.

Let S be a system and $\mathcal{H}$ the set of its histories (i.e., histories of T_S). An _orchestrator_ for S is a function $P : \mathcal{H} \times \mathcal{A} \mapsto \{1, \ldots, n, u\}$ that, given a history $h \in \mathcal{H}$ and an action $a \in \mathcal{A}$, selects a behavior, by returning its index, to delegate a to for execution. For technical convenience, a special value u ("undefined") can be returned, to make P a total function defined also on irrelevant histories or actions that no behavior can perform after a given history.

The problem we are interested in is the following: given a system $S = \langle \mathcal{B}_1, \ldots, \mathcal{B}_n, \mathcal{E} \rangle$ and a deterministic *target* behavior $\mathcal{B}_t$ over $\mathcal{E}$, synthesize an orchestrator P that realizes the target behavior $\mathcal{B}_t$ by suitably delegating each action requested by

$\mathcal{B}_t$ to one of the available behaviors $\mathcal{B}_i$ in $\mathcal{S}$. A solution to such problem is called a _composition_.

Intuitively, the orchestrator realizes a target if for every trace of the enacted target and a requested action, the orchestrator returns the index of an available behavior able to perform the requested action. Observe that these orchestrators are somewhat akin to an advanced form of conditional plans and, in fact, the problem itself is related to planning, being both synthesis tasks. Here, though, plans do not select the next action, but _who shall execute the next action_.

One can formally define when an orchestrator realizes the target behavior, as in [18]. To this end, one first needs to define when an orchestrator P _realizes a trace_ of the target $\mathcal{B}_t$. Then, since the target behavior is a deterministic transition system, and thus its behavior is completely characterized by the set of its traces, we can define that an _orchestrator_ P _realizes the target behavior_ $\mathcal{B}_t$ iff it realizes all of its traces.

8.3.4 Composition via Simulation

Let us next present our approach for synthesizing a composition, based on the notion of _simulation_ [22]. Intuitively, a transition system S_1 "simulates" a system S_2 if S_1 is able to _match_ all of S_2 moves. Due to the (devilish) nondeterminism of the available behaviors and the environment, we cannot use the off-the-shelf notion of simulation, but we need a variant, here called _ND-simulation_.

Let $\mathcal{S} = \langle \mathcal{B}_1, \ldots, \mathcal{B}_n, \mathcal{E} \rangle$ be a system, $\mathcal{B}_t$ a target behavior over $\mathcal{E}$, and let $\mathcal{T}_\mathcal{S} = \langle S_\mathcal{S}, \mathcal{A}, \{1, \ldots, n\}, s_{\mathcal{S}0}, \delta_\mathcal{S} \rangle$ and $\mathcal{T}_t = \langle S_t, \mathcal{A}, s_{t0}, \delta_t \rangle$ the enacted system and enacted target behaviors corresponding to $\mathcal{S}$ and $\mathcal{B}_t$, respectively.

An _ND-simulation relation_ of $\mathcal{T}_t$ by $\mathcal{T}_\mathcal{S}$ is a relation $R \subseteq S_t \times S_\mathcal{S}$, such that $\langle s_t, s_\mathcal{S} \rangle \in R$ implies:

1. $env(s_t) = env(s_\mathcal{S})$;

2. for all $a \in \mathcal{A}$, there exists a $k \in \{1, \ldots, n\}$ such that for all transitions $s_t \xrightarrow{a} s'_t$ in $\mathcal{T}_t$:

   - there exists a transition $s_\mathcal{S} \xrightarrow{a,k} s'_\mathcal{S}$ in $\mathcal{T}_\mathcal{S}$ with $env(s'_\mathcal{S}) = env(s'_t)$; and

   - for all transitions $s_\mathcal{S} \xrightarrow{a,k} s'_\mathcal{S}$ in $\mathcal{T}_\mathcal{S}$ with $env(s'_\mathcal{S}) = env(s'_t)$, we have $\langle s'_t, s'_\mathcal{S} \rangle \in R$.

In words, if a pair is in the ND-simulation, then (i) the component states share the same environment and (ii) for any possible move of the target from its state in the pair, there exists a behavior $\mathcal{B}_k$ able to match the move, while guaranteeing preservation of the ND-simulation.

We say that a state $s_t \in S_t$ is _ND-simulated by_ a state $s_\mathcal{S} \in S_\mathcal{S}$ (or $s_\mathcal{S}$ _ND-simulates_ s_t), denoted $s_t \preceq s_\mathcal{S}$, iff there exists an ND-simulation R of $\mathcal{T}_t$ by $\mathcal{T}_\mathcal{S}$ such that $\langle s_t, s_\mathcal{S} \rangle \in R$. Observe that this is a coinductive definition, thus the relation $\preceq$ is itself an ND-simulation, and in fact the _largest ND-simulation relation_ w.r.t. set containment. Such a relation can be computed by the following _NDS_ algorithm.

Roughly speaking, the algorithm works by iteratively removing those tuples for which the conditions of the ND-simulation definition do not apply.

Algorithm 1 $NDS(\mathcal{T}_t, \mathcal{T}_S)$ – Largest ND-Simulation

---

$\mathcal{R} := S_t \times S_S \setminus \{\langle s_t, s_S \rangle \mid env(s_t) \neq env(s_S)\}$
repeat

$\mathcal{R} := (\mathcal{R} \setminus \mathcal{C})$, where $\mathcal{C}$ is the set of $\langle s_t, s_S \rangle \in \mathcal{R}$ such that there exists $a \in \mathcal{A}$ for which for each k there is a transition $s_t \xrightarrow{a} s_t'$ in $\mathcal{T}_t$ such that either:

(a) there is no transition $s_S \xrightarrow{a,k} s_S'$ in $\mathcal{T}_S$ such that $env(s_t') = env(s_S')$; or

(b) there exists a transition $s_S \xrightarrow{a,k} s_S'$ in $\mathcal{T}_S$ such that $env(s_t') = env(s_S')$ but $\langle s_t', s_S' \rangle \notin \mathcal{R}$.

until $(\mathcal{C} = \emptyset)$
return $\mathcal{R}$

The next result shows that checking for the existence of a composition can be reduced to checking whether there exists an ND-simulation between the enacted target and the enacted system that includes their respective initial states.

Theorem 8.1 *Let $\mathcal{S} = \langle \mathcal{B}_1, \ldots, \mathcal{B}_n, \mathcal{E} \rangle$ be a system and $\mathcal{B}_t$ a target behavior over $\mathcal{E}$. Let $\mathcal{T}_t = \langle S_t, \mathcal{A}, s_{t0}, \delta_t \rangle$ and $\mathcal{T}_S = \langle S_S, \mathcal{A}, \{1, \ldots, n\}, s_{S0}, \delta_S \rangle$ be the enacted target behavior and the enacted system behavior for $\mathcal{B}_t$ and $\mathcal{S}$, respectively. An orchestrator P for a system $\mathcal{S}$ that is a composition of the target behavior $\mathcal{B}_t$ over $\mathcal{E}$ exists iff $s_{t0} \preceq s_{S0}$.*

Theorem 8.1 provides us with a straightforward procedure to check the existence of a composition. Namely, (i) compute the largest ND-simulation relation of $\mathcal{T}_t$ by $\mathcal{T}_S$ and (ii) check whether $\langle s_{t0}, s_{S0} \rangle$ occurs in the relation.

From the computational point of view, the algorithm NDS above computes the largest ND-simulation relation $\preceq$ between $\mathcal{T}_t$ and $\mathcal{T}_S$ in polynomial time in the size of $\mathcal{T}_t$ and $\mathcal{T}_S$. Since in our case the number of states of $\mathcal{T}_S$ is exponential in the number of available behaviors $\mathcal{B}_1, \ldots, \mathcal{B}_n$, we get that $\preceq$ can be computed in exponential time in the *number of available behaviors*.

Theorem 8.2 *The existence of compositions can be checked in polynomial time in the number of states of the available behaviors, of the environment, and of the target behavior, and in exponential time in the number of available behaviors.*

Since the composition problem is EXPTIME-hard [32], the obtained bound is tight.

With the ND-simulation at hand we can *synthesize* an orchestrator. In fact, there is a well-defined procedure that, given an ND-simulation, builds a finite-state program that returns, at each point, the set of available behaviors capable of performing a target-conformant action, and guarantee the preservation of the ND-simulation. We call such a program *orchestrator generator*. Let $\mathcal{S}$ be a system, $\mathcal{B}_t$ a target behavior over $\mathcal{E}$, and let $\mathcal{T}_S$ and $\mathcal{T}_t$ be the enacted system behavior and the enacted target behavior corresponding, respectively, to $\mathcal{S}$ and $\mathcal{B}_t$. The *orchestrator generator* of $\mathcal{S}$ for $\mathcal{B}_t$ is a tuple $OG = \langle \Sigma, \mathcal{A}, \{1, \ldots, n\}, \partial, \omega \rangle$, where:

1. $\Sigma = \{\langle s_t, s_S \rangle \in S_t \times S_S \mid s_t \preceq s_S\}$ is the set of states of OG, formed by those pairs of $\mathcal{T}_t$ and $\mathcal{T}_S$ states that are in the largest ND-simulation relation; given a state $\sigma = \langle s_t, s_S \rangle$ we denote s_t by $com_t(\sigma)$ and s_S by $com_S(\sigma)$.
2. $\mathcal{A}$ is the finite set of shared actions.
3. $\{1, \ldots, n\}$ is the finite set of available behavior indexes.
4. $\partial \subseteq \Sigma \times \mathcal{A} \times \{1, \ldots, n\} \times \Sigma$ is the *transition relation*, where $\langle \sigma, a, k, \sigma' \rangle \in \partial$, or $\sigma \xrightarrow{a,k} \sigma'$ in OG, iff

   - $com_t(\sigma) \xrightarrow{a} com_t(\sigma')$ in $\mathcal{T}_t$;
   - $com_S(\sigma) \xrightarrow{a,k} com_S(\sigma')$ in $\mathcal{T}_S$;
   - for all $com_S(\sigma) \xrightarrow{a,k} s_S'$ in $\mathcal{T}_S$, $\langle com_t(\sigma'), s_S' \rangle \in \Sigma$.

5. $\omega : \Sigma \times \mathcal{A} \mapsto 2^{\{1,\ldots,n\}}$ is the *output function*, where $\omega(\sigma, a) = \{k \mid \exists \sigma' \text{ s.t. } \sigma \xrightarrow{a,k} \sigma' \text{ in } OG\}$.

Thus, OG is a finite state transducer that, given an action a (compliant with the target behavior, and according to the system state corresponding to the current OG state), outputs, through ω, the set of *all* available behaviors that can perform a next while preserving the ND-simulation $\preceq$. Observe that computing OG from the relation $\preceq$ is easy, as it involves checking *local* conditions only.

Coming back to our example, when the user asks for action *hot air on*, the OG outputs the index that represents the bathroom heating device, which is the only one that can perform the requested action. If many bathrooms are available, thanks to the guards and to function ω, the composition layer can instruct one bathroom or another to perform the action, depending on realtime conditions, such as availability of a particular bathroom or device.

If there exists a composition of $\mathcal{B}_t$ by S, then $s_{t0} \preceq s_{S0}$ and OG does include the state $\sigma_0 = \langle s_{t0}, s_{S0} \rangle$. In such cases, we get actual orchestrators, called *generated orchestrators*, which are compositions of $\mathcal{B}_t$ by S, by picking up, at each step, one available behavior among those returned by ω. More precisely, we proceed as follows. A *trace for OG* starting from σ^0 is a finite or infinite sequence $\sigma^0 \xrightarrow{a^1,k^1} \sigma^1 \xrightarrow{a^2,k^2} \cdots$, such that $\sigma_j \xrightarrow{a^{j+1},k^{j+1}} \sigma_{j+1}$ in OG, for all j. A *history for OG* starting from state σ^0 is a prefix of a trace starting from σ^0. By using histories, one can introduce *OG -orchestrators*, which are functions $CGP_{\text{CHOOSE}} : \mathcal{H}_{OG} \times \mathcal{A} \mapsto \{1, \ldots, n, u\}$, where $\mathcal{H}_{OG}$ is the set of OG histories starting from any state in Σ, and defined as follows: $CGP_{\text{CHOOSE}}(h_{OG}, a) = \text{CHOOSE}(\omega(last(h_{OG}), a))$, for all $h_{OG} \in \mathcal{H}_{OG}$, where CHOOSE stands for a choice function that chooses one element among those returned by $\omega(last(h_{OG}), a))$. Assuming that OG (of S for $\mathcal{B}_t$) includes $\sigma_0 = \langle s_{t0}, s_{S0} \rangle$, for any OG history $h_{OG} = \sigma^0 \xrightarrow{a^1,k^1} \cdots \xrightarrow{a^\ell,k^\ell} \sigma^\ell$ starting from $\sigma^0 = \sigma_0$, we can obtain the corresponding system history $proj_S(h_{OG})$, called the *projected system history*, as follows:

$proj_S(h_{OG}) = com_S(\sigma^0) \xrightarrow{a^1,k^1} \cdots \xrightarrow{a^\ell,k^\ell} com_S(\sigma^\ell)$, i.e., we take the "system" component of each OG state σ^i in the history.

Moreover, from a OG-orchestrator CGP_{CHOOSE}, we obtain the corresponding *generated orchestrator* as the function $P_{\text{CHOOSE}} : \mathcal{H} \times \mathcal{A} \mapsto \{1, \ldots, n, u\}$, where $\mathcal{H}$ is the set of system histories starting from s_{S0}, defined as follows. For each system history h and action a: (i) if $h = proj_S(h_{OG})$ for some OG history h_{OG}, then $P_{\text{CHOOSE}}(h, a) = CGP_{\text{CHOOSE}}(h_{OG}, a)$; else (ii) $P_{\text{CHOOSE}}(h, a) = u$.

Through generated orchestrators, we can relate OGs to compositions and show that one gets *all* orchestrators that are compositions by considering all choice functions for CHOOSE. Notably, while each specific composition may be an infinite state program, the orchestrator generator OG, which includes all of them, is always finite.

We have the following central result, which states soundness and completeness of the orchestrator generation defined above.

Theorem 8.3 *If OG includes the state $\sigma_0 = \langle s_{t0}, s_{S0} \rangle$, then every orchestrator generated by OG is a composition of the target behavior $\mathcal{B}_t$ by system S. Moreover, every orchestrator that is a composition of the target behavior $\mathcal{B}_t$ by system S can be generated by OG.*

8.4 A Practical Application in Smart Homes

As previously stated, a concrete case of application of automated service composition with the Roman Model has been performed in the SM4ALL EU research project, recently and successfully concluded.[6]

8.4.1 Software Architecture, Service and Data Models

The goal of SM4ALL is to seamlessly integrate devices, in order to simplify the access to the services that they expose, and dynamically compose such services in order to offer the end users more complex functionalities and a richer experience with the domotic environment. In SM4ALL, all the devices make their functionalities available as SOAP-based Web services, according to a rich *service model*[7] consisting

---

[6] SM4All—Smart hoMes for All, is an FP7 project running from 1 September 2008 to 31 August 2011. Cf. the WWW site http://www.sm4all-project.eu/ and news on major international televisions: Globo TV—http://video.globo.com/Videos/Player/Noticias/0,,GIM1751401-7823-CASA+INTELIGENTE+E+MOVIDA+A+PENSAMENTO+NA+ITALIA,00.html, Channel 1 Russia—http://www.1tv.ru/news/other/191509, Italian Rai3—http://www.youtube.com/watch?v=a9F72_E4mT0 and http://rai.it/dl/tg3/rubriche/PublishingBlock-79554b45-1e4c-41a8-a474-ad3e22ab750f.html#, Ability Channel—http://www.abilitychannel.tv/video/casa-domotica-sm4all/ .

[7] Cf. http://www.dis.uniroma1.it/~cdc/sm4all/proposals/servicemodel/latest.

not only of the service interface specification, but also, e.g., of its conversational description and of the related graphical widgets (i.e., icons) to be presented in the user layer. *Proxies* are indeed the software components offering such services by "wrapping" and abstracting the real devices offering the functionalities. Services are not necessarily offered by hardware devices, but could be also realized through a human intervention; in this case, the proxy exposes a SOAP-based service to the platform, whereas it interacts with the service provider (i.e., the human) by means of a dedicated GUI, when executing the requested operations.

During their run time, services continuously change their status, both in terms of values of sensed/actuating variables (e.g., a service wrapping a temperature sensor reports the current detected temperature, a service wrapping windows blinds report whether the blinds are open, closed, half-way, etc.) and in terms of their conversational state. The definition of the sensed/actuating variables, representing the "state" of the domotic environment, is performed in accordance with the *data model*.[8]

The SM4ALL architecture, described in details in [20], consists of a *Pervasive Controller* and a *Discovery Framework*, which are in charge, when a new device joins the system, to dynamically load and deploy the appropriate service, and to register all the relevant information into the *Service Semantic Repository*. All of the status information, both in terms of (i) service conversational states and (ii) values of the environmental variables, are kept available in the *Context Awareness Manager*, through a publish&subscribe mechanism. On the basis of the service descriptions, *Composition Engines* are in charge of providing complex services by suitably composing the available ones. In SM4ALL, three different types of approaches are provided, each providing different functionalities and therefore complementing one another, in order to provide a rich and novel environment to the users:

- *Off-line synthesis* (provided through the Off-line Synthesis Engine). In the off-line mode, at design/deployment time of the house, a desiderata (i.e., not really existing) target service is defined, as a kind of complex routine, and the synthesis engine synthesizes a suitable orchestration of the available services realizing the target one. Such an orchestration specification is used at execution-time (i.e., when the user chooses to invoke the composite/desiderata service) by the Orchestration Engine in order to coordinate the available services (i.e., to interact with the user on one hand and to schedule service invocations on the other hand). In this approach, the orchestration specification is synthesized off-line (i.e., not triggered by user requests, at run time) and executed on-line as if it were a real service of the home. The off-line mode is based on the Roman Model. The Off-line Synthesis Engine produces what in SM4ALL is referred to as a *routine*.
- *On-line planning* (provided through the On-line Planning Engine). The user, during its interaction with the home, may decide not to invoke a specific service (either available/real or composite), but rather to ask the home to realize a *goal*; in such a case, the engine, on the basis of specific planning techniques [25],

---

[8] Cf. http://www.dis.uniroma1.it/~cdc/sm4all/proposals/datamodel/latest.

synthesizes and executes available service invocations in order to reach such a goal.

- *Visual design of complex services* (provided through the Compound Service Workbench). A skilled user may want to define a *compound service*, by visually composing services offered by proxies, in a way similar to what currently happen in technologies like WS-BPEL. The compound service offers an aggregated operation, which is the result of the proper orchestration of operations offered by other services. Also in this case, the synthesis is performed off-line, but differently from the previous case, it is not supported by automatic techniques, but by a visual workbench. Both routines and compound services fall under the category of "composite services".

The *Orchestration Engine* interprets the specification of a composite service (either synthesized automatically, through the Off-line Synthesis Engine, or visually by the user, through the Compound Service Workbench) and consequently orchestrates the set of component services. In the case of the On-line Planning Engine, due to the need of continuously planning and monitoring services during plan executions, the Orchestration Engine is bypassed and services are directly invoked by the planner itself.

Users are able to interact with the home and the platform through different kinds of user interfaces, e.g., a home control station accessible through a touchscreen in the living room. In particular, Brain Computer Interfaces (BCIs, [28]) allow also people with disabilities to interact with the system. Of course, users can still control the home equipment as if there were not the SM4ALL platform, e.g., a user is obviously allowed to switch the living room light on directly from the manual switcher on the wall, without using any BCI and/or touchscreen; in such a case, the platform, through the specific proxy wrapping the light/switcher as a service, is notified of the specific variable value change. De facto, the event is equivalent, due to the engineering of the platform, to the one of clicking a specific button on the touchscreen and/or selecting the icon on the BCI. Users are able, trough the interfaces, to invoke actions offered by services (either simple of composite) and to achieve goals, in order to reach specific situations that they would like to be realized in the home. Moreover, through the interfaces, they receive the feedback about state changes in the home, as well as requests for further inputs (in case additional parameters are needed for some actions to be executed), notifications about action/service completions, etc.

Going into implementation details of the Off-line Synthesis and Orchestration Engines, they have been realized as Java modules, realizing the techniques presented in Sect. 8.3. In particular, the Off-line Synthesis Engine is built around TLV (Temporal Logic Verifier),[9] an environment for verification of finite state systems; we defined a set of modules that make TLV compute the orchestration generator. Starting from XML descriptions of services (according to the service model), target service and variables, we had to devise a suitable translation into the TLV input language. After the orchestrator generator (see Sect. 8.3) has been computed, it is converted into our

---

[9] http://www.wisdom.weizmann.ac.il/~verify/tlv/

XML orchestration language (we named CBL—Composition Behavioral Language) which is interpreted by the Orchestration Engine, thus really executing at runtime the automatically synthesized composition. Further technical details can be found in [24].

As discussed in Sect. 8.3, the service model focuses on the behavior of services, in terms of conversational states that they traverse during the execution of the exposed actions, as well as on the way they (i) affect the environment and (ii) are inhibited (allowed) in the execution by the environment (respectively, by the expression of post-conditions and pre-conditions on top of the variables). The smart home environment is populated by many deployed *service instances*, which are actual occurrences of given *service types* (also *services* for sake of brevity). Indeed a developer can produce many instances showing the same behavior: e.g., many lamps of the same product series, installed in different rooms, are different instances of the same service type. Therefore, every service instance can be identified by one or more *properties*, which are deployment characteristics (such as the location in the house, the power consumption, etc.).

The *data model* is an extensible framework of variable types. They concern the specific environmental information used by reasoning engines only. I.e., free parameters such as, e.g., name in an operation cheers(name: string): string may not adhere to the data model. Nevertheless, in case the developer wants (i) to describe the effects on the environment once a service action is invoked (post-condition), or (ii) to express the conditions that must hold in the context for an action to take place (pre-condition), she has to write statements formulated on top of variables whose type is coherent with the data model.

This is due to the fact that the platform should be able to cope with a predefined uniform set of common data types, so that the interaction with the environment is clear, despite of the service developer. We call *variable types* (or simply *types*) the types, and *variables* are the entities whose type is a *variable type*. The data model is an XML standard, i.e., it is based on XML Schemata to define value spaces. Each service developer can define her own types, provided that (i) they are described in XML Schema documents identified by a unique *namespace*, and (i) they extend, directly or indirectly, the SM4ALL *base types*.[10] Indeed, types in the data model are derived by XML Schema native ones, and are designed to be extended by SM4ALL system service designers. The data model allows XML Schema simple types only as SM4ALL variable types, according to the XML Schema definition: complex types are not considered. Common variable types are enumerations on top of the numeric type. This allows the ordering over the possible values, as inherited from the basic integer type. In such cases, the insertion of a documentation tag for each enumerated value, provides also a human-readable form. The documentation node is intended to contain the information to (possibly) show the users. That is to say: if, e.g., a variable of type temperatureLevel reaches the value 3, the reasoning engines are informed of it, whereas the users are notified of a new "warm" status. Having enumerations over variables with finite sets of possible values makes feasible and effective the

---

[10] Base types are identified by the http://www.sm4all-project.eu/datamodel/base namespace.

reasoning tasks of the composition engines (as discussed in Sect. 8.3, the approach requires that the set of environmental states is finite).

8.4.2 Discussion and Lessons Learned

Applying automated composition in practice allowed to gain interesting lessons learned, about the performances and the acceptability of the approach by users. As stated in Sect. 8.3, computing an orchestrator generator is EXPTIME-complete, so an interesting question is which are the real dimensions of problems that can be practically solved by the approach. In the SM4ALL project, a testbed/showcase has been realized in a real domotic house located in Roma, Italy, equipped with about 20 sensors, some human-based services (e.g., a nurse assisting a disabled person) and some routines computed with the proposed approach. Table 8.1 reports the average times (over 20 runs) for computing such routines used in the testbed, by using the Off-line Synthesis Engine on a Intel Pentium 4 M, 512 Mb RAM, Ubuntu 10.04 32 bit. The available services amount to 18, whereas the column "services" reports how many services (over the 18 available) are effectively given as input of the problem. The reader should note the low features of the machine, as in a real smart home scenario, a platform like SM4ALL should run on a low-end hardware of type "set-top-box" (e.g., a multimedia player, an EEEBox, etc.) and not on an high-end server. Such times are appropriate, as the reader should remind that the routines are computed off-line, i.e., at design/deployment time of the smart home, and not during run-time, i.e., while living inhabitants exploit the platform.

In order to keep the number of variables and of services (effectively considered in the community given as input to the problem) as low as possible, a careful decomposition approach should be undertaken when defining service descriptions. The reader should note that if a variable should be considered in a composition, then also all possible services affecting such a variable should be considered as input to the problem. Indeed in our testbed, naively the *nurse* service was affecting

Table 8.1 Average times for synthesis

Target	Transitions	States	Variables	Services	Avrg. time (millis)
WakeUp	332	84	3	5	1240.9
CheckIngredients	2704	352	5	3	3340.8
SetAlarm	48	29	1	3	305.3
WakeUpLite	101	41	2	4	487.75
EscapeRoutine	597	93	3	4	1126
RestoreFromWakeUp	85	25	2	3	320.5
RelaxModeSetup	4437	357	4	5	7806.3
FootbalMatchSetupN	2263	215	4	5	3257.75
FootbalMatchSetupW	301	53	3	4	643.95

7 variables, with the result that all routines require, during the composition, to consider as input community all the 18 available services, finally making the computation not practically feasible (after 3 days of running, no composition has been computed yet). Conversely, considering *nurse4bedroom*, *nurse4kitchen* and *nurse4livingRoom* distinct services, each one affecting different variables, we were finally able to keep the number of input services and of variables low, obtaining the above results.

As far as user acceptability, assuming that a designer is willing to provide a target service as input for the composition revealed difficult in many cases, especially if the target is quite complex; on the other side, defining goals is widely accepted, even if in many cases a more fine-grained control over possible intermediate goals is desiderated. To this aim, we started investigating a novel model, which in some sense merges the conversational approach of the Roman model with the "goal-based" approach typical of automated composition based on planning; preliminary results can be found in [14, 15, 17].

Acknowledgments The authors would like to thank all the persons who contributed over the years to the Roman model: Daniela Berardi, Diego Calvanese, Maurizio Lenzerini, Richard Hull, Alessandro Iuliani, Damiano Pozzi, Fahima Cheikh, Valerio Colaianni, Sebastian Sardiña, Claudio Di Ciccio, Riccardo De Masellis, Paolo Felli, Ettore Iacomussi, Vincenzo Forte, Mario Caruso. We also would like to acknowledge the support of the projects MAIS and Brindisys (Italian), SemanticGov and TONES (EU FP6), SM4All, GreenerBuildings and ACSI (EU FP7).

References

1. Baligand, F., Rivierre, N., Ledoux, T.: A declarative approach for QoS-aware web service compositions. In: Proceedings of ICSOC (2007)
2. Beauche, S., Poizat, P.: Automated service composition with adaptive planning. In: Proceedings of ICSOC (2008)
3. Benatallah, B., Casati, F., Toumani, F.: Web service conversation modeling: a cornerstone for e-business automation. IEEE Internet Comput. 8(1), 46–54 (2004)
4. Benatallah, B., Sheng, Q.Z., Dumas, M.: The Self-Serv environment for web services composition. IEEE Internet Comput. 7(1), 40–48 (2003)
5. Berardi, D., Calvanese, D., De Giacomo, G., Hull, R., Mecella, M.: Automatic composition of transition-based semantic web services with messaging. In: Proceedings of VLDB (2005)
6. Berardi, D., Calvanese, D., De Giacomo, G., Lenzerini, M., Mecella, M.: Automatic composition of e-Services that export their behavior. In: Proceedings of ICSOC (2003)
7. Berardi, D., Calvanese, D., De Giacomo, G., Lenzerini, M., Mecella, M.: Synthesis of underspecified composite e-Services based on automated reasoning. In: Proceedings of ICSOC (2004)
8. Berardi, D., Calvanese, D., De Giacomo, G., Lenzerini, M., Mecella, M.: Automatic service composition based on behavioural descriptions. Int. J. Coop. Inf. Syst. 14(4), 333–376 (2005)
9. Berardi, D., Calvanese, D., De Giacomo, G., Mecella, M.: Composition of services with non-deterministic observable behavior. In: Proceedings of ICSOC (2005)
10. Berardi, D., Cheikh, F., De Giacomo, G., Patrizi, F.: Automatic service composition via simulation. Int. J. Found. Comput. Sci. 19(2), 429–451 (2008)
11. Bultan, T., Fu, X., Hull, R., Su, J.: Conversation specification: a new approach to design and analysis of e-Service composition. In: Proceedings of WWW (2003)

12. Cardoso, J., Sheth, A.: Introduction to semantic web services and web process composition. In: Proceedings of 1st International Workshop on Semantic Web Services and Web Process Composition (SWSWPC 2004) (2004)
13. Cheikh, F., De Giacomo, G., Mecella, M.: Automatic web services composition in trustaware communities. In: Proceedings of 3rd ACM Workshop On Secure Web Services (SWS 2006) (2006)
14. De Giacomo, G., Di Ciccio, C., Felli, P., Hu, Y., Mecella, M.: Goal-based composition of stateful services for smart homes. In: Proceedings of CoopIS (2012)
15. De Giacomo, G., Felli, P., Patrizi, F., Sardiña, S.: Two-player game structures for generalized planning and agent composition. In: Proceedings of AAAI (2010)
16. De Giacomo, G., De Masellis, R., Patrizi, F.: Composition of partially observable services exporting their behaviour. In: Proceedings of ICAPS (2009)
17. De Giacomo, G., Patrizi, F., Sardiña, S.: Agent programming via planning programs. In: Proceedings of AAMAS (2010)
18. De Giacomo, G., Sardiña, S.: Automatic synthesis of new behaviors from a library of available behaviors. In: Proceedings of IJCAI (2007)
19. De Paoli, F., Lulli, G., Maurino, A.: Design of quality-based composite web services. In: Proceedings of ICSOC (2006)
20. Di Ciccio, C., Mecella, M., Caruso, M., Forte, V., Iacomussi, E., Rasch, K., Querzoni, L., Santucci, G., Tino, G.: The homes of tomorrow: service composition and advanced user interfaces. ICST Trans. Ambient Syst. 11(10–12), e2 (2011)
21. Gerede, C., Hull, R., Ibarra, O.H., Su, J.: Automated composition of e-Services: Lookaheads. In: Proceedings of ICSOC (2004)
22. Henzinger, M.R., Henzinger, T.A., Kopke, P.W.: Computing simulations on finite and infinite graphs. In: Proceedings of FOCS (1995)
23. Hull, R.: Web services composition: a story of models, automata, and logics. In: Proceedings of SCC (2005)
24. Iacomussi, E.: Service based architectures for smart homes and the SM4All project. The component for the automatic synthesis of conversational services. Master thesis, Sapienza Università di Roma (2011). A copy can be obtained by writing an email to authors
25. Kaldeli, E., Lazovik, A., Aiello, M.: Extended goals for composing services. In: Proceedings of ICAPS (2009)
26. Klein, A., Ishikawa, F., Honiden, S.: Efficient QoS-aware service composition with a probabilistic service selection policy. In: Proceedings of ICSOC (2010)
27. Lenzerini, M.: Data integration: a theoretical perspective. In: Proceedings of PODS (2002)
28. McFarland, D.J., Wolpaw, J.R.: Brain-computer interfaces for communication and control. Commun. ACM 54(5), 60–66 (2011)
29. McIlraith, S., Son, T.: Adapting golog for composition of semantic web services. In: Proceedings of KR (2002)
30. Medjahed, B., Bouguettaya, A., Elmagarmid, A.: Composing web services on the semantic web. Very Large Data Base J. 12(4), 333–351 (2003)
31. Michalowski, M., Ambite, J., Thakkar, S., Tuchinda, R., Knoblock, C., Minton, S.: Retrieving and semantically integrating heterogeneous data from the web. IEEE Int. Syst. 19(3), 72–79 (2004)
32. Muscholl, A., Walukiewicz, I.: A lower bound on web services composition. Logical Methods Comput. Sci. 4(5), 1–14 (2008). doi:10.2168/LMCS-4, http://www.lmcs-online.org/ojs/viewarticle.php?id=359
33. Pistore, M., Marconi, A., Bertoli, P., Traverso, P.: Automated composition of web services by planning at the knowledge level. In: Proceedings of IJCAI (2005)
34. Sardiña, S., De Giacomo, G., Patrizi, F.: Behavior composition in the presence of failure. In: Proceedings of KR (2008)
35. Sardiña, S., Patrizi, F., De Giacomo, G.: Automatic synthesis of a global behavior from multiple distributed behaviors. In: Proceedings of AAAI (2007)

36. Schuller, D., Miede, A., Eckert, J., Lampe, U., Papageorgiou, A., Steinmetz, R.: Qos-based optimization of service compositions for complex workflows. In: Proceedings of ICSOC (2010)
37. Wang, H., Zhou, X., Zhou, X., Liu, W., Li, W., Bouguettaya, A.: Adaptive service composition based on reinforcement learning. In: Proceedings of ICSOC (2010)
38. Wu, D., Parsia, B., Sirin, E., Hendler, J., Nau, D.: Automating DAML-S web services composition using SHOP2. In: Proceedings of ISWC (2003)
39. Yang, J., Papazoglou, M.: Service components for managing the life-cycle of service compositions. Inf. Syst. **29**(2), 97–125 (2004)
40. Zhao, H., Doshi, P.: A hierarchical framework for composing nested web processes. In: Proceedings of ICSOC (2006)

Chapter 9
Behavioral Service Substitution

Christian Stahl and Wil M. P. van der Aalst

Abstract Service-oriented design supports system evolution and encourages reuse
and modularization. A key ingredient of service orientation is the ability to *substitute*
one service by another without reconfiguring the overall system. This chapter aims
to give an overview of the state of the art and open challenges in the area of *service
substitution*. Thereby, we restrict ourselves to changes of the *service behavior*. We
present a formal model of service behavior, formalize service substitution, study
algorithms to decide service substitution, and provide rules to construct services
that are correct by design. Beside analysis at *design time*, we also investigate analysis at *runtime*, where we measure the deviation of a running service (or collection
of services) from its specification based on recorded event data (e.g., message or
transaction logs).

9.1 Introduction

Today's enterprises are challenged to continuously change their systems to address
changes in their environment. On the one hand, systems are highly complex, run
in heterogeneous environments, and are often distributed over several enterprises.
On the other hand, because of the extensively growing acceptance of the Internet
and Internet-related technologies, enterprises consider themselves to be exposed to
intense competition and, therefore, have to act dynamically and to change and adapt
their systems whenever necessary. For example, when some new functionality is
added or some quality parameter of some functionality is improved, this causes a

C. Stahl (✉) · W. M. P. van der Aalst
Department of Mathematics and Computer Science, Technische Universiteit Eindhoven,
PO Box 513, 5600 MB Eindhoven, The Netherlands
e-mail: c.stahl@tue.nl

W. M. P. van der Aalst
e-mail: w.m.p.v.d.aalst@tue.nl

A. Bouguettaya et al. (eds.), *Web Services Foundations*,
DOI: 10.1007/978-1-4614-7518-7_9,
© Springer Science+Business Media New York 2014

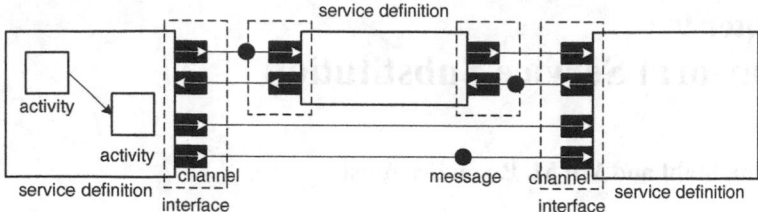

Fig. 9.1 An illustration showing the main terms used to describe services

change in system development. Instead of designing a system from scratch, existing systems need to be redesigned and improved iteratively.

Service orientation [40] is a paradigm to design a complex distributed system by composing it from smaller building blocks called *services*. A service is an autonomous system that has an interface to interact with other services via message passing. As services are composed into more complex services, a service is usually *stateful*. The behavior of a service is described by a set of *activities*. An activity is the atomic unit of work in a service. The execution of an activity is either internal to the service or yields the sending or the receiving of a message. A service can be executed; that is, an *instance* of this service is created. An instance can execute activities. Figure 9.1 illustrates these terms.

An important property of a service composition is *compositionality*; that is, the composition is again a service. To achieve compositionality, a service composition must be *compatible*. The modular design of services enables enterprises to substitute one service by another one rather than changing the entire system. Substituting one service by another one should preserve compatibility of the overall system. Verification of compatibility is challenging, as one wants to derive correctness of the overall system from the correctness of the correctness of its services. *Service substitution*—that is, deciding whether a service can substitute another service—is considered to be one of the grand challenges [42].

In this chapter, we give an overview of the state of the art and open challenges in the area of service substitution. We thereby *restrict ourselves to changes of the service behavior*, which are also known as *business protocol changes* [41]. This restriction implies that we assume that nonfunctional and semantical properties are not violated when changing a service to another service; that is, we abstract from resources and consider only data and message types and not their content. Figure 9.2 illustrates how we approach this topic.

First, in Sect. 9.2, we formalize service behavior according to the illustration in Fig. 9.1. We introduce *open nets*, Petri nets extended with an interface, as a service model and formalize terms such as *compatibility*. Suitability of this model has been demonstrated by feature-complete open-net semantics for various languages such as BPMN and WS-BPEL [29].

In Sect. 9.3, we present two variants of service substitution and formalize them using a refinement relation between the specified (i.e., the old) service *Spec* and the

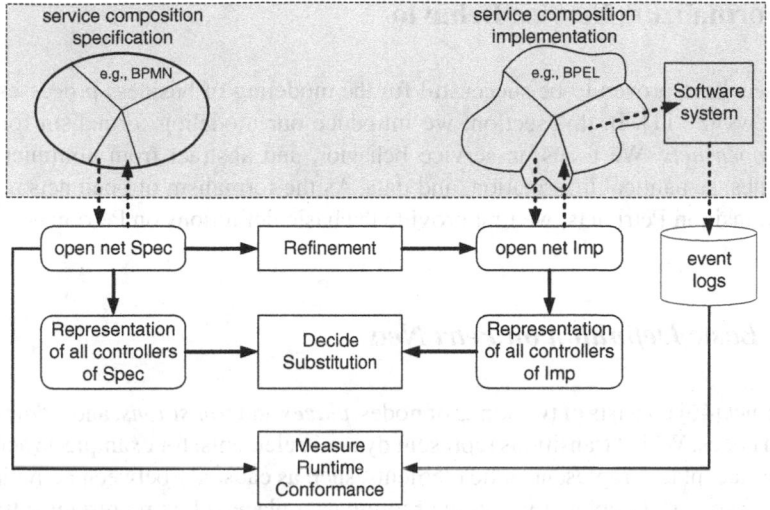

Fig. 9.2 Illustration of the proposed approach

implemented (i.e., the new) service *Impl*. A naive way to ensure correctness during service substitution is to compare the sets of all controllers (i.e., admissible contexts) of *Spec* and *Impl*. Only if all controllers of *Spec* are included in the set of controllers of *Impl*, compatibility is ensured. As these sets of controllers may be infinite, we introduce a *finite representation* of these sets to decide substitution. We also consider service substitution in a setting where a running instance of the old service has to be migrated to the new service.

Besides checking whether a service can actually be substituted by another one, one can also guide the construction of services that are *correct by design*. This approach can then be integrated in design tools and helps to speed up the design process. We investigate such techniques in Sect. 9.4.

Compatibility and substitutability can be studied at *design time* under the assumption that services behave as modeled. However, organizations may—deliberately or accidently—implement a different service or services may evolve over time. As a result, the real service behavior deviates from the modeled behavior. The availability of event logs of the actually implemented service *Impl* and the existence of the specified service *Spec* enables us to check *conformance at runtime*; that is, we investigate to what extent "the real *Impl*" deviates from *Spec*. In Sect. 9.5, we present techniques for *offline* conformance checking (diagnosis of deviations based on historic event data) and *online* conformance checking (generating alerts the moment a deviation occurs).

Section 9.6 concludes the chapter by summarizing our main findings and by discussing open research challenges.

9.2 Formalizing Service Behavior

Petri nets have proven to be successful for the modeling of business processes and workflows [8, 11]. In this section, we introduce our modeling formalism for services, *open nets*. We focus on service behavior, and abstract from nonfunctional properties, semantical information, and data. As the formalism of open nets refines place/transition Petri nets, we first provide the basic definitions on Petri nets.

9.2.1 Basic Definition on Petri Nets

A Petri net [46] consists of two kinds of nodes, *places* and *transitions*, and a *flow relation* on nodes. Whilst transitions represent dynamic elements, for example an activity in a service, places represent static elements, such as causality between activities or an interface port. Graphically, a circle represents a place, a box represents a transition, and the directed arcs between places and transitions represent the flow relation. A *state* of the Petri net is represented by a marking. A marking is a distribution of tokens over the places. Graphically, a black dot represents a token.

Definition 9.1 (**Net**). A *net* $N = (P, T, F, m_N, \Omega)$ consists of

- a finite set P of *places*,
- a finite set T of *transitions* such that P and T are disjoint,
- a *flow relation* $F \subseteq (P \times T) \cup (T \times P)$,
- an *initial marking* m_N, where a marking $m \in \mathcal{B}(P)$ is a multiset over P, and
- a set Ω of final markings.

A *labeled net* is a net N together with an *alphabet* $\mathcal{A}$ of actions and a *labeling function* $l \in T \to \mathcal{A} \cup \{\tau\}$, where $\tau \notin \mathcal{A}$ represents an invisible, internal action.

Let $x \in P \cup T$ be a node of a net N. As usual, $^\bullet x = \{y \mid (y, x) \in F\}$ denotes the *preset* of x and $x^\bullet = \{y \mid (x, y) \in F\}$ the *postset* of x. We interpret presets and postsets as multisets when used in operations also involving multisets.

A marking $m \in \mathcal{B}(P)$ is a multiset over the set P of places; for example, $[p_1, 2p_2]$ denotes a marking m with $m(p_1) = 1$, $m(p_2) = 2$, and $m(p) = 0$ for $p \in P \setminus \{p_1, p_2\}$. We define $+$ and $-$ for the sum and the difference of two markings and $=, <, >, \leq, \geq$ for comparison of markings in the standard way. If $m_1 \in \mathcal{B}(P_1)$ and $m_2 \in \mathcal{B}(P_2)$, then $m_1 + m_2 \in \mathcal{B}(P_1 \cup P_2)$ (i.e., the underlying set of elements is adjusted when needed).

The *behavior* of a net N relies on changing the markings of N by firing transitions of N. A transition $t \in T$ is *enabled* at a marking m, denoted by $m \xrightarrow{t}$, if for all $p \in {^\bullet t}, m(p) > 0$. If t is enabled at m, it can *fire*, thereby changing the marking m to a marking $m' = m - {^\bullet t} + t^\bullet$. The firing of t is denoted by $m \xrightarrow{t} m'$; that is, t is enabled at m and firing it results in m'.

The behavior of N can be extended to sequences: $m_1 \xrightarrow{t_1} \ldots \xrightarrow{t_{k-1}} m_k$ is a *run* of N if for all $0 < i < k$, $m_i \xrightarrow{t_i} m_{i+1}$. A marking m' is *reachable from* a marking m if there exists a (possibly empty) run $m_1 \xrightarrow{t_1} \ldots \xrightarrow{t_{k-1}} m_k$ with $m = m_1$ and $m' = m_k$; for $w = \langle t_1 \ldots t_{k-1} \rangle$, we also write $m \xrightarrow{w} m'$. Marking m' is *reachable* if $m_N = m$. The set M_N represents the set of all reachable markings of N, and the set of runs of N from the initial marking to a final marking is $Ru(N) = \{w \in T^* \mid \exists m_f \in \Omega : m_N \xrightarrow{w} m_f\}$.

In the case of labeled nets, we lift runs to traces: If $m \xrightarrow{w} m'$ and v is obtained from w by replacing each transition by its label and removing all τ-labels, we write $m \xRightarrow{v} m'$. For example, if $w = \langle t_1, t_1, t_2, t_1, t_2, t_3 \rangle$, $l(t_1) = a$, $l(t_2) = \tau$, and $l(t_3) = b$, and $m \xrightarrow{w} m'$, then $m \xRightarrow{v} m'$ with $v = \langle a, a, a, b \rangle$. We refer to v as a *trace* whenever $m_N \xRightarrow{v} m_f$ with $m_f \in \Omega$ and $Tr(N) = \{\sigma \in \mathcal{A}^* \mid \exists m_f \in \Omega : m_N \xRightarrow{\sigma} m_f\}$ is the set of all traces of N.

A net N is *bounded* if there exists a bound $b \in I\!N$ such that for all reachable markings $m \in M_N$ and $p \in P$, $m(p) \leq b$. A reachable marking $m \notin \Omega$ of N is a *deadlock* if no transition $t \in T$ of N is enabled at m. Net N is *deadlock free* if at least one transition of N is enabled at every reachable non-final marking.

9.2.2 Open Nets

A service consists of a control structure describing its behavior and an interface to communicate asynchronously with other services. Thereby an interface consists of a set of input and output *ports*. In order that two services can interact with each other, an input port of the one service has to be connected with an output port of the other service. These connected ports then form a *channel*.

The control structure of a service can be adequately modeled as a net. We use the set of final markings of a net to model the states, in which a service may successfully terminate. In addition, it is necessary to model ports. To this end, we add an *interface* to our model. The service interface is reflected by two disjoint sets of *input and output places*. Thereby, each interface place corresponds to a port. An input place has an empty preset and is used for receiving messages from a distinguished channel, whereas an output place has an empty postset and is used for sending messages via a distinguished channel. In the model, we abstract from data and identify each message by the label of its message channel. The resulting service models are *open nets* [28, 53].

Definition 9.2 (Open net). An *open net* N is a tuple $(P, T, F, m_N, I, O, \Omega)$ with

- $(P \cup I \cup O, T, F, m_N, \Omega)$ is a net such that P, I, O are pairwise disjoint;
- for all $p \in I \cup O$, $m_N(p) = 0$, and for all $m \in \Omega$ and $p \in I \cup O$, $m(p) = 0$;
- the set I of *input places* satisfies for all $p \in I$, ${}^\bullet p = \emptyset$; and
- the set O of *output places* satisfies for all $p \in O$, $p^\bullet = \emptyset$.

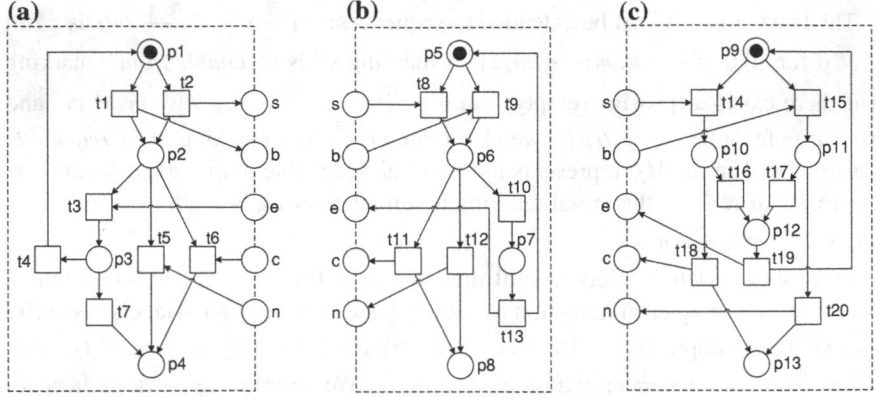

Fig. 9.3 Open nets modeling a customer ($\Omega_C = \{[p_1], [p_4]\}$) and two translation services ($\Omega_T = \{[p_5], [p_8]\}$ and $\Omega_B = \{[p_9], [p_{13}]\}$). **a** Customer N_C. **b** Translator N_T. **c** Translator N_B

If $I = O = \emptyset$, then N is a *closed net*. The net *inner*(N) results from removing the interface places and their adjacent arcs from N. Two open nets are *interface equivalent* if they have the same sets of input and output places.

A closed net can be used to model a service choreography, whereas the inner of an open net reflects the interior of a service. Graphically, we represent an open net like a net with a dashed frame around it. The interface places are depicted on the frame.

Figure 9.3 depicts our running example. It is a simplified (behavioral) model of a translation service. The example is inspired by the translation APIs offered by Bing and Google. The service in Fig. 9.3b receives a text file that must be translated. Our example allows customers to send a small or a large file, modeled by messages s and b, respectively. Depending on the pricing model used, the service asks for a cheap or a normal price (messages c and n). Sometimes the service may not work properly, for example, if too many requests are sent. In this case, the service sends an error message e. After having successfully translated a text file, the service enters a final state. In addition, also the initial state is a final state to allow customers to stop at any time if the translation service does not work properly. Figure 9.3a depicts the open net of a customer who may send small and large file and, in the case of an error, may send the file again or terminate (final marking $[p_1]$).

Communication between two services takes place by connecting pairs of ports using a channel and exchanging messages via these channels. We model this by composing the respective open nets, thereby merging shared interface places and turn these places into internal places. Such a merged interface place models a channel and a token on such a place corresponds to a pending message in the respective channel.

For the composition of open nets, we assume that the sets of transitions are pairwise disjoint and that no internal place of an open net is a place of any other open net. In contrast, the interfaces intentionally overlap. We require that all communication is

Fig. 9.4 Open net modeling a contract

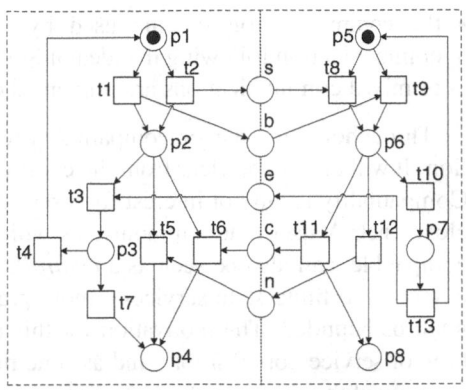

bilateral and *directed*; that is, every shared place p has only one open net that sends into p and one open net that receives from p. We refer to open nets that fulfill these properties as *composable*.

Definition 9.3 (Open net composition). Open nets N_1 and N_2 are *composable* if $(P_1 \cup T_1 \cup I_1 \cup O_1) \cap (P_2 \cup T_2 \cup I_2 \cup O_2) = (I_1 \cap O_2) \cup (I_2 \cap O_1)$. The *composition* of two composable open nets N_1 and N_2 is the open net $N_1 \oplus N_2 = (P, T, F, m_N, I, O, \Omega)$ where

- $P = P_1 \cup P_2 \cup (I_1 \cap O_2) \cup (I_2 \cap O_1)$;
- $T = T_1 \cup T_2$;
- $F = F_1 \cup F_2$;
- $m_N = m_{N_1} + m_{N_2}$;
- $I = (I_1 \cup I_2) \setminus (O_1 \cup O_2)$;
- $O = (O_1 \cup O_2) \setminus (I_1 \cup I_2)$; and
- $\Omega = \{m_1 + m_2 \mid m_1 \in \Omega_1 \wedge m_2 \in \Omega_2\}$.

Ignoring the dotted line along the former interface places, Fig. 9.4 shows the composition of the two open nets N_C and N_T of Fig. 9.3.

Open net composition models asynchronous message passing. Asynchronous message passing means that communication is nonblocking; that is, after a service has sent a message it can continue its execution and does not have to wait until this message is received. Furthermore, messages can 'overtake' each other; that is, the order in which the messages are sent is not necessarily the order in which they are received.

We want the composition of a set of services to be *compatible*. There exist a multitude of compatibility notions in the literature, making it is impossible to list them all. However, almost all of these notions can be classified into three dimensions:

- the composition terminates (e.g., deadlock freedom or the possibility to always reach a final marking, i.e., weak termination);
- the composition fulfills a scenario (e.g., a client must always pay by credit card); and

- the communication schema used by the composition (beside asynchronous communication following the idea of SOA, in practice also synchronous, queued, or mixed communications are implemented).

Throughout this chapter, compatibility refers deadlock freedom or weak termination. It will always be clear from the context, which of the two notions we consider. Compatibility is only of interest for a service choreography, which is modeled by a closed net. A user that communicates with a service, such that the composition is compatible, can also be seen as a *controller* of the service. In addition, we restrict ourselves to finite state services—more precisely, a composition with a controller must be bounded. The motivation for this restriction is that we model the control flow of service compositions and assume finitely many control states and a (finite) capacity of the message channels. For a reasonable concept of a service, we assume the inner of an open net, modeling the service interior, to be finite state. To ensure boundedness in the composition, controllers must not send a message if there the bound in the respective message channel has been reached already. Technically, this enforces that the composition has a finite number of reachable states. Pragmatically, it could either represent a reasonable buffer size in the middleware—for example, the result of a static analysis of the communication behavior of a service—or be chosen sufficiently large.

Definition 9.4 (Controllability). An open net C is a *controller* of an open net N if the composition $N \oplus C$ is closed, compatible (i.e., deadlock free or weakly terminating), and bounded. If such a C exists, then N is *controllable*.

If N is not controllable, then N is obviously ill-designed because it cannot properly interact with any other open net.

The contract in Fig. 9.4 is closed, 1-bounded, and weakly terminating (i.e., it is always possible to reach a final marking). As a consequence, open net N_C is a controller of open net N_T, and vice versa.

Later in this chapter, we want to analyze the behavior of a service modeled as an open net. The behavior of an open net is basically the reachability graph of its inner. To highlight which transitions are sending and receiving actions and which are only internal actions, we label each transition of an open net. The idea is to add to each transition adjacent to an interface place the respective place label and to all other transitions the label τ (denoting the internal action). To simplify the labeling, we restrict ourselves to open nets where each transition is connected to at most one interface place. We refer to those open nets as *elementary communicating*. That way, a transition is labeled by a single label rather than a set. This restriction is not significant as every open net can be transformed into an equivalent elementary communicating open net [28]. The respective inner is a labeled net to which we refer as *the synchronous environment*.

The behavior of an open net N can now be defined by the reachability graph $RG(env^s(N))$ of its synchronous environment. This graph has reachable markings $M_{env^s(N)}$ as its nodes and a $l(t)$-labeled edge from m to m' whenever $m \xrightarrow{t} m'$.

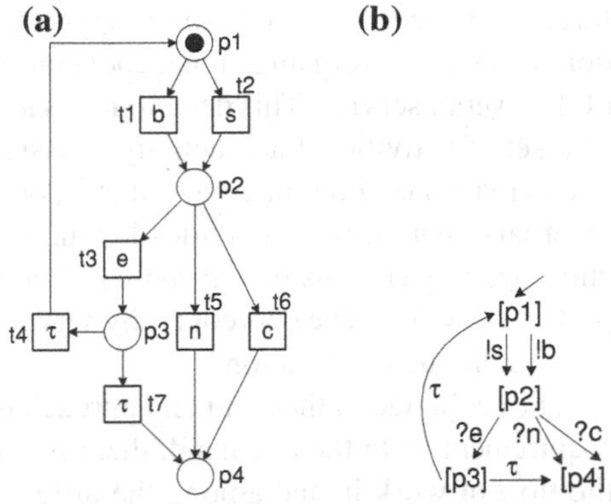

Fig. 9.5 Synchronous environment of the customer and its reachability graph. Symbol "?" denotes a receiving and "!" a sending event of N_C.
a $env^s(N_C)$. **b** $RG(env^s(N_C))$

Figure 9.5 depicts the synchronous environment $env^s(N_C)$ of the customer service and its behavior described by the reachability graph of $env^s(N_C)$.

We introduced open nets as a formal model for service behavior. Open nets can be used to model service compositions, asynchronous communication, and proper termination. Open nets abstract from data and identify each message by the label of its message channel. This abstraction is necessary, because the analysis techniques that shall be introduced in the forthcoming sections are only applicable for finite state models. However, our approach allows to deal with finite data domains as those domains can be unfolded—for example, if a message returns a Boolean, then we could unfold this domain yielding two channels, one for exchanging value true and the other for value false. There also exist techniques to derive a finite abstraction from an infinite data domain, but they are out of scope for this chapter. To simplify our analysis techniques, open nets also abstract from time information. Moreover, open nets are a well-suited model for service behavior due to their link to workflows [8]. Nevertheless, also other modeling techniques have been successfully applied, for example, transition systems, finite automata, process algebra, and session types.

9.3 Service Substitution

In this section, we formalize multiparty contracts, introduce two substitutability notions and algorithms to decide these notions, and present variants of service substitution.

9.3.1 Multiparty Contracts and Accordance of Services

The service-oriented paradigm enables enterprises to publish their services via the Internet. These services can then be automatically found and used by other enterprises. However, this approach has not become accepted in practice, mainly because enterprises usually cooperate only with enterprises they already know. Therefore, in practice, a more pragmatic approach is used instead. The parties that will participate in an interorganizational cooperation specify together an abstract description of the overall service. This description is a choreography. The choreography consists of a set of activities. Each activity is assigned to one party. A connection between two activities is either internal—that is, both activities belong to the same party—or external—that is, both activities belong to different parties. A party's share of the choreography (i.e., its *public view*) is then the projection of the choreography to the party's activities. The choreography serves as a common *contract* among the parties involved in the cooperation.

The challenge of the contract approach is to balance the following two conflicting requirements: On the one hand, there is a strong need for *coordination* to optimize the flow of work in and among the different parties. On the other hand, the parties involved in the cooperation are essentially *autonomous* and have the freedom to create or modify their services at any point in time. Furthermore, the parties do not want to reveal their trade secrets. Therefore, it has been proposed to use a contract that defines "rules of engagement" without describing the internal services executed within each party [2, 13].

After the parties have specified the contract, each party will implement its public view on its own. The implementation, the *private view*, will usually deviate significantly from its public view. Obviously, these local modifications have to *conform* to the agreed contract. This is, in fact, a nontrivial task, because it may cause global errors, such as deadlocks. As all parties are autonomous, none of them owns the overall service (i.e., the implemented contract). Therefore, none of the parties can verify the overall service. As a result, an approach is needed such that each party can check locally whether its private view guarantees global correctness of the overall service.

The basic idea of the contract approach can be seen in Fig. 9.2. The starting point is the specification on the top left which serves as a contract. It is partitioned into four parties, each illustrated as a fragment of the specification. By substituting each fragment by its implementation, we obtain the implementation on the top right.

Basically, we see a contract as a closed net N, where every transition is assigned to one of the involved parties $X_1, \ldots, X_k$. We impose only one restriction: If a place is accessed by more than one party, it should act as a directed bilateral communication place. This restriction reflects the fact that a party's public view of the contract is a service again. A contract N can be cut into parts $N_1, \ldots, N_k$, each representing the agreed public view of a single party $X_i (1 \leq i \leq k)$. Hence, we define a contract as the composition of the open nets $N_1, \ldots, N_k$.

Definition 9.5 (Multiparty contract). Let $\mathcal{X} = \{X_1, \ldots, X_k\}$ be a set of parties. Let $\{N_1, \ldots, N_k\}$ be a set of pairwise interface compatible open nets such that $N = N_1 \oplus \cdots \oplus N_k$ is a closed net. Then, N is a *contract for* $\mathcal{X}$. For $i = 1, \ldots, k$, open net N_i is the *public view of* X_i *in* N.

Figure 9.4 shows a multiparty contract involving only two parties: a customer and a translation service. The dotted line is used to divide the composition into the two shares, open nets N_C and N_T.

As previously mentioned, we want that every party involved in the contract can independently substitute its public view N_i with a private view N_i'. Clearly, this substitution should not violate compatibility of the contact. Informally spoken, all the other services forming the environment of N_i must not distinguish between N_i and N_i'. This can be achieved if every controller of N_i is also a controller of N_i'. This relation between the two open nets forms a refinement relation to which we refer as *accordance*.

Definition 9.6 (Accordance). Let *Spec* and *Impl* be interface equivalent open nets. Open net *Impl* *accords with* open net *Spec*, denoted by *Impl* $\sqsubseteq_{acc}$ *Spec*, if every controller C of *Spec* is also a controller of *Impl*.

The main result for multiparty contracts is that each party can substitute its public view by a private view independently. If each of the private views accords with the corresponding public view, then compatibility (here deadlock freedom) of the implemented contract is guaranteed.

Theorem 9.7 (Implementation of a contract). *Let N be a contract between parties* $\{X_1, \ldots, X_k\}$ *where N is compatible. If, for all $i \in \{1, \ldots, k\}$, N_i' accords with N_i, then $N' = N_1' \oplus \cdots \oplus N_k'$ is compatible.*

Figure 9.3c depicts a private view N_B of the translation service N_T. This service implements a more concrete pricing model compared to N_T: Translating a small file is cheap whereas for large files a normal price is asked for. If we consider deadlock freedom as a compatibility notion, then N_B accords with N_T. With Theorem 9.7, we conclude that substituting N_T by N_B preserves deadlock freedom. Next we show, how we can decide accordance for two open nets.

9.3.2 Deciding Accordance Using Operating Guidelines

An algorithm to decide accordance for two open nets *Spec* and *Impl* must decide whether every controller of *Spec* is also a controller of *Impl*. As an open net has potentially infinitely many controllers, we must check inclusion of two infinite sets. For *deadlock freedom*, we can overcome this problem, because the set of all controllers of open nets can be represented in a finite manner using a data structure called *operating guideline* [28].

An operating guideline $OG(N)$ of a service N describes how a user should successfully communicate with N; technically, it characterizes the behavior of the possibly infinite set of controllers of N in a finite manner. It is based on the observation that there exists a behavior that has the least restrictions, the *most permissive behavior*. The most permissive behavior is a deterministic transition system TS^* and serves as

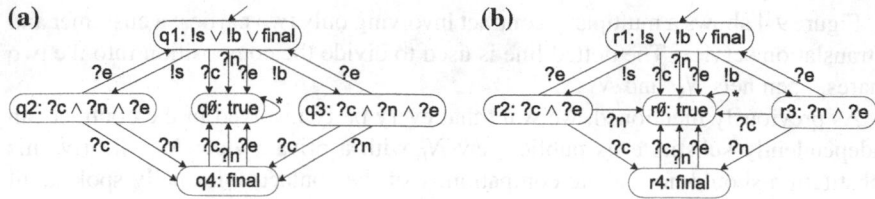

Fig. 9.6 Operating guidelines for the two translator services. Symbol * is a short hand for every element of the alphabet. **a** $OG(N_T)$. **b** $OG(N_B)$

the first ingredient for our operating guideline. Every behavior of any controller is then just a restriction of TS^*. We can specify those restrictions by annotating every state of TS^* with a Boolean formula, specifying which of the outgoing transitions must be present. Thus, a literal of such a Boolean formula is a transition label of N or the literal *final*, specifying that N is in a final state. The Boolean formula are the second ingredient of an operating guideline. Technically, an operating guideline is an annotated automaton.

Figure 9.6a shows the operating guideline of open net N_T. It is a finite automaton with five annotated states and can be read as follows. Initially, a controller of N_T either sends a (small or large) file or is in a final state. After sending for example, a small file (state q_2), the controller must be able to receive messages e, c, and n. The conjunction thereby emphasizes that any of these three messages can be sent and hence has to be received. Receiving e yields the initial state; receiving any of the other messages yields state q_4, where the controller must terminate. State $q_\emptyset$ denotes a nonreachable state: It does not harm if a controller can receive more messages than the service will send. For example, initially N_T will not send the translated file but it is not wrong if a controller can receive such a message.

To determine whether an open net C is a controller of an open net N, we check whether the behavior $TS_C = RG(env^s(C))$ of C *matches* with the operating guideline of N. Matching consists of two steps. First, we check whether TS_C is a potential restriction of TS^* by applying a procedure similar to a weak simulation relation— the difference is, whenever a τ-labeled transition can be performed in TS_C, then TS^* remains in the same state. Second, for each pair (q_C, q^*) of states in the relation, we verify whether the outgoing transitions of q_C and the information whether q_C is a final state or not evaluate the Boolean formula ϕ assigned to q^* to true. That way, we check whether TS_C is a valid restriction of TS^*.

Matching the behavior of the customer N_C with the operating guideline of N_T yields relation $\{([p_1], q_1), ([p_2], q_2), ([p_2], q_3), ([p_3], q_1), ([p_4], q_1), ([p_4], q_4)\}$. For example, in $([p_1], q_1)$, $[p_1]$ assigns true to all three literals of $\phi(q_1)$, thereby evaluating this formula to true. Similar, in $([p_2], q_2)$, $[p_2]$ assigns true to all three literals of $\phi(q_2)$, thereby evaluating this formula to true. The same holds for all other elements of this relation, and therefore we conclude that N_C matches with $OG(N_T)$—which must be the case because N_C is a controller of N_T.

An *operating guideline* $OG(N)$ *of an open net* N *is the annotated automaton that represents all controllers of* N [28]. With the operating guidelines $OG(Spec)$ and $OG(Impl)$ of two open nets $Spec$ and $Impl$, we can decide whether $Impl$ accords with $Spec$.

Theorem 9.8 (Deciding accordance [50]**).** *For open nets Spec and Impl, with operating guidelines* $OG(Spec)$ *and* $OG(Impl)$, *we have that* $Impl \sqsubseteq_{acc} Spec$ *iff there exists a minimal simulation* ϱ *of* $OG(Spec)$ *by* $OG(Impl)$ *and, for each pair of nodes* $(q_{Spec}, q_{Impl}) \in \varrho$, $\phi(q_{Spec})$ *implies* $\phi(q_{Impl})$ *is a tautology.*

Intuitively, the existence of the minimal simulation relation [33] guarantees that $OG(Impl)$ simulates the behavior of every controller of $Spec$, and the implication of the formulae ensures that whenever a service deadlocks with $Impl$ it does so with $Spec$. The operating guideline algorithm has been implemented in the tool Wendy [30] and the accordance check in the tool Cosme [31].

Consider the operating guidelines $OG(N_T)$ and $OG(N_C)$. The minimal simulation relation is $\varrho = \{(q_1, r_1), (q_2, r_2), (q_3, r_3), (q_4, r_4), (q_\emptyset, r_\emptyset)\}$. For each element of ϱ, the tautology holds; for example, for (q_2, r_2) we have $?c \wedge ?n \wedge ?e$ implies $?c \wedge ?e$ is a tautology. Thus, N_B accords with N_T.

9.3.3 Substitution in a Less Restrictive Setting

One of the main drivers for service evolution is that organizations have to increase their profit and therefore continuously improve their services. Service improvement includes figuring out bottlenecks and unprofitable lines of business. On the level of the service behavior, service improvement leads to restructuring the process. Restructuring may also result in excluding some business functionality. For example, the translation service may stop offering the translation of large files if this is not profitable. As a consequence, the improved service may have fewer controllers than the current service. Thus, another refinement notion than accordance is necessary to cope with this scenario. To this end, we introduce *preservation*, a refinement relation in which the implementation preserves only a subset of the controllers of the specification.

Definition 9.9 (Preservation). Let *Spec* and *Impl* be interface equivalent open nets and $\mathcal{C}$ be a set of controllers of *Spec*. Open net *Impl* *accords with open net Spec under preservation of* $\mathcal{C}$, denoted by $Impl \sqsubseteq_{acc,\mathcal{C}} Spec$, if every controller $C \in \mathcal{C}$ is also a controller of *Impl*.

If $Impl \sqsubseteq_{acc,\mathcal{C}} Spec$ then $Impl$ controls every $C \in \mathcal{C}$. This, however, is equivalent to $Impl$ matches with the operating guideline for any C. For a finite set $\mathcal{C}$, we can represent the intersection of the individual sets of services represented by these operating guidelines as one operating guideline. Technically, this operating guideline has the synchronous product of the underlying transition systems as its structure and to every synchronized state we assign the conjunction of the respective Boolean formulae. The following theorem formalizes the informally sketched decision procedure.

Theorem 9.10 (**Deciding preservation** [50]). *Let Spec and Impl be interface equivalent open nets and* $C = \{C_1, \ldots, C_k\}$ *be a set of controllers of Spec. Let* $OG(C_i)$, $1 \leq i \leq k$, *be the operating guideline of* C_i, *and let* $OG_\otimes$ *denote the product of all* $OG(C_i)$. *Then,* $Impl \sqsubseteq_{acc,C} Spec$ *iff Impl matches with* $OG_\otimes$.

The limitation of this result is that set C must be finite. However, it is also possible to constrain the set of controllers of a service by excluding or enforcing certain scenarios. The idea is similar: A constraint can be modeled as an (annotated) automaton. By constructing the product of this automaton and the operating guideline of *Spec*, we can constrain the controllers of *Spec*; see [27, 50]. In addition, [52] shows how certain activities of a service (i.e., transitions in the respective open net) can be covered.

9.3.4 Accordance in a Purely Service-Oriented Setting

In this section, we investigate service substitution in a purely service-oriented setting where services are composed from other published services. We want to decide when a service *Spec* published by some party can be substituted by a modified version *Impl*. Clearly, service *Impl* must accord with *Spec*. The actual challenge is that the party (i.e., a service provider) does not even know in which environment its service is executed. To illustrate that this fact matters, consider a closed net $N \oplus N_1 \oplus Spec$ with N shares interface places with N_1 and *Spec* but N_1 and *Spec* do not share interface places. In the contract setting, the provider of *Spec* knows the public views of N_1 and N and hence can substitute *Spec* by an accordant *Impl*. In the current setting, the provider of *Spec* does not know N nor N_1, but the refinement of *Spec* must be compositional in the sense that an accordant *Impl* must guarantee that also the composition $Impl \oplus N$ accords with $Spec \oplus N$. This argumentation is more difficult, because the two latter open nets are not closed. A refinement relation, such as accordance, that satisfies this property is a *precongruence*. A precongruence is a preorder such that if two open nets *Spec* and *Impl* are related by the precongruence so are $Impl \oplus N$ and $Spec \oplus N$ for any composable open net N. In contrast, the refinement relation necessary for ensuring Theorem 9.7, does not need to be a precongruence but only a preorder. For more details on this setting and a precongruence result for accordance, we refer to [51].

9.3.5 Service Instance Migration

So far, we have considered service substitution on the level of the service definition. However, running services may have long running instances. An example is the service of a life insurance company. A new legal regulation may cause a service to change, while instances of this service have been running for decades. In this case, each running instance of the old service has to be migrated to an instance of the new service. This problem is known as *service instance migration*.

Given a running instance in a state q_{Spec} of *Spec*, instance migration is the task of finding some state q_{Impl} of *Impl* such that resuming the execution in state q_{Impl} does not affect any controller of *Spec*. We call the transition from q_{Spec} to q_{Impl} a *jumper transition*. Clearly, there may be states q_{Spec} for which there does not exist a jumper transition to a state q_{Impl}. Sometimes it might be necessary to continue the instance on *Spec* until a state is reached, where a migration is then possible.

In [26], an algorithm based on operating guidelines has been proposed to calculate jumper transitions for accordance in the case of deadlock freedom. The algorithm has been implemented in the tool Mia. For the translation services N_T and N_B, the following pairs (m_T, m_B) would be calculated: $([p_5], [p_9])$, $([p_6], [p_{10}])$, $([p_6], [p_{11}])$, $([p_7], [p_{12}])$, and $([p_8], [p_{13}])$. For example, if the old instance is in marking $[p_7]$, then it can be migrated to marking $[p_{12}]$, thereby ensuring that no controller of N_T is affected by this migration.

9.3.6 Discussion and Related Work

We introduced two refinement relations, accordance and preservation, and a data structure to decide these relations. The algorithmic solutions are tailored to deadlock freedom, but in recent (yet unpublished) work the procedure has been lifted to weak termination. Case studies in [26, 30] show that our approach is applicable for service models of industrial size. To improve the efficiency of the accordance check, a more compact operating guideline representation has been proposed in [31]. An operating guideline can also be encoded as an automaton without annotations, called the maximal controller in [34]. This allows for another decision procedure for accordance: the composition of the maximal controller of service *Spec* and service *Impl* must be deadlock free. Kaschner and Wolf [23] showed that all noncontrollers of a service can be represented in a finite manner. This result (i.e., controller negation) together with the product of operating guidelines (i.e, intersection of sets of controllers) and an emptiness check yields an algebra on sets of controllers that generalizes the techniques for deciding preservation [23]. An approach to tackle preservation for more general properties has been proposed in [39, 43].

Closest to our work is the work of Vogler [53] who considers a more general notion of composition. Different refinement relations in a process-algebraic setting have been investigated, for example, in [17, 20, 25]. The termination criterion is usually stronger than deadlock freedom but the communication schema is mostly synchronous. Bravetti and Zavattaro [18] consider different communications schemes for weak termination. Benatallah et al. [16] investigate accordance and preservation in a synchronous setting and in [44], results for a timed model are presented. Dumas et al. [19] investigate accordance and preservation using the more expressive π-calculus.

Instance migration has been studied by many researchers, in particular, in the field of workflows; see [5, 45, 47] for an overview. For services, several variants of this problem have been investigated in [49].

9.4 Constructing Substitutable Services

In the previous section, we presented an algorithm to decide for two given open nets *Spec* and *Impl* whether *Impl* accords with *Spec* and thus can substitute *Spec* without violating any controller of *Spec*. However, designing *Impl* is a nontrivial and error-prone task even for experienced service designers. In order to support service designers, we introduce an approach to construct open nets that are *correct by design*.

9.4.1 Approach

Given an open net *Spec*, we want to incrementally transform *Spec* to an open net *Impl* such that every transformation step preserves accordance by construction. To this end, fragments of *Spec* are incrementally substituted by other fragments. In this approach, a fragment Z of *Spec* is substituted by another fragment Z' yielding the open net *Impl*. We prove that if Z' accords with Z, then *Impl* accords with *Spec*.

An open net Z is a *fragment* of an open net N if there is an open net N_{rest} and the composition of Z and N_{rest} is the open net N. The set of interface places of Z is divided into two sets: some interface places of N and some internal places $R \cup S$ of N. We use R to denote these input places and S to denote these output places. For technical reasons, we require that the initial marking of Z is the empty marking and the set of final markings is the singleton set with the empty marking.

Definition 9.11 (Fragment). Let Z be an open net with $m_Z = 0$ and $\Omega = \{[\,]\}$. Open net Z is a *fragment* of an open net N if there exists an open net N_{rest} such that $N = Z \oplus N_{rest}$.

If an open net N has a fragment Z and there is another fragment Z' that accords with Z, then we can substitute Z by Z' without affecting any controller of N. Such transformations can be applied incrementally and thus refine a service specification to an implementation by applying transformation steps. The resulting implementation is correct by construction; that is, it preserves all controllers of the specification.

Theorem 9.12 (Justification [9]). *Let $N_1 \oplus N_2$ be a weakly terminating open net composition. Let Z be a fragment of N_1, and let N_{rest} be an open net such that $N_1 = Z \oplus N_{rest}$. For any open net Z' that accords with Z, the composition $(Z' \oplus N_{rest}) \oplus N_2$ is weakly terminating.*

9.4.2 Transformation Rules

The first three rules correspond to design patterns for extending a service to incorporate new behavior: (1) adding an internal loop, (2) putting a new internal transition in parallel with existing transitions, and (3) inserting an internal transition in-between existing transitions. These rules have been introduced in [5].

We exemplify these rules in Fig. 9.7. Figure 9.7a represents a fragment Z_0 of an open net N. Z_0 contains transitions a, b, and c. By Definition 9.11, there are no other connections of a, b, c, $p1$ and $p2$ than those shown in Fig. 9.7a. Each transition is connected to an input and an output place. However, as indicated by the capital letters, each interface place may correspond to a set of places. Further, A_i, A_o, B_i, B_o, C_i, C_o do not need to be disjoint. Places R and S denote the input and output places to N. Again, R and S may be sets of places. Similar remarks hold for the other three fragments Z_1, Z_2, and Z_3. For example, Z_1 is obtained by adding transition d to Z_0.

The three transformation rules only add (or remove if applied in reverse direction) internal transitions of an open net. However, there are also transformation rules that directly impact the interface behavior. We present four example transformation rules that affect transitions that are adjacent to an interface place.

Rule 4 is depicted in Fig. 9.8a and specifies that a sequence of receiving transitions can be merged, and the messages can be sent simultaneously. It is also possible to reorder a sequence of receiving transitions or to execute them concurrently (not shown). The same rule holds for a sequence of sending transitions. Rule 5 in Fig. 9.8b combines sending and receiving transitions. A receiving transition followed by a sending transition can be executed simultaneously. Due to Rule 4, Rule 5 can be generalized to a sequence of receiving transitions followed by a sequence of sending transitions. Rule 6, depicted in Fig. 9.8c, specifies that first sending and then receiving a message can also be executed concurrently, and vice versa. Rules 4–6 preserve accordance in both directions.

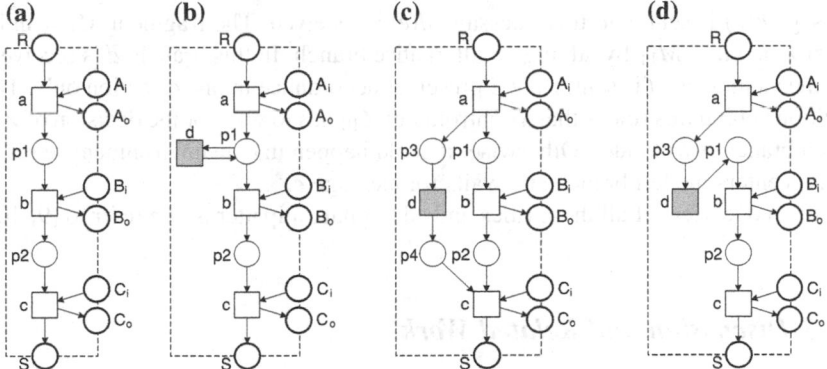

Fig. 9.7 Transformation rules to change internal transitions: transition d is added (when applied *left to right*) or removed (when applied *right to left*). **a** Z_0. **b** Z_1: Adding a loop to Z_0. **c** Z_2: Putting transition d in parallel to b. **d** Z_3: Inserting transition d in-between a and b

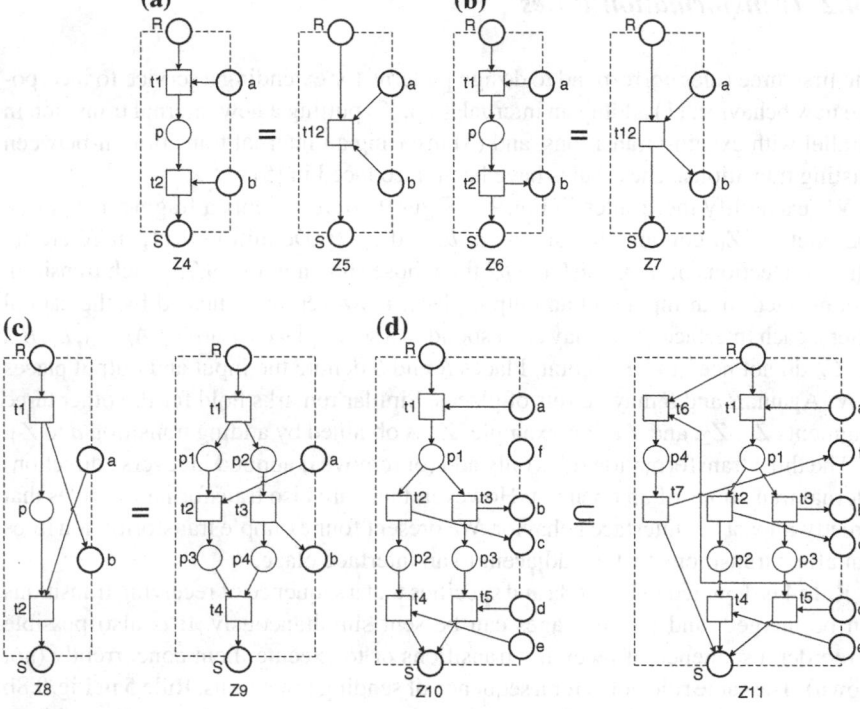

Fig. 9.8 Transformation rules to change interface transitions. **a** Rule 4: $Con(Z_4) = Con(Z_5)$. **b** Rule 5: $Con(Z_6) = Con(Z_7)$. **c** Rule 6: $Con(Z_8) = Con(Z_9)$. **d** Rule 7: $Con(Z_{10}) \subseteq Con(Z_{11})$

This is in contrast to Rule 7 which specifies a way to add an alternative branch to a fragment Z_{10} depicted on the left hand side of Fig. 9.8d. The fragment Z_{10} first receives a and then enters either the left or the right branch. In the left (right) branch, message $b(c)$ is sent, and then message $d(e)$ is received. The fragment M_{10} can be transformed into M_{11} by adding an alternative branch. In this branch, d is received, and then a message f is sent. Rule 7 preserves accordance in one direction only. The intuition behind this rule is that a controller of Z_{10} has to wait for the decision of Z_{10} which branch it will enter. Otherwise, it could happen that an environment sends d, but Z_{10} enters the left branch and waits for message e.

For an overview of all these rules and additional antipatterns, we refer to [9, 10].

9.4.3 Discussion and Related Work

We presented seven accordance-preserving transformation rules. Six of these rules preserve accordance in both directions and one rule preserves accordance only in one direction. Although these transformation rules are sound (i.e., correctness preserving), they are not complete, meaning they do not cover all possible service implementations. This is actually the weak point when dealing with transformations.

Refinement of Petri nets has been addressed by many researchers. However, most of the results require restricted Petri net classes or Petri nets without interfaces. The Murata rules [38] also maintain accordance, if we consider every input place as a place with some additional incoming arcs, and every output place as a place with some additional outgoing arcs. Refinement of places and transitions in Petri nets that preserves compatibility of the whole net is studied in [53]. These results could be applied in our setting. Soundness preserving transformation rules have been proposed in [1, 5, 54]. The rules proposed by Van Hee et al. [22] refine sets of places in service compositions, but they require additional reachability checks. In [24], the authors show how the presented rules can be translated into BPEL. That way, BPEL processes can directly be refined without transforming them into a formal service model.

9.5 Conformance Checking of Services Based on Observed Behavior

Thus far, we only considered *modeled* service behavior. For example, we described requirements linking the public view of one party in the multiparty contract to the corresponding private view (implementation view). The analysis techniques did not consider actually observed behavior. However, in the context of services it is often not realistic to assume that all parties will indeed execute their processes as agreed upon at design time. Services may have been implemented incorrectly or change over time. Therefore, we now focus on *conformance checking based on events logs* (i.e., recorded behavior).

Process mining is a relatively young research discipline that sits between computational intelligence and data mining on the one hand, and process modeling and analysis on the other hand. Process mining research resulted in mature conformance checking techniques and tools that are able to align observed and modeled behavior [3, 4]. As a result it is possible to detect and quantify deviations.

In the remainder, we first introduce some basic process mining terminology. Then, we show how event log and model can be *aligned*. Based on this, we show how conformance checking techniques can be used to compare observed behavior (i.e., event data) with the public view of one or more parties in the multiparty contract. We also define conformance checking problems in a less restrictive setting where, from a behavioral point of view, parties may deviate from the contract as long as it does not harm the overall choreography.

Initially, we focus on conformance checking based on historic data ("offline" conformance checking). However, all techniques can be applied on-the-fly ("online" conformance checking); that is, streaming event data can be monitored at runtime and deviations can be detected immediately.

9.5.1 Process Mining

Process mining aims to *discover, monitor and improve real processes by extracting knowledge from event logs* readily available in today's information systems [3]. Starting point for process mining is an *event log*. Each event in such a log refers to an *activity* (i.e., a well-defined step in some process) and is related to a particular *case* (i.e., a *process instance*). The events belonging to a case are *ordered* and can be seen as one "run" of the process. An event log contains only *example* behavior; that is, we cannot assume that all possible runs have been observed. In fact, an event log often contains only a fraction of the possible behavior.

In this chapter, we define an event log as a multiset of *traces*. Each trace describes the life-cycle of a particular case in terms of the activities executed.

Definition 9.13 (**Event, Trace, Event log**). Let $\mathcal{A}$ be a set of activities. $\sigma \in \mathcal{A}^*$ is a *trace*, i.e., a sequence of events. $L \in \mathcal{B}(\mathcal{A}^*)$ is an *event log*, i.e., a multiset of traces.

In this simple definition of an event log, an event refers to just an *activity*. Often event logs may store additional information about events. For example, many process mining techniques use extra information, such as the *resource* (i.e., person or device) executing or initiating the activity, the *timestamp* of the event, or *data elements* recorded with the event (e.g., the size of an order). In this paper, we abstract from such information. An example log is $L = [\langle b, c \rangle^{10}, \langle s, e, s, c \rangle^5, \langle s, e, b, n \rangle^5]$. L contains information about 20 cases, e.g., 10 cases followed trace $\langle b, c \rangle$. There are $10 \times 2 + 5 \times 4 + 5 \times 4 = 60$ events in total.

To relate event logs to process models, we use labeled nets. The behavior of such a model is described by the set $Tr(N)$ of traces which is computed from the set $Ru(N)$ of runs leading from the initial marking to a final marking; see Sect. 9.2.1 for a definition.

Figure 9.9c shows the labeled Petri net $env^s(N_B)$. The set of runs of $env^s(N_B)$ is the set $Ru(env^s(N_B)) = \{\langle t_{14}, t_{18} \rangle, \langle t_{15}, t_{20} \rangle, \langle t_{14}, t_{16}, t_{19}, t_{15}, t_{20} \rangle, \langle t_{15}, t_{17}, t_{19}, t_{14}, t_{18} \rangle, \ldots\}$. Every of these runs starts in $[p_9]$ and ends in $[p_{13}]$. The labeled net in Fig. 9.9c is weakly terminating, because all partial runs can be extended into a run in $Ru(env^s(N_B))$. If the labeled net has deadlocks or livelocks, then the problematic traces are simply discarded by $Ru(env^s(N_B))$.

Each trace in $Tr(env^s(N_B))$ corresponds to one or more runs in $Ru(env^s(N_B))$. A transition t is removed from the sequence if $l(t) = \tau$, otherwise it is replaced by $l(t)$. Therefore, $Tr(env^s(N_B)) = \{\langle s, c \rangle, \langle b, n \rangle, \langle s, e, b, n \rangle, \langle b, e, s, c \rangle, \ldots\}$ for the labeled net in Fig. 9.9c. In $Tr(env^s(N_B))$, transitions are mapped onto their corresponding labels and τ transitions are not recorded; that is, t_{16} and t_{17} do not leave a trail in $Tr(env^s(N_B))$.

Event logs can be used to discover, monitor and improve services based on observations rather than hand-made models. There are three main types of process mining:

- *Discovery*: Take an event log and produce a model without using any other a-priori information. There are dozens of techniques to extract a process model from raw event data. For example, the classical α algorithm can discover a labeled net by

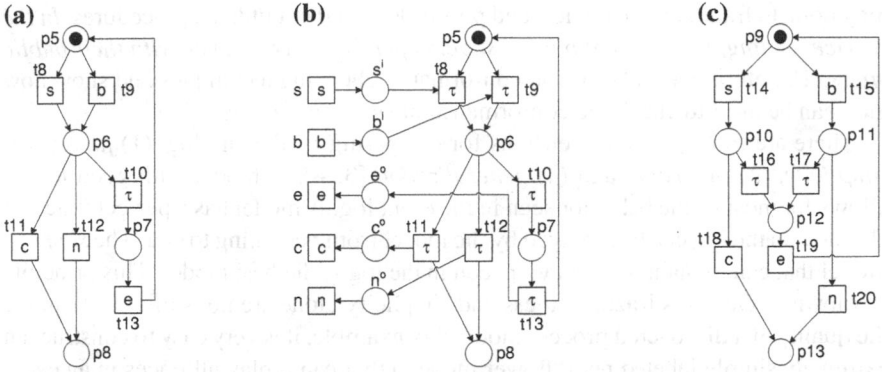

Fig. 9.9 Synchronous and asynchronous environment for open net N_T in Fig. 9.3b ($\Omega = \{[p_5], [p_8]\}$) and synchronous environment for open net N_B in Fig. 9.3c ($\Omega = \{[p_9], [p_{13}]\}$). **a** $env^s(N_T)$. **b** $env^a(N_T)$. **c** $env^s(N_B)$

identifying basic process patterns in an event log [12]. This algorithm takes an event log $L \in \mathcal{B}(\mathcal{A}^*)$ and produces a labeled net N. For many organizations it is surprising to see that existing techniques are indeed able to discover real processes based on merely example executions recorded in event logs. Process discovery is often used as a starting point for other types of analysis.

- *Conformance*: An existing process model is compared with an event log of the same process. For example, an event log $L \in \mathcal{B}(\mathcal{A}^*)$ is compared with the traces of some labeled net N. Ideally, any trace in L also appears in $Tr(N)$. Conformance checking reveals where the real process deviates from the modeled process. Moreover, it is possible to quantify the level of conformance and differences can be diagnosed. Conformance checking can be used to check if reality, as recorded in the log, conforms to the model, and vice versa.

- *Enhancement*: Take an event log and process model and extend or improve the model using the observed events. Whereas conformance checking measures the alignment between model and reality, this third type of process mining aims at changing or extending the a-priori model. For instance, by using timestamps in the event log one can extend the model to show bottlenecks, service levels, throughput times, and frequencies [3].

In the remainder, we focus on the second type of process mining: conformance checking.

9.5.2 Conformance Checking Approaches

Conformance checking techniques investigate how well an event log $L \in \mathcal{B}(A^*)$ and a model—in our case a labeled net—fit together. Conformance checking can be done for various reasons; for example, it may be used to audit processes to see whether reality conforms to some normative or descriptive model [4, 6, 7, 48]. Deviations may point to fraud, inefficiencies, and poorly designed or outdated procedures. *In the services setting, the different parties should operate in accordance with their public views.* Therefore, we elaborate on conformance checking techniques and show how they can be used to check the conformance of *running services*.

There are four quality dimensions for comparing model and log: (1) *fitness*, (2) *simplicity*, (3) *precision*, and (4) *generalization* [3, 4]. A model with good *fitness* allows for most of the behavior seen in the event log. A model has a perfect fitness if all traces in the log can be replayed by the model from beginning to end. The *simplest* model that can explain the behavior seen in the log is the best model. This principle is known as Occam's Razor. Fitness and simplicity alone are not sufficient to judge the quality of a discovered process model. For example, it is very easy to construct an extremely simple labeled net ("flower model") that can replay all traces in an event log (but also any other event log referring to the same set of activities). Similarly, it is undesirable to have a model that only allows for the exact behavior seen in the event log. Remember that the log contains only example behavior and that many traces that are possible may not have been seen yet. A model is *precise* if it does not allow for "too much" behavior. Clearly, the "flower model" lacks precision. A model that is not precise is "underfitting". Underfitting is the problem that the model over-generalizes the example behavior in the log (i.e., the model allows for behaviors very different from what was seen in the log). At the same time, the model should generalize and not restrict behavior to just the examples seen in the log. A model that does not *generalize* is "overfitting". Overfitting is the problem that a very specific model is generated whereas it is obvious that the log only holds example behavior (i.e., the model explains the particular sample log, but there is a high probability that the model is unable to explain the next batch of cases).

In the remainder, we will focus on fitness. Ideally, all traces in the log correspond to a possible run of the model.

Definition 9.14 (Perfectly fitting log). Let $L \in \mathcal{B}(A^*)$ be an event log and let N be a labeled net. L is *perfectly fitting* N if $\{\sigma \in L\} \subseteq Tr(N)$.

Consider the event log $L = [\langle b, c \rangle^{20}, \langle s, e, s, c \rangle^{10}, \langle s, e, b, n \rangle^{10}]$. Clearly, L is perfectly fitting the labeled net $env^s(N_T)$ in Fig. 9.9a but it is not perfectly fitting the labeled net $env^s(N_B)$ in Fig. 9.9c.

There are various ways to quantify fitness [3, 4, 15, 21, 32, 36, 37, 48], typically on a scale from 0 to 1, where 1 means perfect fitness. A naive approach would be to simply count the *fraction of fitting traces*. However, such an approach is too simplistic for two reasons:

- Whether traces in the log "almost" fit the model or not is irrelevant for such a metric. Traces $\sigma_1 = \langle e, b, c \rangle$ and $\sigma_2 = \langle e, e, e, b, c \rangle$ both do not fit the model in Fig. 9.9. However, it is obvious that σ_1 fits "better" than σ_2.
- It is important to also map the non-fitting behavior onto the model in order to do further analysis (performance analysis, predictions, etc.).

To address these issues, we need to *align* traces in the event log to traces of the process model. Some example alignments for L and the labeled net $env^s(N_B)$ are:

$$
\gamma_1 = \begin{array}{|c|c|c|} \hline b & c & \gg \\ \hline b & \gg & n \\ \hline t_{15} & & t_{20} \\ \hline \end{array}
\quad
\gamma_2 = \begin{array}{|c|c|c|c|c|} \hline b & \gg & \gg & \gg & c \\ \hline b & \tau & e & s & c \\ \hline t_{15} & t_{17} & t_{19} & t_{14} & t_{18} \\ \hline \end{array}
\quad
\gamma_3 = \begin{array}{|c|c|c|c|c|} \hline s & \gg & e & s & c \\ \hline s & \tau & e & s & c \\ \hline t_{14} & t_{16} & t_{19} & t_{14} & t_{18} \\ \hline \end{array}
$$

$$
\gamma_4 = \begin{array}{|c|c|c|c|c|} \hline s & \gg & e & b & n \\ \hline s & \tau & e & b & n \\ \hline t_{14} & t_{16} & t_{19} & t_{15} & t_{20} \\ \hline \end{array}
$$

The top row of each alignment corresponds to "moves in the log" and the bottom two rows correspond to "moves in the model". There are two bottom rows because there may be multiple transitions having the same label. If a move in the log cannot be mimicked by a move in the model, then a "$\gg$" ("no move") appears in the bottom row. For example, in γ_1 the model cannot do the c move. If a move in the model cannot be mimicked by a move in the log, then a "$\gg$" ("no move") appears in the top row. For example, all "silent steps" in the model (occurrences of τ transitions) cannot be mimicked by the event log. Moreover, in γ_2 the log did not do an "e move" whereas the model has to make this move to reach the end. Given a trace in the event log there may be many possible alignments. The goal is to find an alignment with the least number of $\gg$ elements, e.g., γ_1 is better than γ_2.

To establish an alignment between process model and event log, we need to relate "moves" in the log to "moves" in the model. However, as shown, there may be some moves in the log that cannot be mimicked by the model, and vice versa. For convenience, we introduce the set $A_L = \mathcal{A} \cup \{\gg\}$ where $x \in A_L \setminus \{\gg\}$ refers to "move x in log" and $\gg \in A_L$ refers to "no move in log". Similarly, we introduce the set $A_M = \{(a, t) \in \mathcal{A} \times T \mid l(t) = a\} \cup \{\gg\}$ where $(a, t) \in A_M$ refers to "move a in model" and $\gg \in A_M$ refers to "no move in model".

One step in an alignment is represented by a pair $(x, y) \in A_L \times A_M$ such that

- (x, y) is a *move in log* if $x \in \mathcal{A}$ and $y = \gg$,
- (x, y) is a *move in model* if $x = \gg$ and $y \in A_M \setminus \{\gg\}$,
- (x, y) is a *move in both* if $x \in \mathcal{A}$ and $y \in A_M \setminus \{\gg\}$, and
- (x, y) is an *illegal move* $x = \gg$ and $y = \gg$.

$A_{LM} = \{(x, y) \in A_L \times A_M \mid x \neq \gg \lor y \neq \gg\}$ is the set of all *legal moves*.

Let $\sigma_L \in L$ be a trace in the event log and let $\sigma_M \in Ru(N)$ be a run from the initial to a final marking of labeled net N. An *alignment* of σ_L and σ_M is a sequence $\gamma \in A_{LM}^*$ such that the projection on the first element (ignoring $\gg$) yields σ_L and the projection on the second element (again ignoring $\gg$ and only considering transitions and not the corresponding labels) yields σ_M. Consider again the four example alignments based on the labeled net $env^s(N_B)$. We represent the moves vertically, e.g., the first move of γ_1 is $(b, (b, t_{15}))$ indicating that both the log and the model make a b move. γ_1 is an alignment of $\sigma_L = \langle b, c \rangle$ and $\sigma_M = \langle t_{15}, t_{20} \rangle$. γ_2 is an alignment of $\sigma_L = \langle b, c \rangle$ and $\sigma_M = \langle t_{15}, t_{17}, t_{19}, t_{14}, t_{18} \rangle$.

To qualify the quality of an alignment, one can define a *distance function* on legal moves: $\delta \in A_{LM} \to I\!N$. The distance function associates costs to moves in an alignment:

- $\delta(a, \gg)$ is the cost of "move a in log" (with $a \in \mathcal{A}$),
- $\delta(\gg, (b, t))$ is the cost of "move b in model" (with $t \in T$ and $l(t) = b$), and
- $\delta(a, (b, t))$ is the cost of "move a in log and move b in model" (with $a \in \mathcal{A}, t \in T$ and $l(t) = b$).

Distance function δ can be generalized to alignments by taking the sum of the costs of all individual moves: $\delta(\gamma) = \sum_{(x,y) \in \gamma} \delta(x, y)$.[1]

We define a *standard distance function* δ_S. For $a \in \mathcal{A}$, $t \in T$, and $b = l(t)$: $\delta_S(a, \gg) = 1$, $\delta_S(\gg, (b, t)) = 1$ if $b \neq \tau$, $\delta_S(\gg, (b, t)) = 0$ if $b = \tau$, $\delta_S(a, (b, t)) = 0$ if $a = b$, and $\delta_S(a, (b, t)) = \infty$ if $a \neq b$. Only moves where log and model agree on the activity or internal τ moves of the model have no associated costs. Moves in just the log or model have cost 1. δ_S associates high costs to moves where both log and model make a move but disagree on the activity. In "$\delta_S(a, (b, t)) = \infty$", ∞ should be read as a number large enough to discard the alignment (see below). Using the standard distance function δ_S: $\delta_S(\gamma_1) = 2$, $\delta_S(\gamma_2) = 2$ (note that the move in model involves a τ transition), $\delta_S(\gamma_3) = 0$, and $\delta_S(\gamma_4) = 0$. So the sum of the costs is $\delta_S(\gamma) = 4$ for $env^s(N_B)$ and $\delta_S(\gamma) = 0$ for $env^s(N_T)$ (because L is a perfectly fitting log for $env^s(N_T)$). Note that δ_S is just an example; various cost functions can be defined.

Thus far we considered a *specific* run (from the initial to a final marking) in the model. However, our goal is to relate traces in the model to the *best matching* run in the model. Therefore, we define the notion of an *optimal alignment*. Let $\sigma_L \in L$ be a trace in event log L and let N be a labeled net. $\Gamma_{\sigma_L,N} = \{\gamma \in A_{LM}^* \mid \exists_{\sigma_M \in Ru(N)} \gamma \text{ is an alignment of } \sigma_L \text{ and } \sigma_M\}$. An alignment $\gamma \in \Gamma_{\sigma_L,N}$ is *optimal* for log trace $\sigma_L \in L$ and model N if for any $\gamma' \in \Gamma_{\sigma_L,N}$: $\delta(\gamma') \geq \delta(\gamma)$.

If $\mathcal{R}(N)$ is not empty, there is at least one (optimal) alignment for any given log trace σ_L. However, there may be multiple optimal alignments for σ_L. Since our goal is to align traces in the event log to traces of the model, we deterministically select an arbitrary optimal alignment. Therefore, we can construct a function λ_M that provides an "oracle": Given a log trace σ_L, λ_M produces *one* best matching run from the initial to a final marking and hence to a best matching trace $\lambda_M(\sigma_L) \in Tr(N)$. In [14, 15], various approaches are given to create an optimal alignment with respect to some predefined distance function. These approaches are based on the A^* algorithm; that is, an algorithm originally invented to find the shortest path between two nodes in a directed graph. The A^* algorithm can be adapted to find an optimal alignment between model and log. The process mining framework *ProM* supports various techniques to create such an alignment and use this for conformance checking and other types of log-based analysis [4].

The alignments produced by the "oracle" λ_M can be used to quantify fitness (typically a number between 0 and 1). If a trace appears multiple times in the event log, the associated costs are also counted multiple times. Moreover, once an optimal alignment has been established for every trace in the event log, these alignments can

---

[1] Summation is generalized to sequences; that is, if the same step occurs k times in γ its costs are counted k times.

be used as a basis to quantify precision and generalization [4, 37]. Such alignments are also a prerequisite for other types of analysis (e.g., performance analysis) [3].

In the remainder, we assume a function $conf$ that computes the fitness of an event log and a model based on an optimal alignment; that is, $conf(L, N)$ yields a number between 0 (poor fitness) and 1 (perfect fitness).

9.5.3 Conformance Checking of the Public View

Earlier we defined a *multiparty contract* as a set of pairwise interface compatible open nets $\{N_1, \ldots, N_k\}$ such that $N = N_1 \oplus \cdots \oplus N_k$ is a closed net. Each of the open nets N_i represents the *public view* of one of the parties. Party i can substitute its public view N_i by a private view N_i'. N_i' may refine N_i but may also change the ordering of some of the activities (see Fig. 9.8). However, ideally, the environment of N_i must not distinguish between N_i and N_i'.

For conformance checking, we need to compare observed behavior (i.e., recorded events in some log L) with modeled behavior (N_i or N_i'). In order to align observed behavior and modeled behavior, we need as input an event log $L \in \mathcal{B}(\mathcal{A}^*)$ and a labeled net $N = (P, T, F, m_N, \Omega, l)$. We cannot simply take some *public view* N_i as input for conformance checking. The public view is an open net with input places I and output places O. Transitions consuming from I are dead when checking the private view N_i in isolation. Tokens produced on places in O cannot be removed by N_i. Hence, $Tr(N_i)$ cannot contain sequences involving interface transitions. Moreover, events need to be related to transitions rather than places.

This triggers the question "What kinds of events can be observed?". Obviously, relevant events are related to the interface places $I \cup O$. However, given the asynchronous nature of open nets, we can take two viewpoints depending on what/when events are actually recorded.

If events are recorded when party i consumes a message from I or produces a message for O, then we can use the *synchronous environment* $env^s(N_i)$ of N_i. As before, we assume (without loss of generality) that a transition is connected to at most one interface place.

However, the environment of party i may be unable to see when a message is consumed from I or produced for O. For example, the environment can put a token in input place $p \in I$, but this does not imply that the token is immediately consumed by party i. Hence, we can only record the event of producing a token for input place p, but not the actual consumption. To this end, we construct the asynchronous environment $env^a(N)$ of an open net N by adding to each interface place p of N a p-labeled transition in $env^a(N)$ and renaming the place p to p^I (p^O) if p is an input (output) place in N. Figure 9.9b illustrates this construction for open net N_T.

To illustrate the difference between both types of environments, consider Fig. 9.9 showing the synchronous environment $env^s(N_T)$ and the asynchronous environment $env^a(N_T)$ for public view N_T in Fig. 9.3b. Which of the two labeled nets is most suitable, depends on the events that are recorded. Consider for example a message passed via input place s. If the event of consuming a message from interface place s is recorded, then $env^s(N_T)$ is more suitable. If the event of producing a message for interface place s is recorded, then $env^a(N_T)$ is more suitable.

The choice of environment matters. Consider for example trace $\langle s, b, e, c \rangle$ which is impossible according to $env^s(N_T)$ but allowed by $env^a(N_T)$. For any labeled net N: $Tr(env^s(N)) \subseteq Tr(env^a(N))$; that is, the asynchronous environment allows for more behavior and will be more "forgiving" under conformance checking. However, the proper choice of environment depends on what is actually logged. In the remainder, we will often abstract from these subtle differences and simply write $env(N)$.

Definition 9.15 (Public view conformance). Let $N = N_1 \oplus \cdots \oplus N_k$ be a multiparty contract and $i \in \{1, \ldots, k\}$ is one of the parties with public view N_i and event log L_i. $conf(L_i, env(N_i))$ is the *public view conformance* for party i.

This discussion thus far assumed that the environment of party i wants to check whether i conforms to its public view N_i. However, it is also possible to reverse roles in the multiparty contract $N = N_1 \oplus \cdots \oplus N_k$ and check whether the partners of i conform to $N_i^{-1} = \bigoplus_{j \neq i} N_j$. Depending what is actually logged on the interface between i and the other parties, one can use synchronous environment $env^s(N_i^{-1})$ or asynchronous environment $env^a(N_i^{-1})$.

Once an event log L and suitably labeled net N (e.g., $env^s(N_i)$, $env^a(N_i)$, $env^s(N_i^{-1})$, or $env^a(N_i^{-1})$) have been determined, we can align each trace in the log with the best fitting execution path of the service(s) under investigation. As discussed earlier, such an alignment can be used to compute a conformance value $conf(L, N)$.

9.5.4 Conformance Checking of the Private View

In the previous section, we showed that it is possible to check whether the observed behavior of party i (or its collaborators) is consistent with the behavior specified in the multiparty contract. However, such a check may be too strict in a services setting.

Theorem 9.7 shows that each party can substitute its public view N_i by a private view N_i' as long as N_i' accords to N_i. Rules 4, 5 and 6 in Fig. 9.8 illustrate that the notion of accordance is different from classical equivalence notions (e.g., trace equivalence). Parties may reorder activities without necessarily jeopardizing accordance. Therefore, it may be inappropriate to directly compare the observed behavior with the contract composed of public views. One party may have changed its behavior without jeopardizing compatibility. Therefore, we can also try to check conformance using some private view N_i' rather than the public view N_i.

Definition 9.16 (Private view conformance). Let $N = N_1 \oplus \cdots \oplus N_k$ be a multiparty contract and $i \in \{1, \ldots, k\}$ is one of the parties with public view N_i and event log L_i.

- $\mathcal{P}(N_i) = \{N \mid N \sqsubseteq_{acc} N_i\}$ is the set of all private views that accord with N_i,
- $N \in \mathcal{P}(N_i)$ is a *best matching private view* for N_i and L_i if for any $N' \in \mathcal{P}(N_i)$: $conf(L_i, env(N)) \geq conf(L_i, env(N'))$,
- $conf(L_i, env(N))$ is the *private view conformance* for party i where $N \in \mathcal{P}(N_i)$ is a best matching private view for N_i and L_i.

Definition 9.16 cannot easily be transformed into an algorithm. The process mining tool ProM provides excellent support for computing optimal alignments between log and model while allowing a variety of distance functions [4, 15]. However, there may be many (if not infinitely many) private views that accord with N_i. Definition 9.16 provides a well-defined conformance notation that can be parameterized with different compatibility notions (e.g., deadlock freedom versus weak termination) and different environments (e.g., $env^s(N)$ or $env^a(N)$). First results to select a best matching private view have been presented in [35].

9.5.5 Beyond Conformance Checking

Conformance can computed by establishing an optimal alignment between an event log and a service model (public view or best matching private view). Moreover, such an alignment can also be used for various other purposes. If conformance is good, alignments will have a high proportion of "move in both" steps. This means that attributes of events can be mapped onto model elements. For example, in most event logs each event has a timestamp. These timestamps can be mapped onto transitions in the corresponding Petri net and can be used to compute how much time tokens spend in places. Since log and model are aligned, waiting times, response times, and service times can be measured easily. This may be used to discover bottlenecks, analyze service-level-agreements, etc. Some logs also contain information about costs, resource usage, errors, etc. Attributes at the level of individual events—just like timestamps—can be associated to model elements using the "move in both" steps.

In this section, we focused on offline conformance checking. For example, we assume a model N_i and an event log L_i containing historic data. However, alignments can be computed on-the-fly; that is, even partially executed traces can be aligned with a model (partial alignments do not need to end in a final marking, but a final marking should remain reachable). This enables *online conformance checking*; that is, streaming event data can be monitored at runtime and deviations can be detected immediately. Similarly, partially aligned traces can be used for *predictions* and *recommendations* at runtime. For example, for a partially handled case we can predict the remaining flow time, predict the probability of a deviation, or recommend a next activity that minimizes costs [3].

9.6 Conclusion

The shift toward service-oriented systems enables enterprises to decompose their systems into several smaller services. That way, service orientation enables for faster changes, because an individual service can be substituted by another service rather than changing the overall system. Service substitution, however, also imposes new challenges as it should not effect compatibility of the overall system. As systems may be distributed over several enterprises, system correctness has to be derived from the correctness of its parts, which is nontrivial.

In this chapter, we have surveyed service substitution at design time and at run-time, thereby restricting ourselves to the service behavior. We have investigated this problem on the level of service models. For design-time support, we introduced several variants of service substitution and illustrated that the problem is parameterized w.r.t. the compatibility notion used. To decide that a service *Impl* can substitute a service *Spec*, we must compare the infinitely many admissible contexts of *Spec* and *Impl*. We proposed decision algorithms based on a finite representation of these sets. In addition, we proposed rules to construct substitutable services that are correct by design. Research challenges are to generalize these techniques to other compatibility notions and, in addition, to incorporate data, time, and resources. Other directions are diagnosing why a service cannot serve as a substitute and ideally propose how it can be repaired.

In this chapter, we did not limit ourselves to comparing *models* of services but also considered the actual behavior recorded in message and transaction logs. The actual service implementation may deviate from its model or the behavior of a service may change over time. We showed that *conformance checking* techniques can be used to detect and diagnose deviations between *observed* service behavior (i.e., event logs) and *modeled* service behavior. As shown, we can define conformance at the level of the public view (contractual level) and at the level of the private view (implementation level). For the public view, we can apply existing conformance checking techniques. However, checking conformance with respect to some unknown implementation is more challenging and requires further research. Moreover, the lion's share of attention has gone to fitness analysis whereas the analysis of "underfitting" and "overfitting" of services is equally important.

References

1. Aalst, W.M.P.v.d.: Workflow verification: finding control-flow errors using Petri-net-based techniques. In: Business Process Management: Models, Techniques, and Empirical Studies, LNCS, vol. 1806, pp. 161–183. Springer (2000)
2. Aalst, W.M.P.v.d.: Inheritance of interorganizational workflows: How to agree to disagree without loosing control? Inf. Technol. Manage. J. 4(4), 345–389 (2003)
3. Aalst, W.M.P.v.d.: Process Mining: Discovery, Conformance and Enhancement of Business Processes. Springer, Berlin (2011)

4. Aalst, W.M.P.v.d., Adriansyah, A., Dongen, B.v.: Replaying History on Process Models for Conformance Checking and Performance Analysis. WIREs Data Min. Knowl. Disc. **2**(2), 182–192 (2012)
5. Aalst, W.M.P.v.d., Basten, T.: Inheritance of workflows: an approach to tackling problems related to change. Theoret. Comput. Sci. **270**(1–2), 125–203 (2002)
6. Aalst, W.M.P.v.d., Dumas, M., Ouyang, C., Rozinat, A., Verbeek, H.: Conformance checking of service behavior. ACM Trans. Internet Technol. **8**(3), 29–59 (2008)
7. Aalst, W.M.P.v.d., Hee, K., Werf, J.v.d., Verdonk, M.: Auditing 2.0: using process mining to support tomorrow's auditor. IEEE Comput. **43**(3), 90–93 (2010)
8. Aalst, W.M.P.v.d., Hee, K.M.v.: Workflow Management: Models, Methods, and Systems. The MIT Press, Cambridge, MA (2004)
9. Aalst, W.M.P.v.d., Lohmann, N., Massuthe, P., Stahl, C., Wolf, K.: From public views to private views—correctness-by-design for services. In: WS-FM 2007, LNCS, vol. 4937, pp. 139–153. Springer (2008)
10. Aalst, W.M.P.v.d., Mooij, A.J., Stahl, C., Wolf, K.: Service interaction: patterns, formalization, and analysis. In: SFM 2009, LNCS, vol. 5569, pp. 42–88. Springer (2009)
11. Aalst, W.M.P.v.d., Stahl, C.: Modeling Business Processes—A Petri Net-Oriented Approach. The MIT Press, Cambridge, MA (2011)
12. Aalst, W.M.P.v.d., Weijters, A., Maruster, L.: Workflow mining: discovering process models from event logs. IEEE Trans. Knowl. Data Eng. **16**(9), 1128–1142 (2004)
13. Aalst, W.M.P.v.d., Weske, M.: The P2P approach to interorganizational workflows. In: CAiSE 2001, LNCS, vol. 2068, pp. 140–156. Springer (2001)
14. Adriansyah, A., Dongen, B.F.v., Aalst, W.M.P.v.d.: Towards Robust conformance checking. In: BPI 2010, LNBIP, vol. 66, pp. 122–133. Springer (2011)
15. Adriansyah, A., Dongen, B.v., Aalst, W.M.P.v.d.: Conformance checking using cost-based fitness analysis. In: EDOC 2011, pp. 55–64. IEEE Computer Society (2011)
16. Benatallah, B., Casati, F., Toumani, F.: Representing, analysing and managing Web service protocols. Data Knowl. Eng. **58**(3), 327–357 (2006)
17. Bravetti, M., Zavattaro, G.: Contract based multi-party service composition. In: FSEN 2007, LNCS, vol. 4767, pp. 207–222. Springer (2007)
18. Bravetti, M., Zavattaro, G.: Contract-based discovery and composition of web services. In: SFM 2009, LNCS, vol. 5569, pp. 261–295. Springer (2009)
19. Dumas, M., Yang, Y., Zhang, L.: Towards a formalization of contracts for service substitution. In: SERVICES 2010, pp. 423–430. IEEE Computer Society (2010)
20. Fournet, C., Hoare, C.A.R., Rajamani, S.K., Rehof, J.: Stuck-free conformance. In: CAV 2004, LNCS, vol. 3114, pp. 242–254. Springer (2004)
21. Goedertier, S., Martens, D., Vanthienen, J., Baesens, B.: Robust process discovery with artificial negative events. J. Mach. Learn. Res. **10**, 1305–1340 (2009)
22. Hee, K.M.v., Sidorova, N., Werf, J.M.E.M.v.d.: Refinement of synchronizable places with multi-workflow nets—weak termination preserved! In: PETRI NETS 2011, LNCS, vol. 6709, pp. 149–168. Springer (2011)
23. Kaschner, K., Wolf, K.: Set algebra for service behavior: applications and constructions. In: BPM 2009, LNCS, vol. 5701, pp. 193–210. Springer (2009)
24. König, D., Lohmann, N., Moser, S., Stahl, C., Wolf, K.: Extending the compatibility notion for abstract ws-bpel processes. In: WWW 2008, pp. 785–794. ACM (2008)
25. Laneve, C., Padovani, L.: The must preorder revisited. In: CONCUR 2007, LNCS, vol. 4703, pp. 212–225. Springer (2007)
26. Liske, N., Lohmann, N., Stahl, C., Wolf, K.: Another approach to service instance migration. In: ICSOC 2009, LNCS, vol. 5900, pp. 607–621. Springer (2009)
27. Lohmann, N., Massuthe, P., Wolf, K.: Behavioral constraints for services. In: BPM 2007, LNCS, vol. 4714, pp. 271–287. Springer (2007)
28. Lohmann, N., Massuthe, P., Wolf, K.: Operating guidelines for finite-state services. In: ICATPN 2007, LNCS, vol. 4546, pp. 321–341. Springer (2007)

29. Lohmann, N., Verbeek, H.M.W., Dijkman, R.: Petri net transformations for business processes—a survey. In: ToPNoC II, LNCS 5460, pp. 46–63. Springer (2009)
30. Lohmann, N., Weinberg, D.: Wendy: a tool to synthesize partners for services. Fundam. Inform. **113**, 1–17 (2011)
31. Lohmann, N., Wolf, K.: Compact representations and efficient algorithms for operating guidelines. Fundam. Inform. **108**(1–2), 43–62 (2011)
32. Medeiros, A.K.A.d., Weijters, A., Aalst, W.M.P.v.d.: Genetic process mining: an experimental evaluation. Data Min. Knowl. Disc. **14**(2), 245–304 (2007)
33. Milner, R.: Communication and Concurrency. Prentice-Hall, Inc., Upper Saddle River (1989)
34. Mooij, A.J., Parnjai, J., Stahl, C., Voorhoeve, M.: Constructing replaceable services using operating guidelines and maximal controllers. In: WS-FM 2010, LNCS, vol. 6551, pp. 116–130. Springer (2011)
35. Müller, R., Aalst, W.M.P.v.d., Stahl, C.: Conformance checking of services using the best matching private view. In: WSFM 2012, LNCS, vol. 7843, pp. 49–68 Springer (2013)
36. Munoz-Gama, J., Carmona, J.: A fresh look at precision in process conformance. In: BPM 2010, LNCS, vol. 6336, pp. 211–226. Springer (2010)
37. Munoz-Gama, J., Carmona, J.: Enhancing precision in process conformance: stability, confidence and severity. In: CIDM 2011, IEEE (2011)
38. Murata, T.: Petri nets: properties, analysis and applications. Proc. IEEE **77**(4), 541–580 (1989)
39. Oster, Z.J., Basu, S.: Extending substitutability in composite services by allowing asynchronous communication with message buffers. In: ICTAI 2009, pp. 572–575. IEEE Computer Society (2009)
40. Papazoglou, M.P.: Web Services: Principles and Technology. Pearson - Prentice Hall, Essex (2007)
41. Papazoglou, M.P.: The challenges of service evolution. In: CAiSE 2008, LNCS, vol. 5074, pp. 1–15. Springer (2008)
42. Papazoglou, M.P., Traverso, P., Dustdar, S., Leymann, F.: Service-oriented computing: a research roadmap. Int. J. Cooperative Inf. Syst. **17**(2), 223–255 (2008)
43. Pathak, J., Basu, S., Honavar, V.: On Context-Specific Substitutability of Web Services. In: ICWS 2007, pp. 192–199. IEEE Computer Society (2007)
44. Ponge, J., Benatallah, B., Casati, F., Toumani, F.: Analysis and applications of timed service protocols. ACM Trans. Softw. Eng. Methodol. 19(4), 1–38 (2010)
45. Reichert, M., Rinderle-Ma, S., Dadam, P.: Flexibility in process-aware information systems. In: ToPNoC II, LNCS 5460, pp. 115–135. Springer (2009)
46. Reisig, W., Rozenberg, G. (eds.): Lectures on Petri Nets I: Basic Models, Advances in Petri Nets, LNCS, vol. 1491. Springer (1998)
47. Rinderle, S., Reichert, M., Dadam, P.: Correctness criteria for dynamic changes in workflow systems—a survey. Data Knowl. Eng. **50**(1), 9–34 (2004)
48. Rozinat, A., Aalst, W.M.P.v.d.: Conformance checking of processes based on monitoring real behavior. Inf. Syst. **33**(1), 64–95 (2008)
49. Ryu, S.H., Casati, F., Skogsrud, H., Benatallah, B., Saint-Paul, R.: Supporting the dynamic evolution of web service protocols in service-oriented architectures. TWEB **2**(2), 1–46 (2008)
50. Stahl, C., Massuthe, P., Bretschneider, J.: Deciding substitutability of services with operating guidelines. In: ToPNoC II, LNCS 5460, pp. 172–191. Springer (2009)
51. Stahl, C., Vogler, W.: A trace-based service semantics guaranteeing deadlock freedom. Acta Inf. **49**(2), 69–103 (2012)
52. Stahl, C., Wolf, K.: Deciding service composition and substitutability using extended operating guidelines. Data Knowl. Eng. **68**(9), 819–833 (2009)
53. Vogler, W.: Modular Construction and Partial Order Semantics of Petri Nets, LNCS, vol. 625. Springer (1992)
54. Wynn, M.T., Verbeek, H.M.W., Aalst, W.M.P.v.d., Hofstede, A.H.M.t., Edmond, D.: Soundness-preserving reduction rules for reset workflow nets. Inf. Sci. **179**(6), 769–790 (2009)

Chapter 10
Web Service Adaptation: Mismatch Patterns and Semi-Automated Approach to Mismatch Identification and Adapter Development

Woralak Kongdenfha, Hamid R. Motahari-Nezhad, Boualem Benatallah and Regis Saint-Paul

Abstract The rapid growth of online Web services has led to the proliferation of functionality-wise equivalent services with differences in their descriptions and behaviors, and therefore has given rise to the need for service adaptation. In this chapter, we discuss key challenges for Web service interoperability and adaptation. We present a consolidated framework including a methodology, methods and tools for identifying and tackling service adaptation challenges by characterizing service adaptation issues, their semi-automated identification and resolution for adapter development. The innovative contributions of the our work consist in (i) a taxonomy of common mismatches at the service interfaces and business protocols whose definitions and resolutions are captured in *mismatch patterns*, (ii) a *business protocol-aware* matching of service specifications, and (iii) methods and tools for instantiating mismatch patterns with two different architectural approaches, i.e., standalone adapters and aspect-oriented adaptation. The combination of mismatch patterns, semi-automated mismatch identification, and tools for adapter development presents the foundation for rapid adaptation of Web services.

W. Kongdenfha (✉)
ECPE, Naresuan University, Phitsanulok, Thailand
e-mail: woralakk@gmail.com

H. R. Motahari-Nezhad
HP Labs, Paolo Alto, USA
e-mail: hamid-reza.motahari-nezhad@hp.com

B. Benatallah
CSE, University of New South Wales, Sydney, Australia
e-mail: boualem@cse.unsw.edu.au

R. Saint-Paul
Oceanet Technology, Nantes, France
e-mail: regis.saintpaul@gmail.com

A. Bouguettaya et al. (eds.), *Web Services Foundations*,
DOI: 10.1007/978-1-4614-7518-7_10,
© Springer Science+Business Media New York 2014

10.1 Introduction

The popularity of Web services has resulted in a rapid growth in the number of Web services available on the Internet. Many Web services are functionally equivalent and therefore are interchangeable in principle. However, services with equivalent functionality are often offered using different interface and business protocol specifications. Service interface defines the set of operations that the service provides along with message formats and data types. Business protocol specifies the order in which operations of a service can be invoked [4]. While there exist standard languages (e.g., WSDL and BPEL) to describe service interfaces and business protocols, service specifications may still be different. This is because those languages only provide generic constructs, which may be used differently by independent teams to define functionally equivalent services. This results in the interface- and protocol-level mismatches [8, 30]. Service matching and adapters are therefore necessary for identification and resolution of service mismatches at the level of business interfaces and protocols.

Service adaptation can be considered as a three-step process: *service matching*, *service mapping* and *adaptation code generation*. In the service matching step, the mismatches between web service specifications (i.e., interface and business protocol) are identified, which are differences in terms of operation specification, messages and data types (XML schema) as well as the sequences in which messages need to be exchanged. The service mapping creates a transformation script for resolving mismatches between involving services. Transformations are typically expressed in languages such as XQuery and XSLT, or even general purpose programming language such as Java, C#. Finally, adapters are generated to hide the differences between the two services, incorporating the transformation scripts generated in the mapping phase.

In this chapter, we first characterize the problem of adaptation in Web services and identify challenges in each step of service adaptation process mentioned above (in Sect. 10.2). We then present our contributions in the area of service adaptation [3, 22, 23, 31, 32] as a consolidated framework that helps addressing the identified challenges. Our work consists in a methodology, methods and software platform that help characterizing common mismatches between Web services and, starting from Web service interface and protocol specifications, assist in the identification of mismatches between Web service interface and protocol specifications, and also help programmers in developing service adapters. In particular, in this chapter we present an integrated services adaptation framework, seamlessly integrating various adaptation techniques and tools, developed over the last years and described independently in our previous work.

- We introduce *mismatch patterns* as a systematic method to capture and formalize common differences between Web service specifications. Patterns help developers in identifying the actual differences between interface and protocol specifications and resolving them. Among other information, patterns include *template* of mapping logic for resolving the captured mismatch. This enables the semi-automated code development in which developers can instantiate the template to create adaptation logic rather than developing them from scratch [3, 23].

- We present a *business protocol-aware* matching method for the semi-automated identification of mismatches between Web service specifications. It incorporates the ordering constraints imposed by business protocol definitions on service operations during service interface matching [31, 32].
- We present two approaches for adapter development, i.e., standalone and aspect-oriented approaches. We also provide a comparative study about the two adapter development approaches. This study can also be used as a guideline for adapter developers when deciding on the adapter development approaches [3, 22, 23].

The chapter is organized as follows. In Sect. 10.2, we characterize the problem of adaptation in Web services, discuss service adaptation challenges and review the state of the art in this space. In Sect. 10.3, we present mismatch patterns. We describe the protocol-aware mismatch identification approach in Sect. 10.4. Section 10.5 review our approaches for adaptation code generation, i.e., standalone and aspect-oriented approaches, as well as a comparative study between them. We conclude this chapter in Sect. 10.6.

10.2 Service Adaptation: Requirements, State of the Art and Gaps

In this section, we discuss the requirements of service adaptation. Then we briefly discuss related work in the area, and describe the gaps and how our work address such challenges.

10.2.1 Service Adaptation Requirements

We classify the need for adaptation in Web services into two categories: adaptation for compatibility and adaptation for replaceability. The first category refers to wrapping a service S so that it can interact with another service S_c. For example, consider a service S allowing companies to order office supplies. If the provider of this service wants to be able to do business with a certain retailer (say, *Wal-Mart* or *Target*) having a service S_c, then it needs to adapt its service S so that it can interact with such a retailer service. On the other hand, adaptation for replaceability refers to the modification of a Web service so that it *complies* with (i.e., can be used to replace) another service. This is important especially in the business environment where the interaction has been standardized either de jure or de facto (e.g. due to the presence of a dominant player in the market). For example, the RosettaNet [1] consortium standardizes the external behavior of services in the IT supply chain space. In these cases, service providers may have to adapt their services so that they follow the guidelines prescribed by the standards. Adaptation for replaceability is also needed when a new version of a service is developed, possibly with a different external behavior, but we want to preserve backward compatibility (i.e., an adapter should be provided so that the service is also offered in a version that behaves like the old one).

Replaceability may be *partial* or *total* [4]. Total replaceability occurs when a service S_r behaves externally like another service S. This means that any service that interacts *correctly* (i.e., without generating runtime faults) with S will also be able to interact correctly with S_r (note that the opposite is not necessarily true). Partial replaceability occurs when a service S_r can behave like S only in certain interactions (i.e., S_r behaves like S in some but not all conversations). We refer the reader to [4] for a detailed definition of compatibility and replaceability among services. In this chapter, we mainly focus on the service interoperability at the business interface- and protocol-layer.

10.2.2 State of the Art

The problem of service interface and protocol adaptation has received significant attention recently [3, 5, 15, 16, 22, 34]. In this section, we review existing work in each step of service interface and protocol adaptation process, i.e., matching, mapping and adapter development. We then identify the challenges in each step and present our contributions in addressing such challenges.

10.2.2.1 Service Matching

In the service matching, several approaches have been proposed to find the similarities between function (operation) signatures in a repository of software components [41, 42] or Web services [14, 39] specifications. In the software engineering, these approaches aim for retrieving components similar to a given one from a repository. The work in [41] identifies a measure of similarities between functional signatures considering the parameter name, parameter type, parameter order, etc. In [42], the authors consider the behavior of software components encoded in terms of pre- and post-conditions of functions to identify the matching between them. However, due to the richer interface definitions of Web services comparing to software components, specific approaches for service interface matching are required. In the area of Web services, approaches such as [14, 39] find service similarity based on information retrieval techniques which typically require a collection of service descriptions in finding a measure of similarity. Particularly, Woogle [14] uses a clustering-based approach to measure service similarity. The approach in [39] extends the work in [41] to find an overall measure of similarity not the exact matching as in [41]. In summary, the existing approaches focus on identifying a measure of similarity rather than the identification and resolution of mismatches between service specifications for the purpose of adapter development.

From the literature in service matching, we found that existing automated approaches for service matching focus either on the interface-level (e.g., [14, 34, 39]) or the protocol-level (e.g., [3, 5, 31]). However, we argue that when matching service specifications, interface and business protocols should not be treated independently. Matching protocol specifications in isolation ignores mismatches at the interface level. And correct matchings at the interface level could be specified more effectively considering the ordering constraints that business protocol definitions impose. Consider a given correspondence between messages m and m' may be plausible according to the information available in the (WSDL) interfaces, the protocol specifications may make it clear that it is not a plausible match, e.g., because message m does not arrive in the expected order to enable sending m' to the partner at the required time. In such cases, it may be possible to choose an alternative matching for message m or, even, the required mapping function can be provided by the developer to make the inter-operation possible. As another issue, existing automated service interface matching methods (including our previous work [31]) consider only one-to-one matching of messages. However, a common class of mismatch between service interfaces is one-to-many matches (also called message merge/split mismatch) where one message in an interface is matched to more than one in the other [3, 15]. In this chapter, we therefore, present a *protocol-aware* semi-automated interface matching approach that consider both interface definitions and also the interactions between services according to their business protocols. Moreover, the proposed method supports the identification of the message merge/split class of interface-level mismatches.

10.2.2.2 Service Mapping

After the mismatches between service specifications are identified, the next step that developers need to do is to create mapping to resolve the identified mismatches. Several commercial mapping tools are offered to assist developers in mapping creation tasks such as Microsoft BizTalk Mapper,[1] Stylus Studio XML Mapping Tools,[2] and SAP XI Mapping Editor.[3] However, these mapping tools focus mainly on service interfaces, while business protocols are ignored. Therefore, to address the protocol-level mismatches, developers need to create mapping logic using either procedural programming language (Java, C#, BPEL, etc.) or transformation language (such as XSLT or XQuery). However, the ad-hoc mapping specifications make it difficult to guarantee that they are correctly implemented the adaptation logic for resolving the identified mismatches. Furthermore, the implementation of adaptation logic not only distract developers from their tasks of application development but also delay time-to-market of the intended applications. We therefore introduce *mismatch patterns* as a systematic method to capture and formalize common differences between Web

---

[1] http://www.biztalk.org

[2] http://www.stylusstudio.com

[3] http://www.sap.com/platform/netweaver/components/xi

service specifications. Patterns can help developers in identifying the differences between service interface and protocol specifications and resolving them.

To the best of our knowledge, our work [3] was the first to characterize the problem of Web services adaptation and to propose the concept of mismatch patterns for standalone adapter development. This is a pioneer work that has built the foundation for other recent work in this area. In particular, in addition to the proposed patterns presented in [3], Dumas et al. [15] have identified two other mismatch patterns and Li et al. [24] adopt the mismatch patterns framework to identify five extra mismatch patterns at the interface- and protocol-level in the context of heterogeneous services composition. However, these work only identify mismatches among service interface and protocol specifications, but they did not provide assistance to developers in their adapter development tasks. In contrast, among other information, our mismatch patterns include *template* of mapping logic for resolving the captured mismatch. Our proposed mismatch pattern thus enables the semi-automated code generation in which developers can instantiate the template to create adaptation logic rather than developing them from scratch.

10.2.2.3 Adapter Development

Once mismatches are identified and mapping logic are created, developers need to generate adapters to hide the differences between interacting services, by incorporating the adaptation logic created in the mapping phase. In this chapter, we consider two adapter development approaches, i.e., by developing standalone adapters and via service modification. For the latter, we propose the notion of *adaptation aspects* that, following aspect-oriented programming paradigm and service modification approach, enable the rapid development of service adapters. A large amount of work has been done in integrating AOP in software components [6, 10, 12, 37]. In many of these work (e.g., [10, 12, 37]), aspects are used to adapt the component to a changing environment at the configuration-level and in the case of component evolution. A more recent work in this area [6] also uses aspects to dynamically adapt software components at the interface and protocol-level in the context of component composition and evolution, focusing on the provision of an implementation framework for aspect-oriented adaptation.

The use of AOP in Web services has also been extensively explored. In particular, non-functional properties of services find a natural appeal in AOP programming [25]. The work in [11, 33], aspects are used to adapt services to changing environments. However, in such approaches, aspect weaving is done at compile time thus require the engine (or running process instances) to be restarted for reflecting changes. In [7], Charfi and Mezini propose to use AOP to modularize cross-cutting concerns of BPEL processes. From the literature, we found that existing approaches mainly focus on non-functional properties and do not consider the mismatch identification and resolution. The work in [40] is the only work that we know of that applies AOP to service interoperability issues. They use AOP to transform the content of messages exchanged between services and thus to resolve mismatches at the interface-level.

They however did not consider mismatches at the protocol level. Our work, on the other hand, proposes the use of AOP to assist the service adaptation at both interface- and protocol-level. We also provide a framework that allows developers to semi-automated generate adaptation aspects from the mismatch template. Moreover, our extension to aspect-enable ActiveBPEL engine allows dynamic weaving of aspects at runtime. Finally, to assist service developers in choosing which adapter development approaches, we provide a comparative study between the two of them. The study shows that the standalone adapters are costly to develop and maintain, while the aspect-based approach allows dynamic plug-and-unplug of adaptation logic with the service implementation, it is thus a preferable approach in many cases.

10.3 Mismatch Patterns for Service Mismatch Characterization and Resolution

In this section, we classify common mismatches between service interfaces and business protocols, and then introduce the mismatch patterns for capturing such common mismatches and generic resolutions for resolving them. Particularly, adaptation logic identified in mismatch patterns aims to achieve total replaceability as mentioned in Sect. 10.2.1, i.e., making a service S_r, characterized by interface I_r and protocol P_r, "looks like" another service S that has interface I and protocol P, so that S_r can interact with any clients that S can interact with.

10.3.1 Common Mismatches Between Web Service Specifications

We summarize the mismatches commonly occur between Web services as identified in prior adaptation work (e.g., [3, 23] by the authors, and also some later work by Dumas et al. [15]). The mismatches presented here are classified into interface- and protocol-level mismatches.

Interface-level Mismatches. To characterize mismatches at the interface-level, we use a concrete example of the *Mappoint*[4] (S) and *Arcweb*[5] (S_r) route Web services. They offer similar functionalities (i.e., finding driving routes between two points), but use different WSDL interfaces (operations CalculateRoute and findRoute, respectively). From their specifications, the names, numbers, and types of the input/output parameters of the operations CalculateRoute and findRoute differ. The operation CalculateRoute requires one input parameter called Specification whose type is SegmentSpecification. The operation findRoute requires two parameters: routeStops and routeFinderOptions whose types are RouteStops and

---

[4] www.microsoft.com/mappoint/
[5] www.esri.com/software/arcwebservices/

RouteFinderOptions, respectively. The values of both parameters routeStops and routeFinderOptions can be computed from the value of the parameter Specification.

- *Signature Mismatch*: This type of mismatch occurs when two services with interfaces I and I_r of functionally equivalent operations differ in their operation names, numbers, order or types of input/output parameters. In the above example, the operation CalculateRoute of *Mappoint* requires one input parameter Specification whose type is SegmentSpecification. The operation findRoute of *ArcWeb* requires two parameters: routeStops and routeFinderOptions whose types are RouteStops and RouteFinderOptions, respectively. These two services therefore have a signature mismatch between them.
- *Parameter Constraint Mismatch*: This mismatch occurs when the operation O of interface I imposes constraints on input parameters, which are less restrictive than those of O_r in I_r (e.g., differences in value ranges). For instance, suppose that element Preference (a sub-element of the parameter Specification of operation CalculateRoute) accepts "quickest", "shortest" and "least toll" as possible values, while element RouteType (an element of parameter routeFinderOptions of operation findRoute) accepts only "quickest" and "shortest". Hence, the findRoute operation cannot replace the CalculateRoute in this case.

Protocol-level Mismatches. To describe common mismatches at the protocol-level, we use a supply chain example. Assume that protocol P_r of service S_r expects messages to be exchanged in the following order: clients invoke login, then getCatalogue to receive the catalogue of products including shipping options and preferences (e.g., delivery dates), followed by submitOrder, sendShippingPreferences, issueInvoice, and makePayment operations. In contrast, protocol P of the client allows the following sequence of operations: login, getCatalogue, submitOrder, issueInvoice, makePayment and sendShippingPreferences. As service S_r does not charge differently even the shipping preferences differ, clients can specify their shipping preferences at the final step. We classify protocol-level mismatches as follows.

- *Ordering Mismatch*: This mismatch occurs when protocols P and P_r support the same set of messages but in different orders, as shown in the above example.
- *Extra Message Mismatch*: This mismatch occurs when one or more messages specified in P_r do not have any correspondence in P. In the above supply chain example, assume that protocol P_r sends an acknowledgment after receiving message issueInvoiceIn, but protocol P does not produce it.
- *Missing Message Mismatch*: This mismatch is the opposite case of the Extra Message Mismatch, i.e., one or more message specified in P do not have any correspondence in P_r.
- *One-to-Many Message Mismatch*: This mismatch occurs when protocol P specifies a single message m to achieve a functionality, while protocol P_r requires a sequence of messages $m_1, \ldots, m_n$ for achieving the same function. Suppose protocol P expects purchase order together with shipping preferences in one message

called submitOrderIn, while protocol P_r needs two separate messages for the same purpose, namely, sendShippingPreferencesIn and submitOrderIn.

- *Many-to-One message Mismatch*: This mismatch occurs when protocol P specifies a sequence of messages $m_1, \ldots, m_n$ to achieve a functionality, while protocol P_r requires only a single message m (which can be created by combining messages $m_1, \ldots, m_n$) for the same function. In this type of mismatch, an assumption is required in which all the messages to be aggregated need to be issued consecutively, i.e., there is no other actions waiting for other messages to be sent during this message aggregation. This assumption is required in order to avoid deadlock.
- *Stream-to-Single message Mismatch*: This mismatch occurs when protocol P_r issues a stream of messages until a condition is satisfied, while the protocol P only requires one message to be sent. In the example, assumed protocol P_r sends shipment notification incrementally until the products are delivered, while protocol P only sends a single shipment notification.
- *Single-to-Stream message Mismatch*: This mismatch is the opposite case of the Stream-to-Single message mismatch, in which protocol P_r issues a single message, while protocol P sends a stream of messages until a condition is satisfied.

10.3.2 Mismatch Patterns

In the following, we present the concept of *mismatch patterns*, which is a similar notion to that of *design pattern* in software engineering [17]. Mismatch patterns provide an abstraction for capturing and formalizing common service differences. Besides capturing differences, a mismatch pattern contains parameterized adaptation logic (called *adapter template*) that can be instantiated to resolve the captured mismatch instead of developing them from scratch. Mismatch patterns can therefore be used as a guideline for mismatch identification and adapter development.

Table 10.1 summarizes the structure of a mismatch pattern, which consists of a *name*, a *mismatch type* that provides a description of the mismatch that is captured,

Table 10.1 The structure of a mismatch pattern

Part	Description
Name	Name of the pattern
Mismatch type	A description of the type of difference captured by the pattern
Template parameters	Information that needs to be provided by the user when instantiating an adapter template to derive the adapter code
Adapter template	Code or pseudo-code that describes the implementation of an adapter that can resolve the difference captured by the pattern
Sample usage	The sample usage section contains information that guides the developer in customizing (or manually generating) the adapter, by providing examples on how to instantiate the template

adapter template, *template parameters*, and *sample usage*. The adapter template is parametric, in which the parameters specified in the *template parameters* part needs to be provided by developers when instantiating it. Developers can just directly use the generated adaptation skeleton to deploy the adapter or may want to customize the resulting logic skeleton to add some custom business logic as needed.

The exact specification of adapter templates depends on the adapter development approach. In Sect. 10.5, we discuss two different approaches for adapter development, and present formalisms for the specification of adapter templates. We use the proposed mismatch pattern framework and the adapter template specification to represent the common mismatches identified in Sect. 10.3.1 as a set of built-in patterns. The developers can also add to the built-in patterns if there are specific mismatches that they would like to handle differently or if there are mismatches that are not captured in the built-in set. Patterns can be shared between adapter developers and evolved, especially with the new trend of user-centric sharing of content fostered by Web 2.0 [29]. By provision of adapter templates and the support for adapter template instantiation in prototype tool, our approach offers a platform for rapid development of adapters. Readers may refer to [3, 22] for detailed descriptions of all mismatch patterns and our prototyped tool.

10.4 Semi-Automated Identification and Resolution of Mismatches

In this section, we present the *protocol-aware* interface matching approach that consider both interface definitions and also the interactions between services according to their business protocols when identifying mismatches between two services.

Motivating example. As a motivating example, we consider an adaptation task for services in the management of shopping carts, i.e., *XWebCheckOut*[6] and *Google Checkout*.[7] They provide similar APIs for order creation and management, payment processing, and order cancellation. However, there are differences in the interface definition (message names, number, and types) and how they exchange messages to fulfill a functionality. For example, Fig. 10.1 shows the protocols of the two services for placing an order.[8] One of the main issues to be addressed for the purpose of adapter development is finding the matching between the interfaces of the two Web services, e.g., to find out that AddOrderRequest *is the corresponding message to* Place-Order in Fig. 10.1. For this purpose, considering only the XML schema definitions of these two services is not enough, as in this case AddOrderRequest would be better matched to New-Order-Notification. Indeed, we need to consider

---

[6] http://www.xwebservices.com/Web_Services/XWebCheckOut/

[7] http://code.google.com/apis/checkout/

[8] Note: we only considered XML messages and ignored HTTP messages, as they constitute implementation details. The protocols have been simplified for presentation purposes.

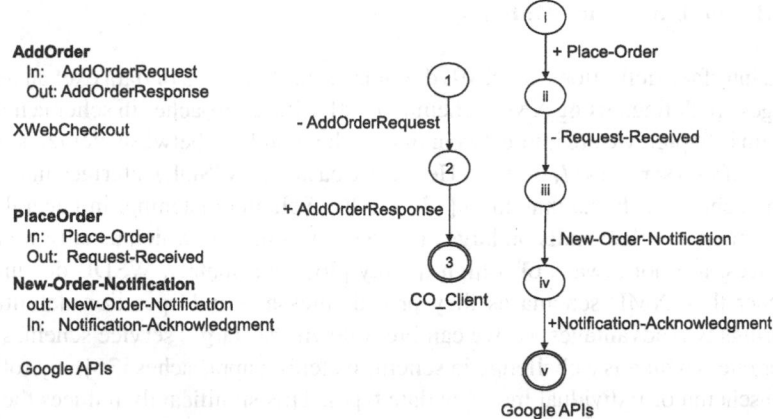

Fig. 10.1 The operations and the corresponding protocols of *CO_Client* (*XWebCheckout*) and *Google checkout APIs* for placing an order

the operation definition information in the WSDL document as well as constraints defined on operation invocation (and directions) at the protocol level.

10.4.1 Protocol-Aware Interface Matching

Interface matching refers to the identification of correspondences between messages in I_s and I_c. Its purpose is to find the set X of parameters of the function $func(X)$ for generating messages m in the two interfaces I_s and I_c. In the interface mapping step, the interface mapping functions $m \leftarrow func(X)$ are implemented. The identification of the set X, (interface matching) is the most important step in specifying $func(X)$.

In this section, we propose three interface matching algorithms: the first one, called *static interface matching*, only considers the information in the WSDL documents including both operation and message definitions and also XML data type definitions. The other two approaches, i.e., *depth-based* and *iterative reference-based*, demonstrate different levels of considering the protocol definitions, on top of the static approach, during interface matching. In particular, the depth-based approach improves the static matching score for messages with a same/close depth (the distance of the transition labeled with the message from the initial state of the protocol) in a protocol, while the reference-based approach propagates the matching score into those of their neighbor messages in the protocols, and also uses already matched message pairs as *references* to reinforce or penalize the matching scores of messages before and after a given pair of matched messages in the protocol.

10.4.1.1 Static Interface Matching

WSDL interface definitions are XML documents, and the type of data exchanged by messages are defined using XML schema [9, 38]. Like approaches in schema matching, in this chapter, we are interested in finding the matching between elements in the schemas of two services (I_s and I_c). Hence, we base our (WSDL) interface matching on approaches in schema matching [13, 35, 36]. Schema matching, in general, is a hard problem and the results on large and arbitrary schemas, which usually we have in services, are not always of a high quality [36]. Fortunately, WSDL documents are richer than XML schema as they provide message and operation definitions. This brings two advantages: (i) we can break down the (large) service schemas into smaller ones (which is a challenge in schema matching approaches [36]), by following the schema of individual message data types. This significantly reduces the size of schemas to be matched, (ii) the association of messages to operation definitions allow to reduce the number of pair-wise matching of schema of messages. Indeed, depending on the type of adaptation (for replaceability, or compatibility) we need to only match input-output messages (compatibility), or input-input and output-output messages together (replaceability) but not all messages. We use these two properties in the presentation of the static interface matching approach as follows: (i) *incorporating message name into the schema*, and (ii) *considering the message direction and adaptation type*.

Algorithm 1 Static Interface Matching Algorithm

Input: I_s, I_c
Output: Message correspondences between I_s, I_c
1: $XSD_m \leftarrow$ XML schema of message m in I_s (I_c)
2: **for** message $m \in I_s$ **do**
3:   **for** message $m' \in I_c$ **do**
4:     match($XSD_m, XSD_{m'}$), considering m and m' directions and adaptation type
5:   **end for**
6: **end for**
7: **for** each message $m_1 \in I_s(I_c)$ **do**
8:   **for** each message $m_2 \in I_c(I_s)$ **do**
9:     **if** $S(m_1, m_2) \geq t_1$ && $matchingElements(m_1, m_2) \geq c_1 * numElements(m_2)$ **then**
10:       m_2 is a component of m_1
11:     **end if**
12:   **end for**
13: **end for**

Algorithm 1 summarizes the interface matching approach, in which I_s and I_c denote WSDL interfaces. We consider messages matching in a pair-wise manner, and $S(m_1, m_2)$ specifies the matching score of message m_1 and $m2$.

10.4.1.2 Depth-Based Approach

The essence of the depth-based approach is incorporating the notion that messages with similar depth in the two protocols P_1 and P_2 are more likely to match. Figure 10.2

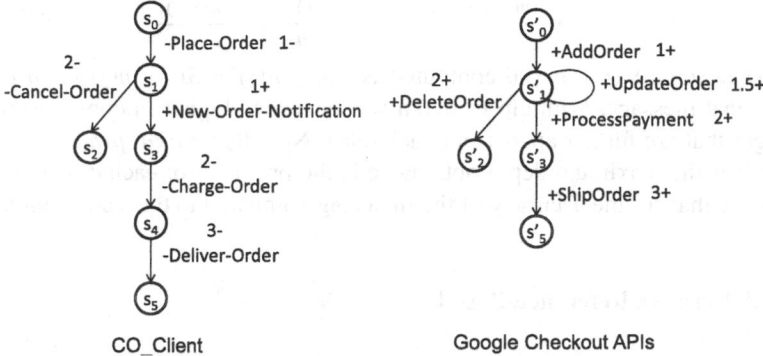

Fig. 10.2 The simplified protocol specifications of *CO_Client* and *Google checkout APIs* associated with respective depth numbering

shows simplified protocols of *CO_Client* and *Google Checkout APIs*. In this example, messages **AddOrder** and **PlaceOrder** which are in the same depth of 1 are more likely to be a correct match. It is useful to consider the direction of messages, i.e., incoming (+) or outgoing (−) in identification of depth, as well.

To avoid going into infinite loops for identifying the depth of a message associated to such transitions, we normalize the protocol into a tree (only self-loops are allowed in this new representation). The normalization process involves traversing each transition and checking whether the outgoing transitions for the target state of the current transitions are already labeled with a smaller depth number. If any of the outgoing transitions meet this criterion, then the normalization process does not continue this path of the protocol. The depth of a message is specified by the number of transitions to be traversed from the initial state s_0 to the message m in this tree-like representation of the protocol.

In this process, messages of each direction are numbered separately. For instance, the message −**Place-Order** gets the number 1−, and the message + **New-Order-Notification** the number 1+. So, as can be seen these numbers are relative but does not show the absolute number of transitions form the initial state. If the protocol P has self-loop, i.e., the source and target states of the transition with the message is the same state (e.g., see message +**UpdateOrder** in Fig. 10.2), we associate the number 1.5+ to show that it is a self-loop (but not the depth of 2).

Once the depth of transitions are identified, we update the static matching scores of messages, computed using the static matching approach (Sect. 10.4.1.1). In fact this process improves the score of each matching considering the depth information as follows. Let $m_1 \in I_1$ and $m_2 \in I_2$, and $S(m_1, m_2)$ be the matching score of messages m_1 and m_2 computed by the schema matching algorithms.[9] The improvement weight for the score in the depth-based approach is shown in Eq. 10.1.

---

[9] Note that $I_1 = I_s(I_c)$ and $I_2 = I_c(I_s)$

$$scale \leftarrow \frac{maxdepth - |depth(m_1) - depth(m_2)|}{maxdepth} \qquad (10.1)$$

The new score $S'(m_1, m_2)$ is computed as $S'(m_1, m_2) = S(m_1, m_2) \times scale$. This ensures that messages with closer depth will be scaled higher in comparison with messages that are further apart from each other. Note that $maxdepth$ is a constant that defines the maximum depth obtainable in the protocol for each direction. This approach enhances the accuracy of the matching compared to the static approach.

10.4.1.3 Iterative Reference-Based Approach

The iterative reference-based approach advances the previous two interface matching approaches by taking into account the following additional protocol-related information.

- *Depth-based score improvement.* Messages with similar depth in protocols P_1 and P_2 are more likely to match, as defined in the depth-based approach.
- *Propagation of similarities to neighbors of a matching pair.* If a pair of messages $m_1 \in I_1$ and $m_2 \in I_2$ matches, then their neighbors are more likely to match too. Neighbor messages are those which are either before or after the message m_1 (respectively, m_2) in the path(s). To incorporate this property, we use the philosophy of *similarity flooding* algorithm [28] to introduce a reinforcement function. When a pair of messages m_1 and m_2 matches, we reinforce the matching scores of their neighbors. The reinforcement is done using a *rate* that controls the pace at which the reinforcement decays that depends on how far the matching messages are from the reference message pair.
- *Penalizing matching pairs leading to deadlock cases.* If the pair of messages $-m_1 \in I_1$ and $+m_2 \in I_2$ match, we observe that, in some cases, if an outgoing (with "$-$" sign) message that has a bigger depth number than m_1 are allowed to match with an incoming (with "$+$" sign) message that has a smaller depth number than m_2, this leads to a deadlock in the interaction between services. Such matching should be identified and their matching score should be penalized. We refer reader to [32] for more details on this topic.

Reference message pair selection. We introduce two methods for selection of reference matching pair: (i) intuitively, the pair with the highest matching score between the two interfaces in each iteration can be selected as the reference, and (ii) in general it is a better approach to start the matching from the messages with small depth and later to the ones, which are deeper. This later approach allows applying the penalization approach more effectively, as messages before a reference pair are more likely to have been matched with messages in the other interface. This approach take messages close to the initial states to find their matching and then proceed to higher depth messages. Nevertheless, if the developer can interfere (approve or refine) in the reference selection process, the accuracy and effectiveness of other steps will be much higher. In general, the success of this approach depends on the quality of selection of reference pairs in each iteration.

Algorithm 2 summarizes the iterative reference-based approach. First, static match scores are computed and reinforced using depth-based approach (line 1). Then, a reference point is specified using one of the approaches explained above (line 2). Next, the message pairs that result in deadlock, based on the selected reference pair, are penalized by multiplying the matching score by the inverse of *scale* (line 11), which is computed according to Eq. 10.1. Otherwise, if the pair of messages are neighbors of reference pairs, their score is reinforced proportional to the difference of their depth with those of messages in the reference pair (line 13). This is done by multiplying their matching score by the reinforcement *rate* (computed in line 9). Afterwards, we look for the next reference pair, if exist. The algorithm will terminate when there are no further reference pairs to be selected.

Algorithm 2 Iterative Reference-based Interface Matching

Input: $mList_1, mList_2$
Output: $mrList$
1: $mrList \leftarrow$ depth-basedMatching($mList_1, mList_2$)
2: $mp \leftarrow$ selectReferencePoint($mList_1, mList_2, mrList$)
3: **while** $mp \neq \emptyset$ **do**
4:    $m_{ref1} \leftarrow mp.m_1, m_{ref2} \leftarrow mp.m_2$
5:    **for** each $m_1 \in mList_1$ **do**
6:      **for** each $m_2 \in mList_2$ **do**
7:        $mr \leftarrow$ getMatchResult($m_1, m_2, mrList$)
8:        $diff \leftarrow max(abs(m_{ref1}.depth-m_1.depth), abs(m_{ref2}.depth- m_2.depth))$
9:        $rate \leftarrow 1 + (maxdepth - diff)/maxdepth$
10:        **if** $[(m1, m2)$ cross $(m_{ref1}, m_{ref2})]$ and *deadlock* **then**
11:          $mr.score \leftarrow mr.score \times 1/scale$
12:        **else if** m_1 (m_2) neighbor of $m_{ref1}(m_{ref1})$ **then**
13:          $mr.score \leftarrow mr.score \times rate$
14:        **end if**
15:      **end for**
16:    **end for**
17:    $mp \leftarrow$ selectReferencePoint($I_1, I_2, mrList$)
18: **end while**

In this algorithm, the short forms of $mList$ refer to list of messages (e.g., $mList_1$ refers to the list of messages in I_1), $mrList$ refers to match result list, mp stands for message pair, and mr stands for match result.

10.4.2 Identification of Protocol-Level Mismatches Through Adapter Simulation

The proposed approaches for interface matching in the previous section allow to perform the matching of two interfaces I_s and I_c using WSDL information (static approach), and also by encoding the protocol information in terms of depth (depth-based approach), and propagation of similarities to neighbor messages, and also disallowing matchings leading to deadlock cases (iterative reference-based approach). While considering protocol information during interface matching increases the

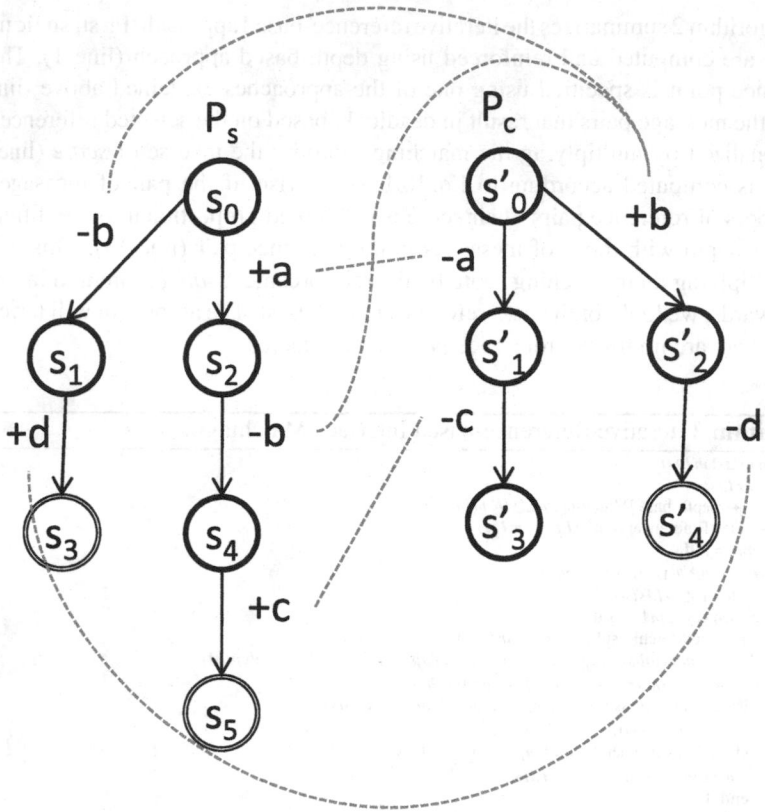

Fig. 10.3 The correspondences between messages of two protocols (shown by *dash lines*) are valid using the protocol-aware interface matching

accuracy of the matching does not completely remove the need for considering the interactions between protocols. A closer look at correspondences between the protocols P_s and P_c in Fig. 10.3, shows that the message $-b$ can be considered as an extra message in its path. In general, extra messages are received by the adapter, but never sent to the other partners, as part of adaptation logic. However, there is a risk for *information loss* that should be considered [20, 26, 27].

Therefore, we propose protocol-level analysis through simulating the interactions between P_s and P_c. In this process, we explore all possible message exchanges between the two services according to P_s and P_c and identify the mismatches between them. This is akin to the adapter generation process, and that is why we refer to it as *adapter simulation* process. The purpose of this process is three folds: (i) identify plausibility of interface matching results by considering the full interactions between protocols, (ii) generating adapter rules for mismatches that do not result in deadlock, and (iii) identification and analyzing mismatches that result in deadlock to examine if it is possible to provide the required interface mappings, and rules, that resolve the deadlocks. For more details in this topic, please refer to [31].

10.5 Adapter Specification, Generation and Deployment

In this section, we describe two approaches for adapter template specification in mismatch patterns, i.e., standalone and aspect-oriented approaches. The adaptation logic typically involves activities such as receiving messages, storing messages, transforming message data, and invoking service operations. These tasks can be very well modeled by process-centric service composition languages such as BPEL. Therefore, we choose BPEL for defining the adapter templates in both approaches. Hereafter, we discuss the two adapter template specification approaches and present a comparative study between them.

10.5.1 Standalone Service Adaptation

In this approach, an adapter A (referred to as a *standal one* adapter) is placed in between a service S implementing protocol P and another service S_r implementing protocol P_r to enable their interactions, as illustrated in Fig. 10.4. In this approach, all messages sent from service S pass through the adapter A, which performs the adaptation logic and invokes operations of protocol P_r from S_r, and vice versa.

We use the *Ordering Constraint Pattern* (OCP) introduced in Sect. 10.3.2 to illustrate how the adaptation logic is specified and implemented in the standalone adapter approach. OCP is associated with an adapter template, shown in Table 10.2, which consists of a set of actions to resolve the ordering mismatch. In particular, OCP takes as its parameters the protocol specifications of two services that have a mismatch, and a message $msg\,O^p$ to be re-ordered. Once instantiated, OCP generates an adapter that resolves an ordering mismatch by receiving message $msg\,O^p$ of protocol P and storing it for later use. When message $msg\,O^{sr}$ is expected by service S_r, the adapter creates it from the value of message $msg\,O^p$. The adapter invokes service S_r with message $msg\,O^{sr}$.

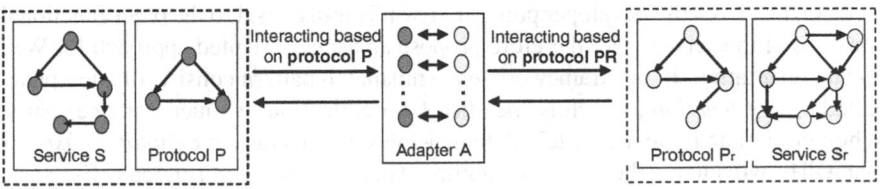

Fig. 10.4 A standalone adapter A for enabling service interoperability

Table 10.2 Ordering constraint mismatch pattern (OCP)

Template parameters	**Protocols P (of service S) and P_r (of service S_r), message $msg\,O^P$ to be re-ordered**
Adapter template	– Passing messages to activities, as prescribed by P, that do not need adaptation (BPEL *receive, invoke, reply* activities);
	– Receive $msg\,O^p$;
	– Assign $msg\,O^a \longleftarrow msg\,O^p$;
	– Assign $msg\,O^{sr} \longleftarrow msg\,O^a$, when $msg\,O^{sr}$ expected;
	– Invoke O^{sr} with $msg\,O^{sr}$

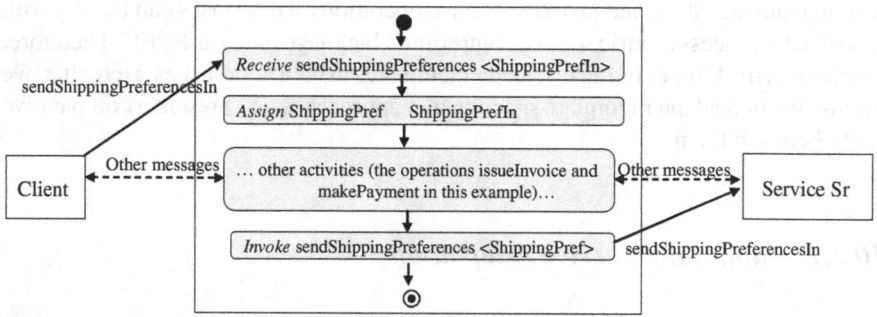

Fig. 10.5 Sample usage of the adapter template specified in the OCP

Figure 10.5 shows the usage of OCP to resolve the ordering constraints of message sendShippingPreferencesIn. In particular, the adapter temporarily stores message sendShippingPreferencesIn sent by the client according to protocol P and forwards it to service S_r according to protocol P_r. Hence, from the client perspective, service S_r looks like service S in this case.

10.5.2 Aspect Oriented Service Adaptation

Aspect-Oriented Programming (AOP) is a technique that allows the separation of concerns in software development, making it possible to modularize cross-cutting concerns of a system [21, 25]. We consider the adaptation logic as a cross-cutting concern, i.e., from the developer point of view it is transversal to the other functional concerns of the service. We therefore propose an aspect-oriented approach for Web service adaptation. In our framework, each mismatch pattern consists of a template, called *aspect template*, which is specified by a collection of ⟨query, advice⟩ pairs. When instantiated, the aspect template generates a collection of *adaptation aspects* that will be woven into the service at runtime. This approach is illustrated in Fig. 10.6, in which adaptation aspects $AS1$, $AS2$, and $AS3$ are integrated as extensions to a running instance of service S_r to enable its interaction with service S. In the following,

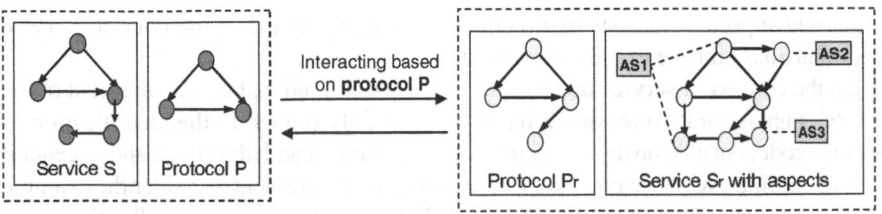

Fig. 10.6 Adaptation aspects $AS1, AS2$, and $AS3$ for enabling service interoperability

we discuss the advice and query part of the aspect template, as well as the deployment of adaptation aspects for resolving mismatches at runtime.

10.5.2.1 Advice

An advice defines the adaptation logic for resolving the difference captured by a mismatch pattern. It requires parameters (e.g., a transformation function to mediate the difference between operation signatures) that are used to generate an adaptation code skeleton from the template. As mentioned before, BPEL provides notations and concepts that are appropriate for the adaptation specification and implementation. We hence chose it as the language to express adaptation advices.

To describe how adaptation logic can be modeled and implemented using aspect-oriented approach, we present the Ordering Constraint Pattern (OCP) in Table 10.3. This pattern is accompanied with an aspect template consisting of two ⟨query, advice⟩ pairs. The first advice, namely OCPStore, comprises of two actions that are used to resolve a mismatch occurs when a message $msg\,O^p$ is sent from service S, but service S_r does not expect it at this state. OCPStore therefore receives and stores message $msg\,O^p$ for later use. When the process execution reaches operation O_j^{sr}, OCPForward assigns the value of message $msg\,O^p$ to message $msg\,O_j^{sr}$ to enable the execution of the operation O_j^{sr}. The exact locations, where these adaptation advices need to be executed, are defined in the query section of the template, and is discussed in Sect. 10.5.2.2.

10.5.2.2 Query

A query expresses a process execution point, also known as *joinpoint* in the context of AOP [21, 25], where a set of actions defined in the advice section of the template will be executed to mediate the differences between services (e.g. when such a message is received, when a message comes from a business partner, etc.) In general, there are two main approaches for joinpoint expression in the context of AOP [25]. A first approach consists in the expression of joinpoints only on the service code constructs.

A second approach consists in directly expressing joinpoints using not only service code but also runtime execution context.

In the context of service adaptation, we have observed that the requirement of the query language for expressing joinpoints is not only limited to the identification of service code, but also on the actual messages exchanged with the client, and in general by the runtime execution context. To illustrate this requirement, consider the example of the supply chain scenario in Sect. 10.3.2. Assume that the service S_r allows two different interaction paths with either unregistered or registered clients. The interaction path for registered clients is as follows: after submitting an order, process S_r allows registered clients to send messages issueInvoice and makePayment respectively. The clients do not need to resend message sendShippingPreferences as it has already been provided and stored in the system when the clients made registrations the first time. In this example, an ordering mismatch between service S_r and its clients only happens when the client takes the unregistered interaction path, otherwise the two services are compatible. Thus it is the choice of interaction path that triggers the adaptation need. This example shows that, for service adaptation, the query language needs to be able to express conditions on the runtime context, i.e., how the service is actually used by a client or how it is executed.

Intuitively, for the purpose of service adaptation, we expect the query language to be able to identify (i) operations (with or without a certain signature) to enable the resolution of interface-level mismatches, and (ii) interaction paths (that are or are not presented in a protocol) to enable the handling of protocol-level mismatches. The latter means that the query language must be able to discriminate between the various execution paths that lead to or follow an activity of the service. In both cases, what is done is the identification of a BPEL activity where adaptation is needed, e.g., the activity where a signature mismatch occurs, or the first activity of a sequence that does not have any correspondence at the protocol level in the client.

Since we assume that services are implemented in BPEL, a query language that operate on BPEL code such as BPQL [2] could be a choice. However, using a query language that focuses on the identification of code constructs would force us to include, as part of the advice, some code to evaluate those runtime conditions. Hence, the approach that expresses runtime conditions directly in the query language

Table 10.3 Ordering Constraint mismatch Pattern (OCP)

Query	Generic adaptation advice
query($\langle$operation$\rangle$,$\langle$sequence$\rangle$) executes *around receive* when $O_i^{sr} = \langle$operation$\rangle$ AND $S_i = \langle$sequence$\rangle$	OCPStore() { Receive $msg O^p$; Assign $msg O^{tmp} \longleftarrow msg O^p$; }
query($\langle$operation$\rangle$,$\langle$sequence$\rangle$) executes *around receive* when $O_j^{sr} = \langle$operation$\rangle$ AND $S_j = \langle$sequence$\rangle$	OCPForward() { Assign $msg O_j^{sr} \longleftarrow msg O^{tmp}$; Reply $msg O_j^{sr}$ }

\<query\>	::=	`query` ([*\<param\>* [,*\<param\>*]*])
		`executes` *\<location\>* *\<activity\>*
		`when`*\<condition\>*
\<param\>	::=	*id[;id]**
\<location\>	::=	*before|after|around*
\<activity\>	::=	*receive|reply|invoke*
\<condition\>	::=	*\<pred\>* [AND *\<pred\>*]
\<pred\>	::=	*\<context object\>*=*\<param\>*
		|\<context object\>!=*\<param\>*
\<context object\>	::=	*partnerLink|portType|operation|inputVariable*
		|outputVariable|inPara|outPara|executionPath

Fig. 10.7 Semi-formal syntax for query language

has been preferred. This is because it groups together all advice execution conditions in the query and frees the advice code from any runtime conditions, and thus results in a more readable code and advices that are more generic.

We therefore propose a joinpoint query language that can express the need of adaptation advices on the service code, as well as runtime execution context. We assume that services are implemented in BPEL, though the concepts and requirements are independent of the specific process language adopted. The query language is therefore designed specifically to BPEL constructs. Figure 10.7 presents the syntax of our query language that satisfies the above requirements. It allows the definition of joinpoints on the BPEL code constructs, such as operation, portType, etc.

While it shares some common characteristics with query languages that operate at the code level such as BPQL, the main differences are: (i) our language can express conditions on service interaction paths, and (ii) our language includes keywords for specifying the relative location of the joinpoint to the BPEL activity that matched the specified conditions (i.e. the *before*, *after* or *around* keywords). These concepts are needed to achieve a self contained query language able to express all the conditions necessary for identifying joinpoints in the service adaptation context.

As shown in Fig. 10.7, the query takes parameters (*param*) that correspond to BPEL constructs (i.e. operation, input variable, output variable, partnerLink and portType), or an execution path (i.e. a sequence of previously exchanged messages). These parameters are matched against some conditions (*context object*) at runtime to identify joinpoints where adaptation advices should be executed. The `executes` statement specifies whether adaptation advice should be executed *before*, *after* or *around* (i.e. in place of) a BPEL activity that matches the joinpoint query.

Consider again the supply chain example, in which the OCP shown in Table 10.3 is used to solve its ordering mismatch. In this case, the OCPStore needs to be executed *around* (instead of) the *receive* activity of operation sendShippingPreference to receive and store the message issueInvoiceIn, which is not expected at this state. As mentioned before that the ordering mismatch only occurs when a specific interaction path (unregistered) is taken, hence the query parameters

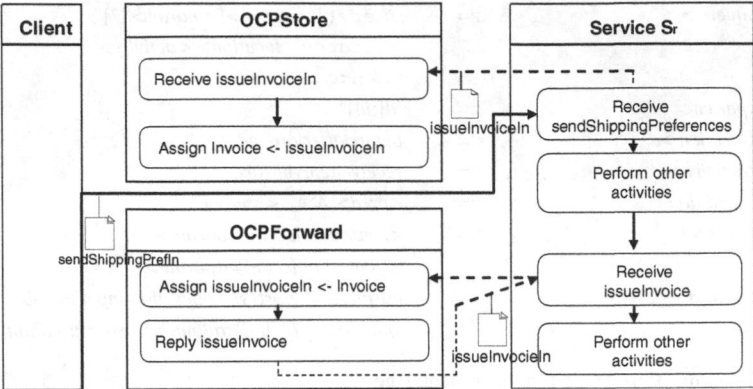

Fig. 10.8 Sample usage of the aspect template specified in the OCP

of the OCPStore in this example are <operation>=sendShippingPreferences and <sequence>=unregistered. These parameters will be evaluated, at runtime, against currently executing operation (O_i^{sr}) and execution path (S_i) of the adapting service.

Figure 10.8 shows a sample usage of OCP at runtime. When the process executes the *receive* activity of operation sendShippingPreferences, OCPStore receives message issueInvoice and stores it in a temporary variable Invoice. After the completion of OCPStore, the process continues to execute the *receive* activity of operation sendShippingPreferences. When the message issueInvoice is required by the S_r, the OCPForward creates it using the value of variable Invoice. OCPForward is executed *around* (instead of) the *receive* activity of operation issueInvoice. Hence, after the completion of OCPForward, the process continues other activities without performing the *receive* activity of operation issueInvoice. This is because the message issueInvoiceIn has already been received by the execution of the OCPForward aspect.

10.5.2.3 Deployment of Adaptation Aspects

The above discussion considers only the query language syntax, not the actual deployment of the solution. Choosing a query language that incorporates runtime conditions also allows for aspect weaving done either at compile-time or at runtime. In the compile-time deployment model, a new BPEL code would be generated with advices preceded by runtime conditions. In a runtime deployment model, a specially modified query engine is required to evaluate runtime conditions based on the execution context it maintains, leaving the original code unmodified. While both models are viable, the first one (compile-time) imposes to incorporate in the advices some additional logic. This logic is not part of adaptation logic but it is required to maintain information regarding the service's execution context (e.g., the interaction path taken by the client). We therefore chose the second (runtime) deployment model which, in addition to its greater simplicity, also allows to dynamically plugging and unplugging adaptation aspects. We refer readers to [22] for the details of the query engine supporting this deployment model.

10.5.3 Aspect-Oriented Versus Standalone Service Adaptation

Figure 10.9 presents a schematic comparison of the standalone and aspect-oriented approaches for adapter development, in cases where a service S_r with protocol P_r has to be adapted to n client services, with heterogeneous protocols $P_1, \ldots, P_n$. In the standalone adapter approach, n adapters, one per each client, have to be developed to make the interactions possible according to protocol P_r. On the other hand, in aspect-oriented approach, the runtime instance that is formed for interacting with each client has to be modified with respective adaptation aspects. Each of these two approaches has characteristics that make them suitable for certain situations.

10.5.3.1 Aspect-Oriented Service Adaptation

Aspect-oriented approach presents several characteristics that make it preferable for the development of adaptation code compared to standalone adapters. In particular, using aspect-oriented approach to realize adapter templates for mismatch patterns further expedites rapid adapter development. This is because there is no need for a new service (i.e., standalone adapter) to be developed, rather instances of the existing service are updated at runtime. Other characteristics are discussed as follows:

- *Possibility of mismatch resolution*: The intertwining of adaptation aspects inside a service allows the aspects to access internal state and variables of the service. This increases the possibility of service adaptations that require contextual information

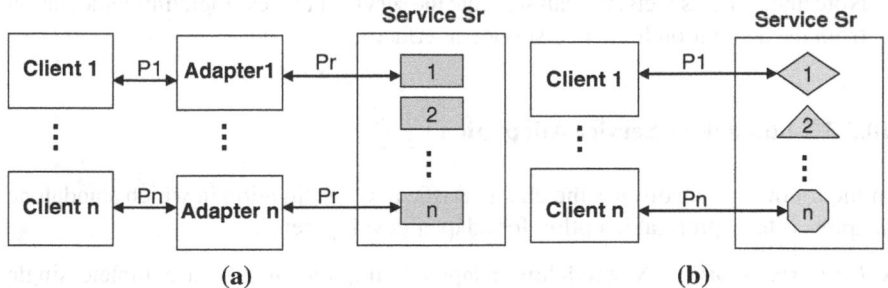

(a) (b)

Fig. 10.9 Schematic comparison of adaptation in standalone and aspect-oriented approaches: (a) service instances 1,...,n are the same, (b) service instances 1,...,n are modified with respective adaptation aspects

of the service, e.g. a message generation that requires internal variables of the service. Note that the patterns are generic and reusable and instantiation of patterns is specific and allows the user to incorporate context information as the input parameters of the pattern.

- *Recovery*: The adaptation aspects share execution context of the adapting service. When an error occurs, the recovery can be performed by analysing the internal state of the service. This is easier than handling exceptions of two separate processes (i.e. adapter and service), which would require correlation of log entries.
- *Reusability*: Aspect-oriented approach promotes reusability of adaptation code when many execution points require the same adaptation logic, e.g., any operations whose messages involve a specific data type can reuse the same aspect for message transformations. There is no need to generate individual adaptation logic for each single message as is the case of the standalone adapter. Consequently, the number of adaptation logic needed to be generated is reduced.
- *Separation of concerns*: The aspect-oriented approach cleanly separates the adaptation concern from the service functionality. The service developers are oblivious to the adaptation concern since they do not need to write gluecode between adaptation logic and service implementation (as is the case in the standalone adapter in which gluecode appear in several places in the service code). The study in [18, 19] also shows that implementing adapters using AOP can better separate the adaptation concern from the functionality of the base programs.

  One may argue that whether it is simpler to modify the business logic of the service (e.g., to re-write the BPEL code) for each new incompatible business partner rather than using the aspect-oriented approach. The former approach translates in creating specialized versions of the service for different (incompatible) partners, which is difficult and expensive to maintain. We can modify the service business logic (BPEL) if we have to cope with only one partner. However, if we have to enable the interactions with many incompatible partners, it would mean creating many versions of the service implementation. The drawback of this approach is that each time that we change the business logic, we would have to replicate the changes in all versions. Nevertheless, in some cases, e.g., for business reasons, it may make sense to create and maintain a customized version of a service for a specific client. Note that using aspects, we can separate the service business logic/implementation from the adaptation logic and service interface.

10.5.3.2 Standalone Service Adaptation

In the following, we discuss the characteristic and the situation in which standalone adapters offer a preferable option for adapter development:

- *Understandability*: A standalone adapter is implemented as a complete single business process comprising of a set of adaptation activities. The interdependencies between these activities are well-defined (comparing to aspect-oriented approach), and thus simplify the understandability.

10.5.3.3 Tradeoffs

In some cases, the intended adaptation scenarios need to be taken into account when selecting the adapter development approaches. These characteristics and situations are discussed as follows:

- *Overhead*: We consider overhead as the time spent by the adapters in performing activities that are not part of the adaptation logic. This characteristic depends on the intended adaptation scenarios, specifically the number of messages that requires adaptation. When such a number is small, the aspect-oriented approach is preferable. This is because the adaptation aspects will be invoked only for those messages that require adaptation, while all messages need to pass through the standalone adapter even if no adaptation is needed. However, aspect-oriented approach introduces overhead for every single message to check if an adaptation is required. Hence, when the number of mismatches is large relative to the total number of messages, the standalone adapter approach might be reasonable.
- *Maintainability*: In the context of service adaptation, we consider maintainability as the impact of changes in the service implementation on the adaptation logic. The impact of changes is spread over multiple aspects comprising the adaptation logic, while it is in one place in the case of standalone adapters. However, in the aspect-oriented approach, the developer can update the adaptation logic by dynamically plug/unplug the aspects, without interrupting the service interactions (as is the case of standalone adapters that need to be suspended and updated).

Table 10.4 provides a high-level comparison of the aspect-oriented and standalone adapter development approaches. It can be used as a guideline for an adapter developer to decide about which adapter development approach to take. It shows that the aspect-oriented adaptation is preferable when developers consider the importance of reusability, relative possible number of mismatches to be resolved, recovery and separation of concerns. On the other hand, when considering the understandability of adaptation logic, developers may consider the use of standalone adapters. In other case, the intended adaptation scenarios need to be taken into consideration. In cases, when we have accesses to service implementation and runtime environment, and the relative number of mismatch is small, the aspect-oriented approach is preferable approach for service adaptation development.

Table 10.4 Comparison of adapter code generation approaches

	Adaptation aspects	Standalone adapters
Possibility of mismatch resolution	+	−
Recovery	+	−
Reusability	+	−
Separation of concern	+	−
Understandability	−	+
Overhead	+/−	+/−
Maintainability	+/−	+/−

10.6 Concluding Remarks and Future Work

This chapter discusses a significant problem in SOA, i.e., service adaptation. We first reviewed the problem of and the state of the art in service adaptation and identified the gaps in each step of service adaptation process, i.e., matching, mapping and adapter development. We found that while functional description of services includes interface, data and behavioral descriptions, existing work on service matching and adaptation often focus only on one of these aspects. However, in reality all these differences are present at the same time, which makes service matching and adaptation more complicated. We presented an integrated framework consisting of a methodology for characterization of service adaptation problem, and approaches that starting from Web service interface and protocol specifications assists in the identification of service mismatches as well as helps developers in adapter code development. We described mismatch patterns which capture and formalize common differences between service specifications and parameterized adaptation logic that can be instantiated for resolving the identified mismatch. We then presented a protocol-aware interface matching approach for the identification of service mismatches. Finally, we provided an overview of a software platform that enables service developers in leveraging mismatch patterns for rapid development of service adapters with two approaches: standalone and aspect-oriented. We also discussed the benefits of each adapter development approach and provided a comparative study between them.

Future work in this area consists of using the proposed framework to identify possible mismatches at other high-level specifications of services, e.g., service policies. We also consider the development of semi-automated mismatch identification of other mismatches in addition to split/merge presented in this chapter. Another area of future work we are considering is to incorporate interface and protocol matching approaches in the composition of Web services as current approaches often do not consider heterogeneities of service specifications while composing services.

References

1. RosettaNet, http://www.rosettanet.org
2. Beeri, C., Eyal, A., Kamenkovich, S., Milo, T.: Querying business processes with BP-QL. In: Proceedings of VLDB'05 (2005)
3. Benatallah, B., Casati, F., Grigori, D., Nezhad, H.R.M., Toumani, F.: Developing adapters for web services integration. In: Proceedings of 17th International Conference on Advanced Information Systems Engineering (CAiSE'05), pp. 415–429 (2005)
4. Benatallah, B., Casati, F., Toumani, F.: Representing, analysing and managing web service protocols. Data Knowl. Eng. **58**(3), 327–357 (2006)
5. Brogi, A., Popescu, R.: Automated generation of BPEL adapters. In: Proceedings of 4th International Conference on Service-Oriented Computing (ICSOC 2006), pp. 27–39 (2006)
6. Cámara, J., Canal, C., Cubo, J., Murillo, J.M.: An aspect-oriented adaptation framework for dynamic component evolution. Electron. Notes Theor. Comput. Sci. **189**, 21–34 (2007)

7. Charfi, A., Mezini, M.: Aspect-oriented web service composition with AO4BPEL. In: Proceedings of ECOWS'04, pp. 168–182 (2004)
8. Chari, K., Seshadri, S.: Demystifying integration. Commun. ACM **47**(7), 58–63 (2004)
9. Chinnici, R., Moreau, J.J., Ryman, A., Weerawarana, S. (eds.): Web Service Description Language (WSDL) Version 2.0. W3C Working draft. http://www.w3.org/TR/wsdl20 (2007)
10. Colyer, A., Clement, A., Bodkin, R., Hugunin, J.: Using AspectJ for component integration in middleware. In: Proceedings of OOPSLA'03, pp. 339–344 (2003)
11. Courbis, C., Finkelstein, A.: Towards aspect weaving applications. In: Proceedings of ICSE'05, pp. 69–77 (2005)
12. Dantas, A., Yoder, J.W., Borba, P., Johnson, R.: Using aspects to make adaptive object-models adaptable. In: Proceedings of RAM-SE'04, pp. 9–19 (2004)
13. Do, H.H., Rahm, E.: COMA—a system for flexible combination of schema matching approaches. In: Proceedings of 28th Conference on Very Large Data, Bases (VLDB'02), pp. 610–621 (2002)
14. Dong, X., Halevy, A.Y., Madhavan, J., Nemes, E., Zhang, J.: Similarity search for web services. In: Proceedings of 30th Conference on Very Large Data, Bases (VLDB'04), pp. 372–383 (2004)
15. Dumas, M., Spork, M., Wang, K.: Adapt or perish: algebra and visual notation for service interface adaptation. In: Proceedings of International Conference on Business Process Management (BPM 2006), pp. 65–80 (2006)
16. Fuchs, M.: Adapting web services in a heterogeneous environment. In: Proceedings of International Conference on Web Services (ICWS'04), p. 656. IEEE CS Press, Washington (2004)
17. Gamma, E., Helm, R., Johnson, R., Vlissides, J.: Design patterns. Addison-Wesley, Boston (1995)
18. Garcia, A., et al.: Modularizing design patterns with aspects: a quantitative study. In: Proceedings of AOSD '05, pp. 3–14 (2005)
19. Hannemann, J., Kiczales, G.: Design pattern implementation in Java and AspectJ. SIGPLAN Not. **37**(11), 161–173 (2002)
20. Kazhamiakin, R., Pistore, M.: Choreography conformance analysis: asynchronous communications and information alignment. In: Proceedings of 3rd International Workshop on Web Services and Formal Methods (WS-FM). Lecture Notes in Computer Science, vol. 4184, pp. 227–241. Springer, Berlin (2006)
21. Kiczales, G., Hilsdale, E., Hugunin, J., Kersten, M., Palm, J., Griswold, W.: An overview of AspectJ. In: Proceedings of ECOOP'01, pp. 327–353 (2001)
22. Kongdenfha, W., Motahari-Nezhad, H.R., Benatallah, B., Casati, F., Saint-Paul, R.: Mismatch patterns and adaptation aspects: a foundation for rapid development of web service adapters. IEEE Trans. Serv. Comput. **2**(2), 94–107 (2009)
23. Kongdenfha, W., Saint-Paul, R., Benatallah, B., Casati, F.: An aspect-oriented framework for service adaptation. In: Proceedings of 4th International Conference on Service-Oriented Computing (ICSOC 2006), pp. 15–26 (2006)
24. Li, X., Fan, Y., Jiang, F.: A classification of service composition mismatches to support service mediation. In: Proceedings of GCC'07, pp. 315–321 (2007)
25. Loughran, N.: Survey of aspect-oriented middleware research. Technical report, Lancaster University, AOSD-Europe-ULANC-10 (2005)
26. Massuthe, P., Wolf, K.: An algorithm for matching non-deterministic services with operating guidelines. Int. J. Bus. Process Integr. Manag. (IJBPIM) **2**(2), 81–90 (2007)
27. McNeile, A.: Dynamic choreography. http://www.metamaxim.com/download/documents/DynChor.pdf (2005)
28. Melnik, S., Garcia-Molina, H., Rahm, E.: Similarity flooding: a versatile graph matching algorithm and its application to schema matching. In: Proceedings of 18th International Conference on Data Engineering (ICDE'02), pp. 117–128 (2002)
29. Murugesan, S.: Understanding Web 2.0. IEEE IT Prof. **9**(4), 34–41 (2007)
30. Nezhad, H.R.M., Benatallah, B., Casati, F., Toumani, F.: Web services interoperability specifications. Computer **39**(5), 24–32 (2006). doi:10.1109/MC.2006.181

31. Nezhad, H.R.M., Benatallah, B., Martens, A., Curbera, F., Casati, F.: Semi-automated adaptation of service interactions. In: Proceedings of 16th World Wide Web Conference (WWW 2007), pp. 993–1002. ACM Press, New York (2007)
32. Nezhad, H.R.M., Xu, G.Y., Benatallah, B.: Protocol-aware matching of web service interfaces for adapter development. In: Proceedings of WWW, pp. 731–740 (2010)
33. Nicoara, A., Alonso, G.: Dynamic AOP with PROSE. In: Proceedings of CAiSE'05, pp. 125–138 (2005)
34. Ponnekanti, S.R., Fox, A.: Interoperability among independently evolving web services. In: Proceedings of 5th ACM/IFIP/USENIX International Conference on Middleware (Middleware'04), pp. 331–351. Springer, New York (2004)
35. Rahm, E., Bernstein, P.A.: A survey of approaches to automatic schema matching. VLDB J. 10(4), 334–350 (2001)
36. Rahm, E., Do, H.H., Massmann, S.: Matching large XML schemas. SIGMOD Rec. 33(4), 26–31 (2004)
37. Soria, C.C., Pérez, J., Carsí, J.A.: Dynamic adaptation of aspect-oriented components. In: Proceedings of CBSE'07, pp. 49–65 (2007)
38. W3C: XML Schema 1.1. W3C recommendation. http://www.w3.org/XML/Schema (2004)
39. Wang, Y., Stroulia, E.: Flexible interface matching for web-service discovery. In: Proceedings of 4th International Conference on Web Information Systems Engineering (WISE 2003), pp. 147–156. IEEE Computer Society, Washington (2003)
40. Wohlstadter, E., Volder, K.: Doxpects: aspects supporting XML transformation interfaces. In: Proceedings of AOSD'06, pp. 99–108 (2006)
41. Zaremski, A.M., Wing, J.M.: Signature matching: a tool for using software libraries. ACM Trans. Softw. Eng. Methodol. (TOSEM) 4(2), 146–170 (1995)
42. Zaremski, A.M., Wing, J.M.: Specification matching of software components. ACM Trans. Softw. Eng. Methodol. (TOSEM) 6(4), 333–369 (1997)

Chapter 11
Transformation Framework for Consistent Evolution of UML Behavioral Elements into BPMN Design Element

Jayeeta Chanda, Ananya Kanjilal, Sabnam Sengupta and Swapan Bhattacharya

Abstract There are many software products that have been developed in the object-oriented paradigm. To incorporate the positive aspects of service-oriented paradigm (SOA) and address the issues related to increasing size and complexity of software products, they need to be evolved to service-oriented domain. There are some proven Object Oriented (OO) Design Tools that can be used for Service Oriented Application design incorporating both the behavioral and structural aspects in a seamless, consistent evolution that can be made from object oriented to service oriented domain. In this chapter, we concentrate on the evolution process of behavioral aspect of design from OO to SOA. Business Process Modeling Notation (BPMN) has become the de-facto standard for modeling business process on a conceptual level. Business processes are an integral part of service-oriented architecture. In service-oriented applications Use cases needs to be ordered along business processes. Business Processes visualize global control-flow across Use cases. Therefore, use of a business process language to visualize the dependencies among different use cases is of high importance. Use case diagram along with activity diagrams represents the behavioral aspect of a system in the analysis phase of an object-oriented system. To enable modeling the relationship among different behavioral aspects and evolve from object oriented domain to service oriented domain, a formal approach would help in establishing the foundation. In order to do that, in this work, we propose a formal framework, FAM (Formalized analysis model), which is a set of grammar

J. Chanda (✉) · A. Kanjilal · S. Sengupta
BPPIMT, 137, VIP Road, Kolkata, India
e-mail: jayeeta.chanda@gmail.com

A. Kanjilal
e-mail: ag_k@rediffmail.com

S. Sengupta
e-mail: sabnamsg@gmail.com

S. Bhattacharya
National Institute of Technology Karnataka , Surathkal, India
e-mail: bswapan2000@yahoo.co.in

A. Bouguettaya et al. (eds.), *Web Services Foundations*,
DOI: 10.1007/978-1-4614-7518-7_11,
© Springer Science+Business Media New York 2014

based formalized Use case and Activity diagram elements of UML and a framework for verification of the diagrams, which includes syntactic correctness and requirement traceability. Along with that, we also propose FAM2BP (Formalized Analysis Model to Business Process) for transformation of Formalized Analysis Model (FAM) of object-oriented systems into BPMN process for SOA application using a set of rules that will help in generating business processes for SOA application directly from object oriented analysis models. This model would help in a consistent evolution of software development paradigms from Object Oriented to Service Oriented systems.

11.1 Introduction

Design and development of software has become much more complex in the last decade, resulting in the evolution of design and development paradigms. Object oriented systems have thus become an integral part of more complex Service Oriented Architecture (SOA) to address complex issues like Separation of Concerns, reusability, granularity, modularity, componentization and interoperability. Evolution of software design and development from OO to SOA domain has become the necessity in this evolving scenario. There are some proven OO design tools that can be used for SOA application design. In object-oriented systems, UML is a widely accepted industry standard for modeling of different aspects of the system under construction. Use case diagrams and activity diagrams are used to model the business functional requirements in the analysis phase. These correlate to the business processes of SOA architecture. In service-oriented architecture, BPMN processes play an important role in the development of services. It is the dynamic behavioral diagrams that are often used for modeling business processes, such as the UML Activity diagram and Use Case diagram . BPMN is related to UML in the sense that it defines a visual notation for business processes that is similar to UML behavioral diagrams. However, BPMN and UML have very different approaches to business process modeling. UML offers an object-oriented approach to the modeling of applications, while BPMN takes a process-centric approach that is more natural and intuitive for the business analyst to use. BPMN also offers the option of explicitly modeling business objects that may be exposed through business services in the process flows. Automatic translation of UML use case and activity models to BPMN design elements is thus necessary to ensure consistent evolution of Object oriented systems to Service oriented paradigm.

In this work, we propose a grammar based framework FAM (Formalized analysis Model) for syntactic and semantic verification of UML diagrams in the analysis phase and a relational model based framework FAM2BP (Formalized Analysis Model to Business Processes) for automated translation of elements of FAM to elements of Business Processes, preserving the use case relationship and dependencies and maintaining the control flow of the Business processes. Our framework would enable a consistent evolution of software systems from object oriented paradigm to service oriented paradigm.

11.2 Related Work

Lots of research work are undertaken presently to address various issues in designing and developing software in service oriented paradigm. We discuss some of the significant contributions and present it in the following two subsections. In the first subsection, we discuss the existing works in the domain of formalization of object oriented design modeled by UML diagrams which forms the basis of automated translation and verification. Our proposed framework FAM is presented subsequently in the context of these existing works. In the second subsection, we discuss the work in the domain of relationship between UML use case model and BPMN process model. This forms the basis of our proposed framework FAM2BP for automated evolution of BPMN process models from UML models.

11.2.1 Formalization Approaches

Formalization of UML has become a prominent domain of research for the last few years. Achievement of automated consistency checking and execution has led the software engineers and researchers to focus in this domain. In this section we will discuss a few works done in this domain related to formalization of UML static and dynamic models. To reduce the risks associated with software development and to increase the safety and the reliability by formalizing the syntax of (a sub-set of the popular UML diagrams (Use Case diagram, Class diagram, and State Machine diagram) using Z specifications has been proposed in [1].

The class diagram being the reference point of the notation, any formalization must start with this diagram. To make it possible to provide computer aided support during the application design phase in order to automatically detect relevant properties, such as inconsistencies and redundancies, in [2], UML class diagram is formalized in terms of a logic belonging to Description Logics, which are subsets of First-Order Logic. An algebraic approach is chosen in [3] because it is more abstract than state-based style languages. UML's class diagram (including type definitions, attributes, operations, aggregation and association) and OCL constraints (syntax and semantics), have been formalized using theorem prover Isabelle using one of its built-in logics, HOL.

RSL (RAISE (Rigorous Approach to Industrial Software) Specification Language) has been used in [4] as a syntactic and semantic reference for UML. An automated tool that implements the translation and the abstract syntax in RSL for the RSL-translatable class diagrams are also presented. The integration of the domain modeling method for analyzing and modeling families of software systems with the SOFL formal specification language is discussed in [5]. A UML 1.5 profile named TURTLE (Timed UML and RT-LOTOS Environment) endowed with a formal semantics given in terms of RT-LOTOS is proposed in [6]. Preliminary results on an approach to formally define UML class diagrams using hierarchical predicate transition nets (HPrTNs) have been presented in [7]. The authors show how to define the main concepts related to class diagrams using HPrTN elements.

The semantics presented in [8] captures the consistency between sequence diagram with class diagram and state diagram. This approach may be useful to develop the model consistent checking functions in UML CASE tools and also to reason about the correctness of a design model with respect to a requirement model. The transformation rules for formalizing UML statechart diagrams have been proposed in [9]. The target language for the transformation is Concurrent Regular Expressions (CREs), which are extensions of regular expression. In [10], the alternative approach of using -calculus to formalize UML activity diagrams is presented to get rich process semantics for activity diagrams. This process model can be automatically verified with the help of -calculus analytical tools. Hoare's CSP (communicating sequential processes) has been used in [1] to formalize the behaviors of UML activity diagrams and provides an approach to model checking during software analysis or design stage. The operational semantics of UML sequence diagrams is specified and this specification is extended to include features for modeling multimedia applications as a case study in [11]. Dynamic Meta modeling has been proposed for specifying operational semantics of UML behavioral diagrams based on UML collaboration diagrams that are interpreted as graph transformation rules. The authors in [12] have defined a template to formalize the structured control constructs of sequence diagram, introduced in UML 2.0.

In all these research works, UML diagrams have been formalized using other formal languages. Our earlier work [13] also used Z to propose a formal model for six UML diagrams. However, Z is a non-executable language and hence automated verification is not possible unless translated or mapped to executable models like XML using ZML. In this work, we use context free grammar to formally define the very widely used UML diagrams namely Use case, Activity and Class. This approach is executable unlike the existing approaches like Z-notation etc and hence can be validated using LEX and YACC.

11.2.2 UML Model and BPMN Model Mapping

There exist some works related to the relationship between use case models and BPMN process model. In [14], Cockburn mentions the possibility of applying Use cases for deriving business processes but no rules are proposed. The field of model-driven development has tried to integrate the concept of Use cases within its UML models. Instead of tabular and textual descriptions, UML sequence diagrams or similar models are used in [15]. In [16], an UML based development of business processes is discussed. Expression of control flow between use cases is missing in this approach.

In [17], it is possible to define control-flow dependencies between Use cases with the introduction of Use case Charts and their formalizations. Use cases are called scenarios that may not have extensions and that are modeled as UML sequence diagrams. However, dependencies between Use cases cannot be derived from the Use Case themselves but have to be modeled explicitly.

In [18], synthesis of state transition graphs from Use Cases is addressing the visualization aspect in a better way. A tabular Use case can be converted to a state transition graph similar to graphical business process languages. In [19], the state transition graphs can be used for simulating one Use case but are not suited for visualizing dependencies between Use Cases. The generation of EPC models from Use Cases is addressed in [20]. EPC models consist of fewer graphical symbol types but are not as powerful as BPMN. BPMN has become the standard business process modeling language in SOA. Therefore, the transformation of Use cases should have BPMN as the target notation and our framework is developed upon this concept.

In [21], an algorithm is proposed that restores the overview of the Use cases and visualizes the control flow of the resulting business process. This approach automatically assembles Use cases to business process. But this work is unable to keep the relationship (includes and extends) among use cases and treated as the flat use case model.

Our work is closely related to these works but improves upon them in several aspects. We capture the use case scenarios as a formalized analysis model (FAM) that is a grammar based representation of UML Use case and Activity models. A formal definition of semantics for the subset of BPMN that is applied here has been presented in [22]. Then, a set of rules are proposed that automatically transforms the FAM to BPMN elements (FAM2BP) maintaining the control flow of scenarios as well as preserving all relationships between the use cases.

11.3 Scope of Work

In this chapter, we propose an integrated framework for automatic evolution of UML analysis models to BPMN design elements of service oriented paradigm. The UML use case and activity diagrams that capture the business functional requirements and their flow of events are formally represented as Formal Analysis Model (FAM) which is the grammar based representation of these artifacts. The elements of UML correspond and correlate to the BPMN elements based on which we have designed the transformation framework FAM2BP. The framework consists of a set of rules to map the UML elements like events and flow of events into BPMN elements like start/stop/intermediate events, parallel/exclusive-OR Gateway, etc. A relational model is proposed to represent the relationship among the artifacts. Finally, an algorithm is presented to automatically transform the UML elements into BPMN elements. The block diagram in Fig. 11.1 depicts our approach.

Fig. 11.1 Our integrated framework

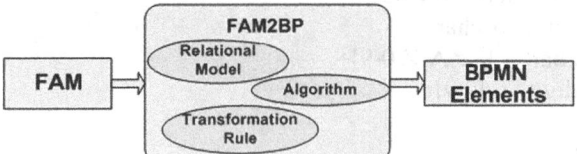

11.4 Formalized Analysis Model

UML, being visual in nature, is easy to understand and communicate, but, it lacks the rigor of formal modeling languages and hence verification of a model specified in UML and ensuring requirement traceability within these models becomes difficult. Formalization of UML diagrams is now a dominant area of research. This section is a work in that direction. We have proposed a formal grammar for the Use case, Activity and Class diagrams. We have considered OMG UML 2.0 standard and proposed formal models for some of its constituent diagrams. The production rules, terminals, non-terminals for the grammars are chosen and proposed accordingly. We have also proposed a set of verification criteria that comprises of syntactic correctness rules and traceability rules.

The consistency rules have been proposed by analyzing the inter-relationships among the diagrams so that they together represent a coherent design. Verification of all the rules has been presented based on the proposed grammar. We have used regular expression features (eg. +, *) in the production rules for simplicity and easy understanding. However, for Lex/YACC implementation, we have used a recursive definition of the grammar. Let, the grammar be G = {S, N, T, P}

where S, N, T, P represent start symbol, non-terminals, terminals and production rules

T= {char, digit, +, -, #, association, generalization, aggregation, (,) , .. ,:, basic, alternate, include, extend}

All other symbols used in the production rule P are non-terminals (N).

Grammar for use case Diagram

P:S → usecase_diagram
usecase_diagram → usecase+ actor* UC_relation* actor_relation*
usecase → UC_id UC_name event+
event → event_ID event_name event_type
event_type → basic | alternate
UC_relation → UC_id UC_reltype UC_id
UC_reltype → ≪include≫ | ≪extend≫ | ≪generalization≫
actor_relation → actor actor_reltype actor
actor_reltype → ≪include≫ | ≪extend≫
event_ID → char
event_name → char
UC_id → char
UC_name → char
actor → char
char→ [a-z A-Z 0-9]+
digit → [0 9]

Grammar for activity diagram

activity_diagram → activity_state+ transition+ objectflow*

activity_state → act_ID event_ID activity_node act_desc
          className pre_element post_element

activity_node → start | end | join | fork | action | decision | merge

pre_element → className prenode

post_element → className postnode

prenode → start | join | fork | action | decision | merge

postnode → end | join | fork | action | decision | merge

transition → tran_ID prenode postnode objectfl_ID
          | tran_ID prenode postnode

objectflow → objectfl_ID objName className preState poststate

preState → objName = statename

postState → objName = statename

act_ID → char

className → char

objName → char

act_desc → char

tran_ID → char

objectfl_ID → char

statename → char

The syntactic rules and traceability rules for the use case diagram and activity diagram are stated as given in the following subsections.

11.4.1 Syntactic Rules

1) The usecase diagram consists of

    a. One or many use cases

    b. Zero or many actors

    c. Zero or many use case relationships

    d. Zero or many actor relationships

2) An usecase consists of One or many events
3) An event has to be of the type basic or alternate.
4) The Use case relationship can be of the type include, extend and generalization.
5) The actor relationship can be of the type include and extend.
6) An activity diagram consists of

    a. A start state

    b. An end state

    c. One or many activity states

    d. Two or many transitions.

7) Zero or many object flows (change in state of an object)
8) Zero or many swimlanes (Transition of state is between two different class)

11.4.2 Traceability Rules

An action/activity state in activity diagram has a one-to-one mapping with an event of a use case in use case diagram.

This traceability rule can be validated using the grammar of use case diagram and activity diagram as stated in the earlier sections.

In this section, we have formalized the analysis phase of OO design elements. These formalized analysis model (FAM) elements are input to the transformation framework FAM2BP. The proposed FAM will establish traceability among the different elements of analysis model. We are establishing traceability in this stage before the transformation because the consistent elements of OO system will generate more robust design elements of the SOA paradigm.

11.5 FAM2BP: Proposed Transformation Model

This section discusses the relational model which maps the artifacts of the two paradigms. The transformation rules and the algorithms for automatic transformation are presented in the following sections.

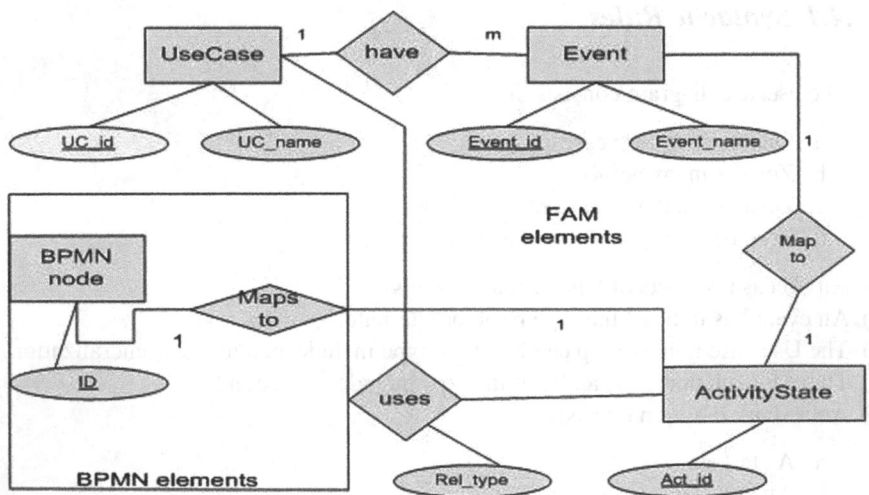

Fig. 11.2 Relational model

11.5.1 Relational Model

The elements of Formalized Analysis Model (FAM) are mapped with the BPMN node. For example, the Use case and Event entity are related to each other. Similarly all other elements of the FAM are related as shown in Fig. 11.2. These elements of FAM model are mapped with the BPMN nodes to ensure automatic transformation from Formalized Analysis Model to Business process. The tables corresponding to this model are generated as follows-

Table Event

(UC_id, event_id, event_name, event_type)

Table ActivityState

(UC_id, event_id, Act_id, activity_node, act_desc, preElement, postElement)

Table ActUCRelation

(Act_ID, UC_id, Rel_type)

Table BPMN_node

(Name, activity_node, Graphical_notation)

The events of the OO behavioral domain are mapped with the BPMN nodes. The SOA behavioral elements BPMN nodes are given below:

- Start Event
- End Event
- Intermediate Event
- Parallel Gateway
- Exclusive-OR Gateway

11.5.2 Transformation Rules

We propose a set of rules to transform Formalized Analysis model into BPMN notation.

Rule 1

The use case activity whose node is marked as *start* will be assigned as the Start Event of the BPMN node. The BPMN node will be labeled as Activity ID (act_ID) of the activity node.

Rule 2

The use case activity whose node is marked as *end* will be assigned as the End Event of the BPMN node. The BPMN node will be labeled as Activity ID (act_ID) of the activity node.

Rule 3

The use case activity whose node is marked as *action / decision* will be assigned as the Intermediate Event of the BPMN node. The BPMN node will be labeled as Activity ID (act_ID) of the activity node.

Rule 4

The use case activity whose node is marked as *fork* will be assigned as the Parallel

Gateway of the BPMN node if both the postElement of the activity node are of the type *basic*. The BPMN node will be labeled as Activity ID (act_ID) of the activity node.

Rule 5

The use case activity whose node is marked as *fork* will be assigned as the Exclusive-OR Gateway of the BPMN node if one the postElement of the activity node are of the type *basic* and the other is of the type *alternate*. The BPMN node will be labeled as Activity ID(act_ID) of the activity node.

These rules are realized in the next section to automate the transformation of Formalized Analysis Model into BPMN nodes.

11.5.3 Algorithm for Automated Transformation

The rules cited in the previous section are realized using two algorithms namely NodeGeneration and FlowGeneration. The flow of the algorithm is as follow:

The elements of Formalized Analysis Model (FAM) in the form of different table schema are used as input to the first algorithm named NodeGeneration The outputs of this algorithm are different BPMN nodes. This output along with the Array FAM_Flow are fed as input to the second algorithm named FlowGeneration. The Array FAM_Flow is formal method of storing the flow information of events of FAM. The FlowGeneration algorithm will generate the BPMN design elements.

11.5.3.1 Algorithm NodeGeneration to Generate BPMN Node

The algorithm NodeGeneration as proposed below will generate the BPMN nodes. We define the algorithm using the tuple relational calculus. The algorithm is proposed as follows-

Query 1:

The following query is the realization of rule 1 of Sect. 11.5.2.It generates the Start of the BPMN node. It selects the *Graphical_notation* from BPMN_node and map that with the *start event* of the activity_node.

$\{t.Graphical\_notation \mid BPMN\_node(t) \land t.ID = 1 \land$

$\quad \exists\, d\, (d.act\_ID \mid ActivityState\,(d) \land d.activity\_node = t.activity\_node \land$

$\quad t.label = d.act\_ID \land d.activity\_node = start)\}$

Query 2:

The following query is the realization of rule 2 of Sect. 11.5.2. It generates the End of the BPMN node. It selects the *Graphical_notation* from BPMN_node and map that with the *end event* of the activity_node.

$\{t.\,Graphical\_notation \mid BPMN\_node(t) \land t.ID = 2 \land$

$\quad \exists\, d(\, d.act\_ID \mid ActivityState(d) \land d.activity\_node =$

t.activity_node ∧ *t.label* = *d.act_ID* ∧ *d.activity_node* = *end)*}

Query 3:

The following query is the realization of rule 3 of Sect. 11.5.2. It generates the
Intermediate Event of the BPMN node. It selects the *Graphical_notation* from
BPMN_node and map that with the action or decision event of the activity_node

{t.Graphical_notation | BPMN_node(t) ∧ t.ID = 3 ∧
   ∧ d(d.act_ID | ActivityState(d) ∧ d.activity_node =
t.activity_node ∧ t.label = d.act_ID ∧ (d.activity_node = action
∨ d.activity_node = decision)) }

Query 4:

The following query is the realization of rule 4 of Sect. 11.5.2. It generates the
graphical notation for Parallel Gateway. It selects the particular *graphical notation*
and map this with that activity_node of ActivityState where activity_node is *fork* and
the event_type of all the postElement of that activity node is basic.

{t.Graphical_notation | BPMN_node(t) ∧ t.ID = 4 ∧
   ∃ q (q.act_ID | ActivityState(q) ∧ q.activity_node = t.activity_node ∧
t.label = q.act_ID ∧ q.activity_node = fork
   ∃ r(r.postElement | ActivityState (t) ∧ r.act_ID = q.act_ID ∧
   ∃ s(s.event_ID | ActivityState(s) ∧ s.act_ID = r.postElement ∧
   ∃ p(p.event_ID | Usecase(p) ∧ p.event_ID = s.cvent_ID ∧
s.event_type = basic))))}

Query 5:

The following query is the realization of rule 5 of Sect. 11.5.2. It generates the graphical notation for Exclusive_OR Gateway. It selects the particular *Graphical notation*
and map this with that activity_node of ActivityState where activity_node is *fork*
and the event_type of the one of postElement of that activity node is *basic* and the
event_type of the other postElement of that activity node is *alternate*.

{t.Graphical_notation | BPMN_node(t) ∧ t.ID = 5 ∧
∃ q(q.act_ID | ActivityState(q) ∧ q.activity_node = t.activity_node ∧
t.label = q.act_ID ∧ q.activity_node = fork ∧
   ∃ r (r.postElement | ActivityState (t) ∧ r.act_ID = q.act_ID ∧
   ∃ s(s.event_ID | ActivityState(s) ∧ s.act_ID = r.postElement ∧
   ∃p(p.event_ID | Usecase(p) ∧ p.event_ID = s. event_ID

In this way, the algorithm *NodeGeneration* described in this section will map the
different nodes of the OO design elements with that of the BPMN design elements.
The algorithm *FlowGeneration* as proposed in the following section will generate
the flows between these nodes that are generated by the algorithm *NodeGeneration*.

11.5.3.2 Algorithm FlowGeneration to Generate the Flow Between BPMN Nodes

We use an array representation FAM_flow to represent the flow between different activity nodes. FAM_flow is a part of our Formalized Analysis Model to depict the flow between different events of use cases of objects oriented systems.

The array FAM_Flow is an [n] [3] array where n is the number of flows in the formalized analysis model.

FAM_Flow [0] [i] lists the source activity node of the flow for i=0 to n

FAM_Flow [1] [i] lists the destination activity node of the flow i= 0 to n

FAM_Flow [2] [i] lists the types of flow between A(0,i) and A(1,i) for i= 0 to n

Entries in FAM_Flow [2, i] are of the following types:

1) S indicates sequential flow
2) D indicates Default Flow
3) C indicates Conditional Flow
4) I indicate Iterative flow

Table BPMN_Flow stores different graphical notations of BPMN flows and are assigned with unique IDs.

Table BPMN_Flow will have the following kind of flows:

1) Sequential Flow (*ID is 1*)
2) Default Flow (*ID is 2*)
3) Conditional Flow (*ID is 3*)
4) Iterative flow (*ID is 4*)

The algorithm FlowGeneration is proposed as follow:
Input:

Output of *Nodegeneration algorithm*, FAM_Flow[n] [3], Table BPMN_Flow.

Algorithm:
```
for( m=0 ; m<=n-1;m++)
{
flow. from = FAM_flow[m] [0] ;
flow. to = FAM_flow[m] [1] ;
If FAM_flow [m] [2] = S
Flow.type = Select BPMN_Flow.Graphical_notation where BPMN_Flow.ID=1
If FAM_flow [m] [2] = D
Flow.type = Select BPMN_Flow.Graphical_notation where BPMN_Flow.ID=2
If FAM_flow [m] [2] = C
Flow.type = Select BPMN_Flow.Graphical_notation where BPMN_Flow.ID=3
If FAM_flow [m] [2] = I
Flow.type = Select BPMN_Flow.Graphical_notation where BPMN_Flow.ID=4
}
```

Output:
Different flows of the BPMN design elements.

In this section, we have proposed and described the transformation framework FAM2BP which is BPMN design elements from the elements of the formalized analysis model. As we have ensured the consistency at the OO level before transformation, this transformation will generate consistent design elements at this stage.

11.6 Case Study

Our proposed Automatic Transformation Model FAM2BP is explained with the help of the case study of a Banking System. We have taken four use cases where use case 2 (UC2) is the primary use case that includes use case (UC1) and use case 3 (UC3) and is extended in specialized case like housing loan by use case 4 (UC4).

These use cases are tabulated in Table 11.1 in the form of Use case Schema as defined in Sect. 11.4.2. The events of individual use cases are stored in Table 11.2 as Event schema which is defined in Sect. 11.4.2. These events will be mapped with the ActivityState. The information regarding ActivityState, will be stored in Table 11.3 as ActivityState schema. Table ActivityState contains the information regarding activity node. The entry in the table will have new activity like fork or join or decision etc apart from normal activity (start/action/end) which are mapped from the events of the Event table. The normal activity will carry the same event_ID as in the table Event. And new event_ID will be generated for the new activity. All the activities will be assigned an unique identifier.

Table 11.4 (Table ActUCRelation) which keeps information regarding any activity that includes any use cases. Table 11.4 can be used for extends relation, as well. Here, UC4 extends UC2 and we can replace this with the relation UC4 includes UC2, which implies that UC4 has all the functionalities of UC2, along with its own functionalities. Henceforth, UC4 will have an activity which will include UC2. The Reuse field in Table 11.3 is used to incorporate reusability (include, extend in terms of include relationship) of use cases. If the Reuse field is Y, then Table 11.4 has to be checked to find which usecase has to be included by checking the UC_id field.

Table activitystate (Table 11.3) contains the information regarding activity node. The entry in the table will have new activity like *fork or join or decision* etc apart from normal activity *(start or action or end)* which are mapped from the events of

Table 11.1 Table use case

UC_id	UC_name
UC1	Verify customer
UC2	Sanction loan
UC3	Determine the maximum limit of loan amount
UC4	Sanction home Loan

Table 11.2 Table event

UC_id	Event_id	Event_name	Event_type
UC1	EV1	A customer has called the bank or visit the bank	Basic
UC1	EV2	The customer will be asked the requisite set of questions	Basic
UC1	EV3	Customer is able answer all verification questions successfully	Basic
UC1	EV4	Customer is unable answer verification questions	Alternate
UC1	EV5	Verification is complete	Basic
UC2	EV1	A customer has called the bank	Basic
UC2	EV2	Includes UC1	Basic
UC2	EV3	Includes UC3	Basic
UC2	EV4	Verify address	Basic
UC2	EV5	Finalization of interest rate	Basic
UC2	EV6	Calculation of EMI	Basic
UC2	EV7	Loan is sanctioned	Basic
UC3	EV1	Customer has applied for loan	Basic
UC3	EV2	Income and other factor are taken as input	Basic
UC3	EV3	The maximum loan limit of the customer is calculated	Basic
UC3	EV4	The maximum calculated limit is less than the requested loan limit	Basic
UC3	EV5	Customer loan amount is sanctioned	Basic
UC4	EV1	Customer has applied for home loan	Basic
UC4	EV2	Customer submit property details etc	Basic
UC4	EV3	The searching of property is done and searching result is satisfactory	Basic
UC4	EV4	The searching of property is done and searching result is not satisfactory	Alternate

the Event table (Table 11.2). The normal activity will carry the same event_ID as in the table Event and new event_ID will be generated for the new activity. All the activities will be assigned an unique identifier. As a result, the different BPMN nodes and flows are generated using Tables 11.1, 11.2, 11.3, 11.4 and the array FAM_flow (defined in the previous section). The Table ActUCRelation (Table 11.4) which keeps information regarding any activity that includes any use cases. Table 11.4 can be used for extends relation as well. Here, UC4 extends UC2 and we can replace this with the relation UC4 that includes UC2, which implies that UC4 has all the functionalities of UC2, along with its own functionalities. Henceforth, UC4 will have an activity which will include UC2.

Table 11.3 Table activity state

UC_id	Event_id	Act_id	Activity_node	preElement	postElement	Reuse
UC1	EV1	AC1	start	——	AC2	N
UC1	EV2	AC2	action	AC1	AC3	N
UC1	F	AC3	fork	AC2	AC4,AC5	N
UC1	EV3	AC4	action	AC3	AC6	N
UC1	EV4	AC5	action	AC3	AC2	N
UC1	J	AC6	join	AC4,AC5	AC7	N
UC1	EV5	AC7	end	AC6	——	N
UC2	EV1	AC8	start	——	AC8	N
UC2	F	AC9	fork	AC8	AC10,AC11	N
UC2	EV2	AC10	action	AC9	AC12	Y
UC2	EV3	AC11	action	AC9	AC12	Y
UC2	J	AC12	join	AC10,AC11	AC13	N
UC2	EV4	AC13	action	AC12	AC14	N
UC2	EV5	AC14	action	AC13	AC15	N
UC2	EV6	AC15	action	AC14	AC16	N
UC2	EV7	AC16	end	AC15	——	N

Table 11.4 Table ActUCRelation

Act_id	UC_id
AC10	UC1
AC11	UC3

11.7 Implementation

In this section, we will discuss the implementation details in the direction of evolution from the OO to the SOA domain. We develop a tool that generates the BPMN design elements of the SOA paradigm from the use case design elements of the OO paradigm. The technical environment for this evolution tool comprises of J2SE 1.6. The Integrated Development Environment (IDE) that is used for developing the tool is Net Beans. The tool is developed as a Multi Document Interface (MDI) desktop application using the Java Swing framework (Fig. 11.3).

The program uses a text file as an input. The text file contains the grammatical constructs that define the pre and post elements for each behavioral artifacts, its type etc of OO domain. The grammatical constructs used in the input file are given below:

Usecase name, Element Name, Event Name, Type, Pre Element, Post Element, Reuse

Example:
UC1,AC1,EV1,START,-,AC2,N
UC1,AC7,EV7,ACTION,AC1,AC2,N
UC1,AC2,EV2,FORK,AC7,AC3,N
UC1,AC2,EV2,FORK,AC7,AC4,Y

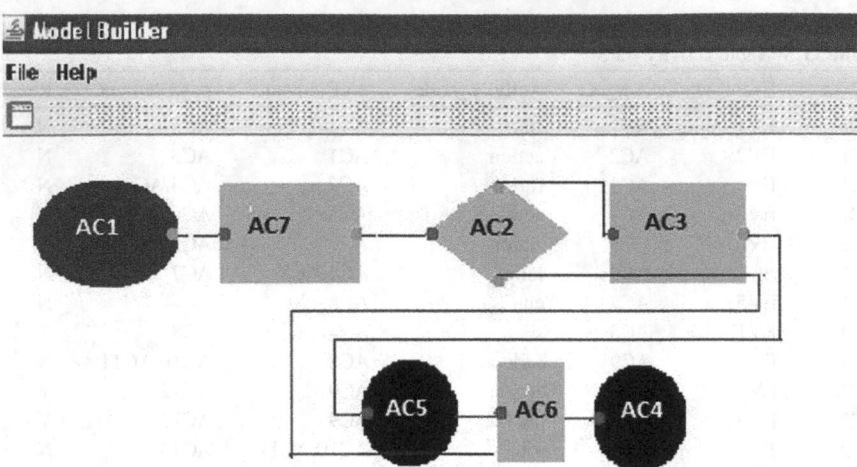

Fig. 11.3 BPMN as generated by our tool

UC1,AC3,EV3,ACTION,AC2,AC5,N
UC1,AC6,EV6,ACTION,AC2,AC4,N
UC1,AC4,EV4,END,AC6,-,N
UC1,AC5,EV5,END,AC3,-,N

11.8 Conclusion

In this chapter, we have proposed an approach for automated translation of Formalized Analysis Models that consists of a formal grammar based description of UML models to Business Processes in the analysis phase. Design and development of software has become much more complex in the last decade resulting in evolution of design and development paradigms. Object oriented systems have thus become an integral part of more complex Service Oriented Architecture (SOA). Evolution of software design and development from the object oriented to the SOA domain has become the necessity in this evolving scenario. This approach would help us in seamless evolution of object oriented systems to the service oriented domain. As this model is based on a formal grammar, this approach can be automated resulting in correct and consistent transformations.

References

1. Mostafa, A.M., Ismail, M.A,. El-Bolok, H., Saad, E.M.: Toward a formalization of UML2.0 metamodel using Z specifications, In: Eighth ACIS International Conference on Software Engineering, Artificial Intelligence, Networking, and Parallel/Distributed Computing, 2007.

SNPD 2007, vol. 1, pp 694–701, July 30–August 1, 2007

2. Cal, A., Calvanese, D., De Giacomo, G., Lenzerini, M.: A formal framework for reasoning on UML Class diagrams. In: Proceedings of the 13th International Symposium on Methodologies for Intelligent Systems (ISMIS 2002), pp. 503–513 (2002)

3. Andre, P., Romanczuk, A., Royer, J.-C.: Checking the consistency of UML class diagrams using Larch prover. In: Rigorous Object Oriented Method (ROOM) (2000)

4. Meng, S., Zhang, N., Aichernig, B.K.: The formal foundations in RSL for UML statechart diagram. Technical Report 299. UNU/IIST, July (2004)

5. Gomaa, H., Liu, S., Shin, M.E.: Integration of the domain modeling method for families of systems with the SOFL formal specification language. In: 6th IEEE International Conference on Complex Computer Systems (ICECCS'00), September 11–15, Tokyo, Japan, pp. 61–71 (2000)

6. Apvrille, L., Courtiat, J.-P., Lohr, C., de Saqui-Sannes, P.: TURTLE: a real-time UML profile supported by a formal validation toolkit. IEEE Trans. Softw. Eng. **30**(7), 473–487 (2004)

7. He, X.: Formalizing UML class diagrams: a hierarchical predicate transition net approach. In: The Twenty-Fourth Annual International Computer Software and Applications Conference, Taipei, Taiwan, 25–28 October 2000

8. Li, X., Liu, Z., He J.: A formal semantics of UML sequence diagram. In: 2004 Australian Software Engineering Conference (ASWEC'04), Melbourne, Australia, 13–16 April 2004

9. Jansamak, S., Surarerks, A.: Formalization of UML statechart models using concurrent regular expressions. In: 27th Australasian Computer Science Conference, The University of Otago, Dunedin, NZ, January (2004)

10. Yang, D., Zhang, s.: Using p - calculus to formalize UML activity diagram. In: 10th IEEE International Conference and Workshop on the Engineering of Computer-Based Systems (ECBS'03), Huntsville, Alabama, 7–10 April 2003

11. Hausmann, J.H., Heckel, R., Sauer, S.: Towards dynamic meta modeling of uml extensions: an extensible semantics for UML sequence diagrams. In: IEEE 2001 Symposia on Human Centric Computing Languages and Environments (HCC'01), Stresa, Italy, 5–7 September 2001

12. Shen, H., Virani, A., Niu, J.: Formalize UML 2 sequence diagrams. In: 11th IEEE High Assurance Systems Engineering Symposium, HASE 2008, pp. 437–440, 3–5 December 2008

13. Sengupta, S., Bhattacharya, S.: Formalization of functional requirements of software development process, In: In the Journal of Foundations of Computing and Decision Sciences (FCDS). Institute of Computing Science, Poznan University of Technology, Poland **33**(1), 83–115 (2008)

14. Cockburn, A.: Writing Effective Use Cases, 14th edn. Addison-Wesley, New York (2005)

15. Object Management Group (2004). Unified Modeling Language: Superstructure. http://www.omg.org/cgibin/doc?formal/05-07-04. Accessed 1 Sept 2007

16. Oestereich, B., Weiss, C., Schroder, C., Weilkiens, T., Lenhard, A.: Objektorientierte Geschftsprozessmodellierungmit der UML. d.punkt Verlag (2003)

17. Whittle, J.: A formal semantics of Use Case charts, Technical Report ISE Dept, George Mason University, ISE-. TR-06-02. http://www.ise.gmu.edu/techrep

18. Some, S.: An approach for the synthesis of State transition graphs from Use Cases. In: Proceedings of the International Conference on Software Engineering Research and Practice, Las Vegas, Nevada, USA, 23–26 June 2003

19. Some, S.: Supporting Use Cases based requirements simulation. In: Proceedings of the International Conference on Software Engineering and Practice (SERP04), Las Vegas, Nevada, USA, 21–24 June 2004

20. Lbke, D.: Transformation of use cases to EPC models. In: Proceedings of the EPK 2006 Workshop (2006)

21. Lubke, D., Schneider, K., Weidlich, M.: Visualizing Use Case sets as BPMN processes. In: Requirements Engineering Visualization (REV'08), Barcelona, Spain, 8–12 September 2008

22. Dijkman, R., Dumas, M., Ouyang, C.: Semantics and analysis of business process models in BPMN. In: Information and Software Technology (IST) (2008)

Chapter 12
Context-Aware Services Engineering
for Service-Oriented Architectures

Dhaminda B. Abeywickrama

Abstract With the proliferation of ubiquitous computing devices and the Internet, *context-aware Web services* continue to evolve from simple proof of concept implementations created in the laboratory to large and complex real-world services developed in industry. Context-awareness capabilities in service interfaces introduce additional challenges to the software engineer. In order to handle the additional complexities associated with these special services, *solid software engineering methodologies* are needed during their development and execution. This chapter proposes a novel software engineering-based approach, which leverages the benefits of model-driven architecture, aspect-oriented modeling, and formal model checking, for engineering context-aware services for service-oriented architectures. The approach has been validated using a real-world case study in intelligent transport. An evaluation framework has been established to validate the main methods and tools employed. We also present two key research directions, extending this work to further benefit the wider service engineering and pervasive computing communities.

12.1 Introduction

Web services are software components that can be distributed over standard internet technologies. They are designed to add interoperability between diverse, distributed and heterogeneous applications. A *context-aware Web service* is a special type of Web service that adapts its behavior or the content it processes to the context of one

---

The work reported here was performed during the author's Ph.D. studies. The author is currently affiliated with the University of Modena and Reggio Emilia, Italy.

D. B. Abeywickrama (✉)
Monash University, Clayton Campus, Wellington Road, Clayton, VIC 3800, Australia
e-mail: dhaminda.abeywickrama@gmail.com

A. Bouguettaya et al. (eds.), *Web Services Foundations*,
DOI: 10.1007/978-1-4614-7518-7_12,
© Springer Science+Business Media New York 2014

or several parameters of a target entity in a transparent way (e.g., restaurant finder services) [20]. Context has been defined by Dey and Abowd ([16], p.3) as:

> any information that can be used to characterize the situation of an entity: an entity is a person, place, or object that is considered relevant to the interaction between a user and an application, including the user and application themselves.

Context information is characterized by several qualities that make the development of context-aware services challenging compared to conventional Web services, such as a highly dynamic nature, real-time requirements, quality of context information and automation. The additional complexities associated with these special services necessitate the use of solid software engineering methodologies during their development and execution. Most state-of-the-art approaches to context-aware services relate to the detailed design or implementation stages [21, 27, 29] of the software life-cycle, such as context-aware Web services. Little work focuses on the early phase of design such as the software architectural level, thus providing motivation for our work.

This novel approach effectively leverages benefits of several software engineering principles such as *model-driven architecture*, separation of concerns through *aspect-oriented modeling*, and formal verification using *model checking*, for engineering context-aware software services. This research adopts model-driven development to represent complex crosscutting context-dependent functionality in service interfaces in a modular manner, and to automate the generation of state machine-based adaptive behavior. The crosscutting context-dependent information of the interacting pervasive services is modeled as aspect-oriented models in UML. Using automated model transformations, we ensure the correct separation of concerns of the crosscutting context-dependent functionality at both semi-formal UML modeling and formal behavioral specification levels. A prototype tool—Aspectual FSP Generation—applying an effective pipeline of model-to-model and model-to-text transformations has been built.

The generated context-dependent adaptive behavior and the core service behavior for the pervasive services are rigorously verified using formal model checking against specified system properties. Model checking is applied, first to check the behavior of the individual pervasive aspects and components, and second to verify the overall behavior of the woven model even if no errors are found in the individual aspects and components. These verification stages can be used to gain confidence before the complex pervasive services are actually implemented. The approach is explored using a real-world case study in intelligent transport. An evaluation framework is established to validate the main methods and tools developed.

This chapter discusses the key features of our overall research work [1, 6] for engineering context-aware services. Also, it presents two key research extensions extending this work to further benefit the wider service engineering and pervasive computing communities. Section 12.2 establishes the motivation for the current study. The case study used to validate our approach is presented in Sect. 12.3. In Sect. 12.4, a high-level description of the methodology proposed for engineering context-aware services is provided. Section 12.5 (models and transformations) and Sect. 12.6

(verification using model checking) address this process in detail. An evaluation framework to validate our work is provided in Sect. 12.7, and Sect. 12.8 discusses two key research extensions to this work. Section 12.9 concludes this chapter.

12.2 Related Work

Previous approaches to the development of context-aware services have largely been at the detailed design or implementation stages [21, 27, 29] of the software life-cycle. In [21], the authors have discussed an approach for the context-aware development of Web applications consisting of Web services. Application modeling has been performed in UML, and a composite Web application targeting different implementation platforms has been generated. Context adaptation takes place on top of the Web application business functionality. Serral et al. [27] introduced a model-driven development method for developing context-aware pervasive systems. A context-aware pervasive system has been specified using a set of models, and automated code generation has been used to generate system Java code. Service adaptation has been performed using an Web Ontology Language specification.

Two main limitations can be identified on state-of-the-art approaches on context-aware services development. First, most existing approaches to representing context-aware services focus on the detailed design or implementation phases of the software life-cycle such as context-aware Web services. Little attention has been given to the early phase of design such as the software architectural level. Building software architectural models of pervasive services provides engineers with a better understanding of how these complex services interoperate and helps uncover any errors during the early stages of the software life-cycle. Second, most of the existing work applies the software engineering techniques of model-driven architecture [7, 9, 28], aspect-oriented modeling [17, 32], and formal model checking [12] in isolation and does not explore the combination of these technologies in the same approach. For example, Sheng and Benatallah [28] have taken no account of any formal verification aspects through techniques such as model checking nor have they applied aspect-oriented modeling in their UML profile. The integration or the synergy of these sound software engineering techniques would mutually complement and augment each other if used in a single approach. While the application of these techniques in isolation can be found in existing work in service engineering, however, an integrated architecture-centric solution aimed at managing the complexities associated with context-aware services is novel, as proposed in this chapter.

12.3 Case Study: Intelligent Transport

This section describes the case study that is used to validate our approach, and the notion of context applied in our work.

The research approach is explored using a real-world case study in intelligent tagging for transport known as the ParcelCall project [14]. The case study describes a scalable, real-time, intelligent, end-to-end tracking and tracing system using radio frequency identification (RFID), sensor networks, and services for transport and logistics. This case study is particularly appealing to the current research as it provides several scenarios for representing software services that interoperate in a pervasive, mobile and distributed environment. A significant subset of the ParcelCall case study is exception handling that needs to be enforced when a transport item's context information violates acceptable threshold values. The reference scenario used in this research describes an awareness monitoring and notification pervasive service, which alerts with regards to any exceptional situations that may arise on transport items, primarily to the vehicle driver of the transport unit. The threshold values for environment status (e.g., temperature, pressure, acceleration) of transport items and route (location) for the vehicle are set by the carrier organization in advance. The service alerts if items' environment status exceeds acceptable levels or if an item is lost or stolen during transport. The primary context parameters modeled in the study include item identity, location, temperature, pressure and acceleration.

The *notion of context* used in our work is based on a definition provided in [8] for context in information modeling. The authors in [8] describe context as a set of objects, each of which is associated with a set of names and another context called its reference. Furthermore, they enhance the definition for context by stating that each object of a context is either a simple object or a link object (attribute, instance-of, ISA) and each object can be related to other objects through attribute, instance-of or ISA links. They use traditional object-oriented abstraction mechanisms of attribution, classification, generalization and encapsulation to structure the contents of a context.

12.4 Context-Aware Services Engineering Process

In this section, we introduce the software engineering process followed for generating context-dependent adaptive behavior for pervasive services (see Fig. 12.1) [3]. Sections 12.5 (models and transformations) and 12.6 (verification) address this further.

The current approach is particularly based on (i) the model-driven development techniques provided by the IBM Rational Software Architect [15], (ii) the formal verification techniques provided by the model checker Labeled Transition System Analyzer (LTSA) [23] and its process calculus Finite State Processes (FSP), and (iii) the LTSA tool's message sequence charts extension (LTSA-MSC). Java Emitter Templates (JET) is an open-source technology developed by IBM. JET is included in IBM Rational Software Architect and it is typically used in the implementation of a code generator [15]. One of the main objectives of the current research is to perform rigorous verification of the pervasive specification using formal model checking. Therefore, we use finite state machines as opposed to other formalisms such as petri-net based models.

The model transformation tool created in this study for adaptive behavior generation is called the Aspectual FSP Generation tool. The crosscutting

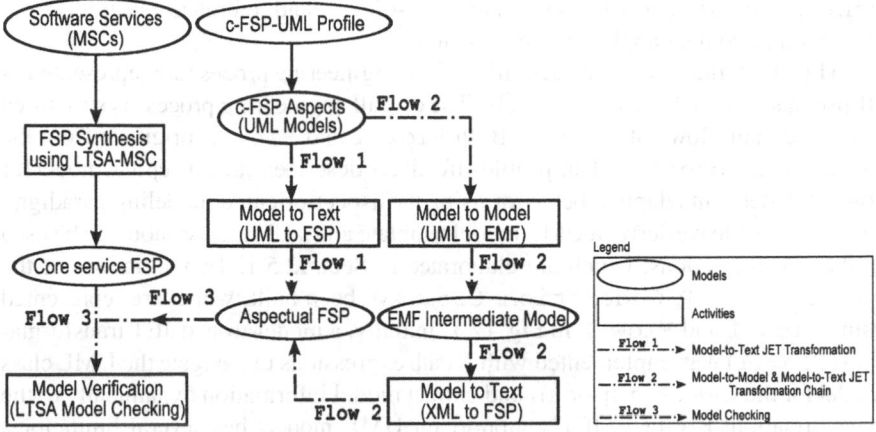

Fig. 12.1 Context-aware services engineering process [3]

context-dependent information of the interacting pervasive services is modeled as aspect-oriented models in UML (`contextual-FSP aspects` or `c-FSP aspects`). Research works related to the aspect-oriented paradigm include composition filters, subject-oriented programming, adaptive programming, multi-dimensional separation of concerns and generative programming. However, compared to these approaches the aspect-oriented paradigm provides better language and tool support, and thus it is widely used in the software engineering community.

We use model transformations to automate the application of design patterns and generate infrastructure code for the `c-FSP aspects` using FSP semantics. The current study explores the strengths of both semi-formal UML meta-level extensions and formal finite state machines for representing the context-dependent behavior of software services, and model transformation techniques are applied as a bridge to enforce correct separation of concerns between these two design abstractions. The main benefits of this approach are: improving the quality and productivity of service development; easing system maintenance and evolution; and increasing the portability of the service design for the pervasive services engineer.

This approach focuses on the application of model-driven development for engineering pervasive services at finite state machine level. An aspect in FSP can be identified as an independent finite state machine that executes concurrently and synchronizes with its base state machine. In general, an aspect in FSP needs to contain synchronization events (transitions) to coordinate with its base state machine and other aspects. Also, each aspect type (e.g., `context`, `trigger` and `recovery`) contains its unique constructs which can be generated automatically using model transformation techniques. For example, a `trigger aspect` requires constructs to alert and send notifications while a `recovery aspect` needs constructs to recover from exception-handling situations. On the other hand, a `context aspect` has attribution, instance-of, ISA and reference constructs from the notion of context applied in this research.

In Fig. 12.1, the models and activities of the engineering process are represented as ellipses and square boxes respectively. The overall engineering process is structured into three main flows of activities. Both `Flow 1` and `Flow 2` originate from the `c-FSP-UML profile`. This profile effectively describes our conceptual model for context-dependent adaptive behavior using the aspect-oriented modeling paradigm. Using the profile we derive a UML model template and a UML class model to be used in the transformations, which are elaborated in Sect. 12.5.1. Two variations of the `Aspectual FSP Generation tool` have been built, which are represented using `Flow 1` and `Flow 2` in Fig. 12.1. Initially, a model-to-text JET transformation (`Flow 1`) was implemented with XPath expressions to navigate the UML class model for the `c-FSP aspects` and extract model information dynamically to the transformation. However, JET's support for UML models has several limitations. Therefore, a more effective solution was implemented as shown by `Flow 2`, which contains an effective pipeline of model-to-model and model-to-text JET transformations. The details of this transformation and its benefits are discussed in Sect. 12.5.2. The LTSA-MSC tool has been used to generate the architecture model in FSP for the service specification from which the core service model was extracted. `Flow 3` contains activities for rigorously verifying the models generated for the core service behavior and the context-dependent adaptive behavior using formal model checking (see Sect. 12.6).

12.5 Models and Transformations

12.5.1 Models: c-FSP-UML Profile and c-FSP Aspects

This subsection elaborates on the `c-FSP-UML profile` and the UML class model created with `c-FSP aspects` to modularize the service architecture (see Figs. 12.2, 12.3) [3].

Using the `c-FSP-UML profile`, we model the core service logic and the context-dependent behavior of a service as two separate concerns within the same model, allowing the modification of the context-dependent behavior without affecting the main functionality. The core service logic of a service is represented by the `State`, `Transition`, `FiniteStateProcess`, `Service` and `Service Specification` classes while the rest of the classes represent the context-dependent functionality. The `c-FSP-UML profile` encompasses constructs of both aspect-orientation and object-orientation aimed at modularizing and reducing the complexity of context-dependent behavior at the service interface level. The use of aspect-oriented modeling in the profile further extends the UML model [2] created previously, which was originally motivated by the ContextUML metamodel [28].

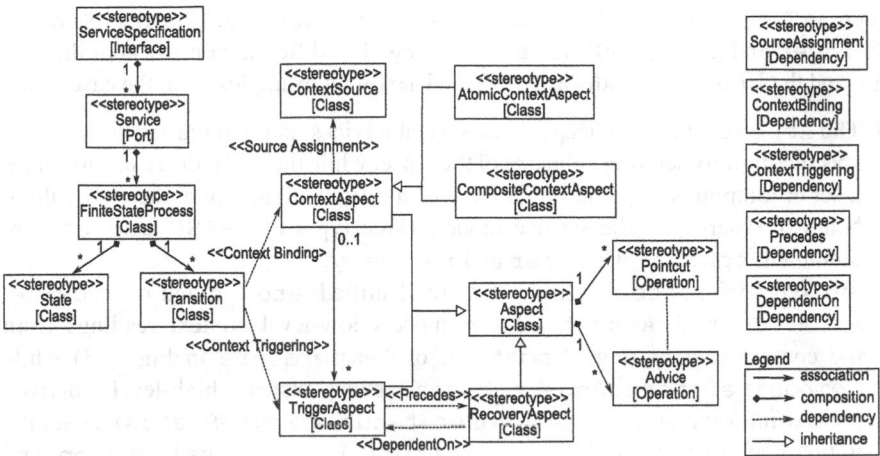

Fig. 12.2 c-FSP-UML profile [3]

The aspect-oriented UML class model provided (see Fig. 12.3) contains several classes on the case study with stereotypes applied from the c-FSP-UML profile. As in the profile, this UML class model contains several constructs for representing the core service behavior, the context-dependent adaptive behavior, and the dependencies between the core service model and the context-dependent model. The core service behavior of the model is represented by classes, such as ParcelCall, InterpretContext, Broadcast, Recovery, ObserveEvents, the FiniteStateProcess classes, and the Transition classes. The c-FSP aspects of the UML class model are represented by several classes,

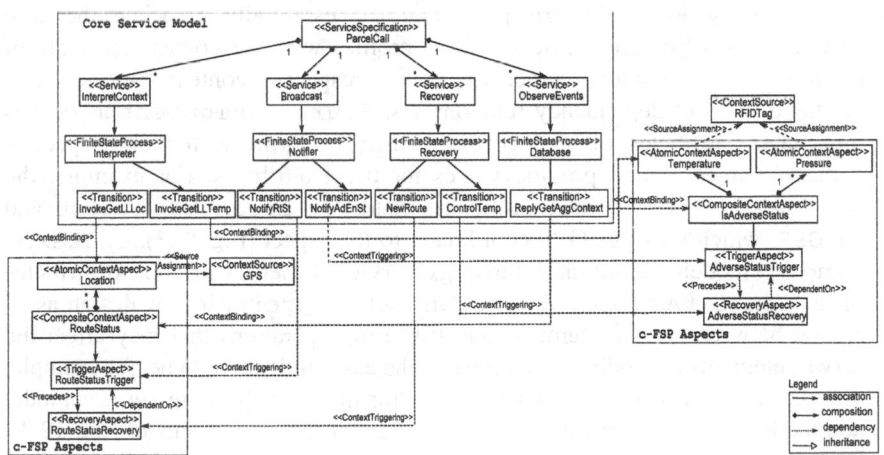

Fig. 12.3 UML class model derived from the profile with c-FSP aspects

such as Temperature, Pressure, IsAdverseStatus, AdverseStatus
Trigger and AdverseStatusRecovery. The different constructs of the profile and the UML class model are described next with examples from the case study.

- The Aspect class encapsulates several advices and pointcuts. The Advice
  specifies the crosscutting behavior of the aspect while the Pointcut encapsulates
  a set of joinpoints. A joinpoint is the location (transition) where the crosscutting
  behavior emerges in the service model. Three types of c-FSP aspects are
  identified: context, trigger and recovery.
- Two types of context aspects are identified: atomic and composite.
  AtomicContextAspect class models low-level context readings from
  the context sources (e.g., Location or Temperature in Fig. 12.3) while
  CompositeContextAspect class encapsulates high-level derived
  context information (e.g., IsAdverseStatus or RouteStatus). Also, the
  notions of attribution, classification, generalization and
  encapsulation from the context definition are applied to structure and link
  the objects defined in the aspects. Thus, both object-oriented and aspect-oriented
  notions are used to represent the complex context-dependent functionality of the
  services.
- The ContextSource class represents the resource from which context information is obtained, for example, RFID Tag or GPS.
- The TriggerAspect class models the contextual adaptation where the service is automatically executed or modified based on context information. For
  example, if isAdverseStatus is true then send an SMS to vehicle driver
  (AdverseStatusTrigger).
- The RecoveryAspect class models recovery actions that follow after an
  exception situation is raised by the trigger aspect. For example, control the
  refrigerator's temperature in the vehicle unit (AdverseStatusRecovery in
  Fig. 12.3).
- Dependency Relationships classes essentially associate the core
  service classes (service elements of the profile) with the context elements of
  the profile, or the context elements with their respective context sources. There
  are three types of dependency relationships. SourceAssignment associates
  the context attributes of a ContextAspect class with their respective
  context sources, which provide values for these attributes. For example, the
  SourceAssignment relationship associates the Location aspect and
  the GPS, which provides GPS coordinates to the aspect (Fig. 12.3). Context-
  Binding models the automatic binding of service elements with context attributes
  of the ContextAspect class. ContextTriggering provides an association between service elements and triggering operations that may affect the
  service elements depending on context. In the case study this can be, for example,
  the association between the NewRoute transition of the core service model
  and the RouteStatusRecovery aspect of the context model (Fig. 12.3).
  Both ContextBinding and ContextTriggering dependency relationships essentially represent the binding of an aspect to its base class.

- `Precedence Relationships` classes explicitly specify how aspect precedence can be enforced at the modeling level to reduce the aspect interference problem. There are two types of precedence relationships. `Precedes` is used to indicate the precedence order for the aspects at a single joinpoint while `DependentOn` is used to specify that an aspect will only be matched on the existence of both aspects at the joinpoint. For example, as shown in Fig. 12.3, the `AdverseStatusRecovery` aspect is executed following the `AdverseStatusTrigger` aspect (`Precedes`), and the existence of both these aspects are required at the joinpoint (`DependentOn`).

12.5.2 Model Transformations

The previous subsection discussed the `c-FSP-UML profile` and aspect-oriented models in UML (`c-FSP aspects`) derived to modularize the service architecture. The current subsection provides the model transformations created to automate the transformation of those UML models to formal behavioral specifications in FSP.

This multi-stage transformation chain describes an effective pipeline of model-to-model and model-to-text JET transformations (see Fig. 12.1, `Flow 2`) [3]. In this solution, first a model-to-model mapping transformation is created which extracts relevant information from the UML model elements and stereotypes, and then a code generator specific Eclipse Modeling Framework (EMF) intermediate model is built which contains only information required for the back-end model-to-text JET transformation. The front-end model-to-model transformation automatically invokes the back-end JET transformation. The benefits of this transformation are:

- As the JET transformation is independent of UML, UML expertise is no longer a requirement for the transformations [15]. This effective multi-stage transformations approach permits the development and validation of pattern implementations independent of any complexities associated with the UML metamodel.
- The JET transformation can be automatically invoked by the front-end model-to-model transformation. Therefore, the software engineer does not have to see or be aware of the back-end JET transformation.

The above factors can make the pattern implementation process a more accessible solution to the software engineer. As a result, this multi-stage transformations approach has been employed in the current research to transform the `c-FSP aspects` into formal FSP code, which has several steps.

- *Build an Intermediate EMF Model.* In this study, an EMF project is created as the intermediate model to be used in the transformations. The intermediate model can be based on EMF or XML. However, EMF has a rich metamodel and with EMF a Java API for the model can be generated [15].
- *Build a UML Profile.* The `c-FSP-UML profile` discussed earlier is used to augment the standard UML with information that is necessary for generation of

aspects in FSP. This profile defines stereotypes identifying core service elements, context-dependent information and dependencies for the pervasive software services. Stereotypes provide an efficient mechanism for extending the information that is stored on UML model elements. As any changes to the stereotypes in the profile affect the underlying UML model elements, it is important to track the profile version. To this effect, the c-FSP-UML profile is released. The profile can be distributed by creating an Eclipse plug-in that publishes the profile. To this end, the existing c-FSP-UML profile project is converted into a plug-in project. By publishing the profile as an Eclipse plug-in, any Eclipse-based product that installs this plug-in has access to the c-FSP-UML profile and its stereotypes.

- *Build a Model-to-Model Mapping Transformation.* After creating the c-FSP-UML profile and the intermediate EMF model, next we create a model-to-model mapping transformation (aspectsFrontendMap) that effectively maps the profile applied UML class model for the c-FSP aspects with the EMF intermediate model. This mapping transformation essentially associates elements of the input model (UML class model with the c-FSP aspects) with elements of the output model, which is the EMF intermediate model (aspectsEMFModel). To this end, several types of maps have been created. A map defines how data from an input type (e.g., a UML class) are copied to an output model type (e.g., an aspect). A map can move data from a source element to a target element using three methods: move transformations, custom transformations and submap transformations. This study uses a combination of *move* and *submap* transformations to associate elements of the UML class model created for c-FSP aspects with the elements of the EMF intermediate model (aspectsEMFModel). In this study, the following maps have been created: (i) UML Model elements to Root elements; (ii) UML Package elements to AspectPackage elements; (iii) UML Class elements to Aspect elements; (iv) UML Operation elements to aspect's Operation elements; and (v) UML Property elements to aspect's Property elements. After creating the mappings, the transformation source code is generated and customized to invoke the back-end model-to-text JET transformation automatically from the front-end model-to-model transformation. To link the model-to-model transformation's output to the back-end model-to-text JET transformation, the TransformationProvider Java file needs to be edited with the ID of the transformation to invoke.
- *Debug and Test.* Finally, we test the transformations created to verify that they are correct and function as required. This involves setting up a test environment called a *run-time workbench*, in which the plug-ins created are installed. Testing using a run-time workbench effectively launches a second copy of the Eclipse-based product. Testing the transformations involves: build the UML class model with c-FSP aspects and apply the c-FSP-UML profile to it; create a transformation configuration and execute the transformation configuration. In the transformations created in this study, the aspect name in UML becomes the process (state machine) name in FSP while operations and properties for the aspect in UML are used for generating states and transitions of the aspectual state machine in FSP. This represents the variable nature (point of variability) of the transformations.

Other than that, as stated previously, the transformations generate infrastructure (skeleton) code for the aspects.

Next the generated context-dependent adaptive behavior and the core service behavior for the pervasive services are rigorously verified using formal model checking against specified system properties.

12.6 Formal Verification

As discussed in Sect. 12.5.1, the crosscutting context-dependent behavior in service interfaces has been modeled using aspect-oriented UML models. To this effect, a custom UML profile (`c-FSP-UML profile`), a UML model template and UML class models (`c-FSP aspects`) have been created to modularize context information with several stereotypes. UML has been a widely applied technique for modeling object-oriented design or core design of a software specification. Also, exploring the meta-level notation of UML or extending the UML notation has been a popular approach used by many researchers for specifying crosscutting concerns. However, one of the main limitations of UML is its lack of support for rigorous verification due to its informal or semi-formal nature.

The expressive power of aspects in design specifications can be potentially harmful. The *crosscutting* nature and the *obliviousness* principle of aspects are two main issues that can introduce an additional correctness problem in an aspect-oriented design specification. These can create several problems or risks such as partial weaving, unknown aspect assumptions, unintended aspect effects, arbitrary aspect precedence, failure to preserve state invariants, and incorrect changes in control dependencies [24, 25]. Therefore, in order to address the main challenges associated with aspect-oriented modeling in software specifications (i.e., the semi-formal nature of UML notations and the expressive power of aspects), tool support such as automatic model checking is highly desirable to ensure the correctness of the specification.

12.6.1 Model Checking Aspectual Pervasive Software Services

In this subsection, we provide an overview of our approach for rigorously verifying the models generated for the context-dependent adaptive behavior and the core service behavior using formal model checking [5] (see Fig. 12.1 (Flow 3), and Fig. 12.4).

The model checking process can be divided into three main tasks: *modeling* (Sects. 12.6.2–12.6.3), *specification* and *verification* (Sect. 12.6.4). Modeling is the task of converting the design into a formalism accepted by a model checking tool [11]. Specification is the stating of the properties that the design needs to satisfy, and verification is the actual validation of the models.

- *Modeling.* The modeling step involves two main tasks that are performed to obtain the context-dependent adaptive behavior and the core service model of the software services. In this study, the `Aspectual FSP Generation tool` is used to generate the context-dependent behavioral code in formal FSP. The LTSA-MSC tool is used to generate the architecture model for the service specification in FSP, which is used to extract the core service model of the services (see Figs. 12.1, 12.4). All service components and aspects are modeled as processes represented as finite state machines in FSP. To verify the pervasive service specification, first the aspects are woven into their base state machines in FSP using an explicit weaving mechanism. Then concurrency and distributed notions (see Sect. 12.6.3) are added to the service specification to facilitate reasoning by the LTSA tool. Abstraction mechanisms are introduced to reduce the size of the woven model.
- *Specification.* Properties provide a way of formalizing and verifying system requirements. Here the properties focus on the required effects of the pervasive aspects, service components and the woven model. Rigorous modeling and specification of properties are very important to identify any defects in the pervasive services early in the software life-cycle before these complex services are actually implemented. According to the system requirements from the case study subset, more than 30 properties have been formalized focusing on the required behavior

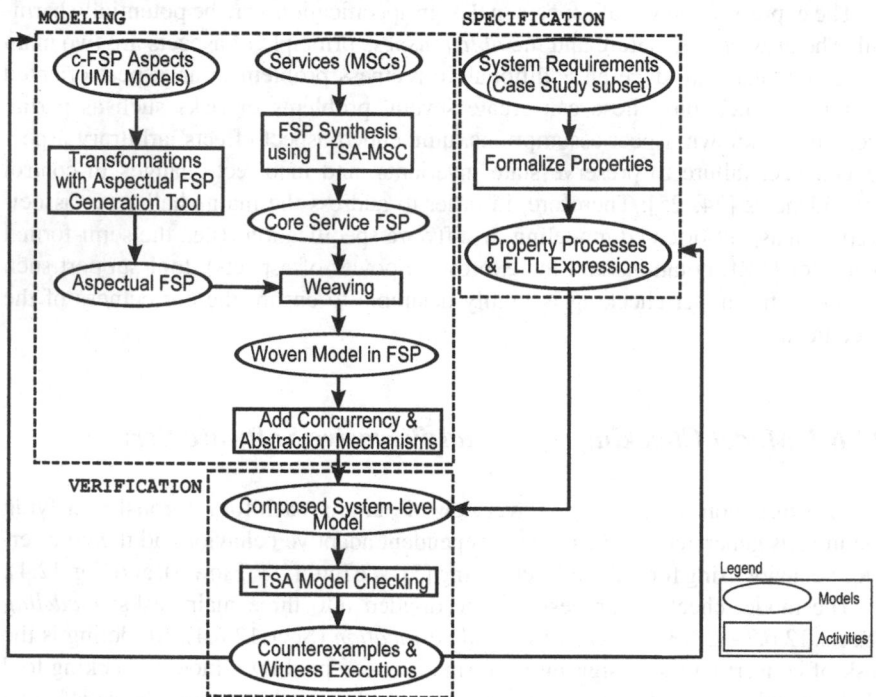

Fig. 12.4 Model checking aspectual pervasive software services [5]

from both service components and aspects. These properties have been expressed as property processes (safety and progress) and fluent linear temporal logic (FLTL) assertions.

- *Verification*. Finally, all behavior and property processes are composed into a system-level process and this process is fed to the LTSA. The LTSA verifies whether any properties are violated and if so it reports a trace to the property violation known as a counterexample. Also, the use of FLTL assertions provides the opportunity to generate examples of traces (witness executions) which satisfy the property. The use of counterexamples and witness executions is exploited to identify and track any errors and their sources in the specification, which consists of several distributed service components and aspects collaborating with each other. Thus, this helps to iteratively improve the state models or the system properties for the aspectual pervasive software services.

12.6.2 Weaving of Pervasive Aspects and Components

Weaving of an aspect to its base state machine is important in order to analyze the overall system behavior. An explicit weaving mechanism is used here, where an aspect is woven into its base state machine using the *parallel composition operator* and *shared actions* in FSP. The main elements of the weaving process are the base program and an aspectual state machine (aspect). In general, the base program is not a single process but it is a combination of several processes. The base program (core service model) is specified as the parallel composition of the constituent base state machines. In order to support explicit parallel composition, the current study injects synchronization events in both the aspectual and base state machines. These events provide an effective mechanism to control the coordination between these state machines. The advice of an aspect contains three logical parts: before advice events, proceed events and after advice events. By using synchronization events the correct execution of these three sequences of actions with the base program can be ensured. Also, weaving of more than one aspect at the same joinpoint is possible using these explicit synchronization events.

The crosscutting elements of the joinpoint model and the weaving process are discussed next using a case study example. Figure 12.5a shows LTSs for three processes. The RFID Tag (RFID_TAG) and the Context Interpreter (CONTEXT_INTERPRETER) components are the base state machines while the Atomic Context Aspect Temperature (ACA_TEMP) is an aspectual state machine. The joinpoints of the base program are specified using the following synchronization events: bf_a (before advice), pr_s (proceed start), pr_e (proceed end), af_a (after advice). A pointcut is a sequence of joinpoints (i.e., the sequence of bf_a, pr_s, pr_e and af_a).

The execution and coordination of the base program and the aspect can be explained as follows (see Fig. 12.5b). The base program (RFID_TAG) emits the bf_a event to the aspect. The aspect performs an initialization operation

Fig. 12.5 Weaving performed. **a** Weaving illustrated using LTSs. **b** Synchronization events

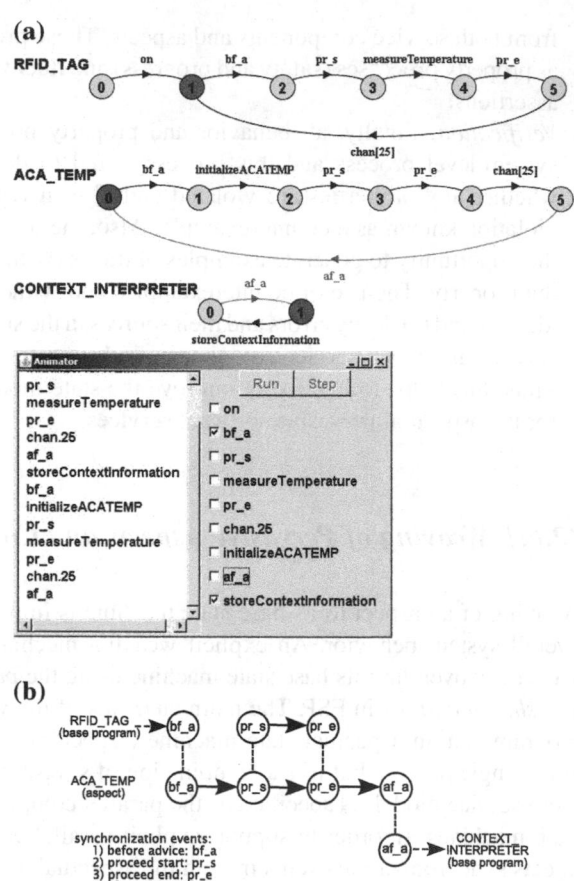

(initializeACATEMP), which is a before advice event. The base program waits for a control event from the aspect, which is a proceed event (pr_s) in this example. The base program performs the measureTemperature event and then emits pr_e to return the control back to the aspect. The aspect performs receiving of temperature readings using message passing, which is its after advice events. Finally, the base program (Context_Interpreter) waits for the end of advice event (af_a) from the aspect, and performs the storeContextInformation action. The woven program is modeled as the parallel composition of the base state machines and the aspect.

12.6.3 Concurrency Modeling

After weaving aspects into their base state machines the concurrency and distributed notions of the interacting pervasive software services are modeled to facilitate reasoning by the LTSA tool, such as message passing, shared objects and mutual exclusion (see Fig. 12.6).

The pervasive service specification includes several distributed service components and aspects collaborating with each other. These components and aspects encompass the active entities of the specification. It also includes shared objects and semaphores, which act as passive entities. All active and passive entities of the specification have been modeled as processes represented as finite state machines in FSP. In the specification, concurrency has been modeled using action interleaving.

This study models the awareness monitoring and notification service as a process-oriented context value chain (see Fig. 12.6). This value chain contains several stages: sensing, refinement, aggregation and contextualization. The context procurement and contextualization tasks of the pervasive service are driven by the c-FSP aspects. The communication between the distributed service components and aspects (e.g., between RFID Tag and Atomic Context Aspect Temperature) has been modeled using the synchronous message passing technique. The environmental readings (e.g., temperature, pressure) from the RFID Tag are sent using a single channel to the receiver (e.g., Atomic Context Aspect Temperature, Atomic Context Aspect Pressure) and the communication is one to one. In addition to using the message passing technique, shared objects have been used to model inter-process communication between the service components and the aspects. The problem of interference has been solved by enforcing mutually exclusive access to the shared objects. This has been modeled using binary semaphores, which are mechanisms for dealing with inter-process synchronization problems. For example, the Atomic Context Aspect Temperature aspect and the Context Interpreter component interact using a shared object for communicating temperature values used in the refinement stage of the context value chain of the pervasive service. The mutually exclusive access to this shared object has been enforced using a semaphore, thus only one process can access it at a given time. The Context Database process has been modeled as a shared resource where the Context Interpreter and the Context Aggregator service components write to it (writers) and the Composite Context Aspect Route Status and the Composite Context Aspect Adverse Environment Status aspects read from it (readers). This scenario has been modeled as a readers-writers problem with writers priority. The readers are denied access if there are writers waiting to acquire access and if a writer is not accessing the database any number of readers can access the database concurrently.

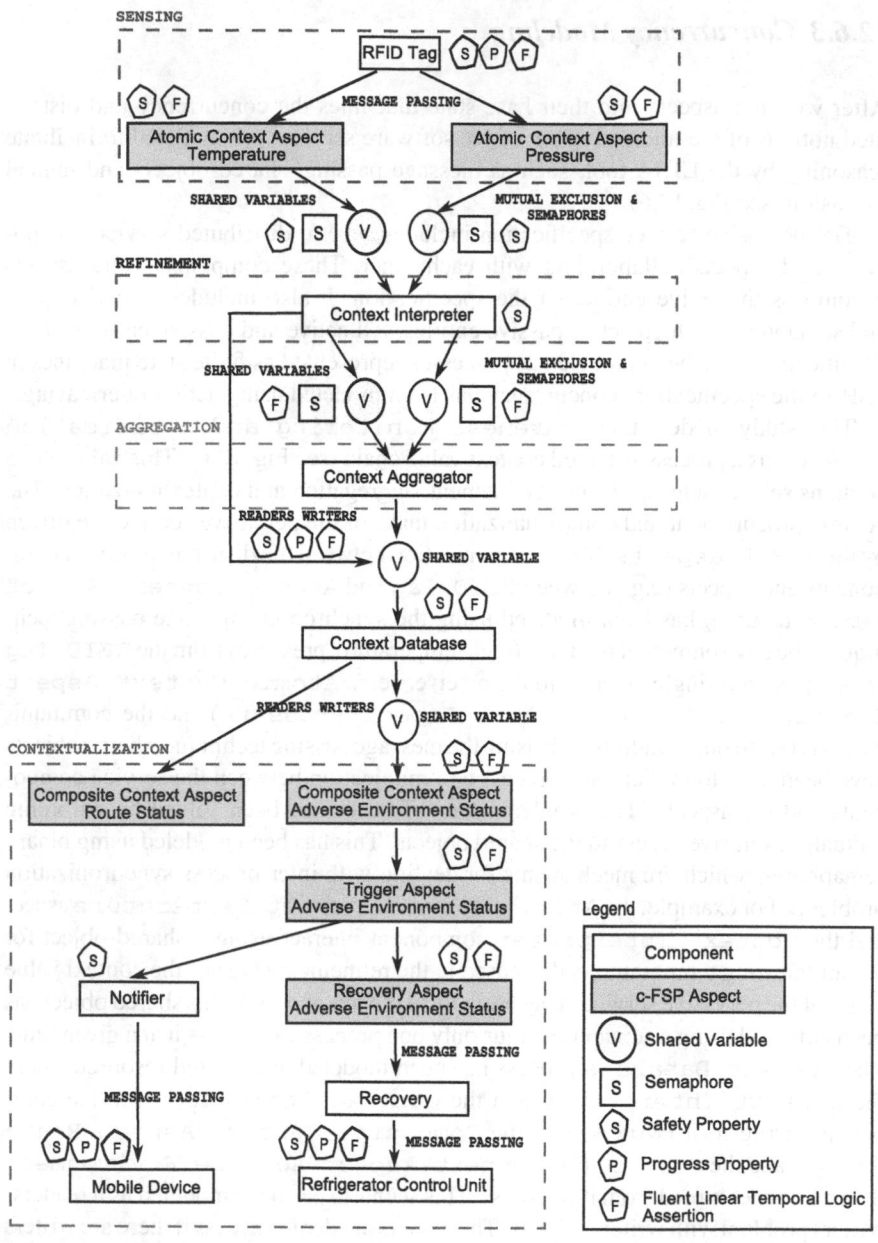

Fig. 12.6 Concurrency modeling between aspects and components [5]

12.6.3.1 Abstraction Mechanisms Applied

These are needed as a woven program may have too many states to be analyzed by the LTSA. One of the main challenges associated with model checking is the *state space explosion problem*. We use action hiding and minimization features available in FSP to reduce the size of the woven model before analyzing using the LTSA tool. For example, the actions modeled in the `Context Interpreter` and `Context Aggregator` components for enforcing mutually exclusive access to their shared variables are not required when modeling the readers-writers problem with writers priority, which involves the same components collaborating with aspects. Also, when executing the entire specification model, the partial order reduction feature has been used to reduce the size of the state space searched by the LTSA.

12.6.4 Properties Specification and Verification

Having discussed the modeling stage of the model checking process, the properties specification and verification stages are briefly addressed next (see [6, 5] for details). Properties have been expressed as property processes (safety and progress) and FLTL assertions.

Safety properties are used in a concurrent program to assert that nothing bad happens during the execution of the program [23]. In the case study subset, several safety properties have been specified for verifying (i) the behavior of the individual aspects and the components, and (ii) the overall behavior of the woven model even if no errors are found in the individual aspects and components. At the individual aspect or component level, a safety property has been defined for the `Trigger Aspect Adverse Environment Status` aspect to verify whether a notification is sent only when environment status is adverse. Another safety property has been defined for the `Context Interpreter` component to verify whether the refinement stage of the pervasive service is performed as expected. At the woven model level, safety properties have been defined to ensure the correct weaving of the base state machines and the aspectual state machines. These properties ensure that the ordering of the synchronization events is correct in the components and aspects of the woven models, thus ensuring the correct weaving of the components and the aspects at the joinpoints in the specification. For example, a safety property has been defined to ensure the correct weaving between the following components and aspects: `RFID Tag`, `Atomic Context Aspect Temperature`, `Atomic Context Aspect Pressure` and `Context Interpreter`. This property is composed with the woven process before performing analysis using the LTSA. LTSA analysis shows that there are no deadlocks or safety violations. Also at the woven model level, safety properties have been created to verify whether the mutually exclusive access to the shared variables is enforced properly.

Unlike safety properties, which are concerned with a program not reaching a bad state, liveness properties are concerned with a program eventually reaching a good state [23]. For example, in the case study subset, *progress properties* have been specified for the readers-writers problem. To this end, two progress properties have been defined to ensure that both readers (i.e., Composite Context Aspect Adverse Environment Status,   Composite Context Aspect Route Status aspects) and writers (i.e., Context Interpreter, Context Aggregator service components) will eventually gain access to the lock to access the Context Database component. A progress analysis for this problem using the LTSA shows no errors.

In addition to safety and progress property processes, properties can be defined as state-based logical propositions in FSP. Fluents in FSP allow the expression of properties about the abstract state of a system at a particular point in time [23]. The current study employs *FLTL assertions* as a method for specifying system requirements of the case study subset. For example, two FLTL assertions have been defined to ensure mutually exclusive access to the shared variables by the Context Interpreter and the Context Aggregator service components. These properties ensure the required mutual exclusion safety property, and an additional liveness property, which asserts that if a process (i.e., Context Interpreter or Context Aggregator) enters the critical section that process should eventually exit before another process can enter. Verification performed for this logical property shows that there are no violations.

The use of FLTL assertions provides the opportunity to generate examples of traces (witness executions), which satisfy the property. This research applies *witness executions* as a means of identifying potential errors in the specification. For example, a FLTL property has been defined to verify the weaving of the base state machines and aspectual state machines in the specification. The negation of this assertion generates a counterexample. By using counterexamples and witness executions, the state models and system properties for the aspectual pervasive services are iteratively improved.

12.7 Evaluation Framework

This section provides the evaluation framework established to validate the research approach.

This evaluation framework [4] mainly validates the main contributions or deliverables of this study against several key evaluation criteria. The main tools used in this study include the Aspectual FSP Generation tool created in this research, the LTSA model checker and the LTSA-MSC tool. The method of evaluation is based on *key feature comparison*. Key feature comparison is used as a credible method for evaluating software engineering-based approaches [30]. The evaluation framework developed here does not produce additions to the research methodology but instead validates the methods and tools used in the research as a whole. The framework comprises a set of detailed criteria for two dimensions or views: *vertical*

Fig. 12.7 Evaluation framework: *vertical* and *horizontal*
views

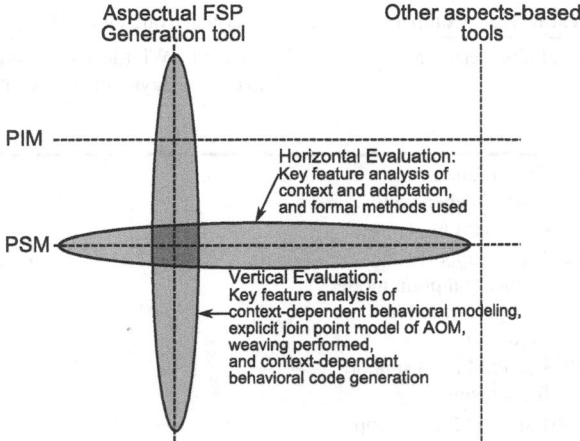

and *horizontal* (see Fig. 12.7). The notions of vertical and horizontal views were
motivated by [30] (p. 14), which also uses a two-dimensional evaluation approach.

12.7.1 Vertical Evaluation of the Research

This evaluation focuses on comparing four tools across the modeling layers of
platform-independent model (PIM) and platform-specific model (PSM) against the
Aspectual FSP Generation tool. The compared tools are Groher and
Schulze [19] approach, Whittle and Jayaraman [31] approach, Motorola WEAVR
[13] and Fuentes et al. [18] approach (see [4] for details). Like the Aspectual
FSP Generation tool, these tools have been developed using commercially
available toolchains of similar area of application such as IBM Rational Software
Modeler, Borland Together, Telelogic Modeller and Topcased [30]. This evaluation
is based on the following criteria: context-dependent behavioral modeling at the PIM
level, explicit joinpoint model of aspect-oriented modeling at the PIM level, weaving
performed at the PIM or PSM level, and context-dependent behavioral code generation from the PIM to PSM level. A particular evaluation criterion can be fully satisfied
(complete cover), partly satisfied (partial cover), or not supported at all.

The results of the vertical evaluation are assuring (see Table 12.1). Like the
Aspectual FSP Generation tool, [13, 18, 19] support an explicit joinpoint model of aspect-oriented modeling at PIM level. Also, all the compared
approaches support PIM or PSM level weaving of aspects. The vertical evaluation
has demonstrated that the Aspectual FSP Generation tool has unique
features on context-dependent behavioral modeling and context-dependent behavioral code generation. Table 12.1 shows that the Aspectual FSP Generation
tool satisfies all the criteria as opposed to the other tools which satisfy only some
criteria.

Table 12.1 Comparison matrix for vertical evaluation [4]

Evaluation criteria	Groher and Schulze	Whittle and Jayaraman	Cottenier et al.	Fuentes et al.	Aspectual FSP generation tool
PIM level support for context-dependent behavioral modeling	–	–	–	*	+
PIM level support for explicit joinpoint model of aspect-oriented modeling	+	–	+	+	+
PIM or PSM level support for weaving	+	+	+	+	+
PIM and PSM level support for context-dependent behavioral code generation	–	–	–	–	+

+ Complete cover of a criterion; * partial cover of a criterion; – no cover of a criterion

12.7.2 Horizontal Evaluation of the Research

In contrast to the vertical evaluation discussed above, the horizontal evaluation is aimed at investigating particular features of our approach at a single modeling level (i.e., the PSM level). These evaluation criteria cover two aspects of the study: the formal methods and tools employed in the study, and the context and adaptation dimensions of the customization approach used in the services.

12.7.2.1 Formal Methods and Tools Used in the Approach

Clarke et al. [10] provide several criteria that formal methods-based approaches and tools need to support. According to [10], although some of these criteria are ideals, it is still considered good to aim for them. The criteria are: early payback, incremental gain for incremental effort, multiple use, integrated use, ease of use, efficiency, ease of learning, orientation toward error detection, focused analysis and evolutionary development. The research methodology of the current study contains three stages: service specification, architecture definition and architecture modularization. In the present study, formal methods and tools (LTSA tool and LTSA-MSC tool) have been applied during the service specification and architecture definition stages of the research methodology, and finally for model checking the aspectual pervasive software services specification. This evaluates the application of the aforementioned formal methods and tools used in the current research against the criteria provided in [10]. Our approach has been evaluated using all the criteria provided by them (see [4]). However, due to space limitations this chapter discusses one key criterion. *Early payback*: this study is focused on the architectural level of the software life-cycle. This architecture-centric approach builds models of pervasive software services and their compositions and verifies their behavior against specified system properties. Building architectural models of pervasive software services allows the software engineers to validate the actual correctness of the services before the services are implemented later in the software life-cycle. Thus, it provides early payback or feedback to the service engineer on the validity of the services.

12.7.2.2 Context and Adaptation of the Customization Approach

Kappel et al. [22] and Schwinger et al. [26] present a comprehensive and uniform evaluation framework, which can be used to compare customization capabilities of approaches originating from the mobile computing and the personalization domains. The notion of customization refers to the adaptation of an applications services toward the current context. Their framework has two orthogonal dimensions, which are context and adaptation, and the mapping between context and adaptation has been represented by the notion of customization. They provide detailed criteria for both the context and adaptation dimensions of the framework. The *context* and *adaptation* dimensions of the customization approach used in the pervasive services of the current research are evaluated using those criteria. The results of this evaluation are summarized in two tables respectively: Tables 12.2 and 12.3. See [4] for a more detailed analysis of these results.

The horizontal evaluation of the approach has shown that the formal methods and tools employed in the research, and the customization approach used in the services, are effective toward the overall objectives of this research.

12.8 Research Extensions

In this section, we discuss two key research directions, extending this work to benefit the broader service engineering and pervasive computing communities.

12.8.1 Aspectual FSP Generation as an Integrated Eclipse Plug-in

The Aspectual FSP Generation tool developed in the current research can be extended as an integrated plug-in to the Eclipse development environment. This will be beneficial as it will allow our tool to be used in conjunction with other plug-ins for engineering context-aware services. Also, it can be leveraged by interested researchers in the wider service engineering community. To the best of our knowledge, such an integrated Eclipse-based plug-in for facilitating the engineering of context-aware software services has not been addressed in existing work.

Table 12.2 Current study's context characteristics [4]

Scope of context	Representation of Context					Acquisition of context				Access of context
Property (C.P.)	Extensibility (C.E.)	Chronology (C.C.)	Validity (C.V.)	Reusability (C.R.)	Abstraction (C.Ab.)	Automation (C.Au.)	Dynamicity (C.D.)		Mechanism (C.M.)	
		History · Future				Manual · Semi-automatic · Automatic	Static · Dynamic		Push · Pull	
Location	+	* *	*	*	+	* * +	* +		+	*
Temperature	+	* *	*	*	+	* * +	* +		+	*
Pressure	+	* *	*	*	+	* * +	* +		+	*
Time	+	* *	*	*	+	* * +	* +		+	*
Device	*	* *	*	*	+	* * +	* +		+	*
Network	*	* *	*	*	+	* * +	* +		+	*
User	*	* *	*	*	+	* * +	* +		+	*
Application	+	* *	*	*	+	* * +	* +		+	*

+ Explicitly supported; * not explicitly supported; − not applicable

Table 12.3 Current study's adaptation characteristics [4]

Kind of adaptation					Subject of adaptation		Process of adaptation			
Operation (A.O.)	Extensibility (A.Ex.)	Effect (A.Ef.)	Complexity (A.C.)	Level (A.L.)	Element (A.El.)	Granularity (A.G.)	Tasks (A.T.)	Automation (A.A.)	Dynamicity (A.D.)	Incrementality (A.I.)
Add Remove Transform		Simple Complex	Content Hyperbase Presentation Others		Text Audio Image Video Link Others	Micro Macro		Automatic Semi-automatic Manual	Static Dynamic	
+ + +	+	* +	+ – – –	–	– – – – – +	+ *	+	+ * *	* *	+

Eclipse is a multi-language software development platform, which comprises an integrated development environment and a plug-in system to extend it. LTSA tool [23], which was originally created as a stand-alone tool, has now been extended to the Eclipse platform. LTSA Eclipse has an extensible architecture which allows extra features to be added by means of extended plug-ins. At present, the following plug-ins are supported which are available from the Eclipse install site: Message Sequence Chart, Architecture, WS-Engineer and SceneBeans. Similarly, the Aspectual FSP Generation tool can be integrated as an editor of the existing Eclipse-based LTSA tool. With this solution, service engineers can use a single integrated development environment to design and verify the pervasive software services specification for any property violations with much ease and confidence. At present, the current research performs the service engineering process using three stand-alone tools: LTSA-MSC tool, Aspectual FSP Generation tool and LTSA tool. In the integrated environment, the Message Sequence Chart plug-in can be used to specify the software services, generate and extract the core service model of the architecture while the Aspectual FSP Generation plug-in can be used to model the context-dependent adaptive behavior of the services using UML models and transform them into behavioral FSP. Finally, the LTSA can be used to perform model checking of the aspectual pervasive software services specification.

The extension of the Aspectual FSP Generation tool as an integrated plug-in to the Eclipse platform can be performed as follows. IBM Rational Software Architect [15], which is the development environment used to create the Aspectual FSP Generation tool, allows exporting of plug-in projects using an export wizard or a mechanism called the Plug-in Development Environment build. The Eclipse platform provides several notions to facilitate extension, which are plug-in, feature and update site [15]. A plug-in is the unit of new function contribution while a feature, which can include one or more plug-ins, is the unit of new function installation. An update site is a mechanism for finding and installing features. An update site can distribute one or more features. The multi-stage transformation chain developed in the current study includes several plug-ins, such as the back-end model-to-text JET transformation, the model-to-model mapping project, the c-FSP-UML profile project, and the EMF project. In order to export these plug-ins, first, a feature project that references those plug-ins needs to be created. Second, an update site needs to be created to distribute the feature created. The created update site can be deployed by copying the required files of the update site to a local or network folder, or to a Web server. Finally, the Eclipse Update Manager can be used to scan update sites for the newly created feature and install it.

12.8.2 Implementing the Model Checked Aspectual Pervasive Services

Service development is considered a very complex process that involves several stages of the software life-cycle, such as requirements analysis, design, implementation, testing and maintenance. In general, a service is validated during the testing phase, which is performed late in the software life-cycle. Testing the service code is considered costly, as any erroneous situations identified during the testing phase essentially require to reperform the design and implementation phases until the expected result is obtained. However, if service implementation can be generated automatically on an already-validated service specification using model transformation techniques, then it reduces or minimizes the need for testing the service code. This essentially reduces implementation time as the code is automatically generated, and the verified design and implementation levels of services are synchronized. Thus, reducing the need for any maintenance by the service engineer. The application of model transformations on an already-verified service design is also appropriate in the context of the current study.

This study has employed rigorous model checking to check whether individual aspects or components, and the woven model, contain any undesired behavior. This model checked pervasive software services specification, which is free of any erroneous behavior, can be fed into a custom model-to-code transformation tool created to automate the generation of executable service code or service implementation. Model-to-text transformations can be employed to generate both core and adaptable code of a service implementation. The core service code is the unchanging or static portion of the service while context handling or the adaptable code is the dynamic portion of the service, which can evolve based on available contextual information. In the current study, at the behavioral modeling level of FSP, the core service behavior and context-dependent information have been treated as separate concerns using the aspect-oriented modeling paradigm (c-FSP aspects). The same separation of concerns can be effectively enforced at the source code level with aspect-oriented programming. Model-to-text transformations can be employed to ensure the correct separation of concerns at both FSP and aspect-oriented programming levels. The service code can be provided using the aspect-oriented version of Java known as AspectJ of aspect-oriented programming and can target readily available software platforms such as Apache Tomcat Web Server and the Axis Simple Object Access Protocol engine. However, one of the main limitations of AspectJ is that it only supports compile time aspect weaving. In this regard, AspectWerkz can be a solution, which is a dynamic, lightweight and high-performing aspect-oriented programming framework for Java.

12.9 Conclusion

In summary, the primary contribution of this chapter is a novel, systematic architecture-centric approach for engineering context-aware services at the software architectural level. Context-awareness capabilities in service interfaces introduce additional challenges to the software engineer. The additional complexities associated with these special services necessitate the use of solid software engineering methodologies during their development and execution. To this end, this chapter has proposed a novel approach which integrates the benefits of solid software engineering principles of model-driven architecture, aspect-oriented modeling and formal model checking for engineering context-aware services. A prototype tool—Aspectual FSP Generation—applying an effective pipeline of model-to-model and model-to-text transformations has been built. The generated formal behavioral models for context-dependent behavior and the core service behavior have been rigorously verified using model checking against desired system properties. The approach has been explored using a real-world case study in intelligent transport, and an evaluation framework has been developed to validate the main methods and tools employed in the study. We have also discussed two key research directions, extending this work to benefit the broader service engineering and pervasive computing communities.

References

1. Abeywickrama, D.B.: Pervasive services engineering for SOAs. Ph.D. thesis, Faculty of IT, Clayton Campus, Monash University, Australia (2010)
2. Abeywickrama, D.B., Ramakrishnan, S.: A model-based approach for engineering pervasive services in SOAs. In: 5th International Conference on Pervasive Services (ICPS'08), Sorrento, Italy, pp. 57–60. ACM (2008)
3. Abeywickrama, D.B., Ramakrishnan, S.: Model-driven development of aspectual pervasive software services. In: 14th IEEE International Enterprise Distributed Object Computing Conference Workshops, Vitoria, Brazil, pp. 49–59. IEEE (2010)
4. Abeywickrama, D.B., Ramakrishnan, S.: An evaluation framework for validating aspectual pervasive software services. In: 6th International Conference on Evaluation of Novel Approaches to Software Engineering conference (ENASE'11), pp. 80–91. SciTePress (2011)
5. Abeywickrama, D.B., Ramakrishnan, S.: Model checking aspectual pervasive software services. In: 35th Annual IEEE International Computer Software and Applications Conference (COMPSAC'11), pp. 253–262. IEEE Computer Society (2011)
6. Abeywickrama, D.B., Ramakrishnan, S.: Context-aware services engineering: models, transformations, and verification. ACM Trans. Internet Technol. J. 11(3), Article 10. ACM (2012)
7. Achilleos, A., Yang, K., Georgalas, N., Azmoodech, M.: Pervasive service creation using a model-driven petri net based approach. In: International Wireless Communications and Mobile Computing Conference, pp. 309–314 (2008)
8. Analyti, A., Theodorakis, M., Spyratos, N., Constantopoulos, P.: Contextualization as an independent abstraction mechanism for conceptual modeling. Inf. Syst. J. 32(1), 24–60. Elsevier Science Ltd., Oxford, UK (2007)
9. Autili, M., Berardinelli, L., Cortellessa, V., Marco, A.D., Ruscio, D.D., Inverardi, P., Tivoli, M.: A development process for self-adapting service-oriented applications. In: International Conference on Service-Oriented Computing, LNCS, vol. 4749, pp. 442–448. Springer (2009)
10. Clarke, E.M., Wing, J.M., Alur, R.: Formal methods: state of the art and future directions. ACM Comput. Surv. 28(4), 626–643. ACM (1996)
11. Clarke, E.M., Grumberg, O., Peled, D.A.: Model Checking. The MIT Press, Cambridge (1999)
12. Colombo, E., Mylopoulos, J., Spoletini, P.: Modeling and analyzing context-aware composition of services. In: International Conference on Service-Oriented Computing, LNCS, vol. 3826, pp. 198–213. Springer (2005)
13. Cottenier, T., van den Berg, A., Elrad, T.: Motorola WEAVR: aspect orientation and model-driven engineering. J. Object Technol. 6(7), 51–88. Chair of Software Engineering, ETH Zurich, Switzerland (2007)
14. Davie, A.: Intelligent tagging for transport and logistics: the ParcelCall approach. Electron. Commun. Eng. J. 14(3), 122–128. Institution of Electrical Engineers, London, UK (2002)

15. DeCarlo, J., Ackerman, L., Elder, P., Busch, C., Lopez-Mancisidor, A., Kimura, J., Balaji. R.S.: Strategic reuse with asset-based development. IBM Corporation (2008)
16. Dey, A.K., Abowd G.D.: Towards a better understanding of context and context-awareness. In: CHI 2000 Workshop on The What, Who, Where, When, Why and How of Context-Awareness (2000)
17. Douence, R., Botlan, D.L., Noye, J., Sudholt, M.: Concurrent aspects. In: 5th International Conference on Generative Programming and Component, Engineering, pp. 79–88 (2006)
18. Fuentes, L., Gamez, N., Sanchez, P.: Aspect-oriented executable UML models for context-aware pervasive applications. In: 2008 5th International Workshop on Model-Based Methodologies for Pervasive and Embedded Software, pp. 34–43, Budapest. IEEE (2008)
19. Groher, I., Schulze, S.: Generating aspect code from UML models. In: 3rd International Workshop on Aspect-Oriented Modeling Co-located with 2nd International Conference on Aspect-Oriented Software Development (AOSD'03), Boston, USA (2003)
20. Hegering, H.-G., Küpper, A., Linnhoff-Popien, C., Reiser, H.: Management challenges of context-aware services in ubiquitous environments. In: Brunner, M., Keller, K. (eds.) Self-Managing Distributed Systems, LNCS, vol. 2867, pp. 321–339. Springer (2003)
21. Kapitsaki, G.M., Kateros, D.A., Prezerakos, G.N., Venieris, I.S.: Model-driven development of composite context-aware web applications. Inf. Softw. Technol. J. 51(8), 1244–1260. Butterworth-Heinemann (2009)
22. Kappel, G., Pröll, B., Retschitzegger, W., Schwinger, W.: Customisation for ubiquitous web applications: a comparison of approaches. Int. J. Web Eng. Technol. 1(1), 79–111. Inderscience Publishers, Geneva, Switzerland (2003)
23. Magee, J., Kramer, J.: Concurrency: State Models and Java Programs, 2nd edn. Wiley, New York (2006)
24. Mceachen, N., Alexander, R.T.: Distributing classes with woven concerns: an exploration of potential fault scenarios. In: 4th International Conference on Aspect-Oriented Software Development, pp. 192–200. ACM (2005)
25. Perez-Toledano, M.A., Navasa, A., Murillo, J.M., Canal, C.: TITAN: a framework for aspect-oriented system evolution. In: International Conference on Software, Engineering Advances, pp. 23–30 (2007)
26. Schwinger, W., Grün, C., Pröll, B., Retschitzegger, W., Schauerhuber, A.: Context-awareness in mobile tourism guides—a comprehensive survey.Technical report, Johannes Kepler University, Linz, Austria (2005)
27. Serral, E., Valderas, P., Pelechano, V.: Towards the model-driven development of context-aware pervasive systems. Pervasive Mobile Comput. J. 6(2), 254–280. Elsevier (2010)
28. Sheng, Q. Z., Benatallah, B.: ContextUML: a UML-based modeling language for model-driven development of context-aware web services. In: International Conference on Mobile, Business, pp. 206–212 (2005)
29. Truong, H., Dustdar, S.: A survey on context-aware web service systems. Int. J. Web Inf. Syst. 5(1), 5–31 (2009)
30. VIsualize all moDel drivEn programming (VIDE), WP 11: Deliverable number D11.3, Supported by the European Commission within Sixth Framework Programme. Polish-Japanese Institute of Information Technology. http://www.vide-ist.eu/download/VIDE_D11.3.pdf. Accessed 16 Sept 2012
31. Whittle, J., Jayaraman, P.: MATA: A tool for aspect-oriented modeling based on graph transformation. In: Giese, H. (ed.) Models in Software Engineering, LNCS, vol. 5002, pp. 16–27. Springer, Berlin(2008)
32. Xu, D., Alsmadi, I., Xu, W.: Model checking aspect-oriented design specification. In: 31st Annual IEEE International Computer Software and Applications Conference, pp. 491–500 (2007)

Part II
Service Selection and Assisted Composition

Chapter 13
Service Selection in Web Service Composition: A Comparative Review of Existing Approaches

Mahboobeh Moghaddam and Joseph G. Davis

Abstract Web service composition (WSC) offers a range of solutions for rapid creation of complex applications in advanced service-oriented systems by facilitating the composition of already existing concrete web services. One critical challenge in WSC is the dynamic selection of concrete services to be bound to the abstract composite service. In this paper, we provide a comprehensive review of the existing proposals for service selection, and a comparative analysis of the optimization and automated negotiation-based approaches.

13.1 Introduction

Service-Oriented Computing (SOC) has emerged as an important computing paradigm in recent years. Its main feature is that it utilizes one or more inter-operable services (software components which implement specific functionalities) as fundamental building blocks to support rapid, low-cost development of distributed applications in heterogeneous environments [23]. SOC represents a new genera-tion of distributed computing platforms which builds on past distributed computing approaches. It is distinguished by the addition of new design layers, governance considerations, and a set of preferred implementation technologies [18].

M. Moghaddam (✉) · J. G. Davis
School of Information Technologies, University of Sydney,
Sydney, NSW 2006, Australia
e-mail: mahboobe@it.usyd.edu.au

M. Moghaddam
National ICT Australia (NICTA), Australian Technology Park,
Eveleigh, NSW 2015, Australia

J.G. Davis
e-mail: joseph.davis@sydney.edu.au

A. Bouguettaya et al. (eds.), *Web Services Foundations*,
DOI: 10.1007/978-1-4614-7518-7_13,

More recently, web services have been advanced as the technology of choice for realizing service oriented computing and its associated set of strategic goals. Web services are self-contained, modular business applications with open, Internet-oriented, standards-based interfaces [52]. The communication between web services is via standards-based technologies which give users the opportunity to access different web services, independent of their hardware, operating system, or even programming environment. This supports organizations with a technology to create services which can be easily discovered and consumed by external users.

One of the critical research challenges in realizing the vision of agile and collaborative software development using web services is *Web Service Composition* (WSC) which involves creating a composite service by combining different web services to provide a new value added service [5]. *Service selection*, as the problem of selecting the most appropriate web services from the pool of available ones that best match the functional and non-functional requirements and constraints specified by the requester has been researched extensively. The primary goal of this paper is to provide a comprehensive review of a range of proposals for service selection in WSC. A comparative analysis of the two dominant approaches based on optimization and automated negotiation is also included.

The remainder of this paper is organized as follows: Sect. 13.2 introduces web service composition lifecycle to provide a common ground on WSC definition. A brief overview of service discovery approaches is presented in Sect. 13.3. In Sect. 13.4, we discuss the main challenges involved in arriving at a service selection solution. A comprehensive review of the existing service selection approaches, optimization-based, negotiation-based, and the hybrid approaches is presented in Sect. 13.5. Section 13.6 includes a comparative analysis of the two main approaches. The paper concludes with a brief summary and an outlook for future research in Sect. 13.7.

13.2 Web Service Composition

Although a single web service has its own value for its users, the functionality offered by the individual web services is limited. The true potential of web services can only be realized through assembling multiple web services into more powerful applications with more sophisticated functionalities; i.e. *Web Service Composition* (WSC). Manual composition of web services is time consuming, error-prone, generally hard and not scalable [5]. Hence, a family of approaches to web service composition aims to fully or partially automate the composition process.

The two main streams in the automatic WSC approaches are: *workflow-based* approaches and *AI planning-based* approaches [5, 47]. Workflow-based approaches are inspired by the similarity of an abstract composite service to an abstract business process, and the similarity of a concrete composite service to a running workflow system. This similarity has helped web service research community to build on the accumulated knowledge that has emerged in the workflow and business process

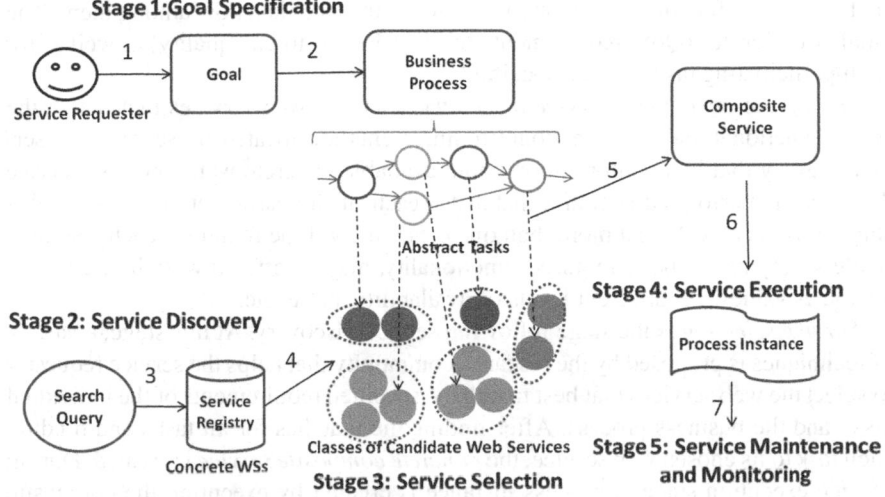

Fig. 13.1 Web service composition lifecycle

design research area [5]. We will discuss this approach in more detail by developing a model of Web Service Composition Lifecycle (Fig. 13.1).

In the AI planning-based approaches, service composition is viewed as a planning problem. Generally, a planning problem has the following elements: description of the *initial state* of the world, definition of the *desired goal state*(s), and a description of the *set of possible actions* which can transform world's state from one to another. The planner agent aims at finding the sequence of actions that will transform the world's state from the initial state to the goal state. In the WSC realm, a composite service is represented as a goal state to be achieved and the available web services are represented as the set of actions that can transform the world (or agent's) states. At the end of a successful planning exercise, a plan is generated. This plan constitutes the chosen web services and the order of their execution in such a way that they, in combination, will deliver the required functionality.

The main difference between the two approaches is that AI planning-based techniques generally do not make any assumption relating an abstract view of the composite service.[1] In contrast, this abstract view is a key element in the workflow-based approaches. In this paper, our focus is on the workflow-based approaches as the research in the business process and workflow-related areas have proven applications in industry, which has, in turn, helped to improve the academic research.

The lifecycle of a typical workflow-based WSC solution is illustrated in Fig. 13.1. In this lifecycle, the first stage is *the goal specification*, where the service requester's goal and preferences are defined. Following this, the goal is decomposed (semi)automatically into an abstract business process (BP) comprising a set of tasks,

---

[1] There are exceptions to this generalization, such as the work of McIlraith and Son [39]. They have a similar concept to an abstract business process, refered to as the high-level generic procedure.

each with clear functionality, along with the control and data flow among them. The Quality of Service (QoS) requirements for the BP (end-to-end quality) as well as for each participating task are also specified.

During the next stage, *service discovery*, concrete web services that match the tasks' functional and non-functional requirements are located by searching a service registry that holds information about available concrete web services. Service discovery is performed to find a match for each of the participating tasks. At this stage, it is very likely that more than one candidate will be found for each task that, while satisfying the basic required functionality, may be offered with different QoS attributes values, i.e. different levels of availability, price, etc.

Service selection is the stage following service discovery. At this stage, a variety of techniques is proposed by the research community that helps the service requester to select the web services that best match the specified requirements of the individual tasks and the business process. After finding the matches for all tasks and binding each task to its chosen web service, the *concrete composite service* is created. During service execution stage, a process instance is created by executing the composite service. The process instance would be continuously monitored for further responses toward any failure or change in its status at the final stage of WSC, i.e. *service maintenance and monitoring*.

Service discovery and selection, as two fundamental steps in the web service composition lifecycle, have been a major focus of service-oriented computing research. Before any interaction happens between service requester and provider, the former needs to locate the web service that best matches her task description. Researchers have mainly focused on service discovery techniques for a single task. In contrast, service selection has been addressed at two levels: for a single task, and for the complex BP. This second level is specifically required during WSC and the complexity level is exacerbated by the fact that service selection is performed for a set of dependent tasks. Hence, many researchers have considered service discovery and service selection as two separate stages to break down the complexity.

Following this approach, service discovery and service selection are treated as two distinct stages in our discussion of WSC lifecycle (Fig. 13.1), where the output of the former is the input to the latter stage. Even though our primary focus is service selection, we present a brief overview of the approaches to service discovery in the next section, before discussing a range of service selection approaches. This will help clarify the expected output of service discovery which is used as the input to service selection.

13.3 Service Discovery Approaches

In WSC, service discovery (also referred to as matchmaking) is the process of finding a concrete service match for each task in the BP. WSC solutions need to define the precise and specific *search criteria* to be executed against the *web service registry* to find the match for each task.

What to include in this search criteria varies among different solutions. The matchmaking algorithm proposed in [15] ranks functionally equivalent services on the basis of their ability to fulfill the service requester's functional and non-functional requirements while maintaining the price below a specified budget. The proposed matchmaking framework in [40] is based on the web service context where context is defined as all the information needed for enabling interactions between the service requester and providers. Semantic and behavioural information are used in [8, 9] for service matchmaking during WSC. Web service behaviour is the order of execution of the service operations or the order of message exchange with a service and the constraints governing the operations' execution sequence [17]. The selection algorithm proposed in [17] takes into account not only the functional requirements but also the transactional properties, and QoS characteristics of web services. Transactional properties guarantee consistent outcome and correct execution of the composite service. An information retrieval approach is suggested in [26] for discovering and ranking web services automatically, given a textual description of the desired services.

The variation in what to include in the search criteria arises from the fact that a web service can be defined from different perpectives, including: *functionality, QoS attributes, interface, semantics, behaviour,* and *context*. Web service interface is an essential aspect in the web service description (W3C working group note on Web Service Architecture [7]). However, what additional aspects to be included in the service definition is largely dependent on the application domain specificities. Service discovery proposals, including the ones mentioned above, have each added one or more aspects to the web service description, in addition to the interface. Elements of service specification affect the criteria included in the search request from the demand side, and the type of information to be stored in the service registry from the supply side.

Based on the search query criteria, service registry returns a number of candidate services. At this point, WSC enters the next stage, namely composite service selection. The input to the composite service selection stage is a set of *classes* of services. Each class contains services that can perform the same functionality, but they may differ on other aspects, such as QoS attributes.

13.4 Service Selection Challenges

In this section, we discuss the main challenges involved in the service selection problem. These challenges are: the NP-hardness of this problem for a composite service and the resulting scalability concern, the need to distinguish the abstract business process from its possible set of execution paths, defining the aggregation functions for the QoS attributes, and elicitation of the service user's preferences about different QoS attributes for the trade-off analysis of the candidate services.

NP-Hardness and Scalability

Composite service selection can be modelled as a multi-dimension multi-choice knapsack problem (MMKP), which is known to be an NP-hard problem in the strong sense [46]. This means that for large problems, it is unlikely that an optimal solution can be found given a reasonable amount of computational effort. Hence, there is a need for heuristic approaches when the problem size is too large to be solved by optimization procedures [46]. A number of heuristic algorithms for the service selection problem have been proposed in the literature; good exemplars include [6, 41, 60]. Some researchers have proposed a Genetic Algorithm approach to solve the scalability problem [10, 29, 37]. An alternative proposal to reduce the computational time of the service selection search algorithm is to shrink the search space. For instance, Alrifai et al. [2] has proposed pruning the service candidates that are not likely to be part of the optimal solution, by computing the service skyline for each service class.[2]

From Business Process to Execution Path

The assumption in workflow-based service composition approaches is that the required composite service is described at an abstract level as a high-level business process [4]. The business process is a collection of generic service tasks with defined control-flow and data-flow dependencies among them. Different languages and models have been used for describing the composite service, or more precisely its equivalent business process, such as UML activity diagram [4], statechart [62], extended BPEL [1], or YAWL [17].

Regardless of the modelling notation, different control-flow constructs are allowed in the existing process modelling languages such as *sequence, loop, parallel execution,* and *conditional branching.* Some control structures such as loop and conditional branching need special consideration. For these, the runtime structure is different from the abstract structure. For instance, only one of the tasks in the conditional branching would be selected for execution. This means that a BP might be executed along different paths, based on the control-flow at runtime. Each possible path of BP execution is called *an execution path.* During service selection, *an execution plan* is created by assigning web services to the tasks of an execution path.

Researchers have used different techniques to translate a BP to its corresponding execution paths, such as *loop peeling* [4], or *loop unfolding* [60, 62] to treat loop structures. In the former approach, every loop is annotated with the expected maxi-

---

[2] For a set of d-dimensional data points, the skyline is a subset of the points where no point in it is dominated by any other member. If $\vec{p}$ $(p_1, ..., p_d)$ and $\vec{q}$ $(q_1, ..., q_d)$ are two points in the d-dimensional data set, p dominates q *iff* $\forall i \in [1, d]$, $p_i \succeq q_i$ and $\exists j \in [1, d]$, $p_j \succ q_j$ [59]. The notation $\succeq$ is defined as being *better than or equal*, and $\succ$ as *better* than. In the service domain, a *service skyline* is the set of providers where no provider is dominated by any other, in terms of the offered values for QoS attributes.

mum number of its iterations, considering a probability distribution for the number of loop iterations. In the latter case, the loop is unfolded by cloning the functions in the loop for a number of times such as the maximal loop count, which can be obtained from process execution history or the process designer.

Aggregation Functions

A critical challenge in service selection is how to measure the end-to-end quality of the composite service. The aggregated value of a QoS attribute should take into account the QoS attribute value of the individual services participating in the composite service, and the business process structure. For example, the overall price of a composite service can be defined as the sum of the prices of all the participating services. However, for execution time, we need a more complex aggregation function, e.g. one that returns the maximum execution time among the parallel services, adds up the execution times of sequential services, and combines these two values if there are both parallel and sequential structures in the BP.

In [30] and its extension [31], Jaeger et al. have proposed aggregation functions for some QoS attributes such as execution time, cost and throughput, supporting a comprehensive set of structural patterns that can be found in workflows. Zeng et al. [62] has proposed aggregation functions for attributes such as execution price, execution duration, and reputation, supporting basic workflow patterns such as loop, sequence, conditional branching, and concurrent threads. Other aggregation functions have been also developed [4, 10, 48, 62].

Defining the Weights of QoS Attributes

There is a general assumption in the literature that the service requester has a clear idea of the importance of a QoS attribute which let her assign a scalar weight to each QoS criterion. But this may not be realistic, especially as the number of QoS attributes involved in the selection criteria increases. Some researchers have challenged this assumption. Wang [54] has proposed a resolution process for determining the linguistic weights of QoS criteria based on a group of participants' preferences. Yu and Bouguettaya [59] has proposed two algorithms for calculating the service skyline. Determining the skyline of a set of data requires pair-wise comparison of all the members of the data set which can be very expensive in terms of computational time and memory usage. The proposed algorithms in [59] exploit the indices of the service operations to compute the skyline more efficiently. The computed skylines guarantee the inclusion of the best user desired service providers without any user intervention.

13.5 Service Selection Spectrum

The input to the service selection stage is a set of classes of web services. The candidate web services in one class provide the same functionality, but they may vary according to other aspects such as QoS attribute values. QoS attributes (or non-functional properties) are the constraints defined over service functionality [45]. They can be categorized as:

- Technical domain-independent attributes,[3] such as: *response time, availability, reliability, robustness* (the ability of the service to continue its work in the presence of invalid, incomplete or conflicting inputs),
- Non-technical domain-independent attributes, such as: *execution price, penalty, discount, reputation,*
- Domain-dependent attributes which are only meaningful in a specific application domain, such as: *refresh time* for a traffic monitoring service [15].

Service QoS profile, provider's offered values for service QoS attributes, plays a central role in service selection research. Different providers may offer the same service at different levels of quality to maintain their competitive advantage over each other [40]. As well, a single provider might offer the same functionality with ranging quality levels to cover a wider range of customers. Moreover, at the composite service level, the QoS of the final composite service is the key factor to ensure service requester's satisfaction [62].

We have surveyed the range of service selection approaches discussed in the literature, based on the underlying assumptions regarding the QoS profile. The variation in the assumptions is illustrated as a spectrum in Fig. 13.2. Corresponding to the two extremes of the spectrum are the two important trends in the service selection literature: *Optimization-based* approaches which typically assume a predetermined not-customizable QoS profiles and, *negotiation-based* approaches which permit QoS profiles to be flexible and negotiable. In the following sections, we provide a

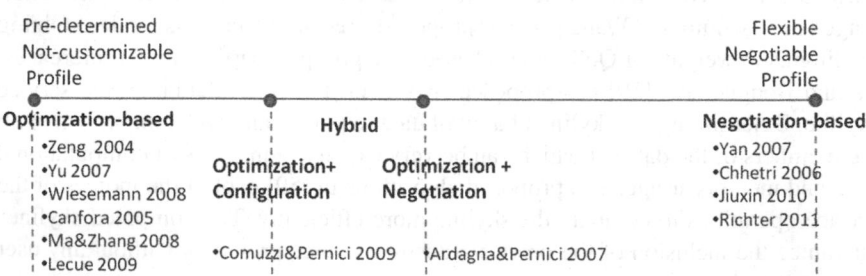

Fig. 13.2 Service selection spectrum based on QoS profile assumptions

---

[3] Due to space limitations, attributes such as privacy, security, and trust are not included in this paper.

comprehensive review of the important contributions on *service selection for a composite service* (or composite service selection).

13.5.1 Optimization-Based Approaches

Service selection can be modelled as an optimization problem. The optimization approach has appeared under different names such as *QoS-driven* or *QoS-aware web service composition, web service composition optimization,* and *optimum concretization.* Optimization can be performed at two levels: *local optimization* for an individual task, approaches such as [1, 17, 44] and *global optimization* for the BP, followed by for example [4, 60, 62].

Local Optimization

At the local level, the best service for individual tasks is chosen, one task at a time, regardless of the task dependencies with other tasks in the BP or the end-to-end quality requirements of the composite service. In this approach, services are ranked based on some criteria, including all service QoS attributes. The dominant technique to rank services is to assign a score to each web service, using utility theory. In utility theory (from microeconomics), the service requester or provider preferences can be mapped to values of utility, where higher utility means greater preferences [56]. To avoid the complexities of multi-dimensional utility function elicitation, each QoS attribute and the price have an independent utility function, based on the assumption of the independence of the outcomes of utility functions originating from *Multi-attribute Utility Theory (MAUT)* [34].

The offered value for the jth QoS attribute, q_j, ($j \in J$: set of all QoS attributes), by web service s, is mapped to a value between 0 and 1 using a single attribute linear utility function, denoted as U_j in Eq. (13.1). In this equation, q_j^{max} and q_j^{min} are the maximum and minimum values offered for q_j by all the candidate web services of the same functionality class.

$$U_j(q_j) = \begin{cases} \frac{q_j - q_j^{min}}{q_j^{max} - q_j^{min}} & \text{if larger } q_j \text{ more desirable} \\ \frac{q_j^{max} - q_j}{q_j^{max} - q_j^{min}} & \text{if smaller } q_j \text{ more desirable} \end{cases} \quad (13.1)$$

To get the aggregated utility of all the QoS attributes offered by service s (denoted as $U(s)$ in Eq. (13.2)), the weighted sum of the individual utility functions is calculated using a normalized weight (w_j) for each attribute specifying its importance. The sum of the normalized weights assigned to different QoS attributes (by service requester) should add up to 1, Eq. (13.3).

$$U(s) = \sum_{j \in J} w_j \times U_j(q_j) \tag{13.2}$$

$$\sum_{j \in J} w_j = 1 \tag{13.3}$$

Global Optimization

Even though the local optimization approach optimizes local service selection, it may not lead to a global optimality for the end-to-end QoS of the BP. Besides, it is not possible to set global constraints for the composite service in the local approach. To overcome these limitations, global optimization approaches have been proposed. In one such approach, optimization is carried out for the overall BP, and the requester can define end-to-end requirements and constraints for the overall BP. It is still possible to have a local selection strategy, beside the global optimization process, to address service requester's concerns about individual task quality. This can be achieved by applying the local QoS constraints as filters to the list of the candidate services returned by the service registry. The realization of the optimization problem's elements for composite service selection is as follows:

- Objective Function: The general objective function illustrated by research community for service selection is to maximize service requester's *satisfaction* from the execution of the composite service. To measure such satisfaction, researchers again draw on utility theory. The objective function is constructed by the weighted sum of the end-to-end QoS attributes' utility functions. An example objective function is presented in Eq. (13.4) below, where the service requester wants to minimize the price (or maximize the price utility, U_P) of the composite service, at the same time, maximizing the availability's utility, U_A.

$$\text{Maximize} \qquad w_P \cdot U_P + w_A \cdot U_A \tag{13.4}$$

$$\text{Subject to:} \qquad U_P = \sum_i \frac{P^{MAX} - \sum_j p_{ij} \cdot x_{ij}}{P^{MAX} - P^{MIN}} \tag{13.5}$$

$$U_A = \sum_i \frac{\prod_j a_{ij} \cdot x_{ij} - A^{MIN}}{A^{MAX} - A^{MIN}} \tag{13.6}$$

$$\sum_{i=1}^{m_j} x_{ij} = 1, \qquad x_{ij} \in 0, 1 \tag{13.7}$$

The price offered by service$_{ij}$ for executing task$_j$ in the BP is denoted as p_{ij}, the aggregation of all the offeres for the tasks in the BP as $\sum_j p_{ij} \cdot x_{ij}$, and the maximum and minimum price offers for the business process as P^{MAX} and P^{MIN}. A similar explanation applies to Eq. (13.6) for availability. Given a BP with J number of tasks, there will be J classes of candidate services where all the m_j candidate services in the jth class, can execute jth task ($j \in J$). Then, the decision variable x_{ij} is defined to be equal to 1 if the candidate web service$_{ij}$, in service class j, is assigned to execute task j or zero otherwise. Equation (13.7) ensures that only one service is selected from each class to execute the related task.

- Constraints: Service requester may have some constraints over the value of the QoS attributes which affects the choice of services for the BP. For example, a maximum budget is available to get the composite service, or the execution time might not exceed a maximum for the composite service to be useful.
- Decision Variables: The choice of what will represent the decision variables determines the type of optimization problem. The dominant approaches are modelling the problem as *Integer Linear Programming (ILP)*, *Genetic Algorithm (GA)*, *Constraint Satisfaction*, and *Stochastic Programming*.

Integer Linear Programming (ILP)

One way of solving this optimization problem is to model it as an integer linear programming problem [4, 62]. In the ILP approach, decision variables are integers representing whether a particular service is selected for executing a specific task or not, similar to x_{ij} in Eq. (13.7).

This approach helps researchers utilize any of the many available ILP solvers today. However, these solvers are effective when the size of the problem is small. An increase in the number of candidate web services leads to the increase of the number of decision variables, which in turn results in the explosion of the search space, and the number of the conditions to be checked. Thus, the ILP approach is limited by how large the BP (number of the tasks) is and how many candidate services exist. Another limitation of the linear programming approach is that both the objective function and the constraints should be *linear*, regardless of the complexity of the QoS attributes and different structures that can be found in the BP.

Genetic Algorithm (GA)

To overcome the limitations of ILP approaches, researchers such as [10, 29, 37] have proposed to apply genetic algorithm for the service selection problem. Any GA starts with encoding the candidate solution in a computer processable manner, called *genome*. The GA creates a *population* of generally random solutions which will be evaluated according to a *fitness function*. Then, based on some selection criteria, some individuals are selected for reproduction. The motive to the reproduction is that the new generation will contain better solutions than the old one. Near optimal solutions can be found by repeating these steps. The algorithm stops when some conditions are met, e.g. a specific number of generations.

In the service selection domain, Canfora et al. [10] and Jaeger and Muehl [29] applied a simple one-dimensional coding schema for the problem representation, while others, including Ma and Zhang [37], have used more complex representations such as a relation matrix coding schema. In the former case, each *individual* represents the assignment of the candidates to the tasks. In the latter one, the matrix can represent all the execution paths of the BP at the same time. The GA's fitness function is designed to maximize some QoS attributes and minimize some others. When dealing with end-to-end QoS attributes, the aggregation function for each QoS attribute needs to be defined. Evidently, there is no need to build "linear" aggregation functions (in contrast to the ILP approach).

GA is an unconstrained search technique [21], making it necessary to find ways for integrating service selection constraints into the search process. The widely used technique is the *additive penalty method* where a penalty cost that is proportional to the total violation of each of the constraints is added to the fitness function [27]. Other techniques to incorporate constraints into the GA search, such as [11] and [42], have not found application in service selection literature.

Constraint Satisfaction

One variant of the optimization approach is presented by Lecue and Mehandjiev [36]. They argue that future semantic web will cater for millions of services, making *scalability* (in terms of the time required for WSC) the main objective to achieve. They proposed a fast selection approach which might not lead to an optimal composition. Modelling service selection as a constraint satisfaction problem, they use a stochastic search method (more precisely, a hill-climbing algorithm) to find the first set of services that satisfy the set of defined constrains (both in terms of functional and non-functional requirements).

Rosenberg et al. [50] has proposed to model the service selection problem as a *Constraint Optimization Problem (COP)*. COP is a generalization of the constraint satisfaction problem where constraints are weighted and the goal is to find a solution maximizing a function of weighted constraints. The main idea in their proposal is that instead of having all the constraints as hard ones, i.e. must be satisfied, there can be defined soft constraints which are optional and it would be "nice" to have them. This will lead to a more flexible composition process. Based on this idea, the proposed CO algorithm does not find the best solution that exists in the search space (in terms of the utility gained by service requester). Rather it searches for the best solution within the boundaries of constraints. They add up all soft constraints to form an objective function, trying to maximize it. However, as they have mentioned, this approach has scalability problem, not suitable for large problems.

Stochastic Programming

Stochastic Programming is another optimization approach to solve the service selection problem in the presence of uncertainty. For example Wiesemann et al. [55] argues that the nature of QoS attributes such as response time and price is *non-deterministic*, and hence the WSC should be treated as a decision problem under *uncertainty*. To incorporate the uncertainty, they assume that the decision maker (the service requester) uses a particular quantile-based risk measure called *average value-at-risk (AVaR)* to quantify the risks associated with time and cost uncertainties. In the optimization objective function, they minimize the AVaR of the random variables defined for the service response time, and invocation cost. More precisely, they build *the worst-case risk functions* corresponding to execution time and price, using the associated AVaR measures. These two criterion functions constitute the optimization's objective function. In their experiment, they compared their risk-aware formulation of WSC in terms of the execution time and the price of the resulted composite services, with those of the deterministic formulation of the problem. According to their findings, for every deterministic composite service, there exists a risk-aware composition with smaller cost and execution time.

13.5.2 *Negotiation-Based Approaches*

Negotiation-based approaches constitute an important stream of contributions to the composite service selection problem. *Negotiation* is a process of reaching an agreement that is beneficial to the involved parties through information exchange and compromises [35]. Negotiating parties usually have different preferences over the negotiation issues and they seek to reconcile these differences through negotiation.

In computer science and related research, negotiation as distributed search through a space of potential agreements [32], has been used for many years to solve a variety of problems, e.g. resource allocation in grid computing, and getting agents to cooperate or compete over a common goal in multi-agent systems. In the context of computer science research, we should make it clear that what we mean by negotiation here is *an automated process* where negotiation is performed automatically by a piece of software such as an agent, a web service, or a third-party broker system. The automated negotiator replaces the human negotiator and performs negotiation on negotiator's behalf.

In the web service domain, researchers have employed negotiation mainly for (semi)automatic creation of *Service Level Agreement (SLA)*. In general terms, SLA is an agreement between the service consumer and the provider. It may also be referred to as *contract, policy,* or *license*. In service oriented infrastructure, SLA is an automatically processable contract between a service and its client, where the client can be an organization, a person, or another service [53]. In *SLA negotiation*, service provider and requester negotiate over SLA terms such as QoS attributes, rewards, penalties, and deliverables, in order to come up with a formal SLA at the end of the process [63]. SLA negotiation solutions are divided by the assumption that the service provider is predetermined before the negotiation or not. The two corresponding approaches are called *pre-contractual SLA negotiation*, and *dynamic provider selection*.

- Per-contractual SLA Negotiation [25]: In this case, the negotiation is performed after service discovery and selection, meaning that the service provider is already determined. Service parameters are negotiated and fixed in order to define the concrete service which will be carried out. This is a one-to-one negotiation process between service requester and the selected service provider. Proposals in this area include, but not limited to [14, 24, 64].
- Dynamic Provider Selection: Here, the negotiation is performed after the service discovery and as a service selection mechanism, aiming at dynamically selecting the service provider that best matches the service requester's non-functional requirements. This is a one-to-many negotiation process between the service requester and the candidate service providers. A successful negotiation output can be used for contract specification.

Basically in the dynamic provider selection approach, a high-level negotiation process (overall negotiation process) is conceptualized that negotiates for the overall BP. It consists of multiple negotiation sub-processes (briefly negotiation process) each associated with one task in the BP. Each negotiation process, in turn, may include multiple negotiation threads, one thread for each candidate provider, to choose the best service for the specific task.

When building an automated negotiation solution, several key components comprising the general negotiation framework [19, 43] should be addressed. These critical components are:

1. Negotiation Object: the set of issues that the parties negotiate to reach an agreement over their values,
2. Negotiation Protocol: the communication and message exchange rules among negotiation parties,
3. Decision-making Model: the rules that the interacting parties follow to decide when to start negotiation, how to prepare an offer, acceptable agreement range, and the time to abandon negotiation.

Meanwhile, when dealing with negotiation at the BP level, negotiation by itself may not be enough for achieving the end-to-end QoS requirement and ensuring a successful overall negotiation. A further management layer, referred to in the literature as coordination [12], becomes necessary. In Fig. 13.3 below, we present a WSC negotiation framework. This extends the general negotiation framework with an additional component i.e. coordination model which includes aspects of coordination strategy and architecture as explained below:

Coordination Strategy: involves decisions on (a) time to initiate negotiation processes for each task: All parallel? Sequential? With what priority?, (b) the type of information to collect from ongoing negotiation processes and/or finished ones to improve the negotiation result, and (c) actions to take for improving the negotiation result or prevent its failure, based on the collected information.

Coordination Architecture: involves how many and what type of negotiators are involved in negotiation (agents, web services, broker systems), and the required number of coordination layers and their configuration.

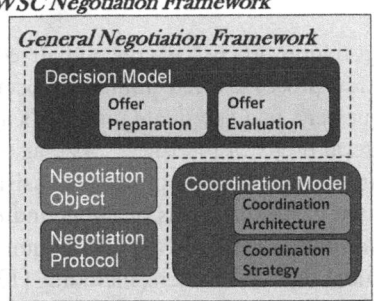

Fig. 13.3 WSC Negotiation framework adapted from the general negotiation framework [19, 43]

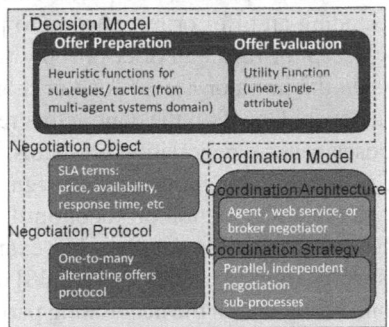

Fig. 13.4 The realization of the WSC negotiation framework based on the current literature

We discuss below the realizations of the key elements of the framework in extant research. A summary of this discussion is included in Fig. 13.4.

Negotiation Object

In service selection, the negotiation object has already been fixed: the service requester negotiates over the value of QoS attributes with different service providers. QoS attributes can be negotiable or non-negotiable. Negotiable attributes are those whose values can be determined at run-time, during service invocation [15]. Negotiation is performed over a range of values for each term; i.e. the service requester and the provider each has a minimum and a maximum admissible value for a QoS attribute. Price, availability, and response time are the more commonly included terms in recent service selection experimental investigations [48, 58, 64]. When the negotiation object includes more than one issue (or attribute), the negotiator needs to know the relative importance of each issue. This is usually realized through a normalized weight for each negotiation issue.

Negotiation Protocol

Although an overall negotiation process is conceptualized for the composite service, the actual negotiation processes that ultimately occur are bilateral negotiation between service requester's and candidate provider's agents. Some researchers have used a general bilateral protocol [4, 14, 24, 49], also called as *bilateral message exchange* or *bargaining*. This general protocol consists of a series of message exchanges between the two parties in terms of *offers* and *counter-offers*, until one of them accepts an offer or withdraws from the negotiation, e.g. due to reaching the maximum negotiation time. Some researchers, including [12, 57, 64], have followed a standard protocol such as *FIPA ICN IP* [22]. This protocol allows multi-round bidding, supporting one-to-many negotiation. Under this protocol, the negotiation initiator issues the initial *call for proposals (CFP)*. The other parties in negotiation (contractors) answer by sending an offer or by refusing to participate in the negotiation. The initiator may accept or reject an offer or reply with a revised CFP. The negotiation terminates when the initiator accepts one or more offers, or refuses all the bids without issuing a new bid, or if all the contractors refuse to bid.

Some researcher proposes *generic* negotiation protocols. The idea is not to bind the negotiation solution to a particular protocol at design time. Rather, delaying the determination of the suitable negotiation protocol until the actual execution of the negotiation process to make a flexible solution. For example, by extending the current WS-Agreement specification [3], Hudert et al. [28] defines a separate stage for protocol determination, during which the negotiating parties agree on a common negotiation protocol before the actual negotiation process starts.

Decision Making Model

The two important parts of a negotiation decision model are: how to evaluate a received offer as to whether accept it or not (*utility function*) and how to prepare a counter-offer (*tactic/strategy*).

(a) Utility Function

Each negotiator needs to specify its preferences about the negotiation object. These preferences guide its decisions during negotiation. In service selection, the dominant approach to express them is through utility theory; referred to in the previous section. Many researchers addressing SLA negotiation have employed single attribute linear utility function to evaluate the value of an individual issue [4, 57, 64]. This utility function is similar to the Eq. (13.1) mentioned in the foregoing. Here, q_j^{max} and q_j^{min} are defined as the maximum and minimum admissible values for jth QoS attribute according to the negotiator's preferences and constraints. The *parametric* single attribute utility function [14], and *multi-attribute* utility function representing the relative preference with respect to each pair of attributes [24] have also been discussed in the literature.

As QoS profile typically involves more than one attribute, the more commonly used technique to measure the utility of a profile with multiple attributes is to assign a normalized weight to each attribute and calculate the overall utility using a weighted linear additive function; similar to the aforementioned Eqs. (13.2) and (13.3).

(b) Negotiation Tactics

The two main approaches discussed in the literature to generate a counter-offer are *concession* and *trade-off*. In the concessionary approach, with every new offer the negotiator concedes to the other side of negotiation (opponent) by preparing an offer that has a lower utility value for itself, and apparently a higher utility value for the opponent. How much concession to make, and the pace of offering concessions to progress the negotiation process are determined by the negotiation influential factors. *Time, resource,* and *opponent behaviour* are three factors proposed by Faratin et al. [19], leading to three families of tactics: *time-dependent, resource-dependent,* and *behaviour-dependent* (or *imitative*).

In contrast, a negotiator with the trade-off approach tries to keep its utility value stable at a desirable level (the *aspiration* level) throughout the negotiation, while generating an offer that has more utility value for the opponent. This can be achieved by trading-off between the values of different issues [20], i.e. lowering the values of some QoS attributes while demanding more on some others. Such a strategy maximizes the chance of the offer to be accepted. Considering the fact that the negotiator usually has no information about the opponent preferences and utility function, the main challenge is how to determine which offer increases the opponent's utility value. The trade-off strategy proposed by Faratin et al. [20] uses the concept of fuzzy similarity [61] to approximate the preferences of the opponent. Assuming that the opponent's last offer reflects its preferences, the negotiator uses it as a reference point and prepares a counter-offer that is most similar to it. In the Yan et al. [57] proposal, the authors take advantage of the one-to-many negotiations occurring for a composite service. The utility value of all the received offers is calculated, and the one with the best utility is used as a reference point for preparing the counter-offer.

Faratin et al. [19, 20] and Comuzzi et al. [13, 14] have proposed heuristic approaches to define the counter offer for bilateral negotiation. Faratin's heuristic functions [19] are widely adopted by researchers, e.g. by [4, 49, 64] due to the clear distinction of tactic families (based on time, resource, and opponent behaviour), the clear mathematical representation, and the analysis of negotiation convergence for different parameters of the model.

The tactics in the Faratin model consider the influential factors in any negotiation. However, negotiation in WSC is a special case of negotiation consisting of multiple one-to-many negotiation processes. This introduces the opportunity for considering other influential factors to define new tactics. For example the Global Negotiation States factor proposed in [33] reduces the need for unnecessary negotiations in a one-to-many negotiation. The received counter-offers are compared to each other, and if all the counter-offers are far from the initial offer, the negotiator should be ready to make bigger compromise. Otherwise, if any counter-offer is more desirable than the negotiator's own offer, negotiator will raise its expectations and prepares the next offer based on the value of this desirable counter-offer.

(c) Negotiation Strategy

Negotiation strategy is another part of the decision model. Conceptualized at a higher level of abstraction than the negotiation tactics, it aims to maximize the utility function of the negotiator for a contract [19], by determining when to use which tactic to prepare the counter-offer, or what combination of tactics to use. More precisely, strategy can be thought of as the pattern of change in the weight of different tactics over time [63]. Taking it to one step further, Di Nitto et al. [16] states that strategy is not just about how to weight different tactics over time, but it can also address the following factors: (a) Changing the importance of negotiation issues over time, e.g. prefer availability over the response time if the latter cannot be improved so far, (b) Changing the severity of the constraint, e.g. relaxing some constraints on the values of some negotiation issues to reflect more concession when the negotiation time is about to expire.

Deciding on the best strategy for a negotiator involves the challenges addressed mostly in game-theory, microeconomics, and multi-agent systems and is outside the scope of this paper.

Coordination Model

To avoid the complexity of dependent negotiation processes, researchers including [33, 48, 57] assume negotiation processes to be independent and concurrent. For the same reason, no information is collected during an ongoing negotiation process.

In the Yan et al. proposal [57], the coordinator takes part only at the end of the process to either confirm or reject the negotiation result. Extending [57], Richter et al. [48, 49] attempted to make the coordinator more actively involved in the negotiation. Thus the coordinator does not wait for all the negotiation processes to finish. Rather, when a negotiation process finishes successfully, the surplus of the negotiation issue is calculated. Surplus is the difference between the actual agreed value and the least desired value (e.g. maximum payable price from the service requester point of view) of the negotiation attribute. Subsequently, it is distributed over failed or unfinished negotiation processes of those tasks which have dependencies to the task producing the surplus. The dependency is determined based on the QoS attribute under negotiation, and the task's position in the process, and is maintained in a tree-format. However, redistributing surplus may prevent the failure of the negotiation process when service requester has severe QoS requirements. It is not helpful in situations where negotiation fails due to the limited negotiation time available.

13.5.3 Hybrid Approach

There are service selection approaches which are not based on pure optimization or negotiation. In this section, we summarize two of the more important contributions.

Optimization + Configuration Approach

One attempt to proceed from a totally predetermined QoS profile to a more flexible one is the work by Comuzzi and Pernici [15]. In their approach, rather than providing a single value for each QoS attribute, the service provider publishes the set of values that they can support for each QoS attribute. For example, a provider offering a Traffic Monitoring Service can publish the offered quality for the refresh time (the time interval between the updates of the traffic information) as $\{2\,h, 1.5\,h, 1\,h, 0.5\,h\}$. This means that refresh time can be offered with any of the intervals of 0.5, 1, 1.5, or 2 hours. Additionally, instead of assuming a single value for the price, they have proposed a pricing model, including a set of pricing functions for the QoS attributes. Each attribute's pricing function determines how much it will cost for the service requester to select a specific level of quality. The web service total price is calculated as the sum of its constituting pricing functions.

The proposed service selection technique is in fact a local optimization where the web service with the lowest price for the *minimum quality profile* is selected. Minimum quality profile of a service consists of the lowest level of quality for each QoS attribute which still satisfies service requester's quality demand. When service selection is completed, a subsequent *agreement configuration* step is performed. During the configuration step, the difference between the price of the low quality profile of the selected service and the service requester's budget is used to improve upon the offered service quality for requester.

This research does not assume a pre-determined QoS profile for neither the service offer nor the service request. Instead, the service provider is able to publish the quality profile in the form of different quality levels that he supports. Besides, a higher level of flexibility is supported for the service price offering with the proposed pricing model. Thus, service requester can receive a personally-configured service, based on her preferences and constraints. However, the flexibility of the QoS profile in negotiation-based approach does not exist here, as no negotiation actually takes place. Rather, a configuration process tailors the service quality based on the requester's preferences and budget.

Optimization + Negotiation Approach

The research by Ardagna and Pernici [4] is another attempt to relax the assumption about a fully pre-determined QoS profile to a more flexible one, by combining optimization with negotiation. They start service selection as a MILP optimization

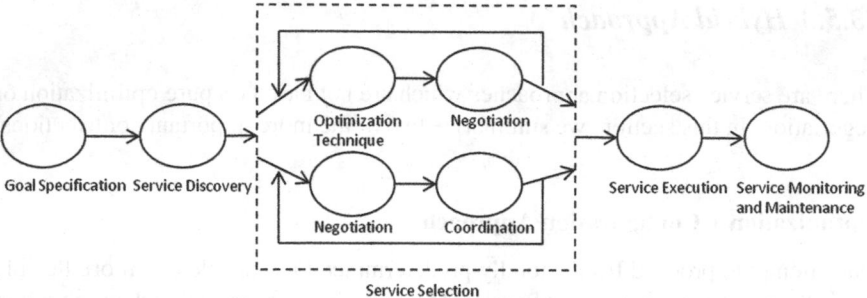

Fig. 13.5 Different perspectives on applying negotiation for service selection during WSC

problem. But if the optimization process fails to find a feasible solution due to sever QoS constraints for example, a negotiation process would initiate.

At the beginning of the negotiation process, first the execution plan that satisfies the maximum number of constraints is identified. Then, negotiation starts with any service provider that contributes to violating the global constraints of this execution plan. After the negotiation is completed, the providers who have agreed to improve their offered quality of service, in return for a higher price, will be added to the optimization space. In other words, negotiation is only used to find new QoS attribute values for web service invocations and it expands the optimization solution domain. As the last step of service selection, optimization is repeated with the new solution domain to find a feasible solution.

As mentioned in their paper, identifying the maximum number of constraints that can be satisfied is an NP-hard problem. Thus, they have assumed the global constraints are limited which allows to find the maximum number of violated constraints through an exhaustive search. Comparing their approach with pure negotiation-based approaches, coordination is not required here (Fig. 13.5). In fact, provider selection is performed through optimization, and not negotiation. However, in contrast to optimization-based approaches, the providers have a chance to improve their offered quality if their existing offers do not satisfy service requester's requirement.

13.6 Comparison

We present a comparison of the optimization and automated negotiation-based approaches to the service selection problem. The bases that we have used for the comparison are the following: the key elements of the proposed solutions, the nature of the QoS profiles in each approach, the reference disciplines that have influenced the literature, the ways in which the methods from the reference disciplines have been applied, the experimental strategies employed to validate the models, and some of the better-known tools.

The key elements in the optimization approach are a range of optimization models which specify one or more objective functions, a set of constraints and decision variables. For automated negotiation, the focus typically is on a set of negotiation objects or issues, a negotiation protocol, a complex decision model required for automated agents to conduct negotiation, and models for coordinating the negotiation process that unfolds over time and for arriving at a final decision on the concrete web services for the composite application.

The use of optimization techniques is generally restricted to situations in which the QoS profiles are pre-determined and fixed. This is somewhat unrealistic in light of the relatively dynamic environments that characterize the selection and composition of web services. Furthermore, it is not clear whether the web service providers will be willing to always create and publish static QoS profiles. The negotiation approach is suited for situations in which, at the very least, the price is negotiable. In many cases, price and at least a subset of the QoS attribute values are flexible which allow for more complex negotiation scenarios.

Automated negotiation approaches for service selection have drawn extensively on the more general agent-based negotiation literature for concepts, functions, and frameworks. These have the potential to address more realistic scenarios in the context of service selection. In particular, the relaxation of the assumption regarding static QoS profiles is an improvement over the less flexible optimization-based approaches. However, the dynamic aspects of negotiation approaches, including the need for a complex decision model and a cordination model, complicate the problem of finding globally optimum solutions. The hybrid models and proposals may offer potentially useful research directions in this regard.

The disciplinary influences that inform the former arise in mathematical and computing sciences whereas the negotiation approach draws on a broader, interdisciplinary body of knowledge. The contributing disciplines to negotiation approaches include computer science and artificial intelligence, behavioral sciences, economics and game theory, and mathematics, to name a few. Synthesizing robust negotiation models poses significant challenges and the results to-date on their applications in web service selection are still in their infancy. Much work still remains to be done on creating effective coordination models for automated negotiation to lead to useful outcomes for composite service selection.

The experiments that have been reported using both optimization and negotiation-based solutions cannot be described as convincing in that they typically incorporate very few QoS attributes to be considered representative of real-world scenarios. While the availability and maturity of available tools for optimization-based approach are very good, the tool space for negotiation is sparse. Though a range of optimization tools are widely available, scaling to larger problem size (in terms of number of tasks involved in BP, number of candidate services for each task, number of QoS attributes involved, number of global constraints etc), will often involve having to settle for feasible solutions, if any.

In general, optimization based approaches tend be more applicable under relatively static conditions in which the QoS profiles are fixed and the attribute values are pre-determined. However, if there is flexibility in the attribute values and tradeoffs

Table 13.1 The comparison of optimization- and negotiation-based approaches

Comparison bases	Optimization-based	Automated negotiation-based
Basic elements of the solution	Objective function, decision variables, constraints	Negotiation object (issues), negotiation protocol, decision model, coordination model
Web service QoS profile	Pre-determined, non-negotiable, not-customizable	Two types of QoS attributes in the profile: negotiable (flexible value), non-negotiable (pre-determined, fixed value)
Disciplinary influences	Well-developed body of knowledge available in optimization area	Automated negotiation approaches still in their infancy; very complex, and multi-disciplinary research area
Application of the original disciplines for compposite service selection	Optimization techniques have been specifically applied for composite service selection, considering the particular constraints and challenges involved in the WSC domain	Need for more inter-disciplinary approaches drawing on game theory, economics (auctions), and coordination theory.
Performed experiments	Typically include four to five QoS attributes in the scenarios.	Fewer QoS attributes included in the experiments. Generally not more than two, in order to manage complexity.
Facilitating tools	(M)ILP :available solvers, GA: well known algorithms, easy to implement	Automated negotiation support tools lacking. Domain-specific tools exist that assist human negotiators, e.g. Kasbah [38], Negoisst [51], CyberSettle[a]

[a] http://www.cybersettle.com/

are possible, a negotiation-based approach involving two or more agents engaging in an iterative communication and decision making process can become feasible. A summary of the comparison of optimization and negotiation-based approaches is presented in Table 13.1.

13.7 Conclusion

As the number of available web services with similar functionality but varying QoS attribute values increases, the problem of discovering and selecting the best web services for composing enterprise applications becomes more challenging. We have presented a comprehensive review of some of the important optimization- and negotiation-based approaches to the service selection problem in WSC. A brief overview of two of the hybrid models is also provided. In conclusion, optimization-based approaches assumption about a pre-determined profile is a hindrance in applying them for real service selection scenarios, considering the dynamic execution environment of web services. While in negotiation-based approaches this assumption is relaxed, the need for a complex decision model that guides the software agents in conducting fully automated negotiation makes their application unrealistic at least for the near future. There is a need for service selection techniques with more realistic assumptions in their service specification, discovery and selection models to make them relevant and useful for the emerging real world service selection scenarios.

References

1. Agarwal, V., Jalote, P.: From specification to adaptation: an integrated QoS-driven approach for dynamic adaptation of web service compositions. In: IEEE International Conference on Web Services (ICWS), pp. 275–282 (2010)
2. Alrifai, M., Skoutas, D., Risse, T.: Selecting skyline services for QoS-based web service composition (2010). doi:10.1145/1772690.1772693
3. Andrieux, A., Czajkowski, K., Dan, A., Keahey, K., Ludwig, H., Nakata, T., Pruyne, J., Rofrano, J., Tuecke, S., Xu, M., (2004¢ 2007), O.G.F.O.: Web services agreement specification (WS-Agreement). Technical report (2007)
4. Ardagna, D., Pernici, B.: Adaptive service composition in flexible processes. IEEE Trans. Softw. Eng. 33(6), 369–384 (2007)
5. Baryannis, G., Danylevych, O., Karastoyanova, D., Kritikos, K., Leitner, P., Rosenberg, F., Wetzstein, B.: Service Composition (2010). www.s-cube-network.eu/results/books/Bookv0.4.pdf
6. Berbner, R., Spahn, M., Repp, N., Heckmann, O., Steinmetz, R.: Heuristics for QoS-aware web service composition. In: International Conference on Web Services (ICWS '06), pp. 72–82 (2006)
7. Booth, D., Haas, H., McCabe, F., Newcomer, E., Champion, M., Ferris, C., Orchard, D.: Web Services Architecture (2004). http://www.w3.org/TR/ws-arch/
8. Brogi, A., Corfini, S.: Behaviour-aware discovery of Web service compositions. Int J Web Serv Res 4(3), 1–25 (2007)
9. Brogi, A., Corfini, S., Popescu, R.: Semantics-based composition-oriented discovery of web services. ACM Trans. Internet Technol. 8(4), 1–39 (2008). doi:10.1145/1391949.1391953
10. Canfora, G., Penta, M.D., Esposito, R., Villani, M.L.: An approach for QoS-aware service composition based on genetic algorithms (2005). doi:http://doi.acm.org/10.1145/1068009.1068189
11. Carlson, S.E.: A general method for handling constraints in genetic algorithms. In: Proceedings of the Joint Conference on Information Science, Citeseer, pp. 663–667 (1995)
12. Chhetri, M.B., Lin, J., Goh, S.K., Yan, J., Zhang, J.Y., Kowalczyk, R.: A coordinated architecture for the agent-based service level agreement negotiation of Web service composition. In: Australian Software Engineering Conference (ASWEC), p. 10 (2006)

13. Comuzzi, M., Francalanci, C., Giacomazzi, P.: Trade-Off Based Negotiation of Traffic Conditioning and Service Level Agreements in DiffServ Networks. In: Chiara, F., Paolo, G. (eds.) International Conference on Advanced Information Networking and Applications, vol. 1, pp. 189–194. Taipei, Taiwan (2005)
14. Comuzzi, M., Pernici, B.: An architecture for flexible Web service QoS negotiation. In: IEEE International Enterprise Computing Conference (EDOC), pp. 70–79 (2005)
15. Comuzzi, M., Pernici, B.: A framework for QoS-based web service contracting. ACM Trans. Web 3(3), 1–52 (2009). doi:10.1145/1541822.1541825
16. Di Nitto, E., Di Penta, M., Gambi, A., Ripa, G., Villani, M.: Negotiation of Service Level Agreements: An Architecture and a Search-Based Approach. In: Krämer, B., Lin, K.J., Narasimhan P (eds.) Service-Oriented Computing ¢ ICSOC 2007, vol. 4749, pp. 295–306. Springer, Berlin (2007). doi:10.1007/978-3-540-74974-5_24
17. El Haddad, J., Manouvrier, M., Rukoz, M.: TQoS: transactional and QoS-aware selection algorithm for automatic web service composition. IEEE Trans Serv Comput 3(1), 73–85 (2010)
18. Erl, T.: SOA: Principles of Service Design. Prentice Hall, USA (2008)
19. Faratin, P., Sierra, C., Jennings, N.R.: Negotiation decision functions for autonomous agents. Int. Journal of, Robot Auton Syst 24(3–4), 159–182 (1998)
20. Faratin, P., Sierra, C., Jennings, N.R.: Using similarity criteria to make issue trade-offs in automated negotiations. Artif Intell 142(2), 205–237 (2002). doi:10.1016/s0004-3702(02)00290-4
21. Fonseca, C.M., Fleming, P.J.: Multiobjective optimization and multiple constraint handling with evolutionary algorithms. I. A unified formulation. IEEE Trans Syst Man Cybernetics Part A: Systems and Humans 28(1), 26–37 (1998)
22. Foundation for Intelligent Physical Agents: FIPA contract net interaction protocol (2000). http://www.fipa.org/specs/fipa00029/SC00029H.pdf
23. Georgakopoulos, D., Papazoglou, M.P.: Service-Oriented Computing. MIT Press, Cambridge (2009)
24. Gimpel, H., Ludwig, H., Dan, A., Kearney, B.: PANDA: Specifying Policies for Automated Negotiations of Service Contracts. In: Orlowska, M.E., Weerawarana, S., Papazoglou, M.P., Yang J. (eds.) Service-Oriented Computing—ICSOC 2003, vol. 2910, pp. 287–302. Springer, Berlin (2003). doi:10.1007/978-3-540-24593-3_20
25. Grimm, S.: Discovery, Identifying Relevant Services. In: Semantic Web Services: Concepts, Technologies, and Applications. Springer, New York (2007)
26. Hao, Y., Zhang, Y., Cao, J.: Web services discovery and rank: an information retrieval approach. Future Gener Comput Syst 26(8), 1053–1062 (2010). doi:10.1016/j.future.2010.04.012
27. Hilton, A.B.C., Culver, T.B.: Constraint handling for genetic algorithms in optimal remediation design. J.Water Resour. Planning Manag 126(3), 128–137 (2000)
28. Hudert, S., Ludwig, H., Wirtz, G.: Negotiating SLAs-An approach for a generic negotiation framework for WS-agreement. Journal Grid Comput 7(2), 225–246 (2009). doi:10.1007/s10723-009-9118-3
29. Jaeger, M.C., Muehl, G.: QoS-based selection of services: the implementation of a genetic algorithm. In: Communication in Distributed Systems (KiVS), 2007 ITG-GI Conference pp. 1–12 (2007)
30. Jaeger, M.C., Rojec-Goldmann, G., Muhl, G.: QoS aggregation for Web service composition using workflow patterns. In: Eighth IEEE International Enterprise Distributed Object Computing Conference (EDOC), pp. 149–159 (2004)
31. Jaeger, M.C., Rojec-Goldmann, G., Muhl, G.: QoS aggregation in web service compositions. In: IEEE International Conference on e-Technology, e-Commerce and e-Service (EEE '05), pp. 181–185 (2005)
32. Jennings, N.R., Faratin, P., Lomuscio, A.R., Parsons, S., Wooldridge, M.J., Sierra, C.: Automated negotiation: prospects, methods and challenges. Group Decis Negot 10(2), 199–215 (2001)
33. Jiuxin, C., Yongsheng, L., Junzhou, L., Bo, M.: Efficient multi-QoS attributes negotiation for service composition in dynamically changeable environments. In: IEEE International Conference on Systems Man and Cybernetics (SMC), pp. 3118–3124 (2010)

34. Keeney, R.L., Raïffa, H.: Decisions with multiple objectives: preferences and value tradeoffs. Cambridge University Press, Cambridge (1993)
35. Kim, J.B., Segev, A., Patankar, A., Cho, M.G.: Web services and bpel4ws for dynamic ebusiness negotiation processes. In: Conference on Web Services, ICWS, vol. 3, pp. 111–117. Citeseer (2003)
36. Lecue, F., Mehandjiev, N.: Towards scalability of quality driven semantic web service composition. In: IEEE Int Conf Web Serv (ICWS), pp. 469–476 (2009)
37. Ma, Y., Zhang, C.: Quick convergence of genetic algorithm for QoS-driven web service selection. Comput Netw **52**(5), 1093–1104 (2008). doi:10.1016/j.comnet.2007.12.003
38. Maes, P., Guttman, R.H., Moukas, A.G.: Agents that buy and sell. Commun. ACM 42(3), 81-ff (1999). doi:10.1145/295685.295716
39. McIlraith, S., Son, T.C.: Adapting golog for composition of semantic web services. In: International Conference on the Principles of Knowledge Representation and Reasoning, pp. 482–496. Citeseer (2002)
40. Medjahed, B., Atif, Y.: Context-based matching for Web service composition. Distrib Parallel Databases **21**(1), 5–37 (2007). doi:10.1007/s10619-006-7003-7
41. Menasce, D.A., Casalicchio, E., Dubey, V.: On optimal service selection in service oriented architectures. Perform. Eval. **67**(8), 659–675 (2010). doi:10.1016/j.peva.2009.07.001
42. Michalewicz, Z.: A survey of constraint handling techniques in evolutionary computation methods. In: Proceedings of the 4th Annual Conference on Evolutionary Programming, pp. 135–155. The MIT Press, Cambridge (1995)
43. Mueller, H.J.: Negotiation principles. In: O'Hare, G.M.P., Jennings, N.R. (eds.) Foundations of Distributed Artificial Intelligence, pp. 211–229. Wiley, New York (1996)
44. Mukhija, A., Dingwall-Smith, A., Rosenblum, D.S.: QoS-Aware service composition in Dino. In: Fifth European Conference on Web Services, pp. 3–12 (2007)
45. O'Sullivan, J., Edmond, D., ter Hofstede, A.: What's in a service? Distrib Parallel Datab **12**(2), 117–133 (2002). doi:10.1023/a:1016547000822
46. Parra-Hernandez, R., Dimopoulos, N.J.: A new heuristic for solving the multichoice multidimensional Knapsack problem. IEEE Trans Syst Man Cybernetics A **35**(5), 708–717 (2005)
47. Rao, J., Su, X.: A Survey of Automated Web Service Composition Methods (2005). doi:10.1007/978-3-540-30581-1_5
48. Richter, J., Baruwal Chhetri, M., Kowalczyk, R., Bao Vo, Q.: Establishing composite SLAs through concurrent QoS negotiation with surplus redistribution. Concurrency Comput Prac Experience (2011). doi:10.1002/cpe.1727
49. Richter, J., Chhetri, M.B., Kowalczyk, R., Bao Quoc, V., Talib, M.A., Colman, A.: Utility decomposition and surplus redistribution in composite SLA negotiation. In: IEEE International Conference on Services Computing (SCC), pp. 627–630 (2010)
50. Rosenberg, F., Celikovic, P., Michlmayr, A., Leitner, P., Dustdar, S.: An End-to-End approach for QoS-Aware service composition. In: IEEE International Enterprise Distributed Object Computing Conference (EDOC '09), pp. 151–160 (2009)
51. Schoop, M., Jertila, A., List, T.: Negoisst: a negotiation support system for electronic business-to-business negotiations in e-commerce. Data Knowl Eng **47**(3), 371–401 (2003). doi:10.1016/s0169-023x(03)00065-x
52. UDDI Consortium: UDDI executive white paper (2001). www.uddi.org/pubs/UDDI_Executive_White_Paper.pdf.
53. Ul Haq, I., Paschke, A., Schikuta, E., Boley, H.: Rule-based validation of SLA choreographies. J Supercomput, pp. 1–22 (2010). doi:10.1007/s11227-010-0492-1
54. Wang, P.: QoS-aware web services selection with intuitionistic fuzzy set under consumer's vague perception. Expert Syst Appl **36**(3, Part 1), 4460–4466 (2009). doi:10.1016/j.eswa.2008.05.007
55. Wiesemann, W., Hochreiter, R., Kuhn, D.: A stochastic programming approach for QoS-aware service composition. In: IEEE International Symposium on Cluster Computing and the Grid (CCGRID '08), pp. 226–233 (2008)

56. Wilkes, J.: Utility Functions, Prices, and Negotiation. In: Buyya, R., Bubendorfer, K. (eds.) Market-Oriented Grid and Utility Computing. Wiley, Hoboken (2009)
57. Yan, J., Kowalczyk, R., Lin, J., Chhetri, M.B., Goh, S.K., Zhang, J.: Autonomous service level agreement negotiation for service composition provision. Future Gener Comput Syst **23**(6), 748–759 (2007). doi:10.1016/j.future.2007.02.004
58. Yan, J., Zhang, J., Lin, J., Chhetri, M.B., Goh, S.K., Kowalczyk, R.: Towards autonomous service level agreement negotiation for adaptive service composition. In: 10th International Conference on Computer Supported Cooperative Work in Design (CSCWD '06), pp. 1–6 (2006)
59. Yu, Q., Bouguettaya, A.: Multi-attribute optimization in service selection. World Wide Web **15**(1), 1–31 (2012). doi:10.1007/s11280-011-0121-9
60. Yu, T., Zhang, Y., Lin, K.J.: Efficient algorithms for web services selection with end-to-end QoS constraints. ACM Trans. Web (TWEB) **1**(1), 6 (2007)
61. Zadeh, L.A.: Similarity relations and fuzzy orderings. Inf Sci **3**(2), 177–200 (1971). doi:10. 1016/s0020-0255(71)80005-1
62. Zeng, L., Benatallah, B., Ngu, A.H.H., Dumas, M., Kalagnanam, J., Chang, H.: QoS-Aware middleware for web services composition. IEEE Trans. Softw. Eng. **30**(5), 311–327 (2004). doi:10.1109/tse.2004.11
63. Zulkernine, F., Martin, P., Craddock, C., Wilson, K.: A policy-based middleware for web services SLA negotiation. In: IEEE International Conference on Web Services ICWS, pp. 1043–1050 (2009)
64. Zulkernine, F.H., Martin, P.: An adaptive and intelligent SLA negotiation system for web services. IEEE Trans. Serv. Comput. **4**(1), 31–43 (2011)

Chapter 14
QoS Analysis in Service Oriented Computing

Huiyuan Zheng, Jian Yang and Weiliang Zhao

Abstract Quality of Service (QoS) is a major concern in the design and management of a composite service. QoS analysis becomes increasingly challenging and important when complex and mission critical applications are built upon services with different QoS. Thus solid models and methods to support for QoS predication in service composition become crucial and will lay a foundation for further analysis of complexity and reliability in developing service oriented distributed applications. In this chapter, we introduce a framework for QoS aggregation in service composition. The QoS of the component services can be single values, discrete values with frequencies, or probability distributions. Experiments are carried out to demonstrate the effectiveness and efficiency of the introduced method.

14.1 Introduction

Service-Oriented Computing (SOC) is a computing paradigm that supports the development of applications in distributed and heterogeneous environments [15]. Techniques of Web services create the opportunity for building composite services by combining existing elementary or complex services (i.e. the component services) from different enterprises and in turn offering them as high-level services or processes (i.e. the composite services) [24]. With more Web services available, QoS is an important selling and differentiating point of Web services [11]. QoS analysis becomes

H. Zheng (✉) · J. Yang
Macquarie University, Sydney, NSW 2109, Australia
e-mail: huiyuan.zheng@mq.edu.au

J. Yang
e-mail: jian.yang@mq.edu.au

W. Zhao
University of Wollongong, Wollongong, NSW 2522, Australia
e-mail: wzhao@uow.edu.au

A. Bouguettaya et al. (eds.), *Web Services Foundations*,
DOI: 10.1007/978-1-4614-7518-7_14,
© Springer Science+Business Media New York 2014

increasingly challenging and important when complex and mission critical applications are built upon services with different QoS. Thus solid model and method support for QoS prediction in service composition will lay a foundation for further analysis of complexity and reliability in developing service oriented distributed applications.

When a QoS metric, such as cost, execution time, of a component service is represented by single or discrete values, aggregation approach is adopted to calculate the QoS for the composite service [4, 8, 9]. When the QoS of component services are represented by standard statistical distributions, simulation approach is applied to compute the distribution of the composite service [5, 17]. The existing aggregation approaches can not handle QoS that are represented as probability distributions. Since simulation approach uses the standard statistical distributions to replace the real QoS distributions for component services, the calculation result can not be accurate by nature. Besides, simulation approach is time consuming. It can only be used in design time when the architecture and component Web services of a service composition are determined. However, the service environment can be highly dynamic [7]. New services coming into market or old ones becoming unavailable happens. Service-based processes should dynamically change to adapt to their environment. Composition engines, such as SELF-SERV [2], are designed for the purpose of run time composition. In these composition engines, QoS of the composite service needs to be estimated in real-time. Simulation method of QoS estimation will become a bottle-neck in real-time scenarios.

In order to overcome the problems mentioned above, we propose a systematic approach to estimate the QoS for composite services. A composite service is built up with four basic composition patterns, which are Sequential Pattern, Parallel Pattern, Conditional Pattern, and Loop Pattern. By recursively replacing patterns with single nodes with the same QoS as the composition patterns, a composite service will finally be represented by one node and the QoS of this node is the QoS of the composite service. Based on the QoS estimation method described above, it can be seen that three techniques are needed to compute the QoS for a Web service composition:

1. Web service compositions and composition patterns modelling, which will be discussed in Sect. 14.3;
2. A QoS calculation method for the four basic composition patterns, which will be discussed in Sect. 14.4;
3. An algorithm to explore the model of a composite service, identify composition patterns, calculate the QoS for the patterns, and get the QoS for the composite service, which will be described in Sect. 14.5.

In the rest of this chapter we will use the term *component QoS* and *composite QoS* to refer to QoS of component service and QoS of composite service respectively. We will also use QoS and QoS metric interchangeably.

This chapter is organised as follows: Sect. 14.2 discusses the work related to QoS estimation. In Sect. 14.3, the methods on modelling a Web service composition and composition patterns are introduced. In Sect. 14.4, QoS calculation methods for composition patterns are designed. In Sect. 14.5, an algorithm is developed to implement QoS estimation for Web service composition. Unstructured or nested composition patterns can be handled by the algorithm. In Sect. 14.6, experiments are carried out and the correctness and performances of the proposed methods are evaluated. Section 14.7 concludes the chapter.

14.2 Related Work

We will first review QoS modeling methods for Web services. Then, QoS monitoring methods for Web services will be summarized. Through these QoS monitoring methods, history QoS, i.e. QoS sample data, of a Web service can be obtained. The QoS sample data is a source of generating probability distributions for Web services. Finally, current QoS estimation methods for service compositions will be discussed.

14.2.1 QoS Models

Existing research in service QoS representation can be categorized as: single values representation, multiple values representation, and standard statistical distributions. In most work, each QoS metric is represented as a constant value [9, 25]. As the QoS of a Web service changes with time and environment settings, single value-modeled QoS does not reflect this variation. Standard statistical distributions are adopted to model QoS to solve the problem [4, 17]. Cardoso et al. [4] mentions that a QoS metric can be specified as a distribution function, such as Exponential, Normal, Weibull, and Uniform. Rosario et al. [17] argues that the contracts between Web service provider and client can be expressed as QoS probability distributions. T location-scale distribution is adopted to fit the original monitored QoS data of Web services. However, the reality is that an actual QoS probability distribution can come in any shape, which may not be able to fit into any well known statistical distributions. A more precise and general QoS modeling method has been proposed in our previous work [27], which is basically a free shaped probability distribution.

14.2.2 QoS Monitoring

The QoS of a Web service can be obtained through QoS monitoring. There are three strategies for QoS monitoring depending on where the measurement takes place:

(1) Client-side monitoring: the measurement of QoS is on the client side. QoS metric that depends on user experience, such as response time, needs to be measured on the client side. Mani and Nagarajan [12] measure response time through recording the time difference between a client receiving and sending out a SOAP

message. Wickramage and Weerawarana [23] illustrate 15 factors that affect response time. By testing the response time of SOAP messages with different complexities and payloads, the performances of different Web service frameworks are compared. Rosenberg et al. [18] develop a client side based method to measure QoS metrics such as response time, latency, etc. A QoS monitoring mechanism is introduced in [10] based on feedback provided by clients. The clients run the monitoring code and periodically report feedback to a trusted centre where the QoS for each provider is gathered and estimated.

(2) Server-side monitoring: the measurement of QoS is on the server side [1]. This technique requires access to the actual Web service implementation, which is not always possible in practice. Michlmayr et al. [13] measure QoS such as payloads of a Web service through their server side based method.

(3) Third party based monitoring: the measurement of QoS is carried out by a third party [28]. Third parties will periodically probes the service from different geographic locations under various network conditions and generate the QoS.

14.2.3 Composite QoS Aggregation

For single values represented QoS, aggregation method [4, 9] is proposed to calculate the composite QoS. A composition can be regarded as being composed of different composition patterns. Formulae to calculate QoS for these patterns are given. But these formulae can only be applied to single values.

For multiple values represented QoS [8], the calculation method is pretty much the same as it is for single values, except that the probability of each QoS value of the composite service are taken into account.

For standard distribution represented QoS [4, 17], simulation approaches are applied to estimate the composite QoS. A simulation needs to be run for thousands of times before a QoS sample for the composite service can be obtained. Simulation method is time consuming. An efficient method is necessary for estimating the QoS probability distributions of composite services, which is the focus of this paper.

14.2.4 Service Modelling and Processing

Aggregation methods [4, 9] are based on the assumption that the process of a Web service composition is well structured so that the composition patterns can be removed out one after another. One node will be left in the process finally, the QoS of which is the QoS of the Web service composition.

The QoS aggregation method [6] extends [4, 9] by handling unstructured patterns including unstructured conditional patterns and some types of loops with single entry and multiple exits. Dumas et al. [6] make use of the Refined Process Structure Tree (RPST) [21] to handle the process of a Web service composition. Specifically, Single Entry Single Exit (SESE) structures in a process can be decomposed recursively from a graph at a complexity of $O(|A|)$ ($|A|$ is the number of arcs in a graph) and a hierarchical tree structure (i.e., the RPST) is generated with the tree root representing the process and the children representing SESE regions. By aggregating the QoS recursively, the QoS of the root of the RPST can be computed, i.e., the QoS of a Web service composition is obtained. Restricted by the fact that the nodes of the RPST have to be SESE regions, the loop handled in [6] has to be in the form that it has only one entry, each exit of the loop goes to a SESE region, and all the SESE regions succeeding the exits of the loop join the same point, i.e., the single-entry-multi-exit loop together with its succeeding exit SESE regions form an SESE region.

An activity graph is proposed in [14] to model the control flows and activities in a WS-BPEL process. Nodes in an activity graph represent activities/scopes/handlers of the WS-BPEL process and the root of the activity graph is the *process* scope. The QoS is calculated from the leaf nodes to the root, the QoS of which is the QoS of the WS-BPEL process. By doing so, unstructured conditional patterns are handled but still leaving unstructured loop patterns an open problem. A directed solid arc in an activity graph represents the target node being an activity/scope/handler within the source node represented activity/scope/handler. A directed dashed arc represents the target node is an activity/scope/handler succeeding the source node represented activity/scope/handler.

The QoS analysis methods in [4, 6, 9, 14] are not able to compute the QoS and probability for each execution path of the Web service composition.

The approach proposed in [29, 26] does not put any constraint on the forms of the loop patterns and is able to handle general loop patterns including MEME loops.

14.3 Composite Service Modelling

Workflow control patterns in real-life business scenarios have been identified in [20]. We choose from [20] the basic patterns that are supported by business process execution language for Web services (BPEL4WS) [3]. These basic patterns include sequential pattern, parallel pattern, conditional pattern, and loop pattern. The process of a Web service composition is assumed to be built upon these four patterns.

We use a *service graph* to represent the process of a Web service composition to compute the QoS. This service graph can be generated from the commonly used process model, such as BPEL and BPMN, with additional information, such as QoS of the component services and transition probabilities. In the following subsections, we will introduce how composite services and composition patterns can be specified by the service graph.

14.3.1 Service Graph

In the graph, vertices represent component services and arcs denote the transitions from one component service to another. Formally:

Definition 14.1 Service Graph: Let S be the set of component services, T be the set of transitions in a composite service, P be the set of transition probabilities between two services linked by a transition, and Q be the set of QoS values of component services. A Service Graph is $G = (V, A)$, where

- $V = S$ are the vertices of the graph;
- $A = T \subseteq V \times \nabla \times V \times P \times Q$ are the arcs of the graph;
- $\nabla = \{-, \|_{split}, \|_{syn-join}, \|_{sng-join}\}$ are connection methods in the graph with

  - '$-$' denoting a sequential connection;
  - '$\|_{split}$' denoting a concurrent split connection;
  - '$\|_{syn-join}$' denoting a synchronised merge connection, i.e., the merge is triggered by the termination of all the concurrent running branches;
  - '$\|_{sng-join}$' denoting a single merge connection, i.e., the merge is triggered by the first finished branch and all the other branches that are still running will be ignored.

- $\forall a \in A$, $a = (v_x \Phi v_y, p)$ (where $\Phi \in \nabla$ and $p \in P$) denotes that the arc from vertex v_x to v_y is a Φ (sequential, concurrent split, synchronised merge, or single merge connection) arc and the transition probability is p.
- $\forall v \in V, q \ (\in Q)$ denotes the QoS of vertex v; and if v_x is not the end vertex of G, there is $\sum_{i_s=1}^{N_s} p_{i_s} + \sum_{i_p=1}^{N_p} p_{i_p} = 1$ where p_{i_s} is the probability of a sequential outgoing arc of v, N_s is the number of sequential outgoing arcs of v, p_{i_p} is the probability of a Parallel Pattern splitting from v, and N_p is the number of Parallel Patterns splitting from v.

The method of deriving the transition probabilities in a composite service has been introduced in [4, 19]. For simplicity, we will not depict the QoS information of the service graph in figures.

14.3.2 Sequential Pattern

In a sequential pattern, one service runs after the completion of another one. Formally,

Definition 14.2 Sequential Pattern (see Fig. 14.1): In $G = (V, A)$, $G' = (V', A')$ is a Sequential Pattern where $V' = \{v_x, v_y | deg^-(v_y) = 1\}$ and $A' = \{(v_x - v_y, 1)\}$. A Sequential Pattern composed of vertices v_x and v_y will be recorded as '$v_x - v_y$' in its replacing vertex with the symbol '$-$' representing the sequential relation between vertex v_x and v_y.

Fig. 14.1 Sequential pattern

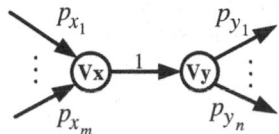

14.3.3 Parallel Pattern

In a composite service, if two or more services split from the same service, execute simultaneously, and converge into a service in synchronisation (referred to as *Parallel Pattern with a synchronised merge*) or the first finished branch triggers the following service (referred to as *Parallel Pattern with a single merge*), then this kind of structure is named as Parallel Pattern. Formally,

Definition 14.3 Parallel Pattern (see Fig. 14.2): In $G = (V, A)$, $G' = (V', A')$ is a Parallel Pattern with n concurrently executing vertices where $V' = \{v_{y_i} | i \in [1, n]\}$ and $A' = \{(v_x ||_{split} v_{y_i}, p) | i \in [1, n]\} \bigcup \{(v_{y_i} ||_{syn-join} v_z, 1) | i \in [1, n]\}$ for Parallel Pattern with a synchronised merge or $A' = \{(v_x ||_{split} v_{y_i}, p) | i \in [1, n]\} \bigcup \{(v_{y_i} ||_{sng-join} v_z, 1) | i \in [1, n]\}$ for Parallel Pattern with a single merge. v_x is the start point of the Parallel Pattern and v_z is the end point of the Parallel Pattern (v_x and v_z are not included in the Parallel Pattern). A Parallel Pattern composed of vertices v_{y_i} ($i \in [1, n]$) will be recorded in its replacing vertex as '$v_{y_1} ||_{syn-join} \cdots ||_{syn-join} v_{y_n}$' for synchronised merge or as '$v_{y_1} ||_{sng-join} \cdots ||_{sng-join} v_{y_n}$' for single merge with the symbols '$||_{syn-join}$' and '$||_{sng-join}$' representing the parallel relation among vertices v_{y_i} ($i \in [1, n]$).

It can be seen from Definition 14.3 that the probability values of the arcs $(v_x ||_{split} v_{y_i}, p)$ of the Parallel Pattern splitting from the start vertex v_x are the same which is p. p is the probability that the Parallel Pattern will be executed. If there is only one Parallel Pattern at vertex v_x, $p = 1$. If there are multiple Parallel Patterns starting at vertex v_x, we assume the execution probabilities for these patterns are different so that different parallel patterns can be distinguished.

For a Parallel Pattern without a start and end points (this could happen in the flow activities of WS-BPEL), i.e. there are only concurrent running Web services v_{y_i} in the pattern, empty actions need to be added as the start and end points for the Parallel

Fig. 14.2 Parallel pattern

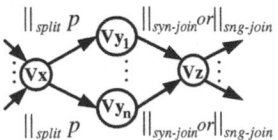

Fig. 14.3 A structured conditional pattern

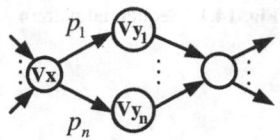

Pattern. The QoS, such as cost and execution time, of the empty action is zero. The
QoS, such as reliability, of the empty action is one.

In Fig. 14.2, the Parallel Pattern is composed of vertices $v_{y_1}, \ldots, v_{y_n}$. The con-
nections between the start point v_x and v_{y_i} is concurrent split '$\|_{split}$' and between v_{y_i}
and the end point v_z is synchronised merge for symbol '$\|_{syn-join}$' or single merge
for symbol '$\|_{sng-join}$'.

14.3.4 Structured Conditional Pattern

In structured conditional patterns, exclusive tasks split from the same task and merge
into another task.

Definition 14.4 Structured Conditional Pattern (see Fig. 14.3): In $G = (V, A)$,
$G' = (V', A')$ is a Structured Conditional Pattern with n exclusively executing
paths (i.e. only one path can be run at a time) where $V' = \{v_{y_i} | i \in [1, n]\}$ and
$A' = \{(v_x - v_{y_i}, p_i) | i \in [1, n]\}$.

14.3.5 Loop Pattern

Definition 14.5 Loop Pattern (see Fig. 14.4): In $G = (V, A)$, $G' = (V', A')$ is
an arbitrary Loop Pattern with n vertices in the Loop where $V' = \{v_i | i \in [1, n]\}$,
$A' = \{(v_i - v_{i \bmod n+1}, p_i) | i \in [1, n]\}$, and $P = \{p_i, p_{I_{ik}}, p_{O_{ij}} | p_i + \sum_{j=1}^{m_i} p_{O_{ij}} = 1\}$
(p_i is the transition probability for an arc within the Loop Pattern, $p_{I_{ik}}$ is the transition

Fig. 14.4 Loop pattern

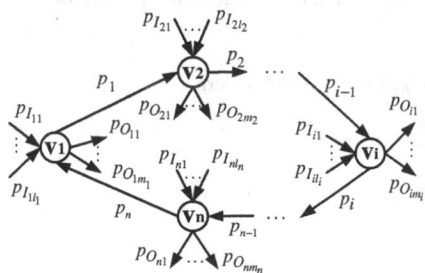

probability for an incoming arc of the Loop Pattern, $p_{o_{ij}}$ is the transition probability for an outgoing arc of the Loop Pattern). A Loop Pattern composed of n vertices v_1, ..., and v_n starting at v_1 will be recorded as '$v_1!v_2 - \cdots - v_i - \cdots - v_n!v_1$' in its replacing vertex.

Definition 14.5 defines a general loop, i.e. a loop with any number of entry and exit points.

Symbol '!' helps distinguish the label of a Loop Pattern from the label of a Sequential Pattern. For example, '$v_1!v_2 - \cdots - v_i - \cdots - v_n!v_1$' is for a Loop Pattern while '$v_1 - v_2 - \cdots - v_i - \cdots - v_n$' is for a Sequential Pattern.

So far, four symbols have been introduced to record the relations between the vertices in a pattern. They are: '$-$', '$||_{syn-join}$', '$||_{sng-join}$', and '!'. Symbol '$-$' has the lowest priority level. Symbols '$||_{syn-join}$', '$||_{sng-join}$', and '!' have the same priority level which are higher than '$-$'.

14.4 QoS Computation for Basic Composition Patterns

QoS aggregation formulae are developed in this section to calculate the QoS for composition patterns.

14.4.1 Approach Overview and Underlying Assumptions

The following assumptions have been made:

(1) The QoS (i.e., the same QoS metric) of different component services are mutually independent, i.e., the QoS of one service has no effect on the QoS of other services.
(2) QoS control is out of the scope of this paper. We only consider the case that the developer of a composite service makes use of the component services but has no control of the QoS of the component services. The QoS probability distributions of a component service are statistically estimated and have already taken into account different QoS influencing factors such as workload.
(3) The transition probabilities from one service to another in a composite service can either be provided according to the experience of the service developer at design time or be statistically estimated based on the execution history of the service. Detailed method of obtaining the transition probabilities in a composite service can be found in [4].
(4) QoS are represented as histograms with the same start point and width of intervals. There is more accurate method of getting the QoS probability distribution based on a QoS sample, which is out of the scope of this paper and can be found in [27].

14.4.2 QoS Probability Distribution Computation for Composition Patterns

14.4.2.1 Classification of QoS Metrics

The QoS metrics are classified into five categories according to their characteristics in different composition patterns, which are: additive, multiplicative, concave (i.e. minimum), convex (i.e. maximum), and weighted additive. For example, the QoS metric execution time reflects an additive behavior in a Sequential Pattern and convex behavior in a Parallel Pattern with synchronized merge. In this paper, the discussion of QoS analysis is based on these categories instead of individual QoS metrics, which makes the QoS analysis approach more general and fits more QoS metrics.

Examples of additive, multiplicative, concave, and convex QoS metrics are cost, reliability, execution time of a parallel pattern with a single merge, and execution time of a parallel pattern with a synchronised merge, respectively.

It is worth mentioning that multiplicative QoS metrics such as availability, reliability, and accessibility, are represented as a statistical percentage value (e.g., 90 %) rather than a distribution. Therefore, only four types of QoS metrics: additive, concave, convex, and weighted additive will be discussed for composite QoS calculation.

14.4.2.2 QoS Calculation Operations

We define four operations on QoS distributions, including QoSSum, QoSMin, QoS-Max, and QoSWeightedSum.

- QoSSum (denoted as ⊛): operates on the component QoS distributions by taking into consideration of the addition of their QoS values;
- QoSMin (denoted as △): operates on the component QoS distributions by taking into consideration of the minimum of their QoS values;
- QoSMax (denoted as ▽): operates on the component QoS distributions by taking into consideration of the maximum of their QoS values;
- QoSWeightedSum (denoted as ⊙): operates on the component QoS distributions by taking into consideration of the addition of their QoS values with path probabilities as weights. It is mainly used in the Conditional and Loop Patterns.

These operations and their relationships with composition patterns and QoS metrics are summarised in Table 14.1.

Formulae are developed for these operations. We introduce the following naming conventions:

- q is a variable representing a QoS metric;
- $f(q)$ denotes the density function of the probability distribution (PDF);
- $F(q)$ denotes the cumulative distribution function (CDF); $F(q)$ and $f(q)$ has the following cumulative relationship: $F(q) = \int_{-\infty}^{q} f(x)dx$ for continuous distributions or $F(q) = \sum_{q_i <= q} f(q_i)$ for discrete distributions.

Table 14.1 Operations for QoS Aggregation

Pattern	Operation	QoS Metric
Sequential	QoSSum	Additive
	QoSMin	Concave
Parallel	QoSSum	Additive
	QoSMin(single-merge)	Concave
	QoSMax(synchronised-merge)	Convex
Conditional	QoSWeightedSum	Any
Loop	QoSSum&QoSWeightedSum	Additive
	QoSMin&QoSWeightedSum	Concave

It should be noted that although the discussion is based on distributions, the developed formulae are also applied to single values. This is because single values can also be represented as distributions with the help of Dirac delta function.[1] For example, if the cost of a Web service is M, then $f(q) = \delta(q - M)$. If the cost of a Web service is N_1 with a probability of p_1 and N_2 with a probability of p_2 ($p_1 + p_2 = 1$), then the distribution of this Web service can be expressed as $f(q) = p_1\delta(q - N_1) + p_2\delta(q - N_2)$.

QoSSum Computing the PDF of the QoSSum of two component QoS distributions is a problem of deducing the PDF of the sum of independent variables, which is the convolution of each of their density functions [16],

$$f(q) = f_1(q) \circledast f_2(q) = (f_1 * f_2)(q) = \int_{\eta=0}^{q} f_1(\eta) f_2(q - \eta) d\eta \qquad (14.1)$$

where $f(q)$ is the PDF of the QoS of a composition pattern, $f_1(q)$ and $f_2(q)$ are the PDFs of the component services.

Let us take a simple example of execution time for a Sequential Pattern. Let the PDFs of the execution time of the two vertices be $f_1(t)$ and $f_2(t)$, respectively. The probability for the execution time of the first one being τ ($\tau \in (0, t)$) and the second one being $t - \tau$ ($t \in (0, +\infty)$) is $f_1(\tau) f_2(t - \tau)$. Therefore, the probability for the Sequential Pattern being finished at time t is the integral of $f_1(\tau) f_2(t - \tau)$ over $(0, t)$ where τ is the variable, i.e., $f(t) = \int_{\tau=0}^{t} f_1(\tau) f_2(t - \tau) d\tau$. The result is the same as what we get from Formula (14.1).

QoSMin The probability distribution of the QoSMin of n component QoS distributions is the distribution of the minimum of n independent variables which can be calculated as [16]:

$$F(q) = F_1(q) \oslash \cdots \oslash F_i(q) \oslash \cdots \oslash F_n(q) = 1 - \prod_{i=1}^{n}[1 - F_i(q)] \qquad (14.2)$$

---

[1] $\delta(x)$ is the Dirac delta function. $\delta(x) = +\infty$ when $x = 0$ and $\delta(x) = 0$ when $x \neq 0$.

where $F(q)$ is the CDF of the QoS of a composition pattern; n is the number of component services within this pattern; and $F_i(q)$ is the CDF of the QoS of the component service i.

Then the PDF can be obtained by differentiating both sides of Formula (14.2) with respect to q:

$$f(q) = f_1(q) \oslash \cdots \oslash f_i(q) \oslash \cdots \oslash f_n(q) = \sum_{i=1}^{n} f_i(q) \prod_{j=1,\cdots,n \& j \neq i} [1 - F_j(q)]$$

(14.3)

where $f(q)$ is the PDF of a composition pattern; n is the number of component services within this pattern; $f_i(q)$ is the PDF of the component service i; and $F_j(q)$ is the CDF of the component service j.

Let us take a QoS metric, response time as an example. Assume that X and Y are two Web services in a parallel pattern with a single merge. The probabilities for them to be finished within time t are $F_X(t)$ and $F_Y(t)$, respectively. The probability for neither of them being able to finish within time t is $(1 - F_X(t))(1 - F_Y(t))$, therefore, the probability for either of them being able to finish within time t is $1 - (1 - F_X(t))(1 - F_Y(t))$. The fact that at least one of the Web services can be finished within t means that t is the shorter execution time of the two Web services.

QoSMax The distribution of the QoSMax of n component QoS distributions is the distribution of the maximum of n independent variables which can be calculated as [16]:

$$F(q) = F_1(q) \oslash \cdots \oslash F_i(q) \oslash \cdots \oslash F_n(q) = \prod_{i=1}^{n} F_i(q) \qquad (14.4)$$

where $F(q)$ is the CDF of the QoS of a composition pattern; n is the number of component services within this pattern; and $F_i(q)$ is the CDF of the QoS of the component service i.

The PDF can be obtained by differentiating both sides of Formula (14.4) with respect to q:

$$f(q) = f_1(q) \oslash \cdots \oslash f_i(q) \oslash \cdots \oslash f_n(q) = \sum_{i=1}^{n} f_i(q) \prod_{j=1,\ldots,n \& j \neq i} F_j(q) \quad (14.5)$$

where $f(q)$ is the PDF of a composition pattern; n is the number of component services within this pattern; $f_i(q)$ is the PDF of the component service i; and $F_j(q)$ is the CDF of the component service j.

Let us take execution time as an example. Assume that X and Y are two concurrently running Web services in a parallel pattern with a synchronised merge. The probability for X and Y to be finished within time t is $F_X(t)$ and $F_Y(t)$, respectively. Therefore, the probability for both of them to be finished within time t is $F_X(t)F_Y(t)$.

The fact that both Web services can be finished within t means that t is the longer execution time of the two Web services.

QoSWeightedSum The QoS distribution for the QoSWeightedSum of component QoS distributions can be calculated as

$$f(q) = f_1(q) \odot \cdots \odot f_i(q) \odot \cdots \odot f_n(q) = \sum_{i=1}^{n} p_i f_i(q) \qquad (14.6)$$

where $f(q)$ is the PDF of a composition pattern; n is the number of component services within this pattern; $f_i(q)$ is the PDF of the component service i; and p_i is the execution probability for the component service i.

Here we can take execution time as an example. Assume X and Y are two Web services within a Conditional Pattern with the execution probabilities being p_1 and p_2, respectively. The probabilities for X and Y to be finished at time t are $f_X(t)$ and $f_Y(t)$, respectively. Therefore, the probability for the path of X to be finished at time t is $p_1 f_X(t)$ and for the path of Y to be finished at time t is $p_2 f_Y(t)$. Therefore, the probability for the Conditional Pattern to be finished at time t is $f(t) = p_1 f_X(t) + p_2 f_Y(t)$.

14.4.3 QoS Probability Distribution Calculation for Composition Patterns

So far, we have discussed the operations and formulae involved in computing composite QoS distributions. In this section, we will explain how component QoS distributions are aggregated for different composition patterns. Here, QoS metrics cost and time (execution time or response time) will be discussed as examples.

For a composition pattern with two component services, assume the probability distribution of composite QoS is $c(q)$ for cost, $t(q)$ for time, and the probability distributions of two component QoS are $c_1(q)$ and $c_2(q)$ for cost, $t_1(q)$ and $t_2(q)$ for time. According to Table 14.1, there are:

- the QoS distribution of a Sequential Pattern is the QoSSum of the QoS distributions of its component services, i.e.,

$$c(q) = c_1(q) \circledast c_2(q) \qquad (14.7)$$
$$t(q) = t_1(q) \circledast t_2(q) \qquad (14.8)$$

- the QoS distribution of a parallel pattern with a synchronised merge is the QoSMax of the QoS distributions of its component services, i.e.,

$$c(q) = c_1(q) \circledast c_2(q) \qquad (14.9)$$
$$t(q) = t_1(q) \oslash t_2(q) \qquad (14.10)$$

- the QoS distribution of a parallel pattern with a single merge is the QoSMin of the
  QoS distributions of its component services, i.e.,

$$c(q) = c_1(q) \circledast c_2(q) \tag{14.11}$$

$$t(q) = t_1(q) \oslash t_2(q) \tag{14.12}$$

- the QoS distribution of a Conditional Pattern is the QoSWeightedSum of the QoS
  distributions of its component services, i.e.,

$$c(q) = c_1(q) \odot c_2(q) \tag{14.13}$$

$$t(q) = t_1(q) \odot t_2(q) \tag{14.14}$$

- in a Loop Pattern:
  The QoS computation for Loop Patterns is more complicated than other patterns.
  Next, we will discuss it in detail.

An arbitrary loop has been defined in Definition 14.5 and shown in Fig. 14.4. We
will study the QoS computation method for the Loop Pattern when vertex v_1 is the
entry point. The QoS calculation method is the same when other vertices are the entry
points. We only use one incoming arc to indicate the entry point of the Loop and
ignore all the other incoming arcs. Doing this does not affect the QoS computation
result. This is because the QoS of a Loop Pattern is affected by the position of an
entry point, i.e., the point where a Loop starts, but not by the transition probabilities
of the incoming arcs of the entry point, i.e., p_I, which indicates the possibility of
entering the Loop and has nothing to do with the repeating of the Loop (which is
determined by p_i) or the jumping out of the Loop (which is determined by p_O).
That is also to say, only the transition probabilities within a Loop (i.e., p_i) and the
transition probabilities of jumping out of a Loop (i.e., p_O) are needed to compute
the probability for each possible execution branch of a Loop Pattern.

Based on the discussion above, the Loop Pattern in Fig. 14.5 is QoS equivalent to
the Loop Pattern in Fig. 14.4 when vertex v_1 is the entry point. Next, we will discuss
the QoS calculation method for it.

A Loop can be seen as a Conditional Pattern with infinite number of branches.
Figure 14.5 can be transformed into a structure shown in Fig. 14.6a. Each branch
$path_{li}$ represents the Loop being executed for l times and left from the ith node

Fig. 14.5 Loop pattern with
v_1 as the entry point

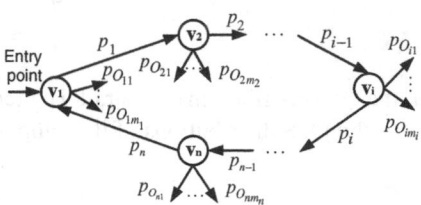

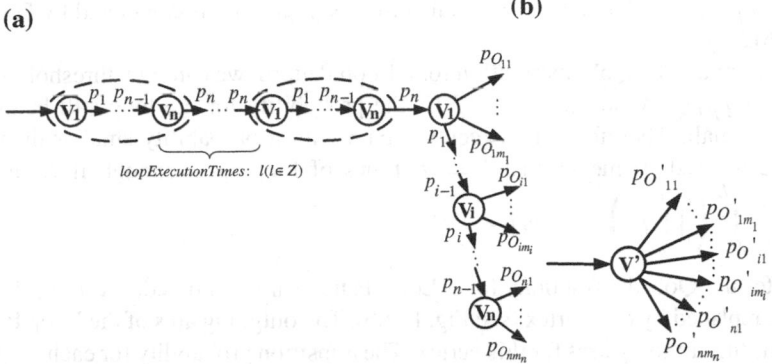

Fig. 14.6 Loop replacement **a** Equivalent Graph. **b** Equivalent Vertex

where $l = 0, 1, \ldots, +\infty$ and $i = 1, 2, \ldots, n$ (n is the number of vertices in the Loop).

The probability of each execution path $path_{li}$ can be calculated based on the transition probability information of each arc of the Loop:

$$P_{path_{li}} = \left(\prod_{k=1}^{n} p_k\right)^l \left(\prod_{k=0}^{i-1} p_k\right)(1 - p_i) \qquad (14.15)$$

where p_k is the transition probability from vertex v_k to v_{k+1} and $p_k = 1$ when $k = 0$, l is the number of times that the Loop is executed, n is the number of vertices in the Loop, and i is the index of the vertex which the Loop is jumped out of.

For both cost and time related QoS metrics, operation QoSSum will be used to calculate the the QoS distribution for each execution path since the vertices in each execution path compose a Sequential Pattern. There is:

$$f_{path_{li}}(q) = \underbrace{((f_1 * \ldots * f_n) * \ldots * (f_1 * \ldots * f_n)}_{l} * f_1 * \ldots * f_i)(q) \qquad (14.16)$$

where $f_k(q)$ is the QoS distribution of vertex k, l is the number of times that the Loop is executed, i is the index of the vertex where the Loop is jumped out of, and n is the number of vertices in the Loop.

Then the QoS distribution of the Loop is the QoSWeightedSum of the QoS of each execution path, i.e.,

$$f_{loop}(q) = \sum_{l=0}^{+\infty} \sum_{i=1}^{n} P_{path_{li}} f_{path_{li}}(q) \qquad (14.17)$$

where $p_{path_{li}}$ is calculated by Formula (14.15), $f_{path_{li}}(q)$ is calculated by Formula (14.16).

To compute the QoS distribution for a Loop Pattern, we can set a threshold value, TH, for $p_{path_{li}}$. When $p_{path_{li}} < TH$, the probability for the loop still being run is quite small. Therefore, the execution path with a probability smaller than TH can be ignored. It means that $l = L$ times of looping is enough if L satisfies

$$\left(\prod_{k=1}^{n} p_k\right)^{L} \left(\prod_{k=0}^{i-1} p_k\right) (1 - p_i) < TH.$$

After the QoS distributions for a Loop Pattern are computed, the Loop Pattern can be replaced by one vertex (see Fig. 14.6b). The outgoing arcs of the Loop Pattern become the outgoing arcs for this vertex. The transition probability for each outgoing arc has to be changed accordingly. The outgoing transition probabilities for the vertex in Fig. 14.6b are calculated as:

$$p'_{O_{ij}} = \sum_{l=0}^{+\infty} \left(\prod_{k=1}^{n} p_k\right)^{l} \left(\prod_{k=0}^{i-1} p_k\right) p_{O_{ij}} = \frac{\left(\prod_{k=0}^{i-1} p_k\right) p_{O_{ij}}}{1 - \prod_{k=1}^{n} p_k} \tag{14.18}$$

where $j \in [1, m_i]$ and $p_{O_{ij}}$ is the transition probability for the jth outgoing arc of vertex i in the Loop Pattern in Fig. 14.4 and $p'_{O_{ij}}$ is the transition probability for the corresponding outgoing arc of the vertex that replaces the Loop Pattern, and other parameters have the same meaning as indicated in Formula (14.15).

14.5 Algorithm to Estimate QoS for Web Service Compositions

To calculate the QoS for a composite service, we need a mechanism which can identify composition patterns in a composite service even if they are nested in each other or there are unstructured conditional patterns. By recursively identifying the composition patterns from a composite service, calculating the QoS for the patterns, removing these patterns, and aggregating the QoS, the QoS of the composite service can be obtained.

14.5.1 Algorithm Overview

The input of the algorithm is the Service Graph of a composite service as well as the probabilistic QoS of the component services. The output is the QoS probability distribution for the composite service. Because of the existence of unstructured patterns, we will first transform the Service Graph from a cyclic graph into an acyclic graph by removing Sequential, Parallel, and Loop Patterns. Then we will transform the acyclic graph into a rooted tree structure.

One way to explore a graph is depth first search (DFS), the time complexity of which is $O(|V| + |E|)$ [22]. We extend the recursive DFS algorithm by a postorder traversal method to handle nested composition patterns. 'Postorder' means that the processing for a composition pattern does not start immediately after this pattern is identified. Instead, it will be conducted after all the direct successors of the start point[2] of the pattern are fully explored. The pattern in the innermost will be identified and processed first while the pattern in the outermost will be identified and processed last. In this way, the problem of the existence of nested patterns is handled.

Three information are needed to identify composition patterns from a Service Graph:

- the status of a vertex, i.e. UNVISITED for a vertex that has not been visited, VISITING for a vertex that is being visited, or VISITED for a vertex that has been visited (i.e. all its successors have been visited);
- the connection way of an arc (see Definition 14.1), i.e. '-' for sequential, '$||_{split}$' for concurrent split, '$||_{syn-join}$' for synchronized merge, and '$||_{sng-join}$' for single merge;
- the transition probability of an arc.

Specifically: let vertex $nxtV$ be the direct successor of vertex $currV$, then $nxtV$ belongs to a

- Sequential Pattern: if there is only one outgoing arc for $currV$ and one incoming arc for $nxtV$ (i.e. the outdegree of $currV$ is 1 and the indegree of $nxtV$ is 1), then $currV$ and $nxtV$ compose a Sequential Pattern.
- Parallel Pattern: if the arc from $currV$ to $nxtV$ is '$||_{split}$', then $nxtV$ is a vertex in one branch of a Parallel Pattern; if the arc from $currV$ to $nxtV$ is '$||_{syn-join}$' or '$||_{sng-join}$', then $nxtV$ is the vertex to which all the branches of a Parallel Pattern join.
- Conditional Pattern: if the arc from $currV$ to $nxtV$ is '-' and the probability is not 1, then $nxtV$ is a vertex in one branch of a Conditional Pattern.
- Join Point for Two Paths: if the status of $nxtV$ is visited, then $nxtV$ is the join point for two paths of a graph, i.e. two paths merge to the same path at $nxtV$.
- Loop Pattern: if the status of $nxtV$ is visiting, then $nxtV$ is the start point of a Loop Pattern and $currV$ is its predecessor in the loop.

14.5.2 Algorithm for the Process of QoS Aggregation

Algorithm 5 gives the solution to calculate the QoS for composite services with arbitrarily combined patterns. The input Service Graph is initialized through function

---

[2] The start point of a Sequential Pattern is the foremost vertex; of a Parallel Pattern is the vertex from which all the branches split; of a Loop Pattern is the entry point of the loop.

Algorithm 1: Algorithm of the Calculation Approach for QoS Analysis

---

```
1   headT = Root of Tree T;
2   headV = Head of Graph G;
3   IniGraph(G); % initialize cyclic graph G;
4   DfsVstGrph(headV); % G is turned into acyclic;
5   IniGraph(G); % initialize acyclic graph G;
6   QoS = DfsVstAcyclcGrph(headV, headT); % calculate the QoS for the composite service;
7   function IniGraph(Grph G)
        foreach vertex currV in Graph G do
            vertex_status[currV] = UNVISITED ;
            loop[currV] = FALSE;


    function DfsVstGrph(GrphNd currV)
8       vertex_status[currV] = VISITING ;
9       EXPLORE1:
10      foreach unvisited outgoing arc of currV do
            Visit the tail vertex of the arc (i.e. nxtV );
11          if vertex_status[nxtV] == UNVISITED then
                DfsVstGrph(nxtV);
12          else if vertex_status[nxtV] == VISITING then
                loop(nxtV) = TRUE;

13      if edge(currV, nxtV) == '||_split' AND edge(nxtV, successor[nxtV]) == '||_{syn-join}' then
            QoS calculation for Parallel Pattern with synchronized merge according to Formulas 14.9 and 14.10;
            Replace pattern by one vertex;
14      if edge(currV, nxtV) == '||_split' AND edge(nxtV, successor[nxtV]) == '||_{sng-join}' then
            QoS calculation for Parallel Pattern with single merge according to Formulas 14.11 and 14.12;
            Replace pattern by one vertex;
15      if loop(currV) == true then
            QoS calculation for Loop Pattern according to Formulas 17 and 18;
            Replace pattern by one vertex;
16      while outdegree(currV) == 1 AND indegree(nxtV) == 1 do
            QoS calculation for Sequential Pattern according to Formulas 14.7 and 14.8;
            Replace pattern by one vertex (i.e. newV);
            Set currV as newV;
            Set nxtV as sucessor[currV];
17      vertex_status[currV] = VISITED ;
18      if indegree(currV) != 0 then
            Visit the most recently explored predecessor (i.e. preV) of currV;
            Set currV as preV;
            GOTO EXPLORE1;


    function DfsVstAcyclcGrph(GrphNd currV, TrNd fatherT)
19      sonT = Generate a tree node for currV;
20      Add sonT to tree T as the child of fatherT;
21      EXPLORE2:
22      foreach unvisited outgoing arc of currV do
            Visit the tail vertex of the arc (i.e. nxtV );
23          if vertex_status[nxtV] == UNVISITED then
                DfsVstAcyclcGrph(nxtV, sonT);
24          else if vertex_status[nxtV] == VISITED then
                Copy the subtree rooted at the tree node of nxtV as the subtree of sonT;
                Obtain one branch of the tree and calculate its QoS and probability;

25      if outdegree(currV) == 0 then
            Obtain one branch of the tree and calculate its QoS and probability;
26      vertex_status[currV] = VISITED ;
27      if indegree(currV) ! = 0 then
            Visit the most recently explored predecessor (i.e. preV) of currV;
            Set currV as preV;
            GOTO EXPLORE2;

28      calculate and return the QoS for the rooted tree;
```

IniGraph (line 16.3). Then, function DfsVstGrph removes all the Sequential, Parallel, and Loop Patterns from the input Service Graph and turns the Service Graph into an acyclic graph with only conditional structures (line 16.4). Next, the acyclic graph is initialized by function IniGraph (line 5). Finally, function DfsVstAcyclcGrph transforms this acyclic graph into a rooted tree and calculates the QoS (line 6). Function IniGraph initializes a graph by setting the statuses of all vertices to UNVISITED and the loop indicator at each vertex to FALSE (line 7).

Function DfsVstGrph performs a recursive depth-first search starting at $currV$ and transforms a Service Graph into an acyclic graph. First, the status of $currV$ will be marked as VISITING (line 8). If $currV$ still has any outgoing arc that has never been explored before, the tail vertex (i.e. $nxtV$) of the outgoing arc will be explored (lines 10–12). If the status of $nxtV$ is UNVISITED, a depth-first search starting at $nxtV$ will be performed by function DfsVstGrph (line 11); else if the status of $nxtV$ is VISITING, the status of the loop indicator at $nxtV$ is changed to TRUE (line 12), which means $nxtV$ is the start point of a Loop Pattern. After all the successors of $currV$ have been visited, the processing of the composition patterns starting at $currV$ begins (lines 13–16). First, the QoS of any Parallel Pattern or Loop Pattern starting at $currV$ will be calculated and the pattern will be replaced by a single vertex with the same QoS (lines 13–15). Then, any direct successor of $currV$ (i.e. $nxtV$) composes a Sequential Pattern with $currV$ will be removed until there is no Sequential Pattern left at $currV$ (line 16). After pattern processing, the status of $currV$ is changed to VISITED (line 17). If $currV$ has incoming arc, the algorithm will backtrack to the most recently explored predecessor of $currV$ (i.e. $preV$), set $currV$ as $preV$, and jump to *EXPLORE1* (at line 9) to explore other successors of $currV$ (line 18). The exploration of the Service Graph ends if $currV$ has no incoming arc, i.e. $currV$ is the start vertex of the Service Graph.

Function DfsVstAcyclcGrph performs recursive depth-first search starting at vertex $currV$ of an acyclic graph and generates a tree rooted at $fatherT$. To distinguish nodes in a graph with nodes in a tree, node is referred as vertex in a graph and is stilled called node in a tree. First, a child node of $fatherT$, i.e. $sonT$, will be generated for $currV$ (lines 19–20). If $currV$ still has any outgoing arc that has never been explored before, the tail vertex (i.e. $nxtV$) of the outgoing arc will be explored (lines 22–24). If the status of $nxtV$ is UNVISITED, a depth-first search starting at $nxtV$ will be performed by function DfsVstAcyclicGrph (line 23); else if the status of $nxtV$ is VISITED, the following will be done: find the tree node for $nxtV$; create the copy of the subtree rooted at this tree node; add the copy to node $sonT$ as the subtree of $sonT$; find the leaf nodes of the subtree of $sonT$, i.e. nodes that have no child; obtain one branch of the rooted tree by backtracking from a leaf node to the root; calculate the QoS and probability for each branch (line 24). If $currV$ is the last vertex of a graph (i.e. outdegree of $currV$ is 1), one branch of the tree can be obtained by backtracking from $sonT$ (which is the tree node for $currV$) to the root of the tree and the QoS and probability of the branch will be calculated (line 25). When all the successors of $currV$ have been visited, the status of $currV$ is changed to VISITED (line 26). If $currV$ is not the start vertex of a graph (i.e. indegree of $currV$ is not 0), the algorithm will backtrack to the most recently explored predecessor of $currV$ (i.e. $preV$), set $currV$ as $preV$, and jump to *EXPLORE2* (at line 21) to explore other successors of $currV$ (line 27). If $currV$ is the start vertex, the QoS of the rooted tree, i.e. the QoS of the composite service, will be calculated and returned (line 28).

14.6 Experiments

In this section, experiments have been done to compare the performance of the proposed QoS calculation method (referred to as *calculation method*) with simulation method. In a simulation method, the execution of a composite service is simulated by exploring the Service Graph of the composite service. One single value for per QoS metric of the composite service is obtained for each run of a simulation by aggregating the QoS of each vertex that has been visited during the exploration of the Service Graph. After running the simulation for a number of times, a QoS sample (containing all the simulated QoS) for the composite service can be obtained. This QoS sample can be used to generate the QoS probability distribution for a composite service.

14.6.1 Validation

First, we shall test the accuracy of the calculation method and the simulation method mentioned earlier.

A composite service and its component services (see Fig. 14.7) are deployed. Experiments have been done to monitor the QoS of the deployed composite service. The monitored QoS are referred to as *experimental result*. By comparing the composite QoS obtained by the simulation method and the calculation method (referred to as *simulation result* and *calculation result*, respectively) with experimental result, the accuracy of the simulation method and the calculation method can be verified. We only consider the QoS metric execution time in the experiments.

The seven component Web services in Fig. 14.7 are developed and deployed on Apache Tomcat 5.5 server. Their execution time distributions follow the distributions in Fig. 14.8.[3] The BPEL process executing the composite service in Fig. 14.7 is developed and deployed on an Active BPEL engine. The detailed information on service deployment is as follows:

(1) The simulation of the QoS probability distribution for a component Web service: An array containing 10,000 values whose distribution conforms to the

Fig. 14.7 An example of a service graph

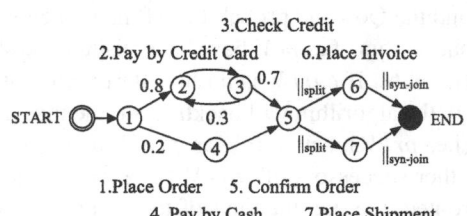

[3] These distributions are generated manually.

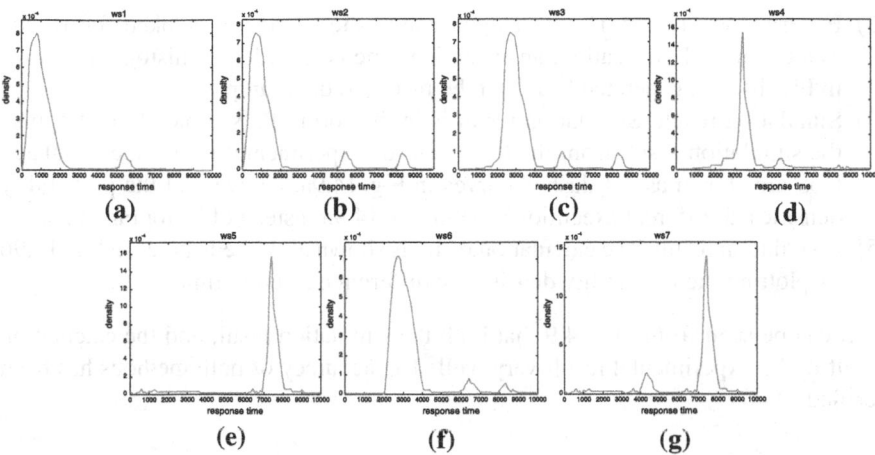

Fig. 14.8 Probability distributions of execution time **a** WS1 **b** WS2 **c** WS3 **d** WS4 **e** WS5 **f** WS6 **g** WS7

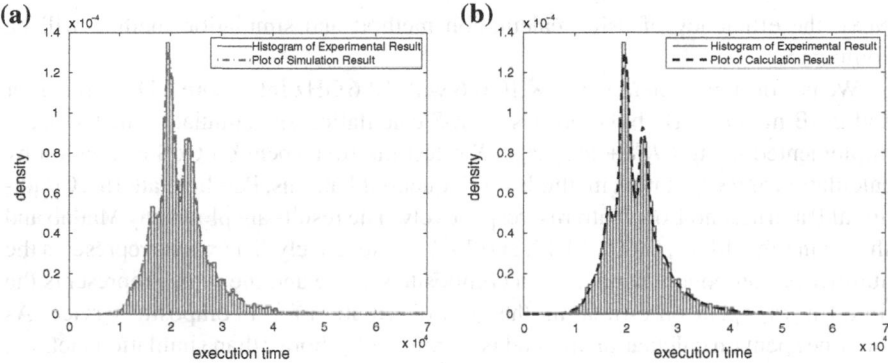

Fig. 14.9 Results of validation **a** Experimental and Simulation Results **b** Experimental and Calculation Results

probability distribution of the Web service is generated and stored in a file. For each execution, the Web service will randomly read one value from the file and suspend for the indicated amount of time before it sends out a response.

(2) The simulation of the transition probabilities within a composite service: A random number generator conforming to a uniform distribution is used. At component service 1 *Place Order*, a random number is generated and compared with 0.8. If it is smaller than 0.8, the output of service 1 is "Credit Card"; otherwise, the output is "Cash". At service 3 *Check Credit*, if the generated number is smaller than 0.7, the output is "Approved"; otherwise, it is "Disapproved".

(3) Experimental result: The developed composite service is invoked for 10,000 times. For each invocation, an execution time is recorded. A histogram, shown in Fig. 14.9, is generated based on the recorded data sample.

(4) Simulation result: Simulation result is in the form of a sample. To distinguish the simulation result from the histogram of experimental result, the simulated QoS are shown as dot-dashed curves in Fig. 14.9a, i.e. we plot the probability densities at different execution time in Fig. 14.9a instead of histogram bars.

(5) Calculation result: The calculation result is shown as dashed curves in Fig. 14.9b by plotting the probability densities at different execution time.

It can be seen from Fig. 14.9 that both the simulation result and the calculation result fit the experimental result very well. The accuracy of both methods has been verified.

14.6.2 Efficiency

Next, the efficiency of using calculation method and simulation method will be compared.

We perform tests on Mac OS X 10.6.6 with 1.86 GHz Intel Core 2 Duo processor and 2 GB memory. Both the proposed QoS calculation and simulation methods are implemented using C/C++ language. We test the time spent on QoS estimation by calculation and simulation methods for Sequential Patterns, Parallel Patterns, Conditional Patterns, and Loop Patterns, respectively. The results are plotted by Matlab and shown in Figs. 14.10, 14.11, 14.12, and 14.13, respectively. The x-axis represents the number of component services in a composite service and the y-axis represents the time (in μs) spent on estimating the QoS distribution for a composite service. As the time spent on calculation method is significantly shorter than simulation method,

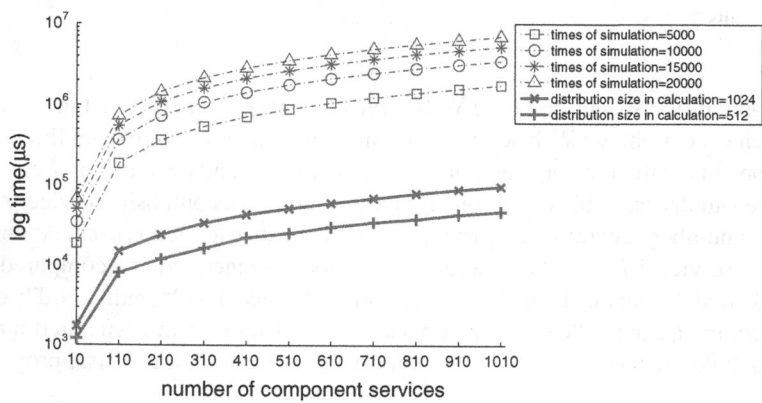

Fig. 14.10 Performance comparison—sequential pattern

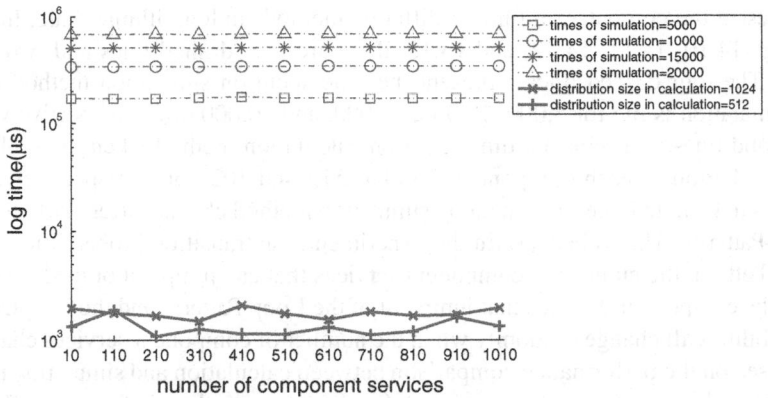

Fig. 14.11 Performance comparison—parallel pattern

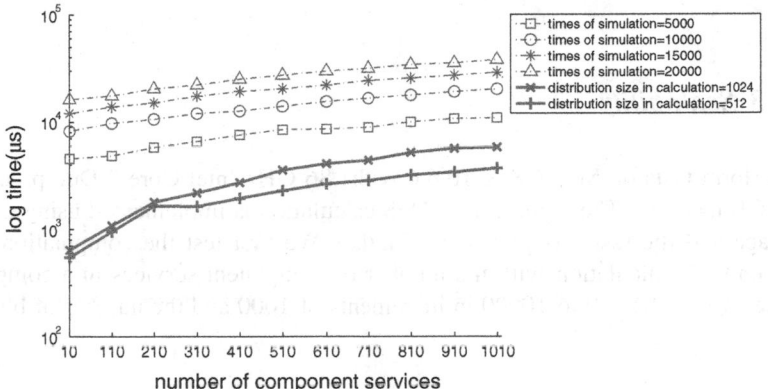

Fig. 14.12 Performance comparison—conditional pattern

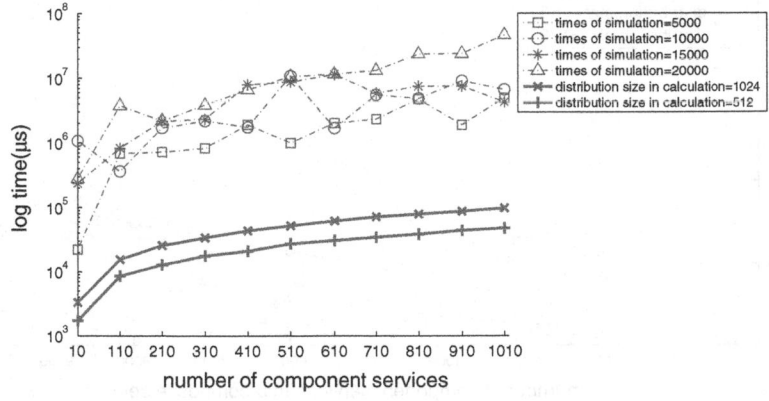

Fig. 14.13 Performance comparison—loop pattern

we present the computation time of different methods in logarithmic scale. In each of Figs. 14.10, 14.11, 14.12, and 14.13, there are four dashed lines and two solid lines. The four dashed lines represent the time spent on simulation method when the simulation is run for 5,000, 10,000, 15,000, and 20,000 times, respectively. The two solid lines represent the time spent on calculation method when the probability distribution of each component QoS has 512 and 1024 bins, respectively. One thing is to be noted: the time spent by simulation method changes irregularly for any Loop Patterns. This is because in the experiment, the transition probabilities in the Loop Pattern, the number of component services that can jump out of the Loop Pattern, the component services that jump out of the Loop Pattern, and the jumping out probabilities all change randomly when the number of component services changes.

Based on the performance comparison between calculation and simulation methods, it can be seen that the proposed QoS calculation method is far more efficient and outperforms simulation method in terms of computing QoS for all the basic composition patterns.

14.6.3 Scalability

We perform tests on Mac OS X 10.6.6 with 1.86 GHz Intel Core 2 Duo processor and 2 GB memory. The algorithm of QoS calculation is implemented using C/C++ language and the result is plotted by Matlab. We first test the computation time spent on QoS calculation with the number of component services in a composite service varying from 0 to 10000 in increments of 1000 and the number of bins for

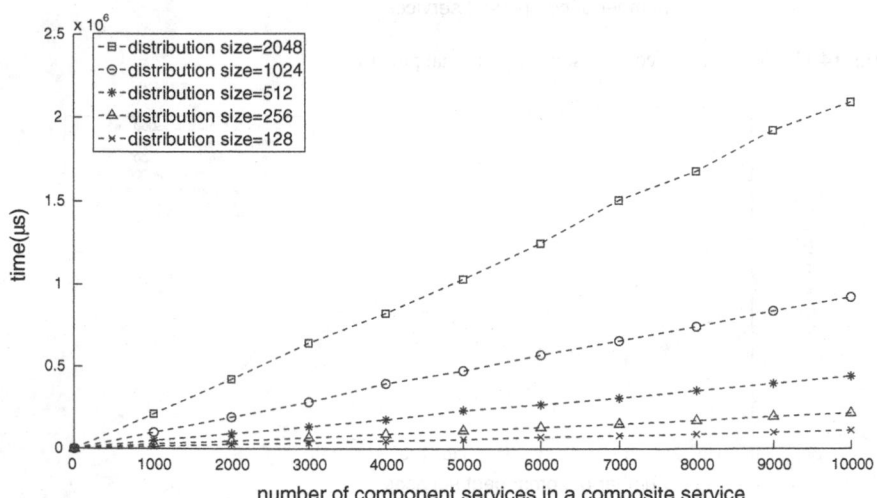

Fig. 14.14 Test of scalability

the probability distribution of each component service (i.e. distribution size) ranging from 128 to 2048 with a common ratio of 2. The result is shown in Fig. 14.14. In Fig. 14.14, there are five lines. For each line, the distribution size is a constant and the number of component services is from 0 to 10000 in increments of 1000. It can be seen that when the distribution size is fixed, computation time increases linearly with the number of component services. Moreover, computation time increases with distribution size when the number of component services is fixed.

It can also be seen from the experimental results that the performance of the proposed QoS calculation method is competent for real-time application since the computation time is less than 0.5 s for a composite service with 10000 component services when the distribution size is 512 or less. In fact, having 512 bins per component QoS distribution is more than enough to evaluate a composite QoS. If we use simulation methods for the same task (simulating QoS for a composite service with 10000 component services and each component QoS with 512 bins), it will take at least 512^{10000} times for the simulation method to get a result at the same precision as the calculation method.

14.7 Conclusions and Future Work

In this chapter, we present a general and systematic QoS analysis framework that is able to provide comprehensive QoS information for a composite service with the existence of complex composition structures. The problems dealt with in the existing methods for QoS aggregation become special cases in the proposed method. Most importantly, the proposed approach is much more efficient compared with existing approaches on estimating QoS based on probabilistic QoS. QoS solution is provided for loop patterns with any number of entry and exit points which has not been touched by existing work in terms of QoS analysis.

The approach introduced in this chapter is based on the following assumptions:

- The QoS of component services and the transition probabilities need to be given as input. This can be derived either from past executions or from domain expert knowledge.
- A composite service is built up upon four basic composition patterns: sequential, parallel, conditional, and loop patterns;
- There are some unstructured patterns that cannot be covered by the proposed method, such as loops containing AND-logic;
- The QoS of the component services are mutually independent and out of the control the composite service;
- The service graph that models the service composition has a single start and a single end node.

Future work needs to be done to relax or remove the restrictive assumptions.

References

1. Artaiam, N., Senivongse, T.: Enhancing service-side qos monitoring for web services. In: ACIS, pp. 765–770 (2008)
2. Benatallah, B., Sheng, Q.Z., Dumas, M.: The self-serv environment for web services composition. IEEE Internet Comput 7(1), 40–48 (2003)
3. Business process execution language for web services version 1.1. Technical Report, IBM, BEA Systems, Microsoft, SAP AG, Siebel Systems (2003)
4. Cardoso, J., Miller, J., Sheth, A., Arnold, J.: Quality of service for workflows and web service processes. J Web Semant 1, 281–308 (2004)
5. Chandrasekaran, S., Silver, G., Miller, J.A., Cardoso, J., Sheth, A.P.: Web service technologies and their synergy with simulation. In: Proceedings of the 2002 Winter Simulation Conference (WSC '02), pp. 606–615. San Diego, California, USA (2002)
6. Dumas, M., García-Bañuelos, L., Polyvyanyy, A., Yang, Y., Zhang, L.: Aggregate quality of service computation for composite services. In: ICSOC, pp. 213–227 (2010)
7. Dustdar, S., Schreiner, W.: A survey on web services composition. Int J Web Grid Serv 1(1), 1–30 (2005)
8. Hwang, S.Y., Wang, H., Tang, J., Srivastava, J.: A probabilistic approach to modeling and estimating the qos of web-services-based workflows. Inf Sci 177, 5484–5503 (2007)
9. Jaeger, M., Rojec-Goldmann, G., Muhl, G.: Qos aggregation for web service composition using workflow patterns. In: Proceedings of the 8th International Enterprise Distributed Object Computing Conference (EDOC '04), pp. 149–159. Monterey, California, USA (2004)
10. Jurca, R., Faltings, B., Binder, W.: Reliable qos monitoring based on client feedback. In: Proceedings of the 16th International World Wide Web Conference (WWW '07), pp. 1003–1012. Banff, Alberta, Canada (2007)
11. Lee, K., Jeon, J., Lee, W., Jeong, S.H., Park, S.W.: Qos for web services: requirements and possible approaches. Technical report, W3C Working, Group (2003)
12. Mani, A., Nagarajan, A.: Understanding Quality of Service for Web Services. IBM Software labs, India. www.ibm.com/developerworks/library/ws-quality.html
13. Michlmayr, A., Rosenberg, F., Leitner, P., Dustdar, S.: Comprehensive qos monitoring of web services and event-based sla violation detection. In: Proceedings of the 4th International Workshop on Middleware for Service Oriented Computing, pp. 1–6. Urbana Champaign, Illinois, USA (2009)
14. Mukherjee, D., Jalote, P., Nanda, M.G.: Determining qos of ws-bpel compositions. In: ICSOC 2008, pp. 378–393 (2008)
15. Papazoglou, M.P., Traverso, P., Dustdar, S., Leymann, F.: Service-oriented computing: a research roadmap. Int J Coop Inf Syst 17(2), 223–255 (2008)
16. Papoulis, A.: Probability, random variables, and stochastic processes. McGraw-Hill, New York (1965)
17. Rosario, S., Benveniste, A., Haar, S., Jard, C.: Probabilistic qos and soft contracts for transaction-based web services orchestrations. IEEE Trans. Serv. Comput. 1(4), 187–200 (2008)
18. Rosenberg, F., Platzer, C., Dustdar, S.: Bootstrapping performance and dependability attributes ofweb services. In: Proceedings of the IEEE International Conference on Web Services, pp. 205–212. IEEE Computer Society, Washington, DC, USA (2006). Doi:10.1109/ICWS.2006. 39. http://portal.acm.org/citation.cfm?id=1172963.1173044
19. Sheth, A., Sheth, A., Cardoso, J., Miller, J., Kochut, K.: Qos for service-oriented middleware. In: Proceedings of the 6th World Multi-Conference on Systemics, Cybernetics and Informatics (WMSCI 2002). Orlando, Florida, USA (2002)
20. van der Aalst, W.M.P., ter Hofstede, A.H.M., Kiepuszewski, B., Barros, A.P.: Workflow patterns. Distrib Parallel Databases 14(1), 5–51 (2003)
21. Vanhatalo, J., Völzer, H., Koehler, J.: The refined process structure tree. In: BPM, pp. 100–115 (2008)

22. Weiss, M.A.: Data structures and algorithm analysis in C, 2nd edn. Addison-Wesley Longman Publishing Co., Inc., USA (1997)
23. Wickramage, N., Weerawarana, S.: A benchmark for web service frameworks. In: Proceedings of the 2005 IEEE International Conference on Services Computing (SCC '05), pp. 233–242. Orlando, Florida, USA (2005)
24. Yang, J., Papazoglou, M.P.: Service components for managing the life-cycle of service compositions. J. Inf. Syst. **29**, 97–125 (2004)
25. Zeng, L., Benatallah, B., Ngu, A., Dumas, M., Kalagnanam, J., Chang, H.: Qos-aware middleware for web services composition. IEEE Trans. Softw. Eng. **30**(5), 311–327 (2004)
26. Zheng, H., Zhao, W., Yang, J., Bouguettaya, A.: Qos analysis for web service composition. In: Proceedings of the 2009 IEEE International Conference on Services Computing (SCC '09), pp. 235–242. Bangalore, India (2009)
27. Zheng, H., Yang, J., Zhao, W.: Qos probability distribution estimation for web services and service compositions. In: Proceedings of the 2010 IEEE International Conference on Service-Oriented Computing and Applications (SOCA '10), pp. 1–8. Perth, Australia (2010)
28. Zheng, Z., Zhang, Y., Lyu, M.R.: Distributed qos evaluation for real-world web services. In: Proceedings of the 2010 IEEE International Conference on Web Services (ICWS '10), pp. 83–90. Miami, Florida, USA (2010)
29. Zheng, H., Yang, J., Zhao, W., Bouguettaya, A.: Qos analysis for web service compositions based on probabilistic qos. In: The 9th International Conference on Service-Oriented Computing (ICSOC '11), pp. 47–61. Paphos, Cyprus (2011)

Chapter 15
QoS-based Service Selection

Fuyuki Ishikawa

Abstract As web services have become widespread, it is essential to ensure not only a service can provide the expected function (e.g., output) but also it can provide it in a "good" way. QoS (Quality of Service) refers to such non-functional aspects of services, including cost, response time, availability, reputation, and so on. QoS is significant for providers to differentiate their services from other functionally-similar services. On the other hand, it is necessary for clients, composers or brokers to assess services in terms of QoS and examine which services they should use. It is often necessary to select multiple services to compose a meaningful workflow or composite service, while balancing different QoS criteria according to preferences and constraints. This chapter introduces foundations for QoS modeling and QoS-based service selection. The foundations have been commonly discussed in recent research literatures, and can work as a basis to deal with specific foundations and to investigate further complex situations and attractive algorithms.

15.1 Introduction

Interoperation of web services has been facilitated through development of (de facto) standard specifications as well as libraries and frameworks to implement the specifications. Thus it is quite common and somewhat easy to run software systems that access functionality provided by remote services. Functionality can be explained in terms of *IOPEs*: obtain designated Output and Effect for given Input and Precondition.

On the other hand, functionality is not the only concern in software systems. For example, it may matter how quickly we can obtain the output after we make a request. *Quality* is the term that comprehensively explains such concerns other than IOPEs,

F. Ishikawa (✉)
National Institute of Informatics, 2-1-2 Hitotsubashi, Chiyoda-ku, Tokyo 101-8430, Japan
e-mail: f-ishikawa@nii.ac.jp

A. Bouguettaya et al. (eds.), *Web Services Foundations*,
DOI: 10.1007/978-1-4614-7518-7_15,
© Springer Science+Business Media New York 2014

involving performance, reliability, and so on. In traditional software engineering, requirements about quality aspects are also called as Non-Functional Requirements (NFR) in contrast with Functional Requirements.

The term *QoS* (*Quality of Service*) has been used to refer to quality aspects of web services, given specific characteristics of web services. Web services are usually considered as "black boxes," whose implementation and operation are encapsulated. It is because they are under control of other parties, or because even in a single party it is desirable to avoid complexity in understanding and managing the whole details of large complex systems. Due to this characteristic, there have been typical criteria such as availability and price. In addition, the characteristic also affects how QoS is analyzed for what kinds of tasks. Specifically, it is not possible to freely determine QoS of a web service provided by another party to meet quality (non-functional) requirements. Instead, it is possible only to select an "adequate" or "best" service from functionally-similar ones, possibly accompanying negotiation with the service providers (*QoS-based service selection*).

As the term refers to a wide range of aspects other than IOPEs, it is significant to clarify what specific aspects, or criteria, are discussed in actual analysis. For example, one may focus on three criteria of price, availability, and response time of services. Moreover, it is necessary to define metrics and models for each criterion. For example, one may want to discuss the worst case or upper bound of response time in milliseconds, instead of modeling continuous changes. Modeling of QoS criteria should be defined according to the purpose and the computational method for intended analysis.

As one of the most significant analyses, QoS-based service selection has been actively investigated in the research community. The problem has been considered significant as the number of published web services has been increasing, implying competition between providers of functionally-similar services [16]. On the other hand, the problem is technically challenging. First, it is necessary to consider multiple criteria of QoS (availability, price, etc.). This fact requires consideration of specific preferences and constraints by a client as well as evaluation of combinations of different QoS criteria. Secondly, an application is composed of multiple activities, and a service to use is selected for each of them. As quality of the whole application matters, it is necessary to evaluate composite or end-to-end QoS, such as the total price for the involved services. This fact leads to a large search space with different combinations of services. It is not adequate to select a service to use for each activity one by one, because such a greedy decision for local optimization may miss global optimization or satisfaction of global constraints (e.g., total budget).

This chapter provides introduction to technical foundations for QoS-based service selection together with underlying QoS modeling. There are two directions in which QoS is modeled as single values or as probability distributions. This chapter focuses on the former, QoS modeling as single values, to give introduction of QoS-based service selection.

In the remainder of the chapter, Sect. 15.2 introduces essential concepts and defines the terminology in this chapter. Section 15.3 describes different criteria of QoS and their expressions. Section 15.4 formalizes the problem of QoS-based service selection, and Sect. 15.5 discusses approaches to tackle the problem. Section 15.6 discusses variations of problem settings, before concluding remarks in Sect. 15.7.

15.2 Terminology

This section clarifies the terminology used in this chapter. Figure 15.1 illustrates the structure of QoS-based service selection. A *workflow* is specified to define a composite service through a meaningful combination of service functions, or *service types*. A *service* that implements each type can be selected according to *QoS* (*values* for a certain set of *attributes*). Details are described below.

15.2.1 Service Type

Suppose we are discussing use of web services in a certain system. It means we believe part of functional requirements for the system can be satisfied by web services that are available publicly or through partnerships. Examples of such functional requirements are "search for available rooms at hotels in a certain city" and "get current stock price for a certain company". In this chapter, the term *service type* is used refer to a specific function satisfied by web services. Other literatures may use different terms, such as service interface, service class, or abstract service (against service instance or concrete service).

This chapter will not provide a comprehensive discussion on how service type is described or how a web service is judged to or not to belong to a service type. For example, WSDL (Web Services Description Language) allows for description of web services [24]. We can consider the "interface" element in WSDL 2.0 defines the

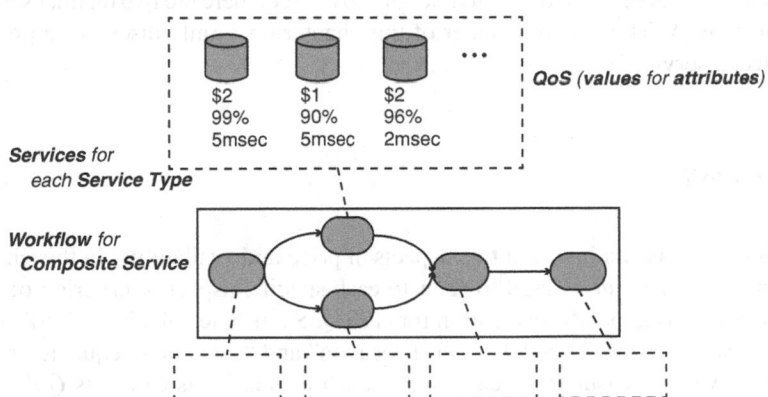

Fig. 15.1 Overview of QoS-based service selection

service type, which only defines provided operations and data types of their inputs and outputs. There can be multiple endpoints that has the equivalent interface with different access points (URLs and protocols). We can further leverage Semantic Web Service technology, to deal with synonyms and homonyms in data types as well as subtype relationships [21].

15.2.2 Service and Service Selection

There can be multiple providers (companies or other kinds of parties) that offer web services satisfactory in terms of the functionality or the service type. To compare the web services with each other, we therefore examine QoS aspects, considering our non-functional requirements. For example, each web service may require fee according to the number of invocations. Then we compare required fees per invocation. As another example, each web service may differ in how it ensures its availability. Then we compare values of ensured availability, or ratio of time periods where the service is available to the total time period.

The above discussion has mentioned different providers of web services satisfactory in terms of the functionality. Actually, each provider may offer a choice regarding what quality is ensured. For example, one provider may offer two plans: "Economy" for lower price with lower availability, and "Advanced" for higher price with higher availability. Another provider may offer a larger choice by allowing for selecting or negotiating detailed options (parameters).

Anyway, we want to distinguish different "ways of implementation" to select from, regardless of what they actually refer to in a specific scenario (provider, plan, or option). In this chapter, the term *service* is used to distinguish a specific QoS setting for a specific function. For example, suppose there are two providers of a certain service type. Company A offers two QoS plans, and Company B does not offer any choice. As a matter of convenience, this situation can be captured as a problem of selection from three services, even if people do not feel there are two distinct services by Company A. Thus the remainder of this chapter uniformly discusses a problem to "select a service".

15.2.3 QoS

The above discussion involved two aspects of price and availability. In this chapter, the term *QoS attribute* is used to refer to each specific aspect or criterion of QoS. Each service has a specific evaluation for each QoS attribute, which is described in a specific way, such as "1 US dollar per invocation" and "availability equal to or more than 95 % when measured for each year." Each evaluation is called as *QoS value*, and a set of evaluations for each service is called as *QoS vector* or merely *QoS*. The way of describing a QoS value is called as *QoS metric*, e.g., cost per invocation in

US dollar. A QoS metric defines how complex states of the real world are abstracted. The term *QoS model* is used to refer to a set of QoS attributes and their metrics, which defines the whole criteria used for comparing services.

This chapter does not rely on specific mechanisms to measure and collect QoS values. Providers often declare QoS values to attract clients by clarifying what they ensure or by offering a possible choice (plans and options). The term *Service Level Agreement (SLA)* is often used for clear specification of QoS to be ensured. The information on SLAs can be used for service selection. In addition, QoS values may be collected or validated through monitoring by clients as well as third-party brokers and rating agencies. Monitoring is significant for clients to be sure that the declared SLA is actually satisfied or to measure values of QoS attributes not included in the SLA. For example, management components are attached with the client and service to exchange SLA and check it by monitoring service invocation requests and responses [15, 22]. For automation and rigor, concrete and machine-processable descriptions are used for QoS metrics (when to measure, in what unit, etc.). A trusted third party may work to evaluate QoS values in place of each client. Such a party may also collect monitoring results from multiple clients to assess "trustworthiness" of the services (one of typical QoS attributes, described as reputation in Sect. 15.3.1.6) [12].

It is notable that the term QoS has been widely used in other communities such as network optimization [5]. Those communities have focused on computational execution and defined attributes such as throughput and availability. QoS for web services include similar attributes as significant aspects, but also consider a wider range of attributes. This is because services usually provide less granular functions, e.g., search for hotels, which are directly related to human personal or business activities. User-oriented attributes (e.g., reputation) appear as well as domain-specific attributes (e.g., the number of hotels the service deals with). In addition, QoS for web services is evaluated typically in the context of service combinations or workflows, which also makes computational difficulties (detailed in the following sections).

15.2.4 Composite Service

It is attractive to compose new services by using existing services, especially by combining functionality of multiple service types. For example, composition of a travel planning service involves a hotel search service, a flight search service, and so on. In this chapter, it is assumed a *workflow* or business process is defined to describe how services of multiple types are invoked to realize the composite service. The workflow defines activities that interact with services of specific types as well as control and data flow among the activities. The workflow definition is abstract in a sense it specifies only the service types involved. When services are selected for all the service types, a workflow becomes an executable *composite service*.

A composite service has a QoS vector that results from QoS vectors of the involved services. A simple example is the price of the composite service, which is total of prices for the involved services. The term *composite QoS* or *end-to-end* QoS is used to refer to QoS of a composite service. The composite QoS depends on QoS of the involved services, thus depending on a proper method for selection of these services.

There have been many languages to define a workflow, such as the WS-BPEL standard (Web Services Business Process Execution Language) [19]. A composite service is realized by allocating specific services to the workflow defined in WS-BPEL. The resulting composite service acts in the same way as an atomic (non-composite) service, which receives a request and returns a response. Thus the clients or brokers do not need to care about the fact it is a composite service. This chapter does not discuss such specific languages. Basic workflow patterns are discussed in terms of QoS, which provide a basis to deal with practical, complex languages such as WS-BPEL.

15.3 QoS Model

This section describes a variety of QoS attributes and their metrics through common examples.

15.3.1 Common Attributes and Metrics

There are a variety of viewpoints, or QoS attributes, for evaluating web services in terms of quality, or other than IOPEs. Sometimes domain-specific QoS attributes are considered. For example, users of a hotel search service may be interested in how many hotels the service deals with in which cities. Nevertheless, there have been several QoS attributes that are considered typical and common for general web services. In this chapter, representative QoS attributes and metrics are introduced from existing literatures, primarily on the basis of [2, 28]. Further QoS models (attributes and metrics) can be defined in a similar way when necessary. Many other literatures have discussed further QoS models [17, 20, 23].

15.3.1.1 Price (Cost)

As web services are often provided by other parties with specific expertise, use of a service often requires fee, especially when QoS is ensured. The attribute *price* describes how much it costs to use the service. An example metric is "fee per invocation in US dollar." Metrics may change depending on the pricing mechanism as well as the currency. For example, when pricing mechanisms are different between providers, a client may estimate his usage amount and consider a "fee for a certain expected amount of requests."

15.3.1.2 Response Time (Execution Duration)

Performance has been considered one of the significant non-functional requirements. The attribute *response time* describes how quickly the response can be obtained from the service after the request is sent. An example metric is "average delay in milliseconds between the moment when a request is sent and the moment when the response is received, in a certain set of trials."

Values of the example metric actually depend on not only QoS of the target service but also quality of the intermediate network. Providers may want to use another metric that refers to the time required for which they are responsible, e.g., delay between the moment when a request is received in their servers and the moment when the response is sent out from them. Each client may then additionally consider the global network latency [14]. Another notable point is response time requires modeling or abstraction of variable experiences about the delay for a certain method of measurement or estimation. The above example mentioned the average, though some clients are concerned about the worst or the variance. In any case, such accumulating metrics are useful to clearly compare complex experiences with different services.

15.3.1.3 Throughput

In actual implementation, it is impossible to ensure a certain response time for any number of requests. The attribute *throughput* describes how highly-frequent requests the service can deal with. An example metric is "the maximum number of requests that can be processed by the service in a certain time period." This metric mentions how the service can bears a burst of requests, possibly from multiple clients.

15.3.1.4 Reliability

When realization of a certain function is delegated to a web service, we want to be sure about its success. The attribute *reliability* describes how it is likely that the service makes the expected response. An example metric is "probability that a successful response for a request is received within a certain time period". This metric mentions a time period suggesting the deadline, because it is nonsense to discuss the possibility that a successful response is made eventually in the far future. In addition, it is practically impossible to distinguish whether the service is taking long time under successful processing or it is freezing.

15.3.1.5 Availability

As operation and maintenance is delegated to a web service, we want to be sure we can use it almost whenever we want. The attribute *availability* describes how it is likely that the service can be accessed. An example metric is "ratio of the time period where the service is available to the total period." Practically, it may be measured by making a periodic request for the service state.

15.3.1.6 Reputation (Trust)

It is difficult to clearly distinguish and separately define all the quality aspects about which clients are concerned. The attribute *reputation* describes how much a service is preferred or trusted by human users. An example metric is "average of ratings given by human users in the range [0, 5]." Such ratings can reflect a variety of aspects, such as integrated evaluation of the QoS vector, evaluation of considerate or poor technical support, and subjective evaluation of provided results (e.g., "natural" translation results).

15.3.1.7 Variations and Other Attributes

The above discussed only representative attributes and metrics for QoS. Different attributes and metrics can be discussed and introduced in a similar way. For example, the above discussion considered a metric for a fixed pricing mechanism. If a dynamic pricing mechanism is considered, as in Spot Instances of Amazon EC2 [1], a metric such as average or worst may be defined (as discussed for response time).

There are significant QoS attributes that have binary or enumeration metrics. For example, an attribute *privacy* may use a metric "certified for satisfaction of a certain guideline." Possible values are binary, "yes" or "no." As another example, an attribute *security authentication* may use a metric "supported authentication protocols." Possible values are enumeration such as "OpenID" or "Kerberos and RADIUS." Enumeration metrics can be decomposed into a set of binary metrics.

QoS attributes presented so far measure positive aspects of services. There are attributes that measure negative aspects of services. Examples include the number of administrative advices received for inadequate operations, the number of specification or SLA changes without prior notice, and reported SLA violations.

15.3.2 Composite QoS

QoS attributes and metrics described in Sect. 15.3.1 can be used for QoS description of composite services as well as atomic services. When we are going to construct a composite service, we want to evaluate a variety of possible combinations of services in complying with the service types involved in the workflow. For this purpose, *QoS aggregation functions* are defined to calculate composite QoS of a composite service by aggregating QoS of involved services.

Suppose a simple workflow consists of sequential execution of n services. Below examples of QoS aggregation functions are shown for each QoS attribute described in Sect. 15.3.1.

- Price: Sum of the values (total fee of all the involved services).
- Response Time: Sum of the values (average of total time required for execution of all the involved services).
- Throughput: Minimum of the values (bottleneck of the involved services).
- Reliability: Product of the values (probability that all the involved services succeed).
- Availability: Product of the values (probability that all the involved services are available).
- Trust: Average of the values (one way to estimate the rating of the composite service).

As another example, suppose a workflow consists of parallel (split-join) execution of n services, where requests are sent to all the services simultaneously and all the responses are waited for. In this case, the aggregation function of response time is the maximum of the values (the workflow needs to wait for the latest service response). The aggregation functions for the other attributes are the same as the ones for sequential execution.

Let's consider a very simple workflow language that only uses two constructs of sequential execution and parallel execution, which can be nested arbitrarily. Figure 15.2 shows an example of a workflow in this language. Suppose services $s1, s2, s3, s4$ are selected to be used for the activities *invoke*1, *invoke*2, *invoke*3, *invoke*4 in the workflow, respectively. In this case, $s1$ is first invoked, then parallely $s2$ and $s3$ are invoked. When both of $s2$ and $s3$ are completed, $s4$ is invoked. In this example, the response time of the composite service is calculated as

$$rt(s1) + max(rt(s2), rt(s3)) + rt(s4)$$

where $rt(si)$ is the response time of each service si. The aggregation function for sequential execution (sum) is applied to three services, in which the second one is a composite service and the aggregation function for parallel execution (maximum) is used. In this way, QoS values for a composite service can be calculated by recursively

Fig. 15.2 Simple example of workflow

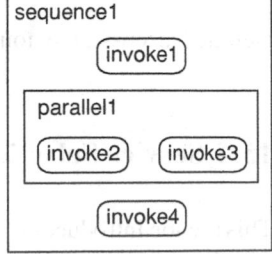

applying aggregation functions for each pattern of execution control (in this example sequential and parallel), and for each attribute.

Practical workflow languages such as WS-BPEL are much more expressive. Below briefly describes how QoS aggregation functions can be defined for other workflow patterns.

- Complex concurrent execution is sometimes described as a control graph, not in the structured way as in the example (e.g., the *flow* activity in WS-BPEL). In a control graph, each directed edge means that one activity can be executed when after another one is completed (restricted to be acyclic). In this case, aggregation functions may be defined over the graph structure. Specifically, the response time is calculated by identifying the longest execution path (the path whose sum of response time for the services on the path is the maximum among the paths in the graph).
- When conditional branches are included, aggregation functions become probabilistic and calculate expected values. For example, aggregation functions for a typical IF-THEN-ELSE control often use the following form.

    Probability the condition holds $*$ QoS value of the THEN sub-workflow
    $+$ Probability the condition does not hold $*$ QoS value of the ELSE sub-workflow

    Loop execution (while) considers expected values with probabilities of how many times the execution is iterated.
- Workflows are often defined to be tolerant of service failures. For example, a fault handler is often defined for invocation failure of a service to continue the workflow execution (not a fault handler that only gives error logs and exits). In that case, the availability of the service is excluded from the aggregation function for availability (the workflow is available even if the service is not available). Instead, a service invocation with a fault hander is considered as a conditional branch and the aggregation function uses the availability of the service as the probability. As another example, join conditions are often defined to denote conditions such as "execution can be continued if at least two of the three services in parallel execution are succeeded." When a join condition is attached with a parallel execution, the aggregation function for availability is changed to reflect it. With the example join condition, the availability of the parallel execution becomes the following (the probability it does not happen that all of the three services s1, s2, s3 are not available).

$$1 - (1 - avai(s1)) * (1 - avai(s2)) * (1 - avai(s3))$$

Detailed discussion is found in literatures such as [7, 18].

15.4 Service Selection Problem

This section introduces notations for the concepts introduced in the previous sections, and then formalizes the problem of QoS-based service selection.

15.4.1 Notations

Below defines notations for the concepts introduced in the previous sections, which defines part of the selection problem.

- Service types in a workflow: Service types involved in the target workflow are denoted by $S_1, S_2, \ldots, S_n$.
- Service candidates for a service type: Services in complying with the service type S_i are denoted by $services(S_i) = s_{i1}, s_{i2}, \ldots, s_{im_i}$.
- Services involved in a composite service: A set of selected services $cs = \{s_1, s_2, \ldots, s_n\}$ denotes a composite service obtained by selecting a service for each service type: $s_i \in services(S_i)$.
- Possible composite services: The set of possible composite services is denoted as $CS = services(S_1) \times services(S_2) \times \cdots \times services(S_n)$.
- QoS attributes: QoS attributes under consideration are denoted by $q_1, q_2, \ldots, q_l$. When specific attributes are significant, attribute names are used in subscript e.g., q_{price} and $q_{availability}$. It is assumed the metric for each q_k is defined.
- QoS: The QoS value of the service s about the attribute q_k is denoted as $q_k(s)$. Thus a service s has QoS, or QoS vector, $QoS(s) = \{q_1(s), q_2(s), \ldots, q_l(s)\}$.
- Composite QoS: Composite QoS for a composite service $cs = \{s_1, s_2, \ldots, s_n\}$ is denoted by $QoS(cs) = \{q_1(cs), q_2(cs), \ldots, q_l(cs)\}$. Each QoS value is calculated by the aggregation function: $q_k(cs) = agg_k(q_k(s_1), q_k(s_2), \ldots, q_k(s_n))$, which is defined by considering the QoS metric and the workflow structure.

We want to select a service for each service type ($s_i \in services(S_i)$, for $i = 1, 2, \ldots, n$) "properly" by considering the composite QoS $QoS(cs)$. Section 15.4.2 defines "acceptable" solutions, and Sect. 15.4.3 defines "best" solutions among "acceptable" ones.

To simplify the following discussion, it is assumed QoS metrics are defined so that higher numeric values mean better quality. This assumptions hold for some of the metrics in Sect. 15.3.1, namely, throughput, reliability, availability, and reputation. The other metrics, price and response time, can be easily converted, for example, by the form $A - bq$ where q is a value in the original metric. Binary metrics can be converted to numeric values, e.g., 1 and 0 (1 means presence of a good option). If this assumption is not introduced, each of the following definitions accompany the different version for the case lower values mean better quality.

15.4.2 Global Constraints

First, *constraints* are introduced to eliminate clearly unacceptable solutions. For example, there may be a limitation in a total budget, which puts the lower bound for the inverse price metric (converted to mean "the higher is the better"). In this way, all the constraints are denoted by lower bounds, given the assumption in Sect. refssec:notation.

Constraints $C = \{c_1, c_2, \ldots, c_l\}$ denote lower bounds for acceptable composite QoS, where each c_k is the lower bound for the metric of q_k. A composite service cs is called as an *acceptable solution* if $q_k(cs) \geq c_k$ holds for all quality attributes q_k.

The term *global constraints* or *end-to-end constraints* may be used to clearly state the fact that the constraints are on composite QoS, not QoS for each involved service. This fact implies it is not sufficient to have a local selection for each of the involved service types as such a greedy selection may miss the possibilities to satisfy the global constraints. This point is later illustrated in Sect. 15.4.4.1.

15.4.3 Utility Function

In addition to constraints, an *utility function* is introduced as a criterion for evaluating and comparing the whole QoS. The criterion reflects preferences of the evaluator, who is going to construct and provide a composite service based on the workflow. One of the popular definitions is described below.

15.4.3.1 Normalization

First of all, QoS values for different attributes, in different metrics, are converted into values in a uniform metric. It is already assumed that QoS metrics are all numeric and mean the higher is the better. Therefore only ranges of the values are adjusted, or normalized into the range [0, 1] for comparison.

In general, given a set of values $vs = \{v_1, v_2, \ldots, v_n\}$, the normalized value $v_{i(nml+)}$ of each v_i is defined as follows.

$$v_{i(nml+)} = \frac{v_i - \min_{v \in vs} v}{\max_{v \in vs} v - \min_{v \in vs} v}$$

This definition is for the case higher values are appreciated. In the other case, the numerator changes as follows.

$$v_{i(nml-)} = \frac{\max_{v \in vs} v - v_i}{\max_{v \in vs} v - \min_{v \in vs} v}$$

Following the assumption made in Sect. 15.4.1, this chapter only uses the *nml+* version.

The normalized QoS value can then be defined for each involved service s_{ij}, for each attribute q_k. This case focuses on (uses the maximum and minimum in) the set of QoS values by services of the same type $s_{i1}, \ldots, s_{im_j}$.

$$q_k(s_{ij})_{nml+} = \frac{q_k(s_{ij}) - \min_{h \in \{1,\ldots,m_i\}} q_k(s_{ih})}{\max_{h \in \{1,\ldots,m_i\}} q_k(s_{ih}) - \min_{h \in \{1,\ldots,m_i\}} q_k(s_{ih})}$$

The normalized QoS value can be similarly defined for a composite service cs. In this case, it is necessary to consider the maximum and minimum values in the set of all the possible composite services. For the aggregation functions described in Sect. 15.3.2, the maximum (minimum) values of possible composite services can be obtained by simply selecting the maximum (minimum) value for each service type. For example, the composite service with the maximum price can be obtained by selecting the most expensive service for each service type. Finally, the normalized QoS value is defined for a composite service cs as follows.

$$q_k(cs)_{nml+} = \frac{q_k(cs) - \text{min} q_k(CS)}{\text{max} q_k(CS) - \text{min} q_k(CS)}$$

where

$$\text{max} q_k(CS) = agg_k(\text{max}_{h \in \{1,...,m_1\}} q_k(s_{1h}), \ldots, \text{max}_{h \subset \{1,...,m_n\}} q_k(s_{nh}))$$
$$\text{min} q_k(CS) = agg_k(\text{min}_{h \in \{1,...,m_1\}} q_k(s_{1h}), \ldots, \text{min}_{h \in \{1,...,m_n\}} q_k(s_{nh}))$$

15.4.3.2 Utility

For the normalized values, *weights* can be used to denote preferences on QoS attributes. Weights $w = \{w_1, w_2, \ldots, w_l\}$ denote that each attribute c_k is weighted by w_k where $0 \le w_k \le 1$ and $\sum w_k = 1$.

A *utility* for a service s_{ij} and that for a composite service cs can be defined.

$$U(s_{ij}) = \sum_k w_k \cdot q_k(s_{ij})_{nml+}$$
$$U(cs) = \sum_k w_k \cdot q_k(cs)_{nml+}$$

As w_k and $q_k(s)_{nml+}$ are defined in $[0, 1]$, the value of $U(s)$ is equal to or less than the number of QoS attributes.

15.4.4 Service Selection Problem

With these definitions, a composite service cs is called as an *optimal solution* if it is an acceptable solution and it maximizes $U(cs)$. QoS-based service selection refers to a problem to find the optimal solution, or near-optimal solutions as it is practically hard to find the optimal solution.

15.4.4.1 Computational Difficulty

One simple approach may come to one's mind, to select the best service for each service type. However, such a solution may not lead to an acceptable solution.

As a very simple example, consider a workflow that consists of two service types, and two QoS attributes are focused on.

- For the service type $S1$, there are two services: s_{11} (price: \$2, availability: 90 %), and s_{12} (price: \$3, availability: 95 %).
- For the service type $S2$, there are two services: s_{21} (price: \$4, availability: 95 %), and s_{22} (price: \$3, availability: 90 %).

Conversion of the price metric (to be "the higher is the better"), as well as normalization, is omitted in the following intuitive discussion.

Suppose a constraint is given that the availability of the composite service must be equal to or more than 85 %. This constraints filters out the cheapest combination, s_{11} and s_{22}, as its aggregated availability is 81 %. It is already clear greedy and local selection based on the utility fuction can fail in some situations. Specifically, suppose the utility function is defined with higher weight on price. It may choose s_{11} and s_{22}, respectively, if a service is selected one by one for each type only by considering the utilify function. However, in that case the (global) constraint is not satisfied.

In this way, the problem requires exploration of all the possible combinations, which are practically unfeasible when the number of services increase as well as that of service types and that of QoS attributes.

15.4.4.2 Service Selection Problem and Well-Known Problems

It should be useful to review a mapping of the selection problem to a well-known mathematical problem, which has been investigated for long time.

For example, knapsack problems are a well-known class of problems to select some items so that their total value is maximized while their total weight is under the constraint. The weight can be considered to denote the amount of a resource required by the item. The service selection problem resembles knapsack problems in a sense items are sleeted by considering maximization under constraint.

Specifically, the service selection problem only with sequential execution can be mapped to multi-dimension multi-choice zero-one knapsack problem (MMKP) [27]. In MMKP, there are groups of items and one item is selected from each of the groups (as a service is selected from the services in complying with each service type). In addition, multiple resources required by each item are considered for constraints (as multiple QoS attributes are considered for constraints). MMKP has been proved to be NP-complete.

Introduction of different settings, e.g., workflow patterns, may change the problem structure. Nevertheless, the service selection problem is often solved by leveraging existing optimization algorithms. On the other hand, specific heuristics are often used to obtain near-optimal solutions efficiently (later discussed in Sect. 15.5.3).

15.5 Approaches to Computation for Service Selection

This section discusses approaches to the problem of QoS-based service selection. Two preliminary approaches are discussed before algorithms to solve the service selection problem. First, some assumptions are discussed to avoid unrealistically complex situations (Sect. 15.5.1). Second, a useful method called skyline is introduced to reduce the problem space (Sect. 15.5.2). Finally, several algorithms for the service selection problem are discussed (Sect. 15.5.3).

15.5.1 Assumptions in Definitions

The definitions in Sect. 15.3 and Sect. 15.4 can be and should be modified or extended if necessary. Nevertheless, it is necessary to notice useful assumptions introduced there.

- Aggregation functions for composite QoS were monotonic for example QoS metrics (Sect. 15.3.2). The higher a QoS value for a component service is, the higher the composite QoS value is for a composite service including the component service. This property was already used to derive the maximum and minimum values of composite QoS (Sect. 15.4.3). Without this property, we may encounter a situation like "when we select a service with higher availability, the decision leads to a composite service with lower availability." With this property, we can be sure it is good to have higher values for component services, as they will lead to higher values for the resulting composite services.
- Similarly, the utility function is defined to be monotonic. We can be sure it is good to have higher values for each QoS attribute, and higher values for each service type, to have higher utility.
- Constraints are defined only in the form of lower bounds. As a counter-example, constraints without apparent rules are difficult to handle efficiently, like "the values 1, 3, 6, 8 are acceptable but the other are not." It seems natural to only consider "better than (no worse than)" constraints. This assumption allows for use of sort of services by QoS values so that a set of services can be found efficiently that are likely to contribute to satisfaction of constraints.

As some algorithms assume and leverage such properties to be efficient, it is significant to be aware of them when modifying or extending the definitions.

15.5.2 Skyline Services

Before exploring the combinations of services, it is useful to filter out as many services as possible, if they are obviously not attractive. This means it is necessary to distinguish services that can be attractive for a certain setting of preferences and constraints.

For example, consider the following 4 services for the same service type.

- s_{i1}: price \$3, availability 90 %, reputation 3.5
- s_{i2}: price \$5, availability 99 %, reputation 3.1
- s_{i3}: price \$4, availability 95 %, reputation 2.5
- s_{i4}: price \$3, availability 85 %, reputation 3.1

In this case, there is no reason to select s_{i4}, as it has the same price as s_{i1}, but worse availability and worse reputation. For any utility function, selecting s_{i1} is better than selecting s_{i4}. There is no situation where s_{i4} satisfies constraints while s_{i1} does not. On the other hand, s_{i1} is better in price than s_{i2} and s_{i3}. Therefore, s_{i1} can be selected in some situations where price is thought significant. This discussion relies on the properties discussed in Sect. 15.5.1.

In this way, it is possible to filter out some unattractive services, before examining specific sets of preferences and constraints. A similar idea has been discussed in the data engineering area, and has been introduced to the service selection problem in [3, 6, 26]. Below outlines the fundamental concepts.

In general, s is said to *dominate* s' if s is equal to or better than s' in all QoS attributes and better in at least one attribute. Under the assumption that the higher is the better for any QoS attributes (Sect. 15.4.1), s dominates s' if $\forall k(q_k(s) \geq q_k(s')) \wedge \exists k(q_k(s) > q_k(s'))$. From the viewpoint of filtering, it is useful to find services that are *dominated* by any other service. In the above example, s_{i4} is dominated by s_{i1}, thus not attractive. On the other hand, s_{i1} is not dominated by any other service, thus attractive.

Attractive services in the above sense are called *skyline services*, derived for each service type. In *services*(S_i), services in complying with a service type, skyline services refers to the set of services each of which is not dominated by any other service in *services*(S_i).

Figure 15.3 illustrates skyline services in the case there are only two QoS attributes $q1$ and $q2$. The points denote QoS vectors of services, and ones at right or upper sides have better quality. Filled points denote skyline services, not dominated by any others, i.e., no other services in its left or upper side. Any of the other services is dominated by another service.

15.5.3 Service Selection Algorithms

As the service selection problem is NP-complete, there have been a lot of studies for algorithms that explores near-optimal solutions. It is very difficult to compare these competing algorithms with other. On one hand, as heuristics are explored in most cases with different focuses, theoretical comparisons are difficult in the form of complexity. On the other hand, empirical evaluations for the algorithms have different purposes and thus different parameters and settings. Existence of various parameters makes both theoretical and empirical comparisons difficult, as each algorithm is evaluated using a specific set of them. Input (setting) parameters for experiments

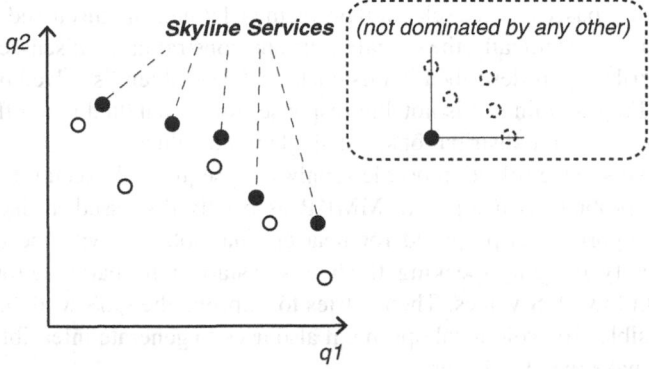

Fig. 15.3 Skyline services

include not only the number of services and that of service types, but also the number of constraints, the number of attributes, shapes of workflows, and distribution of QoS values. Output (compared) parameters are utility values (or their ratios to the optimal solutions) and success rates of constraints satisfaction as well as computation time, memory used, and bandwidth used (in distributed algorithms). Output (compared) parameters are often specific to the algorithm, to evaluate its own ideas.

Nevertheless, this section aims at providing the following intuitions by presenting some of the large number of studies (shown in Table 15.1).

- How the specific focuses of algorithms are different with each other.
- How many services and service types have been considered as experimental settings by existing studies.
- How long time the algorithms take for calculation.

15.5.3.1 Foundations

First, representative initial studies are presented that give solution algorithms for the problem by using algorithms for general optimization problems and often extending them with heuristics.

Table 15.1 Comparison of service selection algorithms

Type	Literature	Base algorithm
Foundational	Zeng, L. 2003 [28]	Linear Programming
	Yu, T. 2007 [27]	Heuristics
	Yu, Q. 2008 [25]	Dynamic Programming
Clustering	Alrifai, M, 2009 [2]	QoS Levels and Distribution
	Alrifai, M. 2010 [3]	Skyline
Meta-Heuristics	Zhang, C. 2007 [29]	Genetic Algorithm
	Dubey, V. K. 2010 [8]	Hill Climbing

In [28], QoS-based service selection problem is defined and discussed intensively for the first time. Specifically, the global utility and constraints are discussed, together with QoS attributes, as described in this chapter. The problem is solved by mapping it to Linear Programming. It is notable response time is handled in a different way, as its values have some distributions, not single fixed values.

In [27], the service selection problem only with sequential execution is first discussed. The problem is mapped to MMKP, as briefly discussed in Sect. 15.4.4.2. A heuristic algorithm is proposed for near-optimal solution with the polynomial time complexity. Roughly speaking, the heuristic starts with searching for a feasible solution with low QoS values. Then it tries to improve the QoS while keeping the solution feasible. To avoid local optima, it also tries to generate infeasible solutions and then to make the QoS lower.

In [27], more complex workflows are also discussed. In this case, possible execution routes (paths) are probabilistically considered, which denote different choices at the branches included in the workflow. The problem is solved by heuristics, after the problem is mapped to Integer Programming.

In [25], a query algebra is defined to formally model and run queries on service types, workflows and QoS (in the terminology of this chapter). It includes the QoS-based service selection problem that optimizes QoS of a composite service. Dynamic Programming is used as the basic approach to the problem, which is extended with a divide-and-conquer strategy.

The initial study in [28] shows a result for good understanding, which used a general solver by IBM. When the number of services in each service type (N) is fixed as 40, computation time increases as the number of service types in a workflow (T) increases: a few hundreds milliseconds ($T = 10$), less than 1 s ($T < 25$), about 3.5 s ($T = 60$) and about 7.5 s ($T = 80$). The solver on established knowledge on Linear Programming can solve the problem somewhat fast, given the fact the full exploration for optimization requires ($O(N^T)$). We can see it can be used for online selection (blocking end users) for $N = 40$ and $T < 25$ (if we consider 1 s is the upper limit).

Following studies often have specific focuses, such as dealing with general workflows in [27]. Then the input parameter changes from T to K, which denotes different execution paths in a workflow (each of them occurs in different probabilities due to conditional branch and other control constructs). Because various algorithms are compared with each other, evaluation of absolute computation time is limited. A similar time range and time increase appear in the evaluation result: less than 1 s for $N = 10$, $K = 10$ but about 9 s for $N = 30$, $K = 30$. Many studies consider smaller numbers for T, e.g., $T = 3$ in [25] with which the algorithm runs within 1 s even with $N = 5000$.

15.5.3.2 Clustering

In [2], the service selection problem is solved in a distributed manner. Global constraints are decomposed into a set of local constraints, which can be then solved efficiently by multiple nodes. For example, the global constraint on the total price is decomposed to range constraints of local prices ("price level" for each service type). It is ensured satisfaction of local constraints lead to satisfaction of global constraints. The constraint decomposition is solved as Mixed Integer Program, whose problem setting is small enough to be solved quickly.

In [3], the notion of skyline services is explored to filter out service candidates. Section 15.5.2 introduced the minimum usage of skyline services. In [3], the service candidates are further reduced through hierarchical clustering. Skyline services can be still large, as a result of a variety of the competitive ways to balance multiple QoS attributes. In addition, an analysis method is presented for identifying improvement required for a service provider to be competitive.

These studies have different purposes from the ones presented in Sect. 15.5.3.1. They use some kind of clustering and filtering so that it does not actually consider all the services. As a result, the computation can be less than 1 s with $N = 2000, T = 5$ and less than 10 s with $N = 500, T = 100$, in [2]. In [3], these pairs of numbers are outstanding. Use of (extended) skylines also shows 10–100 ms with $N = 1000, T = 5$, as N does not matter so much because of the clustering and filtering process.

15.5.3.3 Meta-Heuristics

There have been many other studies, including use of meta-heuristics such as genetic algorithms and Hill-Climbing [8, 29]. Meta-heuristics algorithms define very general ways of exploration for solutions of complex optimization problems, which often work well to some extent. Domain-specific customization is sometimes used to fit more with a specific problem. Due to the nature of meta-heuristics, which relies on iterated exploration with some randomness, it is very difficult to give general characteristics of performance. For example, several variations of algorithms are evaluated in [29], however, the results are somewhat diverse and difficult to compare with other algorithms as in presented in Sect. 15.5.3.1. More experiments seem necessary to discuss the potentials of these algorithms.

15.5.3.4 Notes

As seen in the studies described above, N and T have been considered as important factors, however, there has not been a common agreement on requirements about how large N or T should be handled. Almost all of the data sets in the studies have been generated randomly or by following some distributions. The authors of [2] and [3] have used a data set on (only) QoS with a few thousands of real web services,[1] but the exact values of N or T are unknown. While we need to wait for further analysis on what the real web services are, further directions have been explored for setting or modeling of the problem itself (discussed in the following Sect. 15.6).

[1] http://www.uoguelph.ca/~qmahmoud/qws/index.html

15.6 Directions for Future Research

This section discusses some examples of further extensions in problem settings from existing literatures.

15.6.1 Handling Failures and Runtime Adaptation

The problem discussed in this chapter focused on optimization before execution. Actually, consideration of runtime failures (in advance or at runtime) is necessary, as well as further optimization given runtime situations.

In [11], combination of services for the same service type is discussed. It is often necessary to consider backup services or alternatives for the case the selected service is unavailable or the case it execution fails. Sometimes it may be useful to use multiple services in parallel to obtain merged or selected result. In [11], different ways (workflows) of such combinations of services in the same type are referred to as virtual services. Virtual services can be used in the selection process as if they were atomic services. Composite QoS of virtual services are evaluated in advance, and meaningful ones are left as skyline services.

In [10], proactive adaptation is discussed to improve QoS at runtime. If the execution takes long time, as in logistics, the current status can be monitored and the remaining execution plan (i.e., services to use) can be reconstructed accordingly. Specifically, QoS values for the completed part of the workflow are fixed, and can be compared with the values estimated before execution. For example, the actual response time may be much shorter than the declared one as the worst or the average. Service re-selection in such a situation may be attractive for the remaining part of the workflow, e.g., using cheaper services as it turned out constraints on response time can be loosen.

15.6.2 Refining QoS Models

The problem discussed in this chapter focused on simple metrics with single values. Actual situations can be more complex with changes in quality values, which are conditionally planned, probabilistic, or uncertain.

In [13], QoS metrics refined to express conditional SLAs, e.g., different pricing on peak time. As the QoS values are distributions rather than one numeric value, service selection involves probabilistic simulations. Usage patterns of clients are also considered to examine how they match with the conditional SLAs. The simulation approach also allows for dealing with distributions of response time, without rounding into average or worst.

In [26], the domination relationship is further discussed taking uncertainty into consideration. Specifically, even if a QoS value of a service in an average or worst metric is more than that of another, it does not mean the former always shows a better value than the latter in every instance of execution. Focusing on this point leads to probabilistic modeling of the domination relationships, and an efficient algorithm is proposed for its efficient calculation.

15.6.3 Examining Incentives

The problem discussed in chapter focused on service selection given all reliable information on QoS of each service. Actually, it is necessary to consider incentives of providers or clients for ensuring some kinds of optimality such as social welfare.

In [9], a mechanism is designed to give providers incentives for offering their true cost and capabilities. Roughly speaking without mathematical discussion, such kinds of honesty is promoted by introducing a mechanism to ensure profits of providers, when its offer is attractive and selected. This discourage a provider to declare less attractive QoS by embedding its profits (e.g., setting higher price), as it decreases the possibility the provider is selected.

15.7 Summary

This chapter has described foundations for QoS modeling and QoS-based service selection. The following topics are included.

- How typical aspects of QoS are expressed.
- How QoS of a workflow or composite service is assessed from QoS of involved component services.
- How objective of optimization with multiple QoS attributes is expressed as a utility function.
- How the service selection problem is defined for a workflow or composite service.
- How global constraints make the service selection problem computationally difficult.
- What are exemplary approaches to tackle the difficulty of the service selection problem.

After emergence of web services around 2000, a variety of services are emerging, especially in the paradigm of cloud computing (XaaS: X-as-a-Service) [4]. QoS will continue to be very significant aspects in service-oriented systems. On the other hand, services only allow us to select, not allowing us to determine the quality freely. Further investigation of QoS and service selection methods will be one of the keys to tackle difficulties for quality-assured service-oriented systems.

References

1. Amazon web services. http://aws.amazon.com/
2. Alrifai, M., Risse, T.: Combining global optimization with local selection for efficient QoS-aware service composition. In: The 18th International Conference on World Wide Web (WWW 2009), pp. 881–890 (2009)
3. Alrifai, M., Skoutas, D., Risse, T.: Selecting skyline services for QoS-based web service composition. In: The 19th International Conference on World Wide Web (WWW'10), pp. 11–20 (2010)
4. Armbrust, M., Fox, A., Griffith, R., Joseph, A.D., Katz, R.H., Konwinski, A., Lee, G., Patterson, D.A., Rabkin, A., Stoica, I., Zaharia, M.: Above the clouds: a Berkeley view of cloud. Technical Report UCB/EECS-2009-28, University of California at Berkeley (2009)
5. Aurrecoechea, C., Campbell, A.T., Hauw, L.: A survey of QoS architectures. Multimed. Syst. **6**, 138–151 (1998)
6. Borzsonyi, S., Kossmann, D., Stocker, K.: The skyline operator. In: International Conference on Data Engineering (ICDE 2001), pp. 421–430 (2001)
7. Cardoso, J., Miller, J., Sheth, A., Arnold, J.: Quality of service for workflows and web service processes. J. Web Semant. **1**, 281–308 (2004)
8. Dubey, V.K., Menascé, D.A.: Utility-based optimal service selection for business processes in service oriented architectures. In: The 8th IEEE International Conference on Web Services (ICWS 2010), pp. 542–550 (2010)
9. Gerding, E., Stein, S., Larson, K., Rogers, A., Jennings, N.R.: Scalable mechanism design for the procurement of services with uncertain durations. In: The 9th International Conference on Autonomous Agents and Multiagent Systems (AAMAS'10), pp. 649–656 (2010)
10. He, Q., Yan, J., Jin, H., Yang, Y.: Adaptation of web service composition based on workflow patterns. In: The 6th International Conference on Service-Oriented Computing (ICSOC 2008), pp. 22–37 (2008)
11. Hiratsuka, N., Ishikawa, F., Honiden, S.: Service selection with combinational use of functionally-equivalent services. In: The 9th IEEE International Conference on Web Services (ICWS 2011), pp. 89–96 (2011)
12. Jurca, R., Faltings, B., Binder, W.: Reliable QoS monitoring based on client feedback. In: The 16th International Conference on World Wide Web (WWW 2007), pp. 1003–1012 (2007)
13. Klein, A., Ishikawa, F., Bauer, B.: A probabilistic approach to service selection with conditional contracts and usage patterns. In: The 7th International Conference on Service-Oriented Computing (ICSOC 2009), pp. 253–268 (2009)
14. Klein, A., Ishikawa, F., Honiden, S.: Towards network-aware service composition in the cloud. In: The 21th International World Wide Web Conference (WWW 2012) (2012)
15. Ludwig, H., Dan, A., Kearney, R.: Cremona: an architecture and library for creation and monitoring of WS-agreements. In: The 2nd International Conference on Service Oriented Computing (ICSOC 2004), pp. 65–74 (2004)
16. Masri, E.A., Mahmoud, Q.H.: Investigating web services on the World Wide Web. In: The 17th International World Wide Web Conference (WWW 2008), pp. 795–804 (2008)
17. van Moorsel, A.: Metrics for the internet age: Quality of experience and quality of business. Technical Report HPL-2001-179, HP Labs (2001)
18. Mukherjee, D., Jalote, P., Nanda, M.G.: Determining QoS of WS-BPEL compositions. In: The 6th International Conference on Service-Oriented Computing (ICSOC 2008), pp. 378–393 (2008)
19. OASIS: Web Services Business Process Execution Language Version 2.0. http://docs.oasis-open.org/wsbpel/2.0/OS/wsbpel-v2.0-OS.html (2007)
20. O'Sullivan, J., Edmond, D., ter Hofstede, A.H.M.: What's in a service? Distrib. Parallel Databases **12**(2–3), 117–133 (2002)
21. Paolucci, M., Kawamura, T., Payne, T.R., Sycara, K.: Semantic matching of web services capabilities. In: The 1st International Semantic Web Conference (ISWC 2002), pp. 333–347 (2002)

22. Sahai, A., Machiraju, V., Sayal, M., Jin, L.J., Casati, F.: Automated SLA monitoring for web services. Technical Report HPL-2002-191, HP Labs (2002)
23. Vinek, E., Beran, P.P., Schikuta, E.: Classification and composition of QoS attributes in distributed, heterogeneous systems. In: The 11th IEEE/ACM International Symposium on Cluster, Cloud and Grid Computing (CCGrid 2011), pp. 424–433 (2011)
24. W3C: Web Services Description Language (WSDL) Version 2.0, Part 1: Core Language. http://www.w3.org/TR/wsdl20/ (2007)
25. Yu, Q., Bouguettaya, A.: Framework for web service query algebra and optimization. ACM Trans. Web 2(1), 6 (2008)
26. Yu, Q., Bouguettaya, A.: Computing service skyline from uncertain QoWS. IEEE Trans. Serv. Comput. 3(1), 16–29 (2010)
27. Yu, T., Zhang, Y., Lin, K.J.: Efficient algorithms for web services selection with end-to-end QoS constraints. ACM Trans. Web 1(1), 1–25 (2007)
28. Zeng, L., Benatallah, B., Dumas, M., Kalagnanam, J., Sheng, Q.Z.: Quality driven web services composition. In: The 12th International Conference on World Wide Web (WWW'03), pp. 411–421 (2003)
29. Zhang, C., Su, S., Chen, J.: DiGA: population diversity handling genetic algorithm for QoS-aware web services selection. Comput. Commun. 30(5), 1082–1090 (2007)

Chapter 16
Composition of Web Services: From Qualitative to Quantitative Timed Properties

Nawal Guermouche and Claude Godart

Abstract Dealing with service composition is an important and challenging issue of distributed systems. Existing works investigate mechanisms for analyzing and synthesizing a composition based on qualitative properties which characterize operations and/or messages choreography constraints. Apart from these qualitative properties, quantitative properties such as time related features are a crucial setting to consider. Augmenting service's behavior with timed properties increases the expressiveness and brings new difficult problems. This requires defining rigorous verification and composition primitives for taking into account such properties. In this chapter, we present a formal composition and verification approach which considers quantitative timed properties assigned to qualitative properties. The chapter starts with a general introduction. Then, it introduces the concepts related to timed Web services, timed conversations and protocols. The following section introduces the notion of composition of Web services with emphasis on the temporal dimension, and defines a formal composition approach. This approach relies on the generation of a mediator which aims surpassing timed conflicts. The next section presents validation primitives based on model checking techniques to verify and validate timed compositions. An implementation of the concepts previously introduced is then described. Before concluding with a larger consideration of time implication in Web services definition and composition, and with open issues, we present a study of the state of the art.

N. Guermouche (✉)
CNRS, LAAS, 7 avenue du colonel Roche, Toulouse F-31400, France
e-mail: nawal.guermouche@laas.fr

N. Guermouche
Univ de Toulouse, INSA, LAAS, Toulouse F-31400, France

C. Godart
LORIA-INRIA-UMR 7503, Vandoeuvre-les-Nancy F-54506, France
e-mail: nawal.guermouche@laas.fr

A. Bouguettaya et al. (eds.), *Web Services Foundations*,
DOI: 10.1007/978-1-4614-7518-7_16,
© Springer Science+Business Media New York 2014

16.1 Introduction

Service Oriented Architecture (SOA) is gaining acceptance as a promising architecture for organizations to integrate their business applications. In SOA, application's business logic can be modularized and outsourced as Web services so that these services can be mutually used. Based on standards, Web services promote the composition of loosely coupled applications to integrate them into complex business systems. In this field, many industrial and academic efforts have been done to provide specifications and techniques to allow verification and composition of heterogeneous Web services [4].

Web service description is one of the important ingredients for Web service composition. In fact, selecting, using, and composing services in efficient and correct manner, requires to provide rich specifications for describing various kind of important service properties. Indeed, in real life scenarios, Web services and more particularly Web service composition depends on several properties, such as those related to messages choreography constraints [4], security [15], and *timed properties* [13, 25].

In this chapter, we focus on the Web service composition synthesis problem where we consider *qualitative properties* associated with *quantitative properties*. Qualitative properties define messages choreography constraints and quantitative properties relate to timed properties which specify the *necessary delays* to exchange messages (e.g., in an e-government application a prefecture must send its final decision to grant an handicapped pension to a requester after 7 days and within 14 days). Thus, we consider that building correct compositions requires managing message choreography constraints augmented with timed properties. Few recent works have shown the importance to deal with such timed properties in the compatibility analysis of synchronous [27], asynchronous Web services [14], in checking requirements satisfaction [18], and in calculating temporal thresholds for process activities [25].

Since services are developed autonomously, mismatches can arise and a composition can fail. Mainly, we distinguish two kind of problems: non-timed and timed mismatches. Non-timed problems concern interfaces and sequence messages conflicts which happen when: (1) awaited messages are not produced by other services, (2) awaited and sent messages are not adequate (i.e., they have different names or different data types), and (3) there is a mutual services blocking (e.g., a service Q_1 waits for a message m that must be sent by another service Q_2, which also waits for a message m' from Q_1 to send the awaited message m). Detecting and preventing such composition timed problems is a difficult and challenging problem [13]. In fact, when composing services, dependencies between timed properties can be created and some dependencies can generate timed conflicts. In the context of service composition, it is important to detect and prevent such timed conflicts to anticipate composition failures. To do so, a possible solution, is to build a third party service, called *mediator*. The notion of a *mediator* has been already used to solve many problems as data integration [28, 33], Web semantic heterogeneities [30], adaptation of services interfaces (namely *adaptators*) [2], for discovering appropriate services to satisfy client's preferences [10], and as an interface between Web services [4].

To summarize, the problem we are interested in can be defined as follows: given a timed description of a given need, called *client service* in the following, and a set of discovered timed services, how to build a composition of discovered services to satisfy this client service. Note that we focus on correct interactions of services and we do not consider exception handling which are out of the scope of this chapter. The main contributions of our framework are as follows:

1. Unlike existing composition synthesis models, we propose a formal model of asynchronous Web services that takes into account *qualitative timed properties* associated to messages, data, and data constraints.
2. As we deal with timed properties, when synthesizing a composition, timed conflicts can arise. We propose a mechanism to discover these conflicts.
3. In addition, we propose the use of a mediator based process to anticipate and prevent, when possible, the problem of timed (and non timed) conflicts.
4. We propose a model checking based verification process which can be used to validate Web service compositions.
5. Finally, the primitives described in this chapter have been implemented in a prototype that we have used to perform preliminary tests.

The reminder of the chapter is organized as follows: in Sect. 16.2 we present a global overview of our framework. Section 16.3 describes the model we propose in order to specify the Web services properties we consider. Section 16.4 describes our composition approach steps. Section 16.5 presents a concrete example of composition to illustrate our approach. In Sect. 16.6, we present a verification process which aims at verifying compositions of Web services and an experimental setup. Related work is introduced in Sect. 16.7, and finally Sect. 16.8 concludes.

16.2 Global Overview

In this section, we present an overview of our timed composition framework which relies on the following elements:

- A *client Service*: the first element of our framework is the timed description of the client service. This service specifies timed properties associated to the data flow the client provides and to the data flow he expects without any reference to the operations of available services.
- A *set of discovered services*: we assume that a set of timed Web services can be discovered to answer the client service request.
- A *mediator*: it can access the data yet exchanged by the different services and use them to generate any missing messages.

Case Study: e-government Application

Let us present a part of an e-government application inspired from [21] to illustrate the related issues of the problem we handle. The goal of the e-government application we consider is to manage handicapped pension requests. Such a request involves three organizations: (1) *a prefecture*, (2) *a health authority*, and (3) *a town hall*. We suppose that theses organizations are managed by, respectively, the prefecture service (PS), the health authority service (HAS), and the town hall service (THS).

A high level choreography model of the process is depicted in Fig. 16.1. A citizen can apply for a pension. Once applied, the prefecture solicits the medical entity to deliver an examination report of the requester, and the town hall to deliver the domiciliation attestation. After studying the received files, the prefecture sends the notification of the final decision to the citizen. The interaction between these partners is constrained by timed requirements:

- Once the health authority service proposes meeting dates to the citizen, this one must confirm the meeting within 24 h.
- The prefecture requires at least 48 h and at most 96 h from receiving the file from the requester to notifying the citizen with the final decision.
- The medical report must be sent to the prefecture after at least 120 h and at most 168 h after receiving the request of the medical report.

Notion of Timed Conflicts

Given this set of timed Web services and the client service, our aim is to build a timed composition that satisfies this client service. When building a composition, it

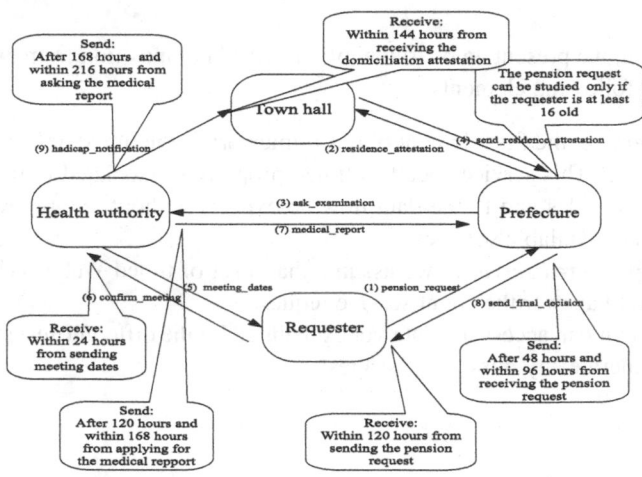

Fig. 16.1 Global view of the e-government application

is mandatory to ensure that data and timed constraints of the involved services are not conflicting. In the context of our work, we do not focus on data type and semantics related analysis problems. We consider simple data which can be simply checked: two data constraints are said to be not conflicting if their solution set is not disjoint. For example, the prefecture studies the pension request only if the requester is at least 16 years old. If we want to create a connection between the requester and the prefecture service to exchange the pension request while the requester is for example at least 18 old, this is possible (i.e., the set of solution of age $\geq 16 \cap$ the set of solution of age $\geq 18 \neq \emptyset$).

While the data constraints we consider can be checked by verifying their set of solutions, timed constraints validation needs more complex investigations. In fact, in a collaboration, timed properties of Web services cannot be checked like simple constraints. In other words, to assert that an interaction is timed deadlock free, it is not sufficient to check timed constraints assigned to sending a message with timed constraints associated to its reception. For example, the prefecture must send its final decision after 48 h and within 96 h from receiving the pension request. On the other side, the requester must receive it within 120 h from sending the request. If we check these two timed constraints as simple constraints, we can conclude that the prefecture and the requester can collaborate together. However, if we examine the progress of the interaction, we can remark that the prefecture can send its final decision only after the medical report has been received. This report must be sent by the medical entity after 120 h and within 168 h from receiving the report request. Since the prefecture must wait for the medical report to send its final decision, i.e., after 120 h, the final decision cannot be sent within 96 h from receiving the pension request. Figure 16.2, illustrates this conflicting interaction. The prefecture sends its decision after 48 h and within 96 h from receiving the pension request. But during this execution, the prefecture must wait for at least 120 h to get the medical report. This presents a simple timed conflict. More complex timed conflicts can arise and can make fail the

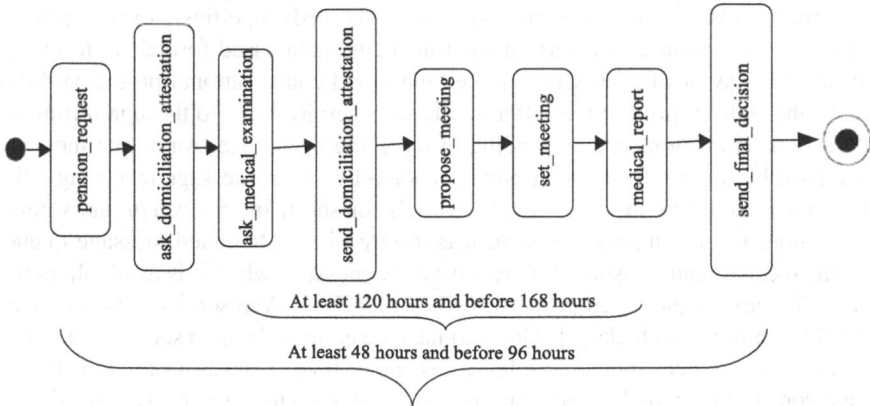

Fig. 16.2 Example of impact of timed properties on web services interaction

composition. As said previously, to succeed the composition, an alternative consists in generating a mediator whose role is to try to prevent these conflicts.

Now, let us check the scenario depicted in Fig. 16.1. We can remark that the town hall has to wait for a medical report of the medical entity before to, for example, deliver an handicapped card. The town hall must receive the report within 144 h, but the medical entity can send its report only after 168 h. So, the town hall cannot receive the report in time and the composition will fail.

But, if we examine the situation in details, we can remark that the medical entity sends its report to the prefecture after 120 h. As a consequence, intuitively, to succeed the collaboration, we can build an indirect connection between the medical entity and the town hall to deliver the medical report within 144 h. This indirect connection can be built by the mediator that generates the message for transmitting the medical report to the town hall in advance. Note that the mediator fails when a required data (i.e., the data involved in the required message) is not available (i.e., the data is not accessible).

To summarize, in this section we have intuitively discussed the impact and the importance to consider timed properties in a composition framework. During a composition, different services with different timed constraints can be involved. Timed properties can give rise to timed conflicts which can make fail the composition. In the following, we propose a formal approach which aims at composing services so that their timed properties are respected.

16.3 Modeling the Timed Behavior of Web Services

As introduced above, one of the important ingredients in a composition framework is the *timed conversational protocol* of Web services which we assume deterministic and able to support synchronous and asynchronous communications. In our framework, the timed conversational protocol specifies the sequences of messages a service supports, the involved data flow, and the associated timed properties to exchange messages. We have adopted a deterministic timed automata based formalism to model the timed behavior of Web services (i.e., the timed conversational protocol). Intuitively, the states represent the different phases a service may go through during its interaction. Transitions enable sending or receiving a message. An output message is denoted by $!m$, whilst an input one is denoted by $?m$. A message involving a list of data is denoted by $m(d_1, \ldots, d_n)$, or $m(\bar{d})$ for short. In an *asynchronous* communication, when a message is sent, it is inserted into a bounded message queue, and the receiver can consume (i.e. receives) the message when it is available in the queue. To capture the timed properties when modelling Web services, we use standard timed automata clocks [1]. The automata are equipped with a set of clocks. The values of these clocks increase with the passing of time. Transitions are labelled by timed constraints, called *guards*, and resets of clocks. The former represent simple conditions over clocks, and the latter are used to reset values of certain clocks to zero. The guards specify that a transition can be fired if the corresponding guards are satisfiable.

Let X be a set of clocks. The set of *constraints* over X, denoted $\Psi(X)$, is defined as follows:

$$\text{true} \mid x \bowtie c \mid \psi_1 \wedge \psi_2, \text{where } \bowtie \in \{\leq, <, =, \neq, >, \geq\}, x \in X, \psi_1, \psi_2 \in \Psi(X),$$

and c is a constant. With that:

Definition 16.1. A *timed conversational protocol* Q is a tuple (S, s_0, F, M, C, X, T) where S is a set of states, s_0 is the initial state, F is a set of final states ($F \subseteq S$), M is a set of messages, C is a set of constraints over data, X is a set of clocks, and T is a set of transitions such that $T \subseteq S \times M \times C \times \Psi(X) \times 2^X \times S$ with an element of the alphabet (exchanged message (M)), a constraint over data (C), a guard over clocks ($\Psi(X)$), and the clocks to be reset (2^X).

The conversational protocols we consider are deterministic. A conversational protocol is said to be deterministic if for each two transitions $(s, \alpha_1, c_1, \psi_1, s'_1)$ and $(s, \alpha_2, c_2, \psi_2, s'_2)$, the following conditions are satisfied:

$$\alpha_1 \neq \alpha_2, \text{ or } c_1 \wedge c_2 = \text{false, or } \psi_1 \wedge \psi_2 = \text{false}$$

Example 16.1 Figure 16.3 illustrates the timed conversational protocol of the PS, THS, HAS services of our use case study, and the client service. In this figure, the initial state of the PS service is p_0, the set of states is $\{p_0, p_1, p_2, p_3, p_4, p_5, p_6, p_7, p_9, p_{10}, p_{11}, p_{12}, p_{13}, p_{14}, p_{15}, p_{16}\}$ and the set of final states is $\{p_7, p_9, p_{16}\}$. This service can send and receive messages. For example, it can send the message $examination\_request(sn, handicap)$, denoted $!examination\_request(sn, handicap)$. This message has as parameters the security number (sn), and the handicap ($handicap$) of the requester. Analogously, this service can consume a message, for example, the message $pension\_request(sn, age, handicap)$, denoted $?pension\_request(sn, age, handicap)$. This message has as parameters the security number (sn), the age (age), and the handicap ($handicap$) of the requester. This service achieves correctly its execution if for each interaction it reaches a final state.

To specify that the prefecture must send its final decision within a delay of 48–96 h after receiving the pension request, we associate to the reception of the request of the pension a reset of a clock t_1 ($t_1 := 0$) and we assign the constraint $48 \leq t_1 \leq 96$ to the sending of the final decision.

16.4 Analyzing the Timed Composition Problem

In this section, we present the algorithm that allows to synthesize a composition of timed Web services. Our framework gathers three steps: (1) creating timed P2P connections between the client service and the discovered services (see Sect. 16.4.1), (2) discovering timed conflicts (see Sect. 16.4.2), (3) generating a *mediator* that tries to step in to succeed a connection (see Sect. 16.4.3).

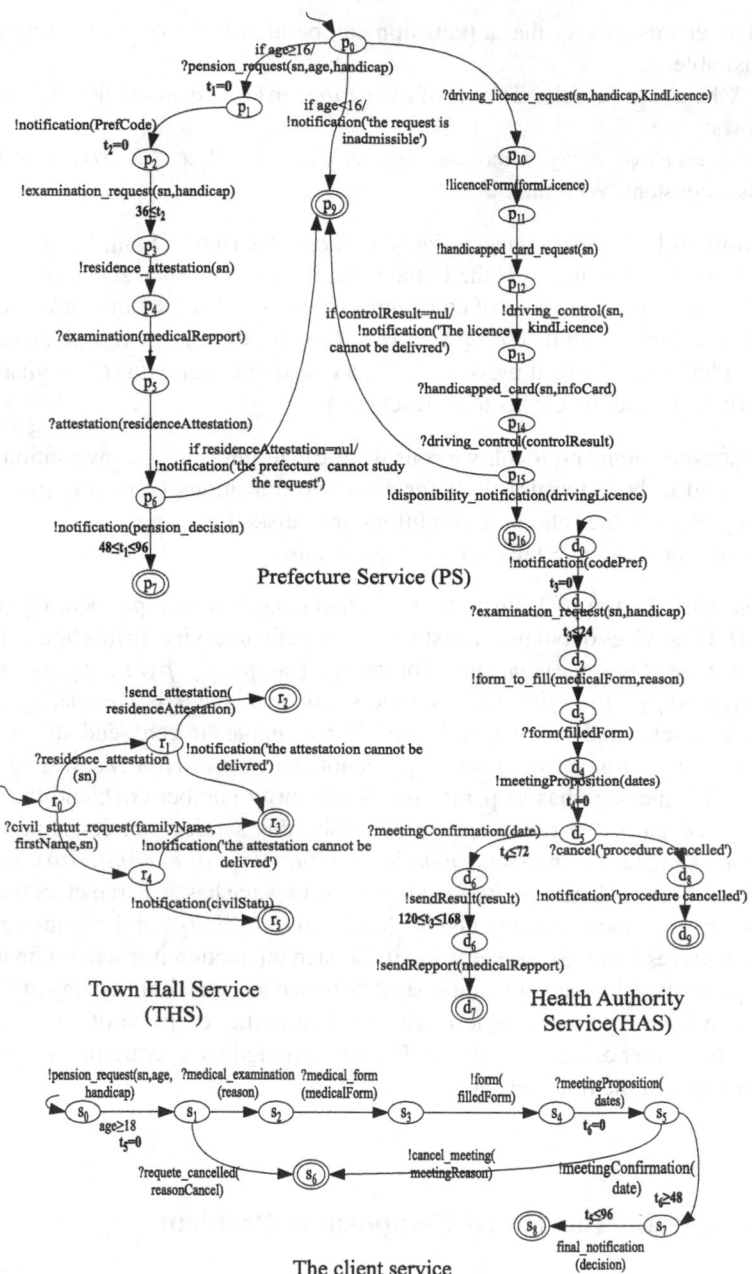

Fig. 16.3 Services of the e-government scenario

16.4.1 *Building Timed P2P Connections*

Given a set of conversational protocols of the services and a client service, our aim is to build a *timed global automaton* that characterizes the *timed composition schema* (the global automaton is called *Timed Composition Schema Automaton TCSA*).

To build this TCSA, we introduce the concept of *configuration* that represents the states of the TCSA at a given time. A configuration defines the evolution of services states when they are interacting together (i.e., connected via channels). In the initial configuration, all the services are in their initial states. Given a source configuration, the TCSA reaches a new configuration when there exists two services that change their states by exchanging a message so that no timed conflict arises.

Definition 16.2. (*A Timed Composition Schema Automaton*)
A *timed composition schema automaton TCSA* is a tuple (S, Q, M, X, L, T) such that S is a set of configurations, Q is a set of services, M is a set of messages, L is a set of channels, X is a set of clocks, and T is a set of TCSA transitions such that $T \subseteq S \times L \times \Psi(X) \times S$. A transition specifies that, from a source configuration, the TCSA reaches a new configuration when a channel can be created to interconnect two services so that the associated (ordered) timed constraints are satisfied. The set of channels L is defined as a set of $(p_s, p_r, m(\overline{d}))$, with $p_s, p_r \in Q$, and the tuple $(p_s, p_r, m(\overline{d}))$ specifies that the service p_s sends the message $m(\overline{d})$, that involves the set of data types $(\overline{d})$, to the service p_r. In our composition framework, a mediator can be generated, hence the set of considered services is $Q = \{R, A, Med\}$, such that R is the client service, A is the set of the available services, and Med is the generated mediator.

Among the transitions of the different services, we distinguish two kinds of transitions: *passive transitions* and *non-passive transitions*.

- A *passive transition* is a timed (resp. non-timed) transition that has timed constraints of the form $x \preceq v$ (resp. $x \prec v$). In fact, these transitions are considered passive because they do not give rise to timed conflicts.
- A *non-passive transition* is a timed transition that has timed constraints of the form $x \geq v$ (resp. $x > v$). In fact, timed conflicts can arise when these transitions precede transitions that have constraints of the form $x \leq v$ (resp. $x < v$).

The approach of composition is based on the Algorithm 1. This algorithm aims to build connections between the different services to try to satisfy the client service. The steps of this algorithm can be described as follows:

From the set of transitions T, it isolates passive transitions T_p and non-passive transitions T_{np}. Initially, it tries to connect each transition of the client service with the transitions of the different services. Note that this algortihm tries to connect passive transitions before non-passive transitions. In fact, the study we have performed shows that timed conflicts can arise when non-passive transitions precede passive transitions. When the connection fails, this algorithm calls the Algorithm 3 that aims at generating the mediator. When a connection is created, the Algorithm 2 checks if the created connection does not give rise to timed conflict. In the following, we present the process of discovering timed conflicts.

16.4.2 Making Explicit the Implicit Timed Constraints Dependencies

As said previously, when creating TCSA transitions, implicit timed dependencies can be created. In that case, timed conflicts can arise. In order to discover timed conflicts when combining services, we need mechanisms for making explicit the implicit timed dependencies. To do so, we propose the *clock ordering* process. The idea behind the *clock ordering* process is to define an order between the different clocks of the services for each new TCSA transition.

To explain why simple checking of timed constraints as simple constraints (called local checking) is not sufficient to detect conflicts, we consider the following example depicted in Fig. 16.4.

Example 16.2 Let us consider the two timed conversational protocols P and P'. We start by building the TCSA of the two conversational protocols by considering the timed constraints as simple constraints, i.e., we check locally the timed constraints of the transitions.

As we can see, the service P sends the message m_0 and resets the clock x. The service P' can receive this message. So we can build the TCSA transition $(s_0 s_0', m_0, x_1 = 0, s_1 s_1')$. Then the service P' sends the message m_1 and resets the clock y. The service P can receive the message m_1. We build the TCSA transition $(s_1 s_1', m_1, y = 0, s_2 s_2')$. Later, the service P sends the message m_2, the service P' can receive it after 20 units of time. Hence, we build the TCSA transition $(s_2 s_2', m_2, y \geq 20, s_3 s_3')$. After that, the service P' sends the message m_3, the service P must receive it within 10 units of time. We build the TCSA transition $(s_3 s_3', m_3, x < 10, s_4 s_4')$. As we can see in Fig. 16.4a, by simply checking timed constraints of transitions, we could build a TCSA.

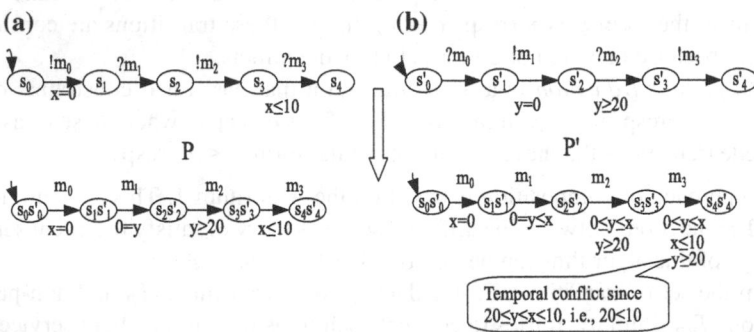

Fig. 16.4 Make explicit the implicit timed constraints dependency. **a** Local checking of the constraints of the transitions. **b** Clock ordering

However, the message m_2 can be exchanged after 20 units of time and m_3 can be exchanged within 10 units of time. As m_3 can be exchanged after exchanging the message m_2, it can be exchanged only after 20 units of time. However, the message m_3 should be exchanged within 10 (i.e., [0, 10]) units of time and after 20 (i.e., [20, ∞)) units of time, which is a contradiction and represents a timed conflict. To cater for such implicit timed properties, we propose to perform a *clock ordering* process. This process allows to define an order between the clocks of the TCSA transitions. Below, we show how we define the clock order.

The two services can exchange the message m_0 via the TCSA transition $(s_0 s_0', m_0, x = 0, s_1 s_1')$. Then when building the TCSA transition $(s_1 s_1', m_1, y = 0, s_2 s_2')$

Algorithm 1: Composition

Input: A client service $Q_g = (S_c, s_{0_c}, F_c, M_c, C_c, X_c, T_c)$, a set of Web services
$\quad Q_i = (S_i, s_{0_i}, F_i, M_i, C_i, X_i, T_i)$, for $i = \{1, .., n\}$
, the initial configuration of the TCSA $\bar{s} = (s_{0_1}, \ldots, s_{0_n})$, the current state of the client service
$s_c = s_{0_c}$

Output: TCSA $= (S, s_0, F, M, C, X, T)$, and the mediator
$\quad\quad Med = (S_{med}, s_{0_{med}}, F_{med}, M_{med}, C_{med}, X_{med}, T_{med})$

begin

  succesComposition=true;
  for *each transition* $t_c = (s_c, \alpha_c, c_c, \psi_c, Y_c, s_c')$ *of each trace of the client service and* **if** *succesComposition* **do**

    $T_{visited} = null$;
    if $(t_c \in T_p)$ *and* $(satisfaction(t_c, \bar{s}))$ **then**
      $s_c = s_c'$;
    else
      if $(t_c \in T_p)$ **then**
        choose one transition t_p of T_p;
        $T_{visited} = T_{visited} \cup t_p$;
        while $T_p \nsubseteq T_{visited}$ *and* $\neg$ *satisfaction*$(t_{sp}, \bar{s})$ **do**
          choose another transition t_{sp} of T_{sp};
          $T_{visited} = T_{visited} \cup t_{sp}$;
        if $\neg$ *satisfaction*$(t_{sp}, \bar{s})$ **then**
          Choose one transition t_{snp} de T_{snp};
          $T_{visited} = T_{visited} \cup t_{snp}$;
          while $T_{snp} \nsubseteq T_{visited}$ *and* $\neg$ *satisfaction*$(t_{snp}, \bar{s})$ **do**
            choose another transition t_{snp} of T_{snp};
            $T_{visited} = T_{visited} \cup t_{snp}$;
          if $\neg$ *satisfaction*$(t_{snp}, \bar{s})$ **then**
            succesComposition=false;

      else
        if $(\psi_a = x > v)$ *or* $(\psi_c \geq v)$ **then**
          choose a transition t_{sp} of T_{sp};
          $T_{visited} = T_{visited} \cup t_{sp}$;
          while $T_{sp} \neq \emptyset$ *and* $\neg satisfaction(T_{sp}, \bar{s})$ **do**
            choose another transition t_{sp} of T_{sp};
            $T_{visited} = T_{visited} \cup t_{sp}$;
          if $\neg$ *satisfaction*$(t_{sp}, \bar{s})$ **then**
            if *satisfaction*$(t_c, \bar{s})$ **then**
              $s_c := s_c'$
            else
              choose a transition t_{snp} of T_{snp};
              $T_{visited} = T_{visited} \cup t_{snp}$;
              while $T_{snp} \neq \emptyset$ *and* $\neg satisfaction(T_{snp}, \bar{s})$ **do**
                choose another transition t_{snp} of T_{snp};
                $T_{visited} = T_{visited} \cup t_{snp}$;
              if $\neg$ *satisfaction*$(t_{snp}, \bar{s})$ **then**
                succesComposition=false;

  if *succesComposition* **then**
    if $\bar{s} \in F$ **then**
      Return ASCT and the mediator;
    else
      'The composition fails because the services do not reach their final states';
  else
    'The composition fails because the client service cannot be satisfied';

we can define the order $y \leq x$ since y is reset after x. So we associate this order to the TCSA transition as follows $(s_1 s_1', m_1, 0 \leq y \leq x, s_2 s_2')$. Then, the service P can send the message m_2 to the service P' which can receive it after 20 units of time. So when the two services exchange the message m_2, $(0 \leq y \leq x) \wedge (y \geq 20)$ must be satisfied. We build the TCSA transition $(s_2 s_2', m_2, 0 \leq y \leq x, y \geq 20, s_3 s_3')$. Until now, there is no timed conflict. Note that we propagate the constraint $y \geq 20$ over the successor transitions. When the service P' sends the message m_3, the service P can receive it within 10 units of time, i.e., $20 \leq y \leq x \leq 10$ must be satisfied. However, this latter induces to a timed conflict $(20 \leq 10)$. As we can see in Fig. 16.4b, by defining a clock ordering when combining services, implicit timed conflicts can be discovered.

The Algorithm 2 allows to define an order between the different clocks of services. Based on the computed order, it detects timed conflicts. This algorithm has as input a candidate TCSA transition $t_i = (s_i, m_i(\overline{d}), c_i, \psi_i, Y_i, s_i')$. To discover timed conflicts, it proceeds as follows.

- It propagates timed constraints, of the form $x > v$ (resp. $x \geq v$), from a predecessor transition t_{i-1} to the transition t_i.
- A clock z which is reset in a predecessor transition t_{i-1}, has a value bigger than a clock y which is reset in the current transition t_i. Hence, it defines the order $y \leq z$.
- In addition, it propagates the order $z_1 \leq \cdots \leq z_n$ of the predecessor transition t_{i-1}.
- If in the transition t_i there exists a constraint of the form $x \leq v$ (resp. $x \geq v$) and at the same time, a clock y is reset, then it defines the order $x - y \leq v$ (resp. $x - y \geq v$). That means, the difference between the two clocks x and y is always less (resp. bigger) than v.
- If among the set of constraints and defined orders, there exists two constraints $x \geq v$ and $x' \geq v'$, and at the same time, there is an order of the form $x - x' \geq v$, it implies the order $x \geq v + v'$. In fact, this order allows to consider the clocks value accumulation.

By applying theses steps when building TCSA transitions, timed conflicts are discovered if at least one of the following conditions is satisfied.

- There exists an order of the form $v \leq x_1 \leq \cdots \leq x_n \leq v'$ where $v' \leq v$.
- There exists three constraints $x \geq v'$ and $y \leq v''$ and $x - y \leq v$ with $v' - v'' > v$ (i.e., following the constraints $x \geq v'$ and $y \geq v''$, the difference $x - y \leq v$ is violated).
- There exists three constraints $x \leq v'$, $y \leq v''$ and $x - y \geq v$ with $v' < v$ (i.e., the constraint $x - y \geq v$ is violated),
- There exists three constraints $x \leq v'$, $y \geq v''$, and $x - y \geq v$ with $v' - v'' < v$ (i.e., the constraint $x - y \geq v$ is violated).

Algorithm 2: Clock_Order

Input: A transition $(s_i, m_i(\overline{d}), \psi_i, Y_i, s'_i)$
Output: boolean
begin
  if s_i *is the initial state* **then**
    | return true;
  else
    for *each* $\varrho_{i-1} \in \psi_{i-1}$, *such as* $\varrho_{i-1} = x \geq v$ *or* $\varrho_{i-1} = x > v$ *of*
    $(s_{i-1}, m_{i-1}(\overline{d}), \psi_{i-1}, Y_{i-1}, s'_{i-1})$ **do**
      $\psi_i = \psi_i \cup \varrho_{i-1}$;
      for *each* $y = 0 \in Y_i$ *and* $z = 0 \in Y_{i-1}$ **do**
        | $\psi_i = \psi_i \cup y \leq z$;
      for *each* $z_1 \leq z_2 \in \psi_{i-1}$ **do**
        | $\psi_i = \psi_i \cup z_1 \leq z_2$;
      for *each* $y \in Y_i$ *et* $\varrho_i \in \psi_i$ **do**
        if $\varrho_i = x \leq v$ **then**
          | $\psi' = x - y \leq v$;
          | $\psi_i = \psi_i \cup \psi'$
        else
          if $\varrho_i = x \geq v$ **then**
            | $\psi' = x - y \geq v$;
            | $\psi_i = \psi_i \cup \psi'$
      if $\exists \varrho_i = x \geq v$ *and* $\varrho'_i = x' \geq v'$ *and* $\varrho''_i = x - x' \geq v$ **then**
        | $\psi' = x \geq v + v'$ $\psi = \psi \cup \psi'$
    if $\exists$ $v \leq y_0 \leq \ldots \leq y_n \leq v' \in \psi_i$ *such as* $v' < v$ **then**
    | return false;
    else
      if $\exists$ $x \geq v' \in \psi_i$ *and* $y \leq v'' \in \psi_i$ *and* $x - y \leq v \in \psi_i$ *such as* $v' - v'' > v$ **then**
      | return false;
      else
        if $\exists$ $x \leq v' \in \psi_i$ *and* $y \leq v'' \in \psi_i$ *and* $x - y \geq v \in \psi_i$ *such as* $v' \geq v''$ *and* $v' < v$
        then
        | return false;
        else
          if $\exists$ $x \leq v' \in \psi_i$ *and* $y \geq v'' \in \psi_i$ *and* $x - y \geq v \in \psi_i$ *such as* $v' - v'' < v$ **then**
          | return false;
          else
          | return true;

The clock ordering process is very important as it allows to predict timed conflicts. A simple technique such as using only a mediator, whose aim is to provide messages without a clock ordering process, will be insufficient and cannot resolve a problem when it arises (i.e., when a timed conflict occurs it means that timed properties are violated). Indeed, our goal is to predict and prevent timed conflicts before they arise. To do so, we use the clock ordering process in association with a mediator.

16.4.3 Generation of a Timed Mediator

As said previously, because of timed (and non-timed) conflicts, a timed P2P connection process can fail. The mediator aims to prevent these conflicts by creating the required messages. In our approach, a required message is created taking the involved data from the history of past exchanged messages, i.e., the current available data (we assume here that data having the same name, have also the same value).

In order to produce the required messages, we check if the involved data are available, i.e, they have been already exchanged. In other terms, the mediator reuses the data historic to produce the required messages.

The mediator is defined using the computed TCSA, by adding input, output and empty messages. As long as the TCSA can be executed, the mediator does nothing. When two services can exchange a message and there are clocks which are reset, the mediator resets the same clocks via an empty transition. In fact, these clocks can be used later by the mediator to consume messages within a defined time window, whilst, when a deadlock can arise, the mediator generates the required message to prevent this deadlock.

Algorithm 3: Generation of a mediator

Input: A transition $t_i = (s_i, \alpha(\overline{d}), c, \psi, Y, s_i')$, the set of exchanged data D_a
Output: A transition
$mediator((s_i, \alpha_i, c_i, \psi_i, Y_i, s_i'), D_a, \overline{s})$;
begin
   if $\alpha = !m(\overline{d_m})$ then
      $M_{med} := M_{med} \cup m(\overline{d})$;
      $S_{med} := S_{med} \cup s_m'$;
      $T_{med} := T_{med} \cup (s_m, ?m(\overline{d}), c_i, \psi_i, Y_i, s_m')$;
      return $(s_m, ?m(\overline{d}), c_i, \psi_i, Y_i, s_m')$;
   else
      if $\alpha = ?m(\overline{d_m}))$ then
         if $\overline{d_m} \subseteq D_a$ then
            $M_{med} := M_{med} \cup m(\overline{d_m})$;
            $S_{med} := S_{med} \cup s_m'$;
            $T_{med} := T_{med} \cup (s_m, !m(\overline{d_m}), c_i, Y_i, s_m')$;
            return $(s_m, ?m(\overline{d}), c_i, Y_i, s_m')$;
         else
            The required data are not available, so the required message cannot be produced;
            return null;

16.5 Back to the Case Study

In order to illustrate the approach presented in this chapter, we propose to show a concrete composition example using the PS, HAS, THS services, and the client service introduced in Sect. 16.2. We first try to build a TCSA (Sect. 5.1, Fig. 16.5a without the timed involvement of a mediator. Then we introduce the mediator (Sect. 5.2, Fig 16.5b to resolve timed problems.

16.5.1 Composition Without the Timed Involvement of the Mediator

As in our framework, a mediator can be involved, we generate an empty mediator that has initially only one state m_0. The initial configuration of the *TCSA* is

(a)

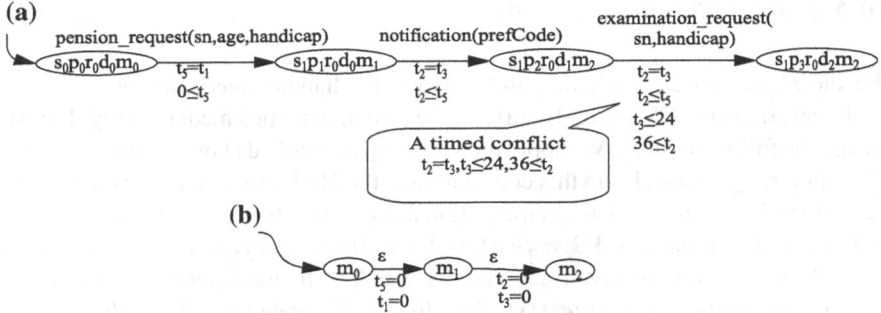

(b)

Fig. 16.5 Composition without the timed involvement of the mediator. **a** A conflicted TCSA. **b** The associated mediator

$s_0 p_0 r_0 d_0 m_0$ (respectively the client service, PS, HAS, THS, and the mediator are in their initial states). From the current state of the client service s_0, the message $!pension\_request(sn, age, handicap)$ can be sent. As we can remark, the PS service waits for this message. Since, the constraints over data ($age \geq 18$ and $age \geq 16$) are not disjoint, we can connect the two transitions (s_0, $!pension\_request(sn, age, handicap), age \geq 18, t_5 = 0, s_1$) and ($p_0$, $?pension\_request$ ($sn, age, handicap), age \geq 16, t_1 = 0, p_1$). When the two transitions are fired, the two clocks t_1 and t_5 are reset. So, we generate an empty mediator transition that allows to reset the same clocks. In fact, theses clocks can be used later to specify constraints to produce or consume messages. We build a global TCSA transition that connects the two transitions of the client and PS services with the transition of the mediator ($s_0 p_0 r_0 d_0 m_0$, $pension\_request(sn, age, handicap), t_1 = t_5 = 0, s_1 p_1 r_0 d_0 m_1$). The new configuration becomes $s_1 p_1 r_0 d_0 m_1$ and the new current state of the client service becomes s_1. From this new configuration, the current transition of the client service is (s_1, $?medical\_examination(reason), s_2$). There is no transition that enables sending the message $medical\_examination(reason)$. So we check if the mediator can produce this message. Since the data $reason$ has not been already exchanged, the mediator cannot generate the message $medical\_examination(reason)$. Among the services transitions, we choose the transition (p_1, $!notification(pre fCode), t_2 = 0, p_2$). Since, the HAS service can consume it, we can connect them. As the clocks t_2 and t_3 are reset, we generate an empty mediator transition that reset the same clocks. We build the TCSA transition ($s_1 p_1 r_0 d_0 m_1$, $notification(pref Code), t_2 \leq t_5, t_2 = t_3, s_1 p_2 r_0 d_1 m_2$). From the new configuration, the HAS service waits for the message $examination\_request(sn, handicap)$ that must be consumed within 24 h from receiving the message $notification(code Pref)$. The message $examination\_request(sn, handicap)$ can be sent by the PS after 36 h from sending the message $notification(code Pref)$. We build the TCSA transition ($s_1 p_2 r_0 d_1 m_2$, $examination\_request(sn, handicap), t_2 = t_3, t_2 \leq t_5, t_3 \leq 24, t_2 \geq 36, s_1 p_3 r_0 d_2 m_2$). This transition is conflicting, since $t_2 = t_3, t_3 \leq 24$ et $t_2 \geq 36$. Thus, we can see that without involving the mediator to handle timed conflicts, the compositions fails.

16.5.2 Involving the Mediator

We show here how the mediator can be involved to handle timed conflicts.

To generate the TCSA (Fig. 16.6a) and the associated timed mediator (Fig. 16.6b), we use the following steps. We apply the same steps described above to reach the configuration $s_1 p_2 r_0 d_1 m_2$. From this configuration, the HAS service can fire the passive transition $(d_1, ?examination\_request(sn, handicap), t_3 \leq 24, d_2)$. Since the corresponding transition of the PS service $(p_2, !examination\_request(sn, handicap), t_2 \geq 36, p_3)$ is a non-passive transition, we check if the mediator can generate the message $examination\_request(sn, handicap)$. The data sn, and $handicap$ have been already exchanged. Hence, the mediator can generate the required message $examination\_request(sn, handicap)$ via the transitions $(m_2, !examination\_req uest(sn, handicap), t_3 \leq 24, m_3)$. When the message is generated, we build the global transition $(s_1 p_2 r_0 d_1 m_2, examination\_request(sn, handicap), t_2 = t_3, t_2 \leq t_5, t_3 \leq 24, s_1 p_2 r_0 d_2 m_3)$. From the new configuration $s_1 p_2 r_0 d_2 m_3$, we choose the passive transition $(d_2, !form\_to\_fill(medical Form, reason), d_3)$ of the HAS service. As there is no service that waits for the message $form\_to\_fill$ $(medical Form, reason)$, we generate the mediator transition to consume this message, i.e., $(m_3, ?form\_to\_fill(medical Form, reason), m_4)$, and then we build the global transition $(s_1 p_2 r_0 d_2 m_3, form\_to\_fill(medical Form, reason), s_1 p_2 r_0 d_3 m_4)$. From the new configuration, the current client transition is $(s_1, ?medic al\_examination(reason), s_2)$. There is no transition that enables sending the message $medical\_examination(reason)$. The mediator can produce the message $medical\_examination(reason)$, via the transition $(m_4, !medical_examination (reason), m_5)$, and then we build the TCSA transition $(s_1 p_2 r_0 d_3 m_4, medical\_examination(reason), s_2 p_2 r_0 d_3 m_5)$. The current transition of the client service is $(s_2, ?medical\_form(medical Form), s_3)$. The data $medical Form$ has been already sent by the HAS service. So, the mediator can generate the missing message

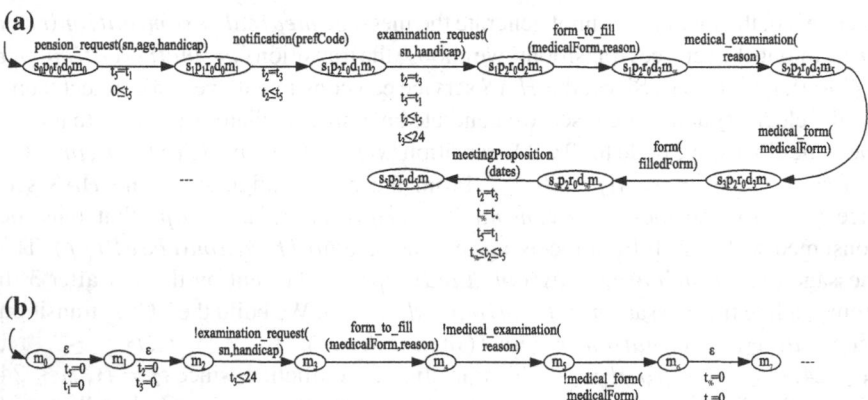

Fig. 16.6 The timed composition schema automaton (TCSA). **a** A part of the generated TCSA. **b** A part of the associated mediator

$medical\_ form(medicalForm)$ via the transition $(m_5, !medical\_ form(medical$
$Form), m_6)$. Once the transition of the mediator is generated, we build the global
transition $(s_2 p_2 r_0 d_3 m_5, medical\_ form(medicalForm), s_3 p_2 r_0 d_3 m_6)$. From the
new configuration, we connect respectively the two transitions of the client and HAS
services $(s_3, !form(filledForm), s_4)$ and $(d_3, !form(filledForm), d_4)$ via the
TCSA transition $(s_3 p_2 r_0 d_3 m_6, form(filledForm), s_4 p_2 r_0 d_4 m_6)$.

By applying the same steps, either we build the TCSA, or we detect a conflict that
cannot be avoided.

16.6 Formal Verification and Validation of the Built Composition

As presented previously, when the composition succeeds, the algorithm generates
a mediator and produces a global timed composition schema TCSA. Such a built
TCSA is an *optimized product* built on the fly: indeed, we build progressively the
product of timed protocols rather than building the whole product.

The built TCSA is correct if it is deadlock free and it satisfies the client service.
Checking that the TCSA is deadlock free can be reduced to checking reachability
properties. This problem is PSPACE-complete in general. The problem of client
service satisfaction checking can be reduced to the *inclusion problem*, which is
decidable [1]. In fact, the formal model of timed conversational protocol that we have
defined relies on a deterministic timed automata for which closure and decidability
properties have been proved [1].

In the following, we present a formal verification process which aims to validate
the built composition. We note that this verification process is generic and can be used
to verify atomic and composite services built automatically or manually. This process
relies on a model checking approach inspired from [14] and using the UPPAAL model
checker.

16.6.1 UPPAAL Overview

UPPAAL is a model checker for the verification and simulation of real time systems [19]. An UPPAAL model is a set of timed automata, clocks, channels for systems
(automata) synchronization, variables and additional elements [19].

Each automaton has one initial state. Synchronization between different processes
can take place using channels. A channel can be written into (denoted as *channel_na
me* !), and can be read (denoted as *channel_name* ?). A channel can be defined as
urgent to specify that the corresponding transition must be fired as soon as possible,
i.e. immediately and without a delay. Variables and clocks can be associated to
processes (automaton). Conditions on these clocks and variables can be associated
to transitions and states of the process. The conditions associated to transitions,
called *guards*, specify that a transition can be fired if the corresponding guards are

satisfiable. The conditions associated to states, called *invariants*, specify that the system can stay in the state while the invariant is satisfiable.

The UPPAAL properties query language is a subset of *Computation Tree Logic* (CTL)[16]. The properties that can be analyzed by UPPAAL are:

- $A[]\psi$: for all the automata' paths, the property ψ is always satisfiable, i.e., for each transition (or a state) of each path, the property ψ is satisfiable.
- $A <> \psi$: for all the automata' paths, the property ψ is eventually satisfiable, i.e., for each path , there is at least one transition (or a state) in which the property ψ is satisfiable.
- $E[]\psi$: there is at least a path in the automata such that the property ψ is always satisfiable, i.e., there is at least one path such that for each transition (or a state), the property ψ is satisfiable.
- $E <> \psi$: there is at least a path in the automata such that the property ψ is eventually satisfiable, i.e., there is at least one transition (or a state) of at least one path in which the property ψ is satisfiable.
- $\psi \leadsto \phi$: when ψ holds, ϕ must hold.

In the following, we present the formal primitives we propose for composition checking.

16.6.2 Verification of Web service Compositions

In this section, we present the verification process we propose using the model checker UPPAAL. The purpose of this verification process is to check if the built composition holds deadlocks. In this context, we define three composition classes: (1) *fully correct composition* , (2) *partially correct composition*, (3) *incorrect composition*.

16.6.2.1 Fully Correct Composition

We say that a composition is correct if it is (timed and non-timed) deadlock free. This is equivalent to check that its corresponding TCSA does not hold timed and non-timed conflicts. Formally, checking that a composition is fully correct is equivalent to check that all the paths of the TCSA lead to a final state.

Let Q be a TCSA and s_f its final state. Q is said to be fully correct, if the following CTL formula is correct:

$$A <> Q.s_f$$ (16.1)

16.6.2.2 Partially Correct Composition

A composition is said to be incorrect if its TCSA is not deadlock free. Formally, a composition is not fully correct if there exists at least a path of the TCSA which does not lead to a final state. This latter can be specified as the following CTL formula:

$$E[] \, not \, Q.s_f \tag{16.2}$$

When the composition is not fully correct, we check if it can achieve at least one correct execution. Formally, a composition can terminate at least one execution if its final state can be reached via at least one path. The former property can be specified as follows.

$$E <> \, Q.s_f \tag{16.3}$$

A composition is said to be partially correct if it is not fully correct (i.e., the property 16.2 is satisfiable) but at the same time it can fulfil at least one execution (i.e., the property 16.3 is satisfiable).

16.6.2.3 Incorrect Composition

When the composition is not even partially correct, we say that the composition is fully incorrect. As specified by the following CTL formula, a composition is said to be fully incorrect if all its TCSA paths do not lead to a final state.

$$A[] \, not \, Q.s_f \tag{16.4}$$

In order to experiment the proposed approach, a prototype has been implemented [12]. Its underlying architecture is depicted in Fig. 16.7. The tool inputs the description of services and the client service as XML documents. The *P2P coordi-*

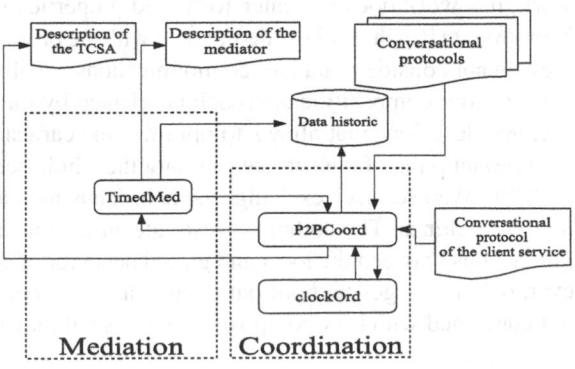

Fig. 16.7 Underlying architecture of the prototype.

nation component tries to build P2P connections (channels) among the services and updates the TCSA description thanks to the Algorithm 1. A third component, the *timed mediator* component, steps in to consume extras messages or to produce, if possible, the required messages using the Algorithm 3. We note that the data historic repository is a database in which we store the involved exchanged data.

16.7 Related Work and Discussion

The research field about how to synthesize automatically a composition is very active. Several research works have been published on automatic service composition, using techniques based on situation calculus [24, 29], transition based systems [9, 23, 11], or symbolic model-checking applied to planning [26]. Unlike the proposed approaches, in our framework we cater for timed properties when composing services.

In [31, 32] the authors consider services as views over data sources. They build on the idea that heterogeneity of data sources may be overcome by exploiting services as wrappers of different information sources, thus providing uniform access to them, exploiting standard protocols such as SOAP and XML. Each data source, i.e., service, is described in terms of input and output parameters (the latter provided by the source), binding patterns and additional constraints on the source. The latter allow to characterize the output data. Analogously, these works consider only atomic services. However, the control flow between data is a crucial aspect. Furthermore, the authors do not consider timed properties.

Like the above works in [20, 22], the considered Web services are atomic. The behavioral aspect is not considered and the timed aspects are not taken into account.

In [6], Web services are described by their BPEL specification. The authors proposed to translate the BPEL specifications into a finite state machine (FSM) specification. As this composition approach is not oriented by the client need (there is no client need notion), the composition consists in performing the product of the whole FSM specification. The composition problem consists then to find paths in the computed cartesian product that satisfies reachability properties. According to our work, this work does not cater for timed properties when building a composition. Moreover, in [6], the authors do not deal with the problem of missing messages, since they do not consider data and communications capabilities as in our framework. In addition, our composition approach is oriented by the client need, defined upon the required data flow, that allows to optimize the cartesian product: we compose only the relevant parts of the services and not the whole services.

In [9], Web services exchange asynchronous messages and they are modelled as Mealy machines. The authors investigate an approach dealing with the unexpected interactions between the local and global behavior of composite Web services. However, only messages without parameters are considered. Moreover, the authors are not concerned with how composing services but they are interested in analyzing the local and global behavior of Web services in a composition. Furthermore, the authors do not deal with timed properties.

An other remark is that, works that consider the control flow, address the composition problem at process level, i.e., they consider the operations the services perform [4, 5, 8, 17]. For example, in [4], one of the important assumptions is that the client need (called *goal service*) is specified upon the operations of the services. The precise specification of the goal service allows for precise matching with available, more elementary services. Nevertheless, in real life scenarios, it is not always possible for a client to precisely specify his need according to the operations of the services. A simple client does not have any preliminary knowledge about the service operations.

Whilst, in our framework, the client need (client service) is specified by the (input and output) data the client expects. Moreover, in [4], the authors do not deal with timed properties when composing services.

The few frameworks that deal with timed properties in Web services specification, focus on compatibility and replaceability analysis [27] and timed model checking a given composition [18]. In both works, the authors consider synchronous Web services. While, in our work, we deal with asynchronous Web services. Furthermore, these works do not deal with the composition synthesis problem of asynchronous timed services. For instance, in [18], the authors assume that the composition is already built.

In [7], the authors focus on the interoperability problem of networked systems where they consider non-functional properties such as the response time (e.g., a consumer who asks for photos must get a list of photos in less than x ms). This work is part of the Connect Integrated Project which aims at enabling continuous composition of networked systems [3]. The non functional properties the author consider are simple and are associated to atomic systems (analogously simple services) which must be connected (analogously composed). Moreover, the approach proposed in [7] aims at monitoring the connected system to check that the non-functional properties such as response time are respected. In our work, we consider timed properties associated to complex services and we handle the problem of building compositions so that timed properties of the involved services are analysed to detect and prevent timed conflicts.

16.8 Conclusion and Perspectives

In this chapter, we present a formal approach to handle timed properties in asynchronous Web services composition. Our framework is oriented by the client data flow. To reach this goal, we first propose a timed automata based formal model of timed conversational protocols. This model provides an operational semantic to consider timed properties of asynchronous communicating Web services. This model gathers: (1) *supported messages*, (2) *data*, (3) *constraints over data*, (4) *timed constraints*, and (5) the *asynchronous conversational aspect* of Web services. Based on this model, we provide an algorithm which aims at building a composition so that no timed conflict arises. In this context, we use *the clock ordering process* that allows to discover implicit timed conflicts that can arise when composing services.

Unfortunately, due to the heterogeneous nature of Web services, timed P2P connections can fail, and the composition too. To tackle this problem, we propose to generate a third party service, called *mediator*. The role of this latter is to avoid conflicts. Obviously, the mediator has a crucial role when composing services, since it contributes to connect the required services by producing the expected messages.

The proposed approach has been implemented in a prototype, which has been used to perform preliminary experiments. Currently, we are trying to carry out fine grained experimentations on a set of richer services.

The framework we presented in this chapter focuses on the composition of timed asynchronous services and considers correct interactions of services. Our ongoing work studies the problem of exceptions handling within the timed composition framework. Moreover, we plan to extend our approach with semantic capabilities in order to support more complex timed properties. This will allow us to construct a composition not only by considering timed properties associated to message exchanges, but also more global constraints.

Another interesting research direction consists in studying dynamic substitution in order to resolve timed conflicts which can be complementary with a mediator based approach. In addition, we plan to extend our approach to support dynamic instantiation when composing timed Web services. In this chapter, we assume that only one instance of each service is required. However, in real scenarios, we can need one or several instances of each service. So, it is interesting to extend the proposed approach to handle such features.

References

1. Alur, R., Dill, D.L.: A theory of timed automata. Theor. Comput. Sci. **126**(2), 183–235 (1994)
2. Benatallah, B., Casati, F., Grigori, D., Nezhad, H.R.M., Toumani, F.: Developing adapters for web services integration. In: CAiSE, pp. 415–429 (2005)
3. Bennaceur, A., Cavallaro, L., Inverardi, P., Issarny, V., Romina Spalazzese Daniel Sykes, M.T.: Dynamic connector synthesis: revised prototype implementation. In: Deliverable D3.3 ICT FET IP Project (2012)
4. Berardi, D., Calvanese, D., Giacomo, G.D., Hull, R., Mecella, M.: Automatic composition of transition-based semantic web services with messaging. In: Proceedings of the 31st International Conference on Very Large Data Bases, pp. 613–624. ACM, 30 August 2005–2 September 2005
5. Berardi, D., Calvanese, D., Giacomo, G.D., Mecella, M.: Composition of services with nondeterministic observable behavior. In: Service-Oriented Computing—ICSOC 2005, Third International Conference (ICSOC), pp. 520–526 (2005)
6. Bertoli, P., Pistore, M., Traverso, P.: Automated web service composition by on-the-fly belief space search. In: Proceedings of the Sixteenth International Conference on Automated Planning and Scheduling, ICAPS 2006, pp. 358–361 (2006)

7. Bertolino, A., Inverardi, P., Issarny, V., Sabetta, A., Spalazzese, R.: On-the-fly interoperability through automated mediator synthesis and monitoring? In: 4th International Symposium on Leveraging Applications of Formal Methods, Verification and Validation (ISoLA'10) (2010)
8. Brogi, A., Popescu, R.: Towards semi-automated workflow-based aggregation of web services. In: Service-Oriented Computing—ICSOC 2005, Third International Conference (ICSOC), pp. 214–227 (2005)
9. Bultan, T., Fu, X., Hull, R., Su, J.: Conversation specification: a new approach to design and analysis of e-service composition. In: Proceedings of the international conference on World Wide Web, WWW 2003, pp. 403–410 (2003)
10. Charif, Y., Sabouret, N.: An overview of semantic web services composition approaches. Electr. Notes Theor. Comput. Sci. **146**(1), 33–41 (2006)
11. Díaz, G., Cambronero, M.E., Pardo, J.J., Valero, V., Cuartero, F.: Automatic generation of correct web services choreographies and orchestrations with model checking techniques. In: Advanced International Conference on Telecommunications and International Conference on Internet and Web Applications and Services (AICT/ICIW'06), p. 186, 19–25 February 2006
12. Guermouche, N.: Timed interation-aware web service composition (wrtiten in french: Etude des interactions temporises dans la composition de services web). Ph.D. thesis, Nancy university, France (2010)
13. Guermouche, N., Godart, C.: Timed properties-aware asynchronous web service composition. In: Proceedings of the 16th International Conference on Cooperative, Information Systems (CoopIS'08) pp. 44–61, 9–14 November 2008
14. Guermouche, N., Godart, C.: Timed model checking based approach for web services analysis. In: IEEE International Conference on Web Services (ICWS'09) (2009)
15. Guermouche, N., Benbernou, S., Coquery, E., Hacid, M.S.: Privacy-aware web service protocol replaceability. In: IEEE International Conference on Web Services (ICWS'07), pp. 1048–1055, 9–13 July 2007
16. Henzinger, T.A., Nicollin, X., Sifakis, J., Yovine, S.: Symbolic model checking for real-time systems. Inf. Comput. **111**(2), 193–244 (1994)
17. Hull, R., Benedikt, M., Christophides, V., Su, J.: E-services: a look behind the curtain. In: Proceedings of the Twenty-Second ACM SIGACT-SIGMOD-SIGART Symposium on Principles of Database Systems (PODS), pp. 1–14 (2003)
18. Kazhamiakin, R., Pandya, P.K., Pistore, M.: Representation, verification, and computation of timed properties in web service compositions. In: Proceedings of the IEEE International Conference on Web Services (ICWS), pp. 497–504 (2006)
19. Larsen, K.G., Pettersson, P., Yi, W.: Uppaal in a nutshell. Int. J. Softw. Tools Technol. Transf. **1**, 134–152 (1997)
20. McIlraith, S.A., Son, T.C.: Adapting golog for composition of semantic web services. In: Proceedings of the 8th International Conference on Principles and Knowledge Representation and Reasoning (KR'02), pp. 482–496, 22–25 April 2002
21. Mecella, M., Batini, C.: Enabling italian e-government through a cooperative architecture. IEEE Comput. **34**(2), 40–45 (2001)
22. Medjahed, B., Bouguettaya, A., Elmagarmid, A.K.: Composing web services on the semantic web. VLDB J. **12**, 333–351 (2003)
23. Muscholl, A., Walukiewicz, I.: A lower bound on web services composition. In: Proceedings of Foundations of Software Science and Computation Structures (FOSSACS), vol. 4423, pp. 274–287. LNCS (2007)
24. Narayanan, S., McIlraith, S.A.: Simulation, verification and automated composition of web services. In: Proceedings of the International Conference on World Wide Web, WWW 2002, pp. 77–88 (2002)
25. Pichler, H., Wenger, M., Eder, J.: Composing time-aware web service orchestrations. In: Proceedings of the 21st International Conference on Advanced Information, Systems Engineering (CAiSE'09), pp. 349–363, 8–12 June 2009
26. Pistore, M., Marconi, A., Bertoli, P., Traverso, P.: Automated composition of web services by planning at the knowledge level. In: IJCAI, pp. 1252–1259 (2005)

27. Ponge, J., Benatallah, B., Casati, F., Toumani, F.: Fine-grained compatibility and replaceability analysis of timed web service protocols. In: The 26th International Conference on Conceptual Modeling (ER) (2007)

28. Sheth, A.P., Larson, J.A.: Federated database systems for managing distributed, heterogeneous, and autonomous databases. ACM Comput. Surv. **22**(3), 183–236 (1990)

29. Sohrabi, S., Prokoshyna, N., McIlraith, S.A.: Web service composition via generic procedures and customizing user preferences. In: International Semantic Web Conference, pp. 597–611 (2006)

30. Stollberg, M., Cimpian, E., Mocan, A., Fensel, D.: A semantic web mediation architecture. In: Canadian, Semantic Web, pp. 3–22 (2006)

31. Thakkar, S., Ambite, J.L., Knoblock, C.A.: A view integration approach to dynamic composition of web services. In: Proceeding of 2003 ICAPS Workshop on Planning for Web Services (2003)

32. Thakkar, S., Ambite, J.L., Knoblock, C.A.: A data integration approach to automatically composing and optimizing web services. In: Proceedings of the 2nd ICAPS International Workshop on Planning and Scheduling for Web and Grid Services (2004)

33. Wiederhold, G.: Mediators in the architecture of future information systems. IEEE Comput. **25**(3), 38–49 (1992)

Chapter 17
Adaptive Composition and QoS Optimization of Conversational Services Through Graph Planning Encoding

Min Chen, Pascal Poizat and Yuhong Yan

Abstract Service-Oriented Computing supports description, publication, discovery, composition of services as well as QoS optimization of service composition to fulfil end-user needs. Yet, service composition processes commonly assume that service descriptions and user needs share the same abstraction level, and that services have been pre-designed to integrate. To release these strong assumptions and to augment the possibilities of composition, we add adaptation features into the service composition process using semantic structures for exchanged data, for service functionalities, and for user needs. Graph planning encodings enable us to retrieve service compositions efficiently. Our composition technique supports conversations for both services and user needs, and it is fully automated and can interact with state-of-the-art graph planning tools. In addition to service composition, QoS optimization aims at satisfying end-user needs about quality requirements. However, most existing work on QoS optimization is studied on the assumption that services are stateless. To obtain a solution with the best QoS value, we propose a QoS-aware service composition method to achieve QoS optimization during the adaptive composition over conversational services. An example is given as a preliminary proof of our QoS-aware service composition method.

M. Chen (✉) · Y. Yan
Concordia University, Montreal, Canada
e-mail: minchen2008halifax@yahoo.com

Y. Yan
e-mail: yuhong@encs.concordia.ca

P. Poizat
Université Nanterre Paris Ouest La Défense, Nanterre, France
e-mail: pascal.poizat@lri.fr

P. Poizat
LIP6 UMR 7606 CNRS, Orsay, France

A. Bouguettaya et al. (eds.), *Web Services Foundations*,
DOI: 10.1007/978-1-4614-7518-7_17,
© Springer Science+Business Media New York 2014

17.1 Introduction

Task-Oriented Computing envisions a user-friendly pervasive world where *user tasks* corresponding to a (potentially mobile) user would be achieved by the automatic assembly of resources available in her/his environment. Service-Oriented Computing [28] (SOC) is a cornerstone towards the realization of this vision, through the abstraction of heterogeneous resources as services and automated composition techniques [17, 22, 30]. However, services being elements of composition developed by different third-parties, their reuse and assembly naturally raises composition mismatch issues [2, 13]. Moreover, Task-Oriented Computing yields a higher description level for the composition requirements, i.e., the user task(s), as the user only has an abstract vision of her/his needs which are usually not described at the service level. These two dimensions of interoperability, namely *horizontal* (communication protocol and data flow between services) and *vertical matching* (correspondence between an abstract user task and concrete service capabilities) should be supported in the composition process.

Software adaptation is a promising technique to augment component reusability and composition possibilities, thanks to the automatic generation of software pieces, called adaptors, solving mismatch out in a non-intrusive way [31]. More recently, adaptation has been applied in SOC to solve mismatch between services and clients (e.g., orchestrators) [12, 23, 27]. In this article we propose to add adaptation features in the service composition process itself. More precisely, we propose an automatic composition technique based on *planning*, a technique which is increasingly applied in SOC [15, 29] as it supports automatic service composition from underspecified requirements, e.g., the data one requires and the data one agrees to give for this, or a set of capabilities one is searching for. Such requirements do not refer to service operations or to the order in which they should be called, which would be ill-suited to end-user composition.

In addition to service composition, QoS optimization aims at satisfying end-user needs about quality requirements. To obtain the solution with the best QoS values for a service composition process, we propose a QoS-aware service composition method to realize QoS optimization during the adaptive service composition.

Outline. Preliminaries on planning are given in Sect. 17.2. After introducing our formal models in Sect. 17.3, Sect. 17.4 presents our encoding of service composition into a planning problem, and Sect. 17.5 proposes a QoS-aware service composition method over conversational services through planning graph as an extension work. Related work is discussed in Sect. 17.6 and we end with conclusions and perspectives.

17.2 Preliminaries

In this section we give a short introduction to AI planning [18].

Definition 17.1. Given a finite set $L = \{p_1, \ldots, p_n\}$ of proposition symbols, a *planning problem* [18] is a triple $P = ((S, A, \gamma), s_0, g)$, where:

- $S \subseteq 2^L$ is a set of states.
- A is a set of actions, an *action* a being a triple $(pre, effect^-, effect^+)$ where $pre(a)$ denotes the preconditions of a, and $effect^-(a)$ and $effect^+(a)$, with $effect^-(a) \cap effect^+(a) = \emptyset$, denote respectively the negative and the positive effects of a.
- γ is a state transition function such that, for any state s where $pre(a) \subseteq s$, $\gamma(s, a) = (s - effect^-(a)) \cup effect^+(a)$.
- $s_0 \in S$ and $g \subseteq L$ are respectively the initial state and the *goal*.

Two actions a and b are *independent* iff $effect^-(a) \cap [pre(b) \cup effect^+(b)] = \emptyset$ and $effect^-(b) \cap [pre(a) \cup effect^+(a)] = \emptyset$. An action set is independent when its actions are pairwise independent. A *plan* is a sequence of actions $\pi = a_1; \ldots; a_k$ such that $\exists s_1, \ldots, s_k \in S$, $s_1 = s_0$, $\forall i \in [1, k]$, $pre(a_i) \subseteq s_{i-1} \wedge \gamma(s_{i-1}, a_i) = s_i$. The definition in [18] takes into account predicates and constant symbols which are then used to define states (ground atoms made with predicates and constants). We directly use propositions here.

Graph Planning [7] is a technique that yields a compact representation of relations between actions and represent the whole problem world. A planning graph $G = (V, E)$ is a directed acyclic leveled graph. It has two kinds of vertices $V = V_A \cup V_P$ where V_A is the vertices representing actions and V_P representing propositions. And edges $E = (V_P \times V_A) \cup (V_A \times V_P)$ connect the vertices. The levels alternate proposition levels P_i and action levels A_i. The initial proposition level P_0 contains the initial propositions (s_0). The planning graph is constructed from P_0 using a polynomial algorithm. An action a is put in layer A_i iff $pre(a) \subseteq P_{i-1}$ and then $effect^+(a) \subseteq P_i$. Specific actions (no-ops) are used to keep data from one layer to the next one, and arcs to relate actions with used data and produced effects. Graph planning also introduces the concept of mutual exclusion (mutex) between non independent actions. Mutual exclusion is reported from a layer to the next one while building the graph. The planning graph actually explores multiple search paths at the same time when expanding the graph, which stops at a layer A_k iff the goal is reached $(g \subseteq A_k)$ or in case of a fixpoint $(A_k = A_{k-1})$. In the former case there exists at least a solution, while in the later there is not. Solution(s) can be obtained using backward search from the goal. Planning graphs whose computation has stopped at level k enable to retrieve all solutions up to this level. Additionally, planning graphs enable to retrieve solutions in a concise form, taking benefit of actions that can be done in parallel (denoted $||$).

An example is given in Fig. 17.1 where we suppose the initial state is $\{a\}$ and the objective is $\{e\}$. Applying U in the first action layer, for example, is possible because a is present; and this produces b and c. The extraction of plans from the graph is performed using a backward chaining technique over action layers, from the final state (objective) back to the initial one. In the example, plans U;Y, Z;Y, (U||Z);Y and (U||Z);S can be obtained (see bold arcs in Fig. 17.1 for U;Y). However, U and Z are in mutual exclusion. Accordingly, since there is no other way to obtain c and d

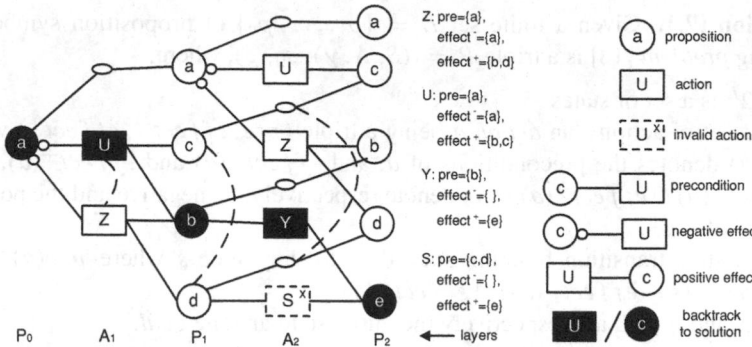

Fig. 17.1 Graphplan example

than with exclusive actions, these two facts are in exclusion in the next (fact) layer, making S impossible. Note that other nodes are indeed in mutual exclusion (such as U and Z in A_1, or two no-ops in A_2 but we have not represented this for clarity).

17.3 Modeling

In this section, we present our formal models, grounding service composition. Table 17.1 lists the symbols used in this section. Both services and composition requirements support conversations. Therefore, we begin with their definition. We then present the structures supporting the definition of semantic data and capabilities. Finally, we present models for services and service composition requirement.

17.3.1 Conversation Modeling

Different models have been proposed to support service discovery, verification, testing, composition or adaptation in presence of service conversations [3, 9, 23]. They

Table 17.1 Summary of symbols

Symbol	Definition	Symbol	Definition
WF^X	A Workflow (WF) over a set of names X	P_A	Activities
P_{so}	XOR-Splits	P_{sa}	AND-Splits
P_{jo}	OR-Joins	P_{ja}	AND-Joins
$\mathcal{D}$	Data Semantic Structure (DSS)	$\mathcal{K}$	Capability Semantic Structure (CSS)
O	A set of operations	W	A set of services

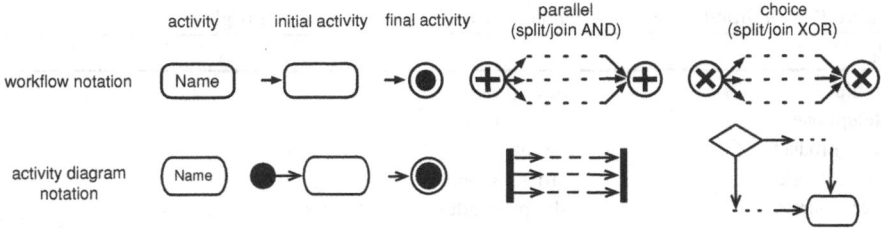

Fig. 17.2 Workflow notation and relation to the UML activity diagrams

mainly differ in their formal grounding (Petri nets, transition systems, or process algebra), and the subset of service languages being supported. Since we target centralized composition (orchestration) with possible parallel service invocation, we choose the workflow model from [19]. An important benefit of workflow models is that they can be related via model transformation to graphical notations that are well-known by the software engineers, e.g., UML activity diagrams (Fig. 17.2) or BPMN. Additionally, workflows are more easily mastered by a non-specialist through pre-defined patterns (sequence, alternative choice, parallel tasks). Transition systems models could yield a simpler encoding as a planning problem but raise issues when it comes to implement the composition models, requiring model filtering to remove parts in the composition models which are not implementable in the target language [23].

Definition 17.2. Given a set of activity names N, a Workflow (WF) [19] is a tuple $WF^N = (P, \rightarrow, Name)$. P is a set of process elements (or workflow nodes) which can be further divided into disjoint sets $P = P_A \cup P_{so} \cup P_{sa} \cup P_{jo} \cup P_{ja}$, where P_A are activities, P_{so} are XOR-Splits, P_{sa} are AND-splits, P_{jo} are OR-Joins, and P_{ja} are AND-Joins. $\rightarrow \subseteq P \times P$ denotes the control flow between nodes. $Name : P_A \rightarrow N$ is a function assigning activity names to activity nodes.

We note $\bullet x = \{y \in P | y \rightarrow x\}$ and $x \bullet = \{y \in P | x \rightarrow y\}$. We require that WF are well-structured [19] and without loop. A significant feature of well-structured workflows is that the XOR-splits and the OR-Joins, and the AND-splits and the AND-splits appear in pairs (Fig. 17.2). Moreover, we require $| \bullet x | \leq 1$ for each x in $P_A \cup P_{sa} \cup P_{so}$ and $|x \bullet | \leq 1$ for each x in $P_A \cup P_{ja} \cup P_{jo}$.

17.3.2 Semantic Structures

In our work we use semantic information to enrich the service composition process and its automation. We have two kinds of semantic information. Capabilities represent the functionalities that are either requested by the end-users or provided by services. They are modelled using a Capability Semantic Structure (CSS). Further, service inputs and outputs are annotated using a Data Semantic Structure (DSS).

Table 17.2 eTablet buying—DSS relations: $d_1 \sqsubseteq d_2$ (left), $d_1 \lhd_x d_2$ (right)

d_1	d_2	
etablet	pear_product	
etelephone	pear_product	
pear_product	product	
product_price	order_amount	
user_address	shipping_addr	
user_address	billing_addr	
user_address	address	

d_1	x	d_2
pear_product_info	price	product_price
pear_product_info	details	product_technical_information
user_info	name	user_name
user_info	address	user_address
user_info	cc	credit_card_info
user_info	pim	pim_wallet
pim_wallet	paypal	paypal_info
pim_wallet	amazon	amazon_info
paypal_info	login	paypal_login
paypal_info	pwd	paypal_pwd
amazon_info	login	amazon_login
amazon_info	pwd	amazon_pwd
credit_card_info	number	credit_card_number
credit_card_info	name	credit_card_holder_name

We define a *Data Semantic Structure (DSS)* as a tuple $(\mathcal{D}, \lhd, \sqsubseteq)$ where $\mathcal{D}$ is a set of concepts (or semantic data type[1]) that represent the semantics of some data, $\lhd$ is a composition relation $((d_1, x, d_2) \in \lhd$, also noted $d_1 \lhd_x d_2$ or simply $d_1 \lhd d_2$ when x is not relevant for the context, means a d_1 is composed of an x of type d_2), and $\sqsubseteq$ is a subtyping relation ($d_1 \sqsubseteq d_2$ means d_1 can be used as a d_2). We require there is no circular composition. DSSs are the support for the automatic decomposition (of d into D if $D = \{d_i \mid d \lhd d_i\}$), composition (of D into d if $D = \{d_i \mid d \lhd d_i\}$) and casting (of d_1 into d_2 if $d_1 \sqsubseteq d_2$) of data types exchanged between services and orchestrator. We also define a *Capability Semantic Structure (CSS)* as a set $\mathcal{K}$ of concepts that correspond to capabilities.

Application. We will illustrate our composition technique on a simple, yet realistic, case study: the online buying of an eTablet. A DSS describes concepts and relations for this case study. For place matters, we only give the relations here (Table 17.2) since concepts can be inferred from these and from the service operation signatures, below.

---

[1] In this paper, the concepts of semantics and type of data are unified.

Table 17.3 eTablet buying—services' operations

Service	Operation	Profile
w_1	order	pear_product $\rightarrow$ pear_product_info, as_sessionid :: product_selection : 20
w_1	cancel	as_sessionid $\rightarrow$ $\emptyset$ :: nil:2
w_1	ship	shipping_addr, as_sessionid $\rightarrow$ $\emptyset$ :: shipping_setup:10
w_1	bill	billing_addr, as_sessionid $\rightarrow$ $\emptyset$ :: billing_setup:25
w_1	charge	credit_card_info, as_sessionid $\rightarrow$ $\emptyset$ :: payment:10
w_1	gift_wrapper	giftcode, as_sessionid $\rightarrow$ $\emptyset$ :: payment:20
w_1	ack	as_sessionid $\rightarrow$ tracking_num :: order_finalization:5
w_2	order	product $\rightarrow$ e_sessionid :: product_selection:5
w_2	ship	shipping_addr, e_sessionid $\rightarrow$ order_amount :: shipping_setup:7
w_2	charge_pp	paypal_trans_id, e_sessionid $\rightarrow$ $\emptyset$ :: nil:12
w_2	charge_cc	credit_card_info, e_sessionid $\rightarrow$ $\emptyset$ :: payment:15
w_2	bill	billing_addr, e_sessionid $\rightarrow$ $\emptyset$ :: billing_setup:8
w_2	finalize	e_sessionid $\rightarrow$ tracking_num :: order_finalization:6
w_3	login	paypal_login, paypal_pwd $\rightarrow$ p_sessionid :: nil:10
w_3	get_credit	order_amount, p_sessionid $\rightarrow$ paypal_trans_id :: payment:20
w_3	ask_bill	address, p_sessionid $\rightarrow$ $\emptyset$ :: billing_setup:8
w_3	logout	p_sessionid $\rightarrow$ $\emptyset$ :: nil:4

17.3.3 Services

A service is a set of operations described in terms of capabilities, inputs, outputs and quality. Additionally, services have a conversation.

Definition 17.3. Given a CSS $\mathcal{K}$ and a DSS $\mathcal{D} = (\mathcal{D}, \lhd, \sqsubset)$, a *service* is a tuple $w = (O, WF^O)$, where O is a set of operations, an operation being a tuple (in, out, k, n) with $in \subseteq \mathcal{D}$, $out \subseteq \mathcal{D}$, $k \in \mathcal{K}$, n is the quality value, and WF^O is a workflow built over O.

For a simple service (without a conversation) w, a trivial conversation can be obtained with a workflow where $P_A = O(w)$ (one activity for each operation), $P_{so} = \{\otimes\}$, $P_{jo} = \{\overline{\otimes}\}$, $P_{sa} = P_{ja} = \emptyset$, and $\forall o \in P_A$, $\{(\otimes, o), (o, \overline{\otimes})\} \subseteq \rightarrow$. This corresponds to a generalized choice between all possible operations. An operation may not have a capability and the quality of the operation may not be given (we then let $k = $ nil). $o = (in, out, k, n)$ is also noted $o : in \rightarrow out :: k : n$. If several quality values are given for operation o, we calculate the aggregated QoS value n as an overall quality for o. How to calculate the aggregated quality value will be introduced in Sect. 17.5.1.

Application. To fulfill the user need, we have three services: **pear_store** (w_1, online store for pear products), **ebay** (w_2, general online shop) and **paypal** (w_3, online payment facilities). Their operations are given in Table 17.3 and their workflows are given in Fig. 17.3. The QoS of each operation in services is supposed to be throughput.

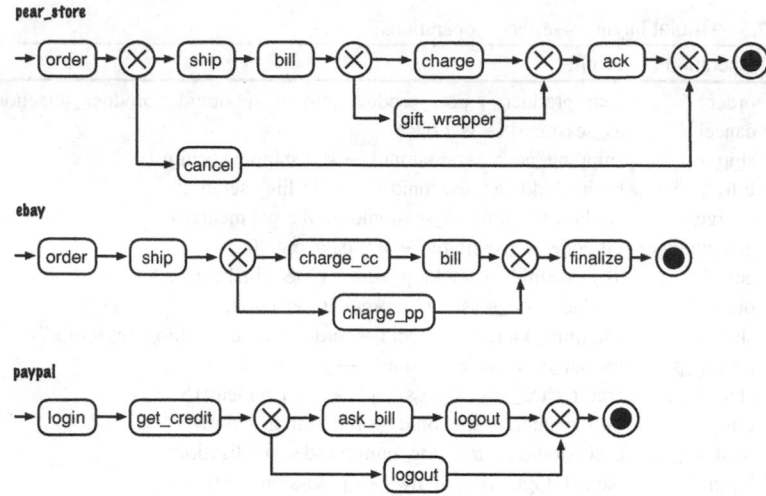

Fig. 17.3 eTablet buying—services' workflows

17.3.4 Composition Requirements

A service composition requirement is given in terms of the inputs the user is ready
to provide and the outputs this user is expecting. Additionally, the capabilities that
are expected from the composition are specified, and their expected ordering given
under the form of a workflow.

Definition 17.4. Given a CSS $\mathcal{K}$ and a DSS $\mathcal{D} = (\mathcal{D}, \vartriangleleft, \sqsubseteq)$, a *composition require-
ment* is a tuple $(D_{\text{in}}, D_{\text{out}}, WF^{\mathcal{K}})$ where $D_{\text{in}} \subseteq \mathcal{D}, D_{\text{out}} \subseteq \mathcal{D}$, and $WF^{\mathcal{K}}$ is a workflow
build over $\mathcal{K}$.

Application. The user requirement in our case study is $(\{etablet, user\_info\}$,
$\{tracking\_num\}, wfc)$. As far as the wfc requirement workflow is concerned,
we have two alternatives for it. The first one (Fig. 17.4, left) requires that payment
is done after shipping and billing have been set up (which can be done in parallel).
The second one (Fig. 17.4, right) is less strict and enables the payment to be done in
parallel to shipping and billing setup.

17.4 Encoding Composition as a Planning Problem

In this section we present how service composition can be encoded as a graph planning problem. We will first explain how DSS can be encoded (to solve out horizontal
adaptation). Then we will present how a generic workflow can be encoded. Based on

Fig. 17.4 eTablet buying—
requirement workflows

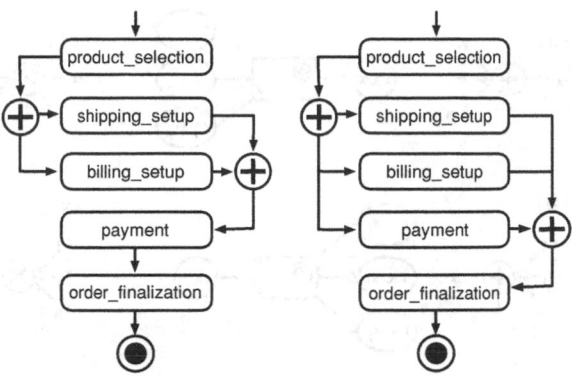

this, we will then explain how services and composition requirements are encoded
(the workflow of the later solving out vertical adaptation).

17.4.1 DSS Encoding

For each $d \lhd \{x_i : d_i\}$ in the DSS we have an action $comp_d(\bigcup_i \{d_i\}, \emptyset, \{d\})$ and an
action $dec_d(\{d\}, \emptyset, \bigcup_i \{d_i\})$ to model possible (de)composition. Moreover, for each
$d \sqsubset d'$ in the DSS we have an action $cast_{d,d'}(\{d\}, \emptyset, \{d'\})$ to model possible casting
from d to d'.

17.4.2 Workflow Encoding

We reuse here a transformation from workflows to Petri net defined in [19]. Instead of
mapping a workflow $(P, \to, Name)$ to a Petri net, we map it to a planning problem.
Let us first define the set of propositions that are used. The behavioral constraints
underlying the workflow semantics (e.g., an action being before/after another one)
are supported through two kinds to propositions: $r_{x,y}$ and $c_{x,y}$. We also have a
proposition I for initial states, and a proposition F for correct termination states.
F will be used both for final states and for initial states (in this case to denote that a
service can be unused). We may then define the actions that are used (Fig. 17.5):

- for each $x \in P_{sa}$, we have an action $a = \oplus x$ (Fig. 17.5a), for each $x \in P_{ja}$, we
  have an action $a = \bar{\oplus} x$ (Fig. 17.5b), and for each $x \in P_A$, we have an action
  $a = [Name(x)]x$ (Fig. 17.5c). In all three cases, we set $pre(a) = effect^-(a) = \bigcup_{y \in \bullet x} \{r_{x,y}\}$, and $effect^+(a) = \bigcup_{y \in x \bullet} \{c_{x,y}\}$.
- for each $x \in P_{so}$, for each $y \in x\bullet$, we have an action $a = \otimes x, y$ (Fig. 17.5d) and
  we set $pre(a) = effect^-(a) = \bigcup_{z \in \bullet x} \{r_{x,z}\}$, and $effect^+(a) = \{c_{x,y}\}$.

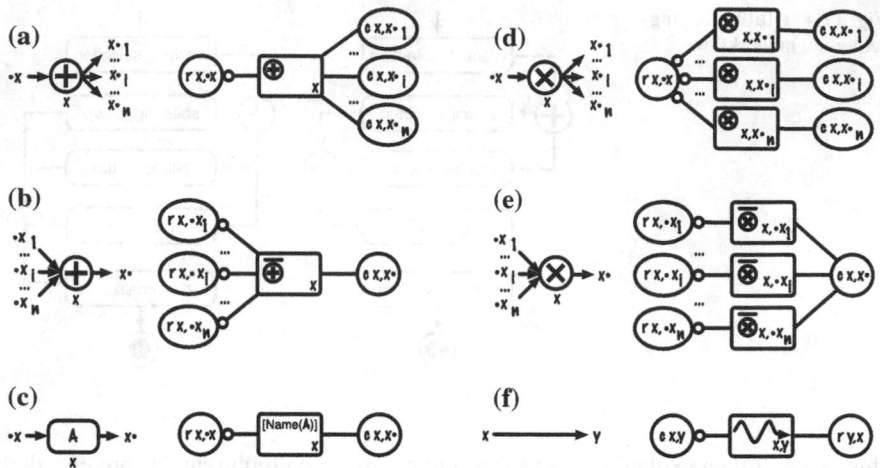

Fig. 17.5 Workflow encoding

- for each $x \in P_{jo}$, for each $y \in \bullet x$, we have an action $a = \bar{\otimes}x, y$ (Fig. 17.5e), and we set $pre(a) = effect^-(a) = r_{x,y}$, and $effect^+(a) = \bigcup_{z \in \bullet x}\{c_{x,z}\}$.
- for each $x \to y$, we have an action $a = \bar{\otimes}x, y$ (Fig. 17.5f) and we set $pre(a) = effect^-(a) = \{c_{x,y}\}$, and $effect^+(a) = \{r_{y,x}\}$.
- additionally, for any initial action a we add $\{I, F\}$ in $pre(a)$ and $effect^-(a)$.
- additionally, for any final action a we add $\{F\}$ in $effect^+(a)$.

17.4.3 Composition Requirements Encoding

A composition requirement $(D_{in}, D_{out}, WF^{\mathcal{K}})$ is encoded as follows. First we compute the set of actions resulting from the encoding of $WF^{\mathcal{K}}$ (see 17.4.2). Then we have to encode the fact that capabilities in the composition requirement encoding should interoperate with operations in service encodings. The idea is the following. Taking a service w, when a capability k is enabled at the current state of execution by $WF^{\mathcal{K}}$ then we should invoke an operation of capability k that is enabled at the current state by $WF^{O(w)}$ before any one of the capability possibly following k could be enabled. Moreover, an operation o with capability k of w can be invoked only iff this is enabled by the current state of execution in $WF^{O(w)}$ and k is enabled in $WF^{\mathcal{K}}$. To achieve this, we replace any action $a = [k]x$ in the encoding of $WF^{\mathcal{K}}$ by two actions, $a' = [k]x$ and $\overline{a'} = [k]\overline{x}$, and we set:

- $pre(a') = pre(a), effect^-(a') = effect^-(a), effect^+(a) = \{e_k, link_x\}$.
- $pre(\overline{a'}) = effect^-(\overline{a'}) = \{link_x, d_k\}, effect^+(\overline{a'}) = effect^+(a)$.

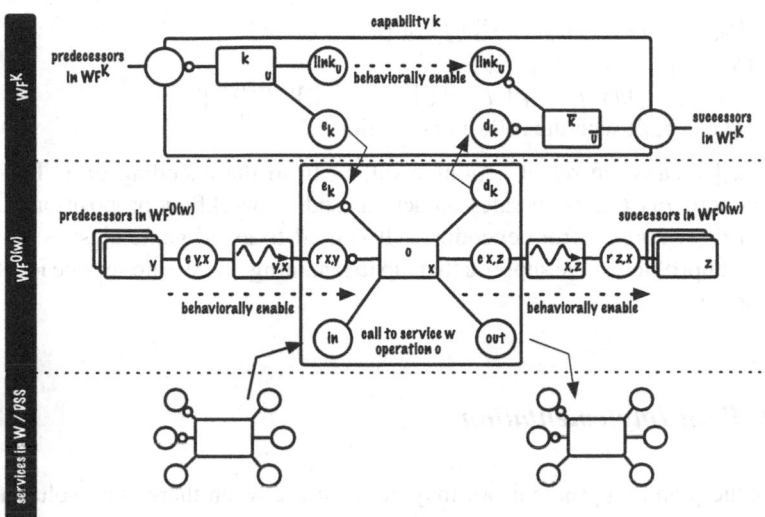

Fig. 17.6 Principle of interaction between service and requirement encodings

e_k and d_k enforce the synchronizing rules between capability workflow (defining when a capability k can be done) and service workflows (defining when an operation with capability k can be done) as presented in Fig. 17.6. $link_k$ ensure that two actions $a_1 = [k]x_1$ and $a_2 = [k]x_2$ with the same capability will not interact incorrectly when x_1 and x_2 are in parallel in a workflow.

17.4.4 Service Encoding

Each service $w = (O, WF^O)$ is encoded as follows. First we encode the workflow WF^O as presented in 17.4.2. Then, for each action $a = [o]x$ in this encoding we add:

- $in(o)$ in $pre(a)$ to model the inputs required by operation o and $out(o)$ in $effect^+(a)$ to model the outputs provided by operation o.
- $e_{k(o)}$ in $pre(a)$ and in $effect^-(a)$ and $d_{k(o)}$ in $effect^+(a)$ to implement the interaction with capabilities presented in 17.4.3 and in Fig. 17.6.

17.4.5 Overall Encoding

Given a DSS $\mathcal{D}$, a set of services W, and a composition requirement $(D_{\text{in}}, D_{\text{out}}, WF^{\mathcal{K}})$, we obtain the planning problem $((S, A, \gamma), s_0, g)$ as follows:

- $s_0 = D_{\text{in}} \cup \{wfc : I, wfc : F\} \bigcup_{w \in W} \{w : I, w : F\}$.
- $g = D_{\text{out}} \cup \{wfc : F\} \bigcup_{w? \in W} \{w : F\}$.
- $A = dss : \|\mathcal{D}\| \cup wfc : \|WF^{\mathcal{K}}\| \bigcup_{w \in W} w : \|WF^{O(w)}\|$.
- S and γ are built with the rules in Definition 17.1.

where $\|x\|$ means the set of actions resulting from the encoding of x. Prefixing (denoted with $prefix$:) operates on actions and on workflow propositions (I, F, $r_{x,y}$, and $c_{x,y}$) coming from encodings. It is used to avoid name clashes between different subproblems. We suppose that, up to renaming, there is no service identified as dss or wfc.

17.4.6 Plan Implementation

Solving the planning problem, we may get a failure when there is no solution satisfying both that (i) a service composition exists to get D_{out} from D_{in}, (ii) using operations/capabilities in an ordering satisfying both used service conversations and capability conversation, (iii) leaving used services in their final state. In other cases, we obtain (see Sect. 17.2) a plan $\pi = L_1; \dots; L_i; \dots; L_n$ where ; is the sequence operator and each L_i is of the form $(P_{i,1}\| \dots \|P_{i,j}\| \dots \|P_{i,m_i})$ where $\|$ is the parallel operator and each $P_{i,j}$ is a workflow process element. First of all, we begin by filtering out π by removing from it all $P_{i,j}$ that is not of the form $dss : \dots$ or $w : [o]x$, i.e., that is a purely structuring item, not corresponding to data transformation or service invocation. Given the filtered plan, we can generate a WS-BPEL implementation for it as done for transitions systems in [23]. Still, we may benefit here from the fact that actions that can be done in parallel are explicited in a graph planning plan (using operation $\|$), while in transition systems we only have interleaving semantics (finding out which actions can be done in parallel is much more complex). Therefore, for the main structure of the <process> ...< /process> element we replace the [23] state machine encoding by a more efficient version using sequence and flows. For π we get:

$$\langle\texttt{sequence}\rangle modeltrans(L_1) \dots modeltrans(L_i) \dots modeltrans(L - n)\langle/\texttt{sequence}\rangle$$

and for each $L_i = (P_{i,1}\| \dots \|P_{i,j}\| \dots \|P_{i,m_i})$ we have:

$$\langle\texttt{flow}\rangle \, modeltrans(P_{i,1}) \dots modeltrans(P_{i,j}) \dots modeltrans(P_{i,m_i})) \, \langle/\texttt{flow}\rangle$$

where $modeltrans$ is the transformation of basic assignment/communication activities defined in [23].

17.4.7 Tool Support

Our composition approach is supported with a tool, **pycompose** (Fig. 17.7), written in the Python language. This tool takes as input a DSS file, several service description files (list of operations and workflow), and the composition requirement (input

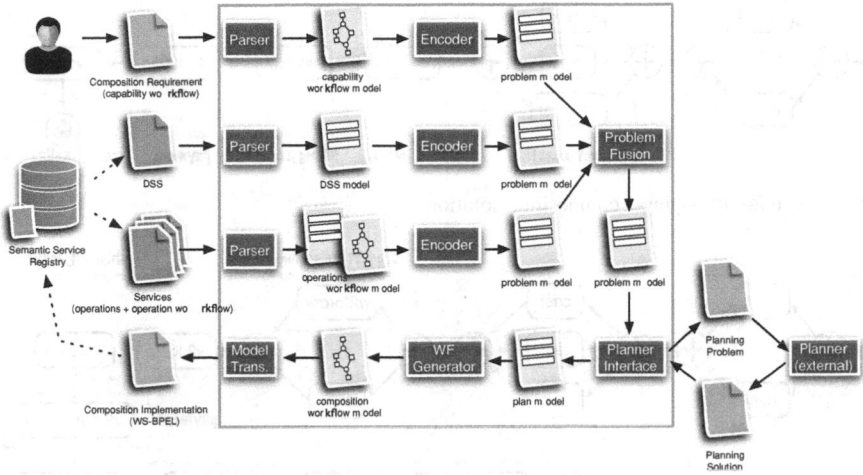

Fig. 17.7 Architecture of the pycompose tool

list, output list, and a workflow file). It then generates the encoding of this composition problem. pycompose supports through a command-line option the use of several planners: the original C implementation of graph planning, graphplan,[2] a Java implementation of it, PDDLGraphPlan,[3] and Blackbox,[4] a planner combining graphplan building and the use of SAT solvers to retrieve plans. The pycompose architecture enables to support other planners through the implementation of a class with two methods: problemToString and run, respectively to output a problem in planner format and to run and parse planner results.

Application. If we run pycompose on our composition problem with the first requirement workflow (Fig. 17.4, left), we get one solution (computed in 0.11 s on a 2.53 GHz Mac Book Pro, including 0.03 s for the planner to retrieve the plan):

(pear_product:=$cast$(etablet) || {user_name,user_address,credit_card_info,pim_wallet}
$:=dec$(user_info)) ;
(shipping_addr:=$cast$(user_address) || billing_addr:=$cast$(user_address) || w_1:order) ;
w_1:ship ; w_1:bill ; w_1:charge ; w_1:ack

The workflow representation of this solution is presented in Fig. 17.8.

However, let us now suppose that the user does not want to give his credit card (user_info $\lhd_{cc}$ credit_card_info is removed from DSS, or the user input is replaced with {etablet,user_name,user_address,pim_wallet}). There is no longer any possible composition: w_1 cannot proceed with payment (no credit card information), moreover, w_2 and w_3 cannot interact since this would yield that capability *payment* is

---

[2] http://www.cs.cmu.edu/avrim/graphplan.html

[3] http://www.cs.bham.ac.uk/zas/software/graphplanner.html

[4] http://www.cs.rochester.edu/kautz/satplan/blackbox/

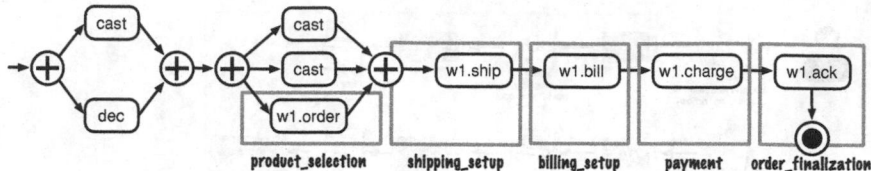

Fig. 17.8 eTablet buying—composition solution

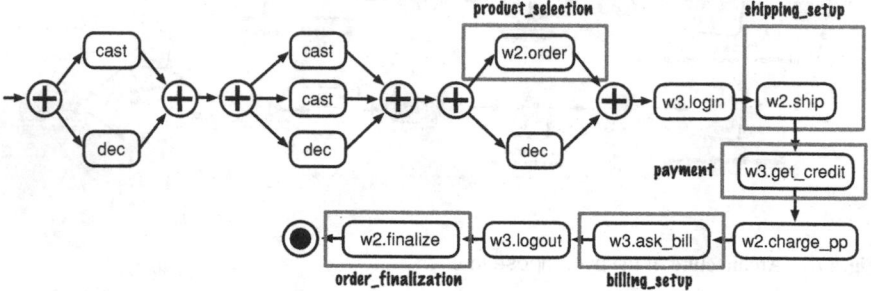

Fig. 17.9 eTablet buying—alternative composition solution

done before capability *billing_setup* (see w_3 workflow in Fig. 17.3 and its operations in Table 17.3) while the requirement workflow forbids it. However, if we let a
more permissive requirement workflow (Fig. 17.4, right) then we get a composition
(computed in 0.11 s on a 2.53 GHz Mac Book Pro, including 0.04 s for the planner
to retrieve the plan) where w_2 and w_3 interact:

(pear_product := *cast*(etablet) || {user_name,user_address,credit_card_info,pim_wallet}
                                    := *dec*(user_info)) ;
(product := *cast*(pear_product) || shipping_addr := *cast*(user_address)
                                    || {paypal_info,amazon_info} := *dec*(pim_wallet)) ;
(w_2:order || {paypal_login,paypal_pwd} := *dec*(paypal_info)) ;
w_3:login ; w_2:ship ; w_3:get_credit ; w_2:charge_pp ; w_3:ask_bill ; w_3:logout ; w_2:finalize

The workflow representation of this second solution is given in Fig. 17.9.

17.5 QoS Optimization of Conversational Service Composition as an Extension

In this section we first introduce how to calculate the aggregation of Quality of
Services (QoS). Then we extend the developed composition method to include QoS
optimization as a non-functional goal.

17.5.1 Aggregation of Quality of Services

A conversational service is composed of a set of operations over which a workflow is specified. Each operation o can be regarded as an elementary service w with certain qualities. For a network of conversational services, we can calculate the QoS of the network as if we have a network of elementary services. Suppose we use $\sigma = w_1, w_2, \ldots, w_n$ to represent a network of connected elementary services. If they are connected in sequence, $\sigma = w_1; w_2; \ldots; w_n$, or in parallel, $\sigma = w_1 || w_2 || \ldots || w_n$. For an elementary service w, a finite set of quality criteria of w is denoted as $Q(w)$. Since our work focuses on throughput and execution price, the two quality criteria for an elementary service w and the aggregated value over σ:

- **Throughput** $Q_1(w)$: the average rate of successful message delivery over a communication channel, e.g., 10 successful invocations per second.

$$Q_1(w_1; \ldots; w_n) = \min Q_1(w_i) \qquad (17.1)$$

$$Q_1(w_1 || \ldots || w_n) = \min Q_1(w_i) \qquad (17.2)$$

- **Execution price** $Q_2(w)$: the fee to invoke w.

$$Q_2(w_1, \ldots, w_n) = \sum Q_2(w_i) \qquad (17.3)$$

Some of the above criteria are negative, i.e., the higher the value, the lower the quality. Execution price and response time are in this category. The other criteria, such as throughput, are positive, i.e., the higher the value, the higher the quality. We want to have a uniform way to compare the qualities, especially with the multiple criteria. We apply a Multiple Criteria Decision Making (MCDM) technique [33] to aggregate QoS value $Q(w)$. Similar to [8] and [36], we first scale the value of a quality i for a service w_j. For negative criteria, e.g., execution price, values are scaled according to Eq. 17.4. For positive criteria, e.g., throughput, values are scaled according to Eq. 17.5. For all the criteria, the higher the quality value, the lower the utility value $U_i(w_j)$. This is because the classic Dijkstra's algorithm finds the "shortest distance"(lowest cost) over a graph.

$$U_i(w_j) = \begin{cases} \frac{Q_i(w_j) - Q_i^{min}}{Q_i^{max} - Q_i^{min}} & \text{if } Q_i^{max} - Q_i^{min} \neq 0 \\ 1 & \text{if } Q_i^{max} - Q_i^{min} = 0 \end{cases} \qquad (17.4)$$

$$U_i(w_j) = \begin{cases} \frac{Q_i^{max} - Q_i(w_j)}{Q_i^{max} - Q_i^{min}} & \text{if } Q_i^{max} - Q_i^{min} \neq 0 \\ 1 & \text{if } Q_i^{max} - Q_i^{min} = 0 \end{cases} \qquad (17.5)$$

The overall quality score for a Web service w_j is defined in Eq. 17.6:

$$U(w_j) = \sum U_i(w_j) \times W_i \qquad (17.6)$$

where $W_i \in [0, 1]$ and $\sum W_i = 1$. W_i represents the weight of criterion i.

For a network of services σ, we would like to do the same conversion. The following equations for defining $U_i(\sigma)$ are the same as those defining $Q_i(\sigma)$, just changing $Q_i(w_i)$ to $U_i(w_i)$, except in Eqs. 17.9 and 17.10, max replaces min, it is because U_2 decreases when Q_1 increases. Thus, the max value of U_1 corresponds to the min value of Q_2.

$$U_1(w_1; \ldots; w_n) = \sum U_1(w_i) \tag{17.7}$$

$$U_1(w_1 || \ldots || w_n) = \max U_1(w_i) \tag{17.8}$$

$$U_2(w_1; \ldots; w_n) = \max U_2(w_i) \tag{17.9}$$

$$U_2(w_1 || \ldots || w_n) = \max U_2(w_i) \tag{17.10}$$

The aggregated utility value for σ is:

$$U(w_1, \ldots, w_n) = \sum U_i(w_1, \ldots, w_n) \times W_i \tag{17.11}$$

With Eqs. 17.7–17.11, we could compare two networks of services by the individual utility values U_i or by the overall score U. The lower the value, the higher the quality of service. We uniform the increasing and decreasing sense of the quality criteria. But the calculation of the precise values are still different for different criteria.

17.5.2 Encoding QoS-Aware Composition as a QoS-Aware Planning Problem

When QoS is given, people expect a solution with the best quality. A QoS-aware service composition is to generate a business process that fulfills the functional goals and optimizes the QoS value simultaneously. We first explain the intuition behind the QoS-aware planning technique. Then we present how to solve QoS-aware composition using QoS-aware planning technique.

17.5.2.1 Motivations

When service composition is encoded as a graph planning problem, the planning graph built by the graph planning technique records all the functional elements, i.e., all the execution paths, to achieve functional goals. If the planning graph can be extended into a QoS-aware planning graph that not only records functional elements but also includes the QoS information, it is possible to solve QoS-aware service composition problem using planning graph technique.

We discover that combining Dijkstra's algorithm with the planning graph technique provides a good way to associate the QoS value with each vertex in a planning graph. Firstly, a planning graph is a compact representation of the whole problem space. All the execution paths that achieve goals can be extracted from the planning graph. We could use a systematic search algorithm like Dijkstra's algorithm to traverse the planning graph from the initial layer to the goals. Secondly, the principle of Dijkstra's algorithm is to calculate the best *cost-to-come* value for a vertex. Since a proposition can be regarded as a vertex of the planning graph, we could use the same principle to calculate the best *cost-to-come* value which is the best QoS value for each proposition. Then, we could get the overall *cost-to-come* for all the goal propositions. And during the search, we could record the best path which is the best plan.

17.5.2.2 QoS-Aware Graph Planning Technique

Our QoS-aware Graph Planning technique builds a Tagged Planning Graph (TPG) instead of a normal planning graph. This technique is firstly developed in our paper [34] for QoS-aware composition problems without negative effects. In this paper we extend it to work with negative effects. A TPG is an extension of a planning graph in the sense that each vertex in the planning graph is assigned with a tag. The affiliated tag records the related QoS information for each vertex. In the following, we present the way to calculate the tag values for action vertices and for proposition vertices respectively.

Actions

When service composition is encoded as a Graph Planning problem, actions in the planning graph come from DSS encoding, workflow encoding, service encoding and composition requirement encoding. The tag for each action vertex is the QoS value of the action. Except the actions encoded from the operations of the conversational services, the other actions, such as decomposition, composition and casting from DSS encoding, P_{so}, P_{sa}, P_{jo} and P_{ja} from service encoding, etc., do not have QoS values. We need to assign a default QoS value to an action vertex which does not have a QoS value in order to facilitate QoS aggregation.

For negative criteria, e.g., execution price, the default QoS value is zero. For position criteria, e.g., throughput, the default QoS value is the maximal value of all actions encoded from operations. These assignments make sense, because these values do not affect the calculation of the aggregated QoS of the resulting composite service.

Propositions

The tag T_p for a proposition vertex p is a set $\{t_1^p, \ldots, t_k^p\}$ ($k = ||T_p||$), which represents all possible execution paths leading to the proposition p. Each tag member t_j^p ($j = 1, \ldots, k$) in T_p is a tuple ($QoSValue, executionpath$) and corresponds to an execution path $executionpath$ with its QoS value $QoSValue$. An $executionpath$ is actually a plan $\Pi = \pi_1; \ldots; \pi_n$ to achieve p, where π_j ($j = 1, \ldots, n$) is a set of actions that can be executed in parallel. When we search a plan for p, we exclude the invalid plans that contain mutex pairs of actions due to the negative effects of actions. Also, we calculate the QoS values for these valid plans at the same time.

For a proposition p at layer P_0, $T_p = \{(U, \{\})\}$ where U is a default QoS value. The assignment of the default QoS value for a proposition at P_0 is similar to the assignment of the default QoS value for actions. For negative criteria, such as response time or execution price, the default QoS value is zero. For position criteria, such as throughput, the default QoS value is the maximal value of all actions encoded from operations. These values do not affect the calculation of the aggregated QoS of the resulting composite service. The $executionpath$ is $\{\}$ since p is provided by service composition query.

Inspired by the Dijkstra's algorithm, we calculate the tag for a p at layer P_i ($i \geq 1$) when the planning graph is constructed. If an action a at layer A_i ($i \geq 1$) produces p at layer P_i ($i \geq 1$), we calculate the tag for p as the following.

- **Calculate the execution paths**. If action a produces p, the combinations of the execution paths of $pre(a)$ (in parallel) appended by a are the execution paths of p. If there are several actions produce p, the execution paths calculated from these actions are all execution paths for p. If these actions are mutex, the execution paths are mutex too.
- **Calculate the QoS value for each execution path**. The calculation of the QoS value for each execution path follows the QoS aggregation formulas. One execution path leading to p is consist of one combination of the execution paths of $pre(a)$ and a. For example, if throughput is the QoS criterion, the throughput of an execution path leading to p is the minimum of the throughput of the combined execution paths and the throughput of a. If execution price is the QoS criterion, that the total execution price of all the combined execution paths plus the execution price of a is the execution price of the execution path leading to p.

After the TPG is constructed, we extract an optimal plan by backtracking the execution path for each goal proposition. An optimal plan is consist of the optimal plans to achieve each individually goal simultaneously. Since a plan cannot contain any mutex pair of actions, we need to consider all the possibilities.

17.5.2.3 QoS-Aware Graph Planning

QoS-aware Graph Planning extends the standard Graph Planning technique. In the construction phase, the QoS tag is calculated and the graph is constructed until a fixedpoint layer, because a longer plan may have a better QoS value. In the backtracking phase, a solution with the best QoS value is extracted. For simplicity, we present our algorithms using throughput as the single quality criterion and the calculation of throughput follows Eqs. 17.1 and 17.2. The calculation of the other QoS criteria is discussed in Sect. 17.5.3.

Algorithm 1 called $QoSGraphPlan$ is the main algorithm QoS-aware Planning Graph. Line 1 sets U as the the maximum throughput of actions. At layer P_0, the multiple tags T_p only contains a tuple of U and an empty set (line 2). Starting from layer 0 (line 3), the algorithm calls $ExpandGraph$ (Algorithm 2) to construct a TPG layer by layer until it reaches $Fixedpoint$ (line 4–7). If the fixed-point layer P_n contains all goal propositions without mutex (line 8), the algorithm calls $ExtractPlan$ (Algorithm 4) (line 9) to extract an optimal plan from the TPG. Otherwise, there is no plan exist (line 11).

Algorithm 1: $QoSGraphPlan(A, s_0, g)$

Data: $G = \langle P_0, A_1, \mu A_1, ..., A_n, \mu A_n, P_i, \mu P_n \rangle$ is a planning graph;

1: $U \leftarrow \max\{cost(a)|a \in A\}$;
2: $P_0 \leftarrow \{(p, T_p)|p \in s_0, T_p \text{ is a multiple-tag set of } p \text{ where } T_p \leftarrow \{(U, \{\})\}\}$;
3: $i \leftarrow 0$;
4: **repeat**
5:   $i \leftarrow i + 1$;
6:   $G \leftarrow ExpandGraph(G)$;
7: **until** $Fixedpoint(G)$
8: **if** $g \subseteq P_n$ and $g^2 \cap \mu P_n = \emptyset$ **then**
9:   **print** $ExtractPlan(G, g)$;
10: **else**
11:   **print** $\emptyset$;
12: **end if**

Algorithm 2 called $ExpandGraph$ expands the TPG by onc layer. A_i gets all the enabled actions at layer i and each actions has a tag t (line 1). The tag t is the QoS value, i.e., throughput, of the action. The enabled actions are those whose inputs are in the previous layer $i - 1$ and there is no mutual exclusion between propositions belonging to the inputs. μA_i is the set of mutex pairs of actions in A_i (line 2). P_i contains positive effects of actions in A_i (line 3). We assign a tag T_p to each $p \in P_i$. T_p is actually a multiple-tag set. Each element $t_j^p \in T_p$ ($j = 1, \ldots, \|T_p\|$) is a tuple $(t_j^p.v, t_j^p.\Pi)$, where $t_j^p.\Pi$ is a execution path that leads to p and $t_j^p.v$ is the QoS value of $t_j^p.\Pi$. It calls $CalMultiTag$ (Algorithm 3) to calculate T_p for p. Line 4 gets the set of mutex pairs of propositions in P_i, denoted as μP_i. Line 5–line 9 create the arcs between actions and propositions.

Algorithm 2: $ExpandGraph(G)$

Data: $G = \langle P_0, A_1, \mu A_1, ..., A_n, \mu A_n, P_i, \mu P_n \rangle$;

1: $A_i \leftarrow \{(a, t) | pre(a) \subseteq P_{i-1}, pre^2(a) \cap \mu P_{i-1}, t = cost(a)\}$;

2: $\mu A_i \leftarrow \{(a, b) \in A_i^2, a \neq b | effects^-(a) \cap [pre(b) \cup effects^+(b)] \neq \emptyset$ or $effects^-(b) \cap [pre(a) \cup effects^+(a)] \neq \emptyset$ or $\exists (p, q) \in \mu P_{i-1} : p \in pre(a), q \in pre(b)\}$;

3: $P_i \leftarrow \{(p, T_p) | \exists a \in A_i : p \in effects^+(a), T_p = CalMultiTag(G, p, i)$ is a multiple-tag set of p where T_p is represented as $\{t_j^p | j = 1, \ldots, ||T_p||$ and $t_j^p = (t_j^p.v, t_j^p.\Pi)\}\}$;

4: $\mu P_i \leftarrow \{(p, q) \in P_i^2, p \neq q | \forall a, b \in A, a \neq b : p \in effects^+(a), q \in effects^+(b) \Rightarrow (a, b) \in \mu A_i\}$;

5: **for** each $a \in A_i$ **do**

6:     link a with precondition arcs to $pre(a)$ in P_{i-1};

7:     link a with positive arcs to each of its $effects^+(a)$ in P_i;

8:     link a with negative arcs to each of its $effects^-(a)$ in P_i;

9: **end for**

10: **return** $(\langle P_0, A_1, \mu A_1 ..., A_n, \mu A_n, P_n, \mu P_n \rangle)$;

Algorithm 3 calculates the tag value for each proposition p. Initially, T is an empty set (line 1). S is a subset of A_i and each action in S produces p as one of its positive effects (line 2). For each pair $(a, t) \in S$, we get a subset of P_{i-1}, denoted as PT. Each element (p, T_p) in PT satisfies $p \in pre(a)$ (line 4). T_p is a multiple-tag set for p where $T_p = \{t_j^p | t_j^p = (t_j^p.v, t_j^p.\Pi)$ is the j-th element of T_p and $j = \{1, \ldots, ||T_p||\}$. For each element t_j^p of T_p, $t_j^p.\Pi$ is a execution path that leads to p and $t_j^p.v$ is the cost, i.e., throughput, of the execution path $t_j^p.\Pi$. Q is the product of all elements in PT (line 5). For a set of execution paths $\{t_m^{p_1}, \ldots, t_h^{p_k}\} \in Q$ (line 6), a new execution path Π' is obtained by combining all the execution paths (line 7). $CheckMutex(G, \Pi')$ is a function to check whether there exists a mutex pair of actions at the same layer $\Pi'.\pi_j$ $(j = 1, \ldots, ||\Pi'||)$. If $CheckMutex(G, \Pi')$ returns true, it means there exists at least a mutex pair of actions in Π' (line 8). In this case, Π' becomes the execution path Π without mutex pairs of actions (line 9). Accordingly, the cost v (line 10) and the multiple-tag set T (line 11) are updated.

Algorithm 4 extracts a plan with optimal QoS value. First, the optimal plan Π is set to be $\langle \rangle$ (line 1). In line 2, all goal propositions obtained from layer P_n are added into S. Line 3 calculates the direct product of all multiple-tag sets in S. The set of possible plans T is initially an empty set (line 4). For each element $\{t_m^{p_1}, \ldots, t_h^{p_k}\} \in Q$ (line 5), a new possible execution path Π' is obtained by combining all the execution paths (line 6). The cost v is the minimum cost of all sub-execution paths that construct Π' (line 7). Line 8 adds (v', Π') into T. The algorithm starts to find an optimal plan from T until T becomes an empty set (lines 10–20). $SelectOptPlan(T)$ is a function to find the current optimal plan with the maximum throughput from T. For every possible optimal plan with the current maximum throughput returned by $SelectOptPlan(T)$ (line 11), $CheckMutex(G, \Pi)$ is to filter out the plans that contain any mutual exclusion pairs of actions.

Algorithm 3: $CalMultiTag(G, p, i)$

Data: $G = \langle P_0, A_1, \mu A_1, ..., A_i, \mu A_i \rangle$;

1: $T \leftarrow \{\}$;
2: $S \leftarrow \{(a, t)|(a, t) \in A_i \text{ and } p \in effects^+(a)\}$;
3: **for** $(a, t) \in S$ **do**
4:     $PT \leftarrow \{(p, T_p)|(p, T_p) \in P_{i-1} \text{ and } p \in pre(a)\}$;
5:     $Q \leftarrow T_{p_1} \times T_{p_2}, \ldots, \times T_{p_k}$ where $(p_j, T_{p_j}) \in PT$ and $j = 1, \ldots, \|PT\|$;
6:     **for** $\{t_m^{p_1}, \ldots, t_h^{p_k}\} \in Q$ **do**
7:         $\Pi' \leftarrow t_m^{p_1}.\Pi.\pi_1\| \ldots \|t_h^{p_k}.\Pi.\pi_1; \ldots; t_m^{p_1}.\Pi.\pi_{i-1}\| \ldots \|t_h^{p_k}.\Pi.\pi_{i-1}$;
8:         **if** $CheckMutex(G, \Pi') = true$ **then**
9:             $\Pi = \Pi'$;
10:            $v \leftarrow \min\{t_j^{p_1}.v|m \le j \le n\}$;
11:            $T \leftarrow T \cup \{(\min\{v, t\}, \Pi; a)\}$;
12:        **end if**
13:    **end for**
14: **end for**
15: **return** T;

Algorithm 4: $ExtractPlan(G, g)$

Data: $G = \langle P_0, A_1, \mu A_1, ..., A_n, \mu A_n, P_n, \mu P_n \rangle$ is a planning graph.

1: $\Pi \leftarrow \langle \rangle$;
2: $S \leftarrow \{(p, T_p)|(p, T_p) \in P_n \text{ and } p \in g\}$;
3: $Q \leftarrow T_{p_1} \times T_{p_2}, \ldots, \times T_{p_k}$ where $(p_j, T_{p_j}) \in S$ and $j = 1, \ldots, \|S\|$;
4: $T \leftarrow \{\}$;
5: **for** $\{t_m^{p_1}, \ldots, t_h^{p_k}\} \in Q$ **do**
6:     $\Pi' \leftarrow t_m^{p_1}.\Pi.\pi_1\| \ldots \|t_h^{p_k}.\Pi.\pi_1; \ldots; t_m^{p_1}.\Pi.\pi_{i-1}\| \ldots \|t_h^{p_k}.\Pi.\pi_{i-1}$;
7:     $v' = \min\{t_m^{p_1}.v, \ldots, t_h^{p_k}.v\}$;
8:     $T \leftarrow T \cup \{(v', \Pi')\}$;
9: **end for**
10: **repeat**
11:    $t \leftarrow SelectOptPlan(T)$;
12:    $\Pi \leftarrow t.\Pi$;
13:    $v \leftarrow t.v$;
14:    **if** $CheckMutex(G, \Pi) = true$ **then**
15:        **return** (Π);
16:    **else**
17:        $\Pi \leftarrow \langle \rangle$;
18:    **end if**
19:    $T \leftarrow T - \{(v, \Pi)\}$
20: **until** $\|T\| = 0$
21: **return** Π;

Application. We have a new service Dangdang (w_4, online store). Suppose Dangdang shares the same workflow and operations with ebay service. The operations "order", "ship", "charge_pp", "charge_cc", "bill", and "finalize" of w_4 have the throughput of 4, 6, 26, 13, 10, and 5 repectively. The requirement in our case

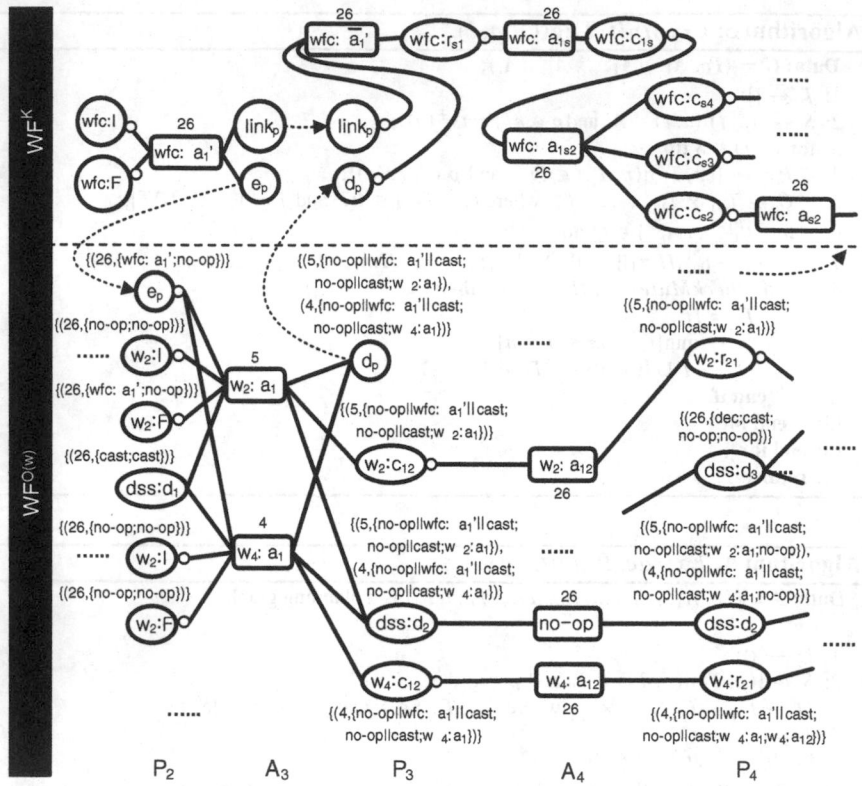

Fig. 17.10 Part of the tagged planning graph

study are $(\{etablet, user\_info\}, \{tracking\_num\}, wfc,)$ and optimization of the throughput of the plan. wfc requires that the payment to be done in parallel to shipping and billing setup as shown in Fig. 17.4 (right). Figure 17.10 presents how to calculate the tag values for each action node in the planning graph. Because the maximum throughput of operations is 26, the tag values of no-op actions and actions that are not encoded from operations are set to be 26. Due to the page limit, we only list part of actions in the planing graph as shown in Table 17.4. Because $effects^-(w_2 : a_1) \cap [pre(w_4 : a_1) \cup effects^+(w_4 : a_1)] = \{e_p\} \neq \emptyset$. The pair $(w_2 : a_1, w_4 : a_1)$ is an element of μA_3. For the proposition d_p in P_3, there are two execution paths without mutex pairs of actions that produce d_p as one of their positive effects. Finally, we remove useless actions from the plan obtained by $Extract Plan$ algorithm such that the plan only contains operation-derived actions. The workflow of the optimal plan is similar to the one in Fig. 17.9 by replacing w_2 with w_4. The throughput of the optimal plan is 4.

Table 17.4 Part of actions encoded from w_2, w_4 and wfc

	Action	Notation	Cost	$pre(a)$	$effect^-(a)$	$effect^+(a)$
	order	$w_2{:}a_1$	5	$w_2{:}I, w_2{:}F, e_p{:}$ product $(d_{ss}{:}d_1)$	$w_2{:}I, w_2{:}F, e_p$	e_sessionid$(d_{ss}{:}d_2), d_p, w_2{:}c_{12}$
w_2	order$\rightarrow$ship	$w_2{:}a_{12}$	26	$w_2{:}c_{12}$	$w_2{:}c_{12}$	$w_2{:}r_{21}$
	ship	$w_2{:}a_2$	7	shipping_addr$(d_{ss}{:}d_3)$, e_sessionid$(d_{ss}{:}d_2), e_s, w_2{:}r_{21}$	$e_s, w_2{:}r_{21}$	$d_s, w_2{:}c_{2s}$, order_amount$(d_{ss}{:}d_4)$
	order	$w_4{:}a_1$	4	$w_4{:}I, w_4{:}F, e_p, d_p, w_4{:}c_{12}$	$w_4{:}I, w_4{:}F, e_p$	e_sessionid$(d_{ss}{:}d_2), d_p, w_4{:}c_{12}$
w_4	order$\rightarrow$ship	$w_4{:}a_{12}$	26	$w_4{:}c_{12}$	$w_4{:}c_{12}$	$w_4{:}r_{21}$
	ship	$w_4{:}a_2$	6	shipping_addr$(d_{ss}{:}d_3)$, e_sessionid$(d_{ss}{:}d_2), e_s, w_4{:}r_{21}$	$e_s, w_4{:}r_{21}$	$d_s, w_4{:}c_{2s}$, order_amount$(d_{ss}{:}d_4)$
	product_selection	$wfc{:}a_1'$	26	$wfc{:}I, wfc{:}F$	$wfc{:}I, wfc{:}F$	$e_p, link_1$
		$wfc{:}\bar{a}_1'$	26	$link_1, d_p$	$link_1, d_p$	$wfc{:}c_{1s}$
wfc	product_selection$\rightarrow$ $\oplus$	$wfc{:}a_{1s}$	26	$wfc{:}c_{1s}$	$wfc{:}c_{1s}$	$wfc{:}r_{s1}$
	$\oplus$	$wfc{:}a_{1s2}$	26	$wfc{:}r_{s1}$	$wfc{:}r_{s1}$	$wfc{:}c_{s2}, wfc{:}c_{s3}, wfc{:}c_{s4}$
	$\oplus$ $\rightarrow$shipping_setup	$wfc{:}a_{s2}$	26	$wfc{:}c_{s2}$	$wfc{:}c_{s2}$	$wfc{:}r_{25}$

$\cdots$

17.5.3 Other QoS Criteria

Up to now, we use throughput as the quality criterion to develop our method. We can also consider how to calculate the other criteria.

For **execution price** (Eq. 17.3), min() function is used. The tag values for the actions encoded from operations are their corresponding execution price. The tag values of other actions are set to be 0. Then, the cost v of a execution path Π is the total execution prices of the plan. Finally, the optimal plan is the plan with the minimum overall execution price.

For **successful execution rate** and **availability**, each service contributes the QoS value in the same way, no matter how they are connected (i.e., sequential or parallel). Here, we focus on throughput and execution price as quality criteria.

17.6 Related Work

Our work is at the intersection of two domains: service composition and software adaptation. Automatic composition is an important issue in Service-Oriented Computing and numerous works have addressed this over the last years [17, 22, 30]. Planning-based approaches have particularly been studied due to their support for underspecified requirements [15, 29]. Automatic composition has also been achieved using matching and graph/automata-based algorithms [4, 11, 25] or logic reasoning [5]. Various criteria could be used to differentiate these approaches, yet, due to our Task-Oriented Computing motivation, we will focus on issues related to service and composition requirement models, and to adaptation.

While both data input/output and capability requirements should be supported, as in our approach, to ensure composition is correct wrt. the user needs, only [6, 25] do, while [4, 11, 16, 20, 21, 37] support data only and [5] supports capabilities only. As far as adaptation is concerned, [4, 16, 21, 25] support a form of horizontal (data) adaptation, using semantics associated to data; and [20] a form of vertical (capability abstraction) adaptation, due to its hierarchical planning inheritance. We combined both techniques to achieve both adaptation kinds. Few approaches support expressive models in which protocols can be described over capabilities—either for the composition requirement [5] or for both composition and services [6, 25] like us. [4, 11, 20, 16, 21] only support conversations over operations (for a given capability).

As opposed to the aforementioned works dealing with orchestration, in [24], the authors present a technique with adaptation features for automatic service choreography. It supports a simple form of horizontal adaptation, however their objective is to maximize data exchange between services but they are not able to compose services depending on an abstract user task.

Most software adaptation works, e.g., [10, 14, 32] are pure model-based approaches whose objective is to solve protocol mismatch between a fixed set of components, and that do not tackle service discovery, composition requirements, or service composition implementation. Few works explicitly add adaptation features to Service-Oriented Computing [12, 23, 27]. They adopt a different and complementary view wrt. ours since their objective is not to integrate adaptation within composition in order to increase the orchestration possibilities, but to tackle protocol adaptation between clients and services, e.g., to react to service replacement.

In an earlier work [1] we already used graph planning to perform service composition with both vertical and horizontal adaptation. With reference to this work, we add support for conversations in both service descriptions and composition requirements. Moreover, adaptation was supported in an ad-hoc fashion, yielding complexity issues when backtracking to get composition solutions. Using encodings, we are able in our work to support adaptation with regular graph planning which enables us to use state-of-the-art graph planning tools.

17.7 Conclusion

Software adaptation is a promising approach to augment service interoperability and composition possibilities. In this paper we have proposed a technique to integrate adaptation features in the service composition process. With reference to related work, we support both horizontal (data exchange between services and orchestrator) and vertical adaptation (abstraction level mismatch between user need and service capabilities). This has been achieved combining semantic descriptions (for data and capabilities) and graph planning. We also support conversations in both service descriptions and composition requirements.

The approach at hand is dedicated to deployment time, where services are discovered and then composed out of a set of services that may change. Yet, in a pervasive environment, services may appear and disappear also during composition execution, e.g., due to the user mobility, yielding broken service compositions. We made a first step towards repairing them in [35], still with a simpler service and composition requirement model (no conversations). A first perspective concerns extending this approach to our new model. Further, we plan to study the integration of our composition and repair algorithms as an optional module in existing runtime monitoring and adaptation frameworks for services composition such as [26].

Acknowledgments This work is supported by project "Service Oriented Systems Integration" (RGPIN/298362-2012) of Canada NSERC Discovery Grant, and by project "Personal Information Management through Internet" (ANR-2010-VERS-0014-03, PIMI) of the French National Agency for Research.

References

1. Beauche, S., Poizat, P.: Automated service composition with adaptive planning, pp. 530–537. In: Proceedings of the ICSOC (2008)

2. Becker, S., Brogi, A., Gorton, I., Overhage, S., Romanovsky, A., Tivoli, M.: Towards an Engineering Approach to Component Adaptation. In: Architecting Systems with Trustworthy Components, vol. 3939. LNCS (2006)

3. ter Beek, M.H., Bucchiarone, A., Gnesi, S.: Formal methods for service composition. Ann. Math. Comput. Teleinf. 1(5), 1–10 (2007)

4. Benigni, F., Brogi, A., Corfini, S.: Discovering service compositions that feature a desired behaviour. In: Proceedings of the ICSOC (2007)

5. Berardi, D., Giacomo, G.D., Lenzerini, M., Mecella, M., Calvanese, D.: Synthesis of underspecified composite e-services based on automated reasoning. In: Proceedings of the ICSOC (2004)

6. Bertoli, P., Pistore, M., Traverso, P.: Automated composition of web services via planning in asynchronous domains. Artif. Intell. 174(3–4), 316–361 (2010)

7. Blum, A.L., Furst, M.L.: Fast planning through planning graph analysis. Artif. Intell. J. 90(1–2), 225–279 (1997)

8. Bouguettaya, A., Yu, Q., Liu, X., Malik, Z.: Service-centric framework for a digital government application. IEEE Trans. Serv. Comput. 4(1), 3–16 (2011)

9. Bozkurt, M., Harman, M., Hassoun, Y.: Testing web services: a survey. Technical Report TR-10-01, Centre for Research on Evolution, Search & Testing, King's College London (2010)

10. Bracciali, A., Brogi, A., Canal, C.: A formal approach to component adaptation. J. Syst. Softw. 74(1), 45–54 (2005)

11. Brogi, A., Popescu, R.: Towards semi-automated workflow-based aggregation of web services. In: Proceedings of the ICSOC (2005)

12. Brogi, A., Popescu, R.: Automated Generation of BPEL Adapters. In: Proceedings of the ICSOC (2006)

13. Canal, C., Murillo, J.M., Poizat, P.: Software adaptation. L'Objet 12, 9–31 (2006)

14. Canal, C., Poizat, P., Salaün, G.: Model-based adaptation of behavioural mismatching components. IEEE Trans. Softw. Eng. 34(4), 546–563 (2008)

15. Chan, K.S.M., Bishop, J., Baresi, L.: Survey and comparison of planning techniques for web service composition. Technical report, Dept Computer Science, University of Pretoria (2007)

16. Constantinescu, I., Binder, W., Faltings, B.: Service composition with directories. In: Proceedings of the SC (2006)

17. Dustdar, S., Schreiner, W.: A survey on web services composition. Int. J. Web Grid Serv. 1(1), 1–30 (2005)

18. Ghallab, M., Nau, D., Traverso, P.: Automated Planning: Theory and Practice. Morgan Kaufmann Publishers, Amsterdam (2004)

19. Kiepuszewski, B.: Expressiveness and suitability of languages for control flow modelling in workflow. PhD thesis, Queensland University of Technology, Brisbane, Australia (2003)

20. Klush, M., Gerber, A., Schmidt, M.: Semantic web service composition planning with OWLS-Xplan. In: Proceedings of the AAAI Fall Symposium on Agents and the Semantic Web (2005)

21. Liu, Z., Ranganathan, A., Riabov, A.: Modeling web services using semantic graph transformation to aid automatic composition. In: Proceedings of the ICWS (2007)

22. Marconi, A., Pistore, M.: Synthesis and composition of web services. In: Proceedings of the 9th International School on Formal Methods for the Design of Computer, Communications and Software Systems: Web Services (SFM)

23. Mateescu, R., Poizat, P., Salaün, G.: Adaptation of service protocols using process algebra and on-the-fly reduction techniques, pp. 84–99. In: Proceedings of the ICSOC (2008)

24. Melliti, T., Poizat, P., Ben Mokhtar, S.: Distributed behavioural adaptation for the automatic composition of semantic services. In: Proceedings of the FASE (2008)

25. Mokhtar, B.S., Georgantas, N., Issarny, V.: COCOA: conversation-based service composition in pervasive computing environments with QoS support. J. Syst. Softw. 80(12), 1941–1955 (2007)

26. Moser, O., Rosenberg, F., Dustdar, S.: Non-intrusive monitoring and service adaptation for ws-bpel, pp. 815–824. In: Proceedings of the WWW (2008)

27. Nezhad, H.R.M., Xu, G.Y., Benatallah, B.: Protocol-aware matching of web service interfaces for adapter development, pp 731–740. In: Proceedings of the WWW (2010)
28. Papazoglou, M.P., Georgakopoulos, D.: Special issue on service-oriented computing. Commun. ACM **46**(10), 25–28 (2003)
29. Peer, J.: Web service composition as AI lanning—a survey. Technical report, University of St.Gallen (2005)
30. Rao, J., Su, X.: A survey of automated web service composition methods. In: Proceedings of the SWSWPC (2004)
31. Seguel, R., Eshuis, R., Grefen, P.: An Overview on Protocol Adaptors for Service Component Integration. Technical report, Eindhoven University of Technology (2008) BETA Working Paper Series WP 265
32. Tivoli, M., Inverardi, P.: Failure-free coordinators synthesis for component-based architectures. Sci. Comput. Program **71**(3), 181–212 (2008)
33. Triantaphyllou, E.: Multi-Criteria Decision Making: A Comparative Study. Springer, New York (2000)
34. Yan, Y., Chen, M.: Anytime QoS optimization over the planGraph for web service composition. In: Proceedings of the ACM SAC, Italy (2012)
35. Yan, Y., Poizat, P., Zhao, L.: Repairing service compositions in a changing world. In: Proceedings of the SERA (2010)
36. Zeng, L., Benatallah, B., Dumas, M., Kalagnanam, J., Sheng, Q.Z.: Quality driven web services composition, pp. 411–421. In: Proceedings of the WWW (2003)
37. Zheng, X., Yan, Y.: An efficient web service composition algorithm based on planning graph, pp 691–699. In: Proceedings of the ICWS (2008)

Chapter 18
Automated Negotiation Among Web services

Khayyam Hashmi, Amal Alhosban, Zaki Malik, Brahim Medjahed and Salima Benbernou

Abstract Automated negotiation among Web services not only provides an effective way for the services to bargain for their optimal customizations, but also allows the discovery of overlooked potential solutions. A number of negotiation supporting techniques have been used to find solutions that are acceptable to all parties in the negotiation. However, employing these solutions for automated negotiations among Web services has its own challenges. In this chapter, we present the design of a Negotiation Web service that would be used by both the consumers and providers of Web services for conducting negotiations. This negotiation service uses a genetic algorithm (GA) based approach for finding acceptable solutions in multi-party and multi-objective negotiations. In addition to the traditional genetic operators of crossover and mutation, the search is enhanced using a new operator called the *Norm*. *Norm* operator represents the cumulative knowledge of all the parties involved in the negotiation process. GA performance with the new *Norm* operator is compared to the traditional GA, hill-climber and random search techniques. Experimental results indicate the practicality of the approach in facilitating the negotiations involved in a Web service composition process. Specifically, the proposed GA with *Norm* operator performs better than other approaches.

K. Hashmi (✉) · A. Alhosban · Z. Malik
Wayne State University, Detroit, Michigan, USA
e-mail: eh2304@wayne.edu

Z. Malik
e-mail: zaki@wayne.edu

A. Alhosban
e-mail: ea1179@wayne.edu

B. Medjahed
The University of Michigan - Dearborn, Dearborn, Michigan, USA
e-mail: brahim@umd.umich.edu

S. Benbernou
Universite Paris Descartes, Paris, France
e-mail: salima.benbernou@parisdescartes.fr

A. Bouguettaya et al. (eds.), *Web Services Foundations*,
DOI: 10.1007/978-1-4614-7518-7_18,
© Springer Science+Business Media New York 2014

451

18.1 Introduction

A Web service is defined as an autonomous and self-contained unit of application that is accessible over a network [83]. In recent years, the number of available Web services has increased, and it is believed that in the near future, we may find multiple services offering the same functionalities [57]. Moreover, with maturing standards (e.g., BPEL [79]) it is now possible to combine several services to formulate a composite solution (selecting the most suitable service for the composite solution from among a pool of competing services). However, this selection process is not straightforward as many inter-related variables of the different services may affect the performance of the service composition. To help facilitate this process we can use automated negotiation to provide an effective way for clients to bargain for an optimal customization of their required variables and to discover any overlooked potential solutions. In this chapter, the research problem of automated negotiation of Quality of Service (QoS) components among Web services is analyzed. The chapter is divided into four sections. The first section serves as an introduction to the service oriented paradigm and the concept of Web services, their underlying QoS specifications, and the process of negotiation. Section two focuses on the communication protocols for automated negotiation, while the third section discusses the different techniques/agents used in the negotiation process. In Sect. 18.4, we discuss the overall service negotiation requirements, show how existing solutions perform in the light of these requirements, and define an approach for solving the automated negotiation problem.

18.1.1 Service Oriented Architecture

Service Oriented Architecture (SOA) is defined as *a paradigm for organizing and utilizing distributed capabilities that may be under the control of different ownership domains* [57]. In other words, boundaries of SOAs are usually *explicit*, i.e., the services need to communicate across boundaries of different geographical zones, ownerships, trust domains, and operating environments. Moreover, explicit message passing is applied in SOAs instead of implicit method invocations. The services in SOAs are *autonomous*, i.e., they are independently deployed, the topology is *dynamic*, i.e., new services may be introduced without advanced acknowledgment, and the applications consuming a service can leave the system or fail without notification [1]. Services in SOAs *share* schema and contracts. The message passing structures are specified by the schema, and message-exchange behaviors are specified by contracts (both implicit or explicit) for each SOA transaction.

Two major entities are involved in any SOA transaction: service customers and service providers. Figure 18.1 represents a typical Web service interaction model. Service providers offer their services by publishing their information (WSDL) in public registries (UDDI) [46, 54]. Customers then query these registries to find the

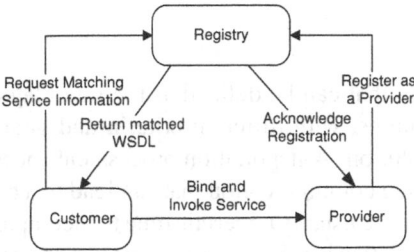

Fig. 18.1 Service-oriented interaction model

required services and then bind to the most suitable service, where input parameters are sent to the service provider and output is returned to the customer [2]. Web service registries thus serve as place holders and provide minimal functional information about a service. Service providers may use $tModels$ [21] to provide any additional information. Since $tModels$ are static place holders for information (service provider may provide a single value or a range for QoS attribute(s)), hence they have limited usability when it comes to negotiating non-functional requirements of the customers (e.g., availability, reliability etc.). A customer looking for a Web service could benefit from a service which if given both functional and non-functional requirements, could provide the most effective solution by simultaneously negotiating with multiple providers.

18.1.2 QoS Specification

The Quality of Service (QoS) is defined as a set of non-functional service attributes that indicate the service's ability to satisfy a stated or implied requirement in an end-to-end fashion [41]. This set of quality attributes not only characterize the service but also any entity used in the path between the service and its client. In a Service Oriented Architecture (SOA), service providers may characterize their services to define both the offered functionalities and the offered quality. Similarly the users may not only express their requirements by listing the desired functionalities, but also define a minimum level of quality that the service must ensure. The main issue here is the subjectiveness of 'quality': the quality of a service from the provider's perspective may be different than the quality experienced by the user. At the same time, the same quality level might be sufficient for a given user and not enough for another one. Hence, QoS parameters consist of both quantitative (availability 99.9 %) and qualitative (privacy, security) parts. Most of the quantitative attributes are not directly proportional in their cost/benefit curve e.g., 99.999 % uptime versus 99.0 % uptime. Hence this non-linear curve naturally generates a disparity among the provided values for these QoS attributes and opens them to negotiation.

18.1.3 Negotiation

Negotiation is a process that can be defined as the interplay of offers and counter-offers between two entities, with different criteria and goals, working to reach a mutually acceptable solution. A negotiation process enhances acquisition opportunities and enables flexible communication that can lead to a better solution [10, 92].

However, negotiation are usually uncertain (due to incomplete information of both parties) and knowledge intensive. Performing negotiations manually is thus ad-hoc and time-consuming. Automated component negotiations (e.g., on the web) are thus valuable not only for the customers and the providers to continuously customize their needs and tailor their offerings, but also to discover overlooked solutions and to maintain documented rationales for future references and reuse.

An automated negotiation mechanism requires at least three components; a high-level protocol, objectives and strategies [47]. The high-level protocol controls the negotiation process depending on types of negotiations (e.g., auction). The objectives of all parties are based on a set of criteria, representing various parameters along with their respective domain values (e.g., price range). Negotiation strategies include mechanisms (rules and knowledge base) that the agent employs to generate and evaluate offers.

Figure 18.2 depicts the state diagram of an automated negotiation process. Typically, negotiation starts when the customer requests for proposals for a component service. After receiving the initial offers from service providers, it would then select some providers to engage in bi-lateral negotiations. This would start a round of offers and counter offers among the customer and selected service providers. Once both the provider and the customer agree on a certain attributes (e.g., price) for the services

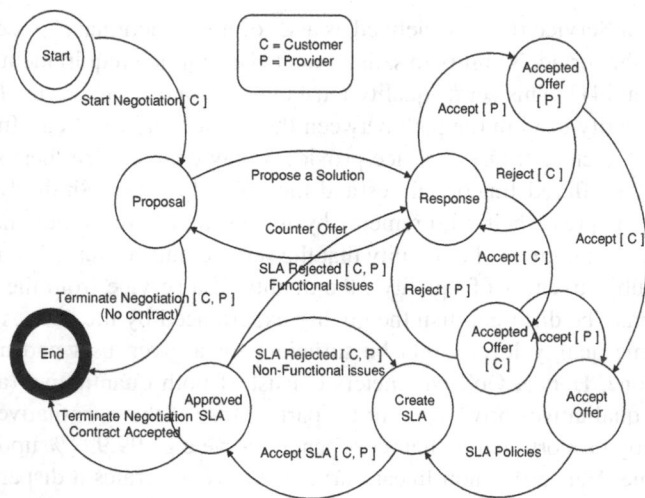

Fig. 18.2 Negotiation state chart

to be provided, they enter into the formal Service Level Agreement (SLA) formation phase. At this point, both parties agree on the terms and conditions of the agreement. These usually include both the functional (service to be provided, cost, etc) and non-functional (QoS parameters, violation terms, penalties, etc). This process could also be modeled as the exchange of offers and counter offers (for SLA terms) among the customer and the selected provider. Once agreed, the parties create/contract an agreement and the services are rendered. If both the parties could not agree on the terms of an SLA the current negotiation session is terminated and a new round of negotiation is started.

18.2 Communication Protocols for Negotiation

A communication protocol defines the syntax, semantics, rules and synchronization of messages exchanged between the partied involved. There are many communication protocols that have been defined to conduct negotiations. This section discusses some of the widely used negotiation protocols applied in the service's domain.

18.2.1 WS-Agreement

WS-Agreement [28] is a protocol for establishing agreements between two parties, such as between a service provider and customer. It uses XML for specifying the nature of the agreement, and agreement templates to facilitate discovery of compatible agreement parties. The specification consists of three parts which may be used in a composable manner: a schema for specifying an agreement, a schema for specifying an agreement template, and a set of port types and operations for managing agreement life-cycle, including creation, expiration, and monitoring of agreement states.

There are two layers of WS-Agreement. The agreement layer provides a Web service-based interface that can be used to create, represent and monitor agreements with respect to provisioning of services implemented in the service layer. The service layer represents the application-specific layer of the service being provided. Although WS-Agreement does not have any negotiation specific structure but there had been discussions for using it in negotiating agreements among parties [5, 87]. An implementation of WS-Agreement to negotiate SLA's for resource orchestration in grids have been presented in [66]. A bilateral WS-Agreement based negotiation process is used to dynamically negotiate SLA templates. One option is for the originating agent to negotiate separately with each Autonomous System (AS) along each potential path to ensure that an end-to-end path is available. The dominant choice, however is to use a cascaded approach where each AS is responsible for the entire path downstream of itself. To rely on WS-Agreement and minimize the extensions to the proposed standard, the idea is not to negotiate SLAs but to negotiate and refine the templates that can be used to create an SLA. An agreement template defines one or more services that are specified by their Service Description Terms (SDT), their Service Property Terms (SPT), and their Guarantee Terms (GT). Additionally an agreement provider can constrain the possible values within the SDTs, SPTs, and GTs by defining appropriate creation constraints within the templates.

Cremona [48] is an agreement management architecture that facilitates (agreement-based) service binding for a variety of services. It uses WS-Agreement as the communication infrastructure. The Cremona architecture separates multiple layers of agreement management, orthogonal to the agreement management functions: the functions associated with an agreement protocol role, initiator or provider, is the Agreement Protocol Role Management (APRM). It comprises, on the agreement provider side, the agreement factory, the agreement instance implementations, the Web services container in which factory and instances are located and interfaces to an agreement template repository, decision-making functionality for *createAgreement* requests and the current state of terms. On the agreement customer side, it comprises proxy functions to interact with an agreement factory and created agreements, template processing functions to create agreement instance document from templates, and interfaces to components initiating agreement establishment, to functions deciding on how to fill an agreement template, and to guarantee monitors. The Agreement Service Role Management (ASRM) is the collection of functions that deals with a party's role in the service relationship, provider or customer, and connects it to the service system. On the service provider's side, this includes the mapping of agreements to provisioning specifications and other input to the service-implementing system—the agreement implementation plan [44].

OpenCCS [35], AgentScape [58] and VIOLA MetaScheduling Service MSS [87] also use negotiation to refine offers and requests in order to create SLAs. As WS-Agreement does not include a protocol for negotiating the terms of an SLA (but an "accept/reject" protocol for the whole SLA), these three approaches currently use proprietary extensions of WS-Agreement for the negotiation.

18.2.2 Contract Net

Contract Net [78] is a generic negotiation protocol. It is viewed as a task having four components (1) it is a local process that does not involve centralized control, (2) there is two-way exchange of information, (3) each party to the negotiation evaluates the information from its own perspective, and (4) the final agreement is achieved by mutual selection.

A contract is established by a process of local mutual selection based on a two-way transfer of information. In brief, available contractors evaluate task announcements made by several managers and submit bids on those for which they are suited. The managers evaluate the bids and award contracts to the nodes they determine to be most appropriate. The negotiation process may then recur. A contractor may further partition a task and award contracts to other nodes. It is then the manager for those contracts. This leads to the hierarchical control structure that is typical of task-sharing. Control is distributed because processing and communication are not focused at particular nodes, but rather every node is capable of accepting and assigning tasks. The basic message constructs of contract protocol are Task Announcement, Task Announcement Processing, Bidding, Bid Processing, Contract Processing, Reporting Results, Termination, and Negotiation Tradeoffs.

A variation of Contract Net protocol for Semantic Web service composition is discussed in [43]. The issue of aligning data flow in semantic web service composition is to ensure the robustness when executing the composed service by preventing any cases when the wrong type of data is passed on from one service to the next is tackled by proposing a unique solution that ensures the robustness of data flow when automatically composing web services through the use of agent-based negotiation between web service providers.

Another variation of Iterative model of Contract Net Protocol (CNP) for negotiation is discussed in [65], where the manager initiates the negotiation process through a call for proposals (CFP) announcing the task specification to the contractors. A contractor receiving the CFP evaluates it and decides whether to answer with a refusal or a proposal to execute the task. The manager receives the contractor's proposals and in turn decides which proposals to accept and which proposals to reject. Rejected contractors consider that the negotiation has terminated, while accepted contractors must expedite the task and send back the results of their work to the manager.

Multiple strategies are implemented using the Iterative model of Contract Net Protocol in [64]. The most basic of them i.e., truth telling strategy, relies on the fact that both the manager and contractors reveal their true preferences. Thus, each CFP is constructed with its preferred value for each issue. A service replies with a proposal where each issue is given its own preferred value for each issue. If the CFP lies outside the reserve values for negotiable issues, then the service's proposal is grounded with the service's reserve values.

18.2.3 WS-Policy

WS-Policy [86] provides a grammar for expressing Web services policies. WS-Policy is used to specify policy information on a broad range of service requirements, preferences, and capabilities. The WS-Policy is represented by a policy expression that is an XML Infoset representation of one or more policy statements. The WS-Policy includes a set of general messaging-related assertions defined in WSPolicyAssertions and a set of security policy assertions related to supporting the WS-Security specification defined in WS-SecurityPolicy.

A framework based on WS-Policy for negotiation of Quality of Service attributes between Web services is proposed in [20]. The approach relies on the definition of an extended SOA in which a service index with QoS information is available. Service provider publishes the non-functional attributes, that may be negotiated by the customer, in the WSDL. This QoS registry could be stored along with WSDL using WSOL, which is a WSDL-compatible language for specifying different service offerings for the same service identified by the different values or constraints on the service QoS attributes [82]. It can include different domain schemas on which the QoS could be defined.

18.2.4 WS-Negotiation

WS-Negotiation [30] is an independent declarative XML language for Web service's providers and customers. In general, WS-Negotiation contains three parts: Negotiation Message, Negotiation Protocol and Decision Making. The Negotiation Message part describes the format of the messages exchanged. Some suggested message types are: Offer, Counter-Offer, Rejected, Accepted, etc. This part of WS-Negotiation tackles the "Initial Contact" and "Offer and Counter-Offer" tasks. Negotiation Protocol describes the mechanism and the rules that the negotiation parties should follow to exchange messages. Messages contain offers and counter-offers and can be exchanged between customer and provider as well as a third-party negotiation service (Negotiation Support System-NSS). Negotiation primitives are also defined in order to coordinate and execute the tasks and events. A negotiation primitive sets the pre and post conditions that should hold as well as rules and constraints that should be applied during the negotiation. Example of negotiation primitives are the "Propose" primitive for proposing an offer/counter-offer to the other party, the "Modify" primitive to modify the sent offer/counter-offer before receiving the other party's reply etc. The Negotiation Decision-making component takes the decisions. It is private and is based on the negotiation strategy each party has chosen (e.g., cost-benefit strategy) and the agreement template. This part of WS-Negotiation tackles the "Evaluation". Negotiation issues vary from one business domain to another but there are some issues that are common or fixed in a domain. Hence, there are several Service Level Agreement (SLA) template models, with domain specific vocabularies, for supporting different types of business negotiations.

WS-AgreementNegotiation [89] describes the re-negotiation of agreements between two parties. It specifies a set of messages and resources that can be used to model several re-negotiation scenarios. WS-AgreementNegotiation sits on top of WS-Agreement, which makes it possible to switch between different negotiation protocol. However, this requires WS-AgreementNegotiation to express negotiation offers in terms of WS-Agreement constructs. This adds a dependency to WS-Agreement. Moreover, it only allows the re-negotiation of existing agreements among two parties and could be initiated by either the provider or the customer.

18.2.5 *Xplore*

Xplore [4] provides a lightweight co-ordination platform focused at multi-party, multi-attribute negotiation. It acts as a "middleware" which aims at addressing general, domain independent requirements on the interaction infrastructure to support negotiation. It is based on the negotiation mechanism which is an extension of the Contract Net protocol [78] with transactional facilities, enabling the coordinated execution of a collection of concurrent, interdependent Contract Nets. It exploits the coordination mechanism provided by CLFMekano [3], a coordination middleware platform designed to integrate negotiation and transaction aspects in distributed systems. CLF contains primitives enabling negotiation and transaction at the lowest level. The primitives are expressed as a set of eight "interaction verbs" a la KQML, similar to speech acts [38]. Xplore extends the unidirectional "announce/collect/ decide" paradigm of CLF to incorporate counter offers by providing a multi-directional "announce/refine/decide" paradigm allowing flexible refinement of the negotiation terms. Xplore's protocol consists of the following negotiation verbs. *Open*, it creates a new node in the negotiation tree i.e., creating a new negotiation branch. *Close*, prevents any further development from the current negotiation branch, effectively closing the negotiation on the current options. *Request*, requests information on an aspect of the parameter passed at the current node of the negotiation tree, retrieving information for making informed proposals along a negotiation branch. *Assert*, is used the describe the aspects of a parameter i.e., refining the negotiation term. *Ready* states that the component is ready to enter in the enactment phase in the condition expressed by the passed node. The *Reserve, Confirm* verbs allow to first reserve and then consume a resource previously returned as an offer. Split in two phases, the operation of resource consumption (Reserve, then Confirm) allows the customer to perform atomic consumption of resources coming from different offers (possibly by different servers), thus realizing the most basic form of transaction. In addition, the *Cancel* verb allows to cancel a reservation, in case other resources in a transaction become unavailable. Finally, the *Insert* verb requests an extension of a service capability by insertion of a new resource.

An example of using Xplore to describe a NegotiAuction is presented in [12]. NegotiAuction [81] is an algorithmic Internet-based auction procedure. It combines various elements from negotiation and auction protocols, supports multiple attributes of the auctioned good and allows both fully automated negotiation as well as semiautomated negotiation process. Each NegotiAuction takes place in a one-to-many market environment. Auction owner sets up the auction and defines the form of auction i.e., reverse or forward and describes the goods and the quantity to be bought (or to be sold) and decides whether the potential bidders should be explicitly invited (closed format), or everybody could qualify for bidding (open format).

Another infrastructure based on Xplore for supporting negotiations in interorganizational alliances in a flexible way with respect to the autonomy of the partners involved is defined as e-Alliance in [15]. It focuses on how to represent decentralized organizations, modeling the coordination of different concurrent interactions, formalization of negotiations, deploying and maintaining an alliance during its life cycle and creating administrative contracts. Similarly, the negotiation middleware CooF supports processes provided by the facilities in the second layer. CooF is the coordinator that supports multi-party, multi-directional, multi-attribute negotiation. This process is modeled by a negotiation graph. This structure captures the dependencies between the negotiation interactions. CooF's job is to coordinate/synchronize these different copies of negotiation graphs. The negotiation process can be considered as a Distributed Constraint Satisfaction Problem [40]. The "distribution" part deals with constraint propagation between nodes, while the "satisfaction" part deals with constraint based reasoning and strategic reasoning at each node.

18.3 Negotiation Agents

A negotiation agent can be termed as the brains behind the negotiation process. This component interacts with the domain knowledge and the system rules to calculate the usefulness of an offer and then generate counter offers against it. Hence, it is responsible for the decision making process. There are different types of negotiation agents that adhere to different types of negotiation (e.g., auction, reverse auction, bilateral negotiation). A brief overview of these follows.

18.3.1 Auction Based Agents

An auction can be described as the simplest form of negotiation where a customer bids on the price of an item and the provider has the option of either accepting the offer or rejecting it. There are multiple types of auctions such as English, Dutch, first-price and Vickery [52]. A service composition agent that both buys components and sells services through auctions has been discussed in [67]. It buys component services by participating in many English auctions. It sells composite services by participating in Request-for-Quotes reverse auctions. Because it does not hold a long-term inventory of component services, it takes risks. It makes offers in reverse auctions prior to purchasing all the components needed, and bids in English auctions prior to having a guaranteed customer for the composite good. The algorithms used are able to manage this risk, by appropriately bidding/offering in many auctions and reverse auctions simultaneously. The algorithms withdraws from one set of possible auctions and moves to another set if this produces a better-expected outcome, but will effectively manage the risk of accidentally winning outstanding bids/offers during the withdrawal process. However only the scenarios with English auction type of negotiation with no one-on-one negotiation are handled. It is assumed that the agent maintains a probabilistic model of expected outcomes of each auction based on past performance of similar auctions. The agent initially identifies the set of options which maximize its a-priori expected utility. These options will consist of a reverse auction for a given composite service, together with a set of English auctions for the required components. It then places bids in these forward/reverse auctions and continues to compete in these auctions, placing more bids when outbid. However, if sufficient competing bids are placed to reduce the expected utility of this set of auctions, then it may change to another set of auctions which can generate the same composite service. It will do this if the expected gain from changing to this new bundle outweighs the expected cost of currently held bids which appear in the old bundle but not in the new bundle. If competing bids are placed in one of the reverse auctions it is participating in, and the expected value of that auction decreases sufficiently it may withdraw from that reverse auction. It may use the associated forward auctions in another option, or may withdraw from them as well. Moreover, the problems of not committing and evaluating each option are solved by limiting the search space to promising offers only.

18.3.2 Trade-Off Based Negotiation Agents

In trade-off based negotiations the concerned parties make tradeoffs on different negotiation parameters based on their respective importance (weights) to the negotiator. Normally each round of negotiation has a slightly different feature vector based on the counter offer generated in the previous negotiation round. This cumulative information is used to generate future offers and hence reach a mutual agreement. A tradeoff based negotiation mechanism for web service procurement using a bilateral protocol to govern interactions between the negotiation parties is used in [63]. Each party can define its own set of evaluation function, utility function and offer generating algorithm. For simplicity both parties share the same generic tradeoff mechanism for automated offer generation while each party can have its own set of objectives and evaluation function. The multi-round negotiation algorithm used contains strategies that focus on generating a set of offers that have the same utility as the current offers and is based on the offers generated by the opponent agent in the previous round. The idea is to exploit the current utility as much as possible. The generated set of offers is presented to opponent agent that chooses the offer that is most suitable to its preferences based on its evaluation function. The negotiation continues until the opponent presents an offer that is of an equal or greater utility than the agent's previous offer. A deadlock condition may be reached if no offer that is of a higher utility to the opponent than the previous offer is being generated. In such a situation the agent reduces its utility expecting to find, in the lower level an offer that satisfies both agents. This strategy ensures that the agent concedes utility in a more rational way.

A trade-offs based agent for multi-dimensional goods for the problem of distributed resource allocation has been presented in [25]. It uses a fuzzy similarity to approximate the preference structure of the other negotiator and then uses a hill-climbing technique to explore the space of possible trade-offs for the one that is most likely to be acceptable. Similar approaches have been discussed in [26] and [51]. Trade-off based agents have also been studied in [17, 50, 97].

18.3.3 Negotiation with Uncertain Data

Having as much information as possible about the other parties is important to strengthen one's negotiation capabilities [60]. Unfortunately, more often than not, we only have partial information about the negotiation context [50]. Hence it is very important to be able to manage different types of unknown parameters about the negotiation. An approach for bilateral negotiation under uncertainty, where a negotiator is uncertain as to what offer or counteroffer to make, at a particular step in the negotiation is presented in [59] and [93]. This uncertainty is resolved by making use of the negotiation experience of reputable parties in [93]. The idea is similar to the scenario where suppose, one has been offered a new employment and it is time to negotiate benefits, including salary. The negotiating parties are yourself and the hiring manager. The fact that mostly salaries are negotiable and often vary with specific job responsibilities, a new hire may not have all the information needed to make a good decision. In this case, a natural course of action, is to seek out others who are trustworthy and who may have negotiated salaries with this company in the past, for similar types of jobs and use their data to make an informed decision. So the main idea is of using the negotiation experiences of trusted parties with matching interests as aids in deciding which negotiating alternatives and offers should be employed.

A model for bilateral negotiations that considers the uncertain and dynamic outside options is defined in [45]. Outside options affect the negotiation strategies via their impact on the reservation price. The model is composed of three modules: single-threaded negotiations, synchronized multi-threaded negotiations, and dynamic multi-threaded negotiations. The single-threaded negotiation model provides negotiation strategies without specifically considering outside options. The model of synchronized multi-threaded negotiations builds on the single-threaded negotiation model and considers the presence of concurrently existing outside options. The model of dynamic multi-threaded negotiations expands the synchronized multi-threaded model by considering the uncertain outside options that may come dynamically in the future. A Poison Process is used to simulate the arrival process of uncertain (dynamic) options.

18.3.4 Genetic Algorithm Based Negotiations

Negotiations are a special class of group decision making problems. Multi-party and multi-objective negotiations add a lot of complexity to the already hard problem of negotiation. Such negotiation problems can thus be formulated as constrained multi-objective optimization problems. The main idea is to optimize a series of objectives simultaneously while considering constraints on the system. The Genetic Algorithm (GA) approach is consistent with the complex nature of real-world negotiations and is, therefore, capable of addressing more realistic negotiation scenarios. Since genetic algorithms and evolutionary algorithms in general search for entire populations of solutions, they are well suited for multi-criterion problems. A weighted sum based genetic algorithm to support multiple-party multiple-objective negotiations have been presented in [71]. The weighted sum approach is used to handle multiple objectives of each participant. Since all the participant start negotiation from a different position hence they will also have different preference for those objectives and are described by how far their current position is from the objective. Hence the objective is to minimize this distance. The genetic algorithm solution is represented as a 2-Dimensional matrix, representing the participants and objectives. Similar approaches have been discussed in [22, 62, 96]. A genetic algorithms based approach that evolve Finite State Machines has been presented in [85]. Each individual in the population of FSMs represents a negotiation strategy that competes against other strategies and is modified over time using traditional operators of mutation and cross over. To mutate an FSM, several different operators are used which include changing the target or source of an edge, changing the output or input symbol of an edge and adding or deleting a state or an edge. A repair algorithm ensures that all the FSMs are valid after mutation or crossover operation. A GA based negotiation model using the traditional operators of mutilation and crossover has been presented in [18]. A special penalty based evaluation function is used that measures the prior concessionary behavior of the opponent agent. A negotiation time aware GA based approach has been presented in [9]. The pace of concession of the agent is proportional to the elapsed negotiation time while considering the opponent's payoff gains and the principal of Pareto optimality. Machine learning and bayesian learning have also been used in conjunction with genetic algorithms to achieve satisfactory results [56, 76].

18.3.5 Combinatorial Negotiations

A combinatorial negotiation is the type of negotiation where entities can negotiate on a combination of items, rather than negotiating independently on each item from a set of items. Combinatorial negotiation stemmed from the traditional combinatorial auctions. In a combinatorial auction, a set M of items, $|M| = m$, is sold to n bidders. The combinatorial character of the auction comes from the fact that each bidder values bundles of items, rather than valuing items directly. The idea is to find such a partition of the items so that the return is maximized for the auctioneer.

A Combinatorial Negotiation based decision-support service (iBundler) for highly constrained negotiation scenarios has been proposed in [69]. iBundler acts as a combinatorial negotiation solver for both multi-item, multi-unit negotiations and auctions. The service can be employed by both negotiating agents and auctioneers in combinatorial auctions. It consists of three main components. The *Manager* agent takes care of all the communication. It provides brokering services of RFQ, collection of bids, winner determination and contracting services. The *Translator* agent perform the necessary XML translations for the Solver and FIPA-compliant descriptions for the *Manager* agent. The *Solver* component extends the *iBundler* with the offering of an XML language for expressing offers, constraints and requirements. The winner determination is modeled as a mixed integer problem similar to the the the binary multi-unit combinatorial reverse auction winner determination problem in [75] with side constraints in [73].

18.4 Discussion

As mentioned earlier an automated negotiation mechanism consists of three main components, namely, a high-level protocol, negotiation objectives, and decision strategies; while the negotiation context dictates the selection and integration of these components [33]. In existing literature, this has usually been accomplished in an ad-hoc manner, which is of minimal interest in SOAs due to the high developmental costs of such solutions, lack of ubiquity, and dynamic participants. Consequently, the prime requirements for developing comprehensive negotiation mechanisms include:

- *Multi-attribute negotiation.* A typical SLA negotiation involves QoS attributes such as *reliability, availability, accessibility* and *response time* [94, 95]. These QoS attributes (and others) influence the negotiation protocol and the customer preferences articulation that the negotiation system must support. Hence there may be more than one combination of these attributes that may be suitable under a specified negotiation context. User preferences could be expressed in a variety of ways, e.g., utility functions [25], combination of attributes [23], or fuzzy constraints [50] etc. The negotiation system should not restrict its user to a single negotiable attribute (e.g., price) rather it should allow the users to express multiple attributes for the negotiation process (REQ 1).

- *Support for heterogeneous negotiation protocols.* In a service oriented system it is very much expected that all the participants using the system may not be similar. They may implement heterogeneous (probably incompatible) negotiation protocols. Thus, there is a need for supporting multiple negotiation protocols (REQ 2), or be able to consent on the negotiation protocol for cases where a participant supports multiple ones.

- *Heterogeneous decision model articulation.* Different participants prefer different negotiation strategies (auction, bargaining etc.) based on their decision models, domains, preferences and history. There are usually two types of decisions that an automated negotiation system has to make. First, it has to generate counter offers in the negotiation by implementing an appropriate algorithm [24, 25, 39, 50]. Second, it has to handle commitment to the new SLA i.e., deciding if the agreement is acceptable and convenient to commit, and in some cases decommitment from previously created SLA [61]. This decision is mostly protocol independent. However, depending upon the negotiation strategy the counter offer generation could be totally different. For instance, in case of a bargaining strategy, there has to be a response for each negotiation message that is received, where as in an auction strategy, bids could be placed at any time. Hence, an automated negotiation system must implement multiple decision models (REQ 3) so that it could support protocol specific negotiations.

- *Dynamic user preferences.* Unlike traditional software environments, SOAs enable delivery of the same service to different customers with varied quality of service (QoS) requirements [23]. Moreover, since negotiation is a dynamic and interactive process, the user preferences could change over time. The user may change the required value of a QoS attribute during the negotiation process, (as it learns new information during the negotiation) or may even add or remove new QoS attributes. Thus, the negotiation system should allow the user preference about the negotiation process to be changed over time (REQ 4).

- *Simultaneous negotiations.* Since services are not stored or downloadable, the market environment tends to be very dynamic [27]. The ability to create on-the-fly dynamic solutions emphasizes the need of conducting simultaneous negotiation (REQ 5) with multiple component services, owned by different parties, at the same time. On one hand, it is necessary for the system to have a global view of all these negotiations to support them properly. However since the preferences of the parties involved in the negotiation could potentially change, it is beneficial for the system to guide the behavior of each negotiation based on the responses generated by other (simultaneous) negotiations. This allows the system to choose the party that would result in the most profitable agreement.

- *Support for dynamic selection of decision making models.* Simultaneous negotiations are desirable in volatile service markets to allow selection of the most profitable agreements for the participants [27]. This entails that the participants are equipped to change their strategies/decisions at runtime (REQ 6), based on market dynamics and changing contexts [70]. The underlying strategy should be robust enough so that it can adapt to different behaviors of participants, and utilize "peripheral knowledge". For instance, information relating to whether the participant tends to concede, participant reputation, etc. may be used to strengthen one's negotiation capabilities [60, 61]. Similarly, in some contexts if a more profitable offer is found, there should be a provision to decommit from the current agreement [74].

Table 18.1 summarizes how the current negotiation systems in the literature perform on the above mentioned requirements. An '✓' in a cell means that the corresponding proposal provides explicit support for the corresponding requirement, whereas a '✗' indicates that the feature is not supported and 'n/a' means that there is no information available. The table shows that most of the existing solutions do not do well when it comes to supporting multiple negotiations at the same time or dynamic selection of decision making models. Moreover, none of the solutions provide any dependency modeling among different QoS components. Howsoever this is is an extended requirement in composite solutions that often have dependent QoS objectives. For example, if we were to have a composite solution consisting of *taskA* and *taskB* and one of the objective was to have services that could handle a load of 1 million transactions per minute. What if we have multiple services offering such a solution for *taskA* but could not find any service for *taskB* that could meet our current

Table 18.1 Summary of automated negotiation systems

Authors	REQ 1	REQ 2	REQ 3	REQ 4	REQ 5	REQ 6
Ashri et al. [6]	✓	✓	n/a	n/a	n/a	n/a
AuctionBot [91]	✗	✗	✓	✓	✗	✗
Bartolini et al. [8]	✓	✓	✗	✗	✗	✗
Benyoucef et al. [11]	n/a	✓	✓	n/a	✗	✗
Bruns et al. [13]	✓	✗	✓	n/a	✓	✗
Comuzzi et al. [19]	✗	✓	✓	✗	✗	✗
Cremona [48]	✓	✗	✓	✓	✗	n/a
DynamiCS [84]	✓	✓	✓	✗	✗	✗
Inspire [36]	✓	✗	✓	✗	n/a	✗
Jonker et al. [34]	✓	n/a	✓	✓	✗	✗
Kasbah [16]	✓	✓	✓	✗	✗	✗
Kim et al. [37]	✓	✓	✗	✗	✗	✗
Lecue et al. [43]	✗	✓	✗	✗	✗	✓
Ludwig et al. [49]	✓	✓	✓	✗	✗	✗
MAGNET [31]	✓	✗	✓	✓	✗	✗
Marco et al. [20]	✓	✓	✗	✓	✗	✗
NegoPlan [72]	✓	✗	✓	✗	✗	✗
Negotiator [14]	✓	✗	✓	✗	✗	✗
PANDA [27]	✓	✓	✓	✓	✗	✗
Paurobally et al. [65]	✓	✗	✗	✗	✗	✗
Rinderle et al. [68]	✓	✓	✗	✗	✗	✗
Skogsrud et al. [77]	✗	✓	✓	✓	✗	✓
Strobel [80]	✓	✓	✗	✗	✗	✗
Tete-a-Tete [42]	✓	✓	✓	✗	✗	✗

objective. It would then be more economical for the composite solution to downgrade *taskA* to the level of *taskB's* solution (since throughput of a system is a composite function of its constituent services). Continuing with this hypothetical scenario, we need the negotiation service to be able to simultaneously negotiate multiple services having multiple objectives with multiple providers. Existing communication protocols [4, 28, 43, 78, 86] lack such capabilities, and a new standard language that could be used to pass on all these constraints and decision model to the negotiation system is required. This leads us to look for a new solution that not only fairs better in comparison with the existing solutions, but also supports all the requirements of a SOA based negotiation system.

18.4.1 A framework for Web Service Negotiation

In this section, we provide an overview of our solution for the service negotiation problem. Figure 18.3 presents a high level architecture of a negotiation system

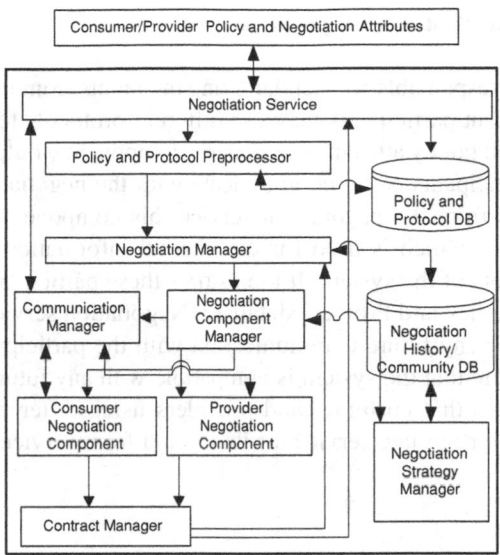

Fig. 18.3   WebNeg system architecture

(defined as *WebNeg*) that is very flexible in terms of its functionality and the services provided. It is primarily targeted to be invoked by the customer searching for a compatible service from a list of service providers providing similar functionalities. The client does not need to implement any negotiation specific component to use the proposed service. The WebNeg architecture is compatible with both the negotiation scenarios i.e., the negotiating participants could either provide their own negotiation component or send all the necessary information to the service, that would handle all the negotiation process. A brief overview of the major modules of the proposed negotiation architecture is as follows:

18.4.1.1 Negotiation Service

The negotiation service layer acts as the interface of the whole system. This layer is responsible for any and all external communication of the system. All the internal components use this service to communicate with both the customer and provider as well as with the community (to be discussed later). Customer invokes the service providing its negotiation attributes, negotiation policy as well its decision model. The service then communicates with potential providers and request their decision model and policy attributes for the negotiation process.

18.4.1.2 Policy and Protocol Preprocessor

This component is responsible for standardizing the inputs from the communicating participants. Different participants may use different protocols for describing their decision models and policy attributes. A generic component would ensure that these heterogeneous participants could communicate with the negotiation service. After receiving this data from the negotiation service this component then translates it into a standard form which is used for the internal information exchange among different components of the system. It then stores these participant communication preference in the Policy and Protocol database. Negotiation service would then use this information for any future communication with the participants. This generic module would ensure that the system is compatible with any future communication protocol and ensures that customer and providers using different communication protocols could still negotiate service attributes and form service level agreements (SLA).

18.4.1.3 Negotiation Manager

Once the service receives a request for negotiation from the customer along with all the necessary data, it then proceeds to the negotiation step. Negotiation manager would then query the Web service directory e.g., UDDI to search for the matching service providers. The customer also has the option of providing its own list of possible providers. Once it has the list of service providers providing similar services, it then ranks these providers based on their ratings, trust and reputation values.

It uses the trust model based on the concept of community [53] where the reputation represents the perception of the users in that community regarding a service. So, the rating of a service represents the average of all the rating provided to the community for that individual service. For the newly starting service that does not have any history, it uses the reputation bootstrapping mechanism defined in [55]. Community is a centralized knowledge base that would be responsible for storing all the data regarding different providers, including reputation, trust and past negotiations. The community ensures that no private information is released to its users but could publish non identifiable data e.g., It does not give out any information about systems that are using lets say *ServiceA*, but could tell the total number of the systems currently running *ServiceA*. These pieces of information combined with the above mentioned methods of trust and reputation assessment, help the negotiation manger in selecting appropriate services, from a number of services providing similar functionalities.

18.4.1.4 Negotiation Component Manager

Since negotiation is a multi-party mechanism, the *WebNeg* system needs to spawn separate components for each customer and provider. In the most basic scenario at any given instance, the systems would have one customer and multiple provider components. These components operate in their separate context and communicate with their original service through the communication manager. The communication manager is responsible for creating and manging these components.

18.4.1.5 Negotiation Strategy Manager

There are multiple strategies available for conducting efficient negotiations. One such strategy is defined below in Sect. 18.4.2 (defined as *WebNeg*). Our system architecture does not restrict the components to any one negotiation strategy. It has multiple strategies for the components to choose from. Participants could opt for using any strategy and could pass on this information as a policy to the system. If none is chosen the system selects one or a combination of strategies for the negotiation process. The negotiation strategy manager selects and binds each component with the appropriate strategy and is responsible for implementing the component policies and decision model in the context of the selected strategy as well as monitoring and storing any transient data related to the negotiation process.

18.4.1.6 Communication Manager

All the external pre-contract communications are handled by this manager. The component may communicate with their respective services for any decision model or policy/guidance queries. Communication manager ensures that all the communication is related to the current negotiation and adheres to the negotiation service's policies.

18.4.1.7 Contract Manager

Once the system identifies perspective negotiation solution(s), it is presented to the respective services, if they agree, contract manager then handles all the formal SLA creation process. If the current selected provider does not agree on the solution, the system would then try the next best available solution, until either an agreement is achieved or the system has ran out of options. If the system could not find a mutually agreeable solution, then the process would be termed as a failure and the customer would be asked to revise its negotiation model.

18.4.2 WebNeg

We present a GA based approach to solving the Web service negotiation problem [29]. We enhance the traditional GA with a new operator called *Norm*. Our proposed approach complements the proposed negotiation framework that is designed towards

Table 18.2 Definition of symbols

Symbol	Definition
f_j	Fitness of the solution s for participant j
F_s	Fitness of the solution s (for all participants)
C_j	The value of jth component of Customer's vector
$C_{j(min)}$	The minimum allowed value of jth component of customer's vector as provided by the customer
$C_{j(max)}$	The maximum allowed value of jth component of customer's vector as provided by the customer
WC_j	The weight of jth component of customer's vector as provided by the customer
P_{ij}	The value of jth component of ith Provider's vector
$P_{ij(min)}$	The minimum allowed value of jth component of ith Provider's vector as provided by the provider
$P_{ij(max)}$	The maximum allowed value of jth component of ith Provider's vector as provided by the provider
WP_{ij}	The weight of jth component of ith Provider's vector as provided by the provider
R_j	Rank for solution j in the system
N_i	Value of Norm i in the system
E_{ij}	The willingness of participant j to exchange objective i
A_{ij}	Amount of resource i exchanged by Web service j
G	Total number of generations
$CrossP_j$	Cross over probability for service j
$AugVal_{ij}$	The value of ith objective to be added or subtracted for Web service j

a scenario where a customer is involved in simultaneous negotiations with multiple providers. Each instance of communication among the customer and service provider is private and holds a lot of information. The proposed *Norm* operator makes it possible to share this private information among all the participants without revealing the source of any of such information. This in turn helps all the agents to adapt quickly and significantly reduces the search space by guiding the negotiation process toward a mutually agreeable solution.

We propose a weighted sum genetic algorithm to support multi-party multi-objective negotiation. All the Web services provide their respective QoS parameters to be negotiated. These are called the component vector of a Web service. Each vector is accompanied by a decision model, i.e., ranges of all the QoS parameters as well as their respective priorities also known as the weights. We assume that all the participating Web services are able to articulate their objectives and prioritize them. Table 18.2 lists the definition of symbols used henceforth.

Since all the Web services (participants) start negotiation from a different position, they have different preferences for those objectives, and are described by how far their current position is from the customer's objective. All the Web services conform to some constraints in the solution. For instance, any QoS vector cannot have a negative value (as shown by Eq. 18.1). The QoS values lie between the maximum and minimum allowable values set by the Web service (as shown by Eq. 18.2). A repair algorithm is applied to GA after each operator, to ensure all these constraints are met.

$$C_j \geq 0, \ P_{ij} \geq 0 \tag{18.1}$$

$$C_{j(min)} \leq C_j \leq C_{j(max)} \text{ and } P_{ij(min)} \leq P_{ij} \leq P_{ij(max)} \tag{18.2}$$

Each gene is a combination of customer and provider chromosomes. If we have n objectives to be negotiated then each gene will have $2n$ chromosomes. The fitness function is a multi-step calculation that evaluates the level of disagreement between the negotiating Web services. A weighted sum approach is used to combine these multiple QoS parameters (objectives). We use a distance function to measure the difference among the proposed solutions of both the customer and provider Web services. Thus, lower fitness values are desired as they translate to lesser disagreement among the participants. Similarly, lower values translate to higher ranks for the solutions among the solution space. Ranks are then used for selection of subsequent steps of the GA [88]. Each solution represents a probable distribution of values that may be agreed upon by the other Web service in the negotiation. The fitness value of a solution is calculated as follows.

$$\Delta_{ij} = \frac{|C_j - P_{ij}|}{C_j} \tag{18.3}$$

$$f_j = \sum_{j=0}^{n}(WC_j * \Delta_{ij} + WP_{ij} * \Delta_{ij}) \tag{18.4}$$

$$F_s = min \sum_{j=0}^{G}(f_j) \tag{18.5}$$

Pareto optimality is not enforced after each generation as it is possible for a Web service to accept a less favorable solution for the time being (in the negotiation process) for a better solution in the long run. However, a secondary population of solutions is kept which is updated after each iteration. This secondary population or *Elitism* is a an important concept in genetic searches [7, 98]. The probabilistic nature of GA does not guarantee that the best solutions would be preserved in the final generation. Hence a secondary population of best solutions is kept through all generations. Below is the algorithm used to determine the optimal solution. Details follow.

Set generation number g equal to zero ($g = 0$)
Generate initial population
Calculate fitness for each member
Store the most fit solution in the secondary population
Rank the solutions
Apply Norm
Select members for crossover using Roulette-Wheel selection method
Perform crossover
Perform random mutations
IF $g = G$ (last generation)
    Ensure Pareto optimality
    exit
ELSE
Set $g = g + 1$
Set Go to step 3

End Algorithm

18.4.2.1 Norm Operator

A new operator *Norm* is implemented to improve the performance of GA and to simulate the exchange of resources based on the common knowledge of the society in a negotiation scenario. The *Norm* operator is based on the observation that in each society people follow certain trends or norms to conduct negotiations. These norms are either informed by the environment or are discovered by the population based on the prior experiences. These norms are transfered through generations and different people follow different norms. Often people are inclined to abandon or follow a new norm on the basis of the facts if they think they are being better off following or deviating from them. Most helpful norms tend to accumulate more followers, which in turn re-enforces that norm. People tend to abandon less useful norms in the favor of useful ones. Once in a while people just hop around trying to find out what works the best for them. These norms serve as a guide for achieving their desired goals. Figure 18.4 shows a scenario that depicts the concept of norm. Assume we have n norms (information sources) in the society and k population subsets. Set 1 may follow *Norm 1*, Set 2 may follow *Norm n* and Set m may choose to follow *Norm 2* while others may not choose to follow any *Norm*. The selection of subsets and *Norm* selections are random. Population in Set 1 is effected by the values of *Norm 1* and they in turn effect the values of the *Norm*. This cycle makes sure that beneficial values are prevailed in the *Norms*.

We have the *Norm* operator behavior defined above in the GA, so that it takes less time to find the solution and to reduce the search space. Each QoS negotiation criteria is represented as a norm and certain members of the population follow a certain norm. After each generation, the followers update the impact factor of their respective norm. If increasing the value of the norm resulted in a better overall fitness value for the member of population, it would influence the norm into increasing its

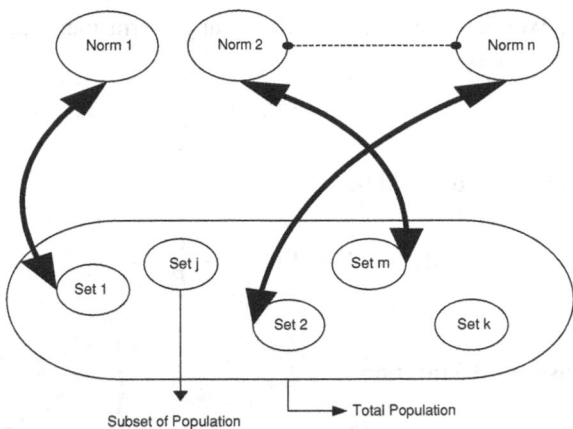

Fig. 18.4 Norm operator in relation to population sets

value. The increase is dependent on the difference of current and previous values of that objective of the reporting individual and the current absolute value of that objective. Both customers and providers share the same influence values of norms. This is an indirect information source for the customer about providers decision model and vice versa. Ideally, we will have one customer and n providers, hence sharing these impact factors does not reveal any trade secrets. These values have the bias of $n+1$ agents and are averaged out.

Norm is implemented for the exchange of recourses among different participant. Exchange must occur between two distinct objectives, participants can trade some or all of their available objectives and there is at most one exchange per pair per generation. Exchange is implemented probabilistically. Each member of population is reviewed for possible exchange. The participants and objectives involved in the exchange are selected randomly. Then it is decided if an exchange will actually occur based on the willingness of participants. The exchange only occurs if both randomly selected participants are willing to make an exchange. Essentially, willingness to exchange is higher if a participant has more of an objective than he ideally wants and if the information source that he is following is influencing a lower value of that specific objective. If the current Web service is following $Norm_m$ then the willingness to exchange is calculated as

$$E_{ij} = |\frac{C_i}{N_m}| \tag{18.6}$$

and the amount exchanged would be

$$A_{ij} = (1 - WC_i)|1 - \frac{C_i}{N_m}| \tag{18.7}$$

If the current Web service is not following any Norm then the willingness to exchange is calculated as

$$E_{ij} = |\frac{C_i}{P_{ij}}| \tag{18.8}$$

and the amount exchanged would be

$$A_{ij} = (1 - WC_i)|1 - \frac{C_i}{P_{ij}}| \tag{18.9}$$

18.4.2.2 Crossover and Mutation

The crossover operator is invoked after applying the Norm operator. Roulette-wheel selection is used for selecting solution pairs for crossover. Roulette-wheel selection is analogous to a roulette wheel where the probability an individual is selected is proportional to its fitness [32].

Solution rankings are used to implement selection. The population is augmented so that solutions with better ranks are more prevalent in the population. We use both ranks and fitness values for our selection technique because ranking indicates the performance of solutions relative to others in the population and minimizes the effect of large disparities in fitness values within the population [88]. Augmentation of the population for roulette-wheel selection is performed as follows:

$$Cross P_j = 1 - \frac{1}{R_j}(R_j - 1) \tag{18.10}$$

Crossover rate is used to determine if crossover will actually occur or if the selected solution will simply be copied over to the next generation. If it is determined that crossover will occur, uniform crossover is implemented on the pair. It has been proved that custom operators provide superior performance for real-valued problems [90].

Mutation is the last operator to act on the population of solutions and is also applied randomly to the elements of the solution, in accordance with the experimentally predetermined mutation rate. A random number is generated for each member in the population and compared to the mutation rate. If the random number is less than or equal to the mutation rate, mutation will occur in that solution. Mutation here involves arbitrarily changing one element of the negotiation vector and then implementing a repair algorithm to ensure that objective values lies within the valid range for that agent.

18.4.2.3 Study and Results

To determine the efficiency to GA with the *Norm* operator we performed experiments covering different scenarios. We compared the performance of GA with *Norm* with other methods of solving similar problems. We used (1) a traditional GA with only mutation and crossover operator, (2) a random search and (3) a hill-climber. We used experiments to determine the GA parameters such as population size, number of generations, crossover rate and mutation rate.

Traditional GA: A traditional GA was implemented by removing the *Norm* operator. It only uses the simple GA operators of crossover and mutation. All the GA parameters are same as that of GA with *Norm* operator.

Random Search: Random search simulates the behavior of arbitrarily exploring the search space in the hope of finding a solution. It is applied on one half of the gene at a time. Either the customer's Web service gene or provider's Web service gene parameters are augmented. This augmentation likelihood is determined randomly. Once selected, a random number is generated for each QoS parameter that lies between the allowable range for that participant. Then all the numbers are aggregated by subtracting their respective minimum values. This summation is then averaged out and either added or subtracted randomly to all the parameters. Then the repair algorithm is applied to ensure that all the constraints from Eqs. 18.1–18.3 are held. Then we add this new solution of our population. The population is then ranked according to their fitness values and members with higher fitness values are taken to the next generation.

Hill-Climber: Hill-climber uses the concept of randomly exchanging the QoS values. It is somewhat similar to the *Norm* operator as both use Eq. 18.10 to determine the amount of the objective to be exchanged. However, the GA with *Norm* uses either Eq. 18.7 or Eq. 18.9 to determine if the exchange will occur, while in hill-climber it is done randomly. Once a gene is randomly selected, the exchange takes place. However, it is guaranteed that only one objective per gene is exchanged and that once selected, that gene does not participate in any other exchange for that generation. We create the initial population and rank them according to their fitness values. We then perform crossover using Roulette-Wheel selection method. Then we apply the mutation operator. After we are done with the basic GA operators we apply the Hill Climbing operator on the population. The repair algorithm ensures that all the constraints from Eqs. 18.1–18.3 are held. All the GA parameters are same as that of GA with *Norm* operator.

Experiment Environment

Our development environment consisted of a Windows server 2008 (SP2) based Quad core machine with 8.0 GB of ram. We developed 1 client and 50 provider Web services running on Microsoft .Net version 3.5 to simulate multi-party negotiations. A large number of similar providers are chosen to show the applicability/scalability of the proposed solution. The client negotiated four QoS components of reliability, availability, throughput and accessibility with the providers. We performed 200 iterations consisting of 500 generations each, for all the four algorithms and analyzed the results for efficiency and completeness.

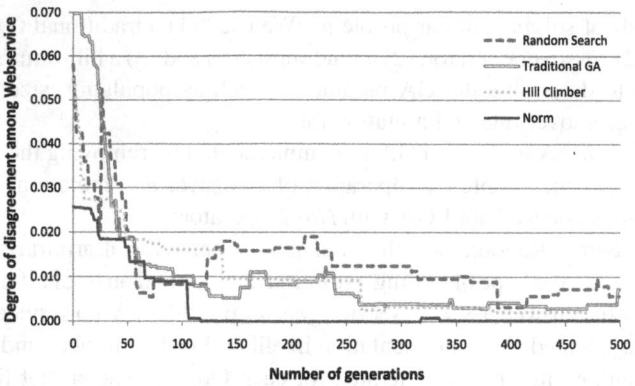

Fig. 18.5 Sample representation of multi-party negotiation

Results

Figure 18.5 shows results of a representative run of the four algorithms after each generation. Note that these are the actual output values without *Elitism* [7, 98]. We have plotted the output of 500 generations (X-axis) against the degree of disagreement (Y-axis) among the client and provider Web services. Lower values of degree of disagreement are desired as they show a higher chance of reaching an agreement e.g., Assume that Web service *A* wants a solution that has an *Availability* value of 98 % and the provider *B* presents a solution that has an *Availability* value of 95 %. The degree of disagreement among the *A* and *B* is small and hence they are more likely to reach a solution. Note that both the customer and provider must have some overlapping search space values for the algorithm to identify a solution. If both the customer and provider have mutually exclusive ranges of QoS parameters, the algorithm fails and no solution is returned.

The graph confirms the assumption that the probabilistic nature of GA does not guarantee that the best solution will be passed on to the next generation. Hence, using *Elitism* to ensure *Pareto optimality* is an important factor. Our proposed technique (GA with *Norm*) takes almost 1/4th the time to reach an agreeable solution. We can see in the graph that *Norm* found a mutually agreeable solution after 100 generations, where as *Hill Climber* took 475 generations, *Traditional GA* took 450 generations and *Random Search* took 375 generations to find their respective best solutions. Hence, we can find the solution faster with our proposed approach. Similarly our proposed approach finds a lot better solution than any of the other techniques.

The probabilistic nature of GA does not guarantee the same solution every time. Hence, it is appropriate to analyze the performance of GA over multiple rounds. Table 18.3 shows that average of 200 runs for all four algorithms.

We can see that the best solution of 0.00002 returned by *Norm* is far better that best solution returned by any other technique. Similarly *Traditional GA* performed better than the *Hill Climber* in finding a more agreeable solution. As far as the worst solution is concerned, *Norm* still performed better than any of the other techniques.

Table 18.3 Average results over 200 iterations

	Random search	Traditional GA	Hill climber	Norm
Min	0.00568	0.00027	0.00041	0.00002
Max	0.06153	0.08547	0.05171	0.03163
Mean	0.02718	0.02192	0.01461	0.00925
Std. dev	0.01663	0.02177	0.01668	0.01157

The worst solution of 0.03163 returned by *Norm* is almost twice as good as that of *Hill Climber*, the second best technique. The average solution returned by *Norm* shows a remarkable improvement from the next best i.e., *Hill Climber* technique, depicting that the *Norm* also has the best average case performance among the compared techniques. Similarly our proposed technique has the lowest standard deviation of 0.01157. Lowest mean value combined with the lowest standard deviation indicates that our technique performs consistently better than other techniques.

These results suggest that our approach outperforms other compared methods in terms of finding the optimal solution in the amount of time it takes to find that solution.

18.5 Conclusion and Future Directions

Designing an automated, flexible and efficient negotiation system that facilitates the Web service selection process, is challenging. None of the existing solutions meet all the requirements for a completely automated solution for Web service negotiation. One of the limitations of the presented techniques involve the assumption of a static environment, where the Web service procurement time window is so small that the user preferences do not change during the course of negotiations. Secondly, most of the solutions use a priori decision model articulation, which requires that all the negotiating participants can identify and share their preferences at the beginning of the negotiation. However, some of these limitations involved with the static environment assumption could be overcome, if participants decide to provide their own negotiating component rather than only articulating their preferences. However, this limits the effectiveness of sharing private information. Therefore, we need to design a negotiation system that can support multiple communication protocols for enabling interactions among different customers and providers as well as supporting multiple negotiation strategies for an optimized solution. The solution should support multiple simultaneous negotiations and provide mechanisms to model the dependency relationships among different component services to achieve an optimal solution.

In this chapter we have presented the framework for Web services negotiation to enable customers and providers negotiating QoS parameters in SLA's. The presented architecture uses a GA based approach to conduct multi-party multi-objective negotiations. Our approach integrates the concepts of Pareto optimality and multiple decision making preferences of the participants. We have enhanced the traditional

GA with a new operator called *Norm*. This operator is based on the concept of cumulative knowledge of the society over a period of time. This accumulated knowledge influences the decision making process of negotiating participants. Furthermore, *Norm* provides a platform for sharing private information of all the participants of the negotiation in such a manner that allows for using this shared knowledge for the overall gain of the society, without revealing the identity of information providers. We have compared *Norm's* performance with similar optimization techniques i.e., Traditional GA, Hill-Climbing and Random Search. The results show that our proposed technique performs better than any of the above mentioned techniques, and that applying a genetic algorithm based approach to complex negotiation for Web service composition problems is a viable option.

We are currently investigating on enhancing the effectiveness of private information sharing by exploring the possibilities of having people follow multiple information sources rather than following just one source. This is motivated by the fact that composite solutions often have dependent objectives. We want to further extend our approach to incorporate these dependencies among the different QoS parameters of multiple services to formulate optimized solutions. We need to be able to use the information sources of *Norm* operator to share such information. We need the negotiation service to be able to simultaneously negotiate multiple service having multiple objectives with multiple providers. Existing communication protocols [4, 28, 43, 78, 86] lack such capabilities. This requires a new standard language that could be used to pass on all these dependency constraints and decision model to *WebNeg*. We are exploring the options of extending WS-Negotiation [30] and WS-AgreementNegotiation [89] by adding the support of complex logical functions for articulating these and similar complex decision models. We are also working on a solution that moves away from the centralized approach in the favor of a more adaptive distributed model.

References

1. Alhosban, A., Hashmi, K., Malik, Z., Medjahed, B.: Assessing fault occurrence likelihood for service-oriented systems. In: Proceedings of the 11th International Conference on Web, Engineering, pp. 59–73 (2011)
2. Alhosban, A., Hashmi, K., Malik, Z., Medjahed, B.: S2r: a semantic web service similarity and ranking approach. Int. J. Next-Gener. Comput. 3(2) (2012). http://perpetualinnovation.net/ojs/index.php/ijngc/article/view/145
3. Andreoli, J., Arregui, D., Pacull, F., Rivire, M., Vion-dury, J., Willamowski, J.: Clfmekano: a framework for building virtual-enterprise applications. In: Proceedings of the EDOC'99 (1999)
4. Andreoli, J.M., Castellani, S.: Towards a flexible middleware negotiation facility for distributed components. In: International Workshop on Database and Expert Systems Applications 0732 (2001)
5. Andrieux, A., Dan, A., Keahy, K., Ludwig, H., Rofrano, J.: From ws-agreement to sla negotiation (2004). http://www.mcs.anl.gov/keahey/Meetings/GRAAP/WS-AgreementNegotiabilityConstrains.pdf
6. Ashri, R., Rahwan, I., Luck, M.: Architectures for negotiating agents. In: Proceedings of the 3rd Central and Eastern European conference on Multi-agent systems, pp. 136–146 (2003)

7. Baker, J.E.: Adaptive selection methods for genetic algorithms. In: Proceedings of the 1st International Conference on Genetic Algorithms, pp. 101–111 (1985)
8. Bartolini, C., Preist, C., Jennings, N.R.: A software framework for automated negotiation. In: SELMAS, Lecture Notes in Computer Science, vol. 3390, pp. 213–235. Springer (2004)
9. Beheshti, R., Rahmani, A.T.: A multi-objective genetic algorithm method to support multi-agent negotiations. In: Second International Conference on Future Information Technology and Management Engineering, 2009. FITME '09, pp. 596–599 (2009). doi:10.1109/FITME.2009.154
10. Benbernou, S., Brandic, I., Cappiello, C., Carro, M., Comuzzi, M., Kertész, A., Kritikos, K., Parkin, M., Pernici, B., Plebani, P.: Modeling and negotiating service quality, in service research challenges and solutions for the future internet—s-cube—towards engineering, managing and adapting service-based systems. In: Papazoglou, M.P., Pohl, K., Parkin, M., Metzger A. (eds.) S-CUBE Book, Lecture Notes in Computer Science, vol. 6500, pp. 157–208. Springer (2010)
11. Benyoucef, M., Verrons, M.H.: Configurable enegotiation systems for large scale and transparent decision making. Group Decis Negot **17**(3), 211–224 (2008)
12. Brandl, R., Andreoli, J., Castellani, S.: Ubiquitous negotiation games: a case study. In: Proceedings of the DEXA e-negotiations, Workshop (2003)
13. Bruns, G., Cortes, M.: A hierarchical approach to service negotiation. In: IEEE International Conference on Web Services, pp. 460–467 (2011)
14. Bui, T.X., Shakun, M.F.: Negotiation processes, evolutionary systems design, and negotiator. Group Decis Negot **5**(10), 339–353 (1996)
15. Castellani, S., Andreoli, J., Bratu, M., Boissier, O., Alloui, I., Megzari, K.: E-alliance: a negotiation infrastructure for virtual alliances (2002)
16. Chavez, A., Maes, P.: Kasbah: an agent marketplace for buying and selling goods. In: Proceedings of the First International Conference on the Practical Application of Intelligent Agents and Multi-Agent Technology, pp. 75–90 (1996)
17. Cheung, S.C., Hung, P.C.K., Chiu, D.K.: On the e-negotiation of unmatched logrolling views. In: Proceedings of the 36th Hawaii International Conference on System Sciences (HICSS-36) (2003)
18. Choi, S.P.M., Liu, J., Chan, S.: A genetic agent-based negotiation system. Comput. Netw. **37**(2), 195–204 (2001)
19. Comuzzi, M., Pernici, B.: Negotiation support for web service selection. In: TES (2004)
20. Comuzzi, M., Pernici, B.: An architecture for flexible web service qos negotiation. In: Proceedings of the Ninth IEEE International EDOC Enterprise Computing Conference, pp. 70–82 (2005)
21. Curbera, F., Duftler, M., Khalaf, R., Nagy, W., Mukhi, N., Weerawarana, S.: Unraveling the web services web: an introduction to soap, wsdl, and uddi. Internet Comput. IEEE **6**(2), 86–93 (2002)
22. Deng, M.D., Li, J.: An agent negotiation system based on adaptive genetic algorithm. In: 2009 5th International Conference on Wireless Communications Networking and Mobile Computing, vol. 18, pp. 5307–5310 (2009)
23. Elfatatry, A., Layzell, P.J.: A negotiation description language. Softw. Pract. Exp. **35**(4), 323–343 (2005)
24. Faratin, P., Sierra, C., Jennings, R.: Negotiation decision functions for autonomous agents. Robot. Auton. Syst. **24**(3–4), 159–182 (1998). http://eprints.ecs.soton.ac.uk/2117/
25. Faratin, P., Sierra, C., Jennings, N.R.: Using similarity criteria to make issue trade-offs in automated negotiations. Artif. Intell. **142**, 205–237 (2002)
26. Freuder, E.C., O'Sullivan, B.: Modeling and generating tradeoffs for constraint-based configuration (2001)
27. Gimpel, H., Ludwig, H., Dan, A., Kearney, B.: Panda: specifying policies for automated negotiations of service contracts, pp. 287–302 (2003)
28. (GRAAP) G.R.A.A.P.: Wsagreement (2007). http://www.ogf.org/documents/GFD.107.pdf
29. Hashmi, K., Alhosban, A., Malik, Z., Medjahed, B.: Webneg: A genetic algorithm based approach for service negotiation. In: Proceedings of the 2011 IEEE International Conference

on Web Services, ICWS '11, pp. 105–112. IEEE Computer Society, Washington, DC, USA (2011). doi:10.1109/ICWS.2011.55.http://dx.doi.org/10.1109/ICWS.2011.55

30. Hung, P.C.K., Li, H., Jeng, J.: Ws-negotiation: an overview of research issues. In: Proceedings of the 37th Hawaii International Conference on System Sciences (2004)

31. Jaiswal, A., Kim, Y., Gini, M.L.: Design and implementation of a secure multi-agent marketplace. Electron. Commer. Res. Appl. **3**(4), 355–368 (2004)

32. James, E.B.: Reducing bias and inefficiency in the selection algorithm. In: Proceedings of the Second International Conference on Genetic Algorithms and their application, pp. 14–21 (1987)

33. Jennings, N.R., Faratin, P., Lomuscio, A.R., Parsons, S., Sierra, C., Wooldridge, M.: Automated negotiation: prospects, methods and challenges. Int. J. Group Decis. Negot. **10**(2), 199–215 (2001). http://eprints.ecs.soton.ac.uk/4231/

34. Jonker, C., Robu, V., Treur, J.: An agent architecture for multi-attribute negotiation using incomplete preference information. Auton. Agents MultiAgent Syst. **15**, 221–252 (2007)

35. Keller, A.: openccs: Computing center software. Technical report, Aderborn Center for Parallel Computing (2007)

36. Kersten, G.E., Noronha, S.J.: Www based negotiation support: design, implementation and use. Decis. Support Syst. **25**(2), 135–154 (1999)

37. Kim, J., Segev, A.: A web services-enabled marketplace architecture for negotiation process management. Decis. Support Syst. **40**, 71–87 (2005)

38. Kit, C.M., Woo, C.C.: A speech-act-based negotiation protocol: design, implementation, and test use. ACM Trans. Inf. Syst. **12**(4), 360–382 (1994)

39. Kowalczyk, R.: Fuzzy e-negotiation agents. Soft Computing—a fusion of foundations, methodologies and applications **6**, 337–347 (2002). doi:10.1007/s00500-002-0187-5

40. Kowalczyk, R., Bui, V.: Jfsolver: a tool for modeling and solving fuzzy constraint satisfaction problems. In: FUZZ-IEEE, pp. 304–307 (2001)

41. Kritikos, K., Plexousakis, D.: Requirements for qos-based web service description and discovery. IEEE Trans. Serv. Comput. **2**(4), 320–337 (2009). doi:10.1109/TSC.2009.26

42. Lab, M.M.: Teteatete (2000). Online: ecommerce.media.mit.edu.

43. Lecue, F., Wajid, U., Mehandjiev, N.: Negotiating robustness in semanticweb service composition. In: Seventh IEEE European Conference on Web Services (2009)

44. Levy, R., Nagarajarao, J., Pacifici, G., Spreitzer, M., N.Tantawi, A., Youssef, A.: Performance management for cluster based web services. In: IFIP/IEEE 8th International Symposium on Integrated Network Management (2003)

45. Li, C., Giampapa, J., Sycara, K.: Bilateral negotiation decisions with uncertain dynamic outside options. IEEE Trans. Syst. Man Cybern. **36**(1), 45–55 (2006)

46. Lin, C., Lu, S., Lai, Z., Chebotko, A., Fei, X., Hua, J., Fotouhi, F.: Service-oriented architecture for view: a visual scientific workflow management system. In: SCC '08, Proceedings of the 2008 IEEE International Conference on Services Computing, pp. 335–342. IEEE Computer Society, Washington, DC, USA (2008). http://dx.doi.org/10.1109/SCC.2008.118

47. Lomuscio, A.R., Wooldridge, M., Jennings, N.R.: A classification scheme for negotiation in electronic commerce. Group Decis. Negot. **12**(1), 31–56 (2004)

48. Ludwig, H., Dan, A., Kearney, R.: Cremona: an architecture and library for creation and monitoring of ws-agreements. In: 2nd International Conference on Service Oriented Computing (2004)

49. Ludwig, A., Braun, P., Kowalczyk, R., Franczyk, B.: A framework for automated negotiation of service level agreements in services grids. In: Bussler, C., Haller, A. (eds.) Business Process Management Workshops 2005, vol. 3812, pp. 89–101 (2005)

50. Luo, X., Jennings, N.R., Shadbolt, N., Leung, H., Lee, J.: A fuzzy constraint based model for bilateral multi-issue negotiations in semi-competitive environments. Artif. Intell. J. **148**(1–2), 53–102 (2003)

51. Luo, X., Jennings, N.R., Shadbolt, N.: Acquiring user strategies and preferences for negotiating agents: a default then adjust method. Int. J. Human Comput. Stud. **64**(4), 304–321 (2006)

52. Maasland, E., Onderstal, S.: Going, going, gone! a swift tour of auction theory and its applications. De Economist **154**, 197–249 (2006). http://dx.doi.org/10.1007/s10645-006-9002-5. doi:10.1007/s10645-006-9002-5
53. Malik, Z., Bouguettaya, A.: Evaluating rater credibility for reputation assessment of web services. In: WISE'07: Proceedings of the 8th International Conference on Web Information Systems Engineering, pp. 38–49. Springer (2007)
54. Malik, Z., Bouguettaya, A.: Rateweb: reputation assessment for trust establishment among web services. VLDB J. **18**(4), 885–911 (2009). doi:dx.doi.org/10.1007/s00778-009-0138-1
55. Malik, Z., Bouguettaya, A.: Reputation bootstrapping for trust establishment among web services. Internet Comput. IEEE **13**(1), 40–47 (2009)
56. Matwin, S., Szapiro, T., Haigh, K.: Genetic algorithms approach to a negotiation support system. IEEE Trans. Syst. Man Cybern **21**(1), 102–114 (1991)
57. Michlmayr, A., Rosenberg, F., Leitner, P., Dustdar, S.: End-to-end support for qos-aware service selection, binding, and mediation in vresco. IEEE Trans. Serv. Comput. **3**(3), 193–205 (2010)
58. Mobach, D., Overeinder, B., Brazier, F.: A ws-agreement based resource negotiation framework for mobile agents. Scalable Comput. Pract. Exp. **7**(1), pp. 23–26 (2006)
59. Mudgal, C., Vassileva, J.: Bilateral negotiation with incomplete and uncertain information: a decision-theoretic approach using a model of the opponent. In: Klusch, M., Kerschberg, L. (Eds.) Cooperative Information Agents IV, LNAI, pp. 107–118. Springer-Verlag (2000)
60. Nguyen, T.D., Jennings, N.R.: Bayesian learning in negotiation. Int. J. Hum.-Comput. Stud. **48**(1), pp. 125–141 (1998)
61. Nguyen, T.D., Jennings, N.R.: Managing commitments in multiple concurrent negotiations. Electron. Commer. Res. Appl. **4**(4), 362–376 (2005)
62. Niu, X., Wang, S.: Genetic algorithm for automatic negotiation based on agent. In: 7th World Congress on Intelligent Control and Automation, 2008. WCICA 2008, pp. 3834–3838 (2008)
63. Patankar, V., Hewett, R.: Automated negotiation in web service procurement. In: Proceedings of the Third International Conference on Internet and Web Applications and Services (2008)
64. Paurobally, S., Aart, C.V., Tamma, V., Wooldridge, M., Hapert, P.V.: Web services negotiation in an insurance grid. In: Proceedings of the 6th International Joint Conference on Autonomous Agents and Multiagent Systems (2007)
65. Paurobally, S., Tamma, V., Wooldrdige, M.: A framework for web service negotiation. ACM Transactions on Autonomous and Adaptive Systems (TAAS) 2(4) (2007)
66. Pichot, A., Waldrich, O., Ziegler, W., Wieder, P.: Towards dynamic service level agreement negotiation: an approach based on ws-agreement. In: 4th International Conference on Web Information Systems and Technologies, WEBIST 2008, Funchal, Madeira, Portugal (2008)
67. Preist, C., Bartolini, C., Byde, A.: Agentbased service composition through simultaneous negotiation in forward and reverse auctions. In: Proceedings of the 4th ACM conference on Electronic commerce, pp. 55–63. ACM (2003)
68. Rinderle, S., Benyoucef, M.: Towards the automation of e-negotiation processes based on web services a modeling approach. In: WISE 05, pp. 443–453 (2005)
69. Rodrguez-Aguilar, J.A., Giovanucci, A., Reyes-Moro, A., Noria, F.X., Cerquides, J.: Agentbased decision support for actual-world procurement scenarios. In: Proceedings of the IEEE/WIC International Conference on Intelligent Agent Technology (2003)
70. Ros, R., Sierra, C.: A negotiation meta strategy combining trade-off and concession moves. J. Auton. Agent Multiagent Syst. **12**, 163–181 (2006)
71. Rubenstein-Montano, B., Malaga, R.A.: A weighted sum genetic algorithm to support multiple-party multiple-objective negotiations. IEEE Trans. Evol. Comput. **6**(4), 366–377 (2002)
72. Matwin, S., Szpakowicz, S., Koperczak, Z.: Negoplan: an expert system shell for negotiation support. IEEE Expert **4**(4), 50–62 (1996)
73. Sandholm, T., Suri, S.: Side constraints and non-price attributes in markets. In: International Joint Conference on Artificial Intelligence (IJCAI), (2001)
74. Sandholm, T.W., Lesser, V.R.: Leveled commitment contracts and strategic breach. Games Econ. Behav. **35**, 212–270 (2001)

75. Sandholm, T., Suri, S., Gilpin, A., Levine, D.: Winner determination in combinatorial auction generalizations. In: Proceedings of the First International Joint Conference on Autonomous Agents and Multiagent Systems (2002)
76. Sim, K.M., Guo, Y., Shi, B.: Blgan: Bayesian learning and genetic algorithm for supporting negotiation with incomplete information. IEEE Trans. Syst. Man Cybern. B **39**(1), 198–211 (2009)
77. Skogsrud, H., Motahari-Nezhad, H., Benatallah, B., Casati, F.: Modeling trust negotiation for web services. Computer **42**(2), 54–61 (2009). doi:10.1109/MC.2009.56
78. Smith, R.G.: The contract net protocol: high-level communication and control in a distributed problem solver. IEEE Trans. Comput. **C-29**(12), 1104-1113 (1980)
79. Standard, O.: Wsbpel (2005). http://docs.oasis-open.org/wsbpel/2.0/wsbpel-v2.0.html.
80. Strobel, M.: Design of roles and protocols for electronic negotiations. Electron. Commer. Res. **1**, 335–353 (2001)
81. Teich, J., Wallenius, H., Wallenius, J., Zaitsev, A.: An internet-based procedure for reverse auctions combining aspects of negotiations and auctions. In: DEXA '00: Proceedings of the 11th International Workshop on Database and Expert Systems Applications (2000)
82. Tosic, V., Bernard, P., Kruti, P., Babak, E., Wei, M.: Management applications of the web service offerings language (wsol). Inf. Syst. **30**(7), 564–586 (2005)
83. Treiber, M., Andrikopoulos, V., Dustdar, S.: Calculating service fitness in service networks. In: ICSOC/ServiceWave Workshops, pp. 283–292 (2009)
84. Tu, M., Seebode, C., Griffel, F., Lamersdorf, W.: Dynamics: an actor-based framework for negotiating mobile agents **1**, 101–117 (2001)
85. Tu, M.T., Wolff, E., Lamersdorf, W.: Genetic algorithms for automated negotiations: a fsm-based application approach. In: Proceedings of the 11th International Workshop on Database and Expert Systems Applications, pp. 1029–1033 (2000)
86. (W3C) W.W.W.C.: Wspolicy (2006). http://www.w3.org/Submission/WS-Policy/.
87. Waldrich, O., Wieder, P., Ziegler, W.: A meta-scheduling service for co-allocating arbitrary types of resources. In: Parallel Processing and Applied Mathematics. Lecture Notes in Computer Science, vol. 3911/2006. Springer, Berlin (2006)
88. Whitley, D.: The genitor algorithm and selection pressure: why rank-based allocation of reproductive trials is best. In: Proceedings of the third international conference on Genetic algorithms, pp. 116–121. Morgan Kaufmann Publishers Inc., San Francisco (1989)
89. Wieder, P.: Ws-agreementnegotiation (2010). http://forge.gridforum.org/sf/go/doc15831
90. Wolpert, D.H., Macready, W.G.: No free lunch theorems for optimization. IEEE Trans. Evol. Comput. **1**(1), 67–82 (1997)
91. Wurman, P.R., Wellman, M.P., Walsh, W.E.: The michigan internet auctionbot: a configurable auction. In: Second International Conference On Autonomous Agents, pp. 301–308 (1998)
92. Yao, Y., Yang, F., Su, S.: Evaluating proposals in web services negotiation. In: Computer and Information Sciences ISCIS 2006, pp. 613–621. Springer, Berlin (2006)
93. Yee, G., Korba, L.: Bilateral e-services negotiation under uncertainty. In: Proceedings of the 2003 Symposium on Applications and the Internet (2003)
94. Yu, Q., Liu, X., Bouguettaya, A., Medjahed, B.: Deploying and managing web services: issues, solutions, and directions. VLDB J. **17**(3), 537–572 (2008). doi:dx.doi.org/10.1007/s00778-006-0020-3
95. Zarras, A., Vassiliadis, P., Issarny, V.: Model-driven dependability analysis of webservices. In: Web Services, International Symposium on Distributed Objects and Applications, pp. 69–79 (2004)
96. Zhai, D., Wu, Y., Lu, J., Yan, F.: A fuzzy negotiation model with genetic algorithms. In: I3E (1)'07, pp. 35–43 (2007)
97. Zhu, J.: A buyer-seller game model for selection and negotiation of purchasing bids: extensions and new models. Eur. J. Oper. Res. **154**(1), 150–156 (2004). http://EconPapers.repec.org/RePEc:eee:ejores:v:154:y:2004:i:1:p:150--156
98. Zitzler, E., Deb, K., Thiele, L.: Comparison of multiobjective evolutionary algorithms: empirical results. Evol. Comput. **8**, 173–195 (2000)

Chapter 19
DRAAS: Dynamically Reconfigurable Architecture for Autonomic Services

Emna Mezghani, Riadh Ben Halima and Khalil Drira

Abstract The development and the provisioning of autonomic networked services are essential for enterprises and factories of the future. Endowing services with autonomic properties allows one to maintain at runtime the Quality of Service (QoS) including different parameters related to performance, availability and reputation such as response time and successful execution rate. Handling the autonomic properties requires the ability to deal with permanent requirement evolving and constraint changes. For instance, managing QoS degradation requires the capacity of identifying its possible or actual sources and the capacity of reconfiguration planning and execution. Dealing with these issues is especially challenging for web services since the autonomic solution has to be seamless for the service requesters, ensuring that web services are always usable under the different deployment constraints. To implement such autonomic systems, the literature provides different approaches, varying from the design to the full implementation of autonomic primitives. In this chapter, we present DRAAS: a Dynamically Reconfigurable Architecture for Autonomic Services able to provide autonomic properties for QoS management in web service-based distributed applications. DRAAS has been implemented and experimented successfully with different use cases. It covers the whole cycle of autonomic management including monitoring and analysis of QoS parameters, planning and execution.

E. Mezghani (✉) · K. Drira
CNRS, LAAS, 7 avenue du colonel Roche, Toulouse F-31400, France
e-mail: emna.mezghani@laas.fr

K. Drira
e-mail: khalil.drira@laas.fr

E. Mezghani · R. Ben Halima
ReDCAD, University of Sfax, B.P.W, 3038 Sfax, Tunisia
e-mail: riadh.benhalima@enis.rnu.tn

A. Bouguettaya et al. (eds.), *Web Services Foundations*,
DOI: 10.1007/978-1-4614-7518-7_19,
© Springer Science+Business Media New York 2014

19.1 Introduction

The important data flows, the frequent interactivity, the increasing number of connected devices, and the network unpredictability make critical the management of the new distributed software systems. In one hand, although the reform of verification and validation of software models has not ceased improving, components of the systems may still hide design faults resulting in system failures or come across deadlock that freezes the system. In the other hand, user's requirements are evolving following the end-user technologies evolution as mobile phone emergence (Multimedia mobile and group-enabled application). In the same time, systems constraints are variable as unstable bandwidth and decreasing energy.

Meeting and taking into account these constraints and requirements at runtime is a challenge especially for web service applications which are dynamic and heterogeneous by nature. Indeed, if a web service does not satisfy the user requests in terms of expected QoS, it is considered degraded. So, it becomes necessary to remedy to such QoS degradation, for example, by substituting the degraded service by one or more other services performing equivalent functions or sharing requests on the available services in order to maintain the QoS. More specifically, self-control systems such as elevator control systems or critical systems such as spacecraft navigational systems need robustness to detect anomalies and avoid them by reconfiguring the systems at runtime [48]. For these reasons, research actors are accelerating the work on autonomic systems. Such systems are capable to detect the problems and continue to operate by managing malfunctions without human intervention. Autonomic computing technology does not only reduce potential catastrophic errors, in critical systems for example, but it also minimizes the human intervention. It is applied when reliability and QoS are required. An autonomic system inspects and changes its own architecture and behavior when the evaluation indicates that the intended QoS is not achieved, or when a better functionality or performance is required. As a result, autonomic computing paradigm is crucial for current systems in order to ensure QoS-aware execution.

The autonomic computing architecture is based on the MAPE-K control loop [30]. This loop is composed of four modules (MAPE) that have access to a common knowledge. *Monitoring* which monitors the data exchanged between the managed elements, *Analysis* which detects possible QoS or performance degradations, *Planning* that implements algorithms for selecting and scheduling appropriate elementary reconfiguration actions and *Execution* which performs them.

This autonomic computing paradigm includes the design and implementation of computer systems, as shown in Fig. 19.1. The first step focuses on establishing a detailed design from which results a framework or an architecture. Frameworks present the skeleton of an application that can be customized by the developer. We distinguish two types of framework [12, 14]: black box that does not need a deep understanding of the framework's implementation in order to use it and white box that requires the internal understanding of the framework to use it effectively. Architectures provide high-level abstraction of system components, while enabling easier

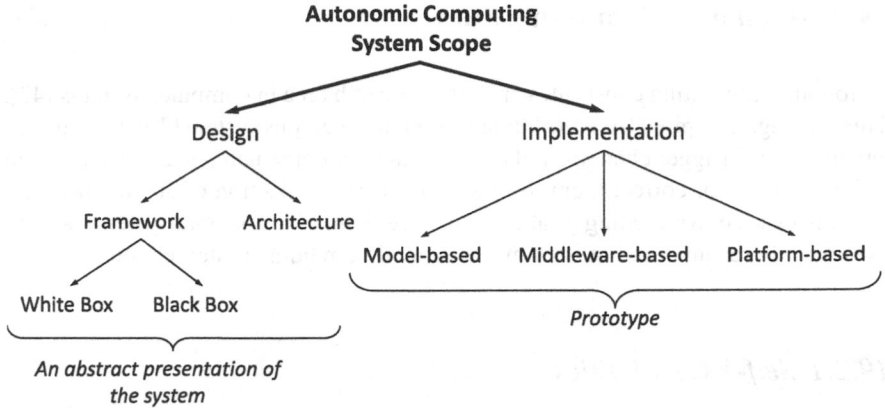

Fig. 19.1 Autonomic computing scope

understanding and interpretation. Furthermore, the architectural approach constraints can be expressed explicitly. The second step concentrates on implementing the architecture or the framework through various techniques. The implementation may be classified into three categories: model-based, middleware-based and platform-based (see Fig. 19.1). Model-based solutions [8, 24, 56] provide explicit implementation of all necessary actions for monitoring, analysis, planning and execution. In this category (model-based), we focus particularly on architectural approaches. Monitoring and analysis are made by testing if the running system conforms to a given architectural style or model. Middlewares, like Bionet [52], AgFlow [58], and OpenORB [4], support dynamic reconfiguration process by offering primitives (like interception) for all autonomic computing modules. Platforms [6, 11, 51] provide developers with already developed autonomic entities.

In this chapter, we propose our DRAAS architecture implementing the autonomic computing to ensure the dynamic reconfiguration of web service-based applications. Then, we evaluate and classify a set of autonomic solutions for web service based application including DRAAS according to criteria such as provided functionalities, managed autonomic steps, applied techniques, programming languages, etc. We aim to provide features which help and guide users to select a suitable solution for implementing autonomic services. However, it is usually difficult to select the appropriate approach to implement an application. We think that this choice depends on the size of the problem to solve, the architecture type (decentralized or centralized), the programming language, the application area (Server or Client, etc.), etc.

This chapter is organized as follows. Section 19.2 presents a survey of the autonomic computing techniques and capabilities. Section 19.3 details our proposed architecture DRAAS for the dynamic reconfiguration and illustrates it by the data load use case. Section 19.4 describes a taxonomy of dynamic reconfiguration implementation approaches focusing on the "model", "middleware" and "platform" categories and gives conclude remarks helping on choosing the appropriate approach. Finally, Sect. 19.5 concludes this chapter and presents our future work.

19.2 Autonomic Computing Survey

Autonomic computing constitutes an active research area in computer systems [42]. This paradigm, inspired from the human autonomic nervous system [30], has a mechanism that can trigger changes in the computing system structures and behaviors in order to bypass or correct them. Furthermore, it is a collection of autonomic components that the overarching goal is to manage themselves, so that systems will be dynamically reconfigured at run time, with minimum human intervention.

19.2.1 Self-* Capabilities

The principles that govern all autonomic computing systems, according to IBM, have been summarized in eight properties [41]:

- Self-Configuring: the ability to dynamically configure components/services following high-policies in order to adjust the system. Such configurations can include the deployment of new components/services or the removal of existing ones [21, 27, 50].
- Self-Healing: the ability of the system to perceive if it does not work correctly. It ensures the necessary adjustments of service properties to restitute it towards its normal state without human intervention [27, 29]. By knowing about the system, it analyzes information, detects service degradations and initiates corrective actions without disrupting its execution.
- Self-Optimizing: the ability of the system to continually enhance its performance. It is a proactive mechanism that detects performance degradation and acts intelligently such as in reallocating resources/services with minimal human intervention [27].
- Self-Protecting: the ability of the system to detect and protect its resources/services from internal and external attacks and maintain its security [27, 30].
- Self-Awareness: the ability of the system to know itself and to be aware of its state and behaviors [41].
- Context Awareness: the ability of the system to know its execution environment and be able to react to its changes [41].
- Open: the ability of the system to work in a heterogeneous world and implement open standards. It should be portable across multiple hardware and software architectures [41].
- Anticipatory: the ability of the system to anticipate its needs and behaviors and to manage itself proactively [41].

19.2.2 Autonomic Computing Techniques

Autonomic computing is based on four main functions [28]: *Monitoring, Analysis, Plan* and *Execution*.

Monitoring is usually defined as the act of listening, carrying out supervision on, and/or recording the activity of a software entity for the purpose of maintaining system reliability and QoS. Monitoring can be ensured using the following techniques as listed in Table 19.1:

- *Interception* represents a hook into exchanged data between a client and a server allowing requests/responses supervision.
- *Assertion* is a set of code lines, introduced in a program, which enables to control and to constrain a program.
- *AOP (Aspect Oriented Programming)* aims to verify system properties and also to configure scope/constraints of each function and discover even a tiny abnormal state.
- *Reflection* enables to discover and to operate on fields and methods of an object at runtime.

Analysis is the process of detecting possible degradation of the system through the evaluation and the examination of monitored data. Analysis compares current system behavior and architecture with a reference model. The following techniques are used by the *Analysis* (see Table 19.1):

- *Architectural Differentiation* refers to compare the obtained architectural model to the architectural style of the system in order to detect non-compliance.
- *Behavioral Differentiation* refers to map the behavior of an implementation to model behavior.
- *QoS Contract* represents explicitly the system requirements under contract between clients and providers.
- *QoS Aware* is based on the historic of the system state. It compares the current state with previous system states.

Table 19.1 MAPE-k loop techniques

Monitoring techniques	Analysis techniques	Plan and Execution techniques
INTERCEPTION [7, 54]	ARCHITECTURAL DIFFEREN-TIATION [9, 35]	SUBSTITUTION [4, 46]
ASSERTION [23, 39]	BEHAVIORAL DIFFERENTIA-TION [45]	WRAPPING [5, 49]
AOP [34, 32, 57]	QoS- CONTRACT (SLA) [38]	LOAD BALANCING[17, 40]
REFLECTION [4, 22]	QoS- AWARE (QoS HISTORIC) [3, 55]	ROLLBACK [59]
		REDUNDANCY AND DUPLICATION [16, 20, 37]

Plan and Execution are complementary. In fact, the plan presents a set of algorithms which refer to concrete reconfiguration actions enforced in the Execution module. The Execution refers to the act/the process of repairing or the condition of being repaired. Also, it may be defined as changes applied to a software entity so that it reaches a desirable state. In distributed systems, several techniques are used to achieve the repair process (see Table 19.1):

- *Substitution* allows replacing a system component by another.
- *Wrapping* consists in substituting a system component by another enveloped which presents the same business logic.
- *Load Balancing* consists in distributing load on available components.
- *Rollback* allows the system to come back to the last stable state.
- *Redundancy* which repeats an action more than one time in order to achieve it.
- *Duplication (replication)* which involves addition of components representing similar functionalities.

19.3 DRAAS: Dynamically Reconfigurable Architecture for Autonomic Services

Based on the previous survey of autonomic computing techniques and capabilities, in this section, we propose to detail our dynamic reconfigurable architecture namely DRAAS, which manages the QoS of web service-based applications at runtime. Firstly, we detail the architecture and describe the different entities composing DRAAS. Then, we illustrate our dynamic reconfigurable architecture with the data load use case.

19.3.1 DRAAS Architecture

DRAAS provides the management of QoS by implementing the virtualization and the autonomic control loop. As shown in Fig. 19.2, DRAAS includes the different autonomic computing functions. The first one is the *Monitoring*. It corresponds to the supervision of the application. In our work, it refers to the supervision of both requesters and providers inflows/outflows and stores the value of the monitored data in the log. Second, the *Analysis* detects the time related QoS degradation. If detected, an alarm signal will be sent to the planning module. Third, the *Planning* identifies the origin of the QoS degradation and calculates the new reconfiguration. Fourth, the *Execution* module executes the reconfiguration actions. In our study, we consider the load balancing as a reconfiguration action. It refers to add/remove connections or activate/deactivate web services in order to reach a QoS objective.

The Fig. 19.2 presents an overview of DRAAS deployed between two *Requesters* and two *Providers*. We assume in our work that "Provider2 is equivalent to Provider1"

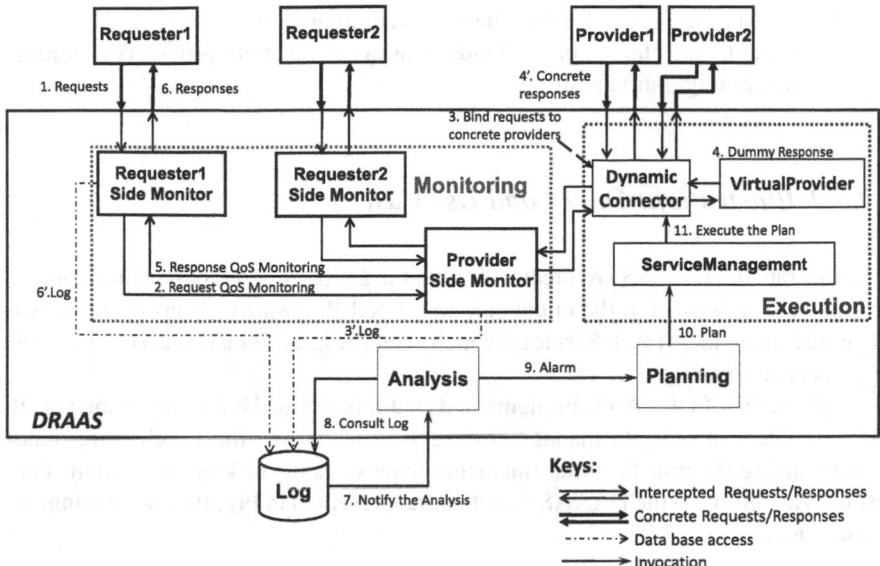

Fig. 19.2 DRAAS architecture

since it offers the same functionalities "business logic" as Provider1. Moreover, Providers are web services, and they are considered as black boxes. The only information provided is their WSDL describing the functional properties. To enable the dynamic reconfiguration, DRAAS defines a set of software entities. In the following, we detail the different entities according to the MAPE loop and we present the used techniques:

- The *Monitoring* module is based on the *interception* technique. Monitors are able to extend SOAP messages exchanged between the service requester and the service provider (Web Service). It is composed of:

  - Requester Side Monitor (RSM) is associated to each requester. It is responsible of intercepting inflow/outflow (Request/Response) of the requester.
  - Provider Side Monitor (PSM), is associated to all providers. It is responsible of intercepting inflow/outflow (Request/Response) of the providers.

- *Analysis* is based on the *QoS-aware* technique. It implements a proactive algorithm for the detection time related QoS degradation.
- *Planning* calculates the new reconfiguration: selecting the web service(s) that will be invoked for the next incoming requests.
- The *Execution* module implements the *Load Balancing* technique. It is composed of:

  - VirtualProvider, is the initial destination of requester requests. It is automatically generated from the concrete providers by parsing their WSDL.

– ServiceManagement, executes the new reconfiguration.
– Dynamic Connector, redirects/binds requests to concrete providers according
   to the reconfiguration plan.

19.3.2 Illustration: Data Load Use Case

We illustrate the DRAAS architecture within the *Data Load* use case which consists
in transferring files from the client side to a Load Repository. Transferring files is
ensured by providers (Web Services) which offer the LoadTransfer service. Each file
is associated to a request.

A prototype of DRAAS is implemented enabling the load balancing among available
providers in order to manage QoS such as response time which corresponds
to minimizing the transfer time. Balancing requests is the task of the dynamic connector.
According to the DRAAS architecture, presented in Fig. 19.2, we distinguish
these actors:

- Requester $\longrightarrow$ Client
- Provider1 $\longrightarrow$ LoadTransferWS1
- Provider2 $\longrightarrow$ LoadTransferWS2
- VirtualProvider $\longrightarrow$ LoadTransferVirtualWS

Initially, (1) the client sends files to the *LoadTransferVirtualWS*. Each one is
encapsulated in a request. (2) Each request is intercepted twice, first by the *RSM*
and second by the *PSM*. The *Dynamic Connector*, associated to the *LoadTransfer-VirtualWS*,
(3) balances the load (requests) by redirecting them to *LoadTransferWS1*
and *LoadTransferWS2*. Each web service provider (*LoadTransfer*) transfers a file
per request. (4, 4′) If the transfer of each file is successfully done, (5) each response
is also intercepted twice as the request but inversely: first by the *PSM* and second
by the *RSM*. (3′, 6′) All monitored data are stored in the log. If (8, 7) the *Analysis*
detects an increase of the transfer time, (9) it sends an alarm to the *Planning* in order
to calculate a new reconfiguration. In this case, the Planning decides to activate an
available *LoadTransferWS3* to participate in the next transfer. (10) It sends this decision
to the *ServiceManagement* to perform it (11). The execution of this decision
will be caught by the *Dynamic Connector*. It will be taken into account for the next
load transfer.

19.3.3 Experimentation

To show the effeciency of DRAAS, we have carried out experiments on the
Data Load. We present in the sequel hardware architecture and tools used for these
experiments.

19.3.3.1 Hardware Architecture and Tools

All test scenarios are assessed under this configuration:

- Operating system: Windows 7, 32 bits
- Processor: Intel Core(TM)2 Duo CPU T5800
- RAM: 2Go

Our implementation is built on the Web Service technology. Analysis, Planning and ServiceManagement are Web Services, while monitors and Dynamic Connector are based on Axis2 handlers. In the following, we cite the technical choices for our implementation:

- Communication level: SOAP
- Web service container/ SOAP Engine: Axis2 1.5
- Web server: Tomcat 6.0.30
- Programming language: Java 1.6
- Monitors and Connectors: Axis2 Handlers
- Logging: MySQL DBMS

19.3.3.2 Assessment

To assess DRAAS performance, we have fixed the global size of the files to be transferred (T=32Mo) and we have prepared six scenarios for testing. All scenarios focused on varying the number of files while maintaining the global size. We present in Table 19.2 the different scenarios used to evaluate DRAAS performance.

In order to show the benefits of DRAAS, we have distinguished two cases for the *Data Load* use case: first, the transfer of files is accomplished without load balancing (only one web service). Second, deploying DRAAS in order to maintain the QoS management, such the transfer time, at runtime.

Without applying DRAAS to the *DataLoad*, the client is connected only to the *LoadTransferWS1* web service and all files are transferred through it, even if there is another Web Service providing the same business logic which is available.

Table 19.2 Load transfer scenarios

	Number of files	File Size
Scenario 1	1	{32Mo}
Scenario 2	2	{17Mo; 15Mo}
Scenario 3	3	{10Mo; 11Mo; 11Mo}
Scenario 4	4	{9Mo; 8Mo; 8Mo; 7Mo}
Scenario 5	8	{3,7Mo; 4,3Mo; 3Mo; 5Mo; 4Mo; 4Mo; 4,2Mo; 3,8Mo}
Scenario 6	10	{3,2Mo; 2,8Mo; 3Mo; 2,8Mo; 3,2Mo; 3,2Mo; 3,2Mo; 3,7Mo; 3,7Mo;}

Table 19.3 Performance measurement

| | Response time (ms) | | | | | |
| | Single web service | | | Two web services (DRAAS) | | |
	Minimum	Maximum	Average	Minimum	Maximum	Average
Scenario 1	4565	5141	4812,6	3748	5168	4700,6
Scenario 2	6210	7669	6717,44	4067	5357	4918
Scenario 3	7780	8228	7920	4520	5583	5039,4
Scenario 4	8790	9609	9153,6	4090	5362	4600
Scenario 5	14592	16326	15451,6	7611	9631	8324,6
Scenario 6	18313	25147	20113,8	8123	8500	8510,4

If the *LoadTransferWS1* Web Service shows a QoS degradation, expressed by an increase of the transfer time, this degradation affects the Data Load application.

However, when we integrate our DRAAS prototype as described in the previews section, the load will be balanced on available web services offering the load transfer service.

We have carried out each scenario experiments at least 5 times. According to obtained values, results are shown in Table 19.3. The average of the response time (transfer time) is equal to the sum of values obtained by tests divided by the number of tests.

Our experiments provided the curves shown in Fig. 19.3. The blue curve describes the average response time related to transferring a variable number of files with a single web service where the global size is maintained constant and equal to 32Mo. However, the red curve describes the same parameters but while using two web services and enabling the load balancing.

It is obvious that transferring files within our DRAAS prototype, using two web services, is more efficient in terms of transfer time than using a single web service. We

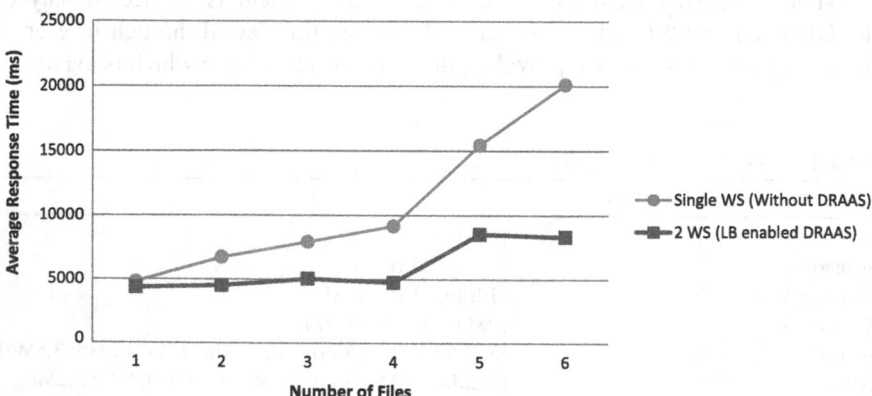

Fig. 19.3 Average response time of DRAAS prototype

noticed that the transfer time (response time) depends on the number of files. In fact, without DRAAS, increasing the number of files while maintaining the overall size leads to increase the response time. However, the DRAAS curve presents a critical point having the following coordinates (4, 4600) for which the average response time is optimal. Moreover, the deployment of DRAAS with a single provider causes the increase of the response time due to an added delay ϵ, epsilon, caused by the virtualization and the communication time between the MAPE modules. This ϵ has no impacts on response time since both the number of requests and the number of providers have exceed two.

Therefore, the deployment of DRAAS is based on a necessary and sufficient assumption which is the presence of at least two providers offering the same business logic. Indeed the presence of a single provider does not allow the dynamic reconfiguration, which is currently based on load balancing. Endowing web-service applications with DRAAS allows the management of the QoS at runtime without human intervention. Applications will run autonomously and will be characterized with the self-healing, self-configuration and self-adaptive capabilities.

19.4 Related Work: Implementation Approaches

In this section, we propose to classify the different existing work including **DRAAS** into three categories of solutions that can be used to implement autonomic systems: the model-based, the middleware-based and the platform-based categories. For the model-based implementations [10, 56], developers start from the scratch and should implement all actions related to autonomic computing modules. For the middleware-based implementations [26, 52, 58], developers build their solutions by adapting basic primitives to their application context. The provided APIs include primitives for monitoring, analysis, planning and possible reconfiguration actions. The platform category provides reusable components to implement autonomic computing strategies [6, 11, 51].

19.4.1 Model-Based Implementation Approaches

Model-based solutions implement all actions starting from the scratch. No primitives are offered. In this category, we focus particularly on architectural approaches in which constraints can be expressed explicitly. Management modules are generally proposed to ensure the dynamic reconfiguration process. These entities enable monitoring, implement analysis and planning, and enforce reconfiguration actions.

The work described in [25] presents a self-monitoring approach for the management of autonomic systems. This approach is not limited to the monitoring function, it includes also the self-diagnostic aspects. In this approach, two models of the self-managed system are distinguished: a structural model and a behavioural model. (i) The structural model describes the software architecture of the distributed object-oriented system. Form the application viewpoint, the structural model refers to runnables, (software) components, classes, and methods. It offers a decomposition of the distributed system that provides a granularity level concerning the monitoring information for the model-based diagnostic. So, a complex web service composed of two or more web services is modelled as a composite managed runnable containing two or more managed runnables, and each web service operation is modelled as a managed method. (ii) The behavioural model consists of the following concepts: jobs, tasks, states, and events. This model refers to a collect of the various use case of the system (the different response to a given request). The dynamic behaviour of a web service can be directly described in OWL as jobs and tasks. These two models help the system to decide where to place sensors. Also, they provide information related to the classification, the moment and the localization of the observation. However, this approach monitors only the state of the web services and does not take into consideration the non-functional requirements such the response of time. Moreover, it does not tackle the reconfiguration of the system if an anomaly is detected.

The work of [1] describes the dynamic and autonomic composition of Grid/ web services. The authors present the Accord Composition Model which is able to to autonomically synthesize composition plans (when possible) from the pool of available services to satisfy dynamically defined composition objectives, policies and constraints. The Accord Composition (ACE) Engine is mainly composed of four modules: ACE translator, Graph Generator, Constraint Analyzer, Plan Generator and Evaluator. Starting from the WSDL describing each service from the pool service, the ACE generates plans according to the request and to constraints. This work tackles the *plan* function of the autonomic computing paradigm. However, in case of more than one plan, the ACE ranks them according to service and link cots rather than performance.

Rainbow [8, 10] is a reusable framework for self-adaptive systems. It is composed of two layers. First, the system layer, which collects information about the system (that can be composed of web services) and enforces reconfiguration plans. Second, the architecture layer, which reflects the current architecture model, checks constraint violations, and determines the required adaptation. The architecture and system layers interact through a *translation infrastructure*. However, experimental work [18] has shown that this externalized approach for self-adaptation causes a significant slowdown of the system behavior. Also, this approach supposes that the target system contains hooks for monitoring and management. The reconfiguration plan is built manually and integrated in the code. No evaluation or validation of this plan is provided.

Other model-based approaches [36] use architectural styles designed to enable autonomic computing. In fact, an architectural style represents a collection of design decisions that have already been made and can be reused. It consists in a few key features and rules for combining these features so that architectural integrity is preserved.

19.4.2 Middleware-Based Implementation Approaches

The middleware-based approaches provide primitives helping developers to implement autonomic computing system. In the following, we present middleware-based implementations. Details about each middleware are presented in Table 19.4.

DynamicTAO [31] is a reflective ORB (an extension of the TAO ORB). It enables detecting changes in environment and reloading new component/service implementations which may be bound to the system at runtime. These features are achieved by the use of a collection of entities known as component *configurators*. These configurators maintain information about the dependencies between the components they manage. The *DynamicConfigurator* inspects implementations and reconfigures system on the fly while loading or removing implementations stored in a *Repository*. The scalability of DynamicTAO is not improved. However, it is only tested with a simple example (*getHello( )*). The DynamicTAO infrastructure includes two management security services. The first is used to crypt/decrypt message contents and the second authenticates communication peers to control access. The security strategy can be loaded and bound dynamically to the system at runtime. This allows the use of a large range of security models.

The work of [2] presents a distributed reflective middleware for service oriented applications. This middleware aimed at proposing solutions to cope with fault tolerance problems in the context of web services composition and choreography based on the Autonomic Computing Architecture. This middleware is divided into two levels: Base Level and Meta Level. The Base level knows the iterations that occur in the choreography and the definitions and rules that govern these iterations. It observes both SOA system (WSDL, OWL-S, etc.) and the SOA application (service consumer, web services providers). The Meta level provides the capacity for reflection, it is instantiated for each service of the choreography. It implements the autonomic control loop in order to dynamically reconfigure the SOA system by changing service properties.

MiniMASC+MiniZinc [33] is a middleware that implements new autonomic business driven decision algorithms for cases when there are multiple running instances of the Web service composition to be adapted. Based on the monitored data from the managed system and WS-Policy4MASC policy assertions, MiniMASC+MiniZinc middleware makes the decision on what assertions to be used. Then according to business metrics, it selects the appropriate one to adapt. It is the role of the Adaptation execution (3rd party module) to perform the chosen adaptation action. The strength of this middleware focuses on its ability to resolve policy conflicts. However, despite using autonomic computing, models in MiniZinc are currently developed by hand which implies human intervention.

Work of [2] and MiniMASC+MiniZinc are developed as an external layer to manage autonomic systems at runtime. However, DynamicTAO can be external or internal. External, in which the monitoring component is supported by applications as an external service. Internal, in which the monitoring component is injected into the application components to provide such service. DynamicTAO does not provide

Table 19.4 Middleware features

Middleware	DynamicTAO	Work of [2]	MiniMASC+MiniZinc
Monitoring	*Event collector*: Observes behavior of components and generates relevant QoS events Collects QoS events and reports abnormal behaviors	*Components monitoring*: Inspect the communication services. QoS parameters of services: The composition response time, throughput, availability and consistency of data exchanged.	*Database of monitored data* technical metrics (measured response time, calculated availability), business metrics (paid prices and penalties), and events
Analysis	*Monitor*: No given details	*Components behavior analysis*: SLA violation (web service fault)	No given details
Planning	*Strategy selectors*: Selects an appropriate adaptation strategy based on feedback from monitors	No given details	*Determining triggered policies and MiniZinc solver*: Decides which WS-Policy4MASC policy assertions can be executed next and select the appropriate one according to business values
Execution	*Strategy activators*: Implements a particular strategy, e.g. by manipulating component graph while preserving the architectural style	*Reparation plan and execution*: Mechanisms for the resolution of faults present in the composition of services repair	*Adaptation execution*: Transfers the system state towards a replica
External/Internal	External or Internal	External	External
Programming language	Python	Java	Java, the PostgreSQL database, and the MiniZinc solver
Application domain	Component/Web service	SOA applications	Web service/ WS composition systems
Reconfiguration strategy	*Structural*: Modifies the architecture	*Behavioral*: Adjusting web service properties	*Structural*: Service composition

entities for fault detections and analysis. The user has to inquire about the application health and to choose the suitable reconfiguration plan. While the Work of [2] does not give any details related to the planning module. Meanwhile, all the steps are automated.

19.4.3 Platform-Based Implementation Approaches

In this section, we present the main suggested platforms employed for developing autonomic applications. The evaluation is based on criteria including provided self-aware, used components and the architecture types supported by these platforms.

Unity [11, 53]: The Unity project is looking for how component behaviors and relationships can support self-management of computing systems. The Unity project implements a prototype of autonomic systems, designed to show the feasibility and to validate the dynamic reconfiguration of the environment. During runtime it reallocates and reconfigures resources/services to optimize its behavior according to specified policies. In this approach, every component incorporates an autonomic part in a way that it becomes autonomic. The different components of Unity are:

- "Application environment manager": which is responsible for the management, communication between components, and predicting the resource/service availability.
- "Resource arbiter": which manages sharing and allocation of resources/services.
- "Registry": which allows locating components/services.
- "Policy repository": which represents administration interfaces.
- "Sentinel": which is used by a component to monitor the functioning of another.
- "Solution manager": which is responsible for the reconfiguration and the maintenance.

The monitoring is enabled by all components, including defective components (if they exist) which can cause system damages. They have to be sure about monitored Data. They should add policies in order to filter gathered data.

SAFDIS [19]: Self-Adaptation For DIstributed Services, enables the dynamic management of service-based architectures. The implementation is built for the OSGi platform, using iPOJO to manage the life-cycle which exposes its functionalities as services . The different components are:

- *Adaptation Manager*: its role concentrates on ensuring the communication between the different components and services responsible of the adaptation of the system.
- *Event Manager*: it collects events from monitors, composes them and keeps a local view of the system. It is the supervisor of the whole system.
- *Analyst*: it is a distributed and a decentralized process. It identifies, analyzes the system changes and decides if an adaptation is needed. Then, it makes an adaptation decision when a need arises. Furthermore, this component is composed of:

– *Decision Maker*: it listens to events coming from the event manager and sends them to the reasoners for analysis.
– *Negotiator*: it is composed of a back end and a front end connected to a remote negotiator of another SAFDIS instance.
– *Negotiation Manager*: it is responsible of managing the multiple negotiations that can happen at the same time.

• *Planner*: it is composed of a set of *Planning Algorithms* and a *Manager* component. According to objectives and constraints, the *Manager* produces simple orderings of actions to reconfigure system.
• *Execution Engine*: it is called to perform planned actions. In SAFDIS, the reconfiguration action moves a service from an execution node to another, which is called the migration of services.

However, SAFDIS does not consider the overload issues of services. It implements only the migration of services as a reconfiguration action.

CAPPUCINO [47] is a platform for executing context-aware Web Services in ubiquitous environments. It combines the strengths of both SCA and COSMOS [13] models to provide a versatile infrastructure for supporting context-aware adaptations in SOA environments. It implements the MAPE control loop distributed in ubiquitous environments as SCA components. Although this work deals with Web Services, it remains restricted to the ubiquitous environments. The reconfiguration is based on deploying new communication protocols and new context collectors.

CODA [44]: Complex Organic Distributed Architecture: CODA applies concepts such as self-organization, self-regulation and viability to derive an intelligent architecture that can be composed of web services. It reacts to operation failures and proactively searches for successful patterns of behavior. CODA is a layered approach. It contains five layers:

• "Operations": which represents business operations of a system.
• "Monitor Operations": which performs internal monitoring.
• "Monitor of the Monitors": which performs external monitoring.
• "Control": which learns about faults and predicts reconfiguration actions.
• "Command": which recognizes threats and makes decisions.

MAIS [6]: Mobile Adaptive Information Systems: The MAIS project studies adaptability at all levels in information systems, from application level to network and device levels (PCs, laptops, cellular phones, and so on). Several levels of adaptability are considered: the upper level (Application level), the middle level (web service level) and the bottom level (Infrastructure & Middleware level). MAIS provides an environment to run composite, multi-channel, mobile, and context-aware web services in an adaptive way. The MAIS architecture implements a runtime service-oriented fault analysis and recovery actions. It detects faults by inspecting request and response messages and analyzing them through a diagnoser component. This architecture provides four modules to handle reconfiguration actions, namely: "reallocation", "substitution", "wrapper generator" and "quality modules".

Jade [15]: Jade is an autonomous administration platform for software infrastructure. It provides an abstract view of the application and acts when a failure occurs on a part of the system. It uses duplication to maintain the service availability and to handle the resource allocation according to the load variation in order to manage scalability. Jade is composed of two parts:

- *Managed Element*: which wraps each software (web service) and provides an administration interface;
- *Autonomic Manager*: which implements the administration management policies (repair and optimization). It monitors and acts on system through the *Managed Elements* interfaces.

DRAAS, **D**ynamically **R**econfigurable **A**rchitecture for **A**utonomic **S**ervices, as detailed in Sect. 19.3, is a reusable architecture for the dynamic reconfiguration of web-service application. DRAAS is based on the autonomic computing and the virtualization for the management of the time related QoS. It implements the structural reconfiguration by ensuring the load balancing.

In Table 19.5, we summarize properties of each platform. Most platforms do not allow any interaction between human or administrator and application except for Unity and MAIS. The programming language supported by all platforms is Java. CODA, Unity, CAPPUCINO, MAIS and **DRAAS** support web services based dynamic reconfiguration. The others may investigate to support them by encapsulating web services in components. The originality of DRAAS, compared to the previous solutions, focuses on its ability to dynamically reconfigure distributed web services applications without modifying the providers sides (e.g. by adding components). Moreover, DRAAS can be easily integrated to existing applications, the only information required is the interface of providers WSDL.

19.4.4 Concluding Remarks

19.4.4.1 Internal Versus External Autonomic Computing

All cited implementations have as goal the dynamic reconfiguration of the system which allows it to evolve incrementally from one state to another at run-time in order to accommodate to changes. The dynamic reconfiguration activities, based on autonomic computing, can be carried out either internally or externally to the application. In internal, codes responsible of the reconfiguration are merged with the application codes, while in external, they are separated from the application codes [43].

In an **internal** autonomic mechanism, it is difficult to add a new code or a new strategy to a black-box component; we must know about the component design in order to govern it. The Unity [11], CODA [44] and DynamicTAO [31] projects present a prototype enabling dynamic reconfiguration, based on internal mechanisms.

Table 19.5 Platform features

Platform names	Unity	CAPPUCINO	CODA	MAIS	Jade	SAFDIS	DRAAS
Centralized/Decentralized	Decentralized	Decentralized	Centralized	Centralized	Centralized	Decentralized	Decentralized
Human intervention	Minimal	No	No	Interaction	No	No	No
Self-aware	Self-configuration, self-optimizing, self-protecting, self-healing	Self-awareness, self-managing, self-adaptive, self-configuration	Self-organization, self-regulation, self-monitoring	Self-adaptation, self-optimizing	Self-adaptation, self-optimizing	Self-adaptation, self-optimizing	Self-healing, self-configuration, self-adaptive
External/Internal	Internal	External	Internal, external	Internal, external	External	External	External
Programming language	Java	Various programming language	Java	Java	Java	Java	Java
Presentation	GUI	No	No	No	Monitoring visualizator	No	No
Monitoring	Sentinel	No given details	Monitor operations, monitor of the monitors	Diagnoser and inspector	Monitor	Event manager	Requester side monitor and provider side monitor: Interception of time related QoS
Execution	Solution manager	CAPPUCINO adaptation runtime: FraSCAti kernel	Command	Recovery actions	Connector: Duplication of services	Migration of services	Dynamic Connector: Request redirection (load balancing)
Level	Application	Application (client/server)	Application	Application, network and device	Application	Application	Application

External mechanism is appropriate when it is so difficult to modify application codes. We generally deploy components in heterogeneous context; therefore, if we use an internal strategy, we have to develop a new component version (with specific self-healing mechanism) for each context. Also, externalized mechanisms allow the reuse of autonomic components and make easy their update, since they are localized. In addition, external mechanism allows us to divide the task of the application implementation between the component developers and managers. DRAAS, Rainbow [8], the work of [2] and MiniMASC+MiniZinc [33] built their systems based on external mechanisms.

Each component may include autonomic mechanisms in order to heal itself. Designed systems have to inquire into problems and ask components to reconfigure their structure or behavior. Furthermore, dynamic reconfiguration strategy must not cause significant slowdown to the execution process and especially for the real time application. It must react in order to repair crashes while the variance of global system response time is kept in limited bounds. In order to reach a suitable and adaptable system which makes system resilient to faults, we have to apply autonomic computing techniques which cover all levels: hardware and software. But this solution may be very expensive and it requires combination of various mechanisms.

19.4.4.2 Behavioral Versus Structural Autonomic Computing

We can distinguish two strategies of the dynamic reconfiguration in the Execution level. In fact, reconfiguration actions act on the system either behaviorally or structurally.

Following the first strategy , it is related to the **behavioral** dimension of the system in general; otherwise, it focuses on its internal behavior. Indeed, we speak about such approach when service behavior is customizable or modifiable. So, when degradation is detected, the installed reconfiguration infrastructure is brought to repair the process at runtime, by applying the reconfiguration actions to the concerned services. This reconfiguration is considered as a direct adjustment, because its actions are supposed to modify at once the internal composition of system services in order to correct it further to a problem. The work of [2] adjusts the service properties in order to dynamically reconfigure the web service choreography.

Following the second one, it is related to the **structural** dimension of the system. So that systems services are observed during the execution of this later. Several symptoms are stored before taking the decision of activating or not reconfiguration actions. In this case, the reconfiguration is done by applying basis actions such as adding or removing services or their connections. The structural adaption refers to "run-time" when the reconfiguration is scheduled during execution. DRAAS, DynamicTAO [31] and MiniMASC+MiniZinc [33] implement the structural reconfiguration.

19.5 Conclusion

In this chapter, we mainly focused on the dynamic reconfiguration supported by the autonomic computing paradigm. We presented our DRAAS architecture to bring dynamic reconfiguration capabilities to distributed web service-based applications. A prototype of DRAAS has been implemented to assess the applicability of the monitoring and reconfiguration within the designed architecture. The repair action is based on the structural reconfiguration providing load balancing for web services at the origin of the QoS degradation. Then, we presented a classification and a comparative study of existing approaches including DRAAS. The classification follows three categories of implementation a model-based, middleware-based and platform-based solution. We conclude that the model-based is usually suitable for a small system and platform-based solutions are appropriated for systems in which only generic QoS properties are required. The new objectives are oriented towards the deployment and the execution of distributed applications on heterogeneous platforms (PC, smart devices, Smart card, etc).

We aim to improve our DRAAS architecture's to support the service composition (orchestration/choreography)and adding new reconfiguration actions such as substitution. Moreover, we target to manage dynamically MAPE-K loop components while enabling flexibility by changing their behaviors at runtime in order to include new features, such as new monitors or new analysis algorithms.

References

1. Agarwal, M., Parashar, M.: Enabling autonomic compositions in grid environments. In: Proceedings of Fourth International Workshop on Grid Computing, pp. 34–41, Nov. 2003
2. Aguilar, J., Vizcarrondo, J., Ernesto Exposito.: Reflective middleware for automatic management of service-oriented applications using the theory of signatures of failure. In: 14th WSEAS International Conference on Mathematical Methods, Computational Techniques and Intelligent Systems (MAMECTIS '12), pp. 183–188. July 2012
3. Ben-Halima, R., Drira, K., Guennoun, K., Jmaiel, M.: Non-intrusive qos monitoring and analysis for self-healing web services. In: First IEEE International Conference on the Applications of Digital Information and Web Technologies (ICADIWT 2008), IEEE Computer Society, Ostrava, 4–6 Aug 2008
4. Blair, G.S., Coulson, G., Blair, L., Duran-Limon, H., Grace, P., Moreira, R., Parlavantzas, N.: Reflection, self-awareness and self-healing in openorb. In: WOSS '02 Proceedings of the First Workshop on Self-Healing systems, pp. 9–14. ACM Press, New York (2002)
5. Bouchenak, S., Boyer, F., Krakowiak, S., Hagimont, D., Mos, A., Jean-Bernard, S., de Palma, N., Quema, V.: Architecture-based autonomous repair management: an application to J2EE clusters. In: SRDS '05 Proceedings of the 24th IEEE Symposium on Reliable Distributed Systems, pp. 13–24. IEEE Computer Society, Orlando (2005)
6. Cappiello, C., Missier, P., Pernici, B., Plebani, P., Batini, C.: Qos in multichannel is: the mais approach. In: Engineering Advanced Web Applications, Proceedings of Workshops in Connection with the 4th International Conference on Web Engineering (ICWE 2004), pp. 255–268. Munich, 28–30 July 2004
7. Chang, F., Karamcheti, V., Automatic configuration and run-time adaptation of distributed applications. In HPDC '00 Proceedings of the Ninth IEEE International Symposium on High

Performance Distributed Computing (HPDC'00), pp. 11. IEEE Computer Society, Washington, DC, USA (2000)

8. Cheng, S.-W., Garlan, D., Schmerl, BR.: Making self-adaptation an engineering reality. In: Self-Star Properties in Complex Information Systems, Conceptual and Practical Foundations [the book is a result from a workshop at Bertinoro, Italy, Summer 2004], vol. 3460, pp. 158–173. Lecture Notes in Computer Science, Springer (2005)

9. Cheng, S.-W., Garlan, D., Schmerl, B.R., Sousa, J.P., Spitnagel, B., Steenkiste, P.: Using architectural style as a basis for system self-repair. In: WICAS3 Proceedings of the IFIP 17th World Computer Congress—TC2 Stream/3rd IEEE/IFIP Conference on Software Architecture, pp. 45–59. Kluwer, B.V., Deventer (2002)

10. Cheng, S.-W., Huang, A.-C., Garlan, D., Schmerl, B.R., Steenkiste, P.: An architecture for coordinating multiple self-management systems. In: 4th Working IEEE/IFIP Conference on Software Architecture (WICSA 2004), pp. 243–254. Oslo. IEEE Computer Society, Washington, DC, USA, 12–15 June 2004

11. Chess, D.M., Segal, A., Whalley, I., White, S.R.: Unity: experiences with a prototype autonomic computing system. In: 1st International Conference on Autonomic Computing (ICAC 2004), pp. 140–147. IEEE Computer Society, New York, 17–19 May 2004

12. Ciupa, I.: Study on whitebox frameworks in java (2003)

13. Conan, D., Rouvoy, R., Seinturier, L., Projet Jacquard Lifl.: Scalable processing of context information with cosmos (2007)

14. Conte, A., Anquetil, L.-P.: A black box framework for an application protocol stack. In: Proceedings of the 3rd IEEE Symposium on, Application-Specific Systems and Software Engineering Technology, pp. 96–101. IEEE Computer Society, 2000

15. de Palma, N., Bouchenak, S., Hagimont, D., Sicard, S., Taton, C.: Jade : Un Environnement d'Administration Autonome. Techniques et Sciences Informatiques 27(9–10), 1225–1252 (2008)

16. Diaconescu, A.: A framework for using component redundancy for self-adapting and self-optimising component-based enterprise systems. In: OOPSLA '03 Companion of the 18th Annual ACM SIGPLAN Conference on Object-Oriented Programming, Systems, Languages, and Applications, pp. 390–391. ACM Press, New York (2003)

17. Ewing, J.M., Menascea, D.A.: Business-oriented autonomic load balancing for multitiered web sites. In: Modeling, Analysis Simulation of Computer and Telecommunication Systems, MASCOTS '09. IEEE International Symposium, pp. 1–10, Sept 2009

18. Garlan, D., Cheng, S.-W., Schmerl, B.R.: Increasing system dependability through architecture-based self-repair. In: WADS, vol. 2677, pp. 61–89. Lecture Notes in Computer Science, Springer (2002)

19. Gauvrit, G., Daubert, E., Safdis, F.A.: A framework to bring self-adaptability to service-based distributed applications. In: SEAA'10 Proceedings of the 2010 36th EUROMICRO Conference on, Software Engineering and Advanced Applications, pp. 211–218. IEEE Computer Society, 2010

20. George, S., Evans, D., Marchette, S.: A biological programming model for self-healing. In: SSRS '03 Proceedings of the 2003 ACM Workshop on Survivable and Self-Regenerative Systems, pp. 72–81. ACM Press, New York (2003)

21. Giroux, S., Gouin-Vallerand, C., Abdulrazak, B.: Toward a self-configuration middleware for smart spaces. In: FGCN '08 Proceedings of the 2008 Second International Conference on Future Generation Communication and Networking, vol. 2, pp. 463–468. IEEE Computer Society, 2008

22. Grace, P., Blair, G.S., Samuel, S.: Remmoc: a reflective middleware to support mobile client interoperability. In: On The Move to Meaningful Internet Systems 2003: CoopIS, DOA, and ODBASE—OTM Confederated International Conferences, CoopIS, DOA, and ODBASE 2003, vol. 2888, pp. 1170–1187. Lecture Notes in Computer Science, Springer, Catania, 3–7 Nov 2003

23. Guinea, S.: Self-healing web service compositions. In: ICSE '05: Proceedings of the 27th International Conference on Software Engineering, pp. 655–655. ACM Press.... 1q, New York (2005)

24. Gurguis S.A., Zeid A.: Towards autonomic web services: Achieving self-healing using web services. In: DEAS '05: Proceedings of the 2005 Workshop on Design and Evolution of Autonomic Application Software, pp. 1–5. ACM Press, New York (2005)

25. Haydarlou, A.R., Oey, M.A., Overeinder, B.J., Brazier, F.M.T.: Use case driven approach to self-monitoring in autonomic systems. In: Autonomic and Autonomous Systems, 2007. ICAS07. Third International Conference on, p. 50. (2007)

26. Huebscher M.C., McCann J.A., Adaptive middleware for context-aware applications in smarthomes. In: Proceedings of the 2nd workshop on Middleware for pervasive and ad-hoc computing, pp. 111–116. ACM Press, New York (2004)

27. Huebscher, M.C., McCann, J.A.: A survey of autonomic computing -degrees, models, and applications. ACM Comput. Surv. **40**(3), 7:1–7:28 (2008)

28. IBM Corp.: An architectural blueprint for autonomic computing. IBM Corp., USA (2004)

29. Jmaiel, M., Ben-Halima, R., Drira, K.: Survey a qos-oriented reconfigurable middleware for self-healing web services. In: ICWS '08: Proceedings of the 2008 IEEE International Conference on Web Services, vol. 1. pp. 104–111. IEEE Computer Society, 2008

30. Kephart, J.O., Chess, DM.: The vision of autonomic computing. Computer **36**(1), 41–50 (2003)

31. Kon, F., Román, M., Liu, P., Mao J., Yamame T., Magalhaes, L.C.: Monitoring, security, and dynamic configuration with the dynamictao reflective orb. In: Middleware 2000, Proceedings of the IFIP/ACM International Conference on Distributed Systems Platforms, New York, April 2000. Lecture Notes in Computer Science. vol. 1795, pp. 121–143. Springer (2000)

32. Lee, K.S., Lee C.-G., Model-driven monitoring of time-critical systems based on aspect-oriented programming. In: Secure Software Integration and Reliability Improvement (SSIRI), 2011 Fifth International Conference on, pp. 80–87. IEEE Computer Society, 2011

33. Lu, Q., Tosic, V.: Minimasc+minizinc: An autonomic business-driven decision making middleware for adaptation of web service compositions. In: Proceedings of the 2010 Symposia and Workshops on Ubiquitous, Autonomic and Trusted Computing (UIC-ATC '10). pp. 474–477. IEEE Computer Society, Washington (2010)

34. Mdhaffar, A., Ben-Halima, R., Juhnke, E., Jmaiel, M., Freisleben, B.: An Aspect-Oriented Programming Approach for Cloud Service Monitoring (AOP4CSM). In: Proceedings of the 11th IEEE International Conference on Computer and Information Technology. pp. 363–370. IEEE Press (2011)

35. Medvidovic, N., Mikic-Rakic, M.: Programming-in-the-many: a software engineering paradigm for the 21st century. Research and Applications. In: Workshop on New Visions for Software Design and Productivity, Nashville (2001)

36. Mikic-Rakic, M., Mehta, N., Medvidovic, N.: Architectural style requirements for self-healing systems. In: Proceedings of the first workshop on Self-healing systems (WOSS '02), pp. 49–54. ACM Press, New York (2002)

37. Moo-Mena, F., Drira, K.: Reconfiguration of web services architectures: A model-based approach. In: 12th IEEE Symposium on Computers and Communications, (ISCC 2007), pp. 357–362. IEEE Computer Society, 2007

38. Mostafaei, F.S., Amani, N., Hajipour, P.: Proposing a new qos/sla management model by regulatory authority. In: Telecommunications (IST), 2010 5th International Symposium on, pp. 508–512. IEEE Computer Society, 2010

39. Oreizy, P., Gorlick, M.M., Taylor, R.N., Heimbigner, D., Johnson, G., Medvidovic, N., Quilici, A., Rosenblum, D.S., Wolf, A.L.: An architecture-based approach to self-adaptive software. IEEE Intell Syst **14**(3), 54–62 (1999)

40. Orleans, L.F., Furtado, P.N.: Optimization for qos on web-service-based systems with tasks deadlines. In: Autonomic and Autonomous Systems, ICAS07. Third International Conference on, p. 6 (2007)

41. Parashar, M., Hariri, S.: Autonomic computing : An overview. pp. 247–259 (2005)

42. Paulson, L.D.: Computer system, heal thyself. Computer **35**(8), 20–22 (2002)

43. Qun, Y., Xian-Chun, Y., Man-Wu, X.: A framework for dynamic software architecture-based self-healing. SIGSOFT Softw. Eng. Notes **30**(4), 1–4 (2005)

44. Ribeiro-Justo, G.R., Karran, T.: Modelling organic adaptable service-oriented enterprise architectures. In: On The Move to Meaningful Internet Systems 2003: OTM 2003 Workshops, OTM Confederated International Workshops, HCI-SWWA, IPW, JTRES, WORM, WMS, and WRSM 2003, Catania, Sicily, Italy, 3–7 Nov 2003, Proceedings, Vol. 2889 of Lecture Notes in Computer Science, pp. 123–136. Springer (2003)
45. Richters, M., Gogolla, M.: Aspect-oriented monitoring of uml and ocl constraints. In: AOSD Modeling With UML Workshop, 6th International Conference on the Unified Modeling Language (UML, 2003)
46. Schmidt, H.: Trustworthy components-compositionality and prediction. J. Syst. Softw. **65**(3), 215–225 (2003)
47. Sheng, Q.Z., Yu, J., Dustdar, S.: Enabling Context-Aware Web Services: Methods, Architectures, and Technologies. Chapman & Hall/CRC, 1st edn. (2010)
48. Shin, M.E.: Self-healing components in robust software architecture for concurrent and distributed systems. J. Sci. Comput. Program. **57**(1), 27–44 (July 2005)
49. Sridhar, N., Pike, S.M., Weide, B.W.: Dynamic module replacement in distributed protocols. In: Distributed Computing Systems. Proceedings 23rd International Conference on, pp. 620–627. IEEE Computer Society, 2003
50. Srivastava, P.K., Sahu, S.: Secured remote tracking of critical autonomic computing applications. published in IEEE E-Tech, Karachi, Pakistan (2004)
51. Sterritt, R., Bantz, D.F.: Pac-men: Personal autonomic computing monitoring environment. In 15th International Workshop on Database and Expert Systems Applications (DEXA 2004), Zaragoza, Spain, pp. 737–741. IEEE Computer Society, 2004
52. Suzuki, J., Suda, T.: A middleware platform for a biologically inspired network architecture supporting autonomous and adaptive applications. IEEE J. Select. Areas Commun. **23**(2), 249–260 (February 2005)
53. Tesauro, G., Chess, D.M., Walsh, W.E., Das, R., Segal, A., Whalley, I., Kephart, J.O., White, S.R.: A multi-agent systems approach to autonomic computing. In: 3rd International Joint Conference on Autonomous Agents and Multiagent Systems (AAMAS 2004), 19–23 Aug 2004, New York, pp. 464–471. IEEE Computer Society, 2004
54. Tosic, V., Pagurek, B., Patel, K., Esfandiari, B., Ma, W.: Management applications of the web service offerings language (wsol). In: Advanced Information Systems Engineering, 15th International Conference, CAiSE 2003, Klagenfurt, Austria, 16–18 June 2003, Proceedings, Vol. 2681 of Lecture Notes in Computer Science, pp. 468–484. Springer (2003)
55. Truong, H.-L., Samborski, R., Fahringer, T.: Towards a framework for monitoring and analyzing qos metrics of grid services. In: e-Science and Grid Computing. e-Science '06. Second IEEE International Conference on, pp. 65–73. IEEE Computer Society, 2006
56. Wile, D.S., Egyed, A.: An externalized infrastructure for self-healing systems. In: WICSA '04: Proceedings of the Fourth Working IEEE/IFIP Conference on Software Architecture (WICSA'04), p. 285, Washington. IEEE Computer Society, 2004
57. Yoo, G., Lee, E.: Monitoring methodology using aspect oriented programming in functional based system. In: Advanced Communication Technology (ICACT), 2010 The 12th International Conference on, Vol. 1, pp. 783–786. IEEE Computer Society, 2010
58. Zeng, L., Benatallah, B.: Anne H.H. Ngu, Marlon Dumas, Jayant Kalagnanam, and Henry Chang. Qos-aware middleware for web services composition. IEEE Trans. Softw. Eng. **30**(5), 311–327 (2004)
59. Zhang, H., Urtado, C., Vauttier, S.: Connector-driven process for the gradual evolution of component-based software. In: Software Engineering Conference, ASWEC '09. Australian, pp. 246–255. IEEE Computer Society, 2009

Chapter 20
Comprehensive Variability Modeling and Management for Customizable Process-Based Service Compositions

Tuan Nguyen, Alan Colman and Jun Han

Abstract Variability in process-based service compositions needs to be explicitly modeled and managed in order to facilitate service/process customization and increase reuse in service/process development. While related work has been able to capture variability and variability dependencies within a composition, these approaches fail to capture variability dependencies between the composition and partner services. Consequently, these approaches cannot address the situation when a customizable composite service is orchestrated from partner services which themselves are customizable. In this article, we describe a feature-based approach that is able to effectively model variability within and across compositions. The approach is supported by a process development methodology that enables the systematic reuse and management of variability. A prototype system supporting extended BPMN 2.0 is used to demonstrate the feasibility of the approach.

20.1 Introduction

Process-based service compositions are prevalent approaches for developing composite services using process modeling techniques. The two widely used standards for this purpose are Business Process Model and Notation (BPMN) [24] for modeling purposes and Business Process Execution Language (BPEL) [23] for execution purposes. In general, in both techniques, a composite service is described by a business

T. Nguyen (✉) · A. Colman · J. Han
Faculty of Information and Communication Technology,
Swinburne University of Technology, Melbourne, Australia
e-mail: tmnguyen@swin.edu.au

A. Colman
e-mail: acolman@swin.edu.au

J. Han
e-mail: jhan@swin.edu.au

A. Bouguettaya et al. (eds.), *Web Services Foundations*,
DOI: 10.1007/978-1-4614-7518-7_20,
© Springer Science+Business Media New York 2014

process capturing the flow of activities (i.e. *control flow*), the interaction between the process and partner services (i.e. *message flow*), and the way data is manipulated throughout the process (i.e. *data flow*).

Due to the diversity in service consumption, service variability has become an important factor in the lifecycle of service development [1, 10, 30]. Service variability is defined as the ability of a service or process to be efficiently extended, changed, customized or configured for use in a particular context [31]. Such variability originates either from service providers wishing to provide different versions of the same service for different market segments, or from service consumers wishing to customize a service to match their particular business requirements.

Service variability brings about a new type of services, namely *customizable services*, in service ecosystems. A *customizable service* is a service whose *runtime customization* by a consumer will result in a particular service variant matching the consumer's requirements [17, 20, 29]. For services with a large number of service variants, the use of customizable services, instead of conventional services, delivers much benefit to service consumers. This is because there are disadvantages with either deploying an all-in-one non-customizable service or deploying all service variants separately. In the first case, the non-customizable service has a large service description most of which is not relevant to one particular consumer. Such redundancy in service description hinders the efficient consumption of services. In the second case, it is difficult for service consumers to recognize the similarities and the differences among those service variants in order to select the most appropriate one.

While a customizable service might be either a composite service or an atomic service, we focus on customizable composite services in this article. In particular, the focal point is on customizable process-based service compositions. For this reason, throughout the article, the term *"customizable services"* is used interchangeably to the term *"customizable composite services"* unless otherwise stated.

To facilitate the development and consumption of customizable services, their variability needs to be explicitly modeled and managed. To this end, there are two key concerns [27]. Firstly, how to model *variation points* and *variants*? Secondly, how to capture *dependencies* among those variants? A *variation point* represents any place in a business process where variation may occur. Each *variation point* is associated with a set of *variants* from which one or several will be bound to the *variation point* when variability is resolved. And variability dependencies are restrictions on variant selections of one or more variation points. These dependencies are often specified in terms of *requires* and *excludes* relations and expressed as "the binding of variant A1 to variation point A requires/excludes the binding of variant B1 to variation point B".

There are two types of variability dependencies in service computing: *variability intra-dependencies* and *variability inter-dependencies* [21]. *Variability intra-dependencies* represent dependencies within a service composition, while *variability inter-dependencies* represent dependencies between the composition and its customizable partner services. Variability inter-dependencies reflect the situation when the runtime resolution of variability in the composition requires the runtime resolution of variability at partner services. And these dependencies may have *ripple effect* in service ecosystems *since service composition is recursive*.

Software Product Line (SPL) is a successful paradigm for systematic identification and management of variability [25]. Therefore, many works have exploited concepts and techniques from SPL in addressing variability in process-based service compositions, e.g. [9, 16, 19, 26]. These approaches are able to capture variability and variability dependencies within the control flow and the data flow of a process model. However, all these efforts fail to capture variability inter-dependencies. Consequently, these approaches are not capable of managing variability in such service compositions that are aggregations of customizable partner services.

In this article, we describe an approach for the comprehensive modeling and management of variability in customizable process-based service compositions. With regard to variability modeling, we present our extension to BPMN 2.0 for incorporating variation points and variants in all three aspects of service composition: control flow, data flow, and message flow. We then describe our extension of a feature modeling technique from SPL for capturing variability dependencies within and across service compositions. Based on these extensions, we specify a process development methodology that enables the systematic reuse of service variability.

With regard to variability management, we exploit our extension of WSDL, namely Web Service Variability description Language (WSVL) [22], to describe the service interface of customizable composite services. A WSVL description is generated from modeling elements to facilitate service consumers in consuming the composite service (e.g. requesting service customization). In addition, we explain how process variants are derived from composite services as a result of customization processes. While the previous work considers the application of WSVL to customizable *atomic services* [22], this work focuses on the use of WSVL in supporting customizable *composite services*. In addition, our variability modeling technique requires that each customizable partner service is accompanied with a WSVL description no matter whether the partner service is atomic or composite. This requirement enables the recursive consumption of customizable services.

This article is structured as follows. Section 20.2 presents a discussion of related work. The description of a motivating example and feature-level service variability modeling is the topic of Sect. 20.3. Section 20.4 explains the techniques underpinning our approach. Section 20.5 presents our approach for modeling variability and variability dependencies. We describe the development and customization of process-based service compositions in Sect. 20.6. The prototype system is described in Sect. 20.7 before our conclusion of the article in Sect. 20.8.

20.2 Related Work

There have been many approaches to modeling and managing variability in process-based service composition [4, 9–12, 16, 18, 19, 26, 28, 30, 32]. Due to the widespread adoption of BPMN and BPEL as, respectively, languages for modeling and executing business processes, most of these works are extensions of these languages. UML activity diagrams have also been extended to model variable processes in a similar fashion to BPMN although they lack the rich set of constructs of BPMN.

There are various ways to extend BPEL. For instance, some approaches extend the BPEL XML schema in order to incorporate information about variation points and variants [4, 11, 16]. The selection of variants will be driven by configuration parameters [16], a decision model [4], or context data collected from runtime events [11]. In contrast, the approach in [19] uses a separate variability descriptor to define the location of variation points in a BPEL definition and possible variants. From the variability descriptor, a separate BPEL process is generated to facilitate consumers in deciding variants to be bound. In addition, the approach in [12] defines notations based on Eclipse Modeling Framework (EMF) [7] for representing BPEL process models with modifiable elements. Separate context model and linkage model help to decide what, when, and how to modify the process (e.g. adding new process elements or deleting existing elements) to generate a particular process variant. In general, the advantage of extending BPEL is that an executable process variant can be automatically derived by resolving all variation points. However, the modeling of variability at the process implementation level results in the complexity issue due to the large number of variation points and their dependencies.

In contrast to BPEL, BPMN and UML Activity diagrams enable the capturing of business processes at the modeling level. At this high-level of abstraction, the number of variation points is much fewer than the one at the process definition level. A number of works have focused on extending BPMN or UML Activity diagrams for supporting variability [9, 10, 18, 26, 28, 30, 32]. In these approaches, various ways are defined for extending BPMN/UML. For instance, some approaches mark variability-related nodes with stereotypes [26, 28, 30], some define operations that can be applied to modify process models [9, 10, 18], while others introduce new variability elements into the BPMN metamodel [32]. However, with the exception of [26, 28], these works focus only on variation of *control flow* of process models. To derive executable process variants, variation in *data flow* needs to be modelled as well, as in [26, 28].

Although *variability intra-dependencies* have been considered, e.g. [10, 16], a major shortcoming of works in both categories is that they are not able to capture *variability inter-dependencies*. All previous approaches assume that partner services are non-customizable. Consequently, those approaches are not applicable to composite services orchestrated from customizable partner services.

20.3 Motivating Example and Feature-Level Variability Modeling

Swinsure Insurance is a wholesale insurance company that provides building insurance business to various insurance brokers. These insurance brokers will be responsible for selling insurance services to end-users. This article considers the claim handling process that brokers use to handle insurance claims from end-users. Insurance brokers have different requirements on the process. Therefore, each broker requires a variant of the process for its own business. As described in the Introduction, to increase efficiency in process development and consumption, the Swinsure Insurance will develop a customizable process from which brokers are able to derive their needed variants. To this end, the Swinsure Insurance needs to capture and manage variability in the process.

20.3.1 Feature Modeling

To capture variability in broker requirements, Swinsure Insurance uses a feature model (cf. Fig. 20.1). Feature models are used in SPL for capturing at high level of abstraction the commonalities and the differences among a family of related software products [25]. In our case, a feature model defines a family of claim handling processes each of which serves one broker. While there are many variations of feature modeling techniques (e.g. [2, 8, 14, 15]), we utilize the Cardinality-Based Feature Modeling (CBFM) technique which provides a complete semantics for capturing service variability [5]. The key characteristics of these feature models are:

- *Features*—represents a business functionality encapsulating broker requirements.
- *Feature hierarchy*—denotes a tree of features with *composed-of* relationships. For instance, the feature *"Claim handling process"* is composed of four features: *"Cover type"*, *"Bill payer"*, *"Extra cover"*, and *"Excess"*.

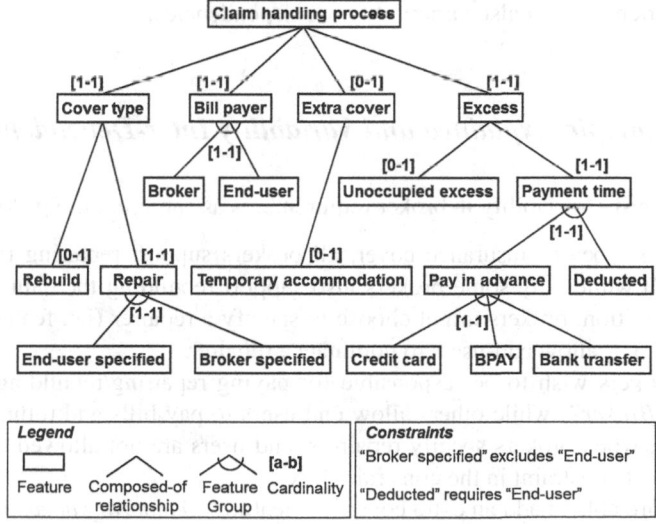

Fig. 20.1 A feature model representing variability of the claim handling process

- *Feature cardinality*—determines the lower and upper bounds for the feature to appear in one *feature configuration*. For instance, the cardinality [0-1] annotation above the feature "*Extra cover*" implies an optional feature, while the cardinality [1-1] for the feature "*Cover type*" defines a mandatory feature.
- *Feature configuration*—is derived from a feature model by resolving all variability within the feature model. For instance, a feature configuration might disable the optional feature "*Extra cover*". A feature configuration represents the requirement set of one broker.
- *Group cardinality*—limits the number of child features in one feature configuration when the parent feature is selected. For instance, the group cardinality [1-1] annotation below the parent feature "*Bill payer*" implies that only one feature among "*Broker*" and "*End-user*" will be selected in one feature configuration.
- *Feature constraints*—describe the inclusive and exclusive dependencies among features across the tree (cf. the constraint box).

To model and manage variability in process-based service compositions, we exploit concepts of variability management in SPL as follows:

1. We use feature models to capture variability in broker requirements.
2. Feature models are used to manage variability in process models. In particular, variant features (i.e. features with cardinality different from [1-1] or features belonging to a feature group) and their constraints will help to identify, capture and manage variability as well as variability dependencies in process models.

Compared to variability management techniques which have been proposed in the SPL research, our approach has two key contributions. Firstly, we define a novel way for introducing variation points and variants into process models. Secondly, we extend the feature modeling technique to capture not only variability intra-dependencies, but also variability inter-dependencies.

20.3.2 Example Explained and Variability Inter-Dependencies

We first describe variability in broker requirements as captured in Fig. 20.1.

- Regarding types of insurance cover, all brokers support repairing (i.e. feature "*Repair*") while only some brokers also support rebuilding the damaged building. In addition, brokers might choose to specify a repairer (i.e. feature "*Broker specified*") or allow end-users to nominate a repairer.
- Some brokers wish to be responsible for paying repairing/rebuilding bills (i.e. feature "*Broker*") while others allow end-users to pay bills and refund the cost. However, when brokers specify repairers, end-users are not allowed to pay bills (cf. the first constraint in the constraint box).
- Brokers are able to add an extra cover (i.e. feature "*Temporary accommodation*") for arranging a temporary property while the insured one is being repaired.

Fig. 20.2 A feature model representing variability of the Swinpay WS

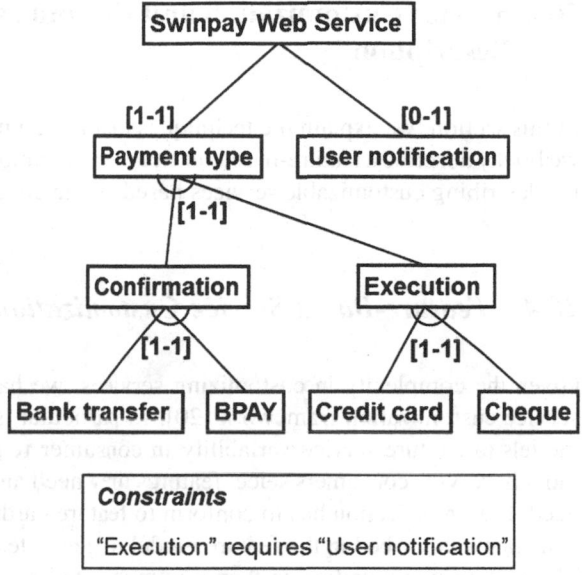

Since an insured building is at greater risk of damage if it is not occupied for a lengthy period, some brokers want to enforce additional unoccupied excess (i.e. feature *"Unoccupied excess"*).

Some brokers ask end-users to pay an excess fee in advance (i.e. feature *"Pay in advance"*) which might be through the use of credit card, BPAY (i.e. a bill payment service) or bank transfer. In contrast, others allow the deduction of the fee from bills paid by end-users, but if the end-user pays the bill (i.e. feature *"End-user"*) (cf. the second constraint in the constraint box)

There are many services available that the Swinsure Insurance may reuse in implementing its process. In this example, the Swinsure Insurance utilizes a customizable partner service, namely Swinpay service (aka Swinpay WS), for dealing with end-user payments. Figure 20.2 presents a feature model capturing the variability of the Swinpay WS. To implement variability in its own process (i.e. realizing different options for *"Pay in advance"*), Swinsure uses three different variants from Swinpay WS. Two variants facilitate payment confirmation through bank transfer and BPAY without notifying end-user of the transaction (i.e. the feature *"User notification"* is disabled). The third variant supports payment execution through Credit card with end-user notification. For the last variant, the feature *"User notification"* is automatically selected due to the *"require"* dependency between *"Execution"* and *"User notification"*. Reusing the Swinpay WS frees the Swinsure Insurance from the overhead of implementing variability in its own process. However, variability in the claim handling process will depend on the variability in the Swinpay WS. In other words, depending on the type of payment a broker prefers, the process needs to invoke a corresponding variant of the Swinpay WS.

20.4 Service Customization and Customizable Service Description

In this section, we explain the techniques that underpin our approach. In particular, we briefly describe a feature-based service customization framework and our solution for describing customizable services based on the concept of features.

20.4.1 Feature-Based Service Customization Framework

Given the complexity in customizing services, we have proposed a feature-based service customization framework [20]. In particular, service providers use feature models to capture service variability in consumer requirements. Based on feature models, service consumers select features they need and disable features they do not need. Feature selection has to conform to feature cardinality, group cardinality and constraints described in the feature model to generate a valid feature configuration. The feature configuration is then communicated back to the service provider so that the service provider can derive and dynamically deploy a service variant that the consumer can invoke. The use of feature models helps to reduce the number of customization options, as well as formally capture dependencies among such options. In addition, it helps consumers to focus on what a variant can achieve, rather than how to technically invoke the capability.

In previous work [20], we have focused on how to model, manage and instantiate variability at the service interface level. The work in this article complements that work in addressing the issues of how to model and manage variability in the service implementation (i.e. business process), and then generating a variant based on a particular feature configuration. In addition, the work in this article also exploits that technique for customizing partner services.

20.4.2 Customizable Service Description

A customizable service needs to be described so that consumers know its variability and how to customize it. To this end, we have defined Web Service Variability description Language (WSVL) as an extension of WSDL for describing customizable services [22]. The language builds upon the concept of the feature-based service customization framework. WSVL helps to formalize the customization interface using the XML technology. *In addition, it loosens the coupling between service providers and service consumers in the provisioning and consumption of customizable services.* In this subsection, we describe the key information captured by WSVL using an excerpt of the WSVL description for the Swinpay WS (Fig. 20.3).

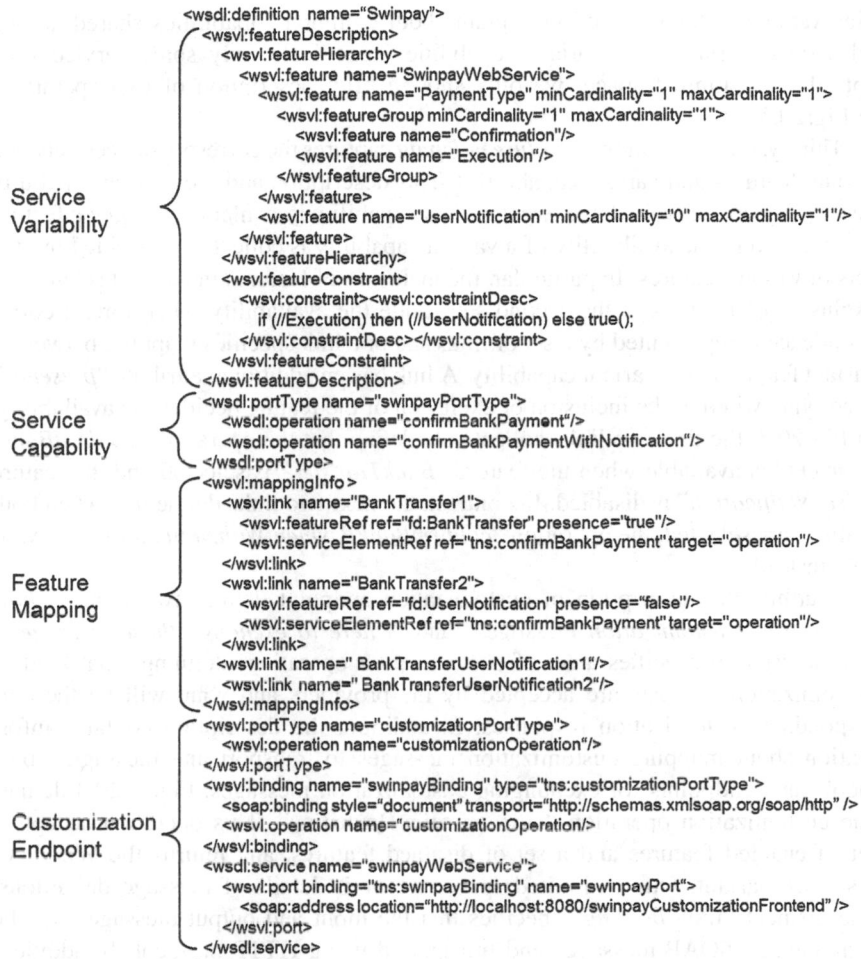

```
                    <wsdl:definition name="Swinpay">
                     <wsvl:featureDescription>
                        <wsvl:featureHierarchy>
                           <wsvl:feature name="SwinpayWebService">
                              <wsvl:feature name="PaymentType" minCardinality="1" maxCardinality="1">
                                 <wsvl:featureGroup minCardinality="1" maxCardinality="1">
                                    <wsvl:feature name="Confirmation"/>
                                    <wsvl:feature name="Execution"/>
                                 </wsvl:featureGroup>
   Service                        </wsvl:feature>
   Variability                    <wsvl:feature name="UserNotification" minCardinality="0" maxCardinality="1"/>
                              </wsvl:feature>
                        </wsvl:featureHierarchy>
                        <wsvl:featureConstraint>
                           <wsvl:constraint><wsvl:constraintDesc>
                              if (//Execution) then (//UserNotification) else true();
                           </wsvl:constraintDesc></wsvl:constraint>
                        </wsvl:featureConstraint>
                     </wsvl:featureDescription>
   Service          <wsdl:portType name="swinpayPortType">
   Capability          <wsdl:operation name="confirmBankPayment"/>
                        <wsdl:operation name="confirmBankPaymentWithNotification"/>
                     </wsdl:portType>
                     <wsvl:mappingInfo>
                        <wsvl:link name="BankTransfer1">
                           <wsvl:featureRef ref="fd:BankTransfer" presence="true"/>
                           <wsvl:serviceElementRef ref="tns:confirmBankPayment" target="operation"/>
                        </wsvl:link>
   Feature           <wsvl:link name="BankTransfer2">
   Mapping              <wsvl:featureRef ref="fd:UserNotification" presence="false"/>
                           <wsvl:serviceElementRef ref="tns:confirmBankPayment" target="operation"/>
                        </wsvl:link>
                        <wsvl:link name=" BankTransferUserNotification1"/>
                        <wsvl:link name=" BankTransferUserNotification2"/>
                     </wsvl:mappingInfo>
                     <wsvl:portType name="customizationPortType">
                        <wsvl:operation name="customizationOperation"/>
                     </wsvl:portType>
                     <wsvl:binding name="swinpayBinding" type="tns:customizationPortType">
                        <soap:binding style="document" transport="http://schemas.xmlsoap.org/soap/http" />
   Customization      <wsvl:operation name="customizationOperation/>
   Endpoint          </wsvl:binding>
                     <wsdl:service name="swinpayWebService">
                        <wsvl:port binding="tns:swinpayBinding" name="swinpayPort">
                           <soap:address location="http://localhost:8080/swinpayCustomizationFrontend" />
                        </wsvl:port>
                     </wsdl:service>
                    </wsdl:definition>
```

Fig. 20.3 An excerpt of the WSVL description for the Swinpay WS

WSVL defines XML notations for capturing four pieces of information: *service variability*, *service capability*, *feature mapping*, and *customization endpoint*. Firstly, the description of *service variability* specifies "*What customization options are*". It is actually the XML representation of the feature model. The element "*wsvl:featureHierarchy*" defines the hierarchical organization of features, while the element "*wsvl:featureConstraint*" denotes cross-tree constraints. The service variability description in Fig. 20.3 represents a part of the feature model demonstrated in Fig. 20.2. In this example, all extended XML notations use the prefix "*wsvl:*" to separate themselves from XML notations defined by the WSDL XML schema.

Secondly, the description of *service capability* defines in standard WSDL the superset of abstract capability (i.e. portType, operations, and data types) of all service variants. This description contains both common capabilities shared among all service variants and variant capabilities specific to only some service variants. Due to limited space, we only show a brief description of two operations in Fig. 20.3.

Thirdly, the description of *feature mapping* captures the correspondences between variant features and variant capabilities. This description and the service capability description collectively define what variant capability is available for a given feature configuration. The availability of a variant capability is collectively decided by two sets of variant features. In particular, the inclusion of features in the first set and the exclusion of features in the second set decide the availability. Therefore, a correspondence is represented by a set of links and one link specifies mapping between a variant feature and a variant capability. A link has an additional attribute "*presence*" specifying whether the inclusion or exclusion of the feature decides the availability. In Fig. 20.3, the first two links collectively define that the operation "*confirmBank-Payment*" is available when the feature "*BankTransfer*" is selected and the feature "*UserNotification*" is disabled. In contrast, the next two links define that when both features are selected, the operation "*confirmBankPaymentWithNotification*" is available instead.

Fourthly, the description of customization endpoint defines two things: "*how to construct customization messages*" and "*where to exchange those messages*". The description specifies a set of customization operations defining what kind of customization requests are accepted by the providers and what will be the corresponding customization responses. In addition, the description contains information about mapping customization messages to transport and messaging protocols, and endpoints for exchanging customization messages. Figure 20.3 defines one customization operation "*customizationOperation*". This operation accepts a set of enabled features and a set of disabled features, and returns the WSDL of a service variant. Due to limited space, we omit details of message definitions. The element "*wsvl:binding*" specifies that the input and output messages will be formatted as SOAP messages and transported using HTTP protocol. In addition, the element "*wsvl:port*" defines the endpoint at which customization messages are exchanged.

Given this description, a service consumer, for instance the Swinsure Insurance, is able to comprehend the variability of the Swinpay WS and request a particular variant by deciding a feature configuration and sending it to the Swinpay WS.

20.5 Modeling Variability and Variability Dependencies in Process-Based Service Compositions

In our approach, we extend the BPMN 2.0 metamodel with new elements for representing variation points and variants within process models. BPMN has the advantage of providing a language rich, business-level description of processes that can be readily translated to an executable BPEL definition.

Fig. 20.4 Variability
metamodel

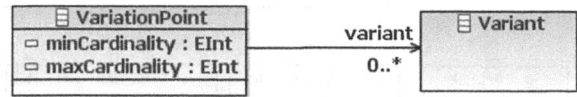

20.5.1 Extending BPMN for Representing Variation Points and Variants

Figure 20.4 presents the variability metamodel which captures the general concept of variability in process models. A **VariationPoint** represents any place in the process model where variability can occur. Each **VariationPoint** is associated with a set of **Variants** from which one or several will be bound to **VariationPoint** when the variability is resolved. The attributes *minCardinality* and *maxCardinality* define how many **Variants** should be bound to one **VariationPoint**. These attributes have the same semantics as the cardinality concept in the feature modeling technique adopted. Note that in the variability metamodel, we do not specify when a variant is bound to the variation point. In our approach, such conditions (aka. *presence condition*) are managed in a separate model.

In the following sub-sections, we explain the specialization of this metamodel to represent variability in control flow, data flow, and message flow. As such, our approach supports the comprehensive modeling of variability in all three aspects of service compositions while related work only focuses on control flow and data flow. The comprehensive modeling of variability not only enables the capturing of variability inter-dependencies, but also facilitates the derivation of executable process variants based on consumers' customization (i.e. consumers' selected feature configurations). Note that while new modeling elements are introduced to capture variability, a process variant resulted from resolving variability in our extended process model is a conventional BPMN model without extended elements. This property enables the use of mapping between BPMN elements and BPEL elements defined in the BPMN 2.0 specification to generate executable process variants.

20.5.1.1 Modeling Variability in Control Flow

Figure 20.5 presents our metamodel extension for modeling variability in control flow. In this metamodel, BPMN elements are written in *italic bold* font, while our extended elements are written in **regular bold** font. We also use this convention when describing BPMN elements and extended elements throughout this article.

A control flow (represented by *Process* element) is a *FlowElementsContainer* which is composed of *FlowElement*. A *FlowElement* can be either a *FlowNode* or a *SequenceFlow* connecting two *FlowNodes*. Three types of *FlowNode* are *Activity*, *Gateway*, and *Event*. An *Activity* can be further specialized to a *Task* or a *SubProcess*. While a *Task* represents an atomic activity, a *SubProcess* denotes a composite activity

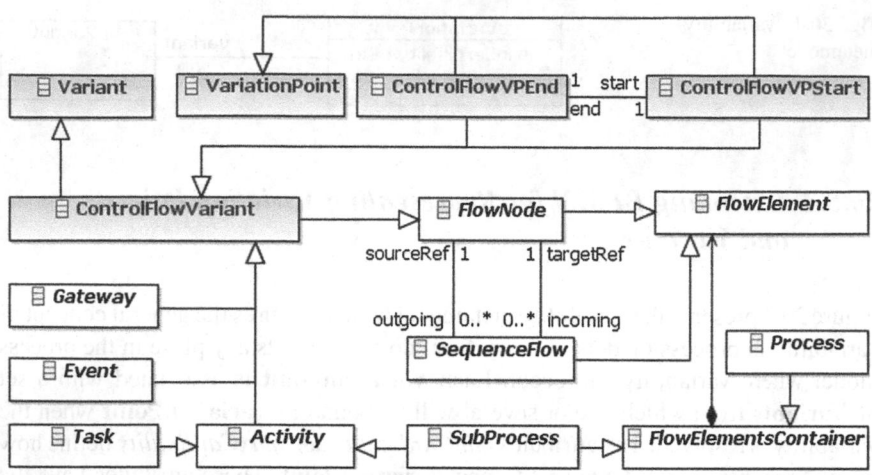

Fig. 20.5 Metamodel extension for variability in control flow

whose details are modeled using *Activities*, *Gateways*, *Events* and *SequenceFlows*. That is, a *SubProcess* is also a *FlowElementsContainer*.

To model variability in control flow, we need to consider how to represent control flow variation points and variants. To this end, we observe that any variability in control flow can be interpreted as a location in the process model at which different process fragments (i.e. variants) can be used. Therefore, we define two new elements, namely **ControlFlowVPStart** and **ControlFlowVPEnd**, as a pair for representing the starting point and the ending point of a control flow variation point. Both elements inherit properties of *FlowNode* (through **ControlFlowVariant**) so that they can be used within a BPMN model. A control flow variant might be a *Task*, a *SubProcess*, or a general fragment which begins and ends with *FlowNodes*. Therefore, we make all existing *FlowNodes* (i.e. *Activity*, *Gateway*, *Event*) inherit **ControlFlowVariant** so that they can be used as control flow variants. Another consideration is related to embedding one control flow variation point within another. In this regard, it is required to use **ControlFlowVPStart** and **ControlFlowVPEnd** as control flow variants. To this end, we also make these two elements inherit from **ControlFlowVariant**. Lastly, control flow variation points and variants are specialized from previously defined **VariationPoint** and **Variant** (cf. Fig. 20.4).

Figure 20.6 presents an example of modeling variability in the control flow. This is an excerpt of the sub-process for finalizing repairing cost. This screenshot is taken from our process modeling tool (detailed later). *VPS6* and *VPE6* are **ControlFlowVPStart** and **ControlFlowVPEnd** respectively. They represent a control flow variation point which has two variants. In our process modeling tool, dashed lines are used to connect variation points to associated variants. By this, the first variant is the upper process fragment after *VPS6* while the second variant is the lower fragment. The first variant is selected when a broker selects the feature "*End-user*", while the second variant is used when the feature "*Broker*" is selected. We use anno-

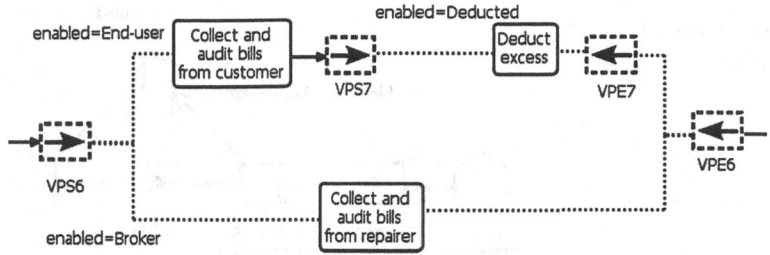

Fig. 20.6 Example of modeling variability in control flow

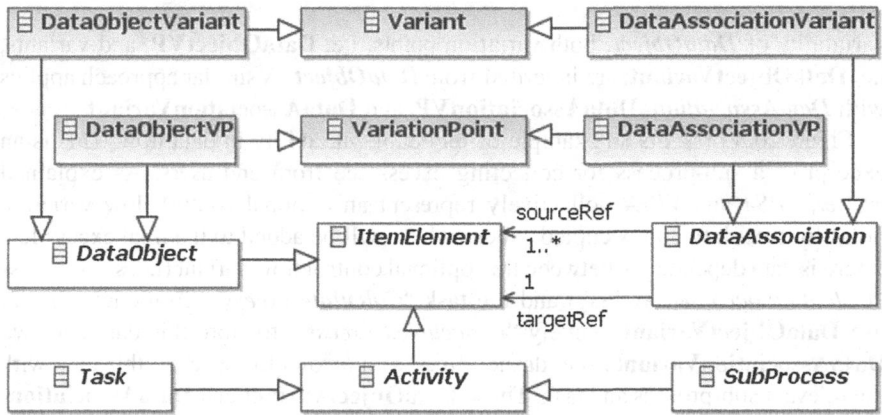

Fig. 20.7 Metamodel extension for variability in data flow

tation in the process model to denote this information. Within the first variant, there is one optional control flow variation point represented as *VPS7* and *VPE7*. The variant is present when the feature *"Deducted"* is selected. This example demonstrates how one control flow variation point can be embedded within another.

20.5.1.2 Modeling Variability in Data Flow

Figure 20.7 presents our metamodel extension for modeling variability in data flow. Capturing data flow involves the modeling of information items that are created, manipulated, and consumed during the execution of a process. In general, it refers to the use of *DataObject* for storing data and *DataAssociation* for moving data from one or many source *ItemElements* to one target *ItemElement*. In this way, data can be instantiated and moved between *Activity* (i.e. *Task*, *SubProcess*) and *DataObject*.

Variability in data flow can be considered as different information (i.e. *DataObject*) to be stored or different ways for moving data around (i.e. *DataAssociation*). In addition, variants in data flow are alternatives. Therefore, we model both variation points and variants as elements inherited from the same element type. That is, for

Fig. 20.8 Example of modeling variability in data flow

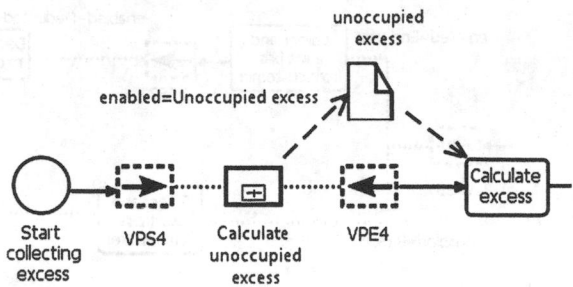

variability of *DataObject*, both variation points, i.e. **DataObjectVP**, and variants, i.e. **DataObjectVariant**, are inherited from *DataObject*. A similar approach applies with *DataAssociation*, **DataAssociationVP**, and **DataAssociationVariant**.

Figure 20.8 presents an example of modeling variability in data flow. This is an excerpt of a sub-process for collecting excess fee from end-users. As explained earlier, *VPS4* and *VPE4* collectively represent an optional control flow variation point for calculating unoccupied excess which will be added to the final excess fee. There is data dependency between this optional control flow variant (i.e. sub-process "*Calculate occupied excess*") and the task "*Calculate excess*". To model this, we use **DataObjectVariant**, namely "*unoccupied excess*", to store this data and two **DataAssociationVariants** (i.e. dashed lines with arrow) to associate this data with the relevant sub-process and task. These **DataObjectVariant** and **DataAssociation-Variants** are optional and are included in a process variant only when the feature "*Unoccupied excess*" is selected (as denoted by the annotation).

20.5.1.3 Modeling Variability in Message Flow

Figure 20.9 presents the extension for modeling variability in message flow. In BPMN, message flow is used to capture interactions between a process and partner processes/services. Each interaction is modeled as a *Conversation* which is composed of either one or two *MessageFlows* depending on whether the interaction is one- or two-way. Each *MessageFlow* carries a *Message* from one *InteractionNode* (e.g. *Task*) in one process to another *InteractionNode* in another process.

Variability in message flow can be seen as alternative *Conversations* between two parties, i.e. the process and a partner service (or a consumer). Therefore, in a similar fashion to modeling variability in data flow, we model both variation points, i.e. **ConversationVP**, and variants, i.e. **ConversationVariant**, as elements inherited from *Conversation*. In addition, we introduce new elements, namely **PartnerTask** and **AbstractPartnerTask**. A **PartnerTask** models a task performed by a part-ner service. An **AbstractPartnerTask** is a variation point associated with a set of alternative **PartnerTasks** from the same partner service. **AbstractPartnerTask** rep-resents a variable capability provided by a partner service. The introduction of

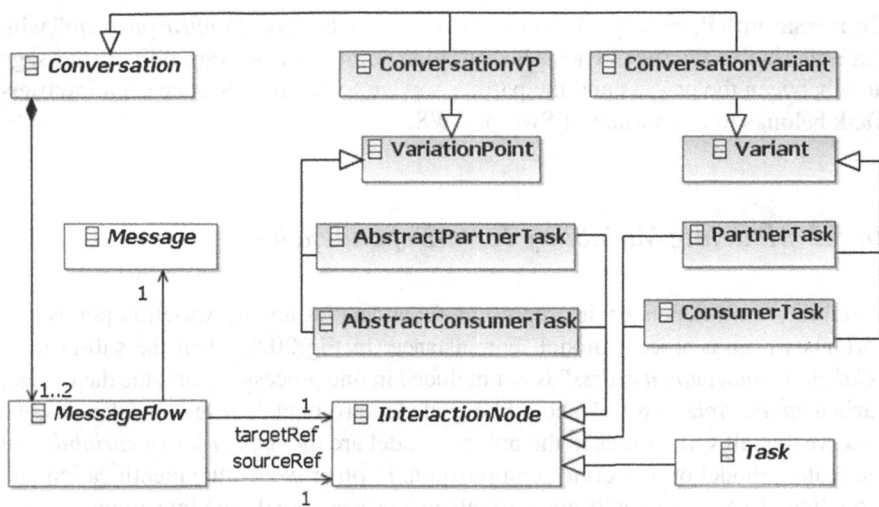

Fig. 20.9 Metamodel extension for variability in message flow

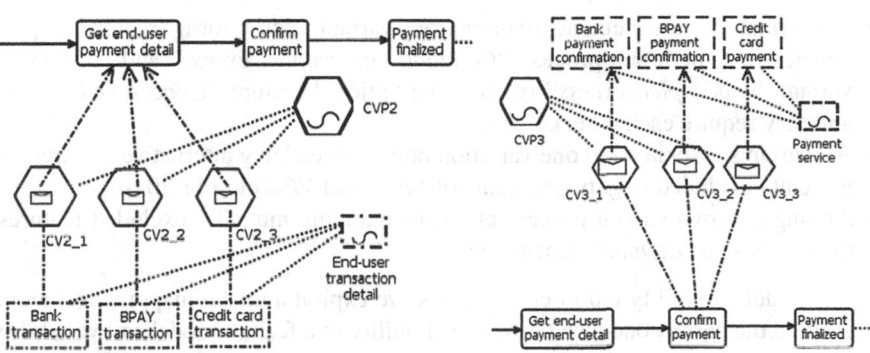

Fig. 20.10 Example of modeling variability in message flow

PartnerTask and **AbstractPartnerTask** facilitates the modeling of variability inter-dependencies as described in the following subsection. Similarly, we introduce **Con-sumerTask** and **AbstractConsumerTask** for the interaction between the business process and its consumers. These elements facilitate the generation of the service variability description (i.e. WSVL description) for this service composition.

Figure 20.10 presents an excerpt of the sub-process for collecting excess fee. The left figure shows a **ConversationVP**, namely *CVP2*, which associates three **ConversationVariants**, namely *CV2_1*, *CV2_2*, *CV2_3* respectively. Each **Coversa-tionVariant** represents an interaction between the same task "*Get end-user payment detail*" with a **ConsumerTask**. They correspond to three alternative features ("*Credit Card*", "*BPAY*" and "*Bank transfer*") and collectively describe variability in message flow between the process and end-users. In addition, the right figure shows another

ConversationVP, namely *CVP3*, which associates the task "*Confirm payment*" with three alternative **PartnerTasks**. This variation point describes variability in message flow between the process and the partner service Swinpay WS since each **Partner-Task** belongs to one variant of Swinpay WS.

20.5.2 Modeling Variability Intra-Dependencies

Variability intra-dependencies represent dependencies among variation points and variants within a process model. For instance, in Fig. 20.8, when the sub-process "*Calculate unoccupied excess*" is not included in one process variant, the data object variant "*unoccupied excess*" should be excluded. To model these dependencies, we observe that all variabilities in the process model are the *realization of variability* in the feature model of the service composition. In other words, the identification and modeling of variation points and variants in a process are driven by variant features in the feature model. *And variability intra-dependencies among different variants exist purely because of constraints among variant features.* In particular:

- All variant process elements realizing one variant feature form "*require*" dependencies (e.g. both sub-process "*Calculate unoccupied excess*" and data object variant "*unoccupied excess*" realizes the optional feature "*Unoccupied excess*" and they require each other).
- All variants associated to one variation point for realizing alternative features are mutually excluded (e.g. two variants of *VPS6* and *VPE6* in Fig. 20.6).
- Among any two variant process elements realizing mutually excluded features, there exists an "*exclude*" dependency.

To model variability intra-dependencies, we exploit a model mapping technique to capture the correspondence between variability in a feature model and variability in a process model. Figure 20.11 shows the mapping metamodel for this purpose. A *MappingModel* relates variant features in a feature model, referenced by *Feature-*

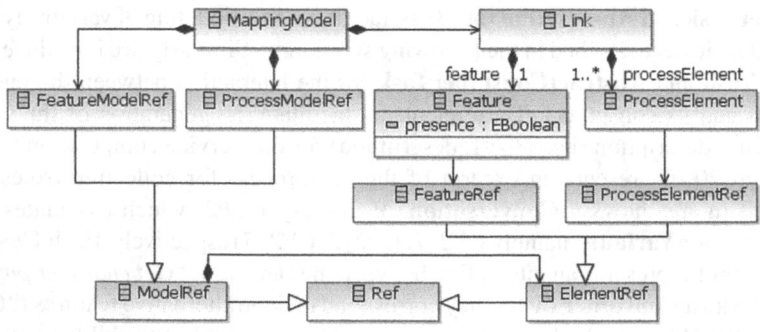

Fig. 20.11 Mapping metamodel

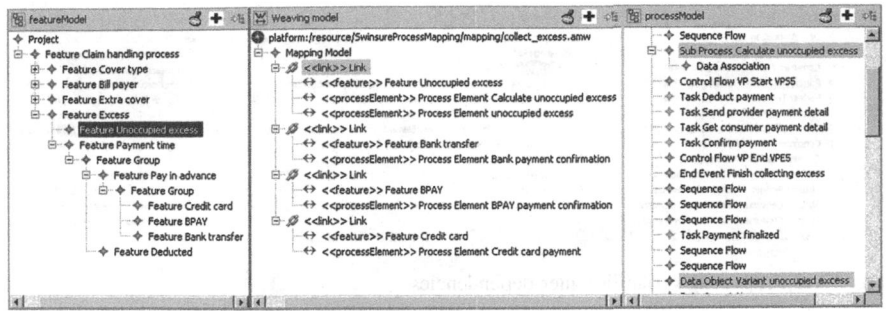

Fig. 20.12 Capturing variability intra-dependencies

ModelRef, with variants in a process model, referenced by *ProcessModelRef*. It is composed of *Links* and each *Link* consists of a *Feature* and at least one *ProcessElement*. *Feature* and *ProcessElement* reference elements in the feature model and the process model respectively. In addition, a *Feature* has a boolean property "*presence*" to define whether the selection or un-selection of the *Feature* is associated with a *ProcessElement*. Each *Link* enables a feature to be mapped to one or several variant process elements in the process model. In addition, by defining multiple links associating multiple features with the same process element, it is possible to specify *the presence condition* of the process element as a logical expression of features.

Figure 20.12 depicts a mapping model capturing variability intra-dependencies within the sub-process for collecting excess fee. This screenshot is taken from our model mapping tool. The left panel shows the feature model. The right panel displays the process model. And the middle panel presents the mapping model. There are four links in this mapping model. The first link associates feature "*Unoccupied excess*" with two variants (one control flow variant and one data object variant) shown in Fig. 20.8. As the result, the link captures the "*require*" dependency between the two variants. The other three links associate each child feature of the feature group "*Pay in advance*" with one **PartnerTask**. Consequently, the links represent mutually exclusive dependencies among the three **PartnerTasks**.

This mapping model is referred to as *FeatureTask mapping model*. Due to the *realization relationships*, the mapping along with feature constraints in the feature model accounts for all variability intra-dependencies. In addition, the use of mapping models has the following advantages in comparison with embedding constraints in the process definition. On the one hand, it helps to separate variability constraint information from the process model, thus simplifies the definition. On the other hand, the validation of process configuration is led to the validation of a feature configuration, which is well-studied in SPL [3].

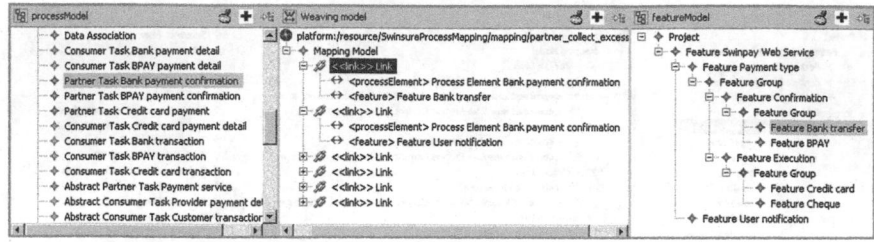

Fig. 20.13 Capturing variability inter-dependencies

20.5.3 Modeling Variability Inter-Dependencies

Variability inter-dependencies represent dependencies between variability in the process model and variability in partner services. For instance, in Fig. 20.10, each **PartnerTask** associated with the **AbstractPartnerTask** *"Payment service"* is performed by one variant of the Swinpay WS. Since the variability of partner services is described using their feature models (cf. Fig. 20.3), in a similar fashion to modeling variability intra-dependencies, we exploit the model mapping technique to model variability inter-dependencies. The main difference between the mapping model for variability intra-dependencies and the one for variability inter-dependencies is the origin of variant features. While variability intra-dependencies is modeled with respect to variant features in the feature model of the service composition, variability inter-dependencies is modeled with respect to variant partner features.

In particular, a mapping model for variability inter-dependencies captures the correspondence between **PartnerTasks** within the process model and variant partner features. We refer to this mapping model as *PartnerTaskFeature mapping model.* Figure 20.13 presents an example of this mapping model in which the **PartnerTask** *"Bank payment confirmation"* in Fig. 20.10 is mapped to two features of the Swinpay WS using two links. The first link refers to the feature *"Bank transfer"* with *"presence=true"*, while the second refers to the feature *"User notification"* with *"presence=false"*. Consequently, this **PartnerTask** is performed by the variant of the Swinpay WS for which the feature *"Bank transfer"* is selected and *"User notification"* is disabled. Comparing to the WSVL description of the Swinpay WS in Fig. 20.3, it means that the **PartnerTask** *"Bank payment confirmation"* is equivalent to the operation *"confirmBankPayment"* provided by the Swinpay WS.

Note that the positions of the feature model and the process model are swapped in the mapping tool for variability inter-dependencies (Fig. 20.13) compared to the one for variability intra-dependencies (Fig. 20.12). This swapping reflects the difference in the origin of features as discussed above. In addition, when reading from the left to the right, one is able to recognise *the realization relationships* (i.e. variability at the feature level is further refined to variability at the process model level) in the mapping tool for variability intra-dependencies. Similarly, when reading from the left to the right in the mapping tool for variability inter-dependencies, one is able to see the common arrangement between a service composition and a partner service.

It should be noted that between **PartnerTasks** and variant partner features, there does not exist a *"natural realization relationship"* as the ones for variability intra-dependencies. If the identification and modeling of **PartnerTasks** and **Abstract-PartnerTasks** are driven by the variant partner features, such *realization relationships* exist. Otherwise, *realization relationships* may not exist and variability inter-dependencies exist by chance. Therefore, the higher the inter-dependency between a composition and partner services is, the better the reuse of service variability from partner services toward the composition will be. In a later section, we describe a process development methodology that systematically increases the reusability of service variability.

Since variability in the feature model of the business process is mapped to variability in the process model, i.e. *FeatureTask mapping model*, and a part of variability in the process model, i.e. **PartnerTasks**, is mapped to variability in partner feature models, i.e. *PartnerTaskFeature mapping model*, it is possible to generate the mapping from variant features in the feature model of the service composition to variant partner features. This mapping model conforms to a mapping metamodel that is similar to the one shown in Fig. 20.11 and allows us to capture variability inter-dependencies at the highest level of abstraction, i.e. the feature level. We refer to this type of mapping model as *FeatureFeature mapping model*. In summary, there are two types of feature mapping models for representing variability inter-dependencies: *PartnerTaskFeature* and *FeatureFeature mapping models*.

20.6 The Development and Customization of Process-Based Service Compositions

In this section, we describe a methodology for developing service compositions with systematic management and reuse of variability. The methodology explicitly utilizes variability information from partner services in driving the identification and modeling of variability within business processes. Consequently, it facilitates the reuse of service variability provided by partner services. In addition, we elaborate how WSVL descriptions for customizable composite services are generated from process modeling elements. The description facilitates service consumers in customizing composite services. To demonstrate this, we describe how process variants are derived from composite services as a result of a customization process.

20.6.1 Process Development Methodology

Figure 20.14 presents the overview of our development methodology. In the first activity, the capability of the service composition is modeled using the feature modeling technique. The result of this activity is a feature model capturing commonalities

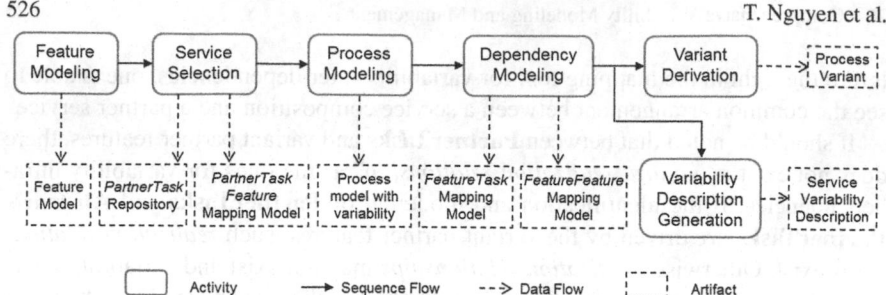

Fig. 20.14 Overview of developing process-based service compositions

and variabilities of the composite service to be. Given a model of desired features, the next activity will be the selection of partner services that can be used for the service composition. For instance, the Swinsure Insurance selects the Swinpay WS for processing end-user payment. There are two types of partner services: *(conventional) non-customizable partner services* and *customizable partner services*. The explicit selection of customizable partner services helps to reduce overhead of addressing variability within the service composition. Customizable partner services come with WSVL-based service descriptions.

During the second activity, both non-customizable partner services and customizable partner services are transformed into a set of partner tasks that will be selectable for modeling the process. *As explained, a partner task is an operation provided by a partner service that is responsible for an atomic message flow between the partner service and the service composition.* While non-customizable partner services are transformed to a set of non-customizable partner tasks, results of transforming customizable partner services are sets of alternative partner tasks. For each set of alternative partner tasks, we also generate an abstract partner task representing all partner tasks in the set. Since the variability of customizable partner services are expressed as feature models with mapping to variant capabilities, we also derive mapping models that represent the correspondence between alternative partner tasks and variant partner features, i.e. *PartnerTaskFeature mapping models*. Consequently, results of the service selection activity are a repository of (alternative) partner tasks, abstract partner tasks and *PartnerTaskFeature mapping models*. It should be noted that in this methodology, the *PartnerTaskFeature mapping models* are intentionally generated before modeling the process.

In the third activity, the business process for the service composition is modeled using the extended metamodel. The identification of variation points and variants are based on the feature model identified in the first activity. Tasks from the partner task repository will be used to model the message flow between the service composition and partner services. The selection of (alternative) partner tasks and abstract partner tasks from the partner task repository will not only facilitate the reuse of variability provided by partner services in the process modeling, but also enable the use of already generated *PartnerTaskFeature mapping model* in capturing variability inter-dependencies. In addition, variability in the message flow between the service composition and consumers is captured by means of consumer tasks. The result of this activity is a process model with variability.

In the next activity, the model mapping technique is exploited to first model variability intra-dependencies. That is, all variation points and variants in a process model are mapped to variant features in the feature model of the business process. The result is a *FeatureTask mapping model*. Since the *PartnerTaskFeature mapping model* is already produced, model transformation techniques are utilized to automatically generate *FeatureFeature mapping model* as described in Sect. 20.5.3.

The resulting software artifacts of the first four activities will be used in two different ways. Firstly, they are used to generate the variability description of the resulting service composition (i.e. *Variability Description Generation* activity) which can contribute to other service compositions. Secondly, those software artifacts are used for the derivation of process variants given a particular feature configuration as the result of a customization (i.e. *Variant Derivation* activity). We elaborate the details of these two activities in the next two sections.

20.6.2 Deriving WSVL Description

As explained in Sect. 20.4.2, the WSVL description of a process facilitates brokers in customizing the process. To derive the WSVL description from modeling elements, we define the following derivation rules:

1. The description of service variability is an XML representation of the feature model for the process (cf. Fig. 20.1) following the WSVL XML schema.
2. The description of service capability is generated from **ConsumerTasks**. In particular, the description contains all **ConsumerTasks** defined in the process model as service capability. **ConsumerTasks** associated with **AbstractConsumerTasks** will become variant capabilities, while other **ConsumerTasks** are common capabilities among all variants.
3. The description of feature mapping is an XML representation of all links associating variant features with **ConsumerTasks** in the *FeatureTask mapping model*.
4. The description of customization endpoint is specific to the process engine and the service platform that the composite service provider uses. Therefore, it is out of the scope of these derivation rules. However its general semantics (i.e. accepting a set of variant features and returning information related to one customized process) is specified in the WSVL XML schema.

Figure 20.15 presents an excerpt of the WSVL description for the claim handling process. The service capability description contains 4 variant operations. The feature mapping description defines that the first two operations are available when the feature "*Bank transfer*" is selected while the following two operations depends on the feature "*BPAY*". This description is based on modeled **ConsumerTasks** (as shown in Fig. 20.10 and complemented by Fig. 20.18), as well as links between these **ConsumerTasks** and variant features in the *FeatureTask mapping model*.

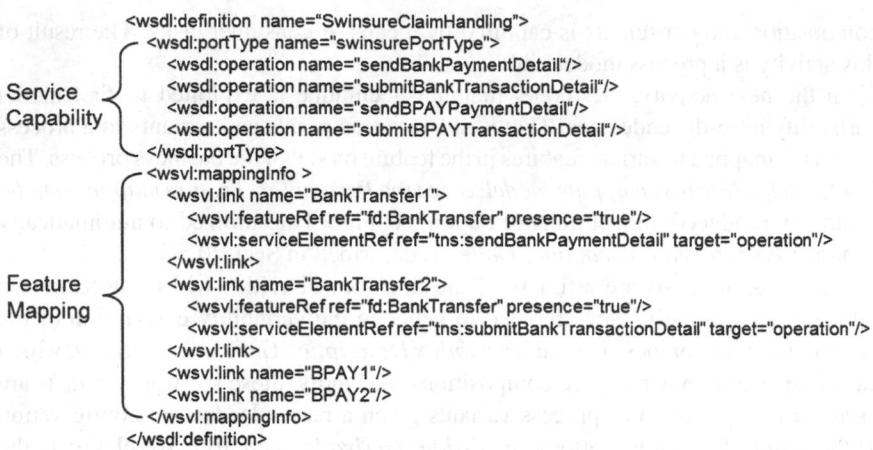

```
                   <wsdl:definition name="SwinsureClaimHandling">
                     <wsdl:portType name="swinsurePortType">
                        <wsdl:operation name="sendBankPaymentDetail"/>
     Service          <wsdl:operation name="submitBankTransactionDetail"/>
     Capability        <wsdl:operation name="sendBPAYPaymentDetail"/>
                        <wsdl:operation name="submitBPAYTransactionDetail"/>
                     </wsdl:portType>
                     <wsvl:mappingInfo >
                        <wsvl:link name="BankTransfer1">
                           <wsvl:featureRef ref="fd:BankTransfer" presence="true"/>
                           <wsvl:serviceElementRef ref="tns:sendBankPaymentDetail" target="operation"/>
                        </wsvl:link>
     Feature          <wsvl:link name="BankTransfer2">
     Mapping             <wsvl:featureRef ref="fd:BankTransfer" presence="true"/>
                           <wsvl:serviceElementRef ref="tns:submitBankTransactionDetail" target="operation"/>
                        </wsvl:link>
                        <wsvl:link name="BPAY1"/>
                        <wsvl:link name="BPAY2"/>
                     </wsvl:mappingInfo>
                   </wsdl:definition>
```

Fig. 20.15 An excerpt of the WSVL description for the claim handling process

20.6.3 Deriving Executable Process Variants

While the modeling of variability and variability dependencies is a design time process, the derivation of an executable process variant happens at either design time or runtime. This is triggered when the service composition is customized by brokers or the provider itself. As explained, the customization is performed using the feature model of the service composition (cf. Sect. 20.4.1) and generally requires the runtime customization of respective partner services. For instance, Fig. 20.16 presents a possible feature configuration which is the result of a broker's customization.

Given a feature configuration, we exploit model transformation techniques as follows to derive a particular executable process variant:

1. The *FeatureTask mapping model* is referenced for specializing the process model. The process model is actually a model template which is the superset of all process variants. Therefore, each variant process element is evaluated against the set of features associated with the element. If the evaluation is true, the process element is kept. Otherwise, the process element is purged from the process model. The result of this task is an abstract process variant which does not have variability but still contains partner tasks and consumer tasks. Figure 20.17 presents a variant of the sub-process for collecting excess fee which corresponds to the feature configuration in Fig. 20.16.
2. The *FeatureFeature mapping model* is referenced for generating a feature configuration for each customizable partner service. These feature configurations are used to customize partner services and produce partner service variants. Given the feature configuration in Fig. 20.16, Swinpay WS will be customized with selected features as "*Confirmation*", "*Bank transfer*", and disabled features as "*BPAY*", "*Execution*", "*Credit card*", "*Cheque*", and "*User notification*".

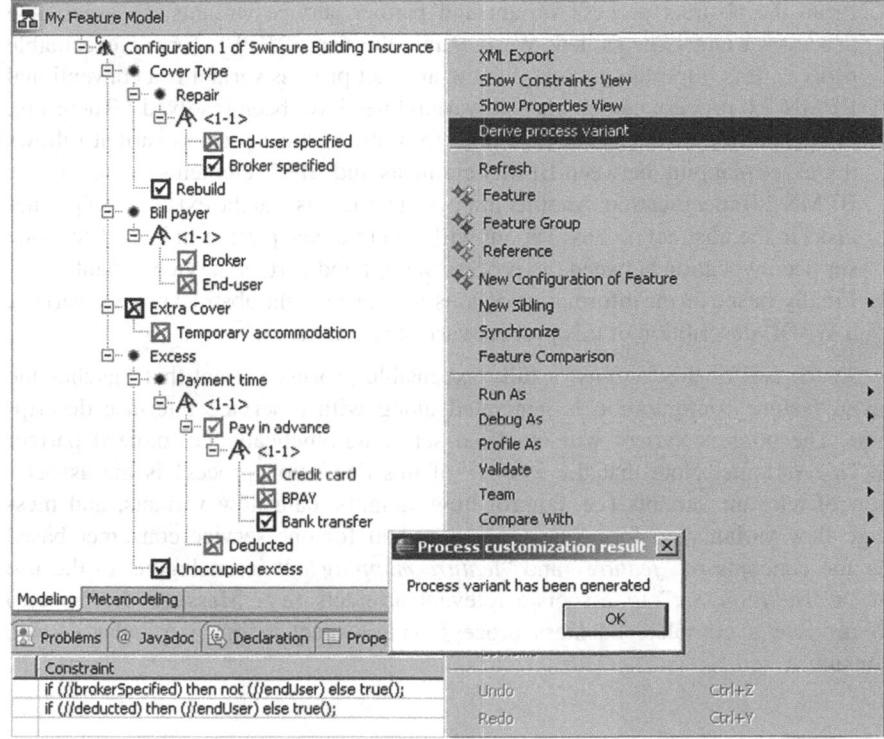

Fig. 20.16 A feature configuration for the claim handling process

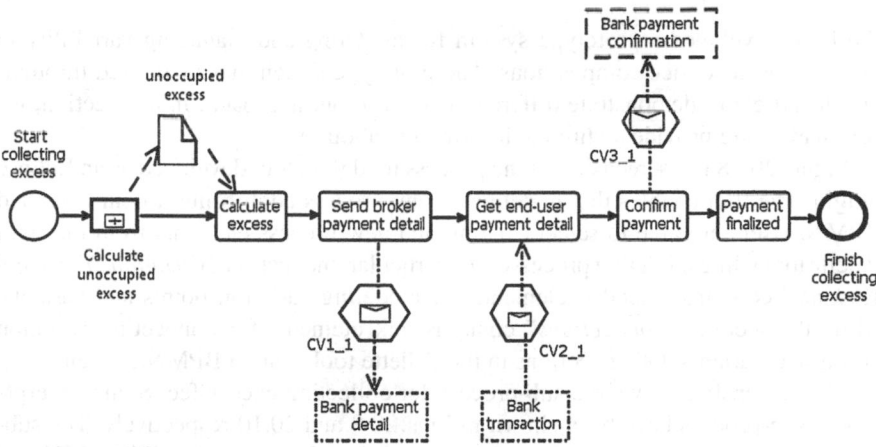

Fig. 20.17 A variant of the sub-process for collecting excess fee

3. From the abstract process variant and partner service variants, an executable process variant is generated. We presume the use of BPEL for the executable process. It is important to note that the abstract process variant is a conventional BPMN 2.0 process model since all variabilities have been resolved.[1] Therefore, the generation of the BPEL definition from the abstract process variant follows the exact mapping between BPMN elements and BPEL elements defined in the BPMN 2.0 specification. Another important remark is that the existence of partner tasks in the abstract process variant will help to create partner links and accurate service invocation between the process variant and partner service variants.

4. Finally, based on the information of consumer tasks in the abstract process variant, a WSDL description of this process variant is generated.

At the end of this activity, a fully executable process variant that matches the given feature configuration is generated along with a service interface description. The process variant will invoke a set of automatically customized partner service variants. Note that the essence of this derivation process is the association of relevant variants (i.e. control flow variants, data flow variants, and message flow variants) to form one process variant for one service consumer based on the concepts of "*feature*" and "*feature mapping*". It is analogous to the use of "*Correlation Set*" to associate relevant artefacts (e.g. **Message** or **Process**) to produce a complete business process with respect to one particular service consumer.

20.7 Prototype Implementation

We have developed a prototype system for modeling and managing variability in process-based service compositions. The prototype system has been used throughout the article to demonstrate different aspects of our approach. In this section, we summarize and provide additional information about it.

Figure 20.18 is a screenshot of the process modeling tool developed as an Eclipse plugin. The tool enables the modeling of any process conforming to our extended BPMN. Users are able to select existing and new process elements from the right Palette tool while modeling processes. In particular, the section "*Variation Points and Variants*" contains extended elements for modeling variation points and variants, while the section "*Connections*" contains link elements for connecting variation points and variants. Other sections in the Pallette tool contain BPMN elements.

The screenshot shows the sub-process for collecting excess fee. Some excerpts of this sub-process have been shown in Figs. 20.8 and 20.10 respectively. The sub-process demonstrates two control flow variation points, namely *VPS4/VPE4* and

---

[1] Strictly speaking, abstract process variants still contain new modeling elements such as **DataObjectVariant**, **ConversationVariant**, or **PartnerTask**. However, these elements are inherited from BPMN elements without additional properties. They are regarded as BPMN elements in generating BPEL definition

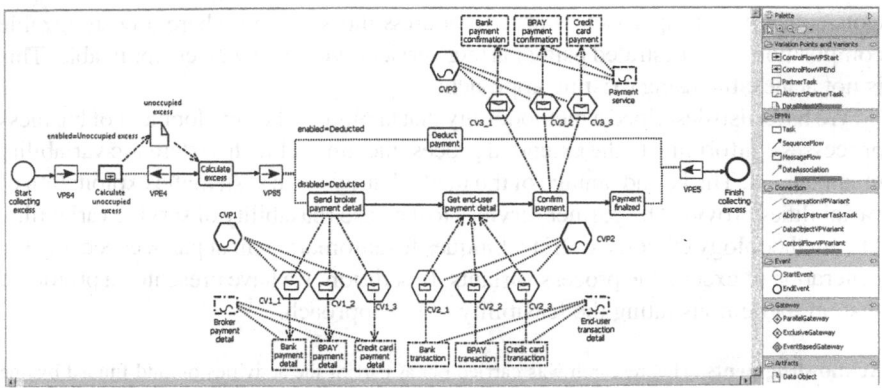

Fig. 20.18 A screenshot of the process modeling tool

VPS5/VPE5, one data flow variation point, namely *"Unoccupied excess"*, and three message flow variation points, namely *CVP1*, *CVP2*, and *CVP3*. *CVP1* and *CVP2* model the message flow between the process and end-users, while *CVP3* models the message flow between the process and the partner service Swinpay WS. The elements **PartnerTasks** and **AbstractPartnerTask**, as well as the *PartnerTaskFeature mapping model* for *CVP3* are derived from Swinpay WSVL as explained in the process development methodology section. Modeling variability in this way enables the capturing of variability inter-dependencies between the process and Swinpay WS.

The tools for capturing variability intra-dependencies and inter-dependencies (cf. Figs. 20.12, 20.13) are implemented as extensions to Atlas Model Weaver (AMW) [6]. Model transformations are performed using Atlas Tranformation Language (ATL) [13] to derive the *FeatureFeature mapping model* for variability inter-dependencies. In addition, there is a tool for initiating process customization (cf. Fig. 20.16).

20.8 Conclusion

In this paper, we have described a feature-oriented approach to modeling and managing variability in process-based service compositions. We have extended the BPMN 2.0 metamodel for introducing variation points and variants in all three aspects of service compositions, i.e. control flow, data flow, and message flow. These extensions enable not only comprehensive modeling of variability, but also the generation of executable process variants as the result of a service customization. In addition, we have introduced a feature mapping technique for capturing not only variability intra-dependencies among variants within a process model, but also variability inter-dependencies between variants in a process model and variants in partner services.

Consequently, our approach is able to address the situation where a customizable composition is orchestrated using partner services which may be customizable. This is not achievable using existing approaches.

We have also described a methodology that facilitates the development of business processes conforming to the extended process metamodel with systematic variability management. The key advantage of the methodology is the systematic exploitation of variabilities provided by partner services to increase reusability of service variability. The methodology exploits MDE techniques for automating most parts, especially the generation of executable process variants. In addition, we have presented a prototype system for demonstrating the feasibility of our approach.

Acknowledgments This research was carried out as part of the activities of, and funded by, the Smart Services Cooperative Research Centre (CRC) through the Australian Government's CRC Programme (Department of Innovation, Industry, Science and Research).

References

1. Barros, A., Allgaier, M., Charfi, A., et al.: Diversified service provisioning in global business networks. In: Annual SRII Global Conference, pp. 716–728 (2011)
2. Batory, D.: Feature models, grammars, and propositional formulas. In: Proceedings of the 9th International Software Product Line Conference, SPLC '05, vol. 3714, pp. 7–20 (2005)
3. Benavides, D., Segura, S., Ruiz-Corts, A.: Automated analysis of feature models 20 years later: a literature review. Inf. Syst. **35**(6), 615–636 (2010)
4. Chang, S.H., et al.: A variability modeling method for adaptable services in service-oriented computing. In: 11th International Software Product Line Conference, pp. 261–268 (2007)
5. Czarnecki, K., et al.: Formalizing cardinality-based feature models and their specialization. Softw. Process Improv. Pract. **10**(1), 7–29 (2005)
6. Didonet, M., Fabro, D., Bzivin, J., Valduriez, P.: Weaving models with the eclipse amw plugin. In: Eclipse Modeling Symposium, Eclipse Summit Europe (2006)
7. Eclipse Project: Eclipse Modeling Framework (EMF). http://eclipse.org/modeling/emf/ (2012). Accessed 30 April 2012
8. Griss, M., Favaro, J., d'Alessandro, M.: Integrating feature modeling with the rseb. In: Proceedings of the Fifth International Conference on Software Reuse, pp. 76–85 (1998)
9. Hadaytullah, H., et al.: Using model customization for variability management in service compositions. In: 7th IEEE International Conference on Web Services (ICWS), pp. 687–694 (2009)
10. Hallerbach, A., et al.: Capturing variability in business process models: the provop approach. Soft. Maintenance Evol. Res. Pract. **22**(6–7), 519–546 (2010)
11. Hermosillo, G., et al.: Creating Context-Adaptive Business Processes. In: Maglio, P., et al. (eds.) Service-Oriented Computing, LNCS, vol. 6470, pp. 228–242. Springer (2010)
12. Jaroucheh, Z., et al.: Apto: A mdd-based generic framework for context-aware deeply adaptive service-based processes. In: IEEE International Conference on Web Services (ICWS), pp. 219–226 (2010)
13. Jouault, F., Allilaire, F., Bzivin, J., Kurtev, I.: Atl: a model transformation tool. Sci. Comput. Program. **72**(12), 31–39 (2008)
14. Kang, K.C., et al.: Feature-oriented domain analysis (foda) feasibility study. Carnegie-Mellon University Software Engineering Institute, Technical report (1990)
15. Kang, K., et al.: Form: a feature-oriented reuse method with domain-specific reference architectures. Ann. Softw. Eng. **5**, 143–168 (1998)

16. Koning, M., ai Sun, C., Sinnema, M., Avgeriou, P.: Vxbpel: supporting variability for web services in bpel. Inf. Softw. Technol. **51**(2), 258–269 (2009)
17. Liang, H., Sun, W., Zhang, X., et al.: A policy framework for collaborative web service customization. In: IEEE International Symposium on Service-Oriented System, Engineering, pp. 197–204 (2006)
18. Machado, I., et al.: Managing variability in business processes: an aspect-oriented approach. In: International Workshop on Early Aspects, pp. 25–30 (2011)
19. Mietzner, R., et al.: Generation of bpel customization processes for saas applications from variability descriptors. In: 5th IEEE International Conference on Services, Computing, pp. 359–366 (2008)
20. Nguyen, T., Colman, A.: A feature-oriented approach for web service customization. In: The 8th IEEE International Conference on Web Services (ICWS), pp. 393–400 (2010)
21. Nguyen, T., Colman, A., Talib, M.A., Han, J.: Managing service variability: state of the art and open issues. In: The 5th International Workshop on Variability Modeling of Software-Intensive Systems (VaMoS), pp. 165–173 (2011)
22. Nguyen, T., Colman, A., Han, J.: Enabling the delivery of customizable web services. In: IEEE 19th International Conference on Web Services (ICWS), pp. 138–145 (2012)
23. OASIS: Web Services Business Process Execution Language (BPEL) Version 2.0. http://docs.oasis-open.org/wsbpel/2.0/wsbpel-v2.0.html (2007). Accessed 30 April 2012
24. Object Management Group (OMG): Business Process Model and Notation (BPMN) Version 2.0. http://www.omg.org/spec/BPMN/2.0/ (2011). Accessed 30 April 2012
25. Pohl, K., Böckle, G., van der Linden, F.J.: Software Product Line Engineering: Foundations, Principles and Techniques, 1st edn. Springer, New York (2005)
26. Razavian, M., et al.: Modeling variability in business process models using uml. In: 5th International Conference on Information Technology: New Generations (ITNG), pp. 82–87 (2008)
27. Schmid, K., John, I.: A customizable approach to full lifecycle variability management. Sci. Comput. Program. **53**(3), 259–284 (2004)
28. Schnieders, A., et al.: Variability mechanisms in e-business process families. In: International Conference on Business Information Systems (BIS), pp. 583–601 (2006)
29. Stollberg, M., Muth, M.: Efficient business service consumption by customization with variability modelling. J. Syst. Integr. **1**(3), 17–32 (2010)
30. ai Sun, C., Rossing, R., Sinnema, M., et al.: Modeling and managing the variability of web service-based systems. J. Syst. Softw. **83**(3), 502–516 (2010)
31. Svahnberg, M., van Gurp, J., Bosch, J.: A taxonomy of variability realization techniques. Softw. Pract. Exp. **35**(8), 705–754 (2005)
32. Weidmann, M., et al.: Adaptive business process modeling in the internet of services (abis). In: International Conference on Internet and Web Applications and Services, pp. 29–34 (2011)

Chapter 21
Software Product Line Engineering to Develop Variant-Rich Web Services

Bardia Mohabbati, Mohsen Asadi, Dragan Gašević and Jaejoon Lee

Abstract Service-Oriented Architecture (SOA) enables enterprise for distributed and flexible software development. SOA aims at promoting effective software asset reuse by means of encapsulating functionalities as reusable services accessible through well-defined interfaces. However, one of the challenging problems for the realization of this vision is an need for design and management of variants of SOA-based solutions. Such SOA-based solutions require customization to meet stake-holders' individual functional and non-functional requirements. In this chapter, a methodological foundation for modeling and developing variant-rich SOA-solutions by incorporating the principles of Software Product Line Engineering (SPLE) into the SOA development life cycle.

21.1 Introduction

Nowadays enterprises and companies deal with several challenges for developing SOA-based solutions. To stay relevant with the global competition, they need to rapidly and cost effectively develop and deploy stockholder-tailored services. On the other hand, enterprises often have to design and develop services which fit to a wide variety of stakeholders (i.e., consumers) within a particular domain or targeted

B. Mohabbati (✉) · M. Asadi · D. Gašević
Simon Fraser University, Burnaby, Canada
e-mail: mohabbati@sfu.ca

M. Asadi
e-mail: masadi@sfu.ca

D. Gašević
Athabasca University, Burnaby, Canada
e-mail: dgasevic@acm.org

J. Lee
Lancaster University, Lancaster, UK
e-mail: j.lee@comp.lancs.ac.uk

A. Bouguettaya et al. (eds.), *Web Services Foundations*,
DOI: 10.1007/978-1-4614-7518-7_21,
© Springer Science+Business Media New York 2014

market sectors. These challenges motivate enterprises to shift from mass software production to mass software customization. A trend inclines towards developing software applications composed from *reusable software assets* that can be re-targeted for different requirement sets. To enable mass customization in the context of Service-Oriented Architectures (SOAs), innovative software engineering methods and models need :(1) to capture the knowledge of variable requirements and reflect variability in services (2) support reuse not only reuse of service, but also in all other software development assets (3) enable service customization and management according to different stakeholders' functional and non-functional requirements [2, 13, 36].

Software Product Line Engineering (SPLE) is one of the most promising and well-established paradigms, focusing on the development of software product lines [12, 49] based on the principles of variability modeling and mass-customization. SPLE research has proposed numerous approaches and techniques for the efficient production of similar software systems (i.e., also known as software families). Hence, the adaptation of SPLE approaches for mass-customization have received much practical attention and have already been applied successfully in many enterprises [39]. Employing SPLE techniques results in the reduction of costs, efforts, and time-to-market and the improvement of quality. This is done by decreasing the complexity of the design and by alleviating customization, maintenance, and evolution of software products [12, 44, 49].

Adopting SPLE offers promising prospects to provide scalable solutions to the current challenges of the development, management and customization of Web services and generally SOA-based systems [13, 14, 35, 36]. to which we refer as *Service-Oriented Software Product Lines* (*SOSPLs*). In this chapter, we firstly provide a comparison of SPL and SOA from different perspectives. We then present a method for a systematic development of a family of SOA-based applications (i.e., SOSPL). The underlying idea of the described method is to guide the development process of an SOSPL and which extends the conventional SPLE life-cycle to support modeling, developing and managing variant-rich service-oriented applications.

This chapter is organized as follows: Section 21.2 introduces the basic concepts of SPLE and outlines some of the main SPLE activities. Section 21.3 presents a holistic comparison of SPL and SOA, which focuses on reuse, architectural and variability aspects of the two paradigms. Section 21.4 introduces the end-to-end methodology for SOSPL development by focusing on the main engineering activities of the approach. Before concluding the paper in Section 21.6, we provide a detailed discussion of the proposed approach in Section. 21.5.

21.2 Software Product Line Engineering (SPLE)

SPLE addresses the issues of software reuse and mass-customization. An SPL or a software product family is defined as: "*a set of software-intensive systems, sharing a common, managed set of features that satisfy the specific needs of a particular market segment or mission and are developed from a common set of core assets in a prescribed way*" [12]. The 'particular market segment' refers to a domain (i.e., a business area) and the business strategies of an enterprise or organization whose objectives of the business area are determined based on changes in its stakeholders' requirements.

A key idea in SPLE is to capture the essential concepts of 'commonality' and 'variability' among a set of similar software products belonging to the same domain. Therefore, rather than describing a single software system, the model of software product lines describes the set of products in the same domain. A product line includes predicted variations that are introduced by tailoring the core assets using variation mechanisms. Variability introduced in SPLE is an abstraction that enables and facilitates customization. It empowers product derivation of different applications by explicit modeling and management of variation points [49, 57]. which define decision points determining how the product family members may differ from each other. Variations along with their possible choices, functions or qualities, can be defined at each level of abstraction (e.g., requirements, architecture, or components).

SPLE relies on a fundamental distinction of *development for reuse* and *development with reuse* with aims at maximizing reusability and eliminating wasteful generic development of components used only once. This insight can be leveraged to improve software development life-cycle [12, 49] that SPLE shifts from the development of a specific application or individual system to a domain, in turn, leads to two characterized development processes commonly referred to as *domain engineering* and *application engineering*. Domain engineering models variability among product family members and develops the reusable software platform by focusing on *developing-for-reuse*. The software platform encompasses all software development artifacts that are liable to be recycle. On the other hand, application engineering adopts the *developing-with-reuse* approach, where products are customized and derived from product family and reference platform which is constructed and developed in the domain engineering phase. Reuse of the software platform and binding variability for different applications are then enacted in application engineering. Differentiating these two development lifecycles allows for establishing the software platform, application customization, and product derivation.

Approaches to the analysis and construction of SPLs can be classified into three strategies: (i) proactive, (ii) reactive, and (iii) extractive [22]. A proactive strategy is similar to the waterfall approach in conventional software engineering, where all product variations on the foreseeable horizon are analyzed and designed, while architectures for the target domain are defined and implemented upfront. This approach is suited for enterprises that to foresee and plan ahead of their product line requirements well and that have available resource and time for a long development cycle. A reactive strategy is an incremental approach where only the product-line reusable assets needed in immediate terms are developed and built. Hence, this approach typically requires less upfront efforts than proactive. In a reactive strategy, one or several variations of software products can be analyzed, designed and implemented in each development spiral. Such an approach is suitable where the upfront requirements for product variations cannot be predicted well in advance or where enterprises have to maintain an aggressive product schedule, which is usually limited in time and resources, through the transition to an SPLE approach. An extractive strategy is between proactive and reactive ones and reuses existing software products as the product line initial baseline.

21.3 Comparison of SPL and SOA

SPL and conventional SOA-based approaches to software development share common goals. With both promoting the concepts of reuse and foster organizations to reuse existing assets and capabilities rather than repeatedly redeveloping them for new software systems. Recent years have witnessed growth of research in the exploration of the synergies of the combination of SPL and SOA in recent years [9, 13, 14, 23, 26, 36, 59]. Even though two paradigms support software reuse there are different perspectives and outlooks [37]. In this section, commonalities and differences corresponding to the two paradigms are discussed, helping to enlighten how SPLE can be adopted and leveraged for the development and customization of a family of SOA-based applications. To compare SPL and SOA, we consider four main aspects including development processes, reusability notions, architectural styles, and variability modeling and management.

21.3.1 Development Processes

SPL and SOA follow different engineering goals. Therefor, the activities associated with their software development life-cycles are different. One of the main objectives of SPLs is to reduce the overall engineering efforts required to produce a set of similar software applications by capitalizing on the commonality and by managing the knowledge of variability and customization. Therefore, the engineering goal of SPL is remarked as the systematic development and management of core assets and software platform in order to achieve the high level of reusability [12, 22, 44, 49]. In contrast, service-oriented approaches set the goal of achieving system agility and of enabling automation to cope with integration, inteoperability and dynamic execution in heterogeneous environments, and providing runtime flexibility [6, 20, 48]. Table 21.1 shows a summary of major life-cycle phases of two paradigms essentially including requirement and domain analysis, design and implementation, and deployment.

- **Requirement and Domain Analysis:** Service-oriented design and development are basically based on an iterative and incremental process. The process is initiated with planning proportional to the requirements which, for a new application, are investigated through the analysis phase. This process comprises of reviewing business goals and objectives that derive the modeling and development of business processes. In the analysis phase, business processes and services are identified and specified in a stepwise manner [20, 47] with the main objective of it to facil-

Table 21.1 Comparison of the major engineering activities of software product line engineering and service orientation

Engineering paradigm	Requirement analysis	Design and implementation	Deployment and maintenance	Main engineering goals
Service-oriented engineering	• Planning and requirement analysis • Business process models • Service identification	• Business process specifications • Service construction	• Service publishing • Service matching	• Integration and Interoperability • System agility through run-time flexibility • Dynamic execution
Software product line engineering — Domain engineering: *Development for reuse*	• Product line scoping • Product line requirement analysis • Variability analysis	• Domain design • Domain realization • Domain testing	• Execution and monitoring • Product line maintenance evolution	• Variability modeling • Variability management • Systematic reuse of assets for development of a software product family • Mass customization
Application engineering: *Development with reuse*	• Application requirement analysis	• Application design • Application realization • Application testing	• Application deployment	

itate the reuse (or reproposing) of the business process functionality through the identification and orchestration of services when constructing new applications.

The requirement-analysis phase in SPLE also consists of determining the requirements and using domain information. Nonetheless , SPLE focuses on the analysis and specification of requirements for the entire product family (i.e., product line). To this end, domain engineering of SPLE mainly concentrates on a systematic analysis and the settlement of the variability of both functional and non-functional (quality) prerequisites performed by scoping the product line, by analysing product line requirements, and identifying commonalities and variabilities among product line members. Requirement analysis in the application engineering life-cycle further focuses on the analysis and determination of prerequisites of individual stakeholders. In the application engineering life-cycle, requirement analysis is established for configuring reusable software assets developed and produced in the domain engineering life-cycle.

- **Design and Implementation:** Service-oriented design and implementation is followed by the design and specification of business processes and service components corresponding to the requirements. Service implementation and testing involves discovery of existing available services through local or remote service repositories; and development of services by using the specifications developed in the design phase.

  In SPL, domain design and implementation involve the detailed design and realizing the reusable software components for the entire product family. It starts with the domain design sub-process which consists of (1) defining and modeling the commonality and variability based on the domain-specific requirements identified in the requirement engineering phase; (2) specifying the reference architecture of the product family; the reference architecture provides a common, high-level structure for all product line applications. Furthermore, the domain design incorporates configuration mechanisms into the reference architecture for supporting variability management in order to enable further product customization and derivation. The domain realization sub-process focuses on the implementation and testing of each component which is planned and designed for the reuse in different contexts (i.e., the applications of the product line). The application design sub-process in the application engineering life-cycle employs the reference architecture to refine and instantiate the application architecture and incorporates application specific adaptations. Afterward, the application realization sub-process focuses on the selection and configuration of reusable software components and testing for specific application, which are already contained product line architecture developed in domain engineering phase.

- **Deployment and Maintenance:** In this phase, service-oriented development deals with packaging, provisioning, publishing services, service-matching based on requirements of stakeholders, executing stakeholders-acceptance testing, and monitoring performance in the production environment. TheSPLE development phase including the configuration and deployment of a final product is associated with application engineering with activities for building and customizing systems according to the result of domain engineering.

21.3.2 Reuse in SPL Versus SOA

Software reuse, as one of the important goals in software engineering, can improve the quality and productivity of software development. For this purpose, several software reuse approaches have been devised. Component-based software engineering (CBSE) facilitates software reuse and promotes quality and productivity. The aims of CBSE are to achieve interoperability, reusability, and extensibility. These objectives are intended to facilitate fast-paced delivery of scalable evolving software systems [33]. Research on SOA is a modern instance of this vision [6, 46]. SOA leverages a logical framework by decoupling several logical units of functionality (i.e., services), which facilitate reuse by eliminating the recreation of common services. Thereby, business goals are achieved through loosely connected services with their variability is guided by SOA policies.

Reuse in SPL versus services in SOA have different characteristics (cf. Table 21.2). As mentioned, reusable assets in SPL encompass all the reusable software artifacts. A core asset is the most essential element of SPL since it is a common asset which is reused within multiple products and the reusability of which will largely determine the success of the whole product line [49]. For instance, the most distinguishable reusable assets in SPL context are as follows [12]:

- *Analysis and design models*: including the requirements and variability models, which describe the common and variable features for all family members
- *Domain models*: describing and representing all the entities and concepts that can be utilized in the context of software product families
- *Architectures*: specifying and determining which of the reusable components are needed for configuring executable applications and how to configure software families that best satisfy non-functional requirements
- *Design decision models*: specifying the family configuration model and determining how to derive software products based on specific requirements
- *Software components*: supporting variation points and implementing the required functionalities of software families
- *Interfaces*: enabling different implementation of the same functionality
- *Test artifacts*: reusing test plans, test cases and scenarios, and test data

Table 21.2 Reuse in SPL and SOA

Reuse characteristic	Reuse in SPL	Reuse in SOA
Reuse units	Analysis and design models (requirement models), domain models, architectures, decision models, software components, composition models, interfaces, test cases, documentations	Service, business processes or collaboration templates, application templates, data schema and data provenance, policies and business rules, test scripts, interfaces
Reuse context	Software family members	Various contexts
Coupling with reuse	Tightly coupled	Loosely coupled
Reuse method	Instantiation	Service invocation composition

In SOA, service, on the other hand, are intended to be reusable building blocks and units of sharable software assets for different applications which implement different business processes. As a consequence, services can be orchestrated to construct composite services through business processes.

Core assets in SPL including a generic architecture and components are used to develop applications, whereas services are basic building blocks in SOA to support software development by composition. In SOA, business processes or application templates specify entire applications through the definition of execution sequences of valid workflows. Services can be reusable artifacts which enable rapid SOA application development [56].

Assets and applications are generally tightly coupled in SPL, while services are loosely coupled which is one of the most pronounced properties of services in SOA research [48]. Services maintain a relationship that minimizes the decency to the context or state of other services.

Software components often operate within a context defined by a generic architecture for product family members in SPLs. SOA is grounded on the idea of open integration of business processes by means of shared services where services are described through standard-interface and are intended for reuse in different contexts. Nevertheless, services can also be developed and reused for internal processes within organizations. In essence, SOA basically envisages and focuses on large scale reuse [28] because SOA promotes services to be seamlessly consumed by diverse applications where they can be published, discovered and invoked through standardized specifications [6].

Unlike core assets are reused in application development time which is often static, while services can be reused at design time but reconfigured at run-time [9].

21.3.3 Architectural Aspects of SPL Versus SOA

Both SPL and SOA require defining the architectural context and composition rules with SPL architecture is often characterized as centralized, static, and specialized into concrete products, but SOA is characterized as decentralized. Composition rules are predefined in SPL, which describe common and variable behavioral characteristics of architecture, while in SOA composition or business rules are generally defined to govern the way in which a composition is constructed. SPL basically aims at providing a common architecture for reuse, whereas SOA lacks enough support for large grained software reuse at the architectural level.

Gomaa et al. [24, 53] discuss software architectural issues in SOA and describe various practices to develop reusable services in order compose systems from services efficiently. They draw attention that the architectural solution space offered by SOA promises to provide potentially significant benefits for reutilization. However, achieving SOA's benefits may not be guaranteed just by implementing based on the SOA solution. Accordingly, the important software architecture and reuse issues should be addressed prior to creating a SOA [53]. Tsai et al. propose a classification schema of architectures for SOA-based applications in order to evaluate variety of architectures [56]. The slackly coupling characteristic and platform-independent view inherited in SOA may address many architectural issues that are open-design and integration problems. Furthermore, architecture style offered by SOA is potential to maximize reuse beside interoperability and flexibility; however, SOA lacks support to manage variability at the architectural level [13, 36]. Whereas SPL enables managing variability to improve reutilization reuse at such level.

21.3.4 Variability in SPL and SOA

The concept of *variability* refers to the ability of software systems or artifacts to be efficiently extended, modified, specialized, or configured (customized) for *(re)use* in the specific context for a particular application [57]. This characteristic enables for applying changes at different levels ranging from software architecture to implementation. Two important concepts related to variability discussed in the literature are variation points and variants [49, 57] with the former being placed in the design or implementation at which variants occur. Variants are the alternatives that can be selected at those variation points. Therefore, variability can specify a part of an architecture which remains variable, as variation points, or what is not completed at design time. Variability can be implemented at design time or run-time [54]. It is noteworthy that variability and flexibility are closely interconnected. Flexibility offers adaptation and changes of architecture, while variability deals with various version of architecture.

Variability in SPL encompasses all software artifacts from requirements to code [12, 57]. Therefore, there are numerous modeling methods proposed that with the objective of modeling variability within software artifacts and at different levels of abstraction. Van Gurp et al. discuss about the notion of variability in SPL [57], where variability is exposed at different levels: platform technologies and user expectations, requirements specifications, designs, component source code, compiled code, linked code, and running code. Variability in this context refers to the ability to select among these artifacts at various stages during product derivations.

Effective management of variability is essential for the success of SPLs [57]. It determines how flexibly new members of a given SPL can be obtained and defines SPL boundaries. The distinction between variability modeling and other techniques is based on the diversity between variability modeling and variability mechanism. Variability modeling techniques model the variability provided by the product line artifacts while variability mechanisms are commonly considered ways to introduce or implement variability in those artifacts. Several of these mechanisms have been proposed in the literature such as conditional compilation, patterns, generative programming, macro programming, and aspect-oriented programming.

Accordingly, variability in SPL is an essential concern in all phases of development life-cycle. Variability identification, modeling and management is rather a large field of research in SPL [11]. Most current works address identification and management of variability by modeling the concepts as *features* which considered as the first-class representation of variability and in terms of which the major advantages of discussing a software system in terms of features is that the concept of feature bridges the gap between the requirements and technical design decisions because software components rarely address a single requirement but rather an entire set of essentials (details are given in Sect. 21.5). There are number of well-studied feature-oriented approaches for domain analysis and modeling common and variable requirements in SPLE such as FODA (Feature-Oriented Domain Analysis) [29] and its extension FORM (Feature-Oriented Reuse Method) [30], RSEB (Reuse-Driven Software Engineering Business) [25], GPM (Generative Programming Methods) [16] and PLUSS (Product Line Use case modeling for Systems and Software engineering) [19]. Every method generally shares feature as the common concept used in the analyses of commonality and variability. Some approaches are architecture-centric such as Hoek [27], Koalish [4], and Thiel [55] some of which are configuration-based, e.g., COVAMOF [50] and Koalish [4]. Some of the approaches extend UML to model variability like VPM [58]. Some proposed approaches focus on separating variability representation from the representation of various SPL artifacts such as Bachmann [5].

The development of SOA-based applications is accomplished through different abstraction layers: business process or orchestration layer, service interface layer, and service implementation or component layer [47] with the business process layer or orchestration layer consists of composite services implementing coarse-grained business activities, or even an entire business process. The service layer is composed of self-contained and business-aligned services, which provide the implementation for fine-grained business activities. The service interface layer comprises the interface of services published by a service provider. Finally, the component layer (i.e., implementation layer) consists of a set of components that realize service interfaces and provide the implementation for services. Variability in SOA affects these different layers thoroughly. Chang and Kim [9] discuss four types of variation points which occur in a general four-layered SOA architecture: workflow variability, composition variability, interface variability, and business logic variability. Workflow variability is identified as variation of the control flow of a business process, i.e., tasks can be alternatively and optionally completed in a workflow depending on the individual service user. Composition variability is identified as variability when there is more than one possible service interfaces for activity construct in the business process which implement the service with either different logic or quality attributes. Interface variability occurs when the candidate services interfaces are different. Finally, components which realize and implement service interfaces by different logic impose logic variability.

Granularity Levels: Granularity in SPL refers to the degree of detail and precision of variability as produced by design or implementation artifacts. SPL variability may exist at different levels of granularity ranging from entire components to single lines of code [16, 31]. SPLE takes a top-down approach and decomposes artifacts into fine grained artifacts, whereas a bottom-up compositional approach is often adopted in SOA to combine artifacts into larger entities-service into composite services (i.e., business processes) that finally form the application. Decomposition or top-down modeling means that an SPL architecture specifies the decomposition of a family into architectural components. However, there are also hybrid approaches, such as product populations modeled using Koala [45], where the mixture of bottom-up and top-down approaches are leveraged. In SOA, generally there is no particular architecture specifying the decomposition.

In SOA, granularity specifies the scope of variability in functionality exposed by a service. A component which provides an implementation for a service interface can be of various granularity levels that software developers can always encapsulate the entire functionality of a solution into a single service is possible due to the well-known 'fractal' nature of services, where a higher-level service can encapsulate lower-level services to any level of granularity [8]. However, a fine-grained service is more easily reused; in distinction, coarse-grained service is more difficult to be reused [47, 53]. Nevertheless, services with high-level interfaces increase the reusability because providing interfaces with a coarse-grained granularity masks specialized or implementation-specific methods, thereby, this enables a service adaptable and reusable by multiple applications. Moreover, from the perspective of service-oriented design and development, creating and designing high-level, coarse grained interfaces that implement a complete business process is desirable [47, 20]. However, there is a trade-off between fine-grained and coarse-grained.

Services at different levels of granularity can be generally classified into different categories [34]: basic services, intermediary services, process-centric services and public enterprise services. Basic services that represent the elements of a vertical domain are simple logic-centric or data-centric services. Data-centric services handle persistent data and logic-centric services encapsulate algorithms for complex calculations or business rules. Intermediary services are designed to bridge a technical gasp in architecture. They provide service links with other services or application front-ends and services in gateways, adapters (mapping message formats to enable interoperability), facades (providing a different view on one or more services), and other functionality-adding services (extending functionality of existing services without altering them internally). In SOA, process-centric services to control and maintain the state of the enterprises business processes which uses basic or intermediary services to perform task and deal with business data. These services separate process logic from representation layer and encapsulate the process complexity for a single point of administration. A common example is an online shopping process, which includes filling the shopping cart, ordering products, and executing billing. Public enterprise services offered to partner companies as an in-house-system interface which, in turn, have the granularity of business documents and are coarse-grained integrate enterprises (B2B).

21.4 Running Example

To illustrate the concepts and the approach presented in the following sections, we
select a part of case study of a family of online marketplace portals providing applications for online trading like eBay.[1] The portal, as an SOSPL, can be customized
and deployed based on different business requirements of targeted stakeholders.
Figure 21.1a presents a service scenario of e-payment processes-part of a large product family that defines a common framework for online payment provided in online
marketplace. For the simplicity, a high-level view of the payment process is represented, and the details are omitted.

Different methods of online payment can be considered for different instances
of products from a family. Therefore, the number of possible payment method variations of a reference payment process, as a catalog and template, can be derived
and customized according to the stakeholders' requirements and business objectives. Some services are indispensable and prerequisite of the payment process (e.g.,
Credit Card payment feature as the dominant online payment), which should be
included for all the stakeholders' service product instance where as, some functional services (e.g., Smart Card e-Check and Debit Card) or extra-functional
services (e.g., Logging and Monitoring) can be determined as optional that can
be included or excluded based on stakeholders' needs (see Fig. 21.1b). As a case
in point, Stakeholder A may require additional features for having highly-secured
payment transactions by including a fraud protection service, whereas this service
is not required to be included in the payment process of the final customized portal
for Stakeholder B. In another scenario, Stakeholder C could ask the payment
process to be supported by a Mobile-based Notification service in addition to
the common payment notification services such as the Mail-based Notification

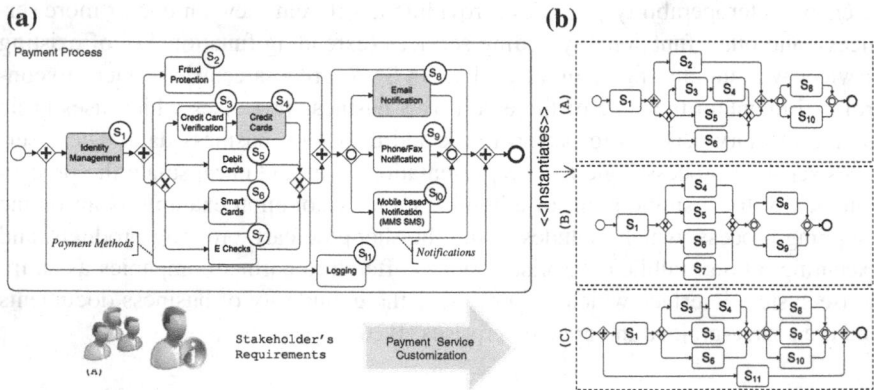

Fig. 21.1 a) A holistic view of e-Payment process family. **b)** e-Payment process variants example

---

[1] http://www.ebayinc.com/

service. Therefore, in the context of a product family, a business process should be imposed inevitably by variants (optional and mandatory services) which are required to be managed, specialized and customized in order to meet different stakeholders' functional or quality requirements.

21.5 Applying SPLE for Development of Service-Oriented Software Product Lines

It is already mentioned that even though SOA has been widely adopted, there are still no systematic methods to support modeling and managing variability during the development of SOA-based applications and further service management, which calls for a well-defined development process and understanding variability in functional and non-functional requirements in the course of development.

This section outlines the activities of a proactive methodology. The proposed method is an extension of a traditional software product-line life-cycle in order to support development and customization of a family of SOA-based applications. The proposed top-down method follows a two-life-cycle approach that separates two core activities related to *Service-Domain Engineering* and *Service-Application Engineering* (see Figs. 21.2 and 21.6). Service-domain engineering constructs and evolves the reuse infrastructure by analyzing the requirements and scoping the product line as a whole and producing any common , reusable business processes and services. On the other hand, service-application engineering derives individual services (i.e., customized services) from the reference architecture. Domain and application engineering life-cycles can rely on fundamentally different processes, namely, plan-driven and agile methods. In the following, we describe the major activities and their artifacts for three major development phases: (1) analysis (requirement engineering), (2) design, and (3) implementation and testing.

21.5.1 Service-Domain Engineering

The overall service-domain engineering processes of an SOSPL is depicted in Fig. 21.2. These activities (D1–D6 in Fig. 21.2) are performed iteratively. Domain analysis in SOSPL mainly encompasses product-line requirements engineering stage (D1) along with the analysis of variability by using feature modeling (D2). A feature model, as a software artifact outcome of the feature modeling process, includes the knowledge of variability associated to the functional and non-functional requirements and describes the permissible configuration space further guiding the customization process and determining how the reference business process model should be tailored according to the stakeholders' requirements in the application engineering life-cycle. During the domain design phase (D3), a reference business process model

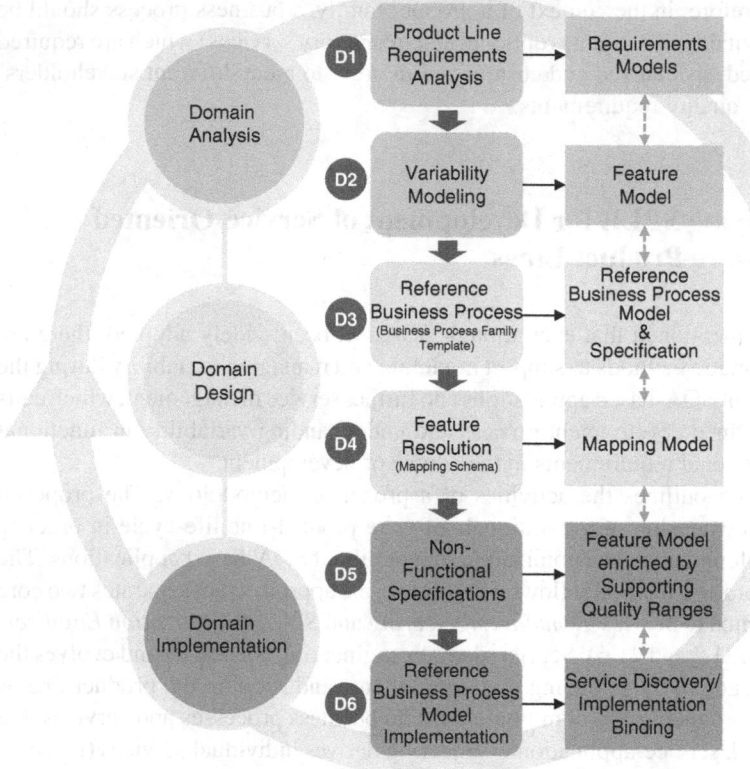

Fig. 21.2 Service-Domain Engineering of an Service-Oriented Software Product Line

(also known as business process family) is designed and constructed for the product line architecture based upon the outcomes of the requirement engineering phase (D1). The model mapping (D4) establishes the mapping relationships between the features within the feature model and the corresponding activities specified within the reference business process model. The activities of the reference business process are delegated to the service(s) in SOSPLs. In as much as non-functional (quality) requirements may also vary for different stakeholders, variability in the quality properties of services should also be captured and specified during the construction of an SOSPL (D5). To this end, features in the feature model are annotated by quality ranges which are supported by the entire product line architecture [40], progressively helping service engineer and developers to evaluate the impact of variant features selected according to the quality characteristics that services provide. In the final phase, the reference business process model is realized and implemented either by binding to the existing services or by developing new services. In the following, we detail these activities.

21.5.1.1 Product Line Requirements Analysis

Similar to traditional requirements engineering, domain requirements engineering should at least include the following activities [52]: (1) *elicitation* in which the product line business goals and stakeholders' requirements are discovered and scoped; (2) *specifications* in which the requirements are analyzed in detail; (3) *validation* in which the requirements are validated and consistency and completeness are checked, and (4) *management* in which the requirements can be managed in terms of changes or refinements. In addition to these activities, domain requirements engineering captures commonality and variability between the requirements of several stakeholders. Moreover, an important activity of the requirements analysis of an SOSPL is to define the product line scope [13, 49, 44] and decide on the boundary of the product line.

A successful scoping which is determined by factors such as the knowledge of similar domain services and future stakeholders' demands is required to be performed carefully because a scope-either too large or too small-will impair the capability of a SOSPL in achieving the goals of stakeholders [12]. A goal-oriented domain analysis can be employed at the early stage of the requirement analysis in order to capture the product line goals for requirement elicitation and to further align the final service products with the business goals and intentions of both the stakeholders and service providers. This is accomplished at the different levels of abstraction by goal modeling about which interested readers can further read in [3]. The outcome of this phase is the requirements models which can be described by goal models, use-cases, documentations and details, which are used subsequently for the variability analysis of the product line under development.

21.5.1.2 Variability Analysis and Modeling

The product line requirement engineering activity follows the variability analysis and modeling of the entire family in order to identify common and variable features. A *feature* is commonly defined as a visible incremental functionality and quality in software system(s) [29]. Nevertheless, depending on the stage of development it may also refer to a requirement or a coarse-grained or fine-grained component in the system(s) which provide the required functionality from different technical views. The emphasis in the variability (i.e., feature) analysis is on optional features, because optional features substantially differentiating one member of the family from the others.

In SOA, services constituting the orthogonal concept to the components notion, are characterized as the loosely coupled building blocks of software. A services encapsulates functionality and provides individual non-functional properties (i.e., QoS) through a well-described and published interfaces. From this view in the context of SOSPL, we define a feature as an increment in service functionality [1], which reflects stakeholders' both functional and non-functional requirements; wherefore, a feature, based on the granularity levels, a feature can be realized and associated to a composite service at the high-level business processes, or associated and realized by an atomic service at the lower-level.

Feature-oriented development [16, 29, 30] is widely employed as a means for analysis, management, and visualization of commonality and variability in SPLE in terms of features at different abstraction levels. In essence, feature modeling organizes features of a software product family into a model called *feature* residing between the requirement model and the design specification model (i.e., the reference business process model described in Sect. 21.5.1.3). Figure 21.3 shows a part of a feature model representing the variants (e.g., optional and alternative features) that characterize a requirements model. These features are selected to derive service products during the application engineering. Moreover, this model serves as a catalog of the variability space offered by a product family to accommodate the idiosyncrasies of the stakeholder enterprise or company.

Feature Model: A feature model consists of both formal semantics and graphical representation (e.g., feature diagram) and encompasses the knowledge of configuration (i.e., customization) for a product line. A feature model is a hierarchical decomposition of features in terms of parent-child relations on different levels of abstraction. As some of the features are not assumed to be present in every product during the application engineering, this differentiation is expressed by the indication of feature types and their relationships. Contrary to a mandatory feature is always selected if their parent is selected , an optional feature may or may not be selected. For instance, in Fig. 21.3, all the products should include the Credit Card feature as a mandatory feature. Other payment methods Fig. 21.3 are specified as optional features.

A feature cardinality and group cardinality can also be determined in cardinality-based feature modeling [17]. A cardinality associated to a feature determines the lower and upper bound of the number of features required in any product in a product family. In the SOSPL context, this attribute specifies the number of service instances that should be linked to a given service at run time. Cardinality can be defined as an interval, from zero to a given value.

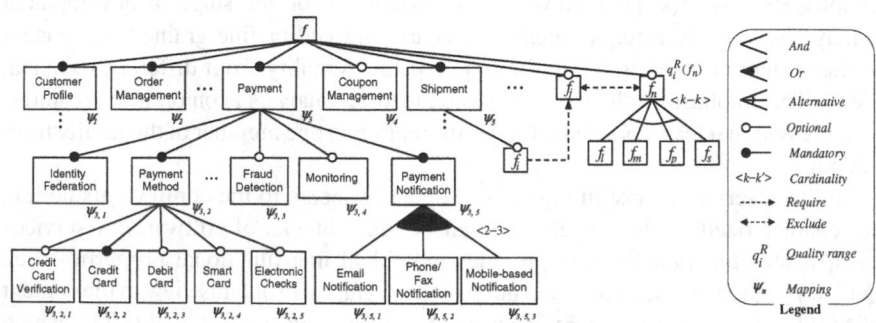

Fig. 21.3 Feature model of e-Payment (conforming stakeholders' requirements model)

Or feature groups with defined cardinality indicate that at least k and at most k' features that can be included out of the n features ($k \leq k' \leq n$) in a group if the parent is selected. Moreover, *Alternative feature groups* with specified the cardinality indicate that that only k out of n features in the group must be included if the parent is selected. Back to the simplified feature model example from Fig. 21.3, all the products should include the Payment Notification features. Also, all the final derived service products should include at least two methods of notification according to the feature model.

Furthermore, because features are not always independent *integrity constraints* (i.e., the *includes and excludes*) can be defined over features of a feature model to model dependencies and relations among them. They are the means to describe that the presence of a certain feature in the product imposes the presence or exclusion of another feature (see Fig. 21.3).

Feature models are an efficient abstraction of variability derived from the domain and stakeholders' requirements. They also help to derive the design and the development of variability through all the stages of the development including service identification and design, and further customization [13, 41].

In the feature-oriented analysis phase, which subsequently guides the identification of candidate services with right granularity, we organize feature based on the following criteria:

- Features supporting a particular business process can be grouped and abstracted as a higher-level feature on a coarse-grained level (e.g., Payment)
- Features supporting specific functional or non-functional services can be grouped and abstracted as a higher-level feature (e.g., Payment Notification and Logging services)
- A feature which incrementally realize a feature at the upper-level, then becomes as a sub-feature at the lower-level
- Features at the leaf-level are realized by fine-grained services

21.5.1.3 Reference Business Process Model

The previous activities, domain decomposition, top-down variability analysis and modeling provide an insight into a target domain in terms of product features. A feature model is generated as an output of the domain analysis. This model is then used to derive reference architecture and develop reusable components (business processes and services) in the course of the domain design. The activities of the design phase produce an architecture-independent model that defines reference architecture as the behavioural model of features for the entire family and specifies how features are composed at run-time.

A template-based approach has been widely adopted in SPLE for creating reference models. In the case of SOSPLs, such a reference model is designed as a template for the entire service products family in a superimposed way [15]. A reference business process model, as a model template, describes and specifies the execution

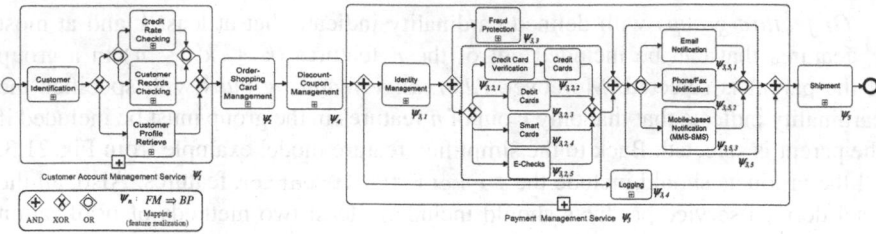

Fig. 21.4 A part of reference business process model

sequence of services for all instances of the product line. That is, a reference business process model is a union of all the business processes of the product line. It provides the common business logic for orchestration and choreography of services, which implement features. The reference model comprises functional interfaces specifying services capabilities, pre and post conditions of the services, and configuration properties representing the data needed to configure a service before its use, and service bindings. The reference business process model can be modeled by using process-oriented modeling languages (e.g., BPMN, EPC, and/or YAWL), and incrementally refined and optimized. For example, Fig. 21.4 illustrates a part of reference business process model, where variability and configuration knowledge have been modeled and encapsulated in given feature model in Fig. 21.3.

The reference business process model configured through the selection/elimination of features from the feature model during the application engineering and executive instances are derived (see Fig. 21.1b). In other words, due to the fact that architectural variations in the reference model are encoded as features, various parts of the reference business process model are organized in variation points. These variation points are managed and configured by means of feature models. It should be noted that we distinguish between design and runtime variability. Feature models capture and encapsulate only architectural variability at design time. In contrast, business process models describe behavioral variability, i.e., how features are composed, which drives runtime variability through composition patterns (discussed in the next section).

Furthermore, feature model configuration (i.e., specialization and customization) is performed during the build-time. The configuration can be done through the process of staged-configuration [18] where features further are prioritized and selected according to the (non-)functional requirements of the stakeholders [41]. All configured service products, which are instances of the family, have to conform to the reference architecture.

21.5.1.4 Feature Resolution and Mapping Model

During the design phase, feature resolution is the activity of analysing and connecting the feature model and the reference business process model in order to specify explicit mapping links between the two models: feature and reference business process models. The outcome of this activity constitutes a mapping model including links between features in the feature model activities in the reference business process model. This mapping model enables the configuration of the reference business process model through feature section during application engineering. From one point of view, this mapping model also provides the traceability links between the requirements and implementation [15, 51].

A mapping model can simply consist of boolean expressions specifying presence or removal of a modeling element (e.g., activity (abstract service)) in a model template (i.e., a reference business process model in our case) based on the selection of features in the feature model [15]. In our approach, we consider a boolean variable ψ_i corresponding to each feature f_i. This approach uses *presence conditions* (PC) as annotation properties for each activity within the reference business process model. The PC of an activity is formulated as a boolean expression of ψ_i variables corresponding to the features mapped to the activity (see Fig. 21.3 and 21.4). Both the feature and activity constructs refer to model elements of feature models and reference business process models. Thereby, when domain engineers map features to activities, the activities' PCs are defined. In application engineering, when a feature f_i are removed from the configuration, their corresponding ψ variables are set to *false*.

Feature resolution also helps to identify cross-cutting concerns related to general non-functional requirements. For example, feature Monitoring with given mapping annotation ψ_i in Fig. 21.3 is mapped to activity Monitoring as an extra-functional abstract service in the reference business process model (see Fig. 21.4). Based on the selection of features from the feature model in application engineering, the reference business process model is configured (Fig. 21.1b).

21.5.1.5 Non-functional Specifications

The domain design phase is also followed by the specification of non-functional properties based on the non-functional requirements (NFRs) analysis. This is due to the fact that NFRs are interlaced and related to functional requirements. Variability in NFRs influences the SOSPL design and implementation. Non-functional variations often exhibit different types and levels of quality properties (e.g., normal and strong authentication or security). For instance, NFRs for feature Credit Card can include *cost, security, availability* and *reliability* or they can also entail defined domain-specific non-functional aspects such as *usability* and *convenience of use*. Furthermore, in application engineering, non-functional variations directly impact the selection of appropriate services from candidate services, all of which provide equivalent functionalities but with different degree of non-functional properties related to the service quality specification. To this end, there are a number of proposals [7], in which feature models are extended to support feature attributes. Such attributes can comprise non-functional properties which can be measured (e.g., cost, availability, latency, bandwidth, etc).

In the context of SOSPL, these non-functional properties can be viewed as QoS properties, which are associated to each feature. Mapping models interconnecting feature and business process models enable for propagation of quality property values of concrete service sets, which are bounded to activities (abstract services) within in the process model. Based on the underlying implementation of a set of functionally equivalent services, which may be available for each feature, ranges of values of quality properties can be further specified and aggregated for each feature. Particularly, during the domain engineering lifecycle, determining the implied QoS ranges q^R for individual features f_n helps domain engineers ensure that the product line architecture will fulfill and deliver the upper and lower bounds of the values of the quality requirements requested by the stakeholders. Moreover, quality range computation enables for keeping track of the product line quality ranges even after the specification of the service quality has changed. For example, in Fig. 21.5, sets of candidate services provide different range of quality q^R for each features. The range of the kth quality property for feature f_n can be hierarchically computed. In [40], we introduce a generic evaluation model and method for aggregation and computation of ranges of quantified values of quality properties defined for product line architectures.

21.5.1.6 Reference Business Process Model Implementation

The domain design phase produces a reference business process model and architecture for a family of service products (i.e, SOSPL). In the domain implementation and realization, the reference business process model is realized and implemented. This activity involves implementing and testing the detailed architecture of the family modeled by reference model. Abstract services specified by the reference business process model are implemented by using component models such as Java class, Enterprise Java Beans, or .Net components. However, some of the services needed

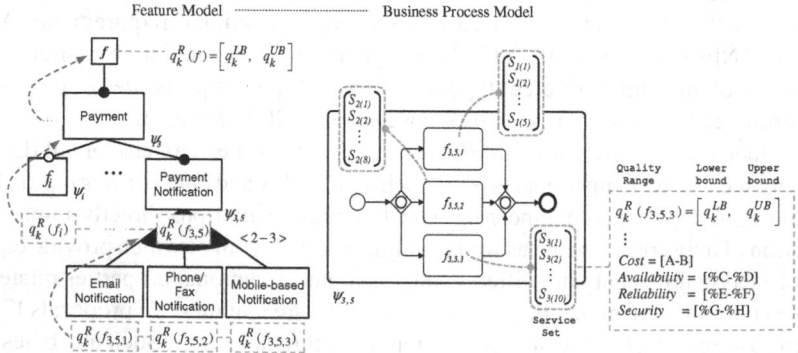

Fig. 21.5 Non-functional specification and aggregation for evaluating quality range supports by product line architecture

for the implementation might already be available; for instance, can be either found in a service catalog or retrieved through a service discovery process, and some of the services could potentially be built by partly reusing or modifying existing solutions.

21.5.2 Service-Application Engineering

This section describes a holistic view to the application engineering life-cycle. This lifecycle includes the major phases of service customization and derivation from the business process family. Regardless of the chosen variability modeling approach, the ultimate of in-service-application engineering is to employ the variability defined in domain engineering by selecting shared assets similarly developed in domain engineering. Figure 21.6 depicts a high-level application engineering process which starts with the elicitation and capturing of both the functional and non-functional requirements of an individual stakeholder through the application-requirement-analysis phase (A1). In the application design phase (A2), features are prioritized based on the stakeholder's captured preferences and business objectives concerning the optional features and quality needs. There after, the feature model is specialized through the

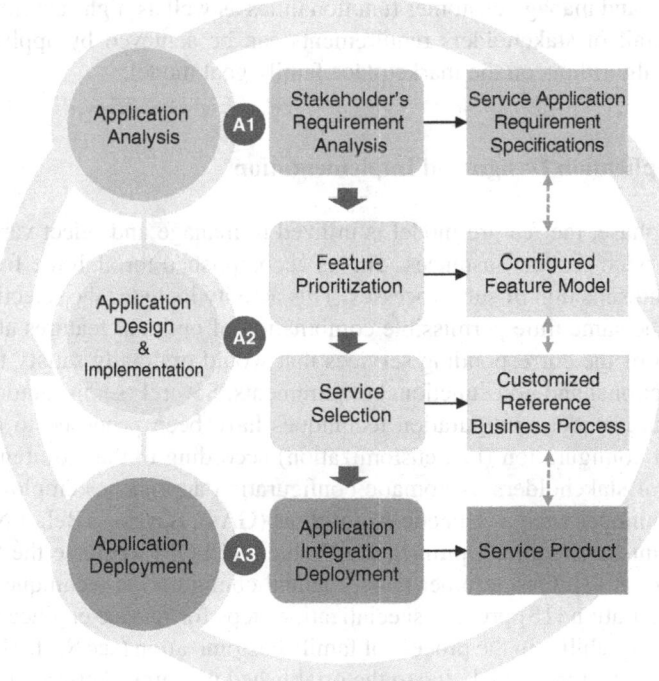

Fig. 21.6 Application Engineering of an Service-Oriented Product Line

decision-making process of selecting optional features. Subsequently, the reference business process model is configured and corresponding services are selected and bound in the deployment and integration phase (A3). The details of these application engineering phases can be found in [41].

21.5.2.1 Application Analysis

This phase focuses on the elicitation of requirements of a particular stakeholder for deriving customized process variants, which can be deployed as the final product. The preferences of the stakeholder are captured and later utilized for feature prioritization and selection. Similar to the requirements engineering phase in service engineering methodologies like SOMA [2], activities in the application analysis phase capture requirements for a single service (application). However, the application analysis activities reuse the family requirements models to develop requirements models of a target service. For example, assuming a family requirement model is represented in a goal model, the service goal model is developed through reasoning on the family goal model based on the inputs of current stakeholders [3]. Validation and verification of the application requirements model with respect to the stakeholder's needs and product line constraints are performed. In the context of marketplace portals, stakeholders of a target service application may request payment, shipment, order management, and manage customer functionalities as well as high security and low cost. The detail of stakeholders requirements can be achieved by applying label propagation algorithms on the marketplace family goal model.

21.5.2.2 Application Design and Implementation

During this phase, the feature model is utilized to manage and select variants that constitute service product instances. This is accomplished through the feature prioritization and selection of sub-processes. This activity includes the selection of the best and at the same time permissible combination of optional features along with the selection of the corresponding services that would optimally satisfy the stakeholder's functional and non-functional requirements. Several (semi-) automatic and manual feature model configuration techniques have been proposed to guide the final product configuration (i.e., customization) according to the requirements and preferences of stakeholders. Automatic configuration approaches employ AI optimization techniques such as Genetic Algorithms (GAs), Bayesian Belief Networks, and Constraint Satisfaction Optimization Problem (CSOP) to create the final customized product [7]. On the other hand, manual configuration techniques through staged-configuration [18] provide specialization steps for service engineers helping them resolve variability in the process of family customization (see Sect. 21.6). After configuring the feature model, due to the established mappings between the feature model and the reference business process model, a concrete business process for a target service-oriented application and its realizations are derived from the family design and implementation models. However, since there may be some requirements which could not be satisfied by existing assets (i.e., services) contained in the developed SOSPL architecture, further refinement of instantiated service products from the reference model can be performed, and new required services can be implemented. In our running example, according to the requirements of the current application derived in the previous stage, application engineers can configure marketplace feature model and derive a business process model for the service-oriented application under development. Also, proper services based on the requested quality of services (e.g. high security and low cost) are selected.

21.5.2.3 Application Deployment

This phase focuses on creating an executable business process and deployment of the customized services in the production environment after validating the customized services against the application requirement specification. After the deployment of the final service product on to the stakeholders' environment, the execution of the customized services is monitored to ensure the compliance of the service execution to stakeholders' requirements and any service level agreements.

21.6 Discussion

The development, management and evolution of many modern software systems rely on the notion of variability and suitable design techniques. SPLE research has devoted a considerable amount of resources to the development of various approaches to dealing with variability analysis, modeling, management, customization and related challenges over the last decade. These approaches can be employed in the design and development of variant-rich service-oriented applications (referred to as SOSPLs in this chapter).

Feature-oriented analysis enables for capturing variability in services at different levels of abstraction in order to support managing variability and leverage it for customization. Variability can be considered in terms of four different general levels of abstractions in service-oriented development [47]: requirements, business process models, service interface model and service component. In that sense, variability at a lower-level of abstraction realizes variability at a higher level. As described earlier in the chapter, we leveraged feature modeling for managing variability by focusing on the requirements and business processes at the higher levels of abstraction. However, feature models also can be employed for modeling, representing and managing variability at the levels of service components, service interface to support efficient service management. For instance, in [21], Fantinato et al. employed feature modeling to manage and enable customization in service contracts.

Nguyen and Colman [42] propose a feature-based service customization framework for modeling and managing variability of complex Web service specifications.

The proposed approach employed feature models as an extension to service description artifacts in order to facilitate the customization of service interfaces. In [43], the same authors adopt a feature-oriented approach to modelling variability in process-based service compositions and to enabling process customization. The approach extends the BPMN 2.0 metamodel to allow for defining variation points and variants within business process models. The extension is focused on modeling variability of three aspect of business process: control flow, data flow, and message flow. A variation point in a control flow is interpreted as any location in a process model at which different execution paths can be take place, and variants can be arbitrary process fragments. Variability in data flow is considered as a different way for storing data objects. Variability in message flow is identified as alternative conversations and interactions between two parties, i.e. the process and a partner service (or a consumer).

Koning et al. [32] investigate how variability can be incorporated into service-based systems in order to enable variability modeling and management. They describe how variability management helps to support run-time reconfiguration of systems by service replacement corresponding to the non-functional requirements of stakeholders. VxBPEL is proposed as an extension of Business Process Execution Language (BPEL) for to the process description and definition. VxBPEL allows for run-time variability and variability management in Web service-based systems. Variability information is defined in-line with the process definition. VxBPEL builds upon COVAMOF [50], a framework for modeling variability. Koning et al. note that the architectural modeling and management of variability in Web service-based systems provides the following advantages: enhances the extensibility of systems through service replacement; improves run-time flexibility for reconfiguration and rebinding of services (e.g., being able to optimize quality attributes through reconfiguration).

As already mentioned, improving reusability in service-oriented development is an often-stated goal in the literature. There are a number of important concerns that can influence highly-important analysis and design decision for the quality of service design. The major concerns include analysis and design for service reuse, service granularity management, and design of composable service [47]. Hence, several challenges have been unveiled for the development of service-oriented systems such as how to identify reusable services at the right level of granularity in order to facilitate service composition. Hence, the identification of service candidates is a challenging task in services engineering [2, 47]. SPL approaches can be adopted to consolidate design principles and service identification during the course of service engineering.

Lee et al. [38] present a feature-oriented approach to the analysis, identification and development in order to improve reusability of service-based systems. The proposed approach provides guidelines about how to address the key issue of granularity and orchestration of services by using feature models. They show how reusable service can be identified and specified based on software features. The proposed method is based on analysis of features that may vary from a user's point of view and will be subject to reconfigurations at runtime. Another approach to using feature-oriented analysis for service identification during the analysis and design phases is proposed by Chen et al. [10] whose main focus is re-engineering towards service-oriented systems and the remark of whom that feature-oriented analysis bridges the gap between the abstract architectural and source code level, whereas business processes are excluded.

Service-Oriented Modeling and Architecture (SOMA) proposed by IBM [2] has been developed as a generic development method for SOA-based applications. SOMA provides the guidelines for identification and specialization of services that realize and implement business processes through service composition. The authors of SOMA remarks that variability analysis in the practical SOA solution design is crucial for the initial finding-binding relationships between a service consumer (i.e., stakeholder) and a service provider. Moreover, it was noted that the publishing and discovery of relationships are often affected by variations, which are identified later in the design process. Hence, such variations may cause expensive fundamental re-design of SOA-based solutions [2]. To address this problem, the authors remark that a development life-cycle for SOA-based solutions should be extended by a variation-oriented analysis as an extra dimension that should be performed.

21.7 Conclusion

We can observe that the convergence of service-oriented and software product line engineering is gaining a considerable amount of attention and rapidly emerging as a viable and important software development paradigm. As we have discussed in this chapter, they both share common goals and promises to collaborate in the development of flexible, cost-effective software systems and to support a high level of reuse. Yet, their main goals are somewhat different. In this chapter, we discussed that how service-oriented development can benefit from SPLE approaches for variability modeling and management in the process of identification and design of variant-rich service-oriented applications.

By combining ideas of service-oriented development and SPLE, we expect to derive new software engineering approaches to make use of the best from both paradigms: (a) development of generic software architectures for highly adaptive Web services that can respond effectively to fluctuations in stakeholders' (non-) functional requirements, and (b) development of shared architectures that could be reused in different instances (benefits from the SPLE principles).

References

1. Apel, S., Kaestner, C., Lengauer, C.: Research challenges in the tension between features and services. In: Proceedings of the 2nd International Workshop on Systems Development in SOA Environments, pp. 53–58. ACM (2008)
2. Arsanjani, A., Ghosh, S., Allam, A., Abdollah, T., Ganapathy, S., Holley, K.: SOMA: a method for developing service-oriented solutions. IBM Syst. J. **47**(3), 377–396 (2008)
3. Asadi, M., Bagheri, E., Gašević, D., Hatala, M., Mohabbati, B.: Goal-driven software product line engineering. In: SAC '11, pp. 691–698. ACM, NY, USA (2011)

4. Asikainen, T., Soininen, T., Männistö, T.: A Koala-based approach for modelling and deploying configurable software product families, pp. 225–249. Software Product-Family Engineering (2004)
5. Bachmann, F., Goedicke, M., Leite, J., Nord, R., Pohl, K., Ramesh, B., Vilbig, A.: A meta-model for representing variability in product family development, pp. 66–80. Software Product-Family Engineering (2004)
6. Benatallah, B., Nezhad, H.M.: Service oriented architecture: overview and directions. In: Advances in Software Engineering, Lecture Notes in Computer Science, vol. 5316, pp. 116–130. Springer, Berlin (2008)
7. Benavides, D., Segura, S., Cortés, A.R.: Automated analysis of feature models 20 years later: a literature review. Inf. Syst. **35**(6), 615–636 (2010)
8. Bussler, C.: The fractal nature of web services. Computer **40**, 93–95 (2007)
9. Chang, S.H., Kim, S.D.: A variability modeling method for adaptable services in service-oriented computing. In: SPLC '07: Proceedings of the 11th International Software Product Line Conference, pp. 261–268. IEEE Computer Society, DC, USA (2007)
10. Chen, F., Li, S., Chu, W.C.C.: Feature analysis for service-oriented reengineering. In: APSEC '05: Proceedings of the 12th Asia-Pacific Software Engineering Conference, pp. 201–208. IEEE Computer Society (2005)
11. Chen, L., Ali Babar, M., Ali, N.: Variability management in software product lines: a systematic review. In: Proceedings of the 13th International Software Product Line Conference, pp. 81–90. CMU (2009)
12. Clements, P., Northrop, L.: Software Product Lines: Practices and Patterns. Addison-Wesley, Reading (2001)
13. Cohen, S.G., Krut, R.: Managing variation in services in a software product line context. Technical Report SEI-2010-TN-007, CMU (2010)
14. Cohen, S.G.S., Krut, R.W.: Proceedings of the 1st workshop on service-oriented architectures and product lines: what is the connection? Technical Report CMU/SEI-2008-SR-006 (2008)
15. Czarnecki, K.: Mapping features to models: a template approach based on superimposed variants. In: GPCE 2005, pp. 422–437. Springer (2005)
16. Czarnecki, K., Eisenecker, U.: Generative Programming: Methods, Tools, and Applications. Addison-Wesley Professional, Reading (2000)
17. Czarnecki, K., Helsen, S., Eisenecker, U.: Formalizing cardinality-based feature models and their specialization. Softw. Process: Improve. Pract. **10**(1), 7–29 (2005)
18. Czarnecki, K., Helsen, S., Eisenecker, U.W.: Staged configuration through specialization and multilevel configuration of feature models. Softw. Process: Improve. Pract. **10**(2), 143–169 (2005)
19. Eriksson, M., Börstler, J., Borg, K.: The PLUSS approach—domain modeling with features, use cases and use case realizations, pp. 33–44. SPLC (2005)
20. Erl, T.: Service-Oriented Architecture: Concepts, Technology, and Design. Prentice Hall PTR, Upper Saddle River (2005)
21. Fantinato, M., de Toledo, M.B.F., de Souza Gimenes, I.M.: Ws-contract establishment with QoS: an approach based on feature modeling. Int. J. Cooperative Inf. Syst. **17**(3), 373–407 (2008)
22. Frakes, W.B., Kang, K.: Software reuse research: status and future. IEEE Trans. Softw. Eng. **31**, 529–536 (2005)
23. Galster, M.: Describing variability in service-oriented software product lines. In: Proceedings of the Fourth European Conference on Software Architecture: Companion Volume, pp. 344–350 (2010)
24. Gomaa, H.: Advances in software design methods for concurrent, real-time and distributed applications. In: Software Engineering Advances, 2008. ICSEA'08. The 3rd International Conference on, pp. 451–456. IEEE (2008)
25. Griss, M.L., Favaro, J., Alessandro, M.d.: Integrating feature modeling with the RSEB. In: Proceedings of the 5th International Conference on Software Reuse, ICSR '98, p. 76. IEEE Computer Society, Washington, DC, USA (1998)

26. Helferich, A., Herzwurm, G., Jesse, S., Mikusz, M.: Software product lines, service-oriented architecture and frameworks: worlds apart or ideal partners? In: Trends in Enterprise Application Architecture, pp. 187–201. IEEE Computer Society (2007)
27. van der Hoek, A.: Design-time product line architectures for any-time variability. Sci. Comput. Program. **53**(3), 285–304 (2004)
28. Huhns, M., Singh, M.: Service-oriented computing: key concepts and principles. IEEE Internet Comput. **9**(1), 75–81 (2005)
29. Kang, K., Cohen, S., Hess, J., Novak, W., Peterson, A.: Feature-oriented domain analysis (FODA) feasibility study (1990)
30. Kang, K., Kim, S., Lee, J., Kim, K., Shin, E., Huh, M.: FORM: a feature-oriented reuse method with domain-specific reference architectures. Ann. Softw. Eng. **5**, 143–168 (1998)
31. Kästner, C., Apel, S., Kuhlemann, M.: Granularity in software product lines. In: Proceedings of the 30th International Conference on Software Engineering, pp. 311–320. ACM (2008)
32. Koning, M., Sun, C., Sinnema, M., Avgeriou, P.: VxBPEL: supporting variability for Web services in BPEL. Inf. Softw. Technol. **51**(2), 258–269 (2009)
33. Kozaczynski, W., Booch, G.: Component-based software engineering. IEEE Softw. **15**(5), 34–36 (1998)
34. Krafzig, D., Banke, K., Slama, D.: Enterprise SOA: Service-Oriented Architecture Best Practices. Prentice Hall PTR, Englewood Cliffs (2005)
35. Krut, R.W., Cohen, S.G.: 2nd Workshop on Service-Oriented Architectures and Software Product Lines: Putting Both Together, pp. 115–147. CMU (2009)
36. Krut, R.W., Cohen, S.G.: 3rd Workshop on Service-Oriented Architectures and Software Product Lines: Enhancing Variation, pp. 301–302. CMU (2009)
37. Lee, J., Kotonya, G.: Combining service-orientation with product line engineering. IEEE Softw. **27**, 35–41 (2010)
38. Lee, J., Muthig, D., Naab, M.: A feature-oriented approach for developing reusable product line assets of service-based systems. J. Syst. Softw. **83**(7), 1123–1136 (2010)
39. McGregor, J., Muthig, D., Yoshimura, K., Jensen, P.: Guest editors' introduction: successful software product line practices. IEEE Softw. **27**(3), 16–21 (2010)
40. Mohabbati, B., Gašević, D., Hatala, M., Asadi, M., Bagheri, E., Bošković, M.: A quality aggregation model for service-oriented software product lines based on variability and composition patterns. In: ICSOC, pp. 436–451 (2011)
41. Mohabbati, B., Hatala, M., Gašević, D., Asadi, M., Bošković, M.: Development and configuration of service-oriented systems families. SAC '11, pp. 1606–1613, NY, USA (2011)
42. Nguyen, T., Colman, A.: A feature-oriented approach for Web service customization. In: 2010 IEEE International Conference on Web Services, pp. 393–400. IEEE (2010)
43. Nguyen, T., Colman, A., Han, J.: Modeling and managing variability in process-based service compositions. In: Proceedings of the 9th International Conference on Service-Oriented Computing, ICSOC'11, pp. 404–420. Springer, Berlin (2011)
44. Northrop, L.: Sei's software product line tenets. IEEE Softw. **19**(4), 32–40 (2002)
45. van Ommering, R.: Building product populations with software components. In: ICSE '02, pp. 255–265. ACM (2002)
46. Papazoglou, M., Traverso, P., Dustdar, S., Leymann, F.: Service-oriented computing: a research roadmap. Int. J. Cooperative Inf. Syst. **17**(2), 223–255 (2008)
47. Papazoglou, M., Van Den Heuvel, W.: Service-oriented design and development methodology. Int. J. Web Eng. Technol. **2**(4), 412–442 (2006)
48. Papazoglou, M.P.: Service-oriented computing: concepts, characteristics and directions. Web Information Systems Engineering, International Conference on, vol. 0, p. 3 (2003)
49. Pohl, K., Böckle, G., van der Linden, F.J.: Software Product Line Engineering: Foundations, Principles and Techniques. Springer, New York (2005)
50. Sinnema, M., Deelstra, S., Nijhuis, J., Bosch, J.: COVAMOF: A framework for modeling variability in software product families. SPLC'04 pp. 25–27 (2004)
51. Sochos, P., Riebisch, M.: Feature-oriented development of software product lines: mapping feature models to the architecture. In: Object-Oriented and Internet-Based Technologies, pp. 138–152. Springer (2004)

52. Sommerville, I., Sawyer, P.: Requirements Engineering. Wiley, London (1997)
53. Street, J., Gomaa, H.: Software architectural reuse issues in service-oriented architectures. In: HICSS, p. 316. IEEE Computer Society (2008)
54. Svahnberg, M., Van Gurp, J., Bosch, J.: A taxonomy of variability realization techniques. Softw.: Pract. Exp. **35**(8), 705–754 (2005)
55. Thiel, S., Hein, A.: Systematic integration of variability into product line architecture design. Software Product Lines, pp. 67–102 (2002)
56. Tsai, W., Jin, Z., Wang, P., Wu, B.: Requirement engineering in service-oriented system engineering. In: e-Business Engineering, 2007. ICEBE 2007. IEEE International Conference on, pp. 661–668. IEEE (2007)
57. Van Gurp, J., Bosch, J., Svahnberg, M.: On the notion of variability in software product lines. In: Proceedings of the Working IEEE/IFIP Conference on Software Architecture, p. 45 (2001)
58. Webber, D.L., Gomaa, H.: Modeling variability in software product lines with the variation point model. Sci. Comput. Program. **53**(3), 305–331 (2004)
59. Ye, E., Moon, M., Kim, Y., Yeom, K.: An approach to designing service-oriented product-line architecture for business process families. In: Advanced Communication Technology, The 9th International Conference on, vol. 2, pp. 1002, 999 (2007)

Chapter 22
QoS-Aware Web Service Recommendation via Collaborative Filtering

Xi Chen, Zibin Zheng and Michael R. Lyu

Abstract With the increasing number of Web services on the Internet, selecting appropriate services to build one's application becomes a nontrivial issue. When searching Web services, users are often overwhelmed by a bunch of candidates with similar functionalities. Quality-of-Service (QoS), the non-functional characteristics of Web services, has become an important factor to distinguish the functionally equivalent ones. In this paper, we introduce two collaborative filtering based Web service recommendation approaches to help users select Web service with optimal QoS performance. The basic idea is to leverage user experience provided by similar users and generate recommendation for the target user. Experiments with large scale real world Web services show the effectiveness and efficiency of the two approaches.

22.1 Introduction

Web service, a method of communication between two machines over a network, has been widely adopted as a delivery mode in both industry and academia. This adoption has fostered a new paradigm shift from development of monolithic application to the dynamic set-up of business process. The increasing usage of Web services on the World Wide Web calls for effective recommendation techniques, which help end

X. Chen
Schlumberger Technologies (Beijing) Ltd., Beijing, China
e-mail: bargittachen@gmail.com

Z. Zheng (✉) · M. R. Lyu
Department of Computer Science and Engineering, The Chinese University of Hong Kong, Shatin, Hong Kong, China
e-mail: zbzheng@cse.cuhk.edu.hk

M. R. Lyu
e-mail: lyu@cse.cuhk.edu.hk

A. Bouguettaya et al. (eds.), *Web Services Foundations*,
DOI: 10.1007/978-1-4614-7518-7_22,
© Springer Science+Business Media New York 2014

users choose the optimal Web service from a large number of functionally equivalent candidates.

In services computing, QoS is a set of properties describing the non-functional characteristics of Web services, such as price, response time, reliability, etc. Some QoS properties have relatively constant value, e.g., the published pricing model of Amazon Web Service (AWS), while other properties like response time vary seriously from user to user, influenced by the unpredictable Internet connections and heterogeneous environments. In this chapter, we focus on the QoS properties that are prone to change and can be easily obtained and objectively measured by individual users, such as response time and availability.

QoS plays an important role in service selection and recommendation [37, 36]. However, it is impractical for users to acquire QoS information by evaluating all the service candidates by themselves. Conducting real world Web service invocation is time-consuming and resource-consuming. Moreover, measuring some QoS properties (e.g., *reliability*) requires long time observation and large number of invocations. Besides client-side evaluation, acquiring QoS information from service providers may not be applicable, because QoS performance is susceptible to the uncertain Internet environment and user context (e.g., user location, user network condition, etc.). Therefore, QoS values evaluated by one user cannot be used directly by another in service selection and recommendation.

To make personalized QoS-aware service recommendation to different users, we introduce two collaborative filtering (CF) based Web service recommendation algorithms in this chapter. Our Web service recommender system collects user observed QoS records and matches together users who share the same information needs or same tastes [10]. Users of our recommender system share their observed QoS performance of Web services, and in return, the system provides accurate personalized service recommendations for them. Section 22.2 and Sect. 22.3 present our proposed recommendation approaches; Sect. 22.4 shows our large scale real world experiments; Sect. 22.5 discusses related work, and Sect. 22.6 concludes our work.

22.2 WSRec: A Neighborhood-Based Web Service Recommendation Algorithm

WSRec employs the concept of *user-collaboration* for Web service QoS information sharing between service users. Similar to sharing videos on *YouTube* or knowledge on *Wikipedia*, service users are encouraged to contribute their past Web service user experience to the system. We assume that users are trustworthy, and all submitted records are correct. The more QoS records users contribute, the more accurate the recommendation will be. Figure 22.1 shows the architecture of WSRec system, which includes the following procedures:

- A service user submits Web service QoS data to the centralized server of WSRec. Users who submit QoS records to WSRec are called *training users*. Users who

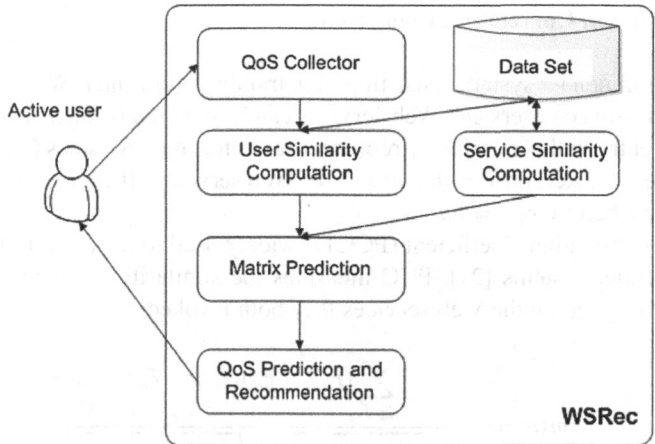

Fig. 22.1 Procedures of QoS value prediction

Table 22.1 An illustration of response time dataset

User	Service 1	Service 2	Service 3	Service 4	Service 5	Service 6	Service 7
Amy	5000 ms	?	2000 ms	?	?	?	2800 ms
Bob	600 ms	3300 ms	?	3300 ms	2000 ms	?	?
Carol	650 ms	2600 ms	200 ms	?	?	?	?
David	600 ms	2500 ms	2000 ms	5000 ms	?	2000 ms	?

require Web service recommendation are called *active users*. Table 22.1 shows an example of the recommendation system data set. There are four users and seven services in the data set. Each user provides some QoS values (response time) they observed, and ? indicates that the user does not use the service.

- WSRec matches the active user with existing training users to find similar users and Web services with similar QoS (details will be introduced in Sect. 22.2.1).
- WSRec predicts QoS values of candidate Web services for the active user (details will be introduced in Sect. 22.2.2).
- WSRec makes Web service recommendation based on the predicted QoS values of Web services (details will be discussed in Sect. 22.2.3).
- The active user receives the predicted QoS values as well as the recommendation results, which can be employed to assist decision making (e.g., service selection, service composition, service ranking, etc.).

22.2.1 Similarity Computation

Similarity computation is used to find users with similar experience as well as Web services with similar QoS in the WSRec system.

22.2.1.1 Pearson Correlation Coefficient

Given a recommender system consisting of m training users and n Web services, the relationship between users and Web services can be denoted by an $m \times n$ user-item matrix. An entry in this matrix $r_{u,i}$ represents a vector of QoS values (e.g., response time, failure rate, etc.) observed by user u of Web service i. If user u has never used Web service i before, $r_{u,i} = null$.

Pearson Correlation Coefficient (PCC) is widely used to measure user similarity in recommender systems [21]. PCC measures the similarity between two service users a and u based on the Web services they both invoked:

$$Sim(a, u) = \frac{\sum_{i \in I} (r_{a,i} - \overline{r}_a)(r_{u,i} - \overline{r}_u)}{\sqrt{\sum_{i \in I} (r_{a,i} - \overline{r}_a)^2} \sqrt{\sum_{i \in I} (r_{u,i} - \overline{r}_u)^2}}, \tag{22.1}$$

where $I = I_a \cap I_u$ is the set of Web services invoked by both user a and user u, $r_{a,i}$ is the QoS values of Web service i observed by service user a, $\overline{r}_a$ and $\overline{r}_u$ represent the average QoS values observed by service user a and u respectively. The PCC similarity of two service users, $Sim(a, u)$ ranges from -1 to 1. Positive PCC value indicates that the two users have similar preferences, while negative PCC value means that the two user preferences are opposite. $Sim(a, u) = null$ when two users have no Web service intersection.

PCC is used to measure the similarity between Web services in WSRec as well. The similarity computation of two Web services i and j can be calculated by:

$$Sim(i, j) = \frac{\sum_{u \in U} (r_{u,i} - \overline{r}_i)(r_{u,j} - \overline{r}_j)}{\sqrt{\sum_{u \in U} (r_{u,i} - \overline{r}_i)^2} \sqrt{\sum_{u \in U} (r_{u,j} - \overline{r}_j)^2}}, \tag{22.2}$$

where $Sim(i, j)$ is the similarity between Web services i and j, $U = U_i \cap U_j$ is the set of users who have invoked both Web services i and j, $\overline{r}_i$ represents the average QoS values of Web service i submitted by all users. The range of $Sim(i, j)$ is $[-1, 1]$. $Sim(i, j) = null$ when there is no user who have used both services.

22.2.1.2 Significance Weight

PCC only considers the QoS difference between services invoked by both users. It can overestimate the similarity of two users that are not similar, but happen to have a few services with very similar QoS records [21]. To devalue the overestimated similarity, we add a correlation significance weight to PCC. An adjusted PCC for user similarity is defined as:

$$Sim'(a, u) = \frac{2 \times |I_a \cap I_u|}{|I_a| + |I_u|} Sim(a, u), \tag{22.3}$$

where $Sim'(a, u)$ is the adjusted similarity value, $|I_a \cap I_u|$ is the number of services invoked by both users (co-invoked services), $|I_a|$ and $|I_u|$ are the number of Web services invoked by user a and user u, respectively. When the number of co-invoked Web service $|I_a \cap I_u|$ is small, the significance weight $\frac{2 \times |I_a \cap I_u|}{|I_a| + |I_u|}$ will decrease the similarity estimation between users a and u. Since the value of $\frac{2 \times |I_a \cap I_u|}{|I_a| + |I_u|}$ is in the interval of $[0, 1]$, $Sim(a, u)$ is in the interval of $[-1, 1]$, the value of $Sim'(a, u)$ is in the interval of $[-1, 1]$.

Similar to Eq. (22.3), an adjusted PCC for the Web service similarity is defined as:

$$Sim'(i, j) = \frac{2 \times |U_i \cap U_j|}{|U_i| + |U_j|} Sim(i, j), \tag{22.4}$$

where $|U_i \cap U_j|$ is the number of service users who invoked both Web services i and j. The range of $Sim'(i, j)$ is $[-1, 1]$.

22.2.2 QoS Value Prediction

In reality, the user-item matrix is usually very sparse, since service users usually have QoS values on a small number of services. Predicting missing values for the user-item matrix can improve the prediction accuracy of active users. In this section, we present a missing value prediction approach to tackle this problem by making the matrix denser.

22.2.2.1 Neighbor Selection

To predict missing values, we first need to find the underlying relationship between the missing values and the existing ones, and then use this information to predict the missing ones. In the user-item matrix of WSRec system, each missing entry $r_{u,i}$ is associated with two sets of neighbors: a set of similar users $S(u)$ and a set of similar items (services) $S(i)$, which can be found by the following equations:

$$S(u) = \{u_a | u_a \in T(u), Sim'(u_a, u) > 0, u_a \neq u\}, \tag{22.5}$$
$$S(i) = \{i_k | i_k \in T(i), Sim'(i_k, i) > 0, i_k \neq i\}, \tag{22.6}$$

where $T(u)$ is a set of similar users to the user u, and $T(i)$ is a set of similar items to the item i. Both $T(u)$ and $T(i)$ are selected using enhanced PCC (Eq. (22.3) and

Eq. (22.4)). Neighbors without correlations or with negative ones are discarded from the neighbor sets.

22.2.2.2 Missing Value Prediction

For each missing entry, we use both its user neighbors and item neighbors to predict the missing value. User-based CF methods (UPCC) employ similar users to predict the missing QoS values:

$$\widehat{r_{u,i}} = \overline{u} + \frac{\sum\limits_{u_a \in S(u)} Sim'(u_a, u)(r_{u_a,i} - \overline{u}_a)}{\sum\limits_{u_a \in S(u)} Sim'(u_a, u)}, \tag{22.7}$$

where $\widehat{r_{u,i}}$ is the predicted QoS vector of service i for user u, $\overline{u}$ and $\overline{u}_a$ are vectors of average QoS values of all Web services observed by active user u and neighbor user u_a respectively.

Item-based CF methods (IPCC) [8, 17, 27] apply similar Web services to predict the missing value:

$$\widehat{r_{u,i}} = \overline{i} + \frac{\sum\limits_{i_k \in S(i)} Sim'(i_k, i)(r_{u,i_k} - \overline{i}_k)}{\sum\limits_{i_k \in S(i)} Sim'(i_k, i)}, \tag{22.8}$$

where $\overline{i}$ is a vector of average QoS values of Web service i observed by all service users.

When a missing entry only has user neighbors or item neighbors, we will employ either Eqs. (22.7) or (22.8) to predict the value. When it has both type of neighbors, we combine the two methods to make prediction. We will not predict the value if it has no neighbors.

User-based method and item-based method may have different prediction accuracy, we use *confidence weights*, con_u and con_i, to reflect our confidence in the two prediction methods. For example, assuming a missing entry has three similar users with PCC similarities $\{1, 1, 1\}$ and three similar items with $\{0.1, 0.1, 0.1\}$. Intuitively, we have more confidence in the prediction by user-based method rather than item-based one. We define con_u as:

$$con_u = \sum\limits_{u_a \in S(u)} \frac{Sim'(u_a, u)}{\sum_{u_a \in S(u)} Sim'(u_a, u)} \times Sim'(u_a, u), \tag{22.9}$$

and con_i as:

$$con_i = \sum_{i_k \in S(i)} \frac{Sim'(i_k, i)}{\sum_{i_k \in S(i)} Sim'(i_k, i)} \times Sim'(i_k, i), \tag{22.10}$$

where con_u and con_i are the prediction confidences of the user-based method and item-based method respectively. The higher the value, the more confidence we have in the predicted value $\widehat{r_{u,i}}$.

Since different datasets may inherit their own data distribution and correlation natures, a parameter λ $(0 \le \lambda \le 1)$ is employed to tune the the final result combining both user-based method and item-based method. When $S(u) \ne \emptyset \wedge S(i) \ne \emptyset$, our method predicts the missing QoS value $r_{u,i}$ by employing the following equation:

$$\widehat{r_{u,i}} = w_u \times \left(\bar{u} + \frac{\sum\limits_{u_a \in S(u)} Sim'(u_a, u)(r_{u_a,i} - \bar{u}_a)}{\sum\limits_{u_a \in S(u)} Sim'(u_a, u)} \right)$$
$$+ w_i \times \left(\bar{i} + \frac{\sum\limits_{i_k \in S(i)} Sim'(i_k, i)(r_{u,i_k} - \bar{i}_k)}{\sum\limits_{i_k \in S(i)} Sim'(i_k, i)} \right), \tag{22.11}$$

where w_u and w_i are the weights of the user-based method and the item-based method respectively ($w_u + w_i = 1$). w_u is defined as:

$$w_u = \frac{con_u \times \lambda}{con_u \times \lambda + con_i \times (1 - \lambda)}, \tag{22.12}$$

and w_i is defined as:

$$w_i = \frac{con_i \times (1 - \lambda)}{con_u \times \lambda + con_i \times (1 - \lambda)}. \tag{22.13}$$

The prediction confidence of the missing value $\widehat{r_{u,i}}$ by our approach using Eq. (22.11) can be calculated by equation:

$$con = w_u \times con_u + w_i \times con_i. \tag{22.14}$$

22.2.3 Recommendation for Active Users

We use the matrix with predicted missing values to generate recommendations for active users. We first predict Web service QoS values for the active user, which is similar to the missing value prediction in Sect. 22.2.2.2. The only difference is that when $S(u) = \emptyset \wedge S(i) = \emptyset$, we predict the QoS values with user-mean (UMEAN) and item-mean (IMEAN). UMEAN is a vector of average QoS values of all the Web services observed by the active user a and IMEAN is a vector of average QoS values of Web service i observed by all service users. The prediction formula is defined as:

$$\widehat{r_{a,i}} = w_u \times \bar{r}_a + w_i \times \bar{r}_i, \tag{22.15}$$

where $\bar{r}_a$ is the average QoS submitted by user a, and $\bar{r}_i$ is the average QoS of service i. In this case, the confidence of the predicted value is $con = 0$.

The predicted QoS values can be used in the following ways: (1) For a set of functionally equivalent Web services, the one with optimal predicted QoS values is recommended to the active user. (2) For Web services with different functionalities, the top k best performing ones will be recommended to service users to help them discover potential Web services.

22.2.4 Time Complexity Analysis

Worst-case analysis of the QoS value prediction algorithm is presented in this section. The input is a full user-item matrix with m users and n Web services.

22.2.4.1 Time Complexity of Similarity Computation

In Sect. 22.2.1, the time complexity of user similarity $Sim(a, u)$ is $O(n)$, since there are at most n intersected services between user a and u. The time complexity of service similarity $Sim(i, j)$ is $O(m)$ with at most m users who used both Web service i and j.

22.2.4.2 Time Complexity of UPCC

To predict missing values with UPCC (Eq. 22.7), we need to first compute similarities of the active user with all users in the matrix (totally m similarity computations). As discussed in Sect. 22.2.4.1, the time complexity of each similarity computation is $O(n)$. Therefore, the complexity of similarity computation is $O(mn)$.

The time complexity of each missing value prediction is $O(m)$, since at most m similar users are employed in the prediction. The complexity of the value prediction for an active user is $O(mn)$ with at most n missing values. Thus the time complexity of UPCC (including similarity computation and value prediction) is $O(mn)$.

22.2.4.3 Time Complexity of IPCC

To predict missing values with IPCC (Eq. (22.8)), we need to compute similarities of the current Web service with all Web services in the matrix (totally n similarity computations). As discussed in Sect. 22.2.4.1, the time complexity of each similarity computation is $O(m)$. Therefore, the complexity of similarity computation is $O(mn)$.

The missing value prediction computational complexity is $O(n)$, since at most n similar Web services are employed for prediction. The complexity of the value prediction for a Web service is $O(mn)$ with at most m users. Therefore, the time complexity of IPCC is $O(mn)$.

22.2.4.4 Time Complexity of Training Matrix Prediction

Training matrix prediction is an offline process, which helps reduce the sparseness of the training matrix and improve the prediction accuracy (Sect. 22.2.2.2). This process is a linear combination of UPCC and IPCC. For UPCC approach, the computational complexity is $O(m^2n)$, since there are at most m rows (users) need prediction. For IPCC approach, the complexity is $O(mn^2)$, because there are at most n columns (Web services) to be predicted. Therefore, the time complexity of matrix prediction is $O(m^2n + mn^2)$.

22.2.4.5 Time Complexity of Active User Prediction

As discussed in Sect. 22.2.4.2, the computational complexity of UPCC for predicting values of an active user is $O(mn)$. When employing IPCC, the similarities of different columns (Web services) can be computed offline, and there are at most n missing values in the active user. For the prediction of each missing value, the computational complexity is $O(n)$, since at most n similar Web services will be employed for the prediction. Therefore, the computational complexity of IPCC for an active user is $O(n^2)$. Since our online QoS value prediction approach is a linear combination of UPCC and IPCC, the complexity of our approach for an active user is $O(mn + n^2)$.

22.3 A Region-Based Web Service Recommendation Algorithm

We present a region-based Web service recommendation algorithm in this section. The main hypothesis is that some QoS properties vary according to users' physical locations. Through the analysis of a real world Web service data set (see Sect. 22.4), which contains 1.5 millions service invocation records evaluated by users from more than twenty countries, we discover that some QoS properties like response time highly relate to users' physical locations. For example, the response time of a service observed by users who are closely located with each other usually fluctuates mildly around a certain value, while it sometimes varies significantly between users far away from each other.

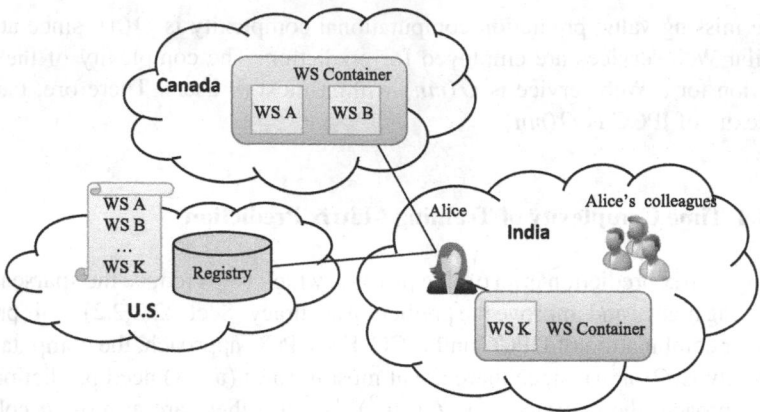

Fig. 22.2 A motivating scenario

22.3.1 A Motivating Scenario

Alice is a software engineer working in India. She needs an email validation service to filter emails. By querying a registry in U.S, she gets a list of service candidates and sorts the services in ascending order of the response time. Alice then tries the first two services provided by a Canadian company. However, she finds that the response time is much higher than her expectation. She then realizes that the response time is based on the evaluation conducted by servers in U.S., and it can vary greatly due to different user contexts, such as user location, user network conditions, etc. Alice then turns to her colleagues for suggestion. They suggest a local service though ranked lower in the previous search result. After trying it, Alice finds that that service has good performance and meets her requirements.

Intuitively, users closely located with each other are more likely to have similar service experience than those who are far away from each other. Our recommendation approach is designed as a two-phase process. In the first phase, we divide users into different regions based on their physical locations and historical Web service QoS experience. In the second phase, we find similar users for the active user, make QoS predictions for the unused services, and finally recommend the one with best predicted value to the user.

22.3.2 Phase One: Region Creation

A *region* is defined as a group of users who are closely located with each other and likely to have similar QoS profiles. Each user is a member of exactly one region. Regions need to be internally coherent, but clearly different from each other. To create regions, we first form small regions by putting users with similar locations

together and extract region features. Then we aggregate highly correlated regions
to form a certain number of large regions. Steps to create regions are presented in
Sect. 22.3.2.1–22.3.2.2 respectively.

22.3.2.1 Region Features

Region center is used to reflect the average performance of Web services observed
by users of one region. Region center is defined as the median vector of all QoS
vectors associated with the region users. The element i of the center is the median
QoS value of service i observed by users from the region. Median is the numeric
value separating the higher half of a sample from the lower half. Besides the average
Web service QoS performance, QoS fluctuation is another feature deserves our attention. From large real data analysis, we discover that user-dependent QoS properties
(e.g., response time) usually varies from region to region. Some services have unexpected long response time, and some are even inaccessible to a few regions. Inspired
by the three-sigma rule which is often used to test outliers, we use similar method to
distinguish services with unstable performance and regard them as region-sensitive
services.

We pick one QoS property r (response time) to simplify the description of this
approach. The set of non-zero QoS values of service s, $r_{.s} = \{r_{1,s}, r_{2,s}, \ldots, r_{k,s}\}$,
$1 \leq k \leq m$, collected from users of all regions is a sample from the population of
service s QoS property R. To estimate the mean μ and the standard deviation σ of
the population, we use two robust measures: median and Median Absolute Deviation
(MAD). MAD is defined as the median of the absolute deviations from the sample's
median.

$$MAD = median_i(|r_{i,s} - median_j(r_{j,s})|), i = 1, \ldots, k, j = 1, \ldots, k \quad (22.16)$$

Based on median and MAD, the two estimators can be calculated by:

$$\widehat{\mu} = median_i(r_{i,s}), i = 1, \ldots, k \quad (22.17)$$
$$\widehat{\sigma} = MAD_i(r_{i,s}), i = 1, \ldots, k \quad (22.18)$$

Definition 22.1 Let $r_{.s} = \{r_{1,s}, r_{2,s}, \ldots, r_{k,s}\}$, $1 \leq k \leq m$ be the set of Web service
s QoS values provided by all users. Service s is a sensitive service to region M
iff $\exists r_{j,s} \in r_{.s}((r_{j,s} > \widehat{\mu} + 3\widehat{\sigma}) \wedge region(j) = M)$, where $\widehat{\mu} = median(r_{.s})$,
$\widehat{\sigma} = MAD(r_{.s})$ and $region(u)$ function defines the region of user u.

Definition 22.2 The sensitivity of region r_m is the fraction between the number of
sensitive services in region r_m over the total number of services.

Definition 22.3 Region r_m is a sensitive region iff its region sensitivity exceeds the
sensitivity threshold λ.

22.3.2.2 Region Aggregation

Each region formed by users' physical locations at the outset always has a very sparse QoS dataset, since the amounts of users and QoS records are relatively small. In this case, it is difficult to find similar users and predict missing QoS records. To solve this problem, we aggregate these small regions based on the similarity of their features. The similarity of two regions r_m and r_n is measured by the similarity of their region centers c_{r_m} and c_{r_n} using Eq. (22.3).

We use a bottom-up hierarchical clustering algorithm to aggregate regions [20]. The input is a set of small regions $r_1, \ldots, r_l$. Each region consists of users with similar locations. The algorithm successively aggregates pairs of the most similar non-sensitive regions until the stopping criterion is met. The result is stored as a list of aggregates in A.

Step one: Initialization

1. Compute the similarity between each two regions with Eq. (22.3), store the similarity and the similar region index in the similarity matrix C.
2. Calculate the sensitivity of each region and identify whether it can be aggregated. Store the result in the indicator vector I. $I[k].sensitivity$ indicates whether region k is sensitive, and $I[k].aggregate$ indicates whether region k can be aggregated.
3. Use a set of priority queues P to sort the rows of C in decreasing order of the similarity. Function $P[k].MAX()$ returns the index of the region that is most similar to region k.

Step two: Aggregation

1. In each iteration, select the two most similar and non-sensitive regions from the priority queues if their similarity exceeds threshold μ, otherwise return A.
2. Aggregate the selected two regions and store their region index in result list A. Use the smaller region index of the two as the new region index and compute the new region center. Mark the indicator vector I of the aggregated region.
3. Calculate the sensitivity of the new region and set indicator I. If it is sensitive and cannot be aggregated, remove this region from other regions' priority queues. Otherwise, update the elements of both priority queues and similarity matrix related to the aggregated two regions. Repeat the above three steps.

22.3.3 Phase Two: QoS Prediction and Recommendation

The region aggregation step clusters thousands of users into a certain number of regions based on their physical locations and historical QoS similarities. With the compressed QoS data, searching neighbors and making predictions for an active user can be computed faster than the conventional methods. Instead of computing the similarity between the active user and each existing user, we only compute the similarity

---

Algorithm 1: Region Aggregation Algorithm

Input: a list of regions $r_1, \ldots r_l$
Output: result list A
foreach $n \leftarrow 1$ *to* $l - 1$ **do**
   foreach $i \leftarrow n + 1$ *to* N **do**
      $C[n][i].sim \leftarrow SIM(r_n, r_i)$;
      $C[n][i].index \leftarrow i$;
   $I[n].sensitivity \leftarrow ISSENSITIVE(r_n)$;
   if $I[n].sensitivity = 0$ **then**
      $I[n].aggregate \leftarrow 1$;
   $I[n].aggregate \leftarrow 0$;
   $P[n] \leftarrow$ priority queue for $C[n]$ sorted on sim;
calculate the sensitivity and aggregate of $I[l]$;
$A \leftarrow []$;
while *true* **do**
   $k_1 \leftarrow argmax_{k:I[k].aggregate=1} P[k].MAX().sim$;
   if $k_1 = null$ *or* $sim < \mu$ **then**
      return A;
   $k_2 \leftarrow P[k_1].MAX().index$;
   $A.APPEND(< k_1, k_2 >)$ and compute k_1 center;
   $I[k_2].aggregate \leftarrow 0$;
   $P[k_1] \leftarrow []$;
   $I[k_1].sensitivity \leftarrow ISSENSITIVE(k_1)$;
   if $I[k_1].sensitivity = 1$ **then**
      $I[k_1].aggregate \leftarrow 0$;
      foreach i *with* $I[i].aggregate = 1$ **do**
         $P[i].DELETE(C[i][k_1])$;
         $P[i].DELETE(C[i][k_2])$;
   else
   foreach i *with* $I[i].aggregate = 1 \wedge i \neq k_1$ **do**
      $P[i].DELETE(C[i][k_1])$;
      $P[i].DELETE(C[i][k_2])$;
      $C[i][k_1].sim \leftarrow SIM(i, k_1)$;
      $P[i].INSERT(C[i][k_1])$;
      $C[k_1][i].sim \leftarrow SIM(i, k_1)$;
      $P[k_1].INSERT(C[k_1][i])$;

---

between the active user and each region center. Moreover, it is more reasonable to predict the QoS value based on one's region, for users in the same region are more likely to have similar QoS experience on the same Web service, especially on those region-sensitive ones. To predict the unused Web service s's QoS value for an active user a, we take the following steps:

- Find the region of the active user a by IP address. If no appropriate region is found, the active user will be treated as a member of a new region.
- Identify whether service s is sensitive to user a's region. If region-sensitive, then the prediction is generated from the region center, because QoS of service s observed by users from this region is significantly different from others.

$$\widehat{r_{a,s}} = r_{c,s} \tag{22.19}$$

- Otherwise, use Eq. (22.3) to compute the similarity between the active user and each region center that has evaluated service s, and find up to k most similar centers $c_1, c_2, \ldots, c_k$. We discuss how to choose k (also called top k) in Sect. 22.4.
- If the active user's region center has QoS value of s, the prediction is computed using the following equation:

$$\widehat{r_{a,s}} = r_{c,s} + \frac{\sum_{j=1}^{k} Sim'(a, c_j)(r_{c_j,s} - \overline{r_{c_j}})}{\sum_{j=1}^{k} Sim'(a, c_j)} \tag{22.20}$$

where $r_{c_j,s}$ is the QoS of service s provided by center c_j, and $\overline{r_{c_j}}$ is the average QoS of center c_j. The prediction is composed of two parts. One is the QoS value of the active user's region center $r_{c,s}$, which denotes the average QoS of service s observed by this region users. The other part is the normalized weighted sum of the deviations of the k most similar neighbors.

- Otherwise, we use the service QoS observed by the k neighbors to compute the prediction. The more similar the active user a and the neighbor c_j are, the more weights the QoS of c_j will carry in the prediction.

$$\widehat{r_{a,s}} = \frac{\sum_{j=1}^{k} Sim'(a, c_j)r_{c_j,s}}{\sum_{j=1}^{k} Sim'(a, c_j)} \tag{22.21}$$

22.3.4 Time Complexity Analysis

We discuss the worst-case time complexity of the region-based Web service recommendation algorithm. We analyze the two phases, region creation and QoS value prediction respectively in Sect. 22.3.4.1 and 22.3.4.2. We assume the input is a full matrix with n users and m Web services.

22.3.4.1 Time Complexity of Region Creation

Time complexity of calculating the median and MAD of each service is $O(n \log n)$. For m services, the time complexity is $O(mn \log n)$. With MAD and median, we identify the region-sensitive services from the service perspective. Since there are at most n records for each service, the time complexity of each service is $O(n)$

using Definition 22.1. Therefore, the total time complexity of region-sensitive service identification is $O(mn \log n + mn) = O(mn \log n)$.

In terms of the region aggregation part, we assume there are l_0 regions in the beginning. Since there are at most m services used by both regions, the time complexity of the region similarity is $O(m)$ using Eq. (22.3), and the complexity for computing similarity matrix C is $O(l_0^2 m)$.

The aggregation of two regions will execute at most $l_0 - 1$ times, in case that all regions are non-sensitive, extremely correlate to each other and finally aggregate into one region. In each iteration, we first compare at most $l_0 - 1$ heads of the priority queues to find the most similar pairs. Since the number of regions that can be aggregated decreases with iteration, the real search time will be less than $l_0 - 1$ the following iterations. For the selected pair of regions, we calculate the new center and update their similar regions. Because the number of users involved in the two regions are uncertain, we use the number of all users as the upper bound and the complexity is $O(mn \log n)$. The insertion and deletion of a similar region is $O(\log l_0)$, since we employ the priority queue to sort similar regions. Thus, the time complexity is $O(l_0^2(\log l_0 + mn \log n)) = O(l_0^2 mn \log n)$.

As the above steps are linearly combined, the total time complexity of the offline part is $O(l_0^2 mn \log n)$.

22.3.4.2 Time Complexity of QoS Prediction

Let l_1 be the number of regions after the region creation. To predict QoS value for an active user, $O(l_1)$ similarity calculations between the active user and region centers are needed, each of which takes $O(m)$ time. Therefore the time complexity of similarity computation is $O(l_1 m)$.

For each service the active user has not evaluated, the QoS value prediction complexity is $O(l_1)$, because at most l_1 centers are employed in the prediction as Eqs. (22.20) and (22.21) state. There are at most m services without QoS values, so the time complexity of the prediction for an active user is $O(l_1 m)$. Thus the time complexity for online phase including similarity computation and missing value prediction is $O(l_1 m) \approx O(m)$ (l_1 is rather small compared to m or n). Compared to the memory-based CF algorithm used in previous work with $O(mn)$ online time-complexity, our approach is more efficient and well suited for large dataset.

22.4 Experiments

22.4.1 Experiment Setup

In this experiment, 21,197 publicly available Web services are crawled from three sources (1) well-known companies (e.g., *Google, Amazon, etc.*); (2) portals listing publicly available Web services (e.g., *xmethods.net, webservicex.net, etc.*); and (3)

Web service searching engines (e.g., *seekda.com, esynaps.com, etc.*). 18,102 Web services stubs with 343,917 Java classes are generated using *WSDL2Java* tool of *Axis2* package. Failures to generate client stub are mainly caused by *network connection problems* (e.g., connection timeout, HTTP 400, 401, 403, 500, 502 and 503), *FileNotFoundException* and *InvalidWSDLFiles*.

To monitor Web service performance, we randomly select 100 Web services located in 22 countries for our experiments. 150 computers in 24 countries from Planet-Lab [7] are employed to monitor and collect QoS information of the selected Web services. The result set contains about 1.5 millions Web service invocation records.

By processing the experimental results, we obtain a 150×100 user-item matrix, where each entry in the matrix is a vector including two QoS values, i.e., *response time* and *failure rate*. *Response time* represents the time duration between the client sending a request and receiving a response, while *failure rate* represents the ratio between the number of invocation failures and the total number of invocations. In our experiments, each service user invokes each Web service for 100 times. Figure 22.3a, b show the value distributions of *response time* and *failure rate* of the 15,000 entries in the matrix, respectively. Figure 22.3a shows that the means of response times of most entries are smaller than 5000 milliseconds and different Web service invocations contain large variances in real environment. Figure 22.3b shows that failure probabilities of most entries (85.68%) are less than 1%, while failure probabilities of a small part of entries (8.34%) are larger than 16%. We divide the 150 service users into two parts, one part as training users and the other part as active users. For the training matrix, we randomly remove entries to generate a series of sparse matrices (e.g., with density 10, 20%, ect.). For an active user, we also randomly remove several entries and name the number of remaining entries as *given number*, which denotes the number of entries (QoS values) provided by the active user. The original values of the removed entries are used as the expected values to study the prediction accuracy.

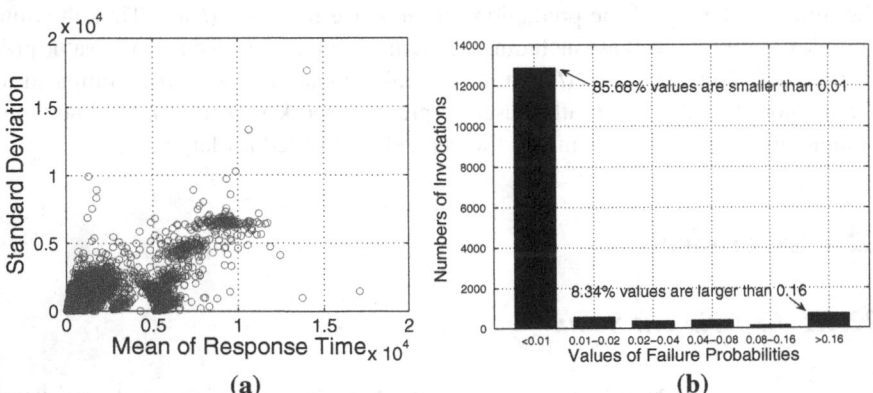

(a) (b)

Fig. 22.3 Value distributions of the user-item matrix

We use Mean Absolute Error (MAE) to measure the prediction quality of the recommendation algorithms. MAE is the average absolute deviation of predictions to the ground truth data. Smaller MAE indicates better prediction accuracy.

$$MAE = \frac{\sum_{i,j} |r_{i,j} - \widehat{r}_{i,j}|}{N},$$ (22.22)

where $r_{i,j}$ denotes the expected QoS value of Web service j observed by user i, $\widehat{r}_{i,j}$ is the predicted QoS value, and N is the number of predicted values. MAE reflects how close predictions are to the eventual outcomes on average, which gives an overview of the prediction quality.

22.4.2 WSRec Performance Evaluation

To study the prediction performance, we compare our approach (*WSRec*) with user-based prediction algorithm using PCC (*UPCC*) [3], and item-based algorithm using PCC (*IPCC*) [27]. UPCC employs similar users for QoS performance prediction (Eqs. (22.1) and (22.7)), while IPCC employs similar Web services for prediction (Eqs. (22.2) and (22.8)).

Table 22.2 shows the MAE result of different prediction methods on *response time* and *failure rate* employing matrices with 10, 20, and 30 % density. We vary the number of QoS values (*given number*) provided by the active user from 10, 20 to 30 (named as G10, G20, and G30 in Table 22.2). We also vary the number of training users as 100 and 140. We set $\lambda = 0.1$, since the item-based approach achieves better prediction accuracy than the user-based approach in our Web service QoS dataset. The detailed investigation of λ value setting will be shown in Sect. 22.4.2.2.

Table 22.2 MAE performance comparison (smaller MAE value means better prediction accuracy)

		Training users = 100									Training users = 140							
		Response time			Failure rate			Response time			Failure rate							
Den %	Method	G10	G20	G30	G10 %	G20 %	G30 %	G10	G20	G30	G10 %	G20 %	G30 %					
	UPCC	1148	877	810	4.85	4.20	3.86	968	782	684	4.11	3.47	3.28					
	IPCC	768	736	736	2.24	2.16	2.21	585	596	605	1.39	1.33	1.42					
10	**WSRec**	**758**	**700**	**672**	**2.21**	**2.08**	**2.08**	**560**	**533**	**500**	**1.36**	**1.26**	**1.24**					
	UPCC	904	722	626	4.40	3.43	2.85	794	626	540	3.93	2.96	2.43					
	IPCC	606	610	639	2.01	1.98	1.98	479	509	538	1.17	1.22	1.28					
20	**WSRec**	**586**	**551**	**546**	**1.93**	**1.80**	**1.70**	**445**	**428**	**416**	**1.10**	**1.08**	**1.07**					
	UPCC	915	671	572	4.25	3.25	2.58	803	576	491	3.76	2.86	2.06					
	IPCC	563	566	602	1.84	1.83	1.86	439	467	507	1.10	1.12	1.17					
30	**WSRec**	**538**	**504**	**499**	**1.78**	**1.69**	**1.63**	**405**	**385**	**378**	**1.05**	**1.00**	**0.98**					

Each experiment is run for 50 times and the average MAE value is reported. The experimental results of Table 22.2 shows that:

- *WSRec* method consistently outperforms other algorithms under all experimental settings.
- The performance of all approaches enhances significantly with the increase of matrix density, the number of training users as well as the number of QoS values provided by active users.
- The item-based approach (IPCC) outperforms the user-based approach (UPCC). This observation indicates that similar Web services provide more information to the prediction than similar users do.

22.4.2.1 Impact of Missing Value Prediction

The *missing value prediction* in Sect. 22.2.2.2 makes use of the similar users and similar items to predict the missing values of the training matrix to make it denser. To study the impact of the *missing value prediction*, we implement two versions of *WSRec*. One version employs missing value prediction (*WSRec**), while the other version does not (*WSRec*). We vary the *given number* of the active users from 5 to 50 with a step of 5 and vary the values of *training users* from 20 to 140 with a step value of 20. We set $density = 10\%$ and $TopK = 10$, which means that the top 10 neighbors will be employed for value prediction.

Figure 22.4 shows the experimental results, where Fig. 22.4a–b show the experimental results of *response time* and Fig. 22.4c–d show the experimental results of *failure rate*. Figure 22.4 shows that predicting the missing values of the training matrix will improve the overall prediction accuracy.

22.4.2.2 Impact of λ

Different datasets have different data characteristics. Parameter λ makes our prediction method feasible and adaptable to different datasets. If $\lambda = 1$, we only extract information from similar users, and if $\lambda = 0$, we only consider valuable information from similar services. In other cases, we leverage both similar users and services to predict missing values for active users.

To study the impact of λ on our collaborative filtering method, we set $Top\ K = 10$ and $training\ users = 140$. We vary the value of λ from 0 to 1 with a step of 0.1. Figure 22.5a, c show the results of $given\ number = 10$, $given\ number = 20$ and $given\ number = 30$ with 20% density training matrix of *response time* and *failure rate*, respectively. Figure 22.5b, d show the results of $density = 10\%$, $density = 20\%$ and $density = 30\%$ with $given\ number = 20$ of *response time* and *failure rate*, respectively.

The experiment shows that λ impacts the recommendation results significantly, and a proper λ value will provide better prediction accuracy. For both the *response*

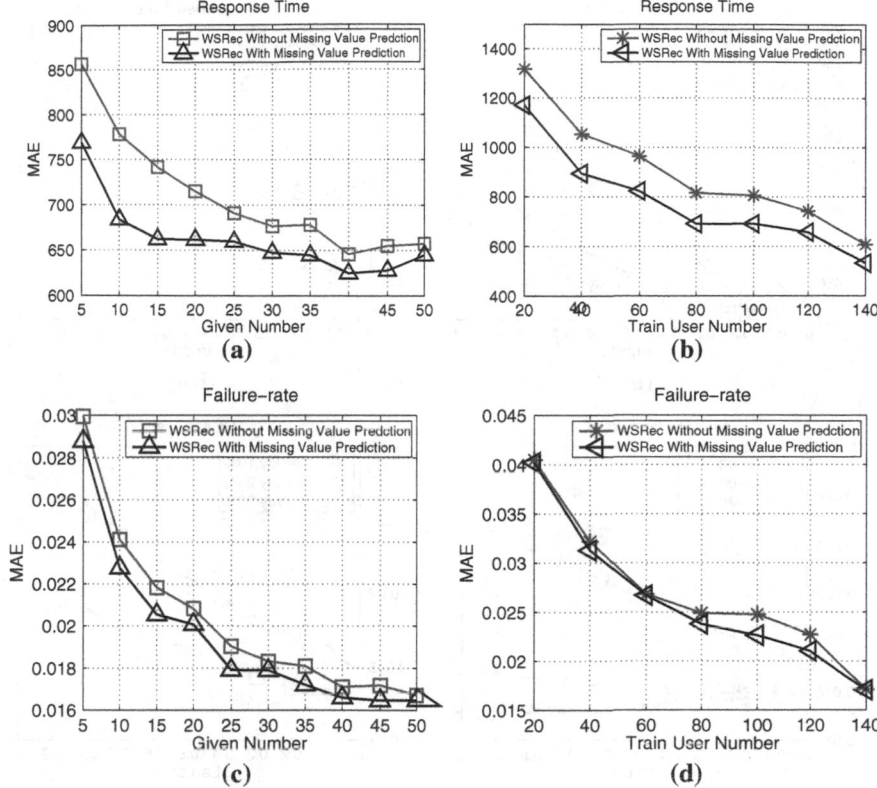

Fig. 22.4 Impact of the training matrix prediction

time and *failure rate*, similar Web services are more important than similar users in prediction QoS when limited QoS values are given by active users, while the similar users become more important when more QoS values are available from active users. As shown in Fig. 22.5b, d, with the given number of 20, all the three curves (*Density* 10, 20, *and* 30 %) of *response time* and *failure rate* obtain the best prediction performance with the same λ value ($\lambda = 0.2$ for *response time* and $\lambda = 0$ for *failure rate*), indicating that the optimal λ value is not influenced by the training matrix density.

22.4.3 Region-Based Recommender System Performance Evaluation

As mentioned in Sect. 22.4.1, QoS records are collected by 150 nodes from the Planet-Lab. For each node, there are more than 100 QoS profiles, and each profile contains

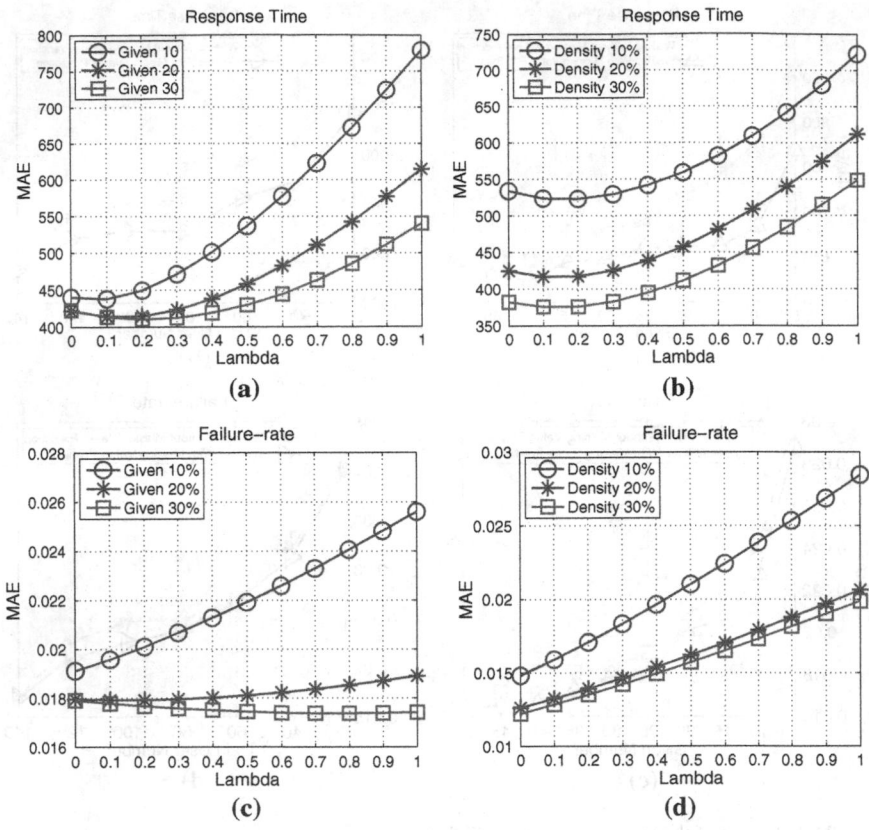

Fig. 22.5 Impact of the lambda

the response time (also called Round Trip Time, RTT) records of 100 services. We randomly extract 20 profiles from each node, and obtain 3000 users with RTTs ranging from 2 to 31407 milliseconds.

We randomly remove 90 and 80 % RTTs of the initial training matrix to generate two sparse matrices with density 10 and 20 % respectively. We vary the number of RTT values given by active users from 10, 20 to 30. The removed records of active users are used to study the prediction accuracy. In this experiment, we set $\mu = 0.3$, $\lambda = 0.8$, and $top - k = 10$. To get a reliable error estimate, we use 10 times 10-fold cross-validation [32] to evaluate the prediction accuracy and report the average MAE value.

Table 22.3 shows the prediction performance of different methods employing the 10 and 20 % density training matrix. It shows that our method (RBCF) significantly improves the prediction accuracy, and outperforms others consistently. The performance of UPCC, WSRec and our approach enhances significantly with the increase of matrix density as well as the number of QoS values provided by active users (given number).

Table 22.3 MAE comparison on response time (smaller value means better performance)

Method	Density = 10%			Density = 20%		
	G10	G20	G30	G10	G20	G30
IPCC	1179.32	1170.73	1160.45	1104.02	1094.63	1086.08
UPCC	1280.95	1145.80	1085.85	1167.84	846.54	674.32
WSRec	976.01	805.60	772.34	968.69	788.37	742.15
RBCF	**638.21**	**624.51**	**623.90**	**573.85**	**560.13**	**556.75**

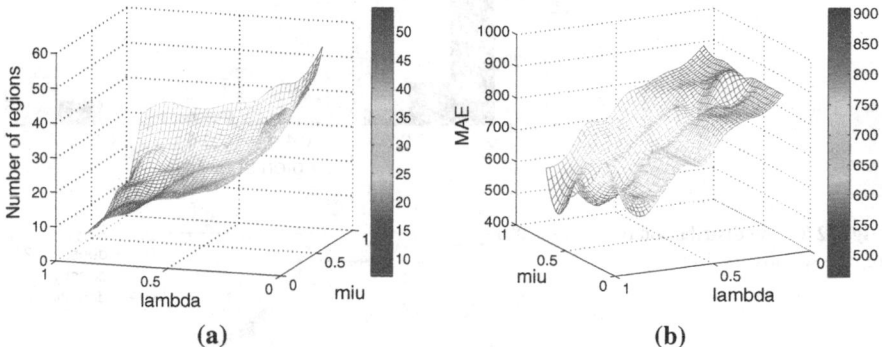

(a)   (b)

Fig. 22.6 Impact of thresholds λ and μ. **a** Impact on the number of regions. **b** Impact on the prediction performance (MAE)

22.4.3.1 Impact of λ and μ

In region creation phase, the two thresholds λ and μ play a very important role in determining the number of regions and can impact the final performance of the prediction. As mentioned in Sect. 22.3.2.2, only regions with similarity higher than μ and sensitivity less than λ can be aggregated into one region. We test the impact of λ and μ on a sparse matrix with 2700 training users and 300 active users. We set $density = 0.2$, $given = 10$ and employ all the neighbors with positive PCC for QoS prediction. We vary the two thresholds λ and μ both from 0.1 to 0.9 with a step of 0.1. Figure 22.6 shows how the two thresholds affect the number of regions and the final prediction accuracy. It shows that lower μ and higher λ result in fewer regions, but fewer regions does not necessarily mean better prediction accuracy. For this dataset, better prediction accuracy is achieved with higher λ and μ. Note that the optimal value of λ is related to the sensitivity of the original regions at the outset. Figure 22.7 shows the distribution of the region sensitivity before aggregation. It shows that the sensitivity of most regions (81.3 %) is less than 0.1, while the sensitivity of a few regions (4.67 %) is around 0.8. Higher λ and μ allow very similar regions with high sensitivity to be aggregated and achieve good performance in this experiment. Figure 22.8 shows the relation between μ and prediction accuracy with training matrix density 0.2, 0.5 and 1. We employ all the neighbors with positive PCC values for QoS prediction and set $\lambda = 1$, so that we do not consider the factor

Fig. 22.7 The distribution of region sensitivity

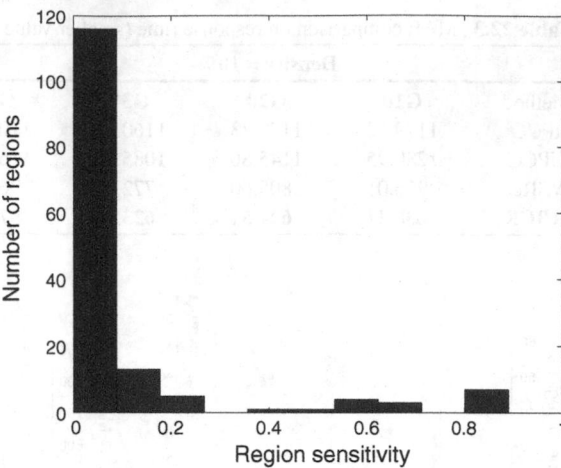

Fig. 22.8 The distribution of region sensitivity

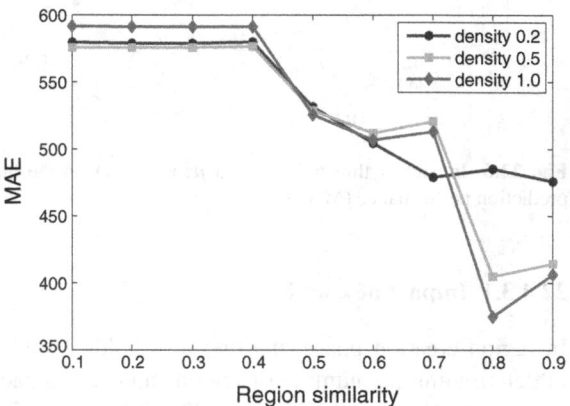

of sensitivity in region aggregation. Similarity becomes the single factor. Obviously, for denser matrix, with higher μ we obtain a set of coherent regions, and better prediction accuracy.

22.5 Related Work

22.5.1 Collaborative Filtering

Collaborative Filtering is firstly proposed by Rich [25] and widely used in commercial recommender systems, such as Amazon.com [4, 17, 19, 24]. The basic idea of CF is to predict and recommend the potential favorite items for a particular user by leveraging rating data collected from similar users. Essentially, CF is based on processing the user-item matrix. Breese et al. [3] divide the CF algorithms into two broad classes: memory-based algorithms and model-based algorithms. The most analyzed examples of memory-based collaborative filtering include user-based approaches [3, 10, 14], item-based approaches [8, 17, 27], and their fusion [37, 31]. User-based approaches predict the ratings of active users based on the ratings of their similar users, and item-based approaches predict the ratings of active users based on the computed information of items similar to those chosen by the active users. These algorithms are easy to implement, require little or no training cost, and can easily take new users's ratings into account. However, memory-based algorithms cannot cope well with large number of users and items, since their online performance is often slow.

Model-based CF algorithms learn the model from the dataset using statistical and machine learning techniques. Examples include clustering model [33], latent semantic models [11, 12] and latent factor model [5]. These algorithms can quickly generate recommendations and achieve good online performance. However, the model must be performed anew when new users or items are added to the system.

22.5.2 Web Service Selection and Recommendation

Web service selection and recommendation has been extensively studied to facilitate Web service composition in recent years. El Hadad et al. [9] propose a selection method considering both the transactional properties and QoS characteristics of a Web service. Hwang et al. [13] find that both composite and individual web services constrain the sequences of invoking operations. They use finite state machine to model the permitted invocation sequences of Web service operations, and propose two strategies to select Web services that are likely to successfully complete the execution of a given sequence of operations. Kang et al. [15] propose AWSR system to recommend services based on users' historical functional interests and QoS preferences. Barakat [2] models the quality dependencies among services and propose a Web service selection method for Web service composition. Alrifai and Risse [1] propose a method to meet a user's end-to-end QoS requirement. Their method consists of two steps: first, they use mixed integer programming (MIP) to find the optimal decomposition of global QoS constraints into local constraints. After that they use distributed local selection to find the best web services that satisfy the local constraints. This approach achieves suboptimal results, but it is more efficient than solutions based on global optimization.

A large amount of work has been done to apply CF to Web service recommendation. Shao et al. [28] use a user-based CF algorithm to predict QoS values. Work [16, 29] apply the idea of CF in their systems, and use MovieLens data for experimental analysis. Combination of different type of CF algorithms are also used in Web service recommendation. Zheng et al. [40] combine the user-based and item-based CF algorithms to recommend Web services; They also integrate Neighborhood approach with Matrix Factorization in work [39]. Qi [23] presents a strategy that integrates matrix factorization with decision tree learning to bootstrap service recommendation systems. Meanwhile, several work employs location information to Web service recommendation. Chen et al. [6] first use a region-based CF algorithm to make Web service recommendations. To help users know more about Web service performance, they also propose a visualization method showing recommendation results on a map . Lo et al. [18] employs the user location in matrix factorization model to predict QoS values. Tang et al. [30] consider the impact of both user location and Web service location on QoS values and propose a CF recommendation approach based on that.

22.6 Conclusion and Future Work

We have presented two Web service recommendation approaches in this chapter. The basic ideas of the two are the same: to predict Web service future QoS performance and recommend the best one for active users by using historical QoS data from similar users. The difference is how the two approaches find similar users. Neighborhood-based approach searches users and Web services in the entire data set to find similar ones. It is straightforward and easy to implement. Moreover, this approach can easily handle new data (new users, Web services and submitted QoS values) by adding new rows or columns to the data set. On the other hand, region-based approach leverages location information to find similar users and achieves better online performance. The drawback of this approach is that we need to recompute the region model when a certain amount of new data coming in. For example, when one normal region becomes sensitive or when a lot of new users go to one region and make it not coherent, we will regenerate all the regions.

In our future work, we will consider several aspects to further improve the proposed Web service recommendation approaches. In terms of the recommendation accuracy, we find that contextual information can greatly influence Web service QoS performance, such as server workload, network condition and the tasks that users carry out with Web services (e.g., computation-intensive or I/O-intensive task). Besides physical location, we will take these factors into account and refine the steps of similarity computation and region aggregation. In terms of the experiment, we use MAE to measure the overall recommendation accuracy currently. Similar to web page search results, users may only consider and try the top three or five recommended services. Thus improving the accuracy of top-k recommended services is another task to investigate. Our future work also includes the study of QoS characteristic. We plan to investigate the distribution of response time and the correlation between different QoS properties such as response time and reliability.

References

1. Alrifai, M., Risse, T.: Combining global optimization with local selection for efficient QoS-aware service composition. In: Proceedings of the 18th International Conference on World Wide Web (WWW'09), pp. 881–890 (2009)
2. Barakat, L.: Efficient correlation-aware service selection. In: Proceedings of the 19th International Conference on Web Services (ICWS'12), pp. 1–8 (2012)
3. Breese, J.S., Heckerman, D., Kadie C.: Empirical analysis of predictive algorithms for collaborative filtering. In: Proceedings of the 14th Annual Conference Uncertainty in Artificial Intelligence (UAI'98), pp. 43–52 (1998)
4. Burke, R.: Hybrid recommender systems: survey and experiments. User Model. User-Adap. Inter. 12(4), 331–370 (2002)
5. Canny J.: Collaborative filtering with privacy via factor analysis. In: Proceedings of the 25th International ACM SIGIR Conference on Research and Development in Information Retrieval (SIGIR'02), pp. 238–245 (2002)
6. Chen, X., Zheng, Z., Liu, X., Huang, Z., Sun, H.: Personalized QoS-aware web service recommendation and visualization. IEEE Trans. Serv Comput. 6(1), 35–47(2013)
7. Chun, B., Culler, D., Roscoe, T., Bavier, A., Peterson, L., Wawrzoniak, M., Bowman, M.: Planetlab: an overlay testbed for broad-coverage services. ACM SIGCOMM Comput. Commun. Rev. 33(3), 3–12 (2003)
8. Deshpande, M., Karypis, G.: Item-based top-n recommendation. ACM Trans. Inf. Syst. 22(1), 143–177 (2004)
9. El Hadad, J., Manouvrier, M., Rukoz, M.: TQoS: transactional and QoS-aware selection algorithm for automatic Web service composition. IEEE Trans. Serv. Comput. 3(1), 73–85 (2010)
10. Herlocker, J.L., Konstan, J.A., Borchers, A., Riedl, J.: An algorithmic framework for performing collaborative filtering. In: Proceedings of the 22nd International ACM SIGIR Conference on Research and Development in Information Retrieval (SIGIR'99), pp. 230–237 (1999)
11. Hofmann, T.: Collaborative filtering via gaussian probabilistic latent semantic analysis. In: Proceedings of the 26th International ACM SIGIR Conference on Research and Development in Information Retrieval (SIGIR'03), pp. 259–266 (2003)
12. Hofmann, T.: Latent semantic models for collaborative filtering. ACM Trans. Inf. Syst. 22(1), 89–115 (2004)
13. Hwang, S., Lim, E., Lee, C., Chen, C.: Dynamic web service selection for reliable web service composition. IEEE Trans. Serv. Comput. 1(2), 104–116 (2008)
14. Jin, R., Chai, J.Y., Si, L.: An automatic weighting scheme for collaborative filtering. In: Proceedings of the 27th International ACM SIGIR Conference on Research and Development in Information Retrieval (SIGIR'04), pp. 337–344 (2004)
15. Kang, G., Liu, J., Tang, M., Liu, X., Cao, B., Xu, Y.: AWSR: active web service recommendation based on usage history. In: Proceedings of the 19th International Conference on Web Services (ICWS'12), pp. 186–193 (2012)
16. Karta, K.: An investigation on personalized collaborative filtering for web service selection. Honours Programme thesis, University of Western Australia, Brisbane (2005)
17. Linden, G., Smith, B., York, J.: Amazon.com recommendations: Item-to-item collaborative filtering. IEEE Internet Comput. 7(1), 76–80 (2003)
18. Lo, W., Yin, J., Deng, S., Li, Y., Wu, Z.: Collaborative web service QoS prediction with location-based regularization. In: Proceedings of the 19th International Conference on Web Services (ICWS'12), pp. 464–471 (2012)
19. Ma, H., King, I., Lyu, M.R.: Effective missing data prediction for collaborative filtering. In: Proceedings of the 30th International ACM SIGIR Conference on Research and Development in Information Retrieval (SIGIR'07), pp. 39–46 (2007)
20. Manning, C.D., Raghavan, P., Schtze H.: An Introduction to Information Retrieval. Cambridge University Press, Cambridge (2009)

21. McLaughlin M.R., Herlocker J. L.: A collaborative filtering algorithm and evaluation metric that accurately model the user experience. In: Proceedings of the 27th International ACM SIGIR Conference on Research and Development in Information Retrieval (SIGIR'04), pp. 329–336 (2004)
22. Ouzzani, M., Bouguettaya, A.: Efficient access to web services. IEEE Internet Comput. **8**(2), 34–44 (2004)
23. Qi, Y.: Decision tree learning from incomplete QoS to bootstrap service recommendation. In: Proceedings of the 19th International Conference on Web Services (ICWS'12), pp. 194–201 (2012)
24. Resnick, P., Iacovou, N., Suchak, M., Bergstrom, P., Riedl, J.: Grouplens: an open architecture for collaborative filtering of netnews. In: Proceedings of ACM Conference on Computer Supported Cooperative, Work, pp. 175–186 (1994)
25. Rich, E.: User modeling via stereotypes. Cognitive Sci. **3**(4), 329–354 (1979)
26. Rosario, S., Benveniste, A., Haar, S., Jard, C.: Probabilistic Qos and soft contracts for transaction-based web services orchestrations. IEEE Trans. Serv. Comput. **1**(4), 187–200 (2008)
27. Sarwar, B., Karypis, G., Konstan, J., Riedl, J.: Item-based collaborative filtering recommendation algorithms. In: Proceedings of the 10th International Conference on World Wide Web (WWW'01), pp. 285–295 (2001)
28. Shao, L., Zhang, J., Wei, Y., Zhao, J., Xie, B., Mei, H.: Personalized qos prediction for web services via collaborative filtering. In: Proceedings of the 5th International Conference on Web Services (ICWS'07), pp. 439–446 (2007)
29. Sreenath, R.M., Singh, M.P.: Agent-based service selection. J. Web Seman **1**(3), 261–279 (2003)
30. Tang, M., Jin, Y., Liu, J., Liu, X.: Location-aware collaborative filtering for QoS-based service recommendation. In: Proceedings of the 19th International Conference on Web Services (ICWS'12), pp. 202–209 (2012)
31. Wang, J., de Vries, A.P., Reinders, M.J.T.: Unifying user-based and item-based collaborative filtering approaches by similarity fusion. In: Proceedings of the 29th International ACM SIGIR Conference on Research and Development in Information Retrieval (SIGIR'06), pp. 501–508 (2006)
32. Witten, I.H., Frank, E.: Data Mining: Practical Machine Learning Tools and Techniques, vol. 2. Elsevier, Amsterdam (2005)
33. Xue, G., Lin, C., Yang, Q., Xi, W., Zeng, H., Yu, Y., Chen, Z.: Scalable collaborative filtering using cluster-based smoothing. In: Proceedings of the 28th International ACM SIGIR Conference on Research and Development in Information Retrieval (SIGIR'05), pp. 114–121 (2005)
34. Yu, T., Zhang, Y., Lin, K.-J.: Efficient algorithms for web services selection with end-to-end qos constraints. ACM Trans. Web **1**(1), 1–26 (2007)
35. Zeng, L., Benatallah, B., Ngu, A.H.H., Dumas, M., Kalagnanam, J., Chang, H.: Qos-aware middleware for web services composition. IEEE Trans. Softw Eng **30**(5), 311–327 (2004)
36. Zhang, L.-J., Zhang, J., Cai, H.: Services Computing. Springer and Tsinghua University Press, New York and Beijing (2007)
37. Zheng, Z., Ma, H., Lyu, M.R., King I.: Wsrec: a collaborative filtering based web service recommender system. In: Proceedings of the 7th International Conference Web Services (ICWS'09), pp. 437–444 (2009)
38. Zheng, Z., Zhang, Y., Lyu, M.: CloudRank: A QoS-Driven component ranking framework for cloud computing. In: Proceedings of the International Symposium Reliable Distributed Systems (SRDS'10), pp. 184–193 (2010)
39. Zheng, Z., Ma, H., Lyu, M., King, I.: Collaborative web service QoS prediction via neighborhood integrated matrix factorization. IEEE Trans. Serv. Comput. (2011)
40. Zheng, Z., Ma, H., Lyu, M., King, I.: Qos-aware web service recommendation by collaborative filtering. IEEE Trans. Serv. Comput. **4**(2), 140–152 (2011)

Chapter 23
On Bootstrapping Web Service Recommendation

Qi Yu

Abstract We present a novel framework to bootstrap Web Service recommendation. Service recommendation has become an effective means to achieve personalized service selection. It leverages past user-service interaction information to accurately predict user preference on previously unknown services. However, one key impediment has been the incompetence of current service recommendation systems in dealing with new users and services. Since a recommendation system has no knowledge about new users and services, it may completely fail to provide any recommendation or provide very poor ones. The proposed framework uses an agile interview process to quickly profile new users and services. The interview is structured by a decision tree that enables adaptive, intuitive, and rapid querying of users or services. We propose to exploit Non-negative Matrix Tri-Factorization (NMTF) to simultaneously partition users and services into a set of user and service groups. The group structure helps estimate the missing interaction information and also provides class labels to construct decision trees for both users and services, which will be used in the interview process. We conduct extensive experiments to assess the effectiveness of the proposed framework for bootstrapping service recommendation.

23.1 Introduction

Service Oriented Computing (SOC) offers an attractive paradigm for the provisioning and consuming of computing resources across a wide spectrum of domains. The large number of applications expected to heavily take advantage of SOC will lead to the deployment of substantial software services on the Web. Many Web services may also offer similar functionalities but vary from each other in terms of the Quality of Service (QoS) they deliver [16]. The QoS is mainly made of user centered quality

Q. Yu (✉)
Rochester Institute of Technology, Rochester, USA
e-mail: qi.yu@rit.edu

A. Bouguettaya et al. (eds.), *Web Services Foundations*,
DOI: 10.1007/978-1-4614-7518-7_23,
© Springer Science+Business Media New York 2014

parameters and examples include availability, response time, throughput, and so on. As the number of Web services is expected to grow far beyond the reach of any manual effort, a key challenge is to automatically assess the QoS of large-scale Web services. This will enable casual service users to easily select the Web service that best fulfills their QoS requirements [17].

The distributed and dynamic SOC environment leads to very diverse QoS experience for service users. Users may locate in different network environments and have different physical distances with the Web services they access. These discrepancies imply that different users may receive significantly different QoS from the same Web service. Service recommendation systems explicitly consider user discrepancies by leveraging a Collaborative Filtering (CF) scheme [5, 11, 15, 18, 19]. CF assumes that users who have common QoS experiences with some services may share similar experiences with other services. It exploits similar users' QoS experience to accurately predict the QoS that an active user may receive from previously unknown services. In this way, personalized service selection can be achieved that enables users to conveniently choose the most suitable services from a large number of previously unknown candidates.

Service recommendation systems rely on the historical user-service interaction to make QoS predictions. The similarity between two users is measured based on the QoS of their commonly invoked services. Similarly, the similarity between two services is evaluated by the QoS received by the set of users that invoke both services. Sufficient historical QoS information increases the chance to identify similar users or services, which is central to the effectiveness of CF based recommendation systems. Therefore, the more knowledge the system has on the users and services, the more accurate QoS prediction can it provide. Existing service recommendation systems perform reasonably well on warm-start users for which they possess adequate information. One key impediment has been their incompetence in dealing with new users and services, which is usually referred to as the cold start issue. As the system possesses very little or no historical QoS information from new users and services, it may fail to provide any recommendation or provide very poor ones.

Due to the wide adoption of SOC in both industry and government, new services are being increasingly deployed and new users keep entering the SOC market. Hence, effectively dealing with the cold-start issue is critical in attracting new users and service providers, which is instrumental for SOC to reach its full potential. An initial interview process is commonly used to elicit user's information in many recommendation systems. User profiles are constructed based on the interview results, which will then be used for recommendation. The initial interview process should be both short and intuitive so that a new user won't get bored or lost. Another desirable feature of the interview process is to adaptively query the user based on the results of prior interview questions [3, 9].

Decision trees have been employed to conduct initial interviews to bootstrap e-commerce recommendation systems (e.g., Amazon and Netflix) [4, 21]. A ternary tree is recursively constructed by selecting an item to split existing users assigned to a tree node into its three child nodes along branches, labeled as "like", "dislike", and "unknown", respectively. During the interview, the new user is expected to rate an item chosen by the decision tree at each given step. Based on the rating, she will be directed to one of the child nodes. The interview continues until the new user is assigned to a leaf node, which represents a homogeneous group of existing users. These users are considered to be as the similar users and will be used to predict the new user's preferences on different items.

Bootstrapping service recommendation poses some new challenges, which hinder a direct application of ternary decision trees. In e-commerce recommendation systems, users' preferences on items are typically represented by few categorical rating values, (e.g., 1–5). This enables a straightforward way to assign users into different groups based on their ratings on an item. For example, the ternary tree assigns a user into the "like" group if her rating is no less than a predefined threshold (e.g., 3) and "dislike" group if otherwise. In contrast, the QoS data used in service recommendation is described by continuous attributes (e.g., 1.2 s response time and 0.95 availability). Therefore, dividing users into groups is less intuitive and demands some principled criterion.

Dealing with incomplete QoS data gives rise to the second key challenge. Since an existing user may only invoke a limited number of services, only a small subset of QoS data is observed. The ternary tree introduces the "unknown" tree node to group together users with no ratings on the selected item. Users in this node share a similar opinion on the item, which may be interpreted as either "not know" or "no interest". Correspondingly, no response is also allowed during the interview process, which directs the new user into the "unknown" node. When bootstrapping service recommendation, a new user is expected to invoke a small number of selected services during the interview.[1] Invoking a service always generates a response. Even when the service is down, a "time out" message is returned, indicating that the service is not available. This is different from rating an item (e.g., a product or a movie), which may result in no response when the user does not know or has no interest in the item. In contrast, no response is no longer an option during the interview for service recommendation. If a ternary tree is used, the "unknown" nodes will never be visited during the interview. This in essence ignores a large number of users that are assigned into these nodes and hence dramatically reduces the chance to locate similar users.

We develop a novel framework to bootstrap Web service recommendation. In a preliminary version of this paper, we developed a strategy to provide high-quality service recommendations for new service users [14]. One key extension of the proposed framework has been the ability to deal with new services. In this way, it provides a complete solution to the cold-start issue in service recommendation by tackling both new users and services. In particular, we propose to exploit Non-negative Matrix Tri-Factorization (NMTF) to simultaneously partition users and services into a set of user and service groups. The group structure helps estimate the missing interaction information and also provides class labels to construct decision trees for both users and services. The decision tree is used to structure an initial interview that

---

[1] The service invocation code can be wrapped as a small software toolkit that is easily accessed by end users.

enables adaptive, intuitive, and rapid querying of users or services. At the end of the interview, a new user or service will be classified into one of the user or service groups obtained by NMTF. Since the group is deemed to be comprised of users or services that are similar to the new user or service, the QoS of the new user or service can be predicted based on the QoS of its similar users or services. One challenging issue that is particular to profiling new services is that the interview process requires to query existing users. However, a selected user may not want to participate in the interview process. The user groups resulted from NMTF enable us to choose alternative users that are similar to the selected users to work as surrogates in the decision tree. Experimental results clearly demonstrate the effectiveness of the surrogate user strategy in profiling new services.

The remainder of the paper is organized as follows. We review some existing works that are most relevant to ours in Sect. 23.2. We describe in detail the proposed framework for bootstrapping service recommendation systems in Sect. 23.3. We assess the effectiveness of the proposed framework via a set of experiments in Sect. 23.4. We conclude in Sect. 23.5.

23.2 Related Work

The ever increasing number of Web services demands systematic approaches to facilitate service users in efficiently and accurately retrieving services that match both their functional and non-functional requirements. Collaborative Filtering (CF) based techniques have been recently adopted to provide personalized service recommendation to users [5, 11, 18, 19]. Shao et. al. present a service recommendation system by assuming that similar users tend to receive similar QoS from similar services [11]. This is in essence a standard user-based CF algorithm. Zheng et. al. enhance the user-based approach by integrating item-based CF, which results in a hybrid algorithm with better prediction accuracy [19]. Complementary information, such as users' locations [1, 2], invocation frequencies of services [10], and query histories of users [18], has also been leveraged to improve the quality of recommendation.

Both user- and item-based approaches follow the neighborhood centric strategy in CF, which explores the local neighborhood to identify similar users or items for recommendation. Zheng et. al. recently proposed a model based CF algorithm that achieves higher prediction accuracy [20]. The proposed algorithm uses the user-based approach as a precursor to identify top-k similar users. Based on the user neighborhood information, matrix factorization is employed to construct a global model, which can be used to predict unobserved QoS data. Different from our strategy, an unconstrained version of matrix factorization is used, which does not discover the user groups.

All existing service recommendation approaches focus on predicting QoS for warm-start users. To our best knowledge, there is no existing work that provides a systematic approach for cold-start service recommendation. Dealing with cold-start users has received considerable attention in e-commerce recommendation systems.

An initial interview has been suggested as an effective way to quickly build new users' profiles. Based on how the seed questions are selected, there are two types of interviews. The first type of interview chooses a static seed set based on some principled criteria, such as coverage [3], popularity [8], and discriminative power [9]. Users always answer a fixed set of questions, which does not fully leverage the interactive nature of the interview process. Recent works propose to adaptively query users based on their responses to the prior interview questions [9, 4, 21]. Decision trees appear as an ideal vehicle to carry out the adaptive initial interview. A ternary tree suits perfectly for the rating-based recommendation systems, which are commonly used in e-commerce. As discussed in Sect. 23.1, service recommendation poses some new challenges that make a ternary tree inapplicable. In particular, since the "unknown" nodes in a ternary tree will never be visited during the interview, valuable information carried by existing users cannot be fully leveraged to provide high quality recommendations.

23.3 Cold-start Service Recommendation

We present the framework for bootstrapping service recommendation in this section. The proposed framework simultaneously deals with both new users and services. It exploits Non-negative Matrix Tri-Factorization (NMTF) to discover the user and service group structures from a set of incomplete QoS data that captures the historical user-service interactions. The tree learning algorithm then constructs two decision trees to partition the users and services, respectively, to fit the group structure discovered by NMTF. The simple structure and interpretability of the decision tree serve ideally for an initial interview process, which adaptively queries new users and services for rapid profiling.

23.3.1 NMTF for User and Service Group Discovery

Before delving into the technical details, we first describe the symbols and notations that are used throughout the paper. Assume that there are n existing users and m Web services. The QoS attribute (e.g., response time, reliability, and availability) under consideration takes positive real values. We use a matrix $A \in \mathbb{R}_+^{m \times n}$ to denote the QoS data, where A_{ij} represents the QoS that service i delivered to user j. In this regard, the i-th row of A represents service s_i while the j-th column of A represents user u_j. This essentially models user u_j as an m-dimensional feature vector, in which each element u_{jq} signifies u_j's interaction with s_q.

NMTF computes three low-rank matrices, the service coefficient matrix $F \in \mathbb{R}_+^{m \times k}$, the prototype matrix $B \in \mathbb{R}_+^{k \times l}$, and the service coefficient matrix $G \in \mathbb{R}_+^{n \times l}$ to approximate the original QoS matrix A, i.e., $A \approx FBG'$. In particular, the $k \times l$ prototype matrix B is deemed to provide a compact representation for the original QoS matrix A with a $k \times l$ block structure. In this regard, the columns of B, $\{b_1, ..., b_l\}$, correspond to the l different types of users and the rows of B, $\{b'_1, ..., b'_k\}$, correspond to the k different types of services.

Let $v_q = Fb_q$ denote the q-th column vector of $V = FB$, where $q = 1, ..., l$. The m dimensional vector $v_q \in \mathbb{R}^m$ reflects how each service interacts with the q-th type of users. Therefore, the columns of V are considered to form a new basis, where each basis vector captures the QoS related latent feature of one (out of l) type of users. Consequently, the user coefficient matrix G is the new representation of the users under this new basis. G can also be regarded as a projection of A onto the latent user feature space V. More specifically,

$$a_j \approx \sum_{q=1}^{l} G_{jq} v_q \qquad (23.1)$$

where a_j is the j-th column vector in A, representing user u_j. Equation (23.1) shows that each user vector a_j is approximated by a linear combination of the column vectors in V weighted by the components of G. Similarly, the service coefficient matrix F is a projection of A' onto the latent service feature space $R' = GB'$,[2] i.e., $a'_i \approx \sum_{p=1}^{k} F_{ip} r'_p$.

The latent user feature space V together with the new representation matrix G should provide a good approximation of the original QoS data matrix A. Since only a small subset of QoS data is observed, we introduce a weight matrix W, where $W_{ij} = 1$ if A_{ij} is observable and $W_{ij} = 0$ otherwise. Therefore, we compute F, B, and G by solving the following optimization problem:

$$\min_{F \geq 0, G \geq 0} J = \left\| W; (A - FBG') \right\|^2 \qquad (23.2)$$

$$= \sum_{i=1}^{m} \sum_{j=1}^{n} W_{ij} \left(A_{ij} - \left(FBG' \right)_{ij} \right)^2 \qquad (23.3)$$

where ; is component-wise matrix product and $|| \cdot ||$ is matrix norm. Since all the components of A take non-negative values, we also enforce a non-negative constraint on matrices F, B, and G. As can be seen from Eq. (23.1), the nonnegative constraint ensures that a user vector is an additive linear combination of the new basis vectors. This allows a more intuitive interpretation than other matrix factorization approaches, such as Singular Value Decomposition (SVD), where negative values are allowed in the matrix components.

---

[2] Along the same lines, a'_i, the i-th row vector in A, representing service s_i, is approximated by a linear combination of the row vectors in BG' weighted by the components of F: $a'_i \approx \sum_{p=1}^{k} F_{ip} r'_p$. $r'_p = b'_p G'$ is the p-th row of BG', which reflects how each user interacts with the p-th type of services

23.3.2 Decision Tree Learning for User and Service Profiling

Due to its simplicity, interpretability, and the ability to adaptively query users, decision tree becomes an ideal tool to perform the initial interview via which a new user's profile can be constructed. As motivated in Sect. 23.1, the continuous nature of the QoS attributes and the limited observable QoS data pose key challenges to build a decision tree. The latent feature space discovered via matrix factorization carries rich information that is instrumental to understand the interaction patterns between users and services. It plays a critical role in learning a decision tree from a set of incomplete QoS data. More specifically, the latent feature space enables us to:

- discover homogeneous user and service groups that contain similar users and services;
- estimate the unobserved entries in the QoS matrix A.

Since the matrix G (or F) is a projection onto the latent user (or service) feature space, it naturally captures the user (or service) group structure. More intuitively, users (or services) that share similar latent features should have similar representations in the latent feature space. To make sure that each user (or service) is assigned to only one user (or service) group (i.e., hard group membership), we enforce constraints $GG' = \text{diag}(|\mathcal{U}_1|, ..., |\mathcal{U}_l|)$ and $FF' = \text{diag}(|\mathcal{S}_1|, ..., |\mathcal{S}_k|)$. This makes G (or F) a user (or service) group indicator matrix:

$$G_{jq} = \begin{cases} 1 \text{ if } u_j \in \mathcal{U}_q \\ 0 \text{ otherwise} \end{cases} \tag{23.4}$$

$$F_{ip} = \begin{cases} 1 \text{ if } s_i \in \mathcal{S}_p \\ 0 \text{ otherwise} \end{cases} \tag{23.5}$$

where $\mathcal{U}_q$ is the q-th user group and $|\mathcal{U}_q|$ denotes the number of users assigned to the group. Similarly, $\mathcal{S}_p$ is the p-th service group and $|\mathcal{S}_p|$ denotes the number of services assigned to the group. These constraints ensure that each row of G (or F) has only one non-zero element, which denotes the group that the user (or service) is assigned to.

The second key usage of the latent feature space is to estimate the missing QoS entries. If the latent features indeed capture the interaction patterns between users and services, they are expected to provide a good estimation of the unobserved QoS data. More specifically, the QoS that an unknown service s_i will deliver to a user u_j can be estimated as:

$$A_{ij} \approx \hat{A}_{ij} = \sum_{p=1}^{k} \sum_{q=1}^{k} V_{ip} G_{jq} \tag{23.6}$$

The j-th column vector of the completed matrix $\hat{A}$ corresponds to user u_j and the j-th row vector of matrix G encodes the class (or group) label for the user. The class labels from G allow us to exploit the classical information gain as the principled criterion to select services to be used as the tree nodes. Using the completed matrix $\hat{A}$ avoids the generation of "unknown" nodes, which are never visited during the initial interview for service recommendation. Instead of a ternary tree, our tree learning algorithm generates a binary decision tree, via which all existing user information can be leveraged to construct a new user's profile. To ensure a concise interview process, we employ two strategies to control the depth of the tree. First, we stop splitting the a node if the number users assigned to it is less than a predefined threshold value. Second, we exploit a standard pruning process to merge and join leaf nodes after the tree is fully grown.

Figure 23.1 shows an example decision tree constructed from a real-world QoS dataset obtained from [19]. Each internal node of the tree represents a service. Based on the QoS value, users are directed to one of its child nodes. For example, if the response time that a user received from service s_{53} is less than 0.74 s, she will be directed to child node s_{59}. At this node, the response time of the user will be evaluated against the service in the node. This process continues until the user reaches one of the leaf nodes, which corresponds to one of the user groups.

In what follows, we present an important property of the binary decision tree as constructed by following the above procedure. This helps justify why it can provide high-quality service recommendations for cold-start users and services.

Theorem 23.1 *A decision tree that exploits class labels provided by matrix G partitions users into cohesive user groups, where G is computed by minimizing objective function J with constraint in Eq. (23.4).*

Proof Since each column vector of A corresponds to a user, we reformulate the objective function J using column vectors of A.

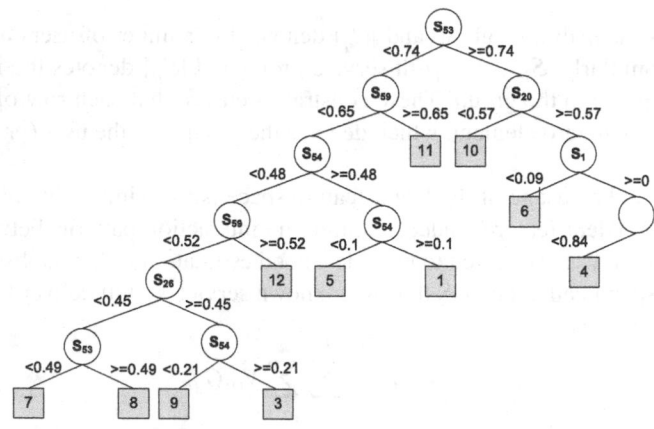

Fig. 23.1 An example decision tree for new user interview

$$J = \sum_{j=1}^{n} \left\| w_j; [a_j - \sum_{q=1}^{k} G_{jq} v_q] \right\|^2 \tag{23.7}$$

$$= \sum_{j=1}^{n} \left\| \sum_{q=1}^{k} G_{jq} [w_j; (a_j - v_q)] \right\|^2 \tag{23.8}$$

$$= \sum_{j=1}^{n} \sum_{q=1}^{k} G_{jq} \left\| w_j; (a_j - v_q) \right\|^2 \tag{23.9}$$

$$= \sum_{q=1}^{k} \sum_{u_j \in \mathcal{U}_q} \left\| w_j; (a_j - v_q) \right\|^2 \tag{23.10}$$

where w_j is the j-th column of W and $\circ$ is element-wise vector product. Due to Eq. (23.4) and the fact that one user is assigned to only one group, we have $\sum_{q=1}^{k} G_{jq} = 1$, which leads Eqs. (23.7) – (23.8). From Eqs. (23.8) – (23.9), we use the fact $G_{jq}^2 = G_{jq}$ since $G_{jq} = 1$ or 0. Finally, $G_{jq} = 1$ only when $u_j \in \mathcal{U}_q$ gives Eq. (23.10).

Minimizing objective function J is equivalent to find the optimal set $\{(\mathcal{U}_q, v_q) | q \in (1, k)\}$ that minimizes Eq. (23.10). We know that $\mathcal{U}_q$ denotes the q-th user group and the group membership is encoded by G. If we can find out what the latent feature vector v_d denotes, we are able to interpret what matrix factorization actually achieves under constraint specified in Eq. (23.4). Since the optimal V minimizes J, in order to find out V, we take the partial derivative of J with respect to V:

$$\frac{\partial J}{\partial V} = -2(W; A)G + 2(W; (VG'))G \tag{23.11}$$

$$= -2(W; (-A + VG'))G \tag{23.12}$$

Setting $\frac{\partial J}{\partial V} = 0$ gives $-A + VG' = 0$. Multiplying both sides by G gives $VG'G = AG$. Using the fact $GG' = \mathrm{diag}(|\mathcal{U}_1|, ..., |\mathcal{U}_k|)$, we get

$$|\mathcal{U}_q| v_q = \sum_{j=1}^{n} G_{jq} a_j \tag{23.13}$$

$$v_q = \frac{1}{|\mathcal{U}_q|} \sum_{j=1}^{n} G_{jq} a_j \tag{23.14}$$

$$= \frac{1}{|\mathcal{U}_q|} \sum_{u_j \in \mathcal{U}_q} G_{jq} a_j \tag{23.15}$$

We exploit Eq. (23.4) in the last step of derivation.

Equation (23.13) reveals that v_q is actually the centroid of the q-th user group. Hence, we conclude that minimizing J with constraint in (23.4) is equivalent to performing k-means clustering on the existing users. The result is a set of cohesive user groups with minimal total squared deviation from their group means (or centroids). As G encodes the group memberships, our tree learning algorithm aims to construct a decision tree that partitions users into the same set of cohesive user groups.

Theorem 23.2 *A decision tree that exploits class labels provided by matrix F partitions services into cohesive service groups, where F is computed by minimizing objective function J with constraint in Eq. (23.5).*

23.3.2.1 Profiling New Users and Services

Profiling a new user is straightforward by following an initial interview structured by a decision tree like the one in Fig. 23.1. During the interview, the user invokes the services on the tree nodes until being directed into one of the leaf nodes, which represents a user group. The new user hence is expected to share similar QoS experience with other users in the same group. To make the interview process painless, the service invocation code can be wrapped as a small software toolkit that is easily accessed by end users.

Profiling a new service, on the other hand, is a little bit more complicated. In the decision tree for new service interview, each internal tree node represents a user. During the interview process, the users on the tree nodes need to invoke the new service and report their QoS. Since a number of users are involved in the interview process, it will take longer than interviewing new users, which just invokes a set of services. In fact, rapidness of the interview process is not critical for profiling new services as it makes sense that introducing a new service into the market may take some time. However, the key issue is that there might be some users that do not want to participate in the interview. One possible solution is to adopt some bonus mechanism to stimulate users. In addition, we propose to use a surrogate user strategy to improve the response rate of service users. The surrogate user strategy benefits from the co-clustering nature of NMTF, which simultaneously clusters both users and services. While the goal of new service profiling is to classify a new service into one of the service groups obtained by NMTF, the user groups provide options to choose alternative users when a selected user is not willing to participate in the interview. More specifically, when a user u_i fails to provide QoS information on the new service s_t, we randomly choose another user u_j from user group $\mathcal{U}_q$, where $u_i \in \mathcal{U}_q$, to replace u_i. Since u_j and u_i are from the same user group, they are expected to receive similar QoS from s_t. Therefore, it is highly probable that s_t will be directed to the same path in the decision tree when u_j is queried instead of u_i. This will have the effect of leading s_t to the same service group as when u_i is queried during the interview. Our experimental results in Sect. 23.4 demonstrate the effectiveness of the surrogate user strategy.

23.3.3 Computing G, B, and F

Matrices G, B and F play key roles in both decision tree learning and cold-start service recommendation. G, B and F can be derived by solving the optimization problem in Eq. (23.2). However, minimizing J under constraints specified by Eq. (23.4) and Eq. (23.5) is non-trivial. Since there is no analytical solution for that, we develop an iterative algorithm to efficiently compute G, B and F.

The constraints in Eq. (23.4) and Eq. (23.5) require binary values on the components of G and F, which makes the optimization problem unsolvable [12]. To resolve this issue, we instead enforce the following constraints: $G1 = 1$ and $F1 = 1$. This is equivalent to enforcing a soft group membership. Take the user group as an example and the same idea is applied to the service group. From $G1 = 1$, we have $\sum_{q=1}^{k} G_{jq} = 1, \forall j \in [1, n]$. Hence, G_{jq} can be interpreted as the probability that u_j belongs to group $\mathcal{U}_q$. User u_j will be assigned to group $\mathcal{U}_{\hat{q}}$, where

$$\hat{q} = \arg\max_{q}\{G_{jq} | 1 \leq q \leq k\}$$

We incorporate these new constraints into objective function J as penalty terms, which lead to the following objective function:

$$\min_{F \geq 0, B \geq 0, G \geq 0} J(G, B, F) = \left\| W; (A - FBG') \right\|^2 + \alpha \| G1 - 1 \|^2 + \beta \| F1 - 1 \|^2$$

$$(23.16)$$

In order to minimize $J(G, B, F)$, the proposed iterative algorithm updates G, B and F alternatively. That is, while $J(G, B, F)$ is minimized with respect to G, B and F will be fixed and vice versa. The update of G, B and F is performed by using a set of update rules, which guarantee the convergence of the iterative algorithm. The update rules are derived based on a set of auxiliary functions of objective function $J(G, B, F)$, which are formally defined as follows.

Definition 23.1 $Z(G, \tilde{G})$ is an auxiliary function of function $J(G)$ if it satisfies the following conditions for any G and $\tilde{G}$: $Z(G, \tilde{G}) \geq J(G)$; $Z(G, G) = J(G)$ [6].

Now, let's plug the auxiliary function into our iterative algorithm and see how we can exploit it to derive the update rules. Let $J(G)$ denote the part of $J(G, F)$ that is only relevant to G. Assume that $\{G^{(1)}, ..., G^{(t)}, ...\}$ is a set of matrices obtained by the iterative algorithm, where (t) denotes the t-th iteration. Assume that G is updated using the following update rule:

$$G^{(t+1)} = \arg\min_{G} Z(G, G^{(t)}) \tag{23.17}$$

where $G^{(t)}$ and $G^{(t+1)}$ are matrix G at the t-th and $(t + 1)$-th iterations, respectively. It is straightforward to show that $J(G)$ monotonically decreases under update rule in Eq. (23.17):

$$J(G^{(t)}) = Z(G^{(t)}, G^{(t)}) \geq Z(G^{(t)}, G^{(t+1)}) \geq J(G^{(t+1)})$$

Following the same lines, we can use similar update rules for B and F. Since the iterative algorithm updates G, B and F in turn, we have

$$J(F^{(t)}, B^{(t)}, G^{(t)}) \geq J(F^{(t+1)}, B^{(t)}, G^{(t)}) \geq J(F^{(t+1)}, B^{(t+1)}, G^{(t)})$$
$$\geq J(F^{(t+1)}, B^{(t+1)}, G^{(t+1)})$$

As $J(G, B, F)$ is apparently lower bounded, it is guaranteed to converge under the above update rules. What remains is to derive the update rules, which requires to find suitable auxiliary functions for $J(G, B, F)$ and compute their global minima.

Theorem 23.3 *Let*

$$J(G) = \left\| W; (A - FBG') \right\|^2 + \alpha \|G1 - 1\|^2 \qquad (23.18)$$

The auxiliary function of $J(G)$ is given by

$$Z(G, \tilde{G}) = Z_1(G, \tilde{G}) + Z_2(G, \tilde{G}) \qquad (23.19)$$

where,

$$Z_1(G, \tilde{G}) = \sum_{ij} W_{ij} \left[A_{ij}^2 - 2 \sum_{pq} A_{ij} F_{ip} B_{pq} \tilde{G}_{jq} \left(1 + \log \frac{G_{jq}}{\tilde{G}_{jq}} \right) \right.$$
$$\left. + \sum_{pq} [FB\tilde{G}']_{ij} F_{ip} B_{pq} \frac{G_{jq}^2}{\tilde{G}_{jq}} \right] \qquad (23.20)$$

$$Z_2(G, \tilde{G}) = \alpha \sum_{jq} \left([\tilde{G}1]_j \frac{G_{jq}^2}{\tilde{G}_{jq}} \right)$$
$$- \alpha \sum_{jq} 2\tilde{G}_{jq} \left(1 + \log \frac{G_{jq}}{\tilde{G}_{jq}} \right) + n\alpha \qquad (23.21)$$

The global minimum of $Z(G, \tilde{G})$ is

$$G_{jq} = \tilde{G}_{jq} \left[\frac{[(W; A)' FB]_{jq} + \alpha}{[(W; (FB\tilde{G}'))' FB + \alpha \tilde{G}E]_{jq}} \right]^{\frac{1}{2}} \qquad (23.22)$$

Proof Sketch It is straightforward to show that $Z(G, G) = J(G)$. Furthermore, $J(G)$ has two quadratic terms. Applying Jensen's inequality and inequality $x \geq 1 + \log x, \forall x > 0$ when expanding both terms, we get

$$\|W; (A - FBG')\|^2 \le Z_1(G, \tilde{G}) \qquad (23.23)$$

$$\alpha\|G1 - 1\|^2 \le Z_2(G, \tilde{G}) \qquad (23.24)$$

From Eqs. (23.23) and (23.24), we have $Z(G, \tilde{G}) \ge J(G)$. Hence, we prove that $Z(G, \tilde{G})$ is an auxiliary function of $J(G)$.

To show that Eq. (23.22) gives the global minimum of $Z(G, \tilde{G})$, we need to first prove that $Z(G, \tilde{G})$ indeed has a global minimum. This can be achieved by showing that $Z(G, \tilde{G})$ is a convex function on G. We compute the second order derivative of $Z(G, \tilde{G})$ with respect to G, which gives the Hessian matrix of $Z(G, \tilde{G})$:

$$\frac{\partial^2 Z(G, \tilde{G})}{\partial G_{jq} \partial G_{pr}} = \delta_{jp}\delta_{qr} \left(\frac{2[W; AFB]_{jq}\tilde{G}_{jq} + 2\alpha\tilde{G}_{jq}}{G_{jq}^2} \right.$$

$$\left. + \frac{2[W; (FB\tilde{G}')FB]_{jq} + 2\alpha[\tilde{G}E]_{jq}}{\tilde{G}_{jq}} \right)$$

where $\delta_{ab} = 1$ when $a = b$ and 0 otherwise. Hence, the Hessian is a diagonal matrix with positive diagonal elements, which makes it positive definite. Therefore, $Z(G, \tilde{G})$ is a convex function on G. To compute the global minimum, it is sufficient to compute its local minimum. We set $\frac{\partial Z(G,\tilde{G})}{\partial G_{jq}} = 0$ and through some algebra, we get Eq. (23.22).

Following the same lines, we can derive the update rules for F and B:

$$F_{iq} = \tilde{F}_{iq} \left[\frac{[W; ABG']_{ip} + \beta}{[W; (\tilde{F}BG')BG' + \beta\tilde{F}E]_{ip}} \right]^{\frac{1}{2}} \qquad (23.25)$$

$$B_{pq} = \tilde{B}_{pq} \left[\frac{[F'(W; A)G]_{pq}}{[F'(W; (F\tilde{B}G'))G]_{pq}} \right]^{\frac{1}{2}} \qquad (23.26)$$

Having update rules (23.22), (23.25), and (23.26), the iterative algorithm essentially updates F, B and G alternatively in each iteration. The algorithm continues until it converges or a predefined number of iterations is reached.

23.4 Experiments

We carry out a set of experiments to evaluate the effectiveness of the proposed framework for boostrapping service recommendation. The experiments are conduced on a real-world QoS dataset that consists of 1.5 million service invocation records. 150 computer nodes from the Planet-Lab,[3] which are located in over twenty countries, are

---

[3] http://www.planet-lab.org

leveraged to automatically invoke a hundred selected Web services. These services are distributed across more than twenty countries. Each computer node invokes each service for 100 times and the average Round-Trip Time (RTT) is used as the QoS dataset in our experiments.

23.4.1 Experiment Design

We organize the QoS data into a 100×150 matrix A, in which entry A_{ij} denotes the averaged RTT that user j used to invoke service i. We randomly remove a certain percentage (80–96 %) of entries from A to simulate a real-world QoS dataset, where only a small subset of entries are observed. To assess the proposed bootstrapping strategy, we follow a similar design as in [21], which splits users (or services) into two disjoint subsets: the training set and the test set, consisting of 80 and 20 % users (or services), respectively. We apply NMTF to the training set to discover the user and service groups and estimate the missing QoS entires. We then construct the decision tree for the initial interview. The actual RTT records of the test users are used to simulate the results of invoking the services in the decision tree.

We employ Mean Absolute Error (MAE), one of the most widely used metric in recommendation systems, to assess the quality of recommendation:

$$MAE = \sum_{i,j} \frac{|A_{ij} - \hat{A}_{ij}|}{N} \tag{23.27}$$

where A_{ij} and $\hat{A}_{ij}$ denote the actual and estimated RTT respectively. N is the total number of estimated QoS entries. Since the RTT entries are randomly removed, all the results reported below are obtained by computing the average over 20 runs. The numbers of user and service groups are 30 and 20, respectively. The default value for the penalty terms α and β are both set to 10. These default values will be used in all the experiments unless specified otherwise.

23.4.2 Quality of Cold-start Recommendation

To our best knowledge, there is no existing work on providing service recommendation for cold-start users. As discussed in Sect. 23.1, the ternary tree approach presented in [4, 21] is not suitable for the initial interview of service recommendation, either. To demonstrate the effectiveness of the proposed bootstrapping strategy, we implemented four representative collaborative filtering methods, including:

- the user based algorithms using both Pearson Correlation Coefficient (UPCC) and cosine similarity (referred to as UCOS) as similarity measures [11];

- the item based algorithm using Pearson Correlation Coefficient (IPCC) as similarity measure;
- the hybrid collaborative algorithm that combines both user and item based approaches using their prediction accuracy as the aggregation weights (referred to as WSRec) [19].
- the constrained matrix factorization model (referred to as NMTF), as discussed in Sect. 23.3, in which Eq. (23.6) is utilized to make the prediction after the model is constructed.

We apply the above methods to the warm-start users and use the obtained result as the baseline to assess our cold-start performance. As indicated in [21], using a ternary tree model, the cold-start performance is always worse than the warm-start performance considering that more information is available for the warm-start users. Therefore, the relative warm/cold start performance is a good indicator about the effectiveness of the bootstrapping process.

Figure 23.2 compares the warm-start MAE performance from the four representative CF algorithms with the MAE performance for cold-start users from the proposed bootstrapping framework (referred to as NMTF-DT). We vary the sparsity ratio of the QoS matrix A from 80 to 96 % and achieve two important observations. First, the cold-start performance of NMTF-DT outperforms the warm-start performance of other algorithms in all cases. This clearly demonstrates the effectiveness of the bootstrapping strategy. As can be seen later in Fig. 23.6, a new user only needs to invoke few services (3–6 on average) during the interview process. This is usually much smaller than the number of services invoked by a warm-start user. For example, if the sparsity of A is 80 %, since we have 100 services in total, each existing user invoked 20 services on average. The fundamental reason for this is that the integration of MF with decision tree learning identifies the most important few services to invoke for the new user. The QoS collected from these services captures the key

Fig. 23.2 Cold-start user MAE performance comparison

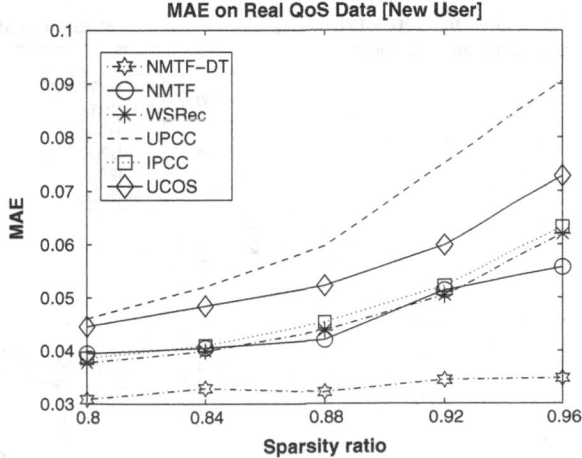

(latent) features of the user. This is critical to discover the most similar user group, which is used to predict the QoS from other services that are unknown to the new user.

Second, as the sparsity of A increases, the performance advantage of NMTF-DT becomes more significant. This is because the warm-start performance drops quickly when less information is available for users. For a very sparse QoS dataset, most users may invoke very few or even zero services. In fact, these algorithms essentially suffer from the cold-start problem, which we aim to resolve in this paper. The MAE performance of NMTF-DF also drops as sparsity increases because it relies on the similar user groups to make the prediction. However, the performance goes down much slower than other algorithms. It is also interesting to note that NMTF suffers less than other algorithms for the cold-start issue. This also contributes to the good performance of NMTF-DT, in which NMTF serves as a precursor of the entire bootstrapping process.

Figure 23.3 shows the results on cold-start services. In this set of experiments, we randomly choose 80 % rows from matrix A, which represent 80 % of the services, and use these services as the training set. The remaining rows are used as the test set. The results show a very similar trend as in Fig. 23.2. The MAE performance on cold-start services is a little bit worse than the performance on cold-start users but it is still comparable with the warm-start performance achieved by NMTF. Furthermore, it outperforms NMTF when the data becomes very sparse.

Figure 23.4 demonstrates the effectiveness of the proposed surrogate user mechanism for profiling new services. In this set of experiments, we randomly choose a user from the query path and replace it with a user that is randomly chosen from the user group where the original user belongs to. As can be seen, using the surrogate user delivers a MAE performance, which is almost identical to using the original user. It is also interesting to see that using the surrogate user sometimes even achieves better MAE performance. This may be due to some noises that affect the QoS delivery

Fig. 23.3 Cold-start service MAE performance comparison

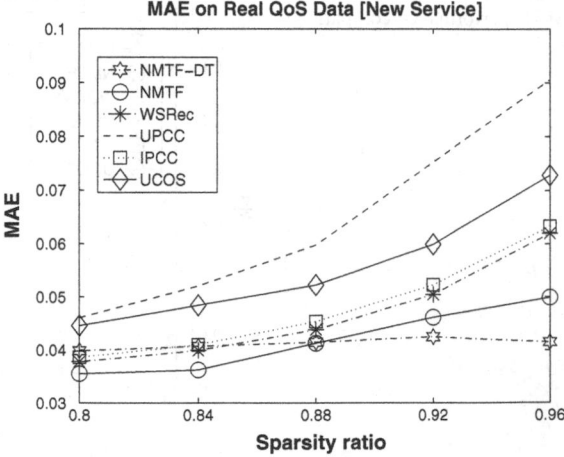

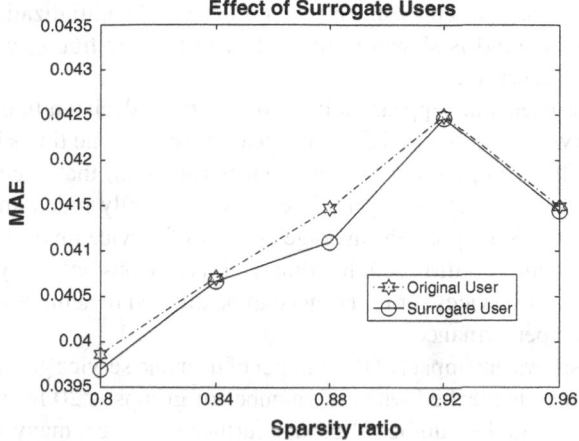

Fig. 23.4 Effectiveness of surrogate users

to the original user. The surrogate user may not be affected by these noises, which contributes to a better estimation of the QoS of the new service.

23.4.3 Impact of Parameters

We investigate the impact of two important parameters in this section, including the height of the decision tree and the number of user groups. The sparsity ratio of A is kept as 80 %.

We control the height of the decision tree by restricting the minimum number of services per leaf node, referred to as min_ leaf_ size. As shown in the left chart of Fig. 23.5, when we vary min_ leaf_ size from 1 to 10, the average tree height decreases from 13.36 to 6.16. The MAE performance on cold-start users also decreases slowly as tree height decreases although there are some small fluctuations

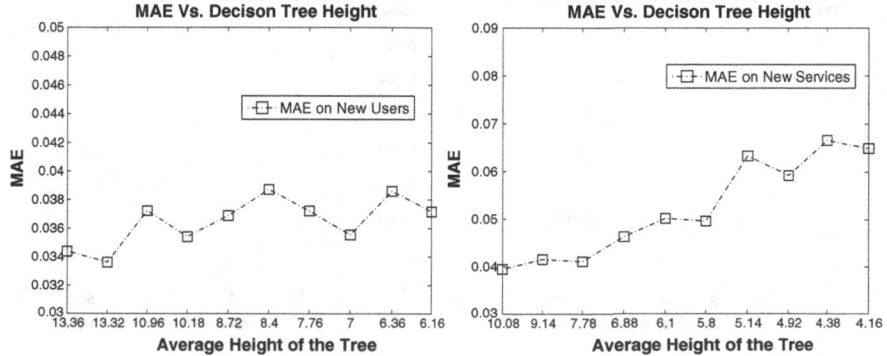

Fig. 23.5 Impact of decision tree height

due to the randomness in removing entries from A and the initialization of F, B and G. A very similar trend is shown in the right chart of the figure, which gives the result on cold-start services.

A service (or user) may appear multiple times in the decision tree. For example, in Fig. 23.1, services S_{53}, S_{59} and S_{54} all appear more than one times in the example decision tree. Therefore, the number of services (or users) that need to be queried by a new user (or service) during the interview is actually much smaller than the tree height. Figure 23.6 reports the average number of service invocations versus the min_ leaf_ size, which confirms our hypothesis. It is obvious only very small number (3–6 on average) of services (or users) need to be queried to achieve good cold-start recommendation performance.

Figure 23.7 shows the impact of the number of user and service groups. An optimal MAE performance is reached when the number of groups is 20 for both new users and new services. As the number of groups further increases, many smaller groups will be generated. Restricted by the group size, similar users or services may be spitted into different groups, which will lower the prediction accuracy.

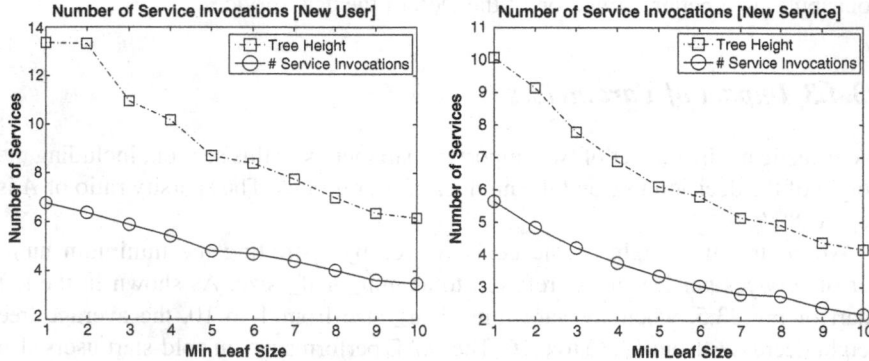

Fig. 23.6 Number of service invocations

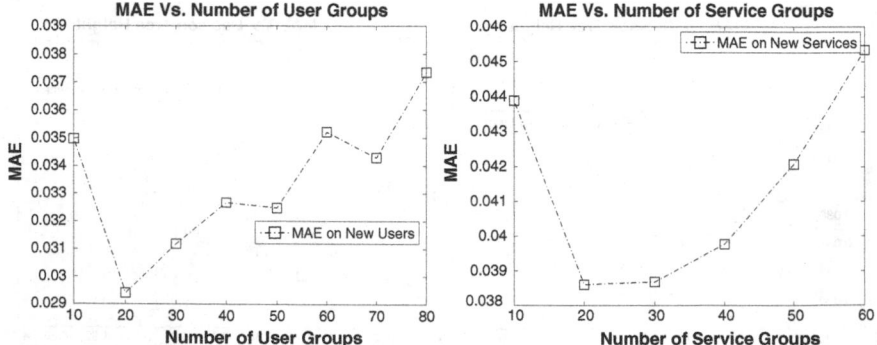

Fig. 23.7 Impact of number of user and service groups

23.5 Conclusion and Future Work

We develop a novel framework for bootstrapping service recommendation. The proposed framework offers a complete solution that tackles both new users and services. The framework is underpinned by Non-negative Matrix Tri-Factorization (NMTF) that simultaneously clusters users and services into a set of user and service groups. The group structure helps estimate the missing interaction information and also provides class labels to construct decision trees for both users and services. An initial interview is conducted to adaptively query users or services for rapid profiling. We propose to exploit surrogate users obtained from the user groups to improve the user response rate for profiling new services. The effectiveness of the proposed framework has been demonstrated via experiments on a real-world QoS dataset and through comparison with competitive collaborative filtering algorithms. An interesting future direction is to exploit existing work on reputation and trust management [7, 13] in service computing to get high-quality QoS data from users to further improve the quality of the recommendation result.

References

1. Chen, X., Liu, X., Huang, Z., Sun, H.: Regionknn: A scalable hybrid collaborative filtering algorithm for personalized web service recommendation. In: ICWS, pp. 9–16 (2010)
2. Chen, X., Zheng, Z., Liu, X., Huang, Z., Sun, H.: Personalized qos-aware web service recommendation and visualization. IEEE Trans. Serv. Comput. 99(PrePrints) (2011). http://doi.ieeecomputersociety.org/10.1109/TSC.2011.35
3. Golbandi, N., Koren, Y., Lempel, R.: On bootstrapping recommender systems. In: Proceedings of the 19th ACM International Conference on Information and Knowledge Management, CIKM '10, pp. 1805–1808. ACM, New York (2010). doi:doi.acm.org/10.1145/1871437.1871734
4. Golbandi, N., Koren, Y., Lempel, R.: Adaptive bootstrapping of recommender systems using decision trees. In: Proceedings of the Fourth ACM International Conference on Web Search and Data Mining, WSDM '11, pp. 595–604. ACM, New York (2011). doi:doi.acm.org/10.1145/1935826.1935910
5. Jiang, Y., Liu, J., Tang, M., Liu, X.F.: An effective web service recommendation method based on personalized collaborative filtering. In: ICWS, pp. 211–218 (2011)
6. Lee, D.D., Seung, H.S.: Algorithms for non-negative matrix factorization. In: NIPS, pp. 556–562 (2000). http://citeseer.ist.psu.edu/lee01algorithms
7. Malik, Z., Bouguettaya, A.: Rateweb: Reputation assessment for trust establishment among web services. VLDB J. 18(4), 885–911 (2009)
8. Rashid, A.M., Albert, I., Cosley, D., Lam, S.K., McNee, S.M., Konstan, J.A., Riedl, J.: Getting to know you: learning new user preferences in recommender systems. In: Proceedings of the 7th International Conference on Intelligent User Interfaces, IUI '02, pp. 127–134. ACM, New York (2002). doi:doi.acm.org/10.1145/502716.502737
9. Rashid, A.M., Karypis, G., Riedl, J.: Learning preferences of new users in recommender systems: an information theoretic approach. SIGKDD Explor. Newsl. 10, 90–100 (2008). doi:doi.acm.org/10.1145/1540276.1540302
10. Rong, W., Liu, K., Liang, L.: Personalized web service ranking via user group combining association rule. IEEE Int. Conf. Web Serv. 0, 445–452 (2009). doi:doi.ieeecomputersociety.org/10.1109/ICWS.2009.113

11. Shao, L., Zhang, J., Wei, Y., Zhao, J., Xie, B., Mei, H.: Personalized qos prediction forweb services via collaborative filtering. In: ICWS, pp. 439–446 (2007)
12. Wang, F., Li, T., Zhang, C.: Semi-supervised clustering via matrix factorization. In: SDM, pp. 1–12 (2008)
13. Yahyaoui, H., Zhioua, S.: Bootstrapping trust of web services through behavior observation. In: Auer, S., Díaz, O., Papadopoulos G.A. (eds.) ICWE, Lecture Notes in Computer Science, vol. 6757, pp. 319–330. Springer (2011)
14. Yu, Q.: Decision tree learning from incomplete qos to bootstrap service recommendation. In: ICWS '12: Proceedings of the 2012 IEEE International Conference on Web Services (2012)
15. Yu, Q.: Qos-aware service selection via collaborative qos evaluation (accepted to appear). The World Wide Web Journal (WWWJ) (2012) http://link.springer.com/article/10.1007%2Fs11280-012-0186-0
16. Yu, Q., Bouguettaya, A.: Framework for web service query algebra and optimization. TWEB **2**(1), 1–35 (2008)
17. Yu, Q., Rege, M., Bouguettaya, A., Medjahed, B., Ouzzani, M.: A two-phase framework for quality-awareweb service selection. Serv. Oriented Comput. Appl. **4**(2), 63–79 (2010)
18. Zhang, Q., Ding, C., Chi, C.H.: Collaborative filtering based service ranking using invocation histories. In: ICWS, pp. 195–202 (2011)
19. Zheng, Z., Ma, H., Lyu, M.R., King, I.: Wsrec: A collaborative filtering based web service recommender system. In: ICWS, pp. 437–444 (2009)
20. Zheng, Z., Ma, H., Lyu, M.R., King, I.: Collaborative web service qos prediction via neighborhood integrated matrix factorization. IEEE Trans. Serv. Comput. 99(PrePrints) (2011). doi:doi.ieeecomputersociety.org/10.1109/TSC.2011.35
21. Zhou, K., Yang, S.H., Zha, H.: Functional matrix factorizations for cold-start recommendation. In: Proceedings of the 34th International ACM SIGIR Conference on Research and Development in Information Retrieval, SIGIR '11, pp. 315–324. ACM, New York (2011). doi:doi.acm.org/10.1145/2009916.2009961

Chapter 24
An Approach for Service Discovery and Recommendation Using Contexts

Hua Xiao and Ying Zou

Abstract Given the large amount of existing Web services nowadays, it is time-consuming for users to find appropriate Web services to satisfy their diversity requirements. Context-aware techniques provide a promising way to help users obtain their desired services by automatically analyzing a user's context and recommending services for the user. Most existing context-aware techniques require system designers to manually define reactions to contexts based on context types (e.g., location) and context values (e.g., Toronto). Those context-aware techniques have limited support for dynamic adaptation to new context types and values. Due to the diversity of user's environments, the available context types and potential context values are changing overtime. It is challenging to anticipate a complete set of context types with various potential context values to provide corresponding reactions. In this chapter, we present an approach which analyzes dynamic changing context types and values, and formulates search criteria to discover desired services for users. More specifically, we use ontologies to enhance the meaning of a user's context values and automatically identify the relations among different context values. Based on the relations among context values, we infer the potential tasks that a user might be interested in, then recommend related services. A case study is conducted to evaluate the effectiveness of our approach. The results show that our approach can use contexts to automatically detect a user's requirements in given context scenarios and recommend desired services with high precision and recall.

H. Xiao (✉)
IBM Canada Laboratory, Markham, ON, Canada
e-mail: huaxiao@ca.ibm.com

Y. Zou
Department of Electrical and Computer Engineering, Queen's University,
Kingston, ON, Canada
e-mail: ying.zou@queensu.ca

A. Bouguettaya et al. (eds.), *Web Services Foundations*,
DOI: 10.1007/978-1-4614-7518-7_24,
© Springer Science+Business Media New York 2014

24.1 Introduction

With the growing prevalence of Service Oriented Architecture (SOA), more Web services become available for users to enrich their daily online experience. It is time consuming for users to find appropriate services to satisfy their various requirements. Context-aware techniques provide a promising way to help users obtain their desired services by automatically analyzing a user's context and recommending services for the user. Specifically, a context characterizes the situation of a person, place or the interactions between humans, applications and the environment [13]. One way to model contexts is to use pairs of context types and context values. A context type describes a characteristic of the context. A context type is associated with a specific context value. For example, "location", "identity", and "time" are context types of a user. "New York" is a context value of the context type "location". Furthermore, a context scenario is the combination of different context types with specific values to reflect a user's situation. To manage different context types and values captured by a context-aware system, a context model is used to specify the relations and the storage structure of various context types and values.

Context-aware systems are designed to react to a user's context without their intervention. A context aware system generally consists of two parts: sensing a context scenario, and adapting the system to the changing context scenario. Most context-aware systems require the designer of context-aware systems to predict the context types. Moreover, the designer needs to manually establish the relation between the sensed context scenario and the corresponding reactions in the form of IF-THEN rules which specify how a system should respond to context changes. However, due to the diversity of user's environments, the available context types and potential context values are changing overtime. For example, if a user travels from her home to another city "Los Angeles". The user's environment changes accordingly. The location is changed from "home" which is a context value of context type "location" to "Los Angeles". And the activity of the user in the new location is "driving", whereas the context-aware system may not detect the activity of the user when she was at home. It is challenging to anticipate a complete set of context types with various potential context values to provide corresponding reactions. Moreover, fixed rules are not flexible enough to accommodate the changing environment and various personal interests. To recommend services for a context scenario, this chapter presents an approach which analyzes dynamic changing context types and values, and formulates search criteria to discover desired services for users. Different from existing approaches which depend on static context models to know the relations among context types (or values) and use predefined rules to infer user's requirements, we seek an automatic approach to recognize the relations between context values and a user's requirements. For example, luxury hotel and limited budget are two context values in conflict. Therefore, the services for booking luxury hotels are automatically filtered when a user has limited budget. We expect that such relations can be used to express more accurate searching criteria that better reflect a user's context. When a new value of a user is detected, our approach can automatically compute the relations between the new context value with existing context values. Instead of manually defining IF-THEN rules using specific context values as the traditional context-aware systems [10], our approach automatically identifies the semantic relations among context values to infer user's requirements. Then we generate service searching criteria based on user's requirements to discover and recommend services. This book chapter extends our earlier work [27] published in the International Conference on Web Services (ICWS) 2010. We enhance our earlier publication at ICWS 2010 in the following aspects:

1. Improve the algorithm for identifying the relations among different context values by considering domain knowledge and semantics of phrases used to describe the meaning of context values;
2. Extend the approach for generating service searching criteria to search for desired services; and
3. Conduct a larger case study to evaluate our extended approach.

To facilitate the presentation of this chapter, we use the following travel scenario as an illustrative example throughout this chapter. Tom is a graduate student living in Toronto. Tom is interested in watching Hollywood movies and National Basketball Association (NBA) games. Especially, Tom is a fan of Kobe Bryant who is an American professional basketball player and plays for the NBA team, Los Angeles Lakers. Tom plans to travel to Los Angeles and spend his vacation in Los Angeles next month. When examining the context in this scenario, we find that some contextual information can be helpful for Tom to plan his trip. For example, as a graduate student who has low income, Tom might prefer budget hotel for the trip. As a fan of NBA, Tom might be glad to know the NBA game schedules of "Los Angeles Lakers" when he is in Los Angeles.

The remainder of this chapter is organized as follows. Section 24.2 gives an overview of our approach. Section 24.3 introduces the background of ontologies. Section 24.4 presents our approach to find matching ontologies from ontologies databases. Section 24.5 discusses the details of inferring relations among different context values. Section 24.6 presents our approach that identifies user's requirements in a given context scenario and generates searching criteria to search for services. Sections 24.7 and 24.8 present an overview of our prototype and discuss the case study. In Sect. 24.9, we present the related work. Finally, Sect. 24.10 concludes the chapter and presents the future work.

24.2 Overview of Our Approach

Figure 24.1 gives an overview of our approach. Context types and context values can be dynamically added and removed to reflect a user's situation. The value of a context type can also be changed over time. To correctly model relations among context values, it is critical to understand the semantic meanings of each context value. Ontologies capture the information related to a particular concept using expert

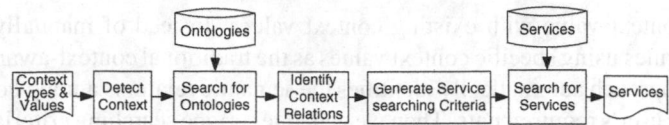

Fig. 24.1 Steps for context-aware service recommendation

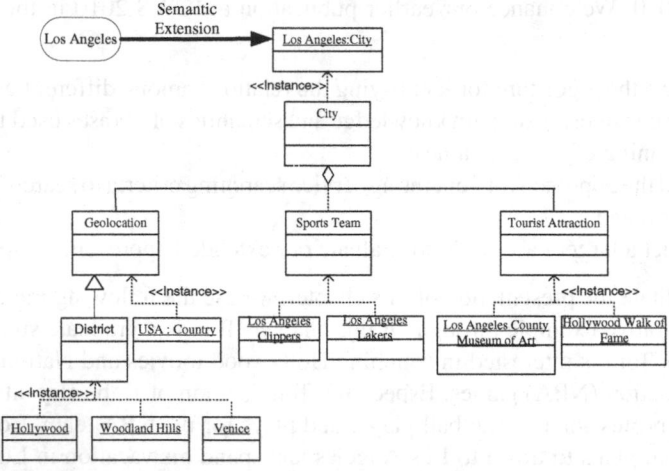

Fig. 24.2 An example of extending context value using ontology

knowledge. To identify the semantics of a context value, we search for publicly available ontologies to extend the meaning of the context value. Figure 24.2 illustrates an example ontology for defining the concept "Los Angeles". In particular, "Los Angeles" is a context value for the context type "Location". The ontology of "Los Angeles" shown in Fig. 24.2 expands the semantic meaning of "Los Angeles" with additional information, such as "Geographic Location", "Sports Team", and "Tourist Attraction". When a new context value for a user is detected, our approach automatically searches for ontologies that expand the semantic meanings of the new value and computes the relations with other context types and values.

We use the identified context relations to discover user's requirements for a given context scenario and generate the corresponding service searching criteria. For example, when the semantics (i.e. ontologies) of several context values share a same concept, the common concept might reflect the potential requirements of the user. In the travel scenario, Tom is going to travel to "Los Angeles", and he is interested in watching NBA games. The ontologies of "Los Angeles" and "NBA" have a same concept "Los Angeles Lakers". It indicates a high likelihood that Tom would be interested in watching the basketball game played by "Los Angeles Lakers". Finally, we use the generated service searching criteria to discover and recommend services to the user.

24.3 Background of Ontology

Ontologies are described using ontology specification languages, such as Web Ontology Language (OWL) [24], Resource Description Framework (RDF) [20] and DAML+OIL [17]. We use ontologies to understand the meanings of context values. The ontologies found for context values can be described in different ontology specification languages. To ease the inference of the relations among context values, we define a simplified model which summarizes the structures and concepts of ontologies needed for our context analysis. Figure 24.3 illustrates the major entities in our ontology definition model. Essentially, our ontology definition model contains the following four major components.

- Class is an abstract description of a group of concepts with similar characteristics. A class has a name and a set of properties that describe the characteristics of the class. For example shown in Fig. 24.2, "Tourist Attraction" as a class contains the common characteristics of tourist attractions. Class is also called "concept", "type", "category" or "kind" in ontology specification languages.
- Individual refers to an instance of a class. For example, "Hollywood Walk of Fame" in Fig. 24.2 is an instance of class "Tourist Attraction" and therefore it is an individual.
- Property describes an attribute of a class or an individual. A property can also be composed by other properties. Atomic properties are the lowest level of properties without other properties. Atomic properties include property name and property value. In our ontology definition model, we use properties to express specific relations among classes and among individuals. For instance, to express that "Los Angeles" is in "USA", we define a property "isIn" for "Los Angeles" and assign it with the value "USA". Property is also referred to as "attribute", "feature" or "characteristic" in ontology specification languages.
- Relation defines ways in which classes or individuals can be associated with each other. In our ontology definition model, the types of relations are predefined. Four types of relations are defined to connect classes and individuals: (1) Subclass extends an abstract class to convey more concrete knowledge; (2) PartOf means a

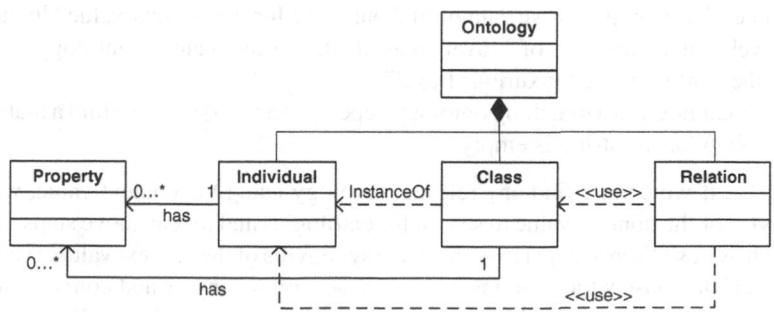

Fig. 24.3 Major entities defined in ontologies

class or an individual is a part of another class or individual. For example, class "Tourist Attractions" is a part of the class "Location"; (3) Complement expresses that the instances of a class do not belong to another class; and the two classes together contain all the instances in a given domain; and (4) Equivalence means that two classes, individuals or properties are the same. For example, class "Nation" could have an equivalence relation with "Country". To express specific relations (e.g., isIn) other than the four types of relations between classes or individuals, we use properties.

24.4 Searching for Matching Ontologies

There are few ontologies named using long phrases, such as "Plan a trip to Los Angeles" which is the context value for context type "activity". We use the following steps to find an annotated ontology for each context value.

1. We treat the context value as a searching string, and use the entire searching string to search for ontologies from ontology databases, such as Freebase [2]. Freebase is an ontology database which extracts structured information from Wikipedia [8]. If we can find a matching ontology, we annotate this ontology to this context value. Otherwise, we go to step 2.

2. We use an adjective and adverb dictionary to identify and remove the first adjective or adverb in the searching string. Adjectives and adverbs are constraints for the describing entity. Therefore, we can keep the important information in the searching string without the adjectives and adverbs. Meanwhile, if the phrase of a context value contains another context value, we remove the repeated words from the long phrase. Thus, in our example, we can remove "Los Angeles" from the context value "plan a trip to Los Angeles". If the removed word is followed by a stop word, we also remove the stop word. A stop word is a commonly used word (such as "by", "the", and "about") that does not contain important significance and some search engines have been set to ignore. Then we use the remainder part of the searching string to search for ontologies.

3. If we can find a matching ontology, we annotate this ontology to the context value. For example, if we cannot find ontology for the context value "luxurious travel" but an ontology of "travel" is available, we annotate the ontology "travel" to the context value "luxurious travel".

4. If we cannot find a matching ontology, repeat (2) and (3) until we find a matching ontology or the string is empty.

Finally, if we cannot find any relevant ontology using the context value, we use synonyms of the context value to search for ontologies and repeat above steps. In our research, we use WordNet [5] to identify the synonyms of the context value. WordNet is a lexical database which groups words into sets of synonyms and connects words to each other via semantic relations. After trying above steps, if we still cannot find

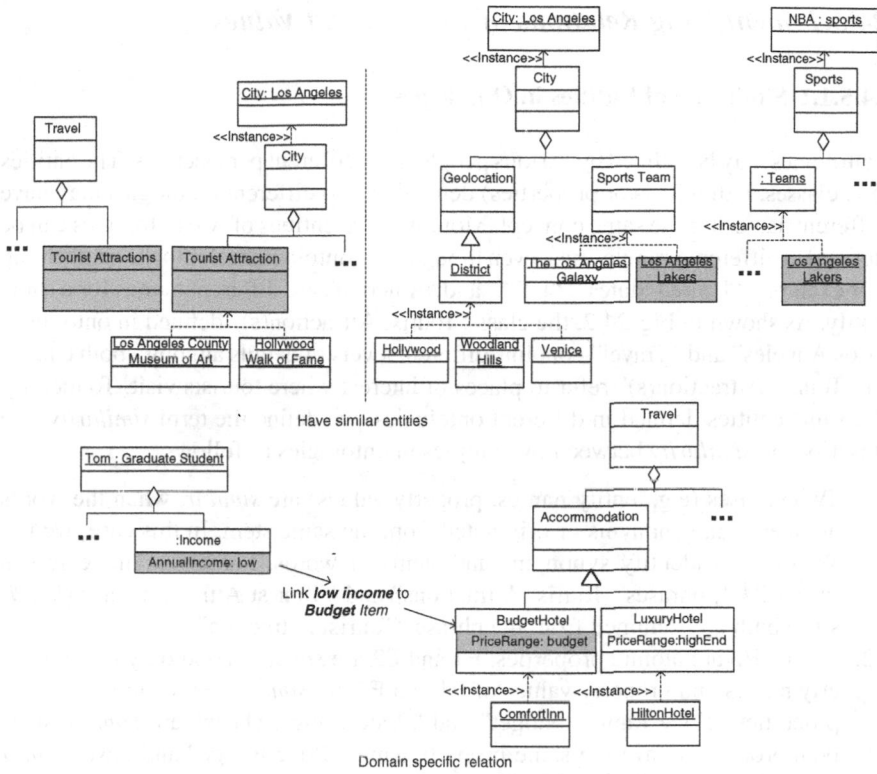

Fig. 24.4 Examples of relations between two context values

any matching ontologies for a context value, we create an empty ontology and set the context value as the only entity of the new ontology.

24.5 Identifying Context Relations

Our approach uses the relations among context values to identify a user's requirements in the given context scenarios. We use two steps to identify the relations among multiple context values.

1. *Identifying the relations between two context values.* We compare the corresponding ontologies which represent the semantics of context values to identify the relations between two context values.
2. *Integrating all the relations of two context values.* To get the relations among multiple context values, we integrate the relations between two context values to construct a relation map that describes the relations of multiple context values.

24.5.1 Identifying Relations of Two Context Values

24.5.1.1 Similarity of Entities in Ontologies

Ontologies may be defined by various people from different perspectives. The entities (i.e. classes, individuals or properties) defined in two different ontologies may have different names for the same concept. Moreover, the entities of two ontologies can be defined in different granularities, even though both ontologies refer to the same thing. For example, "United States", "USA" and "America" are different names for a same entity. As shown in Fig. 24.2, the class "Tourist Attraction(s)" defined in ontologies "Los Angeles" and "Travel" contains different levels of details although both classes of "Tourist Attraction(s)" refer to places of interest where tourists visit. To identify the same entities defined in different ontologies, we define the term *similarity*. We describe the *similarity* between two entities in ontologies as follows:

1. Two phrases (e.g., entity names, property values) are *similar*, when the words are identical, synonyms or originated from the same stem. In this case, we use WordNet to identify synonyms and stems of words. For the example shown in Fig. 24.4, phrases "Tourist Attractions" and "Tourist Attraction" are *similar* since both are stemmed from the phrase "Tourist Attraction".
2. E1 and E2 are atomic properties. E1 and E2 are *similar* if and only if the property names and property values of E1 and E2 are *similar*. For example, atomic properties "Price Range: budget" and "Price Range: cheap" are *similar* since both properties have the same property name "Price Range" and have *similar* properties values "budget" and "cheap".
3. E1 and E2 are classes, individuals or non-atomic properties. E1 and E2 are *similar* if and only if

   a. The names of E1 and E2 are *similar*; and
   b. All the properties defined in entity E1 exist in entity E2, or all the properties defined in entity E2 exist in E1.

   For example, class "Tourist Attractions" with properties "location: Los Angeles" and another class "Tourist Attraction" which does not have properties are *similar*, since the class name "Tourist Attractions" and "Tourist Attraction" are *similar*, and the properties defined in the latter class (i.e. no properties) belong to the former class.

We use WordNet [5] to identify the synonyms and stem of words. WordNet is a lexical database which groups words into sets of synonyms and connects words to each other via semantic relations. By considering the synonyms and stems of words, we can discover that two entities are *similar* even if the entities are not described using the same words. In (3), E1 and E2 might have different numbers of properties. When describing the same entity, some ontologies may provide more detailed information than others due to the different levels of granularity in ontologies. If the properties of E1 (i.e. class or individual) are a subset of the properties of E2, E1 and E2 are treated as *similar* entities.

24.5.1.2 User-Defined Relations Using Domain Knowledge

By comparing the similarity of entities, we can discover the semantic relations between context values. However, the similarity of entities cannot identify the relations which require domain knowledge. For example, in the travel scenario, Tom is a graduate student with low income. We can infer that he might prefer budget hotel instead of luxury hotel while he is traveling. From the ontology of graduate students, we may know that graduate students have low income, but the ontology of graduate students would not specify that he prefers budget hotels. To overcome this problem, we use LinQL language [18] to specify links between entities. LinQL is an extension of SQL and defines the conditions that two given entities must satisfy before a link of two entities can be established.

$$Linkspec\_stmt = CREATE\ LINKSPEC\ linkspec\_name$$
$$AS\ link\_method\ opt\_args\ opt\_limit. \qquad (24.1)$$

Equation (24.1) shows the main structure of defining a link specification statement (linkspec for short) using LinQL. As shown in Eq. (24.1), a CREATE LINKSPEC statement defines a new linkspec which specifies the name of the linkspec and a method to establish the link. For example, Eq. (24.2) defines that if a person's income is low, then the person would prefer economical consumption style.

$$CREATE\ LINKSPEC\ consumption\_style$$
$$AS\ LINK\ low\_income\ WITH\ target$$
$$WHERE\ synonym(term, economy) \qquad (24.2)$$
$$AND$$
$$target\ LIKE\ '\%term\%'$$

The economical consumption style is defined as terms with a property of economy. The details of defining LinQL are described in the publication of Hassanzadeh et al. [18]. In our approach, the administrator of the context-aware system can use LinQL to provide the domain knowledge. Meanwhile, we could develop a graphic user interface to visualize LinQL and enable users to create some simple relations using their knowledge.

24.5.1.3 Relations Between Two Context Values

Based on the definitions of similarity and user-defined relations, we identify the following 5 types of relations between two context values extended by ontologies:

1. Intersection: refers to the fact that the ontologies of two context values contain similar entities (i.e. classes or individuals). Figure 24.4 shows three examples of intersection relations. In Fig. 24.4, the context value "travel" (i.e. its relevant context type is "activity") and context value "Los Angeles" share the same

entity "Tourist Attraction". Context values, "Los Angeles" and "NBA", contain a common entity, "Los Angeles Lakers". When a context value is a part of another context value, such context values are in an intersection relation. In the travel example, ontology "Los Angeles" contains an entity "Hollywood". Therefore, "Hollywood" is a part of "Los Angeles". The context values "Hollywood" and "Los Angeles" have an intersection relation.

We use entity names, properties and individuals to describe the common entities among two ontologies. The children entities (e.g., sub-classes, and individuals of sub-classes) of the common entities are ignored if the children entities are not defined in one of the ontologies. This can make the description of common classes simple, since children entities contain too many details and could become noises of the common entities.

2. Complement: indicates that all members (i.e. classes or individuals) defined in one ontology do not belong to another; and both context ontologies define all the elements in a given domain. The complement relations can be directly derived from the ontology definitions. For example, context values "Economy Hotel" and "Luxury Hotel" have a complement relation as defined in the ontology of "Travel".

3. Equivalence: defines that two context values describe the same concept. Equivalence relations should be explicitly defined in one of the ontologies. Explicit defined equal entities are treated as similar entities when we compare the entities from two different ontologies.

4. Domain Specific relation: means that the corresponding ontologies of two context values contain entities which are linked by user-defined relations. As shown in Fig. 24.4 (3), the domain specific relation is identified by a user-defined relation which links the low income to budget items, i.e. budget hotel in the travel scenario.

5. Independence: means that two context values do not have any connection.

24.5.2 Inferring Relations Among Multiple Context Values

We use entity-relationship (E-R) diagrams [16] to create a global view of relations among multiple context values. E-R diagrams provide a formal description for a set of entities and relationships among entities.

For each relation of two context values, we convert the two context values into two entities in the E-R diagrams. The relation type (e.g., intersection and complement) is converted into a relationship node in the E-R diagrams. A relationship node connects its relevant entities. If the relation type is *intersection*, the common entities are converted into attributes of the *intersection* relationship in the E-R diagram. *Equivalence* relations are used to combine entities in the E-R diagram. To simplify an E-R diagram, *independence* relations are not explicitly described in an E-R diagram.

If two entities are not connected by a relation node in the E-R diagram, it indicates that the entities are *independent*.

We integrate the relations of two context values into an integrated E-R diagram in the following steps:

1. Initialize the integrated E-R diagram as empty.
2. For each relation in the relation list, we repeat the following steps:

   a. Convert a relation of two context values into an E-R diagram.
   b. Add the E-R diagram created in step 2.a to the integrated E-R diagram. If there exist *similarity* or *equivalence* entities, we merge the *similarity* and *equivalence* entities by keeping the one with the richer information in the E-R diagram. If there exist *subset* or *complement* relations, we add a relationship node in the integrated E-R diagram to indicate the corresponding relation. If two relationship nodes contain the same relation type and relationship attributes, we merge them into one relationship node.

Following the aforementioned steps, all the context values are converted into entities in the integrated E-R diagram and the entities which are associated to relations of context values are transformed into properties in the E-R diagram. Figure 24.5 shows an example of an integrated E-R diagram for the context values in the travel scenario. In Fig. 24.5, context ontologies "Student" and "Travel" have an domain specific relation due to a user-defined relation which links "Income: Low" to "Budget Hotel". The NBA team "Los Angeles Lakers" is shared by three context values "Los Angeles", "Kobe Bryant" and "NBA". Context ontology "travel" shares the same class "Tourist Attractions" with ontology "Los Angeles". Class "Tourist Attractions" contains a set of individuals such as "Hollywood Walk of Fame" and "Los Angeles County Museum of Art". We can use the individuals to recommend specific tourist attractions (i.e. services) in Los Angeles.

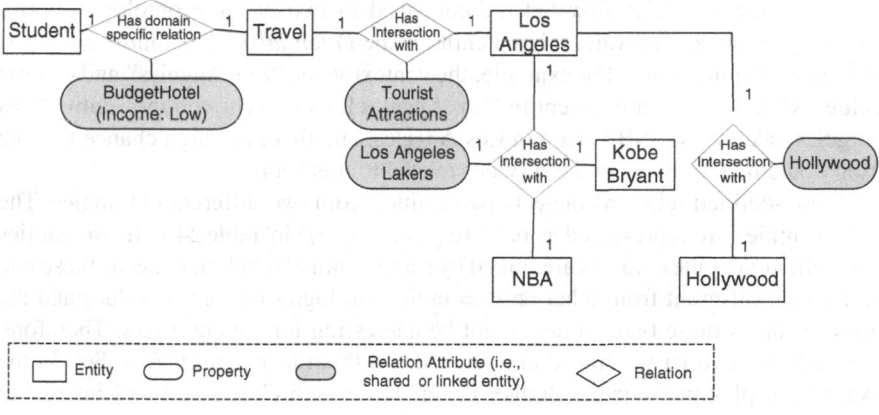

Fig. 24.5 An example integrated E-R diagram

24.6 Generating Service Searching Criteria

To recommend services, we need to identify user's requirements, and then generate searching criteria to search for services. A user's requirements describe the potential tasks to perform in a given context scenario. We define generic rules to infer user's requirements from the E-R diagram. Then we extract service searching criteria from the description of user's requirements to search for services.

24.6.1 Identify User's Requirements in Given Context Scenarios

In our approach, the requirements of a user in a context scenario are identified based on the relations among different context values. However, some relations among context values generally exist in all the scenarios of a user due to the long-term existence of certain context values or the inherent relations of context types. For instance, in the travel scenario, Tom's preferences involve "NBA" and "Kobe Bryant". These preferences can be explicitly specified by Tom and generally exist for a long time. Our approach might always need to recommend the service of "Los Angeles Lakers" since the ontologies of "NBA" and "Kobe Bryant" share the same entity "Los Angeles Lakers". Another example is a case where, the current "city" (e.g., Toronto) always belongs to the current "country" (e.g., Canada). To avoid repeated recommendations, we ignore the relations among context values when the relations are derived from the context values that exist for a long time or inherently exist in the associated context types.

We design 3 generic rules to derive user's requirements from the integrated E-R diagram as shown in Table 24.1. Suppose $E_{c1}, E_{c2}, \ldots, E_{cn}$ are entities in the integrated E-R diagram. Potential Task Set represents a set of a user's requirements.

Rule 1 collects the common entities and properties from the E-R diagram. The entities in the *Potential Task* Set are contained in two or more ontologies corresponding to the context values. Each entity in the *Potential Task* Set indicates a part of a user's requirements. For example, the context value "Los Angeles" and context value "NBA" have a common entity "Los Angeles Lakers". The common entity "Los Angeles Lakers" is a NBA team in Los Angeles, and there is a high chance that the user would be interested in the services related to this team.

A user-defined relation connects two entities from two different ontologies. The linked entities are represented as pairs (e.g., $e_{1i} \rightarrow e_{2i}$) in Table 24.1. If two entities from different context values are linked by a user-defined relation, it means these two entities are different from other entities in the ontologies of context values and the information in these two entities might be interesting for the end-users. Therefore, in rule 2, we extract the linked entities and add them to *Potential Task* Set. In the example of planning a trip, "Budget Hotel" has a high chance to be of interest to Tom since the entity "Budget Hotel" is linked by an attribute of the occupation of the user.

Table 24.1 Generic rules to derive user's requirements

Rule number	Relations	Potential Task Set	Description
1	Intersection relations: $E_{C1} \cap E_{C2} \ldots \cap E_{Cm} = \{e_1, e_2, \ldots, e_k\} \neq \emptyset$	$\{e_1, e_2, \ldots, e_k\}$	$E_{c1}, E_{c2}, \ldots, E_{cm}$ are entities in the integrated E-R diagram. $e_1, e_2, \ldots, e_k$ are entities or relationship attributes in the integrated E-R diagram
2	Domain specific relations: E_{C1} is linked to E_{C2} by user-defined relations $\{(e_{11} \rightarrow e_{21}), \ldots, (e_{1k} \rightarrow e_{2k})\}$	$\{(e_{11} \rightarrow e_{21}), \ldots, (e_{1k} \rightarrow e_{2k})\}$	$E_{c1}, E_{c2}, \ldots, E_{cn}$ are entities in the integrated E-R diagram, and $(e_{1i} \rightarrow e_{2i})$ are a pair of linked entities between entity E_{c1} and entity E_{c2}. In the E-R diagram, $(e_{1i} \rightarrow e_{2i})$ represents a property of the user-defined relation
3	Complement relations: $\bar{E}_{ci} = E_{cj}, e_1 \in E_{ci}$, $e_2 \in E_{cj}$ and $e_1, e_2 \in$ *potential Task Set*	e_1 and e_2 have an OR relation	E_{ci} and E_{cj} are entities in the integrated E-R diagram. e_1 and e_2 are entities or relationship attributes in the integrated E-R diagram; and $\bar{E}$ represents the complement of entity E

Complement relations show that two entities cannot co-exist at the same time. In Rule 3, we use complement relations to split the entities in *Potential Task* Set and identify them as "OR" relation. For example, if a *Potential Task* Set contains both the entities "Budget Hotel" and "Luxury Hotel", we can use the complement relations to identify them as a "OR" relations. Therefore, when an end-user choose one recommendation (e.g., Budget Hotel), we stop to recommend the complement recommendation (e.g., Luxury Hotel) since the user has made a decision between these two types of hotels.

Once the rules are applied on the E-R diagram, we obtain a *Potential Task* Set which contains a set of entities and properties of the entities in the E-R diagram. Some entities in the *Potential Task* Set may describe the same concept at different levels of details. For example, one entity can be a subclass of another entity. To reduce the redundancy of service recommendations, we classify the entities in a *Potential Task* Set t into different groups to merge similar user's needs. Each group maps to a specific service searching criterion.

24.6.2 Generate Service Searching Criteria

The entities and properties in a user's requirements (e.g., *Potential Task* Set) are described using structured data defined in ontologies. We use the mapping rules specified in Table 24.2 to convert structured data to service searching criteria. A class name in Table 24.2 refers to the name of a class defined in an ontology. Furthermore, the generated searching criteria are submitted to existing search engines, such as Google [3].

In Table 24.2, the first column contains the entities from the extracted user's requirements (i.e. *Potential Task* Set). The second column lists the associated query to find matching Web services described in WSDL. The third column shows the generated query submitted to a Web search engine. As shown in Table 24.2, a class contains a class name and prosperities. In a WSDL query, a class name is used to match a service name or operation name in a WSDL document since the class name is the major object name involved in a Web service and it is generally used to describe service names and operation names in WSDL. In most cases, a service name and an operation name are not identical to the class name defined in ontologies. For example, an operation used to search for budget hotels can be named as "GetBudgetHotel" or "BookBudgetHotel". The operation names contain the class name "BudgetHotel" with additional verbs (i.e. "Get" or "Book"). Therefore, in the generated WSDL query, instead of specifying that we need to find a WSDL having the service name or operation exactly matching with the class name, we check if a class name appears in the service name or the operation name. We apply the same requirements to other ontology entities in the conversion process.

Properties of a class specify the detailed attributes of the class. There is a high chance that the properties of classes are required input for performing an operation or are the output data after executing an operation in WSDL services. For example, in our travel scenario, the property "price" in class "Budget Hotel" becomes a parameter of the operation "BookBudgetHotel". As listed in Table 24.2, the names of the properties are used to match parameters of operations in WSDL service. However, a service may not need to use all the properties defined in the class. Therefore, we use the OR relation to connect all the properties. The searching criteria for Web search engines are focused on keywords. In column 3, we convert the class name into a keyword and the properties of classes to the optional (i.e. OR relations) keywords in the query. For the individuals in the *Potential Task* Set, we use the same way as classes of ontologies to convert them to two different queries.

When we specify user-defined relations, entities with more generic meanings are generally used to search for specific entities. For example, we use the generic entity "low income" to find all the budget (or economic, cheap) items. The entity with relevantly more specific meanings plays a more important role in identifying a potential task since the specific entity contains more concrete information. Therefore, we convert the specific entity instead of the general entity to search query as shown in the fourth row of Table 24.2.

Table 24.2 Mapping ontology entities in *potential task* set to WSDL query and general query

Type	Entities in the *Potential Task Set* Involved data	WSDL query	General query for WebPages
Class	Class name: $name_{class}$	$(name_{class} \sqsubseteq (name_{operation} \cup name_{service}))$ && $(name_{property_i} \sqsubseteq (name_{inputPar} \cup name_{outputPar}))$ where $name_{property_i} \in (\cup name_{property})$	$involvedContextValue$ AND $name_{class}$ AND $(property_1$ OR $property_2$ ... OR $property_k)$
	Property names of the class: $\cup name_{property}$		
Individual	Individual name: $name_{individual}$	$(name_{individual} \sqsubseteq (name_{operation} \cup name_{service}))$ && $(name_{property_i} \sqsubseteq (name_{inputPar} \cup name_{outputPar}))$ where $name_{property_i} \in (\cup name_{property})$	$involvedContextValue$ AND $name_{individual}$ AND $(property_1$ OR $property_2$ ... OR $property_k)$
	Property names of the class: $\cup name_{property}$		
User-defined relation ($e_1 \rightarrow e_2$)	Name of the class that entity e_2 belongs to: $name_{class}$	$(name_{class} \sqsubseteq (name_{operation} \cup name_{service}))$ && $(name_{property_i} \sqsubseteq (name_{inputPar} \cup name_{outputPar}))$	$involvedContextValue$ AND $name_{individual}$ AND $(property_1$ OR $property_2$ ... OR$property_k)$
	Properties of entity e_2: $\cup name_{property}$		

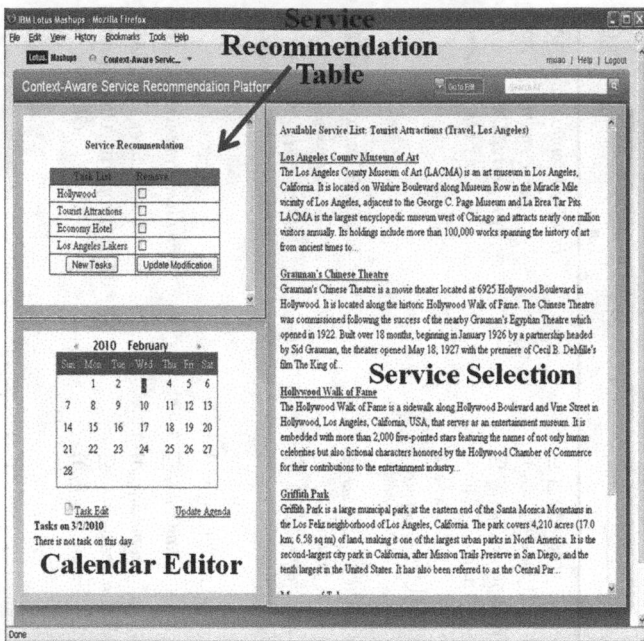

Fig. 24.6 An annotated screenshot for our service recommendation page

24.7 Implementation

A prototype of the proposed approach was implemented. The prototype is developed in Java and uses OWL API [4] as the ontology/RDF parser. To evaluate the WSDL query generated by our approach, we implemented a component to support advanced search based on elements of WSDL (i.e. service name, operation name and input/output parameters). Figure 24.6 shows an annotated screenshot of our service recommendation page. A list of services of potential interest to the user is provided in the services recommendation table. A service in the services recommendation table can be associated with one or more concrete services as shown in Fig. 24.6. Once a user selects the "Tourist Attractions" in the service recommendation table, the associated services (e.g., a list of tourist attractions in Los Angeles) are automatically displayed in the service selection panel on the right side of the Web page. The user can select the services the best fit its requirements.

We use Freebase [2] as the ontology database. In Freebase, there are common entities shared by most of the ontologies, such as "type.object.key", "namespace", and "common.topic". Those entities are used to organize the resources in the database, but are not useful for identifying user's requirements. To increase the accuracy of relation identification, we manually analyze the schema of ontologies defined in Freebase to identify and filter out those meaningless entities.

24.8 Case Study

The objective of our case study is to evaluate the effectiveness of our approach. In particular, we want to examine: (1) whether our approach can effectively recommend useful tasks represented as classes, individuals and properties in the set *Potential Task Set*; and (2) whether the generated searching criteria can find the desired services.

24.8.1 Setup

Table 24.3 lists the context types used in our case study. By providing different context values for each context type, we can create different user scenarios. Each scenario is composed of the context types listed in Table 24.3 with assigned context values. For each scenario, our approach automatically detects various potential tasks for the user and recommends different services. In our case study, we provide 5 different context values for each context type. Using different combinations of these context values, we generate 600 different context scenarios for our case study.

Due to the limitation of time and resources, we cannot evaluate all the 600 scenarios. In our case study, we randomly select 2 % (i.e., 12) context scenarios from the 600 context scenarios to evaluate our approach. To evaluate the identified potential tasks and the service searching criteria generated by our approach in different scenarios, we recruited 6 graduate students to participate in our case study. These graduate students have many years of experiences using online services and possess basic knowledge on the context values that appeared in the context scenarios.

24.8.2 Evaluation Criteria

Precision and *recall* are widely used in information retrieval. We use *precision* and *recall* to measure our approach. *Precision* and *recall* are defined as follows.

Table 24.3 Context types used in our case study

Context types	
Previous environment	Location (city and county)
Current environment	Location (city and country)
	Activity (described by keywords)
Future environment	Location (city and country)
	Activity (provided by calendar, described using keywords)
User's preferences and background	Favorite sports
	Favorite food
	Favorite celebrities
	Major
	Other preferences
	Income

$$Precision = \frac{|\{relevant\ items\} \bigcap \{retrieved\ items\}|}{|\{retrieved\ items\}|}, \qquad (24.3)$$

$$Recall = \frac{|\{relevant\ items\} \bigcap \{retrieved\ items\}|}{|\{relevant\ items\}|} \qquad (24.4)$$

Precision and *recall* are defined in terms of a set of retrieved items (e.g. the set of potential tasks found by our prototype for a given context scenario) and a set of relevant items (e.g. the set of potential tasks existing in the context scenario). *Precision* is the ratio of the number of returned relevant items to the total number of returned items of a query. *Recall* is the ratio of the number of returned relevant items to the total number of existing relevant items.

24.8.3 Experiment Procedure

To evaluate the potential tasks identified by our approach, we assign 2 context scenarios to each subject described in the previous section. For each scenario, a subject manually examines the context values and uses her knowledge to identify the potential tasks that she would like to perform. Independent from the manual evaluation, we also use our prototype to automatically identify the potential tasks by analyzing the context values and the relations among context values. We compare the task sets produced by the subjects and the ones generated by our prototype tool to calculate the precision and recall of each scenario.

To evaluate the service searching criteria generated by our approach, we use the approach described in Sect. 24.6 to generate the service searching criteria, then we submit the searching criteria to search engines Google [3] and Seekda [6] to search for online services. Seekda is a search engine to search for Web services described using WSDL. One of the authors manually examined the available services in Seekda for each scenario. If there are available Web services in Seekda for a given topic, we use Seekda. Otherwise, we use Google to search for services. We use the keywords in the generated searching criteria to search for services. In both cases, we use the generated WSDL query to check the top 20 returned services to identify the matching services. For each query, our prototype chooses the top two returned services to recommend to the subject. The 6 aforementioned subjects manually provided the description of desired services based on the given context scenarios. One of the authors manually compared the services recommended by our prototype with the desired services described by the subjects to evaluate if our prototype can correctly recommend services to a subject for a given context scenario.

24.8.4 Result Analysis

In the 12 context scenarios, 2 scenarios do not have any tasks recommended according to the results from the subjects as well as the results of our prototype. We manually examined both scenarios. We found that the context values in both scenarios do not

Table 24.4 Recall and precision for detecting potential tasks

Scenarios	# of retrieved tasks	# of retrieved relevant tasks	# of relevant tasks	Recall (%)	Precision (%)
1	2	2	2	100	100
2	1	1	1	100	100
3	3	2	3	67	67
4	3	3	4	75	100
5	2	2	2	100	100
6	3	1	1	100	33
7	3	3	3	100	100
8	3	2	2	100	67
9	4	4	4	100	100
10	1	1	1	100	100
Average				94	87

have any relations. Table 24.4 shows the results for detecting potential tasks from the remainder 10 scenarios. We notice that some tasks in certain scenarios are not included in the result from the subjects due to the limitation of subject's knowledge. However, such tasks are identified by our prototype. For example, in a travel scenario, "Michael Jordan" is a favorite celebrity of a subject, and one of the context values is the city "New York". Our prototype can identify that "New York" is the birth place of "Michael Jordan". As a fan of Michael Jordan, the subject would be interested to know this information and purchase the related souvenirs using an on line shopping service. However, such information is overlooked by the subject. When calculating recall and precision, we add the missed tasks into the relevant items set and treat the missed tasks as desired potential tasks. The 94 % of recall reveals that our approach can identify most of the potential tasks based on the semantics of context values. Moreover, our prototype can identify the tasks that are overlooked by the subjects.

Table 24.5 lists the evaluation results of service recommendation. The results show that our approach can recommend most of the needed services desired by subjects. However, as listed in Table 24.5, the recall and precision are not very high in some context scenarios. Here are some reasons which we plan to address in our future work:

1. Some ontologies do not describe all the aspects of a context value. The incomplete ontologies cause incomplete service recommendation. Meanwhile, we only define one user-defined relation which is Eq. (24.2) to capture the domain knowledge of "Income: low". If we add more domain knowledge using user-defined relations, it could increase the recall and precision. For example, one subject in our case study lists "Tickets for Museums at Miami" as a potential task for a context scenario which specifies that the subject majors in "Art" and will attend a conference in "Miami". Due to the lack of domain knowledge of "Art", it is difficult for our prototype to automatically establish the relations between "Art" and "Museums".

Table 24.5 Evaluation Results of service recommendation

Scenarios	Total # of retrieved services	Total # of retrieved relevant services	Total # of relevant services	Recall (%)	Precision (%)
1	4	4	4	100	100
2	2	2	2	100	100
3	6	4	6	67	67
4	6	6	8	75	100
5	4	3	4	75	75
6	6	2	2	100	33
7	6	5	6	83	83
8	6	4	4	100	67
9	8	8	8	100	100
10	2	2	2	100	100
Average				90	83

2. Although WordNet can provide stems and synonyms for a single word, it cannot give the synonyms of phrases (i.e. two or more words in sequences to represent a specific meaning) which are the most common expressions of entities in ontologies. The lack of phrases in our semantic analysis database (i.e. WordNet) makes it challenging for our prototype to identify the similarity of phrases defined in ontologies.

3. When the number of keywords increases, the results returned by Google or Seekda are likely to diminish. Especially, we may extract general terms from ontologies, such as "people", "person", and "location". Such terms in the searching keywords often result in drastically reduction of the quality of searching results.

24.8.5 Threats to Validity

Construct validity is the degree to which the independent and dependent variables accurately measure the concepts which they are intended to measure. We have carefully designed our case study to avoid the threats of construct validity. To evaluate the effectiveness of identified context relations and recommended services, we use *recall* and *precision* which are well adopted evaluation criteria in literature. However, the potential tasks and relevant services of context scenarios contain subjective issues. For example, one subject may be satisfied by a recommended task while another user may not like the recommended task at all. In our case study, we ask the 6 subjects to provide the potential tasks and evaluate the returned services according to the relations among context values and their understanding of the context scenario. The identified potential tasks and relevant services recommended by the 6 objects may not reflect the potential tasks of all the users in practices. Especially, in our case study, all the 6 subjects are graduate students. In the future, we plan to hire more subjects with different backgrounds to participate in our case study.

External validity refers to the generalization of the results. In our case study, we automatically generated 600 different context scenarios and randomly selected 12 scenarios out of the 600 context scenarios. We believe that the automated generation and random selection of context scenarios can reflect the practical situations. However, there are various context types and many variations of context values in a context-aware system. Our case study only evaluates a limited number of context types and values. In the future, we plan to expand our context scenarios with more context types and values. When the number of context types and values increases in our case study, we expect that the *precision* and *recall* is likely to be lower than the result of our current experiment.

Internal validity is concerned with the cause-effect relationship between independent and dependent variables. In our case study, the retrieved tasks are automatically identified by our prototype, and the relevant potential tasks are identified by subjects who did not observe the results of our prototype. Therefore, we can rule out a learning effect of subjects that may impact the results of our case study.

24.9 Related Work

24.9.1 Context Modeling and Context-Aware Systems

Several context models and context-aware systems are proposed in the literature [10, 14, 19, 23, 24]. Strang and Linnhoff-Popien [25] survey existing context models and classify them into different types based on the data structures. The context models are classified into 6 types: key-value models, markup scheme models, graphical models, object oriented models, logic based models, and ontology based models. The context models are evaluated using six requirements. Ontologies are the most expressive model that can fulfill most of the requirements. Sakurai et al. [23] propose a methodology to interpret and combine sensor outputs with contexts as sets of annotated business rules. Chen and Kotz [14] investigate the research on context-aware mobile computing. Chen and Kotz discuss the types of context used, the ways of using context, the system level support on collecting context, and approaches to adapt to the changing context. Baldauf et al. [10] present a layered conceptual design framework to describe the common architecture principles of context-aware systems. Based on their proposed design framework, Baldauf et al. compare different context-aware systems on various issues: the context sensing, context models, context processing, resource discovery, historical context data, security and privacy. In the aforementioned approaches, the context models are predefined and are not flexible to address the dynamical changing environment. In our approach, we can generate and adjust the context relation model automatically according to different available context values.

24.9.2 Discovering and Recommending Services Using Context

Applying context-aware techniques to discover and recommend services has gained lots of attentions. Yang et al. [15, 28] design an event-driven rule based system to recommend services according to people's context. Yang et al. define an ontology-based context model to represent a context. Requester ontology and service ontology are developed for specifying the context of requesters and services respectively. Using rules, further contextual information can be inferred from the current contextual information. For example, a user's activity at a given time can be derived by examining the time and calendar. When searching for Web services, Yang et al. identify the similarities of inputs/outputs between requests and published services using capability matching. If there are no matched services, a semantic matching component would decompose the request into sub-requests based on requester's contextual information and search for services for each sub-request. Balke and Wagner [11] propose an algorithm to select a Web service based on user's preferences. The algorithm starts with a general query. If there are too many results, it expands the service query using user's preferences. The algorithm expands the query with loose constraints extracted from user's preferences. If there are too many results, it extends the query with restricted constraints and searches for Web services again. By adding constraints step by step, the algorithm narrows down the number of service searching results to a small value. However, aforementioned approaches need to predefine the specific reactions on context scenarios using rules which are hard to provide in practice due to the diversity of context types and values in the real world. Our approach can automatically recommend services based on the semantics of context scenarios without requiring the designer of context-aware systems to provide specific rules.

Xi et al. [26] use a collaborative filtering technique to recommend services based on the Quality of services. Qi et al. [22] combine UDDI and OWL-S to describe semantic Web services. In OWL-S, class "process: local" allows users to define some local parameters. Qi et al. use "process: local" to describe context information. Qi et al. define 6 types of contexts: load of server, performance of server, response time of service, geographical position of client, geographical position of server, and distance between client end and server. Dynamic context can be updated on time. After finding services using semantic matching, Qi et al. use context data to evaluate the quality of services and rank the matching services. Mostefaoui et al. [21] present a CB-SeC (Context-Based Service Composition) service description model. In the CB-SeC service description model, Mostefaoui et al. define an optional part called the context function. The context function represents the context of the service (e.g. the current workload of the service) and is shipped with other service description. The context function is used to select the best services from the matching Web service list if there is more than one matching Web service. The value of context function is not known in advance. It needs to be calculated during run time when it is needed. Different from Chen, Qi and Mostefaoui's approaches which use contexts to select services with high Quality of Service (QoS), our approach is intended to detect the requirements of users and recommend services with desired functions.

Abbar et al. [9] provide an approach to recommend services using the logs of a user and the current context of the user. To select and recommend services, the proposed approach requires historical data which are usually not available in the practice. Our approach only needs the context types and values to recommend services. Blake et al. [12] use an agent to detect the execution of applications and the behavior of human users, such as browsing the Internet. Then the agent extracts the context data from applications and users' behaviors. Based on the contextual data, the agent generates a query to search for available Web services. The agents recommend services by matching the similarity of input/output and the operation name of Web services with the contextual information extracted by the agent. The approach by Blake et al. only analyzes the data that the user is currently processing. Their approach cannot combine and analyze two or more context values to recommend services. Our approach can analyze the relations of multiple context types and values and recommend services based on such relations.

24.10 Conclusion and Future Work

In this chapter, we present an approach to dynamically derive context relations from ontologies and automatically recommend services based on specific context values. By discovering the semantic relations among context values, our approach can identify user's tasks hidden behind the context values and generate searching criteria for service discovery. The case study shows that our approach can identify the context relations and user's potential tasks in different context scenarios with high precision and recall.

Context types and context values are interpreted from the outputs of sensors. For example, a GPS signal is mapped to abstract location such as at home or at work. Our current approach is based on the context types and context values which are provided by third part. In our next step, we plan to extend our approach to use or directly interpret the data from the outputs of different sensors. Meanwhile, we observe that some ontologies in FreeBase are not very suitable for extending the context values. As a result, it reduces the accuracy of service recommendation in our approach. To enhance our approach, we could try to use the ontologies from different ontology databases, such as DBpedia [1] and Swoogle [7]. There may have several matching ontologies for the same context value. Currently, there are no effective criteria to help us select the appropriate ontologies for the purpose of extending the context values. A further study can be conducted to evaluate the effectiveness of different criteria for ontology selection and identify the effective criteria for our work.

Acknowledgments This work is financially supported by NSERC and the IBM Toronto Centre for Advanced Studies (CAS). We would like to thank Mr. Alex Lau, Ms. Joanna Ng and Mr. Leho Nigul at IBM Canada Toronto Laboratory and Dr. Foutse Khomh at Queen's University for their suggestions on this work. IBM and WebSphere are trademarks or registered trademarks of International Business Machines Corporation in the United States, other countries, or both. Other company, product, and service names may be trademarks or service marks of others.

References

1. Dbpedia. http://dbpedia.org/ (2012)
2. Freebase. http://www.freebase.com/ (2012)
3. Google. http://www.google.com (2012)
4. Owl api. http://owlapi.sourceforge.net/ (2012)
5. Princeton University: Wordnet, 2010. http://wordnet.princeton.edu (2012)
6. Seekda. http://webservices.seekda.com/ (2012)
7. Swoogle. http://swoogle.umbc.edu/ (2012)
8. Wikipedia. http://en.wikipedia.org/wiki/Wikipedia:About (2012)
9. Abbar, S., Bouzeghoub, M., Lopez, S.: Context-aware recommendation systems: a service-oriented approach. In: Proceedings of the International Conference on Very Large Data Bases (VLDB) Profile Management and Context Awareness (PersDB) Workshop, Lyon, France (2009)
10. Baldauf, M., Dustdar, S., Rosenberg, F.: A survey on context-aware systems. Int. J. Ad Hoc Ubiquitous Comput. 2(4), 263–277 (2007)
11. Balke, W.T., Wagner, M.: Towards personalized selection of web services. In: WWW (Alternate Paper Tracks) (2003). http://dblp.uni-trier.de/db/conf/www/www2003at.html#BalkeW03
12. Blake, M.B., Kahan, D.R., Nowlan, M.F.: Context-aware agents for user-oriented web services discovery and execution. Distrib. Parallel Databases 21(1), 39–58 (2007). doi:10.1007/s10619-006-7001-9. http://dx.doi.org/10.1007/s10619-006-7001-9
13. Brézillon, P.: Focusing on context in human-centered computing. IEEE Intell. Syst. 18(3), 62–66 (2003). doi:10.1109/MIS.2003.1200731. http://dx.doi.org/10.1109/MIS.2003.1200731
14. Chen, G., Kotz, D.: A survey of context-aware mobile computing research. Technical Report, Hanover, NH, USA (2000)
15. Chen, I., Yang, S., Jia, Z.: Ubiquitous provision of context aware web services. In: Services Computing, 2006. SCC '06. IEEE International Conference on, pp. 60–68 (2006). doi:10.1109/SCC.2006.110
16. Chen, P.P.S.: The entity-relationship model toward a unified view of data. ACM Trans. Database Syst. 1(1), 9–36 (1976). doi:10.1145/320434.320440. http://doi.acm.org/10.1145/320434.320440
17. Connolly, D., Harmelen, F., Horrocks, I., McGuinness, D.L., Patel-Schneider, P.F., Stein, L.A.: DAML+OIL (March 2001) Reference Description, W3C Note 18 December 2001. http://www.w3.org/TR/daml+oil-reference (2011)
18. Hassanzadeh, O., Kementsietsidis, A., Lim, L., Miller, R.J., Wang, M.: A framework for semantic link discovery over relational data. In: Proceedings of the 18th ACM Conference on Information and Knowledge Management, CIKM '09, pp. 1027–1036. ACM, New York, NY, USA (2009). doi:10.1145/1645953.1646084. http://doi.acm.org/10.1145/1645953.1646084
19. Hesselman, C., Tokmakoff, A., Pawar, P., Iacob, S.: Discovery and composition of services for context-aware systems. In: Proceedings of the 1st European Conference on Smart Sensing and Context (EuroSCC'06) (2006)
20. Klyne, G., Carroll, J.J.: Resource Description Framework (RDF): Concepts and Abstract Syntax. W3C Recommendation (2004)
21. Mostefaoui, S., Hirsbrunner, B.: Context aware service provisioning. In: Pervasive Services, 2004. ICPS 2004. IEEE/ACS International Conference on, pp. 71–80 (2004). doi:10.1109/PERSER.2004.13
22. Qi, Y., Qi, S., Zhu, P., Shen, L.: Context-aware semantic web service discovery. In: Semantics, Knowledge and Grid, Third International Conference on, pp. 499–502 (2007). doi:10.1109/SKG.2007.127
23. Sakurai, Y., Takada, K., Anisetti, M., Bellandi, V., Ceravolo, P., Damiani, E., Tsuruta, S.: Toward sensor-based context aware systems. Sensors 12(1), 632–649 (2012). doi:10.3390/s120100632. http://www.mdpi.com/1424-8220/12/1/632
24. Smith, M.K., Welty, C., McGuinness, D.L. (eds.) : Owl Web Ontology Language Guide. W3C Recommendation (2004). http://www.w3.org/TR/owl-guide/ (2012)

25. Strang, T., Linnhoff-Popien, C.: A context modeling survey. In: Workshop on Advanced Context Modelling, Reasoning and Management, UbiComp 2004—The Sixth International Conference on Ubiquitous Computing, Nottingham/England (2004)
26. Xi, C., Xudong, L., Zicheng, H., Hailong, S.: Regionknn: a scalable hybrid collaborative filtering algorithm for personalized web service recommendation. In: Web Services (ICWS), 2010 IEEE International Conference on, pp. 9–16 (2010). doi:10.1109/ICWS.2010.27
27. Xiao, H., Zou, Y., Ng, J., Nigul, L.: An approach for context-aware service discovery and recommendation. In: Web Services (ICWS), 2010 IEEE International Conference on, pp. 163–170 (2010). doi:10.1109/ICWS.2010.95
28. Yang, S.J.H., Zhang, J., Chen, I.Y.L.: A JESS-enabled context elicitation system for providing context-aware web services. Expert Syst. Appl. **34**(4), 2254–2266 (2008). doi:10.1016/j.eswa.2007.03.008. http://dx.doi.org/10.1016/j.eswa.2007.03.008

Chapter 25
Data Transformation Knowledge Reuse in Spreadsheet-Based Mashup Development Platform

Vu Hung, Boualem Benatallah and Angel Lagares Lemos

Abstract Data transformation is a key task in mashup development (e.g., access to heterogeneous services, data flow). It is considered as a labour-intensive and error-prone process. The possibility of reusing previously specified mappings promises a significant reduction in manual and time-consuming transformation tasks, nevertheless its potential has not been fully realized in current approaches and systems. In this chapter, we study the problem of data transformation logic reuse in mashup development platforms. We formulate the problem and propose a solution that features novel reuse abstractions and techniques including spreadsheet templates, mapping generalization, and similarity join. Given a spreadsheet instance that is being mapped to the target schema, we recommend a list of mapping formulas that can be potentially reused for the instance. We implemented a prototype of the proposed solution and evaluated its performance via synthetic datasets.

25.1 Introduction

Mashups are valued-added applications developed by aggregating existing services [1, 2]. Recently, "mashup" has become one of the hottest buzzword in the area of web applications. Several solutions have been proposed to simplify mashups developments by providing both textual and visual development environments, thus avoiding users from writing complex scripts (e.g., Yahoo! Pipes [3], Intel Mash Maker [4]).

V. Hung (✉) · B. Benatallah · A.L. Lemos
University of New South Wales, Sydney, Australia
e-mail: vthung@gmail.com

B. Benatallah
e-mail: boualem@cse.unsw.edu.au

A.L. Lemos
e-mail: angell@cse.unsw.edu.au

A. Bouguettaya et al. (eds.), *Web Services Foundations*,
DOI: 10.1007/978-1-4614-7518-7_25,
© Springer Science+Business Media New York 2014

When developing a mashup, developers face several difficult integration challenges. First, there is a need to specify interactions (i.e., request/response messages) with external services. These external services may use heterogeneous data representation models (i.e., JSON, XML, Relational, ...) and access methods (e.g., SOAP, REST protocols). It is, therefore, necessary to specify data transformations to bridge the heterogeneity between data representation models used by the mashup tools and those used by external services. Second, data flow among services in a mashup may require specifying data transformation logic to bridges semantic heterogeneity between these services. Typical data flow requires reading outputs of a service, transforming the data and using it as input of another service [5].

In our previous work [6, 7], we built a mashup development platform over data services. This platform relies on spreadsheets to specify data flow and data transformations, when interacting with external services. Spreadsheets are ubiquitous tools used for the storage, analysis and manipulation of data [8]. There are several reasons for their popularity. Spreadsheet-based data management offers important flexibility in data formatting over a tabular grid [9]. Spreadsheets do not impose many constraints regarding the data layout. Data can be organized according to subjective importance, preferences, and styles (e.g., by placing important data in the top-left corner or placing related elements of data next to each other). Furthermore, spreadsheets offer a simple, but effective formula language using spatial relationships that shield users from the low-level details of traditional programming [10]. To use the language, a user only needs to master two concepts, namely cells as variables and functions for expressing relations between cells.

The first contribution of the proposed mashup platform was a language that allows users to employ familiar spreadsheet concepts to explore, manipulate, and analyze complex data with a data flow; as well as build fairly sophisticated mashups, involving joining data from multiple Web data services [6]. The second contribution was a language that specifies transformations between spreadsheet data and data formats used by external services [7]. This data transformation language provides an expressive spreadsheet-like formula mapping language. Spreadsheets were used to specify transformations as well because of the following reasons: (i) leveraging existing users' experience in spreadsheet programming and preserve important characteristics of spreadsheet programming; (ii) exploiting frequently used formatting features of spreadsheets to generalize a mapping from instance level to template level; (iii) avoiding cluttering spreadsheet documents with transformations by embedding transformation logic into the language.

As mentioned before, data transformation is a labour-intensive and error-prone process, which includes various non-trivial steps, namely schema matching, mapping specification, code generation, and transformation execution [11, 12]. In existing work, data transformation logic is developed using special transformation and query languages, such as XSLT or XQuery, or even general purpose programming languages, such as Java. Specific data transformation tools (e.g., Clio [13], Clip [14], Altova MapForce [15], IBM Relational Data Architect [16], Microsoft BizTalk Mapper [17]) use textual or visual languages to specify transformations and generate executable code (e.g., XSLT, XQuery, Java transformation logic).

In this chapter, we present our work on extending the data flow and transformation features of the mashup development platform to cater for reuse of previously specified mapping as much as possible, improving the productivity in mashup development. More specifically, we consider the problem of reuse in transforming spreadsheet data to structured formats. The problem is challenging because: (i) Spreadsheet systems do not impose many constraints on spatial layout of data, and users can organize same data according to their own preferences and styles, not in a pre-defined way. Therefore, given two spreadsheet instances, it is programmatically difficult to uncover if they are similar in terms of structure. Mapping a spreadsheet instance to a target schema typically depends on the spatial layout of the instance; (ii) Given a spreadsheet instance and a target schema, there may have multiple ways of mapping the instance to the schema. For instance, an optional attribute of the target schema can be mapped or not mapped to spreadsheet data; (iii) A mapping of a spreadsheet instance to the target schema is only applied exactly to this instance, not to other instances with similar structure that also need to be mapped to the target schema; (iv) Since a mapping repository may contain a large number of mappings (up to a few hundred thousand mappings), the reuse recommendation mechanism should suggest previously specified mappings in an effective and efficient way. To the best of our knowledge, the problem of spreadsheet-based transformation reuse has not been addressed before in the setting we consider here. To address the above issues, we make the following main contributions:

- We formulate the problem of spreadsheet-based transformation reuse as a variant of *similarity join* [18–20], which is a well-known similarity search problem that finds all pairs of objects whose similarity is above a given threshold (Sect. 25.3).
- We define spreadsheet templates that are used to characterize spreadsheet structures. We propose techniques to infer a template from an existing spreadsheet based on common spreadsheet presentation patterns. We then generate the string-based representation of an inferred template (Sect. 25.4).
- We propose an algorithm to recommend previously specified mappings for a new spreadsheet instance that needs to be mapped to the target schema. This relies on computing similarity between string-based representations of templates (Sect. 25.5).
- We design a repository to organize mapping information. We implemented a prototype of the proposed solution. We then evaluated the performance and effectiveness of the solution. The experimental results show the viability and usefulness of our approach (Sects. 25.6, 25.7).

The rest of this chapter is organized as follows. A motivating example is illustrated in Sect. 25.2. Section 25.3 formulate the spreadsheet-based data transformation reuse problem. Next, Sect. 25.4 formally defines spreadsheet templates and infers templates from existing spreadsheets. The reuse recommendation algorithm is described in Sect. 25.5. Section 25.6 presents the prototype implementation. Section 25.7 evaluates the performance of the proposed solution. We discuss related work in Sect. 25.8 and conclude in Sect. 25.9.

25.2 Motivating Example

Figure 25.1 shows the transformation scenario used throughout the whole chapter for illustration purpose. We consider three spreadsheets (in Fig. 25.1a–c) containing similar data that must be mapped to the target schema (Fig. 25.1d). The instance in Fig. 25.1a is a *table presentation* [6] with headers in the first row and data in subsequent rows. The instance in Fig. 25.1b is a vertical *repeater presentation* [6] where different values of tuples (Dept, ID, Name) are presented vertically, each of which is separated by two empty rows. The instance in Fig. 25.1c is also a vertical repeater presentation where different values of tuples (Dept, ID, Address, Name) are presented vertically, each of which is separated by one empty row. Note that spreadsheet data in Fig. 25.1b is similar to the one in Fig. 25.1c in terms of structure, but it does not include address information of employees.

Suppose that the two spreadsheets in Fig. 25.1a, b are already mapped to the target schema. Now the user wants to map the spreadsheet in Fig. 25.1c to this schema. The important question to ask is whether previous mapping efforts can be reused for this new mapping or not. The structure of the spreadsheet in Fig. 25.1b is similar to the one of the spreadsheet in Fig. 25.1c so it is desirable that we can reuse the mapping used to transform the instance in Fig. 25.1b to the target format for the new mapping.

(a)

	A	B	C	D
1	Dept	ID	Name	Address
2	IT	1111	Ann	Sydney
3	Marketing	2222	John	Melbourne
4	Sales	3333	Jeffrey	Adelaide
5	Accounting	4444	Steve	Perth
6		...		

(c)

	A	B	C
1	Dept	IT	
2	ID	1111	
3	Address	Sydney	
4	Name	Ann	
5			
6	Dept	Marketing	
7	ID	2222	
8	Address	Melbourne	
9	Name	John	
10		....	

(b)

	A	B	C
1	Dept	IT	
2	ID	1111	
3	Name	Ann	
4			
5			
6	Dept	Marketing	
7	ID	2222	
8	Name	John	
9		...	

(d)
Target
  Emp [1..*]
    Dept =B1 {*IT*}
    EmployeeID =B2 {*1111*}
    EmployeeName =B3 {*Ann*}
    Address?

Fig. 25.1 Motivating example: **a** employees organized in a table presentation; **b** employees organized in a vertical repeater presentation without address information; **c** employees organized in a vertical repeater presentation with address information; **d** the target schema

In what follows, we review two related state-of-the-art approaches for dealing with this scenario.

The first approach, namely schema-based, helps users specify a schema of a spreadsheet [21]. Then, either low-level transformation languages (e.g., XSLT, XQuery) or visual mapping tools (e.g., Clio [13], Clip [14], +Spicy [22], Altova MapForce [15]) is used for specifying transformation at *schema level*. Finally, the spreadsheet instance is translated into an instance of the target schema. However, users must learn a new language, e.g., by creating correspondences between the source and target elements and annotating these correspondences with one or more unfamiliar functions (e.g., functions of XSLT/XQuery or .NET Framework) in the case of mapping tools [12]. This flowchart-like mapping interface is typically cluttered when schemas are large and mappings are complex [23]. In contrast, spreadsheet users are familiar with formulas and an incremental approach to building applications with instant feedback at each step [10].

The second approach, namely column-based, allows users to specify mappings between target elements and spreadsheet columns via drag-and-drop operations [24, 25]. The user can select a target atomic element and drag it onto a source column to specify a mapping. However, this approach offers no reuse support. For example, to map the spreadsheet in Fig. 25.1a, the user can select target atomic elements: `Dept`, `EmployeeID`, `EmployeeName`, `Address`, and drag them onto source columns: A1:A5, B1:B5, C1:C5, D1:D5, respectively. To map the spreadsheet in Fig. 25.1b, the user must modify the presentation of this spreadsheet in order to conform to the structure shown in Fig. 25.1a (i.e., table presentation) and then repeat the steps described in the case of the spreadsheet in Fig. 25.1a. Regarding the spreadsheet in Fig. 25.1c, again, the user must modify this spreadsheet as in the case of the instance in Fig. 25.1b. It is a tedious and time-consuming process with no reuse support.

25.3 Problem Definition

Given a schema T and a spreadsheet instance I, the corresponding specified mapping M_I from I to T is stored as a tuple (M_I, I, P_I, T) in the mapping repository; P_I is a template of I; M_I consists of template-level mappings that are specified to transform I to a target instance conforming to T. We denote Γ_T as a collection of all tuples containing previously specified mappings from past spreadsheet instances to T. The main technical problem can be formally stated as follows.

Definition 25.3.1 *Given an instance J conforming to template P_J that is currently being mapped to schema T, find in Γ_T all tuples (M_I, I, P_I, T) such that similarity between P_I and P_J is greater than or equal θ where θ is a predefined normalized threshold $(0 < \theta \leq 1)$.*

As presented later, a template is represented as a string generated from a context-free grammar. Therefore, similarity between P_I and P_J can be characterized by a string similarity function sim: $sim(P_I, P_J) \geq \theta$. It is also worth noting that the size of $\Gamma_T(|\Gamma_T|)$ may be large (e.g., a few hundred thousand mappings) so we need a more efficient approach, rather than directly comparing P_J with all templates in Γ_T using a similarity function (i.e., pair-wise comparison), which is costly when template lengths are large.

Given two sets of strings R and R', *similarity join* [18–20] finds in all pairs (x, y) $(x \in R$ and $y \in R')$ such that $sim(x, y) \geq \theta$. *Self-join* is a special case of similarity join when $R = R'$. Instead, given a new string x, we find all $y \in R$ (R') such that $sim(x, y) \geq \theta$. The efficient approach to similarity join is a *filtering* (probe the inverted lists and use the filtering methods to eliminate as much as possible false candidates) and *verification* (check each candidate to find out if the threshold is satisfied) process [20], which is also applicable to the spreadsheet-based transformation reuse problem.

A spreadsheet S may contain multiple instances, not only one: $S = \{I_1, \ldots, I_n\}$. For example, the user can put three instances shown in Fig. 25.1a–c in one spreadsheet, instead of three separate spreadsheets. We assume the existence of procedures to identify and separate I_i $(1 \leq i \leq n)$ from S (See [9] for an example). Mapping from S to the target schema T can be, therefore, divided into individual mappings: $(I_1, T), \ldots, (I_n, T)$. Thus, in this chapter, we assume that S contains only one instance.

25.4 Spreadsheet Template

In Sect. 25.4.1, we formally define the template description language. Section 25.4.2 presents template inference techniques and how to generate the string-based representation of an inferred template.

25.4.1 Template Description Language

In many cases, spreadsheets evolve in a number of predictable ways and various spreadsheets tend to emerge from a common pattern. Structure of spreadsheets can be characterized via the notion of template. We use a variation of the language VITSL developed in [26] with the following context-free grammar to describe templates:

1. $Temp ::= C \mid C^{\rightarrow} \mid Temp \mid Temp$
2. $C ::= B \mid B^{\downarrow} \mid C \mid C$
3. $B ::= F \mid B - B$
4. $F ::= \varepsilon \mid const \mid \beta \mid \Phi(F, \ldots, F)$

N is a set of non-terminal symbols: $N = \{Temp, B, C, F\}$. Σ is a set of terminal symbols: $\Sigma = \varepsilon \cup const \cup \beta \cup \Phi$ and $\varepsilon \cap const \cap \beta \cap \Phi = \emptyset$. S is the start symbol: $S = Temp$.

Template *Temp* is a table given by a horizontal composition ($\mid$) of fixed columns (C) or expandable groups of columns ($C^{\rightarrow}$). A column (C) is given by a vertical composition ($-$) of fixed cells (B) or expandable groups of cells ($B^{\downarrow}$). A cell (B) is given by a formula (F), which consists of an empty value (ε), a constant label (*const*), a basic type (β) (e.g., int, string) of a data cell, or a function ($\Phi(F, \ldots, F)$). Note that cells of a template can be basically classified according to their content into four types: empty cell, label cell (e.g., headers), data cell, and formula cell (i.e., computation cell) [9].

All columns of a template have to vertically align (i.e., same height and same expandable groups of cells). An expandable group of columns is called a horizontal expandable group or *hex group* for short. An expandable group of cells is called a vertical expandable group or *vex group* for short. For comparison purpose, we replace the hex group symbol $C^{\rightarrow}$ and the vex group symbol $B^{\downarrow}$ by $[C]$ and $<B>$, respectively. Let us consider some examples on using this language to describe spreadsheet templates.

For example, the template: Dept $-$ <string> $\mid$ ID $-$ <int> $\mid$ Name $-$ <string> $\mid$ Address $-$ <string>, describes a class of tabular spreadsheet instances with four fixed columns, each of which consists of a description label (i.e., header, such as Dept, ID, Name, Address) at the top and a set of subsequent text/numeric data cells (represented by types string, int, ...). The spreadsheet in Fig. 25.1a is an instance of this template.

The template: <Dept $-$ ID $-$ Name $- \varepsilon - \varepsilon$> $\mid$ <string $-$ int $-$ string $- \varepsilon - \varepsilon$>, describes a class of spreadsheet instances with two fixed columns; the first column contains groups of labels, each of which contains three labels and two empty cells; the second column contains groups of data cells adjacent to labels, each of which contains three data cells and two empty cells. The spreadsheet in Fig. 25.1b is an instance of this template. Similarly, the spreadsheet in Fig. 25.1c is an instance of the template: <Dept $-$ ID $-$ Address $-$ Name $- \varepsilon$> $\mid$ <string $-$ int $-$ string $-$ string $- \varepsilon$>.

25.4.2 Inferring Templates

Given a spreadsheet, it is desirable to infer a template that characterizes its structure. The problem is challenging since spreadsheets may not impose any restrictions on how to organize data over a tabular grid. In fact, the spreadsheet may not have enough information for inferring a template. Therefore, template inference is typically ambiguous and users generally need to provide input to resolve ambiguities during inference process [27].

Abraham and Erwig [27] presents an inference technique based on the cells containing similar formulas to identify hex and vex groups. However, there are numerous spreadsheets in which formula cells are not available [28] (e.g., spreadsheets in Fig. 25.1a–c). As a result, in addition to that technique, we also provide an inference technique based on the common spreadsheet presentation patterns we proposed

Fig. 25.2 Inferred template of the instance in Fig. 25.1b in a new worksheet

	A	B	C	D
1	Dept	IT		
2	ID	1111		
3	Name	Ann		
4				
5				
6				
7				

in [6], including the table, repeater, and hierarchical presentations. For instance, the inference algorithm for a repeater presentation in the vertical direction is shown in Algorithm 1. Recall that a vertical repeater presentation contains two columns, each of which contains instances of a vex group. Algorithm 1 extracts the two first instances, which characterize these vex groups, based on identifying the last empty row of the two instances. By using this algorithm, the template of the instance in Fig. 25.1b is inferred as shown in Fig. 25.2 in a new worksheet (table A1:B5), where the two vex groups with some default values are shaded light orange (vex groups A1:A5 and B1:B5).

Algorithm 1: Template inference for a vertical repeater presentation.

Input: Start and end coordinates of the instance: (x, y) and $(x + 1, y')$
Output: Start and end coordinates of the inferred template
begin
    $i \leftarrow 0$;
    repeat
        $i \leftarrow i + 1$;
    until $(x, y + i) = \varepsilon$ *and* $(x, y + i + 1) \neq \varepsilon$;
    return (x, y) *and* $(x + 1, y + i)$

To generate a string-based representation of an inferred template (e.g., the template in Fig. 25.2), the following main steps are performed:

- First, stand at the start coordinate (i.e., top-left cell) of the inferred template (e.g., cell A1 in Fig. 25.2).
- Then, traverse all columns of the template from left to right. If meet a hex group, generate a pair of ("[","]") and put the result of traversing each column in the hex group in this pair. Between two columns (e.g., columns A1:A5 and B1:B5 in Fig. 25.2), a column and a hex group, or two hex groups, generate "|".

- For each column, traverse all cells of the column from top to bottom. If meet a vex group, then generate a pair of ("<", ">") and put the result of traversing each cell in the vex group in this pair. Between two cells (e.g., cells A1 and A2 in Fig. 25.2), a cell and a vex group, or two vex groups, generate "−".

- For each cell : (i) If the cell contains a formula f, generate "f"; (ii) If the cell is an empty cell, generate "ε"; (iii) If the cell contains a label l, generate "l"; (iv) If the cell is a data cell, generate its type. To decide whether a cell inside a hex group/vex group is a data cell or a label, we rely on the observation: If the cell is referenced by a formula or values of the cell are changed in instances of the hex group/vex group in the original spreadsheet (i.e., the spreadsheet from which the template is inferred), it is a data cell; otherwise, it is a label. For example, in Fig. 25.2, cell B1 is a data cell (since its values are changed in vex group instances in the original spreadsheet in Fig. 25.1b), while cell A1 is a label. For a cell outside vex groups/hex groups, if the cell is referenced by a formula, it is a data cell; otherwise, it is a label.

Note that each generated token is separated from the other tokens by a single whitespace that is convenient for tokenizing later. By applying the above steps, the string-based representation of the template in Fig. 25.2 is generated as "<Dept − ID − Name − ε − ε> | <string − int − string − ε − ε>". This string is then shown up to the user for validation and editing.

25.5 Reuse Recommendation Algorithm

There are numerous similarity functions for measuring similarities, but no single function is known to be the best one, basically depending on the application domain. There are mainly two relevant approaches, namely *character-based* and *token-based* similarity metrics [29]. Character-based approach relies on the notion of *edit distance* which measures the minimum number of edit operations needed to transform one string to the other. Edit operation is an insertion, deletion, or substitution of a single character.

For example, the edit distance between "microsoft" and "mcrosoft" is 1, with one delete operation. Edit distance captures well typographical errors (words with alternative spellings). However, when there is a rearrangement of words in a string, character-based metrics fail to capture the similarity (e.g., "Bill Gates" and "Gates, Bill"). Token-based approach is designed to solve this problem, in which strings are tokenized according to word boundaries and popular *set-based* similarity measures (e.g., Jaccard and Cosine) are then used to compute similarity.

Regarding algorithm illustration, we specifically focus on the Jaccard similarity, a commonly used function for defining similarity between sets. It has been shown that supporting Jaccard similarity efficiently leads to sound implementations of other similarity functions (e.g., edit distance and Cosine similarities) [18–20]. As mentioned earlier (Sect. 25.3), we find in Γ_T all templates that are similar to P_J, instead of looking for all similar template pairs in the set of templates $\Gamma_T \cup \{P_J\}$ as in the case of similarity join. Therefore, our algorithm is designed based on modifying the recently proposed algorithm *PPJoin+* [20, 30], which has been shown to outperform previous ones on similarity join. The main steps of the algorithm are sketched in Algorithm 2.

We will intuitively illustrate these steps in via the motivating example. Suppose that Γ_T already contains the mappings of the instance I_0 (Fig. 25.1a) and the instance I_1 (Fig. 25.1b) to the target schema (Fig. 25.1d). The specified template-level mapping formulas are:

- $Emp = A2:D(value = \text{empty})$ (for I_0)
- $Dept = B1:B(next = bottom(Dept) + 5)$ (for I_1)
- $EmployeeID = B2:B(next = bottom(EmployeeID) + 5)$ (for I_1)
- $EmployeeName = B3:B(next = bottom(EmployeeName) + 5)$ (for I_1)

The user now wants to map instance J in Fig. 25.1c to the target schema.
The templates of the three instances are described in Sect. 25.4:

1. P_{I_0} = "Dept − <string> ι ID − <int> ι Name − <string> ι Address − <string>"
2. P_{I_1} = "<Dept−ID−Name−ε−ε> ι <string−int−string−ε−ε>"
3. P_J = "<Dept−ID−Address−Name−ε> ι <string−int−string− string − ε>"

The threshold to be set is 0.8: $\theta = 0.8$.

Algorithm 2: The algorithm for reuse recommendation.

Input: A collection of specified mappings Γ_T;
A new instance J conforming to template P_J;
Jaccard similarity function f and threshold θ
Output: All pairs (P_I, P_J), $P_I \in \Gamma_T$ such that $f(P_I, P_J) \geq \theta$
begin
    1. Tokenize templates in Γ_T and template P_J into sets of tokens (i.e., records).
    2. Records are canonicalized according to the document frequency ordering $\mathcal{O}_{df}$
    3. Create inverted lists on tokens that appear in templates in Γ_T and generate candidates for P_J by probing these inverted lists.
    4. Reduce candidate size for P_J using size filtering and positional filtering.
    5. Verify final candidates using similarity function f such that $f \geq \theta$.

At first step, we transform each template into a set of tokens according to the delimiter whitespace. Since tokens may occur multiple times in a string, we will convert a multiset of tokens into a set of tokens by treating each subsequent occurrence of the same token as a new token [19]. Such a set of tokens is called a *record*. For example:

1. $P_{I_0} = \{\text{Dept}_0, -_0, <_0, \text{string}_0, >_0, |_0, \text{ID}_0, -_1, <_1, \text{int}_0, >_1, |_1, \text{Name}_0, -_2, <_2, \text{string}_1, >_2, |_2, \text{Address}_0, -_3, <_3, \text{string}_2, >_3\}$
2. $P_{I_1} = \{<_0, \text{Dept}_0, -_0, \text{ID}_0, -_1, \text{Name}_0, -_2, \varepsilon_0, -_3, \varepsilon_1, >_0, |_0, <_1, \text{string}_0, -_4, \text{int}_0, -_5, \text{string}_1, -_6, \varepsilon_2, -_7, \varepsilon_3, >_1\}$
3. $P_J = \{<_0, \text{Dept}_0, -_0, \text{ID}_0, -_1, \text{Address}_0, -_2, \text{Name}_0, -_3, \varepsilon_0, >_0, |_0, <_1, \text{string}_0, -_4, \text{int}_0, -_5, \text{string}_1, -_6, \text{string}_2, -_7, \varepsilon_1, >_1\}$

In the second step, to compare records, a record is *canonicalized* by sorting its tokens according to a certain global ordering $\mathcal{O}$ defined on the token universe $\mathcal{U}$. The document frequency of a token is the number of records containing the token. A document frequency ordering $\mathcal{O}_{df}$ arranges the tokens of a record according to the increasing order of tokens' document frequencies. $\mathcal{O}_{df}$ favors rare tokens in prefixes and hence produces a small candidate size as presented in next steps. For example, the token universe, the tokens' document frequencies, and token's orders of P_{I_0}, P_{I_1}, and P_J are presented in Tables 25.1 and 25.2 (DF is the abbreviation for "Document Frequency").

Consequently, P_{I_0}, P_{I_1}, and P_J are canonicalized according to $\mathcal{O}_{df}$ with the following results:

1. $P_{I_0} = \{|_1, <_2, >_2, |_2, <_3, >_3, \text{Address}_0, \text{string}_2, \text{Dept}_0, -_0, <_0, \text{string}_0, >_0, |_0, \text{ID}_0, -_1, <_1, \text{int}_0, >_1, \text{Name}_0, -_2, \text{string}_1, -_3\}$
2. $P_{I_1} = \{\varepsilon_2, \varepsilon_3, \varepsilon_0, \varepsilon_1, -_4, -_5, -_6, -_7, \text{Dept}_0, -_0, <_0, \text{string}_0, >_0, |_0, \text{ID}_0, -_1, <_1, \text{int}_0, >_1, \text{Name}_0, -_2, \text{string}_1, -_3\}$
3. $P_J = \{\text{Address}_0, \text{string}_2, \varepsilon_0, \varepsilon_1, -_4, -_5, -_6, -_7, \text{Dept}_0, -_0, <_0, \text{string}_0, >_0, |_0, \text{ID}_0, -_1, <_1, \text{int}_0, >_1, \text{Name}_0, -_2, \text{string}_1, -_3\}$

In the third step, given two canonicalized records x and y with $O(x, y) = |x \cap y|$, by using the transformation $|x \cup y| = |x| + |y| - |x \cap y|$, we have:

$$Jaccard(x, y) = \frac{|x \cap y|}{|x \cup y|} \geq \theta \Leftrightarrow O(x, y) \geq \alpha = \frac{\theta}{\theta + 1} * (|x| + |y|) \quad (25.1)$$

$$Jaccard(x, y) \geq \theta \Rightarrow \theta * |x| \leq |y|, \theta * |y| \leq |x| \quad (25.2)$$

Table 25.1 Tokens' document frequencies and token's orders of P_{I_0}, P_{I_1}, and P_J (Part 1)

Token	Dept_0	$-_0$	$<_0$	string_0	$>_0$	$|_0$	ID_0	$-_1$	$<_1$	int_0	$>_1$	$|_1$	Name_0	$-_2$	$<_2$
DF	3	3	3	3	3	3	3	3	3	3	1	3	3	1	
Order	17	18	19	20	21	22	23	24	25	26	27	1	28	29	2

Table 25.2 Tokens' document frequencies and token's orders of P_{I_0}, P_{I_1}, and P_J (Part 2)

Token	string_1	$>_2$	$|_2$	Address_0	$-_3$	$<_3$	string_2	$>_3$	$-_4$	$-_5$	$-_6$	$-_7$	ε_0	ε_1	ε_2	ε_3
DF	3	1	1	2	3	1	2	1	2	2	2	2	2	2	1	1
Order	30		3	4 9	31	5	10		6	13	14	15	16	11	12 7	8

Let *p-prefix* of a record x be the first p tokens of x. *Prefix-filtering principle* [19] states that $(|x| - \alpha + 1)$-prefix of x and $(|y| - \alpha + 1)$-prefix of y must share at least one token if (x, y) are a candidate pair. The prefix-filtering principle is used in building *inverted lists* (i.e., inverted indices). In terms of information retrieval, input template P_J can be seen as a query and the templates in Γ_T can be considered as the set of matching documents. The key idea is that we create inverted lists for each token of existing templates in Γ_T and we index prefixes with certain lengths, instead of the whole records. Obviously, if two records x, y are a candidate pair (x, y), then they share at least one token. Given a candidate pair (x, y), the prefix of length $|x| - \lceil \theta * |x| \rceil + 1$ of x and the prefix of length $|y| - \lceil \theta * |y| \rceil + 1$ of y must share at least one token. This is because $|x| - \lceil \theta * |x| \rceil + 1 \geq |x| - \alpha + 1$ and $|y| - \lceil \theta * |y| \rceil + 1 \geq |y| - \alpha + 1$ (based on Eq. 25.2).

Therefore, given a template P_I in Γ_T, we only need to index a prefix of length $|P_I| - \lceil \theta * |P_I| \rceil + 1$. We index both tokens and their positions in the prefixes so that positional filtering can be applied later. Then, with respect to the input template P_J, we match each token of the $(|P_J| - \lceil \theta * |P_J| \rceil + 1)$-prefix of P_J against the inverted lists and generate candidates for P_J by union the matched lists.

For example, the 5-prefix of P_{I_0} to be indexed is $\{\iota_1, <_2, >_2, \iota_2, <_3\}$ with the following lists: $list(\iota_1) = \{(P_{I_0}, 1)\}$; $list(<_2) = \{(P_{I_0}, 2)\}$; $list(>_2) = \{(P_{I_0}, 3)\}$; $list(\iota_2) = \{(P_{I_0}, 4)\}$; $list(<_3) = \{(P_{I_0}, 5)\}$. Also, 5-prefix of P_{I_1} to be indexed is $\{\varepsilon_2, \varepsilon_3, \varepsilon_0, \varepsilon_1, -_4\}$ with the following lists: $list(\varepsilon_2) = \{(P_{I_1}, 1)\}$; $list(\varepsilon_3) = \{(P_{I_1}, 2)\}$; $list(\varepsilon_0) = \{(P_{I_1}, 3)\}$; $list(\varepsilon_1) = \{(P_{I_1}, 4)\}$; $list(-_4) = \{(P_{I_1}, 5)\}$. Next, each token in the 5-prefix of $P_J = \{Address_0, string_2, \varepsilon_0, \varepsilon_1, -_4\}$ is matched against the above lists. Finally, the candidate set is created by applying the union operation on the matched lists: $list(\varepsilon_0) \cup list(\varepsilon_1) \cup list(-_4) = \{(P_{I_1}, 3), (P_{I_1}, 4), (P_{I_1}, 5)\}$. As can be seen, P_{I_0} is filtered out and only P_{I_1} is passed to the next step.

In the fourth step, given a candidate pair (x, y), we reduce the candidate size based on size filtering (see Eq. 25.2) and positional filtering. The positional filtering is stated as follows:

- Let token $\omega = x[i]$, ω partitions the record x into the left partition $x_l(\omega) = x[1..i]$ and the right partition $x_r(\omega) = x[i + 1..|x|]$. If $O(x, y) \geq \alpha$, then for every token $\omega \in x \cap y$, $O(x_l(\omega), y_l(\omega)) + min(|x_r(\omega)|, |y_r(\omega)|) \geq \alpha$.

We have $|P_{I_1}| = |P_J| = 23$ so size filtering is satisfied. For the common token 'ε_0', $O(P_{I_1 l}(\varepsilon_0), P_{J l}(\varepsilon_0)) + min(|P_{I_1 r}(\varepsilon_0)|, |P_{J r}(\varepsilon_0)|) = 1 + min(20, 20) = 21 > \alpha = 20.44$. Similarly, positional filtering is also valid for the other common tokens 'ε_1' and '$-_4$' since:

- $O(P_{I_1 l}(\varepsilon_1), P_{J l}(\varepsilon_1)) + min(|P_{I_1 r}(\varepsilon_1)|, |P_{J r}(\varepsilon_1)|) = 2 + min(19, 19) = 21 > \alpha = 20.44$
- $O(P_{I_1 l}(-_4), P_{J l}(-_4)) + min(|P_{I_1 r}(-_4)|, |P_{J r}(-_4)|) = 3 + min(18, 18) = 21 > \alpha = 20.44$

Hence, the pair (P_{I_1}, P_J) can be passed to the final step for verification. Note that for really large datasets, *suffix filtering* [20] can also be used to prune more candidates. This filtering method is a generalization of the positional filtering to the suffixes of the records by converting the overlap constraint to the equivalent Hamming distance constraint.

Our example has $|P_{I_1}| = |P_J| = 23$ so size filtering is satisfied. For the common token 'ε_0', $O(P_{I_1l}(\varepsilon_0), P_{Jl}(\varepsilon_0)) + min(|P_{I_1r}(\varepsilon_0)|, |P_{Jr}(\varepsilon_0)|) = 1 + min(20, 20) = 21 > \alpha = 20.44$. Positional filtering is also valid for the other common tokens 'ε_1' and '$-_4$' because: $min(|P_{I_1r}(\varepsilon_1)|, |P_{Jr}(\varepsilon_1)|) = 2 + min(19, 19) = 21$ and $min(|P_{I_1r}(-_4)|, |P_{Jr}(-_4)|) = 3 + min(18, 18) = 21$. As a result, the pair (P_{I_1}, P_J) can be passed to the final step for verification.

In the final step, Jaccard similarity function is computed to verify the candidate pair (P_{I_1}, P_J). Recall that threshold θ can be equivalently converted to the overlap threshold α according to Eq. (25.1). $Jaccard(P_{I_1}, P_J) = \frac{|P_{I_1} \cap P_J|}{|P_{I_1} \cup P_J|} = \frac{21}{25} = 0.84 > \theta \Leftrightarrow O(P_{I_1}, P_J) = 21 > \alpha$. Thus, M_{I_1} can be potentially reused for M_J. In particular, the two following mapping formulas are reused completely:

- $Dept = B1{:}B(next = bottom(Dept) + 5)$
- $EmployeeID = B2{:}B(next = bottom(EmployeeID) + 5)$.

The mapping formula $EmployeeName = B3{:}B(next = bottom(EmployeeName) + 5)$ needs to be modified to $EmployeeName = B4{:}B(next = bottom(Employee Name) + 5)$. In addition to that, the user needs to write a new mapping formula for the optional label $Address$: $Address = B3{:}B(next = bottom(Address) + 5)$. M_J is then stored in the mapping repository for future reuse.

It is worth noting that the $start$ $coordinate$ (i.e., top-left cell) of an instance is important in reuse. In the above example, starting coordinates of P_{I_1} and P_J are both $(1, 1)$ so we do not need to change mapping formulas in a recommendation. Suppose that the starting coordinate of P_J is now $(2, 2)$, then mapping formulas of P_{I_1} should be offset based on the row and column differences between two start coordinates. For example, two mappings that can be reused completely are offset as follows: $Dept = C2{:}C(next = bottom(Dept) + 5)$ and $ID = C3 : C(next = bottom(ID) + 5)$.

The algorithm we presented above can be easily switched to other similarity metrics [20]. In the case of cosine similarity, the length of prefix to be indexed for a string x is $|x| - [\theta * |x|] + 1$; the size filtering threshold is $[\theta^2 * |x|]$; overlap threshold for positional filtering is $\alpha = [\theta * \sqrt{|x| * |y|}]$. The algorithm is also applicable to the edit distance with threshold δ if we tokenize strings to q-$grams$. The necessary condition for two strings (x, y) satisfying the threshold δ is their corresponding q-gram sets must have overlap no less than $\alpha = (max(|x|, |y|) + q - 1) - q * \delta$ [31]. Hence, prefix to be indexed for a string x is $q * \delta + 1$; the filtering size threshold is $|x| - \delta$; threshold for positional filtering is $x - q * \delta$.

25.6 Implementation

TranSheet has been implemented as an Excel plug-in using C# 3.0 and Visual Studio 2008.

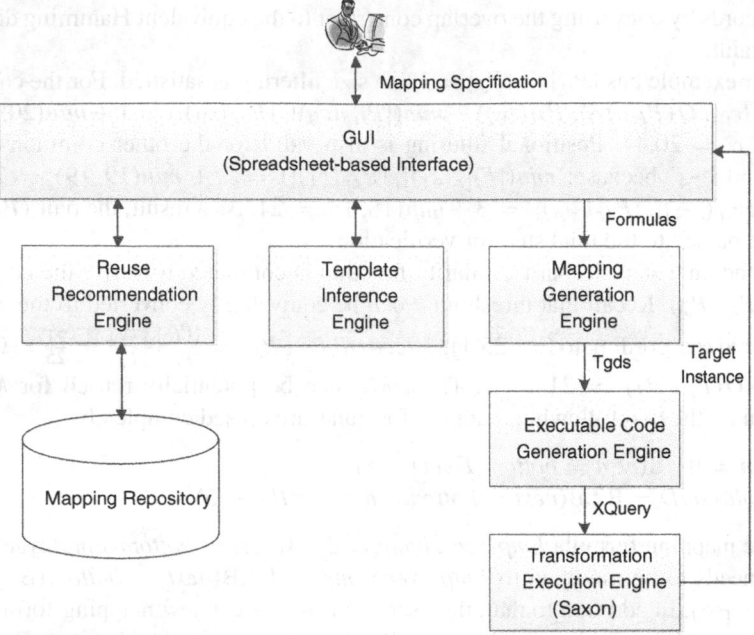

Fig. 25.3 TranSheet architecture for spreadsheet-based data transformation reuse

Architecture. The architecture (Fig. 25.3) contains several components that we developed previously: (i) GUI enables users to specify mappings via formulas. While spreadsheet data is imported using the built-in functionality of Excel, target schemas are imported using TranSheet functionality; (ii) Mapping generation engine takes input mapping formulas from GUI and generates corresponding tuple generating dependencies (tgds); (iii) Query generation engine generates XQuery from input tgds; (iv) Execution engine is responsible for executing input XQuery and then returning the transformation result to GUI for validation. For the work presented in this chapter, the architecture was extended by adding the following components: (i) Template inference engine infers the template of an existing spreadsheet and generates the corresponding string (Sect. 25.4); (ii) Mapping repository stores specified mapping information (presented below); (iii) Reuse recommendation engine uses information stored in the mapping repository and recommends specified mapping formulas for reuse (Sect. 25.5).

Mapping Repository Organization. The main tables that form the basis for designing the mapping repository are as follows:

- `Mappings(MId, InstanceId, TemplateId, SchemaId)`
- `MappingFormulas(MEId, MId, EId, MappingFormula)`
- `Schemas(SchemaId, SchemaName)`
- `Elements(EId, Name, Type, Parent, SchemaId)`

Mappings

MId	InstanceId	TemplateId	SchemaId
M0	I0	P0	Sch0
M1	I1	P1	Sch0

Schemas

SchemaId	SchemaName
Sch0	Employees

Elements

EId	Name	Type	Parent	SchemaId
E0	Target	Rcd	-	Sch0
E1	Emp	Set	E0	Sch0
E2	*	Rcd	E1	Sch0
E3	Dept	Str	E2	Sch0
E4	ID	Int	E2	Sch0
E5	Name	Str	E2	Sch0
E6	Address	Str	E2	Sch0

MappingFormulas

MEId	MId	EId	MappingFormula
ME0	M0	E1	A2:D(value=empty)
ME1	M1	E3	B1:B(next=bottom(Dept)+5)
ME2	M1	E4	B2:B(next=bottom(EmployeeID)+5)
ME3	M1	E5	B3:B(next=bottom(EmployeeName)+5)

Templates

TemplateId	Representation
P0	Dept - < string > - | ID - < int >| Name...
P1	< Dept - ID - Name - ε - ε > | < string -...

Cells

CellId	Coordinate	Value	Formula	InstanceId
C0	A1	Dept	Dept	I0
C1	B1	ID	ID	I0
C2	C1	Name	Name	I0
C3	D1	Address	Address	I0
		...		

Instances

InstanceId	Start Coordinate	End Coordinate
I0	A1	D5
I1	A1	B13

Fig. 25.4 Mapping Repository Organization

- Instances(InstanceId, StartCoordinate, EndCoordinate)
- Cells(CellId, Coordinate, Value, Formula, InstanceId)
- Templates(TemplateId, Representation)

Table Mappings encodes mappings from spreadsheet instances to target schemas where attributes MId, InstanceId, TemplateId, and SchemaId are a mapping identifier, an instance identifier, a template identifier, and a target schema identifier, respectively. Each mapping in table Mappings consists of a set of mapping formulas stored in table MappingFormulas, in which attributes MEId, MId, EId, and MappingFormula are a mapping formula identifier, a mapping identifier, a schema element identifier, and a mapping formula, respectively.

Tables Schemas and Elements encode the target schemas and their corresponding elements, respectively. Table Schemas stores a schema identifier SchemaId and a schema name SchemaName. Table Elements represents the graph representation of a target schema. Each tuple of this table corresponds to a node of the graph where attributes Name, Type, Parent, and SchemaId specify a node's label, a node's type, a node's parent, and an identifier of a target schema, respectively.

Tables Instances and Cells are used to model a spreadsheet instance and its non-empty cells. Table Templates stores a template identifier TemplateId and its corresponding string representation Representation. For example, tables in Fig. 25.4 are created for mapping instances I_0 in Fig. 25.1a and I_1 in Fig. 25.1b to the target schema in Fig. 25.1d.

25.7 Evaluation

For the evaluation we have put the focus on the performance and the effectiveness of the system. We use the EUSES spreadsheet corpus [28], which consists of 4498 spreadsheets collected from various sources (e.g., teaching courses, personal databases, and financial data), for evaluation. This corpus was widely used by many works on spreadsheet research and spreadsheet template inference(e.g., [27]).

25.7.1 Performance

The performance is to be evaluated for Jaccard and Cosine similarities with different thresholds and variants of the template.

Experimental setup. We select 10 spreadsheets in the corpus whose templates can be inferred using techniques presented in Sect. 25.4. The average length of these templates is 104. For each spreadsheet S, the corresponding template $Temp_S$ is modified based on small incremental changes to generate 25000, 50000, 100000, and 200000 variants of it. The following operations are applied: (i) Insert a new column (row) inside a hex group (vex group) of $Temp_S$ at an arbitrary position; (ii) Insert a new column (row) outside the hex groups (vex groups) of $Temp_S$ at an arbitrary position; (iii) Delete an existing column (row) inside a hex group (vex group) of $Temp_S$; (iv) Delete an existing column (row) outside the hex groups (vex groups) of $Temp_S$. Then, apply these operations again to the newly generated templates and so on. All experiments were performed on a laptop with Intel Core 2 Duo 2.1 GHz, 3 GB RAM, and Windows Vista Home Premium SP2.

Methodology. Template $Temp_S$ of spreadsheet S is matched against its generated variants stored in the mapping repository. We measure the running time of this matching for each fixed threshold. We use four thresholds, namely 0.9, 0.85, 0.8, and 0.75. Each experiment covers two similarity measures, namely Jaccard and Cosine. We then average the results of the 10 above selected spreadsheets.

Observations. The experimental results on performance are shown in Figs. 25.5 and 25.6. There was no problem with the amount of available memory during experimentation (e.g., out of memory error). Consider the performance graph for Jaccard similarity in Fig. 25.5. As can be seen, the running time increases when the threshold decreases and this trend is clearer when the number of variants is larger. This can be explained by two main reasons: (i) the number of inverted lists is larger for a small threshold so it takes more time to build and probe them; (ii) the candidate size increases for a smaller threshold. Basically, the running time grows almost linearly with the increase of the number of variants for each threshold.

Regarding Cosine similarity (Fig. 25.6), the findings are essentially similar to those of Jaccard similarity. However, for each threshold, the running time is generally longer since the constraints of Cosine (e.g., length of the prefix, size filtering

Fig. 25.5 Performance graph
of Jaccard similarity

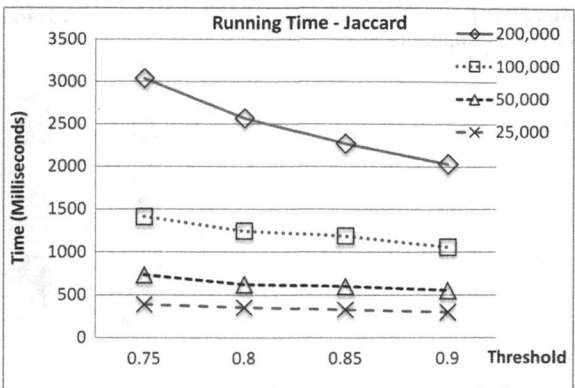

Fig. 25.6 Performance graph
of Cosine similarity

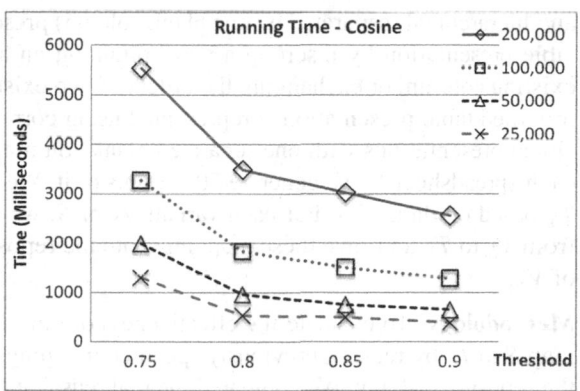

threshold and overlap threshold) are looser than those of Jaccard. Furthermore, the running time increases considerably when changing from threshold 0.8 to 0.75 due to a surge of the candidate size at threshold 0.75, while it is a modest growth for other threshold changes, namely from 0.9 to 0.85 and from 0.85 to 0.8.

25.7.2 Effectiveness

The objective of the experiment to evaluate the effectiveness is to contrast the capability of the system of producing the desired result with different configurations.

Experimental setup. Since the size of the above repository (See Sect. 25.7.1) is quite big, to properly evaluate the reuse effectiveness, we create a smaller repository as the following. We select 10 spreadsheets from the EUSES corpus. For each spreadsheet, we represent it using table, repeater (separated by one blank column),

Fig. 25.7 Reuse effectiveness of Jaccard similarity

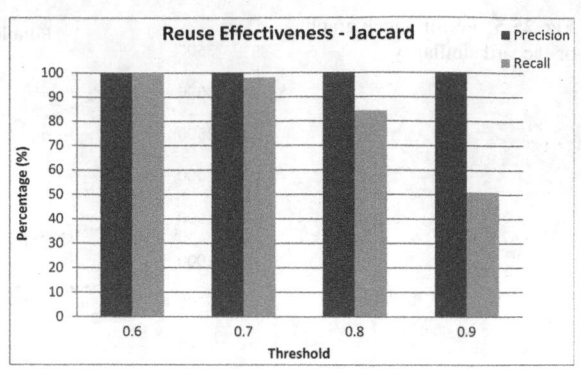

and hierarchical (separated by one blank column) presentations. We then modify the table presentation by inserting a new column at an arbitrary position, deleting an existing column, or exchanging the orders of two existing columns. Afterwards, the modified table presentation is represented using corresponding repeater and hierarchical presentations with one separated blank column. Based on this procedure, for each spreadsheet S, we generate 50 variants of it. We also design the target schema T_S based on data of S. For each variant V_S of S, we manually write the mappings from V_S to T_S and save these mappings into the repository along with the template of V_S.

Methodology. To evaluate the effectiveness of our algorithm in the repository, we map S to T_S by reusing previously specified mappings of the variants of S stored in the repository, if any. We compared the real reusable mappings R (found manually) and the recommended mappings P found by our algorithm at four thresholds, namely 0.9, 0.8, 0.7, and 0.6. Let $I = R \cap P$, we use the quality measures employed by popular information retrieval studies [32, 33]:

- *precision* $= |I|/|P|$
- *recall* $= |I|/|R|$

Similar to the performance experiments, each experiment covers the Jaccard and Cosine similarities. The results of the 10 selected spreadsheets are averaged.

Observations. The experimental results on reuse effectiveness are shown in Figs. 25.7 and 25.8 for Jaccard and Cosine similarities, respectively. Consider the reuse effectiveness graph for Jaccard similarity shown in Fig. 25.7. Precisions for all thresholds are all 100 %. Meanwhile, the recall is higher when the threshold is smaller; at threshold 0.6, recall is 100 %. This is because for a larger threshold, more reusable mappings are filtered out.

Since the constraints of Cosine similarity are looser, the reuse effectiveness results of Cosine (Fig. 25.8) are slightly different from those of Jaccard. Precisions for all thresholds, except threshold 0.6 (recall is nearly 40 %), are 100 %. Some unusable recommended mappings appear at threshold 0.6. Except threshold 0.9 (recall is more than 80 %), recalls for all thresholds are 100 %.

Fig. 25.8 Reuse effectiveness
of Cosine similarity

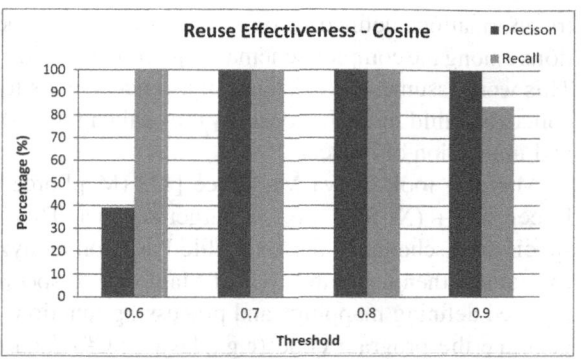

25.8 Related Work

Reusing mapping information is first discussed in the survey of Rahm and Bernstein [34] on schema matching (i.e., find semantic correspondences between the elements of two schemas). It is expected that in many cases schemas being matched can be very similar. Therefore, when matching different but similar schemas to the same destination schema (e.g., integrating new data sources into a data warehouse), it is possible to reuse existing mappings for entire schema structures, which results in significant savings of manual effort.

Inspired by that, COMA [32] proposes the MatchCompose operation for performing a join-like operation on a mapping path consisting of two or more mappings to deduce a new mapping (e.g., combine A–B, B–C, and C–D to derive a new mapping between A and D). COMA++ [35] extends COMA to deal with the cases where such mapping paths are unnecessary (i.e., one or multiple existing mappings can be reused for the given match problem) or not available(i.e., searching for mapping paths which are not available yet, but may be computed with less effort than a direct matching). To handle large and complex schemas, COMA++ also introduces the fragment-based matching approach, in which the source and target schemas are divided into fragments and each pair of source and target fragments are then compared to detect the best matching pairs.

Madhavan et al. [33] leverage the knowledge in a corpus of schemas and mappings to improve schema matching results, in addition to the evidence that is available in the two schemas being matched. The corpus is used to augment the evidence about elements in the schemas being matched. Statistics gleaned from the corpus is used to infer domain constraints, which are crucial in achieving high matching accuracy. The reuse, however, is limited to element-to-element match, rather than larger concepts.

Recent work by Saha et al. [36] introduces the schema covering problem as a first step towards transformation reuse, which is an extension of Clio project [11, 37]. Given a complex schema, schema covering identifies a collection of common concepts (i.e., business objects) in a repository and creates a cover of the schema by these concepts. When a complex schema can be divided into smaller concepts, simple transformations defined among these concepts can be reused to define transformations among the complex schemas (e.g., by composing these simple transformations). This work assumes the existence of a concept repository and transformations among concepts. Building such repository is a challenging task including selection, cleaning, and unification of objects.

Mapping tool Altova MapForce [15] (MapForce for short) allows mapping an Excel 2007+ (XLSX) file to a target schema. This is done by first helping users specify the schema of the Excel file based on analyzing the file's OpenXML [38] format and then using the GUI of MapForce to specify mappings. Once users have finished defining mappings and processing functions, MapForce can automatically generate the program code (e.g., Java or C#) for transforming Excel data to the format required by an external application. The generated code can be reused for future mappings. However, this kind of reuse must be performed manually by users.

Our work focuses on reusing transformations from spreadsheet data to XML. We have extended the spreadsheet-like formula mapping language we presented in our previous work [7] to solve this problem. With respect to the aforementioned reuse approaches, the main difference is that we allow users to specify mappings using spreadsheet-like formulas and then reuse previously specified mapping formulas for a new spreadsheet instance that needs to be mapped to the target schema. Note that our work basically transforms data located on the tabular grid of a spreadsheet to XML, instead of extracting data from the spreadsheet, including macros and formulas. The recently proposed file format, namely OpenXML [38], allows external applications to easily extract data from Excel 2007 files (XLSX).

25.9 Summary

Transformation reuse is an important topic in information integration for both data integration and data exchange. In this chapter, we have considered the problem of reuse in transforming spreadsheet data to XML. We formulated the problem and proposed a solution based on the notions of spreadsheet template, mapping generalization, and similarity join. We extended the formula mapping language developed in our previous work. Given a spreadsheet instance, our algorithm recommended a list of previously specified mappings that can be reused for the instance. We implemented a prototype and evaluated the efficiency and effectiveness of the proposed solution via synthetic datasets. The experimental results confirmed the usefulness and viability of our approach. We truly believe the work presented within this chapter is an important step in building a simple and reusable data transformation framework (as outlined in the Clio project [11, 36]) in the context of spreadsheet-based data transformation.

References

1. Merrill, D.: Mashups: The new breed of web app. IBM Web Architecture Technical Library, pp. 1–13 (2006)
2. Yu, J., Benatallah, B., Casati, F., Daniel, F.: Understanding mashup development. IEEE Internet Comput. **12**(5), 44–52 (2008)
3. Y. Corp. Yahoo! pipes. http://pipes.yahoo.com/pipes. Accessed 03 July 2012
4. Intel Mash Maker. http://mashmaker.intel.com. Accessed 15 June 2012
5. Kovanovic, V., Djuric, D.: Highway: a domain specific language for enterprise application integration. In: Proceedings of the 5th India Software Engineering Conference, pp. 33–36. ACM (2012)
6. Kongdenfha, W., Benatallah, B., Vayssière, J., Saint-Paul, R., Casati, F.: Rapid development of spreadsheet-based web mashups. In: Proceedings of the 18th International Conference on World Wide Web, pp. 851–860. ACM (2009)
7. Hung, V., Benatallah, B., Saint-Paul, R.: Spreadsheet-based complex data transformation. In: Proceedings of the 20th ACM International Conference on Information and Knowledge Management (CIKM), pp. 1749–1754. ACM (2011)
8. Scaffidi, C., Shaw, M., Myers, B.: Estimating the numbers of end users and end user programmers. In: VLHCC '05: Proceedings of the 2005 IEEE Symposium on Visual Languages and Human-Centric Computing, pp. 207–214. IEEE Computer Society, Washington, DC, USA (2005)
9. Abraham, R., Erwig, M.: Header and unit inference for spreadsheets through spatial analyses. In: VLHCC '04: Proceedings of the 2004 IEEE Symposium on Visual Languages—Human Centric Computing, pp. 165–172. IEEE Computer Society, Washington, DC, USA (2004)
10. Jones, S., Blackwell, A., Burnett, M.: A user-centered approach to functions in excel. In: Proceedings of the 8th ACM SIGPLAN International Conference on Functional Programming, pp. 165–176. ACM Press (2003)
11. Haas, L.M., Hernández, M.A., Ho, H., Popa, L., Roth, M.: Clio grows up: from research prototype to industrial tool. In: SIGMOD '05: Proceedings of the 2005 ACM SIGMOD International Conference on Management of Data, pp. 805–810. ACM, New York, NY, USA (2005)
12. Roth, M., Hernandez, M.A., Coulthard, P., Yan, L., Popa, L., Ho, H.C.-T., Salter, C.C.: Xml mapping technology: making connections in an xml-centric world. IBM Syst. J. **45**(2), 389–409 (2006)
13. Hernandez, M., Miller, R., Haas, L.: Clio: a semi-automatic tool for schema mapping. In: SIGMOD '01: Proceedings of the 2001 ACM SIGMOD International Conference on Management of Data. Association for Computing Machinery, Inc., One Astor Plaza, 1515 Broadway, New York, NY, 10036-5701, USA (2001)
14. Raffio, A., Braga, D., Ceri, S., Papotti, P., Hernandez, M.: Clip: a visual language for explicit schema mappings. In: 24th International Conference on Data Engineering (2008)
15. Altova. Mapforce—graphical data mapping, conversion, and integration tool. http://www.altova.com/mapforce.html. Accessed 25 May 2011
16. IBM. Infosphere Data Architect. http://www-01.ibm.com/software/data/optim/data-architect/. Accessed 25 Oct 2010
17. Microsoft. Creating Maps Using Biztalk Mapper. http://msdn.microsoft.com/en-us/library/aa559261(v=BTS.70).aspx. Accessed 13 Apr 2011
18. Arasu, A., Ganti, V., Kaushik, R.: Efficient exact set-similarity joins. In: Proceedings of the 32nd International Conference on Very Large Data Bases, pp. 918–929. VLDB Endowment (2006)
19. Chaudhuri, S., Ganti, V., Kaushik, R., A primitive operator for similarity joins in data cleaning. In: Data Engineering, 2006. ICDE'06. Proceedings of the 22nd International Conference on, p. 5. IEEE (2006)
20. Xiao, C., Wang, W., Lin, X., Yu, J., Wang, G.: Efficient similarity joins for near-duplicate detection. ACM Trans. Database Syst. **36**(3), 15 (2011)

21. Lakshmanan, L.V.S., Subramanian, S.N., Goyal, N., Krishnamurthy, R.: On query spreadsheets. In: ICDE '98: Proceedings of the Fourteenth International Conference on Data Engineering, pp. 134–141. IEEE Computer Society, Washington, DC, USA (1998)
22. Mecca, G., Papotti, P., Raunich, S.: Core schema mappings. In: SIGMOD (2009)
23. Robertson, G.G., Czerwinski, M.P., Churchill, J.E.: Visualization of mappings between schemas. In: CHI '05: Proceedings of the SIGCHI Conference on Human Factors in Computing Systems, pp. 431–439. ACM, New York, NY, USA (2005)
24. Rice, F.: Creating xml mappings in excel 2003. Technical Report, Microsoft Corporation (2005)
25. Brauer, B.: Next evolution of data integration into microsoft excel. Technical Report, StrikeIron (2005)
26. Erwig, M., Abraham, R., Cooperstein, I., Kollmansberger, S.: Automatic generation and maintenance of correct spreadsheets. In: ICSE '05: Proceedings of the 27th International Conference on Software Engineering, pp. 136–145. ACM, New York, NY, USA (2005)
27. Abraham, R., Erwig, M.: Inferring templates from spreadsheets. In: ICSE '06: Proceedings of the 28th International Conference on Software Engineering, pp. 182–191. ACM, New York, NY, USA (2006)
28. Fisher, M., Rothermel, G.: The EUSES spreadsheet corpus: a shared resource for supporting experimentation with spreadsheet dependability mechanisms. In: ACM SIGSOFT Software Engineering Notes, vol. 30, no. 4, pp. 1–5. ACM (2005)
29. Elmagarmid, A.K., Ipeirotis, P.G., Verykios, V.S.: Duplicate record detection: a survey. IEEE Trans. Knowl. Data Eng. **19**, 1–16 (2007)
30. Köpcke, H., Thor, A., Rahm, E.: Evaluation of entity resolution approaches on real-world match problems. Proc. VLDB Endow. **3**, 484–493 (2010)
31. Gravano, L., Ipeirotis, P., Jagadish, H., Koudas, N., Muthukrishnan, S., Srivastava, D.: Approximate string joins in a database (almost) for free. In: Proceedings of the International Conference on Very Large Data Bases, pp. 491–500 (2001)
32. Do, H.-H., Rahm, E.: COMA: a system for flexible combination of schema matching approaches. In: VLDB '02: Proceedings of the 28th International Conference on Very Large Data Bases, pp. 610–621. VLDB Endowment (2002)
33. Madhavan, J., Bernstein, P.A., Doan, A., Halevy, A.: Corpus-based schema matching. In: ICDE '05: Proceedings of the 21st International Conference on Data Engineering, pp. 57–68. IEEE Computer Society, Washington, DC, USA (2005)
34. Rahm, E., Bernstein, P.A.: A survey of approaches to automatic schema matching. VLDB J.: Very Large Data Bases **10**(4), 334–350 (2001)
35. Aumueller, D., Do, H.-H., Massmann, S., Rahm, E.: Schema and ontology matching with COMA++. In: SIGMOD '05: Proceedings of the 2005 ACM SIGMOD International Conference on Management of Data, pp. 906–908. ACM, New York, NY, USA (2005)
36. Saha, B., Stanoi, I., Clarkson, K.L.: Schema covering: a step towards enabling reuse in information integration. In: ICDE, pp. 285–296 (2010)
37. Fuxman, A., Hernandez, M.A., Ho, H., Miller, R.J., Papotti, P., Popa, L.: Nested mappings: schema mapping reloaded. In: VLDB '06: Proceedings of the 32nd International Conference on Very Large Data Bases, pp. 67–78. VLDB Endowment (2006)
38. Rice, F.: Introducing the office (2007) open xml file formats. Technical Report, Microsoft Corporation (2006)

Chapter 26
A Unified RGPS-Based Approach Supporting Service-Oriented Process Customization

Jian Wang, Zaiwen Feng, Jia Zhang, Patrick C. K. Hung, Keqing He
and Liang-Jie Zhang

Abstract Software as a Service (SaaS) aims to provide utility-oriented software delivery and provisioning. While software being published as reusable Web APIs, users can quickly compose multiple services into a new value-added process: a mashup. However, various users may have different requirements, thus preferring to compose the same set of services in different ways. Therefore, there is a need to provide a unified way for users to configure and compose services. RGPS (Role, Goal, Process, and Service) is an ongoing ISO-standard meta-model framework for describing service usage requirements. This chapter presents an approach of leveraging RGPS to help users configure a personalized service-based mashup. Based on users' requirements, a hierarchical goal tree is generated for users to further refine their business goals. According to mappings between goals and variation points in business process templates, a personalized business process will be created. One task in a business process may be realized by an external service. Corresponding

J. Wang (✉) · Z. Feng · K. He
State Key Laboratory of Software Engineering, School of Computer,
Wuhan University, Wuhan, China
e-mail: jianwang@whu.edu.cn

Z. Feng
e-mail: fengzaiwen@whu.edu.cn

K. He
e-mail: hekeqing@whu.edu.cn

J. Zhang
Carnegie Mellon University—Silicon Valley, Silicon Valley, CA, USA
e-mail: jia.zhang@sv.cmu.edu

P. C. K. Hung
University of Ontario Institute of Technology, Oshawa, ON, Canada
e-mail: patrick.hung@uoit.ca

L.-J. Zhang
Kingdee International Software Group Co. Ltd., Shenzhen, China
e-mail: zhanglj@ieee.org

A. Bouguettaya et al. (eds.), *Web Services Foundations*,
DOI: 10.1007/978-1-4614-7518-7_26,
© Springer Science+Business Media New York 2014

visualization tools are introduced to assist users. This chapter also describes a case study of customizing a mashup over an established service supermarket.

26.1 Introduction

Cloud computing is defined as a model for enabling ubiquitous, convenient, on-demand network access to a shared pool of configurable computing resources [16]. This has created significant improvements in terms of software development. Software as a Service (SaaS) is a core objective of cloud computing, aiming to provide utility-oriented software delivery and provisioning. Increasing amounts of software have been published as reusable Web APIs or Web services (e.g., over 28,000 services and 7,000 APIs have been published in Seekda![1] and ProgrammableWeb[2] by September 2012, respectively), allowing users to quickly compose multiple services into a new value-added process, also known as a composite service or a mashup. However, various users may have personalized requirements, thus preferring to compose the same set of software services in different ways. Meanwhile, the large amount of available services makes it difficult for end-users to select suitable services. Therefore, there is a need to provide a unified way for users to configure and compose software services according to their personalized requirements.

WS-BPEL [19] is the most widely adopted standard for building business processes using Web services. Many works have extended WS-BPEL to achieve more flexible and customizable process modeling. For example, Mietzner et al. transform variability descriptors into a WS-BPEL process model to guide a customer through the customization of an SaaS application [17]; Lazovik et al. define a formal model to guide obtaining customer-specific process instantiations by a series of customization steps over reference processes [12]; Van der Aalst et al. investigate the workflow variants within the context of configurable workflow models [21]. However, these works do not consider service-oriented process customization in terms of various end users' requirements. The works [4, 10] establish relationships between process models and requirements models such as KAOS and i*, followed by generating, validating and configuring process models. Compared with these works, our work will focus on customizing service-based processes in a holistic way by connecting the requirements models (role and goal models), process models, and services.

The RGPS (Role-Goal-Process-Service) meta-model framework [6, 22] has been proposed for describing personalized requirements involving domain-related services, toward an ultimate goal of enabling on-demand service provisioning. RGPS is an integral part of the ISO Meta-model Framework for Interoperability (MFI[3]). This chapter presents an approach that leverages RGPS to help users dynamically configure a personalized service-based mashup. RGPS-based domain modeling is used to

---

[1] http://webservices.seekda.com/

[2] http://www.programmableweb.com

[3] http://metadata-stds.org/19763/index.html

create domain models that will be reused in the subsequent process customization. Faced with users' specified requirements, a hierarchical goal tree can be generated for users to refine their specific business goals. According to mappings between goals and variation points in business process templates, a personalized business process model will be created. Afterwards, each task in the process model may be realized by an external service.

Based on the proposed approach, corresponding visualization prototypes including a domain modeling tool and a service supermarket are introduced to assist users in such a RGPS-based service-oriented process configuration. This chapter also describes a case study of customizing a mashup over an established service supermarket consisting of a set of Web services, including a contact service, Delivery-100 API, Check RFID service, Baidu map API, and Yahoo! weather API.

The remainder of the chapter is organized as follows. Section 26.2 introduces our motivation followed by an overview of our approach. Section 26.3 gives an introduction of the RGPS meta-model framework. The RGPS-based service-oriented process customization approach is presented in Sect. 26.4. Section 26.5 shows the visualization prototypes that support the proposed approach. A case study is given in Sect. 26.6. Section 26.7 concludes the chapter.

26.2 Motivation and Overall Approach

In this section, a motivating example will be given, followed by an overview of our approach.

26.2.1 A Motivating Example

The following scenario in the Customer Relationship Management (CRM) domain shows a motivating example of our work. Suppose a salesman in a company plans to deliver goods to his customer. First, he needs to acquire the recipient's shipping information such as address, phone, and postcode. He then will select a shipping company to send these goods and generate a shipping order. After that, he will use a payment service to pay for the order. Finally, after the goods is sent to the shipping company, he can track the shipping status of his goods. Usually, the user can query the order to get the status of the goods in text. However, many salesmen may have additional requirements in tracking the order. For example, some people may want to view the current location of the goods on a map during the shipping process, while some people may hope to know the current weather information of the cities in the shipping route, which can be used to judge whether their goods can arrive at the destination in time. In addition, if the goods are expensive and brittle, some salesmen may hope to check the integrity of these goods during the shipping process.

From this simple scenario, we can see that different users' requirements may be different towards the same goal of "delivering goods to customers". Moreover, initial requirements may be incomplete, and additional requirements may be added or refined during the process of requirements analysis. So it is almost impossible to find a single service that can satisfy the salesman's requirements. Automatic service composition will also be hard to work due to the variability and incompleteness of users' personalized requirements. Therefore, there is a need to provide a unified way for users to configure and compose services according to users' requirements.

26.2.2 Overall Approach

Towards the above-mentioned problem, we propose a RGPS-based service-oriented process customization solution. The RGPS meta-model framework describes requirements and service-based solution in a holistic way using four key elements: Role, Goal, Process, and Service, which provides a guideline for our approach. Our approach is a domain-oriented solution, since domain knowledge can be used to supplement the incomplete requirements and serve as a communication bridge between users and developers to avoid ambiguity. Moreover, many researchers have shown that it is more suitable to reuse software assets in a specific domain [18], and services as important software assets are no exception. Therefore, domain modeling will play an important role during process customization.

As shown in Fig. 26.1, the RGPS meta-model framework will provide a guideline for our approach. Based on users' common requirements in a specific domain, domain models can be created by identifying the commonality and variability of domain knowledge. Then, faced with a user' personalized requirements, RGPS-based service-oriented process customization process can be conducted to provide solutions based on domain models. The result of customization process will in turn

Fig. 26.1 Our overall approach

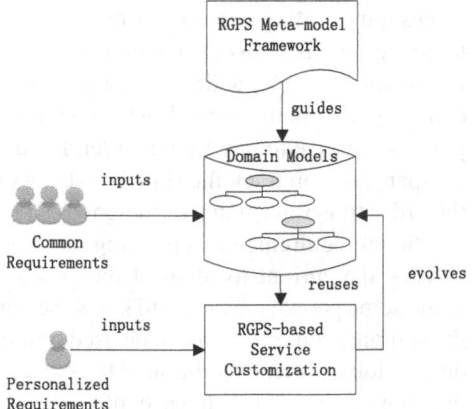

contribute to the evolution of domain models. Note that in this chapter, we mainly describe how to customize service-oriented processes, and do not introduce the detail of the evolution of domain models. We will explain our approach using the motivating example in Sect. 26.2.1 throughout the chapter.

26.3 The RGPS Meta-Model Framework

To support service-oriented software development, we have proposed a meta-model framework named RGPS (Role-Goal-Process-Service) [22]. The role represents the abstract characterization of user behaviors and responsibilities within specified organizational context or domain, which can be used to distinguish different user groups. The goal denotes a descriptive statement of intent of a user or an organization, and can be viewed as an objective that the solution under consideration should achieve. The process is defined as a collection of related, structured activities or tasks that achieve a particular business goal. The service is used to denote a kind of Web-based application such as Web service or Web API, which encapsulates certain computing module and can be accessed by certain interface.

The relations among the four elements are shown in Fig. 26.2. Roles undertake their corresponding role goals, and actors prefer their respective personal goals.

Fig. 26.2 Relations among RGPS

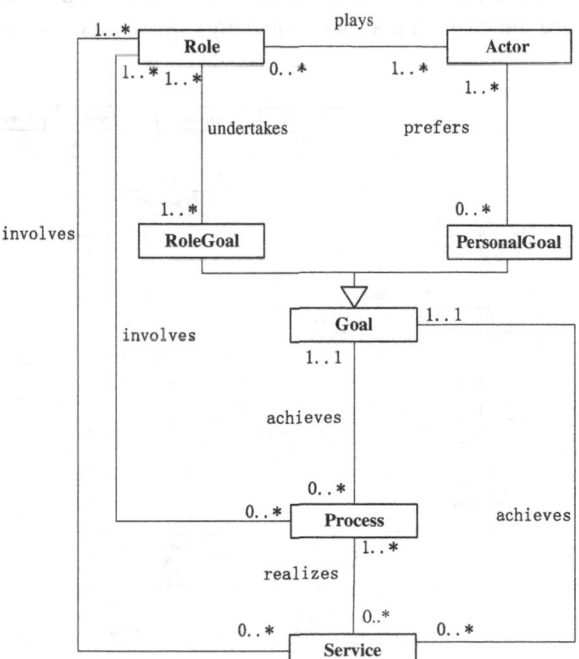

Processes can directly or collaboratively achieve goals. Services can realize certain processes. Roles can be involved in the processes and services. In this way, RGPS can be viewed as a hierarchical modeling framework that can contribute to describe and analyze users' requirements, and provide service-based solutions for requirements.

Here, we will briefly introduce the meta-models in RGPS, shown in UML class diagrams. Since roles and goals are closely related, we prefer to model them together. Then, we will introduce the RGPS-based domain modeling, which can be used to created domain models in a specific domain.

26.3.1 The Role and Goal Meta-Model

The role and goal meta-model is shown in Fig. 26.3. In [15], the definition of roles was described as: (1) a role is a property assigned to humans that can change dynamically, and (2) humans can have multiple roles simultaneously. In [3], a role was used as a definitive factor in task or service selection, and two kinds of roles were presented, i.e., social role and task role. In RGPS, the roles are mainly used to distinguish different user groups. Users who play the same role are likely to share similar business goals and behavior patterns. Once a user's role in a certain context is recognized, the services closely related to the role may be considered to be recommended to the user.

A role can be played by different actors. In an organizational context, role goals are the goals that a role is in charge of. Actors also have their personal preferences,

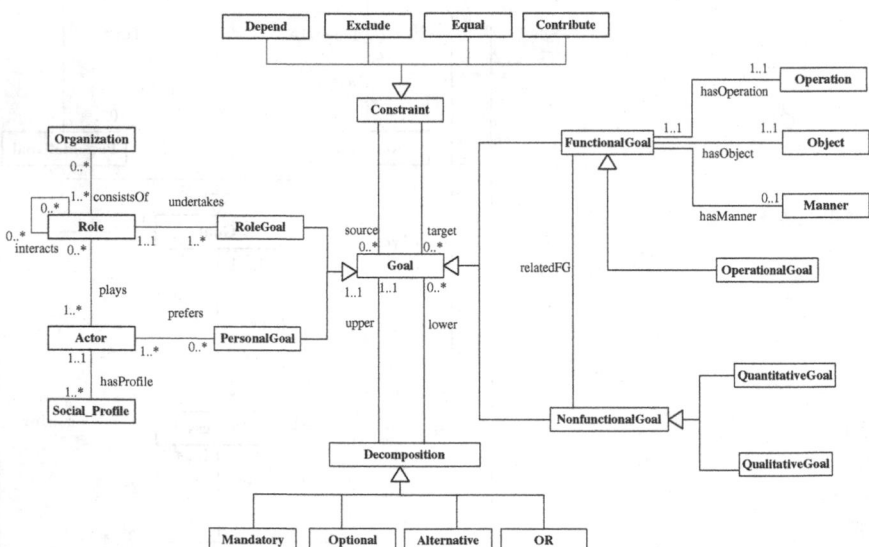

Fig. 26.3 The role and goal meta-model

and these personal preferences are modeled as personal goals. An organization is composed of a collection of related roles.

Goals can be either functional or nonfunctional. Functional goals describe the functions that a system or a solution must achieve, and nonfunctional goals are used to describe how well the functional goals are exercised. The description of a functional goal consists of three parts: a verb that indicates the operation, a noun that indicates the object dealt with by the operation, and the manner that is either a prefix or a suffix to indicate how the operation affects the object. Each operation can be annotated by a verb concept of domain ontology. Similarly, each object can be annotated by a noun concept of domain ontology. Nonfunctional goals can be classified into quantitative goals and qualitative goals according to their description manner.

Usually, a goal is a high-level statement when it is first proposed, and needs to be decomposed in order to get a concrete and operational description [7, 11]. Goal decomposition or refinement depicts how an upper goal can be decomposed into lower goals, and the process will not stop until all the leaf-level sub-goals are operational goals. Each operational goal is the goal that can be directly achieved by an atomic process in the process model. The feature decomposition strategy in FODA (Feature-Oriented Domain Analysis) [8] is adopted during the goal refinement process to support the variability modeling. The decomposition relations between an upper goal and a lower goal set can be classified into four types: *mandatory, optional, alternative,* and *OR.* When an upper goal g is selected by a user, the lower goal set that has the *mandatory* relation with g must also be selected; the lower goal set that has the *optional* relation with g may be or not be selected; exactly one goal from the lower goal set that has the *alternative* relation with g must be selected; and at least one goal from the lower goal set that has the *OR* relation with g must be selected.

In addition, the constraint relation between goals can be classified into *depend, exclude, equal,* and *contribute* relations. The *depend* relation means that the realization of a goal depends on the realization of another one; the *exclude* relation means that two goals cannot be satisfied simultaneously; the *equal* relation means that two goals are the same in semantics; and the *contribute* relation means that the realization of a goal can contribute to the realization of another one.

Figure 26.4 shows an example of how the role and goal meta-model can be used to describe a role and goal model. The model comes from the motivating example in Sect. 26.2.1. The role goal of the role "Salesman" is "Deliver Goods", which is composed of a *mandatory* sub-goal "Send Goods" and an *optional* sub-goal "Track Goods". "Send Goods" can be further refined into four *mandatory* sub-goals: "Acquire Recipient Info", "Select Express Company", "Generate Order", and "Pay Order". "Track Goods" can be refined into two *mandatory* sub-goals: "Inquire Order" and "Display Order". The goal "Display Order" can be further decomposed into four *OR* sub-goals: "Display Order by Text", "Display Order by Map", "Display Integrity of Goods", and "Display Weather". Note that all the leaf-level goals are operational goals, while other goals are functional goals. Moreover, five dependences exist between five pairs of goals: between "Select Express Company" and "Acquire Recipient Info", between "Generate Order" and "Select Express Company", between

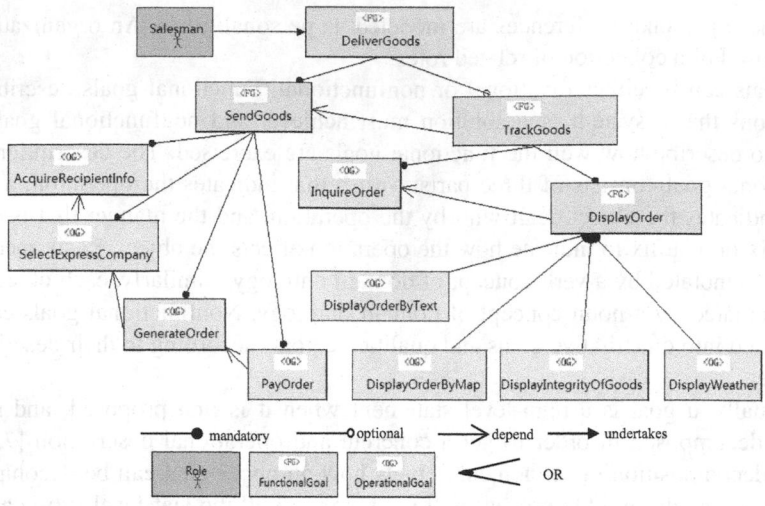

Fig. 26.4 A role and goal model

"Pay Order" and "Generate Order", between "Track Goods" and "Send Goods", and between "Display Order" and "Inquire Order".

26.3.2 The Process Meta-Model

The process meta-model is shown in Fig. 26.5. A process can be either an atomic process or a composite process. The difference between them is that the composite process consists of at least one control structure. Five typical control structures are defined: *sequence, loop, choice, split-join* and *any order*.

A process can achieve certain functional goals, and contribute to some nonfunctional goals. A process has four basic attributes: input, output, precondition and effect. Input and output represent the data flow transformed by the process. Precondition and effect indicate the constraints to be held before the process starts and after the process is normally finished, respectively.

In addition, a process may have nonfunctional expectations including quality expectation and contextual expectation. The former describes the quality requirements (e.g., the range of the response time); the latter describes contextual requirements (e.g., the range of the distance to the office) of the process.

Figure 26.6 illustrates how the process meta-model can be used to describe a process model. We use the modeling notations adapted from [2] to represent the process model. The process model consists of two composite processes "SendGoods" and "TrackGoods", connected by a control structure *sequence*. The details of these composite processes are shown in the dashed ellipses. "SendGoods" consists of four

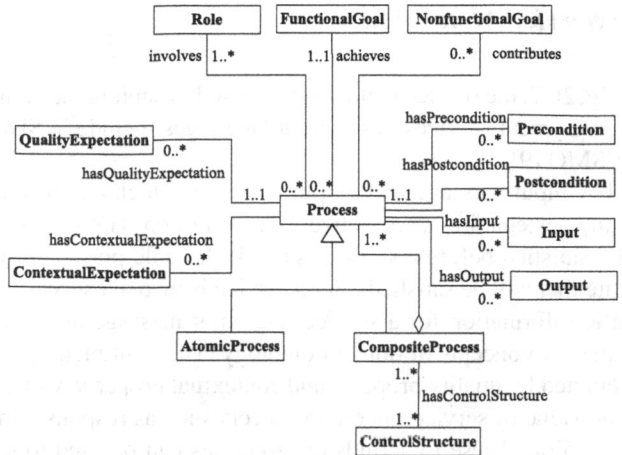

Fig. 26.5 The process meta-model

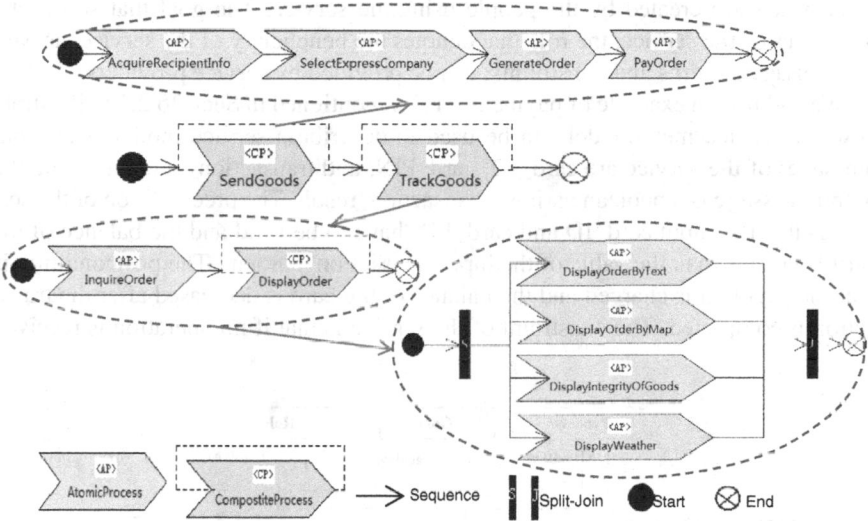

Fig. 26.6 A process model

atomic processes connected by a control structure *sequence*. "TrackGoods" consists of an atomic process "InquireOrder" and a composite process "DisplayOrder" connected by a control structure *sequence*. The composite process "DisplayOrder" consists of four atomic processes connected by a control structure *split-join*.

666

J. Wang et al.

26.3.3 The Service Meta-Model

As shown in Fig. 26.7, the service meta-model is used to capture the common semantics of services. Typical services description languages include WSDL [1], OWL-S [14], and WSMO [9].

A service has input message and output message, which can be constrained by precondition and postcondition, respectively. Precondition is used to specify the state that have to be satisfied before a service is invoked, while postcondition is used to specify the state that will be satisfied after a service is invoked successfully. In order to add semantic information for a service, the input message and output message can be annotated by concepts of domain ontology. The nonfunctional semantics of a service is depicted by quality property and contextual property, which can be used to represent the value of service in certain aspects such as response time, cost, and contextual restriction. These two kinds of properties can be used to match against the quality expectation and contextual expectation of processes, respectively.

As an embodiment of Web 2.0, a service can be annotated by comments or social tags, which are created by the people using the service. The goal that shows the objectives of the service, the role that denotes the beneficiary of the service, as well as the usage patterns and constraints, can be provided by service providers.

We will use an example of payment service mentioned in Sect. 26.2.1 to illustrate how the service meta-model can be used to describe a service model. The input messages of the service are card_ID, card_PIN, and transaction_amount, while the output message is a boolean variable transaction_result. The precondition of the service is that the input card_ID and card_PIN have to be valid and the balance of the card is greater than the value of the input transaction_amount. The postcondition is that the payment is charged and the balance of the card is decreased after the transaction is completed. The constraint of the service is that if no operation is received

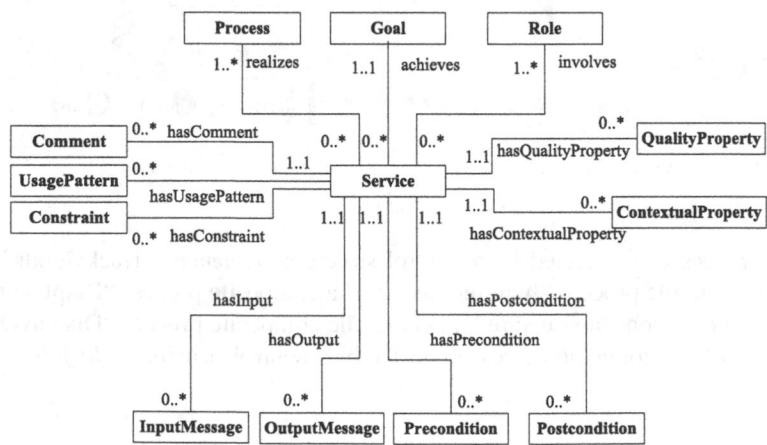

Fig. 26.7 The service meta-model

from users for 15 min during the execution process of the service, the connection will be expired for security reasons. The usage pattern indicates that the service is usually used followed by a shipping service if a merchandize is involved. The quality property denotes that the security of the service is guaranteed. The contextual property denotes that the service is only available in China. The comments can be ad hoc fragmental documents such as social tags and user comments (e.g., good user experience and free of charge).

26.3.4 Domain Modeling

Based on the RGPS meta-model framework, we propose an ontology-based domain modeling approach named O-RGPS. O-RGPS aims to provide a method to construct and manage domain models according to common requirements in a specific domain, which can be reused in requirements analysis and process customization.

In O-RGPS, domain ontologies including domain entity ontology and domain operation ontology are the basis for domain modeling, which can provide semantic annotation for domain models. Based on the domain ontologies, domain models can be created following the RGPS meta-models. More specifically, this approach can be generalized as the following steps:

1. Construct domain entity ontology and domain operation ontology. The domain entity ontology describes entity (noun) concepts and relationships among them, while domain operation ontology describes the operation (verb) concepts and relationships among them.
2. Construct role and goal models and annotate the models using domain ontologies. A role and goal model can be described in OWL and stored into domain model repository.
3. Construct process models and annotate the models using domain ontologies. A process model can be described in extended OWL-S and stored into domain model repository.
4. Construct service models and annotate the models using domain ontologies. Besides the information extracted from service description files such as WSDL, some other information will be modeled as attributes of the service including the role that closely related to the service, the goal that the service can achieve, and the process that the service can realize. A service model can be described in extended OWL-S and stored into domain model repository.
5. Classify and group all the domain models according to different domain problems they are related to, and create the relations among domain models in a group so as to improve the efficiency of searching models.

26.4 RGPS-Based Process Customization Approach

The approach of requirements driven process customization will be introduced in detail in this section.

26.4.1 Procedure of Customization

Based on the domain models created according to the common requirements in a specific domain, users' personalized requirements can be analyzed and corresponding customized service-oriented solutions will be constructed. As shown in Fig. 26.8, the following steps are used to complete the procedure: (1) elicit and parse users' requirements; (2) match the requirements with domain goals; (3) supplement and refine goals; (4) configure processes; and (5) discover services.

Users' requirements can be expressed in two ways. In the first way, the requirements can be represented in SORL, a pseudo natural language to be introduced in Sect. 26.4.2. Then users' requirements can be elicited and parsed, and the output will become the initial goals. The other way is to define some domain requirements templates for users to select from. That is, users can browse all domain models in templates and manually choose the domain, role, and goal information that they prefer step by step. For the initial goals, we need to match them with domain goals in Step 2. If the goals can be matched, it will go to Step 3 for further supplement

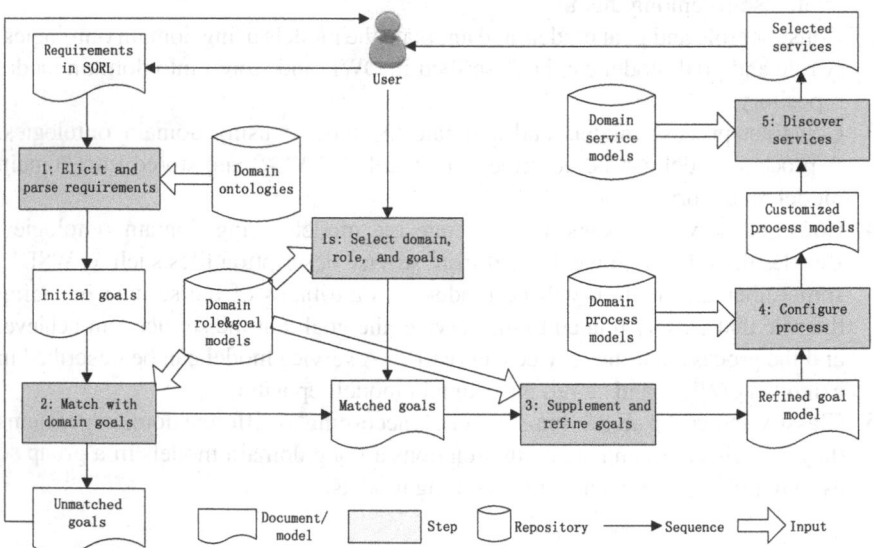

Fig. 26.8 Procedure of RGPS-based process customization

and refinement. Otherwise, the unmatched goals will be returned to users to revise their requirements. Once the goal model is refined, we will go to Step 4 to configure processes by leveraging the mapping between the goal model and process model. It is worth noting that the process configuration in this chapter mainly refers to removing, adding or modifying process model elements to meet the given requirements. When the process models are customized, we need to discover services from our service supermarket or publicly accessible service registries based on the process models. Finally, the selected services will be returned to users. Note that users will be involved in Steps 3, 4, and 5.

26.4.2 Elicit Users' Requirements

Based on the natural language patterns and RGPS, a requirements elicitation language named Service Oriented Requirements Language (SORL) [13] has been designed for eliciting users' requirements. In SORL, two kinds of sentence patterns are defined: domain-independent sentence pattern and domain-specific sentence pattern. We have defined 16 domain-independent sentence patterns that cover the description of functional goals, nonfunctional goals, and so on. For example, the sentence "the salesman will deliver goods to his customer" belongs to the functional pattern. Here, we just list part of them.

Domain-independent Pattern : := Functional Pattern | NonFunctional Pattern;
Functional Pattern : := [Role] Verb Noun;
NonFunctional Pattern : := Qualitative Description Pattern | Quantitative Description Pattern;
Qualitative Description Pattern : := Noun be Adjective;
Quantitative Description Pattern : := Noun Comparison-Operator Number [Unit]; ⋯

The domain-independent sentence patterns are defined according to the role and goal meta-model. The domain-specific sentence pattern is summarized from the characteristics of the domain-specific expressions, which are varied among different domains.

Following these sentence patterns in SORL, users' requirements can be expressed. Firstly, some natural language processing techniques, such as segmentation and stemming, are applied to normalize the requirements text. Next, several steps are taken to parse the normalized requirements text: the requirements text will be tagged by the grammatical item in SORL; the sentence patterns can be recognized based on the finite state automata; and the roles and goals can be extracted based on the mapping between SORL grammatical item and elements in the role and goal meta-model. In this way, an initial goal list can be identified.

Another candidate way is for users to manually select related elements from domain models according to a series of requirements templates. Providing a series of requirements elicitation templates, users can select a domain from the first template that lists all domains. Afterwards, the user can select a role that he hopes to play in the domain from the second template that lists all possible roles in the selected domain. The goals related to the role will then be listed in the third template, and the user can select the goals from the goal list. With selected specific domain goals, the analysis procedure can move to the goal refinement (Step 3).

26.4.3 Match with Domain Goals

In this step, the goals in the initial goal list will be matched with the goals in domain goal models. The goal-matching problem can be solved by calculating the semantic similarity of the two goals.

The similarity between two goals is calculated based on ontology-based concept similarity, which has been widely investigated [20]. Recall that a goal consists of two mandatory attributes: operation and entity (object). The similarity between two goals thus consists of two parts: the similarity of two operation concepts and the similarity of two entity concepts. The similarity of two operation concepts can be calculated using Formula (1). $Depth(O_1)$ means the length of the path from concept O_1 to the root of the ontology. $C(O_1)$ denotes the number of descendants or hyponymy concepts of concept O_1. $C(O_1) \cap C(O_2)$ denotes the number of the intersection of descendants of concepts O_1 and O_2. $Distance(O_1, O_2)$ denotes the number of edges that link concepts O_1 and O_2 in the domain ontology hierarchy. The principles in Formula (26.1) are as follows: if the semantic overlap between two concepts is higher, then the two concepts are more similar; if the distance of two concepts is larger, then the two concepts are less similar; if the difference between the depth of two concepts is larger, then the two concepts are less similar. Similarly, the similarity of two entity concepts E_1 and E_2 can be calculated in Formula (26.2).

$$OperationSim(O_1, O_2) = \frac{C(O_1) \cap C(O_2)}{(Distance(O_1, O_2) + 1) \times (|Depth(O_1) - Depth(O_2)| + 1)} \tag{26.1}$$

$$EntitySim(E_1, E_2) = \frac{C(E_1) \cap C(E_2)}{(Distance(E_1, E_2) + 1) \times (|Depth(E_1) - Depth(E_2)| + 1)} \tag{26.2}$$

To calculate the similarity of an initial goal G_{ig} and a domain goal G_{dg}, the similarity of operation concepts and the similarity of entity concepts should be combined. Formulas (26.3) and (26.4) show how to calculate the proportions of the operation part and the entity part, respectively. Note that O_{dg} and E_{dg} denote the operation concept and entity concept of the domain goal G_{dg}, respectively. The principle in Formula (26.3) is that if a concept lies in a deeper layer of an ontology, then it will have more specific semantics, and is closer to the meaning of users' requirements.

$$OProportion = \frac{Depth(O_{dg})}{Depth(O_{dg}) + Depth(E_{dg})} \tag{26.3}$$

$$EProportion = \frac{Depth(E_{dg})}{Depth(O_{dg}) + Depth(E_{dg})} \tag{26.4}$$

To sum up, the goal similarity of G_{ig} and G_{dg} can be calculated in Formula (26.5). Considering the range of the goal similarity should be within (0, 1), Formula (26.6) is used to normalize the result of Formula (26.5), where β is a factor whose value is between 0 and 1.

$$GoalSim(G_{ig}, G_{dg})' = OProportion \times OperationSim(O_{ig}, O_{dg})$$
$$+ EProportion \times EntitySim(E_{ig}, E_{dg}) \tag{26.5}$$

$$GoalSim(G_{ig}, G_{dg}) = 1 - \beta^{GoalSim(G_{ig}, G_{dg})'} \tag{26.6}$$

In this way, the initial goals can be matched with the goals in domain goal models according to their similarity. For the unmatched initial goals, two actions will be taken. First, the user can manually browse domain goals according to Step 1s. Second, the unmatched goals will be marked and recorded for further analysis by domain engineers to check whether the domain models should evolve.

26.4.4 Supplement and Refine Goals

According to the RGPS meta-model framework, each goal is associated with a role. Therefore, based on the goals that have matched with domain models, we can determine the role that the user plays. Since users' requirements are usually incomplete, all the goals related to the specific role will be listed for users to select. In this way, more complete relative goals may be identified.

As mentioned before, a goal can be decomposed into more concrete sub-goals according to the hierarchical structure in domain goal model. When a goal list is obtained, we need to check whether the decomposition and constraint relations are satisfied towards their semantics in domain goal models. Examples are *alternative, mandatory, depend*, and *exclude*. For the *mandatory* relation, we need to check whether all goals in the lower goal set have been selected. For the *alternative* relation, we need to check whether one and only one goal from the lower goal set is selected. For the *depend* relation, the goals depended by the selected goals will also be added to supplement users' requirements. For example, if a user has selected a goal "book airline ticket by credit card" that has the *depend* relation with the goal "validate credit card", then the latter must be selected. If two goals that have the *exclude* relation exist in users' selected goal list, then one of them must be removed. Since an operation might cause a new problem, the checking process should be iterated until the semantics of all decomposition and constraint relations are satisfied.

26.4.5 Configure Processes

The configuration of processes will be based on users' operations on the refined goal model. Here we discuss the mapping between the goal model and process model. Three kinds of mappings are defined as shown in Table 26.1: mapping between goals and processes (Row 1 and 2), mapping between the relations in the goal model and the control structures in the process model (Row 3–7), as well as the nonfunctional properties between goals and processes (Row 8).

The operational goal cannot be further decomposed, which is similar to the atomic process in the process model. Therefore, the operational goal can be mapped into the atomic process, while the functional goals can be mapped into the composite process. The goal decomposition relations are used to connect an upper goal and a lower goal set. Since the relations *mandatory* and *optional* can coexist in the decomposition of an upper goal, the related goals in the lower goal set are independent with each other, which indicate that their corresponding processes can be achieved in any order. In other words, the two relations can be both mapped into the control structure *any order*. For the relation *alternative*, one and only one lower goal can be selected, which is similar to the control structure *choice*. For the relation *OR*, at least one lower goal should be selected into the resulting goal set, which is comparable to the control structure *split-join*. In addition, the relation *depend* means that achieving a goal should depend on the achievement of another one, which is similar to the control structure *sequence*. As discussed earlier, a nonfunctional goal can take effect on functional goals, which is similar to the process's constraints defined by the expectations.

The relations *mandatory, optional, alternative*, and *OR* belong to the vertical decomposition relations, while the relation *depend* belongs to the horizontal relation. When there is a crossover between a vertical relation and a horizontal relation, the horizontal relation has a higher priority. For example, assume both goals A and B are *mandatory* goals, and B depends on A. According to the mapping rule in Row 3 of Table 26.1, their corresponding processes will be connected by control structure *any order*. However, according to the mapping rule in Row 7 of Table 26.1, their

Table 26.1 Mapping between the goal model and process model

Elements in goal model	Elements in process model
Functional goal	Composite process
Operational goal	Atomic process
Mandatory	Any order
Optional	Any order
Alternative	Choice
OR	Split-join
Depend	Sequence
Related FG	Expectation of a process

Table 26.2 Mapping between the operations on the goal model and process model

Users' operations on goal model	Configuration of process model
Select or deselect *optional* sub-goals	Add or delete sub-processes within the control structure *any order*
Select or deselect *OR* sub-goals	Add or delete sub-processes within the control structure *split-join*
Reselect an *alternative* sub-goal	Delete sub-processes within the control structure *choice* or modify the condition of *choice*
Add a functional goal that has *depend* relation with existing goals	Add a process connected with an existing process using the control structure *sequence*
Add a functional goal that does not have *depend* relation with existing goals	Add a process connected with existing processes using the control structure *any order*
Delete functional goals	Delete corresponding processes
Add or delete nonfunctional goals	Add or delete the expectation properties of a process

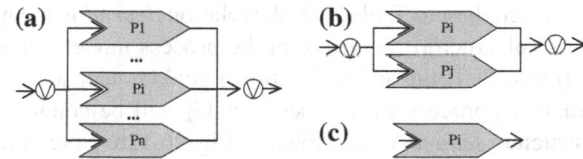

Fig. 26.9 Process customization for *optional* sub-goals

corresponding processes will be connected by *sequence*. In this case, the control structure *sequence* will be selected since the relation *depend* has a higher priority.

Following the mapping between the goal model and process model, we discuss the configuration of process models based on the operations on goal models, as shown in Table 26.2.

1. Select or deselect *optional* sub-goals.

As shown in Fig. 26.9a, the *optional* sub-goals can correspond to the processes P1, . . . , Pn, within the control structure *any order*. If a user only selects the sub-goals that correspond to Pi and Pj, then the result is shown in Fig. 26.9b. If only one goal is selected, then the control structure *any order* will be deleted, and only one process is left, as shown in Fig. 26.9c.

2. Select or deselect *OR* sub-goals.

As shown in Fig. 26.10a, the *OR* sub-goals can correspond to the processes P1, . . . , Pn, within the control structure *split-join*. If a user only selects the sub-goals that correspond to Pi and Pj, then the result is shown in Fig. 26.10b. If only one goal is selected, then the control structure *split-join* will be deleted and only one process is left, as shown in Fig. 26.10c.

3. Reselect an *alternative* sub-goal.

As shown in Fig. 26.11a, the *alternative* sub-goals can correspond to the processes P1, . . . , Pn, within the control structure *choice*. If a user selects the sub-goal that corresponds to Pi, then the other sub-processes within the control structure *choice* as well as the *choice* itself should be deleted, as shown in Fig. 26.11b.

Fig. 26.10 Process customization for *OR* sub-goals

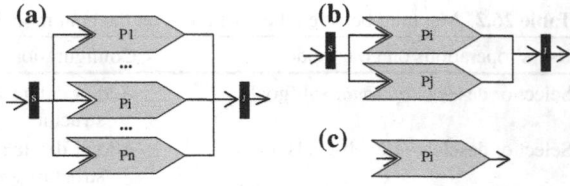

Fig. 26.11 Process customization for an *alternative*
sub-goal

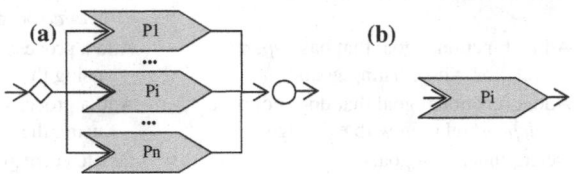

4. Add a functional goal with the *depend* relation.

According to Table 26.1, the relation *depend* in the goal model corresponds to the control structure *sequence* in the process model. Figure 26.12a shows the original process Pi. If the added functional goal Gj depends on the goal that Pi can achieve, then the process Pj that achieves Gj will be connected with Pi using the control structure *sequence*, as shown in Fig. 26.12b. Note that in this example, we use the operation goal to represent the functional goal.

5. Add a functional goal without the *depend* relation.

Figure 26.13a shows the original process Pi, which might be an atomic process or a composite process. If the added functional goal Gj does not depend on any goal that Pi can achieve, then the process Pj that can achieve Gj will be connected with Pi using the control structure *any order*, as shown in Fig. 26.13b. Note that in this example, we use the operation goal to represent the functional goal.

6. Delete functional goals.

When the functional goals are deleted, we just need to delete the corresponding processes that can achieve the functional goals.

7. Add or delete nonfunctional goals.

According to Table 26.1, nonfunctional goals correspond to the nonfunctional expectations of a process. When nonfunctional goals are added or deleted, the non-functional expectations of the corresponding process will be added or deleted accordingly.

26.4.6 Discover Services

After the process models are configured according to users' requirements, the final step is to discover services that can collaboratively realize the processes. During service discovery, two kinds of service registries are considered: our service supermarket and publicly accessible service registries.

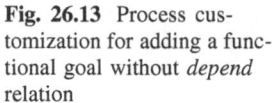 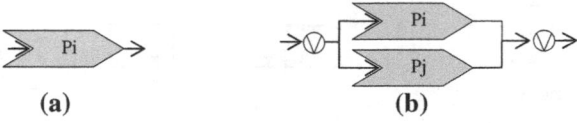

Fig. 26.12 Process customization for adding a functional goal with *depend* relation

Fig. 26.13 Process customization for adding a functional goal without *depend* relation

(a)   (b)

We have developed a service supermarket based on the service meta-model in RGPS. When a service is registered in the service supermarket, besides the information extracted from the WSDL files such as input message and output message, other information can also be registered. Examples include the role that is closely related to the service, the goal that the service can achieve, and the process that the service can realize. Since such additional information is not a mandatory property of services, if they are available, we could use role matching, goal matching or process matching to find corresponding services. Otherwise, we have to make a matchmaking based on the input and output information, as well as the nonfunctional expectations to find corresponding services.

For the publicly accessible service registries such as ProgrammableWeb, we have developed a service categorization method enhanced by incrementally enriched domain knowledge [23]. Using this method, the services in the registry can be classified into different domains. Therefore, the services belonging to the same domain with the proposed requirements will be matched with the processes, which can shorten the searching space of services. The matching is conducted by comparing the similarity between the description of a service and a process based on domain ontology. The services whose similarity with the process is above a given threshold can be selected for further consideration.

In this way, the selected services can be orchestrated according to the customized process model.

26.5 The Visualization Prototypes

To support our approach, we have developed two visualization prototypes: a domain modeling tool and a service supermarket.

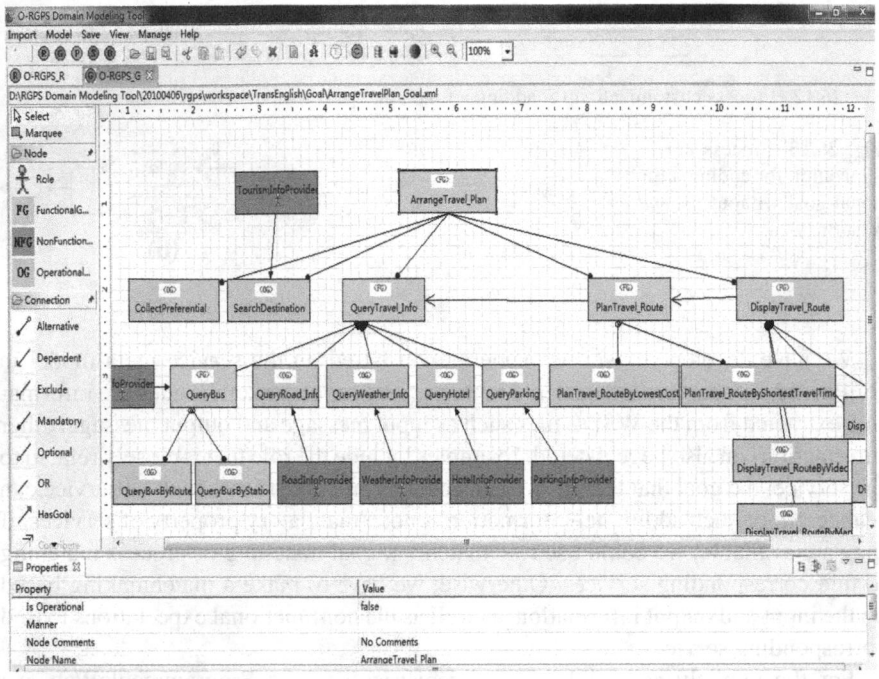

Fig. 26.14 Snapshot of goal modeling interface

26.5.1 O-RGPS Domain Modeling Tool

The O-RGPS domain modeling tool is a plug-in tool, which is similar to the UML modeling tool in Eclipse. It is developed using GEF[4] (Graphical Editor Framework) and EMF[5] (Eclipse Modeling Framework).

By using the tool, three kinds of domain models can be created including role and goal models, process models, and service models. Figure 26.14 shows a snapshot of goal modeling. By dragging the icons listed in the palette into the editing area, domain engineers can create the goal nodes and their relations. They can also set the properties of the goals by editing the "Properties" tab in the part below. The tool also provides a function of flexible reusing goal models in different granularities. Furthermore, if a goal model is properly created, a process model can be automatically transformed, which can greatly alleviate the modeling burden of domain engineers. Our tool can provide semantic support for domain models by importing specific domain ontologies and annotating certain elements of domain models using the concepts of domain ontology.

---

[4] http://www.eclipse.org/gef/
[5] http://www.eclipse.org/modeling/emf/

26.5.2 The Service Supermarket CloudCRM

The service supermarket we have developed is named as CloudCRM[6] since the original services are encapsulated from an open-source software called SugarCRM in the CRM domain. The basic idea of the service supermarket is similar to a supermarket where users can select their goods and receive some recommended products. The service supermarket is more than a service registry that acts as a centralized yellow page to help users find related services [24], since a multi-tenancy architecture is also designed to support users in different tenants using mashups in the supermarket.

26.5.2.1 Services Encapsulation in Service Supermarket

As mentioned before, the original services are encapsulated from SugarCRM that is composed of 14 functional modules. Since SugarCRM is developed using PHP, we firstly create a .php file for each functional module by using SugarCRM API or extracting codes directly from the open-source codes; and then we leverage a tool named Zend Studio for Eclipse to create a .wsdl file from a .php file. Using such a procedure, we have encapsulated some CRM services, such as accounts service, targetLists service, and contact service.

During service encapsulation, multi-tenancy design of these services is also supported. Multi-tenancy is defined as the ability of an application to provide the same service to different tenants [5]. In CloudCRM, separated database is chosen as the solution of data isolation, which means that each tenant will have their separate databases.

Besides the services encapsulated from SugarCRM, we have also registered many Web services into our service supermarket, such as weather forecast service, map service, and flight query service. The services are registered in CloudCRM according to the RGPS meta-model framework, which help improve the precision and efficiency of service query.

26.5.2.2 Users in the Service Supermarket

Since multi-tenancy is an important feature in CloudCRM, users can play three kinds of roles according to their assigned permissions: system administrator, tenant administrator, and end user. The system administrator can manage tenant administrators, while the tenant administrator can manage end users.

For tenant administrators who are the representatives of each organization in CloudCRM, they are responsible for managing the end users in their organizations as well as their subscribed services. More specifically, they can select appropriate services for their organizations; they can allocate available services for each user

---

[6] http://cloud.whu.edu.cn:8080/CloudCrm/login.jsp

according to the business role that the user will play; they can also pause, cancel, and restore the right of an end user to use certain services.

For end users, they are allowed to use the authorized services allocated by the tenant administrators; they can also propose their requirements to use more services. CloudCRM provides a collection of requirements templates to help elicit users' requirements and recommend proper services.

26.6 A Case Study

In this section, we will use the motivating example introduced in Sect. 26.2.1 to show how it can be resolved by our approach on top of the CloudCRM service supermarket.

In our approach, a user's requirements can be defined in two ways. One way is to define the requirements in Service Oriented Requirements Language (SORL). The other way is to configure user requirements templates (i.e., domain, role and goal) created based on domain models. Figure 26.15 is generated by our system based on the domain role and goal model shown in Fig. 26.4. It shows a goal refinement scenario when a user selects the goal "Deliver Goods" as a salesman. During the goal refinement process, the semantics of the decomposition relations have to be satisfied, which will be judged and verified in real time by our system. After the user finishes goal refinement, the constraint relations will be checked.

After the goal refinement process, our system will move forward to the process configuration phase. Based on the configured goals, a mapping between the goal model and the available process models will lead to a recommended template as shown in the left picture of Fig. 26.16. Five atomic processes "Acquire Recipient Info", "Select Express Company", "Generate Order", "Pay Order", and "Inquire

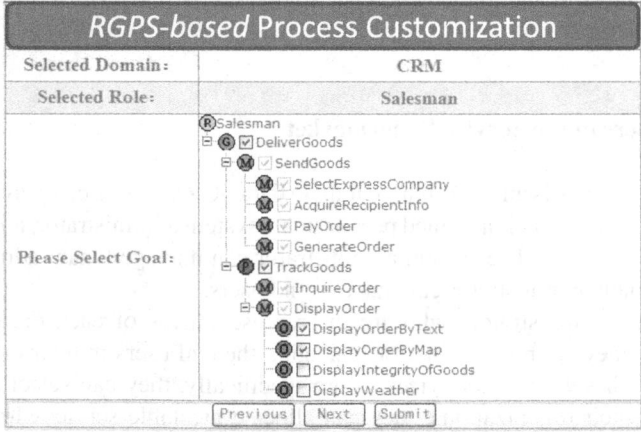

Fig. 26.15 Goal refinement in CloudCRM

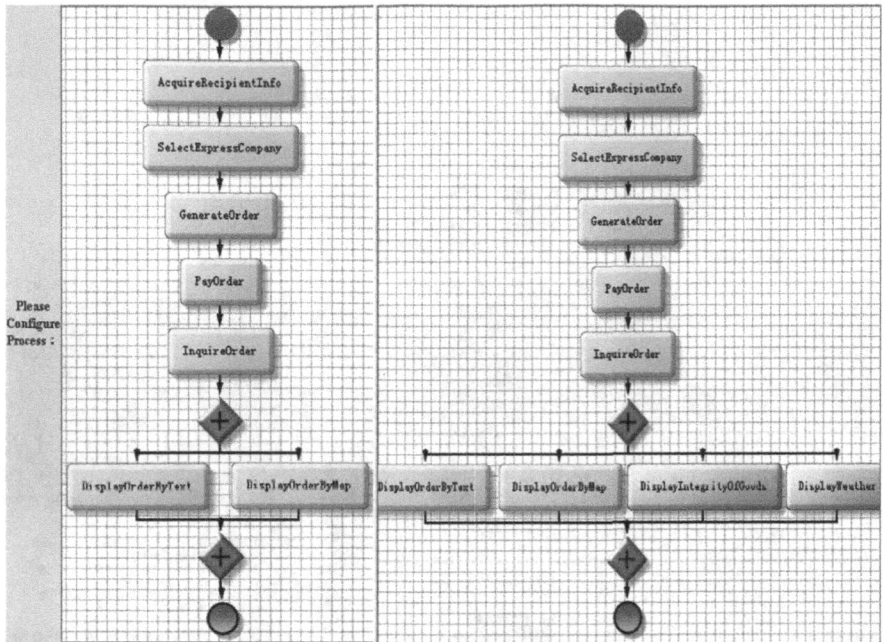

Fig. 26.16   Process configuration in CloudCRM

Order" are connected by a control structure *sequence*, followed by the control structure *split-join* that connects two atomic processes "Display Order by Text" and "Display Order by Map". If the user selects the other two *OR* sub-goals "Display Integrity
of Goods" and "Display Weather" during the goal refinement, the corresponding
atomic processes will be added in the control structure *split-join*, as shown in the
right picture of Fig. 26.16.

Based on the configured process model, some services can be identified from the
service supermarket, such as a contact service, Delivery 100 API, Baidu map API,[7]
Check RFID service, and Yahoo! weather API.[8] The contact service is extracted from
SugarCRM, which can support browsing and searching a recipient's information.
The Delivery 100 API is an open Web API that can support querying orders of most
shipping companies in China. The Check RFID service is a Web service to query
the integrity of expensive goods. If all RFID raw data of the goods collected from
the RFID readers in every transit station is identical, then the goods is considered
to be well maintained during the shipping process. Otherwise, the goods might be
destroyed before reaching a certain station. The Baidu Map API can be used to
display a shipping route in the map. The Yahoo! Weather API can be used to show
weather information of the cities in a shipping route.

---

[7] http://openapi.baidu.com/map/
[8] http://developer.yahoo.com/weather/

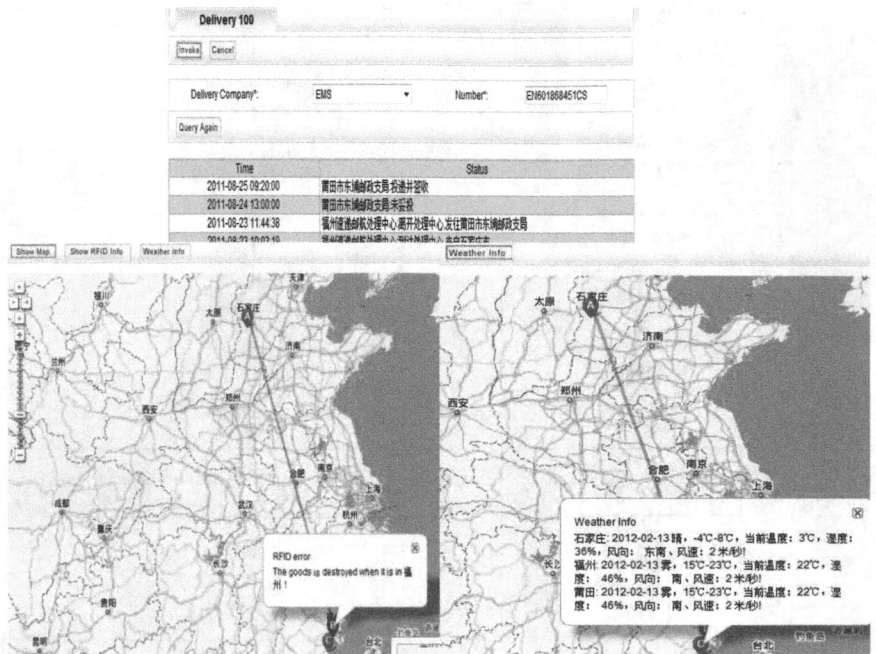

Fig. 26.17 Created mashup

In summary, such services from the service supermarket can be mashed up with other services developed in house (such as "shipping company query service") based on the configured process model. The upper picture in Fig. 26.17 shows a query of a shipping order in China and its results represented in text. Each line in the query result records a shipping status of the goods in a chronological order. For example, the first line shows that the goods arrived at the shipping office on August 25, 2011. The bottom left picture shows the shipping route of the goods as well as the integrity of the order, which alerts the user that the goods might be destroyed before reaching the city "FuZhou", since the RFID raw data in "FuZhou" and that in its previous site are not identical. The bottom right picture lists the current weather information of all cities in the shipping route.

26.7 Conclusions

Service-oriented process customization is a key issue in SaaS. In this chapter, based on the RGPS meta-model framework, we propose a service-oriented process customization approach that can help end-users configure a personalized mashup in design time. Corresponding visualization prototypes are introduced, and a case study illustrates how to follow our approach to customize a shipping mashup. Our approach depends on the quality of domain models to a large extent. If users' requirements cannot be satisfied, their unmatched goals will be recorded, which will in turn contribute to the evolution of domain models. So our approach is an iterative method in essence.

The RGPS meta-models introduced in this chapter have been accepted as several parts of ISO/IEC 19763, that is, ISO/IEC 19763-8 "Metamodel for role and goal registration", ISO/IEC 19763-5 "Metamodel for process model registration", ISO/IEC 19763-7 "Metamodel for service registration", and ISO/IEC 19763-9 "On demand model selection based on RGPS". Currently, these standards are under development.

Our future research will focus on the following directions. First, we will enrich the service supermarket. Second, we will integrate business rules in process customization. Finally, the multi-tenancy architecture and the scalability of the service supermarket will be further explored.

Acknowledgments The work is partially supported by the National Natural Science Foundation of China under Grant No. 61202031, 60970017, 61100017, the National Science and Technology Pillar Program of China under grant No.2012BAH07B01, the central grant funded Cloud Computing demonstration project of China undertaken by Kingdee Software (China).

References

1. Chinnici, R., Moreau, J.-J., Ryman A., et al.: Web Services Description Language (WSDL) Version 2.0, W3C Recommendation. http://www.w3.org/TR/wsdl20/ (2007)
2. Eriksson, H.-E., Penker, M.: Business Modeling with UML: Business Patterns at Work. Wiley, New York (2000)
3. Fukazawa, Y., Naganuma, T., Kurakake, S.: Construction and use of role-ontology for task based service navigation system. In: Proceedings of 2006 International Semantic Web Conference, pp. 806–819 (2006)
4. Ghose, A., Koliadis, G.: Actor eco-systems: from high-level agent models to executable processes via semantic annotations. In: Proceedings of the IEEE International Computer Software and Applications Conference 2007, pp. 177–184 (2007)
5. Grund, M., Schapranow, M., Krueger, J. et al.: Shared table access pattern analysis for multi-tenant applications. In: Proceedings of 2008 Advanced Management of Information for Globalized Enterprises, pp. 1–5 (2008)
6. He, K., Wang, J., Liang, P.: Towards semantic interoperability aggregation in service requirements refinement. J. Comput. Sci. Technol. **25**(6), 1103–1117 (2010)
7. Jureta, I., Faulkner S.: An agent-oriented meta-model for enterprise modeling. In: Proceedings of the ER workshop 2005, LNCS 3770, pp. 151–161. Springer, Heidelberg (2005)
8. Kang, K., Cohen, S., Hess, J., et al.: Feature-oriented domain analysis (FODA): feasibility study. Technical Report: CMU/SEI-90-TR-021, Software Engineering Institute, Carnegie Mellon University (1990)
9. Klusch, M., Kaufer, F.: WSMO-MX: a hybrid semantic web service matchmaker. Web Intell. Agent Syst. **7**(1), 23–42 (2009)
10. Koliadis, G., Ghose, A.: Relating business process models to goal-oriented requirements models in KAOS. In: Advances in Knowledge Acquisition and Management, vol. 4303, pp. 25–39. Springer, Heidelberg (2006)

11. Lamsweerde, A. V.: Goal-oriented requirements engineering: a guided tour. In: Proceedings of the 5th IEEE International Symposium on Requirements Engineering (ER'01), pp. 249–263, Toronto, Canada (2001)
12. Lazovik, A., Ludwig, H.: Managing process customizability and customization: model, language and process. In: Proceedings of the 8th International Conference on Web Information Systems Engineering (WISE). Springer, Heidelberg (2007)
13. Liu, W., He, K., Wang, J., et al.: Heavyweight semantic inducement for requirement elicitation and analysis. In: Proceedings of the 3rd International Conference on Semantics, Knowledge and Grid, pp. 206–211, Xi'an, China (2007)
14. Martin, D., Ankolekar, A., Burstein, M., et al. OWL-S: semantic markup for web services—W3C candidate recommendation. http://www.daml.org/services/owl-s/ (2006)
15. Masolo, C., Vieu, L., Bottazzi, E., et al.: Social roles and their descriptions. In: Proceedings of the 9th International Conference on the Principles of Knowledge Representation and Reasoning, pp. 267–277 (2004)
16. Mell, P., Grance, T.: The NIST definition of cloud computing. National Institute of Science and Technology. http://csrc.nist.gov/publications/nistpubs/800-145/SP800-145.pdf (2009)
17. Mietzner, R., Leymann, F.: Generation of BPEL customization processes for SaaS applications from variability descriptors. In: Proceedings of 2008 IEEE International Conference on Services Computing (SCC), pp. 359–366, Hawaii, U.S. (2008)
18. Mili, H., Mili, F., Mili, A.: Reusing software: issues and research directions. IEEE Trans. Softw. Eng. **21**, 528–562 (1995)
19. OASIS: Web services business process execution language version 2.0, OASIS standard. http://docs.oasis-open.org/wsbpel/2.0/ (2007)
20. Rodriguez, M.A., Egenhofer, M.J.: Determining semantic similarity among entity classes from different ontologies. IEEE Trans. Knowl. Data Eng. **15**(2), 442–456 (2003)
21. Van der Aalst, W.M.P., Dreiling, A., Gottschalk, F., et al.: Configurable process models as a basis for reference modeling. In: Proceedings of the Business Process Management Workshops, pp. 512–518. Springer, Heidelberg (2005)
22. Wang, J., He, K., Gong, P., et al.: RGPS: a unified requirements meta-modeling frame for net-worked software. In: Proceedings of the 3rd International Workshop on Advances and Applications of Problem Frames at 30th ICSE, pp. 29–35. Leipzig, Germany (2008)
23. Wang, J., Zhang, J., Hung, P.C.K., et al.: Leveraging fragmental semantic data to enhance services discovery. In: Proceedings of the 13th IEEE International Conference on High Performance Computing and Communications, pp. 687–694, Banff, Canada (2011)
24. Zhang, L.-J., Zhang, J., Cai, H.: Services Computing. Springer, New York (2007)

Chapter 27
Assisted Mashup Development: On the Discovery and Recommendation of Mashup Composition Knowledge

Carlos Rodríguez, Soudip Roy Chowdhury, Florian Daniel, Hamid R. Motahari Nezhad and Fabio Casati

Abstract Over the past few years, mashup development has been made more accessible with tools such as Yahoo! Pipes that help in making the development task simpler through simplifying technologies. However, mashup development is still a difficult task that requires knowledge about the functionality of web APIs, parameter settings, data mappings, among other development efforts. In this work, we aim at assisting users in the mashup process by recommending development knowledge that comes in the form of *reusable composition knowledge*. This composition knowledge is harvested from a repository of existing mashup models by mining a set of *composition patterns*, which are then used for interactively providing composition recommendations while developing the mashup. When the user accepts a recommendation, it is automatically woven into the partial mashup model by applying modeling actions as if they were performed by the user. In order to demonstrate our approach we have implemented *Baya*, a Firefox plugin for Yahoo! Pipes that shows that it is indeed possible to harvest useful composition patterns from existing mashups, and that we are able to provide complex recommendations that can be automatically woven inside Yahoo! Pipes' web-based mashup editor.

C. Rodríguez (✉) · S. R. Chowdhury · F. Daniel · F. Casati
University of Trento, Via Sommarive 5, 38123 Povo, TN, Italy
e-mail: crodriguez@disi.unitn.it

S. R. Chowdhury
e-mail: rchowdhury@disi.unitn.it

F. Daniel
Dipartimento di Ingegneria e Scienza dell'Informazione, Università di Trento, Povo, Trento, Italy
e-mail: daniel@disi.unitn.it

F. Casati
e-mail: casati@disi.unitn.it

Hamid R. Motahari Nezhad
Hewlett Packard Labs, Palo Alto, CA, USA
e-mail: hamid.motahari@hp.com

A. Bouguettaya et al. (eds.), *Web Services Foundations*,
DOI: 10.1007/978-1-4614-7518-7_27,
© Springer Science+Business Media New York 2014

27.1 Introduction

Mashup tools, such as Yahoo! Pipes (http://pipes.yahoo.com/pipes/) or JackBe Presto Wires (http://www.jackbe.com), generally promise easy development tools and lightweight runtime environments, both typically running inside the client browser. By now, mashup tools undoubtedly simplified some complex composition tasks, such as the integration of web services or user interfaces. Yet, despite these advances in simplifying technology, mashup development is still a *complex task* that can only be managed by skilled developers.

People without the necessary programming experience may not be able to profitably use mashup tools like Pipes—to their dissatisfaction. For instance, we think of *tech-savvy people*, who like exploring software features, authoring and sharing own content on the Web, that would like to mash up other contents in new ways, but that don't have programming skills. They might lack appropriate awareness of which composable elements a tool provides, of their specific functionality, of how to combine them, of how to propagate data, and so on. In short, these are people that do not have software development knowledge. The problem is analogous in the context of web service composition (e.g., with BPEL) or business process modeling (e.g., with BPMN), where modelers are typically more skilled, but still may not know all the features or typical modeling patterns of their tools.

What people (also programmers) typically do when they don't know how to solve a tricky modeling problem is searching for *help*, e.g., by asking more skilled friends or by querying the Web for solutions to analogous problems. In this latter case, examples of ready mashup models are one of the most effective pieces of information—provided that suitable examples can be found, i.e., examples that have an analogy with the modeling situation faced by the modeler. Yet, searching for help does not always lead to success, and retrieved information is only seldom immediately usable as is, since the retrieved pieces of information are not contextual, i.e., immediately applicable to the given modeling problem.

For instance, Fig. 27.1 illustrates a Yahoo! Pipes model that encodes how to plot news items on a map. Besides showing how to connect components and fill parameters, the key lesson that can be learned from this pipe is that plotting news onto a map requires first enriching the news feed with geo-coordinates, then fetching the actual news items, and only then handing the items over to the map. Understanding this logic is neither trivial nor intuitive.

Driven by a user study on how end users imagine assistance during mashup development [4], we aim to automatically offer them help pro-actively and interactively. Specifically, we are working toward the *interactive, contextual recommendation of reusable composition knowledge*, in order to assist the modeler in each step of his development task, e.g., by suggesting a candidate next component or a whole chain of tasks. The knowledge we want to recommend is re-usable *composition patterns*, i.e., model fragments that bear knowledge about how to compose mashups, such as the pattern in Fig. 27.1. Such knowledge may come from a variety of possible

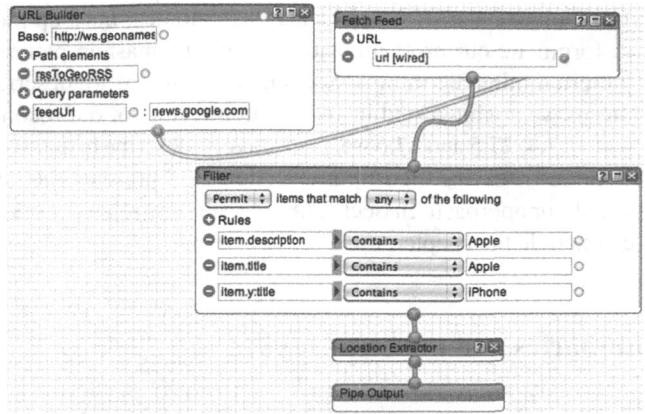

Fig. 27.1 A typical pattern in yahoo! Pipes

sources. In this work, we specifically focus on community composition knowledge and mine recurrent model fragments from a repository of given mashup models.

The **vision** is that of enabling the development of assisted, web-based mashup environments that deliver composition knowledge much like Google's Instant feature delivers search results already while still typing keywords into the search field.

In this chapter, we approach two core **challenges** of this vision, i.e., the *discovery* of reusable composition knowledge from a repository of ready mashup models and the *reuse* of such knowledge inside mashup tools, a feature that we call *weaving*. Together with the ability to search and retrieve composition patterns contextually when modeling a new mashup, a problem we approached in [10] and that we summarize in this chapter, these two features represent the key enablers of the vision of assisted development. We specifically provide the following **contributions**:

- We describe a *canonical mashup model* that is able to represent in a single modeling formalism a variety of data flow mashup languages. The goal is to mine composition knowledge from multiple source languages by implementing the necessary algorithms only once.
- Based on our canonical mashup model, we define a set of *mashup pattern types* that resemble the modeling actions of typical mashup environments.
- We describe an *architecture* of our knowledge recommender that can be used to equip any mashup environment with interactive assistance for its developers.
- We develop a set of *data mining algorithms* that discover composition knowledge in the form of reusable mashup patterns from a repository of mashup models.
- We present our *pattern recommendation* and *pattern weaving* algorithms. The former aims at recommending composition patterns based on the user actions on the design canvas. The later aims at automatically appying patterns to mashup models, allowing the developer to progress in his development task.

In the next section, we start by introducing the canonical mashup model, which will help us to formulate our problem statement, define mashup pattern types and describe our pattern mining algorithms. Section 27.3 is where we describe the types of mashup patterns we are interested in and the architecture of our recommendation platform. In Sects. 27.4, 27.5 and 27.6 we, respectively, describe in details the mining, recommendation, and weaving algorithms. Section 27.7 presents the details of the implementation of our approach. In Sect. 27.8 we overview related work. Then, with Sect. 27.9, we conclude the chapter.

27.2 Preliminaries and Problem

The development of a data mining algorithm strongly depends on the data to be mined. The data in our case are the mashup models. Since in our work we do not only aim at the reuse of knowledge but also at the reuse of our algorithms across different platforms, we strive for the development of algorithms that are able to accommodate different mashup models in input. Next, we therefore describe a *canonical mashup model* that allows us to concisely express multiple data mashup models and to implement mining algorithms that intrinsically support multiple mashup platforms. The canonical model is not meant to be executed; it rather serves as description format.

As a first step toward generic modeling environments, in this chapter we focus on data flow based mashup models. Although relatively simple, they are the basis of a significant number of mashup environments, and the approach can easily be extended toward other mashup environments.

27.2.1 A Canonical Mashup Model

Let CT be a set of *component types* of the form $ctype = \langle type, IP, IN, OP, OUT, is\_embedding \rangle$, where *type* identifies the type of component (e.g., RSS feed, filter, or similar), IP is the set of input ports of the component type (for the specification of data flows), IN is the set of input parameters of the component type, OP is the set of output ports, OUT is the set of output attributes,[1] and $is\_embedding \in \{yes, no\}$ tells whether the component type allows the embedding of components or not (e.g., to model a loop). We distinguish three types of components:

- *Source* components fetch data from the web (e.g., from an RSS feed) or the local machine (e.g., from a spreadsheet), or they collect user inputs at runtime. They don't have input ports, i.e., $IP = \emptyset$.
- *Data processing* components consume data in input and produce processed data in output. Therefore: $IP, OP \neq \emptyset$. Filter components, operators, and data transformers are examples of data processing components.

---

[1] We use the term *attribute* to denote data attributes produced as output by a component or flowing through a data flow connector and the term *parameter* to denote input parameters of a component.

- *Sink* components publish the output of a mashup, e.g., by printing it onto the screen (e.g., a pie chart) or providing an API toward it, such as an RSS or RESTful resource. Sinks don't have outputs, i.e., $OP = \emptyset$.

Given a set of component types, we are able to instantiate components in a modeling canvas and to compose mashups. We express the respective **canonical mashup model** as a tuple $m = \langle name, id, src, C, GP, DF, RES \rangle$, where *name* is the name of the mashup in the canonical representation, *id* a unique identifier, $src \in \{$"Pipes","Wires","myCocktail", ...$\}$ keeps track of the source platform of the mashup, *C* is the set of components, *GP* is a set of global parameters, *DF* is a set of data flow connectors propagating data among components, and *RES* is a set of result parameters of the mashup. Specifically:

- $GP = \{gp_i | gp_i = \langle name_i, value_i \rangle\}$ is a set of **global parameters** that can be consumed by components, $name_i$ is the name of a given parameter, $value_i \in (STR \cup NUM \cup \{null\})$ is its value, with *STR* and *NUM* representing the sets of possible string or numeric values, respectively. The use of global parameters inside data flow languages is not very common, yet tools like Presto Wires or myCocktail (http://www.ict-romulus.eu/web/mycocktail) support the design-time definition of globally reusable variables.
- $DF = \{df_j | df_j = \langle srccid_j, srcop_j, tgtcid_j, tgtip_j \rangle\}$ is a set of **data flow connectors** that, each, assign the output port $srcop_j$ of a source component with identifier $srccid_j$ to an input port $tgtip_j$ of a target component identified by $tgtcid_j$, such that $srccid \neq tgtcid$. Source components don't have connectors in input; sink components don't have connectors in output.
- $C = \{c_k | c_k = \langle name_k, id_k, type_k, IP_k, IN_k, DM_k, VA_k, OP_k, OUT_k, E_k \rangle\}$ is the set of **components**, such that $c_k = instanceOf(ctype)$,[2] $ctype \in CT$ and $name_k$ is the name of the component in the mashup (e.g., its label), id_k uniquely identifies the component, $type_k = ctype.type$,[3] $IP_k = ctype.IP$, $IN_k = ctype.IN$, $OP_k = ctype.OP$, $OUT_k = ctype.OUT$, and:

  - $DM_k \subseteq IN_k \times (\bigcup_{ip \in IP_k} ip.source.OUT)$ is the set of **data mappings** that map attributes of the input data flows of c_k to input parameters of c_k.
  - $VA_k \subseteq IN_k \times (STR \cup NUM \cup GP)$ is the set of **value assignments** for the input parameters of c_k; values are either filled manually or taken from global parameters.
  - $E_k = \{cid_{kl}\}$ is the set of identifiers of the **embedded components**. If the component does not support embedded components, $E_k = \emptyset$.

- $RES \subseteq \bigcup_{c \in C} c.OUT$ is the set of **mashup outputs** computed by the mashup.

---

[2] To keep models and algorithms simple, we opt for a *self-describing* instance model for components, which presents both type and instance properties.

[3] We use a *dot notation* to refer to sub-elements of structured elements; *ctype.type* therefore refers to the *type* attribute of the component type *ctype*.

Without loss of generality, throughout this chapter we exemplify our ideas and solutions in the context of Yahoo! Pipes, which is well known and comes with a large body of readily available mashup models that we can analyze. Pipes is very similar to our canonical mashup model, with two key differences: it does not have global parameters, and the outputs of the mashup are specified by using a dedicated *Pipe Output* component (see Fig. 27.1). Hence, $GP, RES = \emptyset$ and a pipe corresponds to a restricted canonical mashup of the form $m = \langle name, id, \text{"Pipes"}, C, \emptyset, DF, \emptyset \rangle$ with the attributes as specified above. In general, we refer to the generic canonical model; we explicitly state where instead we use the restricted Pipes model.

27.2.2 Problem Statement

Given the above canonical mashup model, the problem we want to address in this chapter is understanding (i) which *kind of knowledge* can be extracted from the canonical mashup model so as to automatically assist users in developing their mashups, (ii) what *algorithms* we need to develop in order to be able to discover such knowledge from existing mashup models, (iii) how to *interactively recommend* discovered patterns inside mashup tools in order to guide users with the next modeling step/s and (iv) how to automatically apply (*weave*) the selected recommendation inside the current mashup design.

27.3 Approach

The current trend in modeling environments in general, and in mashup tools in particular, is toward intuitive, web-based solutions. The key principles of our work are therefore to conceive solutions that *resemble the modeling paradigm* of graphical modeling tools, to develop them so that they can *run inside the client browser*, and to specifically *tune their performance* so that they do not annoy the developer while modeling. These principles affect the nature of the knowledge we are interested in and the architecture and implementation of the respective recommendation infrastructure.

27.3.1 Composition Knowledge Patterns

Starting from the canonical mashup model, we define composition knowledge as reusable **composition patterns** for mashups of type m, i.e., model fragments that provide insight into how to solve specific modeling problems, such as the one illustrated in Fig. 27.1. In general, we are in the presence of a set of composition pattern types PT, where each pattern type is of the form $ptype = \langle C, GP, DF, RES \rangle$, where C, GP, DF, RES are as defined for m.

The size of a pattern may vary from a single component with a value assignment for one input parameter to an entire, executable mashup. The most *basic patterns* are those that represent a co-occurrence of two elements out of C, GP, DF or RES. For instance, two components that recur often together form a basic pattern; given one of the components, we are able to recommend the other component. Similarly, an input parameter plus its value form a basic pattern, given the parameter, we can recommend a possible value for it. As such, the most basic patterns are similar to *association rules*, which, given one piece of information, are able to suggest another piece of information.

Aiming, however, to help a developer refine his mashup model step by step with as less own effort as possible, we are able to identify a set of pattern types that allow the developer to obtain more practical and meaningful composition knowledge. Such knowledge is represented by sensible combinations of basic patterns, i.e., by *composite patterns*.

Considering the typical modeling steps performed by a developer (e.g., filling input fields, connecting components, copying/pasting model fragments), we specifically identify the following set *PT* of *pattern types*:

Parameter value pattern. The parameter value pattern represents a set of recurrent value assignments *VA* for the input fields *IN* of a component c:

$ptype^{par} = \langle \{c\}, GP, \emptyset, \emptyset \rangle$;
$c = \langle name, 0, type, \emptyset, IN, \emptyset, \emptyset, VA, \emptyset, \emptyset \rangle$[4];
$GP \neq \emptyset$ if *VA* also assigns global parameters to *IN*;
$GP = \emptyset$ if *VA* assigns only strings or numeric constants.

This pattern helps filling input fields of a component that require explicit user input.

Connector pattern. The connector pattern represents a recurrent connector df_{xy}, given two components c_x and c_y, along with the respective data mapping DM_y of the output attributes OUT_x to the input parameters IN_y:

$ptype^{con} = \langle \{c_x, c_y\}, \emptyset, \{df_{xy}\}, \emptyset \rangle$;
$c_x = \langle name_x, 0, type_x, \emptyset, \emptyset, \emptyset, \emptyset, \{op_x\}, OUT_x, \emptyset \rangle$;
$c_y = \langle name_y, 1, type_y, \{ip_y\}, IN_y, DM_y, \emptyset, \emptyset, \emptyset, \emptyset \rangle$.

This pattern helps connecting a newly placed component to the partial mashup model in the canvas.

Connector co-occurrence pattern. The connector co-occurrence pattern captures which connectors df_{xy} and df_{yz} occur together, also including their data mappings:

$ptype^{coo} = \langle \{c_x, c_y, c_z\}, \emptyset, \{df_{xy}, df_{yz}\}, \emptyset \rangle$;
$c_x = \langle name_x, 0, type_x, \emptyset, \emptyset, \emptyset, \emptyset, \{op_x\}, OUT_x, \emptyset \rangle$;

---

[4] The identifier $c.id = 0$ does not represent recurrent information. Identifiers in patterns rather represent internal, system-generated information that is necessary to correctly maintain the structure of patterns. When mining patterns, the actual identifiers are lost; when weaving patterns, they need to be re-generated in the target mashup model.

$c_y = \langle name_y, 1, type_y, \{ip_y\}, IN_y, DM_y, \emptyset, \{op_y\},$
$OUT_y, \emptyset \rangle$
$c_z = \langle name_z, 2, type_z, \{ip_z\}, IN_z, DM_z, \emptyset, \emptyset, \emptyset, \emptyset \rangle.$

This pattern helps connecting components. It is particularly valuable in those cases where people, rather than developing their mashup model in an incremental but connected fashion, proceed by first selecting the desired functionalities (the components) and only then by connecting them.

Component co-occurrence pattern. Similarly, the component co-occurrence pattern captures couples of components that occur together. It comes with two components c_x and c_y as well as with their connector, global parameters, parameter values, and c_y's data mapping logic:

$ptype^{com} = \langle \{c_x, c_y\}, GP, \{df_{xy}\}, \emptyset \rangle;$
$c_x = \langle name_x, 0, type_x, \emptyset, IN_x, \{op_x\}, OUT_x, VA_x, \emptyset, \emptyset \rangle;$
$c_y = \langle name_y, 1, type_y, \{ip_y\}, IN_y, DM_y, VA_y, \emptyset, \emptyset, \emptyset \rangle.$

This pattern helps developing a mashup model incrementally, producing at each step a connected mashup model.

Component embedding pattern. The component embedding pattern captures which component c_z is typically embedded into a component c_y preceded by a component c_x. The pattern has three components, in that both the embedded and the embedding component have access to the outputs of the preceding component. How these outputs are jointly used is valuable information. The pattern, hence, contains the three components with their connectors, data mappings, global parameters, and parameter values:

$ptype^{emb} = \langle \{c_x, c_y, c_z\}, GP, \{df_{xy}, df_{xz}, df_{zy}\}, \emptyset \rangle;$
$c_x = \langle name_x, 0, type_x, \emptyset, \emptyset, \{op_x\}, OUT_x, \emptyset, \emptyset, \emptyset \rangle;$
$c_y = \langle name_y, 1, type_y, \{ip_y\}, IN_y, DM_y, VA_y, \emptyset, \emptyset, \emptyset \rangle;$
$c_z = \langle name_z, 2, type_z, \{ip_z\}, IN_z, DM_z, VA_z, \{op_z\},$
$OUT_z, \emptyset \rangle.$

This pattern helps, for instance, modeling cycles, a task that is usually not trivial to non-experts.

Multi-component pattern. The multi-component pattern represents recurrent model fragments that are generically composed of multiple components. It represents more complex patterns, such as the one in Fig. 27.1, that are not yet captured by the other pattern types alone. It allows us to obtain a full model fragment, given any of its sub-elements, typically, a set of components or connectors:

$ptype^{mul} = \langle C, GP, DF, RES \rangle;$
$C = \{c_i | c_i.id = i; i = 0, 1, 2, ...\}.$

Besides providing significant modeling support, this pattern helps understanding domain knowledge and best practices as well as keeping agreed-upon modeling conventions.

This list of pattern types is extensible, and what actually matters is the way we specify and process them. However, this set of pattern types, at the same time, leverages on the interactive modeling paradigm of the mashup tools (the patterns represent modeling actions that could also be performed by the developer) and provides as much information as possible (we do not only tell simple associations of constructs, but also show how these are used together in terms of connectors, parameter values, and data mappings).

Given a set of pattern types, an actual pattern can therefore be seen as an ***instance*** of any of these types. We model a composition pattern as $cp = instanceOf(ptype)$, $ptype \in PT$, where $cp = \langle type, src, C, GP, DF, RES, usage, date \rangle$, $type \in \{$"Par", "Con","Coo","Com","Emb","Mul"$\}$, $src \in \{$"Pipes", "Wires","myCockail", ...$\}$ specifies the target platform of the pattern, C, GP, DF, RES, src are as defined for the pattern's $ptype$, $usage$ counts how many times the pattern has been used (e.g., to compute rankings), and $date$ is the creation date of the pattern.

27.3.2 Architecture

Figure 27.2 details the internals of our knowledge discovery and recommendation prototype. We distinguish between client and server side, where the discovery logic is located in the server and the recommendation and weaving logic resides in the client.

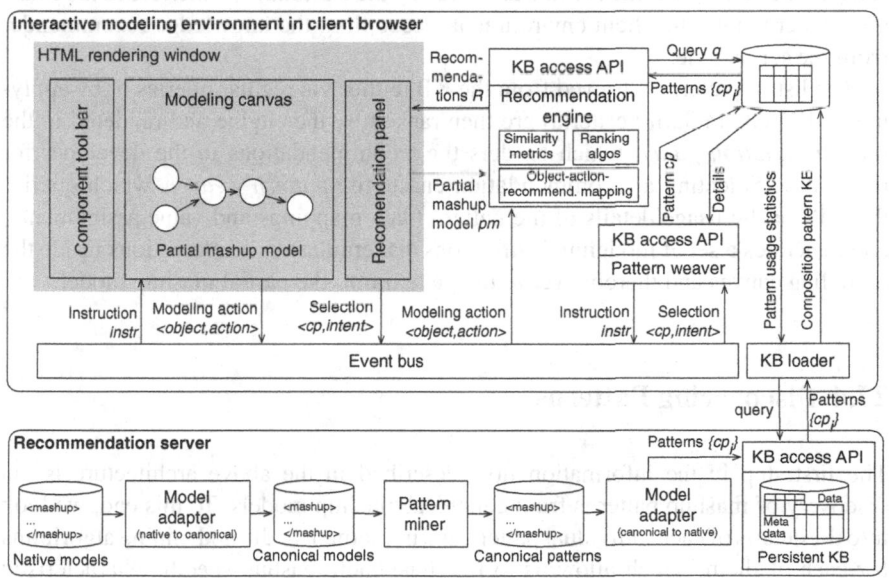

Fig. 27.2 Functional architecture of the composition knowledge discovery and recommendation approach

In the *recommendation server*, a *model adapter* imports the native mashup models into the canonical format. The *pattern miner* then extracts reusable composition knowledge in the form of composition patterns, which is then handed to a second *model adapter* to convert the canonical patterns into native patterns and load them into a knowledge base (KB). This KB is structured to maximize the performance of pattern retrieval at runtime.

In the client, we have the *interactive modeling environment*, in which the developer can visually compose components (in the *modeling canvas*) taken from the *component tool bar*. It is here where patterns are queried for and delivered in response to modeling actions performed by the modeler in the modeling canvas. In visual modeling environments, we typically have *action* $\in$ {*"select"*, *"drag"*, *"drop"*,*"connect"*,*"delete"*, *"fill"*, *"map"*,...}, where the *action* is performed on a modeling construct in the canvas; we call this construct the *object* of the action. For instance, we can *drop* a component onto the canvas, or we can *select* a parameter to fill it with a value, we can *connect* a data flow with a target component, or we can *select* a set of components and connectors. Upon each interaction, the *action* and its *object* are published on a browser-internal *event bus*, which forwards them to the *recommendation engine*. Given a modeling *action*, the *object* it has been applied to, and the partial mashup model *pm*, the engine queries the *client-side pattern KB* via the *KB access API* for recommendations (pattern representations). An *object-action-recommendation mapping* (*OAR*) tells the engine which types of recommendations are to be retrieved for each modeling action on a given object (for example, when selecting an input field, only recommending possible values makes sense). The client-side KB is filled at startup by the *KB loader*, which loads the available patterns into the client environment, decoupling the knowledge recommender from the server side.

The list of patterns retrieved from the KB (either via regular queries or by applying dedicated similarity criteria) are then ranked by the engine and rendered in the *recommendation panel*, which renders the recommendations to the developer for inspection. Selecting a recommendation enacts the *pattern weaver*, which queries the KB for the usage details of the pattern (data mappings and value assignments) and generates a set of modeling instructions that emulate user interactions inside the modeling canvas and thereby weave the pattern into the partial mashup model.

27.4 Discovering Patterns

The first step in the information flow described in the above architecture is the discovery of mashup patterns from canonical mashup models. To this end, we look into the details of each individual pattern and implement dedicated mining algorithms for each of them, which allow us to fine-tune each mashup-specific characteristic (e.g., to treat threshold values for parameter value assignments and data mappings differently). The pattern mining algorithms make use of standard statistics as well as frequent itemset and subgraph mining algorithms [13].

27.4.1 Mining Algorithms

For each of the pattern types identified in Sect. 27.3.1, we have implemented a respective pattern mining algorithm, the details of which we provide in the following.

Parameter value pattern. In the case of the parameter value pattern, we are interested in finding suitable values for the input fields in a given component. Most of the components in mashup compositions contain more than one parameter and more often than not the values of these parameters are related to one another and therefore we need take into account the co-occurrence of parameter values. In order to discover such co-occurrences, we map this problem to the well-known problem of itemset mining [13]. Algorithm 1 outlines the approach for finding parameter value patterns. Here, we first get all component instances from the mashups in the mashup repository (line 2) and group them together by their type (line 5–6) and then perform the parameter value pattern mining by component type (line 7). Finally, we construct the actual set of patterns that consists in tuples $\langle ct, VA \rangle$, where ct represents a component type and VA represents the value assignment for its parameters.

Algorithm 1: mineParameterValues

Data: repository of mashup compositions M and minimun support ($minsupp_{par}$) for the frequent itemset mining
Result: set of parameter value patterns $\langle ct, VA \rangle$.

1   $Patterns = set()$;
2   $C = $ set of component instances in M;
3   $CT = $ array();
4   $Patterns = set()$;
5   **foreach** *type of component ct in C* **do**
6      $CT[ct] = c_x.VA$ with $c_x \in C$ such that $c_x.type = ct$;   // get all the parameter value assignments of component instances of type ct
7      $FI = $ mineFrequentItemsets($CT[ct]$, $minsupp_{par}$);
8   **foreach** $VA \in FI$ **do**
9          $Patterns = Patterns \cup \{\langle ct, VA \rangle\}$;

10   **return** *Patterns*;

Connector pattern. A connector pattern is composed of two components, the source component c_x and the target component c_y, their data flow connector df_{xy}, and the data mapping DM_y of the target component. Given a repository of mashup models $M = \{m_i\}$ and the minimum support levels for the data flow connectors and data mappings, the pseudo-code in Algorithm 2 shows how we mine connector patterns.

We start the mining task by getting the list of all recurrent connectors in M (line 1). The respective function *getRecurrentConnectors* is explained in Algorithm 3; in essence, it computes a recurrence distribution for all connectors and returns only those that exceed the threshold $minsupp_{df}$. The function returns a set of connector types without repetitions and without information about the instances that generated them. Given this set, we construct a database of concrete instances of each connector type (using the *getConnectorInstances* function in line 5 and described in Algorithm 4) and, for each connector type, derive a database of the data mappings for

---

Algorithm 2: mineConnectors

Data: repository of mashup models M, minimum support of data flow connectors ($minsupp_{df}$) and data mappings ($minsupp_{dm}$)
Result: set of connectors with their corresponding data mappings $\{\langle df_{xy,i}, DM_{y,i}\rangle\}$

1 F_{df} = getRecurrentConnectors(M, $minsupp_{df}$);
2 DB = array();   // database of recurrent connector instances
3 $Patterns$ = set();   // set of connector patterns
4 **foreach** $df_{xy} \in F_{df}$ **do**
5 | $DB[df_{xy}]$ = getConnectorInstances(M, df_{xy});
   | // create database for frequent itemset mining
6 | $DBDM_y$ = array();
7 | **foreach** $df_{ixy} \in DB[df_{xy}]$ **do**
8 | | c_y = target component of df_{xy};
9 | | append($DBDM_y$, $c_y.DM$);
10 | FI_{dy} = mineFrequentItemsets($DBDM_y$, $minsupp_{dm}$);
   | // construct the connector patterns
11 | **foreach** $DM_y \in FI_{dy}$ **do**
12 | | $Patterns$ = $Patterns \cup \{\langle df_{xy}, DM_y\rangle\}$;

13 **return** $Patterns$;

Algorithm 3: getRecurrentConnectors

Data: repository of mashup models M, minimum support of data flow connectors ($minsupp_{df}$)
Result: set of recurrent connectors F_{df}

1 DB_{df} = array();   // database of data flow connector instances
2 **foreach** $m_i \in M$ **do**
3 | append(DB_{df}, $m_i.DF$);   // fill with instances

4 F_{df} = set();   // set of recurrent data flow connectors
5 **foreach** $df_{xy} \in DB_{df}$ **do**
6 | **if** computeSupport(df_{xy}, DB_{df}) $\geq$ $minsupp_{df}$ **then**
7 | | F_{df} = $F_{df} \cup \{df_{xy}\}$;

8 **return** F_{df};

---

the connectors' target component c_y (lines 7–9). We feed the so constructed database into a standard *mineFrequentItemsets* function [13], in order to obtain a set of recurrent data mappings for each connector type. Finally, for each identified data mapping DM_y, we construct a tuple $\langle df_{xy}, DM_y\rangle$ (lines 11–12), which concisely represents the connector pattern structure introduced in Sect. 27.3.1; the rest of the pattern comes from the component definitions.

Connector co-occurrence pattern. The *connector pattern* introduced previously is about how pairs of components are connected together. *The connector co-occurrence pattern* goes a step further: it tells how connectors between different pairs of components co-occur together in compositions and how data mappings are defined for them. Algorithm 5 presents the logic for computing *connector co-occurrence patterns*. The main difference with respect to Algorithm 2 is that, instead of computing the frequency of individual dataflow connectors between pairs of components, we compute frequent itemsets of dataflow connectors (lines 2–4).

Algorithm 4: getConnectorInstances

Data: repository of mashup models M, reference connector df_{xy}
Result: array of connector instances DB_{xy}

1 DB_{xy} = array();   // database of data flow connector instances
2 **foreach** $m_i \in M$ **do**
3   append(DB_{xy}], $m_i.DF \cap \{df_{xy}\}$); // fill with instances of the reference connector type
4 **return** DB_{xy};

Algorithm 5: mineConnectorCooccurrences

Data: repository of mashup compositions M, minimun support for dataflow connectors ($minsupp_{df}$) and data mappings ($minsupp_{dm}$)
Result: list of connector patterns with their corresponding data mappings $\langle DF_{xy}, DM_y \rangle$

   // find the co-occurrence of dataflow connectors
1 DB_{df} = array();
2 **foreach** $m_i \in M$ **do**
3   append(DB_{df}, $m_i.DF$);
4 F_{df} = mineFrequentItemsets(DB_{df}, $minsupp_{df}$);

5 DB_{ci} = array();
6 **foreach** $m_i \in M$ **do**
7   **foreach** $DF_{xy} \in F_{df}$ **do**
8   **if** $DF_{xy} \cap m_i.DF = DF_{xy}$ **then**
9   **foreach** $df_{xy} \in DF_{xy}$ **do**
10   append($DB_{ci}[DF_{xy}]$, getConnectorInstances($\{m_i\}$, df_{xy}));

   // find data mappings for the frequent dataflow connectors obtained above
11 $DBDM_y$ = array();
12 **foreach** $DF_{xy} \in DB_{ci}$ **do**
13   **foreach** $df_{xy} \in DF_{xy}$ **do**
14   c_y = target component of df_{xy};
15   append($DBDM_y$, $c_y.DM$);

16 FI_{dy} = mineFrequentItemsets($DBDM_y$, $minsupp_{dm}$);

   // construct the connector patterns
17 $Patterns$ = set();
18 **foreach** $DM_y \in FI_{dy}$ **do**
19     $Patterns = Patterns \cup \{\langle DF_{xy}, DM_y \rangle\}$;
20 **return** $Patterns$;

Component co-occurrence pattern. The component co-occurrence pattern is an extension of the connector pattern; in addition to the connectors and data mappings, it also contains the parameter value assignments of the two components involved in the connector. As shown in Algorithm 6, the respective mining logic is similar to the one of the connector pattern, with two major differences: in lines 6–17 we also mine the recurrent parameter value assignments of c_x and c_y, and in lines 18–21 we consider only those combinations of VA_x, VA_y and DM_y that co-occur in mashup instances for the given connector. Notice that, for the purpose of explaining this algorithm, we perform a cartesian product of VA_x, VA_y and DM_y in line 22. Doing this can be computational expensive if implemented as-is. In practice, the implementation of this algorithm is performed in such a way that we do not have to explore the whole

---

Algorithm 6: mineComponentCooccurrences

Data: repository of mashup models M, minimum support of data flow connectors ($minsupp_{df}$), data mappings ($minsupp_{dm}$), parameter value assignments ($minsupp_{va}$) and pattern co-occurrence ($minsupp_{pc}$).
Result: set of component co-occurrence patterns with their corresponding dataflow connectors, data mappings and parameter values $\{\langle df_{xy,i}, VA_{x,i}, VA_{y,i}, DM_{y,i}\rangle\}$

1   F_{df} = getRecurrentConnectors(M, $minsupp_{df}$);

2   DB = array();   // database of recurrent connector instances
3   $Patterns$ = set();   // set of component co-occurrence patterns

4   **foreach** $df_{xy} \in F_{df}$ **do**
5     $DB[df_{xy}]$ = getConnectorInstances(M, df_{xy});

      // create databases for frequent itemset mining
6     $DBVA_x$ = array();
7     $DBVA_y$ = array();
8     $DBDM_y$ = array();
9   **foreach** df_{ixy} in $DB[df_{xy}]$ **do**
10   c_x = source component of df_{ixy};
11   c_y = target component of df_{ixy};
12   append($DBVA_x$, $c_x.VA$);
13   append($DBVA_y$, $c_y.VA$);
14   append($DBDM_y$, $c_y.DM$);

15   FI_{vx} = mineFrequentItemsets($DBVA_x$, $minsupp_{par}$);
16   FI_{vy} = mineFrequentItemsets($DBVA_y$, $minsupp_{par}$);
17   FI_{dy} = mineFrequentItemsets($DBDM_y$, $minsupp_{dm}$);

      // keep only those combinations of value assignments and data mappings
      // that occur together in mashup instances
18   Coo = set();
19   **foreach** $\langle VA_x, VA_y, DM_y\rangle \in FI_{vx} \times FI_{vy} \times FI_{dy}$ **do**
20   **if** $computeSupport(\langle VA_x, VA_y, DM_y\rangle, DB[df_{xy}]) \geq minsupp_{pc}$ **then**
21         $Coo = Coo \cup \{\langle VA_x, VA_y, DM_y\rangle\}$;

      // construct the component co-occurrence patterns
22   **foreach** $\langle VA_x, VA_y, DM_y\rangle \in Coo$ **do**
23       $Patterns = Patterns \cup \{\langle df_{xy}, VA_x, VA_y, DM_y\rangle\}$;

24   **return** $Patterns$;

---

search space. This comment also applies to the rest of the algorithms presented in this section.

Component embedding pattern. Mashup composition tools typically allow for the embedding of components inside other components. However, not all components present this capability. A common example is the *loop* component: it takes as input a set of data items and then loops over them executing the operations provided by the embedded component (e.g., a *filter* component). Embedding one component into another is not a trivial task, as there may be complex dataflow connectors and data mappings between the outer and inner component as well as between the last two and the component that proceeds the outer component in the composition flow. Algorithm 7 shows the logic for mining component embedding patterns. First, we get the instances of component embeddings from the mashup repository and then we keep only those that have a support greater or equal to $minsupp_{em}$ (lines 2–10). Using these *frequent embeddings*, we look for *frequent dataflows* that involve these embeddings (lines 11–17). For these patterns, we are also interested in finding

---

Algorithm 7: mineComponentEmbeddings

Data: repository of mashup compositions M, minimum supports for component embeddings ($minsupp_{em}$), data flows ($minsupp_{df}$), data mappings ($minsupp_{dm}$), parameter value ($minsupp_{par}$) and pattern co-occurrence ($minsupp_{pc}$)

Result: list of component embedding patterns with their corresponding components, dataflow connectors, data mappings and parameter value assignments $\langle \{c_x, c_y, c_z\}, DF, DM, VA \rangle$

```
    // get the list of component embeddings
 1  DB_em = array();
 2  foreach m_i ∈ M do
 3      foreach ⟨c_x, c_y, c_z⟩ ∈ m_i.C × m_i.C do
 4          if (c_x preceeds c_y) and (c_y embeds c_z) then
 5              em_xyz = ⟨c_x, c_y, c_z⟩;
 6              append(DB_em, em_xyz);

    // find the frequent component embeddings
 7  F_em = set();
 8  foreach em_xyz ∈ DB_em do
 9      if computeSupport(em_xyz, DB_em) ≥ minsupp_em then
10          append(F_em, em_xyz);

    // get dataflows involving the frequent component embeddings
11  DB_df = array();
12  F_df = array();
13  foreach m_i ∈ M do
14      foreach em_xyz ∈ F_em do
15          if em_xyz ∈ m_i then
16              append(DB_df[em_xyz], ⟨m_i.df_xy, m_i.df_xz, m_i.df_yz⟩);

17      F_df = mineFrequentItemsets(DB_df, minsupp_df);

    // get parameter value and data mapping instances and compute the
    // corresponding frequent itemsets
18  DB_va = array(); DB_dm = array();
19  foreach m_i ∈ M do
20      foreach ⟨df_xy, df_xz, df_yz⟩ ∈ F_df do
21          if ⟨df_xy, df_xz, df_yz⟩ ∈ m_i then
22              c_x = component instance c_x ∈ m_i corresponding to df_xy;
23              c_y = component instance c_y ∈ m_i corresponding to df_xy;
24              c_z = component instance c_z ∈ m_i corresponding to df_yz;
25              VA_x = c_x.VA; DM_x = c_x.DM;
26              VA_y = c_y.VA; DM_y = c_y.DM;
27              VA_z = c_z.VA; DM_z = c_z.DM;
28              append(DB_va, VA_x ∪ VA_y ∪ VA_z);
29              append(DB_dm, DM_x ∪ DM_y ∪ DM_z);

30  F_va = mineFrequentItemsets(DB_va, minsupp_par);
31  F_dm = mineFrequentItemsets(DB_dm, minsupp_dm);
    // construct the component embedding pattern
32  Patterns = set();
33  foreach ⟨EM, DF, DM, VA⟩ ∈ F_em × F_df × F_dm × F_va do
34      if computeSupport(⟨EM, DF, DM, VA⟩, M) ≥ minsupp_pc then
35          c_x, c_y, c_z = components corresponding to the dataflows df ∈ DF;
36          Patterns = Patterns ∪ {⟨{c_x, c_y, c_z}, DF, DM, VA⟩};

37  return Patterns;
```

---

data mapping and parameter value patterns and thus we proceed as in the previous algorithms to mine them (lines 18–31). In the last part of the algorithm (lines 32–37), we proceed with building the actual patterns with tuples $\langle \{c_x, c_y, c_z\}, DF, DM, VA \rangle$

that include information about the components involved in the pattern as well as the dataflow connectors, data mappings and parameter value assignments.

Multi-component pattern. The multi-component pattern represents recurrent model fragments that are composed of multiple components. It represents more complex patterns, which are not yet captured by the other pattern types alone. This pattern helps understanding domain knowledge and best practices as well as keeping modeling conventions. Multi-component patterns consists in a combination of the patterns we have introduced before. Algorithm 8 provides the details of the mining algorithm. We start by obtaining the graph representation of the mashups in the repository and mining frequent sub-graphs out of them (lines 2–5). For the sub-graph mining we can choose among the state of the art sub-graph mining algorithms [13]. Then, we get from the mashup repository the list of mashup fragments that match the frequent sub-graphs mined in the previous step (lines 6–11). We do this, so that next we can mine both the parameter value and data mapping patterns using again standard itemset mining algorithms (lines 13–21). Finally, we build the actual multicomponent patterns by going through the mashup repository and keeping only those combinations of patterns that co-occur in the mashup instances (lines 22–25).

27.5 Recommending Patterns

Recommending patterns is non-trivial, in that the size of the knowledge base may be large, and the search for composition patterns may be complex; yet, recommendations are to be delivered at high speed, without slowing down the modeler's composition pace. Recommending patterns is platform-specific. The following explanations therefore refer to the specific case of Pipes-like mashup models. In [10], we show all the details of our approach; in the following we summarize its key aspects.

27.5.1 Pattern Knowledge Base

The core of the interactive recommender is the pattern KB. In order to enable the incremental and fast recommendation of patterns, we *decompose* them into their constituent parts and focus only on those aspects that are necessary to convey the meaning of a pattern. That is, we leverage on the observation that, in order to convey the structure of a pattern, already its components and connectors enable the developer to choose in an informed fashion. Data mappings and value assignments, unless explicitly requested by the developer, are then delivered only during the weaving phase upon the selection of a specific pattern by the developer.

This strategy leads us to the *KB* illustrated in Fig. 27.3, whose structure enables the retrieval of each of the patterns introduced in Sect. 27.3.1 with a one-shot query over a single table. For instance, let's focus on the component co-occurrence

---

Algorithm 8: mineMulticomponentPatterns

Data: repository of mashup compositions M and minimun support for multi-components ($minsupp_{mc}$), parameter value ($minsupp_{par}$) and data mapping ($minsupp_{dm}$) patterns.
Result: set of multi-component patterns $\langle mf.C, mf.DF, VA, DM \rangle$.

1 DB_g = array() ;   // database of graph representations of mashups
2 **foreach** $m_i \in M$ **do**
   // get a graph representation of mashup m_i where the nodes represent
       components and arcs represent dataflows; here, the arcs are labeled
       with the output and input ports involved in the dataflow
3 | g_i = getGraphRepresentation(m_i);
4 | append(DB_g, g_i);

5 FG = mineFrequentSubraphs($DB_g, minsupp_{mc}$);
6 DB_{mc} = array();
7 **foreach** $m_i \in M$ **do**
8 | **foreach** $fg_i \in FG$ **do**
9 | | **if** *getGraphRepresentation(m_i) contains fg_i* **then**
       | | // get the fragment mf from mashup instance m_i that matches fg_i;
                   notice that mf is represented as a canonical mashup model
10 | | | mf = getSubgraphInstance(m_i, fg_i);
11 | | | append($DB_{mc}[fg_i], mf$)

12 $Patterns$ = set();
13 **foreach** $MC \in DB_{mc}$ **do**
   // get parameter values and data mappings and compute the corresponding
       frequent itemsets
14 | $DBVA$ = array();
15 | $DBDM$ = array();
16 | **foreach** $mf \in MC$ **do**
17 | | **foreach** $c_x \in mf.C$ **do**
18 | | | append($DBVA, c_x.VA$);
19 | | | append($DBDM, c_x.DM$);

20 | FI_{va} = mineFrequentItemsets($DBVA, minsupp_{par}$);
21 | FI_{dm} = mineFrequentItemsets($DBDM, minsupp_{dm}$);
   // construct the multi-component pattern
22 | **foreach** $\langle VA, DM \rangle \in FI_{va} \times FI_{dm}$ **do**
23 | | **foreach** $mf \in MC$ **do**
24 | | | **if** $\langle VA, DM \rangle \in mf$ **then**
25 | | | | $Patterns = Patterns \cup \{\langle mf.C, mf.DF, VA, DM \rangle\}$;   // using mf, build the
                   patterns with its components ($mf.C$), dataflows ($mf.DF$), value
                   assignments ($mf.VA$) and data mappings ($mf.DM$)

26 **return** $Patterns$;

---

pattern: to retrieve its representation, it is enough to query the *ComponentCooccur* entity for the *SourceComponent* and the *TargetComponent* attributes. The query is assembled automatically upon interactions in the modeling canvas and is of the form $q = \langle object, action, pm \rangle$. Only weaving the pattern into the mashup model requires querying *ComponentCooccur* $\bowtie$ *Connectors* $\bowtie$ *DataMapping* and *ComponentCooccur* $\bowtie$ *ParameterValues*.

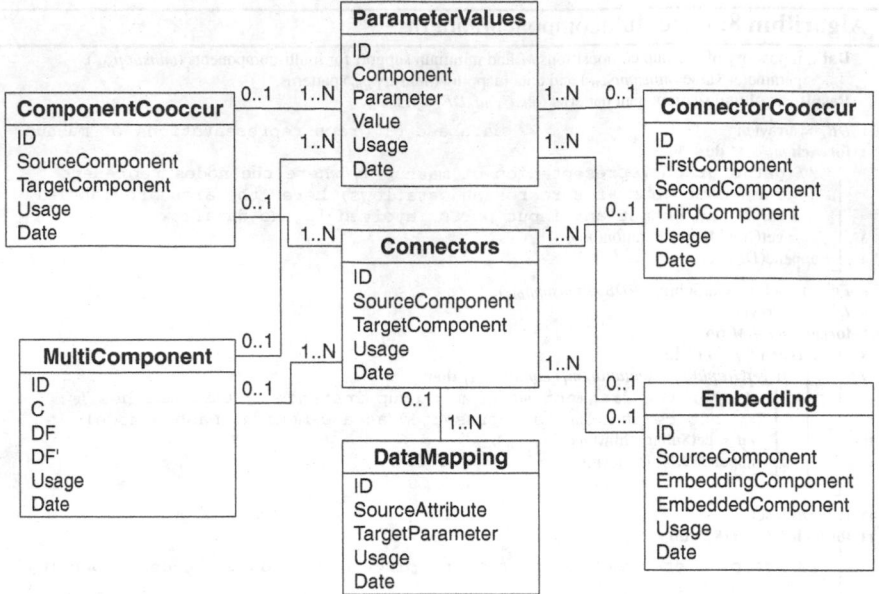

Fig. 27.3 KB structure optimized for pipes

27.5.2 *Exact and Approximate Pattern Matching*

The described KB supports both *exact queries* for the patterns with pre-defined structure and *approximate matching* for multi-component patterns whose structure is not known a priori. Patterns are queried for or matched against the *object* of the query, i.e., the last modeling construct manipulated by the developer. Conceptually, all recommendations could be retrieved via similarity search, but for performance reasons we apply it only when strictly necessary.

Algorithm 9 details this **strategy** and summarizes the logic implemented by the recommendation engine. In line 3, we retrieve the types of recommendations that can be given (*getSuitableRecTypes* function), given an *object-action* combination. Then, for each recommendation type, we either query for patterns (the *queryPatterns* function can be seen like a traditional SQL query) or we do a similarity search (*get-SimilarPatterns* function). For each retrieved pattern, we compute a rank, e.g., based on the pattern description (e.g., containing *usage* and *date*), the computed similarity, and the usefulness of the pattern inside the partial mashup, order and group the recommendations by type, and filter out the best *n* patterns for each recommendation type.

As for the retrieval of **similar patterns**, we give preference to exact matches of components and connectors in *object* and allow candidate patterns to differ for the insertion, deletion, or substitution of at most one component in a given path in *object*. Among the non-matching components, we give preference to functionally

---

Algorithm 9: getRecommendations

Data: query $q = \langle object, action, pm \rangle$, knowledge base KB, object-action-recommendation mapping OAR, component similarity matrix $CompSim$, similarity threshold T_{sim}, ranking threshold T_{rank}, number n of recommendations per recommendation type

Result: recommendations $R = [\langle cp_i, rank_i \rangle]$

1 R = array();
2 $Patterns$ = set();
3 $recTypeToBeGiven$ = getRecTypes($object, action, OAR$);
4 **foreach** $recType \in recTypeToBeGiven$ **do**
5   **if** $recType \neq$ "Mul" **then**
6        $Patterns = Patterns \cup$ queryPatterns($object, KB, recType$) ;   // exact query
7   **else**
8        $Patterns = Patterns \cup$ getSimilarPatterns($object$, $KB, CompSim, T_{sim}$) ;   // similarity search

9 **foreach** $pat \in Patterns$ **do**
10   **if** $rank(pat.cp, pat.sim, pm) \geq T_{rank}$ **then**
11   append($R, \langle pat.cp, rank(pat.cp, pat.sim, pm) \rangle$) ;   // rank, threshold, remember

12 orderByRank(R);
13 groupByType(R);
14 truncateByGroup(R, n);
15 **return** R;

---

similar components (e.g., it may be reasonable to allow a Yahoo! Map instead of a Google Map); we track this similarity in a dedicated *CompSim* matrix. For the detailed explanation of the approximate matching logic we refer the reader to [10].

27.6 Weaving Patterns

Weaving a given composition pattern *cp* into a partial mashup model *pm* is not straightforward and requires a thorough analysis of both *cp* and *pm*, in order to understand how to connect the pattern to the constructs already present in *pm*. In essence, weaving a pattern means emulating developer interactions inside the modeling canvas, so as to connect a pattern to the partial mashup. The problem is not as simple as just copying and pasting the pattern, in that new identifiers of all constructs of *cp* need to be generated, connectors must be rewritten based on the new identifiers, and connections with existing constructs may be required.

We approach the problem of pattern weaving by first defining a *basic weaving strategy* that is independent of *pm* and then deriving a *contextual weaving strategy* that instead takes into account the structure of *pm*.

27.6.1 Basic Weaving Strategy

Given an *object* and a pattern *cp* of a recommendation, the **basic weaving strategy** *BS* provides the sequence of mashup operations that are necessary to weave *cp* into the *object*. The basic weaving strategy does not use *pm*; it tells how to expand *object* into *cp* (*object* being a part of *cp*). This basic strategy is *static* for each pattern type and it consists a set of **mashup operations** that resemble the operations a developer can typically perform manually in the modeling canvas. Typical examples of mashup operations are *addComponent* that corresponds to adding a new component to *pm*, *addConnector* that corresponds to adding a connector between two selected components in *pm*, *assignValues* that corresponds to assigning values to configuration parameters of a component, and similar. Mashup operations are applied on the partial mashup *pm* and result in an updated *pm'*. All operations assume that the *pm* is globally accessible. The internal logic of these operations are highly platform-specific, in that they need to operate inside the target modeling environment.

For instance, the basic weaving strategy for a component co-occurrence pattern of type $ptype^{comp}$ is as follows (we assume $object = comp$ with $comp.type = c_x.type$, c_x being one of the components of the pattern):

1 $newcid^5$=addComponent($c_y.type$);
2 addConnector($\langle comp.id, c_x.op, \$newcid, c_y.ip \rangle$);
3 assignDataMapping($newcid, c_y.DM$);
4 assignValues($comp.id, c_x.VA$);
5 assignValues($newcid, c_y.VA$);

That is, given a component c_x, we add the other component c_y (line 1) as mentioned in the selected pattern to the *pm*, connect c_x and c_y together (line 2) and then apply the respective data mappings (line 3) and value assignments (line 4 and line 5). Note that, the basic strategy is not yet applied to *pm*; it represents an array of basic modeling operations to be further processed before being able to weave the pattern.

27.6.2 Contextual Weaving Strategy

Given an object *object*, a pattern *cp*, and a partial mashup *pm*, the **contextual weaving strategy** *WS* is derived by applying the mashup operations in the *basic weaving strategy* to the current partial mashup model and thus by weaving the selected *cp* into *pm*. The *WS* is *dynamically* built at runtime by taking into consideration the structure of the partial mashup (the context).

Applying the mashup operations in the basic weaving strategy may require the resolution of possible **conflicts** among the constructs of *pm* and those of *cp*. For instance, if we want to add a new component of type *ctype* to *pm* but *pm* already contains an instance of type *ctype*, say *comp*, we are in the presence of a conflict: either we decide that we reuse *comp*, which is already there, or we decide to create a new instance of *ctype*. In the former case, we say we apply a *soft* conflict resolution policy, in the latter case a *hard* policy:

---

[5] We highlight identifier place holders (variables) that can only be resolved when executing the operation with a "$" prefix.

Algorithm 10: getWeavingStrategy

Data: partial mashup model *pm*, composition pattern *cp*, object *object* that triggered the recommendation
Result: weaving strategy *WS*, i.e., a sequence of abstract mashup operations; updated mashup model *pm'*

1   *WS* = array();
2   *BS* = getBasicStrategy(*cp*, *object*);
3   **foreach** *instr* ∈ *BS* **do**
4   *CtxInstr* = resolveConflict(*pm*, *instr*);
5   *pm* = apply(*pm*, *CtxInstr*);
6   append(*WS*, *CtxInstr*);
7   **return** ⟨*WS*, *pm*⟩;

Soft: substitute("var=addComponent(*ctype*)") with "$var = comp.id$"

Hard: substitute("var=addComponent(*ctype*)") with "var=addComponent (*ctype*)"

Formally, the conflict resolution policy corresponds to a function **resolveConflict**(*pm*, *instr*) → *CtxInstr*, where *instr* is the mashup operation to be applied to *pm* and *CtxInstr* is the set of instructions that replace *instr*. Only in the case of a conflict, *instr* is replaced; otherwise the function returns *instr* again.

In Algorithm 10 we describe the logic of our pattern weaver. First, it derives a basic strategy *BS* for the given composition pattern *cp* and the *object* from *pm* (line 2). Then, for each of the mashup operations *instr* in the basic strategy, it checks for possible conflicts with the current modeling context *pm* (line 4). In case of a conflict, the function resolveConflict(*pm*, *instr*) derives the corresponding contextual weaving instructions *CtxInstr* replacing the conflicting, basic operation *instr*. *CtxInstr* is then applied to the current *pm* to compute the updated mashup model *pm'* (line 5), which is then used as basis for weaving the next *instr* of *BS*. The contextual weaving structure *WS* is constructed as concatenation of all conflict-free instructions *CtxInstr*.

Note that Algorithm 10 returns both the list of contextual weaving instructions *WS* and the final updated mashup model *pm'*. The former can be used to interactively weave *cp* into *pm*, the latter to convert *pm'* into native formats.

27.7 Implementation and Evaluation

We have implemented our prototype system, *Baya* [11], as Mozilla Firefox (http://mozilla.com/firefox) extension for Yahoo! Pipes to demonstrate the viability of our interactive recommendation approach. The **design goals** behind Baya can be summarized as follows: We didn't want to develop *yet another* mashup environment; so we opted for an extension of existing and working solutions (so far, we focused on Yahoo! Pipes; other tools will follow). Modelers should not be required to *ask* for help; we therefore pro-actively and interactively recommend contextual composition patterns. We did not want the *reuse* to be limited to simple copy/paste of patterns, but knowledge should be *actionable*, and therefore, Baya automatically weaves patterns.

In Baya we have implemented the *model adapters* (see Fig. 27.2) in Java (1.6), which are able to convert Yahoo! Pipes's JSON representation into our canonical mashup model and back. All the mining algorithms are also implemented in Java. For the frequent itemset mining we used the tool Carpenter (http://www.borgelt.net/carpenter.html), while for graph mining we used the tool MoSS (http://www.borgelt.net/moss.html). The resulting patterns are expressed in terms of canonical mashup models, which are then converted to native models (in this case, Yahoo! Pipes JSON representations) by our canonical-to-native model adapter and loaded into the pattern KB.

For testing our mining algorithms, we used a dataset of 970 pipes definitions from Yahoo! Pipes that were retrieved using YQL Console (http://developer.yahoo.com/yql/console/). We selected pipes from the list of "most popular" pipes, as popular pipes are more likely to be functioning and useful. The average numbers of components, connectors and input parameters are 11.1, 11.0 and 4.1, respectively, which is an indication that we are dealing with fairly complex pipes.

The results obtained from running our algorithms on the selected dataset show that we are able to discover recurrent practices for building mashups. Table 27.1 reports on the list of pattern types and their Upper Threshold for *minsupp* (UTm). The UTm tells us what is the upper threshold for the *minsupp* values at which we start finding patterns of a given type and for a given dataset. In the cases where we use more than one type of *minsupp* (such as in the component co-occurrence pattern where we use $minsupp_{df}$, $minsupp_{dm}$ and $minsupp_{par}$), the *minsupp* we consider is the one corresponding to the pattern that is first computed in the algorithm. For our dataset, in Table 27.1 we can see that we are always able to find parameter value patterns for some component types. For example, this is the case of Yahoo! Pipes' component *YQL* that has the parameter *raw* with a default value *Results only* that is always kept as-is by the users. From the table we can also notice that the connector and component co-occurrence patterns have the same UTm value. This is because in both cases their corresponding algorithms compute first the frequent dataflow connectors and thus the reference minimum support for the UTm is $minsupp_{df}$. Finally, for the Multi-component pattern we have a UTm of 0.021, a relatively low value, when we consider patterns with at least 4 components. However, considering that here we are talking about complex patterns with at least 4 components that, furthermore, include dataflow connectors, data mappings and parameter value assignments, we can say that, even with a relatively low support value, these patterns still captures recurrent modeling practices for fairly complex settings.

The discovered patterns are transformed and stored in a knowledge base that is optimized for fast pattern retrieval at runtime. The implementation of the persistent pattern KB at server side, is based on MySQL (http://www.mysql.com/). Via a dedicated Java RESTful API, at startup of the recommendation panel the KB loader synchronizes the server-side KB with the client-side KB, which instead is based on SQLite (http://www.sqlite.org). The pattern matching and retrieval algorithms are implemented in JavaScript and triggered by events generated by the event listeners monitoring the DOM changes related to the mashup model.

Pattern type	UTm
Table 27.1 Summary of pattern types with their corresponding UTm	
Parameter value pattern	1
Connector pattern	0.257
Connector co-occurrence pattern	0.072
Component co-occurrence pattern	0.257
Component embedding pattern	0.124
Multi-component pattern	0.021

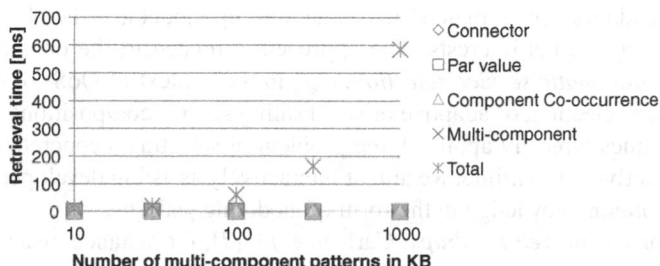

Fig. 27.4 Recommendation types and times in response to a new component added to the canvas

The weaving algorithms are also implemented in JavaScript. Upon the selection of a recommendation from the panel, they derive the contextual weaving strategy that is necessary to weave the respective pattern into the partial mashup model. Each of the instructions in the weaving strategy refers to a modeling action, where modeling actions are implemented as JavaScript manipulations of the mashup model's JSON representation. Both the weaving strategies (basic and contextual) are encoded as JSON arrays, which enables us to use the native eval() command for fast and easy parsing of the weaving logic.

Figure 27.4 illustrates the performance of the interactive recommendation algorithm of Baya as described in Algorithm 9 in response to the user placing a new component into the canvas, a typical modeling situation. Based on the object-action-recommendation mapping, the algorithm retrieves parameter value, connector, component co-occurrence, and multi-component patterns. As expected, the response times of the simple queries can be neglected compared to the one of the similarity search for multi-component patterns, which basically dominates the whole recommendation performance. During the performance evaluation for Baya, we have also observed that the time required for weaving a pattern is negligible with respect to the total time required for the pattern recommendation and weaving.

27.8 Related Work

Traditionally, *recommender systems* focus on the retrieval of information of likely interest to a given user, e.g., newspaper articles or books. The likelihood of interest is typically computed based on a *user profile* containing the user's areas of interest, and retrieved results may be further refined with collaborative filtering techniques. In our work, as for now we focus less on the user and more on the partial mashup under development (we will take user preferences into account in a later stage), that is, recommendations must match the partial mashup model and the object the user is focusing on, not his interests. The approach is related to the one followed by research on *automatic service selection*, e.g., in the context of QoS- or reputation-aware service selection, or adaptive or self-healing service compositions. Yet, while these techniques typically approach the problem of selecting a concrete service for an abstract activity at runtime, we aim at interactively assisting developers at design time with domain knowledge in the form of modeling patterns.

In the context of *web mashups*, Carlson et al. [2], for instance, react to a user's selection of a component with a recommendation for the next component to be used; the approach is based on semantic annotations of component descriptors and makes use of WordNet for disambiguation. Greenshpan et al. [6] propose an auto-completion approach that recommends components and connectors (so-called glue patterns) in response to the user providing a set of desired components; the approach computes top-k recommendations out of a graph-structured knowledge base containing components and glue patterns (the nodes) and their relationships (the arcs). While in this approach the actual structure (the graph) of the knowledge base is hidden to the user, Chen et al. [3] allow the user to mashup components by navigating a graph of components and connectors; the graph is generated in response to the user's query in form of descriptive keywords. Riabov et al. [9] also follow a keyword-based approach to express user goals, which they use to feed an automated planner that derives candidate mashups; according to the authors, obtaining a plan may require several seconds. Elmeleegy et al. [5] propose MashupAdvisor, a system that, starting from a component placed by the user, recommends a set of related components (based on conditional co-occurrence probabilities and semantic matching); upon selection of a component, MashupAdvisor uses automatic planning to derive how to connect the selected component with the partial mashup, a process that may also take more than one minute. Beauche and Poizat [1] use automatic planning in *service composition*. The planner generates a candidate composition starting from a user task and a set of user-specified services.

The *business process management* (BPM) community more strongly focuses on patterns as a means of knowledge reuse. For instance, Smirnov et al. [12] provide so-called co-occurrence action patterns in response to action/task specifications by the user; recommendations are provided based on label similarity, and also come with the necessary control flow logic to connect the suggested action. Hornung et al. [8] provide users with a keyword search facility that allows them to retrieve process models whose labels are related to the provided keywords; the algorithm applies the traditional TF-IDF technique from information retrieval to process models, turning the repository of process models into a keyword vector space. Gschwind et al. [7] allow users to use the control flow patterns introduced by Van der Aalst et al. [14], just like other modeling elements. The system does not provide interactive recommendations and rather focuses on the correct insertion of patterns.

In summary, assisted mashup and service composition approaches either focus on single components or connectors, or they aim to auto-complete compositions starting from user goals by using AI Planning techniques. The BPM approaches do focus on patterns, but most of the times pattern similarity is based on label/text similarity, not on structural compatibility. In our work, we consider that if components have been used together successfully multiple times, very likely their joint use is both syntactically and semantically meaningful. Hence, there is no need to further model complex ontologies or composition rules. Another key difference is that we leverage on the *interactive recommendation* of composition patterns to assists users step-by-step based on their actions on the design canvas. We do not only tell users which patterns may be applied to progress in the mashup composition process, but we also *automatically weave* recommended patterns on behalf of the users.

27.9 Conclusions

With this work, we aim to pave the road for assisted development in web-based composition environments. We represent *reusable knowledge* as patterns, explain how to automatically *discover* patterns from existing mashup models, describe how to *recommend* patterns fast, and how to *weave* them into partial mashup models. We therefore provide the *basic technology* for assisted development, demonstrating that the solutions proposed indeed work in practice.

As for the discovery of patterns, it is important to note that even patterns with very low support carry valuable information. Of course, they do not represent generally valid solutions or complex best practices in a given domain, but still they show *how* its constructs have been used in the past. This property is a positive side-effect of the sensible, a-priori design of the pattern structures we are looking for. Without that, discovered patterns would require much higher support values, so as to provide evidence that also their pattern structure is meaningful. Our analysis of the patterns discovered by our algorithms shows that, in order to get the best out them, domain knowledge inside the mashup models is crucial. Domain-specific mashups, in which composition elements and constructs have specific domain semantics, are a thread of research we are already following. As a next step, we will also extend the canonical model toward more generic mashup languages, e.g., including UI synchronization.

The results of our tests of the pattern recommendation approach even outperform our own expectations, also for large numbers of patterns. In practice, however, the number of really meaningful patterns in a given modeling domain will only unlikely grow beyond several dozens. The described recommending approach will therefore work well also in the context of other browser-based modeling tools, e.g., business process or service composition instruments (which are also model-based and of similar complexity), while very likely it will perform even better in desktop-based modeling tools like the various Eclipse-based visual editors. Recommendation retrieval times of fractions of seconds and negligible pattern weaving times will definitely allow us—and others—to develop more sophisticated, assisted composition environments. This is, of course, our goal for the future—next to going back to the users of our initial study and testing the effectiveness of assisted development in practice.

Acknowledgments This work was supported by the European Commission (project OMELETTE, contract 257635).

References

1. Beauche, S., Poizat, P.: Automated service composition with adaptive planning. In: ICSOC'08, pp. 530–537. Springer (2008). doi:10.1007/978-3-540-89652-4_42
2. Carlson, M.P., Ngu, A.H., Podorozhny, R., Zeng, L.: Automatic mash up of composite applications. In: ICSOC'08, pp. 317–330, Springer (2008). doi:10.1007/978-3-540-89652-4_25
3. Chen, H., Lu, B., Ni, Y., Xie, G., Zhou, C., Mi, J., Wu, Z.: Mashup by surfing a web of data apis. In: VLDB'09, vol. 2, pp. 1602–1605 (2009). http://portal.acm.org/citation.cfm?id=1687553. 1687602
4. De Angeli, A., Battocchi, A., Roy Chowdhury, S., Rodríguez, C., Daniel, F., Casati, F.: End-user requirements for wisdom-aware eud. In: IS-EUD'11. Springer (2011)
5. Elmeleegy, H., Ivan, A., Akkiraju, R., Goodwin, R.: Mashup advisor: A recommendation tool for mashup development. In: ICWS'08, pp. 337–344. IEEE Computer Society (2008). doi:10. 1109/ICWS.2008.128. http://portal.acm.org/citation.cfm?id=1474549.1474748
6. Greenshpan, O., Milo, T., Polyzotis, N.: Autocompletion for mashups. In: VLDB'09, vol. 2, pp. 538–549 (2009). http://portal.acm.org/citation.cfm?id=1687627.1687689
7. Gschwind, T., Koehler, J., Wong, J.: Applying patterns during business process modeling. In: BPM'08, pp. 4–19. Springer (2008). doi:10.1007/978-3-540-85758-7_4
8. Hornung, T., Koschmider, A., Lausen, G.: Recommendation based process modeling support: method and user experience. In: ER'08, pp. 265–278. Springer (2008)
9. Riabov, A.V., Boillet, E., Feblowitz, M.D., Liu, Z., Ranganathan, A.: Wishful search: interactive composition of data mashups. In: WWW'08, pp. 775–784. ACM (2008). doi:10.1145/1367497. 1367602
10. Roy Chowdhury, S., Daniel, F., Casati, F.: Efficient, interactive recommendation of mashup composition knowledge. In: ICSOC'11, pp. 374–388. Springer (2011)
11. Roy Chowdhury, S., Rodríguez, C., Daniel, F., Casati, F.: Baya: assisted mashup development as a service. In: WWW'12 (2012)
12. Smirnov, S., Weidlich, M., Mendling, J., Weske, M.: Action patterns in business process models. In: ICSOC-ServiceWave'09, pp. 115–129. Springer (2009). doi:10.1007/978-3-642-10383-4_8
13. Tan, P., Steinbach, M., Kumar, V.: Introduction to Data Mining. Addison-Wesley, Boston (2005)
14. Van Der Aalst, W.M.P., Ter Hofstede, A.H.M., Kiepuszewski, B., Barros, A.P.: Workflow patterns. Distrib. Parallel Databases **14**, 5–51 (2003)

Chapter 28
End Users Developing Mashups

Nikolay Mehandjiev, Abdallah Namoun, Freddy Lécué, Usman Wajid and Georgia Kleanthous

Abstract Mashups can open up access to the wealth of on-line information, allowing information-providing services to be discovered, integrated and presented in a manner tuned to current user needs. Their uptake is hindered by the fact that most information consumers do not have programming background and thus find it difficult to work with the current systems which are technology-driven. Many researchers attempt to help such non-programmers by replacing programming scripts with interactive visual representations to connect different information-providing service components into an assembly. However, the underlying programming techniques such as event-driven processing still shape the visual interface and make it difficult to understand for non-programmers. In contrast, we did not start with the technology but with the users—service producers and consumers, and studied the core issues which should be resolved before non-programmers can assemble meaningful mashups, over and above the presentation-level integration offered by current mashup environments. The result is an approach to assisted service composition designed for end users, which uses semantic technologies to shield users from the irrelevant complexity of service technology, from the heterogeneity of the information and from the need to

N. Mehandjiev (✉) · A. Namoun · U. Wajid · G. Kleanthous
Manchester Centre for Service Research,
University of Manchester,
Manchester M60 1QD, UK
e-mail: n.mehandjiev@manchester.ac.uk

A. Namoun
e-mail: abdallah.namoune@mbs.ac.uk

U. Wajid
e-mail: usman.wajid@manchester.ac.uk

G. Kleanthous
e-mail: georgia.kleanthous@gmail.com

F. Lécué
IBM Research, Dublin, Ireland
e-mail: freddy.lecue@ie.ibm.com

A. Bouguettaya et al. (eds.), *Web Services Foundations*,
DOI: 10.1007/978-1-4614-7518-7_28,
© Springer Science+Business Media New York 2014

manually resolve dependencies between services. A tool has been developed to help us validate the approach through two observational studies of non-programmers. The studies confirmed the enabling effect of the approach, and generated suggestions for further work at the levels of both the approach and the tool.

28.1 Introduction

The empowering influence of the World Wide Web in terms of fast and convenient access to information and services from all areas of human knowledge and culture, and from any corner of the globe, is universally accepted. This is taken a step further with the idea of mashups, allowing users to combine information from different sources, process it and present it in a finely-tuned manner by composing information-providing services. These have developed from simple web pages aggregating information from different sources and presenting it side-by-side without any integration, such as iGoogle and myYahoo!, to sophisticated mashups where information is passed through a number of processing steps in a workflow-type fashion, for example Gravity[1] and MarcoFlow [11].

Given the clear potential for benefiting from such activities in terms of unleashing creativity and providing services at the point of need, the limited uptake of mashup environments is somehow puzzling. A closer look at the currently available commercial environments and research systems reveals one potential reason—the technology-driven approach underpinning them. The design of such systems would typically start from an integration technique such as event-driven processing, and a visual front-end would be constructed to present this technique to the users through a (hopefully) easy-to-understand metaphor.

However, people trained in programming and able to manage the complexity of contemporary software technologies are a small fraction of all the users who can benefit from mashup technology. Mashup environments constructed around an integration technique such as event-driven processing would not be easily accessible for the latter type of general users, despite the visual front-ends. Indeed, from the existing mashup systems (a selection of which is reviewed in Sect. 28.2), the successful ones (such as iGogle and myYahoo!) are the simplest, presenting information side-by-side in separate panels without any integration between different information sources.

In contrast to the majority of existing mashup approaches, we started from a user-driven perspective, and studied the mental models of general users with regards to mashup activities, and the issues which prevent them from assembling services into meaningful compositions processing information in a non-trivial manner. The results, reported in Sect. 28.3 of this paper, suggest we need to reduce learning costs by making the composition as transparent as possible, hide any technical details which are not relevant to the task of the user, and provide immediate feedback in

---

[1] Available from http://www.sdn.sap.com/irj/scn/weblogs?blog=/pub/wlg/17826.

respect to any design decisions by end users. We also gained insight into our users' mental models regarding software services and their composition.

These activities helped us to create a novel task-oriented approach to composing services into mashups, where users are shielded from the underlying technology and from the heterogeneity of the information processed, and only asked to select from a number of alternative information-providing or processing services for different parts of the composition. Semantic reasoning takes over mundane technical details such as aligning service inputs and outputs and resolving inter-service dependencies, and composition templates allow "best-practice" sharing of mashups specific to the application domain and to the tasks which are to be supported by the mashup.

The approach, called *assisted service composition for end users* and described in detail in Sect. 28.4, comprises the following two contributions:

1. A template-based process with three stages: assisted composition, template adaptation and learning (generalising user-adapted innovative applications into templates). Here we focus on the stage of assisted composition since it targets the widest audience of general users.
2. A semantic technique of service alignment, alleviating the need for data integration between constituent services, and shielding users from inter-service dependencies and from the technical complexity of service technology.

To validate the approach, we have developed a prototype tool which supports the approach and allows users to compose mashups by using "point and click" to select services. The tool uses semantic (monotonic) reasoning to resolve the dependencies between services, and advises the user regarding compatability between services. We used this tool in two observational studies with non-programmers. The observational studies, reported in Sect. 28.5, confirmed the enabling effect of the approach, and generated suggestions for further work at the levels of both the approach and the tool.

28.2 Related Research

28.2.1 Mashups and Service Composition Environments

A number of environments exist which allow the composition of information-provision services in some form of a mashup. The simplest are from presentation-level mashups which display information from different services side-by-side in widgets. The widgets support uniform user interface framework and allow the creation of personalised portal pages. These environments are mainstream and enjoy a large number of users, for example iGoogle and myYahoo.

The next level of sophistication supports the exchange of data between different components of the mashup such as RSS data sources, information processing services, search services and display components, allowing the creation of

functionality over and above the capabilities of the individual reusable components. Some researchers start their mashup classifications from this category of data
mashups, omitting the previous presentation-level maships, for example Daniel et al.
consider them in the "Simple Mashups" category [10], where we have a single page, a
single user and no support for processing workflow. Often cited examples here are the
commercial environments Yahoo!Pipes[2] and MashMaker [13]). Yahoo!Pipes uses
pipe-and-filter-style composition where information sources and processing components are linked with dataflow pipes, and focuses on facilitating reuse of composition
templates by allowing users to publish the pipes they have created and to adapt the
pipes of others. Intel's MashMaker takes a more direct approach, analysing the web
sites visited by users to extract data which are being displayed, and suggesting how
this data can be combined to achieve new output. There are also some research systems of varying degrees of maturity in this space, for example MashArt [9] uses
event-based mechanisms and dataflow between different types of components to
allow the construction of complex applications. Other systems using dataflow-based
integration include [26, 47, 49] and others, including systems advising on appropriate next steps for the composition [18], and supporting navigation through complex
mashups [12].

In contrast to the first two groups, the third group of process mashups focus on the
flow of control between the different components of the mashup, using visual representation of BPEL or BPMN-style constructs linking these components. Examples
of such systems are [11, 27]. At the process composition level, bpmn.org reports
62 tools for wiring services together using the Business Process Modelling Notation
(BPMN). The approach reported here belongs to this group, yet the process representations used are hidden from the naive users. In common with other approaches
in this group, we focus on the way mashup components interact in the course of a
business process, and presume that the presentation integration will be handled using
another existing approach.

Inspired by the underlying implementation technology and often validated by case
study implementations, only a few of these systems have been evaluated in terms of
usability and cognitive effectiveness. We focus on these criteria in the next section.

28.2.2 User-Centric Approaches to Service Composition

The academic field of End User Development (EUD) [25, 44] takes a user-centric
approach to creating tools which can enable non-technical users to develop sophisticated applications. Main EUD results include theoretical models such as the tradeoff-
based "Attention Investment Model" [4] and the lifecycle model of Meta-Design [16].
There are also a number of well-known practical successes such as spreadsheets and
database form painters.

---

[2] http://pipes.yahoo.com/pipes/

Service-focused work in this field, however, is focused on professional programmers [2], or on web mashups rather than fully fledged service composition [51]. An exemplary user-driven design process is reported in [41], yet it is focused on conventional web applications rather than web services.

Interesting conclusions in this field include the need for supporting end users by hiding irrelevant technical details and complexity from them, providing them instead with task-oriented languages [37]; and the view of end user environments as a medium of continuous collaboration between end users and developers, resulting in the evolution of the environment itself to reflect evolving user skills and requirements [33]. The concept of "Power Users" (technology-savvy end users) as a third side to this collaboration is also important since they are often leaders of user-driven application innovation. Our studies, reported in Sect. 28.3, confirmed the validity of some of these conclusions for the domain of user-driven service composition.

28.2.3 Automating Service Composition

Taken to its extreme, the idea of supporting end users in service composition would translate into the aim of fully automating the composition. Indeed, many AI-inspired approaches [3, 20, 28, 40] address the issue of automated web service composition. Full automation, however, even if it were feasible, would miss the chance for user-led innovation and fine-tuning services to user needs.

Only a handful of approaches have the users in the driving seat and support them by resolving technical details such as data integration and other service dependencies. For example, Carlson et al. [7] introduce an approach where users can drag a service onto a canvas, and this narrows down all discovered services to only those which have compatible inputs and outputs with the service thus selected by the user. A more structured support of the composition process is provided by the composition tool reported in [42], where the process is step-by-step, guided by the tool. Both approaches use semantic tagging of services, and limited semantic reasoning with the data thus available. However, neither of them uses templates and thus cannot support reuse of composition knowledge.

Semantic reasoning underpins such selection of compatible services. This can use basic semantic matching types [24, 39], the difference operator [5, 45] or Concept Abduction [8]. Different approaches differ in performance and scalability, and we need to consider the correct approach based on the expected scale of compositions and number of candidate services. This paper does not address research challenges related to ontology matching [14], which is out of the scope of this paper.

28.3 Challenges to Users Attempting to Compose Services

Our user-centric approach to enabling mashup composition by general users necessitated gaining insight into the mental models of services and service composition held by our target user groups, and understanding the main issues which may impede their uptake of service composition. This was achieved through a number of focus groups involving 64 users of mixed background—technical and non-technical. Whilst details of the full study are published elsewhere [30, 36], here we focus on the main challenges faced by users from non-programming background when attempting service composition into mashups.

28.3.1 Realistic Complexity is Overwhelming

Participants quickly extrapolated the simplistic examples used to ones of realistic complexity, which may involve up to "2000 services for each task", and a sizeable number of tasks involved. Our target end users did not consider themselves able (or indeed interested) to handle such complexity, and to manage the complex dependencies existing between different tasks. Some users also did not consider themselves at ease with having to "think in sequence".

The use of "best practice" applications and composition templates was suggested to address some of the complexity issues and allow the sharing of process knowledge between users. A further challenge associated with this approach would be to manage the evolution of both the task and the available services, indeed a successful mashup tool should be able to accommodate frequent new tasks and services.

28.3.2 Heterogeneous Data and Dependencies Between Serviecs

When participants were presented with diagrams showing the flow of data between services in a mashup, a number of them pointed out that the high number of connections linking services makes the interactions "difficult to understand" and hard to figure out "what is going on". The "spaghetti"-like nature of such diagrams made it diffucult to work out where "to put a new service". Also some participants commented on data dependencies as being not "natural".

The alternative of control-flow-based diagram connecting services was felt to "lack the level of detail that is required to make it work". Abstracting away data from these diagrams was felt by the technical users to introduce potential for errors in terms of data mismatch between services. Indeed, a number of users pointed out the different standards and formats of data (XML versus text for example), and the potential for error this would create. These problems were not foreseen by non-technical users who ranked control flow very high and disliked the complexity which stems from explicitly representing data flow between services.

Related discussion points covered the need to specify the semantics of the services using standard semantic notations. This, however, was expected to bring complexity to service descriptions, so we also need to have different ways of representing the composition to people with different skill levels. We need the tool to be "flexible enough to allow composition without worrying about low-level details", whilst we need some "expert mode" for people with technical skills. The tool should support the users by validating the services chosen, ensuring there are no mistakes.

28.4 The Assisted Composition Approach

The approach we have developed can support non-technical end users in creating actual service compositions starting from abstract descriptions of the composition in a template. Those "power users" who are happier to engage with software are then enabled to further customise such compositions by changing the abstract templates and creating innovative variations of standard service composition tasks, customised to specific application domain or social context. In the third stage, a number of similar innovative variations would be generalised into a new reusable template by software developers, thus ensuring the growth of the overall system, allowing innovative compositions to be reused by non-technical users. This three-stage lifecycle of user-driven composition is shown in Fig. 28.1. Here we focus on the left side of the cycle, which involves end users binding concrete services to reusable templates.

Our work with end users (see Sect. 28.3) asserts that users should be shielded from technical details of service assembly such as data dependencies between services. We therefore hide from end users both control flow dependencies and data dependencies between tasks within the template processes. These aspects of the composition are instead considered behind the scene using semantic reasoning.

This section describes in further detail these aspects of our approach, using a formal model of semantic connections between services. The process of assisted composition is then presented. But first we describe a short motivating example.

Fig. 28.1 Lifecycle of user-developed service applications

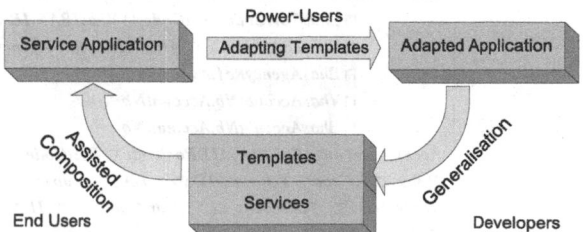

28.4.1 Motivating Scenario

The following scenario is one of the several we used within SOA4All. It targets the arrival of an overseas student to the UK. Students search for suitable universities and register for a course upon arrival. They use the acceptance letter to open a bank account and submit tax exemption letters. The bank account is then used to set up payment for University fees.

There are dependencies between the different registration tasks, often unknown to the arrivals, which cause delays and repeated visits, leading to frustration. A composite reusable service can alleviate this by guiding the process and passing the relevant data through.

Here is a list of tasks required to achieve student registration:

- `SearchForAUniversity` that returns some `Universities` and their descriptions (e.g., `UniversityID`, `Name`, `Postcode`, `Course` and their `Fees`) given a `PostCode` as a location and some subjects of courses `Subject`;
- `RegisterForACourseInUK` that returns an `AcceptanceLetter` and a `StudentID` given a `Person` and an `UKUniversity`;
- `OpenBankAccount` that returns a `BankAccount` given a `Person` and an `AcceptanceLetter`;

All input and output parameters above refer to concepts from a domain ontology, an example portion of which is shown in Fig. 28.2. The particular ontology, which is based on the Description Logics DLs $\mathcal{ALE}$—Attributive language with Atomic nega-

$$
\begin{aligned}
University \equiv{} & Institution \sqcap \forall hasID.UniversityID \\
& \sqcap \exists hasID.UniversityID \sqcap \forall hasName.Name \\
& \sqcap \exists hasName.Name \sqcap \forall hasPostcode.Postcode \\
& \sqcap \exists hasPostcode.Postcode \sqcap \exists hasCourse.Course \\
UKUniversity \equiv{} & University \sqcap \forall hasPostcode.UKPostcode \\
& \sqcap \exists hasPostcode.UKPostcode \\
Course \equiv{} & \exists hasFees.Fees \sqcap \exists hasID.CourseID \sqcap \exists Subject \\
Person \equiv{} & \exists hasPostcode.Postcode \sqcap \exists hasFirstName.Name \\
& \sqcap \exists hasLastName.Name \\
Student \equiv{} & Person \sqcap \exists hasID.StudentID \\
BankAccount \equiv{} & Account \sqcap \forall hasSortCode.SortCode \\
& \sqcap \exists hasSortCode.SortCode \sqcap \forall hasIBAN.IBAN \\
& \sqcap \exists hasIBAN.IBAN \sqcap \forall hasAgencyRef.AgencyRef \\
& \sqcap \exists hasAgencyRef.AgencyRef \\
& \sqcap \forall hasAccoubtNb.AccountNb \\
& \sqcap \exists hasAccoubtNb.AccountNb \\
AcceptanceLetter &\sqsubseteq Letter, UKPostcode \sqsubseteq PostCode \\
Name &\sqsubseteq \top, Fees \sqsubseteq \top, CourseID \sqsubseteq \top, ID \sqsubseteq \top, Subject \sqsubseteq \top, \\
StudentID &\sqsubseteq \top, Account \sqsubseteq \top, SortCode \sqsubseteq \top, IBAN \sqsubseteq \top, AgencyRef \sqsubseteq \\
\top, &AccountNb \sqsubseteq \top
\end{aligned}
$$

Fig. 28.2 Part of an $\mathcal{ALE}$ TBox

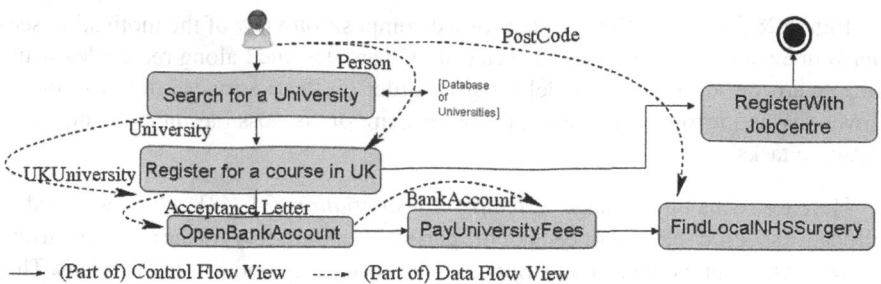

Fig. 28.3 Template-based composition view of the motivating scenario

tion, Concept intersection, Universal restrictions and Existential quantification [1], is part from a larger pair $\langle \mathcal{T}, \mathcal{A} \rangle$. $\mathcal{T}$ and $\mathcal{A}$ refer respectively to a Terminological Box (or TBox i.e., intentional knowledge) and an Assertional Box (or ABox i.e., extensional knowledge) in DL systems. In the following, we will focus on the TBox $\mathcal{T}$ that supports inference on service parameters by means of DL reasoning. An example of inference models concept is subsumption (i.e., concept-based hierarchy checking) for evaluating specialization and generalization of services parameters.

This scenario illustrates the need for user involvement at the level of service customisation. Even if the mashup application was developed by software professionals, each student will have different requirements in terms of need to register with the police, desire to obtain work permit, children to enroll in local schools, etc. This variability motivates direct user control of the composition in terms of user tailoring of the tasks included and which services should be used for each task.

28.4.2 Template-Based Service Composition

An intuitive view to service composition would see it as aiming to satisfy the need for a (non-existing) service by bringing together existing ones. This integration can be done manually, yet this would involve the alignment of numerous inputs and outputs, considering a number of pre- and post-conditions, and dealing with other technical issues of grounding, etc, which are clearly outside of the skills and interests of our end users. Since we allow end users to tune a composition to their own needs, we do not need to have complete automation "from scratch" using program synthesis and AI planning techniques [28].

Instead we opt to reuse composition knowledge and provide a starting template for the users. This composition knowledge can be based on past successful compositions, and can be seeded by formalising domain-specific knowledge about how the problem addressed by the sought service would decompose into sub-problems [46], and task-specific knowledge about the core types of information processing activities [43].

Example 1 (Template-Based Service Composition)

Figure 28.3 presents the template-based composition view of the motivating scenario in Sect. 28.4.1. Tasks (or "service slots") are designed along rectangles while simple arrows are used to model a partial order on these services (i.e., its control flow). Dashed arrows refer to data flow description as possible interdependencies between tasks.

Here we focus on the stage of *template instantiation* [34, 48], where we need to allocate a specific service for each of the generic "service slots" in the template, using knowledge about the data connections and pre- and post-conditions of services. This is the 'Assisted Composition' arrow in Fig. 28.1. Note that the overall approach also includes the stages of template adaptation, where power users can create innovative solutions; and generalisation, or converting the useful innovative adaptations into new templates, helping the library of templates grow. The last stage addresses the issue of feasibility of providing a realistic library of templates—once the library is seeded for a particular domain using generic task scripts, user community will "fill the gaps" by creating numerous innovative applications, mirroring the processes currently underway on Facebook and Yahoo!Pipes.

The focus of supporting end users means that, contrary to existing work in the area (e.g. [22, 29]), we leave control in the hands of our users, and aim to provide expert guidance regarding three parts of the process: selecting suitable services for each task, ranking them according to user profile and working out compatibilities between services in terms of data flow, pre- and post-conditions. The users are involved in selecting one or more services from the shortlist for each task, according to their preferences and knowledge. Because we ensure that users have chosen compatible services, and because these services are tagged semantically, we can automate the mapping of data from one service to the other at execution time behind the scenes, without having to involve users in this.

In this paper we focus only on the aspects of selecting a set of appropriate service candidates for each task, and on working out compatibilities between services in terms of data flow in order to show to the end user the consequences of them selecting a given instance. We use semantic reasoning for both aspects, for example once a user selects a service s_i^j for task T_i, we use semantic reasoning to tag as eligible for further selection only those service candidates for the other tasks in the template which are compatible with s_j^i. Before providing further details in Sect. 28.4.4, we need to describe the semantic reasoning taking place behind the scene.

28.4.3 Semantic Connections of Services

Using tasks specifications of inputs, outputs, pre- and post-conditions of templates, we should be able to infer additional dependencies between tasks, for example we can infer data flow dependencies between tasks using their input and output specifications. In the following we present such dependencies as *semantic links* [22] between services. Then we describe our *semantic-link-based composition model*.

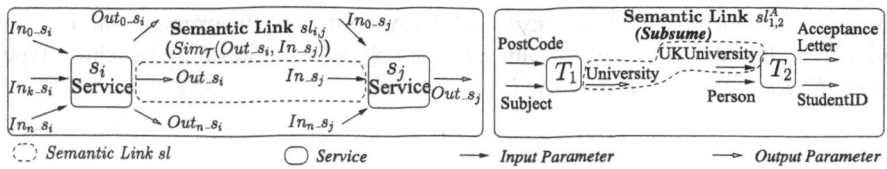

Fig. 28.4 A semantic link $sl_{i,j}$ and its illustration on the motivating scenario

28.4.3.1 Semantic Links

Since input and output parameters of semantic web services are specified using concepts from a common ontology[3] or Terminology $\mathcal{T}$ (an example of such is given in Fig. 28.2), retrieving links between output parameters $Out\_s_i \in \mathcal{T}$ of services s_i and input parameters $In\_s_j \in \mathcal{T}$ of other services s_j could be achieved by using a DL reasoner such as Fact++[4] [19]. Such a link, also known as semantic link [22] $sl_{i,j}$ (Fig. 28.4) between two functional parameters of s_i and s_j is formalized as

$$\langle s_i, Sim_\mathcal{T}(Out\_s_i, In\_s_j), s_j \rangle \tag{28.1}$$

Thereby s_i and s_j are partially linked according to a matching function $Sim_\mathcal{T}$. This function expresses which matching type is employed to chain services. The range of $Sim_\mathcal{T}$ is reduced to the four well known matching type introduced by [39] and the extra type Intersection [24]:

- **Exact** If the output parameter Out_s_i of s_i and the input parameter In_s_j of s_j are equivalent; formally, $\mathcal{T} \models Out\_s_i \equiv In\_s_j$.
- **PlugIn** If Out_s_i is sub-concept of In_s_j; formally, $\mathcal{T} \models Out\_s_i \sqsubseteq In\_s_j$.
- **Subsume** If Out_s_i is super-concept of In_s_j; formally, $\mathcal{T} \models In\_s_j \sqsubseteq Out\_s_i$.
- **Intersection** If the intersection of Out_s_i and In_s_j is satisfiable; formally, $\mathcal{T} \not\models Out\_s_i \sqcap In\_s_j \sqsubseteq \bot$.
- **Disjoint** If Out_s_i and In_s_j are incompatible i.e., $\mathcal{T} \models Out\_s_i \sqcap In\_s_j \sqsubseteq \bot$.

Following the definition of semantic links $sl_{i,j}$ between web service instances s_i and s_j, we also define abstract semantic links $sl_{i,j}^A$ between tasks T_i and T_j.

Example 2 (Semantic Link and Subsume Matching Type) Suppose T_1 and T_2 are respectively tasks related to `SearchForAUniversity` and `RegisterFor` `ACourseInUK` in Fig. 28.4 (right part) of the motivating scenario in Sect. 28.4.1. In such a case, the output parameter `University` of T_1 is semantically linked to

---

[3] Distributed ontologies are not considered here but are largely independent of the problem addressed in this work.

[4] http://owl.man.ac.uk/factplusplus/

the input parameter UniversityUK of T_2. According to the example ontology in Fig. 28.2, this abstract semantic link $sl_{1,2}^A$ is valued by a Subsume matching type since $University \sqsupseteq UKUniversity$.

28.4.3.2 Semantic Link Composition Model

When composing services in mashups, we need to be able to reason about the quality of composition, using aggregation from the quality of individual semantic links. We conceptualise the process model of web service composition as a directed graph which has the web service specifications s_i as its nodes, and the semantic links $sl_{i,j}$ (data dependencies) as its edges.

We can generalise this model to template-based compositions, pre-computed for instance by *template-based* and *parametric-design-based* approaches [34, 48]. The composition graph there has the tasks specifications T_i as its nodes, and abstract semantic links $sl_{i,j}^A$ as its edges.

28.4.4 Helping Users Choose Services Through Semantic Reasoning

Given a template-based composition, semantic descriptions of the tasks in the template and of the candidate services, our approach can help users to instantiate templates with candidate services to optimise the quality of the composition. This is done using the semantic link composition models, where the data flow in the composition is automatically inferred from the DL descriptions of services parameters and from the template of how the composition breaks down into tasks. Optimising the composition models is done at the background and remains hidden from the end users, following [23]. However existing state-of-the-art approaches can be employed for performing optimization using different techniques [6, 52] on different parameters e.g., QoS only [50]. The quality estimate generated is used to provide feedback to users about their selection decisions as follows:

Once a user selects a service, the tool will grey out all service candidates which are incompatible (have a low quality of the semantic links with the selected service instance), and highlight the compatible ones (the instances for which the quality model computes high values). As illustrated in Fig. 28.5, our abstract visualisation hides all details related to control and data flow in the composition, and deals with them in the background.

Example 3 (Abstract Visualisation of Composition) Figure 28.5 illustrates a template-based composition where the user has selected a goal from the taxonomy on the left panel. All related details to data and control flow are abstracted away, and end-users could simply interpret compositions as a list of tasks (first row in Fig. 28.5) wherein each tasks could be instantiated by services (columns in Fig. 28.5). This is a

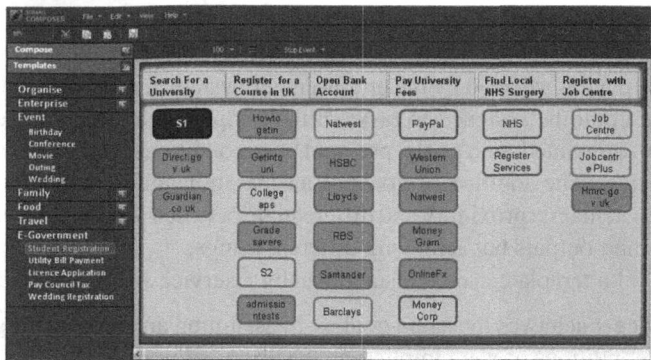

Fig. 28.5 Abstract visualisation of composition

snapshot from a low-tech mock-up we developed early on to test the idea with users, a snapshot of the actual tool is provided in Fig. 28.8.

The overall approach is descibed from two different perspectives: end users interacting with our tool, and actual back-end reasoning.

28.4.4.1 From the End-User Perspective

First of all, the user is responsible for selecting a template from a set of available ones, all organised in a domain taxonomy. The abstract visualisation of the template is then automatically generated by simply extracting its tasks and discovering relevant candidate services for each of them.

The user will proceed to select any service in any column. This selection step assigns the selected service(s) for the considered task. The system reduces the list of candidate services for each task to those which are compatible with the selection and gets back to the users with (only) services that could be assigned to other tasks. This reduction is based on both the previous selection and how the selected services can be semantically linked to candidate services of other tasks. This is repeated until each task is assigned to a service.

Example 4 (Assisted Composition from the End-User Perspective) Figure 28.5 illustrates the instantiation procedure of template after the selection of service s_1 for task `SearchForAUniversity`. Services `CollegeApps` and s_2 of task `RegisterForACourseInUK` are highlighted (in blue) because of (semantic) compatible data flow (Sect. 28.4.3) between them and s_1, while `GradeSavers` (in grey) is not because of its incompability with s_1.

During each step of the template instantiation, the end-user can backtrack and even manually remove some services from any candidates' list.

28.4.4.2 From the Back-End Perspective

Once the template is selected by the end-user, our system aims to discover candidate services that could be assigned to tasks of the template. Note that all services and templates are annotated with goals, pre- and post-conditions, and input- and output-parameter types. The addition of goals as a separate tagging element allows us to estimate their semantic proximity and differentiate between tasks and services having same inputs and outputs but achieving different things.

A task T of a template can be instantiated by a service s if and only if:

1. The service s achieves the same goal as T, assuming an ontology of goals [15].
2. The pre-conditions of s are implied by the pre-conditions of T.
3. The post-conditions of s imply the post-conditions of T.
4. The matching type between the input specification In_T of T and the input specification In_s of s i.e., $Sim_T(In\_T, In\_s)$ is PlugIn.
5. The matching type between the output specification Out_s of s and the output specification Out_T of T i.e., $Sim_T(Out\_s, Out\_T)$ is PlugIn.

Conditions (1)–(3) above ensure the candidate service s has the desired effect of the target task T, whilst conditions (4) and (5) ensure the semantic (functional) fit between the candidate service and the target task. Condition (4) ensures that all the data which can be passed onto T can be procesed by s. Condition (5) ensures that the output of s fits within the output specifications of T.

Once a service is selected by the user, our system retrieves its semantic descriptions and computes all its potential incoming and outgoing semantic links with services of other tasks. The computation is based on the abstract semantic links in the template and the actual service descriptions. Services can be then linked with many services depending on the data flow description of the composition. As previously mentioned, only services linked with a semantic link of value *Exact* or *PlugIn* are consided for robustness reasons. Therefore, these services are highlighted, others are greyed out in the abstract visualisation of the composition.

Example 5 (Assisted Composition from the Back-end Perspective) According to Example 4 and Fig. 28.5, s_1 has been selected to achieved task `Search-For AUniversity`. Our system dynamically reduces the candidates' list of other tasks such as `RegisterForACourseInUK` or `OpenBankAccount` depending on quality of semantic links between services. For instance, the service `GradeSavers` (for `RegisterForACourseInUK` task) is discarded because $T \not\models Out\_Search For AUniversity \sqcap In\_Register For ACourseInUK \sqsubseteq \perp$ while the service s_2 is highlighted because $T \models Out\_Search For AUniversity \sqsubseteq In\_Register For ACour\text{-}seInUK$.

In our approach, the user can assign more than one service to a task, implying parallel execution of services from the back-end perspective. Therefore, the control flow of the template can be even modified on the fly, by adding new parallel branches. Such a modification is transparent to the end user, who are not interested in interacting with real control flow model of composition.

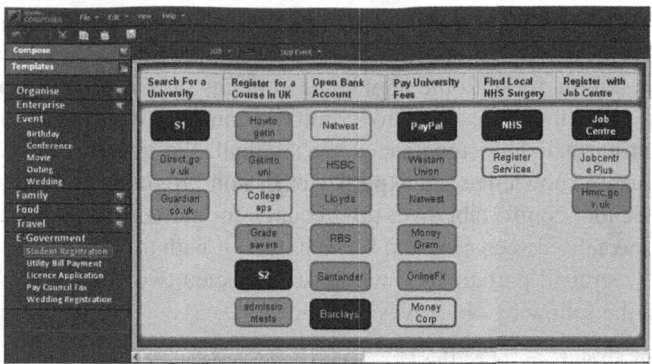

Fig. 28.6   Final composition

In case of parallel branches in the composition, the back-end tool is able to filter and merge data from these branches and connect them to the correct services. The latter is supported by the semantic link presented in (1).

Once the user has assigned services to every task of the template-based composition, the instantiation procedure is complete. Then, the composition is ready to be deployed and executed according to the the control and data flow information automatically elaborated respectively by the template description and the semantic links. Figure 28.6 depicts the final composition we obtain in our motivating scenario i.e., services in black are used to achieve the composition in Fig. 28.3.

Once the template is instantiated by the services selected by the user, the final process is ready to be deployed and then executed. In our approach the process is generated in BPEL4SWS [38] for subsequent analysis and processing by the service orchestrator. The orchestrator is responsible for scheduling, initiating, and monitoring the invocations to the tasks of the composite service during its execution, and for routing events and data items between these components.

28.5 Summative Evaluation of User Assisted Composition Tool

We have implemented a proof-of-concept implementation of the approach presented in the previous section as a module within the EC-funded integrated project SOA4All.[5] Following the technical development, we opted to test the usability and suitability of the User Assisted Composition tool (for short, UAC tool) for our target end users, non-programmers. These are people whose primary function in their jobs is not writing programming code; nonetheless, they might be involved in customising a software application to serve their personal or professional needs.

---

[5] More information on http://www.servicedesign.org.uk, last accessed on 30th Sept 2012.

Our selection of the participants was driven by (a) their profile which should match closely the target group of non-programmers developing process-oriented mashups, and (b) their familiarity with the applicaton domains of University enrollment and shopping. We have therefore aimed to recruit students from the Manchester Business School ensuring their IT competences are minimal. We hypothesise that with the sufficient domain knowledge and expertise other non-programmers will also be able to operate the tool comfortably, yet this requires further testing for which we need to develop specialised scenarios and services that fit with these settings.

Once we recruited participants, we have conducted two consecutive evaluation studies with the following objectives in mind:

- Assess the effectiveness of the User-Assisted Composition approach by analysing composition performance.
- Test the applicability and suitability of the tool in two differing scenarios, a shopping scenario and a university scenario.
- Gauge users positive views and negative views following direct interaction with the UAC tool; thus identifying the merits of user-assisted composition approach on the one hand and the limitations and problems on the other hand.
- Capture user impressions, satisfaction and acceptance of the UAC tool through a usability questionnaire.

The UAC approach provides a number of unique features as follows:

- The composition uses activity-based templates.
- Only simple user interface interaction skills, such as clicking, selecting etc, are required to operate the tool.
- The composition is mainly system-driven using semantic reasoning.
- Services are represented via boxes. No user interface is attached to them.
- No data flow or process flow connections are required. Instead the user can re-arrange the order of activities, and assign services for each activity through "point-and-click" interaction.
- User friendly error messages are displayed in case of mistakes.

28.5.1 Evaluation Tasks

Each evaluation session in both studies took approximately 50 min, and participants went through the same steps with the only variation to the evaluation scenario, where the first study focused on a shopping context and the second study focused on an education context. In our evaluation strategy, we selected scenarios that suit the profile of our target end users by recruiting participants who have sufficient knowledge about the tasks composing the shopping and university scenarios but who have no software programming or development experience. Our participant sample contained students from Manchester Business School enrolled for undergraduate and postgraduate courses. It is worth noting that for each study we recruited a different set of participants to ensure no learning effects are carried over to the second study. All studies were moderated by the same researcher.

The evaluation studies consisted of three common phases: training, task-undertaking, and debriefing interview phase.

- **Training phase**: in 10 min the moderator demonstrated the UAC tool, explained its various features, and encouraged participants to ask questions in case of ambiguity.
- **Task-undertaking phase**: in this phase participants read the scenario and performed the designed tasks. During the interaction with the tool, participants communicated their mental thoughts using the think-aloud protocol [21]. Think-aloud protocol is a research technique used to capture users inner thinking about the way they undertake tasks and the type of problems they encounter. Participants spent around 30 min to complete the designated tasks.
- **Debriefing interview phase**: in this phase participants reported their individual views and opinions about the UAC tool, and rated their satisfaction toward numerous aspects of the UAC tool by scoring a set of questions on a 5-point Likert scale.

28.5.2 Analysis Methods

Throughout the two studies we recorded participants opinions and interaction using SnagIt software, a screen capturing program, and their ratings using a paper questionnaire. The video recordings were reviewed and transcribed into Microsoft Word for follow-up thematic analysis [17], whilst rating scores were inserted into SPSS (i.e. a statistical software package) for calculating descriptive statistics such as the mean and standard deviation.

28.5.3 Evaluation Study One

In the first study, we recruited a total of six students who included five males and one female (mean age = 26.5). These participants were enrolled for a postgraduate degree in Manchester Business School. This study aimed to gauge initial qualitative impressions and reactions from potential end users which justifies the small sample. A pre-test questionnaire to capture participants software development background showed that our sample fits well the definition of non-programmers as depicted in Fig. 28.7. Five participants had no or basic software development background whilst one participant had a strong software development background. Participants rated pre-test questions on a 5-point Likert scale where '1' signifies 'none', and '5' signifies 'expert'. Average scores for all programming and software development experience questions were less than 2.33.

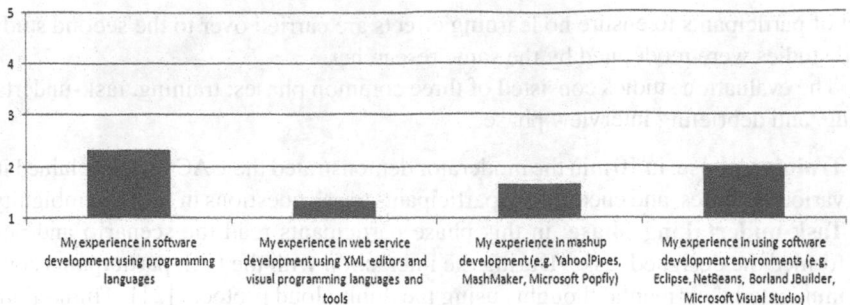

Fig. 28.7 Average scores of pre-test questionnaire

Next, each participant was instructed to go through two scenarios of varying complexity and perform the subsequent tasks:

1. **Scenario One**: suppose you own a reseller business/web shop. Your aim is to create a composition which gets the updated catalogues from clothing suppliers, aggregates the catalogues and publishes them in social networks and/or web shops. Your task is to compose a simple application which allows you to do the following:

   - Select the clothing suppliers whose catalogues you want to update.
   - Select the social networks(s)/web shop(s) where you want to aggregate and publish the desired catalogues.

2. **Scenario Two**: this time you want to build a composition which allows you to retrieve product descriptions and prices from specific suppliers and aggregate updated catalogues accordingly. Your task is to compose an application which allows you to achieve the following activities:

   - Update and aggregate catalogues from various clothing suppliers.
   - Get list of products from the desired footwear suppliers.
   - For each product get the product data and product price.
   - Aggregate the footwear products to the catalogue.
   - Retrieve list of product descriptions and prices and aggregate them to the catalogue.

In both scenarios, concurrent think-aloud protocol [21] was followed to get rich insights into the mental models of our users.

28.5.4 Results of Study One

In respect to user performance, all participants successfully completed the two scenarios using the UAC tool. It is worthwhile to note that in this study we were not

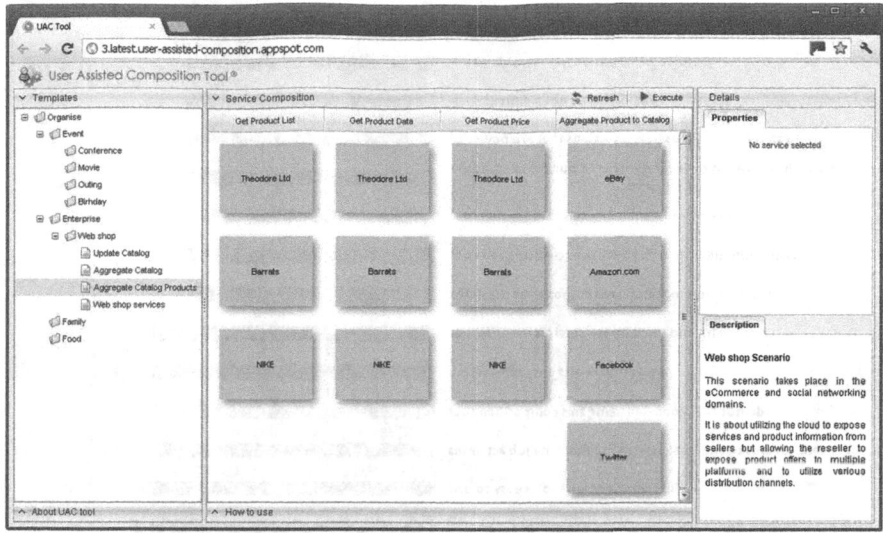

Fig. 28.8 User-assisted composition tool showing aggregate catalog products template

too concerned about the time taken to complete the tasks of the two scenarios but rather focused on user comments in relation to the composition approach and specific problems and ways to improve the tool.

Participants' feedback praised the ease by which they could operate the tool and navigate through the different sections. Also of increasing interest is the ability to compose service using the tool with no need to master programming concepts and paradigms, thus saving money and time. Instead participants were able to manage the composition with only a small number of clicks.

On the negative side participants were confused about the names of the services and activities, and found it difficult to match that to the requirements of the tasks. They also were unsure about why certain incompatible services can still be selected.

Following the composition, participants provided recommendations to help improve the tool. Among which were:

- Add a rating and description to services to empower end users to make an educated selection.
- Sort services alphabetically to facilitate search.
- Use self-explanatory names for the activities of templates to clarify their purpose.
- Enable end users to customise templates by re-arranging the sequence of activities.
- Use clear and distinct colours for selecting and de-selecting incompatible services.

Finally, participants rated their agreement with a number of statements to assess the usability of the UAC tool and their overall experience with service composition on a 5-point Likert scale, where '1' signifies disagree, '3' signifies neutral and '5' signifies agree. Indeed participants perceived the UAC tool as easy to use (with a mean m = 3.83) and navigate (m = 3.66), and did not find the notations used

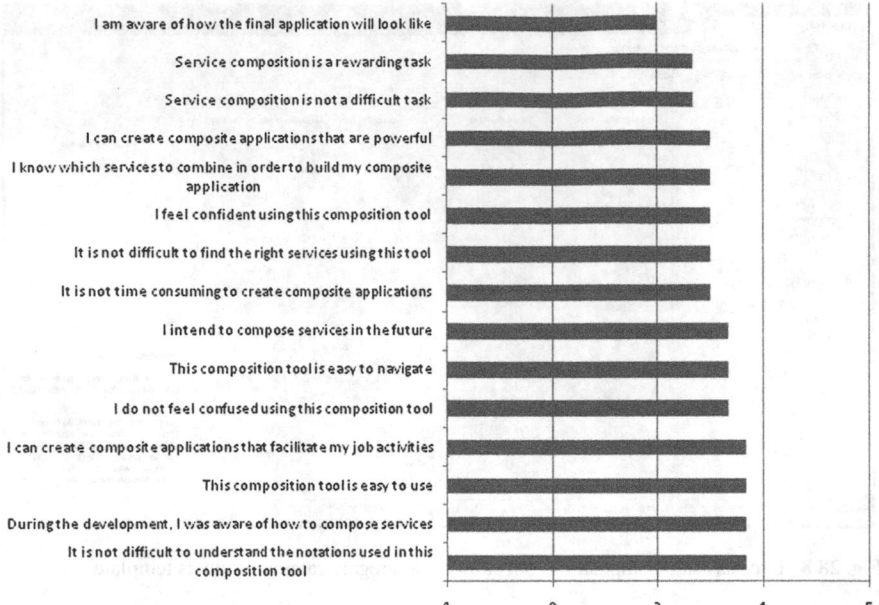

Fig. 28.9 Average rating scores of UAC tool

within the tool difficult to use. This experience improved user confidence that the tool allows end users to create composite applications which facilitate job functions (m = 3.83). However, participants expressed uncertainty in regard to the look and feel, and behaviour of the final application as depicted in Fig. 28.9. Similarly it was difficult for participants to evaluate how rewarding service composition is for they did not see the final application.

28.5.5 Evaluation Study Two

In the second study, we recruited a total of 12 Manchester University students by sending a screening questionnaire to the University student mailing list. The questionnaire collected information about programming and development experience, service modelling experience, background knowledge of software development environments and modelling tools, and general demographic information. We purposefully selected participants whose questionnaire scores match our requirements. Our sample included seven males and five females who study for non-Computer Science degrees such as: Business and Management, International Human Resource Management, Marketing, and Managerial Psychology. Participants rated their experience in respect to seven software development questions of the screening questionnaire on a 5-point Likert scale where '1' signifies Extremely poor, '3' signifies Average, and

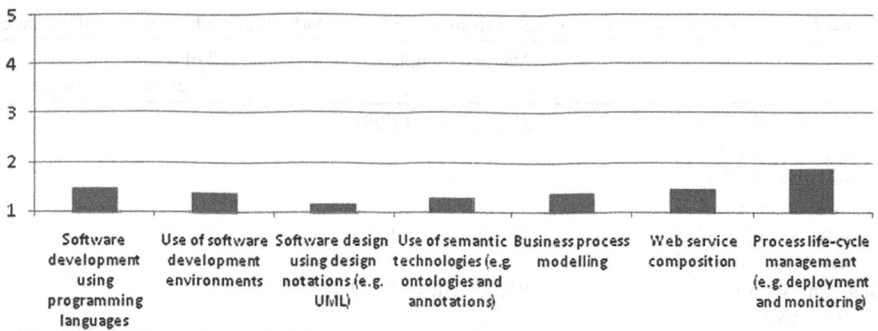

Fig. 28.10 Average scores of software development background questionnaire

'5' signifies Excellent. All scores averaged less than 1.9 as depicted in Fig. 28.10, indicating that our selected participants truly represent people who are not programmers.

We created a scenario with which our participants are familiar as it envisages the process they go through when applying to study at a particular UK university. The test scenario details the registration process overseas students go through while getting admission in UK universities as follows: Your goal is to complete an overseas student registration process. For this you need to develop a software application which allows you to search for a UK university, register for a course in the university and find an accommodation. There are two ways for paying the university fee, the first way is to open a bank account and get funds transferred into that account. The bank account can be used to make payment for the university fee. In the second way you can request a letter from a sponsor and submit that letter to the university. You must choose only one way to pay the university fee. After paying the university fee you will register with the NHS.

To accomplish the above scenario, participants were instructed to complete three primary tasks:

- **Task One**: Navigate to and load the appropriate activity-based template.
- **Task Two**: Remove the police registration activity from the template.
- **Task Three**: Select relevant services for each activity in the template according to the requirements of the test scenario.

During these development tasks, participants were continuously encouraged to express their views.

28.5.6 Results of Study Two

The objective evaluation of the UAC tool focused on measuring the average time taken to complete each task, along with the number of participants who have successfully

Table 28.1 Task completion time in seconds and number of participants who completed the task

Task	Average completion time (s)	# of users who completed the task
Finding and navigating to the right activity-based template Student Registration	21.25 (std = 12.99)	12
Removing 'Police Registration' activity from template	47.33 (std = 39.29)	11
Selecting appropriate services for activities	192.75 (std = 88.29)	12

Table 28.2 Average number of problems, positive comments and suggestions for the user assisted composition tool (STD: Standard Deviation)

Task	Average	STD
Positive comments	3.25	2.22
Overall problems	1.83	1.70
Conceptual problems	0.92	1.24
Usability problems	0.92	1.24
Suggestions	1.25	1.86

completed the tasks. The descriptive statistics revealed that participants spent the longest time inspecting the available services and selecting a relevant service for each template activity. However, participants were quicker to find the relevant template, and remove the police registration activity as summarised in Table 28.1. Of major interest is the ability of all of our participants to successfully complete the three tasks apart from one participant who did not manage to perform task 2 primarily due to the location of the remove button which was encapsulated within a pop-up menu. This high task completion rate reflects the effectiveness of the tool.

In regard to self-reported data, participants feedback and comments were analysed using thematic analysis [17], and classified into four categories; conceptual problems, usability problems, positive comments, and suggestions. Thematic analysis technique is qualitative in nature as a researcher goes through textual representation of an interaction, codes data segments, and creates general themes for the specific codes [17]. The results showed that, on average, participants were positive about the UAC tool, with 3.25 positive comments per participant as summarised in Table 28.2. As for problems, participants reported the same number of conceptual and usability problems, with an average of 0.92 negative comment per participant. Each participant provided at least one comment for ameliorating the UAC tool.

The positive feedback appreciated the presence of a 'how to use' section within the tool to help novice users grasp an understanding of the user assisted composition approach. They also found the tool intuitive, e.g. "it is easy to follow the logical steps", and easy to operate, e.g. "I just need to select the right services". The clickable nature of services and the ability to remove activities as well as services were appreciated by our end users. Finally, participants praised the structure and the way services are laid out within the tool.

Among the conceptual problems that emerged was the ambiguity of how to start the composition process which could be attributed to participants unfamiliarity with the tool, e.g. "What should I do now? I do not know". A total of 5 participants read the how-to-use section to help them get started with the tool. Another issue participants brought up was the inability to view the outcome of their development efforts and test the developed application, e.g. "I can not see the results", "It was easy but I wish I could see the end result so I could understand what I have done". This is aligned with the findings of [35] where users emphasised the need to see runtime results as the development process unfolds. It is quite important to inspect the behaviour of the application and debug any unapparent problems. Some participants proclaimed that the terminology and language used in the 'help and how to use the tool' sections were somewhat technical and complex, for instance: "press execute to deploy composition". Finally, participants highlighted that the tool does not provide any explanation as to why certain services get excluded upon selecting others.

In respect to usability problems, participants complained about the lack of text to describe the purpose of each service. This could greatly enhance their choice of target services and allocation of those to template activities. Some participants were uncertain as to why some services were greyed out upon selecting a particular service. However, this confusion diminished as soon as the experimenter explained that the greying out feature is used to highlight any incompatible services. The context menu for removing activities from the template was not apparent to one participant, and it proved to be cumbersome to find its location. Another aspect that worried our participants is the inconvenience that could be caused by the presence of many activities and their associated services in which case they would have to scroll horizontally and vertically to view them. Table 28.3 summarises the issues participants encountered when using the UAC tool.

To resolve the aforementioned issues and improve the overall composition experience using the UAC tool, participants recommended and discussed a number of potential solutions as follows:

R1 Supplement the activities and services with further details (e.g. service properties and provider information) to allow users to differentiate between services and make an educated selection of services. These details could be shown, for example, in the form of tool tips when mouse hovering upon services. Indeed

Table 28.3 Conceptual and usability issues emerging from UAC tool	Conceptual	Usability
	Runtime effect	Lack of text description
	Terminology and language	Invisible options (e.g. removal of activities)
	Compatibility of services	Scalability of the service template
		Unclear use of colour codes

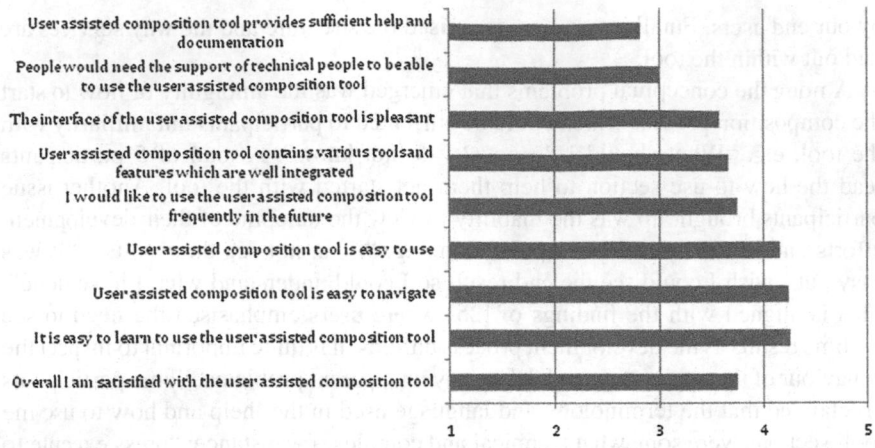

Fig. 28.11 Average rating scores of user-assisted composition tool

the composition process is highly-reliant on the careful selection of relevant services which, in turn, necessitates direct comparison of the features of multiple services accomplishing the same activity.

R2 Simplify the terminology used in the how to use section, and make it as close as possible to end user language.

R3 Provide explanation as to why certain services are incompatible, and couple this with distinct and clear use of colours.

R4 Provide a wizard to guide developers through the selection process of services and activities, especially at the start of the composition.

R5 Add a quick option (e.g. x in windows or a removal button) on the right corner of each activity column to allow fast removal of activities.

R6 Include runtime effects in the composition to empower end users to debug and test their application on the go.

Finally, participants concluded their user-assisted composition interaction tasks by rating a number of usability questions to assess ease of use, ease of learning, ease of navigation, user interface, help and documentation, and overall satisfaction with the tool on a 5-point Likert scale, where '1' signifies disagree, '3' signifies neutral, and '5' signifies agree.

There was a common consensus among our participants that the User Assisted Composition tool is easy to learn (m = 4.27, std = 0.90) and easy to use (m = 4.16, std = 0.93) as shown in Fig. 28.11. Similarly, participants agreed that the UAC tool is easy to navigate (m = 4.25, std = 0.96) and did not think that support from technical people is required to operate the tool (m = 3.00, std = 1.04). These scores confirm that end users can exploit the advantages of user-assisted composition approach without the need to master the underlying technical details of service composition and process modelling. Our participants also expressed strong willingness to use the

UAC tool more frequently in the future (m = 3.75, std = 1.28), and overall were satisfied with the tool (m = 3.75, std = 0.86).

28.6 Conclusion

We have established, through two summative evaluation studies, the effectiveness and suitability of the user assisted composition approach for non-programmers. The simplicity of point and click approach enabled our participants to complete the composition tasks with no major issues despite the short training they received. A number of interesting points emerged, including R1 to R6 listed above and especially the visibility of runtime operation. These will shape our future research directions. Every time participants were to select a service for an activity of the template, they expressed uncertainty and indicated that more service information should be displayed to assist them. In our view, text description of what the service does alone is not sufficient to overcome this issue, but rather more quality characteristics and criteria, such as reliability, reputation, and usability, should be exposed to enable informed service selection.

Our studies including the findings, however, have some limitations. First, it was not possible to demonstrate and test the final composite application which we believe would have strongly influenced user perception in regard to the overall composition experience. Indeed our participants found the composition process easy to perform and straight forward using the UAC tool; however, participants primary concern focused on showing runtime effects and ability to examine the final application.

Secondly, it is quite challenging for the moment to achieve a meaningful comparison between the UAC tool and other existing mashup and service development tools due to a number of qualifying reasons. First experimental design necessitates changing one variable whilst keeping the rest constant to study the influence of the variable. This means creating two similar versions of the UAC tool and varying one feature to test its influence. Testing the UAC tool against another totally different service development tool would not allow us to establish causal relationships but instead inspect mainly user interface issues. Moreover, the selected tools for comparison should be able to accomplish the same scenario and employ the same services for the comparison to be valid, or at least recruit scenarios of similar complexity. In addition, the purpose of this paper was to detail the approach and validate its feasibility with representative end users as an initial step rather than to compare the proposed tool against other tools. We argue that comparing different tools which support the same type of composition (e.g. service composition using service frond-ends) would not yield interesting results, but rather shed light on only usability issues. For the comparison to be scientific and valid, the plan is to extend the current UAC tool with other composition approaches. Thus, we intend in the future to conduct a series of comparative studies where we contrast overall service development experience using differing service development paradigms within a single tool. In particular we aim to investigate user interface based composition, process based composition, and dataflow based composition. The concepts behind these paradigms and how they support the service development process are indeed interesting and worthwhile to explore.

In light of these limitations, we plan to undertake various steps to improve and qualify our research in the future in addition to these comparative studies. To start with, we will recruit participants who are domain experts and practitioners in various sectors such as the public and health sector, and increase our sample size to a satisfactory number. Moreover, in the next evaluations we will empower end users to see and test the final application of their composition, interact with it, and debug it throughout the composition.

In summary, the qualitative and the quantitative feedback obtained demonstrate that our end users understood the principles of the assisted composition approach, were positive about it and were able to accomplish the tasks set to them. Following our earlier work [31, 32], we believe that this is partially due to the benefits expected from service composition in terms of producing mashups which are finely tuned to the user needs, and partially due to the reduction of the learning costs as perceived by the user. The reduction in learning costs is attributed to our two main contributions presented in this paper: the approach of hiding technical complexity using semantic reasoning, and the reuse possible by the template-based development process.

References

1. Baader, F., Nutt, W.: In: The Description Logic Handbook: Theory, Implementation, and Applications. Cambridge University Press, Cambridge (2003)
2. Beaton, J.K., Myers, B.A., Stylos, J., Jeong, S.Y.S., Xie, Y.C.: Usability evaluation for enterprise SOA APIs. In: SDSOA '08: Proceedings of the 2nd International Workshop on Systems Development in SOA Environments, pp. 29–34. ACM, New York (2008). doi:10.1145/1370916.1370924
3. Berardi, D., Calvanese, D., Giacomo, G.D., Lenzerini, M., Mecella, M.: Automatic composition of e-services that export their behavior. In: Proceedings of the 1st International Conference on Service Oriented Computing (ICSOC), pp. 43–58 (2003)
4. Blackwell, A.F.: First steps in programming: a rationale for attention investment models. In: Proceedings of HCC '02, p. 2. IEEE CS, Washington (2002)
5. Brandt, S., Kusters, R., Turhan, A.: Approximation and difference in description logics. In: Proceedings of KR, pp. 203–214 (2002). http://www.citeseer.ist.psu.edu/brandt02approximation.html
6. Canfora, G., Penta, M.D., Esposito, R., Villani, M.L.: An approach for qos-aware service composition based on genetic algorithms. In: Proceedings of GECCO, pp. 1069–1075 (2005)
7. Carlson, M.P., Ngu, A.H., Podorozhny, R., Zeng, L.: Automatic mash up of composite applications. In: Proceedings of the 6th International Conference on Service-Oriented Computing, ICSOC '08, pp. 317–330. Springer, Berlin (2008). doi:10.1007/978-3-540-89652-4_25
8. Colucci, S., Noia, T.D., Sciascio, E.D., Donini, F.M., Mongiello, M.: Concept abduction and contraction for semantic-based discovery of matches and negotiation spaces in an e-marketplace. Electron. Commer. Res. Appl. 4(4), 345–361 (2005)
9. Daniel, F., Casati, F., Benatallah, B., Shan, M.C.: Hosted universal composition: models, languages and infrastructure in mashart. In: Laender, A., Castano, S., Dayal, U., Casati, F., de Oliveira, J. (eds.) Conceptual Modeling—ER 2009. Lecture Notes in Computer Science, vol.

5829, pp. 428–443. Springer, Berlin (2009). http://dx.doi.org/10.1007/978-3-642-04840-1_32. doi:10.1007/978-3-642-04840-1_32

10. Daniel, F., Koschmider, A., Nestler, T., Roy, M., Namoun, A.: Toward process mashups: key ingredients and open research challenges. In: Proceedings of the 3rd and 4th International Workshop on Web APIs and Services Mashups, Mashups '09/'10, pp. 9:1–9:8. ACM, New York (2010). doi:10.1145/1944999.1945008. http://doi.acm.org/10.1145/1944999.1945008

11. Daniel, F., Soi, S., Casati, F.: Distributed user interface orchestration: on the composition of multi-user (search) applications. In: Ceri, S., Brambilla, M. (eds.) Search Computing, Lecture Notes in Computer Science, vol. 6585, pp. 182–191. Springer, Berlin (2011). http://dx.doi.org/10.1007/978-3-642-19668-3_17. doi:10.1007/978-3-642-19668-3_17

12. Deutch, D., Greenshpan, O., Milo, T.: Navigating in complex mashed-up applications. Proc. VLDB Endow. 3(1–2), 320–329 (2010). http://dl.acm.org/citation.cfm?id=1920841.1920885

13. Ennals, R.J., Garofalakis, M.N.: Mashmaker: mashups for the masses. In: Proceedings of the 2007 ACM SIGMOD International Conference on Management of Data, SIGMOD '07, pp. 1116–1118. ACM, New York (2007). doi:10.1145/1247480.1247626

14. Euzenat, J., Shvaiko, P.: Ontology Matching. Springer, Berlin (2007)

15. Fensel, D., Kifer, M., de Bruijn, J., Domingue, J.: Web service modeling ontology submission, w3c submission (2005)

16. Fischer, G., Nakakoji, K., Ye, Y.: Metadesign: guidelines for supporting domain experts in software development. IEEE Softw. 26(5), 37–44 (2009). doi:10.1109/MS.2009.134

17. Guest, G., MacQueen, M.K., Namey, E.: Applied Thematic Analysis. SAGE Publications Inc, New Delhi (2012)

18. Han, J., Han, Y., Jin, Y., Wang, J., Yu, J.: Personalized active service spaces for end-user service composition. In: IEEE International Conference on Services Computing, 2006, SCC '06, pp. 198–205 (2006). doi:10.1109/SCC.2006.80

19. Horrocks, I.: Using an expressive description logic: Fact or fiction? In: Proceedings of KR, pp. 636–649 (1998)

20. Hull, R., Benedikt, M., Christophides, V., Su, J.: E-services: a look behind the curtain. In: Proceedings of the 22nd ACM SIGMOD-SIGACT-SIGART Symposium on Principles of Database Systems, PODS '03, pp. 1–14. ACM, New York (2003). doi:10.1145/773153.773154

21. Kuusela, H., Paul, P.: A comparison of concurrent and retrospective verbal protocal analysis. Am. J. Psychol. 113(3), 387–404 (2000)

22. Lécué, F., Léger, A.: A formal model for semantic web service composition. In: Proceedings of ISWC, pp. 385–398 (2006)

23. Lécué, F., Mehandjiev, N.: Seeking quality of web service composition in a semantic dimension. IEEE Trans. Knowl. Data Eng. 23(6), 942–959 (2011)

24. Li, L., Horrocks, I.: A software framework for matchmaking based on semantic web technology. In: Proceedings of WWW, pp. 331–339 (2003)

25. Lieberman, H., Paternò, F., Klann, M., Wulf, V.: End-User Development: An Emerging Paradigm, Human-Computer Interaction Series, vol. 9. Springer, Netherlands (2006). doi:10.1007/1-4020-5386-X_1. http://dx.doi.org/10.1007/1-4020-5386-X_1

26. Liu, X., Hui, Y., Sun, W., Liang, H.: Towards service composition based on mashup. In: Proceedings of IEEE Congress on Services, pp. 332–339 (2007). doi:10.1109/SERVICES.2007.67

27. Martinez, A., Patino-Martinez, M., Jimenez-Peris, R., Perez-Sorrosal, F.: Zenflow: a visual web service composition tool for BPEL4WS. In: Proceedings of VLHCC'05, pp. 181–188. IEEE Computer Society, Washington, (2005). doi:10.1109/VLHCC.2005.74

28. McIlraith, S.A., Son, T.C.: Adapting Golog for composition of semantic web services. In: Proceedings of KR, pp. 482–496 (2002)

29. Mehandjiev, N., Lécué, F., Wajid, U.: Provider-composer negotiations for semantic robustness in service compositions. In: Proceedings of ICSOC/ServiceWave, pp. 205–220 (2009)

30. Mehandjiev, N., Namoun, A., Wajid, U., Macaulay, L., Sutcliffe, A.: End user service composition—perceptions and requirements. In: Proceedings of 8th IEEE European Conference on Web Services ECOWS'2010 (2010, to appear)

31. Mehandjiev, N., Stoitsev, T., Grebner, O., Scheidl, S., Riss, U.: End-user development for task management: Survey of attitudes and practices. In: Proceedings of VLHCC '08, pp. 166–174. IEEE Computer Society, Washington (2008). doi:10.1109/VLHCC.2008.4639079
32. Mehandjiev, N., Sutcliffe, A., Lee, D.: Organizational view of end-user development. In: Lieberman, H., Paternò, F., Wulf, V. (eds.) End User Development, Human-Computer Interaction Series, vol. 9, chap. 17, pp. 371–399. Springer, Netherlands (2006). doi:10.1007/1-4020-5386-X_17. http://dx.doi.org/10.1007/1-4020-5386-X_17
33. Mørch, A.I., Mehandjiev, N.D.: Tailoring as collaboration: the mediating role of multiple representations and applicationunits. Comput. Support. Coop. Work **9**(1), 75–100 (2000). doi:10.1023/A:1008713826637
34. Motta, E.: Parametric Design Problem Solving—Reusable Components for Knowledge Modelling Case Studies. IOS Press, Amsterdam (1999)
35. Namoun, A., Nestler, T., De Angeli, A.: Service composition for non-programmers: prospects, problems, and design recommendations. In: Proceedings of IEEE 8th European Conference on Web Services (ECOWS), pp. 123–130 (2010). doi:10.1109/ECOWS.2010.17
36. Namoun, A., Wajid, U., Mehandjiev, N.: A comparative study: application development by ordinary internet users and it-professionals. In: Proceedings of ServiceWave'2010. Springer, Berlin (2010, to appear)
37. Nardi, B.A.: A Small Matter of Programming: Perspectives on End User Computing. MIT Press, Cambridge (1993)
38. Nitzsche, J., Norton, B.: Ontology Based Data Mediation in BPEL (for Semantic Web Services). Springer, New York (2008)
39. Paolucci, M., Kawamura, T., Payne, T., Sycara, K.: Semantic matching of web services capabilities. In: Proceedings of ISWC, pp. 333–347 (2002)
40. Pistore, M., Roberti, P., Traverso, P.: Process-level composition of executable web services: "on-the-fly" versus "once-for-all" composition. In: Proceedings of ESWC, pp. 62–77 (2005)
41. Rode, J., Rosson, M.B., Pérez-Qui nones, M.A.: End-users' mental models of concepts critical to web application development. In: Proceedings of VLHCC '04, pp. 215–222. IEEE Computer Society, Washington (2004). doi:10.1109/VLHCC.2004.25
42. Sirin, E., Hendler, J.A., Parsia, B.: Semi-automatic composition of web services using semantic descriptions. In: Proceedings of WSMAI, pp. 17–24 (2003)
43. Sutcliffe, A.: Domain Theory: Patterns for Knowledge and Software Reuse. L. Erlbaum Associates Inc., Hillsdale (2002)
44. Sutcliffe, A., Mehandjiev, N.: Introduction. Commun. ACM **47**(9), 31–32 (2004). doi:10.1145/1015864.1015883
45. Teege, G.: Making the difference: a subtraction operation for description logics. In: Proceedings of KR, pp. 540–550 (1994). http://www.citeseer.ist.psu.edu/teege94making.html
46. ten Teije, A., van Harmelen, F., Wielinga, B.: Configuration of web services as parametric design. In: Motta, E., et al. (ed.) Proceedings of EKAW-2004, LNAI, vol. 3257, pp. 321–336. Springer, Heidelberg (2004). ISBN 3-540-23340-7
47. Westerski, A.: Integrated environment for visual data-level mashup development. In: Proceedings of WISE '09, pp. 481–487. Springer, Berlin (2009). doi:10.1007/978-3-642-04409-0_47
48. Wielinga, B., Schreiber, G.: Configuration-design problem solving. IEEE Expert Intell. Syst. Appl. **12**(2), 49–56 (1997)
49. Wong, J., Hong, J.I.: Making mashups with Marmite: towards end-user programming for the web. In: Proceedings of the SIGCHI Conference on Human Factors in Computing Systems, CHI '07, pp. 1435–1444. ACM, New York (2007). doi:10.1145/1240624.1240842
50. Yu, T., Lin, K.J.: Service selection algorithms for composing complex services with multiple QoS constraints. In: Proceedings of ICSOC, pp. 130–143 (2005)
51. Zang, N., Beth, R.M.: What's in a mashup? And why? Studying the perceptions of web-active end users. In: Proceedings of VLHCC'08, pp. 31–38. IEEE Computer Society, Washington (2008). doi:10.1109/VLHCC.2008.4639055
52. Zeng, L., Benatallah, B., Dumas, M., Kalagnanam, J., Sheng, Q.Z.: Quality driven web services composition. In: Proceedings of WWW, pp. 411–421 (2003)

Index

A. Bouguettaya et al. (eds.), *Web Services Foundations*,
DOI: 10.1007/978-1-4614-7518-7,
© Springer Science+Business Media New York 2014

Printed in the United States
By Bookmasters